SECOND EDITION

HEALTH CARE MANAGEMENT AND THE LAW

Donna K. Hammaker

Director, National Institute Health Care Management & Law
MGA, Wharton School of the University of Pennsylvania; JD, Temple University School of Law
Hebrew University Faculty of Law and London School of Economics
Former Adjunct Professor of Health Law, MBA Program in Biotechnology & Health Industry Management,
Pennsylvania State University
Former President & Chief Executive Officer, Collegiate Health Care Corp.

Thomas M. Knadig

Hospice Chaplain, Hospital of the University of Pennsylvania Health Care System
MDiv, St. Mary's Seminary & University; MA, Notre Dame University; EdD, Widener University
Oxford University, Massachusetts Institute of Technology, and University of California, Berkeley
Adjunct Professor of Humanities, Widener University
Former Board Chairman, Collegiate Health Care Corp.

with Sarah J. Tomlinson

Office of the General Counsel, Fox Rothschild LLP
Health Policy Doctoral Student, Temple University College of Public Health
JD, Villanova University School of Law; MBA, Pennsylvania State University
Adjunct Professor of Health Law, Immaculata University

JONES & BARTLETT
LEARNING

World Headquarters
Jones & Bartlett Learning
5 Wall Street
Burlington, MA 01803
978-443-5000
info@jblearning.com
www.jblearning.com

Jones & Bartlett Learning books and products are available through most bookstores and online booksellers. To contact Jones & Bartlett Learning directly, call 800-832-0034, fax 978-443-8000, or visit our website, www.jblearning.com.

Substantial discounts on bulk quantities of Jones & Bartlett Learning publications are available to corporations, professional associations, and other qualified organizations. For details and specific discount information, contact the special sales department at Jones & Bartlett Learning via the above contact information or send an email to specialsales@jblearning.com.

Production Credits

VP, Executive Publisher: David D. Cella
Publisher: Michael Brown
Associate Editor: Lindsey M. Sousa
Senior Production Editor: Amanda Clerkin
Senior Marketing Manager: Sophie Fleck Teague
Manufacturing and Inventory Control Supervisor: Amy Bacus
Composition: Integra Software Services Pvt. Ltd.

Cover Design: Timothy Dziewit
Rights & Media Specialist: Merideth Tumasz
Media Development Editor: Shannon Sheehan
Cover Image: © Mettus/Shutterstock
Printing and Binding: Edwards Brothers Malloy
Cover Printing: Edwards Brothers Malloy

To order this product, use ISBN: 9781284117349

Library of Congress Cataloging-in-Publication Data
Names: Hammaker, Donna K., author. | Knadig, Thomas M., author.
Title: Health Care Management and the Law / Donna K. Hammaker, Thomas M. Knadig.
Description: Second edition. | Burlington, MA : Jones & Barlett Learning,
  [2018] | Includes bibliographical references.
Identifiers: LCCN 2016054984 | ISBN 9781284134551
Subjects: | MESH: Health Services Administration--legislation & jurisprudence
  | Delivery of Health Care--legislation & jurisprudence | Legislation,
  Medical | United States
Classification: LCC KF3821 | NLM W 32.5 AA1 | DDC 174.2--dc23 LC record available at https://lccn.loc.gov/2016054984

6048

Printed in the United States of America
21 20 19 18 17   10 9 8 7 6 5 4 3 2 1

Contents

PART VII. IMPROVING THE QUALITY OF HEALTH CARE   441

PART VIII. OUR HEALTH CARE SYSTEM'S RESPONSE TO ILLNESS   499

Preface

"With respect to excellence, it is not enough to know, but we must learn to have and use it."

— **Aristotle** (384 BC–322 BC), Greek philosopher, from *Nichomachean Ethics*

Health Care Management and the Law: Principles and Applications is a core law text for readers who will be managers in health care organizations, whether managing in an administrative or clinical role. Health care managers need the knowledge base set forth herein. This text gives readers the opportunity to gain a strong general foundation in health law, as well as strengthens their ability to make legally and ethically sound decisions as health care managers. Students will learn the core fundamentals of health law necessary to meet the challenges that will confront them in their careers, plus specialized, cutting-edge knowledge of emerging issues that will arise in the future, as well as the familiarity with legal principles needed to communicate effectively with legal counsel.

The challenges now facing health care organizations are more dramatic than almost anything faced by managers in years past. Consumers of health care are gaining unprecedented power as health care is increasingly seen as a basic human right that must be treated as such. Provider competition and regulation have gone from wind level to storm level to hurricane level. Medical products firms are discovering not just new biopharmaceuticals but new health needs.

To thrive in this new environment of mushrooming cost, inadequate availability, and uneven quality, health care organizations must rethink everything. They need to consult with consumers of health care so that they can view themselves from the "outside in" as Peter Drucker would have said. They must develop new sources of talent and focus on their core competencies.

Authors' Vision

Throughout this text are two strong recurring themes: namely, that overarching reforms must continue to be implemented to improve the U.S. health care system and that the nation's health laws must continue to be reformed to create a system that works properly. The time for make changes is now. A related premise is that the convergence of many health care sectors is rapidly changing the laws governing provider competition and regulation. These changes require the U.S. legal system to expand the boundaries of health law as it recognizes what is next and what is essential in U.S. health care. Scientifically advanced U.S. medical institutions, with their elaborate systems of specialized knowledge, advanced technologies, and rules of behavior, contain some of the best elements of the U.S. health care system.

While each industry segment faces unique challenges, more and more of these challenges overlap with established legal principles and the hard rules of law. Health care organizations are increasingly shifting strategies to stay ahead of the emerging issues and government regulations. Providers are constructing new breakthroughs in health care delivery. Established pharmaceutical manufacturers are investing heavily in biotechnology and medical devices. Traditional medical research-focused firms are venturing into the realm of commercialization. Together they are seeking to reclaim some of the mislaid status of American medicine and return to the ideals of reason through modern science. All of this active change is taking place amid innovative U.S. reform initiatives, and an increasing focus on global health. Health law should challenge these dynamic changes with a stern but fair message about limits.

This text does not distinguish between access to health care for resident citizens and resident noncitizens or more specifically, those in the United States without status, sometimes labeled undocumented, unauthorized, or illegal immigrants. Whether or not there is agreement on their right to do so, those without status access the U.S. health care system, including its emergency rooms and public clinics. Therefore, it only made sense to include noncitizen residents in the discussion and the proposed solutions. It is assumed that this segment of the U.S. population accesses health care to the same extent as U.S. citizens; therefore, all materials addressed herein encompass citizens and noncitizens alike.

Text Approach

Current practices and advances in health care are summarized, with attention directed to the management issues facing today's health care professionals. Basic legal principles are reviewed and practical applications of the law in health care delivery and practice are presented. The focus is on both the meaning and the effects of the law, so that the legal implications of court decisions and their effect on the evolution of the law are understood. How the Affordable Care Act and implementation of comprehensive reforms of the U.S. health care system are evolving is highlighted throughout.

Real-World Knowledge

Bridging research and practice, this text reflects new, real-world knowledge of the health care industry and government agencies. The health law concepts are practical; application of the concepts seeks to provide health care managers with sufficient knowledge of the law to become intelligent, critical thinkers in professional practice. Students are not being prepared to become health law attorneys; rather they will gain a sense of when and why they should consider consulting attorneys.

 This is a practical health law overview relevant to undergraduate readers seeking the basic management skills required to work in health care organizations, as well as graduate readers currently working in health care organizations as administrators, physicians, nurses, pharmacists, therapists, scientists, and other administrative and clinical managers. This text is also relevant to those general health care consumers who are simply attempting to navigate the complex U.S. health care system. Every attempt is made within the text to support health law and management theory with practical applications.

Depth and Breadth

Readers are not overwhelmed with legal theory; instead, the text covers basic legal principles and then focuses on practical applications of the law in the real world of health care delivery and practice. Challenging, current administrative and judicial decisions are presented. Students can customize their learning experience by selecting from 37 topic chapters or studying a specific topic in-depth, using the chapter references and multiple resources provided. There is a focus on interpretation, insight and ideas; in other words, the focus is more on the meaning of the law, not only what occurs pursuant to it.

Management and Law Learning

The practice and theory of the law is an underlying theme woven throughout this text. Students can develop and strengthen their management skills through the examination of the difficult, and often unresolved, legal and ethical conflicts presented. They can build a framework within which to think through the legal implications of management decisions.

Best Practices

This text seeks to apply the best practices to the health care industry. Students are exposed to management principles and their evolution in a legal context, whether when seeking new ways to overcome the failure of markets and governments to provide the highest-quality medical care to every member of society, or when searching for ways to better understand the complex and quickly evolving medical products industry. Management, leadership, and the dynamics of competition in U.S. health care are emphasized. Students learn about key elements that allow the U.S. health care culture to operate and thrive in a competitive space.

Management Principles

There is a focus on interpretation and insight into management principles for decision-making. Principles underlying the law are intertwined throughout this text as reference points. Students can develop and strengthen their management skills through examination of the difficult considerations of the law that are presented in each chapter. Traditional management principles will, however, only serve as a reference. Students are encouraged to be disciplined and independent in their decision-making and discover new ways for arriving at management decisions. Students can think through the implications of management issues based on normative law standards.

Normative Law Standards

What sets this text apart from other texts on health care management is its focus on the normative standards of the law. In contrast to most traditional texts on health care management, the prescribed rules of law in almost every recent court decision of first impression are examined. Cases of first impression set forth completely original issues of law for decision by the courts. This method of selecting court decisions to ascertain management underpinnings, which is unique to this text, highlights the changing nature of the law and its current effect on the health care industry. Significant U.S. Supreme Court cases, as well as landmark cases from the U.S. Courts of Appeal and the highest state courts with established precedents, will also be examined where the decisions are still good law and relevant. Each of the court decisions reviewed addresses new, important, and substantive issues involving health care management.

Court decisions are examined with a focus on how legal principles underlying the law are currently being applied, the correctness of traditional assumptions and choices, and what might be done differently in future similar situations. Although the role of the courts is to interpret and apply existing law, their decisions often prompt legislators to write new laws in response to new thinking and changes in society. Additionally, although it is not the role of the courts to make judgments about how to manage the U.S. health care system, their decisions certainly contain assumptions about best practices. Therefore, in an effort to provide some help to the reader in making management decisions, this text employs a methodology of examining recent U.S. court decisions for ideas about management practices. The courts are in no way dictating management practices, but their decisions may indicate the direction society is moving in terms of its accepting or rejecting certain actions and whether those actions are tolerable or desirable from a management point of view. It should be emphasized that "legal" does not equal a "best practice," but it provides some indications about what is considered best for management of the U.S. health system.

State-of-the-Art Research

This text is traditional legal scholarship written with state-of-the-art research methods, using searchable online databases that are revolutionizing research on health care management and the law, including foremost:

- Knowledge@Wharton (The Wharton School of the University of Pennsylvania)
- LexisNexis
- NLM (National Library of Medicine)
- Online Wall Street Journal
- OVRC (Opposing Viewpoints Research Center)
- ProQuest

The health care statistics come from various components of the Centers for Disease Control's National Center for Health Statistics National Health Care Surveys, unless otherwise cited. This text reviews jurisprudence and seeks common themes as well as conflicts. Knowledge of the innovations transforming health care industry practices and public policy are clearly explained so that readers' minds can be opened to new possibilities in order to apply what they learn.

Primary Research with Health Care Industry Experts

Background information was obtained from a comprehensive search of published literature and reports obtained from various business, law, and medical trade journals. Secondary research of peer-reviewed journals is included in the references for each chapter; some reference is made to government reports and policy papers. This research, in turn, was supplemented with reviews by a panel of more than 30 health care professionals from all aspects of the health care industry. Their shared opinions and insights helped supplement the online databases with first-hand knowledge on current and future trends in health care management and the law. They identified matters that have the most social significance to them as leaders in the health care industry. This review process resulted in chapters having importance for real-world issues, present-day events, and the current state of U.S. health care reforms.

Organization of This Text

The dual goals of this text are to engage those readers who will be leading and shaping 21st century health care organizations and to raise questions about health law issues such as:

- Emergence of the United States as a player in the global health care industry
- Innovative new approaches to the health care delivery model
- Regenerative and precision medicine
- The future of tailored therapeutics

This text is divided into 12 broad parts:

Part I. Introduction to Health Care Management, provides a brief overview of U.S. health care.

Chapter 1. *Processes for Thinking About the U.S. Health Care System*, explains how the greatest obstacle to transforming the U.S. health care system may be the nation's collective thinking.

Chapter 2. *Introduction to Health Law*, describes how the U.S. legal system functions through the separation of governmental powers that is central to the U.S. Constitution.

Part II. Access to Health Care, addresses Americans' resolve to obtain the best health care for as little as possible.

Chapter 3. *Access to Affordable Health Insurance*, draws attention to the challenge of finding a way to provide medical coverage for the uninsured and every member of society.

Chapter 4. *Medicaid Insurance and Access to Medically Necessary Care*, examines the way to provide basic health care to everyone.

Chapter 5. *Medicare Insurance Reforms*, looks at the complexities of Medicare and the challenge of reforming the system, including Medicare's prescription drug coverage plan.

Part III. Affordable Health Care, investigates how to ensure that as parts of the U.S. health care system offer some of the best health care of any place in the world to those who can afford it, the masses are not left behind.

Chapter 6. *Affordable Care and Tax-Exempt Hospitals*, explores whether not-for-profit hospitals are required to provide mutually affordable health care in return for substantial tax exemptions.

Chapter 7. *Patient Rights and Responsibilities*, reviews the patient bill of rights, the comparative effectiveness of medical treatments, and universal coverage.

Chapter 8. *Medical Malpractice*, covers how malpractice occurs, as well as peer review processes and medical standards of care, tort reform, and malpractice insurance.

Part IV. Staffing of Health Care Systems, concentrates on staffing of U.S. health care systems and the laws affecting the management of employees.

Chapter 9. *Human Resources Departments*, compares two views of human resources in the health care industry: first, as a strategic department that works directly with senior management to improve organizational effectiveness, and second, in its traditional role, with involvement in many responsibilities now being outsourced.

Chapter 10. *Employers' Health Care Costs*, deals with the growing efforts to trim employers' health care costs with particular attention directed to the growing prevalence of obesity, smoking, and non-adherence to treatment regiments.

Chapter 11. *Management and Labor Relations*, outlines fundamental topics, such as unionization of physicians and nurses, as well as the newer concerns of nurse workload management, the hiring of foreign physicians and nurses, and the use of contingent employees to meet unmet staffing needs.

Part V. Strategic Health Care Restructurings, describes how the health care and insurance industries are being pressured to move toward fewer restrictions on care instead of more.

Chapter 12. *Trends in Health Care Restructurings*, examines the movement of the U.S. health care system into integrated delivery systems that are multi-tiered based on the ability to pay for one's health care.

Chapter 13. *Strategic Restructurings in Health Care: Mergers/Acquisitions and Bankruptcies*, looks at two sides of the restructuring coinage: on one side, the mergers of physician practices and acquisitions of medical facilities in order to corner patient markets and on the other side, the bankruptcy of a large, statewide integrated delivery system.

Chapter 14. *Antitrust and Regulation of Health Care Providers*, addresses how antitrust affects health care financing, hospitals, and the consumer-driven health care sector.

Chapter 15. *Global Supply Chain Management*, explores a rapidly expanding integration and outsourcing industry that is offering the health care industry services, such as finance, accounting, claims processing, customer relationship management, and data analytics.

Part VI. Producers of Medical Products, reviews the producers of medical products: pharmaceuticals, biopharmaceuticals, medical devices, and health information technology.

Chapter 16. *Pharmaceuticals*, recognizes that while the industry is frequently criticized by patients, consumer groups, and others for charging high prices and making too much money, a more balanced view of the pharmaceutical industry involves the interplay of high-risk and long timelines for development.

Chapter 17. *Biopharmaceuticals*, explains the laws affecting gene therapy and other biological science fields such as genomics, bioinformatics, and proteomics that hold the potential for breakthroughs that could transform the delivery of health care.

Chapter 18. *Medical Devices*, describes how the use of implantable devices to treat heart disease, orthopedic complaints and other conditions is growing strongly because of advancing technology; the continued prevalence of diseases from an aging and overweight population, and greater acceptance by physicians and patients of implantation as an alternative or a complement to prescription drugs.

Chapter 19. *Clinical Trials*, provides an overview of the complex and multistage pathways to Food and Drug Administration approval of the end results of medical product research and development.

Chapter 20. *Information Management and Telehealth Technologies*, examines how technology is reshaping the ways hospitals, physicians, consumers, and the health insurance industry interact with one another.

Part VII. Improving the Quality of Health Care, covers four areas where broad agreement exists regarding what should be done to combat rising health care costs and improve the quality of care that patients receive.

Chapter 21. *Population Health Management*, reports on the demand for greater transparency about how physicians effectively treat patients and the concomitant drive to develop clinical information technology databases and other processes to assist health care providers in making responsible medical treatment decisions.

Chapter 22. *Evidence-Based Medicine*, explores a discipline that has been around for a little more than a decade and is at the top of the list of industry improvements in the United States to help rein in health care costs and provide more reliable medical treatment.

Chapter 23. *Improving Patient Safety and Quality of Health Care*, reviews programs targeting patient safety to prevent dangerous lapses in care, such as when providers fail to explain and monitor medical product use, deliver test results, or schedule follow-up care.

Part VIII. Our Health Care System's Response to Illness, takes a systematic look at mortality and other dimensions of ill health in the United States, with a focus on the costs of living with a disease or disability.

Chapter 24, *Human Body Parts Industry*, illuminates a billion dollar business intertwined with the U.S. health care system.

Chapter 25. *Organ and Tissue Procurement and Transplantation*, explains the principles of organ procurement and transplantation and further describes the billion-dollar body parts industry.

Chapter 26. *AIDS Pandemic*, depicts the devastating global pandemic, as attention is increasingly focused on U.S. firms holding patents and controlling prices for prescription drugs to treat AIDS and HIV, the virus that causes AIDS.

Chapter 27. *Mental Health*, focuses on the health care system's response to mental illness, and charts the costs of living with disease or mental disability.

Part IX. End-of-Life Health Care, is comprised of three chapters dealing with the right-to-die controversy.

Chapter 28. *Hospice Care*, defines a specialized and growing niche in the health care economy.

Chapter 29. *Mature Minor Rights to Refuse Life-Sustaining Treatment*, analyzes the question of whether mature minors have the right to refuse life-sustaining treatment.

Chapter 30. *Care of the Critically Ill and Dying*, deals with the question of whether human beings have the right to die at a time and place, and in a manner, of their own choosing.

Part X. Our Health Care Systems' Response to Biomedicine, examines emerging discoveries in regenerative and precision medicine, new technologies that have the potential to take health care in a whole new direction.

Chapter 31. *Stem Cells and Regenerative Medicine*, explores the potential of stem cell therapy and the controversy surrounding the use of embryonic stem cells.

Chapter 32. *Cellular Therapeutics and Precision Medicine*, discusses cellular therapeutics, at the intersection of precision medicine and genetics, as well as synthetic biology, both of which are rapidly taking genetic techniques, ingredients, and diagnostic tools, and reengineering precision treatments that have the potential to revolutionize the delivery of health care.

Part XI. Additional Pressing Issues Facing Our Health Care System, is comprised of four chapters describing pivotal issues and real-world pitfalls that every member of society may confront.

Chapter 33. *Pandemics and Public Health Emergency Threats*, details community health and safety in the event of a pandemic or bioterrorist attack, and the appearance of novel or previously controlled or eradicated infectious agents or biological toxins.

Chapter 34. *Women's Reproductive Rights*, focuses on the disparate provision of health care for procreation concerns, and addresses reproductive issues against the backdrop of how the newer forms of contraception and comprehensive maternity care coverage are falling out of reach for more women in the United States.

Chapter 35. *Nutrition and Food Safety*, examines the debate between the food industry and public health advocates over junk food, advertising and obesity.

Chapter 36. *Violence and Gun Injury Prevention*, addresses the quandary of the modern U.S. health care system, that while it is the most expensive in the world, Americans are neither healthier nor do they live longer than citizens in other countries.

Part XII. Conclusion, provides a brief overview of how the Affordable Care Act illustrates preventable behaviors and conditions and how the role of individual responsibility to maintain one's health is one of the most important issues the United States is confronting in terms of politics, economics, and the law.

Chapter 37. *Future Prospects: Health Care Management and the Law*, summarizes the principles in Chapters 1 through 36 of this text and provides an overview of the shifts that are occurring and that are required to develop policy frameworks for instituting changes in health care management and the law in each of the major health care sectors: life sciences, health care delivery, and medical products.

How to Use This Text

One of the strengths of the text is the consistent approach to topics in each chapter. Each chapter has been methodically developed so readers have the opportunity to understand what the law is, as well as the management principles that act as a foundation for the law. It can be used at both the introductory and advanced levels by changing the amount of guidance provided in each chapter. The same format is used in each chapter:

- **Learning Objectives** provide an overview of what is to be learned in each chapter.
- **Key Terms** are listed at the start of each chapter and are expanded upon in the text and Glossary.
- **Fact or Fiction** sections at the beginning of each chapter are short vignettes pulled from in-depth articles or drawn from actual court decisions pertinent to the chapter, demonstrating that society cannot always separate what is lawful conduct from what is wrongful or always know what the best course of action is.
- **Principles and Applications** explain the basics of management decision-making for those with little or no training in the law, namely: the importance of the law, its basic principles, and how it applies to practical management applications. Specific court decisions illustrate how management issues are currently being identified and legal principles applied to decisions in the real world. Understanding the legal reasoning of these court decisions will assist in reaching the best management decisions, particularly when such decisions may involve transforming the current legal order.
- **Management and Law Issues** dispersed throughout each chapter offer readers the opportunity to apply their decision-making skills on both sides of a policy issue to rationally arrive at management decisions.
- **Law Fact** revisits the *Fact or Fiction* that introduces every chapter at the end, and applies what has been put forth and decided by the courts thus far in each chapter.
- **Chapter Summary** summarizes the most important issues and principles covered in each chapter, pulling together practical knowledge and insight on emerging trends in reform of the U.S. health care industry.
- **Law Notes** provide more detailed material about the research cited in each chapter.
- **References** list the extensive body of current research that provides the foundation of this text.

Teaching Materials

The technology-enhanced learning tools accompanying this text are available via the online companion website, which hosts an extensive 2,000 + term glossary and two appendices.

Dramatic changes in the health care industry marketplace have pushed forward new questions about value creation. Because the global health care industry is a uniquely regulated environment, and there are genuine medical issues with people's lives at risk, integrity is very important. This text with help instructors prepare their readers for these challenges. A range of instructional tools will meet virtually every instructor's needs.

Instructor's Resources

The Instructor's Resources are computerized tools for instructional needs. These comprehensive and convenient online materials, available for download via the text's catalog page, are designed to enhance class discussion and measure reader progress. They provide a wide variety of valuable items to help instructors plan their courses and implement activities by chapter. The availability of these resources in an electronic format increases their value as teaching resources. They include:

- **Instructor Manuals** are provided for every chapter and include the following features:
  - **Learning Objectives**
  - **Key Terms**
  - **Review Questions** to help readers' assess their knowledge.
  - **Management and Law Issues** ask readers to analyze selected questions by reference to management principles and the law. This is where readers can reach reasoned conclusions based on the information in each chapter.
  - **Analysis of "New" Court Decisions** as they are decided.
  - **Further Your Knowledge** provides detailed material citing the research supporting the chapter narrative in the main text. At times, this section expands upon the ideas described in the main text, explains important caveats, or offers additional examples of a compelling fact. This section will help readers if they want to investigate certain topics in more depth.
  - **Web Links** provide the opportunity to do further research on the topics presented in each chapter.

- Short vignettes of actual court decisions pertinent to each chapter
- Group and individual activities, including summaries of film and television documentaries
- Links to websites providing additional materials to research cited in the chapter References in both the text and the study guide
- **PowerPoint presentations** are available to visually enhance lectures and aid readers in note taking
- **Computerized test bank** contains short answer, multiple choice, and true/false questions from each chapter. This versatile program enables instructors to create their own tests and to write additional questions

About the Authors

Donna K. Hammaker, a health law attorney, held a faculty appointment in the MBA program in biotechnology and health care industry management at the Pennsylvania State University where she taught health care management and health law for five years. She earned graduate degrees in law and government administration from Temple University School of Law and the Wharton School at the University of Pennsylvania, and completed graduate studies at the Hebrew University Faculty of Law and the London School of Economics. Before entering academia, Hammaker was a member of the Pennsylvania Bar, admitted to practice before the U.S. District Court for the Eastern District of Pennsylvania and the U.S. Court of Appeals for the Third Circuit. Hammaker was also president and chief executive officer of Collegiate Health Care, the nation's first inter-university managed care organization; co-founder of the College Consortium, a preferred provider organization serving the higher education market; counsel to Crozer-Chester Health System, the nation's 12th top grossing hospital system with over $5 billion in revenue, and counsel to West Pharmaceutical Services, a leading global packaging manufacturer for the medical products industry. Hammaker also served as a director at IMS Health, a leading global information and technology company, and Laventhol and Horwath (now Crowe Horwath), one of the nation's largest public accounting, consulting, and technology firms. A County Board of Assistance administrator in Pennsylvania's Medicaid program, Hammaker started her health care career as a traditional midwife. She has served on the adjunct faculty and taught graduate management and health law at Immaculata University, Rutgers University, Saint Joseph's University, Temple University, and Widener University. Hammaker and Thomas M. Knadig recently authored the text, *Health Care Ethics and the Law* (Jones & Bartlett Learning, 2016) with Sarah J. Tomlinson. The first edition of *Health Care Management and the Law* was authored with Sarah J. Tomlinson (Cengage, 2011). Hammaker is a member of the National Health Lawyers Association, Society of Hospital Attorneys, American Association of Nurse Attorneys, and the Pennsylvania and American Bar Associations.

Thomas M. Knadig, a Templeton scholar in science and religion, is a hospice chaplain with the University of Pennsylvania Health Care System and holds an adjunct faculty appointment at Widener University. He earned graduate degrees in education administration, philosophy, and theology from Widener University, University of Notre Dame, and Saint Mary's Seminary and University. Knadig completed post-doctoral studies at Oxford University in England, Massachusetts Institute of Technology, and the University of California-Berkeley. A former ordained Jesuit priest, Knadig was board chairman of Collegiate Health Care and executive director of the College Consortium. He has served on the adjunct faculty and taught core undergraduate ethics and religion courses at Immaculata University, LaSalle University, Saint Joseph's University, and Wheeling College. This is Knadig's second text publication on U.S. health care. Knadig is a member of the American Academy of Hospice and Palliative Medicine and the International Society for Science and Religion.

Hammaker and Knadig are members of the American College of Healthcare Executives.

Sarah J. Tomlinson is an attorney with the Office of the General Counsel of Fox Rothschild, LLP, a national law firm with over 700 attorneys in 22 offices nationwide. The firm has extensive experience as counsel to health care facilities and organizations and advises hundreds of physicians, medical groups, and health care institutions on litigation, corporate, regulatory, and transactional matters. Tomlinson, a member of the Pennsylvania Bar, is a doctoral student in public health with a focus on health policy at Temple University's College of Public Health, and has earned graduate degrees in law and business administration from Villanova University School of Law and Pennsylvania State University. She is also a member of the adjunct faculty at Immaculata University, where she teaches legal and social aspects of health care administration and nursing law. This is Tomlinson's third textbook publication involving health law.

Interaction with the Authors

The standard for this text is excellence. Therefore, every instructor that adopts it must have an excellent experience with both the core text and its ancillary teaching materials. The authors can be contacted with any questions regarding materials herein, to offer suggestions, or share teaching concerns. If we, as instructors of the next generation of health care managers, can somehow help our readers to reclaim a supple awareness of the hard and permanent truths of medicine, our health care system may gain back some of its lost status. Tocqueville believed that the greatest task facing his generation was not to erase the past and reconstruct the present but to recognize what was best in the past—what was essential—and to carry it forward. Our health care system will thrive again when the United States learns to acknowledge the force of Tocqueville's insight. But if our health care system is seen as nothing but a collection of arbitrary processes ripe for complete re-engineering, and social forces are treated as obstacles to be overcome rather than as boundaries to be reckoned with, the U.S. health care system will stay in its current crisis mode. Health law should not be a wholly owned subsidiary of any one management ideology. Instead, health law should both support and challenge all management ideologies.

Donna K. Hammaker
and
Thomas M. Knadig
with
Sarah J. Tomlinson

Acknowledgments

This text has been reviewed by individuals chosen for their diverse perspectives of the health industry and technical expertise. Joseph L. Fink, III, health law attorney and pharmacist, who is Professor of Pharmacy Law and Policy at the University of Kentucky College of Pharmacy, with joint faculty appointments as Professor of Health Services Management in the UK College of Public Health, Professor of Health Administration in the Martin School of Public Policy and Administration, and as Professor of Clinical Leadership and Management in the UK College of Health Sciences, reviewed and provided clear perspective on every chapter in the text. Emma Hopkins, a Tulane University student and research intern with the National Institute on Health Care Management and the Law, reviewed every chapter and provided student perspectives on key terms defining the U.S. health care system. The purpose of these independent reviews was to provide critical comments that would assist in making this text as sound as possible and to ensure objectivity. Yilmaz C. Kaymak, resident fellow with the National Institute on Health Care Management and the Law, managed the process of producing this text and contributed to Part VI of this text on Strategic Health Care Restructurings. At the start, research support for this text was provided by the Penn State University-Great Valley MBA program in Biotechnology and Health Industry Management under the leadership of Dr. Janice L. Dreachslin. The authors are also indebted to the following individuals for their assistance and review:

1. Anderson, Brent: Siemens Medical Services
2. Arujuna, Vinod: Boston Scientific
3. Benning, Shawn: McNeil Consumer Healthcare
4. Bezio, Timothy: Teva Pharmaceuticals
5. Bilo, Michael: Pfizer
6. Bogdanoff, Douglas: University of Pennsylvania Health Care System-Penn Home Care and Hospice
7. Burhams, Sara Baumler: Shire Pharmaceutical
8. Caranfa, Justin: Volcano Corporation
9. Cavanaugh, Jessica Choper: Zoetis
10. Crowland, Keith: Kaiser Permanente
11. Enright, Patty: ROI Performance Solutions
12. Epelbaum, Gleb: Fellheiner & Eichen LLP
13. Ertl, Melissa: Sodexo for SmithKlineBeecham
14. Hardy, Chris: Pfizer
15. Hopkins, Patrick: JP Morgan (formerly with Genzyme and Johnson & Johnson)
16. Jordan, William: Sanofi-Aventis
17. Klein, Jordan: University of Pennsylvania Health Care System-Pennsylvania Hospital
18. Liu, Jeffrey: Johnson & Johnson
19. MacGregor, John: University of Pennsylvania Health Care System-Hospital of the University of Pennsylvania and Perelman School of Medicine
20. McHale, Wendy Wesoloskie: Merck
21. Mennor, Robert: Siemens Medical Services
22. Mullen, Eliose: United Food and Commercial Workers Union (Ret.)
23. Nelson, Ginny: AmeriHealth
24. Spinks, Scott: Bristol Myers Squibb
25. Turnbull, Kathy: Independence Blue Cross
26. Weber, Michael: Janssen Pharmaceuticals, Inc., of Johnson & Johnson
27. Wright, Peter: ReMed
28. Wu, Jason (Jisheng): Frontage Clinical Services

How to Use This Text

One of the strengths of this text is the consistent approach to topics in each chapter. Each chapter has been methodically developed for use at both the introductory and advanced levels by merely changing the amount of guidance provided. The same format is used in each chapter:

IN BRIEF
provides a succinct overview of each chapter.

> ## IN BRIEF[LN1]
> This chapter describes how the greatest obstacle to transforming the U.S. health care system may be the nation's collective thinking. A simple idea in theory—that what is seen and acted upon is more a product of what is inside our heads than what is out in the world—has far-reaching implications for the nation's approach to health care. The nation's mental models may both create and limit opportunities.

FACT OR FICTION
sections at the beginning of each chapter are short vignettes of in-depth articles pulled from the headlines or drawn from actual court cases pertinent to the chapter, demonstrating that society cannot always separate fact from fiction or always know what the law is.

> ## FACT OR FICTION
>
> ### Gorillas in Our Field of Vision
>
> *When thinking of the U.S. health care system, the question to keep in mind is: are we failing to see the gorillas moving through our field of vision?*
>
> Human memory and perception are very malleable and can be much more so than we think. For instance, in one research study, subjects were asked to watch a video and count the number of times players with white shirts passed a basketball. Most of the subjects achieved a fairly accurate account of the passes, but less than half saw something more important: a person in a black gorilla costume walking right into the center of the action and then moving off. More than half the subjects were so involved in the counting task that they could not see the gorilla, an entire gorilla, right in front of their eyes!
>
> It is sobering to consider. Mental models and attention create blinders that limit what our human brain sees. We should be asking ourselves, what is it that makes mental models (relationships and concepts) of the U.S. health care system so difficult to recognize and change?
>
> — *See* Law Fact at the end of this chapter for the answer.

LAW FACT
explains the outcome of the "Fact or Fiction" section that introduces every chapter and applies what is put forth and has been decided thus far in each chapter.

> ## LAW FACT
>
> ### Gorillas in Our Field of Vision
>
> *When thinking of the U.S. health care system, the question to keep in mind is: are we failing to see the gorillas moving through our field of vision?*
>
> Yes. The gorillas in our nation's collective field of vision can be seen in cognitive neuroscience. Neural activity due to sensory stimuli disappears in the cortex. The sensory stimuli cease to exist. We do not really take in what we see. Stimulation flows into our brains, evoking an internal pattern, which our brains use to represent the external situation. We think we see and understand the "real" world of medical care in the United States, but we actually see what is already in our own minds: we see pre-existing mental models (relationships and concepts) of the U.S. health care system.
>
> — Chabris & Simons (2010); Wind & Crook (2007).

MANAGEMENT AND LAW ISSUES
dispersed throughout each chapter offer readers the opportunity to apply relevant court decisions on both sides of a health law issue to specific problems. Readers are then asked to describe and analyze selected controversies. This is where readers can reinforce practical insights gained in the chapter to assess or improve the outcome of timely issues facing the U.S. health care system.

> ## MANAGEMENT AND LAW ISSUES
>
> 1. Should Americans be concerned about the fact that the average tenure of U.S. Supreme Court Justices has increased to almost 30 years, when every other major court of its kind in the world has rejected life tenure and 49 out of 50 states have rejected it for their state supreme courts?
> 2. Is life tenure for a U.S. Supreme Court Justice a good idea or is it an 18th-century anachronism?

PRINCIPLES AND APPLICATIONS
is the heart of each chapter. It explains the basics of health law for readers with little or no legal background – namely, the importance of health law, its basic principles, and how it applies to practical management applications. Specific examples and cases illustrate how health law principles are applied in the real world.

Principles and Applications

A new business model is needed for the delivery of health care in the 21st century. A model that is less focused on treating diseases and more focused on public health needs and the prevention of disease is required. The focus of consumer-driven health care must move away from just costs and bottom lines and return to a place where science and innovation are once again the focal points of medicine. This would mean focusing on managing the health care of consumers as opposed to just focusing on managing costs.

LAW NOTES
at the conclusion of each chapter provide detailed endnotes citing the research supporting the "Principles and Applications" section in the main text. At times, the Law Notes expand upon the ideas described in the main text, explain important caveats, or offer additional examples of a compelling fact. The Law Notes are for those readers who want to investigate certain topics in more depth.

LAW NOTES

1. Valued employees create engaged external customers who foster organizational success by delivering positive financial outcomes (Dau-Schmidt, 2011). Companies where employees are valued outperform their competitors. Based on the results of 2.5 million employee surveys at 28 companies employing 920,000 employees, the share price of companies where employees felt they were valued increased an average of 16%, compared to an industry average of 6% (Dau-Schmidt & Haley, 2007). Where employees do not feel valued, firms saw their share prices increase by only 3% (Sirota & Klein, 2013) (*See generally* Dau-Schmidt, 2011; Dau-Schmidt et al., 2011).
2. Internal Revenue Code § 162m was designed to sharply limit discretion in setting performance-based pay. Compensation agreements are expected to specify objective compensation criteria tied to objective performance goals (*See* Treasury Regulation § 1.162-27(e)(2)(ii)). Discretion to adjust compensation amounts is severely limited; performance-pay compensation agreements can be reduced by the board or the compensation committee, but they cannot be increased after-the-fact (*See* Treasury Regulation § 1.162-27(e)(2)(iii)(A)).

COURT DECISION
challenging current administrative and judicial decisions are presented which focus on practical applications of the law in the real world of health care delivery and practice.

COURT DECISION
Right to Off-Label Access of Prescription Drugs

Sorrell v. IMS Health Inc.
[Attorney General of Vermont v. Data Miner]
564 U.S. 552 (U.S. Supreme Court 2011)

List of Court Decisions

AARP v. EEOC, 489 F.3d 558 (U.S. Court of Appeals for the 3rd Circuit 2007), *cert. denied*, 552 U.S. 1279 (U.S. Supreme Court 2008) (Medicare coverage in Chapter 5). Followed by *Fulghum v. Embarq Corp.*, 778 F.3d 1147 (U.S. Court of Appeals for the 10th Circuit 2015), *cert. denied*, 136 S.Ct. 537 (U.S. Supreme Court 2015). pp. **88, 95**

Abdullahi v. Pfizer, Inc., 562 F.3d 163 (U.S. Court of Appeals for the 2nd Circuit 2009), *cert. denied*, 561 U.S. 1041 (U.S. Supreme Court 2010) (clinical trials in developing nations in Chapter 19). pp. **390, 409–410**

Abigail Alliance v. Von Eschenbach, 495 F.3d 695 (U.S. Court of Appeals for the D.C. Circuit 2007), *cert. denied*, 552 U.S. 1159 (U.S. Supreme Court 2008) (patients' right to lifesaving experimental medications in Chapter 19). pp. **396–397**

Abney v. Amgen, Inc., 443 F.3d 540 (U.S. Court of Appeals for the 6th Circuit 2006) (obligation to provide experimental drugs to clinical trial participants in Chapter 19). pp. **398–399**

Acuna v. Turkish, 930 A.2d 416 (Supreme Court of New Jersey 2007), *cert. denied*, 555 U.S. 813 (U.S. Supreme Court 2008) (informed consent for abortions in Chapter 34). Followed by *Doe v. Planned Parenthood/Chicago Area*, *infra*. p. **732**

Addington v. Texas, 441 U.S. 418 (U.S. Supreme Court 1979) (legal standard to prove dangerous mental illness in Chapter 27). p. **584**

Aetna Health Inc. v. Davila, 542 U.S. 200 (U.S. Supreme Court 2004) (right to sue employers in Chapter 7; disruptive innovation in Chapter 8). pp. **40, 162**

Allen v. Illinois, 478 U.S. 364, 366 (U.S. Supreme Court 1986) (legal standard for confinement of dangerous mentally ill individuals in Chapter 27). p. **591**

Alliance for Bio-Integrity v. Shalala, 116 F.Supp.2d 166 (U.S. District Court for the District of Columbia 2000) (labeling of genetically modified foods in Chapter 35). Followed by *Humane Society of the United States v. Johanns*, 520 F.Supp.2d 8 (U.S. District Court for the District of Columbia 2007).

Allied Chemical & Alkali Workers of America v. Pittsburgh Plate Glass Co., 404 U.S. 157 (U.S. Supreme Court 1971) (employees' bargaining power in Chapter 11). p. **222**

American Chiropractic Association, Inc. v. Leavitt, 431 F.3d 812 (U.S. Court of Appeals for the D.C. Circuit 2005) (competitive managed care restrictions in Chapter 14). Followed by *Banner Health v. Burwell*, 126 F.Supp.3d 28 (U.S. District Court for the District of Columbia 2015). p. **288**

Anderson v. City of Hermosa Beach, 621 F.3d 1051 (U.S. Court of Appeals for the 9th Circuit 2010) (containment of HIV and highly contagious tuberculosis infections in Chapter 26). Followed by *Coleman v. City of Mesa*, 284 p.3d 863 (Supreme Court of Arizona 2012). pp. **553–554**

Arnett Physician Group, p.C. v. Greater Lafayette Health Services, Inc., 382 F.Supp.2d 1092 (U.S. District Court for the Northern District of Indiana 2005) (termination of hospital privileges by physician-owners of specialty hospital in Chapter 14). Followed by *Mercatus Group, LLC v. Lake Forest Hospital*, 695 F.Supp.2d 811 (U.S. District Court for the Northern District of Illinois 2010), *affirmed*, 641 F.3d 834 (U.S. Court of Appeals for the 7th Circuit 2011). p. **284**

Astra USA, Inc. v. Santa Clara County, 563 U.S. 110 (U.S. Supreme Court 2011) (affordable access to health care in Chapter 3). Followed by *Sioux Honey Association v. Hartford Fire Insurance Company*, 672 F.3d 1041 (U.S. Court of Appeals for the Federal Circuit 2012), *cert. denied*, 133 S.Ct. 126 (U.S. Supreme Court 2012). p. **59**

Atkins v. Virginia, 536 U.S. 304 (U.S. Supreme Court 2002) (defining intellectual disability in Chapter 27). p. **582**

Aventis Pasteur, Inc. v. Skevofilax, 914 A.2d 113 (Court of Appeals of Maryland 2007) (medical expert testimony in Chapter 22). p. **478**

Ayotte v. Planned Parenthood of Northern New England, 546 U.S. 320 (U.S. Supreme Court 2006) (parental notification for abortions in Chapter 34). Followed by *Toghill v. Commonwealth of Virginia*, 768 S.E.2d 674 (Supreme Court of Virginia 2015). pp. **727–728, 733**

Baxter v. State of Montana, 2009 MT 449 (Supreme Court of Montana 2009) (physician-assisted dying in Chapter 30). p. **632–634**

Bearder v. State of Minnesota, 806 N.W.2d 766 (Supreme Court of Minnesota 2011) (genetic privacy in newborn screening programs in Chapter 19). pp. **405–406**

Beeman v. Anthem Prescription Management, LLC, 564 Fed.Appx. 332 (U.S. Court of Appeals for the 9th Circuit 2014), *cert. denied*, 135 S.Ct. 476 (U.S. Supreme Court 2014) (constitutional protection of information held by retail pharmacies in Chapter 7). pp. **145–146**

Cutter v. Wilkinson, 544 U.S. 709, 719 (U.S. Supreme Court 2005) (free exercise of religion in Chapter 34). p. **716**

Daniel v. American Board of Emergency Medicine, 428 F.3d 408 (U.S. Court of Appeals for the 2nd Circuit 2005) (physician credentialing in Chapter 14). Followed by *Hessein v. American Board of Anesthesiology, Inc.*, 628 Fed. Appx. 116 (U.S. Court of Appeals for the 3rd Circuit 2015). pp. **285–286**

Daubert v. Merrell Dow Pharmaceuticals, Inc., 509 U.S. 579 (U.S. Supreme Court 1993) (scientific evidence in court proceedings in Chapters 16 and 22). pp. **327, 340, 476, 477**

Davis v. Rennie, 264 F.3d 86 (U.S. Court of Appeals for the 1st Circuit 2001), *cert. denied*, 535 U.S. 1053 (U.S. Supreme Court 2002) (violation of patient rights in Chapter 27). Followed by *Clifford v. Maine General Medical Center*, 91f A.3d 567 (Supreme Court of Maine 2014). pp. **587–588**

DeJesus v. U.S. Department of Veterans Affairs, 479 F.3d 271 (U.S. Court of Appeals for the 3rd Circuit 2007) (liability for deaths caused after negligently discharging mentally ill patient from treatment in Chapter 27). Followed by *Squeo v. Norwalk Hospital Association,* 113 A.3d 932 (Supreme Court of Connecticut 2015). pp. **579–580**

Diamond v. Chakrabarty, 447 U.S. 303 (U.S. Supreme Court 1980) (gene patents in Chapter 32). p. **8**

DiCarlo v. St. Mary Hospital, 530 F.3d 255 (U.S. Court of Appeals for the 3rd Circuit 2008) (hospital charges for the uninsured in Chapter 6). Followed by *Limberg v. Sanford Medical Center Fargo*, 2016 N.D. LEXIS 123 (Supreme Court of North Dakota 2016). pp. **112–113**

District of Columbia v. Heller, 554 U.S. 570 (U.S. Supreme Court 2008) *affirmed in related proceedings*, 801 F.3d 264 (U.S. Court of Appeals for the D.C. Circuit 2015), *rehearing denied*, 2016 U.S. App. LEXIS 3678 (U.S. Court of Appeals for the D.C. Circuit 2016) (federal regulations of firearms in Chapter 36).

Doe v. Planned Parenthood/Chicago Area, 956 N.E.2d 564, 572 (Appellate Court of Illinois, First District, Sixth Division 2011), *appeal denied*, 962 N.E.2d 481 (Supreme Court of Illinois 2011) (duty of doctors to advise patients prior to an abortion in Chapter 34). pp. **731,732**

Doe v. Shalala, 122 Fed. Appx. 600 (U.S. Court of Appeals for the 4th Circuit 2004), *cert denied*, 546 U.S. 822 (U.S. Supreme Court 2005) (research on human embryonic stem cells in Chapter 31). pp. **648, 671**

Doe ex rel. Tarlow v. District of Columbia, 489 F.3d 376 (U.S. Court of Appeals for the D.C. Circuit 2007), *reconsideration denied*, 2007 U.S. App. LEXIS 26150 (U.S. Court of Appeals for the D.C. Circuit 2007) (abortion decisions on behalf of intellectually disabled people in Chapter 27). pp. **580–581**

Drug Mart Pharmacy Corp. v. American Home Products. Corp., 472 F.Supp.2d 385 (U.S. District Court for the Eastern District of New York 2007), *affirmed, Cash & Henderson Drugs, Inc. v. Johnson & Johnson*, 799 F.3d 202 (U.S. Court of Appeals for the 2nd Circuit 2015) (antitrust compliance in Chapter 14). p. **290**

Eastern Railroad Presidents Conference v. Noerr Motor Freight, Inc., 365 U.S. 127 (U.S. Supreme Court 1961) (First Amendment protection of no-compete agreements with generic manufacturers in Chapter 16). p. **330**

EEOC v. Watkins Motor Lines, Inc., 463 F.3d 436 (U.S. Court of Appeals for the 6th Circuit 2006), *superseded by statute*, Americans with Disabilities Act Amendments of 2008, 42 U.S.C.A. § 12101, *et seq.* (2009) (lifestyle discrimination: obesity in Chapter 10). pp. **196, 210**

Enloe Medical Center v. National Labor Relations Board, 433 F.3d 834 (U.S. Court of Appeals for the D.C. Circuit 2005) (management's refusal to bargain in Chapter 11). Followed by *Heartland Plymouth Court MI, LLC v. National Labor Relations Board*, 2016 U.S. App. LEXIS 8164 (U.S. Court of Appeals for the D.C. Circuit 2016). pp. **218, 232**

Equal Access for El Paso, Inc. v. Hawkins, 509 F.3d 697 (U.S. Court of Appeals for the 5th Circuit 2007), *cert. denied*, 555 U.S. 811 (U.S. Supreme Court 2008), *on remand*, 562 F.3d 724 (U.S. Court of Appeals for the 5th Circuit 2009) (equal access to medically necessary care in Chapter 4). pp. **74–75, 83**

Ernst J. v. Stone, 452 F.3d 186 (U.S. Court of Appeals for the 2nd Circuit 2006) (involuntary commitment of mentally ill people in Chapter 27). pp. **582–583**

Finch v. Commonwealth Health Insurance Connector Authority, 959 N.E.2d 970 (Supreme Judicial Court of Massachusetts 2012) (charitable care accountability in Chapter 6). p. **121**

First National Maintenance Corp. v. National Labor Relations Board, 452 U.S. 666 (U.S. Supreme Court 1981) (employees' bargaining power in Chapter 11). p. **222**

Fleischman v. Albany Medical Center, 639 F.3d 28 (U.S. Court of Appeals for the 2nd Circuit 2011) (antitrust compliance in Chapter 14). p. **290**

Florida v. U.S. Department of Health and Human Services, 648 F.3d 1235 (U.S. Court of Appeals for the 11th Circuit 2011), *affirmed in part and reversed in part*, 132 S.Ct. 2566 (U.S. Supreme Court 2012) (cost of insurance regulation; access to affordable health insurance in Chapter 3 challenges to health care reform in Chapter 12). pp. **42, 57, 60, 245**

Flynn v. Holder, 684 F.3d 852 (U.S. Court of Appeals for the 9th Circuit 2011) (compensation of bone marrow donors in Chapter 31). p. **662–667**

PART I

INTRODUCTION TO HEALTH CARE MANAGEMENT

Part I provides an overview of the management issues facing the U.S. health care system.

CHAPTER 1

Processes for Thinking About the U.S. Health Care System

"How strange is the lot of us mortals? Each of us is here for a brief sojourn; for what purpose he knows not, though he sometimes thinks he senses it. But without deeper reflection one knows from daily life that one exists for other people—first of all for those upon whose smiles and well-being our own happiness is wholly dependent, and then for the many, unknown to us, to whose destinies we are bound by the ties of sympathy. A hundred times every day I remind myself that my inner and outer life are based on the labors of other men, living and dead, and that I must exert myself in order to give in the same measure as I have received and am still receiving...."

— **Albert Einstein** From The World as I See It by Albert Einstein. Copyright 1956 1984 The Estate of Albert Einstein. All Rights Reserved.

IN BRIEF[LN1]

This chapter describes how the greatest obstacle to transforming the U.S. health care system may be the nation's collective thinking. A simple idea in theory—that what is seen and acted upon is more a product of what is inside our heads than what is out in the world—has far-reaching implications for the nation's approach to health care. The nation's mental models may both create and limit opportunities.

LEARNING OBJECTIVES

Upon completion of this chapter readers should be able to:

1. Explain how the nation's collective thinking may be the greatest obstacle to transforming the U.S. health care system.
2. Understand the fallacy of imputing internal mental models to correspond with external sensory stimuli.
3. Begin to cultivate how best to see things differently in the health care industry.
4. Consider new ideas while retaining the best of the old and current ideas.
5. Uncover sources for new ideas to transform the U.S. health care system.
6. Establish and evaluate various perspectives from which to understand the U.S. health care system.

KEY TERMS

Adaptive disconnects	Compliance overhead	Deductibles
Affordable Care Act of 2010	Copays	Electronic health records
Cognitive neuroscience	Cost limits	End-users
Coinsurance	Cost-shifting	Evidence-based medicine

Fairness
Federal tax code
Genomics
Health care delivery systems
Health information network
Health Information Technology and
   Economic and Clinical Health Act
   of 2009

Health status
High-deductible health insurance
   plans
Incentives
Internal models
Mental models
Micro-trends
Minimum coverage provision

National Organization for Rare
   Disorders
Neuroscience of mental models
Orphan Drug Act of 1983
Precision medicine
Private health insurance premiums
Reprocessed medical devices
Right to health care

FACT OR FICTION

Gorillas in Our Field of Vision

When thinking of the U.S. health care system, the question to keep in mind is: are we failing to see the gorillas moving through our field of vision?

   Human memory and perception are very malleable and can be much more so than we think. For instance, in one research study, subjects were asked to watch a video and count the number of times players with white shirts passed a basketball. Most of the subjects achieved a fairly accurate account of the passes, but less than half saw something more important: a person in a black gorilla costume walking right into the center of the action and then moving off. More than half the subjects were so involved in the counting task that they could not see the gorilla, an entire gorilla, right in front of their eyes!

   It is sobering to consider. Mental models and attention create blinders that limit what our human brain sees. We should be asking ourselves, what is it that makes mental models (relationships and concepts) of the U.S. health care system so difficult to recognize and change?

— *See* Law Fact at the end of this chapter for the answer.

Principles and Applications

The gorillas that we see (or fail to see) in our field of vision are determined by our **mental models**, or the hypotheses in our minds as to what exists (subjects in shirts passing a basketball or something more). This text defines mental models in terms of **cognitive neuroscience**. Mental models are internal patterns in the brain evoked by neural activity. Sensory stimuli flow into the cortex and evoke internal patterns, which the brain uses to represent the external situation. We think we see the real world, but we actually see the neural patterns or mental models (or structured relationships and concepts) already in our minds. We do not see the sensory stimuli we take in; we see the mental models evoked by our neural activity (*See generally* Freeman, 2001 and 1995).[LN2]

   The focus of this chapter and, indeed, this text is how we can best cultivate an ability to see health care differently, without casting aside all new ideas as preposterous, and without losing all perspective on the past and present. The goal is to embark on a journey toward discovering a better U.S. health care system by considering new ideas while retaining the best of the old and present ideas. For instance, we should be asking:

- What fresh perspectives can be discovered by exploring new medical technologies, new medical products, and new and different systems of delivering health care to different consumer segments?
- What wisdom and opportunities can be found in seemingly out-of-the-ordinary ideas?
- Where should these new ideas come from?
- Which perspectives should be retained in order to make sense of new ones?

The nation's collective thinking may be the obstacle to the impossible concept of an effective, efficient, high-quality health care system that is accessible to every member of society. To transform the nation's health care organizations to achieve this quality health care for everyone will require a transformation of our idea of what constitutes health (Keith, 2015).

New Approach to Health Care

Changing the nation's thinking about health care creates powerful opportunities for action. The health care industry plays a major role in the U.S. economy and by almost any objective account, a highly positive role. The health care industry employs over 12 million Americans and accounts for 1 out of 8 jobs in the United States (BLS, 2014). Admitting blindness in completely understanding such a complex system could be the beginning of newfound wisdom; in other words, any reform of the U.S. health care system will first require acknowledging the gorilla in the room.

The debate about the **right to health care**, access, **fairness**, efficiency, and quality are the players in the white shirts. The gorilla is the $2.6 trillion in health care spending each year (CMS, 2015). The total effective cost for health care is funded from the following:

- Federal budget
- Out-of-pocket costs covered by consumers
- Private, third-party health insurers
- State budgets

The federal budget funds nearly three-quarters of the total health care spending, up from over half ten years ago (CBO, 2016). Clearly, health care costs are being shifted to the federal government. While **private health insurance premiums** have increased to $849 billion (CMS, 2015), health care costs are increasingly being shifted to individuals. As **high-deductible health insurance plans** are taking more of the market share, out-of-pocket spending for health care increased to $311 billion (CMS, 2015).

Health care costs are obfuscated by **cost-shifting** from the government programs (Medicare, Medicaid, and the Children's Health Insurance Program) and the subsidizing of employer-provided health insurance under the **federal tax code**. These two hidden sources of funds hide the true costs of health care (Pasquale, 2014). Health care costs were 18% of the gross domestic product when the gross domestic product was $17.4 trillion in 2014 (CMS, 2015; World Bank, 2016). Obviously, this percentage for health care spending could not have continued to grow indefinitely without comprehensive reforms; the danger was that the U.S. health care system, if left as it was before the **Affordable Care Act of 2010**, would have resolved this cost problem by gradually denying basic coverage to more and more people (*See* 42 U.S.C.A. §§ 18001 *et seq.*).

Nevertheless, questions about funding and the increased shifting of costs to consumers indicate the U.S. health care system is still not sustainable in its current form (Altman, 2015). Much of the escalating costs are attributable to the development of new treatments and other medical technologies (Krause & Saver, 2014). Today, people get joints replaced and have laparoscopic surgery to repair damage that past generations simply learned to live with; health care costs are increasing because there are now more expensive medical products and ways of using old products. On a per-capita basis, the United States spends about twice as much as most other industrialized economies without garnering any tangible benefits on health, infant mortality, or longevity.

How do insured consumers make sense of data like this when:

- 20% of American households face problems paying their insurance **copays**, **deductibles**, or **coinsurance**
- 43% postpone needed medical care
- 41% do not fill their prescriptions
- 62% procrastinate about dental care

(Kaiser, 2015).

Is the U.S. health care system working as well as it could or do the mental models about what is going on need to be modified?

Data Driven

We often think the world is how we see it and that the facts are the facts as we know them. Each of the data-driven facts in this chapter is explained in the remaining chapters of this text, along with citations to their sources of authority. The management principles and the laws surrounding these facts are also described.

Hypothesis Driven

Although we are data driven, we are also driven by hypotheses, or our mental models. Consider what you think about once you read these facts. Are there any underlying hypotheses behind these facts?

FEATURE BOX 1-1

What Is in Our Nation's Collective Mind?

1. *What is the meaning of these data-driven facts?*

   - About one-tenth of the U.S. population has no health insurance, and most of them are earning middle-class incomes; this lack of basic coverage causes two deaths every hour.
   - Although **evidence-based medicine** can help pinpoint which treatments are best for which conditions, patients often still do not receive the best available treatment because physicians are not aware of the best treatment or have their own reasons for not using it.
   - Estimates indicate 90 million people in the United States live with a preventable chronic disease, the ongoing care for which amounts to 75% of the annual $2.6 trillion health care budget.
   - From the estimated $1.9 trillion employers spend on health care costs each year, over 60% of the costs go toward treating tobacco-related illnesses.
   - **Reprocessed medical devices** are a cause for concern, as the FDA standards are not always strictly adhered to, patients are not necessarily informed they are receiving a reprocessed device, and such devices are often obtained from unregulated sources, such as the Internet.
   - Top executives at the U.S. health care systems are compensated with multimillion-dollar salaries and lavish benefits, seemingly without regard to performance, while top-performing lower wage employees are often not paid living wages.
   - While tax-exempt hospitals receive over $12.6 billion in tax exemptions each year, they are not necessarily required to offer free or reduced-cost care to the uninsured or underinsured in return for their tax exemption.
   - Almost one-third of the surgeries performed on Medicare patients are unnecessary.
   - One-third of medical spending is devoted to services that do not improve health or the quality of care, much of which may actually make things worse for patients?
   - Reproductive health needs are not adequately met in the United States, as evidenced by the high rate of teen pregnancies, unintended pregnancies, abortions of unwanted pregnancies, and the lack of access to birth control.
   - The largest portion of hospital expenses are incurred in the last few weeks of life.
   - The recent increase in weight-related chronic illnesses in the United States coincides with the change in American eating habits, with dietary intake consisting mostly of highly processed, prepackaged, and ready-made meals high in carbohydrates and sodium content; fully one-third of the daily Calories Americans eat are from outside the home at fast-food and chain restaurants.
   - While the biggest burdens to the U.S. health care system are depression and gun violence, they receive scant attention in the health care reform debates; yet the cost of gun violence in the United States exceeds to the cost of illnesses from smoking and obesity combined.

2. *What is the explanation underlying these facts and what needs further investigation?*

   - The United States spends more on health care than any other country in the world, yet ranks 28th in life expectancy: is this because we are the only industrialized nation in the world that does not provide medically needed care for everyone, or could it be the open immigration and economic policies of the United States?
   - Should the United States bear the highest burden in the world for research and development of prescription drugs because it has one of the world's highest incomes per capita?

3. *Should the nation's leaders examine the hypotheses underlying some of these facts as they undertake reform of the U.S. health care system, or would they simply be reinventing the wheel based on prior reform efforts and the Affordable Care Act?*

FEATURE BOX 1-1 (CONTINUED)

- If the nation's health laws and regulations are complex, exceedingly nuanced, and incomplete, does this regulatory complexity drive up health care costs and **compliance overhead**? If so, is this one reason why at least one-third of the U.S. health care costs are the result of management and administrative overhead expenses, or is this one-third ratio the norm for U.S. service industries in general?
- Should the United States spend $770 billion every year to administer a heavily regulated, mostly private entity-based health care system, where the government covers almost three-fourths of the costs?

4. *Is there a single, coherent hypothesis that makes sense of all these assorted facts?*

- Should the nation grant hospitals over $13 billion in tax exemptions each year, while their executives are paid multimillion dollar salaries and granted lavish benefits, regardless of performance?
- Or are hospital administrators at the nation's leading tax-exempt health care systems being paid a rate comparable to executives in other sectors of the economy, and if so, is health care different?

5. *Is the United States being mindful of the process of transforming its health care system?*

- The United States has one of the highest infant mortality rates in the world; is this because reproductive services are not available to many women or because more babies survive high-risk pregnancies?
- If evidence-based medicine is not being used by most health care providers, is this why one-third of the nation's medical spending is devoted to services that do not improve health or the quality of care, and may make things worse, or is this a faulty association?

6. *Should the United States rush to implement health care reforms given the rapidly escalating costs of a stressed health care system?*

- When the United States decided to provide medical coverage to every member of society, what happened when tens of millions of people were suddenly added to the health care system?
- Did such a change greatly increase the need for primary care physicians, physician assistants, nurse practitioners, and advance practice nurses?
- Can the nation's staffing needs continue to be met, even with imports of foreign health care professionals?

(*E.g.,* Gregory et al., 2014; Johnson & Stukel, 2016; NBGH, 2012; Surgeon General, 2010.)

Mind Barriers

There is a need to continually examine the mental models that shape thinking on health care reform (*Cf.* Wind & Crook, 2007). We may think the barriers to reform are too complex or that established interests are too entrenched to change, but often these barriers to creating the health care system this nation should have are simply in the nation's collective mind (*See* Wharton, 2005). For instance, consider rare diseases. Abbey Meyers' son suffered from Tourette syndrome but was being helped by an experimental medication manufactured by McNeil Consumer Healthcare, a division of Johnson & Johnson. When McNeil dropped the medication because the patient population was too small to be profitable, Abbey Meyers became a consumer advocate. Her crusade: change the law to create incentives for the pharmaceutical industry to develop brand-name drugs for rare diseases. She founded the **National Organization for Rare Disorders**, and, within two years, the FDA approved a medication for her son's Tourette syndrome. But Abbey Meyers did not stop crusading once her son's health needs were met. She continued to pull together other consumers with rare diseases, and, together, they made their voices heard. Congress responded to the group's call for new treatments with the **Orphan Drug Act of 1983**, giving the pharmaceutical industry a seven-year monopoly for bringing new products for rare diseases to market (Thomas, 2015). *See* Orphan Drug Act of 1983, 21 U.S.C.A. §§ 301 *et seq.*

The mental model of a modest sideline envisioned for the pharmaceutical industry has instead become a multibillion-dollar business. What changed? The impossible: the medical products industry discovered they could profit in small markets. The Orphan Drug Act became a powerful boost to the emerging biotechnology industry.

Today, more than half of the biopharmaceutical products manufactured by the biotechnology industry are for rare diseases. Amgen and Genentech, two of the largest biotechnology firms in the world, were built on orphan drugs for rare diseases. What changed? The impossible: collective thinking about how to provide incentives to the medical products industry worked to motivate the industry to develop new drugs.

New mental models were created and orphan drugs to treat rare diseases suddenly became profitable. Abbey Meyers never envisioned such monumental changes would arise from her simple efforts to obtain the right medication for her son's Tourette syndrome (Lee, 2014). Meyers proved the impossible was possible. The only barriers to achieving her goal were in McNeil's corporate mind. Consider:

- How can the nation challenge the forces that block health care reforms?
- What are the challenges and risks of adopting new mental models of health care, and is the nation ready for them?
- What are the potential blind spots in the U.S. health care system?
- What is holding back implementation of U.S. health care reforms?
- What possibilities would be revealed if barriers to reform no longer existed?
- How can the nation rid itself of obstacles and barriers to change?

Testing Reality

Instead of accepting the U.S. health care system as it is, extensive testing must be conducted continuously to find out what the system really consists of, which parts of it are working, and which parts of it can be improved. Areas that are being explored today include:

- How can the health care system motivate individuals to adopt behaviors that prevent most chronic diseases and illnesses?
- What incentives can be created to insure the uninsured and provide access to affordable health insurance to every member of society?
- What will induce health care providers to use evidence-based medicine?

It is not impossible to create the right insurance incentives; the nation simply needs to change its thinking, like Abbey Meyers did when she needed a medication for her son. Perhaps new hypotheses and new mental models should be developed to achieve universal medical coverage with:

- A **minimum coverage provision**
- Management of risks that can prove profitable
- Mechanisms to ensure insurance availability
- Subsidies to ensure affordability

Neurology of Internal Patterns

Neurology has shown that we do not take in what we really see. You likely did not really see the data-driven facts at the start of this chapter. As stimulation flows into the brain, it evokes an internal pattern the brain uses to represent the external situation, so we are not aware that what we are purportedly seeing and thinking is what is actually already in our own minds (Wind & Crook, 2007).

Walter Freeman, a biologist, theoretical neuroscientist, and philosopher at the University of California at Berkeley, has conducted pioneering research on how brains generate meaning (Freeman, 1975). Freeman discovered that the neural activity due to sensory stimuli disappears in the cortex. It disappears! Humans do not really take in what they actually see (Wharton, 2005). We do not always see the gorilla in the room. When stimulation flows into the brain, it evokes in its place an internal pattern, which the brain uses to represent the external situation. We think we see the real world, but we actually see what is already in our minds (*See generally* Freeman, 2001 and 2000). We should ask ourselves:

- Does this text cause indigestion from too much data or does it cause hunger because it does not provide enough information, and what needs to be done to respond to both sets of feelings?
- How can this text be used to come up with different ways of viewing health care?
- What chapters are limited by an overly broad perspective, and is it possible to zoom in to examine the details more closely?
- What chapters are overwhelming with information, and is it possible to zoom out to look at the broader context?

Power of Internal Models

If we are not aware of the power of our **internal models**, we may just accept what we think we see as reality. This misunderstanding of reality can be limiting, and sometimes even dangerous (Wharton, 2005). We tend to be comfortable and dependent upon our current mental models (Wind & Crook, 2007). Comprehensive changes to the U.S. health care system opened everyone up to uncertainty and risk, along with perhaps your job, or your provider's or employer's way of doing business.

Most people and organizations are risk averse, staying within their comfort zones, even if it causes increasing problems (Wind & Crook, 2007). For instance, Merck stayed with its blockbuster drug marketing model, even when patients died from Vioxx. The biotechnology industry continues to sell its orphan drugs at exorbitantly high prices even as Congress debates changing the laws that enabled biotechnology to evolve into a multibillion-dollar business, using the same mental models the pharmaceutical industry used when the generic drug industry arose to challenge its pricing of brand-name drugs.

Filtered Thinking

Once we know our view of health care is shaped and filtered by our own thinking, we recognize the need to constantly test our mental models against the health care system this nation *should* have (*See* Wharton, 2005). We need to examine our collective thinking and ask:

- Do the medical services most Americans think they have meet the expectations of what Americans want and need in health care?[LN3]
- Does the U.S. health care system meet the needs of most Americans, and do most Americans think it will continue to do so?
- How can the current health care system design new experiments to test the limits of mental models or gain new insights that might suggest new models for implementing reforms of the U.S. health care system?
- Is the U.S. health care system worth the costs, and how might the health care system look without this cost limitation?

Test Mental Models

Individuals and organizations must constantly test their mental models instead of simply accepting what they think things are. This testing and retesting will help determine what the facts are and what works. We may take two steps forward and one rational step back.

Medical Experimentation and Innovation

The unmet medical needs facing the U.S. health care system are considerable. For instance:

- About 1,600 people die every day from cancer.
- An estimated 5.3 million Americans have Alzheimer's disease, a number that is projected to double by 2025.

- There are approximately 27 million heart disease patients and about 70 people die every hour with the disease as their primary diagnosis.
- About 770,000 people are injured every year because of adverse drug events.
- Thousands of patients today suffer from rare genetic disorders; most people have never even heard of these diseases, but they traumatize patients, and leave behind a trail of broken, frustrated families.

(Alzheimer's Association, 2016; Deyette, 2015; NCHS, 2015a and 2015b).

Yet, the system attributes the growth in health care costs to the development of new treatments and other medical technologies (CBO, 2016). How should the U.S. health care system reconcile the need for medical innovation to treat cancer, Alzheimer's disease, heart disease, and rare genetic disorders with the need to reduce or slow cost growth? The unspoken hypothesis—that rationing or controlling spending on medical innovation is one way to control health care costs—shows the need to consider whether the nation's current mental models, which focus on spending, still fit in a world of rapid medical innovation.

Ideally, American medical innovation should not be limited because of costs. There has to be a way to remove this restraint. What possibilities might be obtainable if health care costs were no longer a limitation? U.S. consumers will not stand for a decrease in the pace of adoption of new medical treatments or procedures or limiting the breadth of their application (Lechleiter, 2016). In all likelihood, the United States is not going to ration medical care as has been done in Europe. The United States will always allow Americans to buy what they want; however, they may only be allowed to buy the most innovative treatments with their own money, especially care for preventable health conditions.

Preventable Health Conditions Versus Treatable Conditions

What if the U.S. health care system focused on where the $2.6 trillion in health care costs are being spent? According to the World Health Organization's Commission on the Social Determinants of Health, 50% of health status, or what makes individuals ill or well, is determined by health behavior (CSDH, 2008; Davidson, 2015). This supports the research findings that most chronic illnesses are preventable (Fleck, 2014; Sage & McIlhattan, 2014).

As shown in **FIGURE 1-1**, of the $2.6 trillion spent annually on health care, 80% is devoted to the 10% that determines individuals' **health status**; less than 4% is devoted to improving health behavior and preventive medicine (Schoen et al., 2015). At issue is whether the nation's priorities should be realigned so that 80% of the spending is

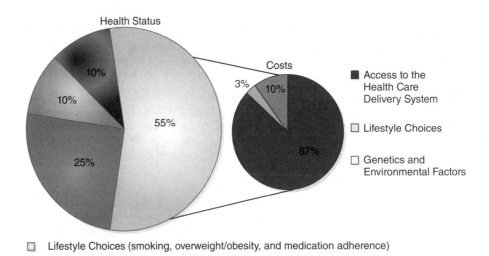

FIGURE 1-1 Attributes of Individual Health Status Compared to Health Care Costs

Data from: Schoen, C., et al. (2015). *State trends in the cost of employer health insurance coverage.* New York, NY: The Commonwealth Fund; Solar, O., & Irwin, A. (2010). *A conceptual framework for analysis and action on the social determinants of health.* Geneva, Switzerland: World Health Organization, Commission on Social Determinants of Health.

directed to the 50% that determines health status. If the focus of health care were to change, some issues to consider might become:

- What health conditions are preventable?
- What level of health care will be provided for preventable health conditions, so as to provide a financial incentive for people to change their behaviors to prevent chronic disease and illness in the first place?
- When are health conditions preventable

The hypotheses to modify health behaviors and prevent health conditions from ever occurring are different from the mental model to access the health care delivery system to treat these same conditions only after they have developed.

World of Constant Change and Evolution

Debates in neuroscience focus on the brain as a computer versus an evolutionary-based biological system, and the influence of nature versus nurture in shaping thinking (Wind & Crook, 2007). The human brain constantly changes and evolves over time. Over one billion neurons continually die and regenerate. Several trillion synapses are continually destroyed and re-created. The human brain selects and reinforces or weakens certain synapses to forge the complex neural structures that determine thinking (Wind & Crook, 2007). Individuals reshape their neural models every day through their day-to-day experiences and thinking.

Individual Micro-Trends

This idea of reshaping the brain's neural models day-by-day brings the issue of **micro-trends** to the forefront. Forget about huge, sweeping universal changes in health care (mega-trends); the biggest trends today are micro: small, under-the-radar patterns of individual behaviors that take on real power when propelled by modern communications and an increasingly independently minded population (Penn & Zalesne, 2009). In the United States, intense identity groups (micro-trends) can:

- Create new markets for risk management of health care costs
- Produce political change to bring about universal health care or more evidence-based medicine or financial incentives for observing healthy diet and exercise
- Spark a social movement that focuses on behavioral change and preventive medicine

The chapters in this text attempt to identify important health care trends in the law as they are happening. Small patterns of change and reform can be detected in state legislatures and in the appellate federal and state courts (Helveston, 2015), and even sometimes in Congress.

Power of Impossible Thinking

Practical steps to understand, and perhaps change, thinking about the U.S. health care system, include:

- Becoming explicitly aware of why people see the U.S. health care system the way they do and what that implies
- Testing the relevance of current mental models against the rapidly changing health care space and seeing if they still fit or whether the models need to change and new ones need to be generated
- Developing a portfolio of mental models, which:
  - Minimizes the risk of switching models entirely
  - Allows the use of models that work best for particular situations
  - Prevents new models from becoming dogma, an absolute transformation, or revolution
- Overcoming the inhibitors to change and reform by reshaping the infrastructure that supports the old mental models and changing the thinking of others
- Quickly generating and acting upon new mental models by experimenting and continuing to assess and strengthen hypotheses and models

(*See generally* Wind & Crook, 2007).

Adaptive Disconnects

Adaptive disconnects in the U.S. health care system occur when *everyone* adapts their thinking at different rates. This is shown by:

- Differences in facts and opinions as to what health care reforms are needed or not needed
- Differences in perspectives between health insurers and the insured
- Different perceptions of what should be done from varying disciplines in the medical products industry, such as product development, finance, operations, and marketing
- Distinction between the goals and priorities of regulators and the regulated
- Divergence of views within **health care delivery systems** between administrative and clinical staff, and among health care professionals and consumers
- Variations between what is considered ethical and unethical, right and wrong, legal and illegal

To arrive at acceptance of real reform of the U.S. health care system, perhaps someone should seek out the most complex and sophisticated minds and put them in a room together, and have them ask each other the questions they are asking themselves. For instance, directing more than a billion dollars in federal funds for comparative effectiveness research to help determine whether medical treatments and devices are worth the money is much easier than coming up with new thinking about the need for these treatments in the first place.

Support of Old Mental Models

The practical infrastructures and routines that support *old* mental models must be addressed. It is significantly more difficult to shift the nation's emphasis upstream from managing diseases to preventing them; this is not how the U.S. health care system is currently structured. It is not enough to simply change one's thinking about health care, we also need to ask:

- How does the choice of mental models shape each health care sector's position on issues and their decisions about them?
- What mental models does the U.S. health care system currently use?
- What other mental models could each of the health care sectors use?

(*See generally* Wind & Crook, 2007).

Misaligned Incentives

Similarly, **incentives** in place in the U.S. health care system are sometimes misaligned, making it difficult for new medical products and technologies to gain acceptance. While a new medical product or technology might produce better outcomes than an existing treatment, there can be resistance to its adoption. An example of this misalignment is the introduction of Gleevec, a drug produced by Novartis Pharmaceuticals, to fight chronic myeloid leukemia. While Gleevec is expensive (at about $76,000 per year), it can obviate the need for a $360,000 bone marrow transplant. The drug is potentially beneficial to patients, but economic calculations as to how much money a medication saves are not always made when it prevents patients from having surgery (McClellan, 2016). The health care system does not always reflect economic benefits to individual patients and we need to ask:

- What mental models underlie the decisions and actions of Novartis and hospital transplant centers or insurers and leukemia patients?
- What are some varied mental models for diagnosing chronic myeloid leukemia, and how do they change the treatment options available?
- Will there be a market for $360,000 bone marrow transplants in the foreseeable future?

Zooming In and Zooming Out

In light of the immense complexity of the nation's health care industry, leaders must learn to both zoom in and zoom out. When examined in detail, parts of a complex system, like almost any phenomenon, will seem to be unstable, even fluctuating wildly. For instance, it is important for the biotechnology industry to develop the ability to zoom in and zoom out in its thinking. Zooming in focuses on details underlying core medical technologies. Zooming out is a sense of how those technologies will play out in the larger health care space, such as how society will pay for the advanced medical technologies being developed.

Process of Making Sense of Things

Cognitive neuroscience studies how the brain works. We must focus on what to do with the facts and data we receive and understand the process of making sense of things. While genetics provides the basis of whom we are as individuals, experience strengthens and weakens genetic capabilities.

Understanding the Forces

Health care systems, like individuals, can focus on the forces that shape and reshape the mental models of their space. For instance, $35 billion is being directed to health information technology by the federal government for implementation of a national health information network (*See* **Health Information Technology and Economic and Clinical Health Act of 2009**, 42 U.S.C.A. §§ 17931 *et seq.*). Yet there is no evidence that this investment is achieving its goals of increasing efficiency, reducing costs, or improving the quality of health care (Deyette, 2015). To ensure success, focus should be directed to:

- Developing rewards and incentives for implementation
- Education on how **electronic health records** have been shown to reduce medical errors and costs to counterbalance forces claiming turmoil from this effort to modernize the nation's inefficient, paper-clogged health care system
- Influencing others (the **end-users**: primary care physicians, physician assistants, nurse practitioners, advance practice nurses, and nurses; the providers: hospitals and medical products industries)

Studies by the National Center for Policy Analysis indicate that when electronic health records are combined with the emerging field of **genomics**, a force will be unleashed that will throw open the door to **precision medicine**, new medical treatments, and ultimately, more affordable health care (NCPA, 2015). However, this advancement in technology is by no means the hoped-for fix for rising health care spending. Moreover, electronic health records and a national **health information network** could be powerfully disruptive for some lucrative sectors in the medical products industry, such as affecting so-called blockbuster drugs. A national health information network would include electronic health records that would allow health providers and others to track outcomes for medical products, eventually resulting in the pharmaceutical, biotechnology, and medical device industries making fewer decisions about treatments. Much of the information physicians now use comes from studies paid for by the medical products industry. The more information is independently generated, analyzed, and distributed, the more the blockbuster model for drugs is in doubt. The medical products industry will have to decide:

- What are the implications of these forces for drug development, and will the new model that emerges be sustainable?
- What impact will these changes have on the current commercial models for the pharmaceutical, biotechnology, and medical device industries?
- Will there be a market for blockbuster drugs in the future?

Information is a dual-edged sword in health care. Better information might blow apart some of the blockbuster markets in the medical products industry. It might also increase demand for other products in smaller, more focused markets. If so, will there be a future market for stand-alone firms in the medical products industry?

New Approach to Decision-Making

There are several ways to change the nation's approach to decision-making about health care, including:

- Recognizing the difficulties in setting **cost limits** and seeing things differently
- Implicitly understanding the neurology of internal patterns
- Understanding, in terms of mental models, the process for making sense of the U.S. health care system

Only then can the national framework for decision making be transformed by:

- Evaluating alternative actions from various perspectives
- Gathering the relevant facts
- Making decisions
- Putting *all* the mental models on the table
- Recognizing issues
- Repeating the process all over again
- Testing *every* mental model
- Testing the results of those decisions

(*See* Wind & Crook, 2007).

Practical Implications of the New Neuroscience

The practical implications are limitless for the *new* **neuroscience of mental models**. There is great risk in changing old views of the U.S. health care system, with its focus on models of managed cost. At the same time, there are great possibilities in the unprecedented opportunities to blend the best of the old and the new (Wind & Crook, 2007).

As you read the following chapters, always ask the following questions:

- How do the mental models change the options available?
- What are some different mental models for looking at the same situations outlined in each chapter?
- What mental models underlie the court decisions and health care actions reported?

Pay particular attention to how different mental models often define the battle lines on issues.

LAW FACT

Gorillas in Our Field of Vision

When thinking of the U.S. health care system, the question to keep in mind is: are we failing to see the gorillas moving through our field of vision?

Yes. The gorillas in our nation's collective field of vision can be seen in cognitive neuroscience. Neural activity due to sensory stimuli disappears in the cortex. The sensory stimuli cease to exist. We do not really take in what we see. Stimulation flows into our brains, evoking an internal pattern, which our brains use to represent the external situation. We think we see and understand the "real" world of medical care in the United States, but we actually see what is already in our own minds: we see pre-existing mental models (relationships and concepts) of the U.S. health care system.

— Chabris & Simons, 2010; Wind & Crook, 2007.

CHAPTER SUMMARY

- Ideally, the development of a better U.S. health care system would be accomplished by considering new ideas, while retaining the best of the old and present ideas.
- The obstacle to an effective, efficient, high-quality health care system accessible to all U.S. residents may be the nation's collective thinking.
- The United States spends about twice as much on health care as most other industrialized economies without garnering any tangible benefits on health, infant mortality, or longevity.
- Americans may think the barriers to reform are too complex, or that established interests are too entrenched to change, but often these barriers to creating an ideal health care system are simply in the nation's collective mind.

- People are not aware that what they are actually seeing and thinking is what is already in their own minds, due to the way the brain interprets new information.
- Many readers may not have fully absorbed the arguably shocking facts presented in this chapter because we tend to be unwilling to change our mental models.
- In order to improve health care in the United States, individuals and organizations must constantly test their mental models instead of simply accepting what they think things are.
- The United States must find a way to reconcile the cost of health care with what consumers actually need; for instance, it may not make sense to spend the most money on developing new and innovative medical technology when consumers cannot access existing technology.
- Instead of rationing health care across the board, Americans would likely prefer to ration it for preventable conditions or for highly innovative and overly expensive medical treatments.
- Another possible way to control costs would be to focus more heavily on preventive care and consumers' lifestyle behaviors, particularly smoking, weight control, medication adherence, and gun ownership.
- Adaptive disconnects in the U.S. health care system occur when everyone adapts their thinking at different rates.
- In light of the immense complexity of the nation's health care industry, participants must learn to see and understand both the minute details and the broader context in order to effect change.
- Neuroscience can be helpful in understanding how the brain works to create and preserve mental models and how to change the framework for decision-making in order to develop new mental models.

LAW NOTES

1. The theoretical perspective of this chapter was developed by two Nobel laureates in experimental psychology and cognitive science, Daniel Simons, professor in the Department of Psychology and the Beckman Institute for Advanced Science and Technology at the University of Illinois, and Christopher Chabris, visiting scholar at the MIT Center for Collective Intelligence and adjunct professor of neurology at Albany Medical College (Chabris & Simons, 2010; Simons & Chabris, 1999). Wharton marketing professor Yoram ("Jerry") Wind and Colin Crook applied the brain theory developed by Chabris and Simons to business settings (*See generally* Wind & Crook, 2007; Wharton, 2005).

2. Mental models of the U.S. health care system are the images, assumptions, and stories people carry in their minds of themselves, other people in the health care industry, and every aspect of the U.S. health care system. The nature of the mind exerts a significant effect on our perceptions of the U.S. health care system. People's view of health care is dependent both on the way the health care system is and on the way they are (Wicks & Keevil, 2014).

3. There is a sharp distinction between the mental model Americans have of the U.S. health care system and the model of how the system is serving their own personal medical needs. Americans believe the U.S. health care system needs reform, particularly when it comes to health insurance coverage and costs (Rasmussen, 2016). At the same time, they are generally pleased with the quality of medical treatment, and are generally satisfied with the quality of their current health care and health insurance coverage; they like its choices and its intensive, high technology approach to curing their ailments. On balance, Americans still favor maintaining their current mental models of health care, 50 to 44% (Newport, 2015). In a word, the American public seems to be calling for surgery on the current mental model of the U.S. health care system (essentially reforms to expand medical coverage to those who need it and actions to rein in costs), rather than an entire transplant operation to uproot the current system.

REFERENCES

Altman, D. (2015, January 5). How health-care bills hinder millions of Americans. *The Wall Street Journal: Washington Wire*, p. A1.

Alzheimer's Association. (2016). *Alzheimer's disease facts and figures*. Chicago, IL: Alzheimer's Association-National Office.

BLS (Bureau of Labor Statistics). (2014). *State occupational employment statistics survey*. Washington, DC: U.S. Department of Labor.

CBO (Congressional Budget Office). (2016). *Health care: Projections for major health care programs for FY 2015*. Washington, DC: CBO.

Chabris, C. F., & Simons, D. (2010). *The invisible gorilla: And other ways our intuitions deceive us*. New York, NY: Crown Publishing Group.

CMS (Centers for Medicare and Medicaid Services). (2015). *National health expenditure report*. Washington, DC: CMS.

CSDH (Commission on Social Determinants of Health). (2008). *Closing the gap in a generation: Health equity through action on the social determinants of health. Final report of the Commission on Social Determinants of Health*. Geneva, Switzerland: World Health Organization.

Davidson, A. (2015). *Social determinants of health: A comparative approach*. New York, NY: Oxford University Press.

Deyette, K. (2015). HITECH Act: Building an infrastructure for health information organizations and a new health care delivery system. *Saint Louis University Journal of Health Law and Policy, 8*, 375–420.

Fleck, L. M. (2014). Just caring: Do the indolent, the inebriated and the irresponsible deserve equal access to needed health care? *Indiana Health Law Review, 11*, 555–589.

Freeman, W. (2001). *How brains make up their minds*. New York, NY: Columbia University Press.

___. (2000). *Neurodynamics: An exploration in mesoscopic brain dynamics (perspectives in neural computing)*. Philadelphia, PA: Springer.

___. (1995). *Societies of brains. A study in the neuroscience of love and hate (The International Neural Networks Society)*. New York, NY: Routledge-Lawrence Erlbaum Taylor and Francis Group.

___. (1975). *Mass action in the nervous system: Examination of neurophysiological basis of adaptive behavior through the ego*. St. Louis, MO: Elsevier-Science and Technology Academic Press.

Gregory, E. C. W. et al. (2014). *NCHS data brief: Trends in infant mortality in the United States*. Hyattsville, MD: Centers for Disease Control and Prevention, National Center for Health Statistics (NCHS).

Helveston, M. N. (2015). Judicial deregulation of consumer markets. *Cardozo Law Review, 36*, 1739–1782.

Johnson, A., & Stukel, T. A. (2016). *Medical practice variations*. New York, NY: Springer.

Kaiser (Kaiser Family Foundation). (2015). *New Kaiser/New York Times survey finds one in five working-age Americans with health insurance report problems paying medical bills*. Menlo Park, CA: Kaiser.

Keith, J., Principal, Deloitte Consulting. (2015, February 20). Keynote Address at the 2015 Wharton Health Care Business Conference–Disruption Amidst Uncertainty: Adapting and Innovating for the Future at the Union League, Philadelphia, PA.

Krause, J. H., & Saver, R. S. (2014). Health care decisions in the new era of health care reform. *North Carolina Law Review, 92*, 1445–1459.

Lechleiter, J. C., Chairman, President and Chief Executive Office, Eli Lilly and Company. (2016, February 19). Keynote Speaker on the Innovation Game: The Race Between Entrants+Incumbents at the 2016 Wharton Health Care Business Conference, Philadelphia, PA.

Lee, S. B. (2014). The drug shortage crisis: When generic manufacturers just say no. *Oregon Law Review, 93*, 355–401.

McClellan, M., Senior Fellow and Director of the Health Care Innovation and Value Initiative at the Brookings Institution, Former Administrator of the Centers for Medicare and Medicaid Services, and Former Commissioner of the U.S. Food and Drug Administration. (2016, February 19). Closing Discussion/Debate at the Wharton Health Care Business Conference: The Innovation Game: The Race Between Entrants+Incumbents, Philadelphia, PA.

NBGH (National Business Group on Health). (2012). *Strategies for driving employee engagement in wellness, health care and job performance*. Washington, DC: NBGH.

NCHS (National Center for Health Statistics). (2015a). *Health, United States*. Hyattsville, MD Centers for Disease Control and Prevention.

___. (2015b). *Heart disease*.

NCPA (National Center for Policy Analysis). (2015). *Roll back the federal 10-year strategic plan for health information technology* (Issue Brief 157). Dallas, TX: NCPA.

Newport, F. (2015, April 8). *Americans slightly more positive toward Affordable Care Act*. Washington, DC: Gallup.

Pasquale, F. (2014). The hidden costs of health care cost-cutting: Toward a post-neoliberal health-reform agenda. *Law and Contemporary Problems, 77*, 171–193.

Penn, M., & Zalesne, E. K. (2009). *Microtrends: The small forces behind tomorrow's big changes*. New York, NY: Hachette Book Group-Twelve.

Rasmussen Reports. (2016, January 6). *Health care law: Voters still want feds out of health care*. Asbury Park, NJ: Rasmussen Reports.

Sage, W. M., & McIlhattan, K. (2014). The buying and selling of health care: Upstream health law. *Journal of Law, Medicine and Ethics, 42*, 535–547.

Schoen, C., et al. (2015). *State trends in the cost of employer health insurance coverage*. New York, NY: The Commonwealth Fund.

Simons, D. J., & Chabris, C. F. (1999). Gorillas in our midst: Sustained *inattentional blindness* for dynamic events. *Perception, 28*, 1059–1074.

Surgeon General, U.S. (2010). *The Surgeon General's vision for a healthy and fit nation*. Washington, DC: U.S. Surgeon General.

Thomas, J. R. (2015). Reflections on current food and drug law issues: The end of "patent medicines"? Thoughts on the rise of regulatory exclusivities. *Food and Drug Law Journal, 70*, 39–53.

Wharton (Wharton School at the University of Pennsylvania). (2005). What's behind the 4-minute mile, Starbucks and the moon landing? The power of impossible thinking. *Knowledge@Wharton*. http://knowledge.wharton.upenn.edu/article/whats-behind-the-4-minute-mile-starbucks-and-the-moon-landing-the-power-of-impossible-thinking/

Wicks, A. C., & Keevil, A. A. C. (2014). The buying and selling of health care: When worlds collide; medicine, business, the Affordable Care Act and the future of health care in the U.S. *Journal of Law, Medicine and Ethics, 42*, 420–429.

Wind, J. R., & Crook, C. (2007). *The power of impossible thinking: Transform the business of your life and the life of your business*. Philadelphia, PA: Pearson Prentice Hall-Wharton School Publishing.

World Bank. (2016). *GDP at market prices (current US$)*. Washington, DC: World Bank.

CHAPTER 2

Introduction to Health Law

"We the People of the United States, in Order to form a more perfect Union, establish Justice, insure domestic Tranquility, provide for the common defense, promote the general Welfare, and secure the Blessings of Liberty to ourselves and our Posterity, do ordain and establish this Constitution for the United States of America."

— **Preamble**, Constitution of the United States of America (1776).

IN BRIEF

This chapter describes how the U.S. legal system functions through the separation of governmental powers that is central to the U.S. Constitution. The role of "the People" and the agencies the federal government uses to administer and enforce U.S. health laws is reviewed. Particular attention is directed to the U.S. Department of Health and Human Services and the Food and Drug Administration, the agency that regulates about one-fourth of the U.S. economy. Crucial public health issues currently facing relevant federal agencies are outlined in the Law Notes and subsequently addressed in greater detail throughout this text.

LEARNING OBJECTIVES

Upon completion of this chapter readers should be able to:

1. Explain the general concept of the separation of powers.
2. Outline the principles flowing from the Declaration of Independence that form the basis of the Constitution and Bill of Rights.
3. Describe the difference between enumerated rights and unenumerated rights and the function of the Ninth Amendment in resolving these with *tacit rights*.
4. Show how the Bill of Rights was conceived to meet various objections to the original Constitution.
5. Describe the three separate but equal branches of government.
6. Discuss the distribution of powers between the federal and state governments.
7. Differentiate among various types of laws: common, statutory, administrative, and constitutional.

KEY TERMS

Affordable Care Act of 2010
Adversarial system
Adverse Events Reporting System
Agency guidelines
Appellate courts
Autonomy
Ballot measures
Bicameralism
Bill of Rights
Boycotts

Budget reconciliation
Case of first impression
Common law
Compassion
Competition
Complementary health care
 practices
Consent of the governed
Democratic legitimacy
Earmarking

Emergency Medical Treatment and
 Labor Act of 1986
Enumerated rights
Equality of opportunity
Exclusive dealing
Exclusive jurisdiction
Expressed powers
Food, Drug, and Cosmetic Act of
 1938
Gainsharing agreements

Horizontal price-fixing
Illegal combinations of competitors
Illegal monopoly
Inalienable rights
Initiatives
Joint ventures
Justice
Legislative measures
Liberty
Limited government
Market discrimination
Medical devices
Medical product error
Medicare Advantage
MedWatch

Nanotechnology
Natural rights
Necessary and Proper clause
Ninth Amendment
Nonbinding policy statements
Nonvaccine biologics
Offset
Part D prescription drug plans
Pay-as-you-go
People, the
Personal health records
Price-fixing agreements
Pricing discrimination
Referendums
Representative democracy

Retail-based health clinics
Rule of law
Separation of powers doctrine
Tax expenditures
Therapeutic inequivalence
Trade restraints
Tradition
Trial courts
Truth in Lending Simplification and
    Reform Act of 1980
Tying arrangements
Unenumerated rights
Unfair methods of competition
Valid insurance claim
Value-based payment system

FACT OR FICTION

Comprehensive Health Care Reform

Should comprehensive health care reforms, as well as repeal of the reforms, be passed through Congress's budget reconciliation process?

Created in 1974, the omnibus **budget reconciliation** process allows federal legislation dealing with entitlement programs, such as parts of the health care reform, to be enacted by Congress upon a simple majority vote after 20 hours of debate. This process precludes a filibuster in the Senate and makes it more difficult for individual Senators to amend legislation on the floor, which might unravel deals struck in congressional committees (Cannan, 2013). Critics of budget reconciliation maintain the process is an attack on federalism, since the Senate has historically been the arena where smaller states have significant influence. One issue being debated is whether the budget reconciliation process shifts too much power to congressional committees and away from members of Congress.

Under the principle of federalism, one of the founding principles of the U.S. Constitution, the federal and state governments should share the power to govern. The federal government has certain **expressed powers** (also called *enumerated powers*). The Constitution's **Necessary and Proper clause** gives Congress (and by delegation the executive branch) the implied power to pass any law *necessary and proper* for the execution of its express powers (*McCulloch v. Maryland*, 17 U.S. 316 (U.S. Supreme Court 1819); Sassman, 2015). Opponents of universal health care believe the federal government has grown beyond the bounds permitted by its expressed powers. One fear is the federal government may be increasing too greatly in both its size and its influence on the everyday lives of Americans and in its expansion relative to the state governments. One side of this debate asserts the provision of universal health care by the federal government may exceed Congress' power, a power rightly belonging to the states. The other side maintains the states are legally subject to the dictates of the federal government when there is a national need to regulate an industry such as the health and insurance industries that span state borders.

It appears a large majority of Americans believe the U.S. Constitution implies that every member of society has a fundamental right to medically necessary care. If so, then the country may be ready for the federal government to comprehensively overhaul U.S. health care and provide access to affordable health insurance for everyone. While implementation of health care reform legislation will require significant intergovernmental mandates for decades to come, the current debate centers on whether there should be a social consensus in Congress for comprehensive reform, or whether health care reform is too important to be stalled by congressional protocol.

— *See* Law Fact at the end of this chapter for the answer.

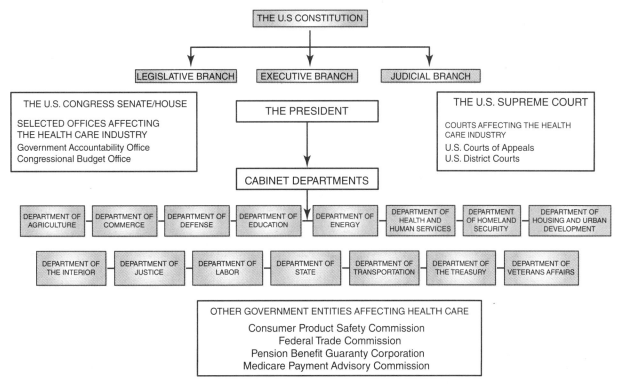

FIGURE 2-1 Organization of the Federal Government

Modified from: Government Manual, The U.S. (2016). Washington, DC: U.S. Government Printing Office.

Principles and Applications

To understand health law, it helps to have a basic understanding of the following:

- **Bill of Rights** (the first 10 Amendments to the U.S. Constitution)
- Declaration of Independence
- Distribution of governmental powers between the federal and state governments
- Three separate branches of government: judicial, legislative, and executive
- U.S. Constitution

This chapter focuses on the facets of the federal government with the most impact on the health care industry as illustrated in **FIGURE 2-1**. Most of the 50 states have created similar organizations and government agencies.

The Declaration of Independence

The Declaration of Independence is the nation's keystone document (Presser & Zainaldin, 2013); its principles form the basis of the U.S. Constitution and the Bill of Rights. The **inalienable rights** concept, embodied in the Declaration of Independence, is the foundation of the fundamental rights of all Americans and the basis for the concept of a **limited government** in the United States.

> *We hold these truths to be self-evident, that all men are created equal, that they are endowed by their Creator with certain unalienable Rights, that among these are Life, Liberty and the pursuit of Happiness.—That to secure these rights, Governments are instituted among Men, deriving their just powers from the consent of the governed.*
>
> — The Declaration of Independence, paragraphs 2–3 (1776)

Three fundamental and inherent rights are listed: *life, liberty,* and *the pursuit of happiness* (meaning a life lived to its full potential); these are basic rights to which everyone is equally entitled. The very idea that people have rights that precede and are superior to government is based on the self-evident truths articulated in the Declaration of Independence (Hamburger, 2015).

U.S. Constitution and Bill of Rights

The U.S. Constitution and Bill of Rights, along with the Declaration of Independence, are salient expressions of the unique character of American democracy (Smith & Gallena, 2014). When the U.S. Constitution was sent to the states for ratification, several states insisted a Bill of Rights be added, but no such bill could list all of the rights intended to be protected; the failure to do so, however, raised the implication that only the **enumerated rights** were to be preserved in this emerging democracy. So the **Ninth Amendment** was ratified, stating **unenumerated rights** are protected in addition to the rights enumerated and protected in the Bill of Rights.

The Ninth Amendment states individuals have tacit rights, in addition to the rights explicit in the Bill of Rights. The legislative branch was given the authority to enumerate the unenumerated rights by using the power to set forth laws that would bring the rights to fruition through the executive branch and that would be subject to review through the judicial branch. These creative powers are not unique to the Ninth Amendment; for instance, the First Amendment's enumerated rights also require the three separate branches of government to balance and protect the rights to freedom of speech, property, and due process of law.

Underlying this **separation of powers doctrine** regarding enumerated and unenumerated rights are the Constitution's **natural rights** and **common law** foundations. When laws become removed from these foundations, the result is often divisive controversies, such as the right to life-sustaining drugs and the right-to-die debates, and even the right to health care debate itself. Confusion reigns until the balance is restored to its grounding in the consent of the governed.

Judicial Branch

In any democracy, there are many sides to the evolving debate over rights. On one side of this ongoing debate is the judicial branch with judges who sometimes become impatient (often justifiably) with the founding principles of the U.S. Constitution and who use their powers to create rights based on their self-conceptions of evolving social values. On the other side of this debate are judges who go overboard in recognizing only those rights specifically expressed in the Constitution. Both extreme sides of this democratic debate ignore the presumptions at the very foundation of the Constitution (Fishkin & Forbath, 2014). These are the uniquely American beliefs in:

- Free markets
- Independence (limited government)
- Individual **autonomy** (personal responsibility)
- Individual freedom
- **Liberty (representative democracy)**

The Constitution no more authorizes the judicial branch to invent rights than it allows the judiciary to ignore rights meant to be protected when it addresses the most difficult, sometimes divisive, cases that arise. Nevertheless, the law must be ascertained and applied by the bench, as opposed to invented from behind it (Blackstone, 2011/1765). Generally the judicial branch gets it right, even if a case must go through several levels of appeal to arrive at the correct interpretation of the law.

Organization of the Judicial Branch

The judicial branch is divided into **trial courts** (courts of first instance) and **appellate courts**. Trial courts function with a judge and often a jury. Juries make findings of fact while judges decide conclusions of law (jury trials), or judges make decisions of both fact and law without a jury (bench trials). Whether or not a jury is selected depends upon the case and whether any of the parties has requested a jury. In the common law system, courts follow the **adversarial system**. Procedural law governs the rules by which courts operate: civil procedure for private disputes; criminal procedure for violation of criminal laws; and administrative procedure for government proceedings.

Federal Courts

The federal courts, as illustrated in **FIGURE 2-2**, are composed of:

- U.S. Courts of Appeals
- U.S. District Courts
- The U.S. Supreme Court

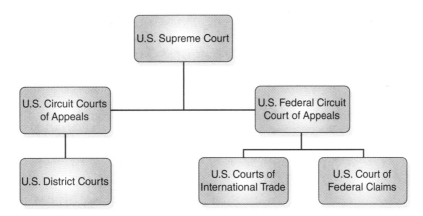

FIGURE 2-2 Organization of the Federal Court System
Modified from: Government Manual, The U.S. (2016). Washington, DC: U.S. Government Printing Office.

Every health law **case of first impression** that has been decided by the U.S. Courts of Appeals within the last five years is summarized in the *Principles and Applications* sections of this text or its ancillary materials. The health law cases decided by the U.S. Supreme Court within the past five years are also examined.

<u>U.S. Supreme Court</u>   Article III, § 1 of the U.S. Constitution provides that the "judicial Power of the United States, shall be vested in one supreme Court, and in such inferior Courts as the Congress may from time to time ordain and establish." The U.S. Supreme Court was created in accordance with this provision in 1790 and is comprised of the Chief Justice and such number of Associate Justices as may be determined by Congress, which in 2016 was eight, for a total of nine Justices (*See* 28 U.S.C.A. § 1). The President nominates the Justices with the advice and consent of the Senate.

The term of the U.S. Supreme Court begins on the first Monday in October and lasts until the first Monday in October of the following year. Approximately 8,000 cases are filed with the Court in the course of a term; some 1,000 applications are filed each year that can be acted upon by a single Justice (*Government Manual*, 2016). While appellate jurisdiction has been conferred upon the U.S. Supreme Court by Congress, Congress has no authority to change the original jurisdiction of the Court as defined in Article III, § 2 of the U.S. Constitution (*See* 28 U.S.C.A. §§ 1251, 1253–1254, 1257–1259, and various special laws). This means that the Supreme Court can only review certain kinds of cases and has no authority to review other kinds, and Congress cannot alter the Supreme Court's authority to hear certain kinds of cases.

<u>U.S. Courts of Appeals</u>   The 94 District Courts are organized into 12 circuits, each of which has a corresponding U.S. Court of Appeals. Courts of Appeal hear appeals from the District Courts located within their regional circuit, as well as appeals from decisions of federal administrative agencies, the Bankruptcy Courts, and the U.S. Tax Court. In addition, the U.S. Federal Circuit Court of Appeals hears appeals in specialized cases:

- U.S. Court of Customs and Patent Appeals (such as disputes between providers of medical products)
- U.S. Court of Federal Claims (such as vaccine injury claims)
- U.S. Court of International Trade (such as counterfeit medical product cases)

<u>U.S. District Courts</u>   The U.S. District Courts are the trial courts of the federal court system. Within limits set by Congress and the U.S. Constitution, the District Courts hear civil and criminal federal cases.

MANAGEMENT AND LAW ISSUES

1. Should Americans be concerned about the fact that the average tenure of U.S. Supreme Court Justices has increased to almost 30 years, when every other major court of its kind in the world has rejected life tenure and 49 out of 50 states have rejected it for their state supreme courts?
2. Is life tenure for a U.S. Supreme Court Justice a good idea or is it an 18th-century anachronism?

U.S. Bankruptcy Courts and the U.S. Vaccine Court are separate units of the District Courts. Federal courts have **exclusive jurisdiction** over bankruptcy and vaccine cases, which means bankruptcy and vaccine cases cannot be filed in state courts. The Vaccine Court, with one chief special master and seven associate special masters, hears cases of children injured as a result of compulsory childhood vaccines and, like the Bankruptcy Courts, was established by Congress to bypass traditional civil malpractice litigation (*See* National Childhood Vaccine Injury Act of 1986, 42 U.S.C.A. §§ 300aa-2 *et seq.*).

State Courts

The organization of each state's judiciary is patterned after the federal judicial system. As in the federal courts, every health law case of first impression that has been decided by the highest state courts within the last five years is summarized in this text and its ancillary materials.

The People and the Judicial Branch

Americans have always been interested in questions related to **the People**, which is the Constitution's term of art referring to the citizenry, and the judicial branch. With hundreds of **ballot measures** in almost every state, **initiatives**, **referendums**, and **legislative measures** are becoming more a part of political discourse than ever before, with spending on such polling approaching a half-billion dollars each election year (Smith, 2014). What role the People retain in the U.S. Constitutional order is not just a theoretical issue; the increasing number of ballot measures addressed to voters has made it a debate with real consequences. The breadth of this debate is not limited to the topic of the right to gay marriage. The People may also play a role in deciding health care issues such as the following:

- Abortion rights
- Food regulations
- Physician-assisted death
- Right to basic health care
- Right to end-of-life medical treatments
- Right to medical marijuana
- Rights of adolescents
- Rights of women to contraception, including the morning-after pill
- Smoking measures

Although there is no provision for legislative measures at the national level, initiatives and referendums are available in thousands of counties, cities, and towns across the nation and are used far more frequently than their statewide counterparts (Smith, 2014 Perhaps more important, the way ordinary Americans choose to live and die gives meaning to the **rule of law**. Because the U.S. legal system often takes its cue from **tradition**, it is critical to decide when the judicial branch should defer to customary practice, both when interpreting the U.S. Constitution and when applying legislation and the rules of law that govern most health care decisions in the United States.

Legislative Branch

Congress makes the controlling choices in policy debates and establishes the acknowledged standards of law (*See Panama Refining Co. v. Ryan*, 293 U.S. 388, 426 (U.S. Supreme Court 1935)). This principle of legislation is grounded in the notion of **democratic legitimacy** (Barnard, 2003). Democratic legitimacy is the concept, first coined by F. M. Barnard, professor emeritus at the University of Western Ontario, that political accountability is as important to the democratic ethic as political participation. Barnard argues that laws must be tempered by a sense of universal humanity. In a democracy, the People's role does not begin and end in the voting booth when members of Congress are elected to take legislative action on behalf of the public; legitimacy assumes ongoing public involvement and regular public deliberation regarding issues of national concern. Democratic legitimacy depends on the nature of the congressional debate that precedes decision-making as much as the actual vote to enact legislation. To be legitimate, laws adopted by the legislative branch should comply with well-reasoned and recognized rules and tradition. The legitimacy of laws is challenged, as need be, through the judicial branch.

These democratic principles extend equally to the executive and judicial branches when they execute and apply the laws emanating from the legislative branch. Execution of the legislative laws by the executive branch should be well reasoned and in compliance with recognized standards of **compassion**, **justice**, and **equality of opportunity** (Rawls, 1999/1971). The judicial branch's interpretation of the policy choices made by both the legislative and executive branches should comply with well-reasoned rules that are consistent with the democratic traditions in the U.S. Constitution, which, in turn, reflects the Founders' beliefs in the universality of the human race (Nozick, 2013/1974).

Failure to comply with a health law does not necessarily indicate malicious intent or lack of compassion. Compliance with the law is required simply because the legislative branch of government has determined it is the law. The law is the policy choice made by Congress based on what it, as the People's representative, determines to be in the nation's best interests.

Organization of the U.S. Congress

Congress was created by Article I, § 1, of the U.S. Constitution, providing that "All legislative Powers herein granted shall be vested in a Congress of the U.S., which shall consist of a Senate and House of Representatives." The Senate is composed of 100 Senators, two from each state elected by its citizens to serve for six-year terms. There are three classes of Senators; a new class is elected every two years. The House of Representatives is composed of 435 members, a number determined by the population in each state. Representatives are elected by their state's citizens for two-year terms, all terms running for the same period.

Delegated Enactment of Laws

Congress cannot transfer the power of making laws to any other hands, for it is a delegated power from the People. They who have it cannot pass it over to others (Locke, 2015/1689). This principle is a fundamental democratic concern arising out of the ideal that significant policy decisions should be grounded in the **consent of the governed**.

Government Accountability Office

The Government Accountability Office (GAO), established in 1921, is the investigative arm of Congress charged with examining all matters relating to the receipt and disbursement of government funds (*See* 31 U.S.C.A. § 702). An independent, nonpartisan agency, the GAO works for Congress and is often referred to as the congressional watchdog because it investigates how the federal government spends society's dollars. The GAO gathers information to help Congress determine how effectively the executive branch is doing its job. The GAO's work routinely answers such basic questions as whether government health care programs are meeting their legislative objectives or providing effective service to the public (*Government Manual*, 2016).

With virtually the entire federal government subject to its review (*Government Manual*, 2016), the GAO issues a steady stream of reports and testimonies by its officials. Its reports help Congress better understand newly emerging issues with far-reaching impacts. For instance, privacy of the National Health Information Network has always been a GAO concern (GAO, 2015, 2014(a-c) and 2007).

Congressional Budget Office

The Congressional Budget Office, established in 1974, provides Congress with economic analyses of fiscal, budgetary, and program policy issues, as well as with information and estimates required for the congressional budget process (*See* 2 U.S.C.A. § 601 (2004)). This enables Congress to have an overview of the federal budget and to make overall decisions regarding spending and taxing levels and the deficit these levels incur.

One of the most controversial activities of the Congressional Budget Office is its projection of costs and savings from proposed legislation. Congressional budget rules allow the rate of mandatory spending and tax spending to grow automatically. If the cost of health care grows, spending will automatically grow. Instead of limiting the growth of health care programs, Congress has limited itself in its ability to pass legislation that would increase spending, known as **pay-as-you-go** (Paygo) (Kamin, 2015).

Paygo restricts Congress to passing only legislation with a net estimated cost of zero, or projected to result in additional revenue for the government. If a new program would increase spending above the current level (a term that, incidentally, has never been defined), Congress would have to either reduce other programs or increase tax revenues. While total government borrowing, in the form of Treasury bonds and notes, could pass $544 billion in 2016 (76% of the gross national product), borrowed funds are not an **offset** for Paygo (CBO, 2016). Paygo estimates the official costs of legislation; a score that is too costly makes new programs harder to pass. Paygo assumes that the future effects of programs can be estimated. For instance, if legislation is proposed to make a new health service available under Medicare, the Congressional Budget Office estimates the increased costs of this proposal over the expected year-to-year automatic increases. In doing so, the Congressional Budget Office also offsets increases with any expected decreases. For instance, if legislation would require Medicare coverage for a drug, scorekeeping would include both the costs of the drug and any offsetting reductions in the need for hospital care (Kamin, 2015). It is debatable whether any supposed cost offsets ever materialize.

Executive Branch

Three issues face the executive branch. They include its:

- Encroachment into the judicial and legislative branches of a federal system established on the Separation of Powers doctrine
- Long-term fiscal gap resultant from expansion of social spending and congressional **earmarking** unprecedented growth of entitlement programs

(CBO, 2015; Lowi et al., 2013).

Expansive Growth and Resultant Long-Term Fiscal Gap

The executive branch faces a long-term fiscal gap driven largely by health care and Social Security entitlements and interest payments (CBO, 2015). Meanwhile, the federal government continues to expand with congressional earmarking without regard for merit, need, or any scrutiny (Nussle & Orszag, 2015). Earmarks skyrocketed to over 16,000 in the middle of the last decade according to the Congressional Research Service (Orszag, 2010; White House, 2009). As a result of these forces, federal expenditures have increased from $1.8 trillion in 2000 to $3.9 trillion in 2016 (CBO, 2016).

Decline of Governance by Separation of Powers

With the growth of the executive branch, agency-promulgated guidelines have become universal in the federal government. There is debate, however, over whether **agency guidelines** and **nonbinding policy statements** are resulting in a diminution of the separation of powers doctrine, particularly for the judicial branch. The actual impact of agency guidelines and their voluntary and cooperative enforcement procedures is often unspoken. Often the issuing agencies declare the guidelines to be nonbinding, even for themselves. Notwithstanding this disclaimer, the health care industry and the judicial branch frequently rely upon agency guidelines in a precedent-like manner. The guidelines often become valued far more than the persuasive power of their ideas. This raises the more general concern as to whether the judicial branch is ceding its role as the check on the executive branch (Moncrieff, 2010). Such questions regarding the judiciary's role in the separation of powers are broadly analogous to those raised regarding Congress's role in the legislative process. Congress is often criticized for writing nonspecific legislation with delegation that arguably transfers legislative power to the executive and judicial branches (Lowi et al., 2013).

MANAGEMENT AND LAW ISSUES

3. Should the independent federal regulatory agencies be truly independent and free of executive and legislative branch control?

Executive Branch Departments and Agencies Affecting the Health Care Industry

Eleven departments exist in the executive branch that are part of the President's Cabinet and report to the President. The U.S. Department of Health and Human Services has the most direct impact on the health care industry, particularly the Food and Drug Administration (FDA) and the Centers for Medicare and Medicaid Services. The Internal Revenue Service (IRS), within the U.S. Department of the Treasury, and the Federal Trade Commission also have significant impacts on health care.

Organization of the U.S. Department of Health and Human Services

Funding for the U.S. Department of Health and Human Services is greater than all the other federal agencies combined, with 86% of the outlays for government health insurance programs (*Government Manual*, 2016). The $1.1 trillion size of the departmental budget is more than double the size of the budget of global retailer Walmart; by comparison and in terms of revenue, the department is equal to more than 13 IBMs.[1] Created in 1798 as a Cabinet-level department, the Department of Health and Human Services is composed of the following 11 agencies that report to the Secretary:

- Administration for Children and Families
- Administration on Aging
- Agency for Healthcare Research and Quality
- Agency for Toxic Substances and Disease Registry
- Centers for Disease Control and Prevention (CDC)
- Centers for Medicare and Medicaid Services (CMS)
- Food and Drug Administration (FDA)
- Health Resources and Services Administration
- Indian Health Service
- National Institutes of Health (NIH)
- Substance Abuse and Mental Health Services Administration

Administration for Children and Families

The Administration for Children and Families is the second largest agency in the Department of Health and Human Services. The agency deals primarily with:

- Adoptions
- Child abuse and neglect
- Child support
- Developmental disabilities
- Family assistance (welfare)
- Foster care[LN1]
- Head Start
- Human trafficking
- Legalized aliens
- Native American assistance
- Refugee resettlement and unaccompanied children's services

(*Government Manual*, 2016).

Today, welfare programs are substantially controlled by federal legislation. Every five years, the agency conducts reviews of state programs to ensure they are in conformity with federal requirements; most states are not. At the same time, the agency is criticized for failing to adequately monitor state programs and its inability to sufficiently hold states accountable. Although states may be penalized for noncompliance or failure to comply with federal reporting requirements, a state would only lose a small portion of its federally allotted money for noncompliance. Congressional influence on the agency's oversight role, without exception, results in new promises of future compliance by the noncompliant states but no cutbacks in funding.

---

[1] In 2015, the revenue of IBM was $81.7 billion (IBM, 2015); the revenue of Walmart was $485 billion (Walmart, 2016).

Administration on Aging

The Administration on Aging helps Americans aged 65 and over to maintain independence in their homes through comprehensive community-based systems of care. This population of 45 million comprised about 14% of the population in 2014 and is expected to more than double by 2060 (AOA, 2014). Three health care issues are of special importance to the population served by the agency. They include the following:

- Inadequate efficacy and affordability of medicines[LN2]
- Limited access to and increased non-affordability of basic health care[LN3]
- Unreported elder abuse and neglect with lack of protective services[LN4]

In partnership with the National Aging Network (which consists of over 50 state agencies on aging, almost 900 area agencies on aging, and 29,000 service providers), the Administration on Aging seeks to promote the development of all-inclusive structures encompassing:

- Home health care
- Hospice services
- Long-term nursing care

Agency for Healthcare Research and Quality

Since 2005, the Agency for Healthcare Research and Quality has issued comprehensive annual reports that address statistical compliance on a range of issues and highlight how the United States could improve the quality, safety, efficiency, and effectiveness of the nation's health care.[LN5] In addition, health services research to improve the quality of health care and promote evidence-based decision-making is supported by the agency, including research on:

- Access to quality health care for minorities and people of lower socioeconomic status;
- Emerging standards in national health care information technology
- Patient injuries caused by medical errors[LN6]
- Payments for the routine costs of clinical trials and treatment of trial-related complications[LN7]
- Physician compliance with clinical guidelines[LN8]
- Provision of emergency contraception in the nation's hospital emergency rooms[LN9]

Centers for Disease Control and Prevention

The Centers for Disease Control and Prevention is charged with protecting the public health of the nation by providing leadership and direction in the prevention and control of diseases and preventable conditions, and responding to public health emergencies (*Government Manual*, 2016). Within the Centers for Disease Control and Prevention are the following centers, institutes, and offices:

- CDC Washington Office
- Center for Global Health
- Office for State, Tribal, Local and Territorial Support
- Office of Equal Employment Opportunity
- Office of Infectious Diseases

  - National Center for Emerging and Zoonotic Infectious Diseases
  - National Center for HIV/AIDS, Viral Hepatitis, STD, and TB Prevention
  - National Center for Immunization and Respiratory Diseases

- Office of Minority Health and Health Equity
- Office of Noncommunicable Diseases, Injury and Environmental Health

  - National Center for Chronic Disease Prevention and Health Promotion
  - National Center for Environmental Health/Agency for Toxic Substances and Disease Registry
  - National Center for Injury Prevention and Control
  - National Center on Birth Defects and Developmental Disabilities

- Office of Public Health Preparedness and Response
- Office of Public Health Science Services

  ◦ Center for Surveillance, Epidemiology and Laboratory Services
  ◦ National Center for Health Statistics

- Office of the Associate Director for Communication
- Office of the Associate Director for Laboratory Science and Safety
- Office of the Associate Director for Policy
- Office of the Associate Director for Science
- Office of the Chief of Staff
- Office of the Chief Operating Officer

Health law is a foundational public health tool for disease prevention and health promotion. For many traditional public health problems, both acute and chronic, the role of law has been crucial in attaining public health goals, both framing and complementing the roles of epidemiology and laboratory science. Recently, law has played a fundamental role in the control and prevention of emerging health problems such as the threat of pandemic influenza, food safety, and gun violence. The agency's Public Health Law Program assists the centers, institutes, and offices to improve their understanding and use of law as a public health tool. CDC law initiatives have been developed in **personal health records** and **retail-based health clinics**.

Centers for Medicare and Medicaid Services

The Centers for Medicare and Medicaid Services administers Medicare, Medicaid, and related government health insurance programs. These programs serve one in three Americans, with over 1.2 billion claims per year, making the federal government the nation's largest purchaser of health care (*Government Manual*, 2016). The definition of what constitutes a **valid insurance claim** for payment by the government is an ever-present source of contention.[LN10]

The agency is attempting to transition its $927.7 billion insurance program to a **value-based payment system** (CMS, 2015). Hospitals are being solicited to enter into **gainsharing agreements** with physicians in order to reduce costs while also improving care. Under standard gainsharing agreements, hospitals pay physicians a share of any reduction in a hospital's costs attributable to the physicians' cost-saving efforts in providing care (Greaney, 2014). The merits of value-based payments are controversial (Santo, 2014).

On one hand, properly structured arrangements could offer opportunities for hospitals to reduce costs without causing inappropriate reductions in health care or rewarding patient referrals. On the other hand, gainsharing could reduce physician choice of medical devices and diagnostic tests and thus limit access to the most appropriate care (Fendell, 2014). The medical device and diagnostic industries claim gainsharing decreases incentives to invest in newer, more expensive technology and treatment procedures. While the U.S. Department of Justice, which enforces health care fraud and abuse laws, does not prosecute gainsharing agreements authorized by the Centers for Medicare & Medicaid Services (Farringer, 2015), this conditioned exception could vanish should gainsharing not produce positive results.

Food and Drug Administration

The Food and Drug Administration (FDA), the oldest federal regulatory agency in the nation, has garnered more than a century of scientific expertise. Federal concern for drugs started with the establishment of U.S. customs laboratories to administer the Import Drugs Act of 1848 (*See* 9 Stat. 237). The agency's roots date back to 1862, when the Division of Chemistry was created in the newly formed U.S. Department of Agriculture to analyze the food supply and provide advice on agricultural chemistry.

Regulation of a $4.4 Trillion Market

Growth in the medical products and food industries has resulted in the FDA regulating about $4.4 trillion of the U.S. economy (*Government Manual*, 2016; World Bank, 2015). The FDA is responsible for protecting the public health by ensuring the safety, efficacy, and security of the nation's food supply and the following eight categories of products:

- Biologics
- Cosmetics (including color additives found in makeup and other personal care products, skin moisturizers and cleansers, nail polish and perfume)

- Foods (including dietary supplements, bottled water, food additives, and infant formulas)
- Pharmaceuticals or human therapeutic drugs
- Medical devices (simple items, complex technologies such as heart pacemakers, dental devices, and surgical implants and prosthetics)
- Products that emit radiation
- Tobacco products (including cigarettes, cigarette tobacco, roll-your-own tobacco, and smokeless tobacco)
- Veterinary products (including livestock feeds, pet foods, and veterinary drugs and devices)

The FDA plays a significant role in addressing the following functions:

- Advertising of medical products with the Federal Trade Commission
- Consumer products that pose a hazard with the Consumer Product Safety Commission
- Counterterrorism capabilities
- Drinking water standards with the Environmental Protection Agency
- Security of the nation's food supply with the U.S. Department of Agriculture's Food and Safety Service

(*Government Manual*, 2016).

Incremental Regulation

In the last 70 years, the federal **Food, Drug, and Cosmetic Act of 1938** has been amended several hundred times to narrow the broad mandates the FDA was originally given. This incremental approach to regulation has resulted in enormously complex ambiguities.[LN11] Yet, Congress has not engaged in a comprehensive review of the Food, Drug, and Cosmetic Act since 1938, choosing instead to revise it word by word, provision by provision (Melnick, 2014). Today, the Food, Drug, and Cosmetic Act has slowly become inconsistent in both its terms and scope, specifically:

- Conflicting enforcement powers are provided for comparable violations
- Different words are used to mean the same thing in different parts of the law
- Inconsistent types of authority are granted with respect to similar matters
- Relationships among all of the provisions in the law are increasingly ambiguous

Drug Safety: Premarket Approval Process

Before a new medical product is introduced into the marketplace, the FDA must be provided reasonable assurances that the product is both safe and effective (Kramer et al., 2014). These assurances may be provided through the FDA's premarket approval process. The process permits the FDA to demand the submission of detailed information regarding the safety and effectiveness of the product under review (*See* 21 U.S.C.A. § 360e (describing the required contents of a premarket approval application)). The FDA then spends substantial time and resources reviewing these applications, with the average submission requiring 1,200 hours of review (over nine months of review time). Ordinarily, the FDA refers the product to an independent panel of experts, which prepares a report and recommendation on whether to approve marketing of the product. The FDA may also advise a medical products firm of any measures necessary to put its product in approvable form. Once the FDA determines the required reasonable assurances have been provided, an order is issued permitting product marketing, exactly as approved. Thereafter, changes affecting the safety or effectiveness of the product may not be made to the approved labeling, manufacturing process, or product design. The FDA may withdraw its marketing approval if any such changes are made without prior approval. The U.S. Court of Appeals for the 11th Circuit provided a summary description of the premarket approval process in *Goodlin v. Medtronic, Inc.*, 167 F.3d 1367, 1369-70 (U.S. Court of Appeals for the 11th Circuit 1999) that has since been cited by federal courts and the U.S. Supreme Court.

Post-Marketing Surveillance

Despite premarket review of medical products, active post-marketing surveillance for adverse effects is essential. Because all possible side effects of a product cannot be anticipated based on preapproval studies involving only several hundred to several thousand patients, the FDA maintains a system of post-marketing surveillance to identify adverse events that did not appear during the approval process. The FDA monitors adverse events such as reactions and poisonings and uses this information to update labeling and, on rare occasions, to reevaluate or revoke product approvals or marketing decisions.

Product Safety and Adverse Event Reporting

The FDA's **MedWatch** program provides an avenue for health care professionals and the public to voluntarily report serious reactions and problems with medical products. It also ensures that new safety information is rapidly communicated to the health care community. All data contained on the MedWatch form is entered into the **Adverse Events Reporting System**, a computerized information database of safety reports that supports the FDA's post-marketing safety surveillance program for all approved medical products.

Industry Surveillance

After a product is approved and marketed, FDA field investigators and analysts conduct unannounced inspections of drug production and control facilities to assure that firms adhere to the terms and conditions of approval described in the application. Investigators also determine if the drug or product is manufactured in a consistent and controlled manner.

Product Errors

Drug manufacturers are required by regulation to submit adverse event reports to the FDA. The MedWatch website provides information on mandatory reporting by manufacturers. In addition, manufacturers must submit either error and accident reports or drug quality reports when deviation from current good manufacturing practice regulations occurs.

The FDA receives error reports on marketed human drugs (including brand-name and generic prescription drugs as well as non-prescription over-the-counter drugs) and **nonvaccine biologics** and **medical devices**. A **medical product error** is defined as any preventable event that may cause or lead to inappropriate product use or patient harm. Such events may be related to professional practice or the medical products (including prescribing, product labeling, packaging, compounding, dispensing, distribution, administration, education, monitoring, and use).

Medical Product Shortages

It is the FDA's policy to attempt to prevent or alleviate shortages of medically necessary products. Medical product shortages may arise from varying causes, such as the unavailability of raw materials or packaging components, marketing decisions, and enforcement issues.

Drug Therapeutic Inequivalence Reporting

In the past 10 years, the FDA has received an increase in reports of **therapeutic inequivalence** or medical products that fail to work in patients because they simply have no effect or are toxic. These problems are usually attributed to switching brands of pharmaceuticals (brand-name to generic or one generic to another generic manufacturer). As a result, the FDA created the Therapeutic Inequivalence Action Coordinating Committee to identify and evaluate reports of therapeutic failures and toxicity that could indicate that one medical product is not equivalent to another similar product.

National Institutes of Health

The National Institutes of Health is the largest source of funding for medical research in the world. As the nation's medical research agency, the National Institutes of Health:

- Conducts research in its own campus laboratories and clinics across the United States
- Distributes public health information
- Facilitates the integration of safe and effective **complementary health care practices** into mainstream Western or conventional medicine
- Supports biomedical and behavioral research domestically and abroad
- Trains research scientists internally, as well as at universities and other institutions across the United States

Most of the agency's $30 billion in funding is awarded through competitive grants to more than 300,000 researchers at over 3,000 universities, medical schools, and other research institutions in every state and around the world (*Government Manual*, 2016). There are 27 national institutes and centers, including the following 18 national institutes that focus on particular diseases or body systems:

- Aging
- Alcohol Abuse and Alcoholism
- Allergy and Infectious Diseases

- Arthritis and Musculoskeletal and Skin Diseases
- Biomedical Imaging and Bioengineering
- Child Health and Human Development
- Deafness and Other Communication Disorders
- Dental and Craniofacial Diseases
- Diabetes and Digestive and Kidney Diseases
- Drug Abuse
- Environmental Health Sciences
- Eye (Ophthalmological Diseases)
- General Medical Sciences
- Heart, Lung, and Blood Diseases
- Human Genome Research
- Mental Health
- Neurological Disorders and Strokes
- Nursing Research

Internal Revenue Service Within the U.S. Department of the Treasury

U.S. tax laws have a significant effect on the health care industry, affecting the payment for and delivery of health care. Many of the provisions in the Internal revenue laws and related laws are direct government expenditures but are not included in the federal budget. For this reason, they are termed **tax expenditures**. In recent years, tax expenditures have amounted to almost half the federal budget outlays. For instance, employer-paid health insurance benefits are nontaxable income. The federal government is forgoing taxes on health insurance premiums to promote a policy of encouraging employers to provide their workers with health insurance as opposed to higher salaries and wages. This policy was implemented after World War II in the 1950s when the economy shifted from workers being self-employed or working in family-run farms or businesses to industrial and urban wage-based jobs instead.

Limited Government

The architects of the U.S. Constitution took great care to form a limited government founded on personal responsibility and individual liberty. A fundamental policy issue facing the nation right now is whether the U.S. internal revenue laws promote or undermine these founding principles. When more than $3.3 trillion is collected in federal tax revenue each year, by over 100,000 government employees, the meaning of *limited* arguably takes on an altogether different connotation (*Government Manual*, 2016; OMB, 2016).

MANAGEMENT AND LAW ISSUES

4. Do Americans still have a limited government that exists to preserve freedom, and, for the most part, does this principle still apply to health care?

Social Policy Vehicle

An ongoing debate is whether the U.S. internal revenue laws are an appropriate vehicle for implementing sweeping social policies. If tax fairness is placed ahead of economic progress, will either be achieved? The perennial question is whether the wealthiest class of Americans and corporations should pay higher tax rates to help the poor and middle classes. Congress first received authority to levy taxes on the income of individuals and corporations in 1913, pursuant to the Sixteenth Amendment of the U.S. Constitution. The percentage of tax filers paying no federal taxes has risen from about 18% in the 1980s to over 45% in 2015 (CBO, 2016). The Tax Policy Center estimated that in 2015 nearly 78 million filers had no federal income tax liability (TPC, 2015). There is serious debate about whether the removal of millions of taxpayers from the federal tax rolls is wise social policy.

Other Government Entities Affecting Health Care

Debate about whether the 59 independent federal regulatory agencies and government corporations are truly independent is ever-present. There are at least three such agencies that significantly impact and regulate the health care industry:

- Federal Trade Commission (FTC)
- National Science and Technology Council, which regulates emerging technologies such as **nanotechnology**[LN12]
- The Consumer Product Safety Commission, which tries to prevent harms before they occur; nevertheless, over 36,000 deaths and almost 14 million injuries are related to consumer products each year

By placing limits on the President's power to appoint and remove independent agency heads as well as mandating limits on the number of the President's own partisans that can be appointed, Congress has sought to limit presidential control of independent agencies (Krotoszynski et al., 2015; Lewis & Selin, 2015). Whether this independence is effective is debatable.

Federal Trade Commission

The Federal Trade Commission (FTC) was established by the Federal Trade Commission Act, 15 U.S.C.A. §§ 41–58. The following eight principal FTC functions affect the health care industry:

- Barring interlocking directorates' or officers' positions that may restrain competition
- Compelling hospitals and other health care providers to disclose in writing certain cost information, such as the annual percentage rate for deferred payments, before patients enter into credit transactions, as required by the **Truth in Lending Simplification and Reform Act of 1980** (*See* 15 U.S.C.A. §§ 1601 *et seq.*)
- Prohibiting the dissemination of false or deceptive advertisements of health care products and services as well as other unfair or deceptive practices
- Promoting competition through the prevention of general **trade restraints** such as **price-fixing agreements, boycotts, illegal combinations of competitors,** and other **unfair methods of competition**
- Proscribing **pricing discrimination, exclusive dealing, tying arrangements** (where buyers desiring to purchase one product must purchase a second product that they may or may not want), and **market discrimination** among competing health care providers and medical products firms
- Protecting patients with medical debt against circulation of inaccurate or obsolete credit reports and ensuring that credit bureaus, consumer reporting agencies, credit grantors, and bill collectors exercise their responsibilities in a fair and equitable manner
- Safeguarding the privacy of patients' personal information to prevent illegal or unwanted use of health data
- Stopping corporate mergers, acquisitions, or **joint ventures** that may substantially lessen **competition** or tend to create an **illegal monopoly**

(*Government Manual*, 2015).

Competition in Health Care

One of the two major missions of the FTC is to encourage competition in the delivery of health care. The FTC seeks to prevent unfair practices that undermine competition and attempts to prevent mergers or acquisitions of health care systems if the results would inappropriately lessen competition. It is the only federal agency with jurisdiction to enhance health care welfare and protect competition in broad sectors of the health care economy by:

- Enforcing laws that prohibit industry practices that are anticompetitive, deceptive, or unfair to health care entities if the results would inappropriately lessen competition

- Challenging attempts by independent practice associations, hospital-contracting networks, physician-contracting networks, and preferred provider organizations to impede competition and prohibiting physicians from discriminating among themselves in terms of price or other services provided
- Denying payment to physicians providing services to consumer-driven health care organizations
- Negotiating jointly with the health insurance industry and health care providers when they act in a manner that constitutes unlawful **horizontal price-fixing**

(DOJ & FTC, 2004; FTC, 2013).

The FTC is the only federal agency from which the American Medical Association has sought special exemption from jurisdiction (Blair & Durrance, 2015). The House passed a bill placing a moratorium on FTC investigations and lawsuits against physicians until Congress expressly approved such activity, but the bill was defeated in the Senate when the FTC challenged the rules banning physicians from engaging in contract medicine.

Health Care Advertising and Marketing

Health care consumer protection is the second of the two main missions of the FTC. The FTC works to:

- Ensure advertising is truthful and not false or misleading
- Prevent hospital and other health care providers from using unlawful practices when granting credit, maintaining credit information, collecting debts, and/or operating credit systems
- Reduce instances of fraudulent, deceptive, or unfair marketing and promotional practices

(DOJ & FTC, 2004).

The FTC initiates investigations in areas of concern to consumers of health care, including health and nutrition claims in advertising. The rapid expansion of medical testing, especially the direct-to-consumer advertising of genetic testing, raises questions about the accuracy of such tests and their consequences for even the most educated of consumers (Hartzog & Solove, 2015).

Medicare Advantage and Part D Prescription Drug Plan Compliance Activities

The deceptive sales tactics of private insurers running **Medicare Advantage** and **Part D prescription drug plans** victimize Medicare beneficiaries (Reiss et al., 2013). FTC audits of health-benefit options approved by Medicare, but sold and administered by private insurers, show widespread violations of patients' rights. Since 2006, when private Medicare coverage began, abuse of Medicare beneficiaries has grown as access to needed drugs or coverage of medical treatments has been restricted under the private Medicare plans. This problem is not limited to a few rogue insurance agents; rather, insurers provide lucrative incentives to producers who sell the private plans and then fail to supervise their agents (Pasquale & Ragone, 2014).

Unfortunately, weak federal regulations preempt stronger state law protections (*See* 42 U.S.C.A. §§ 139w-26(b)(3)-112(g) (pre-empting all state laws and regulations related to private Medicare plans)). Through systematic review of the marketing of Medicare's private plans, the FTC is obtaining and maintaining compliance with its cease-and-desist orders. All private insurers against whom such orders have been issued are required to file reports with the FTC to substantiate their compliance. In the event compliance is not obtained or if the order is subsequently violated, civil penalty proceedings may be instituted.

Agency Guidelines and Cooperative Procedures

Since the late 1960s, the FTC (like the FDA and Consumer Products Safety Commission) has relied increasingly on guidelines (Krishnakumar, 2015). A debate is ensuing in the health care industry about whether greater transparency is needed in the FTC's use of discretion. In carrying out its congressional directive to prevent unfair methods of competition or unfair or deceptive practices, the FTC makes extensive use of voluntary and cooperative procedures. Through these procedures, the health care industry obtains authoritative guidance and a substantial measure of certainty as to what it may do under the laws administered by the FTC. Guidelines provide the basis for voluntary abandonment of unlawful practices, while failure to comply with the guidelines may result in corrective action by the FTC.

Agency Investigations

Investigations by the FTC may originate through a complaint by a health care provider, competitor, Congress, or from federal, state, or local government agencies. Also, the FTC itself may initiate an investigation into possible violations of

MANAGEMENT AND LAW ISSUES

6.   How should the benefits of private development and public regulation be balanced?

the laws it administers. No formality is required in submitting a complaint[LN13]. It is the general policy of the FTC not to disclose the identity of the health care provider of any complainant, except as required by law or FTC rules. Upon receipt of a complaint, various criteria are applied in determining whether the particular matter should be investigated. An order issued after an administrative proceeding that requires the respondent to cease and desist or take other corrective action may be appealed. Appeals may go as far as the U.S. Supreme Court. In addition to, or in lieu of, the administrative proceeding initiated by a formal complaint, the FTC may request a U.S. district court to issue a preliminary or permanent injunction to:

- Halt the use of unfair or deceptive practices
- Prevent an anticompetitive merger or unfair methods of competition
- Stop violations of any law enforced by the FTC

Recently, the FTC initiated an investigation into children's advertising practices and the link between unhealthy food ads and childhood obesity. The consolidation of generic drug manufacturers is another area of ongoing FTC investigation as generics face a growing pressure to reduce costs. Lastly, the FTC is investigating the entire private equity industry, which may impact the pace of future acquisition deals.

Use of Governmental Powers

The federal government is continually developing new health care programs and expanding its regulation of the health care industry. However, this evolution has created overlap and excessive complexity in administrative responsibilities and regulatory powers. Further, there is confusion regarding how the federal government should construct health care spending plans that meet long-term objectives while helping put the economy on a path to budget balance. This is particularly true following the comprehensive health care reforms that were instituted with the **Affordable Care Act of 2010** (42 U.S.C.A. §§ 18001 *et seq.*).

LAW FACT

Comprehensive Health Care Reform

Should comprehensive health care reforms, as well as repeal of the reforms, be passed through Congress's budget reconciliation process?

No, generally but not always necessarily. The Supremacy Clause of the U.S. Constitution is a powerful protection of the principle of federalism because it allows federal action only if the precise procedures for lawmaking are followed (Rubenstein, 2015). Budget reconciliation eliminates and lessens some of the major hurdles to enacting comprehensive federal legislation. Omnibus budget reconciliation acts, which typically include changes to revenue laws and entitlement programs, cannot be filibustered in the Senate; instead, a reconciliation bill is considered under rules that limit debate and allow passage by a simple majority (Perkins, 2014). While budget reconciliation bills still must meet the constitutional requirements of **bicameralism** and pre-sentment to the President for enactment, congressional passage is more likely because it eliminates internal impediments of the minority (Kysar, 2014).

— 2 U.S.C.A. §§ 601-688, 900-907d (primary governing laws for the federal budget process).

CHAPTER SUMMARY

- U.S. health care law has evolved out of the interpretation and application by the judicial, legislative, and executive branches of government of the fundamental principles contained in the country's founding documents: the Declaration of Independence, the U.S. Constitution, and the Bill of Rights.
- The separation of governmental powers is central to the U.S. Constitution.
- Americans have rights beyond those enumerated in the founding documents; this is based on the notions that it would be impossible to set forth every possible right and that some rights supersede the government.
- It is the province and duty of the judicial branch to interpret and apply the laws enacted by the legislative branch; the judiciary sometimes struggles to say what the law is, not what it should be.
- The U.S. Supreme Court is the nation's highest court, but it may only hear certain kinds of cases.
- The People are attempting to increase their influence upon their government, particularly through ballot initiatives and citizen movements.
- The legislative branch consists of Congress, which is comprised of the U.S. Senate and House of Representatives, who jointly draft and enact legislation.
- The Government Accountability Office and the Congressional Budget Office help to advise Congress and provide oversight and guidance.
- The executive branch is comprised of the President and various government agencies that administer and enforce legislation; two ongoing priorities have been to address health care fraud and drug safety issues.
- The U.S. Department of Health and Human Services has a pervasive influence on the U.S. health care industry; its budget is greater than all of the other federal agencies combined.
- The nine Department of Health and Human Services agencies that significantly impact the U.S. health care industry are the Administration for Children and Families, Administration on Aging, Agency for Healthcare Research and Quality, Centers for Medicare and Medicaid Services, Food and Drug Administration, Health Resources and Services Administration, National Institutes of Health, Public Health Service, and Substance Abuse and Mental Health Services Administration.
- The Food and Drug Administration regulates approximately one-fourth of the U.S. economy by ensuring the safety and efficacy of food, cosmetics, dietary supplements, therapeutic drugs, medical devices, radioactive products, and veterinary drugs.
- Beyond the U.S. Department of Health and Human Services, federal tax laws also influence how health care is paid for and delivered.
- Nanotechnology provides the first opportunity since the formation of the Food and Drug Administration for governance to develop simultaneously with emerging technology.
- The Federal Trade Commission protects U.S. health care by preventing unfair competition and deceptive business practices and protecting consumers.
- The Food and Drug Administration further protects consumers by requiring medical products manufacturers to prove that their products are safe and effective prior to marketing.

LAW NOTES

1. For decades, the Administration for Children and Families has met criticism for the nation's lack of oversight of state-administered foster programs. Recent concerns have been directed at how foster youth are generally unable to live independently once they reach 18 years of age, with some youth resorting to sleeping in hospital emergency rooms (Beam, 2014; Dixon et al., 2011). Today, a child welfare issue involving transitions out of foster care has evolved into a health care issue.
2. Medicines produced by the medical products industry have helped to increase the life expectancy of Americans 65 and over, to 20 years longer than their predecessors (NBER, 2016). Therefore, as a significant portion of the U.S. population grows older, the Administration on Aging will be placed under greater scrutiny to ensure the nation's medical products are safe, as well as efficacious and affordable for older Americans.
3. Americans 65 and over spend twice as much on health care compared to the rest of the population (Kaiser, 2014). While the majority Americans over 65 have health insurance coverage through Medicare, nearly half of all health care costs come from non-Medicare sources. This places a heavy burden on this population, considering that nearly 45% of Americans over the age of 65 are also socioeconomically deprived with limited access to health care (Cubanski et al., 2015 and 2014).

4. Elder abuse is so pervasive it qualifies as a major public health problem in the United States (Marcus, 2015). The Administration on Aging estimates that over 4 million Americans 65 and older have been the victims of some form of abuse. At the same time, the National Center on Elder Abuse believes the reporting of elder abuse and neglect is as low as 1 in 14 cases, despite mandatory reporting in all 50 states. Systems to address this public health issue simply do not exist in most communities (Kapp, 2014).

5. The Quality and Disparity Report measures differences in the availability and use of health care services in various populations. Differences in quality and access to health care do exist. People of lower socioeconomic status are less likely to receive high-quality health care; they also spend more money to get inferior care, suffer poorer health outcomes, and die earlier than their more affluent peers (AHRQ, 2014; Matthew, 2015).

6. New research estimating the rate of injuries caused by medical errors suggests that U.S. hospitals and health care providers bear some of the responsibility for as many as 440,000 deaths each year (James, 2013); a finding consistent with studies by the Agency for Healthcare Research and Quality (Landrigan, 2010), the Office of the Inspector General at the U.S. Department of Health and Human Services (Levinson, 2012; OIG-HHS, 2010), and the Institute of Medicine (IOM, 2010). The Agency for Healthcare Research and Quality continuously monitors this phenomenon using outcomes research. For instance, the Agency for Healthcare Research and Quality and the Centers for Disease Control and Prevention recently found that two-thirds of the serious injuries and deaths to newborn infants in the delivery room are the result of human error (CDC, 2013). Once the Agency for Healthcare Research and Quality makes discoveries like this, national guidelines for common medical procedures are produced to address the problem (*See* Welch et al., 2012). Compliance with applicable guidelines is in turn monitored by The Joint Commission on Accreditation of Healthcare Organizations. Noncompliance could cause a health care provider to lose accreditation, which could provide grounds for insurers to deny payment for medical treatments provided to patients (including government insurance programs like Medicare and Medicaidinsurance).

7. Health insurance coverage for the routine costs of qualifying clinical trials, and medically reasonable and necessary services used to diagnose and treat clinical trial-related complications, is inconsistent and denials are plentiful. The General Accounting Office estimates that the medical coverage denial rate for experimental and investigational treatment is one in four of all claims (GAO, 2011). The Agency for Healthcare Research and Quality, the Centers for Medicare and Medicaid Services, and the FDA are working with the health insurance industry and patients to resolve this payment issue (Lee, 2014).

8. Quality and Disparity Reports, from the Agency for Healthcare Research and Quality, on the terms of statistical compliance with clinical guidelines has demonstrated that even with clear-cut clinical guidelines, physicians ignore the guidelines more times than not. As a result, Americans receive the care that is recommended by the best available information only about 54% of the time (IOM, 2012). To improve physician compliance, the Agency for Healthcare Research and Quality and the Institute of Medicine have recommended the need for a conceptual framework to analyze physician performance (Avraham, 2014 and 2011; IOM, 2012).

9. Research from the Agency for Healthcare Research and Quality found the personal beliefs of physicians often supersede the proper care of sexual assault victims (Hrobak & Wilson, 2014; Mulla, 2014). Although the FDA approved over-the-counter access to emergency contraception for those over age 18 in the pharmacy setting, few states have enacted explicit emergency contraception laws to require hospital emergency rooms to provide sexual assault victims with information regarding emergency contraception and then to furnish it in the hospital upon request. The Agency for Healthcare Research and Quality has been clear in advising states that hospital emergency rooms must inform rape survivors of the availability of emergency contraception and provide information on how to access it, even though they may refer the patient to another facility to secure it (Deutsch, 2015).

10. Across the nation hospital debts are mounting due to the unreimbursed care that is given to the 11 million undocumented immigrants (Berlinger et al., 2015; Gusmano, 2012). While the Centers for Medicare and Medicaid Services funds Emergency Medicaid and promulgates policies the states must follow in administration of their own plans, defining emergency care has proven to be a problem (*See* **Emergency Medical Treatment and Labor Act of 1986**, 42 U.S.C.A. § 1395dd). Several states are funding chemotherapy for immigrants regardless of status and are requesting payment from the federal government. This argument over whether chemotherapy should be covered under Emergency Medicaid highlights the ambiguity of the government policy of only offering financial assistance for emergencies. Immigrants diagnosed with cancer suffer emergencies as the disease takes its course, but any emergency care given ultimately does little good because necessary follow-up treatment is unavailable. Hospitals often wind up with large bills of uncompensated care if chemotherapy is part of any treatment intervention (Price, 2012).

11. The FDA prohibits the medical products industry from promoting the unapproved use of its pharmaceutical, biologic, and device products, maintaining that this information is detrimental to public health (Abbott & Ayres, 2014). At the same time, the FDA mandates that the industry provide open access to available data about unapproved uses so medical decision-making can be safe (LaSalle, 2011). One policy prohibits the same speech that another policy mandates. Despite these regulatory inconsistencies, the significance of the FDA's role in the U.S. economy continues to increase.

12. Nanotechnology offers the possibility of revolutionizing health care. Though a number of nanotechnology products are already on the market, the major developments are yet to come. Most discussion presents a polarized debate between those seeking rapid development unfettered by excessive regulation and those who advocate a stringent regulatory regime to protect against nanotechnology risks. For the second time in history, there is the opportunity for a federal governance system to develop simultaneously with an emerging technology, the first time being the FDA (Cortez, 2014). The governance model that is emerging for nanotechnology could provide important insights for reforming governance systems in general.

13. The FTC's law enforcement work falls into two general categories: actions to foster voluntary compliance with the law, and formal administrative or federal court litigation leading to mandatory orders against offenders. Compliance with the law may be obtained through:

- Formal advisory opinions;
- Guides and policy statements outlining legal requirements as to industry practices; and
- Voluntary and cooperative action in response to nonbinding staff advice.

Formal litigation is instituted either by issuing an administrative complaint or by filing a federal district court complaint charging a health care provider or a medical products firm with violating one or more of the laws administered by the FTC. If the charges in an administrative matter are not contested, or if the charges are found to be true after an administrative hearing in a contested case, an order may be issued requiring discontinuance of the unlawful practices.

REFERENCES

Abbott, R., & Ayres, I. (2014). Evidence and extrapolation: Mechanisms for regulating off-label uses of drugs and devices. *Duke Law Journal, 64*, 377–435.

AHRQ (Agency for Healthcare Research and Quality). (2014). *National Healthcare Quality and Disparities Report*. Rockville, MD: AHRQ.

AOA (Administration on the Aging). (2014). *A profile of older Americans*. Washington, DC: AOA.

Avraham, R. (2014). Overlooked and underused: Clinical practice guidelines and malpractice liability for independent physicians. *Connecticut Insurance Law Journal, 20*, 273–333.

Barnard, F. M. (2003). *Democratic legitimacy: Plural values and political power*. Montreal, Canada: McGill-Queen's University Press.

Beam, C. (2014). *To the end of June: The intimate life of American foster care*. Boston, MA: Mariner Books-Houghton Mifflin Harcourt.

Berlinger, N., et al. (2015). *Undocumented immigrants and access to health care in New York City: Identifying fair, effective, and sustainable local policy solutions*. New York, NY: New York Immigration Coalition and Garrison, NY: Hastings Center.

Blackstone, W. (2011). *The commentaries of Sir William Blackstone, Knight, on the laws and constitution of England*. Chicago, IL: American Bar Association (Original work published 1765).

Blair, R. D., & Durrance, C. P. (2015). Licensing health care professionals, state action and antitrust policy. *Iowa Law Review, 100*, 1943–1967.

Cannan, J. (2013). A legislative history of the Affordable Care Act: How legislative procedure shapes legislative history. *Law Library Journal, 105*, 131–173.

CBO (Congressional Budget Office). (2016). *The budget and economic outlook: 2016 to 2026*. Washington, DC: CBO.

___. (2015). The 2015 long-term budget outlook.

CDC (Centers for Disease Control and Prevention). (2013, August 9). CDC grand rounds: Public health approaches to reducing U.S. infant mortality. *Morbidity and Mortality Weekly Report (MMWR), 62*(31), 625–628.

Cortez, N. (2014). Regulating disruptive innovation. *Berkeley Technology Law Journal, 29*, 175–228.

Cubanski, J., et al. (2015). *Poverty among seniors: An updated analysis of national and state level poverty rates under the official and supplemental poverty measures*.

___. (2014). *Health care on a budget: The financial burden of health care spending by Medicare households*.

Deutsch, E. B. (2015). Expanding conscience, shrinking care: The crisis in access to reproductive care and the Affordable Care Act's nondiscrimination mandate. *Yale Law Journal, 124*, 2470–2514.

Dixon, J., et al. (2011). The politics of protecting children. *Tennessee Journal of Law and Policy, 7*, 218–263.

DOJ & FTC (U.S. Department of Justice & Federal Trade Commission). (2004). *Improving health care: A dose of competition*. Washington, DC: DOJ & FTC.

Farringer, D. R. (2015). Keeping our eyes on the prize: Examining Minnesota as a means for assuring achievement of the "triple aim" under the ACA. *Hamline Law Review, 38,* 177–225.

Fendell, S. (2014). The unintended results of payment reform and electronic medical records. *Health and Biomedical Law Society, 10,* 173–200.

Fishkin, J., & Forbath, W. E. (2014). The great society and the constitution of opportunity. *Drake Law Review, 62,* 1017–1054.

FTC (Federal Trade Commission). (2013). *Overview of FTC antitrust actions in health care services and products.* Washington, DC: FTC.

GAO (General Accountability Office). (2015). *Cybersecurity: Recent data breaches illustrate need for strong controls across federal agencies.* Washington, DC: GAO.

___. (2014a). *Healthcare.Gov: Information security and privacy controls should be enhanced to address weaknesses.*

___. (2014b). *Healthcare.Gov: Actions needed to address weaknesses in information security and privacy controls.*

___. (2014c). *Electronic health records: HHS strategy to address information exchange challenges lacks specific prioritized actions and milestones.*

___. (2011). *Private health insurance: Data on application and coverage denials.*

Government Manual, The U.S. (2016). Washington, DC: U.S. Government Printing Office.

Greaney, T. L. (2014). Regulators as market-makers: Accountable care organizations and competition policy. *Arizona State Law Journal, 46,* 1–40.

Gusmano, M. K. (2012). *Undocumented immigrants in the United States: U.S. health policy and access to care.* Garrison, NY: The Hastings Center.

Hamburger, P. (2015). The inversion of rights and power. *Buffalo Law Review, 63,* 731–832.

Hartzog, W., & Solove, D. J. (2015). The scope and potential of FTC data protection. *The George Washington Law Review, 83,* 2230–2300.

Hrobak, R. M., & Wilson, R. F. (2014). Emergency contraceptives or "abortion-inducing" drugs? Empowering women to make informed decisions. *Washington and Lee Law Review, 71,* 1385–1428.

IBM. (2015). *Annual report,* Armonk, NY: IBM.

IOM (Institute of Medicine). (2012). *Best care at lower cost: The path to continuously learning health care in America.* Washington, DC: The National Academies Press.

___. (2010). *Redesigning continuing education in the health professions.*

James, J. T. (2013). A new, evidence-based estimate of patient harms associated with hospital care. *Journal of Patient Safety, 9*(3), 122–128.

Kaiser Family Foundation. (2014). *Medicare at a glance.* Menlo Park, CA: Kaiser.

Kamin, D. (2015). Basing budget baselines. *William and Mary Law Review, 57,* 143–219.

Kapp, M. B. (2014). Home and community-based long-term services and supports: Health reform's most enduring legacy? *Saint Louis University Journal of Health Law and Policy, 8,* 9–32.

Kramer, D. B., et al. (2014). Ensuring medical device effectiveness and safety: A cross-national comparison of approaches to regulation. *Food and Drug Law Journal, 69,* 1–23.

Krishnakumar, A. S. (2015). Longstanding agency interpretations. *Fordham Law Review, 83,* 1823–1903.

Krotoszynski, R. J., et al. (2015). Partisan balance requirements in the age of new formalism. *Notre Dame Law Review, 90,* 941–1017.

Kysar, R. M. (2014). The shell bill game: Avoidance and the origination clause. *Washington University Law Review, 91,* 659–720.

Landrigan, C. P. (2010). Temporal trends in rates of patient harm resulting from medical care. *New England Journal of Medicine, 363,* 2124–2134.

LaSalle, K. (2011). A prescription for change: *Citizens United's* implications for regulation of off-label promotion of prescription pharmaceuticals. *Journal of Law and Policy, 19,* 867–911.

Lee, W. B. (2014). Recalibrating "experimental treatment exclusion": An empirical analysis. *University of Cincinnati Law Review, 83,* 171–201.

Levinson, D. R. (2012). *Hospital incident reporting systems do not capture most patient harm.* Washington, DC: U.S. Department of Health and Human Services, Office of the Inspector General.

Lewis, D. E., & Selin, J. L. (2015). Political control and the forms of agency independence. *The George Washington Law Review, 83,* 1487–1516.

Locke, J. (2015). *The second treatise of civil government.* Peterborough, Canada: Broadview Press (original work published 1689).

Lowi, T. J., et al. (2013). *American government: Power and purpose* (13th ed.). New York, NY: W. W. Norton and Company.

Marcus, I. (2015). Gaps and barriers: Elder abuse qualifies as a major public health problem in the United States. *Montana Lawyer, 40*(7), 20–22.

Matthew, D. B. (2015). Toward a structural theory of implicit racial and ethnic bias in health care. *Health Matrix: Journal of Law Medicine, 25,* 61–85.

Melnick, R. S. (2014). Has the Constitution exacerbated the crisis of governance? The conventional misdiagnosis: Why "gridlock" is not our central problem and constitutional revision is not the solution. *Boston University Law Review, 94,* 767–793.

Moncrieff, A. R. (2010). The Supreme Court's assault on litigation: Why (and how) it might be good for health law. *Boston University Law Review, 90,* 2323–2382.

Mulla, S. (2014). *The violence of care: Rape victims, forensic nurses, and sexual assault intervention.* New York, NY: New York University Press.

NBER (National Bureau of Economic Research). (2016). *The impact of new drug launches on longevity: Evidence from longitudinal, disease-level data from 52 countries.* Cambridge, MA: NBER.

Nozick, R. (2013). *Anarchy, state, and utopia.* New York, NY: Basic Books-Perseus Book Group (original work published 1974).

Nussle, J., & Orszag, P. (2015). *Moneyball for government* (2nd ed.). Disruption Books: Amazon Digital Services.

OIG-HHS (Office of the Inspector General, U.S. Department of Health and Human Services). (2010). *Adverse events in hospitals: National incidence among Medicare beneficiaries.* Washington, DC: HHS, OIG.

OMB (Office of Management and Budget). (2016). *Budget of the U.S. government.* Washington, DC: OMB.

Orszag, P. R. (2010). *Changing the trend for earmarks.* Washington, DC: Office of Management and Budget.

Pasquale, F., & Ragone, T. A. (2014). Protecting health privacy in an era of big data processing and cloud computing. *Stanford Technology Law Review, 17,* 595–653.

Perkins, R. H. (2014). Breaking the spell of tax budget magic. *Columbia Journal of Tax Law, 6,* 1–32.

Presser, S. B., & Zainaldin, J. S. (2013). *Cases and materials on law and jurisprudence in American history* (8th ed.). St. Paul, MN: West Academic Publishing.

Price, R. (2012). The killer mandate: EMTALA and its financial effects on hospitals and immigrants. *UMKC [University of Missouri-Kansas City] Law Review, 80,* 881–903.

Rawls, J. (1999). *Theory of justice.* Cambridge, MA: Belknap Press-Harvard University Press (original work published 1971).

Reiss, J. B., et al. (2013). Your business in court and at federal agencies. *Food and Drug Law Journal, 68,* 1–51.

Rubenstein, D. S. (2015). Administrative federalism as separation of powers. *Washington and Lee Law Review, 72,* 171–254.

Santo, C. (2014). Walking a tightrope: Regulating Medicare fraud and abuse and the transition to value-based payment. *Case Western Reserve Law Review, 64,* 1377–1417.

Sassman, W. G. (2015). Applying originalism. *UCLA Law Review Discourse, 63,* 154–171.

Smith, Jr., F. O. (2014). Due process, republicanism, and direct democracy. *New York University Law Review, 89,* 582–665.

Smith, G. P., & Gallena, R. P. (2014). Re-negotiating a theory of social contract for universal health care in America or, securing the regulatory state? *Catholic University Law Review, 63,* 423–463.

TPC (Tax Policy Center). (2015). *The numbers: Tax units with zero or negative income tax.* Washington, DC: Urban Institute and Brookings Institution.

Walmart. (2016). *Annual report.* Bentonville, AR: Walmart.

Welch, H. G., et al. (2012). *Over-diagnosed—Making people sick in the pursuit of health.* Boston, MA: Beacon Press.

White House, The. (2009). *Press release: Remarks by the President on earmark reform.* Washington, DC: The White House.

World Bank. (2015). *GDP at market prices (current US$).* Washington, DC: World Bank.

PART II

ACCESS TO HEALTH CARE

Part II addresses Americans' resolve to obtain the best health care system for as little investment as possible.

CHAPTER 3

© Andy Dean Photography/ShutterStock, Inc.

Access to Affordable Health Insurance

"To me our country is a living, breathing presence, unimpressed by what others say is impossible, proud of its own success, generous, yes, and naive, sometimes wrong, never mean, and always impatient to provide a better life for its people in a framework of a basic fairness and freedom."

— **Ronald Reagan** (1911–2004), 40th President of the United States

IN BRIEF

This chapter draws attention to the challenge of finding a way to provide access to affordable health insurance for everyone. A description of the economics of insurance is followed by an explanation of distributive justice, the political philosophy underlying recent health care reforms and the consequent pooling of health risks and responsibility to pay for society's health care within each of our communities. Risk-pooling programs that provide effective and affordable medical coverage to millions of Americans are examined. Also discussed are plans for the uninsured that cut through the ideological spectrum, from fair play legislation that mandates universal medical coverage to federal subsidies that offset much of the cost of buying health insurance policies from private insurance companies and public exchanges.

LEARNING OBJECTIVES

Upon completion of this chapter readers should be able to:

1. Describe the reasons the uninsured and underinsured lack insurance
2. Explain the basic purposes of insurance
3. Define health risks in conjunction with allocation of limited resources
4. Outline the principles of economic fairness
5. Understand health insurance risk pooling
6. Contrast consumer-directed health care with high-deductible health plans

KEY TERMS

Affordable Care Act of 2010
340B drug pricing program
Autonomy
Average and best prices
Benefit
Cost-shifting
Distributive justice
Drug rebate program
Economic fairness
Employee Retirement Income
    Security Act of 1974 (ERISA)
Equality of opportunity
Expected utility maximization

Expected utility model
Guaranteed issue
Health insurance exchange
Health outcomes
Health risk
Health risks and responsibility
Individual mandate
Insurance
Insurance risk pools
Medicaid insurance
Medically necessary care
Minimum essential health insurance
    coverage

Patent
People, the ("We the People")
Patient assistance programs
Principles
Privilege
Purchase rebates
Refundable tax credits
Rights
Shared responsibility payment
Social contracts
Tax credits
Tax-exempt
Utility

FACT OR FICTION

Access to Affordable Health Insurance

Should everyone be required to maintain health insurance as an economic imperative of national health care reform?

Four uninsured Michigan residents, along with the Thomas More Law Center, a public interest law firm that provides health insurance to its employees, claimed that the **individual mandate** (or minimum coverage provision) of the **Affordable Care Act of 2010** (42 U.S.C.A. §§ 18001 *et seq.*) unconstitutionally compels them to purchase health insurance. Each of them objects to being compelled by the federal government to purchase medical coverage or to pay a **shared responsibility payment** for failure to maintain basic coverage based on household income. This annual penalty is accessed on anyone who does not purchase or maintain a certain level of coverage.

In reviewing the individual mandate, the court noted how Congress determined that this provision was an essential part of the Affordable Care Act. The court then provided background on the legislation and explained the five interrelated parts of the law that were designed to improve affordable access to health insurance and minimize the **cost-shifting** that occurs whenever insurers charge more for certain services and medical products in order to subsidize services and products that are provided at or below cost. The following is accomplished by the Affordable Care Act:

- Enlarges **insurance risk pools** by building upon the existing nationwide system of employer-based health **insurance** to spread the costs of illness and disease across U.S. society by:
  - Establishing tax incentives for employer-provided health insurance for small businesses and individuals
  - Requiring large employers to offer health insurance coverage to expand the pooling of **health risks** by insurers to help pay for the costs of their employees' health care
- Provides for the creation of **health insurance exchanges** that allow individuals and small businesses to leverage their collective buying power to obtain competitively priced health insurance
- Expands eligibility for **Medicaid insurance** and offers federal **tax credits** for payment of health insurance premiums
- Provides for **guaranteed issue** of health insurance by prohibiting insurers from denying basic coverage to anyone with preexisting conditions and bars them from charging higher rates to people based on their medical history
- Requires everyone to obtain **minimum essential health insurance coverage**, the so-called **individual mandate**

The court further explained the Congressional findings accompanying the individual mandate requiring almost all U.S. residents to maintain health insurance, thereby automatically enrolling virtually everyone in the United States into an insurance risk pool for medical coverage financed through broad-based premiums and tax subsidies for those unable to pay the premium costs. Ideally, under the Affordable Care Act, the costs of illness and disease will be spread across an entire society as government and private health insurers pool the nation's health risks and the responsibility to help pay for everyone's health care expenses.

— *See* Law Fact at the end of this chapter for the answer.

Principles and Applications

The Affordable Care Act, the biggest change in health care since **Medicare** and Medicaid insurance were established in 1965, is reversing uninsured trends and lowering cost barriers (Collins et al., 2015). For the first time in decades, the number of people who report cost-related access problems and medical-related financial difficulties has declined (Commonwealth Fund, 2016). The number of adults who did not get needed health care because of cost declined by over 16 million in 2014 and 2015 (Commonwealth Fund, 2016). The number of adults who reported problems paying their medical bills declined by 11 million (Commonwealth Fund, 2015).

Despite this progress, health care access and reimbursement for health care remain at the forefront of public concern (Wiley, 2016). There is near unanimous agreement that the lack of universal access to health care is one of the principal

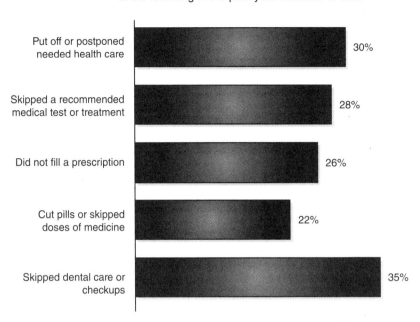

FIGURE 3-1 Lack of Access to Health Care

Data from: Commonwealth Fund. (2015). The problem of underinsurance and how rising deductibles will make it worse. New York, NY; Kaiser Family Foundation. (2015). Employer health benefits survey. Menlo Park, CA: Kaiser.

shortcomings of the U.S. health system, relative to health systems in other similar high-income, developed countries. Lack of access is believed to be the most significant contributor to the underperformance of the U.S. health system in terms of broad population health measures, such as life expectancy (Sugden, 2012). As illustrated in **FIGURE 3-1**, about 39 million working-age Americans still report cost as a barrier to receiving needed health care (Kaiser, 2015b). The uninsured experience the most consistent erosion in access to care, resulting in a widening gap in general health between the insured and uninsured (Commonwealth Fund, 2015).

Minimum Essential Coverage for the Uninsured

One of the most intractable problems facing public policy makers for years is how to provide medical coverage in a way that is both effective and affordable. For more than half a century, there has been discussion about the fundamental question of how many households are uninsured and whether the uninsured are actually harmed due to lack of coverage (IOM, 2004; Wiley, 2016). Today, there appears to be near universal agreement about the three *W*'s of health insurance:

- Who the uninsured are
- What happens to the uninsured when they need health care or when the medical expense of the underinsured exceeds their coverage and ability to pay for care
- Why the uninsured are uninsured

About 27 million Americans, or 1 in 9 people in the United States, have no health insurance (CBO, 2016b), and most of them have middle-class incomes (Kaiser, 2014).[LN1] The uninsured population is not static; Americans fall into and out of coverage for various periods of time (Martinez & Cohen, 2015). For the other higher income uninsured, their higher income or lack of insurance is transient (CBO, 2016b).

The effect of having 27 million Americans uninsured is considerable (CBO, 2016b). For one thing, the uninsured risk serious illness or death by delaying necessary health care. Although expanding insurance coverage is associated with a 6% drop in unnecessary deaths (Sommers et al., 2012), the precise effect of insurance status remains uncertain (Collins et al., 2015; O'Neill & O'Neill, 2009).

FEATURE BOX 3-1

Facts About the Uninsured

- About 6 in 10 of the uninsured have at least one full-time worker in their family, while 1 in 5 have only part-time workers.
- About 7 in 10 uninsured adults cite unemployment or high costs as a major barrier to purchasing health insurance coverage, compared to 2 in 10 adults who say they are uninsured because they do not need basic coverage.
- Children are the least likely to be uninsured because they are more likely to qualify for government coverage through Medicaid insurance or the Children's Health Insurance Program (CHIP).
- Most of the uninsured are in a working family with low or moderate-middle-class incomes (meaning a family of four earning less than $88,000/year) and cannot afford family premiums without employer contributions.
- Nearly three-quarters of the uninsured have been unemployed and uninsured for more than a year.

Note: Includes adults under age 65 who are not eligible for Medicare insurance coverage.

Data from: AHRQ, 2015; CDC/NCHS, 2015; Kaiser, 2015a and 2014; Majerol et al., 2015; Martinez & Cohen, 2015.

Economics of the Uninsured

The purpose of health insurance is to pool risks in order to provide access to affordable health care for all. The insured pay into insurance risk pools, also known as guaranteed access programs, hoping they will never have to use it.

Societal costs in this situation, from the uninsured and the underinsured, may take noneconomic forms such as a more unproductive workforce. Whether health insurance is effective in reducing societal costs is not clear (Blake, 2015; Mantel, 2015); however, the Affordable Care Act potentially could lift millions out of poverty by eliminating medical expenses that are now covered by insurance. Moreover, what is clear is that the long-term uninsured of sufficient means that can afford health insurance, but choose not to purchase coverage, are shifting their share of the insurance risk pools to everyone else. Even if an individual is generally healthy, they still cannot predict an expensive serious illness or injury.

Spillover Effect from the Uninsured

While the health care costs of the uninsured, in terms of uncompensated care, are driving up overall costs, the spillover effect of not being insured is more disturbing. As illustrated in **FIGURE 3-2**, 1% of the U.S. population is responsible for about one-fourth of the nation's health care spending, and the top 5% accounted for half of the spending (Majerol et al., 2015; Martinez & Cohen, 2015). One widespread characteristic of this patient population is the seriousness and chronic nature of their illnesses. Moreover, their health conditions often arise from a general failure to receive preventive health care and seek timely care, which are two common attributes of being uninsured (Fleck, 2011). These hidden costs must be more visible and better controlled.

In addition, there is another spillover effect beyond the uninsured. In communities with large numbers of uninsured, even those who have insurance experience less availability of health care and receive lower quality care

FEATURE BOX 3-2

How Does the Issue of the Uninsured Affect the Insured?

Everyone who pays into insurance risk pools is forced to pay higher health insurance premiums because it costs more to treat the uninsured when they become seriously ill as a result of a lack of routine, preventive care. Higher premiums lead to the insured being underinsured, who then do not have adequate coverage when a catastrophic injury or illness hits.

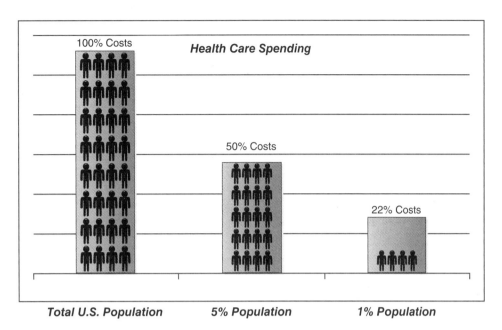

FIGURE 3-2 Disproportionate Health Care Spending

Data from: Majerol, M., et al. (2015). *The uninsured: A primer—key facts about health insurance and the uninsured on the eve of coverage expansions.* Menlo, CA: Kaiser Family Foundation; Martinez, M. E., & Cohen, R. A. (2015). *Health insurance coverage: Early release of estimates from the national health interview survey.* Atlanta, GA: Centers for Disease Control and Prevention's National Center for Health Statistics.

than people who live in communities with few uninsured individuals (Leifer et al., 2014; Satz, 2015). For instance, the burden on the charity care system is much higher because the uninsured often go to the emergency room for preventable illnesses (Morrell & Krouse, 2014).

Economic Cycle of Health Insurance

The best, most highly trained physicians are also often some of the most highly compensated citizens in the nation; the United States richly rewards its most skilled health care professionals. The most highly regarded medical institutions in the United States are able to attract and retain the best physicians in the world with attractive compensation packages. These respected medical institutions, in turn, are part of comprehensive health care delivery systems with significant revenues; each of the top 12 hospital systems have gross revenues of more than $6 billion a year (American Hospital Directory, 2015).

In turn, these health care delivery systems maintain their earnings from strategies pursued to increase revenues, including demanding upfront payments from patients and hiking list prices for health care to several times their actual cost (Weisblatt, 2014). The uninsured are generally unable to afford this type of health care with its requirements for upfront cash payments and high prices (those with health insurance are required to pay their deductibles and co-payments before service is ever rendered). The economic circle of health care follows the money: the highest-quality health care is physically located near those patients who can afford the care, who are the insured.

By comparison, most of the hospitals under financial strain are in communities handling large numbers of uninsured. In turn, these hospitals are not often able to attract the best, most highly trained physicians with attractive compensation packages, nor are they able to invest in the latest medical technologies. Medical institutions with limited financial resources and average-skilled physicians and mediocre equipment often provide lower quality health care. It is the classic cycle of economic poverty: the least advantaged of society receive the least, despite needing the most.

Reframing Choices About Health Insurance

In seeking to address the challenge of insuring the uninsured, the Affordable Care Act adopted three different scenarios:

- Employer and individual mandates to purchase health insurance
- Federal and state exchanges with standardized, competitive health insurance plans
- Targeted tax subsidies to purchase health insurance

No matter what solutions were adopted to deal with the uninsured, **health risks and responsibility** continue to occupy center stage in reform of U.S. health care (Maher, 2011). While the Affordable Care Act adopted the European style of maximizing **health outcomes** by focusing on the effect of treatment interventions on patient health status, the health insurance marketplace continues on its course of allocating health risks and financial responsibility. There may be better ways of defining the objectives of health care policy or ways of framing the choices about health insurance. Hopefully, the nation will battle its deeply entrenched ideas about health risks and responsibility to pay for those risks when they materialize in order to bring about additional reforms.

Defining Health Risks

The allocation of health risks and financial responsibility is a dominant force in the U.S. health care system (Wiley, 2016). The term *health risks* come up frequently when medicine and health care are discussed. What are the risks and responsibility of:

- Dying from a complication of surgery or a medical procedure?
- Experiencing a life-threatening reaction to a medication or innovative treatment?
- Going without health insurance if healthy?
- Experiencing a preventable medical emergency or serious illness?

Most people do not necessarily use the term *health risks* in the same way health professionals and insurance experts do, which is a fact that can potentially lead to less than optimal policy decisions about health care (Wharton, 2007). The language that describes access to health care, the uninsured and underinsured, and health spending sometimes gets in the way of clear thinking and sometimes implicitly reflects quite different ways of thinking (Blake, 2015; Pauly & Pagan, 2007). There is no better example of this language confusion than use of the term *health risks*. Debates about health risk occur often as if there were consensus on the meaning of the term but, in reality, everyone in the room uses the term in a variety of ways:

- Analyzing health risks in clinical decisions
- Pooling health risks through insurance
- Trading off between the health risks and benefits of medical interventions
- Assessing the likelihood of realizing the consequences of health risks

Expected Utility Maximization

Flawed thinking about health risks can cause faulty decisions. One decision-making model that is increasingly followed to make decisions about risks is known as **expected utility maximization**, or benefit–cost analysis (Zamir, 2012). In the health care industry, **utility** is a measure of the relative satisfaction from consumption of health care. Used primarily by economists and antitrust attorneys in the health care industry, the **expected utility model** values risks as a weighted average of the possible outcomes with the:

- Weights being the probabilities of risks for any given medical intervention
- Values being the utility attached to changes in a patient's health and well-being, in each intervention

  (Gayer et al., 2014; Kreps, 2012).

For instance, at the individual level, when a patient makes a subjective decision about what type of medical intervention to accept, each treatment outcome would be ranked. Suppose the patient could:

- Do nothing
- Change their behavior and take medicine
- Have surgery and take medicine

If patients elect to change their behavior, then patients strictly prefer changing their behavior to having surgery or are indifferent between them. In this situation, if the medical interventions are ranked by the preferred treatment outcomes:

- Do nothing = 0
- Behavior change = 1

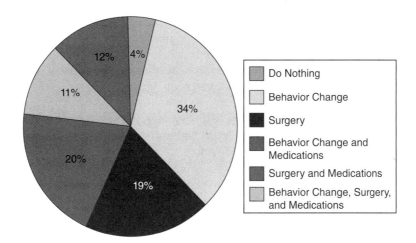

FIGURE 3-3 Expected Utility Maximization

Data from: Enemark, D. (2013). Modeling human decision-making in the law: Can legal actors play equilibrium strategies? Two dubious assumptions in the game-theoretic analysis of the law. *Southern California Law Review, 86,* 449–458; Gayer, et al. (2014). Pareto efficiency with different beliefs. *The Journal of Legal Studies, 43,* 151–170; Kreps, D. M. (2012). Microeconomic foundations: Choice and competitive markets. Princeton, NJ: Princeton University Press; Zamir, E. (2012). Loss Aversion and the law. *Vanderbilt Law Review, 65,* 829–894.

- Behavior change and medicine = 2
- Surgery = 3
- Surgery and medicine = 3
- Behavior change, surgery, and medicine = 4

Then, as illustrated in **FIGURE 3-3**, this patient prefers behavior change over surgery (with *one* being the most preferred choice), but prefers behavior change and taking medicine over surgery and taking medicine. Though research in this area is still in its infancy, many decisions about treatment interventions are subject to these behavioral factors (Enemark, 2013).

When deciding what can be done to address the challenges of health care access and reimbursement for health care, all the things that can be done at the systems level could be treated in the same manner. That is, when confronted with a range of options, the preferences are rank ordered, taking into consideration the probability of achieving each option, the most efficient means to the desired end (access to affordable health insurance for everyone) is then chosen. In this instance, the patient is the U.S. health care system and the treatment interventions are:

- Consumer-directed health care plans
- Corporate taxes on excessive profits related to any activities subsidized with government funds
- Discounted medication programs
- Expansion of government insurance programs
- Individual and employer mandates to purchase health insurance
- Regulatory reform of state insurance laws
- Targeted federal tax subsidies on health insurance premiums
- Taxes on excessive total compensation of individual executives in the health care industry whose organizations receive any type of tax subsidies (through their tax-exempt status or acceptance of employer-provided insurance that receives tax preferential treatment), government health insurance payments, or government grants

If the maximization of utility is the criterion for organization of the U.S. health care system, one may speak meaningfully of determining a choice of action by increasing or decreasing utility. Although the complexity of the U.S. health care system may diverge from strict expected utility maximization, this decision model could help explain the behavior of consumers in terms of their consumption of health care (*See* Kant, 2005/1797).

Political Philosophy of Distributive Justice

The theory of **distributive justice** (Rawls, 2005/1971)[LN2] underlies the expected utility model. Distributive justice concerns what is just with respect to the allocation of health risks and responsibility. In this instance, if everyone were provided access to affordable health insurance, the U.S. health care system would be considered guided by the principles of distributive justice. This theory is key to reform of the nation's health insurance system whereby health care is financed by individuals on the basis of their ability to pay, but is available to all who need health care on more or less equal terms. Distributive justice suggests most Americans have a harmony of interests and responsibilities that are integral to living as a citizen of the United States, as opposed to alone as individuals with no interest in or obligation to anyone other than themselves. In other words, Americans as a society have implicitly agreed to give up some personal autonomy in favor of the benefits to society at large.

For instance, what principles could Congress agree to if one side of the aisle cooperates with the other side of the aisle, but each side still prefers more of the benefits and less of the burdens associated with cooperation? What decisions about access to affordable health insurance are both rational and reasonable, and according to whom? Assuming legislators are rational, they have ends they want to achieve, but are also reasonable and open to compromise insofar as they would be glad to achieve these ends together if they could, in accord with principles that are mutually acceptable. Given how different the needs and aspirations are on each side of the aisle, how can Congress find principles that are acceptable to both sides? One decision-making model for this choice is expected utility maximization. The ideal health care reform would therefore be an overlapping consensus because different and often conflicting needs and aspirations will always overlap with each other (*See generally* Rawls, 2005/1971 and 2001).

Fairness to the Least Advantaged

The theoretical approach to this decision-making model is based on the notion that inequalities should work to the benefit of the least advantaged in society. A fair health care system provides **medically necessary care** to the healthiest people as well as to people who are suffering the most from disease and illness. This policy approach is framed around two theories: the theory of **social contracts** and the theory of **economic fairness**.

Social Contracts

In a just society there is an imaginary social contract between the governed and their government. A social contract implies that a nation's citizens give up some **rights** to their government in order to receive and jointly preserve social order, the theoretical groundwork of democracy (Locke, 2008/1689). For John Locke, the purpose of government is to serve and benefit **the people**; government must be controlled by the people for which the government was made. For Jean-Jacques Rousseau, citizens of a nation place themselves and their authority under the supreme direction of the general will, and the group receives each individual as an indivisible part of the whole. As the U.S. Supreme Court has stated: a *"fundamental principle of the social compact [is] that the whole people covenants with each citizen, and each citizen with the whole people, that all shall be governed by certain laws for the common good."* Jacobson v. Massachusetts, 197 U.S. 11, 27 (U.S. Supreme Court 1905).

Most people in the world believe their government has a social contract to provide health care, a belief that is shared by the majority of the citizens in every democracy in the world, and a commitment that was accepted by the United States with adoption of the Affordable Care Act. Access to health care was always considered a **privilege** in the United States, which was usually expressed as a **benefit** of employment, while in other democracies access is considered a right of citizenship. This chapter is about the parameters of this social contract and how it has developed and is developing in the United States. For instance, a social contract exists between the health care industry and society that gives the public a legitimate expectation that the companies, in return for their corporate existence provided by the people through their government, will respond by providing access to affordable health insurance. In return for the benefits of:

- FDA market approval, the medical products industry is obligated to comply with the nation's anti-fraud laws
- **Patent** protection, the medical products industry will respond with prescription drugs, biologics, and medical devices that are reasonably accessible to the public
- Tax subsidies on employee health insurance plans, the insurance industry will provide risk pools that offer affordable access to health insurance
- **Tax-exempt** status, hospitals will make access to charitable health care available to patients in financial need

Economic Fairness

In making any decision, the essential question must always be: Is this fair and does it make economic sense (Rawls, 2005/1971)? There can be no fairness if something does not make economic sense. Wherever one ends up in society, one wants the transactions that affect their life to be reasonably just and understandable; the activities in one's life

FEATURE BOX 3-3

Fairness Based on John Rawls' Political Philosophy

First Principle: Universal Health Insurance

- Each person is free to select the health care system and providers for their health care
- Everyone has an equal claim to access affordable health insurance
- Health care providers are guaranteed to receive fair value for the services they provide
- The means to access medically necessary care must be the same for everyone

Second Principle: Pooled Risk

- Inequalities brought about by the inability to pay fair value for health care are permissible if the following two conditions are met:
  - Affordable health insurance must be accessible to everyone based on the fairness principle; in other words, access to health care must be based on medical need and equality of opportunity
  - The greatest assistance to access affordable health insurance must be given to the least advantaged

Data from: Rawls, J. 2005/1971.

should be able to be transacted according to fair and socially acceptable rules that are in accordance with what is expected. In addressing access to affordable health insurance, one framework for the decision process might be the concept of fairness based on John Rawls' political philosophy.

Equality of Health Opportunities

While Americans have decided to act collectively so that everyone can access health care when in need, regardless of income or health status, adoption of the **equality of opportunity** principle is not the same as mandating that everyone have access to exactly the same health care. Achieving this would offend American notions of individual **autonomy** and responsibility. Nonetheless, access to affordable health insurance is assured, but there will always be freedom to pursue additional health care based on the ability to pay fair value for that care (*See generally* Rawls, 1971/2005).

MANAGEMENT AND LAW ISSUES

1. If the law requires consistency in the way individuals are treated, what legal standards are prevailing for accessing health care in the United States today?
2. Should the uninsured, underinsured, and Medicaid-insured have the same rights to access health care as the privately insured? Alternatively, is it better yet to offer a cafeteria approach so individual employees can make their own decisions to meet their specific health care needs?

Hierarchy of Principles

The first principle of universal health insurance has priority over the second principle of pooled health risks, and the first half of the second principle has priority over the latter half. The claim for universal health insurance would have priority over the claim for pooled health risks. The right to medically necessary care has a greater weight than the cost of the care. The ability to pay fair value for health care would have priority over the assistance provided to access the needed care (*See generally* Rawls, 1971/2005).

Relationship Between Principles and Their Application

The **principles** and their application are two distinct but related issues. The principles are not validated or invalidated by the ability or inability to apply them. For instance, just because the U.S. health care system cannot have equal application of the principles does not mean the principles are not valid. If these principles were applied perfectly and if the United States could find a way to pay for universal health care without any limitations, there would be no inequalities.

If the United States had the ability to pay for every medical technology and every medicine needed by everyone, inequalities of access to health care would not exist. Essentially, if the United States had unlimited resources there would be no inequalities. The point is that the United States does not have the financial resources to pay for everything. The scarcity of resources mandates that available financial resources be maximized. So, the nation must decide who gets what.

Application of the Principles: Health Risks and Responsibility

The expected utility maximization model could be used by employers to decide what type of health insurance coverage to offer their employees.

The key questions about health risks and responsibility are:

- Which preferences should government use in designing medical interventions?
- Should the United States implement economically sensible solutions that may benefit only a fraction of the public?
- Or should the United States adopt less than optimal economic policies that are preferred by a wider constituency?

By definition, health risks involve uncertainty. Uncertainty makes people uneasy. It is not just that people do not like bad outcomes; rather, they do not like not knowing what the outcome will be (Morag-Levine, 2014). In the achievement of health and the use of health care, health risks seem to be everywhere at once. Questions about these risks and uncertainties include:

- What will anyone's health be in the future?
- What accident or illness might occur?
- If sick:
  - What will be the outcome of treatments, prescription drugs, or biologics?
  - What adverse side effects could occur?
  - What future medical bills might arise?

While health economists use the expected utility model to explain how the public tends to make decisions in risky situations, in the real world, people do not always make decisions this way (Zamir, 2012). There is still a lot of smoking in the United States, and there are many people who eat fast food every day. Moreover, consumers often misconstrue health risks when they are deciding among various treatment options. Should they try an experimental drug or biologic or accept a more standard treatment? Or what type and level of coverage should they select when deciding whether to purchase health insurance?

FEATURE BOX 3-4

Health Insurance Coverage Options

Is it better to offer employees a health insurance policy with a:

- High deductible but excellent catastrophic coverage?
- Low deductible with more coverage for routine, lower-end expenses such as preventive care and routine provider visits?

Or is it best to offer both options to employees and let them choose which policy fits their needs?

Data from: Enemark, 2013; Gayer et al., 2014.

Americans seem to value health insurance that reimburses them, so they get a return on their premium payments (Gonzales & Stuart, 2014). This perception is different than viewing health insurance as protection against the health risks of a catastrophic accident or illness that probably will not happen but that could mean financial disaster if it did occur. Most people reason that because they paid for insurance for so many years and hardly ever used it, that the purchase was a bad financial decision (Wharton, 2007). The expected utility model says that was not a bad decision. If something catastrophic had happened, they would benefit so much from the insurance that it would offset all the years of paying and getting nothing back.

Less Extensive Coverage for the Uninsured of Limited Means

The Affordable Care Act prohibits limited-benefit insurance plans (Herrick, 2014). Although most health insurance policies offer coverage for inpatient hospitalization, some insurers attempted to attract the uninsured with low premiums that covered some outpatient services which are more likely to be needed, while leaving less likely but far more expensive hospital costs uncovered or only partially covered. This reduced treatments of minimal value, while enrollees faced higher cost-sharing or tighter control of their health care (Korobkin, 2014).

While limited-benefit plans were perhaps appealing to the uninsured of limited means, this approach to health insurance was problematic from an economic standpoint (Wharton, 2007). Even though the uninsured are less likely to be hospitalized than require a physician's visit, everyone should be protected against hospital costs (Brown, 2015). While individuals with less extensive coverage may be treated fairly from an economic perspective, they are not being treated fairly in terms of access to coverage.

Mutual Health Insurance Plans

Healthy people, in particular, fail to weigh health risks and responsibility optimally, thinking they should not spend money on health insurance because their chances of falling seriously ill are small. In this case, one possible solution is designing health plans exclusively for healthy people who are unlikely to have preventable health conditions: for instance, nonsmokers who are not obese. The uninsured who are healthy could contribute insurance premiums into mutual health insurance plans, in return for the promise that if they are right and everyone is a low-user of health care services, premiums would be refunded. Mutual health insurance plans would pay dividends to policyholders if benefits payouts were low; these dividend payments would, in turn, be used to lower future premiums. Thus, healthy people would be in a risk pool with other healthy people like themselves who have the same health risks as they do, whatever that health risk really is.

Private Insurance Debate on Health Risks and Responsibility

The current controversy over employer-provided insurance increases speculation that individual health insurance will soon become a possibility for more Americans under the Affordable Care Act (Levitt et al., 2015). Research on the relationship between premiums and expected medical expenses across the three major sources of private health insurance in the United States has exposed some common misconceptions about how the following insurance markets work:

- Individual health insurance
- Large employer-provided insurance
- Small-group insurance

Employer-provided insurance may not be as performing as well, nor individual health insurance performing as poorly, as is generally believed (Pauly & Pagan, 2007; Pollitz, 2016). While the number of Americans covered by employer-provided insurance has been declining since 1997, the leading source of health insurance held by more than 147 million Americans is still employment based (Kaiser, 2015b). Conventional wisdom gives high marks to employer-provided insurance, asserting it manages to pool health risks and responsibility across all consumers. Individual health insurance, on the other hand, which is held by about 16 million Americans, gets the worst grade for supposedly seeking out low-risk customers while avoiding those considered high-risk (Levitt et al., 2015). While this information may be correct, the appearances that give rise to these judgments may be quite deceiving (Majerol et al., 2015; Pauly & Pagan, 2007).

Perceptions (or Misconceptions) About Health Risks and Responsibility

Perceptions (or misperceptions) about health risks and responsibility affect the debate about how to best provide coverage for the uninsured and underinsured. It is hard to override public misperceptions, especially misperceptions about health risks and responsibility (Pauly & Pagan, 2007). There are at least three prevalent misconceptions:

- High-risk individuals with higher than average health risks pay higher health insurance premiums
- Individual health insurance policies carry higher premiums because of their high administrative costs
- Individual policies are not the best type of health insurance

High-Risk Individuals

First, do individual nongroup insurers segment health risks and responsibility? If so, does the health insurance industry rate people based on risks, and do high-risk individuals pay more? There is no relationship between individual health risks and the premiums people pay. While insurers attempt to segment health risks and responsibility, the segmentation has never worked. Individuals holding individual insurance, whose anticipated medical expenses are twice the average, pay premiums only about 20 to 40% higher than other individual insurance customers (Wharton, 2007).

The result of these market forces in the individual nongroup market is that health insurance premiums paid by those with chronic conditions are not consistently greater than those paid by healthy people. What is more, there is no conclusive evidence that anyone seeking health insurance in the nongroup market is deterred from obtaining coverage because they have higher than average health risks. Anecdotal reports exist, but, on an aggregate scale, this misconception does not appear to be supported by the facts.

Insurance Risk Pools

Second, do employer-provided insurance policies pool health risks almost completely? The governance and distribution of risks are what drive the health care system. Interconnected policies and give-and-take practices are evident everywhere. All actors within the system (health insurers, health care providers, and consumers) take on aspects of risk, and the system's viability is contingent on allocating these pool risks (Gruisin, 2015).

In large employer groups, high-risk individuals pay somewhat more either through higher premiums or lower wages because they exhibit some risk factors that influence their expected health expenses, such as age. Employees receive lower wages over their careers when they obtain employer-based health insurance than when in organizations where they do not (Wharton, 2007). Thus, through lower wages over time, the more senior employees effectively pay more for their health insurance.

In addition, there is evidence that location also plays a role in the premium rates employees pay (for instance, in New York, physicians and hospitals are more expensive than in Iowa, resulting in higher premiums for New Yorkers) (Rausch, 2012). Accordingly, the Affordable Care Act requires the health insurance industry to base premiums on community ratings (42 U.S.C.S. § 300gg(a)). Moreover, high-risk, low-wage employees in small groups are less likely to obtain health insurance than others. With employer-provided insurance there is, of course, also a freedom of choice issue. There is currently a managed care backlash where employees are unhappy with what their employers are offering. Insurers stung by the cost in goodwill from this have developed consumer-driven product lines that shift elevated levels of risks and responsibility to their employees through health savings accounts and higher co-payments and deductibles (Kaiser, 2015b).

Employer Mandates or Taxes to Provide Health Insurance

The Affordable Care Act all but eliminates the likelihood that state or local governments will undertake significant health care reform in the short term, but it does not eliminate the importance of clarifying the scope of employer spending mandates. Growing numbers of state and local governments continue to experiment with universal health care plans (Bignami & Spivac, 2016). The basic similarity of these experiments is that like the Affordable Care Act, most state and local government reforms feature additional employer mandates or taxes aimed at changing employee health insurance plans; they seek to require all employers to provide adequate levels of coverage for their employees (including small business employers that are exempt from the Affordable Care Act mandates) (Frankenfield, 2010).

MANAGEMENT AND LAW ISSUES

6. Who should be included and excluded in any insurance risk-pooling process?
7. What type of systems of accountability and checks and balances should be sufficient to produce an insurance risk-pooling system that is equitable, as well as efficient and flexible?
8. What standards should govern access to health care?

Fair Share (Pay or Play) Employer Mandates

The Affordable Care Act does not eliminate the importance of employer spending mandates as a financing component for state and local governments to expand access to health care. The gap between the uninsured and access to health care remains. How well state and local governments are able to perform that role, however, depends upon the extent to which ERISA continues to impede state and local health care reforms (Frankenfield, 2010).

In American legal scholarship, experiments in democracy are closely associated with a collaborative approach to health law that emphasizes regulatory initiatives (Starr, 1983). If Justice Louis Brandeis were to witness San Francisco's experiment with universal health care legislation, he might amend his characterization of the states as laboratories of democracy to include municipalities as well. San Francisco is seeking to provide access to affordable health care to the city's estimated 80,000 uninsured residents, roughly half of whom work.

COURT CASE
Fair Share Health Reform Measure

Golden Gate Restaurant Association v. City and County of San Francisco
[Opponents of "Pay or Play" Reform v. Municipal Reformers]
546 F.3d 639 (U.S. Court of Appeals for the 9th Circuit 2008),
cert. denied, 561 U.S. 1024 (U.S. Supreme Court 2010)

Facts: In San Francisco, where 10% of the City residents have no health insurance and 15% of businesses provide no medical coverage for their employees, the Board of Supervisors passed the San Francisco Health Care Security law, which funds a network of primary care services for uninsured residents (S.F. Admin. Code § 14.2(d)). While the law met with general approval, its provision mandating contributions from local businesses that do not meet minimum health spending requirements was the subject of litigation. The law, adopted unanimously, creates a health access program designed to make health care services available to the City's more than 80,000 uninsured residents. Funding for the program, which provides primary care for the uninsured at both public and private facilities throughout the City, comes from:

- Mandatory contributions from businesses that do not meet designated health care contribution levels for their employees
- Municipal, state, and federal government grants
- Payments from individual enrollees

Employers can meet their required contribution levels in a variety of ways, by:

- Contributing to employee health savings accounts
- Donating to the City's new health access program
- Paying a third party for health care delivery for their employees
- Reimbursing their employees directly for their health care expenses

Such contribution provisions are often called pay or play because employers must either help *pay* for government-sponsored health care programs or *play* by providing their employees with health insurance themselves.

Golden Gate Restaurant Association, representing the interests of over 800 San Francisco restaurants, brought an action challenging the law. The Association claimed the federal **Employee Retirement Income Security Act of 1974** (ERISA) preempted the law's fair share employer spending requirement (29 U.S.C.A. §§ 1001 *et seq.*). ERISA sets minimum standards for a wide array of employer-provided benefit plans including most employer health insurance plans. ERISA explicitly preempts state and local laws that relate to employee benefit plans regulated by ERISA.

Issue: Does federal ERISA preempt the Fair Share law that requires employers in San Francisco to spend a minimum percentage of their revenues on health care plans for their employees?

Holding and Decision: No. ERISA does not preempt San Francisco's Fair Share law.

Analysis: The court unanimously decided that the public interest would be best served by allowing the Fair Share law to go forward in its entirety. The court emphasized there was a presumption against ERISA preemption where laws fall within the state's traditional police power to regulate health and safety. It was unlikely, according to the court, that the Fair Share law had an impermissible connection with an ERISA plan, because the law did not require employers to:

- Adopt an ERISA plan
- Change the administrative practices of such plans
- Provide specific benefits through an existing ERISA plan

While employers would face an administrative burden in the form of required record maintenance, the court noted this burden fell equally on employers who had ERISA plans and those who did not. In addition, it was unlikely the Fair Share law would be preempted because of a reference to an ERISA plan (since the law may take ERISA health plan spending into account when calculating the required contribution of employers). The Fair Share law does not refer to ERISA plans specifically and it could operate effectively, whether or not such plans existed. Furthermore, the court expressed confidence in the Fair Share law's political legitimacy given that the San Francisco Board of Supervisors passed the law unanimously with the support of the Mayor of San Francisco. Citing the U.S. Supreme Court, the court concluded federal courts of equity should exercise their discretionary power with proper regard for the rightful independence of local governments in carrying out their domestic policy.

Rule of Law: The spending requirements of San Francisco's Fair Share law do not establish an ERISA plan, nor do they have an impermissible connection with employers' ERISA plans, or make an impermissible reference to such plans.

References discussing this court decision: Frankenfield, 2010; Hoffmann, 2014.

The San Francisco Fair Share law has forced retail and restaurant businesses with large populations of uninsured employees to adjust. While some businesses raised prices and curtailed hiring, the Fair Share law did what it was intended to do: it pushed employers to defray medical costs for more of their employees who could not afford coverage (Dvorak, 2008; Serota & Singer, 2011). What is less clear is the extent to which mandated health insurance laws affect the cost of coverage to employers (Strine, 2015).

Mandates for Universal Health Care Coverage

After a yearlong struggle to provide universal health insurance to all state citizens, the California legislature defeated the measure. Today, California continues to grapple with one of the highest uninsured rates in the nation, with one in five citizens uninsured (Litchfield, 2012). Like the San Francisco law, the proposed California plan for universal health care coverage was explicit in requiring all employers to provide health insurance or pay a tax. The California law was to have applied to all employers with 10 or more employees to provide adequate employee health care benefits or pay a 4% state tax.

The Massachusetts plan for universal health insurance, a state with one of the lowest uninsured rates in the nation, is slightly different than the California plan; it does not feature a percentage tax. Massachusetts charges a $295-a-head fee to employers who do not provide employees with health insurance. Employers in Massachusetts are also liable for the catastrophic medical expenses of uninsured employees. Moreover, the incentive in the Massachusetts law is not significant enough to force employers to make changes to their ERISA plans. Unlike with the Maryland law, discussed below, the rational action for employers to take in Massachusetts would be to pay the $295 per employee fee, a much less expensive option than making a fair and reasonable contribution to employee medical coverage. Because the incentive under the Massachusetts law does not function as a mandate, the Massachusetts law is likely to survive any preemption challenge.

On the other hand, universal health insurance attempts by Maryland and Suffolk County, New York, to require employers to provide adequate health insurance coverage for all their employees were overturned by the federal courts following challenges by the retail industry (Jensen, 2011). Maryland's legislation would have required employers with over 10,000 employees to spend at least 8% of their payroll on employee health care or remit such amount to the state (Jost & Hall, 2013). Although Maryland's percentage requirement was less than half what most employers in the United States pay to provide employee health insurance, it did not survive a preemption challenge.

The average employer in the United States spends at least 17% of its payroll providing health insurance coverage (Kaiser, 2015b). Suffolk County sought to require large retail stores selling groceries to pay a penalty for not providing health insurance that was equivalent to the cost incurred by the public health care system of providing health care to one uninsured employee. Both the Maryland and Suffolk County provisions would have largely affected Walmart employees who were uninsured (Strine, 2015).

Common Law Barriers to Health Care Reforms

ERISA opponents claim the law accomplishes its goal of regulatory uniformity at the expense of state and local governments' ability to provide innovative health care reforms. Although ERISA's legislative history makes it clear Congress intended to craft a broad preemption provision, it is unclear whether Congress ever anticipated the comprehensive influence the law has had on health care. There were sound reasons Congress decided to create a uniform national regulatory framework in 1974; employers were meant to be freed from the administrative burden of having to comply with a multitude of state and local requirements, leaving them with more money to spend on actual health care and other employee benefits. The question is whether enough small businesses are providing adequate health insurance to justify continued use of ERISA preemption. In 2015, the Kaiser Family Foundation annual survey of employers found:

- Employees pay an average of $1,050 month toward family coverage, which is more than one-third what they paid 10 years ago
- Employers with the highest percentage of low-wage workers (defined as earning $23,000 or less annually) contributed the lowest percentage for coverage for their employees
- Low-wage workers are generally required to pay 41% of their health insurance premiums
- Low-wage workers have higher annual deductibles and higher cost-sharing than higher-wage workers
- The cost shift has been most dramatic for employers in small businesses, where more than one in three covered employees must pay at least $1,700 out of pocket before their plan will start to pay a share of their health care bills
- While almost all business with more than 200 employees provided employee health insurance, less than half the small businesses provided coverage

(Kaiser, 2015b).

If the U.S. Supreme Court gives ERISA preemption, most, if not all, fair share laws could be overturned. The resulting common law barrier to innovative solutions at the state and local levels would no doubt increase the already significant demands for a federal solution to the challenge of providing more equitable access to health care (Lewis, 2014).

Limited ERISA Preemption

Not all state governments are willing to accept the minimum provisions of the Affordable Care Act. Many states do not want to exempt small business employers from providing health insurance or exempt the uninsured from access to health insurance due to affordability (as the Affordable Care Act has) (Blum et al., 2015). Other states are not willing to have their insured citizens unable to access necessary health care due to costs (cost-shifting with unaffordable high deductibles and co-payments) or be unjustly denied or delayed claims for coverage under ERISA health insurance plans (Lewis, 2014; Vukadin, 2014).

The U.S. Supreme Court accepted the San Francisco experiment by declining to hear the case, permitting the *Golden Gate Restaurant Association v. City and County of San Francisco* decision to stand. Consequently, the nation is likely to see a proliferation of state and local government provisions similar to the San Francisco law. At least 30 states are considering legislation that requires all employers either to provide access to minimum levels of health care to all their employees or to pay the shortfall into state health care programs (Vukadin, 2014).

Federal Fair Share Mandate

ERISA only preempts state and local law; therefore, a federal fair share mandate could avoid this particular difficulty. The ultimate result of this ERISA litigation, therefore, may be to increase the demand for federal universal health care reform (Lewis, 2014).

Tax Subsidies to Encourage the Purchase of Health Insurance

Before the Affordable Care Act, federal tax subsidies to encourage the purchase of private health insurance exceeded $307 billion a year (IRS, 2015; Lowry, 2014; Rae et al., 2014). This system, however, was upside-down for half a century (Gruisin, 2015). For instance, employer coverage premiums are excludable from income taxed at the federal and state levels. Therefore, for employees with high marginal tax rates (totaling over 50% for the highest wage earners), the tax incentive was high. With the health insurance subsidy decreasing according to marginal tax rates, the lowest wage earners with lower marginal tax rates had little tax incentive to purchase health insurance.

The working poor received no benefit from tax subsidies before the Affordable Care Act. In other words, employees in the 50% tax category saved half the cost of their premiums for health insurance. This compared to the 40% of Americans who do not pay any federal taxes and therefore saved little when they purchased the same insurance. Thus, the prior system provided the greatest tax benefits to persons who needed it the least. In this instance, the middle class got the smallest subsidy, but paid the highest share of their income for health insurance.

Federal tax credits are one way to provide coverage for the uninsured and help correct this upside-down system. Estimates are that the cost of this latest scheme will add at least another $100 billion to the existing $307 billion tab as more individuals enroll in subsidized coverage under the Affordable Care Act (Lowry, 2014; Rae et al., 2014). Problems in states with large-scale compulsory proposals for covering the uninsured set the stage for the use of flexible, well-designed targeted federal subsidies, such as the Affordable Care Act's **refundable tax credits** to cover part of the premiums for health insurance. A refundable tax credit is simply a credit that allows payments to taxpayers to exceed their tax obligations.

Proposals that are now gaining acceptance are plans under which individuals or businesses take advantage of federal tax credits for basic coverage that would vary inversely with income (IRS, 2015; Rae et al., 2014). The Health Care Coalition for the Uninsured, an organization composed of 16 of the nation's largest health care and community organizations, endorsed the Affordable Care Act program of tax credits that offsets a large part of the cost of buying policies from the health insurance industry or from public insurance exchanges.

Tax credits or targeted subsidies permit the uninsured to buy mainstream insurance and use mainstream health care; this will, in turn, improve quality for the insured by unleashing the power of the competitive market to provide more choices when it comes to securing affordable, quality coverage (CBO, 2016b). The insured may gain the most from helping the uninsured if the assistance is not targeted specifically at providing services to the uninsured only (Pauly & Pagan, 2007). While there is debate over the use of tax credits to provide health insurance versus expansion of Medicaid, proponents of this approach claim targeted tax subsidies best address the issues of effectiveness and affordability (Auerbach, 2014; CBO, 2016b; *Contra* Archambault, 2014).

Insurance Regulation

The United States spends a greater percentage of its gross domestic product on health care than any other industrialized country; its system of insurance regulation is partly to blame for this (Hoffman, 2010).

While the federal government regulates nearly all employer-provided insurance coverage, states retain the power to regulate insurance contracts issued to their residents (*See* McCarran-Ferguson Act, 15 U.S.C.A. §§ 1011-1015). As a result, employers who purchase insurance to cover their health plan benefits are subject to both federal and state regulation, while employers who self-insure plan benefits are exempt from all state insurance regulations and subject to only federal regulations.

Employers who purchase insurance to cover their health plans are covered by federal insurance laws, such as the Mental Health Parity Act (*See* 29 U.S.C.A. § 1185a and 42 U.S.C.A. § 300gg-5) requiring employers to provide the same health insurance coverage for health and mental health conditions and the Newborns' and Mothers' Health Protection Act (*See* 42 U.S.C.A. § 300gg-4) requiring coverage for a minimum hospital stay of 48 hours following childbirth.

States regulate the amount of financial reserves an insurance company must maintain. Employers subject to the state-based regulatory system have significantly higher compliance costs and have to comply with as many as 50 different sets of state laws. While insurance companies are likely to bear the brunt of the burden of technical compliance with individual state laws, having separate insurance contracts in different states does raise costs for multistate employers.

Regulatory Disparity

Employers who self-insure, as most employers with more than 200 employees do, enjoy nearly complete freedom to structure their health plans. Those who purchase insurance, as most small firms and individual purchasers do, are often heavily regulated by their state (Monahan, 2012). This disparity in insurance regulation is difficult to justify.

In both types of employer-provided insurance plans, the insurance company typically processes all initial claims. However, employers have the ultimate authority to decide a claim on appeal from a self-insured plan, whereas the insurance company will decide all levels of an appealed claim in an insured plan pursuant to state law and regulations. While about one-third of Americans are covered by self-insured plans (Kaiser, 2015a), most court cases challenging claim appeals appear to come from the more regulated health insurance plans rather than the self-insured plans.

The Congressional Budget Office found that health insurance would likely cost about 6% less if the insurance industry were allowed to get out from under some of the outmoded state insurance regulations (CBO, 2016a). Insurance

---

FEATURE BOX 3-5

Costs of Insurance Regulation

$90 billion for underwriting
$156 billion administrative costs from redundancy and inefficiency
$210 billion for the health insurance claims system

Data from: *Florida, et al. v. U.S. Department of Health and Human Services*, 648 F.3d 1235 (U.S. Court of Appeals for the 11th Circuit 2011), *affirmed in part and reversed in part*, 132 S.Ct. 2566 (U.S. Supreme Court 2012); Schwarcz & Schwarcz, 2014.

regulations provide employers who are most likely to provide medical coverage with the lowest regulatory burden, while imposing a significant regulatory burden on smaller employers who are already least likely to provide medical coverage to their employees (Hoffman, 2010). It is estimated that as much as one-fourth of the uninsured lack coverage due to overregulation of the insurance industry (Ben-Shahar & Logue, 2012).

Access to Prescription Drugs and Biologics

Unlike other nations, the United States does not directly regulate the prices that the medical products industry can charge for their products. A federal pricing scheme would establish the prices that patients and health insurers pay for prescription drugs and biologics. In addition to federal pricing, patent protection and market exclusivity shield the medical products industry from normal market competition, giving the industry significantly greater bargaining power over prices than patients or insurers. Without any competition or additional regulation of prices (other than the federal pricing scheme), prescription prices are simply what the medical products industry sets for its products.

Yet, at a time when more than half of all Americans and 90% of the Medicare insured take prescription drugs or biologics (NCHS, 2015), there are no enforceable rights for charging too much. This federal pricing policy is difficult to justify when patients and insurers often pay exorbitant prices for their prescriptions, even for brand products that are no more effective than less expensive generic options (Spiro et al., 2015). The issue that must be addressed is: how can the medical products industry overcharge purchasers of their products and be subject to virtually nonexistent federal administrative oversight (Greve, 2011)?

Surely, this lack of enforceable rights for overcharging cannot be compatible with the statutory objectives of federal pricing. Supporters of the existing statutory scheme maintain that the current system ensures compliance by the medical products industry and spreads the enforcement burden beyond government. Nevertheless, without enforceable rights for overcharging, prices for prescription drugs and biologics may have risen to rates that are unsustainable in the absence of intervention and better negotiation by the federal government.

COURT DECISION
Product Pricing by the Pharmaceutical Industry

Astra USA, Inc. v. Santa Clara County
[Pharmaceutical Manufacturer v. Local Government]
563 U.S. 110 (U.S. Supreme Court 2011);
followed by *Sioux Honey Association v. Hartford Fire Insurance Company*,
672 F.3d 1041 (U.S. Court of Appeals for the Federal Circuit 2012), *cert. denied*,
133 S.Ct. 126 (U.S. Supreme Court 2012)

Facts: The federal **drug rebate program**, created in 1990, governs the manufacturers of prescription pharmaceuticals and biologics who participate in Medicaid insurance programs and requires participating manufacturers to provide **purchase rebates** to the states based on **average and best prices**, which are calculated according to regulatory formulas. In 1992, Congress added the **340B drug pricing program**, which requires manufacturers to offer prescription drugs and biologics to safety-net providers caring for the uninsured and low-income consumers at discounted rates. These rates are determined based on the same average and best price calculations used in the drug rebate program. Participation in the 340B drug pricing program is governed by a form agreement, which lays out the statutory requirements of the program. Santa Clara County, which operates several health care facilities in California, sued nine pharmaceutical manufacturers, claiming they overcharged for products purchased under the 340B drug pricing program.

Issue: Should there be enforceable rights for overcharging by the pharmaceutical industry?

Holding and Decision: Patients and health care providers are not entitled to enforce the drug pricing provisions of a statutorily created agreement between pharmaceutical manufacturers and the federal government.

Analysis: The U.S. Supreme Court began by recognizing the law authorizing the federal drug rebate and 340B drug pricing programs does not allow for private causes of action. Instead, the federal government has oversight authority with power to order reimbursement or terminate manufacturers' participation in the programs. The Court determined that the form agreement served to enroll manufacturers into the 340B drug pricing program and spell out the terms of the law and underlying regulations.

The Court reasoned that, because the obligations under the 340B agreement and under the law are identical, a suit to enforce the agreement would be the same as a suit to enforce the law. This conclusion was supported by the facts of the case where the claims by Santa Clara County were based entirely on statutory obligations embodied in the agreement rather than on any independent substantive obligation unique to the contract. The Court also rejected third-party beneficiary suits as being inconsistent with the legal framework of the 340B drug pricing program, which centralizes enforcement power to avoid fragmented application of the program.

Rule of Law: Health care providers cannot sue pharmaceutical manufacturers as third-party beneficiaries to enforce pricing agreements between the federal government and the manufacturers.

References discussing this court decision: Finegan, 2011; Greve, 2011; NCHS, 2015; Spiro et al., 2015.

Challenges of Access to Affordable Health Insurance

Employer mandates to provide coverage, individual mandates to purchase coverage, reform of state insurance laws, and prescription discount programs are all important steps to incentivize greater medical coverage and to make health insurance more affordable for everyone. Yet, there are continued challenges to the Affordable Care Act with some compromises possible on tax subsidies, Medicaid insurance, and other features, but no prospects of brokered solutions in Congress in the immediate future. At the same time, the health care marketplaces are becoming more efficient and millions of the previously uninsured are now insured (CBO, 2016a).

LAW FACT

Access to Affordable Health Insurance

Should everyone be required to maintain health insurance as an economic imperative of national health care reform?

Yes. The federal requirement that everyone maintain health insurance falls within Congress's constitutional authority over interstate commerce. Everyone will access health care at some point, whether voluntarily or not, and therefore the question is how to pay for it.

— *Thomas More Law Center v. Obama*, 651 F.3d 529 (U.S. Court of Appeals for the 6th Circuit 2011) (holding the individual mandate constitutional), *cert. denied*, 133 S.Ct. 61 (U.S. Supreme Court 2012), *related proceeding at United States Citizens Association v. Sebelius*, 754 F.Supp.2d 903 (U.S. District Court for the Northern District of Ohio 2010), *as amended* 2011 (holding the Association's challenge was not barred). Followed by *Wright v. O'Day*, 706 F.3d 769 (U.S. Court of Appeals for the 6th Circuit 2013). *Compare Mead v. Holder*, 766 F.Supp.2d 16 (U.S. District Court for the District of Columbia 2011) (holding the individual mandate constitutional), *affirmed*, 661 F.3d 1 (U.S. Court of Appeals for the D.C. Circuit 2011), *with Commonwealth of Virginia ex rel. Cuccinelli v. Sebelius*, 656 F.3d 253 (U.S. Court of Appeals for the 4th Circuit 2011) (dismissing Virginia's challenge to the individual mandate for lack of standing), *cert. denied*, 133 S.Ct. 59 (U.S. Supreme Court 2012). *See also National Federation of Independent Business v. Sebelius* and *Florida v. U.S. Department of Health and Human Services*, 648 F.3d 1235 (U.S. Court of Appeals for the 11th Circuit 2011), *affirmed in part and reversed in part*, 132 S.Ct. 2566 (U.S. Supreme Court 2012) (holding the individual mandate and the entire legislation constitutional, except the expansion of the Medicaid program).

See also Blumstein, 2014; Grover, 2011; Kahn, 2014; Leonard, 2012; Maher, 2011; Pratt, 2011; Record, 2012; Willis & Chung, 2012 (discussing this court decision). *Compare* Barnett, 2010 (arguing the individual mandate is unconstitutional), *with* Tribe, 2011 (arguing the individual mandate is constitutional).

CHAPTER SUMMARY

- The lack of access to affordable health insurance was one of the principal shortcomings of the U.S. health care system that the Affordable Care Act sought to address.
- One of the key reasons the United States lags behind other similar nations in terms of health measures is the uniform lack of access to comprehensive health care: *not every member of society has access to medically necessary care.*
- About one in eight Americans have no health insurance, and most of them are earning middle-class incomes.
- Before the Affordable care Act, the reasons some working Americans had no health insurance are because their employers did not offer insurance, they did not qualify for their employer's plans, or they could not afford their employer's plan's premiums.
- Lack of health insurance causes over 18,000 deaths per year and also results in higher health insurance premiums and underinsurance for those with insurance.
- Under the theoretical approach to addressing the nation's health care access problems, known as distributive justice, health care is financed by individuals on the basis of their ability to pay, but is available to all who need health care on more or less equal terms.
- Theoretically, under the principle of distributive justice, the right to medically necessary care has a greater weight than the cost of the care, and the ability to pay fair value for health care would have priority over the assistance provided to access the needed care.
- There is not yet a consensus on whether employer-provided plans or individual plans would provide the best method of reducing costs and allocating risks and responsibility in terms of providing universal, comprehensive health care.
- A major source of the cost of health insurance is the administrative costs necessary to comply with government regulations, especially conflicts between federal and state laws.
- A major source of costs is the rise in treatment prevalence rather than the rise in the cost of treatment itself.
- The pharmaceutical industry has taken steps to address rising drug costs, such as clearinghouse programs, comparison shopping websites, and **patient assistance programs**.
- Other than managed care, consumer-directed health care plans are proven to control health care costs by giving consumers the opportunity to choose what kind of coverage they would like based on their willingness to pay expenses out of pocket.

LAW NOTES

1. While one in three Americans without health insurance lives in a household with income greater than $50,000, this is misleading. These higher-income uninsured people do not fit the profile of people who have the money but are unwilling to buy coverage. The higher income uninsured have low individual incomes, but live with others, and only together are they considered higher income. (*See generally* Smith & Medalia, 2015).
2. John Rawls (1921–2002), Harvard University philosopher, is one of the leading 20th-century figures in American law philosophy and is cited most frequently by the U.S. judiciary, especially the U.S. Supreme Court. Rawls received the National Humanities Medal from former President Bill Clinton in recognition of how his thought process helped a whole generation of learned Americans revive their faith in democracy (*See* Rawls, 1999, 1993, 1971).
3. Many businesses are passing the cost on to customers, with varying degrees of subtlety: A legal staffing agency bills clients a San Francisco health law fee of $1.17 per hour, a cafe adds a 5% surcharge to bills and hands diners fliers describing the City's landmark solution to health care, a Mexican eatery notes a 3.5% charge for San Francisco affordable health care legislation (Dvorak, 2008).
4. The University of Pennsylvania (along with 17 other colleges and universities) were investors and early backers of Collegiate Health Care Corp. (CHCC),[1] the nation's first interuniversity managed care organization. CHCC attempted to develop a mutual health insurance plan for college students. More than 100 schools participated in the nationwide effort before the concept was abandoned, primarily because of its complexity. CHCC attempted to develop this insurance model at the same time as it tried to start an array of other innovative managed care

---

[1] Hammaker is the former President and Chief Executive Officer of CHCC; Knadig is the former Chairman of the Board of CHCC.

services and products, and it could be said it failed because it did not focus on viable priorities in a competitive market. It tried to do it all as a start-up organization, from integrated delivery of campus health care services, to national conferences and online education, to sponsorship of population-specific medical research, to comprehensive inpatient and outpatient substance abuse and mental health services for the collegiate population.

5. Some health experts express concern about the failure of online pharmacies to follow proper prescription procedures. Rogue online pharmacy sites are plagued with hoaxes and fake, tainted, contaminated, or unsafe medicine that the U.S. Customs and Border Protection agency and the U.S. Food and Medication Administration cannot provide even rudimentary controls over. There is also the inherent danger of patients obtaining medicine from a variety of sources, thereby eliminating the potential for pharmacists to prevent duplication and watch for negative interactions. Another concern is the online distribution of medicine subject to licensing in the United States but not subject to licensing elsewhere in the world. The one benefit of online pharmacies is their ability to provide emergency contraception for next-day delivery to women's homes, a need in states where access is restricted by state conscience laws that permit pharmacists to refuse dispensing of contraceptive prescriptions based on their religious convictions (*See generally* Rienzi, 2013).

REFERENCES

AHRQ (Agency for Healthcare Research and Quality). (2015). *Healthcare cost and utilization project.* Rockville, MD: Department of Health and Human Services, AHRQ.

American Hospital Directory. (2015). *Hospital statistics.* Louisville, KY: American Hospital Directory, Inc.

Archambault, J. (2014). What does Massachusetts' RomneyCare tell us to expect for labor market impacts under ObamaCare? *American Journal of Law and Medicine, 40,* 195–214.

Auerbach, D. (2014). Assessing the true impact of the ACA: Revisiting the CBO's initial predictions. *American Journal of Law and Medicine, 40,* 231–236.

Barnett, R. (2010, April 29). Editorial: The insurance mandate in peril. *Wall Street Journal,* p. A19.

Ben-Shahar, O., & Logue, K. D. (2012). Outsourcing regulation: How insurance reduces moral hazard. *Michigan Law Review, 111*(2), 197–248.

Bignami, F., & Spivac, C. (2016). Human rights: Social and economic rights as fundamental rights. *The American Journal of Comparative Law, 62,* 561–587.

Blake, V. (2015). Narrow networks, the very sick, and the Patient Protection and Affordable Care Act: Recalling the purpose of health insurance and reform. *Minnesota Journal of Law, Science and Technology, 16,* 63–142.

Blum, A. B., et al. (2015). Implementing health reform in an era of semi-cooperative federalism: Lessons from the age 26 expansion. *Health and Biomedical Law Society, 10,* 327–361.

Blumstein, J. F. *(2014).* Understanding the faulty predictions regarding the challenges to health reform. *University of Illinois Law Review, 2014,* 1251–1263.

Brown, E. C. F. (2015). Resurrecting health care rate regulation. *Hastings Law Journal, 67,* 85–142.

CBO (Congressional Budget Office). (2016a). *Private health insurance premiums and federal policy.* Washington, DC: CBO.

___. (2016b). *Updated budget projections.*

CDC/NCHS (Centers for Disease Control and Prevention/National Center for Health Statistics). (2015). *National health interview survey.* Atlanta: GA: CDC/NCHS.

Collins, S. R., et al. (2015). *To enroll or not to enroll? Why many Americans have gained insurance under the Affordable Care Act while others have not.* New York, NY: The Commonwealth Fund.

Commonwealth Fund. (2016). *New survey: More Americans could get needed health care and afford to pay their medical bills in first year of ACA enrollment—For the first time, Commonwealth Fund's biennial health insurance survey also finds sharp declines in uninsured rates, particularly among young adults and people with low incomes.* New York, NY: Commonwealth Fund.

Dvorak, P. (2008, May 5). Firms adjust to health care law in San Francisco, businesses move to adapt to costs. *Wall Street Journal,* p. B4.

Enemark, D. (2013). Modeling human decision-making in the law: Can legal actors play equilibrium strategies? Two dubious assumptions in the game-theoretic analysis of the law. *Southern California Law Review, 86,* 449–458.

Finegan, S. (2011). United States Supreme Court update. *Appellate Advocate, 23,* 647.

Fleck, L. M. (2011). Cost and end-of-life-care. Just caring: Health care rationing, terminal illness, and the medically least well off. *Journal of Law, Medicine and Ethics, 39,* 156–168.

Frankenfield, C. J. (2010). The relationship between ERISA, state and local health care experimentation, and the passage of national health care reform. *Journal of Health Care Law and Policy, 13*(2), 423–457.

Gayer, et al. (2014). Pareto efficiency with different beliefs. *The Journal of Legal Studies, 43,* 151–170.

Gonzales, A. R., & Stuart, D. B. (2014). Two years later and counting: The implications of the Supreme Court's taxing power decision on the goals of the Affordable Care Act. *Journal of Health Care Law and Policy, 17,* 219–269.

Greve, M. S. (2011). Atlas croaks. Supreme Court shrugs. *Charleston Law Review, 6,* 15–48.

Grover, S. T. (2011). Religious exemptions to the PPACA's [Patient Protection and Affordable Care Act] health insurance mandate. *American Journal of Law and Medicine, 37,* 624–651.

Gruisin, S. L. (2015). Holding health insurance marketplaces accountable: The unheralded rise and imminent demise of structural reform litigation in health care. *Annals of Health Law, 24,* 337–409.

Herrick, D. M. (2014). *The effects of the Affordable Care Act on small businesses.* Washington, DC: National Center for Policy Analysis.

Hoffman, A. K. (2010). Oil and water: Mixing individual mandates, fragmented markets, and health reform. *American Journal of Law and Medicine, 36,* 7–77.

Hoffmann, J. (2014). Preemption and the MLR provision of the Affordable Care Act. *American Journal of Law and Medicine, 40,* 280–297.

IOM (Institute of Medicine). (2004). *Insuring America's health: Principles and recommendations.* Washington, DC: National Academies Press.

IRS (Internal Revenue Service). (2015). *Employer health care arrangements.* Washington, DC: U.S. Treasury, IRS.

Jensen, M. (2011). Is ERISA preemption superfluous in the new age of health care reform? *Columbia Business Law Review, 2011,* 464–528.

Jost, T. S., & Hall, M. A. (2013). Self-insurance for small employers under the Affordable Care Act: Federal and state regulatory options. *New York University Annual Survey of American Law, 68,* 539–565.

Kahn, J. H. (2014). The individual mandate tax penalty. *University of Michigan Journal of Law Reform, 47,* 319–358.

Kaiser Family Foundation. (2015a). *Survey of low-income Americans and the Affordable Care Act.* Menlo Park, CA: Kaiser.

___. (2015b). *Employer health benefits survey.*

___. (2014). *Key facts about the uninsured population.*

Kant, I. (2005). *Fundamental principles of the metaphysics of morals.* Mineola, NY: Dover. (Original work published 1797.)

Korobkin, R. (2014). Comparative effectiveness research as choice architecture: The behavioral law and economics solution to the health care cost crisis. *Michigan Law Review, 112,* 523–573.

Kreps, D. M. (2012). *Microeconomic foundations: Choice and competitive markets.* Princeton, NJ: Princeton University Press.

Leifer, et al. (2014). Federally-qualified health centers: From safety net provider to cornerstone of health reform? *Journal of Health and Life Sciences Law, 8*(1), 29–50.

Leonard, E. W. (2015). Affordable Care Act litigation: The standing paradox. *American Journal of Law and Medicine, 38,* 410–444.

Levitt, L., et al. (2015). *Data note: How has the individual insurance market grown under the Affordable Care Act?* Menlo Park, CA: Kaiser Family Foundation.

Lewis, J. A. (2014). At the intersection of insurance and tax: Equitable remedies under the Affordable Care Act. *John Marshall Law Review, 47,* 973–989.

Litchfield, C. P. (2012). Taxing youth: Health care reform writes a costly prescription that leaves the young and healthy paying the bill. *Southern California Law Review, 85,* 353–393.

Locke, J. (2008). *Two treatises of government.* Birmingham, AL: Palladium Press. (Original work published 1689.)

Lowry, S. (2014). *Itemized tax deductions for individuals: Data analysis.* Washington, DC: Congressional Research Service.

Maher, B. S. (2011). The benefits of opt-in federalism. *Boston College Law Review, 52,* 1733–1793.

Majerol, M., et al. (2015). *The uninsured: A primer—key facts about health insurance and the uninsured on the eve of coverage expansions.* Menlo, CA: Kaiser Family Foundation.

Mantel, J. (2015). A defense of physicians' gatekeeping role: Balancing patients' needs with society's interests. *Pepperdine Law Review, 42,* 633–726.

Martinez, M. E., & Cohen, R. A. (2015). *Health insurance coverage: Early release of estimates from the national health interview survey.* Atlanta, GA: Centers for Disease Control and Prevention's National Center for Health Statistics.

Monahan, A. (2012). Fairness versus welfare in health insurance content regulation. *University of Illinois Law Review, 2012,* 141–230.

Morag-Levine, N. (2014). The history of precaution. *The American Journal of Comparative Law, 62,* 1095–1131.

Morrell, M. T., & Krouse, A. T. (2014). Accountability partners: Legislated collaboration for health reform. *Indiana Health Law Review, 11,* 225–300.

NCHS (National Center for Health Statistics). (2015). *Health, United States: With special feature on adults aged 55–64.* Washington, DC: U.S. Department of Health and Human Services, NCHS.

O'Neill, J. E., & O'Neill, D. M. (2009). *Who are the uninsured? An analysis of America's uninsured population, their characteristics and their health.* Washington, DC: Employment Policies Institute.

Pauly, M. V., & Pagan, J. A. (2007). Spillovers and vulnerability: The case of community uninsurance. *Health Affairs, 26*(5), 1304–1314.

Pollitz, K. (2016). *Surprise medical bills.* Menlo Park, CA: Kaiser Family Foundation.

Pratt, D. (2011). Health care reform: Will it succeed? *Albany Law Journal of Science and Technology, 21,* 493–589.

Rae, M., et al. (2014). *Tax subsidies for private health insurance.* Menlo Park, CA: Kaiser Family Foundation.

Rausch, R. L. (2012). Health cover(age)ing. *Nebraska Law Review, 90,* 920–970.

Rawls, J. (2005). *A theory of justice.* Cambridge, MA: Harvard University Press. (Original work published 1971.)

___. (2001). *Justice as fairness: A restatement.*

___. (1971). *A theory of justice.* (1999). The law of peoples: With "the idea of public reason revisited."

Reagan, R. (1999, September 29). Remarks at his announcement for presidential candidacy at the University of Texas at Austin. Austin, TX.

Record, K. L. (2012). Litigating the ACA: Securing the right to health within a framework of negative rights. *American Journal of Law and Medicine, 38,* 537–546.

Rienzi, M. L. (2013). God and the profits: Is there religious liberty for moneymakers? *George Mason Law Review, 21,* 59–116.

Satz, A. B. (2015). Fragmentation after health care reform. *Houston Journal of Health Law and Policy, 15,* 171–228.

Schwarcz, D., & Schwarcz, S. L. (2014). Regulating systemic risk in insurance. *University of Chicago Law Review, 81,* 1569–1640.

Serota, M., & Singer, M. (2011). Maintaining healthy laboratories of experimentation: Federalism, health care reform, and ERISA. *California Law Review, 99,* 557–604.

Smith, J. C., & Medalia, C. (2015). *Health insurance in the United States: Current population reports.* Washington, DC: U.S. Census Bureau.

Sommers, et al. (2012). Mortality and access to care among adults after state Medicaid expansions. *New England Journal of Medicine, 367,* 1025–1034.

Spiro, T., et al. (2015). *Enough is enough: The time has come to address sky-high drug prices.* Washington, DC: American Center for Progress.

Starr, P. (1983). *The social transformation of American medicine: The rise of a sovereign profession and the making of a vast industry.* New York, NY: Basic Books.

Strine, L. E. (2015). A job is not a hobby: The judicial revival of corporate paternalism and its problematic implications. *Journal of Corporation Law, 41,* 71–115.

Sugden, R. (2012). Sick and (still) broke: Why the Affordable Care Act won't end medical bankruptcy. *Washington University Journal of Law and Policy*, 38, 441–474.

Tribe, L. (2011, February 8). Op-ed: On health care, justice will prevail. *New York Times*, p. A27.

Vukadin, K. T. (2014). Unfinished business: The Affordable Care Act and the problem of delayed and denied ERISA healthcare claims. *John Marshall Law Review*, 47, 1–33.

Weisblatt, R. (2014). Uncharitable hospitals: Why the IRS needs intermediate sanctions to regulate tax-exempt hospitals. *Boston College Law Review*, 55, 687–717.

Wharton School at the University of Pennsylvania. (2007). A prescription for healthier medical care decisions: Begin by defining health risks. *Knowledge@ Wharton*. http://knowledge.wharton.upenn.edu/article/a-prescription-for-healthier-medical-care-decisions-begin-by-defining-risk/

Wiley, L. F. (2016). From patient rights to health justice: Securing the public's interest in affordable, high-quality health care. *Cardozo Law Review*, 37, 833–889.

Willis, S. J., & Chung, N. (2012). No healthcare penalty? No problem: No due process. *American Journal of Law and Medicine*, 38, 516–536.

Zamir, E. (2012). Loss aversion and the law. *Vanderbilt Law Review*, 65, 829–894.

© Andy Dean Photography/ShutterStock, Inc.

CHAPTER 4

Medicaid Insurance and Access to Medically Necessary Care

"In view of the Constitution, in the eye of the law, there is in this country no superior, dominant, ruling class of citizens. There is no caste here."

— **Justice John Marshall Harlan** (1833–1911), Associate Justice of the U.S. Supreme Court, *Plessy v. Ferguson*, 163 U.S. 537 (U.S. Supreme Court 1896)

IN BRIEF

Following the chapter, *Access to Affordable Health Insurance*, this chapter draws further attention to the challenge of finding a way to provide access to medically necessary care for everyone. Attention is directed toward providing an overview of Medicaid financing and examining the equal access provisions of the federal Medicaid law. Finally, methods used to assess the economic impact of Medicaid insurance are explained.

LEARNING OBJECTIVES

Upon completion of this chapter readers should be able to:

1. Discuss various approaches to providing access to medically necessary health care for the deserving and medically needy.
2. Provide an overview of Medicaid financing.
3. Describe the basics of the equal access provisions of Medicaid insurance.
4. Discuss methods used to determine the economic impact of Medicaid insurance.
5. List the three *W*s of health insurance.
6. List the criteria for Medicaid insurance eligibility.
7. Explain the function of the Children's Health Insurance Program.
8. Discuss why government health insurance is economically necessary.

KEY TERMS

Acquired immunodeficiency syndrome (AIDS)
Affordable Care Act of 2010
Antiretroviral drugs
Children's Health Insurance Program Class action
Cost-sharing rules
Coverage gap
Dual insured
Equal access provision
Expected utility maximization

Gross state product
Human immunodeficiency virus (HIV)
Implied right of action
Input-output models
Intergovernmental mandates
Matching funds
Medicaid insurance
Medically necessary care
Medicare insurance
Multiplier effect

Narrow tailoring requirements
Outreach programs
Permanent residents
Private health insurance premiums
Prohibitive costs
Retroactive period
Safety net
State capacities
Strict scrutiny
Subsidized coverage
Waivers

Access to Medically Necessary Care

Should the judiciary force a solution to shape the legislative dimensions of how to provide access to medically necessary care for everyone, and in particular poor children?

Before 1965, health care in America was dual tracked. The insured received care from private physicians, while the uninsured, if they could access care at all, were treated in ambulatory clinics and emergency rooms (Staszak, 2015). This was meant to change after Congress amended Title XIX of the Social Security Act of 1965 and created **Medicaid insurance** as a means-tested program funded by both the federal and state governments. Since then, courts have examined whether the Medicaid insured have an individually enforceable right to health care. Courts are split on whether the federal Medicaid law creates a federally enforceable right of access to **medically necessary care**, but generally agree U.S. residents eligible for Medicaid insurance have a federal right to financial assistance for:

- Early and periodic screening, diagnostic, and treatment services
- Medical services comparable in amount, duration, and scope to the insured in their geographic community
- Receipt of health care benefits with reasonable promptness

While courts generally hold there is a federally enforceable right to prompt and comparable payment for medical services received by the Medicaid insured, courts have failed to provide a uniform remedy when that right is violated (Chen, 2015). The Oklahoma chapter of the American Academy of Pediatrics, a professional organization of pediatricians and pediatric specialists, the Community Action Project of Tulsa County, and 13 children and their parents representing a class of individuals filed a federal civil rights lawsuit against the State of Oklahoma (*See* 42 U.S.C.A. § 1983). The class maintained the State of Oklahoma and the Oklahoma Health Care Authority violated various provisions of the federal Medicaid law by failing to provide Medicaid-insured children in the state with necessary health care. The claim against the State of Oklahoma was twofold: the class contended state policies and procedures denied or deprived Medicaid-insured children of the health and health care to which they were entitled under federal law, in particular early and periodic screening, diagnostic, and treatment services with reasonable promptness. In addition, they claimed the state failed to have provider reimbursement rates set at a sufficient level to assure Medicaid-insured children equal access to quality health care. The court found the state failed to ensure payments sufficient to enlist enough health providers so that services were available to Medicaid-insured children to the same extent such medical services were available to the general, non-Medicaid-insured population. Second, the state failed to furnish medical assistance with reasonable promptness to Medicaid insurance–eligible children. The State of Oklahoma appealed the court's decision.

— *See* Law Fact at the end of this chapter for the answer.

Principles and Applications

As millions of Americans newly gain health insurance coverage as a result of the **Affordable Care Act**, affordability of coverage remains a persistent problem for some (Saver, 2015). Economic disparities, largely a function of different sources of insurance coverage, still influence access to health care in the United States (Kaiser, 2015). Many technological innovations and health care initiatives are focused on affluent communities and are accessible mainly to people with private health insurance. For the uninsured or people with Medicaid coverage, access to routine medical care is often inadequate and not of the highest quality, if access exists at all.

While health care in the United States improves every year, since new drugs and new technologies appear constantly, health care in the United States also costs more every year and shows no signs of changing course. For those who have comprehensive health insurance and the money to pay their deductibles, coinsurance, and out-of-network

The Three Ws of Government Health Insurance: Who? What? Why?

67

fees as needed, the U.S. health care system offers the best health care available anywhere in the world. For the one out of every four adults who may be without health insurance for part or all of any given year, however, access to this quality health care is simply not affordable (Collins et al., 2015a).

The Three Ws of Government Health Insurance: Who? What? Why?

Medicaid is the nation's government health insurance program for Americans of limited means and the severely disabled. It finances health care and long-term care services for almost 58 million people, many of whom face the highest burden of chronic disease of any population group in the United States, owing to economic hardships (CMS, 2015a). Over the past 50 years, the program has changed significantly; not only has Medicaid eligibility expanded, so also has the scope of its medical services (Owcharenko, 2016). Medicaid insurance now pays $1 out of every $6 spent on health care in the United States (Snyder & Rudowitz, 2015).

Medicaid insurance is the second largest line item in state budgets behind education, with over 19% of state funds being allocated to Medicaid on average (NASBO, 2015). Medicaid funds are also the largest source of federal support for the states (Kaiser, 2013a) accounting for roughly 16% of the nation's health care spending (CMS, 2015c). More than half of all Medicaid spending goes to nursing home and other long-term care (CMS, 2015c).[LN1]

Federal Share of Medicaid Spending

For states that expand Medicaid insurance through the Affordable Care Act, the federal government pays 100% of the costs of those newly eligible from 2014 to 2016; it then phases down to and stays at 90% by 2020 (Snyder & Rudowitz, 2014), well above regular match rates of about 60% (CMS, 2015d). In addition to substantial new federal revenues and increases in coverage from the expansion, state budget savings within and outside of the Medicaid insurance program as well as broader economic effects have been projected in a number of studies.[LN2] As illustrated in **FIGURE 4-1**, states that do not adopt the expansion will forgo substantial federal revenues with the result that low-income adults may fall into a **coverage gap**.

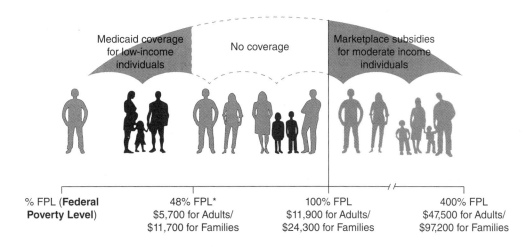

In states that do not expand medicaid insurance, there will be large gaps in coverage, leaving millions of adults with no affordable options

| % FPL (**Federal Poverty Level**) | 48% FPL* $5,700 for Adults/ $11,700 for Families | 100% FPL $11,900 for Adults/ $24,300 for Families | 400% FPL $47,500 for Adults/ $97,200 for Families |

Note: Applies to states that do not expand medicaid. The current median state medicaid eligibility limit for parents is 48% FPL in the 21 states that are not moving forward with the medicid expansion at this time.

FIGURE 4-1 Coverage Gap

Modified from: Kaiser Commission on Medicaid and the Uninsured. (2013a). *Medicaid eligibility for adults*. Washington, DC: Kaiser. Data from: HHS (U.S. Department of Health and Human Services). (2016). *Poverty guidelines*. Washington, DC: HHS; Kaiser Commission on Medicaid and the Uninsured. (2016). *Who is impacted by the coverage gap in states that have not adopted the Medicaid expansion*. Washington, DC: Kaiser.

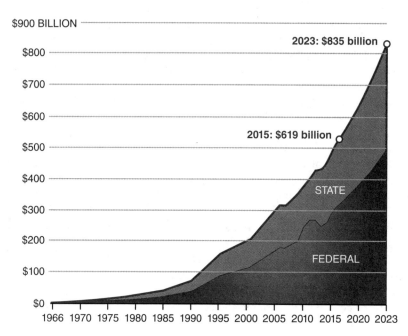

FIGURE 4-2 Medicaid Spending Exceeds Half a Trillion Dollars

Data from: CMS (Centers for Medicare and Medicaid Services). (2015). *National health care expenditure data.* Baltimore, MD: U.S. Department of Health & Human Services, CMS; Modified from: Owcharenko, N. (2016). *Medicaid at 50: Reform is needed to better serve low-income health care needs.* Washington, DC: Heritage Foundation.

Federal contribution varies based on state per capita household income relative to the national income average. The highest federal contribution of 76% goes to Kentucky, one of the poorest states in the deep South with nearly one in five citizens living below the poverty threshold (Census Bureau, 2015 Kaiser, 2014). The federal government and states spent about $529 billion on Medicaid insurance in 2015 (up from $206 billion in 2000). As illustrated in **FIGURE 4-2**, by 2023 total spending will reach $835 billion, of which the federal share will be $497 billion and the state share will be $337 billion (CMS, 2014b).

Who Is Categorically Eligible for Medicaid Insurance?

Without Medicaid insurance, most of the Medicaid insured would be uninsured. To qualify for medical assistance, they must meet financial criteria and also belong to one of the categorically eligible groups, as illustrated in **FIGURE 4-3**. Medicaid insurance is the principal **safety net** for:

- Blind or severely disabled children and adults
- Low-income working families with children
- Medicare-eligible with limited resources, who need assistance with filling gaps in their Medicare coverage
- Uninsured pregnant women

As illustrated in Figure 4-3, low-income adults (earning under $16,500/year) are eligible for Medicaid insurance if their state has expanded coverage under the Affordable Care Act; otherwise they are ineligible (Kaiser, 2016).

Medicaid insurance does not, however, provide coverage for everyone at the bottom of the economic pyramid as shown in **FIGURE 4-4** unless the state expanded traditional coverage. Even under the broadest regulatory provisions, traditional Medicaid insurance does not generally provide coverage for medically necessary care, even for the very poorest persons in society, unless they are in one of the designated eligibility groups. The regulations for counting income and resources vary from state to state and from categorically eligible group to group. There are also special regulations for those who live in nursing homes and for disabled children living at home. The regulatory obfuscations of the Medicaid insurance system, for health providers as well as individuals and families, are one of the most confusing areas of health law.

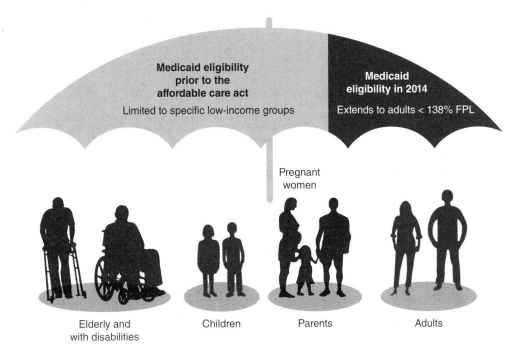

FIGURE 4-3 Categorically Eligible Groups for Medicaid Insurance

Reproduced from: Kaiser Commission on Medicaid and the Uninsured. (2016). *Who is impacted by the coverage gap in states that have not adopted the Medicaid expansion.* Washington, DC: Kaiser.

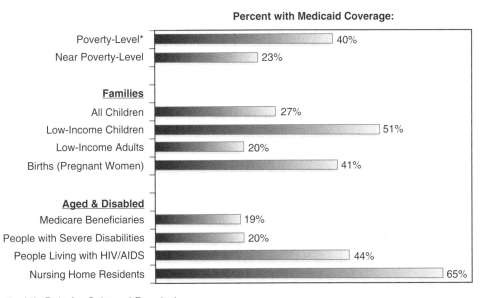

FIGURE 4-4 Medicaid's Role for Selected Populations

Data from: CMS (Centers for Medicare and Medicaid Services). (2016). *Dual eligibility expansion.* Baltimore, MD: U.S. Department of Health and Human Services, CMS (2014b). CMS, 2014). *Medicaid At-a-Glance*; Kaiser Commission on Medicaid and the Uninsured. (2016). *Federal and state share of Medicaid spending.* Washington, DC: Kaiser; NGA (National Governor's Association). (2015). *Maternal and child health (MCH) update.* Washington, DC: NGA; U.S. Census Bureau. (2015b). *Census definitions.* Washington, DC: U.S. Department of Commerce, U.S. Census Bureau.

Most of the Medicaid insured are low-income working parents with children (Kaiser, 2015). Many others are people from the middle class who are retired and now require care in a nursing home or other long-term care facility (MedPAC, 2016). Many of the severely disabled are blind or are infected with the **human immunodeficiency virus (HIV)** and its resulting **acquired immunodeficiency syndrome (AIDS)**. Some 38% of the people living with AIDS are Medicaid insured (NASTAD, 2015).

Disabled Medicare Beneficiaries

One out of four of the Medicaid insured are seriously disabled and receiving Medicare benefits (MedPAC, 2016). This population group accounts for more than 70% of the nation's Medicaid insurance spending (Kaiser, 2015).

Severely Disabled Children and Adults

Medicaid insurance provides health insurance coverage for people with physical and mental disabilities and chronic illnesses, such as symptomatic HIV/AIDS patients. One out of five people who are severely disabled are Medicaid insured (Kaiser, 2015). Almost half of the people living with HIV/AIDS in the United States are covered by Medicaid insurance. Nearly three out of every five Americans infected with HIV/AIDS are symptomatic and dying from what should be a chronic illness with proper medical care; if these Americans could have accessed the health care system before their symptoms manifested, they would not be facing premature deaths (Kaiser, 2013c).

Uninsured Pregnant Women

The birth mothers of 4 out of 10 children born in the United States are covered by Medicaid insurance (Kaiser, 2013c). Medicaid insurance provides access to prenatal care and neonatal intensive care for eligible women and their babies. Most states offer expanded coverage of pregnant women beyond the federal income eligibility level of other Medicaid-insured individuals. Twenty states covered pregnant women up to 185% of the federal poverty level or $16,120 for a single mother in 2008; another 20 states provide eligibility criteria at higher income levels (Kaiser, 2013c). Poverty guidelines are updated periodically by the U.S. Department of Health and Human Services under the authority of 42 U.S.C.A. § 9902(2) (1998), which was set at $11,880 for an individual plus $4,140 for each additional person in 2016 (HHS, 2016).

What Medicaid Insurance Coverage Is Required?

There is no national consensus of the three *W*s of Medicaid insurance: who is deserving of financial assistance, what health care costs should be covered, and why the government should be involved in the first place. The demand for broader state accountability is a constant theme for Medicaid insurance as the three *W*s are debated.

Coverage Issues

Issues surrounding the question of what coverage should be provided by Medicaid insurance is currently being debated in state legislatures and the state and federal appellate courts. Controversies that remain unresolved include:

- Rules for when someone may be eligible for Medicaid insurance coverage (the three-month rule)
- Entitlement of noncitizens, if they are entitled at all, for taxpayer-paid Medicaid insurance
- Identification of what constitutes a life-threatening medical event; Medicaid coverage is always available to the medically needy when they face serious medical emergencies that are life-threatening
- Delivery system inequities between the uninsured/underinsured compared to those with comprehensive health insurance coverage plus the ability to pay their out-of-pocket costs before any non–life-threatening treatment is ever received (e.g., the ever-increasing deductibles and co-payments on health insurance plans)

Three-Month Rule

Coverage may start three months prior to application for Medicaid insurance, if the individual would have been eligible during the **retroactive period** but was unaware of this opportunity or because the nature of their illness prevented them from seeking coverage. With many individuals facing unemployment as a result of serious injuries, illness, or disease, many who are eligible for Medicaid insurance do not take advantage of this opportunity when faced with extraordinary medical bills. Coverage generally stops at the end of the month in which their circumstances change.

The primary reason for this failure to apply for Medicaid insurance is that hospitals and other health providers do not always advise patients of their possible eligibility until after the three-month eligibility period has lapsed. Whether this is simply an oversight or whether they prefer to bill the middle class at a higher rate than is available under the Medicaid fee structure is an issue of much debate (Radley et al., 2014). In addition, states seldom develop **outreach programs** to advise their residents of the benefits of Medicaid insurance, nor do they actively seek to enroll state residents.

Lawful Permanent Residents

Most states have additional charity programs to provide medical assistance to residents who do not qualify for Medicaid insurance, but face extraordinary circumstances requiring that society give them a helping hand. For instance, **permanent residents** are not eligible for Medicaid insurance until they have been in the United States for five years. No federal funds are provided for these charity and patient assistance programs; they are strictly state-funded programs.

COURT DECISION
Eligibility of Permanent Residents for Medicaid Insurance

Finch v. Commonwealth Health Insurance Connector Authority
[Lawful Permanent Residents v. State]
959 N.E.2d 970 [Supreme Judicial Court of Massachusetts 2012]

Facts: A group of lawfully residing permanent residents sued the state when their Medicaid insurance was terminated, alleging that their denial of benefits was based solely on their immigration status and thus, violated their constitutional rights under the state's equal protection provision. Both federal and state funds supported the insurance subsidies for eligible Massachusetts residents. The federal government partially reimbursed the state for expenditures by noncitizen immigrants who were eligible for federal benefits but did not provide reimbursement for federally ineligible noncitizen immigrants (such as permanent residents in the United States for less than five years).

Initially, Massachusetts permitted all legal immigrants to enroll in its Medicaid insurance program, including all permanent residents and refugees or asylum recipients. Without federal **matching funds**, Massachusetts assumed the cost of providing **Medicaid insurance** to approximately 29,000 federally ineligible immigrants. Eventually due to state budgetary constraints, Massachusetts proposed excluding all noncitizens from Medicaid insurance coverage; meaning that permanent residents who were in the United States for less than five years were no longer eligible for Medicaid insurance in Massachusetts.

Issue: Should lawfully residing permanent residents be eligible for Medicaid insurance?

Holding and Decision: State legislative appropriations that deny Medicaid insurance to permanent residents fails **strict scrutiny** and thus violates Massachusetts's equal protection provision.

Analysis: The court held that the immigrant restriction did not meet strict scrutiny. First, the court found that the text, statutory scheme, and legislative history of the state appropriations all suggested that the purpose of restricting Medicaid appropriations was entirely fiscal and not based on an interest in furthering national immigration policies. Since fiscal concerns alone are not adequate to survive strict scrutiny, the court held that the Medicaid appropriation restriction violated the state's equal protection provision.

Second, where a state acts on its own authority, rather than obeying mandatory federal laws regarding the treatment of permanent residents, strict scrutiny applies. Even if the purpose of the state restriction was to further national immigration policies, the state made no effort to implement a law that was narrowly tailored to achieving this purpose. While the court declined to reach the question of whether national immigration policy can ever serve as a compelling state interest, it held that Massachusetts's failure to evaluate whether the Medicaid appropriation restriction was narrowly tailored to achieve federal immigration purposes did not satisfy strict scrutiny.

The court further rejected the state's argument that its adoption of the federal eligibility rules entitled it to bypass the **narrow tailoring requirement** of strict scrutiny. Although strict scrutiny does not apply to uniform national guidelines and policies dictating how states are to regulate and legislate issues relating to permanent residents, the state legislature voluntarily adopted federal eligibility requirements; the strict scrutiny standard thus applies in full force, including the narrow tailoring requirement. Ultimately, the court held that the immigrant restrictions failed strict scrutiny because the purely fiscal purpose was not a compelling state interest and it was not sufficiently narrowly tailored. The restriction thus violated the equal protection provision under the Massachusetts Constitution.

Rule of Law: While protection against discrimination on the basis of national origin does not include protection against discrimination on the basis of immigration status, strict scrutiny applies to a state law distributing economic benefits that discriminates against permanent residents.

References discussing this court decision: Rosenberg, 2014; Sacco, 2016.

The U.S. pharmaceutical industry has assumed a leadership position with their patient assistance programs. Since 2003, the industry has also provided discounted drug programs for legal noncitizen immigrants. Both programs are privately funded, without any government funding.

Definition of Medically Needy

Low income is only one test for Medicaid eligibility; assets and resources are also tested against established thresholds. Resources such as bank accounts, real property, or other items that can be sold for cash, generally must be used before individuals are eligible for Medicaid insurance. The medically needy who would be categorically eligible for Medicaid insurance, except for income or assets, may become eligible for assistance, however, solely because of excessive medical expenses. Medicaid insurance often becomes available to the American middle class facing nursing care or other long-term care costs or home care costs arising from chronic, nonterminal illnesses, such as Parkinson's disease or dementia. The middle class is often covered by Medicaid insurance when their private insurance coverage is exhausted from medical situations, such as when:

- Expenses from a catastrophic injury or illness exceed their ability to pay the limits of their private insurance
- The medical treatments they elect to have are excluded from coverage by private insurers, who deem their care to be experimental

The annual and lifetime caps used by private insurers for high-end users were removed under the Affordable Care Act. Prior to this legislative reform, half of all bankruptcies were tied to illness or injury (Radley et al., 2014).

Emergency Medical Services

One exception for coverage by Medicaid insurance is generally for emergency services. Emergency services must be life-threatening to be covered by Medicaid insurance, and what constitutes a threat to life is determined by state agencies rather than by health providers or injured or sick individuals.

Delivery System Inequities

The federal government and the states jointly finance Medicaid insurance. States increase Medicaid enrollments to qualify for more federal assistance rather than being given incentives to increase efficiency and higher quality. This is theoretically easier said than practically achieved.

At the same time, there are significant differences between states on measures of health care access, quality, costs, and outcomes (Commonwealth Fund, 2015). Additionally, these differences could very well widen in the future as many of the lowest performing states are choosing not to expand their Medicaid insurance programs under the Affordable Care Act. Some states discourage eligible uninsured citizens from purchasing **subsidized coverage** through the federal marketplace, though some uninsured are signing up nonetheless.

Coverage Incentives

One criticism of the current Medicaid delivery system is that coverage has become the end in itself (*See* Keehan et al., 2015). States spread resources widely but thinly, without enough attention to:

- Accessibility
- Accurate and comparable payment rates
- Health outcomes, or whether coverage is actually improving health
- Quality of health care

MANAGEMENT AND LAW ISSUES

1. Should coverage be revoked if it turns out an individual's experience was not life-threatening?
2. Should there be a limit on the total amount of coverage Medicaid insurance will provide?
3. What should be considered life-threatening?

States have no obligation to rigorously evaluate their programs in order to qualify for additional federal funds; funding is based on state demographics. For its part, the federal government has been restrained by coverage regulations when states have attempted to take steps to fix their own Medicaid insurance programs, such as by devising outcome-based standards for evaluating performance and de-emphasizing the goal of growing the number of covered people. Federal regulations also prohibit states from limiting Medicaid enrollments or establishing wait lists for entitlement programs.

State Waivers

States may expand Medicaid insurance and the federal minimum standards, and they have done so to varying degrees. Before expansion of Medicaid insurance under the Affordable Care Act, states could not use federal matching funds to provide insurance coverage to cover nondisabled adults without children, no matter how poor they were. States could use additional state funds, but no federal funds could be used for adults of working age who were not suffering from physical or mental disabilities. As previously illustrated in Figure 4-1, this changed for those states that chose to expand Medicaid insurance under the Affordable Care Act; all low-income adults are now eligible for Medicaid health insurance that is subsidized by the federal government.

A handful of states have received special permission, known as **waivers**, from federal regulators to take incremental steps to improve their Medicaid insurance programs. These include the following:

- Indiana is incorporating personal saving accounts to allow its citizens who are covered by Medicaid insurance greater choice of health providers and is also providing financial incentives to citizens who follow their treatment regimens.
- Louisiana is providing tailored Medicaid services through managed care networks run by private, competing companies that are accountable for improving the health outcomes of its citizens.
- North Carolina created a primary-care-based program that pays physicians to improve coordination of care and gives its citizens more choice by expanding the number of physicians participating in its Medicaid insurance program.
- Pennsylvania has sought to provide universal health coverage to uninsured families by expanding the eligibility requirements to qualify for Medicaid insurance.

The federal government gave states the flexibility to redesign their Medicaid benefits by modeling the programs after managed care plans already offered in particular states (42 U.S.C.A. § 1315[f]). However, creating incentives for broader state accountability makes federal regulations far less significant, which probably means eventually ending the open-ended federal funding for Medicaid insurance all together. Indeed, a series of state waivers finally led to mandatory Medicaid managed care as a way to prevent unnecessary health care expenditures (Huberfeld & Roberts, 2016).

Economics of the Medicaid Insured

Almost three-quarters of the people receiving Medicaid insurance are Medicare insured and seriously disabled (Kaiser, 2013b). With health insurance premiums rising more rapidly than the federal poverty level, the protection offered to the sickest and poorest Americans by Medicaid insurance has not kept pace with rising health insurance costs over time (Kaiser, 2013c). The federal poverty level has increased 30% since 1996; during the same time period, **private health insurance premiums** have increased over 134%. Clearly, the elderly who are medically needy and the disabled are being the least protected by Medicaid insurance. This is one reason that Medicaid per capita spending has grown much more slowly than private health spending per capita.

Access to Medically Necessary Care

While Medicaid insurance is an improvement over being uninsured, it often relegates Medicaid-insured consumers to inferior health care. In recognition of the disparity in health care available to the privately insured and Medicare insured, as compared to the Medicaid insured, vigorous legislative and judicial debate is occurring about what constitutes equal access to health care in the United States.

Eventually the nation will be forced to arrive at a political consensus. Whether the leadership to reach a compromise will arise from the executive branch or the legislative branch will assume its leadership role, is not yet clear. Whether the solution is a federalist approach or an approach arising from the states remains to be seen. What is certain is that major reform of the U.S. health care system will require significant **intergovernmental mandates** for decades to come.

The U.S. Fifth Circuit chose not to advance the rights of those historically denied equal access to health care and treatment in *Equal Access for El Paso, Inc. v. Hawkins*. However, future litigants might seek relief in state courts. Today, it is the state judiciary (not the federal courts) that is expanding protection of individual liberties through interpretation of their own state constitutions. *See generally* Brennan, 1986 and 1977, where a sitting U.S. Supreme Court Justice called for state courts to take a more active role in protecting human rights and ensuring their citizens' health.

COURT DECISION
Equal Access to Medically Necessary Care

Equal Access for El Paso, Inc. v. Hawkins
[Medicaid-Insured Recipients v. Commissioner of the Texas State Medicaid Plan]
509 F.3d 697 (U.S. Court of Appeals for the 5th Circuit 2007),
cert. denied, 555 U.S. 811 (U.S. Supreme Court 2008), *on remand*,
562 F.3d 724 (U.S. Court of Appeals for the 5th Circuit 2009)

Facts: Equal Access for El Paso is a nonprofit corporation designed to increase access to health care for individuals in El Paso County, Texas. Equal Access for El Paso and three health providers (a physician, hospital, and health maintenance organization), all of whom sued on behalf of themselves and Medicaid-insured residents of El Paso County, brought suit against Hawkins, Commissioner of the Texas Health and Human Services Commission and the administrator of the Texas Medicaid insurance plan (Texas).

Equal Access for El Paso claimed Texas set deficient Medicaid reimbursement and capitation rates, in violation of the equal access provision of the federal Medicaid law (*See* 42 U.S.C.A. § 1396a(a)(30)(A)). This deficient reimbursement resulted in inadequate access to health care for Medicaid-insured consumers living in the El Paso area. The inadequacy of the reimbursement and capitation rates, when combined with the disproportionately high percentage of Medicaid-insured consumers in El Paso, created a financial incentive for health providers to practice outside the El Paso area and to seek out patients covered by private health insurance.

Issue: Do Medicaid-insured consumers and health providers have the right to seek federal civil rights remedies for inadequate health care in their local communities under the equal access provision of the federal Medicaid law?

Holding and Decision: No. The equal access provision of the federal Medicaid law does not confer an individual private right of action that is enforceable under the federal civil rights law.

Analysis: The court began its analysis with examination of the federal civil rights law in which § 1983 imposes liability on any person who deprives a citizen of any rights secured by the U.S. Constitution and laws under color of state law or authority. Section 1983 provides in relevant part:

> *Every person who, under color of any law, ordinance, regulation, custom, or usage, of any State or Territory or the District of Columbia, subjects, or causes to be subjected, any citizen of the United States or other person within the jurisdiction thereof to the deprivation of any rights, privileges, or immunities secured by the Constitution and laws, shall be liable to the party injured in an action at law, suit in equity, or other proper proceeding for redress....* 42 U.S.C.A. § 1983.

The U.S. Supreme Court restricted this civil right when it held that § 1983 provides a remedy only for the deprivation of rights secured by the Constitution and laws of the United States, not broader benefits or interests that may be enforced under the federal laws (*See Gonzaga University v. Doe*, 536 U.S. 273 (U.S. Supreme Court 2002)). The circuit court held there was no **implied right of action** in the federal Medicaid law without some rights-creating language showing Congress intended to create a right of equal access to health care. According to the U.S. Supreme Court, it is only violations of rights, not laws, that give rise to § 1983 actions.

The circuit court held the equal access provision of the federal Medicaid law did not show congressional intent to create individualized rights for Medicaid-insured consumers and health providers. The equal access provision was interpreted as covering only institutional policy and practices in terms of the functions that must be performed by the states and the U.S. Department of Health and Human Services (HHS) in giving effect to the federal Medicaid law. The court saw the federal Medicaid law as creating an affirmative duty on the part of states and HHS to enlist enough health providers, so that health care was available to Medicaid-insured consumers to the same extent such care was available to the privately insured population in the El Paso geographic area. The focus of the equal access provision was interpreted as being aggregate, as opposed to individual, which is required to establish a private, individual right of action under § 1983.

As a result, the equal access provision of the federal Medicaid law does not create private, individual rights of action under § 1983. Rather, the equal access provision simply provides that the states and HHS have a legal duty to assure Medicaid-insured consumers as a group have access to health care on the same basis as the privately insured population. The equal access provision is not concerned with whether Medicaid-insured consumers as a group have the right to equal access to health care, or whether any particular Medicaid insured has a right to access health care that is equal to the care provided to the privately insured in El Paso.

Rule of Law: The equal access provision of the federal Medicaid law confers no individual rights and thus cannot be enforced under the federal civil rights law; only laws that clearly confer private, individual rights of action may be enforced under § 1983.

References discussing this court decision: Chen, 2015; Bienstock, 2012; Brendel, 2011; Dwyer, 2013; Huberfeld, 2014; McKennan, 2011.

Following this decision, the majority of the federal circuit courts have found the equal access provision unenforceable under the federal civil rights law (Bienstock, 2012); but *Pediatric Specialty Care* found an enforceable right.

COURT DECISION
Right of Access to Medically Necessary Care

Pediatric Specialty Care, Inc. v. Arkansas Department of Human Services
[Medicaid Insured v. Arkansas Department of Human Services]
443 F.3d 1005 (U.S. Court of Appeals for the 8th Circuit 2006),
vacated in part on other grounds, Selig v. Pediatric Specialty Care, Inc.,
551 U.S. 1142 (U.S. Supreme Court 2007)

Facts: The directors of the Arkansas Medicaid insurance program implemented a policy of prior authorization that reduced the scope and duration of early intervention day treatment for disabled Medicaid-insured children. The primary motivation of the prior authorization policy action was to save money, even though federal Medicaid law requires states to act in the best interest of needy children who are disabled and require medically necessary rehabilitation and health care.

Issue: Do Medicaid-insured children and health providers have the right to seek federal civil rights remedies for inadequate health care in their local communities under the equal access provision of the federal Medicaid law?

Holding and Decision: Yes. The equal access provision of the federal Medicaid insurance law confers an individual private right of action to both health providers and patients that is enforceable under the federal civil rights law.

Analysis: The Circuit Court found that the directors of the Arkansas Medicaid insurance program violated the health providers' and the children's clearly established rights to provide and receive medically necessary care. Medicaid-insured disabled children are entitled to diagnostic, screening, preventive, and rehabilitative services. This includes any medical or remedial services provided in a facility, a home, or other setting, recommended by a physician. The services provided must seek to maximally reduce the physical or mental disability of children. In addition, the services must be continued until disabled children are restored to their best possible functional level. The court held the federal Medicaid law created an enforceable federal right to early intervention treatment when recommended by a physician that cannot be overridden by government policies or regulations.

The **equal access provision** of the federal Medicaid law also requires the states to reimburse medically necessary care and ensure that Medicaid payments are:

- Consistent with efficiency, economy, and quality of care
- Sufficient to enlist enough health providers so that medical services are available to the extent such care is available to the privately insured population in the geographic area

The court further held the equal access provisions of the federal Medicaid law created a clearly established federal right to equal access to quality health care.

Rule of Law: The rights to medically necessary care conferred by the federal Medicaid law are clearly established federal rights, and those provisions of the law are enforceable by both Medicaid-insured children and health providers through federal civil rights causes of action.

References discussing this court decision: Sheffner, 2015.

The conflict between the two decisions in this chapter, the *Equal Access for El Paso* decision and the *Pediatric Specialty Care* decision virtually ensures the U.S. Supreme Court will eventually step in to reconcile the differences. Only the U.S. Eighth Circuit Court has interpreted a right of access for both consumers and health providers (Sheffner, 2015). Judicial interpretations of the law regularly vary in the federal circuits and change over time, often going through conflicting stages of development before maturing into a coherent national policy. It is not uncommon for the federal circuits to go in different directions on the same issue. The role of Medicaid insurance in providing equal access to basic health care is just one instance of this difference.

Economic Inequities

For the medically needy, health care is very different than it is for those with private health insurance coverage. Medicaid reimbursement rates are so low, and billing under the program is so complicated, that it is difficult for Medicaid-insured consumers to access timely medical interventions or specialized care. Accumulating medical data shows that the poor health outcomes of Medicaid-insured consumers are not just a function of their underlying medical conditions, but a more direct consequence of the shortcomings of Medicaid insurance. For instance, Medicaid insurance is replete with paperwork, regulations, and treatment rejections that make the program hard to navigate for health providers, as well as the people it was established to serve, the deserving who need temporary financial assistance to cover their unexpected health care costs.

Medicare/Medicaid Insured

Data from the Medicare Payment Advisory Committee reveal the access problems faced by those who qualify for both Medicare and Medicaid insurance, generally referred to as being **dual insured**. While the next chapter will explain the important protections provided by Medicare insurance, there are significant gaps in Medicare coverage, gaps that many meet with Medicaid insurance and private health insurance. For instance, there are fairly high cost-sharing requirements for covered benefits, and Medicare insurance does not have a stop-loss benefit that limits out-of-pocket spending. Other gaps in Medicare coverage illustrate that:

- 4 out of 10 physicians restrict access, because Medicaid reimbursement rates are so low and payments are often delayed
- About 30% of U.S. physicians refuse to accept new patients with Medicare/Medicaid insurance, while less than 3% refuse to accept new private-insured Medicare patients
- Access for patients with Medicare/Medicaid insurance is most limited in urban areas
- Most of the 6.2 million individuals who are dual-insured face restrictions on access to the latest medical technologies

(MedPAC, 2016).

Medicare consumers who are Medicaid insured are more likely to suffer from cognitive impairments and mental disorders and have higher rates of diabetes, pulmonary disease, stroke, and Alzheimer's disease than peers in their age group who are privately insured (MedPAC, 2016). Nearly 40% are disabled. Relative to the Medicare insured with private insurance, the Medicare/Medicaid insured are:

- 3 times as likely to be in poor health
- Almost 20 times as likely to be institutionalized
- Spending a disproportionate share of Medicaid and Medicare funds

(MedPAC, 2016).

For instance, the Medicare/Medicaid insured account for less than 1% of the Medicare consumers and almost one-third of Medicaid spending (CMS, 2015b, 2015c). The costliest 20% account for more than 77% of Medicare spending (MedPAC, 2016).

Treatment of Serious Heart Conditions

The treatment of heart disease, which is among the most evaluated Medicaid insurance service, discloses clinical disparities that can only be attributable to the influence of insurance status. While the clinical outcomes may have been a result of poorer long-term follow-up care, most studies tried to control for the medical factors believed to influence patients' outcomes. Nevertheless:[LN2]

- National Hospital Discharge Survey data, over a 25-year period, reveal that more than 80% of the hospitalizations for heart failure are patients with Medicare/Medicaid insurance, which is a rate of hospitalization reflecting the lack of timely interventions and medicines
- Patients who are Medicaid-insured face significantly more angina, poorer quality of life, and higher risks of hospitalizations after myocardial infarctions, with nearly twice the increased risk of complications and death
- Patients with Medicaid coverage are almost 50% more likely to die after coronary artery bypass surgery than patients with private health insurance coverage

(*E.g.*, Fichtner, 2014; Silow-Carroll et al., 2011).

Diagnoses of Cancer

As illustrated in **FIGURE 4-5**, the probability of being diagnosed with late-stage cancers is two to almost three times greater for the uninsured and Medicaid insured than it is for people with private insurance coverage and access to health care, even after correcting for differences in the location of the tumor and its stage when diagnosed (Halpern,

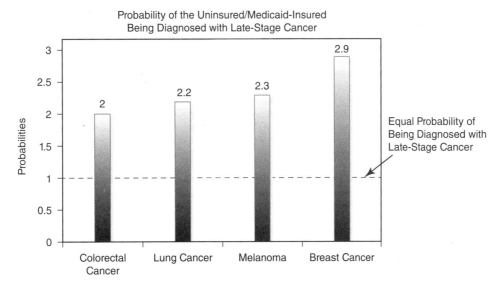

FIGURE 4-5 Diagnosis of Late-Stage Cancer, Uninsured/Medicaid Insured v. Privately Insured

Data from: Halpern M.T., et al. (2008). Association of insurance status and ethnicity with cancer stage at diagnosis for twelve cancer sites: A retrospective analysis. *Lancet Oncology*, *9* (3), 222–231; Kaiser Commission on Medicaid and the Uninsured. (2015). *Fact sheet: Key facts about the uninsured population*. Washington, DC: Kaiser; Orentlicher, D. (2014). The future of the Affordable Care Act: Protecting economic health more than physical health? *Houston Law Review*, 51, 1057–1079.

2008; *See* Orentlicher, 2014). People without private health insurance are unlikely to have access to comprehensive health care or participate in cancer-screening programs. Over the years, everyone in the health care industry knew, and regional studies suggested, that the uninsured and Medicaid insured were more likely to present with advanced-stage cancer than privately insured patients (Halpern, 2008).

However, it was not until 2008 that these regional findings were assessed using national data. A national analysis revealed that patients who were uninsured and Medicaid insured had substantially increased risks of presenting with advanced-stage cancers at diagnosis (Halpern, 2008). Although many factors other than insurance status also affect the quality of care received, adequate insurance is a crucial factor for receiving appropriate cancer screening and timely access to health care. Individuals without medical insurance or with limited insurance are less likely than those with broader insurance coverage to receive preventive services and to seek timely health care. The national analysis examined the association between insurance status and stage at diagnosis among women with breast cancer. These results are consistent with other reports that have documented less use of preventive services, including mammography, among uninsured women and the resulting delays in diagnosis and treatment.

Treatment of HIV/AIDS

The uninsured and underinsured with inadequate prescription plans complain about being denied access to the **antiretroviral drugs** that can prevent their immune systems from being weakened to the point where they are disabled by full-blown acquired immune deficiency syndrome (AIDS) (Castleberry, 2015). While infection with the human immunodeficiency virus (HIV) has become a serious, but manageable, chronic condition for those with the resources to gain access to quality health care, lack of early access to care is the difference between life and death from AIDS (WHO, 2010).

While most young adults are relatively healthy, half of all new HIV infections occur among young people 15–24 years of age. About 20,000 young Americans are newly infected with the virus that causes AIDS annually; this is 55 new infections per day (WHO, 2010). One out of five people living with HIV infections is uninsured (Bradley et al., 2014; Dawson et al., 2016). The cruel irony for them is that they do not qualify for Medicaid insurance and thus are not given access to the antiretroviral drugs that would have prevented their symptoms until they manifest symptoms of the AIDS disease. This means treatment is withheld for many uninsured Americans of limited means until it is too late for preventive health care (Montaner et al., 2006). For the uninsured poor in the United States, HIV/AIDS is still a death sentence.

Children's Health Insurance Program

The **Children's Health Insurance Program** was created in 1997 to address the growing challenge of uninsured children (*See* 42 U.S.C.A. §§ 1397aa-jj). Before the coverage expansions under the Affordable Care Act, the Children's Health Insurance Program was the single largest expansion of health insurance coverage since the Medicare and Medicaid insurance programs were initiated in 1965. The federal government spent $5 billion on this program in 2007 and another $7 billion in 2008 (CMS, 2015d).

The Centers for Medicare and Medicaid Services is in charge of the Children's Health Insurance Program, with joint financing by the federal and state governments. Administered by the states, within broad federal guidelines, each state determines:

- Administrative and operating procedures
- Benefit packages
- Design of its program
- Eligibility groups
- Payment levels for coverage

Who Is Targeted for the Children's Health Insurance Program?

Covering approximately 8.1 million children, the Children's Health Insurance Program plays an important role in reducing the number of uninsured children in the United States, as illustrated in **FIGURE 4-6** (CMS, 2014c). The federal government provides a capped amount of matching funds to states for coverage of children and some parents with household incomes too high to qualify for Medicaid insurance but for whom private health insurance is unavailable or unaffordable. Although the Children's Health Insurance Program is aimed mainly at covering children, under the Affordable Care Act a handful of states have obtained waivers to use funds from the program to cover adults with children.

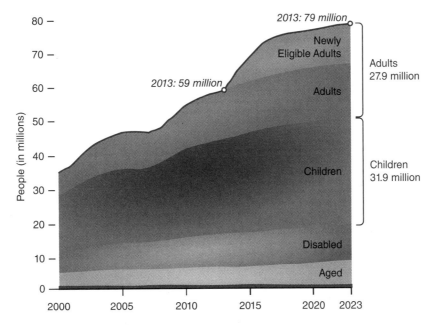

FIGURE 4-6 The Changing Face of Medicaid Insurance

Data from: CMS (Centers for Medicare and Medicaid Services). (2015b). *National health care expenditure data.* Baltimore, MD: U.S. Department of Health and Human Services. CMS.Owcharenko, N. (2016). *Medicaid at 50: Reform is needed to better serve low-income health care needs.* Washington, DC: Heritage Foundation.

MANAGEMENT AND LAW ISSUES

4.   Should states be able to place limitations upon enrollment in Medicaid insurance, such as maintenance of a healthy weight, not smoking, and not abusing drugs?

The Children's Health Insurance Program is designed to provide health insurance coverage to uninsured, low-income children who:

- Reside in a family with household income below 200% of the federal poverty level
- Whose family has a household income 50% higher than the state's Medicaid insurance eligibility threshold

Poverty guidelines are updated periodically in the *Federal Register* by the U.S. Department of Health and Human Services under the authority of 42 U.S.C.A. § 9902(2) (1998): income level to be considered living in poverty was set at $11,880 for an individual plus $4,140 for each additional person in the household in 2016 (HHS, 2016). Certain children cannot be covered under the Children's Health Insurance Program, including children who are:

- Eligible for Medicaid insurance coverage
- Insured under an employer-sponsored health insurance plan or have health insurance coverage through an association or individual plan
- Members of a family eligible for state or local government-sponsored health insurance based on employment with a public agency
- Residing in an institution for those suffering from mental illnesses

Expansion of Medicaid Insurance to Higher Income Households

If a state elects to expand its Medicaid insurance program using the Children's Health Insurance Program, the Medicaid insurance eligibility rules apply, including the inability to:

- Enact lifetime caps
- Enforce residency requirements
- Establish time limits for eligibility

For states that opt for a separate child health program, certain other federal restrictions affecting Medicaid insurance eligibility are optional. States may at their option:

- Choose to offer children one year of continuous eligibility
- Enforce enrollment caps for eligible children
- Have waiting lists for coverage of uninsured children

When screening and enrolling children for the Children's Health Insurance Program, all states must establish a system to determine if children are eligible for Medicaid insurance and provide a mechanism for enrollment into the Medicaid insurance. This is creating a dual system of government insurance eligibility for children. On the one hand, poor children may face more restrictive eligibility determinations and may not be continuously eligible, while children residing in higher income households who are not eligible for Medicaid insurance may face enrollment caps in some states, forcing them to remain uninsured but wait-listed for coverage.

Limitation of Government Insurance Coverage ns

For a period of time, the federal government required the states to restrict the availability of the Children's Health Insurance Program to children who were U.S. citizens. Self-declarations of citizenship were abandoned in 2009; all children residing in the United States who meet need-based requirements for participation are now eligible for the Children's Health Insurance Program.

Need-Based Cost-Sharing

States are permitted to impose different cost-sharing on the Children's Health Insurance Program. More generous **cost-sharing rules** may apply but are not required to apply to children in the poorest households in the nation. While all courts acknowledge these federally imposed requirements, not all courts will offer families a remedy if state agencies or health providers accepting the Children's Health Insurance refuse to follow the program regulations. In other words, some of the poorest insured families in America have unenforceable rights when their children are denied medical coverage.

Middle-Income Families

Costs may not be charged for preventive services or immunizations nor may costs exceed 5% of a family's gross or net household income. States and health providers may determine whether to base their cost-sharing on a gross or net basis, and there is no mandate requiring uniformity. Families must be advised of their maximum annual cost-sharing limit for each child. The state plan must describe the:

- Consequences of not paying cost-sharing charges
- Disenrollment protections for families who cannot pay their cost-sharing obligations
- Methods used to determine cost-sharing amounts

States must permit families to pay their past-due cost-sharing charges before being disenrolled; if household income declines, the failure to meet cost-sharing obligations may be waived, but waivers are not required. Again, some courts will not penalize states if they fail to follow their cost-sharing procedures.

MANAGEMENT AND LAW ISSUES

5. Should participation in the Children's Health Insurance Program be limited to children who are U.S. citizens?

Low-Income Families

Where children reside in households at or below 150% of the federal poverty line, states may not impose more than:

- Nominal cost-sharing fees
- One cost-sharing charge for all services delivered during a single office visit
- One type of cost-sharing for a medical service

What Health Insurance Coverage Is Required for Uninsured Children?

For states that opt to expand Medicaid insurance by participating in the Children's Health Insurance Program, the medical services covered must mirror the medical services covered by Medicaid insurance. States cannot simply restrict Medicaid insurance coverage to focus on improving the health of their children; rather, states are required to offer medical services to eligible individuals and families that meet specified financial criteria. This inability to target limited resources is a major weakness of the nation's government insurance system (Geraghty, 2016, 2007).

Why Is Government Insurance Economically Necessary?

Aside from the economic need to seek **expected utility maximization**, there are at least four additional reasons why government health insurance is economically necessary. In a democratic society like the United States, there is an economic need for the federal government to:

- Enhance state capacities for health insurance coverage
- Help generate economic activity in the states
- Maximize economic impacts on the nation's health care system
- Support the nation's health care system and safety net

(Snyder & Rudowitz, 2014).

Nation's Health Care System and Safety Net

The guarantee of federal financing for Medicaid insurance that matches state spending enables states to respond to:

- Aging population
- Chaotic economic downturns
- Emergencies and disasters
- Increases in health care costs
- Uninsured and underinsured populations

Generation of Economic Activity

As the largest source of federal support to the states, Medicaid insurance is also a major economic engine in state economies. Medicaid insurance supports millions of health care jobs across the nation and provides funding to thousands of health providers who care for the Medicaid insured, including those who work at:

- Community health centers
- Group homes
- Hospitals
- Managed care plans
- Nursing homes and other long-term care facilities.

In turn, Medicaid funds generate economic activity, as follows:

- Additional tax revenues are derived from the health care jobs and household incomes generated
- Economic impact of Medicaid ifunds is intensified because of the federal matching dollars

- Health care jobs generate household income within the health care sector and throughout other sectors of the local economy due to the **multiplier effect**
- Medicaid insurance funding to health providers supports health care jobs and household income
- State spending on behalf of Medicaid-insured consumers for health care pulls federal tax dollars into the state's local economies

Economic Impact on the Health Care System

Government payments to health providers, on behalf of the Medicaid insured, directly impact the health providers by:

- Creating household income
- Promoting consumer purchases associated with the provision of health care
- Supporting health care jobs

Through the multiplier effect, new government spending creates larger impacts because of the influx of additional government funds. Other businesses and industries indirectly benefit from the multiplier effect through the economic chain. For instance, government funding of pharmaceutical drugs affects the downstream drug distributor's supply order, which affects the supply of drugs to the neighborhood retail pharmacy or pharmacy benefit manager, that are purchased by consumers, and so on. Upstream, the pharmaceutical industry's supply order for raw materials to produce and manufacture the drugs affects the intermediates who supply the compounds, which affects the global market for raw materials, and so on. Finally, both the direct and indirect effects produce changes in household consumption. The taxes derived from household income being consumed are returned to the government where the economic cycle repeats itself, each time multiplying the economic impact on the overall economy.

State Capacity for Health Insurance Coverage

Apart from whichever model is used to assess the economic impact of Medicaid funds from the federal and state governments, consumer spending on health care has a positive impact on local economies. The magnitude of the economic impact that can be contributed by Medicaid-insured consumers is dependent on at least three factors:

- Economic conditions of the state economy
- Federal funding to the states for Medicaid insurance
- Level of state funds available for Medicaid ispending on health care

Reductions in Medicaid spending lead to declines in federal funding to the states, which decreases the flow of funds to health providers, and consequently leads to declines in economic activity at the state and local levels. For instance, due to the federal match, a state with a 60% federal share of Medicaid spending must cut overall Medicaid insurance by $2.40 to save $1 in state spending (Kaiser, 2013a).

Unaffordability of Advanced Medicine

The United States has long prided itself on its medical innovations, and the United States is the global leader in medical research and health care technology (Bradley & Taylor, 2013). Unfortunately, these advances provide little consolation for many Americans. One in four Americans cannot afford the costs required to meet their medically needed care (Collins et al., 2015a). **Prohibitive costs** keep advanced medicine completely out of reach for other members of society, including the:

- Low-wage earners
- Medicaid-insured

- Underinsured of limited means
- Uninsured

(Collins, 2015b).

This lack of access because health systems are inadequate and prices are unaffordable has been termed a health care crisis across America. The skyrocketing cost of advanced medical innovations in the United States should be at the top of the congressional priority list (Rosato, 2015); alas, it is not.

LAW FACT

Access to Health Care

Should the judiciary force a solution to shape the legislative dimensions of how to provide access to medically necessary care for everyone, and in particular poor children?

Yes or no, it depends. Courts face real challenges when confronting questions with political implications without an accompanying political consensus on legislation, such as the federal Medicaid law. The role of the judiciary becomes more difficult when it faces making decisions regarding deeply contested health care values. In this **class action**, the court held that the federal Medicaid law imposed no obligation whatsoever on the state of Oklahoma to deliver any health care. Rather, the court concluded the state's obligation under the federal Medicaid law was merely to pay promptly for the medical services of Medicaid-insured children.

— *Oklahoma Chapter of the American Academy of Pediatrics v. Fogarty*, 472 F.3d 1208 (U.S. Court of Appeals for the 10th Circuit 2007), *cert. denied*, 522 U.S. 813 (U.S. Supreme Court 2007). Followed by *Equal Access for El Paso Inc. v. Hawkins*, 509 F.3d 697 (U.S. Court of Appeals for the 5th Circuit 2007), *cert. denied*, 555 U.S. 811 (U.S. Supreme Court 2008), *on remand*, 562 F.3d 724 (U.S. Court of Appeals for the 5th Circuit 2009).

See Brendel, 2011; Herr, 2013; Huberfeld, 2014 and 2011 (discussing these decisions).

CHAPTER SUMMARY

- For those who have comprehensive health insurance and/or money, the U.S. health care system offers the best care in the world; for those at the bottom of the U.S. economic pyramid, access to care is inadequate, if it exists at all.
- Medicaid insurance covers over 60 million Americans of limited means and/or who are severely disabled.
- Medicaid insurance is funded and operated jointly by the federal and state governments; federal contributions to states vary based on state per capita income, and it reached over $400 billion in 2008.
- People who qualify for Medicaid insurance include low-income working families with children, the Medicare-insured with limited resources, the blind or severely disabled, and uninsured pregnant women.
- Medicaid insurance covers services such as dental, preventive, screening, diagnostic, family planning and pregnancy, home health, hospital, laboratory and radiological services, as well as licensed professionals and nursing facilities.
- Problems with obtaining Medicaid insurance coverage include the timeline within which to apply for it, the requirement of being medically needy or suffering a medical emergency, and delivery system inequities.
- Whether equal access to health care in the United States will be developed by the executive branch or legislative branch of the federal government or the states has yet to be seen.
- Even though some low-income people are able to secure Medicaid insurance, they still suffer poor health outcomes due to its shortcomings, including its paperwork, complexity, regulations, low reimbursement rates for health providers, length of time required to obtain care, and lack of complete coverage.
- The Children's Health Insurance Program is similar to Medicaid insurance that is targeted toward covering children in low-income families.
- Medicaid insurance and the Children's Health Insurance Program make good economic sense because they further the federal government's goals of supporting the nation's safety net, generating economic activity, maximizing the impact of dollars spent on health care, and enhancing the states' abilities to provide their own health insurance coverage.

- In resolving the U.S. health care crisis, one of the fundamental questions is whether it remains more consistent with American notions of autonomy and responsibility for the government to simply encourage the desired result and ultimately leave the choice to the individual, or whether the time has come for government to mandate desired health outcomes.

LAW NOTES

1. Medicaid insurance is distinct from **Medicare insurance**. The following chapter will address Medicare, the insurance program for Americans 65 and older and for people with permanent disabilities who are under age 65. Individuals contribute payroll taxes to Medicare throughout their working lives and become eligible for Medicare insurance when they reach 65, regardless of their income.

2. The prevalence and consequences of financial barriers to health care are well documented for patients having a heart attack (myocardial infarction) (CMS, 2015a; Kawecka-Jaszcz et al., 2013; Rodwin et al., 2013). Examination of data from the Hospital Inpatient Quality Reporting program to determine the influence of payer status on use of invasive cardiac procedures and patient outcome shows that Medicaid-insured consumers face up to a 100% increased risk of complications and death after a heart attack (Gaglia et al., 2014 and 2011; Hannan et al., 2013; Parikh, et al., 2011; Smolen et al., 2014). Similar review of data from the Prospective Registry Evaluating Myocardial Infarction Event and Recovery (PREMIER) system showed financial barriers to health care were associated with worse recovery after symptoms manifested (Leifheit-Limson et al., 2012). Review of PREMIER data, an observational, multicenter study of some 2,500 patients who had a heart attack, consistently shows that Medicaid-insured consumers who lack access to necessary health care have significantly more angina, poorer quality of life, and higher risk of rehospitalizations (Arnold et al., 2012; Eaddy et al., 2012; Levine et al., 2013; Parikh et al., 2014; Turk-Adawi et al., 2014). Research looking at early or late coronary artery bypass surgeries found Medicaid-insured consumers have worse late surgery survival than privately insured or Medicare patients. The Medicaid insured are up to 50% more likely to die after coronary artery bypass surgery than patients with private coverage or Medicare alone (Efird et al., 2013; LaPar et al., 2011).

3. To assess economic impact, health economists generally use either the RIMS II (regional dual-insured modeling system) or IMPLAN (impact analysis for planning) **dual-insured models**. Input–output models account for economic relationships that show the relationships between businesses and industries in an economy; the effects of changes in government expenditures can also be estimated. Both models are based on a similar theory: A change in input (Medicaid expenditures) will produce direct impacts that will then ripple through other sectors of the economy, producing indirect and induced impacts (Snyder & Rudowitz, 2014). The differences in the models are related to the types of multipliers each model uses and the approach used to compute the multipliers. A review of studies estimating the impact of the Medicaid expansion on state economies found that, regardless of the economic impact model used, all of the studies anticipated positive increases to state output and **gross state product** (Kaiser, 2013a). The magnitude of the impact depends on the level of current and anticipated new Medicaid funding and the economic conditions within the state (Gilead & Ma, 2013). For instance:

   If Idaho expands Medicaid insurance, an additional 88,000 adults would be newly eligible, and state spending would increase by $246 million/year; for every $1 million change in state Medicaid spending:

   - $2.4 million would be gained in federal dollars
   - $5.2 million would be gained in business activity
   - 69 jobs would be created

   for a $2.5 million total economic impact (Angeles, 2012; CBPP, 2016; Frogner & Spetz, 2013; Henry & Fredericksen, 2013; Holahan et al., 2012; Kenney et. al., 2012; Peterson, 2014).

   If North Carolina expands Medicaid insurance, an additional 568,000 adults would be newly eligible, and state spending would increase by $3.1 billion/year; for every $1 million change in Medicaid spending:

   - $1.7 million would be gained in federal dollars,
   - $5.1 million would be gained in business activity, and
   - 130 jobs would be created,

   for a $6.0 million total economic impact (CBPP, 2016; Holahan et al., 2012; Kenney et. al., 2012).

If Oklahoma expands Medicaid insurance, an additional 204,000 adults would be newly eligible, and state spending would increase by $689 million/year; for every $1 million change in Medicaid spending:

- $1.8 million would be gained in federal dollars,
- $2.4 million would be gained in business activity, and
- 85 jobs would be created,

for a $4.5 million total economic impact (CBPP, 2016; Holahan et al., 2012; Kenney et. al., 2012; Splinter, 2011).

REFERENCES

Angeles, J. (2012). *How health reform's Medicaid expansion will impact state budgets*. Washington, DC: Center on Budget and Policy Priorities.

Arnold, S. V., et al. (2012). Perceived stress in myocardial infarction: Long-term mortality and health status outcomes. *Journal of the American College of Cardiology, 60*(18), 1756–1763.

Bienstock, J. (2012). Administrative oversight of state Medicaid payment policies: Giving teeth to the equal access provision. *Fordham Urban Law Journal, 39*, 805–848.

Bradley, E. H., & Taylor, L. A. (2013). *The American health care paradox: Why spending more is getting us less*. New York, NY: Public Affairs.

Bradley, H., et al. (2014). Centers for Disease Control and Prevention; Vital signs: HIV diagnosis, care, and treatment among persons living with HIV. *Morbidity and Mortality Weekly Report, 63*(47), 1113–1117.

Brendel, M. (2011). When a door closes, a window opens: Using preemption to challenge state Medicaid cutbacks. *Chicago-Kent Law Review, 86*, 925–950.

Brennan Jr., W. J. (1986). The Bill of Rights and the states: The revival of state constitutions as guardians of individual rights. *New York University Law Review, 61*, 535–553.

___. (1977). State constitutions and the protection of individual rights. *Harvard Law Review, 90*, 489–567.

Castleberry, C. (2015). A human right to health: Is there one and, if so, what does it mean? *Intercultural Human Rights Law Review, 10*, 189–232.

CBPP (Center on Budget and Policy Priorities). (2016). *Health reform's Medicaid expansion*. Washington, DC: CBPP.

Census Bureau. (2015). *Income and poverty in the United States*. Washington, DC: U.S. Department of Commerce, U.S. Census Bureau.

Chen, J. (2015). In the nick of time: Using the reasonable promptness provision to challenge Medicaid spending cutbacks. *Yale Journal of Health Policy, Law, and Ethics, 15*(2), 350–376.

CMS (Centers for Medicare and Medicaid Services). (2016). *Dual eligibility expansion*. Baltimore, MD: U.S. Department of Health & Human Services, CMS.

___. (2015a). *Medicaid and Children's Health Insurance Program applications, eligibility determinations, and enrollment report*.

___. (2015b). *National health care expenditure data*.

___. (2015c). *Outcome measures: Acute myocardial infarction*.

___. (2015d). *Improving care for Medicaid consumers with complex needs and high costs*.

___. (2014a). *Statistical enrollment report (Statistical Enrollment Data System)*.

___. (2014b). CMS, 2014). *Medicaid At-a-Glance*.

___. (2014c). *Actuarial report on the financial outlook for Medicaid*.

Collins, S. R., et al. (2015a). *How high is America's health care cost burden? Findings from the Commonwealth Fund health care affordability tracking survey*, New York, NY: Commonwealth Fund.

___. (2015b). *The rise in health care coverage and affordability since health reform took effect*.

Commonwealth Fund. (2015). *Scorecard on state health system performance*. New York, NY: Commonwealth Fund.

Dawson, L., et al. (2016). *The Affordable Care Act and people with HIV: An update*. Menlo Park, CA: Kaiser Family Foundation.

Dwyer, A. M. (2013). Ensuring equal access: Rethinking enforcement of Medicaid's equal access provision. *Minnesota Law Review, 97*, 2320–2351.

Eaddy, M. T., et al. (2012). How patient cost-sharing trends affect adherence and outcomes: A literature review. *Pharmacology and Therapeutics, 37*(1), 45–55.

Efird, J. T., et al. (2013). The effect of race and chronic obstructive pulmonary disease on long-term survival after coronary artery bypass grafting. *Frontiers in Public Health, 1*(1), 4–7.

Fichtner, J. J. (2014). *The economics of Medicaid: Assessing the costs and consequences*. Arlington, VA: Mercatus Center, George Mason University.

Frogner, B., & Spetz, J. (2013). *Affordable Care Act of 2010: Creating job opportunities for racially and ethnically diverse populations*. Washington, DC: Joint Center for Political and Economic Studies.

Gaglia, M. A., et al. (2014). African-American patients are less likely to receive drug-eluting stents during percutaneous coronary intervention. *Cardiovascular Revascularization Medicine, 15*(4), 214–218.

___. (2011). Effect of insurance type on adverse cardiac events after percutaneous coronary intervention. *American Journal of Cardiology, 107*(5), 675–680.

Geraghty, S. (2016). How the criminalization of poverty has become normalized in American culture and why you should care. *Michigan Journal of Race and Law, 21*, 195–203.

Gilead, S., & Ma, S. (2013). *How states stand to gain or lose federal funds by opting in or out of the Medicaid expansion*. New York, NY: The Commonwealth Fund.

Halpern, M. T., et al. (2008). Association of insurance status and ethnicity with cancer stage at diagnosis for twelve cancer sites: A retrospective analysis. *Lancet Oncology, 9*(3), 222–231.

Hannan, E. L., et al. (2013). Underutilization of percutaneous coronary intervention for ST-elevation myocardial infarction in Medicaid patients relative to private insurance patients. *Journal of Interventional Cardiology, 26*(5), 470–481.

Henry, B., & Fredericksen, A. (2013). *Alliance for a Just Society 2013 Job Gap Study: America's changing economy; Searching for work that pays in the new low-income job market.* Washington, DC: Alliance for a Just Society.

Herr, M. (2013). Outsourcing our children: The failure to treat mental illness in-state. *North Carolina Insight,* 56–61.

HHS (U.S. Department of Health and Human Services). (2016). *Poverty guidelines.* Washington, DC: HHS.

Holahan, J., et al. (2012). *The cost and coverage implications of the Affordable Care Act Medicaid expansion: National and state-by-state analysis.* Washington, DC: Urban Institute and Kaiser Commission on Medicaid and the Uninsured.

Huberfeld, N. (2014). Medicaid matters: Where there is a right, there must be a remedy (even in Medicaid). *Kentucky Law Journal, 102,* 327–354.

___. (2011). Federalizing Medicaid. *University of Pennsylvania Journal of Constitutional Law, 14,* 431–484.

Huberfeld, N., & Roberts, J. L. (2016). Health care and the myth of self-reliance. *Boston College Law Review, 57,* 1–60.

___. (2013a). *Medicaid eligibility for adults.*

___. (2013b). *Medicaid/ Children's Health Insurance Program child participation rates.*

___. (2013c). *The role of Medicaid in state economies: A look at the research.*

Kaiser Commission on Medicaid and the Uninsured. (2016). *Who is impacted by the coverage gap in states that have not adopted the Medicaid expansion.* Washington, DC: Kaiser.

___. (2015). *Fact sheet: Key facts about the uninsured population.*

___. (2014). *Federal and state share of Medicaid spending.*

Kawecka-Jaszcz, K., et al. (2013). *Health-related quality of life in cardiovascular patients.* New York, NY: Springer Publishing.

Keehan, S. P., et al. (2015). National health expenditure projections, 2014–24: Spending growth faster than recent trends. *Health Affairs, 34*(8), 1407–1417.

Kenney, G., et al. (2012). *Opting out of the Medicaid expansion under the Affordable Care Act: How many uninsured adults would not be eligible for Medicaid?* Washington, DC: Urban Institute.

LaPar, D. J., et al. (2011). Surgery for coronary artery disease primary payer status is associated with mortality and resource utilization for coronary artery bypass grafting. *Circulation, 126,* 5132–5139.

Leifheit-Limson, E. C., et al. (2012). Changes in social support within the early recovery period and outcomes after acute myocardial infarction. *Journal of Psychosomatic Research, 73*(1), 35–41.

Levine, G., et al. (2013). Recent trends in cost-related medication nonadherence among stroke survivors in the United States. *Annals of Neurology, 73*(2), 180–188.

McKennan, M. (2011). Medicaid access after health reform: The shifting legal basis for equal access. *Seton Hall Circuit Review, 7,* 477–509.

MedPAC (Medicare Payment Advisory Committee). (2016). *MedPAC and MACPAC data book: Beneficiaries dually eligible for Medicare and Medicaid.* Washington, DC: MedPAC.

Montaner, J. S., et al. (2006). The case for expanding access to highly active antiretroviral therapy to curb the growth of the HIV pandemic. *Lancet, 368,* 531–536.

NASBO (National Association State Budget Officers). (2015). *NASBO state expenditure report.* Washington, DC: NASBO.

NASTAD (National Alliance State and Territorial AIDS Directors). (2015). *ADAP (AIDS Drug Assistance Program) supports expanded access to care.* Washington, DC: NASTAD.

Orentlicher, D. (2014). The future of the Affordable Care Act: Protecting economic health more than physical health? *Houston Law Review, 51,* 1057–1079.

Owcharenko, N. (2016). *Medicaid at 50: Reform is needed to better serve low-income health care needs.* Washington, DC: Heritage Foundation.

Parikh, P. B., et al. (2011). Association of health insurance status with presentation and outcomes of coronary artery disease among nonelderly adults undergoing percutaneous coronary intervention. *American Heart Journal, 162*(3), 512–517.

___. (2014). The impact of financial barriers on access to care, quality of care and vascular morbidity among patients with diabetes and coronary heart disease. *Journal of General Internal Medicine, 29*(1), 76–81.

Peterson, S. (2014). *Expanding health coverage with federal funds will create economy-boosting jobs in Idaho.* Boise, ID: Idaho Community Action Network.

Radley, D. C., et al. (2014). *Aiming higher: Results from a scorecard on state health system performance.* New York, NY: Commonwealth Fund.

Rodwin, B. A., et al. (2013). Economics of psychosocial factors in patients with cardiovascular disease. *Progress in Cardiovascular Diseases, 55*(6), 563–573.

Rosato, C. E. (2015). The medical liability exemption: A path to affordable pharmaceuticals. *Florida State University Law Review, 42,* 1067–1097.

Rosenberg, G. T. W. (2014). Alienating aliens: Equal protection violations in the structures of state public-benefit schemes. *University of Pennsylvania Journal of Constitutional Law, 16,* 1417–1475.

Sacco, S. (2016). In defense of the eligible undocumented New Yorker's state constitutional right to public benefits. *New York University Review of Law and Social Change, 40,* 181–244.

Saver, R. S. (2015). Envisioning the future health care system. *Houston Journal of Health Law and Policy, 15,* 1–15.

Sheffner, D. J. (2015). Rate setting after Douglas. *Hamline Law Review, 38,* 57–84.

Silow-Carroll, S., et al. (2011). *Reducing hospital readmissions: Lessons from top-performing hospitals.* New York, NY: The Commonwealth Fund.

Smolen, J. R., et al. (2014). Health insurance and chronic conditions in low-income urban whites. *Journal of Urban Health, 91*(4), 637–647.

Snyder, L., & Rudowitz, R. (2015). Medicaid financing: How *Does it Work and What are the Implications?* Washington, DC: Kaiser Commission on Medicaid and the Uninsured.

Splinter, G. L. (2011). *National health care reform, Impact on Oklahoma.* Tulsa, OK: Oklahoma Health Care Authority.

Staszak, S. (2015). *No day in court: Access to justice and the politics of judicial retrenchment.* New York, NY: Oxford University Press.

Turk-Adawi, K. I., et al. (2014). Cardiac rehabilitation enrollment among referred patients: Patient and organizational factors. *Journal of Cardiopulmonary Rehabilitation and Prevention, 34*(2), 114–122.

WHO (World Health Organization). (2010). *Towards universal access: Scaling up priority HIV/AIDS interventions in the health sector.* Geneva, Switzerland: WHO.

CHAPTER 5

Medicare Insurance Reforms

"Our current national health care system is simple: don't get sick."

— Anonymous

IN BRIEF

This chapter draws attention to the challenge of reforming Medicare insurance, including Medicare's complex prescription drug plan. Debate about how much health care the Medicare-insured should finance versus how much should be financed by society is reviewed. How the federal government might pay for access to better quality health care and medical services is discussed, with a focus on reforming the Medicare Advantage model of managed care.

LEARNING OBJECTIVES

Upon completion of this chapter readers should be able to:

1. Contrast consumer-directed health care with high-deductible health plans.
2. Define health risks in conjunction with allocation of limited resources.
3. Describe the reasons the uninsured and underinsured lack adequate health insurance.
4. Explain the basic purposes of health insurance.
5. Outline the principles of economic fairness.
6. Understand health insurance risk pooling.

KEY TERMS

Affordable Care Act of 2010	Health risks	Payroll taxes
Age Discrimination in Employment Act of 1978	Homebound	Polypharmacy
	Incumbent health insurers	Profit subsidies
Bundled billing	Managed care	Single-payer systems
Catastrophic coverage	Medicare Advantage	Social insurance program
Civil complaint	Medicare eligibility	Social Security
Coinsurance	Medicaid insurance	Special needs program
Cost-sharing	Medicare Part A	Super-users
Coverage gap	Medicare Part B	Supplemental coverage
Deductible	Medicare Part C	Traditional indemnity insurance
Delayed payment reductions	Medicare Part D	
Donut hole coverage	Medigap	Treatment prevalence
Dual-eligible	Out-of-pocket limits	Unbundled billing
Entitlement	Overpayments	

FACT OR FICTION

Medicare Coverage

Are employers allowed to alter and decrease health insurance benefits for Medicare-eligible retired employees to a level below that provided to non-Medicare-eligible retired employees?

The Equal Employment Opportunity Commission proposed that employers be able to decrease their employer-provided health insurance benefits for retirees who reach the age of **Medicare eligibility** after many employers began dropping insurance benefits to avoid liability for age discrimination. Under the **Age Discrimination in Employment Act of 1978**, it is unlawful for employers to provide workers different benefits based on age, therefore making it difficult for employers to coordinate their retiree health insurance benefits with Medicare eligibility (*See* 29 U.S.C.A. §§ 621–634). Although employers are not required to provide retiree benefits, one in five of the Medicare-insured rely on private coverage to supplement Medicare insurance and meet their health care needs, a drop from two in three in just two decades (McArdle et al., 2014). Medicare insurance, on average, provides less generous benefits than employer-provided insurance plans; Medicare has no **out-of-pocket limits** and greater **cost-sharing**, thereby imposing an additional burden on a population group that already assumes a greater share of health care costs. In addition, there is the coverage gap in the Medicare Part D prescription drug benefit, and Medicare insurance does not pay for long-term care, dental care, or vision care.

— *See* Law Fact at the end of this chapter for the answer.

Principles and Applications

The Medicare program is the second largest **social insurance program** in the United States, behind **Social Security**, offering guaranteed health insurance benefits to those eligible by virtue of their Social Security eligibility. Persons eligible for Medicare insurance include:

- Individuals aged 65 and over
- The severely disabled
- Those with end-stage renal disease

(*See* 42 U.S.C.A. § 1395c).

With over 55 million insured and total expected expenditures of $632 billion in 2015, plus an additional 67 million baby-boomers en route to Medicare insurance, the challenge is one of growing needs versus limited federal resources (CBO, 2016; Kaiser, 2016). While the Medicare-insured make up just 17% of the U.S. population, they account for most of the nation's health care costs; the rise in their treatment prevalence, rather than rising treatment costs per case or population growth, accounts for most of the spending growth in the nation's health care costs (Thorpe et al., 2010; *See* Kaiser, 2016). The sickest 25% of the Medicare-insured spend 90% of the U.S. health care dollars with an average of:

- At least one hospitalization yearly
- $181,800 in health care expenditures yearly
- 5 diagnosed medical conditions
- 10 prescriptions
- 12 physicians

(AHRQ, 2016; Lane et al., 2014; Reschovsk et al., 2011).

The sickest 1% of the Medicare-insured account for over 20% of total health care spending (Darragh, 2014). The key to cutting costs lies with the physicians who treat these **super-users** (Kennedy & Blodgett, 2012). What can probably be said about this subgroup of the Medicare-insured is:

- At least two of their chronic medical conditions were preventable
- Their care is not being coordinated by their multiple health care providers

- There is no medical evidence to support the **polypharmacy** (or drug cocktails) they are being prescribed
- They are being over-treated and mistreated

(Thorpe et al., 2010; *See* Lane et al., 2014).

Medicare Reform: Financing by Individuals or Society?

Medicare insurance, originally constructed in the 1960s to mimic the Blue Cross/Blue Shield mainstream approach to medicine, must be changed if it is to be sustained. Its benefits package still closely resembles the standard package available in the mid-1960s; 70% of Medicare enrollees have **traditional indemnity insurance** at a time when less than 2% of the nation's insured have conventional insurance that is not part of a **managed care** plan (Kaiser, 2016). At the same time, Medicare payments are not intended to cover all the medical needs of enrollees, nor should society pay for all these expenses (Wharton, 2004). Only about 1 in 10 individuals over 65 relies solely on Medicare insurance; the rest have:

- **Medicaid insurance**
- Employer-provided coverage
- Supplementary health insurance in addition to Medicare

Although there is substantial variation in the ability of consumers to supplement Medicare's benefits, essential care is available to everyone who qualifies for Medicare.

Complexity of Medicare Insurance

The complexity of Medicare insurance mirrors the nation's broader health care system with overlapping services and convoluted public/private financing. To demonstrate the veracity of this statement, a brief overview of the types of Medicare plans is in order. As illustrated in **FIGURE 5-1**, Medicare payments are organized and paid for in different ways.

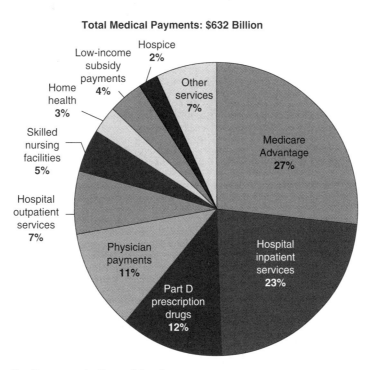

Total Medical Payments: $632 Billion

FIGURE 5-1 Medicare Benefits Payments by Type of Service

Data from: CBO (Congressional Budget Office). (2016). *Medicare baseline*. Washington, DC: CBO; Kaiser Family Foundation. (2016). *Fact sheet: Medicare*. Menlo Park, CA: Kaiser.

Part A: Medicare Hospital, Skilled Nursing, Home Health, and Hospice Care

Medicare Part A (hospital insurance) pays for almost one-fourth of benefits spending (CBO, 2016). Most the Medicare-insured do not pay premiums for this benefit, because they have already paid for it through their **payroll taxes**.[LN1] Part A does not cover custodial or long-term nursing care, and consumers must meet certain eligibility criteria for home health and hospice care.

The home health care benefit is available to individuals certified by their physicians as being **homebound**. Eligibility is determined by the type of services needed (intermittent skilled nursing care, physical therapy, speech-language pathology services, or continued occupational therapy) (CMS, 2015a).The Medicare hospice benefit is available only to individuals whose physicians have certified their expected mortality is less than six months away.

Part B: Medicare Physician, Outpatient, Home Health Care, and Preventive Services

Medicare Part B covers physician visits, outpatient services, preventive services, and some home health visits. Most people pay a monthly premium for this insurance; Medicaid insurance may subsidize premiums based on income eligibility, which varies by state (CMS, 2015a). Services are provided on a medically necessary basis. No **coinsurance** or **deductible** is charged for an annual wellness visit or for preventive services.

Part C: Medicare Advantage Coverage

Medicare Part C refers to **Medicare Advantage**, where the federal government pays a fixed amount per member per month to private insurance companies that then coordinate and finance care. Consumers can select from a variety of private managed care plans and enroll in:

- Health maintenance organizations
- Preferred provider organizations
- Private fee-for-service plans
- Special needs plans

Medicare Advantage has more than doubled its enrollments in the past decade (Wharton, 2014). With 26 Medicare Advantage regions administering these programs, most consumers have a choice of 6 private plans (Kaiser, 2016). About one-third of the Medicare-insured elect a Medicare Advantage plan (CMS, 2015a).

Medicare's Special Needs Program

The Medicare Advantage **special needs program** is restricted to **dual-eligible** Medicare/Medicaid insurance consumers residing in long-term care facilities. There are almost 800 special needs programs coordinating services in all 3,077 Medicaid insurance offices in county boards of assistance with 50 state Medicaid insurance agencies. The special needs program serves about 1.2 million consumers (CMS, 2015a).

Administrative Complexity of Medicare Advantage

With this public/private sector complexity, the federal government has no way to monitor access, use, or performance for the over 165 million consumers enrolled in Medicare Part C. Medicare Advantage insurance plans are not required to:

- Have Medicare review of services
- Negotiate fees
- Report quality measures

(MedPAC, 2016; Newhouse & McGuire, 2014; *See* 42 C.F.R. § 422.152 and CMS, 2015b).

MANAGEMENT AND LAW ISSUES

1. Why is it important to provide health care coverage for the groups Medicare covers?

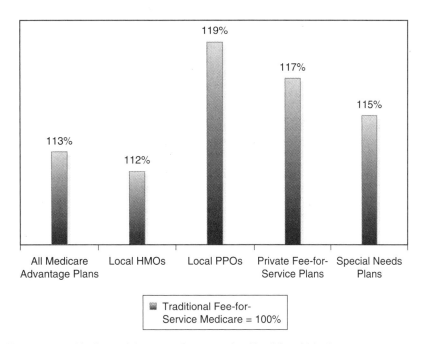

FIGURE 5-2 Average Payments to Medicare Advantage Compared to Traditional Medicare

Data from: AHRQ (Agency for Healthcare Research and Quality). (2016). *Medical expenditure panel survey.* Rockville, MD: AHRQ; MedPAC (Medicare Payment Advisory Commission). (2015a). *Report to the Congress: Medicare and the health care delivery system.* Washington, DC: MedPAC; (2015b). *Report to the Congress: Medicare payment policy.*

The result of this federal policy is shown in **FIGURE 5-2**, where it is illustrated how costs for Medicare Advantage exceed traditional fee-for-service Medicare. Despite increased costs, however, there is little discernible improvement in the quality of Medicare Advantage services (Duggan et al., 2014). The increase in competition generated by higher payments to Medicare Advantage has not translated into better benefits for consumers (Wharton, 2014). As a result of this discrepancy, there has been a significant reduction in the payments to Medicare Advantage over time (*See* Medicare Improvements for Patients and Providers Act, 42 U.S.C.A. 1395w-21 and 1395w-28 *et seq.*); these cuts have not impacted the Medicare-insured aversely. Conversely, paying somewhat more did not necessarily benefit consumers all that much although the health insurance industry shareholders benefited from the **delayed payment reductions** mandated under the **Affordable Care Act of 2010** (Duggan et al., 2014).

Part D: Medicare Prescription Drug Coverage

Medicare Part D prescription drug plans generally have at least two economic objectives:

- Allow the health care system to improve the overall delivery of health care to the Medicare-insured
- Relieve the financial burden on those who have trouble affording their prescription drugs

While the prescription drug program has value, it does not begin to address either of these economic objectives. It does, however, show how public perceptions, or misconceptions, can unduly influence decisions about **health risks**. The Medicare prescription drug plan is an example of health policy based not on a rational response to health risks, but rather on misperceptions of risks (Clements & Coady, 2012). The drug plan, while providing coverage at the lower and upper ends of expenditures, allows for a **coverage gap** in the middle, which is why it has become known as a **donut hole coverage** plan. As illustrated in **FIGURE 5-3**, the drug benefit is not **catastrophic coverage** above a deductible, but rather:

- 75% coverage for a range of expenses, after a modest deductible (or, most of the donut), then
- 100% cost-sharing for beneficiaries (or, the donut hole with zero coverage), before
- A return to 80% donut coverage (or, the rest of the donut)

(CMS, 2016a).

Compared to traditional catastrophic coverage with a deductible, Medicare Part D reduces coverage for people with high expenses (where, in theory, people would have gotten the most economic utility value from coverage) to offer generous coverage for people with low expenses (where, in theory, coverage should be less valuable), to provide most

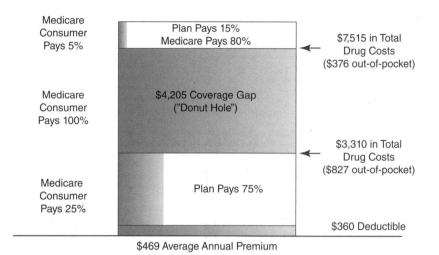

FIGURE 5-3 Standard Medicare Drug Prescription Benefit

Data from: CMS (Centers for Medicare and Medicaid Services). (2016). *Your guide to Medicare prescription drug coverage.* Baltimore, MD: CMS.

consumers with a return on their premium. While concentrating more of the Medicare prescription drug money on upper-end catastrophic coverage makes more sense, the gap in the middle allows the federal government to provide the largest number of people with some benefit from this plan.

Patient Assistance Programs

For enrollees covered by Medicare Part D, the medical products industry offers patient assistance programs that provide access to prescription drugs outside of the Part D benefit without any cost to the Medicare program. Most manufacturers have a data-sharing agreement with the federal government to help coordinate prescription use with plans providing Medicare prescription coverage. Medicare Part D benefit coverage has reduced the load on patient assistance programs, enabling the medical products industry to expand such programs to individuals with complex needs and high costs.

Supplemental Insurance Coverage

Medicare has high cost arrangements, no limit on out-of-pocket spending, and a coverage gap in the Part D prescription drug plan. Employer-sponsored health insurance, Medicaid insurance, and **Medigap** overlay each of the four types of Medicare and help with cost-sharing requirements and benefit gaps. Medigap, a supplemental insurance offered through private insurers, takes care of medical expenses not covered by Medicare. Most of the Medicare-insured have some form of **supplemental coverage**.

Structural Reform of Medicare Insurance

It is important to gather more evidence about the implications of either paying less to Medicare Advantage or other changes in **entitlement** to make the Medicare system more fiscally sustainable.[LN2] Right now, little attention is being directed to the:

- $65 trillion the United States needs to make Medicare whole
- $1 billion that private insurers get in **profit subsidies** from Medicare Advantage plans each year
- $1 trillion in unfunded health care obligations for health care industry retirees (as well as from state and local governments and corporate entities, both profit and nonprofit)

(Duggan et al., 2014; Schultz, 2011; Wharton, 2014).

MANAGEMENT AND LAW ISSUES

2.   Should employers be required to fund retirees' health care costs?

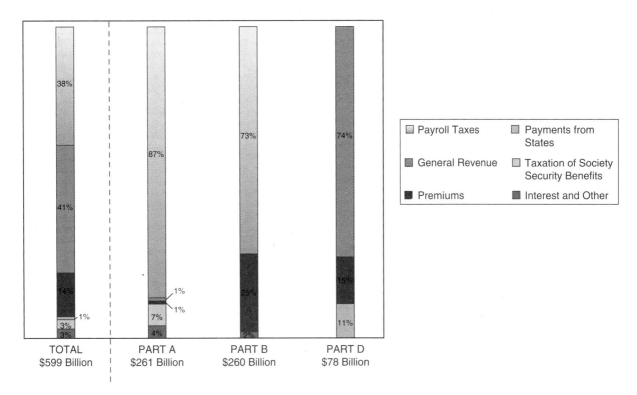

FIGURE 5-4 Estimated Sources of Medicare Revenue

Data from: Medicare Board of Trustees. (2015). *Annual report of the boards of trustees of the federal hospital insurance and federal supplementary medical insurance trust funds.* Washington, DC: Medicare Board of Trustees.

The nation is more focused on the revenue side of the equation than on addressing the growth of benefit obligations. Little attention is directed to insurance industry profits that were to be returned to the Medicare-insured in the form of reduced premiums or additional benefits (MedPAC, 2016). Discussion generally centers on increasing payroll taxes or the premiums for Medicare insurance.[LN3]

Medicare is financed by a combination of sources of revenue, as illustrated in **FIGURE 5-4**. Payroll taxes finance the majority of Part A, while general revenues fund three-quarters of Parts B and D. There is not much talk about the real issue: how to control the growth of Medicare.

COURT DECISION
Common Law Recovery of Medicare Overpayments

United States v. Lahey Clinic Hospital, Inc.
[United States v. Medicare Provider]
399 F.3d 1 (U.S. Court of Appeals for the 1st Circuit 2005),
cert. denied, 546 U.S. 815 (U.S. Supreme Court 2005);
followed by *United States v. Khan*, 2009 U.S. Dist. LEXIS 68546 (U.S. District Court
for the Eastern District of Michigan, Southern Division 2009)

Facts: A **civil complaint** was filed against the Lahey Clinic Hospital, claiming it billed Medicare and received payment for unnecessary tests and other diagnostic procedures for the Medicare-insured. The court was careful to acknowledge that Lahey, a renowned academic medical center, was not arguing that the United States may not recover **overpayments**, only that it has chosen the wrong approach in doing so; similarly, the United States has not alleged fraud on Lahey's part in this action. The United States sought restitution for over $311,000 in overpayments, under common law theories of unjust enrichment and payment under mistake of fact. Lahey maintained the federal Medicare Act and the administrative procedures promulgated by the Secretary of Health and Human Services were the exclusive avenue for recovery of Medicare overpayments and, as such, the federal courts had no subject matter jurisdiction (*See* 42 U.S.C.A. §§ 1395ff(b) and ii).

Issue: Can the federal government sue to recover Medicare overpayments using the common theories of unjust enrichment and payment under mistake of fact?

Holding and Decision: Yes. The federal government may use the .common law to recover Medicare overpayments.

Analysis: The court summarized the background leading to this claim, namely how Medicare's escalating payments for laboratory services became a source of increasing concern. Congress imposed payment caps on laboratory services, yet costs continued to escalate. Medicare was paying twice as much as physicians for the same laboratory tests. Much of the added cost was attributable to laboratories billing Medicare separately and at the full rate for each individual test in chemistry and urinalysis panels (known as **unbundled billing**). When physicians ordered the same panels, they were billed at a reduced rate to account for savings from performing the tests as a group (**bundled billing**). In addition, when physicians ordered certain hematology indices (which can be generated from the results of other tests), the laboratories repeated the test and billed Medicare for the duplicative test. Medicare overpaid laboratories in excess of $43.6 million for these two billing practices during a two-year period in the mid-1990s. Laboratories might have saved an additional $15.6 million billed to Medicare by using available automated technology. Accordingly, the federal government sought to recover the overpayments from unbundled billing and duplicative tests that were medically unnecessary. A number of civil actions were instituted to recover some of these costs under various theories, and this is one of those cases.

The court rejected the argument that the United States could only recover overpayments through the administrative process established under the Medicare Act (*See* 42 U.S.C.A. § 405(g) and (h); *See also* 42 U.S.C.A. § 1395ff(b) and ii). Nothing in the Medicare Act established that the administrative remedy mandated by Congress was the exclusive remedy for recovery of overpayments. The court also rejected the contention that the Medicare Act displaced underlying common law causes of action to recover overpayments.

Rule of Law: The federal government has broad power to recover overpayments wrongly paid from the U.S. Treasury, even absent any express statutory authorization to sue.

Reference discussing this case: Turner, 2015.

Lahey is one example of the federal government attempting to control costs (albeit, after the fact). From the perspective of the Lahey Clinic Hospital, it maximized its revenue; unbundling its laboratory services made perfect economic sense. Medicare regulations did not preclude the practice at the time of the billings by the hospital. The bundling and unbundling practice was not foreseen, and the retesting was not defined as duplicative until later. Once again, the complexity of Medicare presented itself.

Lahey also demonstrates the problems that may arise under **single-payer systems** without competition. Physicians could compete for laboratory services and receive lower rates. Obtaining more revenue for the Medicare program does not solve the issue of the long-term sustainability problem until unnecessary spending like in the *Lahey* case is controlled. While Social Security is still believed to be the most "untouchable" topic in politics, Medicare insurance is a tougher problem politically because it does not involve a simple cash benefit; rather, Medicare puts a price tag on consumers' health, perhaps even their lives.

Reallocating Medical Treatments and Prevalence

Given the higher costs of Medicare Advantage, with no discernible improvement in the quality of its managed care, there may be many opportunities to cut its services, with minimal adverse impact on consumers. The money saved could then be allocated where it may provide more efficient benefits. For instance, as more private insurers enter the Medicare Advantage market and more consumers enroll, advertising expenditures are expanding; but better quality care does not come from advertising (Wharton, 2014).

As mentioned, the rise in **treatment prevalence**, rather than rising treatment costs, accounts for most of the spending growth (Thorpe et al., 2010). Yet, rationing Medicare expenditures is rarely discussed. Politicians do not want to say,

3.   Should some medical services be exempt from Medicare coverage?

"this person's life expectancy is only so many years, so this procedure is not worth the cost." Nevertheless, Americans are going to be forced to have this discussion soon. Perhaps this rationing discussion could occur at the same time as taxpayers decide whether they want the private health insurance industry to get billions of dollars from Medicare Advantage (*Compare* Graham, 2014 (opposing profit subsidies) and Frakt & Mayes, 2012 (supporting profit subsidies)). With educated baby-boomers entering the Medicare system, access to health care is a growing issue. Costs and profit subsidies aside, demands simply for access and for medical freedom may yet breathe new life into the Medicare system (Thorpe et al., 2010; Wharton, 2014).

Overhauling Medicare

There is general consensus on several overhauls of the Medicare system, including:

- Increase payroll taxes and premiums for Medicare insurance to those who can afford to pay more
- Mandate that profit subsidies from Medicare Advantage be returned to consumers in the form of reduced premiums or additional benefits
- Monitor quality use and performance for *all* the Medicare-insured
- Require more competitive bidding for medical services reimbursed by Medicare insurance

(Duggan, 2014; Lane et al., 2014; Walker, 2011).

Everyone pays for hospitalization insurance (Medicare Part A) through payroll taxes during their working lives, but physician payments (Medicare Part B) and prescription drug benefits (Medicare Part D) are voluntary; perhaps those who are better off should pay higher premiums.

An additional potential area for overhaul is the allocation of health risks. Medicare is an inadequate health insurance plan in the sense that it does not protect against long hospital stays or catastrophic expenses. This is not optimal health insurance. Insurance should protect consumers from financial ruin, but Medicare insurance does not do that (Huberfeld & Roberts, 2016). The least likely to purchase supplemental Medicare coverage are financially distressed consumers with complex needs. It is essential that Medicare insurance protects everyone against high costs and catastrophic loss.

LAW FACT

Medicare Coverage

Are employers allowed to alter and decrease health insurance benefits for Medicare-eligible retirees to a level below that provided to non-Medicare-eligible employees?

Yes. Employers can decrease or drop health care benefits for retirees who reach the age of Medicare eligibility.

— *AARP v. EEOC*, 489 F.3d 558 (U.S. Court of Appeals for the 3rd Circuit 2007), *cert. denied*, 552 U.S. 1279 (U.S. Supreme Court 2008). Followed by *Fulghum v. Embarq Corp.*, 778 F.3d 1147 (U.S. Court of Appeals for the 10th Circuit 2015), *cert. denied*, 136 S.Ct. 537 (U.S. Supreme Court 2015).

CHAPTER SUMMARY

- The Medicare insurance program is one of the largest social insurance programs in the United States, behind only Social Security.
- Soon, over 100 million people will be eligible for Medicare insurance, meaning the demand will likely exhaust the resources.
- Rise in treatment prevalence, rather than treatment cost or patient growth, accounts for most of the spending growth for the Medicare insurance program.
- About 90% of those receiving Medicare supplement their insurance benefits with other forms of coverage.
- Medicare is organized into four parts: A (hospital insurance), B (physician insurance), C (Medicare Advantage), and D (prescription drug coverage).
- Medicare insurance is financed by payroll taxes, general federal revenue, premiums from consumers, payments from states, taxation on Social Security benefits, and interest, but still suffers a serious budgetary shortfall.
- Medicare insurance does not protect people from the kinds of medical expenses causing financial ruin, such as long hospital stays or catastrophic illnesses.

LAW NOTES

1. Medicare premiums are $96.40/month; individual consumers with incomes over $85,000 or married couples with incomes over $170,000 pay income-related rates. Medicare Part A consumers pay the first $800 of hospital care and the first $100 of outpatient physician visits in 2016. Part A benefits are subject to an annual deductible ($1,288 in 2016), plus coinsurance amounts for extended inpatient stays in a hospital or skilled nursing facility. If anyone remains in the hospital for more than 60 or 90 days, they could end up paying another $250 per day for hospital care. Medicare Part B benefits are subject to a deductible ($166 in 2016) and a coinsurance of 20% (CMS, 2016b).

2. There are some incumbents, like Aetna and the nonprofit Blue Cross/Blue Shield mainstream insurers, that operate whether Medicare reimbursement is generous or not. But then there are marginal firms like United Health that come in when the government pays somewhat more and leave when reimbursement reductions are forecast. Understanding who these firms are, or whether they offer a somewhat different level of quality—perhaps a lower level of quality than the **incumbent health insurers**—is important if the Medicare system is to be fiscally sustainable (Wharton, 2014).

3. The government collects payroll taxes over time. These vary by individuals' wages and income, while providing a standard benefit to all enrollees. In this way, the program is able to assure access to essential health care for consumers at all levels of income. Medicare is a more progressive program than Social Security when both the contributions and benefits sides are considered; the benefits are the same, while contributions are higher from persons with high incomes (White & Ginsberg et al., 2012).

REFERENCES

AHRQ (Agency for Healthcare Research and Quality). (2016). *Medical expenditure panel survey*. Rockville, MD: AHRQ.

CBO (Congressional Budget Office). (2016). *Medicare baseline*. Washington, DC: CBO.

Clements, B. J., & Coady, D. (2012). *Economics of public health care reform in advanced and emerging economies*. Washington, DC: International Monetary Fund.

CMS (Centers for Medicare and Medicaid Services). (2016a). *Your guide to Medicare prescription drug coverage*. Baltimore, MD: CMS.

___. (2016b). *Medicare and you 2017*.

___. (2015a). *Annual report of the Board of Trustees of the Hospital Insurance Supplementary Medical Insurance Trust Funds*.

___. (2015b). *Medicare Advantage quality improvement (QI) program*.

Darragh, T. (2014). *Sick system. Special report: How hospital super-users account for bulk of health-care spending*. University of California's Annenberg School of Journalism.

Duggan, M., et al. (2014). *Who benefits when the government pays more? Pass-through in the Medicare Advantage program*. Cambridge, MA: National Bureau of Economic Research.

Frakt, A. B., & Mayes, R. (2012). Beyond capitation: How new payment experiments seek to find the "sweet spot" in amount of risk providers and payers bear. *Health Affairs, 31*, 1951–1955.

Graham, J. (2014). *Are Medicare Advantage plans overpaid and corrupt?* Washington, DC: National Center for Policy Analysis.

Huberfeld, N., & Roberts, J. L. (2016). Health care and the myth of self-reliance. *Boston College Law Review, 57*, 1–60.

Kaiser Family Foundation. (2016). *Fact sheet: Medicare*. Menlo Park, CA: Kaiser.

Kennedy, J., & Blodgett, E. (2012). Health insurance: Motivated disability enrollment and the Affordable Care Act. *New England Journal of Medicine, 367,* 16.

Lane, J., et al. (2014). *Privacy, big data, and the public good: Frameworks for engagement.* New York, NY: Cambridge University Press.

McArdle, F., et al. (2014). *Overview of health benefits for pre-65 and Medicare-eligible retirees: Trends among employers offering retiree health benefits.* Menlo Park, CA: Kaiser Family Foundation.

Medicare Board of Trustees. (2015). *Annual report of the Boards of Trustees of the Federal Hospital Insurance and Federal Supplementary Medical Insurance Trust Funds.* Washington, DC: Medicare Board of Trustees.

MedPAC (Medicare Payment Advisory Commission). (2016). *Report to the Congress: Medicare payment policy.* Washington, DC: MedPAC.

Newhouse, J. P., & McGuire, T. B. (2014). Review article: How successful is Medicare Advantage? *Milbank Quarterly, 92*(2), 351–394.

Reschovsk, J. D., et al. (2011). Following the money: Factors associated with the cost of treating high-cost Medicare beneficiaries. *Health Services Research Journal, 46*(4), 1–25.

Schultz, E. E. (2011). *Retirement heist: How companies plunder and profit from the nest eggs of American workers.* New York, NY: Portfolio, Penguin Random House.

Thorpe, K. E., et al. (2010). Chronic conditions account for rise in Medicare spending. *Health Affairs, 29*(4), 718–724.

Turner, C. M. (2015). A path toward an increased role for the United States in patent infringement litigation. *Chicago-Kent Journal of Intellectual Property, 14*(2), 485–520.

Walker, D. M. (2011). *Comeback America.* New York, NY: Random House.

Wharton School at the University of Pennsylvania. (2004). Restructuring Medicare is a riskier operation than first thought. *Knowledge@Wharton.* http://knowledge.wharton.upenn.edu/article/restructuring-medicare-is-a-riskier-operation-than-first-thought/

___. (2014). Why consumers don't gain much from Medicare Advantage. http://knowledge.wharton.upenn.edu/article/medicare-advantage-offer-much-advantage

White, C., & Ginsberg, P. B. (2012). Slower growth in Medicare spending: Is this the new normal? *New England Journal of Medicine, 366,* 1073–1075.

PART III

AFFORDABLE HEALTH CARE

Part III investigates how to ensure that, as parts of the U.S. health care system offer some of the best health care of any place in the world to those who can afford it, the masses are not left behind.

CHAPTER 6

Affordable Care and Tax-Exempt Hospitals

"America is a living, breathing presence, unimpressed by what others say is impossible, proud of its own success; generous, yes, and naive; sometimes wrong, never mean, always impatient to provide a better life for its people in a framework of a basic fairness and freedom."

— **Ronald Reagan** (1911–2004), 40th President of the United States

IN BRIEF

This chapter examines whether tax-exempt hospitals are required to provide fair and reasonable charges for medical services in return for substantial federal, state, and local tax exemptions. Amid growing concern about whether tax-exempt hospitals are doing enough to justify their tax exemptions, Congress and many state legislatures are calling on hospitals to make changes to their charitable care and financial assistance policies, as well as their billing and debt collection practices. It is important to note that while this chapter addresses the nation's tax-exempt hospitals, the pricing, billing, and collection practices and principles are equally applicable to tax-exempt health care systems, of which hospitals are only one part.

LEARNING OBJECTIVES

Upon completion of this chapter readers should be able to:

1. Describe the historical foundation of tax-exempt hospitals.
2. Explain the general idea of affordable health care.
3. Review the history of the social contract for hospital care with special emphasis on the changes that took place starting in the late 1960s.
4. Outline the effects of shifting from nonprofit (charitable) to profit-based hospitals.
5. Explain who comprises the deserving and medically needy.
6. Discuss the health care pricing disparities among the privately insured, Medicare/Medicaid insured, and the uninsured.
7. Describe the ban on extraordinary debt collection practices.
8. Explain the conflict among federal, state, and local governments due to the tax-exempt status of hospitals and other health care elements.
9. Define the chargemaster system of hospital pricing and its effect on the disparity of charges among patient groups with varying health care coverage.
10. Outline the responsibilities of government health care monitoring systems that seek to contain costs.
11. Explain the Emergency Medical Treatment and Active Labor Act of 1986, its impact on cost for health care, and its limitations.

KEY TERMS

Actual prices	Duty of good faith and fair dealing	Model Nonprofit Corporation Act of 1987
Acute and necessary care	Emergency Medical Treatment and Active Labor Act of 1986	Net patient revenue
Affordable Care Act of 2010	Extraordinary debt collection	Not-for-profit
Anti-kickback laws	Federal poverty level	Price discrimination
Available resources (for financial assistance)	Fee-for-service arrangements	Price gouging
Bad debts	Fiduciary duty	Public benefit corporations
Chargemaster	Financial assistance policies	Safety-net hospitals
Charitable care	Illegal immigrants	Securitized medical debt
Charitable care standard	Injunction	Sliding scale payment scheme
Children's Health Insurance Program	Lawful permanent residents	Special fraud alerts
Community benefits standards	List prices	Tax-exempt
Constructive trusts	Market-based for-profit hospital model	Uncompensated care
Critical access hospitals	Means-based discounts	Underinsured
Deserving and medically needy	Medical emergencies	Underutilized hospital resources
Discriminatory pricing	Medically necessary care	Worker's Compensation insurance
		Working age population

FACT OR FICTION

Discriminatory Pricing

Are the uninsured being charged the highest prices for health care?

Carlos Ferlini installed and repaired gutters for a living. Like millions of Americans, he made a decent living, but was not offered health insurance through his employer and could not afford to buy it on his own. This was before enactment of the **Affordable Care Act of 2010** (*See* 42 U.S.C.A. § 18001 *et seq.*) that mandated affordable health insurance be made available to everyone. Ferlini fell while working on a roof and badly injured himself, fracturing his skull and ribs, and puncturing his lung. When he arrived at the hospital, Ferlini was close to death and the last thing on his mind was the cost. After spending 18 days in Saint Joseph Medical Center, a **tax-exempt** hospital in Burbank, California, Carlos and his wife knew the resulting hospital bill was going to be a large amount. They fully intended to pay their bill, but they never expected it to be $246,000.

K. B. Forbes is a community activist who has been pushing to protect uninsured patients' rights. When Ferlini asked him to look into his hospital bill, Forbes explained to him that what happened is very common. According to Forbes, hospitals charge uninsured patients four or five times more than what they would accept as payment in full from insurers. Forbes describes the hospital practice of charging the uninsured $20,000 for an appendectomy, a procedure that normally costs $5,000 for people with health insurance. Forbes investigated Ferlini's hospital bill and found that the Medical Center billed Ferlini $246,000, when slightly less than $50,000 would have been billed to Medicare/Medicaid insurance or a private health insurer for the same exact care if Ferlini had been insured. At the same time, Saint Joseph Medical Center failed to advise Ferlini of his possible eligibility for Medicaid insurance and **Worker's Compensation insurance**, which covers the health care costs of employees injured on the job.

— (*See* Law Fact at the end of this chapter for the answer).

Principles and Applications

At issue in this chapter is how tax-exempt hospitals carry out their charitable mission when attempting to allocate scarce health resources in the most effective way possible. The Affordable Care Act addressed many of the problems traditionally experienced by patients. Under the new law, tax-exempt hospitals are required to:

- Assess the need for **charitable care** in their service areas
- Establish **financial assistance policies** to assist the deserving and medically needy in covering their medical bills
- Report to the Internal Revenue Service on the fulfillment of their charitable care mission

In addition, tax-exempt hospitals are now limited in their ability to bill at the rate of full **list prices** to patients who qualify for financial assistance or to engage in **extraordinary debt collection** against such patients. In this text, charitable care is defined as the unreimbursed cost of providing medical services, as distinguished from the discounted reimbursed rates from financial assistance policies.

Historic Foundation of Tax-Exempt Hospitals

Historically, providing charitable care has been an integral part of hospitals since the Middle Ages, when the first European hospitals were actually shelters for the physically and mentally disabled and the homeless, and a place to isolate portions of the population affected by epidemics. The early hospitals, however, actually provided more in the way of comfort care than medical services. During this era, people who needed medical attention, and who could afford to pay for it, received care at their homes by visiting physicians, surgeons, and nurses. However, with progressive technical advances in 18th-century Europe, in particular the discovery of anesthesia and antiseptics, the concept of the modern-day hospital serving only medical needs began to take hold.

The hospital movement began in England with the dual purpose of caring for the sick and removing the ailing from charity rolls, thereby reducing or removing the financial burden of their care from the community. In turn, hospital patients served as clinical subjects for scientifically oriented physicians. For the same humanitarian, financial, and scientific reasons, the hospital movement spread to the American colonies (Morton & Woodbury, 1895).

The Social Compact for Hospital Care: 1751 to 1960s

The Pennsylvania Hospital in Philadelphia, the first hospital in the United States, was chartered in 1751 from private subscriptions matched by funds from the Pennsylvania legislature. Founded by Benjamin Franklin and Dr. Thomas Bond, the hospital was established to care for the sick, poor, and insane. The story of the Good Samaritan was chosen by Franklin and Bond for the official seal, and the statement of mission was "Take Care of Him and I Will Repay Thee." This ushered in a new attitude of social responsibility in U.S. health care. In fact, Pennsylvania Hospital was established a quarter of a century before the United States emerged as an independent country in 1776, before the U.S. Constitution was created and ratified, and before the federal government was established.

By the mid-19th century, large public hospitals opened in all of the major cities in the United States, along with academic research hospitals affiliated with medical schools. The first public hospitals in the United States were fully charitable and relied almost entirely on government support with no fee structures. The public hospitals provided health care to anyone who needed it and expected no payment in return. While most private hospitals were tax-exempt due to their **not-for-profit** charitable purpose, they provided only a minimum of charitable care in the form of free or discounted health care. All tax-exempt hospitals must be nonprofit, but not all nonprofits need be tax-exempt.

The Social Compact Evolves: 1969 to 2000s

After the Medicare/Medicaid insurance programs were created in 1965 and the government's **Children's Health Insurance Program** was established in 1997, centuries of legal precedent on what constituted charitable purposes for hospitals changed. The hospital industry contended there would no longer be enough demand for charitable care to satisfy the Internal Revenue Service's tax exemption standards because the government programs now reimbursed hospitals for care previously provided free of charge (Buxton, 2014). The industry maintained most Americans would be covered either by the new government insurance programs or by private health insurance and pushed for a more flexible tax exemption standard (Principe et al., 2012). This new standard was known as the **community benefits standard**.

Since then, tax-exempt hospitals have qualified for tax exemption by providing other types of benefits to the communities they serve, such as emergency care and health education as opposed to charitable care. For the first time since 1751, tax-exempt hospitals in the United States were no longer required to offer charitable care directly to the poor and financially distressed (Tahk, 2014). Prior to 1965, hospitals had to be involved in charitable care in order to be tax-exempt. After 1965, the meaning of charitable care evolved from a connotation that tax-exempt hospitals had to provide charitable care to a community benefits standard with a commitment to the federal, state, and local governments to provide a benefit to the community that outweighed the benefits the governments would receive from tax revenue (Buxton, 2014).

Private-Based, For-Profit Approach: 1997 to Present

By the 20th century, the U.S. hospital system was largely private-based with a for-profit approach to providing hospital care; few state-supported public hospitals remained. In the late 20th century, chains of hospitals arose across the United States, sponsored by not-for-profit and for-profit corporations. Until recently, generous payment rates permitted hospitals to provide significant levels of charitable care by cross-subsidizing that care from charges paid by insured patients. Today, as the generosity of insurance payments has tightened, hospitals have become increasingly focused on financial performance and survival, and charitable care was the first casualty. The current debate is whether community benefits justify the tax dollars that governments forgo in granting exemptions to hospitals, as illustrated in **TABLE 6-1**. As the demands for **medically necessary care** intensify, the tax dollars received by tax-exempt hospitals for the community's health are being scrutinized across the United States (Hackney, 2013).

Duty of Tax-Exempt Hospitals to Provide Care

Medically necessary care is undefined within the context of the current health care payment system. Does it mean everyone should be able to receive acute or emergency necessary care? If so, then what defines **acute and necessary care**? Once a consensus is reached on this definition, the next question is how can the United States develop a politically acceptable universal solution to the problem of paying hospital costs for medically necessary care for everyone?

Part of this solution is fair and mutually reasonable payments to hospitals for the costs of health care. The duty of tax-exempt hospitals to provide medically necessary care is at the center of the policy debate about how the United States might provide reasonably priced, comprehensive, and continuous health insurance to everyone. At the core of this controversy is the responsibility of tax-exempt hospitals to provide charitable care (Mayo, 2010).

Congress is investigating tax-exempt hospitals, which represent almost half of the not-for-profit sector's revenue, as part of a broader inquiry into possible abuses of tax exemptions by not-for-profit organizations (Young et al., 2013). Altogether the not-for-profit sector accounts for over $1.7 trillion in revenue in the United States (Urban Institute,

TABLE 6-1 The $51.8 Billion Tax-Exemption to Hospitals

Type of Tax Exemptions	Tax Exemptions
Government subsidies	$32.1 billion
Annual tax exemptions: federal and state corporate income taxes, state and local sales taxes, and local property taxes	$12.6 billion
Tax-deductible charitable contributions	$5.3 billion
Tax-exempt debt financing subsidy	$1.8 billion
Total tax exemptions	$51.8 billion

Note: For-profit hospitals have a cost of capital of about 12.9 cents per dollar of investment, while not-for-profit hospitals have a cost of capital of 10.8 cents per dollar of investment.

Data from: Duke Center for Health Policy and Inequalities Research. (2016). *Nonprofit tax exemption*. Durham, NC: Duke University; IRS (Internal Revenue Service). (2015). *Report to Congress on private tax-exempt, taxable, and government-owned hospitals*. Washington, DC: U.S. Department of Treasury, Internal Revenue Service; NCCS (National Center for Charitable Statistics). (2016). Guidestar: NCCS national nonprofit research database. Washington, DC: Urban Institute; Tahk, S. C. (2014). Tax-exempt hospitals and their communities. *Columbia Journal of Tax Law, 6*, 33–85.

2015). Many lawmakers are concerned about the plight of patients who are labeled as self-pay, which includes the uninsured, in the wake of recent reports that more and more people are being bankrupted by medical debts.[LN1]

The Internal Revenue Service is also checking to see if tax-exempt hospitals provide community benefits that set them apart from for-profit hospitals and justify their tax-exempt status (Buxton, 2014). In addition, some patients have sued tax-exempt hospitals, claiming the hospitals failed in their charitable mission by overcharging them for their care. Some of the lawsuits have been dismissed by federal courts, while others are pending in state courts.

Heightened Scrutiny of Charitable Care Practices

Tax-exempt hospitals have come under intense scrutiny over long-standing practices that often result in charging the highest prices to uninsured patients (Purdy & Siegel, 2012). Recently, several tax-exempt hospitals across the country have been charged with billing the uninsured significantly more than the insured for the same health care, and then using extraordinary collection practices to collect the resultant medical debt. Legal proceedings and class-action lawsuits brought against tax-exempt hospitals highlight the contradictory views underscoring concerns about the rising cost of health care (Helvin, 2013).

Some hospitals chose to enter settlement agreements rather than litigate the myriad of unresolved issues as to what constitutes affordable care. Regardless, this litigation has made hospital pricing, billing, and debt collection issues of public concern. This litigation serves as a signal to tax-exempt hospitals that they should expect closer inspection when dealing with financially distressed patients (Tahk, 2014). Many not-for-profit health care systems are under scrutiny, and some tax-exempt hospitals have already been singled out for:

- **Discriminatory pricing**
- Extraordinary debt-collection
- **Price gouging**

(Bai & Anderson, 2015; Frakt, 2011; Weissman, 2016).

Aggressive patient billing and debt collection practices by the entire hospital industry helped blur the distinction between for-profit and tax-exempt hospitals (Brown, 2015). Now the various levels of government are examining this widespread discontent as they are squeezed by revenue shortfalls and they are eyeing the revenue bases of tax-exempt hospitals and challenging their tax-exemptions (Blodgett et al., 2013).

COURT DECISION
Eligibility for Charitable Care

St. Luke's Magic Valley Regional Medical Center, Ltd. v.
Board of County Commissioners of Gooding County
[Tax-Exempt Hospital v. County Commissioners]
248 P.3d 735 (Supreme Court of Idaho 2011);
followed by *In the Matter of T.A. and T.O. v. Elmore County*
350 P.3d 1025 (Supreme Court of Idaho 2015)

Facts: St. Luke's Magic Valley Regional Medical Center provided emergency medical treatment to Mrs. Freeman with costs totaling over $19,000. Freeman did not have medical insurance or sufficient resources to cover the amount she owed. Freeman subsequently filed an application to the Gooding County Commissioners for charitable care. At the time Freeman filed the application, she was voluntarily unemployed and caring for her two young children. She admitted to being able-bodied and able to work. In the process of making its decision, the county imputed Freeman's potential income, as well as her future tax returns, by assigning her a full-time minimum wage position and averaging her two most recent tax returns. As a result, it was determined that Freeman had reasonable resources to pay the hospital for her medical treatment and thus was denied charitable care.

Issue: Should potential income and future tax returns be considered when determining whether someone qualifies for charitable care?

Holding and Decision: Potential income and past and future tax returns can be considered when determining whether patients qualify for charitable care.

Analysis: The court examined eligibility criteria for charitable care. A patient must have insufficient resources to pay for medically necessary care to be eligible for charitable care. The court decided that a patient's potential future income and future tax returns are within the meaning of available resources.

The court reviewed state charitable care laws and court decisions. Idaho state laws had two components: to provide charitable care and to allow hospitals to obtain compensation for services rendered to patients eligible for charitable care. Hospitals can receive compensation for charitable care only if a patient is determined to be **deserving and medically needy**. Rather than requiring patients to show that they are impoverished, they must only show that they are unable to pay for their medical expenses with their **available resources**. In addition to their financial status, whether the patient or patient's spouse voluntarily quit their job despite being a healthy individual may be considered. The court further interpreted available resources to mean that a patient had:

- Liquid assets that could be readily converted to cash (including cash on hand, cash in checking/savings accounts, stocks and bonds)
- Positive net value assets that were greater than their debt and liabilities (such as real estate values that exceed a home's mortgage/home equity loans)

Future Social Security income could be considered. Until this case, courts had not decided whether assets patients had not yet obtained were within the meaning of available resources. Available does not necessarily mean present ability to pay but rather the ability to pay within a reasonable time. Implicit in this reasoning are considerations of the patient's debts. The court never clarified whether past medical debts should be given more weight than other types of personal debt in determining eligibility for charitable care. It was noted that the uninsured are more likely to accrue medical debt, as they have significantly less ability to pay for necessary health care.

The court considered whether a patient's potential future income contributes to available resources. It was emphasized that everyone, to the maximum extent possible, is responsible for their own health care. The court explained that anyone who receives charitable care must reimburse the county over a reasonable period of time. In seeking charitable care, patients can be required to find employment if they are capable and able to work. The court reasoned that because a patient's ability to work can be considered, a patient's potential income could also be a resource.

Idaho state laws were designed to encourage self-reliance while showing reasonable compassion for the truly needy without impoverishing taxpayers or providing services beyond that affordable by the average taxpayer. This focus on self-reliance and preventing the dilution of government resources (or unnecessary spending of taxpayer funds from hard-working Americans on the undeserving) demonstrates the intent to require that a wide variety of resources be considered to limit who is truly eligible for charitable care. The court did not address whether employment opportunities should be considered in imputing potential income or how potential wages could be determined.

Rule of Law: The county properly imputed the patient's potential income and future income tax returns as factors in finding that the patient was not eligible for charitable care.

Reference discussing this court decision: Thayer, 2011.

As a result of the court's decision, Freeman will likely struggle close to the poverty line in attempting to pay her medical bill over five years. While the scope of this decision may change as the number of uninsured decreases under the Affordable Care Act, the holding in this case will still apply in some instances. Ultimately, this decision should prompt state legislatures to provide clear guidelines regarding eligibility for charitable care and financial assistance programs.

Evolving Health Care Delivery Systems

Propelling this conflicted situation is the changing business structure of tax-exempt hospitals. Their traditional foundation as compassionate caregivers is being transformed as they increasingly evolve into comprehensive health care delivery systems with significant revenues. The size of tax-exempt hospitals' tax exemptions is increasingly criticized, in part because their revenues have risen so sharply in recent years and because they represent such a significant portion of U.S. health care spending. When 31cents of every health care dollar are spent on hospital care (Kaiser, 2012a), tax-exempt hospitals are being scrutinized for:

- Allowing for-profit entities to derive a profit from use of their tax-exempt facilities (food services, anesthesiology practices, physician practices, and parking)
- Charging patients more than the actual cost of health care rendered in order to cover the cost of **unreimbursed care** (the shortfall of contractual payments coming from Medicaid/Medicare insurance)
- Charging uninsured patients the undiscounted cost for health care without regard to ability to pay, while discounting costs for insured patients and patients covered by Medicare/Medicaid insurance
- Failing to use their assets and revenues to provide medically necessary care, while providing luxury facilities and excessive multimillion dollar executive salaries[LN2]
- Refusing to provide emergency services or medically necessary care without regard to the ability to pay

(Ascher, 2014; Buxton, 2014).

Public Benefit Corporations

Tax-exempt hospitals are typically organized under a state's corporate laws. Although corporate laws differ from state to state, the **Model Nonprofit Corporation Act of 1987** has been adopted by most states to provide general uniformity of state laws nationally (Smith, 2016; *See* Model Nonprofit Corporation Act, § 2.02(a)(2)(i-iii)). This uniform law serves to help state autonomy while providing consistent solutions to common not-for-profit matters (Fremont-Smith & Horwitz, 2016).

Public benefit corporations are chartered by states to carry out benefits for the public; they usually receive tax-exempt status but are run almost identically to for-profit corporations. According to the Internal Revenue Code, the definition of a not-for-profit entity is any entity that serves the public interest. A not-for-profit entity is one that does not declare a profit and uses all revenue available after meeting costs to serve the public interest (as opposed to accumulating revenue surpluses or using the surpluses for other than the public interest).

Most not-for-profit entities are incorporated, which means they share many similarities with for-profit entities. Like other not-for-profit corporations, tax-exempt hospitals do not have shareholders or owners to whom any profit can be distributed. Rather, any money they earn from their operations or from financial investments must be channeled back into the organization in some way.

Not-for-profit entities have both paid and voluntary workers, but employment taxes and federal and state worker rules are no different than those applicable to for-profit entities. The perception that not-for-profit organizations are full of volunteers and low-paying jobs is a misconception. In fact, most not-for-profit health care systems maintain salaries and benefits on par with their for-profit competitors. Of the 5,600 hospitals in the United States:

- 59% are not-for-profit, tax-exempt entities
- 21% are for-profit
- 20% are run by the federal government, states, or counties

(AHA, 2016a and 2016c).

MANAGEMENT AND LAW ISSUES

2. Should non-charitable, for-profit entities (physician group practices, pharmacies, cafeterias) be able to derive profits from the use of tax-exempt hospital facilities?
3. What standards should govern the charges that tax-exempt hospitals can charge for health care?

Profitability of Tax-Exempt Hospitals

One-third of the nation's hospitals are losing money because Medicare/Medicaid insurance does not provide enough to cover the actual costs of treating hospital patients. Underpayment by Medicare/Medicaid insurance to U.S. hospitals was $51 billion in 2014. Medicare reimbursed 88 cents and Medicaid reimbursed 90 cents for every dollar hospitals spent caring for these patients (AHA, 2016b). Most of the hospitals that are under financial strain are **safety-net hospitals**, including many large, urban facilities that handle large numbers of uninsured patients. At the same time, more than half the **critical access hospitals** in rural America are vulnerable to closure, which totals nearly 700 hospitals (iVantage, 2015).[LN3]

Solvency

Three out of four tax-exempt hospitals are solvent based on financial stability, patients, and quality indicators. This compares with about 60% of for-profit hospitals. This measure of solvency does not measure how solvent they are, whether they are just barely solvent or highly profitable. Thus, while it appears tax-exempt hospitals may have higher sustainability levels than their for-profit counterparts, no true financial comparison is available.

As illustrated in **TABLE 6-2**, it may be that this apparent disparity in solvency is the result of tax exemptions enjoyed while failing to return those tax benefits to the communities they serve. Nationally, there is a surplus of over $13 billion between the tax exemptions received by hospitals and the community benefits that tax-exempt hospitals return to their communities (Duke, 2016; IRS, 2015; NCCS, 2016; *compare* the $51.8 billion in tax exemptions received in Table 6-1 to the $38.6 billion returned to their communities in Table 6-2). Tax-exempt hospitals are expected to channel the surpluses they generate back into their operations. Many tax-exempt hospitals, however, have used their growing surpluses to:

- Accumulate large cash reserves
- Build expensive new facilities
- Purchase the latest medical equipment and technologies
- Reward their executives with rich pay packages

(Buston, 2014; Tahk, 2014; Westenberger, 2015).

As a result of the way tax-exempt hospitals have used their surpluses, some health care economists argue all hospitals should pay taxes (Westenberger, 2015). They argue that tax-exempt hospitals differ little from for-profit hospitals in the provision of charitable care and, therefore, should either lose their tax-exempt status or adhere to new strict and specific requirements to provide care for the deserving and medically needy (Buxton, 2014).

Enjoying the pricing power that came from a decade of mergers, many tax-exempt hospitals saw earnings soar in recent years. The combined surpluses or profits of the 50 largest tax-exempt hospitals exceed $4 billion a year (*See* Carreyrou & Martinez, 2008; Coffman, 2014). One reason for hospitals' soaring surpluses is a gradual increase in

TABLE 6-2 Levels of Community Benefits Provided by Tax-Exempt Hospitals

Community Benefits Provided	Costs	Average Percent of Operating Expenses-Nationally
Charitable care	$12.0 billion	2.1%
Bad debt expenses	$8.7 billion	1.6%
Unreimbursed costs	$17.9 billion	3.2%
Total community benefits	$ 38.6 billion	6.9%

Note: There is no uniform definition of the terms used to determine community benefits reported to the Internal Revenue Service.

Data from: Duke Center for Health Policy and Inequalities Research. (2016). *Nonprofit tax exemption*. Durham, NC: Duke University; IRS (Internal Revenue Service). (2015). *Report to Congress on private tax-exempt, taxable, and government-owned hospitals*. Washington, DC: U.S. Department of Treasury, Internal Revenue Service; NCCS (National Center for Charitable Statistics). (2016). Guidestar: NCCS national nonprofit research database. Washington, DC: Urban Institute; Tahk, S. C. (2014). Tax-exempt hospitals and their communities. *Columbia Journal of Tax Law, 6*, 33-85.

Medicare payments after federal budget cutbacks during the 1990s. By merging and gaining scale, many tax-exempt hospitals also gained leverage in price negotiations with health insurers. No fewer than 25 tax-exempt hospitals or hospital systems now have surpluses of more than $250 million a year (AHA, 2016a). Much of the hospital industry's earnings growth comes from strategies it pursued to increase revenues. Among them:

- Demanding upfront payments from patients
- Focusing on expensive procedures
- Hiking list prices for procedures and services to several times their actual cost
- Issuing tax-exempt bonds, investing the proceeds in higher-yielding securities, and then keeping the untaxed investment gains
- Securitizing and then selling patients' debts to aggressive third party debt collectors

(Buxton, 2014; Corbett, 2015; Patton, 2014).

Lack of Affordable Health Care

Despite the multibillion-dollar surpluses enjoyed by the hospital industry, the number and proportion of Americans reporting no health care or a delay in obtaining needed health care has increased sharply in recent years. For instance:

- 1 in 9 privately insured adults has a deductible of $3,000 or more; up from 1% a decade earlier
- 31 million working adults have such high out-of-pocket costs or deductibles relative to their incomes that they are considered **underinsured**
- 6 in 10 families cut corners to avoid health care costs
- 80% of the people with poor health and complex needs delay or skip care due to cost

(Collins et al., 2015; Kaiser, 2012a and 2012b).

While access to affordable care has deteriorated for both the insured and uninsured, the insured are experiencing a larger relative increase in access problems compared with the uninsured who lacked much access to begin with (Collins et al., 2015). As illustrated in **FIGURE 6-1**, health insurance no longer guarantees people will be able to access health care.

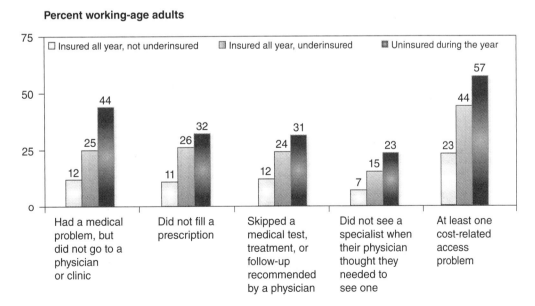

FIGURE 6-1 Health Insurance Is No Guarantee of Access to Health Care

In addition, unmet medical needs increased for low-income children, reversing earlier trends and widening the access gap as compared to higher income children (Hamm, 2015). People reporting access problems increasingly cited:

- Cost as an obstacle to needed health care with rising deductibles and co-payments
- Health system barriers, such as health insurance restrictions and limitations, and the demands for upfront payments before medical services are rendered
- Rising rates of health insurance premiums, leaving little to cover the access fees required to obtain preventive, routine care

(Hamm, 2015; *See* Sanford, 2013).

Uninsured and Underinsured Hospital Patients

With the number of uninsured Americans at 32 million, the safety net tax-exempt hospitals provide is stretched to the breaking point (Kaiser, 2015a and 2015b). The cost of caring for this population by major teaching hospitals is over $6.0 billion a year (Kirch, 2012; *See* Corlette et al., 2016). Health insurance is the most important determinant of access to health care (Collins et al., 2015). People without adequate health care coverage risk financial disaster if they find themselves in need of expensive health care.

Complete lack of health insurance is only one part of the problem today, as even the insured have serious gaps in health care coverage. A growing number of insured Americans also find themselves on shaky financial ground (Vagelos, 2014). Insurance coverage is the ticket into the health care system, but for too many Americans, that ticket does not buy financial security or genuinely affordable access to care. People who have health insurance, but have health care coverage that does not adequately protect them from high health care costs, are generally considered underinsured if they have:

- Deductibles equal to or greater than 5% of their total household income
- Out-of-pocket medical, prescription, dental, and vision costs that amount to 10% or more of their total household income
- Out-of-pocket medical, prescription, dental, and vision costs that amount to 5% or more and their total household income falls below the **federal poverty level** of $11,900 (plus $4,200 for each additional family member)

(Collins et al., 2015; *See* HHS, 2016 and Schoen et al., 2005).

As illustrated in **FIGURE 6-2**, a significant number of Americans face lingering financial problems because of their hospital bills. Almost one-quarter of working-age adults face potential financial exposure from unaffordable care. Much of this growth in the underinsured comes from the middle class. While low-income people remain

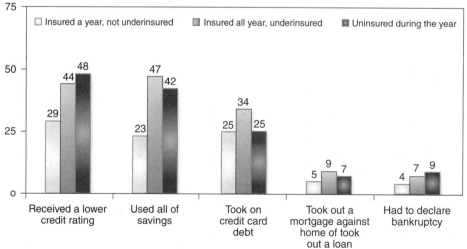

Percent working-age adults with hospital bill problems or accrued hospital debt

Note: Working-age adults who had difficulty paying their hospital bills, were contacted by a collection agency for unpaid hospital bills, had to change their way of life in order to pay hospital bills, or has an outstanding hospital debt.

Commonwealth Fund, 2014.

FIGURE 6-2 Working-Age Americans with Lingering Financial Problems Because of Their Hospital Bills

vulnerable, middle-income families are being hit the hardest. Although adults below the poverty level are at the highest risk of being uninsured or underinsured, insurance erosion has spread up the ladder well into the middle-class range. For those with annual incomes of $40,000 to $59,000, the underinsured percentage rate has reached double digits (*See generally* Commonwealth Fund, 2014).

Uninsured Hospital Patients

People who spend any time without health insurance:

- Are significantly less likely to have a regular family physician
- Are less likely to report that they always or often receive the health care they need when they need it
- Report significantly higher rates of cost-related access problems

(Collins et al., 2015; Garfield & Young, 2015; Long et al., 2015).

The uninsured represent about 18% of the **working age population**, which is a percentage that is steadily decreasing since the Affordable Care Act mandated that everyone purchase health insurance (CBO, 2016). Since implementation of the Affordable Care Act, the number of uninsured has decreased by about 3.5 million (Collins et al., 2015).

The Challenge of Employer-Provided Insurance

Most American families still obtain their health insurance through their employers, but that is not a guaranteed benefit for approximately 150 million employees and their dependents (Collins et al., 2015). In fact, 8 in 10 of the uninsured come from working families (DeNavas-Walt & Proctor, 2015). The working poor compose more than one-third of the uninsured; without employer-sponsored insurance, they cannot afford to pay the premiums themselves.

As the cost of health insurance continues to increase, fewer employers, particularly small firms, are able to provide affordable health insurance to their employees (Collins et al., 2015). In fact, employer-sponsored insurance has decreased to 46% of the population (CBO, 2015). Medicaid insurance has filled some of the gap, but half of the states refuse to expand Medicaid insurance under the Affordable Care Act, leaving many working-age Americans behind (Long et al., 2015).[LN4]

Underinsured Hospital Patients

As illustrated in **TABLE 6-3**, more than 31 million working-age adults are underinsured, up 60% from the 16 million who had inadequate coverage in 2003 (Collins et al., 2015). The rate of underinsurance nearly tripled among middle-income

TABLE 6-3 Underinsurance Rates Doubled in Past Decade

	2003	2005	2010	2012	2014
Out-of-pocket medical, prescription, dental, and vision costs 10% or more of total household income*	14 million	14 million	25 million	23 million	24 million
Deductibles equal to or greater than 5 % of total household income	4 million	4 million	8 million	11 million	14 million
Net increase in millions underinsured because of high deductible	2 million	2 million	5 million	6 million	7 million
Underinsured	16 million	16 million	29 million	30 million	31 million

Note: Out-of-pocket medical, prescription, dental, and vision costs amounts to 5 percent or more and their total household income falls below the federal poverty level of $11,900 (plus $42,00 for each additional family member).

Modified from: Commonwealth Fund, The. (2014). *Biennial health insurance survey.* New York, NY: Commonwealth Fund. Data from: Collins, S. R., et al. (2015). *The problem of underinsurance and how rising deductibles will make it worse: Findings from the Commonwealth Fund Biennial Health Insurance Survey.* New York, NY: Commonwealth Fund.HHS (U.S. Department of Health and Human Services). (2016). *Poverty guidelines: U.S. federal poverty guidelines used to determine financial eligibility for certain federal programs.* Washington, DC: HHS.

families, or those with at least $40,000 in family income. The upward trend in the underinsured rate reflects how much rising health care costs have outpaced wage increases (*See generally* Commonwealth Fund, 2014).

In this instance, the premiums for family coverage jumped 78% in the past decade, wages rose 19%, and general inflation went up 17% (NCSL, 2015). Today, the average annual cost of health insurance for family coverage ($16,800) exceeds the equivalent of a minimum-wage worker's annual wages, at $15,000 (Census Bureau, 2014). Given this state of affairs, even with tax subsidies from the Affordable Care Act, it is understandable why people have little left to cover the access fees required to obtain preventive, routine health care (Collins et al., 2015).

Federal, State, and Local Governments at Odds

While the argument over hospital tax exemption is ongoing at the federal level, the real battle is waged at the state and local levels (Dirlam, 2015). While tax-exempt status is defined by the federal government, tax-exempt hospitals are also exempt from paying state and local taxes. State and local exemptions predate federal exemptions, originating when public hospitals functioned exclusively for financially distressed members of the community. Tax-exempt hospitals relieved state and local governments from operating public hospitals and the burden of caring for those unable to afford health care, which offset the loss in state and local taxes.

Over time, tax-exempt hospitals evolved into huge businesses (Sage, 2016). The tax-exempt hospital changed its image dramatically after a while. In the end, hospitals are no longer looked at as benevolent caregivers that serve their community's best interests. Consequently, state and local governments have a vested interest when it comes to determining tax exemption status for these huge businesses; public officials are actively joining the debate as to what constitutes charitable care (Purdy & Siegel, 2012). In fact, the theories concerning charitable care are sharpened by states and localities and are used to attack or support the federal tax-exempt status of hospitals.

It is clear that the federal approach to this debate differs from state and local approaches because of two opposing viewpoints. While the federal government has a strong incentive to support tax exemption to foster competition between for-profit and not-for-profit entities, states and localities have noted the surpluses these tax-exempt hospitals accumulate and question whether community benefits from these hospitals really outweigh the benefit governments would receive from not only federal income tax revenues, but also state income and property tax revenues and tax-exempt bond financing. Yet, acknowledgement must be made of the fact that the most important benefit tax-exempt hospitals provide to governments is absorbing the unreimbursed costs from Medicare/Medicaid insurance (Tahk, 2014).

Federal Lawsuits

At the same time Congress is questioning the debt collection policies of tax-exempt hospitals, a coordinated effort is under way to file federal lawsuits against the hospital industry (Brown, 2014). Several national law firms with years of experience in mass malpractice litigation are participating in this litigation; several successfully led aggressive, coordinated actions against the tobacco industry in the 1990s (Moskowitz, 2005; *See* Scott, 2014).

For more than a decade, lawsuits alleging the hospital industry has charged the uninsured fees well in excess of those charged to the insured have been initiated in federal courts. However, the consensus from the courts is that these cases do not present viable claims. This consensus is consistent with the U.S. Supreme Court decision, *Eastern Kentucky Welfare Rights Organization v. Simon*, 426 U.S. 26 (U.S. Supreme Court 1976), finding that uninsured patients had no standing to challenge Internal Revenue Service revenue rulings granting tax-exempt status to hospitals.

COURT DECISION
Hospital Charges for the Uninsured

DiCarlo v. St. Mary Hospital
[Uninsured Patient v. Tax-Exempt Hospital]
530 F.3d 255 (U.S. Court of Appeals for the 3rd Circuit 2008);
followed by *Limberg v. Sanford Medical Center Fargo*
2016 N.D. LEXIS 123 (Supreme Court of North Dakota 2016)

Facts: DiCarlo brought a class action lawsuit against an acute care medical/surgical hospital and its nonprofit Catholic health care system operating the hospital, alleging breach of contract, breach of the duty of good faith and fair dealing, unjust enrichment, breach of **fiduciary duty**, and fraud. The hospital accepted discounted payments from various payers, including Medicare/Medicaid insurance, and health insurance plans that negotiated discounts with the hospital. The hospital also provided free or means-tested discounted care to patients eligible for charitable care.

DiCarlo was admitted to the hospital after experiencing an increased heart rate. At the time he was admitted, DiCarlo was uninsured and did not qualify for Medicare/Medicaid insurance or charitable care. Upon his arrival at the hospital, DiCarlo consented to whatever medical treatment was deemed necessary and guaranteed payment of all charges for services rendered. Following his medical treatment, the hospital charged DiCarlo $3,483 excluding separately billed physician fees.

Issue: Is discriminatory pricing that charges the uninsured more than the insured for medical services lawful?

Holding and Decision: Yes. Tax-exempt hospitals may establish discriminatory pricing for their medical services.

Analysis: While the severe economic hardship faced by the uninsured was acknowledged, the courts refused to determine what fair and reasonable hospital costs should be or to decide what should constitute medically necessary care. These issues were seen by the courts as matters for the legislative branch, not the judiciary.

The courts refused to examine the issue. Nor would the courts examine the underlying issues of this case as to whether uninsured patients have the freedom to contract for emergency care, or whether it is fundamentally fair to charge the uninsured greater amounts than those paid by the insured or patients eligible for charitable care.

First, DiCarlo contended he only agreed to pay a reasonable price, which he defined as the Medicare/Medicaid insurance and charitable care rates, not the undiscounted rates charged the uninsured. This breach of contract claim goes directly to the heart of the federal class-action lawsuits: the charges to uninsured hospital patients for medical services. All the same, the court dismissed this breach of contract claim, finding the claim did not reflect how hospital charges are actually set.

Hospitals have a uniform set of charges, known as the **chargemaster**, which applies to all patients. Discounted charges and computations apply in different situations. For instance: differing discounts are negotiated with private insurers, another discount is accepted if patients are covered by Medicare/Medicaid insurance with legislatively imposed discounts, still other means-tested discounts are given to patients eligible for charitable care, while **uncompensated care** is available to deserving patients that demonstrate financial need but are ineligible for any other financial assistance.

Second, the court dismissed the breach of the **duty of good faith and fair dealing** claim built on the breach of contract claim. DiCarlo might have been entitled to relief under the covenant of good faith and fair dealing if his reasonable expectations of what he was obligated to pay were destroyed after he signed the consent form guaranteeing payment for medical services rendered, and if the hospital acted with ill motives and without any legitimate purpose. In signing the consent form, however, DiCarlo promised to pay in full the definite price terms set by the hospital; his obligations were clear.

Third, in order to state a claim for unjust enrichment, the hospital must have received and retained a benefit from DiCarlo that would be unjust. However, DiCarlo did not give anything at all to the hospital. Therefore, the court dismissed this claim against the hospital.

Fourth, the court refused to expand the fiduciary duty of hospitals to their billing practices. Analogizing the practice to the debtor-creditor relationship, the breach of fiduciary duty claim was dismissed.

Finally, in dismissing the fraud claim, the court found the hospital's pricing and billing practices were not covered by state fraud laws. Hospital debt collectors are usually not covered by state consumer fraud laws, so long as they are operating in their professional capacities.

Rule of Law: Tax-exempt hospitals are not required to provide free or reduced rates for medical services to uninsured patients; moreover, it is not unreasonable to charge uninsured patients higher rates merely because various insurers have negotiated to pay lower rates.

Reference citing this decision: Hafemeister & Porter, 2013; Hall, 2015.

How duty of good faith and fair dealing applies, and appropriate remedies for breach of this duty are determined, varies based on the circumstances. Health law issues such as the definition of standards of fair dealing in the hospital industry and the justified expectations of patients are being challenged by Congress and the Internal Revenue Service, who have imposed additional requirements on tax-exempt hospitals under the Affordable Care Act (Thai, 2011; Weisblatt, 2014). Many ongoing litigations center on medically necessary care and are postured against health care systems, of which tax-exempt hospitals are only one part (Crossley, 2012). The American Hospital Association and other individual decision makers (including officers, directors, and attorneys) are often listed as co-conspirators in the lawsuits for having drafted guidelines and provided advice that advanced discriminatory billing practices against the uninsured and underinsured. The complaints:

- Ask courts to impose **constructive trusts** on the hospitals' assets
- Request **injunctions** prohibiting the hospitals from:
  - Billing the uninsured the full, undiscounted cost of health care without using a **sliding scale payment scheme**
  - Charging the uninsured more than the insured for the same medical services
  - Collecting unreasonable fees from patients
  - Prohibiting the use of extraordinary debt collection by third party collection agencies that have acquired **securitized medical debt**
- Seek monetary damages

(Hall, 2015; Weisblatt, 2014).

The current lawsuits are likely part of the larger national debate on what charitable care means and whether hospitals are deserving of their exemption status.

State Lawsuits

In addition to the federal litigation, new pleadings are being filed in state courts (Harrison et al., 2015; Melone & Nation, 2014). These complaints allege that tax-exempt hospitals are overcharging their uninsured patients. Specifically, the uninsured are charged more for the same medical services than the insured. While the exact rate of discount that the insured receive is unknown, many experts estimate that the typical range of discounts nationally is between 45% and 50% (*Infra, Provena Covenant Medical Center v. Department of Revenue,* 925 N.E.2d 1131 (Supreme Court of Illinois 2010)). One nationwide study suggests that the uninsured pay 2.5 times the amount health insurance providers pay for the same medical treatments (Melone & Nation, 2014). The lawsuits also allege that tax-exempt hospitals are overly aggressive and abusive in their debt collection efforts, and that these unrelenting procedures together are followed more for private interests than for financial survival (Berg, 2010).

Heightened Scrutiny of Charitable Care and Community Benefits Standards

There is heightened questioning on how much community benefits tax-exempt hospitals should provide to the communities they serve (Groebe, 2015). There is also debate on what **means-based discounts** tax-exempt hospitals should charge.

Charitable Care Standard

The traditional **charitable care standard** of tax exemption considered the conventional role of public hospitals as health care facilities catering to the financially distressed (Schirra, 2011). The standard required tax-exempt hospitals to be

MANAGEMENT AND LAW ISSUES

4. Should disparate pricing for health care be permissible?

organized as not-for-profit entities whose main purpose was providing health care to the sick. Any surpluses over revenue incurred must never be used to benefit any private shareholder or individual. Under this standard, tax-exempt hospitals must provide health care to anyone, despite their ability to pay. The standard did not deny tax-exempt hospitals the right to charge patients who had the ability to pay; rather, it provided an ethical obligation to provide affordable care to persons unable to pay. In addition, hospitals could charge patients means-based discounts and thereby render charitable care.

This standard came under attack for several reasons, mostly because it was ambiguous. The charitable care standard assumed hospitals could attain tax exemption even if their primary function was providing health care to patients able to pay, as long as they provided free or discounted rates to those with no ability to pay (Tyrrell, 2010). In addition, the standard lacked clarity; it allowed hospitals to enjoy tax-exempt status based on behavior that might not satisfy the requirement that they be operated exclusively for exemption purposes (such as lessening the burdens of government). Also, with the arrival of Medicare/Medicaid insurance, less uncompensated care was required. Ultimately, the Internal Revenue Service found it necessary to modify the ruling.

Community Benefits Standard

In return for not paying taxes, tax-exempt hospitals are expected to provide community benefits, a loosely defined federal requirement whose most important component is charitable care. However, many tax-exempt hospitals incorporate other costs in their community benefits accounting to the Internal Revenue Service, including unpaid patient bills. Often, such hospitals also include the difference between the list prices of health care they provide and what they are paid by Medicare/Medicaid (Lenihan & Hermer, 2014). Excluding those other costs, many tax-exempt hospitals spend less on charitable care than they receive in tax breaks (CBO, 2015).

In 1969, the Internal Revenue Service established the community benefits standard. In determining whether a not-for-profit hospital qualifies for tax exemption, the Internal Revenue Service applies the standards specified under the community benefits standard. The underlying principle of the standards is that federal tax exemption is granted to tax-exempt hospitals that improve the overall health standard for the community, thus providing a benefit to the community. A key component is that the hospitals serve a public instead of a private interest. A tax-exempt hospital can demonstrate adherence to this standard by:

- Establishing a governing board composed of individuals representing the community
- Having an open admissions policy for patients who can pay by personal means or by health insurance
- Maintaining an open medical staff policy whereby any qualified physician can have admitting privileges
- Operating an emergency room that is available to anyone needing health care regardless of ability to pay

(Tahk, 2014).

Although several revisions have been made to the community benefits standard, the Internal Revenue Service never provided a detailed description of what the specific community benefits must be. Therefore, variations to the requirement proliferate as not-for-profit health care systems individually interpret what community benefits means. For instance, the Catholic Health Association, which is comprised of over 1,200 Catholic hospitals, includes five activities when computing community benefits:

- Charges related to community development activities
- Development costs
- Education costs
- Research expenditures
- Unpaid patient bills

(Patton, 2014).

Many want to know how these activities directly benefit the community. Other tax-exempt hospitals have included the salaries of their employees as community benefits, further obscuring the issue of affordable care. At the same time, others maintain the impact of job production is a benefit that should be seen as promoting the community's well-being. New Internal Revenue Service standards require tax-exempt hospitals to explicitly state the specifics of their community benefits contributions. However, the new standards still do not require the tax-exempt hospitals to provide any minimum amount of charitable care.

Not-For-Profit Hospitals Look Similar to For-Profit Hospitals

Not-for-profit hospitals in the health care industry are significant, revenue-seeking enterprises that compete vigorously, and for the most part, successfully, against their for-profit rivals (Klebes, 2015). Often, for-profit hospitals are accused of charging higher prices to patients; however, research shows that the only distinction between tax-exempt and for-profit hospitals in terms of affordable care is market share. The higher the market share, the higher the prices to patients. While for-profit hospital pricing more strongly correlates with market concentration than not-for-profit hospital pricing, price increases for both as the hospitals' market share increases (Rice, 2010; *See* Tyrrell, 2010).

Many contend that the federal government is too far removed from the community to determine whether tax-exempt hospitals are really providing adequate benefits to outweigh the tax revenue benefits the governments give up. Since the federal government bears a large portion of the government subsidies to hospital care, it has a fiscal motive in wanting tax-exempt hospitals to operate at the same efficiency and performance levels as for-profit hospitals. Therefore, the federal government is not stepping in to disrupt the current state of affairs. Moreover, not-for-profit hospitals distinguish themselves from for-profit hospitals by providing traditionally unprofitable but necessary medical services, for instance, burn, neonatal, obstetric, and trauma care (Klebes, 2015; Westenberger, 2015).

States and localities see things differently. They see the public hospital of the past being driven by advances in medicine, technology, and an abundance of money from insurance programs into efficient business enterprises that mimic for-profit hospitals. While tax-exempt hospitals continue to take advantage of their tax-exempt status, states and localities argue they no longer provide meaningful charitable care. They argue such hospitals rarely care for the financially distressed as they used to and, in some cases, deny charitable care altogether (Fleischer, 2015). For instance, the tax-exempt University of Pittsburgh Medical Center and Johns Hopkins Hospital each dedicate only about 2% of their revenues to providing charitable care (Westenberger, 2015).

Discriminatory Pricing

The current hospital pricing system is based on a chargemaster, a list price for every infinitesimal procedure possibly delivered, along with a list price for every conceivable supply item that might be used in the process of the medical treatment. In theory, this list price is updated annually by each hospital based on actual costs; in actuality, the payment rates for Medicare/Medicaid insurance drive the list price. Chargemaster list prices can vary enormously across hospitals, depending on government payment methods, reportedly by a factor of up to 17 even within a single community (Piper, 2016).

While some may debate the prices hospitals charge for individual medical treatments and medical supplies, this is really an unsuitable way to describe how hospital prices are determined because it is based on an incomplete picture of the pricing system. Hospital pricing can be divided into two prices. First, there is the list price, similar to the salary advertised for jobs; it serves only as a beginning point for salary negotiations, for those who have the education and experience to negotiate. From these list prices, private insurers, the government, and other groups negotiate discounts with hospitals to arrive at so-called **actual prices**. Although list prices vary widely, the actual prices paid are relatively static (Frakt, 2011).

Given the list prices in the chargemaster, four general systems are used to actually pay hospitals:

- Commercial health insurers: discounted prices or per diems negotiated separately with each of the insurers from which a hospital accepts payment
- Medicaid/Children's Health Insurance Program: prices set by state governments based on per diem diagnosis-related groups
- Medicare: prices set by the federal government on a diagnosis-related group basis with outlier payments based on charges calculated with charge-to-cost ratios
- Self-paying and uninsured patients: full charges or means-tested discounts

(Moncrieff, 2012; Purdy & Siegel, 2012).

Price discrimination, the practice of charging different prices to different patients for identical medical services even when the actual costs are identical, is standard (Lenihan & Hermer, 2014). Hospital pricing becomes even more complex when it is noted that half of the revenue of most tax-exempt hospitals comes from Medicare/

Medicaid insurance at levels that do not cover the actual costs incurred. Given this pricing complexity, along with the additional out-of-pocket losses for unreimbursed care and **bad debts** (defined as accounts written off as unpaid even though patients have the ability to pay), the rationale of hospitals behind seeking to maximize payments from the remaining segments of their private markets suddenly becomes much more understandable, if not logical (Nussbaum, 2012).

Hospitals' Definition of Charitable Care

The way hospitals define charitable care and the implications of how unreimbursed care is released through bad debt write-offs is under examination. Tax-exempt hospitals have a certain degree of discretion regarding how they classify charitable care. In basic terms, six activities are classified together because of their common revenue character. All six definitions of charitable care can change just by changing how that care is defined.

Most tax-exempt hospitals offer uncompensated care to those demonstrating income up to 200% of the federal poverty level ($23,800; plus $8,400 for each additional family member) (HHS, 2016; *See* New Jersey Charitable Care Program, N.J.A.C. § 10.52-11.8). This represents about 65% of the uninsured (Kaiser, 2015a). While this estimate represents over one-third of the U.S. population (and almost half the population in Arizona, Mississippi, and Nevada) (Census Bureau, 2014), uncompensated care is only provided to patients not eligible for Medicaid insurance or other financial assistance programs.

Bad Debt as a Contribution to Charitable Care

Given the complexity of the health care payment system, controversy ensues when tax-exempt hospitals write off bad debt and classify that write off as a charitable care contribution to the community. In many instances, what is reported as bad debt may be merely a book loss (for accounting purposes) as opposed to an actual cash loss. This complexity appears as a theme in many of the lawsuits on affordable care, particularly the intersection of charitable care, uncompensated care, and bad debt, and how hospitals report these relative costs for the purpose of payment (Groebe, 2015).

FEATURE BOX 6-1

Categories of Charitable Care

- *Bad debt*: charges that cannot be collected from patients who are able to pay
- *Medicare/Medicaid insurance*: or other financial assistance policies
- *Pure charitable care*: hospitals can write off all or part of the list costs of medical services determined prior to providing the services, and then write off the remaining actual costs (if any) after providing the care
- *Total charitable care*: pure charitable care combined with bad debt write-offs and unreimbursed care
- *Uncompensated care (free care)*: bad debt combined with pure charitable care
- *Unreimbursed care*: pure charitable care combined with the shortfall of contractual payments coming from Medicaid/Medicare insurance

Nearly all hospitals that are billing patients and collecting after health care is delivered will incur a certain amount of bad debt. Hospitals make allowances for bad debts and consider the financial implications in their fiscal budgets and forecasts. On average, tax-exempt hospitals charge patients 20% extra in order to make up for bad debt (*See* Gold, 2012; NPR, 2012).

Monitoring Responsibilities of State Governments

State governments monitor not-for-profit health care systems to ensure their tax-exempt hospitals meet prescribed standards required to retain their tax exemption. States ensure charitable care remains a determining factor in allowing tax exemptions. By taking a proactive role, states increase the amount of charitable care tax-exempt hospitals must provide. Most state laws are broad and flexible but still require a minimum level of charitable care. States and localities are generally in the best position to understand what their various communities require. They can also determine whether a tax-exempt hospital in a given community provides adequate charitable benefits to offset the tax revenue the government could otherwise obtain from taxes (Tahk, 2014).

Stricter State Requirements

Many states are debating whether to impose stricter requirements on tax-exempt hospitals (Klebes, 2015). While it is too early to characterize this as a trend (and so far, state legislative efforts to enact new charitable care standards have not generally succeeded), what is clear is that a growing number of states are aggressively using tax exemptions as a means of extracting affordable care (Sage, 2016). Hospitals in Texas are now required to set aside 4% of their **net patient revenues** (patient revenue less total operating costs for patient care) to provide charitable care to retain their tax exemptions (Corbett, 2015; Sage, 2016). Illinois requires tax-exempt hospitals to spend at least 8% of their total operating costs on charitable care each year to retain their state tax exemptions (Patton, 2013; Sage, 2016). A state debt collection law also requires Illinois hospitals to:

- Adhere to serious procedural checks on when hospitals can go forward with debt collection proceedings
- Offer a reasonable payment plan to the deserving and medically needy who cannot pay their medical bills
- Publicize their free care and financial aid programs

(Corbett, 2015; Westenberger, 2015).

Officials in Minnesota and Kansas have also expressed concern about the level of charitable care provided by tax-exempt hospitals and about their billing and debt collection practices (Patton, 2014; Sage, 2016). Utah and Pennsylvania have used the federal government's community benefit standard to place further requirements on their tax-exempt hospitals (Corbett, 2015; Dirlam, 2015).

Charitable Care Accountability

States are beginning to require greater accountability from tax-exempt hospitals than is required by the federal government. Yet, there is no evidence that hospitals cut off the uninsured once they meet the minimum charitable care requirements set by the states. To retain their tax-exemptions, hospitals must provide charitable care at an acceptable level as defined by three federal criteria. These criteria include:

- Benefits the hospitals receive from their exemptions
- Community needs assessments
- Resources at the hospitals' disposal

(Tahk, 2014).

In addition, the Affordable Care Act mandates that charitable care must:

- Be provided in an amount equal to or greater than the hospital's monetary benefit from not having to pay state and local taxes
- Meet at least 4% of total patient revenue (as compared to the government mandates based on total **net patient revenue**).

COURT DECISION
Charitable Obligations of Tax-Exempt Hospitals

Provena Covenant Medical Center v. Department of Revenue
[Tax-Exempt Hospital v. State]
925 N.E.2d 1131 (Supreme Court of Illinois 2010)

Facts: Provena Covenant Medical Center, one of two regional full-service not-for-profit hospitals serving the Midwest college towns of Champaign and Urbana, Illinois, is part of a Catholic health care system with six hospitals and a host of for-profit subsidiaries that are managed and owned by the tax-exempt hospitals to fulfill key hospital functions, including emergency physicians, pharmacies, and hospital cafeterias. While Provena's charitable care program for free or discounted services was typical of many tax-exempt hospitals, charitable care was limited to patients at or below the federal poverty level with discounts for care based on income. Few hospital debtors knew of Provena's charitable care program. If patients failed to respond quickly to their hospital bills, their cases were referred to aggressive debt collection agencies; at that point it was too late to apply for charitable care or discounts.

If a patient did hear about Provena's charitable care program, the application was confusing, the deadline was short, and the processing time was long. Every application had to be approved by a committee in the corporate office, and, even for seniors on fixed incomes, approval only lasted six months. Often patients did not know they owed Provena money until a debt collection agency contacted them or they were sued. Debt collection agencies harassed patients with phone calls and letters, sued financially distressed patients, garnished wages and bank accounts, obtained liens on homes, and asked for arrest warrants when patients failed to keep up with any follow-up enforcement proceedings.

For the tax year in question, Provena had patient revenues of $714 million; of approximately 110,000 admissions, 302 patients received free or discounted care, at a cost to the hospital of $2.5 million, which was $1.3 million less than Provena's local property tax exemption. In other words, the hospital's $2.5 million charitable care program was $1.3 million less than the $3.8 million Provena would have had to pay in local property taxes but for its exemption from taxes other comparable entities paid. Tax-exempt status exempts hospital systems like Provena from payment of federal, state, and local taxes, while enabling them to solicit charitable donations.

Nearly 25,000 people in the surrounding county had incomes below the federal poverty level and an estimated 20,000 were uninsured. Provena claimed $7.1 million of bad debt. Provena always maintained its operations were like every other tax-exempt hospital. Following initial denial of its property exemption by the local county board of review, Provena hung posters in its public restrooms advising of its charitable care program.

Issue: Was Provena entitled to the tax exemptions its hospitals historically received as tax-exempt institutions?

Holding and Decision: No, Provena did not show that its hospitals were charitable institutions. Its hospital revenue was derived mainly from providing medical services for a fee. It did not dispense charitable care to all who asked for it; rather it placed obstacles in the way of hospital patients seeking charitable care.

Analysis: The court adopted five criteria as characteristics of tax-exempt organizations and then ruled that Provena was not entitled to tax exemption because it satisfied only two of the five criteria:

- Dispenses charitable care to all who need it and apply for it
- Does not place any obstacles in the way of those who need and would avail themselves of the charitable benefits it dispenses
- Earns no profits or dividends but rather derives its funds from charitable contributions
- Has no capital, capital stock, or shareholders
- Provides no gain or profit to anyone connected with it

While finding that each of the five conditions must be determined on a case-by-case basis, whether all five factors were required for tax exemption was not addressed. The court simply found that Provena did not have shareholders and was not operated to benefit any private shareholder or individual. Since Provena derived over 95% of its revenues from providing medical services for a fee, the court reasoned that it did not derive its funds mainly from charitable contributions. Additionally, Provena failed to dispense charitable care to all who needed and applied for it. Finally, Provena was not deemed to be tax-exempt by its charitable expenditures.

The court then analyzed each of Provena's six arguments as justification to retain its tax exemption status. First, the court described how Provena may have reduced the burdens faced by the federal and state government in providing health care, but found that Provena failed to lessen the local government's tax burdens. The court stated that Provena was required to demonstrate that it helped alleviate the financial burdens faced by local taxpayers. The court further noted that, even if Provena provided medical services that lessened the local government's burdens, Provena must also prove that its services relieved the burdens of local taxpayers. The court ruled that **fee-for-service arrangements** extended for value do not relieve local taxpayers of their tax burdens.

The court then found that Provena was primarily devoted to the care and treatment of hospital patients in exchange for compensation through private insurance, Medicare/Medicaid insurance, or self-pays. The number of uninsured patients receiving free or discounted care and the dollar value of their care was minimal. The court ruled that hospitals that do not provide a certain level of free or discounted care are not eligible for tax exemptions.

Provena next contended that the bad debts that it incurred should be considered in measuring the value of its charitable care. The court acknowledged that Provena treated all patients requesting services without regard to the person's ability to pay for their care. However, because Provena subsequently sought payment for these services, the court reasoned that as a practical matter, there was little to distinguish the way in which Provena dispensed its charitable care from the way in which for-profit institutions wrote off bad debt. The court ruled that it would not consider bad debts as a form of charitable care.

The court also rejected the argument that discounted care should be viewed as charitable care on the grounds that since the undiscounted rates included a gross profit margin, discounts up to 50% still allowed Provena to cover the costs of its care. Further, the court observed that Provena recouped these discounts through cross-subsidies from the higher fees paid by insured patients. The court held gifts should be without consideration. When hospital patients are treated for a fee, consideration is passed; their care therefore does not qualify as a gift. If it were not a gift, it could not be charitable care. The court viewed any consideration received as full consideration and, therefore, there was no element of a gift and no charitable care.

The court also rejected the argument that the shortfall from Medicare/Medicaid insurance should be characterized as charitable care. The court found that acceptance of Medicare/Medicaid insurance was optional and that these insurance programs:

- Allowed Provena to generate income from potentially **underutilized hospital resources**
- Generated a reliable stream of revenue
- Produced favorable tax treatment under federal law

Similar to discounted care, the court observed that gifts are gratuitous and that Provena did not serve the Medicare/Medicare insured gratuitously.

Lastly, the court rejected the argument that charitable use should include the broader federal concept of community benefits (ambulance service, graduate medical education, behavioral health services, emergency care, and a crisis nursery). The court ruled that community benefits are not the test for tax exemption. The court reasoned that private for-profit hospitals frequently offer comparable services as a community benefit and as a means for generating publicity and goodwill.

Rule of Law: Taxation is the rule and tax exemption the exception; hospitals that do not provide a certain level of charitable care are not eligible for tax exemptions.

References discussing this court decision: Basanta et al., 2010; Brody, 2010; Colinvaux, 2011; Fleischer, 2015; Groebe, 2015; Hazen & Hazen, 2012; Mintz, 2013; Morrell & Krouse, 2014; Sataline, 2010.

Texas requires tax-exempt hospitals to develop community benefit plans by including specific language in their corporate mission statements that clearly shows a commitment to serving the health needs of the community. The statements must identify specific goals and objectives and provide a way to measure the effectiveness of the plans. The benefit plans are to be constructed after consulting and planning with local health departments, private businesses, consumers, and insurance firms. Finally, the plans must provide a time frame and specify budgets for carrying out the plans.

In addition, Texas provides a means to enforce the community benefit rules. Tax-exempt hospitals are audited every year and financial details are provided to the state attorney general and to the state comptroller who look for violations of the community benefit plans. Before strict charitable care requirements were imposed on its tax-exempt hospitals, Texas was one of three states with the highest percentages of uninsured in the United States, along with Arizona and New Mexico (Kaiser, 2015a and 2015b). The debate today is the provision of charitable care to **illegal immigrants** (as compared to the debate over providing Medicaid insurance to **lawful permanent residents**; *See, e.g., Finch v. Commonwealth Health Insurance Connector Authority* 959 N.E.2d 970 (Supreme Judicial Court of Massachusetts 2012)).

Tax-Exempt Hospitals

When the first federal class-action lawsuits were withdrawn or dismissed, there was an opportunity for hospital governing boards to prevent being drawn into the legal battles over what constitutes affordable care. Tax-exempt hospitals now have the opportunity to increase oversight in many aspects of their pricing, billing, and debt collection activities. This includes, among other things:

- Examining how they handle billing for their uninsured and underinsured patients, and determining whether the community is adequately informed about the hospital's charitable care and financial assistance activities
- Exploring in-house debt collection practices and agreements with third party debt collectors to insure that fair and appropriate practices are being followed
- Looking for obstacles that hinder the financially distressed when seeking health care and deciding whether the charge structure and the amounts of charitable care and financial assistance the hospital can provide in light of its overall financial situation should be modified
- Performing a community assessment of the service area and demographics to see if hospital mission statements and community expectations are being appropriately applied to the hospital's patient population
- Reviewing patient intake procedures and policies to determine how charitable care and financial assistance practices are handled

(Tahk, 2014).

For instance, after the Yale-New Haven Hospital was named in a federal class-action lawsuit alleging improper charitable care, it:

- Closed accounts over five years outstanding
- Developed a sliding scale to provide means-tested discounts and uncompensated care to deserving patients below certain incomes
- Removed property liens against former patients

(Helvin, 2013).

This highly publicized case involved a husband who made regular payments to Yale–New Haven Hospital for 20 years after his wife died of cancer at the hospital. He eventually paid $16,000 on the $19,000 charge, but because of compounding interest accumulations, the principal of the debt grew to some $40,000. In instances like this, tax-exempt hospitals may need to rethink their overall role in the communities they serve. In fact, it is their approach to corporate social responsibility and their disregard for community sentiment that has raised questions about the billions of dollars in tax exemptions they receive (Carreyrou & Martinez, 2008).

Financial Viability and Mission

The lawsuits brought against the hospital industry due to its billing and debt collection activities have resulted in some modification to the way tax-exempt hospitals are providing health care to their uninsured and underinsured patients. In fact, most hospitals have recently made changes and clarified their:

- Billing
- Charitable care programs
- Debt collection
- Pricing

(Tahk, 2014).

Some hospitals are making changes quietly so as not to spur additional pressure against already stretched charitable care programs. However, with more than 47 million Americans uninsured or underinsured, tax-exempt hospitals are under tremendous pressure to correctly determine when patients are eligible for charitable care or when patients can afford to pay. While health care should ideally never be compromised due to the ability or inability to pay, tax-exempt hospitals have a responsibility to all of their patients to attempt to obtain payment from those who can afford to pay. These critical distinctions are a constant challenge to tax-exempt hospitals who strive to balance their charitable missions with running a fiscally responsible business.

As court cases show, aggressive pressure on the uninsured to pay more than their insured counterparts is not the way to obtain fiscal health. In fact, adopting aggressive debt collection policies usually requires added collection staff to contact patients for payment, and repeated attempts at cash collections likely turn into consulting sessions with patients on how to pay their medical bills. Extraordinary debt collection often gives way to assisting indebted, discharged patients with enrollment in Medicaid insurance. When debts cannot be collected, these situations should be seen as clear signals that there is something wrong with the way billing is being conducted and, in particular, something is fundamentally wrong with patient access to hospital care. To find the proper balance between a hospital's charitable mission and financial viability, operational principles should be applied, not just to debt collection processes but to the entire hospital business.

Up-Front Billing Practices

Many tax-exempt hospitals make health care contingent on up-front payments. Typically, hospitals bill patients after they receive care. Now, pointing to their rising bad debt and charitable care costs, hospitals are asking patients for money before they receive medical treatment.

A recent survey found about 14% of tax-exempt hospitals required patients to make payments before receiving medical treatment. Hospitals say they have turned to the practice because of a spike in patients who do not pay their medical bills. Since 2000, uncompensated care cost the hospital industry $502 billion (AHA, 2016c). The bad debt is driven by a larger number of Americans who are uninsured or who do not have enough insurance to cover health care costs if a catastrophe strikes. Even among those with adequate insurance, deductibles and co-payments are growing so large that insured patients also have trouble paying hospitals.

Life-Threatening Medical Emergencies

The **Emergency Medical Treatment and Active Labor Act of 1986** creates an illusion about the availability of health care for the uninsured (42 U.S.C.A. § 1395dd). While the law prohibits hospitals from refusing to screen, treat, and stabilize any person who seeks emergency medical treatment, the law does not require hospitals to cover the cost of medical treatment or any post-stabilization care. Hospitals are required to treat **medical emergencies** (such as heart attacks or injuries from accidents); however, the law does not cover conditions that are not immediately life-threatening. With emergency departments at more than half of all urban hospitals and over half of all teaching hospitals at capacity or over their capacity, even if hospitals could provide medically needed care in cases that are not life-threatening, they generally could not do so because they are already over their capacity providing emergency care to more than the maximum number of patients that can be safely taken in (AHA, 2010).

Federal regulations address a hospital's ability to register and collect payment information from a patient seeking emergency services. These regulations allow a hospital to follow reasonable registration processes, including inquiries regarding a patient's insurance status and method of payment as long as such processes do not result in a delay in screening or emergency medical treatment (*See* 42 C.F.R. § 489.24(d)(4)). Since determining credit capability can be done almost instantaneously, hospitals can generally determine whether patients have the capability to guarantee payment of all charges before care is rendered. The law actually allows hospitals to transfer a patient to another hospital for care as long as the patient is in stable condition.

Hospital registration processes, including all information obtained and forms signed by patients, should always be reasonable and not delay life-threatening medical treatment. Medicare-participating hospitals are required to provide a medical screening examination to any person that comes to the emergency room; if a medical condition exists, hospitals are only required to provide stabilization services. Additional medical treatment can be conditioned on a determination of the ability to pay for such care and an agreement to sign contracts agreeing to pay incurred charges.

Medical Billing and Debt Collection Transparency

The regulatory environment makes billing and debt collection for tax-exempt hospitals somewhat difficult. Under the Affordable Care Act, hospitals are:

- Barred from charging low-income patients higher rates than the lowest amounts billed to the insured
- Obligated to widely publicize their financial assistance policies describing who is eligible for free or discounted health care
- Prohibited from enforcing extraordinary debt collections against patients before determining whether they qualify for Medicaid insurance or other financial assistance
- Required to conduct assessments of the health needs of the community they serve and implement a strategy to meet those needs

Social perceptions of acceptable debt collection have changed under the Affordable Care Act. The expectation is that tax-exempt hospitals have a role in their communities beyond just providing health care, a public expectation that can start with improving medical billing (Thai, 2011). Nothing is standardized across the health care industry as a whole when it comes to billing and debt collection transparency; such standardization would be a start in the right direction.

Regulatory Environment

There are several confusing laws intended to prevent discriminatory billing and extraordinary debt collection. For instance, there are Medicare's/Medicaid's bad debt rules and regulations requiring hospitals to make all reasonable attempts to collect payment from a patient before discharging the uncollected debt as uncompensated care or bad debt. There is also the policy adopted by the American Hospital Association that since Medicare pricing policies require hospitals to bill all patients the same charge for each service, this meant the uninsured had to pay full price for their care. Hospitals nationwide chose to interpret this to mean they were precluded from offering means-tested discounts to the uninsured.

Combine these regulations and policies with **special fraud alerts** and **anti-kickback laws** specifying when hospitals can and cannot waive co-payments and deductibles, and the confusion about billing practices expands. The federal compliance program guidance for hospitals and advisory opinions from the Office of the Inspector General singularly and together make it difficult for hospitals to provide any type of means-tested discounts. While these policies do not and never have prohibited hospitals from providing means-tested discounts, they have often been misconstrued to require the uninsured to pay full price for their medical services. These misconceptions also make it more difficult for hospitals to use means-tested discounts or other means of financial assistance (OIG, 2004).

MANAGEMENT AND LAW ISSUES

8. Should tax-exempt hospitals be forced to charge every patient the same price?

Standard Means-Tested Discounts

A critical first step that tax-exempt hospitals should take is a meticulous review of the policies and procedures that touch upon billing the uninsured, and then assuring that there is a standard means-tested discount for all eligible patients. This requires a detailed evaluation of state billing regulations. The American Hospital Association has published a statement of principles and guidelines governing hospital billing. Their principles are:

- Assist the deserving and medically needy who cannot pay for part or all of the health care they receive
- Balance needed financial assistance with broader fiscal responsibilities in order to keep hospitals open and serving the needs of the community
- Serve the emergency care of everyone, regardless of a patient's ability to pay
- Treat all patients equally

Unfortunately, these principles are vague and leave plenty of room for interpretation for hospitals that may want to increase their profits through higher revenues and more effective debt collection policies.

Provision of Price Information

One sound practice that leads to debt collection success is having documentation supporting outstanding medical bills (Beck, 2014). Patients should have an idea in advance of what the amount billed will be (in non-emergency situations) and be able to understand the bill when it arrives. The bill should detail what medical treatment, services, and materials it encompasses and should set forth the expectation of prompt payment by a specified due date.

Consider a scenario in the commercial environment involving billing customers using the same practices as many hospitals use to bill their patients (such as shipping a product to a customer without any discussion regarding the costs of the product and then invoicing the customer for the highest price the vendor can charge). This is unheard of. Instead of collecting the bill promptly, countless hours would be spent negotiating a fair price for what the customer bought. Besides the resulting slow turnover in debt collections, customers would be infuriated over this deceptive practice.

Likewise, hospitals should be obligated to notify prospective patients what the hospital plans to provide them in terms of care and at the very least a reasonable estimate of the total price for the anticipated care. While handing patients detailed hospital charges for each and every conceivable service is unreasonable, patients should have an understanding of the nature of their financial obligations before any non-emergency care is accepted or rendered. Simply put, hospitals should provide patients with price information. One is hard-pressed to find reasons why hospitals should not model their business practices after those that are successful and accepted for cosmetic surgeries and other elective medical surgeries that are self-pay (for instance, laser vision correction surgery).

Some hospital charges are certainly less precise than the price terms of ordinary contracts for goods or services. Hospitals cannot be expected to specify an *exact* amount to be paid when emergency medical treatments are rendered or when unexpected medical conditions arise. While general payment obligations of patients can be set forth for most medical treatments, with emergency care usually nobody knows just what particular condition the patient has, or what will be necessary to remedy the disease, sickness, or injury presented (Johnson, 2014). It is incongruous to expect hospitals to fully perform their ethical obligation to provide emergency care to patients and then not send patients invoices for charges (including charges not covered by their health insurance). This would be an unrealistic expectation. Patients should know, before agreeing to non-emergency care, what is not covered by their health insurance. It bears repeating, price information should be provided before medical treatment is accepted.

Medical and Financial Vulnerabilities

While the United States has favored a **market-based for-profit hospital model**, it has not been as successful as most might have liked. Perhaps it is time to revisit this approach to hospital care. Indeed, debate on medically necessary care suggests that continuing on the path where health care coverage decisions are based on clinical evidence alone, without

MANAGEMENT AND LAW ISSUES

9. Should hospitals be required to explain their means-tested discount policies to all patients?

consideration of costs, may no longer be feasible in the long run. The legal obligation to provide charitable care in lieu of taxes is uncertain.

Determining who should be charged and how much to charge for health care is a complicated issue. The Affordable Care Act has brought major improvements in the U.S. health care system but at a serious risk to the status quo. Everyone knows they are medically vulnerable because no one is going to live forever, but as more Americans realize they are also financially vulnerable, changes and solutions that work financially, medically, and politically will be in order.

LAW FACT

Discriminatory Pricing

Are the uninsured being charged the highest prices for health care?

Yes. A few weeks after probing Saint Joseph Medical Center for an explanation of the charges, the Ferlinis received an adjusted bill for $41,000, less than one-fifth the amount of the original medical bill of $246,000. While charges and computations are based on a uniform set of charges in each hospital's chargemaster, negotiated discount payments may apply in different situations.

— Kuntze, 2008; Rosembaum, 2016; *See* Sadick, 2014 (cutting down on excessive diagnostic testing in emergency departments).

CHAPTER SUMMARY

- In return for federal tax exemption, tax-exempt hospitals are required to render a significant amount of community benefits that do not necessarily consist of charitable care.
- Because the community benefits can constitute almost anything, hospitals are not necessarily required to offer free or reduced-cost care to the uninsured or underinsured.
- While the tax-exempt hospitals are heavily subsidized with over $12.6 billion in tax exemptions and $32 billion in government assistance subsidies each year, many fail to use their assets and revenues to provide affordable care to the uninsured and underinsured.
- Congress is investigating tax-exempt hospitals in light of the number of people bankrupted by medical debt and reports of hospitals abusing their tax exemptions.
- Government agencies at all levels are investigating whether tax-exempt hospitals provide enough community benefits to justify federal, state, and local governments forgoing the tax income they would otherwise receive.
- Patients have begun to sue tax-exempt hospitals, sometimes through class-action lawsuits, claiming the hospitals violate their charitable missions by overcharging the uninsured and underinsured, price gouging, and employing extraordinary debt collection methods; this litigation has encouraged some hospitals to improve their pricing, billing, and debt collection practices before being sued.
- The uninsured and underinsured are often charged four to five times more for the exact same medical services than the insured are charged.
- Today's tax-exempt hospitals compete effectively with for-profit hospitals, and in many cases are nearly indistinguishable, right down to state-of -the-art facilities and medical equipment.
- Medicare/Medicaid insurance often does not reimburse tax-exempt hospitals enough to cover the actual cost of care rendered, forcing such hospitals to write off the remaining uncompensated care.
- One in four Americans are uninsured or underinsured, and nearly one in five Americans reports not seeking or delaying seeking necessary health care; only about half of the American population is able to obtain insurance coverage through employers.
- Many states are beginning to impose stricter regulations upon tax-exempt hospitals in order to ensure that the hospitals are justifying their tax exemption through meaningful benefits to their communities.

- One way tax-exempt hospitals might improve upon collecting their accounts receivable is to familiarize patients in advance of their hospital admission with the costs and, upon discharge, provide clear, detailed bills.
- Other ways tax-exempt hospitals can improve patient payments include better coordinating of their overall business functions: charging patients on a sliding scale or means-tested ability to pay, charging patients up front for care, and modeling their business practices after other industries.

LAW NOTES

1. There are no accurate statistics as to how many personal bankruptcies are due to medical debt; most estimates are that it is as high as 80% (Weissman, 2016). Part of the problem with medical debt is its direct relationship to the consequences of lost income resulting from illness and hospitalizations. Additionally, unplanned spending may lead people to overstate the role of medical problems in their financial crises, as most of the research on bankruptcy filings is conducted by analyzing debtors' explanations. It is certainly more socially acceptable to admit to bankruptcy due to medical bills as opposed to acknowledging a history of undisciplined spending or failure to earn sufficient income to meet one's needs (or wants). The question of determining how many personal bankruptcies are due to medical debt is further complicated by the fact that hospitals routinely accept major credit cards as payment, while other people take out second mortgages to cover their medical bills; therefore, medical debt is often incorporated into regular personal debts (Zimmon, 2015). Thus, the precise number of people for whom medical debts are the primary cause of bankruptcy is unknown and difficult to estimate. What is undisputed is that most of those bankruptcy filers were insured (GAO, 2014).

2. Chief executive officers at the top academic health care systems earn an average of $15 million in total compensation, most of which is non-salary compensation. The average base salary for chief executives for independent health systems is $752,800, while the salary for chief executives of independent hospitals that do not report to a parent organization is $425,200. Hospital administrators earn $267,000 on average. These top earners compare to hospital physicians, who earn an average of $306,000 despite being the most highly trained professionals in the health care industry (*See generally* Gallagher, 2016). Whether multimillion compensation packages may affect inflated costs of health care costs is debatable.

3. Although hospital closures raise concern about access to health care, the general link between a closed hospital and rates of patient mortality rates may be unfounded. There does not appear to be any difference in mortality rates in hospital service areas where there were hospital closures (Joynt et al., 2015).

4. Critical access hospitals may be for-profit and eligible to receive Medicare payments at 101% of their allowed costs (Balance Budge Refinement Act). With a critical access designation, for-profit hospitals are also eligible for Medicare incentives if they adopt certified electronic health records (American Recovery and Reinvestment Act).

5. States that have expanded Medicaid insurance have seen their uncompensated care rates from the uninsured decline by over 30% due to the impact of the Affordable Care Act, while charity expenditures have declined more than a third (Crowe Horwath,[1] 2015).

REFERENCES

AHA (American Hospital Association). (2016a). *AHA hospital statistics*. Chicago, IL: AHA.

___. (2016b). *Underpayment by Medicare and Medicaid fact sheet*.

___. (2016c). *Uncompensated hospital care cost fact sheet*.

___. (2010). *The state of America's hospitals: Taking the pulse; Results of AHA survey of hospital leaders*.

Ascher, M. L. (2014). The role of federal law in private wealth transfer: Federalization of the law of charity. *Vanderbilt Law Review, 67*, 1581–1619.

Bai, G., & Anderson, G. F. (2015). Extreme markup: The fifty U.S. hospitals with the highest charge-to-cost ratios. *Health Affairs, 34*(60), 922–928.

Basanta, W. E., et al. (2010). Survey of Illinois law: Healthcare law. *Southern Illinois University Law Journal, 34*, 1033–1075.

Beck, M. (2014, February 23). How to bring the price of health care into the open: There's a big push to tell patients what they'll pay-before they decide on treatment. *Wall Street Journal*, p. A–1.

Berg, J. (2010). Putting the community back into the "community benefit" standard. *Georgia Law Review, 44*, 375–431.

Blodgett, M. S., et al. (2013). State oversight of nonprofit governance: Confronting the challenge of mission adherence within a multi-dimensional standard. *Journal of Law and Commerce, 32*(1), 81–108.

Brody, E. (2010). All charities are property-tax exempt, but some charities are more exempt than others. *New England Law Review, 44*, 621–732.

Brown, E. C. F. (2015). Resurrecting health care rate regulation. *Hastings Law Journal, 67*, 85–142.

___. (2014). Irrational hospital pricing. *Houston Journal of Health Law and Policy, 14*, 11–56.

---

1. Hammaker is a former employee of Laventhol & Horwath, predecessor to Crowe Horwath.

Buxton, Z. J. (2014). Community benefit 501(r)edux: An analysis of the Patient Protection and Affordable Care Act's limitations under community benefit reform. *Saint Louis University Journal of Health Law and Policy, 7*, 449–484.

Carreyrou, J., & Martinez, B. (2008, April 4). Tax-exempt hospitals, once for the poor, strike it rich with tax-benefits, they out-perform for-profit rivals. *Wall Street Journal*, p. A1.

CBO (Congressional Budget Office). (2016). *Tax-exempt hospitals and the provisions of community-benefits*. Washington, DC: CBO.

___. (2015). *Updated budget projections*.

Census Bureau. (2014). *Poverty thresholds*. Washington, DC: U.S. Department of Commerce, Census Bureau.

Coffman, J., Partner, Bain & Company. (2014, February 21). Remarks at the panel discussion on The Future of Medical Care Delivery: Reimaging Health Care; Driving Change in a Patient Centered World at the 2014 Wharton Health Care Business Conference, Philadelphia, PA.

Colinvaux, R. (2011). Charity in the 21st century: Trending toward decay. *Florida Tax Review, 11*, 1–71.

Collins, S. R., et al. (2015). *The problem of underinsurance and how rising deductibles will make it worse: Findings from the Commonwealth Fund Biennal Health Insurance Survey*. New York, NY: Commonwealth Fund.

Commonwealth Fund, The. (2014). *Biennial health insurance survey*. New York, NY: Commonwealth Fund.

Corbett, T. L. (2015). Healthcare corporate structure and the Affordable Care Act: A need for mission primacy through a new organizational paradigm? *Indiana Health Law Review, 12*, 103–181.

Corlette, S., et al. (2016). Obama administration moves forward with new continuity of care protections; How will they affect existing state laws? New York, NY: The Commonwealth Fund.

Crossley, M. (2012). Tax-exempt hospitals, community health needs and addressing disparities. *Howard Law Journal, 55*, 687–704.

Crowe Horwath. (2015). *Decreasing charity expenditures: Putting Medicaid expansion state hospitals at risk?* Chicago, IL: Crowe Horwath.

DeNavas-Walt, C., & Proctor, B. D. (2015). *Income and poverty in the United States: Current population reports*. Washington, DC: U.S. Department of Commerce, Census Bureau.

Dirlam, B. (2015). Property tax exemptions for institutions of purely public charity after Mesivtah Eitz Chaim of Bobov, Inc. *Duquesne Business Law Journal, 17*, 175–196.

Duke Center for Health Policy and Inequalities Research. (2016). *Nonprofit tax exemption*. Durham, NC: Duke University.

Fleischer, M. P. (2015). Libertarianism and the charitable tax subsidies. *Boston College Law Review, 56*, 1345–1415.

Frakt, A. B. (2011). How much do hospitals cost shift? A review of the evidence. *The Milbank Quarterly, 89*(1), 90–130.

Fremont-Smith, M. R., & Horwitz, J. R. (2016). *Restatement of the law, charitable nonprofit organizations*. Philadelphia, PA: American Law Institute.

Gallagher Benefit Services. (2016). *Integrated healthcare strategies: National healthcare leadership compensation survey*. Minneapolis, MN: Gallagher.

GAO (U.S. Government Accountability Office). (2014). *Credit cards designed for medical services not covered by insurance*. Washington, DC: GAO.

Garfield, R., & Young, K. (2015). Adults who remained uninsured at the end of 2014. Menlo Park, CA.: Henry J. Kaiser Family Foundation.

Gold, J. (2012, April 27). Sued over an $1,800 hospital bill. *Kaiser Health News*. Retrieved from http://khn.org/news/charity-care-nonprofit-hospitals-patient-debt/

Groebe, C. Z. (2015). The evolution of federal courts' healthcare antitrust analysis: Does the [Affordable Care Act] spell the end to hospital mergers? *Washington University Law Review, 92*(6), 1617–1645.

Hackney, P. T. (2013). What we talk about when we talk about tax exemption. *Virginia Tax Review, 33*, 115–167.

Hafemeister, T. L., & Porter, J. H. (2013). Don't let go of the rope: Reducing readmissions by recognizing hospitals' fiduciary duties to their discharged patients. *American University Law Review, 62*, 513–575.

Hall, M. A. (2015). Toward relationship-centered health law. *Wake Forest Law Review, 50*, 233–249.

Hamm, A. (2015). Do not pass go and do not collect $200: Denying medical insurance to parents who register themselves before registering their children. *William and Mary Journal of Women and the Law, 21*, 743–765.

Harrison, S., et al. (2015). Health care fraud. *American Criminal Law Review, 52*, 1223–1288.

Hazen, T. L., & Hazen, L. L. (2012). Punctilios and nonprofit corporate governance: A comprehensive look at nonprofit directors' fiduciary duties. *University of Pennsylvania Journal of Business Law, 14*(2), 347–416.

Helvin, L. K. (2013). Caring for the uninsured: Are not-for-profit hospitals doing their share? *Yale Journal of Health Policy, Law and Ethics, 8*(2), 423–470.

Hermer, L. D., & Lenihan, M. (2014). Medicaid matters: The future of Medicaid supplemental payments: Can they promote patient-centered care? *Kentucky Law Journal, 102*, 287–326.

HHS (U.S. Department of Health and Human Services). (2016). *Poverty guidelines: U.S. federal poverty guidelines used to determine financial eligibility for certain federal programs*. Washington, DC: HHS.

IRS (Internal Revenue Service). (2015). *Report to Congress on private tax-exempt, taxable, and government-owned hospitals*. Washington, DC: U.S. Department of Treasury, Internal Revenue Service.

iVantage Health Analytics. (2015). *Vulnerability to value: Rural relevance under healthcare reform*. Portland, ME: iVantage.

Johnson, A. (2014, July 24). The anatomy of a hospital bill: An appendectomy ran nearly $30,000; Where did the money go? *Wall Street Journal*, p. D1.

Joynt, K. E., et al. (2015). Hospital closures had no measurable impact on local hospitalization rates or mortality rates. *Health Affairs, 34*(50), 765–772.

Kaiser Family Foundation. (2015a). *Key facts about the uninsured population*. Menlo Park, CA.

___. (2015b). *Distribution of the total population by federal poverty level (above and below 200% FPL)*.

___. (2012a). *Kaiser health security watch*.

___. (2012b). *Kaiser health tracking poll*.

Kirch, D. (2012). *Reform is no "either-or": We must fix the payment system along with access*. New York, NY: Modern Healthcare and The Commonwealth Fund.

Klebes, K. (2015). For-profit healthcare in Connecticut: New requirements under the Patient Protection and Affordable Care Act and the emerging for-profit hospital model in Connecticut. *Quinnipiac Health Law Journal, 18*, 239–285.

Kuntze, C. (2008). The fight for equal pricing in health care. *Journal of Legal Medicine, 29*(4), 537–552.

Lenihan, M., & Hermer, L. D. (2014). On the uneasy relationship between Medicaid and charity care. *Notre Dame Journal of Law, Ethics and Public Policy, 28*, 165–208.

Mayo, T. W. (2010). Tax-exempt hospitals: Renewed focus on indigent care. *Journal of Health and Life Sciences Law, 4*(1), 140–152.

Melone & Nation, G. A. (2014). Standing on formality: *Hollingsworth v. Perry* and the efficacy of direct democracy in the United States. *Brigham Young University Journal of Public Law, 29*, 25–98.

Mintz, L. R. (2013). The rules of the fight must be fair: States should pass a uniform code for nonprofit hospital tax exemption of real property. *Journal of Law and Health, 26*, 415–449.

Moncrieff, A. R. (2012). Cost–benefit federalism: Reconciling collective action federalism and libertarian federalism in the Obamacare litigation and beyond. *American Journal of Law and Medicine, 38*, 288–324.

Morrell, M. T., & Krouse, A. T. (2014). Accountability partners: Legislated collaboration for health reform. *Indiana Health Law Review, 11*(1), 225–301.

Morton, T. G., & Woodbury, F. (1895). *The history of the Pennsylvania Hospital, 1751–1895*. Philadelphia, PA: Times Printing House.

Moskowitz, E. (2005). Recent developments in health law: Class-action suits allege improper charitable care practices. *Journal of Law, Medicine and Ethics, 33*, 168–170.

NCCS (National Center for Charitable Statistics). (2016). *Guidestar: NCCS national nonprofit research database*. Washington, DC: Urban Institute.

NCSL (National Conference of State Legislatures). (2015). *Health insurance: Premiums and increases*. Washington, DC: NCLS.

NPR. All things considered: Nonprofit hospitals faulted for stinginess with charity care (NPR radio broadcast April 27, 2012).

Nussbaum, A. (2012). Can Congress make you buy health insurance? The Affordable Care Act, national health care reform, and the constitutionality of the individual mandate. *Duquesne Law Review, 50*, 411–466.

OIG (Office of Inspector General). (2004). *Hospital means-tested discounts offered to patients who cannot afford to pay their medical bills*. Washington, DC: U.S. Department of Health & Human Services.

Patton, T. J. (2014). The calamity of community benefit: Redefining the scope and increasing the accountability of Minnesota's nonprofit hospitals. *Hamline Law Review, 37*, 1–18.

Piper, C. E. (2016). *Healthcare fraud investigation guidebook*. Boca Raton, FL: CRC Press.

Principe, K., et al. (2012). The impact of the individual mandate and Internal Revenue Service Form 990 Schedule H on community benefits from nonprofit hospitals. *American Journal of Public Health, 102*(2), 229–237.

Purdy, J., & Siegel, N. S. (2012). The liberty of free riders: The minimum coverage provision, Mill's "harm principle," and American social morality. *American Journal of Law and Medicine, 38*, 374–396.

Reagan, R. Official announcement of Reagan's candidacy for President of the United States in New York City, NY (1979, November 13).

Rice, E. L. (2010). Evanston's legacy: A prescription for addressing two-stage competition in hospital merger antitrust analysis. *Boston University Law Review, 90*, 431–453.

Rosembaum, M. (2006, March 5). *60 Minutes: Hospitals: Is the price right?* (CBS News television broadcast).

Sadick, B. (2014, February 23). A push for less testing in emergency rooms: Heavy use of imaging scans may drive up costs and risks. *Wall Street Journal*, p. A1.

Sage, W. M. (2016). Assembled products: The key to more effective competition and antitrust oversight in health care. *Cornell Law Review, 101*, 609–700.

Sanford, S. T. (2013). Medicaid matters; Emergency response: A systemic approach to diaper rash, chest pain, and Medicaid in the emergency department. *Kentucky Law Journal, 102*, 441–470.

Sataline, S. (2010, March 19). Illinois high court rules nonprofit hospital can be taxed. *Wall Street Journal*, p. B4.

Schirra, J. J. (2011). A veil of tax exemption? A proposal for the continuation of federal tax-exempt status for "nonprofit" hospitals. *Health Matrix: Journal of Law and Medicine, 21*, 231–277.

Schoen, C., et al. (2005). Insured but not protected: How many adults are underinsured? *Health Affairs*, 289–302. Retrieved from http://content .healthaffairs.org/content/early/2005/06/14/hlthaff.w5.289.short

Scott, C. (2014). Why law pervades medicine: An essay on ethics in health care. *Notre Dame Journal of Law, Ethics and Public Policy, 14*(9), 245–303.

Smith, K. J. H. (2016). Charitable choices: The need for a Uniform Nonprofit Limited Liability Company Act (UNLLCA). *University of Michigan Journal of Law Reform, 49*, 405–466.

Tahk, S. C. (2014). Tax-exempt hospitals and their communities. *Columbia Journal of Tax Law, 6*, 33–85.

Thai, A. W. (2011). Is Senator Grassley our savior? The crusade against "charitable" hospitals attacking patients for unpaid bills. *Iowa Law Review, 96*, 761–789.

Thayer, L. (2011). In determining whether a patient is medically indigent, county boards can impute a patient's potential income and future tax returns: *St. Luke's Magic Valley Regional Medical Center v. Board of County Commissioners of Gooding County*, 237 P.3d 1210 (Idaho 2010). *Journal of Health and Biomedical Law, 7*, 115–123.

Tyrrell, III, J. E. (2010). Non-profits under fire: The effects of minimal charity care requirements legislation on not-for-profit hospitals. *Journal of Contemporary Health Law and Policy, 26*, 373–402.

Urban Institute. (2015). *Nonprofit almanac*. Washington, DC: National Center for Charitable Statistics.

Vagelos, P. R., Chairman of the Board, Regeneron Pharmaceuticals and Retired Chairman and CEO of Merck & Co., Inc. (2014, February 21). Keynote speaker on Reimagining Healthcare: Driving Change in a Patient-Centered World at the 2014 Wharton Health Care Business Conference, Philadelphia, PA.

Weisblatt, R. (2014). Uncharitable hospitals: Why the IRS needs intermediate sanctions to regulate tax-exempt hospitals. *Boston College Law Review, 55*, 687–717.

Weissman, S. I. (2016). Remedies for an epidemic of medical provider price gouging. *Florida Bar Journal, 90*, 22–38.

Westenberger, M. C. (2015). Tax-exempt hospitals and the community benefit standard: A flawed standard and a way forward. *Florida Tax Review, 17*, 407–435.

Young, G. J., et al. (2013). Provision of community benefits by tax-exempt U.S. hospitals. *New England Journal of Medicine, 368*, 1519–1527.

Zimmon, A. J. (2015). Rx for costly credit: Deferred interest medical credit cards do more harm than good. *Boston College Journal of Law and Social Justice, 35*, 319–352.

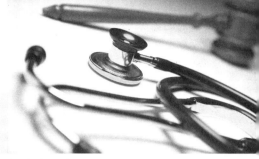

CHAPTER 7

Patient Rights and Responsibilities

"The assault on the national government is represented as a disinterested movement to 'return' power to the people. It transfers power to the historical rival of the national government and the prime cause of its enlargement—the great corporate interests."

— **Arthur Schlesinger, Jr.** (1917–2007), Pulitzer Prize-winning historian and American social critic

IN BRIEF

This chapter looks at patient rights and the responsibility for paying for health care. How do patients protect themselves when seeking health care in today's consumer-driven market? Who is the patient's agent in making health care decisions if it is no longer their physician? This debate underscores the difficult job of trying to hold down health care costs while giving patients more say in the kind of medical treatment they can obtain, though the biggest obstacles to holding down health care costs are the patients who fail to accept responsibility for maintaining a healthy lifestyle and who then demand medical treatments for preventable diseases and illnesses that could have been avoided or delayed, or which are futile. Based on this rights and responsibilities debate involving parties with incredibly divergent interests, this chapter examines the feasibility of providing medically necessary care for every member of society, including those members of society who neglected to avail themselves of the preventive measures they could have taken to reduce their risks of bad health.

LEARNING OBJECTIVES

Upon completion of this chapter readers should be able to:

1. Explain why the American middle class lacks a real safety net for catastrophic medical events.
2. Contrast rights and privileges as applied in the health care debate.
3. Understand the Employee Retirement Income Security Act's preemption of state law claims against the insurance industry and appreciate how state preemption limits patients' recovery for harm suffered as a result of health insurance policies and practices.
4. Recognize how providers are third-party beneficiaries of contracts between the health insurance industry and patients.
5. List elements of the movement involving medical malpractice reform.
6. Explain why total health care spending generates individual and societal benefits far in excess of their total cost while, at the same time, current expenditures for medical services are worth far less than they cost.
7. Relate the legislative history of how the passage of Medicare and Medicaid were conditioned on measures to prevent the government from having any control over the practice of medicine or its compensation of physicians.
8. Show how those who have health care insurance actually pay for the care of those who do not.
9. Understand how the Affordable Care Act established new patient rights and responsibilities.

KEY TERMS

Abigail Alliance for Better Access to Developmental Drugs
Acute care
Affordable Care Act of 2010
Alternative dispute resolution
Arbitration clauses
Benchmark strategy
Charitable care
Commercial speech
Common law
Comparative effectiveness
Compelled speech
Compelled speech doctrine
Compelling interest
Content-based burdens
Credible health insurance coverage
Critical care
Data miners
Detailing
Economic pyramid
Emergency Medical Treatment and Labor Act of 1986
Employee Retirement Income Security Act of 1974 (ERISA)

Equality of opportunity
Essential health insurance
Fairness
Financial assistance programs
Free riders
Fundamental right
General well-being
Health capital
Health Employer Data Information Set
Health-related well-being
Healthy lifestyles
Human entitlements
Informed consent
Insurance
Joint and several liability
Justice
Liberty interest
Medical necessity
Medical screening (in emergency departments)
Medical triage
Medically necessary care
Medically needed care
Medicare fee-for-service

Minimum essential coverage
National Academy of Medicine
Off-label
Patient Bill of Rights
Personal autonomy
Pharmacy benefit managers
Prescriber-identifying data
Pretax income
Privilege
Quality-adjusted life year
Quality of life research
Rational basis
Rationing
Right
Rights through disclosure
Risk pools
Safety net
Safety net hospitals
Section 125 cafeteria plans
Social contract
Social loafers
Uncompensated care
Universal coverage
Wear-aways
World Health Organization

FACT OR FICTION

Right to Emergency Care

Are patients entitled to emergency care?

Carolina Morales was diagnosed with a nonviable ectopic pregnancy. In an ectopic pregnancy, the embryo grows outside the uterus (also called a tubal or an abdominal pregnancy). Ectopic pregnancy can go away without treatment or it can be a medical emergency if the ectopic tissue ruptures (ASM, 2014).

Two days later, while at work, Morales experienced severe abdominal pain accompanied by vomiting. Her employer called an ambulance. After placing Morales inside the ambulance, the ambulance crew set off for the hospital at which Morales's obstetrician regularly practiced. While in transit to the hospital, the paramedics called ahead to the emergency department to notify them of Morales's arrival and her need for emergency treatment. When the hospital received no assurance from the paramedics that Morales was insured, they abruptly terminated the call. The paramedics interpreted this as a refusal to treat Morales at the hospital emergency department. The hospital never claimed to be in diversionary status, that is, without adequate staff or facilities to accept additional emergency patients. Stymied by the actions of the hospital, the paramedics took Morales to a different facility where she was treated. In due course, Morales sued the first hospital and others for violating her legal right to emergency care. The hospital claimed that Morales was never entitled to emergency care since she had never physically come to its emergency department.

— *See* Law Fact at the end of this chapter for the answer.

Principles and Applications

The patient rights debate underscores the difficult job of trying to minimize costs while giving consumers greater freedom of choice in the kind of health care available. The debate largely affects the middle class rather than individuals and families who are often eligible to be covered by Medicaid insurance or other **financial assistance programs** (Wiley, 2016). While uninsured families were often eligible for **charitable care** (or discounted or **uncompensated care**) as needed, prior to enactment of the **Patient Bill of Rights** (*See* 45 C.F.R. §§ 144, 146–147), the middle class insured lacked a real **safety net** for catastrophic events when their deductibles, coinsurance, annual caps, or lifetime limits on health care coverage exceeded their ability to pay for their health care. Before this reform legislation was enacted, the middle class was the only group in the United States that was unprotected, with nowhere to turn for assistance when their legitimate claims for advanced drugs and medical devices exceeded their ability to pay for **medically needed care**, the highest attainable standard of necessary health care and medical treatments.

The fundamental issue in the patient rights debate concerns how patients can protect themselves when confronted by illness or disease. Physicians are no longer patients' agents (Farley, 2016; Wharton, 2008); the U.S. health care system is comprised of parties with conflicting interests. When the U.S. political system took a comprehensive look at this pressing issue, the answer seemed to be a comprehensive system of health insurance where everyone had health care coverage that was fairly broad and deep (Frakt, 2011). For the raison d'être of protecting middle-class America, many have come to favor this system of **universal coverage**. The most important reason for universal coverage, in this sense, is an **insurance** system that provides affordable access to **essential health insurance** for everyone. Deductibles and coinsurance payments are restricted under the Patient Bill of Rights, while annual caps and lifetime limits on health care coverage are prohibited.

Rights or Privileges Debate

The entire subject of patient rights is so complex that it does not lend itself to easy analysis or solutions. The Patient Bill of Rights does not address the issue of whether **medically necessary care** is a **right** or a **privilege**. Furthermore, there is no public consensus on whether health care is a moral entitlement arising from the humanity of people or a legal entitlement freely granted by law.

A right is the inverse of a privilege. If society decides health care is a privilege, then health care is conditioned on the ability to pay or otherwise purchase health insurance that will provide health care coverage for the highest attainable standard of medically necessary care, including advanced drugs and medical devices, and access to the most highly trained specialists. In this instance, medically necessary care may be delayed or not received at all if someone is underinsured and the necessary care is unaffordable because of costs.

On the other hand, if society decides health care is a right, the storyline is very different. Everyone will be provided access to affordable health insurance coverage to obtain medically necessary care with subsidies available to people at the lower end of the **economic pyramid**.

Commonsense economics demanded that the United States address affordable health insurance coverage for one simple reason: it was cost-effective to do so. It is less costly to provide comprehensive health insurance that covers preventive and regularly administered health care than it is to provide delayed charitable care on an as-needed basis (Lipschutz et al., 2015). It simply costs less to provide regular, basic preventive health care than it costs to provide delayed **acute care**, as every other developed economy in the world has long ago discovered.

MANAGEMENT AND LAW ISSUES

1. Is health care a right and not a privilege?
2. Should health care be treated the same as every other service industry (such as restaurants, hotels, and dry cleaning); that is, those who can pay for it may have it?

The Patient Bill of Rights

The Patient Bill of Rights does not address the issue of how to find a way to provide affordable health care coverage to all uninsured Americans, nor does it address Medicare reform. While patient rights are attractive, this issue was really a red herring to avoid dealing with the more serious problems of the rapidly rising use of medical technologies and Medicare (Chandra et al., 2013). The problem of patient rights was attractive to both sides of the political aisle, largely because it affects the middle class.

As illustrated in **FEATURE BOX 7-1**, the standards for patient rights and responsibilities were debated for more than a decade before the Patient Bill of Rights was enacted into law (IOM, 2003). Congressional debate, as well as state legislative and judicial action on the issue of patient rights, had already occurred (Wiley, 2016). Proposals over the issue of patient rights were much like the legislation describing health insurance coverage; consequently, the Patient Bill of Rights is complex, confusing, technical, and legalistic. While it was necessary to give patients a degree of leverage over the health insurance industry, the benefits to be derived from giving patients the right to sue were never resolved (Vukadin, 2014).

FEATURE BOX 7-1

The Standards for Patient Rights and Responsibilities

The **National Academy of Medicine** recommended that the health care industry redesign health care processes in accordance with the following standards (IOM, 2013):

- *Care based on continuous care relationships*: Patients should receive health care as needed and in many forms, not just face-to-face visits, but care provided over the Internet, by telephone, by remote monitoring, and by other technological means. This standard implies health care systems should be responsive at all times.
- *Continuous decrease in waste*: Health care systems should not waste resources or patient time.
- *Cooperation among providers*: Health care providers should actively collaborate and communicate to ensure appropriate exchanges of health information and coordination of care.
- *Customization based on patient needs and values*: Health care systems should be designed to meet the most common types of medical needs, but have the capability to respond to individual patient choices and preferences.
- *Evidence-based practice*: Patients should receive health care based on the best available scientific knowledge. Medical treatments should not significantly vary from one provider to another or from one geographic location to another.
- *Patients as the source of control*: Patients should be given the necessary information and opportunity to exercise a chosen degree of control over health care decisions affecting them and their families. Health care systems should be able to accommodate differences in patient preferences and encourage shared decision-making.
- *Preventive care*: Health care systems should anticipate the health needs of patients, as opposed to simply reacting to medical events.
- *Safety*: Patients should be safe from injury caused by health care systems. Reducing risk and ensuring safety requires greater attention to health care processes that help prevent and mitigate medical errors.
- *Shared knowledge and the free flow of health information*: Patients should have open access to their own medical data and to clinical knowledge. Medical providers and patients should communicate effectively and share information.
- *Transparency*: Health care systems should make health information available to patients and their families to allow for making informed decisions when selecting health insurance plans, hospitals, or physicians, or when choosing among alternative medical treatments. This should include information describing the performance of health care systems on safety, evidence-based practice, and patient satisfaction.

Note: The Institute of Medicine, operating under an 1863 Congressional charter, was renamed the National Academy of Medicine in 2016.

IOM, 2003; *See* Hermer & Lenihan, 2014; Hoffman, 2011; McDonough, 2015.

While patients are overlooked and sometimes even harmed by insurers, physicians, and many others in the health care system, it is not necessarily knowingly. No one purposely wants to do harm to another. But in the course of events, patients do end up hurt (Huberfeld et al., 2013). For instance, cost-shifting hurt not only patients but health care systems. When excessive costs are shifted to patients, many costs go unpaid. For some hospitals, this translated into a drop in funding; for others, it translated into overly aggressive collection actions against patients. For patients who could pay their medical bills by credit cards, it often began a cycle of debt that ended in personal bankruptcy.

Therefore, while the public backlash against the **Affordable Care Act of 2010** may sometimes be justified; the reforms are not as bad as spurious anecdotal stories would indicate (Baker, 2011). Current public debate is characterized less by careful analysis than by unfounded claims and harsh rhetoric (Kevelson, 2012). For instance, the health insurance subsidies may well be one of the most misunderstood parts of the Affordable Care Act (Lovendale, 2014). Attacks on this idea are ruthless, but the subsidies are progressive and provide an incentive for the uninsured to purchase health insurance, a feature that should endear opponents to the proposal.

Patient Bill of Rights

The Patient Bill of Rights sets forth consumer protections patients are entitled to, as illustrated in **FEATURE BOX 7-2**. The Patient Bill of Rights does not address how to find a way to provide health insurance coverage to everyone who needs life-sustaining, advanced care nor does it address Medicare reform. The level of financial obligation required to obtain access to the latest medical technologies and drugs remains an unresolved issue in reform of the U.S. health care system.

Right to Access Essential Health Insurance

The right to access affordable insurance for essential health care is confusing and immersed in exceptions. While health care coverage may exceed what is currently covered as deemed medically necessary by different insurers, limitations

---

FEATURE BOX 7-2

Patient Bill of Rights

- Allows young adults under 26 to stay on a parent's family health insurance policy or be added to it
- Bans insurers from imposing pre-existing condition exclusions
- Enables women to see an OB-GYN without a referral
- Ensures patients can choose the primary care physician or pediatrician they want from their plan's provider network
- Guarantees renewability of health insurance regardless of health status
- Limits rating variation of health insurance based only on age, geographic area, family composition, or tobacco use
- Mandates access to affordable essential health insurance
- Presumes eligibility for Medicaid insurance
- Prevents insurers from requiring prior approvals before seeking emergency care at a hospital outside a plan's provider network
- Prohibits insurers from rescinding or taking away health insurance coverage based on technicalities and unintentional mistakes on an application
- Provides for access to essential health care
- Requires insurers to spend 80 to 85% of their premium dollars on health care
- Restricts the use of annual caps on health care coverage
- Stops insurers from setting lifetime limits on health care coverage
- Warrants health care coverage for individuals participating in clinical trials

Modified from: 45 C.F.R. §§144, 146-147.

FEATURE BOX 7-3

Right to Essential Health Insurance

- Accepted genetic testing
- Conventional medical devices
- Customary tissue and organ repair and replacement
- Established pharmaceuticals
- General surgical procedures
- Predictive tests, such as cholesterol tests
- Traditional diagnostics, including diagnostic imaging (computed or positron emission tomography scans or magnetic resonance imaging)
- Traditional therapies

Dartmouth Institute for Health Policy and Clinical Practice, 2012; Satz, 2013.

are crucial to defining health insurance. By definition, essential health insurance does not extend health care coverage to long-term **critical care** or extensive hospitalizations for acute care (Satz, 2013). Although the right to health insurance is necessarily interpreted relative to traditional diagnostics and short-term acute care of serious disease or trauma (generally less than 25 days of inpatient care), as illustrated in **FEATURE BOX 7-3**, future health care coverage will most likely be driven by prevention.

Prior to health care reform, the focus of health insurance was acute care. Medicaid insurance provided health care coverage for only a narrow set of primary care services, while Medicare expressly excluded preventive services (Dartmouth, 2016). New and emerging predictive technologies that further prevention by enhancing diagnostic and screening options were generally not covered by government health insurance (Satz, 2013). Patients were unwittingly overlooked and sometimes even harmed by this policy, as well as by physicians and others in the current health care system that often focused on limited as opposed to long-term treatment. No one purposely wanted to do harm to others, but in the course of events, patients did end up hurt because they did not receive all the treatment that was clinically effective and needed (Huberfeld et al., 2013).

Right to Emergency Care

Hospitals must provide for a **medical screening** within the capability of the hospital's emergency department to determine whether an emergency health condition exists (*See* 42 U.S.C.A. § 1395dd(a)). Moreover, a patient can obtain care at an emergency room even if the hospital is not affiliated with the patient's insurer. Insurers have recently implemented policies whereby they will not deny payment for a visit to the emergency room, even when it is determined no medical emergency exists.

At the same time, these patient rights are of no consequence for people without access to emergency care at all. A third of the urban acute-care hospitals, which serve higher shares of poor and financially distressed populations, have shut their emergency departments or closed altogether since 1990 (Hsia et al., 2011). One side of the debate about patient rights to emergency care asserts that this is an expression of a healthy marketplace (Schumpeter, 2014/1942). The other side dismisses this assertion, since a large number of people without health insurance or with government insurance could not support the full costs of these hospitals. The result of this loss is that populations served by the closed emergency departments can no longer obtain immediate medical assistance.

No reforms have emerged to replace the bankrupt health care systems that faced economic destruction. The question of whether this loss is defensible when it makes emergency care less accessible, both by increasing the distance that must be traveled or by increasing loads and wait times at accessible hospitals, remains unanswered. One thing is certain: **safety net hospitals** that serve poor and financially distressed patients and that deliver a significant level of uncompensated care to the uninsured require particular attention if emergency care access is to be sustained.

Regrettably, the lack of access to primary care drives up emergency room visits (Frakt, 2011). Nevertheless, the nation has an ethical obligation to ensure that access to emergency trauma care is equitably distributed in the United States when hospital facilities are not always available to patients needing urgent medical treatments, such as for heart attacks (*See generally* Hsia et al., 2011).

Right to Off-Label Access of Prescription Drugs

Patients have the **common law** right to control their medical treatment (*See Union Pacific Railway Company v. Botsford*, 141 U.S. 250 (U.S. Supreme Court 1891)). Terminally ill patients, especially those with cancer, regularly choose to be treated with **off-label** or unapproved treatments. For instance, cancer drugs are ordinarily approved for very narrowly defined diseases; the more narrow the disease population for approved use, the easier it is to obtain approval from the federal Food and Drug Administration (FDA). The wider the defined disease for approved use, the more likely side effects will appear to obstruct regulatory approval. While the FDA generally approves such drugs for specific types of cancer and particular clinical indications; physicians frequently prescribe cancer drugs for off-label uses outside of the narrowly defined indications (Kesselheim, 2011).

This right to off-label access of cancer drugs is based on the doctrine of **informed consent**, under which patients can choose off-label treatments if given sufficient information to understand the consequences, risks and benefits, and alternatives to such treatments (NIH, 2016). The information provided must not only enable patients to make an evaluation of the nature of their chosen treatment and of any substantial risks, but alternative options must be clearly understood by patients, including the option to do nothing. One aspect of this off-label access controversy was recently considered by the U.S. Supreme Court in *Sorrell*.

COURT DECISION
Right to Off-Label Access of Prescription Drugs

Sorrell v. IMS Health Inc.
[Attorney General of Vermont v. Data Miner]
564 U.S. 552 (U.S. Supreme Court 2011)

Facts: The FDA requires pharmacies to record patient prescription data, including the identity of prescribers. This patient-prescriber data is then sold to third parties who use the data to produce prescribing reports that are sold to the pharmaceutical industry for use in their marketing. Pharmaceutical sales representatives, in turn, use the data in the prescribing reports to tailor their face-to-face conversations with individual prescribers, known in the industry as **detailing**.

In 2007, the Vermont State legislature enacted its Prescription Confidentiality Law to address the use of prescriber-identifying data to enhance prescriber detailing. Vermont was concerned that industry sales tactics were influencing prescribers to prescribe newer brand-name drugs over generics. Vermont was also concerned that industry sales tactics were contributing to rising costs for Medicaid insurance. Vermont additionally expressed concern about the protection of patient privacy. The Vermont law mandating the collection of prescriber data provided state funding for counter-detailing to educate physicians on the uses of generics.

The Vermont law only limited pharmaceutical marketing and applied only to pharmacies and the health insurance industry. The law was designed to impact pharmaceutical sales representatives whose speech conflicted with the goals of the government in reducing health care costs. Vermont prohibited the sale of **prescriber-identifying data** and the use of that information for industry marketing. In so doing, Vermont sought to foster more neutral and scientific detailing discussions centered on the safety, effectiveness, and costs of drugs. IMS Health,[1] the medical products industry's leading data miner, challenged the Vermont law as an affront to free speech under the First Amendment.

---

[1]IMS Health is a former employer of Hammaker, co-author of this text.

Issue: Should the government be able to limit the use of patient-prescriber data that was gathered in accordance with state regulations, if this data was subsequently used by the pharmaceutical industry in a way that failed to serve the government's interests in controlling health care costs?

Holding and Decision: No. The Vermont law was a violation of the First Amendment. Although the government may place incidental burdens on **commercial speech**, for instance to protect patient privacy and control costs, the Vermont law was more than a mere incidental burden and thus was subject to strict scrutiny, which the law did not survive.

Analysis: The Court held that the Vermont law contained both content and speaker-based restrictions that were designed to restrict the effectiveness of marketing tactics by the pharmaceutical industry. Indeed, the legislative findings acknowledged that the law's express purpose was to lessen the effectiveness with which the pharmaceutical industry could market their brand-name drugs. The Court saw Vermont's opposition to the industry's targeted marketing as nothing less than viewpoint discrimination aimed at suppressing the industry's commercial messages in favor of Vermont's message of cost effectiveness.

By restricting the use of the patient-prescriber identifying data, Vermont tried to indirectly influence the pharmaceutical industry's promotion of more expensive brand-name drugs over less expensive generics. The effect of detailing on physician prescribing, however, cannot justify restrictions on commercial speech. The fear that patients might make bad decisions if given data about using brand-name drugs as opposed to generics cannot justify **content-based burdens** on speech. First Amendment jurisprudence is especially skeptical of regulations that appear to keep patients in the dark for what the government perceives to be their own good, such as using less expensive generics. Persuasive information alone does not permit the government to quiet the speech or to burden its messengers.

The Court concluded that the debate over detailing and the prescribing of brand-name drugs must be settled by free and uninhibited speech, not by restricting the pharmaceutical industry's ability to promote its pro-brand messages. Accordingly, the Vermont law was struck-down. The Court was not persuaded by Vermont's cost justifications for the law.

Rule of Law: Although the First Amendment right to free speech restricts the government's ability to limit the use of patient-prescriber data, commercial speech may be restricted to protect patient privacy and serve a state's interest of reducing health care costs.

References discussing this court decision: Baron, 2012; Bhagwat, 2012; Blackman, 2014; Blitz, 2014; Brandon, 2012; Dhooge, 2014; Gooch et al., 2013; Hethcoat, 2012; Jacobs, 2014; Janssen, 2014; Joseph et al., 2012; Mermin & Graff, 2013; Pasquale & Ragone, 2014; Schindler & Brame, 2013; Shinar, 2013; Spacapan & Hutchison, 2013; Spears, 2015; Swartz, 2015 and 2012; Thomson, 2013; Wolf, 2013; Young, 2012.

Right to Experimental Medical Treatments

Off-label use of approved drugs raises the related issue of whether the doctrine of informed consent should be extended to allow terminally ill patients to choose experimental drugs that have passed limited safety trials but have not been proven effective by the FDA. Is there a significant distinction between permitting patients to choose to end medical treatment, even if doing so would result in death, and permitting terminally ill patients to choose to have access to potentially lifesaving drugs that have not been approved for efficacy by the FDA (Brandes, 2012)? *See Cruzan v. Director, Missouri Department of Health*, 497 U.S. 261 (U.S. Supreme Court 1990).

The FDA can grant accelerated drug approval based on limited but promising clinical data. Proponents of access maintain the FDA should use fast-track regulations to give terminally ill patients the right to choose lifesaving treatments while more lengthy definitive trials are undertaken (von Eschenbach, 2010). The pharmaceutical industry, however, is concerned about accelerated deaths or harm to patients beyond the harm from their disease or illness, given the ongoing uncertainties on the right to sue for deaths or injuries caused by experimental drugs (Conroy, 2010). Currently, many lawsuits against the pharmaceutical industry are based on state consumer safety regulations that are stronger than federal FDA standards (Lindenfeld & Tran, 2016). Although the U.S. Supreme Court recently ruled in favor of preemption in a medical device case involving Medtronic, Congress may have other ideas to undo preemption and guarantee the right to sue in drug cases (*See Riegel v. Medtronic, Inc.*, 552 U.S. 312 (U.S. Supreme Court 2008)).

COURT DECISION
Right to Access Lifesaving Experimental Drugs

Abigail Alliance v. Von Eschenbach
[Patients v. FDA]
495 F.3d 695 (U.S. Court of Appeals for the District of Columbia Circuit 2007),
cert. denied, 552 U.S. 1159 (U.S. Supreme Court 2008)

Facts: The Abigail Alliance for Better Access to Developmental Drugs, an advocacy group dedicated to terminally ill patients, appeared to have won a victory when a trial court ruled that terminally ill, mentally competent adult patients had a legal right to access experimental drugs that have been deemed safe enough for human testing in Phase I clinical trials but have not reached Phase II to evaluate both the effectiveness of the brand-name drug for a particular indication and its short-term side effects. Victory was short lived, however. The decision was reversed on appeal, marking a setback in the drive for removal of the regulatory barriers that prevent terminally ill patients from gaining early access to early stage experimental drugs.

The reversal represented the latest act in a drama that began when Abigail Burroughs, a 21-year-old college student, ran out of conventional treatment options in her battle against head and neck cancer at Johns Hopkins Hospital. The Alliance filed a citizen petition with the FDA for access to Cetuximab (Erbitus), an experimental drug only available to patients participating in clinical trials for colon cancer. The Alliance's petition proposed adding an early approval regimen that would allow terminally ill patients to gain earlier access to experimental drugs. The FDA failed to respond to the proposal, thus prompting the Alliance to proceed to this judicial challenge. While Cetuximab was approved as a treatment for head and neck cancer shortly after Abigail Burroughs died, this case was not resolved until seven years after her death when the U.S. Supreme Court declined to hear the appeal.

Issue: Do terminally ill patients have a right to access to potentially lifesaving, but also potentially life-threatening, experimental drugs?

Holding and Decision: No. Terminally ill patients do not have a legal right to access experimental drugs.

Analysis: Whether an asserted right constitutes a **fundamental right** and **liberty interest** is extremely important.[LN1] Fundamental rights are **human entitlements** that are deeply rooted in the nation's history and traditions and implicit in the principles of **justice** and liberty, such as the right to **personal autonomy** (or self-determination). If the government wishes to restrict a fundamental right, then the government must prove that it has a **compelling interest** justifying the restriction and that the restriction is narrowly tailored to serve that interest. On the other hand, if the restricted right is not a fundamental right, then the government can justify its intervention by showing instead that there is a **rational basis** for the restriction, an easier standard to meet than the test for restricting fundamental rights.

Since fundamental rights are not explicitly stated in the U.S. Constitution, the U.S. Supreme Court has established a two-pronged test to determine if the asserted right is a fundamental one. This analysis requires proponents of a proposed fundamental right to describe the asserted fundamental liberty interest and show that the asserted right is deeply rooted in the nation's history and tradition, such that neither liberty nor justice would exist if it were sacrificed. The first part of the test is very important: too broad, and a right becomes too comprehensive and impossible to evaluate; too narrow, and a right appears inconsequential.

Rule of Law: The majority opinion described the right of terminally ill patients to access experimental drugs and found no fundamental right to potentially toxic drugs with no proven therapeutic benefit. The dissenting opinion cast the patients' right to experimental drugs in terms of the right of the terminally ill to preserve their lives and found a fundamental right.

References discussing this court decision: Hill, 2012; Janssen, 2014; Mathes, 2012; Pivarnik, 2014.

The issue of access to potentially lifesaving experimental drugs continues to be controversial. The **Abigail Alliance for Better Access to Developmental Drugs** continues to seek expanded access to drugs for terminally ill patients. A bill for expanded access has been in the Committee on Health, Education, Labor, and Pensions for more than a decade. If Congress were to permit terminally ill patients to access experimental drugs, then the FDA would have to create a system to allow that access.[LN2]

Right to Accountability by Health Insurers

One of the most contentious issues in health care deals with when and where patients can take legal action if they feel an insurer wrongly denies them health care coverage and, as a result, causes them harm (Wharton, 2008; *See* Noonan & Boraske, 2015). One side of this debate maintains Congress should make certain insurers are held accountable when they deny treatments recommended by physicians. The other side argues increased liability on insurers will lead to increased costs, which will make health insurance even more costly, which is counter to congressional intent when the **Employee Retirement Income Security Act of 1974 (ERISA)** was adopted in the first place (*See* 29 U.S.C.A.18 §§ 1001 *et seq.*).

The federal courts have constructed substantial barriers to a state's ability to bring ERISA suits on behalf of its citizens (Muir & Stein, 2015). ERISA is viewed primarily as a federal concern outside the parameters of state interference. With a broad preemptive scope to occupy the entire field of regulation of employer-sponsored health plans, ERISA can exclude state laws and regulation.

Patients have simply not found a constructive way to deal with tensions existing in the coverage of medical services by insurers. A mechanism is needed to allow for appropriate cost containment in health care decision-making and increased accountability of the people in charge of that cost containment. There is heated debate about the appropriate way to find a compromise (Wharton, 2008). However, almost everyone agrees (except perhaps trial attorneys) that it is a shame anyone thinks lawsuits are the way to do it.

Alternative Dispute Resolution

There is a strong government preference toward some type of alternative system to resolve health care disputes because of the belief it would be more efficient than litigation, less costly, and a better process for patients suffering some type of harm (*See* U.S. Arbitration Act of 1925, 9 U.S.C.A. §§ 1–15). The U.S. Supreme Court's expansive interpretation of arbitration has further fueled the widespread use of **alternative dispute resolutions** in medical settings and fostered the belief that malpractice law is not the best way to provide incentives for high-quality health care. *See Moses H. Cone Memorial Hospital v. Mercury Construction Corp.*, 460 U.S. 1, 24 (U.S. Supreme Court 1983) (upholding the enforceability of arbitration clauses in contracts). Most Americans find it hard to believe there is not some method superior to litigation for resolving disputes between patients and health providers (Belton & Galle, 2014).

Reasonableness of Arbitration Clauses

Critics of alternative dispute resolution often say that when patients forgo their right to sue, the health care industry strips them of a valuable right at a time when they might be at their most vulnerable (Aragaki, 2011). On this basis of unreasonableness, patients party to health care contracts generally make one of five arguments when attacking **arbitration clauses**:

- Arbitration clauses are non-mutual because they are binding to patients not health care providers
- Arbitration clauses are unreasonable because they reduce patient rights

---

MANAGEMENT AND LAW ISSUES

3. What is the distinction, if any, between requiring informed consent of patients who participate in clinical testing of experimental drugs for FDA approval and requiring informed consent for distribution of potentially lifesaving drugs to terminally ill patients outside the clinical testing context?

- Arbitration is too costly for patients to participate
- Lack of independent or neutral arbitrators
- Patients were coerced to sign arbitration agreements because there was no meaningful choice in obtaining needed medical services

(Bennett, 2014; Mullenix, 2015).

Patients' rights to sue insurers often kicks in only after patients go through administrative review processes established by their insurers. The review processes are designed to provide a way to settle complaints in lieu of litigation. Patients who are able to demonstrate they were irreparably harmed by an insurer's refusal to pay for treatment must nonetheless often wait a period of time before filing a lawsuit. During that time, a panel of independent experts often reviews the case, and the panel's findings are admissible in the court where the lawsuit is being heard (Wharton, 2008).

To better uphold patient agreements to use alternative dispute resolution, the American Bar Association recommends that health care providers:

- Draft terms in the arbitration agreement clearly and unequivocally
- Educate patients about their right to sue insurers
- Encourage patients to ask questions regarding their right to sue
- Make arbitration agreements in insurance contracts optional, revocable, and mutual
- Prevent patients from bearing a large financial burden to arbitrate their claims

(Aragaki, 2014 and 2011; Schleppenbach, 2014).

Potential Conflicts of Interest

Beyond the right to sue insurers is the issue of what constitutes a reasonable mechanism for ascertaining damages (Davis et al., 2011). The U.S. Supreme Court addressed this issue when it examined how conflicts should be taken into account on judicial review of discretionary benefit determinations when administrators of insurers and self-insured health insurance plans both determine and pay patient claims. *See Metropolitan Life Insurance Co. v. Glenn*, 554 U.S. 105 (U.S. Supreme Court 2008). Federal courts reviewing claim denials should take into account the conflicts of interest ERISA plan administrators face when they pay claims out of their own pockets while standing to profit by denying claims (Kolodin, 2015). The question is whether there is a conflict of interest when the same party administering a health insurance plan and paying claims out of its own pocket also stands to profit by denying patient claims.

Malpractice Reform

Legislative alterations to common law doctrines, otherwise known as malpractice reform, have been an intense political issue for at least 30 years. In particular, malpractice law has held a central place on many state legislative agendas with dozens of reforms enacted, struck down, and reenacted over the years. At the national level, legislation to federalize malpractice law, currently governed by state common law, has been debated in Congress (Chang et al., 2015).

The Center for Public Integrity's *Lobby Watch* reports most interest groups agree lawsuits against insurers are acceptable, provided there are safeguards in place to prevent frivolous suits. While proponents of malpractice reform often exaggerate the dangers posed by such lawsuits, the judicial system already has the ability to throw out such cases before they go to trial. Malpractice reformers also often exaggerate the extent to which juries award unwarranted damages that can financially harm insurers. The federal government has found evidence demonstrating that the rhetoric on malpractice reform is intentionally skewed by the American Medical Association (GAO, 2003; Teninbaum & Zimmermann, 2013). When jury awards are excessive they can be, and commonly are, pared back by trial judges or appeals courts (*See* Kerr, 2010).

Limitations on Damages

Limitations on damages are the only malpractice reform that continues to surface as effective (Eisenberg & Engel, 2014). While limitations on noneconomic and punitive damages that could be awarded to patients may be acceptable, there is no simple prescription as to what those limitations should be (Hines & Hines, 2015). Nor is there agreement on whether patient lawsuits should be allowed in state courts as well as federal courts. Should defense costs be recoverable when patient lawsuits are determined frivolous? How high a standard should be set for determining whether patient lawsuits are frivolous? Should there be limitations on **joint and several liability**? Should the collateral source rule be limited?

In federal courts, there are generally no limits on damage awards for lost wages or pain and suffering, but punitive damages are often limited to around $5 million (Sanders, 2013). In state courts, by contrast, patients are generally allowed to file suits if denied health care coverage based on a medical judgment. In state courts, there are no limits on awards for lost wages, pain and suffering, or punitive damages, unless state law imposes limits (Pfander & Dwinell, 2016). Both sides of the malpractice reform movement debate the merits of paying damage awards in installments (O'Gorman, 2014).

Federal Preemption of Malpractice Law

Today, with more decisions in courtrooms made by juries than by judges, more class-action lawsuits, and contingency fees for trial attorneys, policy choices made about the legal system have ramifications in the U.S. health care system (MacMahon, 2013). There is a national reform movement afoot for Congress to take a leadership position and begin addressing malpractice reform. By concluding malpractice is a significant federal issue, perhaps because of its impact on interstate commerce, Congress could enact a law shifting claims to federal courts (*See* O'Malley, 2015).

Once malpractice cases are in the federal system, the national reform effort could then take additional measures. For instance, the federal system could shift malpractice cases within the federal system for consolidated handling by specialized medical courts under the Judicial Panel on Multidistrict Litigation (*See* 28 U.S.C.A. § 1407). Specialized courts may be more knowledgeable about medical treatments and monitoring of conditions, diseases, and disorders (Clark, 2014).

Federal malpractice reform could serve the role of forcing state courts and legislatures to identify more clearly the substantive objectives of malpractice law (Cook, 2013). After all, since the federal government purchases a significant portion of the nation's medical services, it is in a position to make greater use of its spending power to leverage modifications in state laws that would otherwise be politically unfeasible to implement at the state level. Most important, the cost of malpractice has driven OB/GYN specialists and neurosurgeons out of certain geographic areas (Jena et al., 2015), and medical devices are pricier in the United States than anywhere else, all a result of the current U.S. malpractice system (Calabresi, 2016). An issue of critical national importance is malpractice reform, not adequately addressed since the modern state malpractice reform movement began with California's Medical Injury Compensation Reform Act (Liang, 2015).

Right to Sue Employers

Employees cannot sue their employers, unless the employer played a direct role in deciding whether the employee would receive health care. Generally, the courts favor allowing employees the right to sue employers involved in decisions about health care coverage (Kesselheim & Brennan, 2013). If an employed physician of the employer played a significant role in making treatment decisions with regard to an employee, that employer will probably be sued, but employers are only sued if employees are actually harmed (*See Aetna Health Inc. v. Davila*, 542 U.S. 200 (U.S. Supreme Court 2004)).

The most controversial part of malpractice reform is expanding employees' right to sue employers (Kachalia & Mello, 2011). Businesses providing health insurance coverage to their employees are alarmed because they see a scenario in which they are sued, along with physicians and hospitals, when their employees are harmed as patients (Kesselheim & Brennan, 2013). In general, employees have **rights through disclosure** (or acquisition of information) rather than by regulation. Disclosure rights and notice requirements are similar. For instance, if an employer tells its employees they cannot sue them for administration of their health insurance, then employees can make a decision about whether they want to accept the employer's health insurance coverage. In *Davila*, the U.S. Supreme Court volleyed back to Congress the question of whether ERISA beneficiaries should have any remedy for damages caused by decisions about health care coverage. Ironically, the same law that was created to better inform employees of their benefit rights through disclosure has often shielded employers from inequitable results.

COURT DECISION

New Protections for Prospective Retirees with Employer-Provided Health Insurance

Cigna Corp. v. Amara
[Employees v. Health Services Employer]
563 U.S. 421 (U.S. Supreme Court 2011)

Facts: When Cigna Corp. amended its $3.2 billion retirement plan, employees' existing retirement benefits were converted to a hypothetical lump sum, making this their new opening account balance, which would grow by a percentage of their pay each year. Cigna advised employees in handouts and meetings that the amended plan was an overall improvement in their retirement benefits. But Cigna failed to disclose that the opening balances of about 25,000 long-tenured employees were not worth 100% of their old retirement plans, but instead, were now worth as little as half. This meant employee retirement benefits would not increase until the payroll credits in the amended plan built their old retirement savings back to their original value, which could take years (if it ever reached the original value).

Janice Amara, an attorney in Cigna's compliance department, had earned a retirement pension worth $1,833 per month at age 55. But the amended plan produced a pension of about $900 per month. Cigna created underwater opening balances called **wear-aways**, so-called because it was as if Cigna told employees their prior retirement plans had been overpaid, so they would have to work off their debt, or wear it away, before they received new compensation.

The Pension Protection Act banned this widespread wear-away practice in 2006. The lower courts concluded that Cigna had deliberately provided misleading information to employees. Cigna's successful efforts to conceal the pension freeze deprived the employees of the opportunity to take timely action, such as protesting at the time of the change or leaving Cigna for another employer with a more favorable retirement plan.

Issue: By analogy, should employers be required to provide employees the health benefits they were led to believe they had in the same manner as they are required to do for pension and retirement plans?

Holding and Decision: Yes. When employers provide misleading summary information to their employees, employers are required to provide all employees the benefits the employer led them to believe they had.

Analysis: When there is a conflict between summary plan documents given to employees and the plan's formal documents which employees rarely see, employees cannot sue to enforce the terms of the summary as the Cigna employees had done. While courts cannot award benefits that are not in a retirement pension plan when employers breach their fiduciary duty to their employees, courts can order plans to be amended to conform to the terms in the summary plan documents given to employees. This is a significant change in the law since courts had heretofore refused to restore retirement benefits lost as a result of violations of disclosure rules and fiduciary duties.

Before this U.S. Supreme Court decision restored employee protections, remedies had been severely curtailed for nearly two decades beginning in 1993. Three earlier U.S. Supreme Court decisions harshly reduced the remedies available to current and near-term prospective retirees with employer-provided retirement plans who had their benefits curtailed or eliminated outright (*Sereboff v. Mid Atlantic Medical Services, Inc.*, 547 U.S. 356 (U.S. Supreme Court 2006); *Great-West Life & Annuity Ins. Co. v. Knudson*, 534 U.S. 204 (U.S. Supreme Court 2002); *Mertens v. Hewitt Associates*, 508 U.S. 248 (U.S. Supreme Court 1993)). Heretofore, employers faced no consequences for behaving unlawfully or deceitfully, even when their actions resulted in catastrophic financial losses to their employees.

Rule of Law: If employers breach their fiduciary duty by providing misleading information to their employees about their retirement benefits, employers may be required to amend the terms of their benefit plans to conform to the terms in the plan summary as opposed to the less generous benefits described by formal plan documents.

References discussing this court decision: Brunce, 2015; Lewis, 2014; Valenza, 2011.

The Affordable Care Act defines the scope of the **social contract** between individuals and their health insurance plans and expands patient rights and protections. Health insurance now has a role in ensuring the safety net for

Americans. Federal courts seem to agree that health insurance plans must now join pension and retirement plans in protecting the health benefits of their insured (Lewis, 2014). The time has arrived for health insurance to meet the heightened statutory and judicial requirements for protection of the health benefits of the insured just as pension and retirement plans are required to do (Brunce, 2015; Valenza, 2011). The facts of the *Cigna* decision potentially have broad repercussions for employer-provided health insurance (Candeub, 2011).

Rationing and Comparative Effectiveness Analysis

Some commentators distinguish between **rationing**, allocation of resources, and **medical triage** (Syrett, 2007). In this chapter, however, rationing refers to the withholding of scarce resources from specific individuals so the resources will be available for others in the future. The ability of patients to sue helps ensure a level playing field when rationing decisions are made. However, people who think lawsuits are a solution to U.S. health care problems are likely wrong. Lawsuits cannot possibly address the fundamental question at the heart of meaningful health care reform: how much is human life worth (Partnoy, 2012)?

There is a near universal assumption that Americans' desire for health care exceeds their willingness to pay for it or to have others pay for their participation in government health insurance programs. But is this assumption true? There is also a widespread but largely untested perception that Americans are unwilling to accept limits in health care (Mechanic & Alpine, 2010).

Allocation of Scarce Health Resources

The paradox of the U.S. health care system is that total health care spending generates benefits far in excess of its total cost while, at the same time, current expenditures are for medical services worth far less than they cost (Danis et al., 2015). This contradictory statement obviously leads to questions about how to allocate scarce health resources in the most effective way possible (Posner, 1983/1981). The entire issue of affordable health care, however, has become so complex it does not lend itself to easy analysis. Health insurance plans and employers paying premiums for health care coverage are in a tough position. The public wants to cut costs, which inevitably involves rationing care, but then are outraged at the manner in which care is rationed. At the same time, most insurers have gone to excess in cost containment (Gould, 2013; Wharton, 2008).

To analogize, if a system contains excess fat, and if a scalpel is carefully used, the fat can be trimmed without harming the muscle or the nerves. But some insurers have used a meat cleaver to cut out the fat in health care and have harmed patients as a result. Although cost-containment strategies have been used in managing care, using **comparative effectiveness** to prioritize decisions about health care coverage has not been among them (Donnelly, 2010). While comparative effectiveness analysis has the potential to consider a broad range of medical services to determine which medical interventions are most effective for which patients and under what circumstances, it has met with criticism (*See* Davis et al., 2011). Critics disapprove the meat cleaver's potential to restrict access to health care by using criteria that discriminates against age and poor health status (Satz, 2013). This disapproval, however, fails to understand that comparative effectiveness is a **benchmark strategy** to carefully guide decision-making on **health-related well-being**. Comparative effectiveness is used in determining whether the medical needs of individual patients will receive health care coverage as opposed to deciding whether coverage will be provided for treatment of specific diseases. Critics often confuse this approach to management of individual insured patients with health decisions on **general well-being** and the population-based factors that are prioritized in this broader analysis of whether to provide health care coverage. General well-being analysis manages the health risks of insured patient populations to minimize their risks of disease or injury as opposed to deciding whether health care coverage will be provided to insured individuals, a distinction that is often confused.

Quality of Life Research

Quality of life research at the University of Pennsylvania offers guidance to engage in shaping some of the broadest resource allocation questions facing the U.S. health care system (Lee et al., 2009a and 2009b). Based on Medicare kidney dialysis data, analysis shows that on average, $129,000 is spent on each dialysis patient per year. This research used data from the U.S. Renal Data System on outcomes and costs from more than 500,000 patients initiating dialysis as well as from almost 160,000 patients who received a transplant. More important, this research put a value on the comparative effectiveness of dialysis as compared to transplant treatment across the entire end-stage renal disease population in an attempt to develop a benchmark for decisions about health care coverage.[LN3]

Quality-Adjusted Life Year in End-Stage Renal Disease Patients

Dialysis for patients suffering end-stage renal disease is the one service Medicare provides for anyone, regardless of age. The program has been in effect since the 1970s. Health care economists have long considered it a fair substitute for universal health care coverage and the value society places on a year of life as measured by self-reported health and functioning (Muennig & Bounthavong, 2016; Wharton, 2008).

Before the University of Pennsylvania research, the number most commonly used to place a value on a year of quality life was $50,000 (Braithwaite et al., 2008). A Canadian study used an accounting ledger for more than 200 patients with end-stage renal disease during a time span of one year (Molzahn et al., 1996). The University of Pennsylvania research brings this older end-stage renal disease study up to date with costs and modern practices. While the gold standard was $50,000, this figure did not reflect the way dialysis is practiced today or the technology currently in use (Neumann et al., 2014). When it comes to health care, placing a value on life often leads to qualified coverage. Using rankings of the quality of life from medical interventions to make decisions about health care coverage is clear and explicit. Without definite rankings, rationing is implicit because Medicare has a finite budget (Syrett, 2007).

Medicare cannot provide health care coverage for everything. In the end, patients with renal disease will not get everything they want. The mechanism for the rationing is performed in the name of what is medically necessary and reasonable. Medicare coverage is based on a clause stating patients must receive treatments that are necessary and reasonable (Wharton, 2008).

The $129,000 figure determined by the University of Pennsylvania research compares to a range of $50,000 to $100,000 used in other countries running national health care systems, such as Australia and England, in guiding their decisions about health care coverage (Neumann et al., 2014). The **World Health Organization** has proposed $109,000 as the value of a disability-adjusted life year, adding that, even though countries adopt spending thresholds in decisions about health care coverage, they do not apply them without exceptions (Chan, 2010). Moreover, human health is just too unpredictable at the individual level for strict rationing of medical services.

Continuing to base coverage decisions on clinical evidence alone without consideration of costs may not be feasible in the long run. Several researchers argue decisions about health care coverage should be based on quality of life criteria. New technologies with quality of life ratios below $50,000 to $100,000 per incremental **quality-adjusted life year** are deemed suitable for health care coverage, while others with higher ratios may be too expensive (Neumann et al., 2014; Wharton, 2008).

The University of Pennsylvania research concerns employers in several ways including employer and employee health benefit payments, insurance coverage, and malpractice cases. Health care costs are rising for employees, but

---

FEATURE BOX 7-4

Quality-Adjusted Life Year

When is it justified for one person to subsidize the demands and wishes of someone else? The relevant questions are:

- At what point does health care coverage produce too little benefit for the costs demanded?
- How do universal health plans determine the right degree of health care coverage?
- How should preventable, detrimental behaviors and conditions affect all of these decisions?
- What is the acceptability of such limits for both physicians and patients?
- What line-drawing problems exist?

Basu & Philipson, 2010.

employers are also paying more. Health insurance is expensive partly because of the degree of health care coverage. The fact is there are many medical procedures with high prices and minimal medical benefits (Muennig & Bounthavong, 2016).

One practical benchmark is based on end-stage renal disease. To the extent end-stage renal disease, given its unique historical status in the United States, offers a reasonable point of reference for making decisions about health care coverage, the University of Pennsylvania research can be used to guide those decisions. Although the $129,000 figure is substantially higher than the figure of $50,000, using the former as the benchmark does not necessarily mean more funds will be spent (Neumann et al., 2014). What it means is that resources could be allocated using end-stage renal disease as the reference point to define what is comparatively effective and what is not. In the same way, if applied to a case where malpractice cost a patient 10 years of quality-adjusted life years, a figure of $1.29 million could be used as a rough start for settlement negotiations.

Lifestyle Choices in Quality-of-Life Decisions

Quality of life is directly related to leading a responsible lifestyle (Ford et al., 2013). To the extent increased costs attributable to preventable behaviors and conditions are deducted from the $129,000 benchmark figure, increased costs would be borne by those who create the risk of the increased costs rather than by those who do not pose the same economic risk. Research has not addressed how the $129,000 figure would change if costs incumbent in the lifestyles choices of patients were factored into the benchmark, while at the same time relieving patients from bearing costs not attributable to their own behavior. In short, the question is how future research can help make people more accountable for their behavior with health insurance coverage consequences (Posner, 1983/1981).

Prospective Guidance for Allocation Decisions

The quality of life research provides guidance for making allocation decisions. These decisions are hard because they involve social values where there is no clear right or wrong. Given the opportunity to weigh in on normative concerns that surround comparative effectiveness analysis, members of the public are appropriate parties to engage in shaping the broadest resource allocation questions. Public debate should continue on medical value and the difficulties involved.

Determinations of Medical Necessity

The phrase **medical necessity** has been the benchmark by which decisions about health care coverage are made affecting the medical treatment of patients. However, without incorporating the benefit derived from specific medical treatments, it is impossible to know what is medically necessary or reasonable. Moreover, this phrase is highly subjective because the decisions are not based on objective notions of what constitutes a medical benefit (Wharton, 2008).

Regulation intended to improve the flow of health information to patients is unequivocally desirable based on either equity or efficiency grounds (Ho, 2015). Patients need to be able to compare their treatment options with the treatment of others when deciding which health providers achieve the best outcomes. Patients also need health information in determining what is reasonable for insurance coverage.[LN4]

MANAGEMENT AND LAW ISSUES

4. Should patient behavior be taken into account in determining whether a patient is eligible for health insurance? For instance, should a patient who took no steps to stop smoking, in spite of a physician's recommendations, be eligible for private or government health insurance funding of respiratory disease or lung cancer that is directly attributable to their smoking habit?

5. Similarly, should patients who fail to monitor their health with regular routine checkups be compelled to pay higher insurance premiums for their health insurance plans?

Access to Health Information

Health care could be rationed if information measuring the relative quality of providers was collected (Aaron, 2008). If health care is to be rationed, the health insurance industry, in partnership with health providers, needs to produce meaningful information on cost, outcomes, performance of physicians, and quality of hospitals.

Currently, unbiased, easy-to-understand, comparative information evaluating medical services is lacking. For instance, surgical success rates are almost impossible to find. One noteworthy exception is the New York State Department of Health Cardiac Surgery Reporting System, which collects and tracks clinical data on cardiac surgeries performed in New York hospitals.

COURT DECISION

Constitutional Protection of Information Held by Retail Pharmacies

Beeman v. Anthem Prescription Management, LLC
[Retail Pharmacies v. Pharmacy Benefit Managers]
564 Fed.Appx. 332 (U.S. Court of Appeals for the 9th Circuit 2014),
cert. denied, 135 S.Ct. 476 (U.S. Supreme Court 2014)

Facts: **Pharmacy benefit managers** act as intermediaries between retail pharmacies and insurers. They reimburse pharmacies for claims according to a network-wide rate that is lower than the rate generally paid by uninsured customers. California law requires pharmacy benefit managers to report pharmacy fees for uninsured customers to insurers, so insurers can compare the prices that retail pharmacies charge insured customers. Retail pharmacies brought a class action suit to restrict publication of their charges to uninsured customers.

In response, the pharmacy benefit managers argued that compelled disclosures are unconstitutional under the free speech provisions of the U.S. and California Constitutions. The pharmacy benefit managers claimed that the publication of payment rates was contrary to their financial interests. By forcing the pharmacy benefit managers to highlight their lower payment rates, the law turned the pharmacy benefit managers into unwilling advocates for higher payment rates.

Issue: Are courts required to follow First Amendment restraints against compelled commercial speech established by the U.S. Supreme Court that they consider misplaced?

Holding and Decision: No. A California law requiring pharmacy benefit managers to disclose payment rates to insurers does not violate the First Amendment or the California Constitution.

Analysis: The court held that California law only required the pharmacy benefit managers to report factual information; it did not compel them to endorse the findings. The court further held that compelled speech implicates the First Amendment or the California Constitution only if it affects content by forcing the pharmacy benefit managers to endorse a particular viewpoint or by burdening a message they would otherwise make. The pharmacy benefit managers could both comply with the law and discourage increasing payments to retail pharmacies. Therefore, the law did not violate the First Amendment or the California Constitution because it did not restrict the pharmacy benefit managers' ability to independently comment on payment rates.

The U.S. Supreme Court's First Amendment decision in *Sorrell v. IMS Health Inc.*, 564 U.S. 552 (U.S. Supreme Court 2011) is in tension with this California decision. *Sorrell* struck down a Vermont law that restricted the disclosure of factual information similar to the speech compelled by California law. The factual information that was restricted in *Sorrell* was prescriber-identifying information that retail pharmacies receive when they process prescriptions. Pharmacies would sell this information to **data miners** who would use this data to produce reports on prescriber behavior and lease these reports to the pharmaceutical industry. Subsequently, the pharmaceutical industry would rely on prescriber behavior data to market products directly to targeted physicians. The U.S. Supreme Court noted that the First Amendment protects factual information, devoid of advocacy, political relevance, or artistic expression because even factual information conveys messages.

The California court departed from the U.S. Supreme Court's stance in *Sorrell*, claiming that compelled factual speech is different from the prohibition of such speech. The pharmacy benefit managers retained the ability to comment on the compelled speech, distinguishing this case from *Sorrell*, which restricted speech. In this case, the pharmacy benefit managers could still encourage action or inaction or say that the payment rates for uninsured customers were worthless.

Nevertheless, if the U.S. Supreme Court believes that factual information is the beginning point for speech and implicitly contains a message, then the forced publication of this information implicates the First Amendment. The distinction drawn by the California court may be without significance if the First Amendment is broadly understood to guarantee individual freedom of speech, both what to say and what not to say. In other words, there is an individual right to speak and the right to refrain from speaking. Neither Congress nor state governments may collectivize this aspect of society, regardless of what their Constitutions may do elsewhere in regulating economic activities.

Rule of Law: State laws do not implicate the First Amendment or the California Constitution if they compel rather than restrict factual commercial speech.

References discussing this court decision: Boumil, 2012; Post, 2015.

The refusal of the California courts to acknowledge the *Sorrell* decision (that the First Amendment protects factual information) sets the stage for an answer to the question of whether **compelled speech** that is required is different from the restriction of speech. In this instance, the California courts refused to use the **compelled speech doctrine** of the U.S. Supreme Court to invalidate ordinary regulations of the marketplace. The California courts found that constitutional liberty does not encompass a right to be free of constraints in market transactions. They refused to use the *Sorrell* doctrine of compelled commercial speech to strike down mandatory disclosures of pharmacies' pricing by pharmacy benefit managers. The California courts held that since commercial speech reflects market forces that are profit oriented, these market forces prevent commercial speech from being an expression of individual freedom or choice (Post, 2015).

Medicare Database Information

Attempts to access the Medicare database to better understand how health care dollars are being spent met with stiff resistance from the medical establishment and its professional medical associations (*See Consumers' Checkbook v. U.S. Department of Health and Human Services*, 554 F.3d 1046 (U.S. Court of Appeals for the D.C. Circuit 2009), *cert. denied*, 559 U.S. 1067 (U.S. Supreme Court 2010)). Even after the Affordable Care Act provided for restricted access to qualified entities to review the Medicare database (*See* 42 U.S.C.A. §10332), it took years before the data became publically accessible (Cramer, 2015).

The availability of the Medicare database is the beginning of an important patient choice movement that could help contribute to high quality health care and lower costs. Patients can now benefit from a deeper understanding of the risks and benefits of a number of medical treatments provided by different providers. Patients are further empowered to make the best treatment choices, based on consideration of all the relevant factors, including which physicians have the best track records in treating their particular disease or illness. Access to this Medicare health information affects everything from elective procedures for non-serious conditions to complex medical treatment such as open-heart surgery and cancer therapy, since decisions will no longer be made just on the preconceptions of patients' physicians.

Regardless, the Medicare data has a number of limitations. Of particular importance is the fact that the data is not representative of a physician's entire practice as it only includes information on **Medicare fee-for-service** patients. In addition, the data does not indicate the quality of care provided and is not risk-adjusted to account for differences in underlying severity of disease of patient populations (CMS, 2015). Although patients need this information to compare national outcome and cost data in the context of their individual needs and health goals, the data should be supplemented with additional information.

Health Employer Data Information Set

In addition to the information in the Medicare database, health information is vital in the marketplace of consumer-driven health care. In a consumer-driven health care market, patients must estimate how frequently illness will strike and what their needs will be when they do get sick, in addition to estimating how much health care they will be permitted to access each time they need to use their health insurance. Developing uniform sets of performance measures could provide benchmarks and promote the development of standards for quality. Development of the **Health Employer Data Information Set** by the National Committee for Quality Assurance is an important step in this direction (Somers et al., 2011). This data provides a limited but important set of measures of differences in the rates at which patients use key medical services such as pediatric immunization and blood-pressure screening.

Mandated Disclosure of Audited Outcome Data

Driven by patient choice, the federal government could establish an agency that requires the disclosure of audited outcome data from all insurance firms and health providers nationwide (Ball et al., 2012). With access to impartial data comparing health providers, patients could be empowered to make choices based on critical information that has been noticeably lacking in the health care space. For instance, patients could review data on everything from surgeries to treatments for high cholesterol and diabetes, and then determine which physicians and hospitals have the

- Best outcomes
- Least number of complications
- Lowest costs
- Most experience

(Ball et al., 2012; Falit, 2006).

Without government-mandated disclosure requirements, however, it is unclear how health information would ever be sufficiently uniform to produce meaningful results, let alone why the health insurance industry and health providers would ever comply (*See* Lennox & Pittman, 2011).

Universal Coverage and the Right to Access Essential Health Insurance

Most Americans favor a system of universal coverage that provides essential health insurance for every citizen. Just as there is a legal right to emergency care, energy and imagination is being directed to generalizing the right to essential health care (Hill, 2012). One challenge is to define exactly what constitutes this right to access insurance. Much debate is centered on the issue of how the United States should ensure everyone gets the medically necessary care they need. A related debate centers on access to advanced technologies and the most specialized physicians.

Effective Citizenship

Generally, the right to access essential health insurance is based on effective citizenship and **fairness** (ACOG, 2010). Fairness requires that everyone receive the care they medically need and, at the same time, those entrusted with governance of limited health resources must act in a trustworthy and ethical manner. **Equality of opportunity** does not require that every member of society receive the most technologically advanced health care. It compels society to create a system of health care to aid its members in achieving the normal functioning required to enjoy the fundamental right of equal opportunity. Thus, the right to health care imposes an ethical obligation on society to provide health care to all, but does not create an unlimited right for individuals to access medical interventions without regard for effectiveness and resource limitations (Bodenheimer & Grumbach, 2016).

Economic Imperative

In addition to the moral appeal of universal coverage, strong economic arguments can be made for ensuring that no one remains uninsured (Falit, 2006). It usually costs less to provide preventive and regularly administered health care than it does to provide delayed charitable care for what would have otherwise been a preventable medical emergency, or once a medical condition has progressed to a severe level (Rudowitz, 2016). This is especially true when the cost of lost productivity or unemployment as a result of medical problems is also taken into account. There is a quantifiable financial burden associated with the loss of income and quality of life that the uninsured experience because of poorer health and shorter life spans. According to the Institute of Medicine, the aggregate annual amount of lost **health capital** is between $87 billion and $174 billion (IOM, 2003) (calculated to what the dollar is today using the consumer price index with annual inflation of 2.1%).

Health Insurance Plans Approaching Universal Coverage

The Affordable Care Act went into full effect in 2014 with health insurance reforms and new medical coverage options across the country. Prior to 2014, California and Massachusetts expanded their state's Medicaid insurance program and enacted innovative strategies to redesign their safety net hospitals in anticipation of the full expansion of the federal reforms (Kaiser Commission, 2015). California and Massachusetts are two states that now provide health care plans approaching universal medical coverage (*See* Act Providing Access to Affordable, Quality, Accountable Health Care, M.G.L.A. 111M § 2). As illustrated in **TABLE 7-1**, central elements of the Affordable Care Act and the California and Massachusetts state plans rely on the following:

- Employer assessments
- Minimum coverage provisions
- Purchasing pools
- Shared responsibility

TABLE 7-1 Overview of the Affordable Care Act and California and Massachusetts Health Care Reforms

	Affordable Care Act	California Health Care Reforms	Massachusetts Health Care Reforms
Insurance market reforms	• Guarantee issue • Community rating • Essential coverage standards • Affordability standards • Expansion of dependent coverage to age 26 • Elimination of annual and lifetime limits	• Guarantee issue • Community rating • Essential coverage standards	• Guarantee issue • Community rating • Essential coverage standards • Affordability standards • Expansion of dependent coverage to age 26
Subsidies for private coverage	• Subsidized private health insurance coverage on a sliding scale for individuals with incomes up to 400% of the federal poverty level (FPL). • Cost-sharing subsidies are available for those with incomes up to 250% FPL. • An individual's expected contribution will range from 2% to 9.5% depending on household income.	• Subsidized private health insurance coverage on a sliding scale for individuals with incomes up to 400% FPL. • Cost-sharing subsidies are available for those with incomes up to 250% FPL.	• Subsidized private health insurance coverage on a sliding scale for individuals with incomes up to 300% FPL. • Fully subsidized coverage for individuals with incomes below 150% FPL. • For those with incomes between 150 and 300% FPL, individual monthly premiums range from $39 to $116.
Expansion of Medicaid insurance	• Individuals under age 65 with incomes up to 133% FPL (plus a 5% automatic income disregard) based on modified adjusted gross income	• Individuals under age 65 with incomes up to 138% FPL	• Children: family incomes up to 300% FPL • Parents: 133% FPL • Pregnant women: 200% FPL • Long-term unemployed: 100% FPL

	Affordable Care Act	California Health Care Reforms	Massachusetts Health Care Reforms
Minimum coverage provision: Everyone must have health insurance or face a tax penalty.	• $695 year up to $2,085 for a family or 2.5% of household income, whichever is greater	• $695 per year up to $2,085 for a family or 2.5% of household income, whichever is greater	• 50% of the lowest cost premium
Minimum essential coverage	• Deductible: $6,000 • Limits on out-of-pocket expenses: $12,700 • Coinsurance limits: 50%	• Minimum coverage plan costs: $1,200 annually • Deductible: $5,000 • Limits on out-of-pocket expenses: $7,500 • Individual monthly premiums range from $219 to $304	• Minimum coverage plans costs: $3,000 to $6,600 annually • Deductible: $2,000 • Limits on out-of-pocket expenses: $5,000
Employer mandates	• Employers who have 50 or more full-time employees and do not offer coverage are required to pay a fee of $2,000 per employee, excluding the first 30 employees. • Employers with over 200 employees must automatically enroll employees into plans offered by the employer; employees may opt out of coverage.	• Employers who have 50 or more full-time employees and do not offer coverage are required to pay a fee of $2,000 per employee, excluding the first 30 employees. • Employers with over 200 employees must automatically enroll employees into plans offered by the employer; employees may opt out of coverage.	• Employers who have 11 or more employees and do not offer coverage are required to pay a fee of $295 per employee. • Employers are required to offer a cafeteria plan that permits workers to purchase health insurance with pretax dollars. • Employers face a free-rider surcharge if employees make excessive use of uncompensated care.

Note: The federal poverty level for 2016 is $11,880 for individuals and $24,300 for a family of four (HHS (U.S. Department of Health and Human Sevices). (2016). *Poverty guidelines*. Washington, DC: HHS).

Data from: Brooks, T., et al. (2015). Modern era Medicaid: Findings from a 50-state survey of eligibility, enrollment, renewal, and cost-sharing policies in Medicaid and CHIP. Washington, DC: Georgetown University Center for Children and Families and Kaiser Commission on Medicaid and the Uninsured; CAPH (California Association of Public Hospitals and Health Systems) & California Health Care Safety Net Institute. (2015). California's delivery system reform incentive program. Sacramento, CA: CAPH and California Health Care Safety Net Institute; Garfield, R., et al. (2015). Coverage expansions and the remaining uninsured: A look at California during year one of Affordable Care Act implementation. Menlo. Park: Kaiser Family Foundation; Guyer, J., et al. (2015). Key themes from delivery system reform incentive payment (DSRIP) waivers in 4 states. Menlo Park, CA: Kaiser Family Foundation; Kaiser Family Foundation (2012). Massachusetts health care reform: Six years later. Menlo Park, CA: Kaiser; Packard Foundation for Children's Health. (2014). Insure the Uninsured Project: Children's Health Coverage Under the Affordable Care Act. Palo Alto, CA: Packard Foundation.

While health insurance plans are administered by private insurers, they are regulated, coordinated, and sold by the federal exchange and the states. The Affordable Care Act empowers all states to individually determine the fate of expanding Medicaid insurance in their jurisdictions.

The Affordable Care Act, California, and Massachusetts require guaranteed issue and community rating; insurers are prevented from denying health care coverage because of age or health status, or adjusting premiums based on health status. While insurers are required to promote healthy behaviors, other costly mandates have been removed in California and Massachusetts (United Health Foundation, 2016). The use of nurse practitioners, physicians' assistants, retail-based clinics, and telemedicine are encouraged as ways to cut costs. Quality of care is improved through the use of information technology.

Minimum Coverage Provisions

One core problem of the U.S. health care system is that those with health insurance pay for the health care of the uninsured (Kaiser, 2015). To address this free-loader problem, everyone must participate equally. One solution is minimum coverage provisions that require every member of society to purchase health insurance for themselves and their children or face a tax penalty. Under universal coverage, everyone pays through their federal and state progressive tax systems. While the insured are still paying for the uninsured, the health law attempts to reduce the burden of people with a lower ability to pay health insurance premiums and shifts the incidence disproportionately to those with a higher ability to pay.

Affordability Waivers

The Affordable Care Act and Massachusetts's minimum coverage provision include affordability waivers that protect those who are ineligible for premium subsidies yet cannot afford private insurance. Rather than allowing more people to qualify for the subsidy in the first place (given limited health resources), the waiver is directed to assisting the working poor who are not eligible for Medicaid insurance and individuals facing transient financial problems (Guyer et al., 2015). California lacks a safety valve like the Affordable Care Act and Massachusetts, which may affect universal coverage and premium rates (Kaiser Commission, 2015).

Both states provide subsidized insurance programs for the financially distressed while extending eligibility for Medicaid insurance coverage. Nationally, it is estimated that:

- 26% of the uninsured are eligible for Medicaid insurance
- 52% need financial assistance to purchase health insurance
- 22% can afford health insurance coverage

(BLS & Census Bureau, 2014).

Purchasing Pools

Individual and small group insurance markets merged into state-administered purchasing pools to provide a centralized location for individuals to purchase insurance. This consolidation created larger **risk pools**, thereby lowering premium costs.

Employer Assessments

In the context of universal coverage plans, a key issue is the role of employer-sponsored coverage. Such health care coverage has been slowly eroding and has been criticized for providing little meaningful plan choice (Wharton, 2011). Universal coverage plans for individuals could make employer-sponsored plans much less attractive down the road.

Employers in Massachusetts with 10 or more full-time employees must enroll their employees in employer-sponsored health insurance plans or pay a portion of the premiums for employee group insurance plans. Noncompliance results in annual assessments of employers while tax penalties are imposed on uninsured adults without **credible health care coverage**. Employers in Massachusetts must also offer **Section 125 cafeteria plans** allowing employees to purchase insurance with **pretax income** or risk the liability of state-sponsored care used by their employees if that usage exceeds a set limit. Finally, Massachusetts equalizes health care coverage for employees; in contrast, California employers are allowed to offer better plans and higher contributions to their higher paid employees. While the Affordable Care Act establishes **minimum essential coverage** requirements as outlined in **FEATURE BOX 7-5**, neither California nor Massachusetts set quality standards to prevent employers from offering plans that provide little real protection (Blum, 2014). Undocumented immigrants and some lawfully residing immigrants remain ineligible to enroll in Medicaid insurance but can purchase unsubsidized coverage on the California insurance exchanges.

Shared Responsibility

Responsibility for universal coverage is spread more broadly in California than in Massachusetts where not-for-profit insurers dominate the market. With for-profit insurers dominating the national and California markets, the health insurance industry is required to spend most of its premiums on patient care. In Massachusetts, where not-for-profit insurers dominate, there is no such mandate. The Affordable Care Act requires the medical products industry to pay

FEATURE BOX 7-5

Minimum Essential Coverage

- Ambulatory patient services
- Emergency services
- Hospitalization
- Maternity and newborn care
- Mental health and substance use disorder services, including behavioral health treatment
- Prescription drugs
- Rehabilitative services and devices
- Laboratory services
- Preventive and wellness services and chronic care continuum
- Pediatric services, including oral and vision care

Note: States define the benefits in their minimum essential coverage plans.

Data from: 26 U.S.C. A. § 5000A.

a percentage of their revenues to help cover reforms. In California, physicians and hospitals are also required to pay a percentage of their revenues to help cover reforms.

Patient Responsibilities

One of the biggest obstacles to frustrate the Patient's Bill of Rights, and perhaps the most important obstacle to health reform, is the difficulty of patients accepting responsibility to maintain healthy lifestyles. Although there is always the problem of **free riders** who exploit the health care system without due compensation, a far greater problem is **social loafers** who have health insurance but who fail to avail themselves of the preventive measures they could take, which have been shown to reduce the risks associated with bad health (Billauer, 2007; Wharton, 2011). The medical phenomenon of social loafers is often the result of family and environmental factors that do not support **healthy lifestyles** (Johnson, 2009/1758). For instance, overweight and obese people often exert less effort to achieve weight goals when they are around other overweight people, just as smokers exert less effort to stop smoking when they are around other people who smoke (Wharton, 2011).

Patients also have a responsibility to plan for life's medical uncertainties by maintaining health care coverage. While uninsured free riders are real problems in the United States, the social loafers who do have health insurance but freely choose not to avail themselves of it, are more of a problem (Wharton, 2011). Social loafers who refuse to afford themselves the benefits of preventive care increase the national burden of health care costs and force it upon other members of society. Social loafers who do not use screening diagnostics inflate the cost of health care just as free riders do (Billauer, 2007). Free riders and social loafers both refuse to do their part to hold down health care costs; both frustrate reforms under the Patient's Bill of Rights.

MANAGEMENT AND LAW ISSUES

6. While the fear of free riders and social loafers drove some of the opposition to the Patient's Bill of Rights, should people who refuse to maintain healthy lifestyles have the same rights to medical treatments as those who maintain healthy lifestyles? For instance, should the obese be eligible for medical coverage of knee replacements or smokers be eligible for lung transplants?
7. Are not the true free riders those people who decide not to procure health insurance when they can afford it but prefer to purchase other consumer goods instead?

Patients' Rights and Responsibilities

President Franklin D. Roosevelt encouraged the United States to embrace the global recognition of a right to health in his State of the Union address in 1944, while advancing his idea of a second Bill of Rights, including the right to adequate health care and the opportunity to achieve and enjoy good health (Roosevelt, 1944). Although it took 66 years, the nation finally followed through with Roosevelt's overall vision with the passage of the Patient Bill of Rights in 2010.

The Patient Bill of Rights goes a long way toward enacting the measures established by the Institute of Medicine at the start of this chapter (*See* The Standards for Patient Rights and Responsibilities). Patients' hope is that the law will make a real difference.

LAW FACT

Right to Emergency Care

Are patients entitled to emergency care?

Yes. Patients have a legal right to emergency care without physically arriving on the hospital grounds as long as patients are en route to the hospital and the emergency department has been notified of their imminent arrival. Refusal to treat an uninsured patient in an emergency condition because of their insurance status is a violation of the **Emergency Medical Treatment and Labor Act of 1986**.

—*Morales v. Sociedad Espanola de Auxilio Mutuo y Beneficencia*, 524 F.3d 54 (U.S. Court of Appeals for the 1st Circuit 2008), *cert. denied*, 555 U.S. 1097 (U.S. Supreme Court 2009), *criticized by, Penn v. Salina Regional Health Center, Inc.*, 2012 U.S. Dist. LEXIS 64616 (U.S. District Court for the District of Kansas, 2012) (because the patient did not come to the hospital, nor was in a hospital ambulance, nor was being transferred from another hospital, there was no legal right to emergency care).

See Camozzi, 2010; Cicero, 2010; Fillenwarth, 2014; Gundlach, 2010 (discussing these decisions).

CHAPTER SUMMARY

- The main issue in the patient rights debate is how to balance costs with patients' choice of care.
- Many Americans support a system of universal coverage that would provide for basic health needs, with the option of buying additional health care coverage.
- Patient harm seems to occur more often due to problems with the health care system than due to actual malpractice.
- Patients have a right to emergency care, experimental medical treatments in certain situations, and a limited right to sue for these services.
- Under ERISA, a harmed patient can only recover the value of the treatment denied and nothing for any foreseeable injuries as a result of the denial, and states generally do not have standing to sue on behalf of their citizens; however, third parties may file a class-action suit alleging ERISA violations against insurers.
- Lawsuits, and even malpractice reform, are arguably not the best way to resolve problems in health care systems; arbitration and other alternative dispute mechanisms are gaining popularity, but still do not resolve the underlying problems with health care delivery, namely the questions of whether Americans' demand for health care outstrips available resources and how much a human life is worth.
- It is impossible to cut health care costs without rationing care, and it is impossible to ration care in a manner acceptable to all parties involved.
- One possible method of containing and managing health care costs involves cost-effectiveness analysis, but there is not yet a general consensus on how best to determine cost-effectiveness.
- Other methods of managing costs include redefining what is *medical necessity* and providing more public access to health care information.

- Uniform sets of performance measures and mandated disclosure of audited care outcome data would help patients make better health care decisions.
- Massachusetts and California are the closest to providing universal coverage for their citizens, but neither state has a perfect solution to the ethical and financial dilemmas involved in providing such a system.
- The two biggest obstacles to frustrate the Patient's Bill of Rights are patients failing to accept responsibility for maintaining healthy lifestyles and social loafers who have health insurance but freely choose not to avail themselves of preventive measures they could take to reduce the risks of bad health.

LAW NOTES

1. The key question in the Abigail Alliance case was how patients' right to lifesaving experimental drugs is described. If future cases choose to define this right narrowly, courts could infer a narrow right from a broader, established fundamental right. This has been done in the past; for instance, the rights to abortions, to use contraception, and to plan one's family from the broader rights to privacy and freedom from government intrusion (*See generally* Tsakopoulos et al., 2015).

2. A proposal by the Abigail Alliance represents one legislative possibility for addressing patients' right to experimental treatments. The proposal would involve:

   - Granting terminally ill patients who have exhausted all FDA-approved therapies the personal autonomy of selecting post-Phase I experimental drugs with their physicians
   - Lifting the current prohibition of charging any price higher than the cost for experimental drugs
   - By allowing commercialization or charging a price higher than the cost of experimental products, clinical trials would be safeguarded. The intention of this commercialization feature is to create incentives to actively distribute experimental drugs, as opposed to merely recover costs under the current FDA regulation. High prices could, however, act as a barrier to some patients seeking access to experimental drugs, thus forcing them to participate in free clinical trials, which would create disparities in access based on economics.

3. Research from the University of Pennsylvania shows the incremental comparative effectiveness ratio of dialysis in current practice relative to the next least costly alternative is on average $62,000 per year, or about $129,000 for a quality-adjusted life year. A quality-adjusted life year is a measure that combines the length of time that life is extended and the quality of that life. However, the distribution of cost-effectiveness across the entire end-stage renal disease population is wide. For the lowest percentile, it costs about $65,500 to provide an additional quality-adjusted life year. For the top percentile, the figure is about $500,000. The higher costs per quality-adjusted life year were strongly associated with age and additional chronic illnesses in addition to end-stage renal disease. No health economist or the strongest advocate for providing health care coverage would argue $500,000 for one year of life is reasonable. This would inflate health care spending by 10 to 15 times on top of current expenditures. The cost to preserve one year of quality-adjusted life drops to $240,000 in the 90th percentile of expenditures. In effect, if this were to become the threshold, 90% of the dialysis patients could be treated for half what it would cost to treat the sickest for whom heavy expenditures do not effectively improve or extend quality or length of life (Lee et al., 2009a and 2009b).

4. Health insurers determine medical necessity and therefore payments using guidelines published by actuarial firms such as Milliman or InterQual (Polzin, 2014). In reality, medical necessity determinations are made on the basis of statistical calculations of financial benefit, not medical benefit (Dolgin, 2015). Of course, the American Association of Health Plans and the actuarial firms deny their guidelines are based on financial objectives; instead, they claim they are designed to support quality health care. But health insurance carriers often deny payment for health care because of actuarial guidelines, regardless of a patient's medical necessity. Critics of Milliman maintain health insurers seem to be using the actuarial guidelines 100% of the time and only consider the individual medical needs of patients on appeal of denied claims. Thus, claims for payment other than routine claims are generally denied if they do not follow the so-called cookbook guidelines established by the actuarial firms (Mantel, 2015). Milliman claims that health insurers who use their guidelines as a basis for denying payment for health care received are using them inappropriately; they are to be used to determine the risks and benefits of medical treatments (*See generally United States ex rel. Nudelman v. International Rehabilitation Associates*, 2006 U.S. Dist. LEXIS 17958 (U.S. District Court for the Eastern District of Pennsylvania 2006) (whistleblower case that settled for $3.2 million and included a three-year monitoring program of medical necessity determinations)).

REFERENCES

Aaron, H. J. (2008). Health care rationing: Inevitable, but impossible? *Georgetown Law Review, 96*, 539–558.

ACOG (American College of Obstetricians and Gynecologists). (2010). *Forming a just health care system.* Washington, DC: ACOG Committee on Ethics.

Aragaki, H. N. (2014). The Federal Arbitration Act as procedural reform. *New York University Law Review, 89*, 1939–2026.

ASM (American Society for Reproductive Medicine). (2014). *Ectopic pregnancy.* Birmingham, AL: ASM.

Baker, T. (2011). Health insurance, risk, and responsibility after the Patient Protection and Affordable Care Act. *University of Pennsylvania Law Review, 159*(5), 1577–1621.

Ball, R., et al. (2012). Audited financial reporting and voluntary disclosure as complements: A test of the confirmation hypothesis. *Journal of Accounting and Economics, 53*(2012), 136–166.

Baron, J. B. (2012). Property as control: The case of information. *Michigan Telecommunications and Technology Law Review, 18*, 367–418.

Basu, A., & Philipson, T. J. (2010). *The impact of comparative effectiveness research on health and health care spending.* NBER working paper 16633. Cambridge, MA: National Bureau of Economic Research.

Belton, S. E., & Galle, F. P. (2014). How the arbitration-at-all-costs regime ignores and distorts settled law. *Berkeley Journal of Employment and Labor Law, 35*, 135–152.

Bennett, P., IV. (2014). "Waiving" goodbye to arbitration: A contractual approach. *Washington and Lee Law Review, 69*, 1609–1681.

Bhagwat, A. (2012). Details: Specific facts and the First Amendment. *Southern California Law Review, 86*, 1–61.

Billauer, B. P. (2007). Current issues in public policy; The right to health: A holistic health plan for the next administration. *Rutgers Journal of Law and Public Policy, 5*, 234–281.

Blackman, J. (2014). What happens if data is speech? *University of Pennsylvania Journal of Constitutional Law Heightened Scrutiny, 16*, 25–36.

Blitz, M. J. (2014). The Pandora's box of 21st century commercial speech doctrine: *Sorrell, R.A.V.,* and purpose-constrained scrutiny. *Nexus: Chapman's Journal of Law & Policy, 19*, 19–49.

BLS (Bureau of Labor Statistics) & Census Bureau. (2014). *Current population survey.* Washington, DC: U.S. Department of Labor, BLS and U.S. Department of Commerce, U.S. Census Bureau.

Blum, J. D., Principal Deputy Administrator, Centers for Medicare and Medicaid Services. (2014, February 21). Remarks at the panel discussion on Health Care Policy: Untangling Today's Regulatory Environment and Preparing for the Future at the 2014 Wharton Health Care Business Conference, Philadelphia, PA.

Bodenheimer, T., & Grumbach, K. (2016). *Understanding health policy: A clinical approach* (7th ed.). New York, NY: McGraw Hill.

Boumil, M. M., et al. (2012). Prescription data mining, medical privacy and the First Amendment: The U.S. Supreme Court in *Sorrell v. IMS Health Inc. Annals of Health Law, 21*, 447–491.

Braithwaite, R. S., et al. (2008). What does the value of modern medicine say about the $50,000 per quality-adjusted life-year decision rule? *Medical Care, 46*(4), 349–356.

Brandes, P. (2012). Regulation of drugs: A death sentence for the terminally ill? *University of San Francisco Law Review, 46*, 1149–1178.

Brandon, S. C. (2012). What's mine is yours: Targeting privacy issues and determining the best solutions for behavioral advertising. *The John Marshall Journal of Computer and Information Law, 29*, 637–672.

Brooks, T., et al. (2015). *Modern era Medicaid: Findings from a 50-state survey of eligibility, enrollment, renewal, and cost-sharing policies in Medicaid and CHIP.* Washington, DC: Georgetown University Center for Children and Families and Kaiser Commission on Medicaid and the Uninsured.

Brunce, H. M. (2015). Two hats, one head, no heart: The anatomy of the ERISA [Employee Retirement Income and Security Act] settlor/fiduciary distinction. *North Carolina Law Review, 93*, 459–549.

Calabresi, G. (2016). *The future of law and economics: Essays in reform and recollection.* New Haven, CN: Yale University Press.

Camozzi, B. D. (2010). Eleventh annual review of gender and sexuality law: Health care law chapter: Health care access. *The Georgetown Journal of Gender and the Law, 11*, 443–509.

Candeub, A. (2011). Contract, warranty, and the Patient Protection and Affordable Care Act. *Wake Forest Law Review, 46*, 45–93.

CAPH (California Association of Public Hospitals and Health Systems) & California Health Care Safety Net Institute. (2015). *California's delivery system reform incentive program.* Sacramento, CA: CAPH and California Health Care Safety Net Institute.

Chan, M., Director-general of the World Health Organization. (2010, July 16). Remarks at the panel discussion on Creating Synergies Between Intellectual Property Rights and Public Health Intellectual Property at the WHO-WIPO-WTO Joint Technical Symposium: Access to Medicines: Pricing and Procurement Practices, Geneva, Switzerland.

Chandra, A., et al. (2013). *Is this time different? The slowdown in health care spending.* Washington, DC: Brookings Papers on Economic Activity, 261–323.

Chang, Y-C., et al. (2015). Pain and suffering damages in wrongful death cases: An empirical study. *Journal of Empirical Legal Studies, 12*(1), 128–160.

Cicero, R. J. W. (2010). Not worth the paper it's printed on: EMTALA should be repealed and replaced with a federal malpractice statute. *The Review of Litigation, 29*, 417–437.

Clark, S. R. (2014). Avoiding the appearance of impropriety: Missouri and Kansas supreme court decisions on the constitutionality of caps on noneconomic damages demonstrate the need for objective procedures in the selection of special judges. *Albany Law Review, 77*, 1441–1454.

CMS (Centers for Medicare and Medicaid Services). (2015). *Medicare provider utilization and payment data: Physician and other supplier.* Baltimore, MD: CMS.

Conroy, A. (2010). FDA approval and federal preemption after *Riegel* and *Levine. Quinnipiac Health Law Journal, 14*, 285–313.

Cook, A. C. (2013). *Civil justice tort reform.* Washington, DC: The Federalist Society.

Cramer, B. W. (2015). Privacy exceptionalism and confidentiality versus the public interest in uncovering universal service fraud. *Communication Law and Policy, 20*(2), 149–190.

Danis, M., et al. (2015). *Fair resource allocation and rationing at the bedside.* New York, NY: Oxford University Press.

Dartmouth Institute for Health Policy and Clinical Practice. (2016). *Our parents, ourselves: Health care for an aging population.* Lebanon, NH: Dartmouth College.

___. (2012). *Dartmouth Atlas of Health Care: Improving patient decision-making in health care.*

Davis, R. C., et al. (2011). *Cold-case investigations: An analysis of current practices and factors associated with successful outcomes.* Santa Monica, CA: RAND Corp.

Dhooge, L. J. (2014). The First Amendment and disclosure regulations: Compelled speech or corporate opportunism? *American Business Law Journal, 51,* 559–659.

Dolgin, J. L. (2015). Unhealthy determinations: Controlling "medical necessity." *Virginia Journal of Social Policy and the Law, 22,* 435–489.

Donnelly, J. (2010). Comparative effectiveness research. *Health Affairs/Robert Wood Johnson Foundation Health Policy Brief.* Princeton, NJ: Robert Wood Johnson Foundation.

Eisenberg, T., & Engel, C. (2014). Assuring civil damages adequately deter: A public good experiment. *Journal of Empirical Legal Studies, 11,* 301–332.

Falit, B. P. (2006). The Bush administration's health care proposal: The proper establishment of a consumer-driven health care regime. *Journal of Law, Medicine and Ethics, 34,* 632–636.

Farley, T. A. (2016). When is it ethical to withhold prevention? *The New England Journal of Medicine, 374,* 1303–1306.

Fillenwarth, C. (2014). Beyond the emergency room doors: Rejecting patient admittance as satisfaction of hospital obligations under EMTALA [Emergency Medical Treatment and Active Labor Act]. *Indiana Health Law Review, 11*(2), 792–829.

Ford, E. S., et al. (2013). *Co-occurrence of leading lifestyle-related chronic conditions among adults in the United States.* Atlanta, GA: Centers for Disease Control and Prevention.

Frakt, A. B. (2011). How much do hospitals cost shift? A review of the evidence. *The Milbank Quarterly, 89*(1), 90–130.

GAO (General Accountability Office). (2003). *Medical malpractice: Implications of rising premiums on access to health care.* Washington, DC: GAO.

Garfield, R., et al. (2015). *Coverage expansions and the remaining uninsured: A look at California during year one of Affordable Care Act implementation.* Menlo, Park: Kaiser Family Foundation.

Gooch, G. R., et al. (2013). The moral from *Sorrell*: Educate, don't legislate. *Health Matrix: Journal of Law Medicine, 23,* 237–277.

Gould, E. (2013). *Increased health care cost sharing works as intended: It burdens patients who need care the most.* Washington, DC: Economic Policy Institute.

Gundlach, J. (2010). The problem of ambulance diversion, and some potential solutions. *Legislation and Public Policy, 13,* 175–217.

Guyer, J., et al. (2015). *Key themes from delivery system reform incentive payment (DSRIP) waivers in 4 states.* Menlo Park, CA: Kaiser Family Foundation.

Hermer, L. D., & Lenihan, M. (2014). Medicaid matters: The future of Medicaid supplemental payments: Can they promote patient-centered care? *Kentucky Law Journal, 102,* 287–326.

Hethcoat, G. O., III. (2012). Regulating pharmaceutical marketing after *Sorrell v. IMS Health Inc. Quinnipiac Health Law Journal, 15,* 187–208.

HHS (U.S. Department of Health and Human Services). (2016). *Poverty guidelines.* Washington, DC: HHS.

Hill, B. J. (2012). What is the meaning of health? Constitutional implications of defining "medical necessity" and "essential health benefits" under the Affordable Care Act. *American Journal of Law and Medicine, 38,* 445–470.

Hines, L. J., & Hines, N. W. (2015). Constitutional constraints on punitive damages: Clarity, consistency, and the outlier dilemma. *Hastings Law Journal, 66,* 1257–1316.

Ho, C. S. (2015). Exceptions meet absolutism: Outlawing governmental underreach in health law. *Denver University Law Review, 93,* 109–171.

Hoffman, A. K. (2011). Three models of health insurance: The conceptual pluralism of the Patient Protection and Affordable Care Act. *University of Pennsylvania Law Review, 159,* 1873–1954.

Hsia, R. Y., et al. (2011). Factors associated with closures of emergency departments in the United States. *Journal of the American Medical Association, 305*(19), 1978–1987.

Huberfeld, N., et al. (2013). Plunging into endless difficulties: Medicaid and coercion in *National Federation of Independent Business v. Sebelius. Boston University Law Review, 93,* 1–88.

IOM (Institute of Medicine). (2003). *Hidden costs, value lost: Uninsurance in America.* Washington, DC: National Academies Press.

Jacobs, L. G. (2014). Compelled commercial speech as compelled consent speech. *The Journal of Law and Politics, 29,* 517–533.

Janssen, W. M. (2014). A "duty" to continue selling medicines. *American Journal of Law and Medicine, 40,* 330–392.

Jena, A. B., et al. (2015). Physician spending and subsequent risk of malpractice claims: Observational study. *British Medical Journal, 351,* 3–8.

Johnson, S. (2009). The idler. In D. Greene (Ed.), *The major works.* New York, NY: Oxford University Press-Oxford World's Classics. (Original published in 1758.)

Joseph, J. H., et al. (2012). Is *Sorrell* the death knell for FDA's off-label marketing restrictions? *Journal of Health and Life Sciences Law, 5*(2), 1–33.

Kachalia, A., & Mello, M. M. (2011). New directions in medical liability reform. *New England Journal of Medicine, 364,* 1564–1572.

Kaiser Commission on Medicaid and the Uninsured. (2015). *Fact sheet: The California health care landscape.* Washington, DC: Kaiser.

Kaiser Family Foundation. (2015). *Key facts about the uninsured population.* Menlo Park, CA: Kaiser.

___. (2012). *Massachusetts health care reform: Six years later.*

Kerr, J. (2010). *Exxon Shipping Co. v. Baker*: The perils of judicial punitive damages reform. *Emory Law Journal, 59,* 727–768.

Kesselheim, A. S. (2011). Off-label drug use and promotion: Balancing public health goals and commercial speech. *American Journal of Law and Medicine, 37,* 225–257.

Kesselheim, A. S., & Brennan, T. A. (2013). The swinging pendulum: The Supreme Court reverses course on ERISA and consumer-driven health care. *Yale Journal of Health Policy, Law, and Ethics, 5*(1), 451–463.

Kevelson, R. (2012). *Law and semiotics.* New York, NY: Springer Publishing.

Kolodin, Z. J. F. (2015). Standing to challenge regulatory failure in the age of preemption. *New York University Environmental Law Journal, 22,* 157–180.

Lee, C. P., et al. (2009a). An empiric estimate of the value of life: Updating the renal dialysis cost-effectiveness standard. *Value in Health, 12*(1), 80–87.

___. (2009b). Optimal initiation and management of dialysis therapy. *Operations Research, 55*(6), 1428–1449.

Lennox, C. S., & Pittman, J. A. (2011). Voluntary audits versus mandatory audits. *The Accounting Review, 86*(5), 1655–1678.

Lewis, J. A. (2014). At the intersection of insurance and tax: Equitable remedies under the Affordable Care Act. *John Marshall Law Review, 47,* 973–989.

Liang, C-M. (2015). Rethinking the tort liability system and patient safety: From the conventional wisdom to learning from litigation. *Indiana Health Law Review, 12*, 327–381.

Lindenfeld, E., & Tran, J. L. (2016). Prescription drugs and design defect liability: Blanket immunity approach to the increased costs and unavailability of prescription medication. *Drake Law Review, 64*, 111–139.

Lipschutz, D., et al. (2015). *Comparison of consumer protections in three health insurance markets: Medicare advantage, qualified health plans and Medicaid managed care organizations.* Menlo Park, CA: Kaiser Family Foundation.

Lovendale, R. (2014). Tax vs. penalty, round two: Interpreting the ACA's assessable payment as a tax for federal award cost allowances. *Boston College Law Review, 55*, 947–978.

MacMahon, P. (2013). Proceduralism, civil justice, and American legal thought. *University of Pennsylvania Journal of International Law, 34*(3), 545–610.

Mantel, J. (2015). A defense of physicians' gatekeeping role: Balancing patients' needs with society's interests. *Pepperdine Law Review, 42*, 633–726.

Mathes, M. (2012). The next civil rights movement? Health care and the aged: Arguing equality in the absence of a right. *Temple Political and Civil Rights Law Review, 21*, 337–347.

McDonough, M. (2015). Catholic health care and the Affordable Care Act: A matter of social justice. *Intercultural Human Rights Law Review, 10*, 69–116.

Mechanic, D., & Alpine, D. D. (2010). Sociology of health care reform: Building on research and analysis to improve health care. *Journal of Health and Social Behavior, 51*(1), S147–S159.

Mermin, S. E., & Graff, S. K. (2013). The First Amendment and public health, at odds. *American Journal of Law and Medicine, 39*, 298–307.

Molzahn, A. E., et al. (1996). Quality of life with patients with end stage renal disease. A structural equation model. *Quality of Life Research, 5*(4), 1573–2649.

Muennig, P., & Bounthavong, M. (2016). *Cost-effectiveness analysis in health. A practical approach.* New York, NY: John Wiley and Sons, Jossey-Bass.

Muir, D., & Stein, N. (2015). Two hats, one head, no heart: The anatomy of the ERISA settlor/fiduciary distinction. *North Carolina Law Review, 93*, 459–549.

Mullenix, L. S. (2015). Forum selection after Atlantic Marine: Gaming the system; Protecting consumers from unconscionable contractual forum-selection and arbitration clauses. *Hastings Law Journal, 66*, 719–760.

Neumann, P. J., et al. (2014). Updating cost-effectiveness: The curious resilience of the $50,000-per-QALY threshold. *The New England Journal of Medicine, 371*, 796–797.

NIH (National Institutes of Health). (2016). *NIH clinical research trials and you.* Bethesda, MD: NIH.

Noonan, K. G., & Boraske, S. J. (2015). Enforcing mental health parity through the Affordable Care Act's essential health benefit mandate. *Annals of Health Law, 24*, 252–285.

O'Gorman, D. P. (2014). The Restatement (second) of contracts' reasonably certain terms requirement: A model of neoclassical contract law and a model of confusion and inconsistency. *University of Hawaii Law Review, 36*, 169–269.

O'Malley, K. M. (2015). The intensifying national interest in patent litigation. *Marquette Intellectual Property Law Review, 19*, 1–13.

Packard Foundation for Children's Health. (2014). *Insure the Uninsured Project: Children's Health Coverage Under the Affordable Care Act.* Palo Alto, CA: Packard Foundation.

Partnoy, F. (2012). *Wait: The art and science of delay.* New York, NY: Public Affairs.

Pasquale, F., & Ragone, T. A. (2014). Protecting health privacy in an era of big data processing and cloud computing. *Stanford Technology Law Review, 17*, 595–653.

Pfander, J. E., & Dwinell, J. (2016). A declaratory theory of state accountability. *Virginia Law Review, 102*, 153–235.

Pivarnik, G. (2014). Cells as drugs? Regulating the future of medicine. *American Journal of Law and Medicine, 40*, 298–321.

Polzin, R. A. (2014). Short-stay, under observation, or inpatient admission? How CMS' two midnight rule creates more confusion and concern. *Saint Louis University Journal of Health Law and Policy, 8*, 147–188.

Posner, R. A. (1983). *The economics of justice.* Boston, MA: Harvard University Press. (Original work published 1981.)

Post, R. (2015). Compelled commercial speech. *West Virginia Law Review, 117*, 867–919.

Roosevelt, F. D. (1944, January 11). President's message to the 79th Congress on the State of the Union. *Published Papers, 12*, p. 41.

Rudowitz, R. (2016). *Issue brief: A closer look at the remaining uninsured population eligible for Medicaid and CHIP.* Washington, DC: Kaiser Commission on Medicaid and the Uninsured.

Sanders, S. M. (2013). Uncle Sam and the partitioning punitive problem: A federal split-recovery statute or a federal tax? *Pepperdine Law Review, 40*, 785–833.

Satz, A. B. (2013). Towards solving the health care crisis: The paradoxical case for universal access to high technology. *Yale Journal of Health Policy, Law, and Ethics, 8*(1), 93–143.

Schindler, D. S., & Brame, T. (2013). This medication may kill you: Cognitive overload and forced commercial speech. *Whittier Law Review, 35*, 27–78.

Schleppenbach, J. R. (2014). Something old, something new: Recent developments in the enforceability of agreements to arbitrate disputes between nursing homes and their residents. *Elder Law Journal, 22*, 141–174.

Schlesinger, A., Jr. (2003). *The crisis of the old order.* New York, NY: Houghton Mifflin Harcourt-Mariner Books. (Original work published 1957.)

Schumpeter, J. (2014). *Capitalism, socialism, and democracy* (2nd ed.). Manassas Park, VA: Impact Books. (Original work published 1942.)

Sethi, M. K., & Frist, W. H. (2013). *An introduction to health policy: A primer for physicians and medical students.* New York, NY: Springer Publishing.

Shinar, A. (2013). Public employee speech and the privatization of the First Amendment. *Connecticut Law Review, 46*, 1–71.

Somers, S., et al. (2011). Sunshine and accountability: The pursuit of information on quality in Medicaid managed care. *Saint Louis University Journal of Health Law and Policy, 5*, 153–179.

Spacapan, L. T., & Hutchison, J. M. (2013). Prosecutions of pharmaceutical companies for off-label marketing: Fueled by government's desire to modify corporate conduct or pursuit of a lucrative revenue stream? *Annals of Health Law, 22*, 407–444.

Spears, J. M. (2015). Embracing 21st century information sharing: Defining a new paradigm for the Food and Drug Administration's regulation of biopharmaceutical company communications with healthcare professionals. *Food and Drug Law Journal, 70*, 143–160.

Swartz, M. (2015). Are physician-patient communications protected by the First Amendment? *Cardozo Law Review de novo, 2015*, 92–104.

___. (2012). Physician-patient communication and the First Amendment after *Sorrell*. *Michigan State University Journal of Medicine and Law, 17,* 101–125.

Syrett, K. (2007). *Law, legitimacy and the rationing of healthcare: A contextual and comparative perspective*. New York, NY: Cambridge University Press.

Teninbaum, G. H., & Zimmermann, B. R. (2013). A tale of two lawsuits. *Health and Biomedical Law Society, 8,* 443–470.

Thomson, H. B. (2013). Whither Central Hudson? Commercial speech in the wake of *Sorrell v. IMS Health. Columbia Journal of Law and Social Problems, 47,* 171–207.

Tsakopoulos, A., et al. (2015). The right to try: An overview of efforts to obtain expedited access to unapproved treatment for the terminally ill. *Food and Drug Law Journal, 70,* 617–641.

United Health Foundation. (2016). *America's health rankings spotlight: Impact of unhealthy behaviors*. Minnetonka, MN: United Health Foundation.

Valenza, M. A. (2011). *Cigna v. Amara*: Supreme Court resolves several ERISA claim issues while leaving others for the lower courts. *Transactions: The Tennessee Journal of Business Law, 13,* 139–164.

von Eschenbach, A. C. (2010). Continuing the restoration and transformation of the FDA. *Journal of Health Care Law and Policy, 13*(2), 203–209.

Vukadin, K. T. (2014). Unfinished business: The Affordable Care Act and the problem of delayed and denied ERISA healthcare claims. *John Marshall Law Review, 47,* 1–33.

Wharton School at the University of Pennsylvania. (2011). In the health care sector, who should choose which treatment is best? *Knowledge@Wharton.*

___. (2008). Cost-effective medical treatment: Putting an updated dollar value on human life.

Wiley, L. F. (2016). From patient rights to health justice: Securing the public's interest in affordable, high-quality health care. *Cardozo Law Review, 37,* 833–889.

Wolf, A. J. (2013). Detailing commercial speech: What pharmaceutical marketing reveals about bans on commercial speech. *William and Mary Bill of Rights Journal, 21,* 1291–1323.

Young, E. A. (2012). The constitutionality of the Affordable Care Act: Ideas from the academy; Popular constitutionalism and the under-enforcement problem: The case of the national healthcare law. *Law and Contemporary Problems, 75,* 157–201.

© Andy Dean Photography/ShutterStock, Inc.

CHAPTER 8

Medical Malpractice

"Every man is a reformer until reform tramps on his toes."

— **Edgar Watson Howe** (1853–1937), American novelist and newspaper editor

IN BRIEF

This chapter covers medical malpractice as well as peer review processes, standards of care, and liability insurance. Also examined are selected proposals for tort reform, medical review boards, and elimination of provider liability for experimental or cutting-edge treatments that do not meet patient expectations.

LEARNING OBJECTIVES

Upon completion of this chapter readers should be able to:

1. Define medical malpractice.
2. Explain how government health insurance programs affect malpractice reform.
3. Outline the three premises that underlie Medicare/Medicaid insurance regarding the care and competency of health care providers.
4. Explain why malpractice is a non-issue in the total cost of health care.
5. Detail how malpractice occurs.
6. Review myths about malpractice.
7. Discuss proposed solutions offered for malpractice problems.
8. Explain the concept of enterprise liability and its effect on malpractice.
9. Contrast approaching the malpractice issue through systems design as opposed to individual fault.

KEY TERMS

Administrative health courts	Corporate practice prohibitions	Experience rating
Best practices	Creative destruction	Failure to warn
Boundaries of liabilities	Damage awards	Fiduciary duty
Breach of care	Damage caps	Financial incentives
Burdens of proof	Defensive medicine	Financial viability
"But for" test	Deregulation	Fraudulent
Capital maintenance	Disruptive innovation	Free cash flow
Capitalist system	Disruptive regulations	Handoffs
Claims-free policies	Doctrine of agency	Hard liability markets
Clinical practice guidelines	Duty	Health maintenance organizations
Collateral source rule	Duty of care	Institutional practices
Common law	Duty to warn	Intentional tort
Compensation benchmarks	Enterprise liability	Intermediary actor
Contingency fees	Equal protection	Joint liability

FACT OR FICTION

Negligence

Do pharmacies have a **fiduciary duty** *to protect the public from customers who may be abusing prescription drugs?*
     This section discusses a **malpractice** lawsuit against a number of Nevada pharmacies for death and injury caused by Patricia Copening, a pharmacy customer who was abusing prescription drugs with the pharmacies' knowledge. During a 12-month period, Copening received prescriptions for about 4,500 hydrocodone pills at 13 different pharmacies. Hydrocodone is a narcotic used for severe pain relief with a high potential for abuse that may impair one's ability to perform potentially hazardous tasks such as driving a vehicle.
     While under the influence of hydrocodone, Copening struck Gregory Sanchez, Jr. and Robert Martinez with her vehicle while they were on the side of the road, killing Sanchez and leaving Martinez seriously injured. The incident resulted in Copening's arrest for driving under the influence of narcotics. Sanchez's daughters, his widow, the personal representatives of Sanchez's estate, and Martinez and his wife filed a wrongful death and personal injury complaint against Copening. During discovery, it was learned that a state task force designed to protect the general public from unlawful distribution of controlled substances had detected problems with Copening's prescription history. Following review of its computerized tracking program of prescriptions dispensed by pharmacies, the state task force sent a letter informing certain pharmacies about Copening's suspected abuse of narcotics.
     State law provides that narcotic prescriptions should not be honored if a pharmacist deems a prescription to be:

- **Fraudulent**
- Not for a legitimate medical purpose
- Potentially harmful to the customer's health
- Unlawful

     Pharmacists must contact the prescriber before dispensing such prescriptions. If, after the consultation, the pharmacist still reasonably believes that one of the four conditions exists, the narcotic prescription may not be dispensed. Upon discovering the letter about Copening to the pharmacies from the state task force, the original complaint was amended to include the pharmacy chains that dispensed narcotic prescriptions to Copening: Wal-Mart, Long's Drug Stores, Walgreen's, CVS Pharmacy, Rite Aid, Albertson's, and Lam's Pharmacy. All seven of the pharmacy chains had knowledge of Copening's suspected abuse of narcotics when they dispensed her prescriptions.

— *See* Law Fact at the end of this chapter for the answer

Principles and Applications

A **tort** is the legal term for a civil wrong for which a remedy may be obtained. Medical **malpractice** claims are torts that cause injury to patients for which patients may sue for damages. Actions in tort are derived from the **common law**. Common law is derived from court decisions, unlike the laws developed by Congress and state legislatures. Congress and state legislatures, however, can change the common law that governs the **tort system**, and many states have enacted reform laws to reduce the risk of malpractice lawsuits.

Together, the U.S. legal and medical systems must make some difficult trade-offs and policy choices in reforming the nation's tort system. The cost of malpractice, for instance, has driven obstetrician/gynecologist specialists out of certain geographic areas, making health care less accessible (Reyes, 2010). But can it be said that the high cost of the U.S. health care system is the result of a malfunctioning tort system?

Some maintain it is; most, however, maintain malpractice is a **red herring**—named for the aromatic bait that apparently throws bloodhounds off the scent. Malpractice is of little consequence to the total cost of health care, but it is a factor that distracts from implementing real reform of the U.S. health care system. Any real reform must begin with a serious look at malpractice within the context of the largest funder of health care in the United States, Medicare/Medicaid insurance programs that cover care provided to over 113 million Americans (CBO, 2016; CMS, 2015).

Medicare/Medicaid Affect Malpractice Reform

Medicare was enacted in 1965 as part of the nation's federal **social insurance** program, along with need-based Medicaid insurance, with the reluctant support of physicians. The opening section of the legislation enacting Medicare/Medicaid insurance reads:

> *Nothing in this subchapter shall be construed to authorize any Federal officer or employee to exercise any supervision or control over the practice of medicine or the manner in which medical services are provided… or to exercise any supervision or control over the administration or operation of any such institution, agency, or person.*

Social Security Amendments, 42 U.S.C.A. § 1395

The three underlying premises of Medicare/Medicaid insurance, inherent in this Social Security legislation, are:

- Health care providers will always be financially principled
- Patient care will be paramount at all times, as opposed to financial or corporate interests
- Providers will be clinically competent in rendering all care

As it turns out, the three premises are not always true. The theoretical foundation for Medicare/Medicaid insurance was arguably flawed from the start. Today, a half a century after the Medicare/Medicaid insurance programs were first enacted, malpractice is more often than not blamed for the level of difficulty facing health care in the United States. Some of the difficulties include:

- Adherence to **evidence-based clinical practice guidelines** and **best practices** are distressingly low
- Avoidable medical errors are widespread
- Treatment for chronic diseases costs more than $2.2 billion annually
- **Preventable conditions** and chronic disease affect about half of all adults
- Quality of health care is comparably below other similarly developed, high-income countries around the world
- U.S. life expectancy is lower than all other industrialized countries for both women and men
- United States spends more on health care than other high-income countries but has worse outcomes

(CDC, 2016; Commonwealth Fund, 2016; IOM, 2015; Kaiser, 2016).

During the half-century since the decision was made to provide health insurance for Americans 65 and over (the population group most likely to be living in poverty), some lessons have been learned from the nation's largest medical coverage program covering low-income aged, blind, and disabled individuals, as well as parents and their dependent children on welfare. These lessons include:

- Health care delivery systems are important
- **Institutional practices** drive error rates more than individual failings of health care providers
- Coordination of care by physicians is essential to successful health outcomes
- Patient involvement is a factor in medical care quality

- Reliable information about the cost and value of medical services is needed
- Physician complaints seem to be a marker for clinically significant quality lapses in hospitals

(Pyles, 2015; Sage, 2016; Terry, 2014).

While few would defend the tort system as a cost-effective method of either patient compensation or care quality improvement, it has become clear that preventable injuries are a more troubling problem for the U.S. health care system than frivolous lawsuits (Tenner & Ringel, 2014). Choices made about the Medicare/Medicaid insurance programs have ramifications in the legal and health care systems, and these choices must be addressed. Over 58 million American adults have Medicaid coverage, and over 55 million have Medicare coverage (CBO, 2016). Malpractice reform cannot occur without reform of the government health insurance systems that reimburse more than one in three Americans.

Disruptive Innovation

The concept of **disruptive innovation** may be useful for the malpractice sector. The idea known in management circles for the past decade as transformative innovation is what Austrian economist Joseph Schumpeter had in mind when he borrowed the phrase **creative destruction** to describe his theories of how entrepreneurs sustain the **capitalist system** (Schumpeter, 2008/1942). The development of new health insurance products with moderately higher risk sharing and much lower cost may be useful for the **malpractice sector**.

New payment methodologies for providing health insurance that is cheaper and more convenient must be developed if premium costs are to be lowered. Such insurance products are rarely offered, and when they are, as in the case of **health maintenance organizations**, they are subject to intense criticism and resistance from those who have a vested interest in the traditional payment of health care providers. *See Aetna Health Inc. v. Davila*, 542 U.S. 200 (U.S. Supreme Court 2004) (class action suit claiming injuries arising from insurer's decisions not to provide medical coverage for treatment recommended by treating physicians and alleging that the insurer failed to exercise ordinary care in the handling of medical coverage decisions).

Reframing State Regulations

The legal and health care systems have both been guilty of inhibiting discussion of malpractice reform alternatives (McClurg, 2011). While the applicability of the concept of disruptive innovation may be quite limited for regulators given today's political realities, theoretically, the possibility of reframing state insurance regulations could be the innovative change U.S. health care systems need. If there were sufficient changes in framing and regulating **liability insurance** by the states, it might be helpful if government health care programs also went through this process (Hermer, 2014; Smith, 2014).

Reform Market Exit Regulations

One regulatory change that could impact the cost of malpractice insurance is making it more difficult for national insurers to exit the professional liability insurance market in some states while continuing to operate in other states. **Market exits** of insurance carriers from a state leave that carrier's insured clients either uninsured or facing substantial premium increases for the same amount of medical coverage with new insurers (Hermer, 2014). Any hospital or health professional facing an **open claim** or having settled a significant malpractice claim will be uninsurable at comparable rates with a different carrier, regardless of fault.

In addition, switching to a new comparable insurer for the same liability coverage is always more expensive given the experience rating deductions that are based on **claims-free policies**. Policyholders obtain a deduction from their premiums for each year they remain free of filing any claims against their insurance carrier; the more years an insured remains claims-free, the higher the deduction, thus making it prohibitively expensive to switch carriers. When switches must be made, the malpractice premiums start from a higher base.

Reform Claims and Pricing Regulations

Concerns over liability insurance rate hikes appear to have cooled as the industry passes through another cycle. While premiums saw significant rate increases through the late 1990s, the rate hikes have slowed down. Nevertheless, high premiums, at the top of a cycle, will at some point return as an issue (Landry & Landry, 2011). Most state insurance agencies have mediocre controls over claims and pricing to help smooth the behavior of insurers in cyclical markets. State regulators approve high premium increases for one company and then tend to approve increases by other mimicking insurers, creating hot markets.

Compromise Reforms

Liability insurance costs have grown to unprecedented levels for physicians in states where **malpractice reform** has not occurred. After more than 25 years of debate, court battles, lobbying, and even ballot initiatives to amend state constitutions, several compromises are under consideration. They include the following:

- Adopt **noneconomic damage** (pain and suffering) caps on malpractice awards
- Create specialized **administrative health courts**
- Develop **compensation benchmarks** for malpractice payouts
- Develop **medical review panels** where malpractice claimants present their claims before accessing the court system
- Enhance the requirements for insurers to gain entry into state liability insurance markets such as by mandating a greater capital base for entry
- Redefine malpractice by limiting the liability for innovative and experimental medical treatments that do not meet patient expectations
- Extend **enterprise liability** to hospitals and managed care organizations

(*E.g.,* Engstrom, 2015; Hermer, 2014; Kaplow, 2015; Sage, 2016).

No one single compromise is the solution to reducing the risk of malpractice. However, some ideas have fallen by the wayside, including the following:

- Abolishing the common law **collateral source rule** that allows damages to be recovered from third parties for losses already paid by first-party insurance (in other words, attempts to require **damage awards** to be reduced by the amounts received from collateral sources, such as health insurance, have not succeeded)
- Periodic payments of future damage awards (payment of awards periodically rather than in a lump sum)
- Legal limitations on malpractice claims (*See, e.g., Kenyon v. Hammer,* 688 P.2d 961 (Supreme Court of Arizona 1984))
- Limiting **joint liability** and **several liability** (requiring awards for injuries to be proportionately based on the health care provider's level of responsibility when more than one party may be liable for the injury)
- Limits on **punitive damages**
- Restrictions of attorneys' **contingency fees**

(*E.g.,* Laakmann, 2015; Liang, 2015; Popper, 2015; Smith, 2014).

Legislation that has attempted to abolish the common law collateral source rule has generally been struck down under **equal protection** concerns.

How Malpractice Occurs

Malpractice liability occurs when a health care provider:

- Commits an **intentional tort** or wrongful act that injures a patient
- Engages in **negligence** or act that deviates from the accepted **standards of care**

(ALI, 2013).

The core of a malpractice claim is that a health care provider failed to administer the care and skill ordinarily exercised by members of the medical profession. While there are no national standards of care, the United States has moved to a statewide required level of reasonable skill and ability for practicing physicians (*See Gonzales v. Oregon,* 546 U.S. 243 (U.S. Supreme Court 2006) (holding that the federal government does not have the power to declare illegitimate standards for care that are specifically authorized under state laws)).[LN1] Today, evidence-based **clinical practice guidelines** increasingly help define and establish standards of care and help provide a shield against liability.[LN2]

MANAGEMENT AND LAW ISSUES

1. Should there be a limit on the amount of damages permitted for noneconomic pain and suffering, as distinguished from economic damages for costs, such as lost wages?

COURT DECISION
Malpractice

Torres-Lazarini v. United States
[Patient v. Veterans Health Administration]
523 F.3d 69 (U.S. Court of Appeals for the 1st Circuit 2008)

Facts: After Torres-Lazarini injured his shoulder in a fall, he went to a Veterans Health Administration's hospital emergency room in early September 2002 complaining of pain and limited range of motion and was treated by Dr. Rodriguez. Rodriguez examined his shoulder and ordered x-rays of the area. The x-rays revealed no damage from the fall, but did reveal a mild degenerative bone condition indicative of a precursor to osteoporosis. Torres-Lazarini was offered anti-inflammatory drugs but refused them. Rodriguez suggested he apply ice to the shoulder and told him to return in two weeks if there was no improvement.

Torres-Lazarini returned to the hospital with complaints of shoulder pain in three months. Rodriguez reexamined the shoulder and concluded that its condition had worsened. She offered to refer Torres-Lazarini to a physiatrist, a specialist who could determine if an MRI study was required and who would recommend physical therapy, if appropriate. He turned down these suggestions. He returned to the hospital again within a month still complaining of shoulder pain, but refused Rodriguez's offer to evaluate his shoulder.

Eight months later, he had another appointment with Rodriguez but refused further evaluation of his shoulder. Rodriguez recommended that he undergo an MRI, receive physical therapy, and schedule follow-up appointments. Torres-Lazarini underwent an MRI a few weeks later. The MRI revealed osteoarthritis and tearing of several tendons in the shoulder. Torres-Lazarini was told that although surgery would not necessarily help restore his range of motion, it would ease his pain. He declined the surgery and sued the Veterans Health Administration for malpractice.

At trial, an orthopedic surgeon who had never examined Torres-Lazarini testified that Rodriguez breached her duty of care by failing to conduct an orthopedic evaluation shortly after his fall and by waiting two years before conducting an MRI. He also testified that surgery soon after the accident would have restored his range of motion and alleviated his pain. The Veterans Health Administration presented the testimony of its expert, an orthopedic surgeon who physically examined Torres-Lazarini, asserting that severe osteoarthritis was causing the shoulder pain. He stated Rodriguez's recommendation of physical therapy was the proper treatment for loss of motion due to a dislocated shoulder. He further testified that there was no **breach of care** because it was not standard practice to refer a patient with negative x-rays to an orthopedist. Standard procedures were immediately ordering x-rays, recommending a course of anti-inflammatory drugs, and scheduling follow-up appointments. Finally, he stated that Rodriguez's recommendation that he receive evaluation from a physiatrist was proper.

Issue: Did Rodriguez commit malpractice when she did not immediately order an MRI after x-rays came back negative?

Holding and Decision: No. Torres-Lazarini failed to prove that Rodriguez committed malpractice; referral to a physiatrist to determine if an MRI was necessary was not a deviation from standard medical practice.

Analysis: Negligence is defined as conduct that falls below the standard established by law for the protection of others against unreasonable risk of injury. It generally arises from a failure to exercise the appropriate **standard of care**. The court found that the care Torres-Lazarini received for his shoulder was in full compliance with the standards of the medical profession for the type of soft tissue injury he suffered. While health care providers may still be found to have imposed an unreasonable risk on a patient even when they apply the standard diagnoses and carefully evaluate all possible medical treatments, the court also found that Torres-Lazarini refused the conservative treatment offered to him: he missed appointments, rejected physical therapy, and refused to cooperate with Rodriguez in assessing and treating his shoulder injury.

Courts generally use the **"but for" test** to determine the existence of negligence. Courts use the **substantial factor test** when the "but for" test might allow each individual health care provider to escape responsibility because the conduct of one or more of the others would have been sufficient to produce the same result. Under the substantial factor test, a provider's conduct is a cause of the result if it is a substantial factor in bringing it about. In this case, Rodriguez was the only treating physician. Under the "but for" test, proximate cause is established when three elements are proven:

- The injury is a natural and probable result of the negligence
- There is no other relevant intervening cause
- "But for" the negligent action, the injury would not have occurred

While no negligence was found, the court noted the shoulder complications were caused by other intervening factors such as age, multiple other falls, and degenerative joint illness, as opposed to any negligent actions of Rodriguez.

Rule of Law: When a malpractice claim alleges negligence against a health care professional with a duty to provide care, three elements must be demonstrated:

- Generally recognized standard of care
- Deviation from that standard
- The deviation was the cause of any injuries

References discussing this court decision: N/A

Malpractice Myths

The U.S. legal system's use of the tort system is often blamed for the lack of access to quality health care services due to the rising costs of liability insurance. The public is convinced there is a malpractice crisis due to excessive verdicts. Medical malpractice costs account for less than 2% of the nation's health care costs.

Myth: Malpractice Costs Raise the Nation's Health Care Costs

Malpractice costs account for less than 2% of total health care spending (CBO, 2013). This may seem insignificant until one realizes this is 2% of $2.6 trillion, which is the total amount spent on health care each year (CMS, 2016). The national cost of malpractice passed on to consumers now becomes approximately $51 billion (about $160 per capita).

While a 25 to 30% reduction in malpractice costs would lower health care costs by less than half of 1% (about $12 billion), the likely effect on the nation's health care costs would be comparably small (CBO, 2013). It seems that attention should be directed to areas where greater cost savings can be achieved. Malpractice costs are the red herring that diverts attention from the real issue of why many Americans still lack affordable access to quality health care. Where are the cost savings in the remaining $2.5 trillion in total health care spending?

The health care delivery system has diverted its attention to the costs of malpractice, blaming the legal and insurance industries for the nation's rising health care costs, while failing to adequately address the costs associated with its own:

- Excessive administrative expenses
- Inappropriate care
- Inefficiencies
- Inflated prices
- Medical errors
- Poor management
- Waste and fraud

(*E.g.*, Brown, 2014; Hall, 2014; Pardue, 2016; Sage, 2016).

The total cost of malpractice is a valid cost to be examined, but this does not address the more important issue of how over 98% of the *other* health care costs are being spent.

Myth: Malpractice Settlements Are Pervasive and Irrational

Almost two-thirds of all malpractice claims are not meritorious and most such claims are resolved without any payment of money (OIG, 2016). Contrary to popular opinion, empirical research over the past two decades shows malpractice settlements are deliberate and rational. Furthermore, no academic study has ever found a significant volume of successful frivolous malpractice claims (*See* Frakes & Jena, 2014).

The amounts awarded to injured patients generally correlate to the merits of the underlying claims of negligence (Farrow, 2010). Malpractice settlements are the product of an insurance claims process that acts much like **peer review** in evaluating cases arising from negligence or intentional torts. Insurance payments are:

- Least likely when the quality of medical care was high
- Somewhat more likely when the quality of medical care was uncertain
- Most likely when the quality of medical care was inadequate

(Harris et al., 2015; *See* McClurg, 2011).

Medical Review Panels

The idea of medical review panels is an example of **disruptive regulation** that first surfaced in the 1980s but did not survive judicial scrutiny. Different from peer review, these panels conduct preliminary hearings before a malpractice trial to determine the validity of the complaint. Recently, a regulatory proposal to establish a new complaint process for Medicare claimants has given new life to medical review panels (*E.g.,* Ginsberg, 2016).

Modifying Medicare's Complaint Process

Disruptive regulation could occur at key exchange points between the federal government and the Medicare insured to remove well-established but fundamentally misguided biases that diminish the effectiveness of Medicare (Laakmann, 2015). Medicare's **quality improvement organizations** that currently handle complaints by the Medicare insured could be revamped to use medical review panels to:

- Hear and resolve real cases of medical injury
- Mediate discussions with patients
- Award reasonable compensation
- Provide feedback to participating health care providers regarding the safety and quality of their care

(*See* Peer Review Improvement Act, 42 U.S.C.A. §§ 1320c-1320c-12) (authorizing quality improvement organizations).

By modifying the complaint process for the Medicare insured, current peer review practices could be constructively disrupted for a significant patient population. Restructuring the process between patient experience and system response would change the complaint process from one that is relatively weak to one that could produce real results (Ginsberg, 2016).

MANAGEMENT AND LAW ISSUES

2. Should malpractice claims be permitted at all, or should physicians be permitted to make mistakes along with everyone else?
3. Should malpractice claims be permitted when the patient's initial need for medical care arose from the patient's own negligence or misconduct, such as an illegal drug overdose, an accident caused by driving under the influence, or cancer due to smoking?

Financial Incentives Based on Quality and Efficiency

Opponents of Medicare's **financial incentives** maintain that not all patient complications (such as pressure ulcers, ventilator-associated pneumonia, and catheter-associated urinary tract infections) are necessarily reflective of medical errors or poor care. They contend that complete avoidance of such conditions is impossible and complications generally occur with the sickest patients. Opponents claim providers will not want to care for the sickest patients since they will be punished for the patient's poor health when complications arise. Providers can reduce risks, but even with what is considered optimum care, bad things can happen.[LN3] If Medicare aligns financial incentives with the dual goals of improving health care quality and efficiency, however, this might enable collaborative quality improvement (Ginsberg, 2016). For the first time since Medicare was established, health care providers might have the opportunity to promptly identify, resolve, and learn from medical errors as real malpractice cases are resolved through medical review panels (Laakmann, 2015).

Noneconomic Damages Caps

With the national median jury award for malpractice liability approaching half a million dollars (Falk, 2014), noneconomic damages caps appear to reduce malpractice premium growth (Rodwin et al., 2015). States that have enacted caps on awards for noneconomic damages have had significantly lower rates of malpractice premium increases than those without caps. While these facts have proven persuasive to the 35 state legislatures that have placed limits on noneconomic damages (ATRA, 2016), the challenges to this damage cap reform continues. Eight state supreme courts have found a cap on noneconomic damages in wrongful death malpractice cases to be unconstitutional (Menaker, 2014).[LN4]

Determining noneconomic damages is largely left to the discretion of the courts, and juries in particular. Such awards are often based on the following multiples of the economic damages:

- Lost wages
- Medical expenses
- Rehabilitation costs

(Sanders, 2015; Tenner & Ringel, 2014)

Economic damages are not discretionary, as claimed by many opponents of malpractice reform (Rhee, 2012); they must be proven at trial either by expert reports and testimony, or by documentary proof, such as itemized medical bills. Supporters maintain that noneconomic damages caps balance the occasional need for lawsuits with the larger public need for affordable health care.

Limits on Malpractice Awards

Limits on malpractice awards (that include economic and noneconomic damages) have been adopted in all but 15 states. Opponents are challenging noneconomic **damage caps** (showing the principle that no malpractice reform is ever final), arguing that caps violate the **separation of powers principle** and the rights of juries. While these arguments have generally been unsuccessful, the challenges continue (Menaker, 2014). Supporters counter by citing the rule of law that the legislative branch has always been able to alter common law remedies, whether in the form of changing laws by:

- Limiting damage awards
- Refusing to recognize punitive damages
- Shifting the **burdens of proof**

(*E.g.*, Cheng & Yang, 2014; Lens, 2014).

Entry and Exit Restrictions for the Liability Insurance Industry

Evidence on the role of aberrant pricing in the severity of swings between **hard liability markets** (when liability insurance is expensive and difficult to obtain) and **soft liability markets** (when liability insurance is plentiful and prices may become unrealistically low) supports the belief that insurers who undercharge, due to inexperience or excessive risk taking, contribute to excessive competition during soft liability markets. This has resulted in excessive price increases and insurer exits during a hard liability market. It is not the large insurance carriers with over 100 years of experience selling policies and total assets in the hundreds of billions that start the atypical pricing cycles; rather it is the new players who simply have to show **financial viability** to enter today's insurance market (Epstein & Hyman, 2013).

It is only within the last decade of **deregulation** that insurance carriers were no longer required to provide performance guarantees and performance bonds to enter the industry. Appropriate regulatory policies must weigh the competitive benefits of easy entry and exit of new insurance businesses against the costs and disruption to the health care industry of deviations from what is normal pricing of liability insurance. Some restrictions, such as the following that are being returned to the books for the banking industry could also be applied to the liability insurance sector:

- Activities restrictions and regulations
- Guidelines on **capital maintenance** and distributions of **free cash flow**
- Mandates requiring diversification of investments
- Regulation of management quality and investment policy

(*See* Epstein & Hyman, 2013).

Liability Limitations for Innovative and Experimental Medical Treatments

The increasing pace of medical innovation and experimental treatments demands a better definition of malpractice. Physicians should not be liable, absent negligence, if cutting-edge treatments do not meet patient expectations (Chen & Yang, 2014). Complicated medical procedures simply do not always work out due to their complexity (*See* Chapter on Patient Rights and Responsibilities: Patients' Right to Experimental Medical Treatments).

Compensation Benchmarks for Malpractice Payouts

Research on the value of a **quality-adjusted life year** could be used in malpractice litigation, which has an impact on health care costs (Hermer, 2014).[LN5] For instance, the value of each life year is about $150,000; therefore, in a case where negligence costs a patient 10 years of life, a figure of $1.5 million could be used to begin settlement negotiations (*See* Lee et al., 2009) (authors took the $129,000 research figures in the 2009 Lee research and computed it to the 2016 present value of $150,000; *See* Chapter on Patient Rights and Responsibilities: Quality of Life Research). Providing a benchmark is important as it establishes a precedent for how compensation should be set.

A number of malpractice lawsuits have ended in higher payouts that have set new precedents. The costs of malpractice lawsuits hurt the health care system in the sense that physicians and hospitals pay these costs and, ultimately, patients pay the bill (Lee et al., 2009). In order to avoid being hit with a malpractice lawsuit, physicians:

- Curtail or halt their practice of medicine altogether
- Move their practices to more lucrative locations, leaving behind medically underserved areas
- Practice **defensive medicine**, ordering excessive tests and treatments which in turn drives up the overall cost of health care
- Tailor their practices to more lucrative specialties, resulting in a shortage of general physicians

(Hermer, 2014; Wiley, 2016).

Redefining Malpractice

While the benefits of enterprise liability far outweigh its disadvantages, there are differences on a number of issues like the choice between hospitals as the responsible enterprise. Regardless, malpractice could be redefined in terms of:

- **Boundaries of liabilities** or line-drawing where foreseeable harms can arise from negligent conduct, such as the line between exercise of discretion and breach of fiduciary duty
- Physician negligence
- **Corporate practice prohibitions**

- Performance improvement
- **Risk management**
- Patient safety

(Sage, 2016; Tenner & Ringel, 2014).

Boundaries of Liabilities

States must define the boundaries of **vicarious liability** (*See* Cortez, 2011). Courts are combining the **duty to warn** with the **duty of care**, which enlarges the field of physician liability (Schwartz & Appel, 2011). In practice, this combination of duties raises the possibility that physicians may:

- Be on notice of the consequences of **polypharmacy** prescribing, the all too common medical practice of prescribing a multitude of approved drugs for patients in combinations that have never been clinically tested by the pharmaceutical industry for their interactions together
- Over-warn patients about every conceivable side effect of prescription drugs, thereby deterring patients from following their adherence to treatment regimens
- Reconsider prescribing drugs they believe will be effective

Since physicians already owe a duty of care to patients, this does not impose a new **duty**, but perhaps unnecessarily expands a duty to non-patients.

COURT DECISION
Negligence

Coombes v. Florio
[Patient v. Accident Victim]
877 N.E.2d 567 (Supreme Court of Massachusetts 2007);
followed by *Jarmie v. Troncale*, 50 A.2d 802 (Supreme Court of Connecticut 2012)

Facts: Lyn-Ann Coombes brought this lawsuit on behalf of her 10-year-old son, Kevin Coombes, who was killed while standing on the sidewalk with a friend when David Sacca, a patient of Dr. Roland Florio, lost consciousness while driving and struck the boy when his car left the road. Coombes claimed the accident was a result of the side effects caused by the eight prescription drugs Florio prescribed to Sacca. By the date of the accident, Sacca was 75 years old and suffered from several serious health conditions including asbestosis, chronic bronchitis, emphysema, high blood pressure, and metastatic lung cancer. While Florio had warned Sacca not to drive during his cancer treatments, he advised Sacca he could drive again when his treatments ended. Potential side effects of the combination of drugs Florio had prescribed to Sacca at the time of the accident included drowsiness, dizziness, lightheadedness, fainting, altered consciousness, and sedation. Moreover, combining prescription drugs often causes more severe side effects than the side effects resulting from individual use. The standard of care for a primary care physician includes warning elderly or chronically ill patients about the potential side effects of combining prescription drugs and their effect on a patient's ability to drive. Florio did not warn Sacca about any potential side effects of the various drugs prescribed or the possibility they could impair Sacca's ability to drive.

Issue: Does a physician's duty to warn patients of the side effects of prescription drugs extend to foreseeable third party non-patients?

Holding and Decision: Yes. The duty to warn extends to foreseeable third party non-patients.

Analysis: The court made clear this was an ordinary negligence claim and not a medical malpractice claim, which would require a direct physician-patient relationship. Florio was found negligent under ordinary common law negligence principles in prescribing drugs without warning Sacca of their potential side effects. The duty to warn extended to Coombes because his injury was a foreseeable consequence of Florio's negligence.

To bring a negligence claim, Coombes had to show the existence of an act or omission that violated a duty owed to him by Florio. A precondition of the required duty is foreseeability, which means that the risk of the injury which occurred must have been foreseeable to Florio. Physicians have a duty of reasonable care, including the duty to warn their patients about side effects when prescribing drugs. When the side effects involved are likely to impair the patient's **mental capacity**, the foreseeable risk of injury in an automobile accident is not limited to the patient alone.

Turning to similar cases outside the medical context, the duty of reasonable care extends to all those involved when there is a foreseeable risk of an automobile accident. In addition, when the risk involved is large, it is irrelevant whether Florio did foresee, or should have foreseen, the particular circumstances even if Sacca was an **intermediary actor**.

The duty to warn patients about the effects of prescription drugs has generally been limited to drugs taken in a physician's presence. This time, however, this distinction was not made. Instead, the court concluded the risk of potential side effects was foreseeable when the physician issued the prescription, regardless of where the prescribed drugs were taken. Finally, the court determined public policy favors imposing a duty on physicians under these circumstances, reasoning the duty will not impose a heavy burden on physicians because existing duties already require physicians to warn their patients of the side effects of prescription drugs. Additionally, the benefit of imposing the duty is significant because the duty protects the public from the foreseeable risk of known side effects impairing a patient's ability to drive.

In response to Florio's argument that fear of litigation arising from this duty would impose on a physician's decision about course of treatment, the court asserted the duty only involves warning a patient of side effects and does not imply negligence in choosing a course of medical treatment. Florio also argued against increasing malpractice in ways that could become costly for the health care system. Physicians are not, in ordinary circumstances, legally responsible for the safety of others on the highway, or elsewhere, based on medical treatment afforded patients. The duty still resides with patients to know how prescription drugs affect them; under this decision, however, some of that duty of care may be shifted to prescribing physicians. The decision enhances the duty to warn of the potential side effects of all prescribed drugs.

When applying the foregoing analysis to the facts of this case, the court said the number and combination of prescription drugs Sacca took increased the potential severity of any side effects and the likelihood that his driving ability would become impaired. The court further concluded that Florio owed a duty to all those foreseeably put at risk by his **failure to warn**, including Coombes. Ultimately it will be a factual determination for a jury to decide whether Florio breached that duty, but the granting of summary judgment was inappropriately based on a finding of no duty assigned to Coombes. Finally, the court clarified that Coombes did not assert Florio had any affirmative duty to control Sacca's actions and the claim asserted was limited to Florio's duty to warn Sacca of side effects. The court was clear that Florio was not the cause of Coombes's injury; Sacca was responsible for knowing how he was reacting to the prescription drugs he was taking. The jury must decide what degree of responsibility Sacca's prescribing physician, if any, shared.

Rule of Law: The duty to warn patients of the side effects of prescription drugs extends to non-patients foreseeably put at risk by a failure to warn.

References discussing this court decision: *E.g.*, Schwartz & Appel, 2011.

Enterprise Liability

Vicarious liability is an area of ever-expanding liability that arises under the common law **doctrine of agency** (*respondeat superior*). Any third person who has the right, ability, or duty to control the activities of a health care professional whose conduct resulted in an injury might be vicariously liable. All it takes to be liable is that the third party knew or should have known of the conduct and failed to take immediate and appropriate corrective action.

Enterprise liability, a form of vicarious liability, could improve patient safety by changing existing laws to make hospitals or managed care organizations vicariously liable for the malpractice of individual physicians. While states will need to decide such issues as whether patient injuries occurring in outpatient facilities or those caused by medical errors during office visits following hospitalization should be covered by enterprise liability, these state decisions arguably are relatively inconsequential. Most malpractice claims arise out of medical care given inside hospitals (*See* Liang, 2015).

In the rest of the health care industry, the entity that delivers the medical products is vicariously liable for the **medical errors** of its workforce. Medical products manufacturers are liable for defective products, not the individuals on the team who engineered the product. Liability is shifted entirely from individuals to the larger business enterprise. As a practical matter, the medical products industry operates under a system in which the enterprise bears all the costs of legal liability. By contrast, most malpractice claims are brought against physicians and other individual health care providers (Mantel, 2013).

Corporate Practice Prohibitions

Private practice physicians have always been different. Unlike highly trained professionals in the medical products industry, physicians have historically been treated as independent contractors, not employees, and have valued the independence associated with this status. A century ago, when physicians feared that corporate employment of physicians would threaten the prevailing model of private practice, they successfully lobbied for enactment of corporate practice prohibitions. They have resisted corporate influence ever since, most recently in their alliance with patients to limit the power of managed care organizations (*See Davila*, 542 U.S. 200). However, physician independence has a cost.

Hospital-Based Physicians

Some states impose vicarious liability on hospitals for the conduct of physicians who are exclusively hospital-based, such as emergency medicine and anesthesiology physicians (Sage, 2016). Insurance rates are a strong reason against expanding a physician's duty to non-patients by vicarious liability. The courts have asserted, however, that limiting physician liability to reduce malpractice rates is a decision best reserved for Congress and state legislatures.

Attending Physicians

Physicians who are not hospital-based are generally treated as independent contractors rather than as agents or employees of the hospital. Hospitals therefore may escape vicarious liability for the medical errors of attending physicians.

Performance Improvement

Enterprise liability would more optimally use the resources hospitals could bring to system quality activities. Only institutions can muster the resources to bring about systematic improvements in performance (*See* Kahn, 2012). Quality improvement theory, with its emphasis on systems design as opposed to individual fault, focuses on system strategies such as:

- Accommodation of foreseeable human error
- Better monitoring of medical errors
- Examination of **hand-offs** between shifts
- Review of multi-person diagnostic and treatment processes

(Hafemeister & Porter, 2013; Liang, 2015).

Hospitals, of course, do not want any additional liability shifted to their organizations and often oppose enterprise liability. They are content with shifting liability onto individual providers, away from their institutions.

Anesthesiology Innovations

The power of enterprise liability is best illustrated by the late 1990s reduction in anesthesia accidents such as poor reactions to anesthesia or oxygen supply deficiency from errors or faulty equipment. It happened because Harvard University Health Services was looking to lower the payouts made for anesthesia injuries in its nine teaching hospitals. Harvard's risk managers asked hospital anesthesiologists to investigate why their collective experience was so poor. As a result of their investigation, the anesthesiologists collectively devised new techniques and equipment to lower the risk of anesthesiology mishaps.

At the same time, the American Society of Anesthesiologists conducted an intensive study of the causes of anesthesia-related injuries and developed better protocols (ASA, 2016). The improved standards of practice that resulted from these combined efforts have since become the standard of care. As a result, mortality rates from anesthesia accidents dropped from 1 in 10,000 to 1 in about 200,000 today, a 20-fold improvement in less than two decades. Liability insurance premiums for the specialty of anesthesiology went from being among the highest in medicine to among the lowest. These successful innovations in anesthesiology were prompted in part by the system of enterprise liability operating at

Harvard. Like most medical schools, Harvard protected its anesthesiologists from the threat of liability by purchasing liability insurance on their behalf. Having done so, Harvard had a strong incentive to look for ways to bring down the cost of that insurance.

Risk Management

The emphasis presently is on managing risks in health care systems as opposed to focusing on the performance of individual health care providers. The greatest improvements in patient safety come from greater attention to the processes by which health care is delivered, since most medical errors are due to system breakdown, not individual medical errors. Greater attention to the system of delivery, rather than individual medical errors, enables risk managers to identify those stages of the process at which medical errors are most common and to redesign those stages to make medical errors less common, and more swiftly and effectively corrected.

Accomplishing this objective requires both the capacity and the willingness to look at the entire health care delivery system. Hospitals are better situated to accomplish this than individual physicians. The traditional system of individual physician liability greatly reduces the hospital's incentive to take the necessary steps and then weather the possible backlash from physicians about interference with their discretion. Enterprise liability could produce that incentive.

Patient Safety

Many promising safety initiatives are led by hospitals that already operate under a system of enterprise liability. For instance, Kaiser Permanente improves its world-renowned diagnostic accuracy by using tools like computer decision-support systems, to:

- Help order correct tests
- Institute proper follow-up plans
- Obtain complete medical histories
- Perform adequate physical exams

Hospitals like Kaiser, who are at the forefront of patient safety, voluntarily disclose medical errors and also employ and insure their attending physicians (Sage, 2016). Enterprise liability has two advantages regarding patient safety. First, enterprise liability could permit physicians to discuss medical errors and near misses more freely. Enterprise liability is not risk-free; for instance, eliminating individual physician liability could theoretically dilute the effort physicians make to avoid patient injuries. Second is the potential to increase physician participation in patient safety initiatives, along with physician willingness to disclose medical errors to **patient safety committees**. By eliminating individual liability, enterprise liability makes it easier for hospitals to institute a blame-free culture that encourages open discussion of medical errors. Yet, that risk is already diluted by the availability of liability insurance that is not experience-rated and by the belief that physicians are not compensated for avoidance of patient injury (Shieh, 2014).

Experience Rating

Hospitals, unlike individual physicians, can be experience-rated. Insurance rates for hospitals are based on actual claims as opposed to the demographics of their geographic community (like individual physicians). **Experience rating** creates a powerful incentive to reduce medical errors. Health care causes far too many accidental injuries to avoid taking advantage of this potential to enhance patient safety.

While hospitals have an obvious financial reason to resist the transfer of legal responsibility entirely onto their shoulders, the issue is more complex for physicians. On the one hand, enterprise liability would take them out of the shadow of malpractice liability. On the other hand, physicians have traditionally opposed expanding hospital vicarious liability because they fear it will bring greater interference with their medical decision-making. Yet, this objection evokes a health care world that has long since passed. With rare exceptions, physicians already function as part of complex systems, and physicians understand the importance of building those systems carefully. Furthermore, enterprise liability has existed in university hospitals and **staff-model managed care organizations** for many years. Sooner or later, malpractice law must adapt. In hindsight, it is now obvious that the law's delay in doing so has been harmful for both physicians and patients, keeping individual physicians on the front line of malpractice litigation and depriving patients of the safety systems that enterprise liability will produce.

Administrative Health Courts

There is increased momentum to take malpractice cases out of traditional courts and assign them to administrative health courts modeled after the **Vaccine Injury Compensation Program**, a no-fault alternative to the traditional legal system (Engstrom, 2015). Congress has proposed legislation authorizing the creation of such specialized courts, and legislation has also been proposed in about half a dozen states to use expert judges instead of juries to award compensation in medical malpractice cases in which injuries are claimed as a result of medical errors or omissions in medical treatment. Administrative health courts have also been recommended by the Institute of Medicine (*See* IOM, 2013) and the American Medical Association (AMA, 2014).

An Accountable Tort System

The dysfunctional tort system that neither deters medical errors nor consistently recognizes and pays patients who are injured needs to be replaced (Ginsburg & Wright, 2013; Mello et al., 2011). If medical errors and preventable adverse events can be prevented through good organizational design and management, the U.S. health care system has no excuse for not adopting management reforms supported by evidence-based academic research. The new health care reform laws are now refusing to pay the $4.4 billion in annual costs that Medicare always paid for adverse events, which is a significant beginning to reform of the U.S. tort system (*See* Frakes, 2015).

LAW FACT

Negligence

Do pharmacies have a fiduciary duty to protect the public from customers who may be abusing prescription drugs?

No. Pharmacies do not owe a duty to third parties with whom they have no direct relationship. The act of dispensing prescription drugs does not create a legal duty. Therefore, the standards of care imposed on pharmacies do not extend to the public and unidentified third parties under current law.

— *Sanchez v. Wal-Mart Stores, Inc.*, 221 P.3d 1276 (Supreme Court of Nevada 2009).

See, e.g., Stempel, 2014 (discussing this decision).

CHAPTER SUMMARY

- Malpractice claims are civil wrongs caused by negligence or intentional conduct that cause injury for which patients may sue for damages.
- Malpractice claims are blamed for some of the difficulties the U.S. health care system faces, such as quality of health care and relative health of patients being lower than that of similar countries, despite spending more per capita on health care.
- It is suggested that the focus be shifted to preventing injury in the first place and away from the tort system in order to improve quality and patient safety.
- Liability insurance rates are highest in states where malpractice reform has not occurred.
- Some suggestions for reforming malpractice law include the implementation of medical review panels, pain and suffering damage caps, limited liability for experimental treatments, enterprise liability, and specialized administration health courts.
- To prove a malpractice claim, three elements must be demonstrated: 1) generally recognized standard of care, 2) deviation from that standard, and 3) the deviation was the cause of any injuries.

- Malpractice costs account for less than 2% of health care spending and a reduction in such costs would have little effect on insurance premiums.
- Contrary to popular belief, malpractice awards are generally rational and deliberate; they are not usually obtained when the claim is frivolous or lacks merit.
- Despite the legal challenges that the idea of medical review panels has faced, the idea is still pursued by Medicare and states, particularly Wyoming, as a method of reducing malpractice litigation.
- Those other than the patient, who were foreseeably harmed by the patient's medical treatment or lack thereof, may press malpractice claims under some circumstances.
- The greatest improvements in patient safety come from greater attention to risk management, since most medical errors are due to system failures as opposed to individual medical errors.
- Although enterprise liability may eliminate individual physician liability, it has the potential to greatly improve patient safety by increasing physician participation in patient safety initiatives and encouraging open disclosure and resolution of medical errors.

LAW NOTES

1. While health care providers collectively set standards of care, at least three practical realities dispel the notion of national standards. These include:

    - The practical difficulty of proving exactly what the prevailing medical standard is, since the standard is generally custom-based for each patient and can differ by locale and even by provider.
    - To the extent the standard of care is ascertained, by continuing to give such medical care, providers are creating and perpetuating the very standards with which they may not want to comply.
    - Medicine is regulated at the state level where physicians and other health care professionals are licensed to practice within a certain locality.

2. Evidence-based guidelines are published by the Agency for Healthcare Research and Quality, in partnership with the American Medical Association and the American Association of Health Plans, and are available through the National Guideline Clearinghouse.

3. The argument against Medicare's financial incentives is that they are too little, too late. Most non-Medicare markets already bear 100% of the financial costs of any medical errors. For instance, Medicare reimburses health care providers on a fee-for-service basis. This means that if a provider makes a mistake that injures a patient and the patient requires follow-up care, Medicare will pay for both the care that caused the injury and the follow-up care. Medicare thus rewards medical errors with extra payments. In other words, providers are paid more when quality is worse, such as when medical complications occur as the result of medical error. Medicare recently acknowledged this problem and no longer reimburses providers for hospital services attendant to hospital-acquired conditions (such as catheter-associated urinary tract infections) or hospital or physician services attendant to "never events," defined as events that should never happen (such as performing the wrong test on a patient or a duplicate test).

    One alternative to fee-for-service Medicare is the adoption of Medicare prepaid group plans. Medicare would give health care providers a flat amount per Medicare recipient. When combined with an integrated delivery system, where the hospital and all the physicians work for the same entity, prepayment places the cost of avoidable medical errors squarely on providers. Following a medical error, the providers themselves have to pay the cost of any additional care. Under fee-for-service payment, providers lose money if they reduce medical errors; under prepayment, providers profit by reducing medical errors (Starr, 2013). This is how the Veterans Health Administration operates.

4. At least eight state supreme courts—those in Alabama, Florida, Georgia, Illinois, Missouri, New Hampshire, Oregon, and Washington—have struck down statutorily enacted malpractice damage caps for malpractice (Menaker, 2014).

5. The most commonly used compensation benchmark for the value of a quality-adjusted life year is based on end-stage renal disease, the one disease for which Medicare has provided universal health care services since the 1970s. On average, $150,000 is spent per quality-adjusted life year on each kidney dialysis patient suffering from this disease (computed research figures represent present values) (*See generally* Lee, et al., 2009; *See also* Chapter on Patients' Rights and Responsibilities: Quality of Life Research).

REFERENCES

ALI (American Law Institute). (2013). *A concise restatement of torts* (3rd ed.). Philadelphia, PA: ALI.

AMA (American Medical Association). (2014). *Medical liability reform NOW! The facts you need to know to address the broken medical liability system.* Chicago, IL: AMA.

ASA (American Society of Anesthesiologists). (2016). *ASA standards, guidelines and statements.* Park Ridge, IL: ASA.

ATRA (American Tort Reform Association). (2016). *Noneconomic damages reform.* Washington, DC: ATRA.

Brown, E. C. F. (2014). Irrational hospital pricing. *Houston Journal of Health Law and Policy, 14*, 11–58.

CBO (Congressional Budget Office). (2016). *Updated budget projections.* Washington, DC: CBO.

CDC (Centers for Disease Control and Prevention). (2016). *Chronic disease overview.* Atlanta, GA, CDC.

Cheng, B. K., & Yang, C.-Y. (2014). Increased perception of malpractice liability and the practice of defensive medicine. *Journal of Empirical Legal Studies, 11*, 446–476.

CMS (Centers for Medicare/Medicaid Service). (2016). *National health expenditures reports.* Baltimore, MD: CMS.

___. (2015). *Medicaid and CHIP applications,* eligibility determinations, and enrollment report.

Commonwealth Fund. (2016). *U.S. health care from a global perspective.* New York, NY.

Cortez, N. (2011). Embracing the new geography of health care: A novel way to cover those left out of health reform. *Southern California Law Review, 84*, 859–931.

Engstrom, N. F. (2015). A dose of reality for specialized courts: Lessons from the VICP. *University of Pennsylvania Law Review, 163*, 1631–1717.

Epstein, R. A., & Hyman, D. A. (2013). Fixing Obamacare: The virtues of choice, competition, and deregulation. *New York University Annual Survey of American Law, 68*, 493–537.

Falk, J. (2014). Resuscitating noneconomic medical malpractice damage caps in Illinois. *DePaul Law Review, 64*, 185–212.

Farrow, F. L. (2010). The anti-patient psychology of health courts: Prescriptions from a lawyer-physician. *American Journal of Law and Medicine, 36*, 188–219.

Frakes, M. D. (2015). The surprising relevance of medical malpractice law. *University of Chicago Law Review, 82*, 317–391.

Frakes, M. D., & Jena, A. B. (2014). *Does malpractice law improve health care quality?* Cambridge, MA: National Bureau of Economic Research.

Ginsberg, M. D. (2016). The execution of an arbitration provision as a condition precedent to medical treatment: Legally enforceable? Medically ethical? *William Mitchell Law Review, 42*, 273–318.

Ginsburg, D. H., & Wright, D. (2013). Antitrust courts: Specialists versus generalists. *Fordham International Law Journal, 36*, 788–810.

Hafemeister, T. L., & Porter, J. H. (2013). Don't let go of the rope: Reducing readmissions by recognizing hospitals' fiduciary duties to their discharged patients. *American University Law Review, 62*, 513–576.

Hall, M. A. (2014). Evaluating the Affordable Care Act: The eye of the beholder. *Houston Law Review, 51*, 1029–1056.

Harris, W. H., et al. (2015). Legal malpractice damages: Settlement-value as an emerging basis for proving causation and damages. *Houston Lawyer, 53*, 10–13.

Hermer, L. D. (2014). Aligning incentives in accountable care organizations: The role of malpractice reform. *Journal of Health Care Law and Policy, 17*, 271–302.

Howe, E. W. (2015). *Ventures in common sense.* Charlestown, SC: Forgotten Press. (Original work published 1883.)

IOM (Institute of Medicine). (2015). *Improving diagnosis in health care.* Washington, DC: The National Academies Press.

___. (2013). *Geographic variation in health care spending and promotion of high-value care.*

Kahn, W. A. (2012). Accountable care organizations: A response to critical voices. *DePaul Journal of Health Care Law, 14*, 309–339.

Kaiser Family Foundation. (2016). *How does U.S. life expectancy compare to other countries?* Menlo Park, CA: Kaiser.

Kaplow, L. (2015). Information and the aim of adjudication: Truth or consequences? *Stanford Law Review, 67*, 1303–1371.

Laakmann, A. B. (2015). When should physicians be liable for innovation? *Cardozo Law Review, 36*, 913–968.

Landry, A. Y., & Landry III, R. J. (2011). Medical bankruptcy reform: A fallacy of composition. *American Bankruptcy Institute Law Review, 19*, 151–182.

Lee, C. P., et al. (2009). An empiric estimate of the value of life: Updating the renal analysis cost-effectiveness standard. *Value in Health, 12*(1), 80–87.

Lens, J. W. (2014). Tort law's deterrent effect and procedural due process. *Tulsa Law Review, 50*, 115–156.

Liang, C.-M. (2015). Rethinking the tort liability system and patient safety: From the conventional wisdom to learning from litigation. *Indiana Health Law Review, 12*, 327–376.

Mantel, J. (2013). The myth of the independent physician: Implications for health law, policy, and ethics. *Case Western Reserve Law Review, 64*, 455–519.

McClurg, A. J. (2011). Fight club: Doctors vs. lawyers; A peace plan grounded in self-interest. *Temple Law Review, 83*, 309–367.

Mello, M. M., et al. (2011). *Administrative compensation for medical injuries: Lessons from three foreign systems.* New York, NY: The Commonwealth Fund.

Menaker, P. S. (2014). *Litigation news: Caps on noneconomic damages held unconstitutional.* Chicago, IL: American Bar Association.

OIG (Office of Inspector General). (2016). *National practitioner data bank: Malpractice reporting requirements.* Washington, DC: U.S. Department of Health and Human Services, OIG.

Pardue, C. (2016). How will I know? An auditing privilege and health care compliance. *Emory Law Journal, 65*, 1139–1176.

Popper, A. F. (2015). The Affordable Care Act is not tort reform. *Catholic University Law Review, 65*, 1–25.

Pyles, J. C. (2015). A principled approach to healthcare. *Tennessee Journal of Law and Policy, 10*, 9–43.

Reyes, J. W. (2010). *The effect of malpractice liability on the specialty of obstetrics and gynecology.* Cambridge, MA: National Bureau of Economic Research.

Rhee, R. J. (2012). A financial economic theory of punitive damages. *Michigan Law Review, 111*, 33–87.

Rodwin, M. A., et al. (2015). Why the medical malpractice crisis persists even when malpractice insurance premiums fall. *Health Matrix: Journal of Law Medicine, 25*, 163–226.

Sage, W. M. (2016). Assembled products: The key to more effective competition and antitrust oversight in health care. *Cornell Law Review, 101,* 609–699.

Sanders, S. R. (2015). Uncapping compensation in the Gore punitive damage analysis. *William and Mary Bill of Rights Journal, 24,* 37–91.

Schumpeter, J. A. (2008). *Capitalism, socialism, and democracy.* New York, NY: Harper Perennial Modern Classics. (Original work published 1942.)

Schwartz, V. E., & Appel, C. E. (2011). Reshaping the traditional limits of affirmative duties under the third restatement of torts. *John Marshall Law Review, 44,* 319–351.

Shieh, D. (2014). Unintended side effects: Arbitration and the deterrence of medical error. *New York University Law Review, 89,* 1806–1835.

Smith, C. (2014). It's a mistake: Insurer cost cutting, insurer liability, and the lack of ERISA preemption within the individual exchanges. *Cleveland State Law Review, 62,* 75–124.

Starr, P. (2013). *Remedy and reaction: The peculiar American struggle over health care reform* (revised ed.). New Haven, CT: Yale University Press.

Stempel, J. W. (2014). Making liquor immunity worse: Nevada's undue protection of commercial hosts evicting vulnerable and dangerous patrons. *Nevada Law Journal, 14,* 866–895.

Tenner, S., & Ringel, L. (2014). Medical complication compensation law: Improving quality healthcare delivery while providing for injury compensation. *Journal of Health and Biomedical Law, 10,* 55–100.

Terry, N. P. (2014). Pit crews with computers: Can health information technology fix fragmented care? *Houston Journal of Health Law and Policy, 14,* 129–189.

Wiley, L. F. (2016). From patient rights to health justice: Securing the public's interest in affordable, high-quality health care. *Cardozo Law Review, 37,* 833–889.

PART IV

STAFFING OF HEALTH CARE SYSTEMS

Part IV concentrates on staffing U.S. health care systems and the laws affecting the management of employees.

© Andy Dean Photography/ShutterStock, Inc.

CHAPTER 9

Human Resources Departments

"It is not the strongest of the species that survives, nor the most intelligent; it is the one that is most adaptable to change."

— **Attributed to Charles Darwin** (1809–1882), English naturalist

IN BRIEF

Human resources departments are an essential partner in building many of the legal frameworks in this text, from compliance and ethics programs to developing policies that ensure the health care industry adheres to its social missions. This chapter addresses two fundamental ways of viewing human resources: as a legal and technical department that works directly with senior management, providing crucial input into major business transactions, and focused on recruiting talent, promoting mobility and career development, and improving organizational effectiveness, versus the traditional role of administrators that involved many responsibilities that are now being outsourced. The need for the health care industry to become more strategy-driven is emphasized in terms of the issues of pay as it relates to performance and management development.

LEARNING OBJECTIVES

Upon completion of this chapter readers should be able to:

1. Define the role of human resources in the health care industry.
2. Explain the changing nature of the business partnership between the human resources department and top management.
3. Detail the evolution of human resources from administratively assisting and impartially advocating for employees to supporting management.
4. Describe the social contract that previously existed between the organization and its employees, whereby a lifetime of employment was exchanged for employee loyalty and commitment, but which is obsolete now that employees have many employers in their lifetimes.
5. Show how a shift to serving employees as customers could significantly improve the health care industry and benefit those it serves.
6. List the triple roles of human resources.
7. Contrast *employment security* with *employability security*.
8. Understand the issue of pay parity and the continued disparity in pay between men and women.
9. Discuss performance-based pay and its use for individuals, teams, and the organization as a whole.

KEY TERMS

Acquisitions
Backdating
Benchmark salaries

Cafeteria-style benefits
Consulting services
Deferred compensation

Fringe benefits
Human resources
Internal Revenue Code § 162(m)

Mergers
Non-performance-based
   compensation
Performance-based pay

Private equity owners
Restructurings
Risk mitigation
Rubber-stamp

Sarbanes-Oxley
Social contract
Subcontracting

FACT OR FICTION

Executive Compensation

Should human resources have a role in examining executive compensation?

    William McGuire, the former chief executive officer and chairman of the board of directors of UnitedHealth Group, departed from the company at the board's request after he illegally obtained executive compensation by backdating stock options worth over $1 billion. Backdating stock options brings an instant paper gain, which is equivalent to extra pay and thus is a cost to the company; failure to recognize this cost may mean the company overstated its profits, possibly necessitating a restatement of past financial results. **Backdating**, in and of itself, is not illegal as long as it is authorized, fully disclosed and reported, and in keeping with tax rules. At his departure, McGuire was a named defendant in numerous shareholder suits and federal securities class actions. In addition to the $1 billion, McGuire claimed United owed him millions in additional executive compensation. The Securities and Exchange Commission filed its own lawsuit, which was settled when the board's special litigation committee's report was released. McGuire agreed to settle the securities lawsuit against him by returning over $470 million to UnitedHealth and paying a $7 million civil fine. The shareholder lawsuits were settled when McGuire paid an additional $30 million in fines, returned over $3 million in unexercised stock options, and disgorged over $11 million in incentive-based cash bonuses received over the last two years of his employment; UnitedHealth paid over $895 million to shareholders.

— *See* Law Fact at the end of this chapter for the answer.

Principles and Applications

There are two different views of human resources in the health care industry. According to its critics, human resources can be needlessly bureaucratic, obstructionist, stuck in the comfort zone of filling out forms and explaining benefits, and too closely aligned with the interests of management, yet lacking the business knowledge to be effective strategic partners in an organization's success (Sirota & Klein, 2013). Dealing with this type of department is difficult. When employees are asked to rate the quality of different functions within their organization, this type of human resources is repeatedly rated the lowest (Whitney, 2016).

    The more positive view of human resources is that it works directly with senior management, providing crucial input into major business transactions, such as **mergers**, **acquisitions**, and **restructurings**. In this scenario, human resources has moved away from the traditional role of administrators, as many of those responsibilities are now outsourced, and toward a more creative focus on their primary roles, including:

- Improving organizational effectiveness
- Promoting mobility and career development
- Recruiting talent

Unless human resources reports to the chief executive officer, its priorities are likely set in the wrong direction and driven by inappropriate and ineffective motivators. For instance, if human resources reports to the chief financial officer, then it is not in the best position to be successful in today's competitive health care market. Human resources must be in a strategic position to affect and execute policy, not simply farther down the hierarchy and relegated to performing administrative functions and support services (Sirota & Klein, 2013; Wharton, 2005).

Defining the Role of Human Resources in the Health Care Industry

Beginning in the 1920s, human resources was a way to advocate for and protect employees, an orientation that became quite explicit in the 1950s and beyond as part of an effort by the health care industry to prevent unionization. More recently, however, and especially over the past decade, the **social contract** between employees and employers, under which employers provided lifetime employment to their employees in return for loyalty and commitment to the employer, has ended (Useem, 2015).

Recently the health care industry is pushing more and more work onto employees, and human resources is becoming the mechanism for accomplishing this goal. As a result, the idea that human resources represents employees, or at least deals objectively with their concerns, is antiquated. In addition, with the health care industry continuing to cut back employee benefits, human resources has increasingly found itself serving as the bearer of bad news to employees. Meanwhile, human resources issues are very much a part of press coverage.

Business Partnership

Historically, in the health care industry, changes in human resources usually require about a decade to take hold. This includes:

- Establishing health care call centers and service centers
- Integrating work-life balance issues
- Outsourcing of administrative functions

(Wharton, 2015).

FEATURE BOX 9-1

Press Coverage of Human Resources Issues

- In Chicago, Northwestern Memorial Hospital's former chief executive officer received a $16.4 million payout, while less than 2% of the hospital's revenues went to charitable care.
- In New Jersey, the chief executive officer of the Norwell Health System makes over $10 million a year, including a $1.7 million bonus.
- The chief executive officer of Ascension Health earned $2.4 million in salary compensation at the country's largest not-for-profit hospital system, while Ascension closes money-losing hospitals in poor urban areas from Los Angeles to Chicago to Newark, New Jersey, where a large percentage of patients are uninsured.
- The Cleveland Clinic continued to pay its former chief executive officer more than $1 million a year in **deferred compensation**, vacation pay, and **consulting services**, for two years after he retired.
- The University of California San Francisco Medical Center provided its chief executive officer and its chief operating officer low-interest mortgage loans of more than $1 million each.
- The University of Pittsburgh Medical Center paid its chief executive more than $3.3 million, plus almost $37,000 from the hospital to cover a car allowance, spousal travel, and legal and financial counseling.

Corbett, 2015; Rodrigues, 2011; Vincent & Klein, 2015; Carreyrou & Martinez, 2008.

For instance, the health care industry is trying to rapidly transform human resources into a business partner with less emphasis on those administrative functions that can be outsourced. To achieve this, it is vital to help key human resources accelerate their development of business skills. Many health care organizations are doing this, but not very quickly. A tremendous attraction within human resources to the comfort zone of more traditional and functional support-service relationships remains (Etengu & Kwerigira, 2016).

Strategic Restructurings

While medical products manufacturers, hospitals, health insurers, drugstore chains, and pharmacy benefit managers are all in a restructuring frenzy as everyone seeks to gain more leverage in negotiations with payers, there is a shift away from traditional mergers and acquisitions toward affiliations, joint ventures, and partnerships (Smith, 2016). The classic area where human resources can provide tactical input is in anticipating these restructurings. A very well-defined set of human resource opportunities and experiences exists in these strategic areas:

- Assisting in valuing the deals
- Communicating with internal customers (employees)
- Developing integration plans
- Matching talent

(Nussbaum, 2015).

Some human resources departments play a key role here. Others are still only observers. For instance, mergers and acquisitions often involve crucial decisions about the future of small health care systems. One controversial area where human resources plays a critical communications role involves the mergers of Catholic and non-Catholic hospitals (Deutsch, 2015). Such mergers generally result in the elimination of most reproductive health services, including:

- Abortions
- Birth control drugs and devices
- In vitro fertilization
- Sterilizations

(Nejaime & Siegel, 2016; Sawicki, 2016; Smith, 2016).

In California and the Midwest, where mergers between Catholic and non-Catholic hospitals have become increasingly prevalent, access to reproductive health services for isolated rural and economically disadvantaged areas has become a problem. Legislation has therefore been proposed in some states that, among other things, would expressly require all hospitals to provide a full range of reproductive health services as a condition of government funding and merger approval (Deutsch, 2015). Human resource departments become entangled in issues of accommodating Catholic employees who do not want to be involved in the delivery of selected reproductive health services as a matter of conscience, as well as whether Catholic hospitals must employ the employees from the non-Catholic hospital who practice or hold views contrary to Catholic teaching. Then, there is the issue of fostering tolerance of and fairness toward the employees who hold conflicting religious views of health issues in the workplace.

Operational Return on Investment

Over the last 10 to 15 years, human resources has begun to have a serious impact on how the health care industry operates. To put this in perspective, about half of expenses in any health care organization are related to personnel, including:

- **Fringe benefits**
- Incentive plans
- Risk management strategies
- Salaries
- Talent retention programs

(Sirota & Klein, 2013)

MANAGEMENT AND LAW ISSUES

1. Why does the Conference Board survey of human resources directors report job satisfaction in the U.S. health care industry at its lowest level ever?

If the human resources department can effectively manage those dollars, with the goal of the highest possible return on human investment, the department will approach opportunities much differently. Under this scenario, the human resources department would have the operational mandate of:

- Developing leadership
- Growing revenue
- Increasing productivity

(Spivack, 2015; Wharton, 2005)

To effectively meet this mandate, the human resources department should look very similar to any other high-level department in terms of employee skill level. So, when human resources participates in meetings with other departments, it has the capability to talk about the business of delivery of health care as opposed to focusing on human resources services alone (Sirota & Klein, 2013).

Net Supplier of Management Talent

The human resources department should be comprised of business managers and partners, in other words, management professionals who can address the often unspoken critical facts regarding who is best qualified to be responsible for revenue production. Human resources should be included on replacement charts for other areas of the organization when management opportunities arise (when managers are replaced, the replacements could come from within human resources versus the traditional approach of hiring new managers from outside health care organizations). One of the goals of human resources should be to serve as a net supplier of management talent; human resources is where managers:

- Are trained
- Become skilled at understanding how all parts of the health care organization contribute to the whole
- Gain knowledge of the business

Human resources professionals should have the ability to move into managing any part of the organization (Spivack, 2015).

Direct Tie-In with Strategic Development

Without the direct tie to strategy, there is no context for human resources to work within. Human resources practice should be completely focused on aligning policies and procedures to the overall strategy of the health care organization. For instance, if a health care system converts from a not-for-profit to a for-profit entity with **private equity owners**, a radical cultural shift occurs (Smith, 2016; Useem, 2015). Human resources must take the current set of practices and ensure they are consistent with organizational goals (Wharton, 2005). At the simplest level, this means redesigning pay systems not to automatically increase employee pay but to consist of smaller amounts of fixed compensation and to base any further pay largely on performance (Smith, 2016).

Cafeteria-Style Benefits

The health care industry increasingly offers a **cafeteria-style benefits** approach (Morse, 2014). From flexible spending arrangements to health savings accounts, cafeteria benefits are more suited to the type of consumer-driven health care system the health care industry strives to be. In this benefits approach employees occupy the primary decision-making role regarding the type of benefits they receive. Recruiting goals may have to shift and the way new employees are socialized may have to change.

Nevertheless, human resources can do much to align departmental missions from the employee point of view with the strategy of the health care organization. Human resources can help train employees to become:

- Cost-conscious about the employee benefits they and their families need
- More entrepreneurial about the opportunities within their health care organizations
- More involved in their careers within the U.S. health care industry
- More skilled at learning to take charge of their own lives

(Sirota & Klein, 2013; Wharton, 2005).

Leadership Development

Many chief executive officers see human resources as holding the most critical function in their health care organization. Development of managers is the ultimate responsibility of every chief executive officer and thus an integral part of human resources. It is the responsibility of the human resources department to allocate employees and dollars to opportunities. The chief executive officer does not provide health care services or deliver medical products; one of the responsibilities of the chief executive is placing employees in the right jobs, in partnership with human resources (Useem, 2015).

To effectively meet this responsibility in partnership with the chief executive officer, human resources evaluation systems should be:

- Monitored as closely as financial reporting
- Non-bureaucratic
- Rigorous

While many departments of human resources state that their role is to serve as a strategic partner with senior management, critics question whether this is possible given that human resources staff often lack the business skills to understand strategy or their role in implementing it. Furthermore, some senior managers are not interested in having human resources as strategic partners; they simply want the human resources department to hire the employees managers want. If top management does not see value in aligning strategically with its human resources department, and if human resources cannot think creatively in that role, then the partnership will likely never happen (Nussbaum, 2015; Sirota & Klein, 2013).

Of course, becoming a partner with senior management does not happen overnight. The human resources department must earn its way to the table. The key question should always be whether human resources is successful at helping move everyone in the direction the organization wants to go. To do this, human resources has a number of strategic imperatives, such as:

- Hiring the right employees to be in the right places at the right times
- Looking for breadth and depth of leadership talent within the health care organization
- Maintaining the right culture for the organization
- Operational excellence
- **Risk mitigation**

(Nussbaum, 2015).

To meet these imperatives, human resources staff should be out among the employees, patients, and insurers, providing feedback on the pulse of the health care organization. Senior management must see their human resources department as very valuable, especially in the areas of professional development and succession plans.

Branding

The influence of human resources should also extend beyond that department. Outside of the marketing function, human resources has one of the biggest responsibilities related to brand (Arons et al., 2014). For instance, every year, the American health care industry hires more than 3.8 million employees externally (BLS, 2015). This is a branding opportunity to associate 19 to 38 million additional people with a health care service or medical product from a specific health care provider. As a rule of thumb, for every person hired, 5-10 additional people hear detailed information and form personal impressions about the employer (Wharton, 2005).

Each time human resources interviews someone, it should look for talent that can be developed. The interviewee, in turn, has a chance to see the health care industry from an insider's perspective. This is another branding opportunity. When human resources interviews a potential candidate, even if that candidate is not hired, the experience should leave the interviewee with the desire to support the health care provider (Useem, 2015).

A Two-Tiered Human Resources System

Critics of human resources development in the late 2000s suggested that human resources has become a servant of management. Human resources is viewed as being more concerned with carrying out directives from above than supporting the needs of employees (Kern, 2011). While there might be some truth to this claim, it is largely because of the decentralization of human resources functions.

The most common model today in large health care organizations is a smaller, highly expert central staff with human resources support staff distributed throughout the organization. The reporting relationship may either be dual, to the head of the operating office and to the head of the human resources department, or direct. Most often, the power dynamic seems to favor the relationship of human resources support staff to head operational executives. This distribution of the human resources function has many advantages. However, one downside is a decrease in the view of human resources support staff as playing an ombudsman role (Issac, 2014).

Pro-Management Perspective

The change toward the perception of the human resources function as pro-management originated when the health care industry began to outsource the administrative duties traditionally performed by human resources (Weil, 2014). Human resources functions that were generally regarded by employees as positive interactions (such as help with medical insurance, leave, and vacation issues) suddenly disappeared. Today, day-to-day contact between employees and human resources is relegated to either voicemail or e-mail as opposed to conversations. At one time, employees could ask human resources questions about benefits, compensation, and retirement. It was more transactional than strategic, but it was at least personal.

There is also the tendency of the human resources department to treat employees as costs to be controlled rather than as human assets (Wharton, 2005). It is often very difficult for the human resources department not to feel the pressure to cut personnel costs. Given these two forces, it is no wonder employees view human resources as an unnecessary evil (Sirota & Klein, 2013).

Alternative Dispute Resolution System

Human resources systems are more effective when they are two-tiered. An alternative dispute resolution system or some dispute resolution mechanism that gives employees a voice in the organization should be developed in every health care organization (Issac, 2014). Alternative dispute systems that mediate, arbitrate, or resolve workplace conflicts in other ways, in general, have certain advantages, including:

- Added flexibility
- Less focus on an adversarial nature
- Less formality
- More solution-oriented

Employee mediation and resolution of workplace conflicts is still part of the human resources function. Employees need a means to exercise their right to challenge a performance appraisal, salary decision, or other personnel matter. Challenges are often handled in one of two ways:

- Appointment of an independent investigator, assigned by management, to look into the complaint
- A panel, comprised of randomly selected employees and managers, hears and reviews the case and makes a decision

Where these alternative dispute resolution systems are in place, employees use them frequently and are generally satisfied with them (Sirota & Klein, 2013).

Social Contract

The social contract between the organization and its workforce no longer exists today; employees are on their own (Useem, 2015). Employers no longer consent to transfer some of their powers to their employees in order to promote the common good; implied contracts of employment in return for employee service are a thing of the past. What human resources must continually do is offer a compelling case to employees as to why they should want to work for their employer, as opposed to have employees feeling it is a privilege bestowed upon them to work. Things to be emphasized could include:

- Commitment to diversity
- Focus on performance differentiation
- Leadership development
- Leading-edge technology
- Skills training
- Workplace flexibility options

(Kochan, 2013).

Human resources must show employees these opportunities exist with their employer. The most important issue for most health care professionals is the quality of culture and management the health care industry supports. Fundamental respect for employees and a long-term orientation toward them are essential (Sirota & Klein, 2013). In this regard, many human resources departments are seeking policies to assist working families and lower wage employees. Many human resources departments are also working to address the problems faced by temporary/contingent workers and the growing immigrant workforce. There is ongoing debate about how the health care industry as a whole should achieve a more focused set of industry aims (Kochan, 2013).

Serving Employees as the Customers

The health care industry would do well to adopt one rule in the Nordstrom's employee handbook: use your good judgment in all situations (Sirota & Klein, 2013). Many human resources departments are not interested in an open-minded approach when it comes to making exceptions to policies. Instead, they pursue standardization and uniformity in the face of a workforce that is heterogeneous and complex (Clarke, 2011).

Bureaucrats everywhere abhor exceptions, not just because they may lead to charges of bias, but because they require more than rote solutions and are difficult to manage. Rather than sending the message that the organization values high-performing employees and is focused on rewarding and retaining them, human resources bureaucrats often:

- **Benchmark salaries**, function by function and job by job, against industry standards
- Keep salaries (even those of star performers) within a narrow band determined by competitors

(Yingling, 2015).

While human resources departments often forfeit long-term value for short-term cost-efficiency, general principles that value employees are increasingly being adopted for crafting workplace policies that serve employees as the customers. This means valuing employees as people. This is not being soft-hearted or naive, but rather is simply common sense. Valued employees far out-produce and out-perform the average workforce—they step up to do the hard, even impossible tasks.[LN1] For instance, serving employees as the customers is about giving employees what they want most. What employees want most is best summarized in the so-called Three-Factor Theory, which includes:

- Being treated fairly and equitably
- Experiencing teamwork and camaraderie
- Feeling proud of their work and their employer

(Sirota & Klein, 2013).

This sounds simple, but every human resources professional and manager knows how challenging this can be.

Fair and Equitable Treatment

Human resources has a responsibility to assure employees receive fair pay (which is defined as competitive pay), benefits, and job security (Jenoff, 2012). Health insurance is a significant issue. On the non-financial side, human resources must ensure employees are treated respectfully. Unless all these employee needs are met, not much else matters for any health care organization.

Sense of Achievement

The human resources department also has the responsibility to ensure employees have a sense of achievement from their work. Employees must feel proud of what they do and proud of the organization for which they are doing it. Human resources must assure employees understand they are doing meaningful work, which is the primary reason so many employees are attracted to the health care industry in the first place (*See generally* Kitchen, 2012).

Team Camaraderie

Camaraderie involves supporting employees (not as a friend in the traditional sense of camaraderie, but as a valued customer) (Sirota & Klein, 2013). When an employee is sick, human resources must be there. When there are occasions for grief or joy, human resources must ensure the employee is treated accordingly. The human resources department is ultimately responsible for managing this customer service (Arons et al., 2014). This means convincing other managers at the table that the workforce cannot be cut when there are economic uncertainties; trimming employees, without ensuring employees have comparable employment opportunities elsewhere within the health care industry, destroys employees as customers and devastates any sense of camaraderie (Useem, 2015; Wharton, 2005).

Human Resources' Triple Roles

Human resources has three roles in the health care industry:

- Conducting administrative functions
- Serving the employee as a customer
- Acting as a strategic partner

The most important part of this customer-centric approach for human resources involves developing policies, practices, and philosophies geared toward creating a truly motivated and dedicated workforce. Generally speaking, this human resources role is more notable by its absence (Sirota & Klein, 2013).

General Principles for Human Resources Policies, Practices, and Philosophies

U.S. employment regulations overlap with and in most cases agree with the core labor standards adopted by the International Labor Organization Declaration on Fundamental Principles and Rights at Work. Human resources professionals should assist the U.S. health care industry with complying with federal and state employment laws and regulations in order to:

- Ensure a safe and healthy work environment with minimal exposure to safety and health risks (*See* Occupational Safety and Health Act, Mine Safety and Health Act, 29 U.S.C.A. §§ 651 *et seq.*; 42 U.S.C.A. § 3142-1 (establishing black lung disease program), and Drug Free Workplace Act, 41 U.S.C.A. §§ 701–707).
- Ensure basic labor standards (hours of work, overtime compensation) (*See* Fair Labor Standards Act, 2 U.S.C.A. § 60k; 29 U.S.C.A. §§ 201 *et seq.* (establishing national minimum wage, guaranteeing time-and-a-half for overtime in certain jobs, and generally prohibiting employment of minors); Davis-Bacon Act, 40 U.S.C.A. §§ 3141–48; and Walsh-Healy Public Contracts Act, 41 U.S.C.A. §§ 35–45).
- Protect against major downside risks associated with employment and help cushion the impact of globalization and economic downturns, such as loss of pensions or health care benefits (*See* Worker Adjustment & Retraining and Notification Act, 29 U.S.C.A. §§ 2101–2109; Family Medical Leave Act, 5 U.S.C.A. §§ 6381 *et seq.*; Trade Adjustment Assistance Act, 19 U.S.C.A. §§ 2341 *et seq.*).

188

- Protect against workplace bias and discrimination in hiring, promotion, dismissal, and treatment of employees (*See* Equal Pay Act, 29 U.S.C.A. § 206(d) (prohibiting wage differentials based on sex); Executive Order 11246 of 1965 (Equal Employment Opportunity) (prohibiting discrimination and requiring affirmative action to prevent discrimination); Age Discrimination Employment Act, 29 U.S.C.A. §§ 621–634 (2009); Americans with Disabilities Act of 1990, 42 U.S.C.A. §§ 12101 *et seq.*; 47 U.S.C.A. § 225; Rehabilitation Act, 29 U.S.C.A. §§ 701 *et seq.*; Surface Transportation Assistance Act, 49 U.S.C.A. § 31105; and Veterans' Reemployment Rights Act, 38 U.S.C.A. §§ 4301–4307).
- Provide basic mechanisms for employee representation in the workplace (*See* National Labor Relations Act, 29 U.S.C.A. §§ 151–169; Labor Management Reporting and Disclosure Act, 29 U.S.C.A. §§ 401 *et seq.*; and Railway Labor Act, 45 U.S.C.A. §§ 151 *et seq.*).

(ILO, 2010).

These existing labor regulations, however, do not completely and satisfactorily address many human resources challenges involving new practices in the health care industry, such as:

- Outsourcing business processes
- Converting not-for-profit entities to for-profit entities
- Employing independent contractors
- Reneging on long-term employment commitments
- Shifting production offshore
- **Subcontracting**
- Temporary workers
- Utilizing overseas suppliers

(*See* Chapter on Global Supply Chain Management; *See also* Avgoustaki, 2016).

Employee Surveys

When human resources professionals say they want to be business partners, what they often mean is they want to work for management. Most health care organizations say their employees are their greatest asset, but what they really mean is employees are their biggest cost. Human resources professionals should be proactive, actively involved in finding out the issues facing employees. The health care industry regularly surveys patients and external customers; human resources should survey its internal customers—its employees—as well (Watson & Swanberg, 2013).

Employee Advocate

What is missing in the health care industry, as well as in all other workplaces, is the view of human resources as an employee advocate. Human resources should be able to handle hard conversations with employees about what must be done to improve and develop their individual talents on behalf of the organization. Employees must be allowed to question whether human resources will actually provide skills training and leadership development, and whether human resources will help employees move around the organization or get positioned for a promotion, if employees do what is expected (*See generally* Bodie, 2013).

Administration Functions

Human resources tends to push a number of functions onto managers, such as finding and downloading the forms needed when an employee retires. Human resources has delegated a number of jobs to others that they used to do themselves (Useem, 2015). Debate is ongoing about whether this is the direction to take (Sirota & Klein, 2013; Useem, 2015).

MANAGEMENT AND LAW ISSUES

2. Should labor standards be legislated to address these new industry practices?

Layoffs and Restructurings

One of the more difficult human resources responsibilities is dealing with layoffs. The situation should be handled in a very humane way. Where major long-term issues are involved, such as restructurings and joint ventures, human resources should actively be a part of those strategic discussions from the beginning, not just after the management decisions are made (*See generally* Kochan, 2013; Krieger et al., 2015).

Flexible Work Environment

Flexible work in the health care industry is a modern-day paradox. This is perhaps currently more so in the medical products sector because of their highly educated and trained employees, but may be upcoming industry-wide as the health care services sector transforms the delivery of medical treatments (*See generally* Bird, 2015; Watson & Swanberg, 2013).

Current Paradox

Employers are introducing flexible policies needed by their workforces to help them maintain their dual work and family responsibilities. Today, as in the generation of the family farms, work and family are once again almost inseparable. In addition, technology has further blurred the lines between work and personal life. Work in the health care industry must be better organized so employers can make full use of employee skills (Wharton, 2005). Employees must be cross-utilized so human resources can promote mobility and career development (Useem, 2015). The talk is no longer of work-life balance, but of work-life integration (Dau-Schmidt et al., 2011; Wharton, 2005).

However, while flexible employment policies are required to increase or diminish the workforce and reassign and redeploy employees with ease, it is not always clear how this goal is to be accomplished (Bison-Rapp et al., 2010). The health care industry is debating how to adapt and yet preserve employee rights in the face of these challenges. Employers want to motivate employees to contribute their knowledge. Yet the job security and job ladders of the past century, whereby employees had a stake in the well-being of their employers, have been almost entirely dismantled (Gahan et al., 2012; Podgers, 2010). To address this paradox, human resources is devising new organizational structures that embody flexibility while also promoting skill development and fostering employee engagement (Cameron, 2014).

New Employment Relationship

This new employment relationship involves a change in the contract between employees and employers. Today's health care employees do not have a promise of lifetime employment security with a single employer (Riedy & Sperduto, 2014). Instead, employers must promise *employability security* to employees or the ability to acquire skills that will enhance employment opportunities in the health care industry in general (Njoya, 2012).

While today's employers can no longer promise employees orderly promotional opportunities, employers can promise employees opportunities to network and gain skills to prepare for jobs within the health care industry itself. In this new relationship, human resources should be helping employees to manage their own careers in the health care industry as opposed to expecting long-term employment from a single employer. Today, nowhere is this new employment relationship clearer than in the medical products sector; the health care information technology sector has been at the vanguard of this relationship change (Fisk & Barry, 2012).

In-Sourcing

In-sourcing is another strategic imperative for human resources (Kolben, 2015). If someone within a health care organization wants to create a new business opportunity, human resources should be there to negotiate about the employees and programs needed to get there. Health care organizations are increasingly finding new businesses and needs they can provide and meet in-house (Friedman, 2007). A number of health care organizations have established what used to be known as ancillary businesses that sell the expertise they have developed internally, including:

- For-profit pharmacies
- Imaging and diagnostic centers
- Pharmacy benefit management firms
- Physician practice management firms

(Smith, 2016; Wharton, 2005).

The health care industry may also start in-sourcing business process functions that were previously outsourced. For instance, recruiting has generally been outsourced because of the pricing, but the quality has been questionable in many health care organizations. Human resources must always look at trade-offs.

Performance-Based Pay

Given the controversies over compensation packages at tax-exempt hospitals, **performance-based pay** (such as annual bonus plans, stock options, or stock bonus arrangements) continues to be an issue in the health care industry (Walker, 2013). For this very reason, Congress adopted **Internal Revenue Code § 162(m)** in an effort to deter excessive executive pay packages by limiting the deductibility of **non-performance-based compensation** above $1 million (*See* 26 U.S.C.A. 162(m) (2014)).[LN2] While tying compensation to results has been a relatively new focus in health care, performance-based pay represents the latest strategy to help everyone within a health care organization be more inclined to act in the best interest of its real customers: the patients.

Many health care organizations have adopted performance-based pay. Performance-based pay is viewed as one way to help improve the quality of U.S. health care. Simply stated, performance-based pay is an incentive program that measures several defined aspects of work and compensates employees according to the performance achieved by:

- Health care organization as a whole
- Individuals
- Workplace teams

(Griffith, 2016).

The trend is to segment work across the organization as well as to segment the workforce in a way that allows differences to be defined and valued. The compensation system design in the health care industry is an ever-evolving discipline tied closely to quantifiable metrics of value creation. This allows human resources to move away from a system of treating everyone the same, to one where employees can be treated differently, and according to:

- Employee performance
- Individual preferences
- The needs of the health care organization

(Etengu & Kwerigira, 2016; Stabile, 2014).

Individual performance is not the only measurement; team and organizational incentives (such as profit sharing or employee stock options) are also indispensable. A threefold difference in total compensation (based on pay, promotions, or the opportunity for incentive rewards) is the underpinning of performance-based pay (Wharton, 2005).

Board Compensation Committees

Issues of pay and performance are now reaching boards as well. One key factor in the evolution of human resources has been the Sarbanes-Oxley Act of 2002, more commonly simply called **Sarbanes-Oxley**. Sarbanes-Oxley affects the medical products industry, for-profit hospitals, and health care providers in general (*See* 15 U.S.C.A. § 7241(a)(5) adopting the requirement that chief executive officers and chief financial officers must discuss and review certain reports with the board's audit committee before filing). Committee members who **rubber-stamp** reports face liability. For human resources, this has radically changed the relationship with the board compensation committees.

The question arises as to whether a board should obtain guidance on matters of pay and perks from human resources or consultants hired directly by the board. While board compensation committees now often hire consultants to advise them rather than rely solely on internal assessments, human resources still should be performing compensation analysis and bringing information and advice to the board. Issues surrounding pay, including sensitivity to full disclosure of executive perks, are in the forefront for the health care industry as are issues of management development and succession.

Sarbanes-Oxley, an area in which the human resources function plays a key role, has had a profound effect on strengthening boards in the health care industry (Torres-Spelliscy, 2015). After Sarbanes-Oxley, directors are exercising a leadership function in the boardroom and with top management (Wharton, 2014); they are helping the health care industry to change and to go where it has to go (Charan et al., 2013). Leadership at the top is being redefined, as boards take a more active role in decisions on ethics and risks that once belonged solely to management (Useem, 2015).

MANAGEMENT AND LAW ISSUES

3. Why does pay equity remain one of the most violated human resources standards in the health care industry?

Pay Issues and Equality

Pay issues are not always easy to resolve, especially at hospitals, where numerous constituencies believe they take precedence (Tufarolo, 2015). It is often difficult to develop a clear strategy. One approach to setting compensation levels, a leftover from the culture of looking out for employees, is to have a model of equality: treat everyone roughly the same, especially on issues of compensation and benefits (Etengu & Kwerigira, 2016). Of course, organizations that do this get complaints from top managers claiming they lost employees because human resources would not let them pay enough. Top managers, who for the most part are high achievers, believe employees should be paid based on individual performance.

The problem is that perceived inequities drive employees to distraction. It is one thing to view an employee as a star performer and to want to pay some individuals more to prevent them from quitting. It is another to deal with what happens next. Employees who discover someone else is being paid more within an equal pay system object and charges of discrimination arise. So human resources moves to a model where everyone is paid based on performance. However, this approach requires an objective assessment of performance that everyone should be willing to buy into; this is the hard part (Spivack, 2015).

LAW FACT

Executive Compensation

Should human resources have a role in examining executive compensation?

Yes. If human resources is to be strategic business partners in the health care industry, they can no longer only be in partnership with the chief executive officer of a health care organization; the human resources department must also partner with the board and the board compensation committee.

— *In re: UnitedHealth Group Inc. Shareholder Derivative Litigation*, 631 F.Supp.2d 1151 (U.S. District Court for the District of Minnesota 2009), *appeal dismissed*, 631 F.3d 913 (U.S. Court of Appeals for the 8th Circuit 2011); *In re UnitedHealth Group Incorporated PSLRA Litigation*, 754 N.W.2d 544 (Supreme Court of Minnesota 2008).

— *See* Bartholomew, 2015; Lopatka & Smith, 2012 (discussing this decision). *See also* Wilmer Cutler Pickering Hale and Dorr LLP (2006).

CHAPTER SUMMARY

- Human resources can be viewed as either an administrative function or a strategic business partner.
- While human resources departments began as employee advocates and protectors, human resources too often today treats employees as expendable, expensive liabilities.
- The media increasingly focuses upon human resources issues as top executives are compensated seemingly without regard to performance, while top-performing lower-wage employees are often not paid living wages.
- One reason human resources is slow to become an effective strategic business partner is because few human resources professionals have developed business skills necessary for this transition.
- Used effectively, human resources could help health care entities grow revenue, increase productivity, and develop leadership.
- For human resources to become an effective strategic business partner, senior managers must view it as more than just the department that hires and fires employees.

- An additional function human resources could work to improve is that of a mediator between employees and employer; employees need a non-adversarial way to resolve grievances.
- The social contract between a health care organization and its workforce, as far as long-term employment and rewards in return for loyalty, has been broken; employees increasingly feel as if they are on their own and have lost their status as the employer's customers.
- Although human resources is responsible for ensuring compliance with labor and employment laws, these laws do not satisfactorily address many challenges human resources faces, or address them at all in some cases.
- Too many employees lack the motivation to contribute their knowledge to employers due to the lack of job stability, rewards for performance, and flexibility in balancing personal and family obligations with work.
- Performance-based pay is difficult to administer because it is difficult to objectively determine; furthermore, it often subjects employers to distracted employees and charges of discrimination.

LAW NOTES

1. Valued employees create engaged external customers who foster organizational success by delivering positive financial outcomes (Dau-Schmidt, 2011). Companies where employees are valued outperform their competitors. Based on the results of 2.5 million employee surveys at 28 companies employing 920,000 employees, the share price of companies where employees felt they were valued increased an average of 16%, compared to an industry average of 6% (Dau-Schmidt & Haley, 2007). Where employees do not feel valued, firms saw their share prices increase by only 3% (Sirota & Klein, 2013) (*See generally* Dau-Schmidt, 2011; Dau-Schmidt et al., 2011).

2. Internal Revenue Code § 162m was designed to sharply limit discretion in setting performance-based pay. Compensation agreements are expected to specify objective compensation criteria tied to objective performance goals (*See* Treasury Regulation § 1.162-27(e)(2)(ii)). Discretion to adjust compensation amounts is severely limited; performance-pay compensation agreements can be reduced by the board or the compensation committee, but they cannot be increased after-the-fact (*See* Treasury Regulation § 1.162-27(e)(2)(iii)(A)).

REFERENCES

Arons, M., et al. (2014). The ultimate marketing machine. *Harvard Business Review, 4*, 7–11.

Avgoustaki, A. (2016). Work uncertainty and extensive work effort: The mediating role of human resource practices. *Industrial and Labor Relations Review, 69*, 656–678.

Bartholomew, C. P. (2015). Saving charitable settlements. *Fordham Law Review, 83*, 3241–3292.

Bird, R. C. (2015). Why don't more employers adopt flexible working time? *West Virginia Law Review, 118*, 327–367.

Bison-Rapp, S., et al. (2010). Decent work, older workers, and vulnerability in the economic recession: A comparative study of Australia, the United Kingdom, and the United States. *Employment Rights and Employment Policy Journal, 15*(1), 43–121.

BLS (Bureau of Labor Statistics). (2015). *Economic news release: Employment projections: 2014–2024 Summary.* Washington, DC: U.S. Department of Labor, BLS.

Bodie, M. T. (2013). The Roberts Court and the law of human resources. *Berkeley Journal of Employment and Labor Law, 34*, 159–217.

Cameron, C. D. R. (2014). The rule of law goes to work: How collective bargaining may promote access to justice in the United States, Canada, and the rest of the world. *University of California Davis Journal of International Law and Policy, 20*, 211–243.

Carreyrou, J., & Martinez, B. (2008, April 4). Nonprofit hospitals, once for the poor, strike it rich; With tax breaks, they outperform their non-profit rivals. *Wall Street Journal*, p. A1.

Charan, R., et al. (2013). *Boards that lead: When to take charge, when to partner, and when to stay out of the way.* Cambridge, MA: Harvard Business Review Press.

Clarke, J. A. (2011). Beyond equality? Against the universal turn in workplace protections. *Indiana Law Journal, 86*, 1219–1287.

Corbett, T. L. (2015). Healthcare corporate structure and the ACA: A need for mission primacy through a new organizational paradigm? *Indiana Health Law Review, 12*, 103–180.

Darwin, C. (2003). *The origin of species.* New York, NY: Signet, Penguin Random House. (Original work published 1859.)

Dau-Schmidt, K. G. (2011). Promoting employee voice in the American economy: A call for comprehensive reform. *Marquette Law Review, 94*(3), 766–836.

Dau-Schmidt, K. G., & Haley, T. A. (2007). Governance of the workplace: The contemporary regime of individual contract. *Comparative Labor Law and Policy Journal, 28*(2), 313–349.

Dau-Schmidt, K. G., et al. (2011). *Legal protection for the individual employee.* (4th ed.). St. Paul, MN: West Academic Publishing.

Deutsch, E. B. (2015). Expanding conscience, shrinking care: The crisis in access to reproductive care and the Affordable Care Act's nondiscrimination mandate. *Yale Law Journal, 124*, 2470–2514.

Etengu, R. O., & Kwerigira, A. (2016). The relationship between long-term incentives and corporate performance: A theoretical review. *International Journal of Humanities Social Sciences and Education, 3*(3), 23–31.

Fisk, C., & Barry, A. (2012). Contingent loyalty and restricted exit: Commentary on the restatement of employment law. *Employee Rights and Employment Policy Journal, 16*, 413–464.

Friedman, T. L. (2007). *The world if flat: A brief history of the twenty-first century.* New York, NY: Farrar, Straus & Giroux.

Gahan, P. G., et al. (2012). Economic globalisation and convergence in labour market regulation: An empirical assessment. *American Journal of Comparative Law, 60*, 703–742.

Griffith, S. J. (2016). Corporate governance in an era of compliance. *William and Mary Law Review, 57*, 2075–2140.

ILO (International Labor Organization). (2010). *ILO declaration on fundamental principles and rights at work and its follow-up.* Geneva, Switzerland, ILO.

Issac, K. D. (2014). The organizational ombudsman's quest for privileged communications. *Hofstra Labor and Employment Law Journal, 32*, 31–47.

Jenoff, P. (2012). As equal as others? Rethinking access to discrimination law. *University of Cincinnati Law Review, 81*, 85–126.

Kern, P. (2011). *Anticipation and management of restructuring in the United States of America.* London, England: Kings College London, Department of Management.

Kitchen, R. K. (2012). Off-balance: Obama and the work-family agenda. *Employee Rights and Employment Policy Journal, 16*, 211–285.

Kochan, T. A. (2013). The American jobs crisis and its implication for the future of employment policy: A call for a new jobs compact. *Industrial and Labor Relations Review, 66*, 291–312.

Kohn, A. (1999). *Punished by rewards: The trouble with gold stars, incentive plans, A's, praise, and other bribes.* New York, NY: Houghton Mifflin Harcourt, Mariner Books. (Original work published 1993.)

Kolben, K. (2015). Dialogic labor regulation in the global supply chain. *Michigan Journal of International Law, 35*, 425–465.

Krieger, L. H., et al. (2015). When "best practices" win, employees lose: Symbolic compliance and judicial inference in federal equal employment opportunity cases. *Law and Social Inquiry, 40*, 843–868.

Lopatka, J. E., & Smith, D. B. (2012). Class action professional objectors: What to do about them? *Florida State University Law Review, 39*, 865–929.

Morse, E. A. (2014). Health accounts/arrangements: An expanding role under the Affordable Care Act? *John Marshall Law Review, 47*, 1–56.

Nejaime, D., & Siegel, R. B. (2016). Conscience wars: Complicity-based conscience claims in religion and politics. *Yale Law Journal, 124*, 2516–2591.

Njoya, W. (2012). Job security in a flexible labor market: Challenges and possibilities for worker voice. *Comparative Labor Law and Policy Journal, 33*, 459–479.

Nussbaum, S. T., Executive Vice President, Clinical Health Policy, Chief Medical Officer, Anthem. (2015, October 16). Remarks at the Annual Wharton Health Care Management Alumni Leadership Conference, Philadelphia, PA.

Podgers, J. (2010). Playing catch-up: United States lags behind other wealthy nations in rule of law index. *American Bar Association Journal, 96*(12), 58–61.

Riedy, M. K., & Sperduto, K. (2014). At-will fiduciaries? The anomalies of a "duty of loyalty" in the twenty-first century. *Nebraska Law Review, 93*, 267–312.

Rodrigues, U. (2011). Entity and identity. *Emory Law Journal, 60*, 1257–1322.

Sawicki, N. N. (2016). Mandating disclosure of conscience-based limitations on medical practice. *American Journal of Law and Medicine, 42*, 85–128.

Sirota, D., & Klein, D. A. (2013). *The enthusiastic employee: How companies profit by giving workers what they want.* Saddle River, NJ: Pearson Financial Times Press.

Smith, B., Co-Founder and Chief Executive Officer, Aspire Health. (2016, June 16). Remarks at the Keynote Panel on State of the Healthcare Mergers and Acquisitions Industry: The "View-from-36,000 Feet" at the Investment and Mergers and Acquisitions Opportunities in Healthcare Conference, Nashville, TN.

Spivack, M., Managing Director and Co-Head, Health Care Group within KPMG Corporate Finance. (2015, October 16). Remarks at the Annual Wharton Health Care Management Alumni Leadership Conference, Philadelphia, PA.

Stabile, S. J. (2014). Motivating executives: Does performance-based compensation positively affect managerial performance? *University of Pennsylvania Journal of Labor and Employment Law, 2*(2), 227–285.

Torres-Spelliscy, C. (2015). Corporate democracy from say on pay to say on politics. *Constitutional Commentary, 30*, 431–461.

Tufarolo, M. A. (2015). You haven't come a long way, baby: The courts' inability to eliminate the gender wage gap fifty-two years after the passage of the Equal Pay Act. *American University Journal of Gender, Social Policy and the Law, 24*, 305–336.

Useem, M., Professor of Management and Director, Center for Leadership and Change Management at the Wharton School at the University of Pennsylvania. (2015, October 16). Remarks at the Annual Wharton Health Care Management Alumni Leadership Conference, Philadelphia, PA.

Vincent, I., & Klein, M. (2015). This guy makes $10M a year to head a nonprofit. *New York Post*, p. A1.

Walker, D. I. (2013). A tax response to the executive pay problem. *Boston University Law Review, 93*, 325–387.

Watson, L., & Swanberg, J. E. (2013). Flexible workplace solutions for low-wage hourly workers: A framework for a national conversation. *American University Labor and Employment Law Forum, 3*, 380–437.

Weil, D. (2014). *The fissured workplace: Why work became so bad for so many and what can be done to improve it.* Cambridge, MA: Harvard University Press.

Wharton School of the University of Pennsylvania. (2014), Boards revisited: Michael Useem on the new corporate governance. *Knowledge@Wharton.*

___. (2005). Is your HR department friend or foe? Depends on who's asking the question. http://knowledge.wharton.upenn.edu/article/is-your-hr-department-friend-or-foe-depends-on-whos-asking-the-question/

Whitney, H. M. (2016). Rethinking the ban on employer-labor organization cooperation. *Cardozo Law Review, 37*, 1455–1521.

Wilmer Cutler Pickering Hale and Dorr, LLP (2006). *Report to the special committee of the board of directors of UnitedHealth Group, Inc.*, New York, NY.

Yingling, K. (2015). Pay ratio disclosure: Another failed attempt to curtail executive compensation. *University of Pennsylvania Journal of Business Law, 18*, 203–253.

© Andy Dean Photography/ShutterStock, Inc.

CHAPTER 10

Employers' Health Care Costs

"For this is the great error of our day in the treatment of the human body, that physicians separate the soul from the body."

— **Plato** (B.C. 423–347), Greek philosopher

IN BRIEF

This chapter deals with the growing efforts to reduce and fairly allocate employers' health care costs. Particular attention is directed to smoking and the growing prevalence of obesity, which are examples of preventable behaviors that are both recognized as serious health issues that can no longer be ignored, and as problems that can be addressed through environmental interventions. The challenges on the continuum of employer influence are twofold: first, to decide what type of medical interventions are legally permissible for preventable behaviors and conditions that are triggered by daily lifestyle choices, and second, whether the health care industry should be working with employers regarding other preventive self-care issues that cost employers money and affect employee work performance.

LEARNING OBJECTIVES

Upon completion of this chapter readers should be able to:

1. Describe what efforts reduce and fairly allocate employers' health care costs.
2. Explain the effects of smoking and obesity on employers' health care costs.
3. Outline the influences of precision medicine on preventable behaviors and conditions.
4. Understand the primary issues with lifestyle discrimination and choices.
5. List what health laws support lifestyle choices.
6. Describe the disclosure requirement of lifestyle choices.
7. Explain why lifestyle discrimination is good business.

KEY TERMS

20% threshold rule
Affidavit
Americans with Disabilities Act of 1990
Amicus brief
Anti-obesity initiatives
At-will right
Black box warnings
Body mass index
Brand-name drugs
Care continuum
Chronic ailments

Civil liberties
Civil Rights Act of 1964
Computerized physician order entry system
Cost-sharing trend
Deductibles
Demographic health insurance ratings
Developed countries
Disabled individuals
Disclosure requirement of lifestyle choices

Drug-device combination products
Dynamic pricing
E-cigarettes
Employer-provided insurance
Equal Employment Opportunity Commission
Family Smoking Prevention and Tobacco Control Act of 2009
Federal appellate court
Food, Drug, and Cosmetic Act of 1938
Genetic information

Health care costs
Health factor
Health hazard
Health Insurance Portability and
    Accountability Act of 1996 (HIPAA)
Health risk assessments
Health savings accounts
HIPAA wellness rules
Individual medical histories
Inherent right to privacy
Intrusion upon seclusion
Lifestyle discrimination
Non-arbitrary employment
    considerations
Non-therapeutic tobacco products
Obesity

Off-duty activities
Physical or mental impairment
Physiological disorder
Polypharmacy
Population health management
Precision medicine
Predictors of health care costs
Preliminary injunction
Pre-marketing approval
    requirement
Premiums
Preventable behaviors and
    conditions
Preventive care
Primary care
Privacy interests

Prospective medicine
Rate of inflation
Rehabilitation Act
Risk portfolio
Secondhand smoke
Self-identification
Slippery slope arguments
Smoking-cessation program
Social responsibility
Summary judgment
Surcharge
Tobacco-free policy
Tobacco-related illnesses
Vaping
Weight-related conditions
Wellness programs

FACT OR FICTION

Lifestyle Discrimination

Can employees be fired for being obese?

Stephen Grindle weighed about 345 pounds when he was hired as a driver and dock worker with Watkins Motor Lines where he loaded, unloaded, and arranged heavy freight. Following an on-the-job knee injury, he took a medical leave of absence for almost six months. When his medical leave was almost over, Grindle weighed 405 pounds, had a limited range of motion that prevented him from ducking and squatting, and became short-of-breath after a few steps. After his medical leave expired, Watkins fired Grindle, claiming that he could not safely perform his job requirements as a dock worker even though he had performed his job for five years when his weight ranged from 340 to 450 pounds. Grindle claimed that he was fired because of his **obesity**,[LN1] in violation of the **Americans with Disabilities Act of 1990** (42 U.S.C.A. §§ 12101 *et seq.*; 47 U.S.C.A. § 225), which prohibits disability-based job discrimination.

— *See* Law Fact at the end of this chapter for the answer.

Principles and Applications

Preventable behaviors and conditions are often a topic of public conversation and debate, but **preventive care** has not been as successful as hoped for thus far. For instance:

- Employees are not motivated to maintain healthy lifestyles
- Health plans are reluctant to pay for comprehensive preventive care
- Physicians are far more focused on treating than preventing disease

As employers are trying to reduce the cost of their health insurance programs, the epidemics of depression, diabetes, cardiovascular disease, and other **chronic ailments**[LN2] are bringing new urgency to the concept of preventive care. Consequently, employers are taking a much more aggressive look at preventable behaviors and conditions. While preventable chronic diseases such as diabetes, arthritis, and circulatory disorders are responsible for the most direct health care costs among employees, the costliest health condition overall is depression (CMS, 2014; Roehrig, 2016). Depression is more of a burden to the U.S. health care system than any other illness (CDC, 2013a; WHO, 2015). Whether **polypharmacy** causes or contributes to the epidemic of depression is increasingly gaining attention (Thomas et al., 2014).[LN3] Employees are often prescribed drugs before any other non-drug treatment options are explored, resulting in depression drugs being the leading cost among prescription drug expenses (Levkovitz et al., 2011).

Current Quality and Costs Trends

Two current trends in employer-provided insurance suggest that employers are inconsistent about how they want their health plans to work. One trend is investing in improving the quality of employee health care; the other trend is shifting the costs of this improvement to employees. This suggests that while employers want to improve the quality of employee health care, they do not want to foot the increased bill.

Quality Improvements of Employee Health Care

Many employers are investing in new programs to improve the quality of health care. For instance, a coalition of employers called the Leapfrog Group encourages hospitals to adopt **computerized physician order entry systems** for entering orders as a way to prevent errors. General Electric has a program to identify the higher quality physicians and hospitals used by its employees, thereby setting the stage for providing financial incentives for those employees who use better providers. Many employers are willing to invest in quality improvements with the expectation that quality care will, in the long run, lower their health care costs. Increasingly, employers are willing to pay for newer, higher priced **brand-name drugs** that have less adverse side effects so employees will be more compliant in taking their prescribed drugs, thereby promoting better health outcomes (Roebuck et al., 2011).

Shifting Quality Improvement Costs to Employees

At the same time as employers are investing in improving the quality of their employees' health care, more employers are shifting the costs of their health insurance to employees, partly because their health care costs have increased during the past ten years (Long et al., 2016a). The highest profile example of the **cost-sharing trend** has been the move to **health savings accounts**, championed as a way to combat health care inflation by giving consumers incentives to shop more astutely for care (McMahon & McGovern, 2016). Health savings accounts, created early in 2004, allow pretax money to be put into accounts similar to 401(k) retirement accounts. Participants buy health plans with high deductibles, at least $1,000 a year for an individual and $2,000 for a family. High **deductibles** are meant to keep health plan **premiums** as low as possible. Money from the tax-free savings account is used to pay deductibles, and it could build up over the years. Health savings accounts represent a way for employers to make employees more responsible for their own health care (Shepherd, 2016).

High-profile health savings accountsSAs aside, cost-sharing can also be something as simple as increasing employee co-payments.[LN4] While the Affordable Care Act managed to bring basic coverage to almost everyone (about 90% of Americans are now covered), for many employees their average deductible spending has nearly tripled in the past decade (Claxton et al., 2016). A new recent poll shows that for one in four employees, health care costs are a very or somewhat serious problem for them or their families (NPR et al., 2016).

Cost-Sharing Trend

Taken together, the two trends illustrate that employers are struggling to accurately assess how decisions about health insurance affect the bottom line. The cost-sharing trend, in particular, comes at time when information is lacking about whether short-term savings will lead to long-term health problems and added costs. No one knows whether employees will avoid **primary care** for financial reasons, or whether employees will try to stay healthy to avoid paying more if they get sick.

Employers might just have to pay higher wages if health care benefits are reduced. This is not just an assumption of economic theory. Empirical evidence shows that the costs of health care benefits are fully shifted out of the wages employees receive (Wharton, 2015). What is missing in the debate about health care costs is a practical and accurate method to determine how much employers should invest in the health of their employees, and to identify the best health insurance packages designed to encourage appropriate health care delivery and use. When measuring the true cost of **employer-provided insurance**, employers need to accurately measure and consider the payoffs that come from improving the health of their employees.

Forget Big Brother

Employees are always vulnerable to subtle forms of exploitation by their employers (Wharton, 2013). This is one reason for federal privacy legislation known as the **Health Insurance Portability and Accountability Act of 1996** (HIPAA) that in part governs the collection of health care information about individual employees (*See* 18 U.S.C.A. § 24). When dealing with preventable behaviors and conditions to control the costs of employer-provided insurance, it is important for employees not to conjure up images of their employer as "big brother" doing everything in their power to take advantage of them. Even though employers have access to broad-based information about the health conditions of their employees, most do not use it effectively and others do not always analyze it at all. The assumption is that larger self-insured employers with 1,000 or more employees are very effective at understanding all of the different employer health insurance practices; they are not.

Despite the acknowledged benefits of **wellness programs**, employers continue to challenge their value. Most wellness programs require health screenings to develop baseline metrics for **health risk assessments**, such as:

- Blood pressure
- Body mass index
- Cholesterol
- Nicotine use

Yet, these baseline metrics are not always analyzed or evaluated. Employers are not always aware that initial screenings can catch potentially serious health problems in their employees. In addition, aggregate data is seldom analyzed to detect systemic changes that could be made by employers (Wharton, 2013).

Prospective Medicine

The key to cutting employer-provided insurance costs is getting employees involved in their own health care when disease conditions can still be prevented.[LN5] What is really required is personalized prevention. For instance, employers are increasingly making health risk assessments and personalized health plans available to their employees in hopes that they will become directly involved in avoiding preventable behaviors and conditions. In other words, the focus is shifting from treating preventable conditions toward tailoring treatments to individual needs so employees can develop healthy lifestyles and block or delay disease and illness from arising. Although the United States is one of the world's most advanced countries, its population's overall health lags behind other similarly situated countries. This is perhaps because of the lifestyle differences between the United States and other such countries; Americans tend to treat their illness and disease rather than focusing on preventive health. In addition, other countries focus on complementary and alternative therapies (SPA treatments, massages, and acupuncture are routinely covered by health insurance plans in other countries), resulting in lower health care costs for those countries (*See* Miller, 2015).

This new approach to health care is called **prospective medicine** as opposed to *preventive medicine*. It uses **individual medical histories** to identify employees at the greatest risk of developing preventable health conditions, and it takes steps to intervene early to prevent their onset (Synderman & Williams, 2013). The issue for employers is how the value of preventive self-care can be raised so that employees will set priorities for their own health. This is the leading question surrounding the change in how employer-provided insurance will be managed in the future.

Population Health Management

Traditional approaches put employees in **care continuum** programs once a health condition was diagnosed. Today, employers are moving into **population health management** programs with focused, realistic ways to use early detection and early intervention to prevent conditions from ever developing into disease states (Synderman & Williams, 2013). This change does not succeed with a cookie-cutter approach for all employees, but rather by tailoring programs for individual employees. Clearly, employers are driving this prospective change. They provide health plans for 160 million

1. What types of medical interventions are permissible for preventable behaviors and conditions triggered by voluntary lifestyle choices made on a day-to-day basis?

employees (Claxton & Levitt, 2015). With the average cost of a family insurance plan having risen to $17,500 per year, the need to trim employers' health care costs is undisputed (Long et al., 2016b).

Predictors of Health Care Costs

Smoking and obesity are two strong **predictors of health care costs**. The business reason for doing something to diminish smoking and obesity is simply that expenses related to employer-provided insurance would be less. The general trend for most employers is that, sooner or later, the cost of health insurance depends on how expensive employee health needs are. Smoking and obesity in particular have come under attack because both directly relate to rapidly rising health care costs, and both are seen as more easily avoidable than many other preventable diseases and illnesses that drive rising health care costs for employers.

Preventable Behaviors and Conditions

National business advocacy groups and associations now call smoking a preventable behavior and obesity a preventable condition, terminology that recognizes these problems are avoidable and necessary to avert. Almost three-quarters of the adult U.S. population is overweight or obese (CDC, 2016b and 2015b). Among **developed countries**, the United States has the most obese population (WHO, 2015). Americans are much heavier than they were 10 years ago and much heavier than other people around the world. Life expectancy in the United States, which is among the richest countries, only ranks 33rd in the world (World Bank, 2016). Being overweight is comparable to having diabetes or high blood pressure; it is a true diagnosable disease that affects life expectancy (Hodge et al., 2013).

Recently, employers have declared war on smoking and obesity for one simple reason: smoking and obesity are now recognized as two real and largely preventable drains on employer-provided insurance costs. It is not the health behavior and condition of employees that is driving employers to take this seriously; the big driver is really the cost of health care.

Smoking Behaviors: Billion-Dollar Preventable Cost

In 1964, the Surgeon General first released a report stating that smoking is a **health hazard** and a primary contributor to lung disease (HEW, 1964). Since that report, and as illustrated in **FEATURE BOX 10-1**, substantial research has established that smoking dramatically increases the risk of death from a plethora of conditions, compared with the average cost of nonsmoking employees with healthy lifestyles. Despite widespread awareness and acceptance of the risks of smoking, one in six Americans still smokes (HHS, 2014).

From the $1.9 trillion that employers spend on health care each year, estimates are that over 60% of the costs go toward treating **tobacco-related illnesses** (NBGH, 2012; Surgeon General, 2010). In addition to this direct cost, smokers cost the U.S. economy $98 billion a year in lost productivity (HHS, 2014; *See* HEW, 1964). Smokers miss work more often due to illness, take longer to recover from common illnesses, and take many more breaks throughout the average workday than their nonsmoking coworkers, all resulting in lost productivity (Wharton, 2009).

Health care costs for smokers are estimated to be as much as 40% higher than those for nonsmokers (HHS, 2014). Many of the employment costs attributable to smokers, including increased health insurance costs and productivity losses due to absenteeism, are ultimately shared by nonsmoking employees. Employers pay more than $1,400 per smoker per year in increased health insurance costs or they pass these costs on to their employees (Long et al., 2016b). Employees with healthy lifestyles might ask why they are subsidizing the unhealthy choices of their counterparts on a day-to-day basis.

FEATURE BOX 10-1

Smoking Tobacco: The Billion-Dollar Preventable Cost

- Adverse health effects from smoking account for nearly 1 of every 5 deaths
- Smoking is responsible for 440,000 deaths annually
- 90% of the lung cancers, coronary heart disease, and chronic obstructive lung disease is attributable to smoking
- 8.6 million smokers suffer from serious illnesses attributable to smoking

BLS, 2015; CDC, 2015c; HHS, 2014.

Obesity Conditions: Billion-Dollar Preventable Cost

Obesity and **weight-related conditions** are significant contributors to health care costs, contributing as much as $184 billion to the nation's yearly medical bill (CDC, 2015b). Of that $184 billion cost, the total cost of obesity to U.S. employers is estimated at more than $13 billion per year, a price tag that includes:

- $8 billion for added health insurance costs
- $2.4 billion for paid sick leave
- $1.8 billion for life insurance
- $1 billion for disability insurance

(CDC, 2016c; Hammond & Levine, 2010)

As illustrated in **FIGURE 10-1**, obesity levels continue to escalate. Obesity is now considered a greater trigger for health problems and increased health spending than smoking (NBGH, 2012).

The RAND Corporation found that individuals who are obese have 30 to 50% more chronic medical problems than those who smoke (RAND, 2016; *See* Sturm & Ruopeng, 2014). The CDC notes that being overweight increases the risk of many diseases and health conditions, including:

- Cancers (especially breast, colon, and endometrial)
- Dyslipidemia (high total cholesterol or high levels of triglycerides)
- Gallbladder disease
- Heart disease

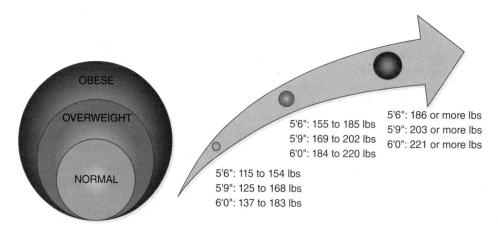

FIGURE 10-1 Overweight and Obese Adults

Data from: CDC (Centers for Disease Control and Prevention). (2016a). *Defining adult overweight and obesity.* Atlanta, GA: U.S. Department of Health and Human Services, CDC, National Center for Health Statistics.

- Hypertension (high blood pressure)
- Osteoarthritis
- Respiratory problems
- Sleep apnea
- Stroke
- Type 2 diabetes

The RAND study used a methodology to match obese nonsmokers with non-obese nonsmokers (and obese smokers with obese nonsmokers) in a fashion that could be described as an apples-to-apples approach that yielded sound results (RAND, 2016; Sturm & Hattori, 2013). When compared to a person of average weight, an obese person accounts for an additional $1,034 every year in health care costs (Cohen, 2014).

As obesity rises in the United States, the preventable conditions associated with obesity have helped trigger an increase in health care costs. The National Business Group notes that obesity accounts for approximately 9% of the health care costs each year and that 8% of employers' medical claims are due to obesity. When analyzing increases in medical spending, the National Coalition on Health Care documented that obesity drove 27% of the increased costs of health care (Russell, 2007).

Lifestyle Discrimination and Choices

There is no doubt that rising health care expenses increase the cost of health care and health plans. The NCHC notes that employer health plan premiums are increasing at nearly three times the **rate of inflation**. In an effort to counter these statistics and to help employees adopt healthier lifestyles, employers are offering a variety of programs and benefits (RAND, 2016).

Every state permits employers to penalize employees for smoking in the workplace or during working hours. Crucially, by law, if a penalty is imposed on employees for smoking, reasonable alternatives must be available to employees who cannot quit smoking. For instance, a smoker addicted to nicotine could avoid being penalized by participating in a **smoking-cessation program**. Thus, employers with company policies on not smoking on company property may lawfully discipline or terminate employees who violate their smoking ban (Martin et al., 2016).

In many states, an increasing number of employers have enacted policies precluding the employment of smokers (Allen, 2015). The only protection from employment discrimination that smokers can rely on exists in the form of state laws prohibiting employment discrimination based on tobacco use, which exist in half the states, but almost all of which are under challenge by public health organizations such as the American Heart Association (Bhatnagar et al., 2014; *See* Hernandez, 2015). For instance, the World Health Organization's hiring policy rejects all applicants who smoke, as do an increasing number of employers from health care organizations to airlines. In contrast to this no-smoking approach by employers in states that tolerate **lifestyle discrimination**, other employers in those states have adopted a middle-of-the-road approach to employee smoking. Those employers, as opposed to prohibiting employment of smokers, have passed on the additional costs attributable to smoking to employees who smoke.

Smoking opened the door for employers to also think about obesity-related issues, the leading preventable cost to the U.S. health care system. Obesity has not been examined critically in the same way as smoking has. Most employers see **anti-obesity initiatives** as beneficial. However, if employers begin to address other preventable behaviors and conditions that are less costly, there might be push-back (Wharton, 2013). For instance, some employers already prevent their executives from participating in extreme sports (skydiving, motor-cross and off-road racing, BMX racing and jumping, mountain and ice climbing, street luge, and adventure racing) and offer cafeteria-style benefits that index employee costs according to the number of children receiving benefits (families with more than one child pay higher health plan premiums) (Rausch, 2012; Wharton, 2009).

MANAGEMENT AND LAW ISSUES

2. Having an unusually high number of children is also a lifestyle choice resulting in higher health care costs for employers. Would charging such employee-parents just as much as smokers and obese employees without children be permissible?

Health Insurance Plan Ratings

There are two restraints on expansion of lifestyle discrimination beyond smoking and obesity:

- **Demographic health insurance ratings** for small employers
- HIPAA

HIPAA Wellness Rules

Lifestyle discrimination is subject to **HIPAA wellness rules** that require all employees covered under the same employer-sponsored insurance plan to pay the same premiums regardless of their health, with certain wellness programs being the exception. Employers can offer financial incentives of as much as 20% off the cost of covering an employee for participating in wellness programs. Two of the most popular incentives have become:

- Discounts to nonsmokers
- Health risk assessments

This chapter focuses on this 20% incentive for employer-sponsored plans. The first restraint is that HIPAA prevents employers from knowing which individual employees suffer from generally preventable diseases such as alcoholism, diabetes, emphysema, and heart disease (Wiley, 2014). Employers have no proof of individual employees' preventable conditions (Ajunwa, 2016).

Credible Versus Demographic Ratings

Second, only larger employers have health plans with health insurance costs credibly based on actual employee claims, and such employers are generally self-insured. They purchase reinsurance and only use health insurers as plan administrators (*See* Turk, 2015). On the other hand, small employers with fewer than 1,000 employees generally purchase health plans based on demographics; their claims history has no relationship to the cost of their health plans (Hall, 2014). In other words, when one or more members in their geographic community develops a costly health condition, all the small employers in that community must pay higher premiums. Small employers cannot effectively manage their disease risk; their disease risks are based on the demographics of their geographic community, not on the actual claims of their employees. In summary, health plan costs for large employers are based on actual claims; for small employers, costs are based on demographics in general. Large employers can effectively manage their employee claims; small employers cannot because they cannot control their risk pools (Cogan, 2016).

Smoking Behaviors: A Lifestyle Choice

While employees have used the courts to challenge employment policies that consider off-duty behavior, such challenges have met with little success. Unless a state prohibits employers from banning participation in specific activities such as smoking, employers have generally been successful in protecting their right to hire and fire employees as they please, meaning that employers can take an employee's health care costs into consideration in a decision to hire or fire that employee (Martin et al., 2016).

Ideally, employee policies should not be arbitrary and should be rationally connected to a legitimate goal. Challenges to policies often come about when a court compares the purpose and intent of a policy with its effect on the individual employee challenging it. The effect has to fit with the purpose. If challenged in a court of law, employers should be able to defend their employment policies and be able to demonstrate that they saw a rational connection between their policies and the specific interests served by the policies. If this connection is arbitrary or irrational, then the policy will fail. For instance, policies prohibiting smoking should apply to all new hires or to current employees within a specific time period. Employers can also require job applicants to sign affidavits stating they have not used tobacco or tobacco products during a specified period preceding their job application if they can show that smoking would interfere with the employee's job performance or the operation of the business (Luff, 2015).

Not all policies precluding the employment of smokers are permissible (Martin et al., 2016). The use of race or gender to somehow target smokers or other such discriminatory treatment is not permitted. In addition, if employers use **dynamic pricing** to set the price of smokers' health plan premiums in such a way that it angers all employees, employers can spark a backlash against any prospective changes. However, dynamic pricing of health plan premiums is ever more common. This is subject to two federal regulatory restrictions: the HIPAA wellness rule and the **20% threshold rule**. Under the wellness rule, group health plans cannot discriminate among individuals in eligibility, benefits, or premiums based on any **health factor** of an individual (health status, preventable conditions, and genetic information are all considered health factors). For instance, employers cannot charge smokers higher health care premiums without offering those with a nicotine addiction access to supplemental wellness programs, such as smoking-cessation activities. Under the 20% threshold rule, employers cannot award employees more than a 20% reduction in their health plan premiums for being healthy (through lower co-payments, deductibles, or cash incentive payments). Increasingly, employees who smoke pay higher premiums to the same insurer than employees who have never smoked.[LN6]

COURT DECISION
Lifestyle Discrimination: Smoking

City of North Miami v. Kurtz
[Employer v. Employee]
653 So.2d 1025 (Supreme Court of Florida 1995),
cert. denied, 516 U.S. 1043 (U.S. Supreme Court 1996);
followed by *Long v. Ballard*, 2013 U.S. Dist. LEXIS 34499 (U.S. District Court for the Southern District of Indiana, Indianapolis Division 2013)

Facts: Arlene Kurtz attempted to apply for a clerk-typist position with the city of North Miami.

At the time of her interview, she was informed that she was required to sign an **affidavit** stating that she had not used tobacco products for one year. Kurtz refused and brought suit.

Issue: Are employees entitled to protection against government intrusion into **off-duty activities**, namely smoking?

Holding and Decision: No. Smoking is not considered a private activity entitled to protection against government-employer consideration.

Analysis: Initially, the trial court held that neither the Florida State Constitution nor the U.S. Constitution afforded Kurtz a right to privacy with respect to off-duty smoking and granted the city's motion for **summary judgment**. On appeal, the trial court decision was reversed, concluding that Kurtz did have a right to privacy with respect to smoking under Florida's state constitution, and that the city of North Miami's interests were insufficient to outweigh the intrusion into her privacy. However, the Florida Supreme Court reversed and remanded with directions to reinstate the trial court's judgment. Florida, together with 10 other states, incorporates privacy rights into its state constitution.

The Florida Supreme Court addressed whether the Florida constitution, with its right to privacy, protected Kurtz from governmental intrusion into non-work-related activities. In concluding that it did not, the court relied on the pervasive public nature of smoking. The court reasoned that smokers must frequently disclose whether they smoke in obtaining seating in restaurants, renting cars, and reserving motel rooms. Accordingly, the court held that smokers did not have an expectation of privacy within the meaning of the Florida constitution.

Turning to the U.S. Constitution, the court again concluded that Kurtz did not have a right of privacy with respect to smoking. First, the court examined whether the right to smoke constituted a recognized fundamental right entitled to protection absent a compelling state interest. The court concluded that smoking did not implicate fundamental rights. Notwithstanding this conclusion, the court concluded that even if the city's policy infringed upon a liberty interest, there was a sufficient rational basis for the rule given the cost savings realized by the city in refusing to hire employees who smoked.

Rule of Law: Smoking is not a fundamental right superseding governmental interests as it relates to employment.

References discussing this court decision: *E.g.*, Hearing & Ussery, 2012; Mariner, 2012; Shamsey, 2014.

Obesity Conditions: A Lifestyle Choice

While Santa Cruz and San Francisco, California, and Washington, DC have passed laws barring employment discrimination because of weight (Shinall, 2016), outside these areas, it remains very difficult for employees and job applicants to bring a successful case against employers for lifestyle discrimination based on obesity. However, a 240-pound aerobics instructor in San Francisco did successfully challenge Jazzercise Inc., which denied her a teaching position because she did not look leaner than the public (Ware, 2013). Each case must be decided on a case-by-case basis with fact-specific and individualized inquiry.

COURT DECISION
Lifestyle Discrimination: Obesity

Cook v. Department of Mental Health, Retardation and Hospitals
[Interviewee v. Interviewer]
10 F.3d 17 (U.S. Court of Appeals for the 1st Circuit 1993);
followed by *U.S. Equal Employment Opportunity Commission v. Resources for Human Development, Inc.*, 827
F.Supp.2d 688 (U.S. District Court for the Eastern District of Louisiana 2011)

Facts: The State of Rhode Island refused to hire Arlene Cook, who weighed over 320 pounds, because of her obesity.

Issue: Can employers refuse to hire people who are obese?

Holding and Decision: No. Obesity need not be a physiological disorder to qualify for health care coverage under the Rehabilitation Act.

Analysis: The trial court held that while obesity can be a disability under the **Rehabilitation Act**, it must be a physiological disorder and cannot be a transitory or self-imposed condition. The trial court found that the state discriminated against Cook because of a physiological disorder. The state appealed the trial court's judgment. In response to the state's appeal, the **Equal Employment Opportunity Commission** (EEOC) filed an **amicus brief** arguing that the issue of whether obesity is a disability must be determined on a case-by-case basis.

The EEOC further argued that obesity may constitute a disability despite not being a physiological disorder; that is, obesity may be considered a physical impairment. The EEOC argued that whether obesity is substantially limiting should be analyzed by considering three factors, the:

* Duration or expected duration of the impairment
* Nature and severity of the impairment
* Permanent or long-term impact resulting from the impairment

Additionally, the EEOC argued that neither the Rehabilitation Act nor the Americans with Disabilities Act (ADA) requires the consideration of how obese individuals become impaired. The EEOC maintained that voluntariness should not preclude the protection of obese individuals under either Act, and should only be relevant if someone could quickly change their weight by altering their behavior.

The court adopted the EEOC's reasoning that obesity need not be a physiological disorder to qualify for health care coverage under the Rehabilitation Act. Morbid obesity is a **physiological disorder**. The medical profession considers individuals morbidly obese if they weigh either more than twice their optimal weight or are more than 100 pounds over their optimal weight. Morbid obesity involves a dysfunction of both the metabolic system and the neurological appetite-suppressing signal system, capable of causing adverse effects within the musculoskeletal, respiratory, and cardiovascular systems. Metabolic dysfunction, which leads to weight gain in the morbidly obese, lingers even after weight loss. Further, the court held that employers cannot deny employment on the grounds that obesity increases their health insurance costs.

Rule of Law: As determined on a case-by-case basis, obesity is a disability protected against discrimination under the Rehabilitation Act.

References discussing the court decision: *E.g.,* Barry et al., 2013; Clarke, 2015; Henry, 2014; Porter, 2014; Shinall, 2016; Ware, 2013; White, 2013.

The First Circuit Court of Appeals was the first **federal appellate court** to recognize that an employer violated the Rehabilitation Act by refusing to hire an obese job applicant. The Rehabilitation Act provides protection from discrimination to handicapped employees; it preceded the ADA. Courts that have subsequently applied and discussed the decision, however, have generally found that obesity fails to meet the definition of a disability under the Rehabilitation Act or the ADA, the Rehabilitation Act's successor. Weight is a real dilemma for employers. They want employees to lose weight, but they do not want to fire them for being overweight. Practically, employers cannot refuse to hire overweight individuals because almost three-quarters of Americans are overweight.

Health Laws Supporting Lifestyle Choices

Disability Legislation

Although some federal laws are specifically aimed at barring lifestyle discrimination, none reach so far as to regulate employer scrutiny of the smoking or weight status of employees. For instance, the ADA prohibits employers from discriminating against **disabled individuals** on the basis of their disability in regard to job application procedures (hiring, advancement, or discharge), compensation, or job training. To be disabled within the meaning of the ADA, employees must establish that they have either a **physical or mental impairment** that substantially limits one or more of their major life activities, a record of an impairment, or that they are regarded by others as having such an impairment (whether or not the employee actually has an impairment). Major life activities include caring for oneself, performing manual tasks, walking, seeing, hearing, speaking, breathing, learning, and working. Other examples of major life activities include sitting, standing, lifting, and mental and emotional processes such as thinking, concentrating, and interacting with others. The ADA prohibits employers from requiring medical examinations or making other disability-related inquiries to determine if an employee is disabled (or the extent of any such disability) unless the examination or inquiry is job-related and consistent with business necessity.

The ADA, with its focus on preventing discrimination against those with a significant physical or mental impairments, is inapplicable to claims brought by employees or job applicants who are not restricted in life activities (Wharton, 2013). Although smoking and obesity may lead to eventual disability, neither, in and of itself, is a disability because neither limits major life activities as required under the ADA. Accordingly, while obese employees faced with lifestyle discrimination have recourse under the ADA, their legal protections are narrow and quite specific (Clarke, 2015). Smokers have no such recourse.

MANAGEMENT AND LAW ISSUES

4. Should employers be permitted to penalize employees for smoking behavior and obesity conditions that increase employers' health care costs? If so, when? If not, why not?

Civil Rights Legislation

The federal **Civil Rights Act of 1964** prohibits discrimination in employment based on race, national origin, color, sex, and religion (42 U.S.C.A.§§ 2000e *et seq.*). Because discrimination against smokers and obese employees does not implicate race, national origin, color, sex, or religion, employees and job applicants subject to discrimination based on smoking or obesity have no recourse under the Civil Rights Act or similar state enactments.

In addition, as a result of the considerable body of evidence concerning the effect of **secondhand smoke**, there has been significant government regulation of smoking (Persad, 2015). For instance, smoking is generally prohibited in the workplace and in public buildings. While policies aimed at protecting nonsmokers from secondhand smoke have not reached so far as to preclude smoking in private or to preclude employer consideration of private, off-duty smoking, absent state legislation, employers in most states are free to exercise their **at-will right** to exclude employees who smoke from their workforce (Clarke, 2015).

Invasion of Privacy

Employers' considerations of smoking and obesity do not usually violate **privacy interests**. Because there is no recognized state or federal constitutional right to be free from **non-arbitrary employment considerations**, absent lifestyle discrimination legislation, employers can implement no-smoking and obesity policies (*See* Hoffman, 2015).

Privacy claims, like the right to be free from **intrusion upon seclusion**, require that an employer's intrusion be unreasonable and intrusive upon private affairs (Froomkin, 2015). The mere fact that smoking may take place in private is insufficient to subject the activity to privacy protection. The same reasoning would apply to eating and/or not exercising.

Courts that have considered whether smoking is a private affair that implicates a legitimate privacy interest have concluded that it is not (Fairfield & Engel, 2016). Today, smokers must reveal that they smoke in almost every aspect of life. No courts have considered whether eating and/or not exercising until obesity occurs is subject to privacy protection. However, claims for intrusion upon seclusion cannot be maintained where activities are habitually disclosed or undertaken in public (Grider, 2015).

Disclosure Requirement of Lifestyle Choices

Most employers who prohibit employee smoking or obesity require that employees agree to disclose their smoking or weight status (Clarke, 2015). This is called a **disclosure requirement of lifestyle choices**. No intrusion into privacy occurs where employers have permission to commit the intrusive act or when the employee is on notice of the employment policy. Thus, where an employer has given notice of a no-smoking policy, the lifestyle smoker is caught between disclosing the smoking and being fired or refusing disclosure and being fired. Obesity is readily apparent, so it is difficult to claim a privacy intrusion.

Even if employees could establish that they had a reasonable expectation of privacy regarding their smoking or weight, employer scrutiny into employee smoking and obesity is reasonable (Wharton, 2009). A balancing test is generally utilized in determining whether an employer's intrusion into an area the employee deems private is unreasonable (Clarke, 2015). Thus, the significance of employee privacy interests is balanced against employer business interests. Assuming that employers have a legitimate business interest in reducing health insurance costs, such as the increased health care costs incurred due to employees who smoke or are obese, employer policies requiring employee self-disclosure are not inherently unreasonable (Wharton, 2013).

Tobacco-Free Policies

Weyco, an Okemos, Michigan, company specializing in employee health insurance plans and health insurance management, became famous as a result of its **tobacco-free policy**. As adopted in 2005, the Weyco policy required current employees to quit smoking or be fired, and employees who were identified as smokers on the target date were terminated. The Weyco policy provided that employees were to be subjected to random breath tests for carbon monoxide. A positive test result would be followed by a confirmatory urine test. After Weyco fully implemented its no-smoking policy, employees were required to maintain a tobacco-free status at all times (Roberts, 2014). Since Weyco, the movement to promote smoke-free workplaces has spread widely in the United States and the rest of the world (Warner, 2014).

Vaping: Gateway Back to Smoking Cigarettes

With the health safety of **e-cigarettes** in doubt, employee **vaping** is the newest preventable behavior. Every day that passes debating about e-cigarettes exposes more and more employees to vapor advertising,[LN7] which, as research shows, means an increasing number of smokers and an opening of the gateway back to cigarettes (Zimlich, 2015). Right now, one can only guess as to how the *Sottera* ruling will affect public health.

COURT DECISION
Regulation of Electronic Cigarettes

Sottera, Inc. v. Food and Drug Administration
[E-Cigarettes Distributor vs. Federal Government]
627 F.3d 891 (U.S. Court of Appeals for the D.C. Circuit 2010),
rehearing denied, 2011 U.S. App. LEXIS 26339
(U.S. Court of Appeals for the D.C. Circuit 2011)

Facts: Sottera is an importer and distributor of electronic cigarettes (e-cigarettes) in the United States. E-cigarettes are manufactured to look similar to conventional cigarettes, cigars, or pipes, but are smokeless, flameless, battery-powered devices that vaporize liquid nicotine for users to inhale. While the nicotine in e-cigarettes is derived from tobacco, the e-cigarette itself contains no tobacco. The products allow users to inhale nicotine vapor without fire, smoke, ash, or carbon monoxide. E-cigarettes thus allow users to satisfy their nicotine craving without ingesting the harmful chemicals contained in traditional tobacco products such as cigarettes, cigars, and smokeless tobacco.

When the Food and Drug Administration (FDA) blocked shipment of Sottera's e-cigarettes from importation into the United States, Sottera filed for a **preliminary injunction**. Sottera sought to bar the FDA from regulating e-cigarettes as **drug-device combination products** and from blocking their importation. Sottera maintained that e-cigarettes served the same purpose as traditional tobacco cigarettes and were marketed without therapeutic claims or as a smoking cessation product and, therefore, they should be regulated under the **Family Smoking Prevention and Tobacco Control Act of 2009** like traditional tobacco cigarettes. The FDA countered that only cigarettes and smokeless tobacco were excluded from its regulation.

Issue: Should e-cigarettes be regulated and distributed subject to the same rigorous safety testing required for nicotine patches and gums or as a tobacco product?

Holding and Decision: The FDA lacks the authority to ban the importation of e-cigarettes into the United States under the federal **Food, Drug, and Cosmetic Act of 1938**.

Analysis: In blocking the imports, the FDA claimed that e-cigarettes were adulterated, misbranded, and unapproved drug-device combinations, thereby falling within the FDA's broad regulatory authority over medical devices, much like nicotine gums and patches. In seeking an injunction against the FDA, Sottera claimed that e-cigarettes were merely tobacco products.

The court based its decision on the fact that the Family Smoking Prevention and Tobacco Control Act provided a regulatory scheme for **non-therapeutic tobacco products**. While the FDA did not challenge Sottera's claim that its e-cigarettes were not marketed for therapeutic uses, the court noted that the FDA might be able to succeed in such a challenge. The FDA's authority over tobacco products allows the FDA to restrict how the products are marketed, manufactured, and distributed. The FDA's authority over drug-device products is more expansive and includes a **pre-marketing approval requirement**. The safety of e-cigarettes is in doubt.

Rule of Law: E-cigarettes and other nicotine-containing products are not drugs or devices unless they are marketed for therapeutic purposes, but they are nicotine-containing products and can therefore be regulated as tobacco products under the Family Smoking Prevention and Tobacco Control Act.

References discussing this court decision: *E.g.*, Allen, 2015; Freiberg, 2012; Lindblom, 2015; Shechtman, 2011; Zimlich, 2015.

Opinion is split about the outcome of this decision. Supporters of the ruling view e-cigarettes as a lesser evil than tobacco cigarettes. The lenient regulatory scheme of the Family Smoking Prevention and Tobacco Control Act (as opposed to the Federal Food, Drug, and Cosmetic Act) ensures that e-cigarettes remain widely available. This is especially important to former heavy smokers seeking to avoid the harmful health effects of chronic tobacco use by replacing tobacco cigarettes with e-cigarettes.

On the other hand, many would prefer to see e-cigarettes subject to the same rigorous testing that is required for nicotine patches and gums. In the meantime, until the FDA issues production and manufacturing standards for e-cigarettes, they will be distributed without government regulation or oversight for quality control. Some public health advocates are concerned that e-cigarettes, which come in a variety of flavors (menthol, tobacco, cherry, coffee, apple, chocolate, almond, and vanilla, among others) will appeal to youths, leading to nicotine and tobacco dependence.

Regulation of Off-Duty Smoking

In response to Weyco's tobacco-free policy, some states enacted laws prohibiting employers from basing employment decisions on off-duty smoking. Although many are broader, most of the laws are aimed at preventing employers from firing, refusing to hire, or otherwise discriminating against those who smoke. Not surprisingly, one of the biggest proponents of the right to smoke is the tobacco industry.

Similarly, the American Civil Liberties Union has denounced lifestyle discrimination based on off-duty smoking as infringing on one's **civil liberties** or **inherent right to privacy**. Both argue that employers' consideration of lifestyle activities constitutes a slippery slope that will lead to discrimination based on other unhealthy or undesirable habits. The slippery slope argument centers on privacy issues and genetic testing.

Concerns about discrimination against employees whose test results could become public already have led most states to prohibit health insurers from using **genetic information**. In addition, federal agencies are prohibited from collecting genetic information from their employees or using such information to make hiring, promotion, or placement decisions (Executive Order, 2000).

Slippery Slope Arguments

A **slippery slope argument** has been defined as one that covers all situations where "A", which might be appealing, ends up materially increasing the probability that other situations will bring about "B," which is opposed. In the context of lifestyle discrimination on the basis of smoking and obesity, the argument is that where "A," the right to smoke in private and to be obese is not protected, then "B," employees will be subject to more offensive intrusions into their private lives.

Employees are always vulnerable to being taking advantage of by their employers. This is the reason for HIPAA privacy laws dealing with the collection of health care information about individual employees (Pike, 2016). What happens when a female employee gains weight during pregnancy and does not lose it right away after delivery? How would Weyco address the Pregnancy Discrimination Act of 1978?

Based on the slippery slope argument, if employers are allowed to discriminate against smokers and the obese, they might start targeting other groups as well. For instance: women who choose to have children might have to pay for the health care costs associated with pregnancy and the costs associated with their children's health; people who break their legs while skiing might have to pay for the cost of the injuries they received as a consequence of their dangerous choice; even people who choose to take a busy highway home from work and then get in a

MANAGEMENT AND LAW ISSUES

5. Could e-cigarettes possibly improve public health by replacing tobacco products and thereby significantly decreasing the number of tobacco users, and thus also the prevalence and severity of tobacco-related health problems for employers?

serious car accident might have to pay for the cost of the injuries they received as a result of choosing to take that particular way home that day. On some level, practically all health care costs are a result of employees' own preventable choices. Based on this slippery slope argument, the only thing health care plans would have to pay for is preventive care.

One of the greatest problems with the slippery slope argument is that it is a convenient way of warning of the dire effects of lifestyle discrimination without actually having to address smoking or obesity (Little, 2016). Thus, proponents argue that while **self-identification** at the outset of no-smoking or obesity policies may suffice, eventually employers will require universal medical testing of employees to enforce the policies. Although most employers who discriminate based on smoking or obesity rely on voluntary disclosures (Pike, 2016), it is true that some employers, such as Weyco, have resorted to more intrusive measures to enforce their policies. However, when more intrusive means of policing off-duty behaviors are used, employers risk claims for invasion of privacy (Clarke, 2015).

Lifestyle Discrimination Is Good Business

It is undisputed that employers incur costs as a result of hiring and retaining employees with unhealthy lifestyles. If employers do not impose a **surcharge** on such employees, then those additional costs are passed onto, or shared with, all employees. There is no doubt that the greatest harm caused by smokers and obese employees is almost entirely self-inflicted. Nonetheless, their lifestyle consequences have a ripple effect resulting in employer consequences. From the employer's perspective, given a choice between a nonsmoker and a smoker or between someone who is obese or non-obese, with all other things being equal, it would be an irrational business decision to choose the lifestyle smoker or obese employee (Wharton, 2009). In dollars and cents, the employer who chooses to hire the lifestyle smoker or obese employee has opted to pay more for services that can be purchased for less. In other words, it is good business to hire nonsmokers and non-obese employees.

Nonetheless, employers who opt for lifestyle discrimination make a business decision to forgo hiring from a segment of the available labor market (DeMuth, 2016). In certain industries, a ban on employment of employees with unhealthy lifestyles may be impracticable. For instance, because the highest incidence of smoking is among young unskilled employees, those businesses seeking a significant pool of unskilled laborers could ultimately limit their applicant pool to a point that any savings in health insurance costs would be offset by the increased wages necessary to broaden the applicant pool (Wharton, 2009).

At the same time, those in favor of lifestyle discrimination claim that no-smoking and obesity policies provide incentives for employees to adopt healthy lifestyles. In fact, there is some, albeit anecdotal, evidence supporting the proposition that no-smoking and healthy weight policies provide incentives for some employees to quit smoking or lose weight. When cast in these terms, employers' concerns for employees' health sounds virtuously noble; numerous news sources quote employees testifying that without incentives from employers, they would have never quit smoking or lost weight. Moreover, evidence is beginning to emerge showing that incentivizing employees to lose weight may be effective (Copp, 2012).

Paying for Lifestyle Choices

There are two sides to the lifestyle discrimination debate. On one hand, there is reluctance to allow employers to intrude into the health of employees with preventable behaviors and conditions. In reality, however, employers have a right to make hiring decisions based on the predicted efficiency of job applicants. Inevitably, employees with unhealthy lifestyles will cost more in employer-provided insurance and be less productive in general due to poor health (Wharton, 2009).

Therefore, the question is whether there are alternatives to lifestyle discrimination. Many employers have opted to pass on **health care costs** attributable to preventable behaviors and conditions to those employees who smoke or are obese (RAND, 2016). Of course, this middle position is available only in those jurisdictions that have not enacted laws prohibiting discrimination and adhere to the premise that employment is at-will (Madison, 2015).

The middle approach of passing on employer costs attributable to preventable behaviors and conditions has two benefits. First, supplemental amounts paid by employees with preventable behaviors and conditions are intended to, and by all accounts do, offset at least some of the employer costs inherent in hiring these employees (Wharton, 2013). Accordingly, to the extent that increased health care costs attributable to preventable behaviors and conditions are passed on to employees, the increased costs are borne by those who create the risk of the increased costs, as opposed to those who do not pose the same economic risk to employers (Wharton, 2009). Second, because it operates as a surcharge, it provides an incentive to employees to adopt healthier lifestyles or stop smoking and lose weight (Wharton, 2013).

Studies confirm that employers believe employees should be held accountable for their own health (RAND, 2016). At the same time, employers believe employees are not held accountable. One of the advantages of the benefits surcharge is that it forces employees to be responsible for the additional costs incumbent on their lifestyles, while at the same time relieving employees from bearing health insurance costs not attributable to their own behavior (Wharton, 2009). In short, it makes employees accountable for their behavior with employment and health consequences (RAND, 2016).

Balancing Costs: Preventable Behaviors and Conditions

Healthy lifestyles constitute a legitimate employment consideration (Wharton, 2009). Employers need to know more about the nature of the risks they face, the likelihood of occurrence, and the health care costs that may result. Self-insured large employers and insurers that provide health insurance plans to small employers are interested because they need to know how to set premiums for different types of risk within the context of their overall **risk portfolio**.

Although some states proscribe employment consideration of obesity and off-duty smoking, a number of states continue the at-will tradition of employment, allowing employers to fire or refuse to hire employees at their option. In the middle are those employers who opt to hire smokers and obese employees, but only on the condition that those who smoke or are obese pay at least some of the health insurance costs attributable to smoking or their weight. The prevailing view of employers is that policies covering preventable behaviors and conditions at the expense of all employees are not fair (RAND, 2016).

No one seriously disputes that smoking and obesity impact health and impose significant health and productivity costs on employers (Pricewaterhouse Coopers & World Economic Forum, 2007). The World Economic Forum calls on business leaders to fight chronic diseases, many of which are related to smoking and obesity, in the workplace, not only to cut direct and indirect costs but as a matter of **social responsibility**. There is considerable evidence that smoking and obesity are directly related to increased employer health care costs (Wharton, 2009). An equitable approach to lifestyle discrimination should balance the concerns of employees with healthy lifestyles with those of employees who have preventable behaviors and conditions.

Attempts should be made to balance individual employee privacy concerns with the cost burdens imposed on employers who are forced to hire employees with preventable behaviors and conditions. Under a balanced approach, employers could proscribe making hiring and firing decisions based on preventable behaviors and conditions. At the same time, legislation could also provide for employers to pass on the costs reasonably associated with the hiring and retention of employees with preventable behaviors and conditions to those specific employees. Under this scheme, it would be legitimate to charge a surcharge for employer-provided insurance to those employees who smoke or are obese (RAND, 2016; Wharton, 2009).

LAW FACT

Lifestyle Discrimination

Can employees be fired for being obese?

No. Employees cannot be fired for being obese if they can show that they were discriminated against because of their obesity. Being obese is considered a protected disability, even without a proven physiological cause; there is no need to show that obesity actually limits or is perceived to limit a major life activity.

— *EEOC v. Watkins Motor Lines, Inc.*, 463 F.3d 436 (U.S. Court of Appeals for the 6th Circuit 2006), *superseded by statute*, ADA Amendments Act of 2008, 42 U.S.C.A. § 12101, *et seq.* (lowering the legal standards for what constitutes a protected disability).

See Browne et al., 2010; Concannon, 2012; Katz, 2010; Liu, 2010; Morris, 2010; Swartz, 2010; Vallor, 2013 (discussing this decision).

CHAPTER SUMMARY

- HIPAA prevents employers from learning of individual employee health conditions.
- Employers may penalize employees for smoking behavior and obesity conditions unless there are state prohibitions against specific lifestyle discrimination activities.
- Lifestyle policies must not be arbitrary and must be rationally connected to a legitimate goal to survive being challenged in court.
- Neither gender nor race can be used to target smokers or obese employees for discriminatory treatment.
- Employers may use dynamic pricing in their health insurance plans and charge smokers and obese employees higher premiums.
- No federal laws regulate employer scrutiny of the smoking or weight status of employees.
- The ADA prohibits employers from discriminating against the disabled in regard to job application procedures (hiring, advancement, or discharge), compensation, and training.
- To be protected as disabled under the ADA, employees must show only that they were discriminated against because of an actual or perceived disability, whether or not that disability limits or is perceived to limit a major life activity.
- The ADA prohibits employers from requiring medical examinations or inquiries to determine if an employee is disabled, unless the examination or inquiry is job-related and consistent with business necessity.
- Because lifestyle discrimination against smoking and obesity does not implicate race, national origin, color, sex, or religion, employees and job applicants have no recourse under the Civil Rights Act or similar state enactments.
- Lifestyle discrimination against smoking and obesity does not violate privacy interests since there is no constitutional right to be free from non-arbitrary employment considerations.
- Employers cannot unreasonably intrude upon the private affairs of employees, but the fact that smoking may take place in private is insufficient to subject the behavior to privacy protection.
- Employers may require employees to agree to disclose their smoking or weight status; no intrusion into privacy occurs where employers have permission to commit the intrusive act or when the employee is on notice of the employment policy.
- Since employers have a legitimate business interest in reducing health insurance costs, employer policies requiring employee self-disclosure are not unreasonable.
- Healthy lifestyles constitute a legitimate employment consideration.

LAW NOTES

1. It is important to note that this chapter addresses only the actual medical diagnosis of obesity, and not simply employees who are "pleasantly plump." For adults, obesity ranges are determined by using weight and height to calculate a number called the **body mass index**, which correlates with their level of body obesity. A person who is 5 feet, 9 inches and weighs between 125 pounds and 168 pounds is considered a healthy weight; the same person weighing between 169 pounds and 202 pounds is overweight; and the same person weighing more than 203 pounds is considered obese (CDC, 2016a).

2. Chronic diseases affect at least 125 million Americans and cost more than $500 billion annually (CMS, 2016 and 2015). The Centers for Disease Control and Prevention warned of an increased burden of heart disease and stroke on the health care system and has called for stronger prevention efforts (Arnett et al., 2014; CDC, 2013b). The federally sponsored U.S. Preventive Services Task Force, which issues recommendations on screening tests, calls for physicians to screen their adult patients for preventable diseases and prescribes intensive behavior therapy to those who need it (AHRQ, 2014).

3. The side effects of all too many prescription drugs have in common the possible side effect of depression (*E.g.*, Thomas et al., 2014). For instance:

   - Anticonvulsant drugs (Walker & Kalviainen, 2011)
   - Asthma drugs (Calapai et al., 2014)
   - Beta-blocker drugs used to treat high blood pressure, especially Inderal (propranolol) (Luijemdijk et al., 2011)
   - Contraceptives including those delivered by vaginal ring or patch (Lopez et al., 2010)

- Corticosteroids (Bhangle et al., 2013)
- Nonnucleoside reverse transcriptase inhibitors for HIV and breast cancer therapies (Simpson et al., 2014)
- Smoking cessation drugs, especially Chantix (varenicline) (FDA, 2016)

The FDA investigates drugs that have reports of depression symptoms as a side effect and then requires **black box warnings** to be clearly printed on the drug's packaging as opposed to regulating or seeking to control the marketing of such drugs. This is law by disclosure as opposed to law by regulation. The regulation of polypharmacy is just beginning to draw attention.

4. Humana, a health insurer in Louisville, Kentucky, asks its employees if they smoke. Those who said they do not smoke get a bonus in their paychecks each pay period. General Mills, Northwest Airlines, Continental Airlines, Sprint Nextel, Nissan, Gannett, and Scotts Miracle-Gro, among others, impose a surcharge on the employer-provided insurance of smokers (Wharton, 2009).

5. Prospective health programs with personalized planning have been around since the mid-2000s. Prospective health care determines the risk for employees to develop specific diseases, detects the disease's earliest onset, and prevents or intervenes early enough to provide maximum health insurance; every employee has a personalized health plan to accomplish this (Synderman & Williams, 2013). Duke University studied this idea in a randomized trial funded by the federal government before offering a prospective health program to its 35,000 employees and their dependents. Emory University and other large academic medical centers and the Association of American Medical Colleges are also implementing prospective health models for their employees. Medical schools that do research and provide health plans to their employees offer the perfect testing ground for this effort.

    Preventive care with more personalized planning is becoming more common in large not-for-profit managed-care groups, such as Seattle's Group Health Cooperative, which covers 560,000 employees and their dependents in the Pacific Northwest. The lawn and gardening products company Scotts Miracle-Gro requires employees to take annual health assessments through a program affiliated with medical information website WebMD Health Corp. or pay extra health insurance costs at a significant level. The health assessment starts with a form filled out online. Then, a health coach contacts the employee and arranges a treatment regimen to address any health issues. The employee must follow through with the recommendations or pay higher premiums. Whole Health Management Inc., a Cleveland company that also works with Continental Airlines, Sprint Nextel, and Nissan, among others, administers the program (Suk, 2011).

6. Vital Measures is one wellness program where credits are issued to employees under a supplemental health plan. Launched by United Healthcare, the program is available to employers in Rhode Island, Pennsylvania, Colorado, and Ohio. Employees usually have a health plan with a $2,500 deductible and can then participate in a free, confidential health screening to establish baseline metrics. For each test that employees pass, they earn a $500 credit toward their deductible, issued under a supplemental plan administered by BeniComp Advantage. The earliest an employee failing a health test can earn the credit is the next year. However, there is an appeals process and employees whose physicians say they cannot meet the standards for medical reasons are offered alternative ways of earning credits such as participation in healthy lifestyle programs (a smoking-cessation program or a weight-loss program) (*See generally* Hodge et al., 2013).

7. The need to address vaping in the absence of government restrictions is illustrated by a recent advertisement for vaping that mimics the banned advertisements of tobacco products put in place in the late 1960s (following the revelation of cigarettes' direct link to lung cancer):

    For us smokers, times have changed. But a few things remain the same: our desire to explore, to adventure, to roam without boundaries. After all, this country was founded on free will; embrace it; take back your freedom. (Zimlich, 2015, p. 483)

REFERENCES

AHRQ (Agency for Healthcare Research and Quality). (2014). *Guide to clinical preventive services: Recommendations of the U.S. Preventive Services Task Force.* Rockville, MD: AHRQ.

Ajunwa, I. (2016). Genetic data and civil rights. *Harvard Civil Rights and Civil Liberties Law Review, 51,* 75–114.

Allen, M. M. (2015). Everybody's vaping for the weekend: Nicotine addiction as a workplace disability. *University of Cincinnati Law Review, 83,* 1393–1422.

Arnett, D. K., et al. (2014). AHA [American Heart Association]/ACC [American College of Cardiology]/HHS [U.S. Department of Health and Human Services] strategies to enhance application of clinical practice guidelines in patients with cardiovascular disease and comorbid conditions. *Circulation, 130,* 1662–1667.

Barry, K., et al. (2013). Pleading disability after the ADAAA [ADA Amendments Act]. *Hofstra Labor and Employment Law Journal, 31,* 1–63.

Bhangle, S. D., et al. (2013). Corticosteroid-induced neuropsychiatric disorders: Review and contrast with neuropsychiatric lupus. *Rheumatology International, 33*(8), 1923–1932.

Bhatnagar, A., et al. (2014). Electronic cigarettes: A policy statement from the American Heart Association. *Circulation, 130*(16), 1418–1438.

BLS (Bureau of Labor Statistics). (2015). *Current employment statistics highlights.* Washington, DC: U.S. Department of Labor: BLS.

Browne, M. N., et al. (2010). Obesity as a protected category: The complexity of personal responsibility for physical attributes. *Michigan State Journal of Medicine & Law, 14,* 1–69.

Calapai, G. (2014). Montelukast-induced adverse drug reactions: A review of case reports in the literature. *Pharmacology, 94*(1–2), 60–70.

CDC (Centers for Disease Control and Prevention). (2016a). *Defining adult overweight and obesity.* Atlanta, GA: U.S. Department of Health and Human Services, CDC, National Center for Health Statistics.

___. (2016b). *Obesity and overweight.*

___. (2016c). *Adult obesity causes and consequences.*

___. (2015a). *Chronic diseases: The leading causes of death and disability in the United States.*

___. (2015b). *Adult obesity facts.*

___. (2015c). State-specific prevalence of current cigarette smoking among adults and secondhand smoke rules and policies in homes and workplaces. *U.S. Morbidity and Mortality Weekly Report, 64*(19), 532–536.

___. (2013a). *Burden of mental illness.*

___. (2013b). *Preventing chronic disease: Public health research, practice, and policy.*

Clarke, J. A. (2015). Against immutability. *Tulane Law Review, 125,* 2–102.

Claxton, G., & Levitt, L. (2015). *How many employers could be affected by the Cadillac plan tax?* Menlo Park, CA: Kaiser Family Foundation.

Claxton, G., et al. (2016). *Peterson-Kaiser health system tracker: Payments for cost sharing increasing rapidly over time.* New York, NY: Peterson Center on Healthcare and Menlo Park, CA: Kaiser Family Foundation.

CMS (Centers for Medicare and Medicaid Services). (2016). *Chronic conditions overview.* Baltimore, MD: CMS.

___. (2015). *HHS initiative on multiple chronic conditions: Optimum health and quality of life for individuals with multiple chronic conditions.*

___. (2014). *National health expenditure data.*

Cogan, J. A. (2016). Health insurance rate review. *Temple Law Review, 88,* 411–471.

Cohen, D. (2014). *A big fat crisis: The hidden forces behind the obesity epidemic and how to end it.* New York, NY: Nation Books.

Concannon, J. (2012). Mind matters: Mental disability and the history and future of the Americans with Disabilities Act. *Law and Psychology Review, 36,* 89–114.

Copp, A. (2012). The ethics and efficacy of a "fat tax" in the form of an insurance surcharge on obese state employees. *Quinnipiac Health Law Journal, 15,* 1–31.

DeMuth, C. (2016). Can the administrative state be tamed? *The Journal of Legal Analysis, 8,* 121–184.

Executive Order No. 13145 (2000, February 8). 65 Federal Register 6877.

Fairfield, J. A. T., & Engel, C. (2016). Privacy as a public good. *Duke Law Journal, 65,* 385–457.

FDA (U.S. Food and Drug Administration). (2016). *FDA drug safety communication: FDA updates label for stop smoking drug Chantix (varenicline) to include potential alcohol interaction, rare risk of seizures, and studies of side effects on mood, behavior, or thinking.* Silver Spring, MD: FDA.

Freiberg, M. (2012). Options for state and local governments to regulate non-cigarette tobacco products. *Annals of Health Law, 21,* 407–445.

Froomkin, A. M. *(2015).* Regulating mass surveillance as privacy pollution: Learning from environmental impact statements. *University of Illinois Law Review, 2015,* 1713–1790.

Grider, K. (2015). The "best of" litigation update 2015: Employment law update. *The Advocate, 70,* 138–255.

Hall, M. A. (2014). Evaluating the Affordable Care Act: The eye of the beholder. *Houston Law Review, 51,* 1029–2015.

Hammond, R. A., & Levine, R. *(2010).* The economic impact of obesity in the United States. *Diabetes, metabolic syndrome and obesity: Targets and therapy, 2010*(3), 285–295.

Hearing, G. A., & Ussery, B. C. (2012). The times they are a changin': The impact of technology and social media on the public workplace. *The Florida Bar Journal, 86,* 20–27.

Henry, A. E. (2014). The ADA Amendments Act of 2008: Why the qualified individual analysis is the new battleground for employment discrimination suits. *Oklahoma Law Review, 67,* 111–148.

Hernandez, S. L. (2015). Let's clear the air: Regulating electronic cigarette use in New York City. *Brooklyn Law Review, 81,* 301–327.

HEW (U.S. Department of Health, Education and Welfare). (1964). *Smoking and health: Report of the Advisory Committee to the Surgeon General of the Public Health Service.* Washington, DC: Public Health Service.

HHS (U.S. Department of Health and Human Services). (2014). *The health consequences of smoking—50 years of progress: A report of the Surgeon General.* Washington, DC: HHS.

Hodge, J. G., et al. (2013). New frontiers in obesity control: Innovative public health legal interventions. *Duke Forum for Law and Social Change, 5,* 1–36.

Hoffman, S. (2015). Citizen science: The law and ethics of public access to medical big data. *Berkeley Technology Law Journal, 30,* 1741–1806.

Katz, M. (2010). Towards a new moral paradigm in health care delivery: Accounting for individuals. *American Journal of Law and Medicine, 36,* 78–135.

Levkovitz, Y., et al. (2011). Antidepressants: A complicated picture. *Journal of Clinical Psychiatry, 72*(4), 509–514.

Lindblom, E. N. (2015). Effectively regulating e-cigarettes and their advertising and the First Amendment. *Food and Drug Law Journal, 70,* 55–92.

Little, J. N. (2016). The weighting game: Do government agencies consider obesity a disability? *Wake Forest Journal of Law and Policy, 6,* 567–583.

Liu, S. (2010). Obesity as an "impairment" for employment discrimination purposes under the Americans with Disabilities Act Amendments Act of 2008. *The Boston University Public Interest Law Journal, 20,* 141–166.

Long, M., et al. (2016a). Kaiser Family Foundation: Eligibility and coverage trends in employer-sponsored insurance. *Journal of the American Medical Association, 315*(17), 1824.

___. (2016b). Kaiser Family Foundation: Recent trends in employer-based health insurance premiums. *Journal of the American Medical Association, 315*(1), 18.

Lopez, L. M., et al. (2010 March 17). Skin patch and vaginal ring versus combined oral contraceptives for contraception. *Cochran Database Systematic Review, 3*.

Luff, P. (2015). Regulating tobacco through litigation. *Arizona State Law Journal, 47*, 125–180.

Luijendijk, H. J., et al. (2011). β-blockers and the risk of incident depression in the elderly. *Journal of Clinical Psychopharmacology, 31*(1), 45–50.

Madison, K. (2015). Employer wellness incentives, the ACA, and the ADA: Reconciling policy objectives. *Willamette Law Review, 51*, 407–457.

Mariner, W. K. (2012). Emerging issues in health care reform at the federal, state, and local levels; The Affordable Care Act and health promotion: The role of insurance in defining responsibility for health risks and costs. *Duquesne Law Review, 50*, 271–331.

Martin, W. J., et al. (2016). Labor and employment law. *Mercer Law Review, 67*, 955–974.

McMahon, M. J., & McGovern, B. A. (2016). Recent developments in federal income taxation. *Florida Tax Review, 18*, 275–481.

Miller, J. S. (2015). Can I call you back? A sustained interaction with biospecimen donors to facilitate advances in research. *Richmond Journal of Law and Technology, 22*, 1–67.

Morris, T. (2010). Civil rights/employment law: States carry weight of employment discrimination protection: Resolving the growing problem of weight bias in the workplace. *Western New England Law Review, 32*, 173–213.

NBGH (National Business Group on Health). (2012). *Strategies for driving employee engagement in wellness, health care and job performance.* Washington, DC: NBGH.

NPR, et al. (National Public Radio). (2016, February). *Patients' perspectives on health care in the United States: A look at seven states and the nation.* Washington, DC: NPR.

Persad, G. (2015). Priority setting, cost-effectiveness, and the Affordable Care Act. *American Journal of Law and Medicine, 41*, 119–166.

Pike, E. R. (2016). Securing sequences: Ensuring adequate protections for genetic samples in the age of big data. *Cardozo Law Review, 37*, 1977–2038.

Plato, & Tuozzo, T. M. (2014). *Plato's Charmides: Positive elenchus in a "Socratic" dialogue.* New York, NY Cambridge University Press. (Original work published 1509–1511.)

Porter, N. B. (2014). The new ADA backlash. *Tennessee Law Review, 82*, 1–81.

Pricewaterhouse Coopers' Health Research Institute & World Economic Forum. (2007). *Working towards wellness: Accelerating the prevention of chronic disease.* New York, NY: Pricewaterhouse Coopers.

RAND Corporation. (2016). *Putting the brakes on the obesity epidemic.* Santa Monica, CA: RAND.

Rausch, R. L. (2012). Health cover(age)ing. *Nebraska Law Review, 90*, 920–970.

Roberts, J. L. (2014). Healthism and the law of employment discrimination. *Iowa Law Review, 99*, 571–635.

Roebuck, M. C., et al. (2011). Medication adherence leads to lower health care use and costs despite increased drug spending. *Health Affairs, 30*(1), 91–99.

Roehrig, C. (2016). Mental disorders top the list of the most costly conditions in the United States: $201 billion. *Health Affairs, 10*, 1377–1387.

Russell, L. B. (2007). *Prevention's potential for slowing the growth of medical spending.* Washington, DC: National Coalition on Health Care (NCHC).

Shamsey, J. K. (2014). Thank you for not smoking … Indoors: The confusing state of local government smoking regulation in Florida. *Stetson Law Review, 43*, 311–324.

Shechtman, M. (2011). Smoking out big tobacco: Can the Family Smoking Prevention and Tobacco Control Act equip the FDA to regulate tobacco without infringing on the First Amendment? *Emory Law Journal, 60*, 705–749.

Shepherd, H. R. (2016). It saves to be healthy: Using the tax code to incentivize employer-provided wellness benefits. *Indiana Law Journal, 91*, 597–616.

Shinall, J. B. (2016). Distaste or disability? Evaluating the legal framework for protecting obese workers. *Berkeley Journal of Employment and Labor Law, 37*, 101–142.

Simpson, K. N., et al. (2014). Costs of adverse events among patients with HIV infection treated with nonnucleoside reverse transcriptase inhibitors. *HIV Medicine, 15*(8), 488–498.

Sturm, R., & Hattori, A. (2013). Morbid obesity rates continue to rise rapidly in the United States. *International Journal of Obesity, 37*(6), 889–891.

Sturm, R., & Ruopeng, A. (2014). Obesity and economic environments. *Cancer: A Cancer Journal for Clinicians, 64*(5), 337–350.

Suk, J. C. (2011). Preventive health at work: A comparative approach. *The American Journal of Comparative Law, 59*, 1089–1134.

Surgeon General, Office of the (2010). *The Surgeon General's vision for a healthy and fit nation.* Rockville, MD: U.S. Department of Health and Human Services, Public Health Service, Office of the Surgeon General.

Swartz, C. J. (2010). The revivification of *in loco parentis* behavioral regulation in public institutions of higher education to combat the obesity epidemic. *New England Law Review, 45*, 101–137.

Synderman, R., & Williams, R. S. (2013). Prospective medicine: The next health care transformation. *Academic Medicine, 78*(11), 1079–1084.

Thomas, K. H., et al. (2014). Reporting of drug induced depression and fatal and non-fatal suicidal behaviour in the UK. *BMC Pharmacology and Toxicology, 15*(54), 1–12.

Turk, M. C. (2015). The convergence of insurance with banking and securities industries, and the limits of regulatory arbitrage in finance. *Columbia Business Law Review, 2015*, 967–1072.

Vallor, J. (2013). Gut check: Why obesity is not a disability under Tennessee law and how the legislature can address the obesity epidemic. *Tennessee Journal of Law and Policy, 9*, 265–326.

Walker, S. D., & Kalviainen, R. (2011). Non-vision adverse events with vigabatrin therapy. *Acta Neurologica Scandinavica, 192*, 72–82.

Ware, D. (2013). Against the weight of authority: Can courts solve the problem of size discrimination? *Alabama Law Review, 64*, 1175–1214.

Warner, K. E. (2014). Tobacco control policies and their impacts. Past, present, and future. *Annals of American Thoracic Society, 11*(2), 227–230.

Watson Wyatt. (2007, November 7). *Press release: More employers to offer workers financial incentives for healthy behavior.* Arlington, VA: Watson Wyatt.

Wharton School of the University of Pennsylvania. (2015). Does employer-sponsored health insurance have a future? *Knowledge@Wharton.*

___. (2013). Using the hunger games to encourage healthier choices.

___. (2009). One way to lower health costs: Pay people to be healthy.

White, J. J. (2013). Perspectives on public health and taxation: Taxing the platypygous. *University of Michigan Journal of Law Reform, 46*, 975–997.

WHO (World Health Organization). (2015). *The global burden of disease*. Geneva, Switzerland: WHO.

Wiley, L. F. (2014). Access to health care as an incentive for healthy behavior? An assessment of the Affordable Care Act's personal responsibility for wellness reforms. *Indiana Health Law Review, 11*, 639–713.

World Bank. (2016). *Life expectancy at birth, total (years)*. Washington, DC: World Bank.

Zimlich, C. M. (2015). What is a cigarette? Electronic cigarettes and the tobacco master settlement agreement. *Wake Forest Law Review, 50*, 483–507.

CHAPTER 11

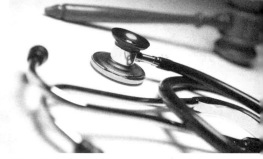

Labor and Management Relations

"All that serves labor serves the nation. All that harms is treason. If a man tells you he trusts America, yet fears labor, he is a fool. There is no America without labor, and to fleece the one is to rob the other."

— Attributed to **Abraham Lincoln** (1809-1865), 16th President of the United States

IN BRIEF

This chapter covers fundamental topics, such as Employee Free Choice reforms and unionization of physicians and nurses in an emerging stakeholder society. Nurse workload management and mandatory overtime are viewed in the context of their most severe consequences: adverse medical care and patient mortality. Health care staffing is placed alongside the recruitment of foreign physicians and scientists who help the United States address high-value staff shortages in its health care systems.

LEARNING OBJECTIVES

Upon completion of this chapter readers should be able to:

1. Explain the details of Employee Free Choice reform.
2. List the issues associated with physician and nurse unionization.
3. Outline how labor and management may work together to improve efficiency and value.
4. Address the problem of nurse shortages.
5. Understand the basis for nurse dissatisfaction.
6. Explain the law and practice of foreign health care staff.

KEY TERMS

Adverse medical care
Adverse occurrences
Bargain in good faith
Binding arbitration
Business Roundtable
Collective bargaining
Conrad program
Contingent employees
Department of Labor
Election process
Employee Free Choice
Exempt employees
Failure to rescue
Fair Labor Standards Act of 1938
Foreign nationals

Globalization
H-1B visas
Income gap
J-1 visas
Joint employer
Labor law
Labor unions
Last, best, and final offers
Licensed, practical nurse-hours or
    aide-hours
Majority sign-up
Managed care
Mandatory on-call
Mandatory ratios
Medical technology

National Labor Relations Act of 1935
National Labor Relations Board
Naturalization
Nurse staffing plans
Nurse-to-patient ratios
Pension payments
Permanent residence
Scope of practice
Service economy
Service Employees International
    Union
Toothless remedies
Treble back pay
Trickle-down economics
Union

Management's Refusal to Bargain

Do labor unions have any recourse when management unilaterally makes decisions affecting represented employees and refuses to bargain over subjects not clearly contained in a collective bargaining agreement?

The California Nurses Association is the **collective bargaining** representative of the nurses at Enloe's facilities in Chico, California. The dispute in this case stems from management's unilateral adoption of a **mandatory on-call** policy that required nurses to work one four-hour on-call shift every four weeks, in addition to their regular shifts; nurses were permitted no more than 30 minutes to report when on call. Management indicated that if any nurse had a problem complying with the time requirement, that nurse should contact Enloe's clinical coordinator in order to make other arrangements.

When the California Nurses Association learned of the on-call policy change, the labor union told Enloe it could not unilaterally make the proposed change without first negotiating with the Association. There is no disagreement that the mandatory on-call policy was unilaterally adopted without consultation with Enloe's employees or their representatives. The collective bargaining agreement included provisions spelling out Enloe's right to:

- Assign duties and hours to nurses
- Compensate nurses for on-call and call-back work
- Establish standards related to patient care
- Manage the schedules of its employees

It also contained a broad management rights clause. There is a fundamental and long-running disagreement as to the appropriate approach to determine whether management has violated federal labor law when it refuses to bargain with its organized union employees over subjects not contained in collective bargaining agreements. Based on management's unilateral imposition of the new on-call policy, the California Nurses Association filed a charge with the **National Labor Relations Board**. The National Labor Relations Board, in turn, issued a complaint against Enloe.

— *See* Law Fact at the end of this chapter for the answer.

Principles and Applications

A new business model is needed for the delivery of health care in the 21st century. A model that is less focused on treating diseases and more focused on public health needs and the prevention of disease is required. The focus of consumer-driven health care must move away from just costs and bottom lines and return to a place where science and innovation are once again the focal points of medicine. This would mean focusing on managing the health care of consumers as opposed to just focusing on managing costs.

Public Perceptions of Labor and Management

Many Americans believe the U.S. health care system is at a crossroads, facing both challenges to its funding and opportunities for accelerating medical advancement (Bagley, 2015). They believe significant reform of the system or even universal health care would be helpful in their struggle to access affordable, quality health care (Baron, 2016). At the same time, a public image of ineffectiveness clouds the health care industry and its regulators. The only way to change this image of ineffectiveness is to change current reality (Neidhardt, 2015).

Both labor and management in the health care industry must appreciate that there are ways in which a partnership can catalyze change to add more value to the U.S. health care system, returning American medicine to its former place of global prominence. Both sides need to:

- Appreciate where each partner can be most helpful: management with reforming the health care system and labor unions with increasing revenue from the public and private sectors to bring about management's systemic reforms
- Level the playing field so medicine is about quality health care and efficiency and not about who can pay the least for staffing
- Understand their local, national, and global rivals that are competing to deliver the best medical care
- Value markets and consumers of health care

(*See generally* Hobbes, 2013/1651; *See also* Rogers, 2012).

Research About the Impact of Labor Unions

Union membership has the following far-reaching effects on labor markets in the U.S. health care industry:

- Higher levels of unionization are associated with increases in employee tenure and therefore less turnover
- Labor unions impact the pay of non-union employees
- The decline in union membership has political ramifications for continued reform of the health care system
- There is a correlation between union decline and the widening income gap

(Wharton, 2012a and 2012b).

Political Ramifications

Labor unions have long been a potent force in American business and politics (Wharton, 2012a). Despite popular claims that labor unions are in decline, unions have maintained reasonably strong public support.[LN1] Although the data indicate that Americans remain skeptical about how much confidence they can place in labor unions and their leaders (the same can be said for management), the public generally recognizes the need for labor unions to protect the rights of employees (Neidhardt, 2015). Moreover, as union membership declines, the effective engagement of the American middle class in the political process is likely to fall as well (Wharton, 2012a). The result is that as union political power has diminished, corporate political power has increased.

Research of both union and non-union private-sector employees shows that if employees were provided the union representation they desired, the unionization rate would be about 58%, or more than five times higher than the actual rate of 11% today (BLS, 2016a; Freeman, 2007). The polls make clear that labor's public support in disputes with business has remained steady over time (Jones, 2011). Nevertheless, even though labor unions may be voicing an opinion that is supported by the majority of Americans, unions are still a small group, basically a special interest (Wharton, 2012a).

Union Decline Affects the Nation's Widening Income Gap

There is a connection between the decline in **union** membership and the widening **income gap** in the United States (Wharton, 2012a). The decline in private sector union membership over the past three decades accounts for between 20 to 30% of the growth in income inequality in the United States (Western & Rosenfeld, 2011). This suggests that labor unions help institutionalize norms of equity and fairness in the U.S. workplace.

Labor Unions Impact Non-Union Pay

Labor unions have an impact on non-union worker pay; employers worried about a unionization drive usually raise their scale to match union pay. Labor unions establish what is considered right and fair in the marketplace when it comes to wages and salaries, and non-union employees benefit from that consideration (Western & Rosenfeld, 2011). Most commentators maintain it is impossible to tackle income inequality without a vibrant labor movement (Wharton, 2012a and 2012b).

Relevance of Labor in the Health Care Industry

A window of opportunity exists for strategic trade-offs between the American labor movement and management. Almost three out of four employees are either underperforming or actively undermining their work (Selmi, 2012). This level of employee disengagement should be a wake-up call to management and opponents of organized labor who believe labor unions are a detriment to the health care industry and the U.S. economy. Organizations with high engagement scores exhibit:

- Better employee productively
- Greater mobility of their employees and less income inequality
- Higher corporate growth
- Improved customer loyalty
- Lower employee turnover
- Superior performance by the organization

(Selmi, 2012; Wharton 2012b).

Today, there is a unique opportunity for labor and management to come together and find new ideas and new solutions to make working in the health care industry pay for everyone, not just the shareholders and the senior management executives. While labor unions have the possibility of being more relevant today than at any time since labor organizing first started in the United States, both labor and management need an attitude adjustment (Fisk & Barry, 2012).

While many American labor unions are losing members, the health care industry is becoming more unionized. Dominated by nurses and low-income immigrant employees hoping for higher pay, health insurance, and retirement benefits, labor unions are successfully organizing nurses, maintenance staff, security staff, and aides in hospitals, nursing homes, and other institutional health care facilities. Labor union membership is high in the nursing profession. Labor unions represent more than 5 million of the total 10 million registered nurses, practical and vocational nurses, paramedics, and aides (BLS, 2016b).

Union employees continue to receive higher wages than non-union employees and have greater access to employer-sponsored employee benefits, a difference that continues to widen (Long, 2013). If an additional 5 million employees in the health care industry joined a union:

- $34 billion in total new wages would flow into the U.S. economy
- 5 million employees would get a 22% raise on average, or an additional $7,000 per year
- 900,000 jobs would be lifted above the poverty wage for a family of four
- Between 1.8 million and 3 million dependent children would share in these benefits

(Mishel, 2012; Vidal, 2009).

While a valid concern regards the increased costs to the health care system from unionization, it might be more appropriate to focus attention on the top of the socioeconomic pyramid as opposed to the bottom. The nation might begin by addressing the merits of the senior executives' multimillion-dollar compensation packages that are so prevalent in the health care industry. As illustrated in **TABLE 11-1**, the average chief executive officer's pay has skyrocketed from 27 times the average employee's wages in the mid-70s to 296 times higher today (Wharton, 2015).

While chief executive officers no doubt contribute to the economic development of the health care industry, there is growing debate about this income disparity when almost half of the 3 million aides are working for poverty wages, as are one in four support staff (BLS, 2016a). Clearly, **trickle-down economics** is not working for everyone, as once anticipated. Perhaps part of the health care reform should begin from this point and have the health care industry focus on reductions in its own employees' poverty and inequality (Wharton, 2015).

Nevertheless, the cost from adding 5 million to the industry's unionized workforce would be $34 billion in new wages added to the nation's health care costs (Mishel, 2012; Vidal, 2009). While this number would be offset by the economic benefits of poverty reduction when 900,000 families would be brought above the poverty level, no definitive study exists to explain how wage increases would affect the nation's health care costs.

MANAGEMENT AND LAW ISSUES

1. How should established health care providers and the medical products industry think about labor and management, given the current economy?

TABLE 11-1   Compensation of the Top Five Chief Executive Officers in Each Health Care Sector

Corporations and State Headquarters	Sales	Average Revenue Growth Rate Past 5 Years	Average Net Income Growth Rate Past 5 Years	Value of CEOs' Total Direct Compensation in 2014
Health Insurance:				
Aetna (CN)	$60.4 billion	+15.75	+4.07	$15.0 million
UnitedHealth Group (MN)	$157.1 billion	+10.85	+2.61	$14.9 million
Cigna (CN)	$38.0 billion	+14.55	+11.56	$14.5 million
Anthem (IN)	$79.2 billion	+6.06	−0.66	$13.5 million
Humana (KY)	$54.3 billion	+9.48	−2.02	$10.1 million
For-Profit Hospitals:				
Community Health Systems (TN)	$19.4 billion	+8.53	−5.09	$26.4 million
Universal Health Services (PA)	$9.4 billion	+4.12	+14.21	$18.3 million
Tenet Healthcare (TX)	$18.6 billion	+22.09	−52.27	$17.9 million
Hospital Corporation of America (TN)	$39.7 billion	+6.74	−2.73	$14.6 million
Mednax (FL)	$2.8 billion	+15.01	+10.86	$9.2 million
Pharmacy Services:				
CVS Health (RI)	$153.3 billion	+8.63	+9.74	$32.3 million
McKesson (CA)	$190.9 billion	+11.11	+12.64	$25.9 million
Express Scripts (PA)	$101.8 billion	+24.12	+18.82	$12.9 million
Cardinal Health (OH)	$102.5 billion	−0.02	+5.09	$12.4 million
Laboratory Corp. America (NC)	$8.7 billion	+11.32	−3.19	$10.5 million
Medical Products:				
Regeneron Pharmaceuticals (NY)	$4.1 billion	+164.10	−77.36	$42.0 million
Bristol-Myers Squibb (NJ)	$16.6 billion	−4.41	−11.56	$27.1 million
Johnson & Johnson (NJ)	$70.2 billion	+1.59	+11.86	$25.0 million
AbbVie (IL) (formerly Abbott)	$22.9 billion	+6.21	+9.82	$22.0 million
Merck (NJ)	$38.8 billion	−3.89	−5.80	$21.4 million

Notes: Total direct compensation is the sum of salary, annual incentives, and long-term incentives.

Data from: Corporate filings with the U.S. Securities and Exchange Commission. Revenue and net income (profit) figures are derived from 2015 and 2000 corporate annual income statements. Compensation data reflects year ended December 31, 2014.

Labor–Management Partnerships

The **Service Employees International Union**, with more than two million members, is feared by management in the health care industry because of its high success rate at waging aggressive organizing campaigns that usually include support from the industry's stakeholders (elected officials, clergy, and community and patient activists), in addition to unremitting publicity (Wharton, 2012a). In the health care industry, however, labor unions have generally shed their adversarial image and created labor-management partnerships. For instance, the Service Employees International Union recently entered into a partnership with the **Business Roundtable**[LN2] to support enactment of the Affordable Care Act and implement its reforms (Goldberg, 2015).

Income Disparities

The need for labor unions is far greater today than almost any time since the 1930s and 1940s (Wharton, 2012b). The compensation disparity between the average employee and the average senior management executive is wider than at any time in American history (BLS, 2016b). Yet, in addition to concerns about management compensation, employees want a voice in their employment with a meaningful channel for expressing their workplace concerns. Employees generally want a role in changing the practices and politics of the organizations to which they belong (Wharton, 2012a).

With 7% of U.S. private-sector employees belonging to labor unions today, down from about 35% a half century ago, the United States has one of the lowest percentages of private-sector employees covered by collective bargaining compared to other democracies around the world (BLS, 2016a). The question is whether labor and management will become partners to respond to what is now a global service economy, or whether they will function as adversaries. Labor unions missed out on the growth of the new **service economy**, so the newest sectors of the health care industry developed without unions, especially the biotechnology and health information technology sectors. Today, as regulatory changes, industry consolidation, and economic globalization are rapidly occurring, there is a unique opportunity for an engaged workforce through non-adversarial partnerships between management and labor (Freeman, 2007; Jones, 2011).

Debate is ongoing about whether management and labor in the health care industry want to address the differences in compensation between lower level employees and senior management executives. This difference in total direct compensation, however, is the tip of the iceberg in seeking a balance between labor and management interests. For instance, on top of differences in total compensation between senior management executives, many employees also bear associated health care costs, such as higher health insurance premiums and reduced wages due to co-payments and coinsurance fees that have a greater effect on them than they do on top executives.

No Remedial Enforcement Without Reforms

Union organizing campaigns are very sophisticated today. There is a wide range of consultants, management and labor lawyers, and strike breakers who are battle-tested. The most significant deficiency, however, is that existing labor law has no remedial enforcement power without legislative reforms. For instance:

- *Allied Chemical & Alkali Workers of America v. Pittsburgh Plate Glass Co.*, 404 U.S. 157 (U.S. Supreme Court 1971) (holding that employers are under no duty to engage in collectively bargaining over retirees' benefits because retirees are not considered employees, thereby restricting the definition of employees covered by the National Labor Relations Board)
- *First National Maintenance Corp. v. National Labor Relations Board*, 452 U.S. 666 (U.S. Supreme Court 1981) (holding that plant closures are not a mandatory subject of bargaining even where employees lose jobs)
- *H. K. Porter Co., Inc. v. National Labor Relations Board*, 397 U.S. 99 (U.S. Supreme Court 1970) (holding that the National Labor Relations Board is not authorized to impose contract terms as a remedy)
- *Pattern Makers' League of North America v. National Labor Relations Board*, 473 U.S. 95 (U.S. Supreme Court 1985) (holding that union members who are strikebreakers have a protected right to resign from the union at any time)
- *Republic Steel Corp. v. National Labor Relations Board*, 311 U.S. 7 (U.S. Supreme Court 1940) (limiting the National Labor Relations Board to remedies designed to make employees harmed by unfair labor practices whole, not remedies designed to deter bad conduct)

Management and labor unions often violate labor laws and intimidate employees without fear of repercussion; **toothless remedies** fail to deter abuses by both management and labor (Louris, 2010). Currently, federal court injunctions are imposed only for violations by labor unions; no such equitable remedy exists for unlawful acts committed by management. When management violates the law by refusing to **bargain in good faith**, the most common remedy

MANAGEMENT AND LAW ISSUES

2. What further innovative labor and management partnerships, if any, might emerge as alternatives to the traditional adversarial model?
3. Who will be the winners and losers under new labor and management partnerships, and how should winning and losing be defined given current budget constraints?
4. Which side do you want to work for, management or labor, and why?

issued by the National Labor Relations Board is for management to promise to act correctly in the future; no actual penalty is imposed on management (Weiss, 2012). It is statutorily impossible under current labor law to impose fines, imprisonment, or punitive damages on management.

Employee Free Choice Reforms

One priority of labor unions is reform of the labor laws adopted in the 1930s and 1940s (*See* Labor Management Relations Act (Taft-Hartley Act), 29 U.S.C.A. §§ 141 *et seq.*). The movement, popularly known as **Employee Free Choice**, is built around three provisions that would:

- Force management to recognize labor unions seeking to represent employees on the basis of a showing of signed authorization cards instead of a secret ballot election administered by the National Labor Relations Board
- Increase penalties for management who hassle and seek to intimidate pro-union employees
- Provide for **binding arbitration** to resolve impasses in contract bargaining

(Andrias, 2015; Bowness, 2014).

In general, Employee Free Choice might rebalance power between labor and management in the context of organizing and collective bargaining for an initial contract (Andrias, 2015). Opponents of Employee Free Choice claim the cost to individuals for this rebalance is too high since secret ballot elections are eliminated. This secret ballot claim, however, misreads Employee Free Choice; its proponents have not, however, successfully explained the distinctions in current labor law and the proposed Employee Free Choice Act (Cowie, 2016).

Many highly regarded health care systems, such as Kaiser Permanente, the largest health care organization in the United States, currently allow their employees to make their own choice in forming labor unions as proposed by the Employee Free Choice. The result is that Kaiser is consistently ranked as one of the best places to work. When Kaiser is compared to its competitors who are non-union, its competitors have much higher employee turnover and work dissatisfaction rates. *See generally* Rogers, 2012.

Signed Authorization Cards Versus Ballot Elections

Under current labor law, a labor union seeking to be certified as the bargaining representative for a group of employees must demonstrate that it has the support of the majority of employees in the group (Cowie, 2016). Usually, labor unions will solicit employees to sign authorization cards showing their support for union representation; if a majority of employees sign cards, the union may present these cards to the employer and ask to be recognized. Management is not, however, obligated to recognize a union on the basis of signed authorization cards. The only way to force management to recognize a union as its employees' representative is through a secret ballot election.

Currently, employers can insist on a secret ballot election if 30% of employees sign authorization cards. Employee Free Choice reforms would change this; if more than 50% of the cards are signed, there is no election because union recognition is automatic. Under Employee Free Choice, employees, as opposed to employers, can request a secret ballot vote when between 31 and 50% of the employees have signed authorization cards (Kochan et al., 2016). Supporters of Employee Free Choice maintain that the secret ballot election is still an option; opponents claim that the secret ballot is theoretical because labor unions will unduly pressure half of the employees to sign cards (Levinson & Sachs, 2015).

Under current labor law, management has an advantage over employees. The choice of whether to use an **election process** or **majority sign-up** to form the union is now exclusively controlled by management (Gould, 2015). From the time a union requests an election and the actual date of the election, which can last indefinitely, management can actively discourage employees from supporting a union. The union, however, is not permitted on company property. Under the Employee Free Choice reforms, this extended pre-election period would vanish.

Financial Penalties

Management who fired or discriminated against pro-union employees would face more significant financial penalties than currently exist. Research shows that one-quarter of union-organizing drives lead to employee terminations, and that one out of every five employees who openly supports a union is terminated. It can take years of hearings to have these employees reinstated, and the penalties management faces are minimal (Hallett, 2015).

Employee Free Choice laws would contain **treble back pay**. Treble back pay increases the amount management is required to pay to three times the amount of the employee's back pay when an employee is discharged or discriminated against during an organizing campaign or first contract drive (Weiss, 2012). They also contain civil penalties, which provide for fines of up to $20,000 per violation for violating employees' rights during an organizing campaign or first contract drive.

Binding Arbitration

Employee Free Choice would further require management to submit to binding arbitration to resolve negotiating impasses. In particular, if the two sides did not reach a first contract within 90 days of the commencement of bargaining, the matter would have to be submitted to an alternative dispute resolution process that could lead to binding arbitration upon the demand of either side. This represents a change from current labor law, which permits management to unilaterally put into place the terms of the **last, best, and final offers** upon reaching an impasse in negotiations. Under current labor rules, management must bargain in good faith with employees, but is not obligated to agree to any terms.

Prospects for Change

While management forces wield extraordinary clout in opposition of Employee Free Choice, business's unity, or lack of it, will decide what happens. Majority sign-up is not a new procedure, as Employee Free Choice opponents claim. Since the inception of the **National Labor Relations Act**, employees have been able to form a union when a majority signs authorization cards indicating their intent to be represented by a union. Currently, employers can demand a secret ballot election even if a majority of the employees have signed authorization cards. Comprehensive labor legislation is necessary to correct the fundamental problems facing management and labor. The most critical focus of this reform should be protecting the right of employees to freely choose whether they wish to be represented (Hallett, 2015).

General Bargaining Principles

Labor unions increase the odds that employees will understand and capitalize on the rights they are entitled to under existing **labor law** (Wharton, 2012a). The general principles outlined in the following legislation could serve as a reasonable starting point for crafting health care industry workplace policies that serve employees (Rogers, 2012):

- Protection against major downside risks associated with employment to cushion the impact of **globalization** on individuals and local communities including loss of pensions or health care benefits and loss of job from major family emergencies:
  - Continuation of Health Benefits Coverage Act (COBRA), 5 U.S.C.A. §§ 8901-8914
  - **Employee Retirement Income Security Act of 1974** (ERISA), 29 U.S.C.A. §§ 1001 *et seq.*
  - Worker Adjustment and Retraining Notification Act of 1988 (WARN) 29 U.S.C.A. §§ 2101-2109
  - Family and Medical Leave Act of 1993, 5 U.S.C.A. §§ 6381 *et seq.*
  - Trade Adjustment Assistance Act of 2015, 19 U.S.C.A. §§ 2341 *et seq.*
  - Unemployment Compensation created by the Social Security Act of 1935, 5 U.S.C.A. §§ 8501-8525

- Assuring basic labor standards, such as hours of work and overtime compensation:
  - Davis-Bacon Act of 1931, 40 U.S.C.A. §§ 3141-48
  - **Fair Labor Standards of 1938**, 2 U.S.C.A. § 60k; 29 U.S.C.A. §§ 201 *et seq.*
  - Minimum Wage Act of 1938, 29 U.S.C.A. § 206
  - Service Contract Act of 1965, 41 U.S.C.A. §§ 351-358
  - Walsh-Healy Act of 1936, 41 U.S.C.A. §§ 35-45

- Ensuring a safe and healthy work environment with low exposure to safety and health risks:
  - Drug Free Workplace Act of 1988, 41 U.S.C.A. §§ 701-707
  - Occupational Safety and Health Act of 1970, 29 U.S.C.A. §§ 651 *et seq.*; 42 U.S.C.A. § 3142-1

- Protection against workplace discrimination in hiring, promotion, dismissal, and treatment of employees:
  - **Age Discrimination Employment Act of 1967**, 29 U.S.C.A. §§ 621-634
  - **Americans With Disabilities Act of 1990** (ADA), 42 U.S.C.A. §§ 12101 *et seq.*; 47 U.S.C.A. § 225
  - **Civil Rights Act of 1964**, 42 U.S.C.A. §§ 2000e *et seq.*
  - Equal Pay Act of 1963, 29 U.S.C.A. § 206d
  - Immigration Reform and Control Act of 1986, 8 U.S.C.A. §§ 1101 *et seq.*
  - **Pregnancy Discrimination Act of 1978**, 42 U.S.C.A. § 2000e(k)

- ◦ **Rehabilitation Act of 1973**, 29 U.S.C.A. §§ 701 *et seq.*; 42 U.S.C.A. § 2000d-7
    - ◦ Uniformed Services Employment and Reemployment Rights Act of 1964, 5 U.S.C.A. § 8432b; 38 U.S.C.A. §§ 4301 *et seq.*
    - ◦ Veterans' Reemployment Rights Act of 1994, 38 U.S.C.A. §§ 4301-4307
- • Providing basic mechanisms for worker representation and voice at the workplace:
    - ◦ Labor Management Reporting and Disclosure Act of 1959, 29 U.S.C.A. §§ 401 *et seq.*
    - ◦ **National Labor Relations Act of 1935**, 29 U.S.C.A. §§ 151-169

Labor unions help make labor law stronger (Wharton, 2012a). The preceding labor legislation was supported by labor unions, with the Employee Retirement Income Security Act (ERISA) being supported by unions and almost no one else, while the Pregnancy Discrimination Act grew out of a U.S. Supreme Court case brought by the International Union of Electrical Radio and Machine Employees. Outside of labor unions, there is no national voice for the average working employee (Bellace, 2011). While some believe this reality may eventually lead to a revival for unionization, others see no resurgence for labor unions unless there is a radical change in the political climate (Wharton, 2012a).

Nurse Workload Management

Nurses represent the largest single group of health care professionals in the nation (BLS, 2015). However, hospitals often struggle to maintain an adequate number of registered nurses on their staff. This staffing struggle is occurring even as the number of young people entering nursing during the past decade has surged (Auerbach et al., 2014). The reasons for this continued staffing struggle are circular. One of the effects of **managed care** cost cutting is understaffing, which leads to overworking existing staff. As hospitals operate with understaffing, nurses are dissatisfied with the working conditions because they believe they cannot provide quality patient care. Thus, nurses leave hospitals for more satisfying positions elsewhere, and hospitals continue to operate with understaffed nursing departments and overworked nurses. It is a perilous cycle.

In the midst of nursing shortages in many hospitals, nurses claim that understaffing represents a danger to patient care. California was the first state to require mandatory **nurse-to-patient ratios** in all hospital units. This change ensured that staffing could no longer be ignored in the dialogue between hospital management and the nursing profession. Staffing concerns include:

- • Fewer registered nurses on staff significantly increases the risk of preventable hospital deaths and complications
- • A direct correlation between increased workload and lower nursing staff retention rates

(Frolik, 2016).

Unfortunately, the shortages of registered nurses that first manifested in the late 1990s in intensive care units and operating rooms, then spread to labor and delivery units and general medical/surgical wards, have not abated everywhere. Hospitals continue to face staffing shortages even though more registered nurses are entering the workforce than anticipated and more nurses are delaying retirement (Auerbach et al., 2014).

Nurse Staffing Research

The nursing shortage in hospitals, with the resulting increase in workloads by registered nurses, has also contributed to high rates of job dissatisfaction within the profession, with one in five trained registered nurses no longer working as nurses (BLS, 2015). Workloads in hospitals have the following effects on nurses and patients:

- • A higher proportion of nurse care, plus more nurse hours per day, results in shorter hospital stays and lower rates of upper gastrointestinal bleeding and urinary tract infections.
- • Almost half of the nurses who reported high levels of burnout and job dissatisfaction intended to leave their jobs within the next year.
- • Decreased nurse staffing at night is related to postoperative complications and increased health care costs.
- • Fewer nurses on the night shift results in an increased risk for complications in intensive care units.
- • A higher professional skill mix, in other words more nurses versus nonprofessional caregivers, results in a lower incidence of **adverse occurrences** in inpatient care units (adverse occurrences include patient falls, medication administration errors, pressure ulcers, nosocomial infections, patient complaints, and mortality).

- Higher proportion of nurse-hours relates to lower rates of **failure to rescue**, a term used by the federal Agency for Healthcare Research and Quality as a patient safety indicator and is defined as the death of a patient with one of six life-threatening complications, which can be largely influenced by early identification and medical intervention:
  - Acute renal failure
  - Deep vein thrombosis or pulmonary embolism (DVT/PE)
  - Gastrointestinal hemorrhage and/or acute ulcer
  - Pneumonia
  - Sepsis
  - Shock and/or cardiac arrest
- Nurses experience job dissatisfaction rates that are four times greater than the average for all other employees of any type in the United States.
- The higher the number of nurse-hours a patient receives, the better the patient care outcome

(*E.g.*, Aiken, 2002; ANA, 2009; Hayes et al., 2012; Needleman et al., 2011).

Although registered nurse-hours affect patient outcome, there was no such connection between lower rates of adverse outcomes and increased numbers of **licensed practical nurse-hours or aide-hours** (Aiken, 2002; IOM, 2004). The most definitive research findings came out of the University of Pennsylvania, where low nurse staffing levels were linked to increased risks of mortality. These findings include:[LN3]

- Applied nationally, some 20,000 deaths could be prevented annually with adequate nurse/patient ratios.
- Heart attack recovery rates were found to be higher in hospitals where nurses were unionized than in non-union hospitals where staffing levels were higher.
- In hospitals with high patient-to-nurse ratios:
  - Surgical patients experience higher risk-adjusted 30-day mortality and failure-to-rescue rates
  - Nurses are more likely to experience burnout and job dissatisfaction.
- Mortality rises by one-third when the nurse workload increases to eight patients.
- Patients' chances of dying within 30 days after admission and the chances of experiencing failure to rescue each increased 7% for every additional patient per nurse.
- When a nurse must care for 6 patients, instead of 4, there is a 14% increase in mortality

(*E.g.*, Aiken, 2002).

Various Approaches to Hospital Understaffing

Approximately 500,000 licensed registered nurses are not practicing nursing (IOM, 2004). There are three approaches to hospital understaffing:

- Combine nurse-staffing plans and legislatively determined nurse-to-patient ratios
- Implement safe staffing plans in hospitals, with input from practicing nurses, to develop safe nurse-to-patient ratios based on evaluations of patient need
- Mandate specific nurse-to-patient ratios through legislation or administrative regulations

Mandatory Nurse-to-Patient Ratios in California

In the legislative preamble to the California nurse-to-patient ratio law, the state legislature declared that the quality of patient care was in jeopardy because of hospital staffing changes implemented in response to managed care. The California legislature found that the quality of patient care was related to the number of nurses at the bedside, and it wished to ensure a minimum number. The mandated nurse-to-patient ratios include:

- 1:1 in trauma
- 1:2 in critical care units, intensive care newborn nursery, and post-anesthesia
- 1:4 in emergency, pediatrics, and telemetry units
- 1:5 in specialty care and step-down units
- 1:6 in medical surgical care units

(*See* 22 California Code of Regulations § 70217).

Regulations prohibit hospitals from assigning certain duties to unlicensed personnel, even if under the direct clinical supervision of nurses; criminal sanctions are authorized for willful or repeated violations. Whether or not patient quality has improved since passage of California's legislation is uncertain (Harless et al., 2013; McHugh et al., 2011).

Nurse Staffing Plans

Nurse staffing plans are based upon the premise, established by the American Nurses Association, that adequate nurse staffing is critical to the delivery of quality patient care (ANA, 2012; *See, e.g.,* Aiken, 2002). This principle calls for an individualized staffing model based upon a measure of unit intensity. The intent is for nurses to help develop these plans based upon a variety of factors, such as:

- Available medical technology
- Experience of the nursing staff
- How sick the patients are
- Support services available to the nurses

(ANA, 2012).

Nurse staffing plans are state law in more than 11 states. The legislation requires nurse staffing plans at all health care facilities. The laws include a variety of components, such as:

- Civil penalties for enforcement purposes
- Daily posting of the numbers of nursing staff responsible for patient care
- Evaluation of the adequacy of the staffing plan through the collection of patient quality outcomes
- Requirement that the American Nurses Association's principles for nurse staffing serve as a basis for development of staffing plans
- Requiring management to adopt and implement staffing plans with input from direct care nurses

(*E.g.,* ANA, 2012).

Nurse staffing plans generally incorporate at least four of the following components:

- Appropriate mix of personnel that will allow nurses to practice according to their legal **scope of practice**
- Ongoing assessment of the severity of the patient's disease, condition, and/or level of impairment or disability, done by nurses
- Professional standards of nursing practice
- Specific unit census to meet the needs of patients in a timely manner

(*E.g.,* ANA, 2012).

Controversy: Merits of Nurse-to-Patient Ratios

Debate is ongoing about the merits of nurse-to-patient ratios. Supporters claim adequate nurse staffing is key to patient care and nurse retention. They also claim the following:

- Costs of implementing safe staffing ratios are offset by the improved quality of care and lives saved
- High turnover rates for nurses are expensive, and they are a direct result of the poor working conditions caused by understaffing
- Understaffing endangers patients' lives
- Understaffing results in longer hospital stays (patients have a 3 to 6% shorter stay in hospitals with a high number of nurses)

(*E.g.,* Cashmore, 2014; Kohn, 2012; Madow, 2013).

Opponents maintain that minimum staffing ratios would only solve one aspect of nurses' job dissatisfaction, and that:

- Costs of meeting the ratios are prohibitive and would decimate the already fragile health care systems in many parts of the nation
- Due to the massive nursing shortage, there are simply not enough nurses to meet mandated ratios, and thus units would be forced to close rather than operate in violation of the ratio mandates

- Management would be stripped of its ability to make judgments about staffing levels
- Ratios do not provide the flexibility necessary to account for the changing needs of hospital patients

(*E.g.*, Carlson, 2010; Cashmore, 2014).

Opponents argue that hospitals would be compelled to cut spending for non-nursing staff to cover the increased costs for nurses. Another issue is the risk that hospitals could focus too narrowly on staffing issues, while ignoring other factors that are also critical to quality patient care. Critics maintain that hospitals with the best patient outcomes have organizational cultures that give nurses an important role in decision-making, the implication being that other factors can play just as important a role as staffing ratios (Satz, 2015). From an economic perspective, although staffing is a major concern, other aspects of the nursing profession are also important, including:

- Control of work schedules
- Input into hospital policy and management decisions
- Opportunities for advancement
- Salaries
- Support from hospital management
- Support staff to perform non-nursing tasks

(*E.g.*, Kohn, 2012; Madow, 2013).

Mandatory Minimum Nurse-to-Patient Ratios

Despite the various arguments put forth by hospitals in favor of shifting staffing plans, there appears to be a need for definitive minimums in order to provide safe, effective patient care. Studies demonstrate the clear threat to patient health when nurses are given too many patients in an effort reduce costs. Ironically, cutting costs have led to increased damage awards against some hospitals and increased mortality for their patients (*E.g.*, Andres, 2016).

Furthermore, the perceived short-term costs that hospitals will avoid absent **mandatory ratios** may be counterproductive when understaffing results in poor patient care. Low staffing levels are a dangerous choice when scientific studies quantitatively identify the increased risks to hospital patients. Cost reductions should not take precedence over adequate patient care (ANA, 2012).

Other Crucial Issues in Health Care Staffing

Four other areas of controversy in the workplace include:

- Mandatory overtime
- Joint employees
- Exempt status
- Worker's compensation

Mandatory Overtime

Problems are associated with mandatory overtime, the most severe consequence being **adverse medical care** (Kugielska & Linke, 2008). Nurses average about 8.5 weeks of total overtime per year; yet few states have mandatory overtime laws that include protection from retaliatory behavior (ANA, 2012). The role of labor unions in negotiating contract provisions limiting mandatory overtime is especially important in states that do not currently have laws banning mandatory overtime.

Some collective bargaining agreements limit mandated overtime to four hours in one shift. Other agreements specify overtime can only be mandated after an unforeseen emergency and limit the shift of any nurse, even those normally working 12 to 13 hours. Other negotiated agreements simply ban mandatory overtime and are aimed at retaining currently employed nurses and attracting new nurses (ANA, 2012).

Joint Employees

The **Department of Labor** issued an opinion letter in response to a question from a health care system about its obligation to pay overtime under the Fair Labor Standards Act (DOL, 2005a). The health care system had a nurse who held positions at two different companies within the system. Based on a review of the facts provided, it was determined that the health care system had to pay overtime to the nurse if the nurse's combined hours at the two companies exceeded 40 hours in a workweek.

The Department of Labor's determination was based on its interpretation of **joint employer** regulations, which state that an employee who performs work that simultaneously benefits two or more hospitals at different times during the workweek generally will be jointly employed, where the hospitals are not completely disassociated with respect to the employment of the particular employee (DOL, 2005a). If the hospitals have common control, especially in personnel matters, they will be treated as the same employer for employment purposes (Garcia, 2016). Separating personnel functions may not be enough to avoid being considered joint employers (Bales et al., 2014). Each hospital within the health care system had its own:

- Federal identification number
- Human resources department
- Payroll system
- Retirement plan

While there was no regular interchange of employees between the hospitals, the Department of Labor found they were joint employers. The Department of Labor looked at the facts and found the following about the two hospitals:

- They had a common president and board of directors
- Non-union employees had common health care plans
- One human resources department occasionally provided administrative support to the other
- Personnel policies were the same, although in different handbooks
- Senior executives and managers had responsibility for more than one entity within the system
- They shared a system for posting job openings

(DOL, 2005a).

Because of these multiple associations, both hospitals were responsible for combining the hours an employee worked at both hospitals for purposes of calculating overtime. The joint employer analysis is fact-sensitive; several factors need to be considered, and each relationship has to be reviewed separately (Garcia, 2016). To avoid being a joint employer, hospitals need to remain as separate as possible and stay away from multiple associations (Bales et al., 2014).

Exempt Status

Issues often arise with regard to exempt and salaried employees. **Exempt employees** are salaried employees who are not subject to overtime compensation under the Fair Labor Standards Act as hourly employees. Whether exempt employees perform the same duties as others within the same job classification that are paid on an hourly basis does not affect the status of salaried employees, assuming those who are considered exempt truly meet the duty and salary basis requirements necessary for the exemption (DOL, 2011b).

One controversial issue is whether paying exempt employees a shift differential for working evenings and weekends affects their salary basis, and therefore invalidates their professional exemption (*See* 29 C.F.R. § 541.300). The Department of Labor's opinion is that the predetermined amount of salary necessary to support an exemption need not include all of the compensation that employees will be paid. Exemptions are not based on job title or classification, but rather upon the salary and duties of employees (*See* 29 C.F.R. § 541.2). Further, the exemption is not lost if employees who are paid a salary also receive additional compensation based on hours worked beyond the normal workweek.

The Department of Labor relied on 29 C.F.R. § 541.602, which states that employees are compensated on a salaried basis if they regularly receive a predetermined amount each pay period that constitutes all or part of their compensation, which amount is not subject to reduction because of variations in the quality or quantity of the work performed. Additional amounts of compensation may be paid on any basis, including:

- Bonus
- Flat amount
- Paid time off
- Straight-time hourly amount
- Time and one-half of a calculated hourly amount

Exempt employees may be paid overtime premiums or shift differentials without invalidating their exempt status (*See* 29 C.F.R. § 541.604a).

Worker's Compensation

COURT DECISION
Exclusive Remedy of Worker's Compensation

Jennings v. St. Vincent Hospital and Health Care Center
[Nurse v. Hospital]
832 N.E.2d 1044 (Court of Appeals of Indiana, 5th District 2005),
transfer denied, 855 N.E.2d 1001 (Supreme Court of Indiana 2006);
followed by *Van Swol v. ISG Burns Harbor, LLC*
2009 Ind. App. Unpub. LEXIS 1031 (Court of Appeals of Indiana 2009)

Facts: Jennings was a nurse who specialized in emergency room care. He was employed by StarMed, a firm that assigned employees to hospitals on a temporary basis. StarMed contracted with St. Vincent to provide St. Vincent with nurses for temporary staffing needs. Jennings allegedly contracted Hepatitis C after being stuck by an angiocatheter while performing nursing duties in the emergency room at St. Vincent Hospital.

Jennings filed a claim for worker's compensation benefits against StarMed. He also filed a civil suit against St. Vincent claiming negligence. St. Vincent responded with a motion to dismiss based on lack of subject matter jurisdiction, claiming that Jennings was a co-employee of St. Vincent and StarMed, thus invoking the protection of the exclusive remedy provision of the Worker's Compensation Act. Under this provision, an injured employee is entitled to worker's compensation benefits only, and he may not sue the employer for damages. The trial court granted St. Vincent's motion, and Jennings appealed that determination.

Issue: Are employees working for health care facilities through a staffing agency in a joint employment situation?

Holding and Decision: Yes, employees working for health care facilities through a staffing agency are employees of both entities and are subject to the exclusive remedy provision in the Worker's Compensation Act.

Analysis: The court held that Jennings was a co-employee of St. Vincent and StarMed. The Worker's Compensation Act explicitly recognizes that a worker may have more than one employer at a given moment. To determine whether a worker was engaged in a joint employment situation, seven factors must be evaluated and weighed as a balancing test. The factors include:

- Belief of the parties in the existence of an employer-employee relationship
- Control over the means used in the results reached
- Establishment of the work boundaries
- Length of employment
- Mode of payment
- Supplying tools or equipment
- The right to discharge

After analyzing each factor, the court determined that St. Vincent's right to discharge Jennings, the tools and equipment that St. Vincent supplied Jennings, and, most important, its control over Jennings's performance of his duties led to the conclusion that Jennings was a co-employee of St. Vincent and StarMed. Weighing against this determination was the belief of the parties in the existence of an employer-employee relationship and the length of employment factors. The court found that the mode of payment factor was not determinative. Because the more significant factors weighed in favor of an employer-employee relationship, the court concluded that both StarMed and St. Vincent were management entities protected by the exclusive remedy provision.

Rule of Law: An injured employee is entitled to worker's compensation benefits only, and may not otherwise sue the employer for damages.

References discussing this court decision: N/A

Recruitment and Rights of Foreign Nationals

Immigration law as it pertains to the recruitment of **foreign nationals** is the subject of renewed focus and contention within the global health care industry. For instance, there are few procedural protections and vague explanations for denials when:

- The information technology industry temporarily employs foreign nationals
- The medical products industry employs foreign national scientists in the United States
- U.S. citizens employ foreign nationals as home health aides
- U.S. citizens sponsor their spouses for lawful **permanent residence** (on green card status) or seek permission for their foreign national spouses to live in the United States
- Valued foreign nationals employed by the U.S. health care industry seek **naturalization** (*See* Family, 2016).

While Congress sets the general categories and quotas, the executive branch fills in the details and actually adjudicates benefit applications.

J-1 Waivers for Foreign National Physicians: Conrad Program

Foreign national medical school graduates usually enter the United States on **J-1 visas** to complete their graduate medical education and graduate training. Upon completion of such programs (often medical residency and fellowship training), the foreign national must return home to satisfy a two-year home residency requirement before becoming eligible for lawful permanent residence (*See* Inadmissible Aliens, 8 U.S.C.A. § 1182(e)). Many foreign national physicians seek a waiver of their home residency requirement to pursue employment in the United States.

Any government may request a waiver on behalf of a foreign national physician (*See* 8 U.S.C.A. § 1184(l)(1)). One waiver option is the **Conrad program**, which allows each state 30 waivers to foreign national physicians. In exchange, the physician must agree to practice medicine for three years in a designated health care shortage area. Once the two-year home residency requirement of the temporary visa status is waived, the physician is able to pursue other immigration options, including permanent residence (*See* 8 U.S.C.A. § 1182(e)).

H-1B Annual Quotas

Although not exclusively affecting the health care industry, the current annual quota of 85,000 **H-1B visas** has caused considerable difficulty for management teams seeking to employ foreign nationals in specialty occupations (*See* 8 U.S.C.A. § 1184(g)(1)(A)). The health care industry regularly uses the H-1B visa category to sponsor foreign national physicians and scientists (8 U.S.C.A. § 1184(i)(1)(B)). The current quota is not sufficient to meet the demand for H-1B foreign nationals, and new legislation to further increase and extend the quota has been the subject of debate for decades (*See* Family, 2016; Funke, 2015; Papa & Whelan, 2015). The inability to secure guaranteed work visas seriously hinders the ability of foreign nationals to work in the United States and meaningfully contribute to the advancement of U.S. science and medicine (Gill, 2014).

Lawful Permanent Residence

The health care industry often sponsors highly skilled and educated foreign nationals for permanent residence (*See* 20 C.F.R. §§ 655 and 656) (Funke, 2015). This avenue of entry to the United States is only available where qualified U.S. employees are not available for the work offered to foreign nationals. For instance, high-skill scientists have long been recognized as a job shortage area.

New Protections for Contingent Employees

Part-time and temporary employees, and independent contractors or employees of a subcontracting employer, are reaching new heights and changing the employment relationship in the health care industry, especially in the medical products sector (Wharton, 2011b). **Contingent employees** face continued downward pressure on their wages with generally no health care or pension benefits and no expectation of long-term employment (Dau-Schmidt, 2015). With jobs that are not well defined, few contingent employees are offered training or educational benefits (Holloway, 2016).

Most contingent employees spend their careers with multiple employers with none of the employment advantages of traditional employees in years past (Wharton, 2011a). One of the most critical impacts on the health care industry is that contingent employees in the U.S. economy often face periods of unemployment between jobs which is a key part of the nation's uninsured problem (Holloway, 2016). Employers, in effect, are shifting their workforce costs to society in the name of flexibility; taxpayers are stuck paying the bill for this business practice.

Employers with high numbers of contingent employees are often more concerned with ensuring low prices than with maintaining a stable workforce. When Manpower is the nation's largest employer with almost 4 million contingent employees worldwide, there is a need for comprehensive reform of U.S. labor law (Dau-Schmidt, 2015). The common misconception is that the federal government or Wal-Mart is the nation's largest employer; however, Wal-Mart employs 1.2 million employees and 1 in 10 of the 1.8 million federal employees are contingent employees (often through Manpower). Clearly, existing labor law no longer improves the plight of American employees or betters the U.S. economy (Wharton, 2012b).

LAW FACT

Management's Refusal to Bargain

Do labor unions have any recourse when management unilaterally makes decisions affecting represented employees and refuses to bargain over subjects not clearly contained in a collective bargaining agreement?

No, if the focus of any dispute is not covered by a collective bargaining agreement, management has the right to adopt and implement employee policies without bargaining with labor unions. The Enloe Medical Center was not required to negotiate over the new mandatory on-call policy or its effect with the labor union.

— *Enloe Medical Center v. National Labor Relations Board*, 433 F.3d 834 (U.S. Court of Appeals for the D.C. Circuit 2005). Followed by *Heartland Plymouth Court MI, LLC v. National Labor Relations Board*, 2016 U.S. App. LEXIS 8164 (U.S. Court of Appeals for the D.C. Circuit 2016) (upholding the contract coverage approach to disputes between labor unions and management; management could reduce employee hours without bargaining).

CHAPTER SUMMARY

- Nurses are the largest single group of health care providers in the country; the most severe consequence of nurse shortages is increased patient mortality.
- Labor and management in the health care industry have the opportunity to work together to improve efficiency and value in the delivery of health care.
- Although many labor unions are losing members, the health care industry is becoming increasingly unionized.
- Labor law has not undergone much reform since it was first enacted in the earlier part of the 20th century; many are calling for reforms that would allow employees to unionize more easily, be prevented from employer backlash, and allow for problem resolution through arbitration.
- The general legal principles that already exist could also serve the health care industry in crafting workplace policies.

- Nurse shortages are a severe problem; unless something changes, the nurse workforce will be nearly 30% below projected requirements within the decade.
- Because of the workload increase due to shortages, nurses have a very high rate of job dissatisfaction; however, simply involving nurses in the workplace discussion tends to reduce dissatisfaction despite the workload.
- California has enacted mandatory minimum nurse-to-patient ratios.
- Although mandatory overtime helps address the nurse shortage issue, it contributes to reduced quality of care for patients.
- One possibility to address the shortage of nurses and other health care employees is to attract foreign employees, but employers face legal and regulatory hurdles in doing so.

LAW NOTES

1. Labor unions compete with corporations in the political process in terms of manpower and maintain reasonably strong public support for their views, as evidenced by polling conducted by:

   - The American National Election Study (Ohio State University)
   - The Current Population Survey (U.S. Bureau of Labor Statistics and U.S. Bureau of the Census)
   - Gallup surveys
   - Hart Research National Opinion surveys
   - Roper Center for Public Opinion Research surveys (University of Connecticut)

2. The Business Roundtable is an association of chief executive officers of leading U.S. corporations with more than $5 trillion in annual revenues and nearly 10 million employees. Member corporations comprise nearly a third of the total value of the U.S. stock markets and pay nearly half of all corporate income taxes paid to the federal government.

3. The landmark Aiken study was a cross-sectional analysis of data from over 10,000 nurses surveyed and over 250,000 general, orthopedic, and vascular surgery patients discharged from 168 general hospitals in Pennsylvania (Aiken, 2002). The Aiken research was subsequently confirmed by international research (*E.g.*, Griffiths et al., 2007 (nurse staffing levels in hospitals in 12 European countries have the same impact on patient outcomes and factors influencing nurse retention as found in the United States by Aiken)) and review of 97 research articles since the 2002 Aiken research (*See* Arling & Mueller, 2014).

REFERENCES

Aiken, L. (2002). Hospital nurse staffing and patient mortality, nurse burnout, and job dissatisfaction. *Journal of the American Medical Association, 288*(16), 1987–1993.

ANA (American Nurses Association). (2012). *Principles for nurse staffing* (2nd ed.). Silver Spring, MD: ANA.

___. (2011). *Mandatory overtime: Summary of state approaches.*

___. (2009). *Utilization guide to the principles on safe staffing.*

Andres, M. N. (2016). Making elder financial exploitation cases part of a sustainable practice: Tips from the experiences of the University of Illinois College of Law's Elder Financial Justice Clinic. *Elder Law Journal, 23*, 297–341.

Andrias, K. (2015). Separations of wealth: Inequality and the erosion of checks and balances. *University of Pennsylvania Journal of Constitutional Law, 18*, 419–503.

Arling, G., & Mueller, C. (2014). Nurse staffing and quality: The unanswered question. *Journal of American Medical Directors Association, 15*(6), 376–378.

Auerbach. D. L., et al. (2014). Registered nurses are delaying retirement, a shift that has contributed to recent growth in the nurse workforce. *Health Affairs, 33*(8), 1–10.

___. (2011). Registered nurse supply grows faster than projected amid surge in new entrants ages 23–26. *Health Affairs, 30*, 2286–2292.

Bagley, N. (2015). Medicine as a public calling. *Michigan Law Review, 114*, 57–106.

Bales, R. A., et al. (2014). A comparative analysis of labor outsourcing. *Arizona Journal of International and Comparative Law, 31*, 579–622.

Baron, R., President and Chief Executive Officer of the American Board of Internal Medicine and the ABIM Foundation. (2016, October 21). Closing Keynote on What Do We Know and Where Do We Go from Here? at the Wharton Health Care Management Alumni Association Annual Conference on The Value Ripple Effect, Philadelphia, PA.

Bellace, J. (2011). Achieving social justice: The nexus between the ILO's fundamental rights and decent work. *Employee Rights and Responsibilities Journal, 15*(1), 101–124.

BLS (Bureau of Labor Statistics). (2016a). *Economic news release: Union members' survey.* Washington, DC: U.S. Department of Labor, BLS.

___. (2016b). *Occupational employment and wages.*

___. (2015). *Occupational outlook handbook: Registered nurses.*

Bowness, M. (2014). Protecting employees from quid pro quo neutrality arrangements. *Emory Law Journal, 63*, 1499–1537.

Carlson, E. M. (2010). Trends and tips in long-term care: Who benefits, or loses, from expanded choices? *The Elder Law Journal, 18*, 191–212.

Cashmore, E. B. (2014). Guarding the golden years: How public guardianship for elders can help states meet the mandates of *Olmstead. Boston College Law Review, 55*, 1217–1251.

Cowie, J. (2016). Labor organizing and the law: Reframing the new deal: The past and future of American labor and the law. *Theoretical Inquiries in Law, 17*, 11–38.

Dau-Schmidt, K. G. (2015). Opportunities for improvement in changing times: The impact of new information technology on the employment relationship and the relevance of the NLRA. *Emory Law Journal, 64*, 1583–1609.

DOL (U.S. Department of Labor). (2005a, April 11). Overtime for joint employees of health care system. *Fair Labor Standards Act Opinion Letter 2005–15*. Washington, DC: Department of Labor, Employment Standards Administration.

____. (2005b, August 19). Exempt status of nurse practitioners. *Fair Labor Standards Act Opinion Letter 2005-20*. Washington, DC: Department of Labor, Employment Standards Administration.

Family, J. E. (2016). The executive power of process in immigration law. *Chicago–Kent Law Review, 91*, 59–87.

Fisk, C., & Barry, A. (2012). Papers from the American Bar Foundation: The labor law group conference on the proposed Restatement of Labor Law: Contingent loyalty and restricted exit: Commentary on the Restatement of Labor Law. *Employee Rights and Employment Policy Journal, 16*, 411–462.

Freeman, R. B. (2007). *Briefing paper: Do employees still want labor unions? More than ever*. Washington, DC: Economic Policy Institute.

Frolik, L. A. (2016). Private long-term care insurance: Not the solution to the high cost of long-term care for the elderly. *Elder Law Journal, 23*, 371–415.

Funke, J. (2015). Supply and demand: Immigration of the highly skilled and educated in the post-9/11 market. *John Marshall Law Review, 48*, 419–452.

Garcia, R. A. (2016). Modern accountability for a modern workplace: reevaluating the National Labor Relations Board's joint employer standard. *The George Washington Law Review, 84*, 741–775.

Gill, J. (2014). Immigration reform = false hope? Examining the current and proposed immigration laws regarding H-1B visas. *University of Missouri-Kansas City Law Review, 83*, 233–255.

Goldberg, M. J. (2015). Democracy in the private sector: The rights of shareholders and union members. *University of Pennsylvania Journal of Business Law, 17*, 393–451.

Gould IV, W. B. (2015. Assessing the NLRB's impact and political effectiveness: Politics and the effect on the National Labor Relations Board's adjudicative and rulemaking processes. *Emory Law Journal, 64*, 1501–1527.

Griffiths, P., et al. (2014). Nurses' shift length and overtime working in 12 European countries: The association with perceived quality of care and patient safety. *Medical Care, 52*(11), 975–981.

Hallett, N. (2015). From the picket line to the courtroom: A labor organizing privilege to protect workers. *New York University Review of Law and Social Change, 39*, 475–524.

Harless, M. B., et al. (2013). California's minimum nurse staffing legislation: Results from a natural experiment. *Health Services Research, 48*(2), 435–454.

Hayes, L. J., et al. (2012). Nurse turnover: A literature review: An update. *International Journal of Nursing Studies, 49*(7), 887–905.

Hobbes, T. (2013). *Leviathan*. Riverside, CA: Renaissance Books (Original work published 1651).

IOM (Institute of Medicine), Committee on the Work Environment for Nurses and Patient Safety. (2004). *Keeping patients safe: Transforming the work environment of nurses*. Washington, DC: IOM.

Jones, J. M. (2011, August 31). *Approval of labor unions holds near its low, at 52%*. Washington, DC: Gallup.

Kane, R. L., et al. (2007). *Evidence report/technology assessment number 151: Nurse staffing and quality of patient care*. Washington, DC: Agency for Health Care Policy and Research.

Kochan, T. A., et al. (2016). Updating the transformation of American industrial relations. *Industrial and Labor Relations Review, 69*, 1281–1284.

Kohn, N. A. (2012). Elder rights: The next civil rights movement. *Temple Political and Civil Rights Law Review, 21*, 321–328.

Holloway, C. (2016). Keeping freedom in freelance: It's time for gig firms and gig workers to update their relationship status. *Wake Forest Journal of Business and Intellectual Property Law, 16*, 298–334.

Kugielska, L., & Linke, M. (2008). Emerging technology and employee privacy: Balancing the Red Cross: An examination of hospital malpractice and the nursing shortage. *Hofstra Labor and Employment Law Journal, 25*, 563–598.

Levinson, D., & Sachs, B. I. (2015). Political entrenchment and public law. *Yale Law Journal, 125*, 400–482.

Long, G. L. (2013). Differences between union and non-union compensation. *Monthly Labor Review, 4*, 16–23.

Louris, T. (2010). The necessary and desirable counterpart: Implementing a Holmesian perspective of labor rights as human rights. *Law and Inequality, 28*, 191–221.

Madow, D. L. (2013). Why many meritorious elder abuse cases in California are not litigated. *University of San Francisco Law Review, 47*, 619–645.

McHugh, M. D., et al. (2011). Contradicting fears, California's nurse-to-patient mandate did not reduce the skill level of the nursing workforce in hospitals. *Health Affairs, 30*(7), 1299–1306.

Mishel, M. (2012). *Labor unions, inequality, and faltering middle-class wages*. Washington, DC: Economic Policy Institute.

Neidhardt, A. W. (2015). The federalist view of right-to-work laws. *University of Pennsylvania Journal of Law and Social Change, 18*, 251–281.

Needleman, J., et al. (2011). Nurse staffing and inpatient hospital mortality. *New England Journal of Medicine, 364*(11), 1037–1045.

Papa, J., & Whelan, J. (2015). Moving to opportunity: Examining the risks and rewards of economic migration: Regaining the economic edge: Policy proposals for high-skill worker and student authorizations. *Indiana International and Comparative Law Review, 25*, 33–44.

Rogers, B. (2012). Passion and reason in labor law. *Harvard Civil Rights-Civil Liberties Law Review, 47*, 311–369.

Satz, A. B. (2015). Fragmentation after health care reform. *Houston Journal of Health Law and Policy, 15*, 171–228.

Selmi, M., Professor of Law, George Washington University. (2012, November 19). Remarks at the panel discussion on Supersize Me: The Restatement's Duty of Loyalty provision at the American Bar Foundation experts' meeting on the Restatement of Labor Law Project, Evanston, IL: Northwestern University Law School.

Vidal, N. (2009). *Organizing prosperity: Union effects on job quality, community betterment, and industry standards.* Washington, DC: Economic Policy Institute.

Weiss, M., Professor of Law, University of Maryland School of Law. (2012, November 19). Remarks at the panel discussion on Conventional and Unconventional Thinking: Drawing on Legislative Developments and Supreme Court Case Law to Imagine a Unified Theory of Labor law Remedies at the American Bar Foundation Experts' Meeting on the Restatement of Labor Law Project, Evanston, IL: Northwestern University Law School.

Western, B., & Rosenfeld, J. (2011). Unions, norms, and the rise in U.S. wage inequality. *American Sociological Review 76*(4), 513–537.

Wharton at the University of Pennsylvania. (2015). The uncomfortable questions you should be asking about pay equity. *Knowledge@Wharton.*

____. (2012a). State of the labor unions: What it means for employees; and everyone else.

____. (2012b). Revisiting the American dream: Is the U.S. providing fewer opportunities to get ahead?

PART V

STRATEGIC HEALTH CARE RESTRUCTURINGS

Part V describes how the health care and insurance industries are being pressured to move toward fewer restrictions on care instead of more.

© Andy Dean Photography/ShutterStock, Inc.

CHAPTER 12

Trends in Health Care Restructurings[1]

"[Professions uphold] as the criterion of success the end for which the profession, whatever it may be, is carried on, and [subordinate] the inclination, appetites and ambition of individuals to the rules of an organization which has as its object to promote the performance of function."

— **R. H. Tawney** (1880-1962), economist, historian, and social critic, from *The Acquisitive Society* (1921)

IN BRIEF

This chapter examines the movement of the U.S. health care system into integrated delivery systems that are multitiered. Within these integrated health care systems are numerous restructured programs, such as the emergence of affordable care organizations, medical homes, retail clinics, and medical tourism.

LEARNING OBJECTIVES

Upon completion of this chapter readers should be able to:

1. Describe trends in managed care and consumer-driven health care.
2. List problems with financial incentives.
3. Discuss issues associated with comparative effectiveness research.
4. Explain the need for medical homes.
5. Describe quality incentives to improve health care.
6. Outline the problems and limits of cost-shifting.
7. Explain the integration process in health care.
8. Compare professional autonomy with collectivization of physicians and other health care professionals.
9. Discuss two health care restructuring directions: retail clinics and medical tourism.
10. Describe the multitiered delivery of health care.

KEY TERMS

Acute care
Administrative power
Adverse event
Affordable Care Act of 2010
Alexandrian solution
Alternative treatments
Bioscience
Bundled payments
Clinical governance

Collectivization
Comorbidity
Comparative efficacy
Comparative effectiveness
Conflict management
Confounding
Contracting vehicles
Cost-shifting
Data mining

Detection signals
Disease management
Disease registries
Diversification
Drug segmentation
Economic pyramid
Effective
Efficacy
Emerging countries

---

[1]Contributor: Yilmaz C. Kaymak, MBA, MSE in finance, innovation, and technology management, The Wharton School of the University of Pennsylvania.

Employer-provided insurance
Executive authority
Financial incentives
Food, Drug, and Cosmetic Act of 1938
Global product standardization
Health outcomes
Horizontal integration
Industry best practice
Integrated care
Integrated health care systems
Joint Commission
Joint Commission International
Legal forum
Long-term care markets
Managed care
Market force
Medical home
Medical tourism

Medically necessary care
Multitiered delivery of health care
Non-group policies
Off-label
Patient-Centered Outcomes
    Research Institute
Patient information
Pay-for-performance
Pharmacovigilance
Physician hospital organizations
Polarities
Polypharmacy
Population health
Post-approval research
Post-marketing surveillance
Preventive services
Primary care
Prospective payment system

Provider networks
Provider segmentation
Public good
Pyramid of health care delivery
Quality Healthcare Resources, Inc.
Quality-of-care scores
Randomized controlled clinical trials
Retail clinics
Risk status
Supplemental private health
    insurance
Tertiary care
Third party payment system
U.S. Agency for Health Care
    Research and Quality
Utilization review
Value-added treatment procedures
Vertical integration

FACT OR FICTION

Comparative Effectiveness Research

Should prescription drugs that are found to be less clinically effective but more expensive than others not be prescribed?

Congress has allocated over $1.1 billion for **comparative effectiveness** research to determine which drugs are best for certain health conditions. Some see this research as a way to help the federal government and the health insurance industry curtail the use of expensive medicines that do poorly in comparative studies, though the official purpose is not cost reduction. The issue is: how should comparative effectiveness research be carried out in the United States? Congress hopes to expand medical coverage while limiting use of medical treatments and drugs that do not work well. There is no political consensus, however, on how to best expand medical coverage while limiting unnecessary health care. Numerous options to achieve optimal effectiveness raise questions:

- Should the pharmaceutical industry reengineer the way drugs are developed?
- Should the **U.S. Agency for Health Care Research and Quality** restructure and enhance its post-approval system for identifying and interpreting **adverse events**? This oversight system is termed **pharmacovigilance**, which is defined as "the science and activities relating to the detection, assessment, understanding and prevention of adverse events or other drug-related problems" (WHO, 2008, p.7).
- Should the U.S. Food and Drug Administration (FDA) be restructured to ratchet up the approval criteria for new drugs?

Selecting the optimal option to achieve effectiveness is not as easy as it may seem:

- About 4 billion prescriptions are written every year in the United States, with close to a half million adverse events reported to the FDA every year.
- Errors in prescribing or administering drugs by prescribing health care professionals, and self-medication with supplements, over-the-counter drugs, and **alternative treatments** by patients, further confound detection of effectiveness.
- Health care spending varies wildly between geographic regions, often with little or no correlation to **health outcomes**.
- More than half of the insured population in the United States is taking prescription drugs, often for more than one drug, and more than 20% of the time the use is **off-label**.

(Alspach, 2016; Bynum et al., 2016; Kleinrock, 2016; Woodcock, 2016).

— *See* Law Fact at the end of this chapter for the answer.

Principles and Applications

The legend of Alexander the Great arriving in the Kingdom of Phrygia in what is now central Turkey is analogous to the quandary of health care in the United States, where everyone has known for more than a decade that about half of what is spent on medical treatments each year is unnecessary (Bynum et al., 2016; *See* Asch et al., 2006). Like Alexander, the United States faces a challenge. In Phrygia, the gods had assisted Gordius, the king, with tying his oxcart to a pole with an intricate knot. The man who could undo the Gordian knot would rule all Asia. When Alexander could not untie the knot, he unsheathed his sword and sliced it with one stroke, producing the **Alexandrian solution**.

Clearly, the U.S. health care system needs an Alexandrian solution if it hopes to develop effective, **integrated health care systems**. The U.S. health care system is like the Gordian knot. Health care in the United States has become a complex, impossible-to-resolve system of interrelated rules and regulations that no one can rationally understand or direct.

Trends in Health Care

With health care reform, the prediction is that three important trends will emerge in the United States:

- Movement toward **multitiered delivery of health care** based on the ability to pay for medically needed care
- Provider segmentation with growth of personalized drugs and **value-added treatment procedures**
- Cost-based payment

Multitiered Delivery of Health Care

The movement of the United States toward a multitiered health care system was first recognized in the mid-1990s (Reinhardt, 1995). Critics maintain this policy direction is contrary to Congressional intent inherent in the Medicaid/Medicare legislation, as well as the reforms in the **Affordable Care Act of 2010**, because both legislative proposals envisioned integrated uniform health care based on medical need. Yet, this uniformity of care is not where the U.S. health care system is moving, as illustrated in **FIGURE 12-1** (*See* Kaiser, 2015; U.S. Census Bureau, 2015). Medically needed health care is increasingly based on the ability to prepay for such care.

For those who are able to pay, there will be a level of service that goes beyond what is now available. For everyone else, who is underinsured or uninsured, they will not always have access to the most innovative and advanced medical technologies.

- The top tier of the pyramid, the high-income wage earners, pays handsomely for access to tomorrow's medical technology; some higher income insured individuals may have high-deductible policies or are insured through individual, **non-group policies**, while some have **employer-provided insurance**.
- In the next tier down, the middle and upper-middle tier of the pyramid, are the employed with employer-sponsored health insurance and the Medicare-insured with **supplemental private health insurance**; they spend more out of pocket to receive health care from **provider networks**.
- At the bottom tier of the pyramid are the uninsured, underinsured, Medicaid-insured, and Medicare-insured without supplemental private health insurance. These individuals are eligible to receive health care wherever they can find it, but more often than not go to public hospitals and clinics or go without specialized care; low Medicaid payment rates generally restrict their choice of health care providers, but if they can find providers who will accept Medicaid, the services and products of those providers will be covered in full.

(Jost, 2007; Reinhardt, 1995; *See* Chou, 2015).

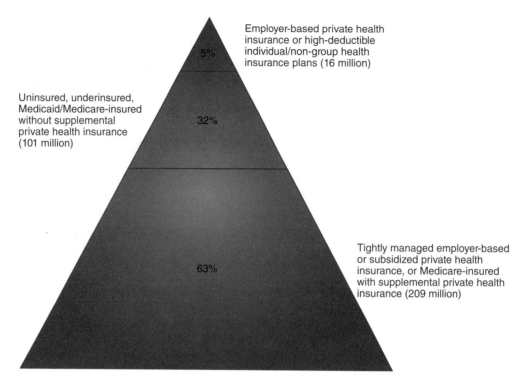

Employer-based private health insurance or high-deductible individual/non-group health insurance plans (16 million)

5%

Uninsured, underinsured, Medicaid/Medicare-insured without supplemental private health insurance (101 million)

32%

Tightly managed employer-based or subsidized private health insurance, or Medicare-insured with supplemental private health insurance (209 million)

63%

Note: Princeton University economist, Reinhardt, was the first to predict emergence of the three-tiered health care system in the United States.

FIGURE 12-1 Multitiered Delivery of Health Care

Data from: Census Bureau, U.S. (2015) *Current population survey: Annual social and economic supplement.* Suitland, MD: U.S. Department of Commerce, U.S. Census Bureau; Jost, T. S. (2007). The Massachusetts health plan: Public insurance for the poor, private insurance for the wealthy, self-insurance for the rest? *University of Kansas Law Review, 55,* 1091-1102; Kaiser Family Foundation. (2015). *State health facts: Medical coverage of the total population.* Menlo Park, CA: Kaiser; Reinhardt, U.E. (1995). Turning our gaze from bread and circus games. *Health Affairs, 14* (1), 33-35 (Princeton University economist first predicted the three-tiered health care system).

Provider Segmentation

Because not everyone receives the same health care, other parts of the health care industry will segment themselves into tiers that make more intelligent use of **patient information** (such as health care delivered, including medical tests, prescriptions, and surgeries) (Wharton, 2002). Some of this will be aimed at more effective use of personalized treatments and drugs. If, for instance, a hospital system has a regional primary care network of 30 physician practices, the system might expand to a national network of 300 specialists and begin accepting referrals from a national network of physician practices. Several levels of fine **provider segmentation** could then occur, and treatment costs could be spread among this larger network of providers (*Cf.* Tawney, 2013/1921 (explaining cost segmentation)).

Personalized Drugs

When prescribing drugs, as opposed to offering patients one drug that fits everyone, different versions of the same drug will be offered at different prices to different groups of patients with different medical needs (Gaddy, 2015). In other words, different versions of a drug will be prescribed to different patient groups based on clear

MANAGEMENT AND LAW ISSUES

1.   If basic health care is provided to everyone, should access to the latest medical technologies be based on need or the ability to pay?

differences in their medical needs. The day of one-size-fits-all drug prescribing will eventually end and drugs will be personalized for different patient groups based on their specific medical needs or levels of functionality. **Drug segmentation** would be similar to Starbucks offering dark, medium, light, and decaffeinated roast versions of their coffee.

Value-Added Treatment Procedures

More than one price could also be set between different providers without significant differences in the costs of providing the care (Hoffman, 2015). With fine provider segmentation, the focus would be on value-added treatment procedures that providers can meet cost-effectively (Nichols, 2011). Some patients may be charged higher prices for treatment procedures with a high level of individualized attention from specialists; other patients will be charged lower prices for the same treatment procedures from a primary care network. Some patients will pay a higher price in return for care that they feel adds value to their health. Provider segmentation enables hospital systems to offer the same treatments, but add features that patients are willing to pay for or remove elements that are not important to patients.

Payment Systems

The more accurately treatment procedures are priced, the better it is for patients with little or no medical coverage at the lower tier of the health care delivery pyramid. For instance, if a patient who requires $700 a month in treatments pays their physician $300, and another patient who needs $50 worth of treatments each month also pays the same physician $300, what the provider is paid can be adjusted to better reflect each patient's **risk status**. In other words, what is the cost difference for treating these two patients with different health conditions? Once this question is answered, the differences in patient costs can be converted into cost differences in what the providers will be paid. *See generally*, Nation, 2016.

Bundled Payments

Instead of reimbursing health care providers a set amount each time a patient is treated for a given medical service, with **bundled payments**, providers are paid for a full treatment cycle (Satz, 2015). This creates an incentive for providers to provide the most effective, innovative care available as opposed to cheaper treatments. As a result, providers are forced to compete in the prevention, diagnosis, and treatment of individual health conditions, disease by disease, and patient by patient. It is here where enormous differences in costs occur.

When bundled payments occur, providers face the choice of becoming low volume, high cost specialists, or high volume, low cost providers of standard health care. Providers can treat both segments with great benefits by lowering the average costs. To do this, however, it must be possible to provide treatments at different prices at the level of the health condition of each patient (Sage, 2016).

Value-Based Payments

Health care costs must match value in each disease and patient segment. Different disease and patient values require different prices to cover different health care costs. Over time, providers will be forced to choose one segment or the other (Mantel, 2015a). The alternative is what we have today with the absence of price differentials: providers are reimbursed below cost in one segment and are non-competitive in another because payment is based on average costs

MANAGEMENT AND LAW ISSUES

2.   Where does value-added personalization and provider segmentation end, and harmful discrimination begin?

that hide more than they disclose. When this occurs, the number of uninsured Americans might decrease and basic preventive care might become more affordable (Wharton, 2006b).

Restructuring Health Care Systems

When the **managed care** movement began in the 1970s, the problems it was supposed to solve were clear: the **financial incentives** associated with the traditional **third party payment system** were inflationary, and the delivery of care across the board was poorly coordinated (Wharton, 2000). Today, it is difficult to reach a political consensus about where the U.S. health care system should go, after almost 40 years of managed care. One thing is certain: given the amount of frustration expressed by the American public, the health care industry does not have it right yet. Many of the different managed care organizations that have been developed have not worked as expected.

In addressing the future of managed care, it is critical to realize that for many people, the term **integrated care** has become synonymous with a number of significant breakdowns in the health care system. Managed care cuts prices without integrating service delivery, which means there was a continued overall lack of coordination and integration in patient treatment. Recent health care reforms are addressing these concerns through different approaches from various ends of the spectrum:

- Comparative effectiveness research
- **Medical home** models at the level of single medical practices
- Quality incentives for improvements in patient health

Comparative Effectiveness Research

Although **comparative efficacy** would be a more precise term, this text uses the term *comparative effectiveness* because it is what is more familiar, even though the two nouns are not synonyms.[LN1] In an era of more and more high-powered and expensive advanced medical technologies, the dissatisfaction with managed care is only going to get worse without fundamental change concerning who has access to research comparing drugs and medical treatments (Choi, 2015). Many argue that comparative effectiveness research should be considered a non-excludable and non-rivalrous **public good** given the degree of government subsidies to the U.S. health care system (Rodwin & Abramson, 2012). The use of research information by the health care industry—especially the claims data held by the health insurance sector and the clinical trials data held by the medical products sector—should not reduce its availability to others, especially to consumers of health care (as well as academics and independent research organizations).

Shifting Decision-Making Away From the Health Insurance Industry

Under managed care, physicians and hospitals have to undergo **utilization review** in an attempt to reduce unnecessary medical treatments and prescriptions for the purpose of controlling costs and monitoring the quality of care (Mantel, 2015b). To address costs and quality issues, 20 Blue Cross health insurance firms joined to create Blue Health Intelligence, a program under which they pool data from about 80 million subscribers. The plan was to share this claims research initially with employers and eventually with consumers, but a decade after the data-sharing program began, external sharing outside of the industry is still in the works (BHI, 2016).

However, the public's dissatisfaction with managed care has caused the health insurance industry to dilute or end most of its cost-control strategies that were implemented starting in the 1980s. Today, it is acknowledged by many that managed care may work only if government is the one safeguarding against unnecessary and inappropriate health care. At the same time, health care costs can be controlled *only* when everyone has affordable access to **medically necessary care** (Dolgin, 2015)

Cost Limitations

As the United States seeks to expand medical coverage, drugs and medical treatments that do not work must be limited, but there is no consensus as how this limitation is to take place (Satz, 2015). One proposal is that drugs and medical treatments found to be less effective but more expensive than others should not be prescribed (*See* Persad, 2015a). Yet any effort to reduce medical coverage based on cost alone still seems to be untenable to most Americans.

Patient-Centered Outcomes Research Institute

No matter what, there is a push to determine which drugs and medical treatments work best at the lowest cost in particular patients (Persad, 2015a and 2015b). This health care reform push was left unharmed by challenges to the Affordable Care Act. *See National Federation of Independent Business. v. Sebelius*, together with, *Florida v. U.S. Department of Health and Human Services*, 132 S.Ct. 2566, 2607-2608 (U.S. Supreme Court 2012).

In 2010, Congress established the **Patient-Centered Outcomes Research Institute**, a national center to integrate information about the relative clinical and cost-effectiveness of alternative treatment options into health care purchasing and coverage decisions (*Cf.* IOM, 2006; Schoen et al., 2007 (recommending establishment of the Institute)). One goal of this institute is to make effectiveness determinations on the best unbiased science possible in cooperation with the National Institutes of Health and other national research institutes. The objective is to analyze error rates and other quality-rated data about physicians and hospitals.

This research into comparative effectiveness will help Medicare/Medicaid insurance and the health insurance industry better direct their dollars to drugs and treatments that are worth the money. While there is concern that useful drugs and treatments risk being subject to limited availability for some patients, or not being made available at all, just because they cost too much, the greatest concern is about conflicts of interest among those asked to generate the research. Despite these contending concerns, there is widespread agreement on the attributes that ideally should be associated with comparative effectiveness research, including:

- Objectivity in the selection of what is studied
- Independence from political pressures generated either by government or by private-sector stakeholders
- Credibility in the findings

(McDonough, 2012).

Before the Affordable Care Act, the medical products industry controlled this clinical trial data and research, how it was reviewed and evaluated, and whether the public and the government even found out about the data and could use it.[LN2] The goal of comparative effectiveness research is to determine how to obtain more value from the nation's health care spending, not how to avoid expensive drugs and medical treatments, a critical distinction that has not always been adequately addressed (*See* Marino et al., 2015). Transparency of health costs, effectiveness, quality, and the ability to use such information are critical prerequisites for coordinated health care and the development of policies that encourage such care.

Patient-Centered Medical Homes

Physicians cannot understand all the health care being provided to their patients because no single physician is responsible for a patient's overall care (Morrell & Krouse, 2014). This indicator is important because having a medical home or regular provider of care is crucial to efforts to ensure access to timely, quality care (Hermer & Lenihan, 2014). Under this model of care, every individual and family has a primary care professional such as a physician, physician's assistant, or nurse practitioner, to:

- Facilitate their timely and integrated health care
- Coordinate referrals for testing and specialty services
- Monitor management of chronic conditions

(Morrell & Krouse, 2014).

From a patient's perspective, this represents an **industry best practice**. Patients benefit from a single point of entry into the health care system, as well as the continuity of a relationship with a primary care professional to direct their plan of care (Satz, 2015). From a systems perspective, emphasizing **primary care** and **preventive services** is widely recognized as producing:

- Fewer hospitalizations
- Improved health outcomes
- Lower health care costs

(Hermer & Lenihan, 2014).

In recent years, working conditions for primary care physicians have deteriorated, with salaries among the lowest and work hours among the longest of all physicians (Hammond, 2014). This combination has resulted in a significant decrease in the number of U.S. medical graduates selecting careers in family medicine and general internal medicine. While foreign medical professionals, as well as nurse practitioners and physician assistants, have filled some of the gaps in the primary care base, this new and important concept of the medical home gives promise to a reconceptualization of primary care (AAFP, 2007).[LN3]

A quality health care system that is affordable will not exist without a robust primary care base that is trained for the job and competitively compensated for the work (Madison, 2014). Payment reforms are required to strengthen primary care to provide better coordination and more accessible and patient-centered care through enhanced medical home approaches that help integrate care (Satz, 2015). Some preferred provider organization medical home networks are being developed, but thus far, primarily for Medicaid-insured populations.

Quality Incentives for Improvements in Patient Health

For health care providers, health care reform is a mixed bag. Sometimes it changes the incentives for doing more by doing less, but not often. The Affordable Care Act provides shared savings to providers for preventive care; as opposed to rewarding providers for providing treatments and drugs for health conditions (Thurman, 2014). For instance, if hospitals develop preventive programs for cardiovascular disease that significantly reduce hospitalizations, they will now share the savings when their patients stay healthy, rather than being penalized in the form of reduced opportunities for reimbursement if less medical care was delivered. When Duke University's hospital system saved $8,000 per patient by creating an integrated program for treating congestive heart failure in 2007, the episode-centered payment system penalized Duke by reducing the compensation its hospital received; as the number of reimbursable episodes fell, so did the hospital's revenue (Madison, 2014). There was no incentive to deliver quality over quantity before the Affordable Care Act. Today, Duke would be rewarded for coordinating patient care across its provider organization to increase quality of care.

Such perverse incentives also affected physicians before the Affordable Care Act. Insurers typically dictated the payment for every discrete episode of care. Since patients with chronic conditions cost physicians more because they required more time, but often did not result in additional revenue per treatment, physicians had an incentive to establish a practice that selected the healthiest patients. Today, payer's payment policies encourage providers to create bundles of related services that patients with chronic conditions typically require. Financial incentives have been realigned to enhance value and achieve savings when physicians provide quality health care that reduces costs (Mantel, 2015a).

Disease Management v. Pay-for-Performance

Medical treatments found to be less effective and in some cases more expensive than others should no longer be prescribed. The U.S. health care system must direct its dollars to treatments that are worth their cost (Wiley, 2016). While the financial pressure on physicians and hospitals has been significant, before the Affordable Care Act became fully implemented, there were few financial incentives for providing coordinated quality health care. The **disease management** movement of the 1990s that was developed by employers slowly became intertwined with the **pay-for-performance** movement developed by the insurance industry; cost savings came to the forefront under the guise of coordinated quality care, which oftentimes cost more (Satz, 2015).

MANAGEMENT AND LAW ISSUES

3. How did pay-for-performance programs debase the disease management efforts of the 1990s?
4. Can the comparative effectiveness movement prevent itself from becoming intertwined with the health insurance industry in the same manner as the pay-for-performance movement did?

Reform Solutions

According to prominent studies, adults in the United States receive the generally accepted standard of preventive, acute, and chronic care only about half the time (Asch et al., 2006; McGlynn et al., 2003). Moreover, one-third of the health care provided does not improve patients' health and may actually harm them (IOM, 2013). What is more, and contrary to popular misconceptions, there is only moderate variation in **quality-of-care scores** among different socioeconomic groups (McGlynn et al., 2003). In other words, the U.S. health care system is uniformly failing to serve everyone at least one-third of the time, and generally half the time people are not receiving the appropriate care they need (Asch et al., 2006; IOM, 2013).

While most Americans understand the need for a better system of affordable health insurance and increased access to health care, a stalemate about implementation of the Affordable Care Act still exists (Woodcock, 2016). Problems have been identified and there was political consensus on what the solutions should be. But Americans seem resolved to wanting the best health care, but are not always willing to pay for it (Wharton, 2006a). What the United States had with managed care was not managed care, but managed costs. What the nation considered with the Affordable Care Act was how to deliver a quality health care system, where health care problems are avoided and where people obtain care before it is too late.

Cost-Shifting

Health care systems can no longer continue to just shift costs. **Cost-shifting** has been going on for a long time. Most health care systems were fine while Medicare reimbursed them all of the costs they incurred in treating individuals with Medicare insurance. Medicare stopped overpaying in 1983 when it implemented the **prospective payment system** for inpatient hospital care. Health care costs had mushroomed partly because hospitals tried to bill Medicare for as many services for each patient as they could (Mantel, 2015a). Under the prospective payment system, Medicare started paying hospitals a predetermined amount for each Medicare patient discharged, based on the patient's diagnoses or procedures. Today, Medicare pays the costs that should be incurred by an efficient health care provider when it provides necessary and appropriate health care.

But it is important to remember that Medicare payments are made not simply to reimburse hospitals for treatment of patients covered by Medicare insurance, but for maintaining a certain level and quality of care, both for the hospital and the community the hospital serves (Marmor & Sullivan, 2016). In practice, what the actual rates of payment are for Medicare is determined as much by political calculations as by hospital costs; there is no rational analysis driving Medicare payments (Nation, 2016). The issue is: what can the political market bear and how does this translate to all the individual payments?

Understanding the Pyramid of Health Care Delivery

Health care researchers and government employees cannot resolve the U.S. health care crisis without understanding the nation's multilevel **pyramid of health care delivery** (Angeli & Jaiswal, 2016). For instance, one health care policy came about by chance. Medicare beneficiaries would not get flu shots until they were completely free, which was not a big budgetary issue, but this understanding came about in a peculiar way. The federal government's fiscal year starts October 1, which is when the Medicare deductible recycles. October is also the start of the flu shot season, but many Medicare participants did not want to use their deductible right away, preferring to save it for something more important. Once flu shots were free, flu shot participation doubled and tripled. This is just one example of how decisions on how to manage health care are complicated in many ways. *See generally*, Underhill, 2016.

People at the bottom of the **economic pyramid** behave the same way with small amounts of dollars as people higher up the socioeconomic pyramid; they save their dollars for something important to them (Wharton, 2006a). In the U.S. health care system, too many people making public policies do not understand that people at different levels of the economic pyramid are no different than they are; they just have different amounts of money, some more and some less. Despite a lack of understanding of this basic economic principle by most people making public policies, health concerns are indeed paramount for most Americans. For instance, it is estimated that 40% of the hits on the Internet are for health care information; most people are going to their physicians and then checking the Internet to find out more, or vice versa (Pew, 2013).

Light at the End of the Tunnel

As amazing as emerging medical technologies are, they will not improve the health care delivery system by themselves. Anyone who sees a light at the end of this tunnel probably is not being realistic. Managed care cannot survive in its present form, if all managed care is doing is cutting costs. The nation must move to a system that recognizes the importance of bringing new **bioscience** into the service of health care delivery (Executive Order 13497, 2009).

Closer Integration of Industry Sectors

The medical products industry is an integral part of the U.S. health care system, yet its value is not understood by rank-and-file health care professionals and consumers of health care (Alspach. 2016). New pharmaceuticals, biopharmaceuticals, medical devices, and health information technologies hold significant promise for patients facing illnesses and diseases, or health conditions that are often life-threatening. All parts of the system will have to pay their fair share for medical treatments, but it will never work until there is more concern about quality than finances (Lewis & Wittlin, 2015). Squeezing one part of the U.S. health care system has unintended impacts on another (*See* Abramowicz et al, 2011).

Integrated Health Care Systems

While debate is occurring about the role of managed care, the uninsured, and rising health care costs, it may be worthwhile to take another look at integrated health care systems. Integrated health care systems emerged in the 1980s, amid promises that they could achieve more cost-effective delivery along with value-added services for patients, and improved provider satisfaction. Today, very few integrated health care systems have delivered on that promise (Sage, 2016).

It could be said that answers were not sought from the right places (Freeman et al., 2015). In pursuit of the perfect integrated health care system, attention went to the various structural vehicles, such as **physician hospital organizations** that have been developed to enable physicians and hospitals to jointly contract with one another (Sage, 2016). Rather than concentrating on the *structures* of integration, focus should have been directed to the *processes* of integration, such as:

- Developing clinical leadership among physicians to advance their personal and professional goals (a process that Kaiser excels in)
- Vertical partnerships with physicians and other health care providers, such as home health agencies and long-term care facilities
- Representing all health care professionals in **clinical governance** where everyone is held accountable for continually improving patient safety and the quality of patient care (*See* Chapter on Improving Patient Safety and Quality of Health Care)

(See Blair et al., 2016).

Integration Processes

Integrated health care systems are built by bringing multiple hospitals, physicians, and other health care professionals together under one system to establish, at least in theory, a single cohesive **market force**. Because hospitals, physicians, and other health care professionals often span various markets, tensions and conflicts often arise from the clash of different cultures and philosophies existing within the different medical stakeholder groups (Blair et al., 2016). In fact, these polarities are inherent to the structure of integrated health care systems and exist at various levels, such as:

- Hospital-to-hospital
- Physician-to-physician
- Physician-to-other health care professionals
- Physician-to-integrated health care system

Acknowledgment of Inherent Polarities

Progress has been stymied in large part because integrated health care systems do not adequately attend to inherent **polarities**. Until they are acknowledged and managed, the future success of integrated health care may be limited. Research has identified numerous polarities that exist in any integrated health care system (Blair et al.,

2016). Generally, they arise because integrated health care systems encompass multiple entities with competing agendas. For instance:

- While integrated health care systems seek interdependence and centralization, physicians and other health care professionals seek decentralization and personal autonomy.
- Hospitals, physicians, and other health care professionals often want to maintain control of their health care services and are threatened by integrated health care systems that seek to centralize activities.
- Hospitals, physicians, and other health care professionals are often reluctant to embrace objectives led by integrated health care systems because they require cooperation with other hospitals and physicians, many of whom were once considered rivals.
- Tensions often arise because physicians and health care professionals are neither informed nor consulted on issues of integration, despite the fact that integrated health care systems need their buy-in.

(*See* Blair et al., 2016; McCann & Vorrasi, 2014).

Not surprisingly, the challenge is addressing and managing these inherent polarities and tensions.

Centralized Standardization

The issues that integrated health care systems face are not unique to the delivery of health care. In fact, much can be learned from members of the medical products industry, such as Johnson & Johnson, a $70.2 billion global pharmaceutical firm that employs some 127,000 employees in 250 operating companies in 57 different countries (Johnson & Johnson, 2016). For Johnson & Johnson, it is critical to achieve **global product standardization** while still maintaining market responsiveness and flexibility at the local level.

Successful global pharmaceutical corporations balance the simultaneous needs to be:

- Both centralized and decentralized
- Both global and local
- Both large and small

One might ask how Johnson & Johnson does this. They do it by using centralized, integrative structures, which appear to be more financially successful than less centralized structures (Blair et al., 2016). Like Johnson & Johnson, integrated health care systems could centralize their **administrative power** within an executive office responsible for policy planning, with **executive authority** residing in the individual hospitals, physicians, and professional groups.

In integrated health care systems, problems often arise when the executive office meddles in the affairs of individual hospitals, physicians, and professional groups, such as drawing up plans over trivial issues. Autonomous hospitals, physicians, and professional groups end up acting as extensions of the executive office, merely executing plans already decided by the executive office. Recognizing that it cannot resolve all the polarities it faces, Johnson & Johnson developed processes that allow the corporation to balance these polarities and pursue their corresponding interests simultaneously.

For instance, the presidents of Johnson & Johnson's operating companies report to both a global head, who has responsibility for a product line, and regional country coordinators who have responsibility for a geographical line. In this way, Johnson & Johnson ensures that neither interest, global or local, is prioritized or ignored, but both have the opportunity to further their agendas. Integrated health care systems face similar challenges when the executive office enters into payment contracts with the health insurance industry and the individual hospitals, physicians, and professional groups encounter utilization barriers as they attempt to provide health care to their insured patients (McCann & Vorrasi, 2014). Everyone must learn to navigate the narrow channels between conflicting objectives.

Collectivization of Physicians and Other Health Care Professionals

In integrated health care systems, a key issue for physicians and other health care professionals is how to maintain professional autonomy in a managed care environment without sacrificing their economic security (Sage, 2016). One way many physicians and other health care professionals have attempted to reconcile these seemingly incompatible interests is through a process called **collectivization**. They organize themselves into medical groups with collective control (by function, such as anesthesiology and physical therapy, or by medical specialty, such as cardiology or orthopedics). Essentially, physicians and other health care professionals organize themselves into collectives, for instance:

- **Contracting vehicles**, such as physician-hospital organizations, provider-sponsored organizations, and other networks of health care providers
- Large physician and professional group practices
- Specialty clinics

(Blair et al., 2016).

Although collectivization requires some sacrifice of personal autonomy at the individual level, the payoff is collective autonomy and increased economic security (McCann & Vorrasi, 2014). The size of the medical group provides increased visibility and leverage for physicians and other health care professionals within integrated health care systems. These medical groups also enjoy enhanced representation in governance and other integrated health care system benefits, such as strategic planning and financial assistance. Integrated health care systems benefit from this process because unorganized physicians and other health care professionals are pressured to form their own collective medical groups (Sage, 2016).

No Formula for Successful Integration

During the mid-1990s, many hospitals pursued several integration efforts, including:

- Development of managed care plans (**vertical integration** into health insurance products)
- Loose alliances with and acquisitions of physician practices (vertical integration into primary care services)
- Mergers and affiliations with other hospitals (**horizontal integration** of health care products and services)

(Blair & Sokol, 2015).

Hospitals pursued these efforts both individually and jointly (Blair et al., 2016). While numerous approaches have been used by integrated health care systems to resolve polarities, there is no formula for successful integration. The structures, or contractual vehicles, however, are never the answer. Processes must be developed to manage the polarities within integrated health care systems in a way that creates meaning for all of the participants (Kleinrock, 2016), including:

- Hospitals
- Integrated health care systems
- Patients
- Physicians and other health care professionals
- Wider service community comprised of consumers of health care

(Blair & Sokol, 2015).

Diversification Strategies

Conceptually, these integrated arrangements represent a variety of **diversification** strategies that expand into new areas of business. Diversification is said to exist when a system operates in two or more markets. Thus, for instance, the hospital diversifies when it begins to produce services in upstream primary care markets, or downstream in **long-term care markets**. Such diversification is typically unrelated to the hospital's core specialty care.

Diversification can also exist when an integrated health care system moves into new geographic markets or related lines of business. In the hospital industry, such diversification can take the form of multihospital systems that cross metropolitan and state lines, with different levels of market risk, as well as hospital systems that combine academic medical centers with outlying community hospitals. In all of these instances, diversification requires changes in administrative mechanisms, which are multidivisional structures, to enable management of the increased number of services and geographic markets in which the integrated health care system operates (Blair et al., 2016).

Conflict Management

Recognition that polarities exist and are interdependent and not always mutually exclusive is key to successful integration. One medical group's position cannot be supported at the expense of another; commonalities must be recognized and developed where possible. **Conflict management** calls for a careful balancing of rival perspectives that, most of the time, requires that multiple directions be simultaneously pursued. The goal should be to create strategic alliances that accomplish the objectives of the integrated health care system while balancing the often divergent needs of individual hospitals, physicians, and professional groups (Schutzbank, 2016).

Restructured Health Care Programs

Two emerging areas of interest are **retail clinics** and **medical tourism**. Two of the major players are profiled: RediClinic, retail health clinics created by America Online founder Steve Case (*See generally* Rozga, 2009), and Apollo Hospitals, the largest health care system in India (*See generally* Muzaurieta, 2015).

Retail Clinics

A new strategic innovation is walk-in medical clinics at retail stores and malls, operated by firms such as RediClinic. Wal-Mart has over 50 retail clinics, and while they may not be profit centers themselves (at least not yet), the clinics boost pharmacy sales and draw shoppers into Wal-Mart. Currently, of those visiting the clinics at Wal-Mart:

- 10 to 20% would have gone without medical treatment
- 20 to 40% would have sought emergency room care
- 30 to 40% are uninsured

(Cortez, 2011; Hoffmann, 2010).

While retail clinics are getting leverage from Wal-Mart, they pose new issues of supply chain management specific to health care, as opposed to product inventory, where Wal-Mart is viewed as the master. It makes sense for Wal-Mart to provide the retail clinics; they complement Wal-Mart's optical and pharmacy services. The challenge for Wal-Mart is managing consistent, quality health care. Health care is consumed as it is produced, unlike a shelf product that sits around until customers want it. Quality health care often rests on the dependability of the health care professionals delivering the care. Consistent, quality health care requires retail clinics to maintain excess capacity during times when they are not busy in order to meet patient needs when they arise. It is still an exercise in balancing supply and demand, but the factors at play are different. Retail clinics also fit into Wal-Mart's push to present itself as a kinder company, particularly after unions generated reports showing that Wal-Mart employees generally lacked medical coverage and that the company's employees were the nation's top users of Medicaid insurance (Americans for Tax Fairness, 2014; O'Connor, 2014).

Medical Tourism

Medical tourism, the phenomenon in which health care providers in emerging markets offer a vacation and surgery together at low prices to patients from the United States, is gaining in popularity. An estimated 1.4 million U.S. citizens seek health care outside the United States, a number that has more than doubled in less than a decade (PBB, 2016). While India lags behind countries like Thailand, as a result of airport infrastructure, health care providers such as Apollo Hospitals are rapidly expanding their medical tourism from the United States and Europe (Muzaurieta, 2015). Costa Rica, India, Israel, Malaysia, Mexico, Singapore, South Korea, Thailand, and Turkey remain the top medical tourism destinations with a market of $45 to $72 billion (PPB, 2016). This billion-dollar market is cash revenue that U.S. hospitals and physicians could be competing to put on their books instead.

Joint Commission International Accreditation

There is high value in terms of health outcomes and high quality care at up to 65% less than the cost of comparable models of care in the United States (Muzaurieta, 2015). Hospitals that are medical tourism sites have **Joint Commission International** accreditation, which puts them on par with hospitals in the rest of the world.[LN4] Today, almost 900 medical centers, hospitals, and primary care providers outside the United States have Joint Commission International accreditation, a number that is growing by about 20% year (JCI, 2016; PBB, 2016). To reiterate, this international market growth in low-priced delivery of health care is a billion-dollar market segment that is just beginning to be challenged by U.S. providers who are developing new reimbursement models that are yielding new innovative models of care (Schutzbank, 2016). At this point in time, it is not clear which U.S. models are best positioned to compete with medical tourism.[LN5]

5. How should governments to respond to medical tourism?

Tertiary and Acute Care in India

The case mix of most of the work that goes to India is **tertiary care** and **acute care**. It is not the plastic surgeries found in Bangkok. It is high-end orthopedic work, cardiology, and some oncology that can be obtained for a fraction of the costs as comparable care in the United States. Apollo Hospitals is developing packages to assist patients to use Indian facilities and is in conversation with private medical insurers for medical coverage (PBB, 2016). Apollo accepts U.S. health insurance. United Group Programs, a Florida-based insurer, with offices in Pennsylvania and Georgia, sells self-insurance policies to small businesses that offer a plan that sends patients to Bumrungrad Hospital in Bangkok. Dunkin' Donuts and Manpower are two United Group clients. Blue Shield of California and Health Net of California offer policies allowing patients to seek treatment in Mexico. Given the high-deductible insurance plans that many Americans now carry, costs are a *real* factor in selecting high-end care (Wharton, 2008). The single hurdle facing U.S. patients going to **emerging countries** for health care is legal liability and the fact that they cannot address their concerns through a **legal forum** in the United States. They can, of course, use the legal system where they receive their health care, but generally patients want a legal system they are familiar with to back them up in case there is a problem (Bennie, 2014). Currently, the incidence of problems is not even 1% at Apollo Hospitals in India; its clinical success rates and health outcomes are also very good (Muzaurieta, 2015). While patients have the same rights in India as they would in the United States, it is a hurdle for India to address the legal forum issue. Apollo Hospitals combines elements of both Western care and Eastern medicine. Allopathic medicine is used for actual treatment in terms of surgery and diagnosis, but where rehab and well-being are concerned, the systems of ayurveda (traditional Indian medicine) and yoga are integrated into patient care. The key here is that many patients find value from integrating ayurveda and yoga with allopathic care and are willing to travel to India to obtain this integration (Conley, 2013).

Frenzy in Health Care Restructurings

The Affordable Care Act has unleashed a frenzy in health care restructurings, with hospitals scrambling to:

- Create organizations capable of managing **population health**
- Improve operational efficiency
- Shore up their market positions

(Cutler & Morton, 2013).

At the same time, a large reduction in use of inpatient care is leading to significant consolidation in the hospital industry (Dafny, 2014; *See* Chapter on Antitrust Regulation of Health Care Providers). Acquisitions of physician groups are also on the rise (Carlin et al., 2015). Additional health care restructurings are inevitable. Like the legend of Alexander the Great at the start of this chapter, the U.S. health care system needs an Alexandrian solution if it hopes to avoid the frenzy of the mid-1990s and a bankruptcy like the Allegheny Health Education and Research Foundation, the largest health care industry failure at restructuring in the United States (*See* Chapter on Strategic Restructurings in Health Care: Mergers/Acquisitions and Bankruptcies).

The restructuring goals remain the same today as they were in the mid-1990s. Health care systems are still seeking to develop effective, integrated health care systems that will efficiently function to provide high quality patient care. To paraphrase R. H. Tawney, a 20th century economist: the criterion of success at the start of the 21st century should "subordinate the inclination, appetites and ambition of individuals to the rules of an organization which has as its object to promote the performance of function" (Tawney, 2013/1921, p. 37). Everyone needs to be alert to the unrequited appetites and ambitions of the few when it comes to the restructuring of the many health care providers.

LAW FACT

Comparative Effectiveness Research

Should prescription drugs that are found to be less clinically effective but more expensive than others not be prescribed?

Yes. Three federal agencies are coordinating the billion-dollar effort for comparative effectiveness research:

- National Institutes of Health
- U.S. Agency for Health Care Research and Quality
- U.S. Department of Health and Human Services

For purposes of effectiveness comparisons in determining which drugs are safe and which ones work, there are two research categories:

- **Post-approval research**
- **Post-marketing surveillance**

Post-marketing surveillance focuses on **detection signals** or warnings that adverse events or other drug-related problems are occurring. Information is collected on health outcomes from health care professionals, patients, and the pharmaceutical and biotechnology industries, as well as generic manufacturers. Such surveillance information is collected through two types of health information systems:

- Passive retrieval systems: adverse event reporting
- Active retrieval systems: **data mining** of health records from the health insurance industry and **disease registries**

Post-approval research consists of surveys, studies, or trials to further ascertain whether a detection signal actually represents a drug-related health effect (as opposed to **confounding** due to background prevalence of symptoms in the patient population or some other cause) and to elicit data that will help to clarify the magnitude and frequency of adverse events as well as mitigating factors, such as:

- **Comorbidity** (multiple cofounding health conditions)
- **Polypharmacy** (use of multiple prescription drugs and self-medications)
- Patient demographics.

— *See* Elmendorf, 2010; Obama, 2016; OMB (2016, 2015, and 2009) (discussing this issue).

CHAPTER SUMMARY

- Managed care was meant to control health care costs and coordinate health care delivery, but four decades after its inception, it has accomplished neither goal.
- Health care providers lack the financial incentives to provide quality care.
- Policymakers should understand that people at the bottom of the economic pyramid behave the same as those at the top; they save their health care dollars to put toward what is important to them.
- Integrated health care systems are meant to combine hospitals and health care providers together into one system.
- Integrated health care systems are difficult to accomplish because of the differences in practice, culture, and philosophy between different medical groups.
- The unresolved polarities and tensions between different medical groups hinder the progress of integrated health care systems; there is no formula for successful integration.
- As with other industries, global health care firms must balance the need to be simultaneously large and small, centralized and decentralized, and global and local.

- Physicians in particular desire to retain personal autonomy within integrated health care systems, and so they organize into collectives in order to maintain their influence.
- A diversification strategy is needed within an integration strategy because once an integrated system comes into existence it is usually operating within more than one market.

LAW NOTES

1. Congress defined the term **effective** in the federal **Food, Drug, and Cosmetic Act of 1938**, declaring that the federal government must prohibit the sale of any drug if "there is a lack of substantial evidence that the drug will have the effect it purports or is represented to have under the conditions of use prescribed, recommended, or suggested in the proposed labeling thereof …" (*See* 21 U.S.C.A. § 355(d)). This meaning of *effective* distinguishes effectiveness from **efficacy**. Efficacy refers to the propensity of a drug to achieve intended, observable clinical improvement. An anti-hypertensive drug is efficacious if it lowers blood pressure. Effectiveness, by contrast, refers to the fit between what happens to patients and what the pharmaceutical manufacturer promises on drug labels. An example of a drug that achieves efficacy but not effectiveness might be an anti-hypertensive drug that functions to lower blood pressure but not by as many millimeters as its manufacturer claims it will (Persad, 2015a).

2. No research studies are considered as critical or useful in determining clinical effectiveness as those using human participants, also known as clinical trials. It is only in the past few decades that the clinical trial has emerged as the preferred method in the evaluation of medical interventions. More specifically, **randomized controlled clinical trials** are considered the gold standard of medical research for evaluation of therapeutic efficacy (Lewellen, 2015). In medical products review, any conclusion regarding a medical product's safety or efficacy depends on what is found in controlled clinical trials on humans. Of course, a number of pieces of information are relevant to the effectiveness analysis. For instance, an explanation of the chemical structure, studies on stability, and descriptions of the physiochemical characteristics can tell scientists much about how a drug will be likely to act in the human body (*See* FDA, 2001).

3. Numerous groups advocate the medical home model to expand and enhance the role of primary care physicians in coordinating care and medical homes, including:

   - The American Academy of Family Physicians
   - The American Academy of Pediatrics
   - The American College of Physician
   - The American Osteopathic Association

   (*E.g.*, Morrell & Krouse, 2014).

4. The Joint Commission International was formed in 1994 by the Joint Commission on Accreditation of Healthcare Organizations and its not-for-profit arm, **Quality Healthcare Resources, Inc.** Four years later, the Joint Commission International launched its international accreditation program in response to growing interest in worldwide accreditation and quality improvement. Today, three Apollo hospitals (Chennai, Hyderabad, and Indraprastha) are ranked shoulder to shoulder with the Mayo Clinic and the Cleveland Clinic (Wharton, 2008).

5. Will the new models of U.S. health care be primary care centered affordable care organizations or the population health schemes being developed by major health systems (*See* Chapter on Population Health Management)? Or a host of new services entirely: retail clinics, telehealth offerings, or on-demand home care (*See* Chapter on Health Information and Telehealth Technologies)? Most importantly: What do these new low-cost models mean for patients in terms of quality and affordable access?

REFERENCES

AAFP (American Academy of Family Physicians), American Academy of Pediatrics, American College Physicians, and American Osteopathic Association. (2007). *Joint principles of the patient-centered medical home.* Leawood, KS: AAFP.

Abramowicz, M. et al. (2011). Randomizing law. *University of Pennsylvania Law Review, 159,* 929–1005.

Alspach, C., Chief Majority Health Counsel, House Energy and Commerce Committee. (2016, June 17). Remarks at the Plenary Session on 21st Century Cures: Which Are the Most Transformative Provisions and How Do They Accomplish Major Change? At the Drug Information Association) Annual Conference, Washington, DC.

Americans for Tax Fairness. (2014). Walmart on tax day: How taxpayers subsidize America's biggest employer and richest family. Washington, DC: Americans for Tax Fairness.

Angeli, F., & Jaiswal, A. K. (2016). Business model innovation for inclusive health care delivery at the bottom of the pyramid. *Organization and Environment, 10*, 1–22.

Asch, S. M., et al. (2006). Who is at greatest risk for receiving poor-quality health care? *New England Journal of Medicine, 354*, 1147–2619.

Bennie, R. (2014). Medical tourism: A look at how medical outsourcing can reshape health care. *Texas International Law Journal, 49*, 583–600.

BHI (Blue Health Intelligence). (2016). *How to build a successful big data analytics program in health care.* Chicago, IL: BHI.

Blair, R. D., & Sokol, D. D. (2015). *The Oxford handbook of international antitrust economics.* New York, NY: Oxford University Press.

Blair, R. D., et al. (2016). Hospital mergers and economic efficiency. *Washington Law Review, 91*, 1–70.

Bynum, J. P. W., et al. (2016). *A report of the Dartmouth Atlas Project: Our parents, ourselves: Health care for an aging population.* Hanover, NH: The Dartmouth Institute for Health Policy and Clinical Practice, Dartmouth College.

Carlin, C. S., et al. (2015). The impact of hospital acquisition of physician practices on referral patterns. *Health Economics, 25*, 439–457.

Choi, R. (2015). Increasing transparency of clinical trial data in the United States and the European Union. *Washington University Global Studies Law Review, 14*, 521–547.

Chou, F. (2015). Implementing medical tourism regulation in the face of the volume shock problem. *Seton Hall Legislative Journal, 40*, 187–217.

Conley, J. (2013). Medicare and medical tourism: Saving Medicare with a global approach to coverage. *Elder Law Journal, 21*, 183–222.

Cortez, N. (2011). Embracing the new geography of health care: A novel way to cover those left out of health reform. *Southern California Law Review, 84*, 859–931.

Cutler, D. M., & Morton, F. S. (2013). Hospitals, market share, and consolidation. *Journal of the American Medical Association, 310*, 1964–2170.

Dafny, L. (2014). Hospital industry consolidation - Still more to come? *New England Journal of Medicine, 370*, 198–207.

Dolgin, J. L. (2015). Unhealthy determinations: Controlling medical necessity. *Virginia Journal of Social Policy and the Law, 22*, 435–490.

Elmendorf, D. W., Director, Congressional Budget Office. (2010, February 10). Key issues and budget options for health reform. Hearing before the Senate Budget Committee, Washington, DC.

FDA (U.S. Food and Drug Administration). (2001). *Guidance for industry: Safety pharmacology studies for human pharmaceuticals.* Bethesda, MD: FDA.

Freeman, D., et al. (2015). Best practices and cost controls: Improving healthcare access through innovation and communication. *Tennessee Journal of Law and Policy, 10*, 108–144.

Gaddy, M. (2015). Uniting all interests: Law and regulation must facilitate pharmacogenomic development. *Annals of Health Law, 25*, 50–63.

Hammond, J. B. (2014). Balance billing and physician reimbursement in an age of austerity. *Health and Biomedical Law Society, 9*, 435–492.

Hermer, L. D., & Lenihan, M. (2014). Medicaid matters: The future of Medicaid supplemental payments: Can they promote patient-centered care? *Kentucky Law Journal, 102*, 287–326.

Hoffmann, A. (2010). Minute medicine: Examining retail clinic legal issues and legislative challenges. *Health Matrix: Journal of Law and Medicine, 20*, 467–497.

Hoffman, S. (2015). Citizen science: The law and ethics of public access to medical big data. *Berkeley Technology Law Journal, 30*, 1741–1803.

IOM (Institute of Medicine). (2013). *Patients charting the course: Citizen engagement in the learning health system.* Washington, DC: National Academies Press.

___. (2009). *Roundtable on evidence-based medicine. Leadership commitments to improve value in health care: Finding common ground.*

___. (2006). *Performance measurement: Accelerating improvement.*

Johnson & Johnson. (2016). *Annual report.* New Brunswick, NJ: Johnson & Johnson.

JCT (Joint Commission International). (2016). *JCI-accredited organizations.* Oak Brook, IL: JCT.

Jost, T. S. (2007). The Massachusetts health plan: Public insurance for the poor, private insurance for the wealthy, self-insurance for the rest? *University of Kansas Law Review, 55*, 1091–1102.

Kaiser Family Foundation. (2015). *State health facts: Medical coverage of the total population.* Menlo Park, CA: Kaiser.

Kleinrock, M., Director, Research Development, IMS Institute for Healthcare Informatics (2016, June 27). Remarks at the Session on The Value of Medicines: How Stakeholders' Differing Views are Reshaping the Use of Medicines at the DIA (Drug Information Association) Annual Conference, Philadelphia, PA.

Lewellen, N. (2015). Beating the odds: The public policy of drug efficacy and safety. *Minnesota Law Review, 99*, 1541–1570.

Lewis, J. I. D., & Wittlin, M. (2015). Entering the innovation twilight zone: How patent and antitrust law must work together. *Vanderbilt Journal of Entertainment and Technology Law, 17*, 517–572.

Madison, K. (2014). Building a better laboratory: The federal role in promoting health system experimentation. *Pepperdine Law Review, 41*, 765–815.

Mantel, J. (2015a). A defense of physicians' gatekeeping role: Balancing patients' needs with society's interests. *Pepperdine Law Review, 42*, 633–726.

___. (2015b). Spending Medicare's dollars wisely: Taking aim at hospitals' cultures of overtreatment. *University of Michigan Journal of Law Reform, 49*, 121–177.

Marino, B., et al. (2015). A case for federal regulation of telemedicine in the wake of the Affordable Care Act. *Columbia Science and Technology Law Review, 16*, 274–347.

Marmor, T. T., & Sullivan, K. (2016). Medicare at 50: Why Medicare-for-all did not take place. *Yale Journal of Health Policy, Law and Ethics, 15*, 141–182.

McCann, R. W., & Vorrasi, K. M. (2014). Antitrust treatment of physician-hospital integration post-*FTC v. St. Luke's. Antitrust: American Bar Association, 28*, 75–81.

McDonough, J. E. (2012). The road ahead for the Affordable Care Act. *New England Journal of Medicine, 367*(3), 199–201.

McGlynn, E., et al. (2003). The quality of health care delivered to adults in the U.S. *New England Journal of Medicine, 348*(26), 2635–2645.

Morrell, M. T., & Krouse, A. T. (2014). Accountability partners: Legislated collaboration for health reform. *Indiana Health Law Review, 11*, 225–301.

Muzaurieta, J. L. (2015). Surgeries and safaris: Creating effective legislation through a comparative look at the policy implications, benefits, and risks of medical tourism for the American patient. *Temple International and Comparative Law Journal, 29*, 115–167.

Nation, III, G. A. (2016). Hospital chargemaster insanity: Heeling the healers. *Pepperdine Law Review, 43*, 745–781.

Nichols, L. M. (2011). Making health markets work better through targeted doses of competition, regulation, and collaboration. *Saint Louis University Journal of Health Law and Policy, 5*, 7–25.

Obama, B. H. (2016, February 9). *The budget message of the President to the Congress of the United States*. Washington, DC: The White House.

O'Connor, C. (2014, April 15). Report: Walmart workers cost taxpayers $6.2 billion in public assistance. *Forbes*, 37–43.

OMB (Office of Management and Budget). (2016). *The President's fiscal year 2017 budget proposal*. Washington, DC: Office of Management and Budget.

___. (2015). *The budget for fiscal year 2016: Investing in America's future*.

___. (2009). *The President's fiscal year 2010 budget proposal*.

PBB (Patients Beyond Borders). (2016). *Medical tourism statistics and facts*. Chapel Hill, NC: Patients Beyond Borders.

Persad, G. (2015a). Priority setting, cost-effectiveness, and the Affordable Care Act. *American Journal of Law and Medicine, 41*, 119–166.

___. (2015b). The medical cost pandemic: Why limiting access to cost-effective treatments hurts the global poor. *Chicago Journal of International Law, 15*, 559–611.

Pew Research Center. (2013). *Health fact sheet: Highlights of the Pew Internet Project's research related to health and health care*. Washington, DC: Pew Research Center, Internet, Science and Tech.

Reid, P. R., et al. (2005). *Building a better delivery system: A new engineering/health care partnership*. Washington, DC: Institute of Medicine and National Academy of Engineering.

Reinhardt, U. E. (1995). Turning our gaze from bread and circus games. *Health Affairs, 14*(1), 33–35.

Rodwin, M. A., & Abramson, J. D. (2012). Clinical trial data as a public good. *Journal of the American Medical Association, 308*, 871–873.

Rozga, K. (2009). Retail health clinics: How the next innovation in market-driven health care is testing state and federal law. *American Journal of Law and Medicine, 35*, 205–231.

Sage, W. M. (2016). Assembled products: The key to more effective competition and antitrust oversight in health care. *Cornell Law Review, 101*, 609–699.

Satz, A. B. (2015). Fragmentation after health care reform. *Houston Journal of Health Law and Policy, 15*, 171–228.

Schoen, C., et al. (2007). *Bending the curve: Options for achieving savings and improving value in U.S. health spending*. New York, NY: Commonwealth Fund.

Schutzbank, A., Vice President of Clinical Development, Iora Health. (2016, February 19). Remarks at the panel discussion on Disruptive Care Delivery; Putting Patients at the Center; The Race to Re-engineer How Care is Delivered at the Wharton Health Care Business Conference on The Innovation Game; The Race Between Entrants+Incumbents, Philadelphia, PA.

Tawney, R. H. (2013). *The acquisitive society*. Eastford, CT: Martino Publishing (Original work published 1921).

Thurman, C. B. (2014). The risk of shared savings in the commercial insurance market. *University of Louisville Law Review, 52*, 559–581.

Underhill, K. (2016). When extrinsic incentives displace intrinsic motivation: Designing legal carrots and sticks to confront the challenge of motivational crowding-out. *Yale Journal on Regulation, 33*, 213–279.

U.S. Census Bureau. (2015) *Current population survey: Annual social and economic supplement*. Suitland, MD: U.S. Department of Commerce, U.S. Census Bureau.

Wharton School at the University of Pennsylvania. (2008). Apollo Hospitals' Suneeta Reddy: Medical tourism is a huge market. *India Knowledge@Wharton*.

Wharton School at the University of Pennsylvania. (2006). A brave new world beckons Indian innovators and entrepreneurs. *Knowledge@Wharton*.

___. (2006a). Wal-Mart: Is there a downside to going upscale?

___. (2002). Business processes are moving from the west to other parts of the world.

___. (2000). Drug prices: Let the competition begin.

WHO (World Health Organization). (2008). *Policy perspectives on medicines: Pharmacovigilance: Ensuring the safe use of medicines*. Geneva, Switzerland: WHO.

Wiley, L. F. (2016). From patient rights to health justice: Securing the public's interest in affordable, high-quality health care. *Cardozo Law Review, 37*, 833–889.

Woodcock, J., Director, Center for Drug Evaluation and Research, FDA (2016, June 17). Remarks at the Plenary Session on 21st Century Cures: Which Are the Most Transformative Provisions and How Do They Accomplish Major Change? At the DIA (Drug Information Association) Annual Conference, Washington, DC.

© Andy Dean Photography/ShutterStock, Inc.

CHAPTER 13

Strategic Restructurings in Health Care: Mergers/Acquisitions and Bankruptcies

"Property is nothing but a basis of expectation of wealth creation."

— **Jeremy Bentham** (1748-1832), British legal and social reformer, founder of modern utilitarianism

IN BRIEF

This chapter looks at the two sides of the restructuring coin: mergers and acquisitions, and bankruptcies. On one side, not-for-profit to for-profit conversions and private equity buyouts in the health care sector have experienced the greatest expansion of any industry group in recent years, with transactions and dollar amounts doubling across the nation. On the other side, the largest not-for-profit health care failure in the United States, the bankruptcy of the Allegheny Health Education and Research Foundation (AHERF), is discussed. A popular integration strategy among academic medical centers, namely that of acquiring hospitals and physicians in order to corner patient markets, is examined. While AHERF did not survive its bankruptcy, the ever-evolving understanding and lessons to be taken from its fall are as relevant today as when it filed for protection from its creditors. It could be said that the demise of AHERF foreshadowed the current financial environment that is impacting the health care industry.

LEARNING OBJECTIVES

Upon completion of this chapter readers should be able to:

1. Describe details of the increase in hospital restructurings and bankruptcies.
2. Explain how managed care failed to solve the health care issues of high costs and poor quality.
3. List the means used and reasons for conversions of not-for-profit hospitals to for-profit hospitals.
4. Discuss private equity buyouts of for-profit and bankrupt hospital restructurings.
5. Explain the processes of health insurance plan conversions.
6. Describe what made underwriting at not-for-profit and for-profit hospitals the same.
7. Detail the reasons why the health care industry has few rewards for quality preventive care.

KEY TERMS

Accountable care organizations
Affordable Care Act of 2010
Bad debt reserves
Bankruptcy
Bond ratings
Capital expenditure budgets
Credit crunch
Debt-to-cash flows

Debt-to-equity ratios
Defined benefit pension plans
Defined contribution plans
Divestment
Dodd-Frank Wall Street Reform and
    Consumer Protection Act of 2010
Economies of scale
Enron era

Equity joint ventures
Full risk, fully capitated contracting
Market capitalization value
MBIA Insurance
Moody's Investor Service
Not-for-profit to for-profit conversion
Payer mix
Primary care

Private equity buyout
Profit margin
Revenue streams
Risk-based payment
Sarbanes-Oxley Act of 2002

State-mandated closures
Strategic alliances
Synergies
Third-party payment system
Uncollectible accounts receivables

Underwriting practice and
   policies
Vertical integration
Zero-sum game posture
Zone of insolvency

FACT OR FICTION

Voluntary Closure of Insolvent Hospitals in Medically Underserved Communities

Are states required to consider the needs of individual patients before approving the closure of insolvent hospitals in medically underserved communities?

St. Vincent's Catholic Medical Centers was one of New York City's most comprehensive health care systems and the largest provider of emergency care in the city. Before filing for **bankruptcy**, St. Vincent's had seven tax-exempt hospitals with 2,500 affiliated physicians and employed 12,500 employees. Over the course of its bankruptcy, St. Vincent's divested itself of all its acute care hospitals, except its flagship hospital in Greenwich Village.

Two communities, Central Brooklyn and Southeast Queens/Jamaica were especially impacted by St. Vincent's **divestment** activities. Both communities suffer from some of the worst health outcomes in the nation. Both Central Brooklyn and Jamaica have an infant mortality rate that is more than quadruple the rate in Greenwich Village. Additionally, the percentage of adults with diabetes in both Central Brooklyn and Jamaica is more than double the percentage in Greenwich Village. New York City designated the Central Brooklyn neighborhoods of Crown Heights, Bedford-Stuyvesant, and East New York/Brownsville as neighborhoods with the most severe health-related problems in the city. Compared to New York City overall, adults in Crown Heights, Bedford-Stuyvesant, and Brownsville have:

- 20% higher rate of heart disease hospitalizations
- 25% higher rate of deaths from cancer
- 35% higher rate of mental illness hospitalizations
- 60% higher rate of drug-related deaths
- 66% higher rate of asthma-related hospitalizations
- More than 70% higher rate of alcohol-related hospitalizations
- More than twice the rate of HIV-related deaths

While similar to Central Brooklyn, Jamaica—which has toxic sites from aluminum, glass, metal, plastics, steel, and textiles manufacturing activities for the aerospace, apparel, automotive, building, computer, electronics, and telecommunications industries—has the second highest asthma hospitalization rate for children, and the highest rate of asthma prevalence for adults in New York City. Jamaica also houses New York City's transitional housing program for homeless men and women living with HIV/AIDS, who in turn relied on a St. Vincent's hospital for their treatment needs. This was the backdrop behind St. Vincent's divestment plans.

Residents in Central Brooklyn and Jamaica claimed the hospital closures in their communities would amount to a health care catastrophe and urged the government to consider their needs in determining the future of the hospitals. Specifically, the residents asked the government to determine whether patients would have alternative sites for medical services, and requested that the public be allowed to participate in the decision-making process before closing hospitals affecting local health care. As part of the bankruptcy reorganization, St. Vincent's directed $800 million in funds derived from the divestment of its six hospitals in Central Brooklyn and Jamaica to reconstruction of its Greenwich Village hospital. St. Vincent's reasons for closing or selling its hospitals were never based on the health needs of the communities, but rather on the need to cover its costs.

— *See* Law Fact at the end of this chapter for the answer.

Principles and Applications

One of the consequences of the **Affordable Care Act of 2010** (42 U.S.C.A. §§ 18001 *et seq.*) is that it has sparked a wave of mergers and acquisitions, a trend that will rapidly continue as health care systems establish more **accountable care organizations** in response to the law (Wharton, 2015). Accountable care organizations tie payment amounts to improvements in quality and reductions in the total cost of care, in essence forcing providers into accepting **risk-based payments**. Health providers have responded to this call to accept more risk by growing and strengthening themselves in numbers, as illustrated in **FIGURE 13-1**.

Health care consolidation could help health providers weather the Affordable Care Act reforms (Gaynor & Town, 2012b). Merged hospitals, however, are struggling to reap efficiency gains with their integration deals, and they are failing to pass along any benefits of size to their end customers, the patients (Town, 2011). It is very sobering (FTC & DOJ, 2015).

Mergers and Acquisitions

Weaker and slower health care systems face a greater chance of restructuring or even bankruptcy in this competitive space (Houle & Fleece, 2011). The hospital industry, in particular, is likely to see a significant rise in restructurings. What is particularly notable about the recent spate of mergers and acquisitions is that it is both horizontal and vertical. Hospitals are not just buying other hospitals; they are also acquiring physician practices, rehabilitation facilities, and other ancillary health providers as well as health insurers (Wharton, 2015).[LN1]

Physician Practice Acquisitions

Combining hospitals with physician practices has raised prices and per-capita costs of care (FTC & DOJ, 2015). So far, hospitals and physician practice mergers have higher costs of care, and their quality is not any better (Wharton, 2015). Similarly, the preponderance of the evidence is that patients lose after hospital mergers. Patients lose because hospitals' prices rise and that gets translated into higher health insurance premiums (Pauly et al., 2015). Mergers and acquisitions also leave patients with fewer health choices, because in this uncertain new world created by the Affordable Care Act, the barriers to entry for new hospitals to start up are just too high (Wharton, 2015). The harm to competition is significant, and it is hard to undo.

At the same time, hospitals acquiring bolt-on services like physician practices are not necessarily a negative in the new world of health care reform. That is because the Affordable Care Act rewards hospitals for reducing readmissions and achieving other goals that reflect a healthier patient base (Gaynor & Town, 2015). Part of the larger landscape here is a shift in the values behind the system: the positive movement toward keeping consumers healthy as opposed to just treating them when they are sick (Wharton, 2015). Consolidations should be viewed in the context of this larger shift. How does an integrated health care system keep a patient population healthy? A scale has to be created in order to meet this objective efficiently and effectively (Town, 2011). Three or four hospitals in a local system may make good strategic sense provided the mergers and acquisitions are not just about hospitals (Gaynor & Town, 2012a). The strategy must include ancillary organizations, rehabilitation facilities, and so on, that are required to keep a population healthy.

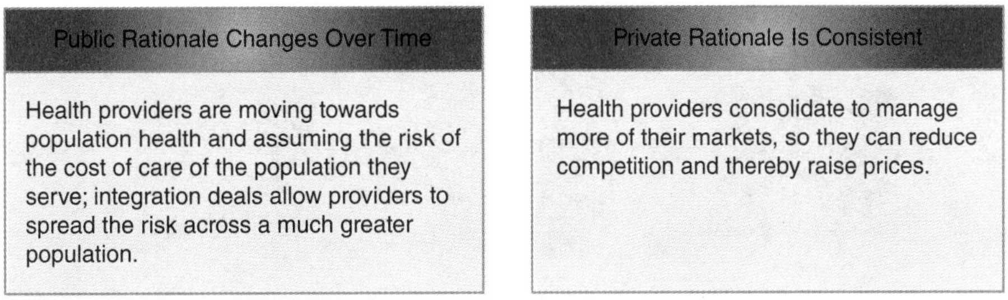

Public Rationale Changes Over Time	Private Rationale Is Consistent
Health providers are moving towards population health and assuming the risk of the cost of care of the population they serve; integration deals allow providers to spread the risk across a much greater population.	Health providers consolidate to manage more of their markets, so they can reduce competition and thereby raise prices.

FIGURE 13-1 Rationalizing Health Providers' Herding Instinct

Strategic Restructurings

The issue of strategic restructurings in this chapter, as illustrated in **FIGURE 13-2**, is substantial and important and explained with broad strokes as opposed to overly technical details. The way in which hospitals choose to change the way they provide medical services will determine the direction of the next movement in the upcoming decade or so. When the managed care movement began, the problems it was supposed to solve were clear:

- Accountability in the health care marketplace was weak.
- Delivery of care was fragmented and poorly coordinated.
- Financial incentives associated with the traditional **third-party payment system** were inflationary.

(Greaney, 2014; Grusin, 2015).

What is considerably harder to determine is where the health care industry will go from where it is at the present. There are really only two sure things: first, the United States does not have it correct yet, and, second, integration deals and other strategic restructurings, particularly hospital bankruptcies, will be part of the next attempt to give Americans the highest standard of care with continued innovation and broader access to new technologies at a lower and more affordable cost (Wharton, 2015).

Competition in Health Care

Several factors contribute to the changing landscape of the health care industry and the increasing need of not-for-profit providers to compete with for-profit providers. With governmental regulation of the industry blurring and market forces becoming more dominant, medicine has taken on a primarily business rather than service orientation. The line between the standards governing for-profit and not-for-profit enterprises has blurred.

Not-For-Profit to For-Profit Conversions

While the current **not-for-profit to for-profit conversion** phenomenon has been characterized as the largest redeployment of charitable assets in the Anglo-American world since Henry VIII closed the monasteries in 1536-1540 (Rizk, 2015), there is no denying the last two decades have seen the proliferation of billion-dollar deals in health care. It is nearly impossible to accurately estimate the number of not-for-profit to for-profit conversions in the health care industry

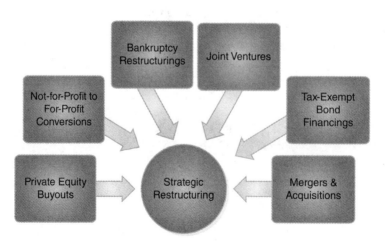

FIGURE 13-2 Strategic Restructurings

(FTC & DOJ, 2015) because they have generally occurred as changes in corporate form rather than as straightforward mergers and acquisitions (*See* Reiser, 2011).

Hospital Conversions

For-profit hospitals unquestionably generate a healthier **profit margin** than other hospitals. For-profit hospitals hover around a 9% profit margin, while the margins for not-for-profits are approximately 4% (MedPAC, 2015). Public hospitals (owned by local governments, states, and the federal government) fall slightly behind the not-for-profits (Rizk, 2015).

Many of the converted not-for-profit hospitals were the victims of insolvencies and bankruptcies. For instance, Tenet Healthcare, the nation's third largest hospital chain behind Community Health Systems and Hospital Corporation of America, obtained ownership of several significant hospital systems affiliated with academic medical centers during bankruptcy proceedings. Tenet Healthcare acquired eight hospitals in eastern Pennsylvania out of the bankruptcy of AHERF and retained two as acute care facilities; the other six hospitals were sold and subsequently converted to other uses such as rehabilitation, skilled nursing, or outpatient-care centers, or closed.[LN2]

It appears that hospital conversions do not generally result in economies of scale and lower prices unless the hospitals are small and the markets are competitive (FTC & DOJ, 2015). As a consequence, there is widespread concern that when hospitals convert, they will focus more on maximizing profits and improving **payer mix**, and less on quality of care or patient outcomes (McPherson, 2014). Yet, there is no evidence that conversions to for-profit status are associated with worsening quality, clinical outcomes, or access to care (Joynt et al., 2013).

Health Plan Conversions

Most of the converted managed care organizations have merged with one another or with historically for-profit insurers. As illustrated in **TABLE 13-1**, five firms now dominate the health insurance market:

Significantly, the regional Blue Cross (covering hospitals) and Blue Shield (covering physicians) plans, which were established during the Depression to provide expansive hospital and physician coverage and were historically not-for-profit in the orientation, recently changed their corporate status by eliminating the requirement that their licensees be organized as not-for-profit corporations (Hazen & Hazen, 2012). When the largest, and often dominant, not-for-profit provider in health care finance or delivery moves toward a for-profit model, the extent of the conversion phenomenon becomes clearer (Fox, 2014; *See* Joynt et al., 2013).

Restrictive Underwriting　The time has passed when not-for-profit Blue Cross plans were more lenient underwriters in assessing the eligibility of individuals to receive health insurance coverage than their for-profit commercial counterparts. **Underwriting practices and policies** at Blue Cross plans are now broadly consistent with those of for-profit insurers (Cogan et al., 2012). Underwriters place similar restrictions on how much health care coverage individuals should receive for their health care and establish comparable ranges of deductibles and co-payments that are available for any given premium. Underwriting decisions on certain individuals with certain diseases and illnesses are the same (Joynt et al., 2013). While the underwriting practices of the converted Blue Cross plans are generally similar in comparison to for-profit insurers, if not more lenient, conversions adversely impacted the risk selection in some states.

TABLE 13-1　Profile of the For-Profit Health Insurance Industry

Corporations and State Headquarters	Sales	1-Year Sales Change	Number of Employees
UnitedHealth Group (MN)	$157.1 billion	20.4%	200,000
Anthem (IN)	$79.2 billion	7.1%	53,000
Aetna (CN)	$60.4 billion	4.1%	50,100
Humana (KY)	$54.3 billion	11.9%	50,100
Cigna (CN)	$38.0 billion	8.7%	39,300

Data from: 2015 Annual Report filings with the U.S. Securities and Exchange Commission (Fiscal Year Ends December 31).

And, although the evidence is mixed, members of Blue Cross plans are more satisfied and receive better service and a somewhat higher quality of care (Cohen, 2014; Fox, 2014).

Increased Profit Incentives   Not-for-profit to for-profit conversions of the Blue Cross plans increased profit incentives. Therefore, such conversions should result in:

- Higher health insurance rates in market segments where Blue Cross plans hold considerable market power and as a result are subject to less aggressive rate regulation
- Improved operational efficiency and customer service
- Lower medical loss ratios, which can be achieved by tougher negotiations with health providers and more refined underwriting and risk selection practices
- Unlocked wealth that can be devoted explicitly to health-related charitable purposes

(Fox, 2014; *See* Hall & Conover, 2006).

For health providers, however, for-profit conversions of Blue Cross and managed care plans remain a jumbled hodgepodge of unrelated profit incentives. Sometimes the conversion changes the incentives, but not often. Also, while the financial pressures on the health care industry are significant, there are still few rewards for providing quality preventive health care.

Private Equity Buyout of For-Profit Hospitals

For-profit hospitals, as illustrated in **TABLE 13-2**, have made attractive private equity buyout targets because many have:

- Endowments that can be used to reduce the debt from going private
- Large **capital expenditure budgets**
- Strong cash flows

(FTC & DOJ, 2015; McCue, 2011).

However, hospitals can also be risky buys, thanks to industry headwinds over the last several years. Some for-profit hospitals are opting to go private because expansion through nontraditional mergers and acquisitions, such as **equity joint ventures** and **strategic alliances**, take time to pay off, which is time they do not have as publicly traded entities.

The Hospital Corporation of America was the first publicly traded for-profit hospital chain to go private in 2006 (HCA, 2015). A trio of private equity firms paid almost $21 billion plus the assumption of about $12 billion in debt. These firms included:

- Bain Capital
- Kohlberg Kravis Roberts
- Merrill Lynch Global Private Equity

TABLE 13-2   Profile of the For-Profit Hospital Industry

Corporations and State Headquarters	Sales	1-Year Sales Change	Number of Hospitals	Number of Beds	Number of Employees
Hospital Corporation of America (TN)	$39.7 billion	7.5%	165	42,900	233,000
Community Health Systems (TN)	$19.4 billion	4.3%	160	27,000	137,000
Tenet Healthcare (TX)	$18.6 billion	12.2%	84	20,800	134,600
Universal Health Services (PA)	$9.4 billion	12.1%	25	N/A	72,600
LifePoint Health (TN)	$5.2 billion	16.3%	71	8,200	40,000

Data from: 2015 Annual Report filings with the U.S. Securities and Exchange Commission.

Within months, the nation's third largest hospital chain, Triad Hospitals, agreed to convert from a public to a private company. Triad had an acquisition agreement with private equity investors, CCMP Capital Advisors, and the private equity arm of Goldman Sachs for $4.7 billion, plus the assumption of about $1.7 billion in debt (Francis, 2007). Before the conversion occurred, Triad changed its mind and merged with Community Health Systems. The combined company has a market capitalization value of about $19 billion (CHS, 2015).

With number two-ranked Tenet Healthcare too heavily leveraged to be attractive, the most likely remaining acquisition candidate is LifePoint Hospitals, with a **market capitalization value** of about $2 billion. A hindrance to future acquisitions, however, may be the growing belief among private equity investors that the payment problems facing the hospital industry will not be solved anytime soon. Buyouts of faltering hospitals cannot cover gaping wounds that continue to get bigger. *See generally* Wallace, 2012.

Bankruptcy Restructurings

Some see the whole hospital industry sliding slowly into insolvency. Before the hospital industry can bottom out, more hospitals will have to seek mergers, buyouts, or bankruptcy restructurings to cure their balance sheets (Wharton, 2015). Most hospitals can get by even if they are insolvent, but they do not have much of a future unless their capital structures are fixed. Growth and recovery both depend on the political aftermath of the Affordable Care Act's implementation. In the meantime, most health care systems are watching costs and raising short-term revenues in whatever ways they can (e.g., Gowrisankaran et al., 2016).

More than half of the U.S. hospitals are not seeing enough insured patients to provide sufficient revenue to fund operations, and many are on the brink of insolvency or already are insolvent. For instance:

- More than 2,000 of the over 5,600 hospitals do not make a profit treating patients
- Nearly 750 hospitals that do turn a profit earn less than what they need to fund day-to-day operations
- One-fifth of the nation's acute-care hospitals do not have enough funds for their most basic capital expenditures, such as making facility repairs or meeting essential maintenance needs
- While many hospitals continue to operate despite insolvency, an increasing number are filing for bankruptcy

(Gowrisankaran et al., 2016; Maizel & Lane, 2011; Pauly et al., 2015).

Moreover, capital expenses are underfunded in the range of $10 billion to $20 billion because hospitals are using capital funds to support their day-to-day operations. While hospital insolvencies and hospital bankruptcies are rampant, the U.S. Trustee Program, the government agency charged with ensuring the integrity of the bankruptcy system, projects there will be continued insolvencies and more bankruptcies moving forward.

A top tier of about 500 to 1,000 hospitals are consistently profitable; they claim a substantial share of the market and have excellent credit ratings. The problem facing the roughly 5,000 hospitals that remain is widespread overcapacity: too many beds and too few insured patients (Houle & Fleece, 2011). Hospitals are now also competing with same-day surgery centers and outpatient clinics and all sorts of innovative ways to deliver health care. While hospital occupancy levels move downward:

- Costs continue to increase
- Payment rates continue to decline
- There is an increasing number of underinsured patients

(FTC & DOJ, 2015).

Hospitals are not immune to the nation's **credit crunch**; they are forced to take on costly loans, if they can get financing at all. Lenders willing to finance a hospital at an amount that was five or six times its cash flow a decade ago are now making loans only in amounts that are double or triple the hospital's cash flow. What was a relatively secure financial environment in health care has now become rather tenuous. Hospitals then turn to other, often unsteady, sources of revenue, including:

- Cash from for-profit subsidiary operations (such as anesthesiology, emergency departments, parking lots)
- Local and state government assistance
- Philanthropists

(Fishman & Schwartz, 2015).

MANAGEMENT AND LAW ISSUES

1. Is it time for hospitals to challenge underpayment by Medicare/Medicaid insurance?
2. Although the government has a legitimate interest in keeping the costs of health care as low as possible, are hospitals being unfairly coerced to accept society's financial burdens when they take a loss on each Medicare/Medicaid-insured patient admitted?

Insurer-Provider Integration

Just as competition is resulting in more **vertical integration** between hospitals and physician practices, hospitals are becoming their own insurance providers (Stilson et al., 2015; Wharton, 2015). Hospital-owned health insurance is appealing in areas where consumers are price sensitive, such as the state-based exchanges where co-branded, provider-specific insurance products have emerged over the last few years (Argue & Stein, 2015; *See* Gaynor & Town, 2012b).[LN3] Hospitals are able to cost-effectively eliminate the middleman; when customers sign up for hospital-owned insurance, the hospitals get them as patients, giving hospitals a return on investment for managing patient care (Gaynor & Town, 2015).

Many integrated health networks have chased the dream of becoming the next Kaiser Permanente, the California-based managed care giant that encompasses hospitals and insurance coverage, but none have succeeded (FTC & DOJ, 2015).[LN4] The current class of consolidators is also running into obstacles. Kaiser was set up in the 1930s and 1940s. It began with physicians and added on a health insurance plan, and the hospitals came later. Most other insurer-provider integrations start with hospitals and bolt physician practices and health insurer services to them (Wharton, 2015). So they start at a different point that is more hospital-focused.

Unfortunately, hospitals that have integrated with health plans do not improve their clinical or financial efficiency (FTC & DOJ, 2015). In fact, the more the hospitals invest in expanding their health care delivery networks, the more likely they are to suffer lower profit margins and return on capital (Wharton 2015). Consumers lose when hospitals also own health insurance plans, because when hospital prices rise it gets translated into higher health insurance premiums (Gaynor & Town, 2015).

The Nation's Largest Not-For-Profit Health Care Bankruptcy

Hospitals have not succeeded in their mission to provide better coordinated care that results in improved health outcomes or lower costs (FTC & DOJ, 2015). The current trends in provider consolidation and provider network strategies are sobering in light of the failure of AHERF (Goldsmith et al., 2015). Before filing for bankruptcy, AHERF and its 53 corporate affiliates:

- Employed almost 30,000 employees
- Enrolled about 3,300 students a year at the nation's largest medical school, the Philadelphia-based Allegheny University of Health Sciences (formerly the Medical College of Pennsylvania and Hahnemann University; now the merged medical schools are known as MCP Hahnemann University of the Health Sciences, managed by Drexel University)
- Reported $2.05 billion in revenues
- Were composed of 15 hospitals in the Philadelphia and Pittsburgh markets with more than 500 physicians

(SEC, 2000; Weinstein, 2000).

When AHERF finally entered bankruptcy, it left behind $1.5 billion in debt and 65,000 creditors. *See In re Allegheny Health, Education and Research Foundation*, 292 B.R. 68 (U.S. Bankruptcy Court for the Western District of Pennsylvania 2003). When bankruptcy proceedings were finally concluded, unsecured creditors received about 12 cents on the dollar from the bankrupt estate (DeMott, 2012). According to the American Bankruptcy Institute, the AHERF bankruptcy meant the dismantling of the nation's largest not-for-profit health care provider. It led to thousands of layoffs and the sale of six Philadelphia hospitals to Tenet Healthcare, an investor-owned corporation. Further, it called into question a popular strategy of acquiring, at almost any cost, physicians, researchers, and medical facilities in order to corner health care markets (Kallenberger, 2015).

Flawed Corporate Strategy

AHERF had a mandate from its board to develop a premier medical education and research system. The strategy was to:

- Achieve synergies among the assets acquired
- Build regional market share to leverage managed care payers
- Develop the nation's first statewide integrated delivery system grounded in academic medicine
- Negotiate contracts from managed care insurers that covered all the costs of enrollees' health care
- Use community/suburban hospitals to refer private-pay patients to AHERF's teaching hospitals

(Maizel & Lane, 2011; SEC, 2000).

For various reasons, all five elements of AHERF's strategy were problematic:

- Academic medical centers had trouble persuading suburbanites to use older teaching hospitals in the cities, especially as suburban hospitals were developing revenue-generating services that attracted urban patients
- Few of its delivery systems had enough market share to leverage managed care payers, especially in markets such as Philadelphia with an excess of hospital beds and physicians
- Hospitals' enthusiasm for assuming risk, and the willingness of managed care to pass it on, meant huge hospital losses
- Pennsylvania had few statewide payers that could contract with a statewide integrated delivery system
- **Synergies** and **economies of scale** through mergers are difficult to realize, especially with rapid expansion

(SEC, 2000; Weinstein, 2000).

While these five assumptions were serious miscalculations, it is important to remember they were common sense wisdom at the time (Pauly et al., 2015). Everyone believed them, consultants were propounding them, and the trade literature was repeating them. After a while, if enough people repeat something, it becomes believable. Other leading academic medical centers, including the University of Pennsylvania Health Care System, went the same route (Wharton, 2015).

The expansion of AHERF into Philadelphia was conducted at a breakneck pace over a 10-year period (mid-1980s to the mid-1990s), with major acquisitions every two years, including the following:

- Graduate Health System and its six hospitals
- Hahnemann Medical College and its hospital
- Medical College of Pennsylvania and its two affiliated hospitals
- United Hospitals' four hospitals and Suburban Medical Associates

(Maizel & Lane, 2011; Sather, 2010).

Breakdown in Accountability

No one single factor led to the bankruptcy of AHERF. Instead, there was a breakdown in accountability at almost every level. Indeed, much of the intrigue of this bankruptcy stems from the fact that so many actors, both inside and outside AHERF, played a part in its demise (SEC, 2000; Weinstein, 2000). AHERF fell behind with its technology and innovation for unmet medical needs on top of everything else. Among those who failed both AHERF and the communities it served were:

- Accountants
- Auditors
- Board of directors
- Bond-rating agencies
- Senior management

(DeMott, 2012).

Even with this cast of hundreds, however, the former AHERF chief executive officer, former chief financial officer, and former general counsel, are particularly deserving of criticism (SEC, 2000; Weinstein, 2000). While they were never found to have used AHERF for their own personal gain, their flawed assumptions, fiscal irresponsibility, and questionable ethical decisions remained the topic of litigation for more than a decade after their downfall (SEC, 2000; Weinstein, 2000).

- The chief executive officer faced nearly 1,500 criminal charges and pleaded no contest to a single misdemeanor count of misusing charitable funds and was sentenced to 11 to 23 months of prison with work-release; he was paroled in three months.
- The chief financial officer paid a $40,000 Securities and Exchange Commission fine and entered an accelerated rehabilitative disposition program that permits non-violent, first-time offenders a chance to wipe their records clean upon completion of program requirements.
- Following the bankruptcy, AHERF's management team and board were the subject of over 60 unsecured creditors' lawsuits.

(Cobb & Hotchkiss, 2004; DeMott, 2012).

Investigations by the Pennsylvania Attorney General and the federal Pension Benefit Guaranty Corporation are still not finalized. Creditors received an undisclosed settlement from AHERF's auditor, Coopers and Lybrand, now part of PricewaterhouseCoopers in 2013. Three auditors were sanctioned by the SEC; one paid a fine of $40,000 (SEC, 2000).

Faulty Integration of Primary Care Practices

As part of its vertical integration strategy, AHERF purchased physician practices in the mistaken belief this would help secure inpatient referrals to the system's hospitals. Unfortunately, its competitors were following the same strategy and the bidding wars that resulted meant physicians were frequently overpaid for their practices. Purchase agreements filed in the Philadelphia Court of Common Pleas showed that physician practices acquired by AHERF generally received:

- $70,000 to $150,000 for their assets irrespective of actual value (which was considerably less in almost all instances)
- 60% of their revenues above $470,000 to $570,000

(Weinstein, 2000; *See In re Allegheny Health, Education and Research Foundation*, 383 F.3d 169 (U.S. Court of Appeals for the 3rd Circuit, 2004)).

Furthermore, the physicians received an average annual salary of $220,000 to $250,000 for five years. In addition, the contracts included no means to monitor practice productivity (SEC, 2000; Weinstein, 2000). Along with aggressively acquiring physician practices, AHERF was also recruiting clinical and research faculty, which it hoped would:

- Attract federal funding
- Enhance its research reputation
- Result in more patients and thus new revenue sources

(SEC, 2000).

Again, high payments were the norm. Before its bankruptcy, AHERF was recruiting three orthopedists a year and guaranteeing salaries of about $3.9 million a year. At the time, the average salary for a surgical orthopedist in Philadelphia was $67,000, which was lower than the national norm because of the regional oversupply of orthopedists.

None of the acquisitions were strong financial performers; most were financial underperformers and highly leveraged. The purchase of the Graduate Health System was the straw that broke the back of AHERF. It was a huge debt load and the Graduate hospitals were marginal performers financially. There was simply no way to manage it all (Evans, 2012).

Overloaded Debt

Debt was a major problem for AHERF. When the newly established AHERF consisted of Pittsburgh-based Allegheny General Hospital in 1983, the hospital had just $67 million in debt. With a teaching affiliation with the University of Pittsburgh Medical Center, Allegheny was one of only a few hospitals nationwide with an 'Aa' bond rating (SEC, 2000; Weinstein, 2000). By 1998, a hugely expanded AHERF, which by then had been using Allegheny General Hospital and other facilities in the western part of the state to subsidize its eastern operations, had a debt of $1.3 billion (*In re Allegheny Health, Education and Research Foundation*, Case No. 98-25773 (U.S. Bankruptcy Court for the Western District of Pennsylvania)). Its margins during the mid-1990s fell to zero, compared to 6 to 12% at competing hospitals.

Dominant Bargaining Power of Payers

While AHERF engaged in **full-risk, fully capitated contracting** with local health insurers, that is, accepting a fixed payment per year for each enrollee for agreed-upon medical services, its precarious financial condition was significantly aggravated by Philadelphia's competitive health care environment. AHERF lost over $100 million each year as it attempted to become a player in the managed care market; during its last year of operation, it was losing $1 million per day (Fishman & Schwartz, 2015). Pittsburgh, in western Pennsylvania, had only five health plans and 15% managed care penetration. By contrast, Philadelphia, in eastern Pennsylvania, had 11 health plans and a 30% managed care penetration. Moreover, two plans (Aetna U.S. Healthcare and Keystone Blue Cross) dominated the managed care market, which meant they had enormous power over health providers in Philadelphia (SEC, 2000; Weinstein, 2000). With five major academic medical centers (and more than 80 teaching and community hospitals vying for market share and research funding,[LN5] Philadelphia was:

- Over-bedded
- Over-doctored
- Over-staffed
- Over-utilized

This competitive environment only increased the bargaining power of insurers. This was all at a time when neither the Federal Trade Commission nor the U.S. Department of Justice pursued antitrust actions against insurers for their managed care activities to control health care markets. Thus, AHERF was receiving insurance premiums that were increasing in number but at a lower rate, while the cost of providing health care for its expanded health care system was escalating (Kallenberger, 2015).

AHERF's expansion occurred just as the state's entire Medicaid population was switched to managed care. At the same time, federal efforts were reducing hospital payments for Medicare patients. On top of all this, insurers were all lowering their payment rates (SEC, 2000; Weinstein, 2000). The combined decline in revenues relentlessly hit an already overextended AHERF. In the end, AHERF spent a lot on building an integrated health care system but achieved little leverage over the payers.

Faulty Financing Mechanisms

Health policy in the United States has, for more than a century, paradoxically incentivized the growth as well as the commercialization of not-for-profit organizations in the health care industry (Kallenberger, 2015). This policy paradox was starkly evident in the operation of AHERF. Months before the bankruptcy, senior management was praising AHERF's:

- Ever-expanding physician networks
- Growing market share
- Organizational growth
- Productivity improvements

What was not disclosed were the financing mechanisms used to fuel AHERF's decade of growth, including:

- Enormous debt from all the acquisitions
- Failing to account for **bad debt reserves** from **uncollectible accounts receivables**
- Hidden internal cash transfers among the 55 affiliated corporations
- Internal subsidies not justified by business activities
- Invasion of restricted funds from employee pension funds
- Misappropriation of funded depreciation and reserve cash accounts for operating expenses
- Misuse of research and scientific grants
- Raids on restricted assets and hospital endowments

(DeMott, 2012; SEC, 2000; Weinstein, 2000; *See Official Committee of Unsecured Creditors of Allegheny Health Education and Research Foundation v. PriceWaterhouseCoopers, LLP*, 989 A.2d 313 (Supreme Court of Pennsylvania 2010)).

Complex Tax-Exempt Hospital Bonds

Economic thinkers have been saying for at least two centuries that the more important a given kind of thing becomes to society, the more likely there will be hard-edged rules to manage it (Komesar, 2001). Ever sharper lines are drawn around rules of entitlements so everyone knows who has what. Unfortunately, the rules surrounding hospital debt and bond-rating mechanisms are complex and little understood; the need for clarity is not lacking.

It is safe to assume many actors, both inside and outside AHERF, failed to understand that the credit ratings given to AHERF's debt referred to the rating of its insurer, not the rating of the health care system. This lack of clarity produced a greater level of misunderstanding for AHERF to resolve, as its hospitals were largely stuck in a **zero-sum game posture** with payers. AHERF was trying to maximize its position with payers, just as funds to reimburse hospitals became scarce, making bond funds more highly valued.

Confusion like this all along the debt line helped conceal AHERF's true financial condition. One example illustrates the complexity involved in debt financing of large integrated health care systems like AHERF (Evans, 2012). **Moody's Investor Service** (Moody's) covered debt issued by five sets of AHERF hospitals, some of which found their debt publicly downgraded as AHERF's financial problems grew (SEC, 2000; Weinstein, 2000).

The hospital debt of the Graduate Health System was junk bond status with a 'Ba2' rating at the time its six hospitals were acquired by AHERF. However, another AHERF affiliate, the Delaware Valley Obligated Group, which consisted of two hospitals affiliated with the Medical College of Pennsylvania, Hahnemann University Hospital, and the four hospitals acquired from United Hospitals, had hospital bonds separately rated as 'Aaa' insured, 'Baa' (barely above investment grade), and 'Ba' (below investment grade). AHERF:

- Called five sets of outstanding bonds on 13 hospitals in Eastern Pennsylvania
- Insured the Delaware Valley Obligated Group bonds using **MBIA Insurance**
- Refinanced the debt on the 13 hospitals
- Reissued new bonds under the Delaware Valley Obligated Group

(SEC, 2000; Weinstein, 2000).

MBIA Insurance, the nation's largest health care bond insurer, was the underwriter of the newly issued bonds. By insuring the debt, AHERF garnered an 'Aaa' rating for the Delaware Valley Obligated Group's debt (the highest quality rating possible). Yet in reality this rating had nothing to do with any improvement in the underlying financial health of the system issuing the bonds. Rather, the rating reflected the underlying health of the insurance company (MBIA's rating by Moody's) to insure that debt. The financial troubles at AHERF thus remained hidden from the public.

Meanwhile, although Moody's internal assessment noted weak operations at AHERF, underlying **bond ratings** are not published unless requested by the issuers. AHERF never requested that its ratings be made public until it was forced to do so. When Moody's finally released its underlying rating of the Delaware Valley Obligated Group, debt that had been rated 'Aaa' suddenly had a publicized underlying rating of 'B3' (not much assurance that bond interest and principal payments will ever be paid). Within days, the Delaware Valley Obligated Group ratings fell to 'Caa1' (poor-quality rating, such issues are dangerous and may be in default), and AHERF was forced to declare bankruptcy (SEC, 2000). During the hospital debt financing, no one apparently examined how Delaware Valley Obligated Group's bond ratings matched up with the following standard financial fundamentals:

- **Debt-to-cash flows**
- **Debt-to-equity ratios**
- Falling or rising **revenue streams**

(SEC, 2000; Weinstein, 2000).

Hidden Cash Transfers

AHERF's use of hidden cash transfers to cope with the system's growing financial problems was another factor leading to the bankruptcy filing. This situation came about because AHERF's corporate bylaws allowed management of the parent company to move cash from one operating affiliate to another, without the consent of the affiliate or the knowledge of the board.

Financial management of AHERF was in boxes, so each person or entity within AHERF could see only one piece of the overall financial position. Moreover, the operating revenues and endowment funds from the scattered operations of AHERF were commingled in a complex structure that permitted funds to be transferred between operating affiliates as needed and financial results to be manipulated to make affiliate operations look as favorable as possible (SEC, 2000; Weinstein, 2000).

AHERF's external auditors gave AHERF a clean bill of health in its last audit before its bankruptcy. *See Official Committee of Unsecured Creditors of Allegheny Health Education and Research Foundation v. PriceWaterhouseCoopers, LLP*, 989 A.2d 313 (Supreme Court of Pennsylvania 2010). Included in this audit was a large, improperly recorded loan and financial statements that were later retracted, precipitating an investigation by the SEC (SEC, 2000; Weinstein, 2000). AHERF was the first not-for-profit health care system the SEC ever pursued (Acquaviva, 2010).

Inadequate Governance Structure

Following AHERF's bankruptcy, hospital governing boards were held to a higher standard of corporate governance (Evans, 2012). The weak governance structure of AHERF included a parent board of between 25 and 35 directors, as opposed to the standard 13 to 17, and a network of 10 different boards responsible for AHERF's various operations (SEC, 2000; Weinstein, 2000). There was little overlap in membership and little diversity in industry experience.

The composition of their boards of directors is an area of debate among hospitals. Should physician practitioners serve on hospital boards? One factor used by the Internal Revenue Service for determining tax-exempt status is board composition. Tax-exempt hospitals operate to serve public rather than private interests. *See* Revenue Ruling 69-545. AHERF also suffered from weak board composition and several inherent conflicts of interest. Two months before the bankruptcy of AHERF, the chief executive officer ordered the repayment of an $89 million loan to a bank consortium including Mellon Bank without board discussion or approval. Five board members were current or former directors or executives with Mellon, including its former chairman, who was AHERF's chairman (SEC, 2000; Weinstein, 2000).

Wealth Destruction

The eight hospitals owned by AHERF in the Philadelphia region were valued between $500 million and $550 million before the bankruptcy filing, based on various bids received from Vanguard, a potential buyer. The final acquisition of the eight Philadelphia hospitals by Tenet Healthcare for $345 million suggests a loss of $200 million. In actuality, eight not-for-profit hospitals were converted to for-profit entities, and then all but two were subsequently sold or closed. In addition, the eight Philadelphia hospitals had more than $206 million in endowments and other restricted accounts that disappeared (*See* Eason, 2010). AHERF's bankruptcy also spelled the demise of its western hospitals in Pittsburgh, including its one-time star performer and flagship, Allegheny General Hospital (SEC, 2000; Weinstein, 2000).

Unfunded Pension Funds

The sale of the Philadelphia hospitals owned by AHERF required termination of its pension plans. *See Burstein v. Retirement Account Plan for Employees of Allegheny Health Education and Research Foundation*, 334 F.3d 365 (U.S. Court of Appeals for the 3rd Circuit 2003). However, AHERF was $40 million short in funds needed to terminate plans in its Philadelphia operations, a shortfall that became the responsibility of the federal Pension Benefit Guaranty Corp.[LN6]

Excess System Capacity

The State of Pennsylvania and local officials in Philadelphia and Pittsburgh overreached their legitimate government roles and stepped in to make sure the AHERF hospitals did not close. In terms of saving jobs, keeping all the existing hospitals open was a good political strategy, but in terms of maintaining efficiency, excess bed capacity was expensive and not needed. The poor performance of AHERF's integration strategies was cloaked by inaccurate, misleading financial results and certain institutional structures that limited the scrutiny and efficient response of the health

Lessons Learned from the Largest Not-For-Profit Health Care Failure in the United States

1. Acquisitions based on the arguments of expansion, greater size, and greater market presence still require prudence and due diligence; there is no substitute for precise financial analysis and close scrutiny.
2. Bankruptcy may not be the best course of action if the troubles are more the product of:

   - Management's unethical and lax behavior
   - Lack of due diligence by the governing board
   - Presence of inflexible and rigid organizational forces

3. Bond insurance masks the underlying credit quality of bonds.
4. Clear and precise financial reports and related disclosures should be made to the governing board to better enable its directors to identify when financially distressed subsidiaries and affiliates may enter the **zone of insolvency**.
5. Commission-based acquisitions in the health care industry provide too strong an incentive to cut deals rapidly; the chief operating officer of AHERF's physician network received a $15,000 commission for each physician practice acquired, which resulted in overpaying for most practices.
6. Corporate governance policies and executive employment agreements should confirm the obligation of management to advise the governing board regularly on financial conditions.
7. Disciplined growth strategies need to be supported by rigorous financial planning and feasibility analysis.
8. Disclosure of the financial performance of all of a health system's operations creates greater transparency and builds credibility.
9. For health care systems with multiple subsidiaries and operating affiliates, intrasystem financial arrangements should be treated as loans from the parent to the affiliates, as appropriate. This enhances the ability of the parent to be treated as a legitimate creditor of the affiliates in the event of any affiliate's bankruptcy or other similar condition.
10. If the troubles of a health care system are the product of managerial decisions that initially succeed but then fail in the face of new market forces, bankruptcy is not necessarily an undesirable outcome.
11. Lack of market knowledge meant that the vertical integration into **primary care** through acquisition of physician practices generally resulted in losses of $75,000 to $100,000 per physician per year for AHERF.
12. Physician integration is critical to grow market share, but it needs to be methodical and measured.
13. Strong governance and oversight of management are needed to ensure accountability.
14. The credit-rating agencies (Standard & Poor's, Moody's, and Fitch Ratings) are constrained in providing ratings to risky health system bonds; financial ratings should be free of political influence.
15. There is no firm evidence that large health care systems understand value chain management and the need for revenue generation in their operations, and there is some evidence that these ideas are completely divorced from patient care.
16. When in the zone of insolvency, governing boards should pay particular attention to the financial impact of proposed corporate transactions; financial advisors should be retained to advise on the fairness of any such transactions.

Gaynor & Town, 2015; *Official Committee of Unsecured Creditors of Allegheny Health Education and Research Foundation v. PricewaterhouseCoopers, LLP*, 989 A.2d 313 (Supreme Court of Pennsylvania 2010); SEC, 2000; *See also, In re: Bankruptcy Appeal of Allegheny Health Education and Research Foundation*, 252 B.R. 309 (U.S. District Court for the Western District of Pennsylvania 1999).

care markets (SEC, 2000; Weinstein, 2000). Nevertheless, actions were taken for political and regulatory reasons, not economic reasons.

Message to Other Health Care Systems

The larger question of what AHERF's bankruptcy means for the health care industry is not easily answered. But not much has changed since AHERF went bankrupt. Hospitals are still justifying mergers in much the same way as AHERF did during the mergers and acquisitions boom of the 1990s, when the rapid spread of managed care left hospitals desperate to maintain market share (Wharton, 2015).

While few health care systems, if any, operate in exactly the same way AHERF did, there is a significant segment of the hospital industry that continues to face multimillion-dollar losses and financial trouble due to practices similar to AHERF's:

- Continued pressure on reimbursement payments
- Eroded hospital endowments and investments from stock-market turbulence
- Growing competition from specialty care centers, such as diagnostic imaging boutiques
- High costs of hiring top physicians
- Increasing costs of keeping up with medical technology
- Mounting debt collection problems and defaults by patients unable to pay their medical bills
- Paucity of gifts and pledges depended upon over the past decade

(Kallenberger, 2015; Pauly et al., 2015).

It should be kept in mind that what happened at AHERF occurred years before the financial crises and the corporate scandals of the so-called **Enron era** of inflated corporate revenues were brought to light (*See* **Sarbanes-Oxley Act of 2002**, 15 U.S.C.A. §§ 7201 *et seq.* (federal legislation that was enacted to oversee the financial reporting landscape); *See also* **Dodd-Frank Wall Street Reform and Consumer Protection Act of 2010** (12 U.S.C.A. §§ 1021 *et seq.* (federal legislation that reshaped credit ratings regulation of financial products, corporate governance and disclosure, and transparency)). Health care entities are well advised to stay grounded and do honest business even in times of relentless frustration and financial stress.

Basis of Expectations

The finance rules in this chapter are the beliefs that:

- Bankruptcy restructurings repair capital structures
- Not-for-profit to for-profit conversions improve profit margins
- **Private equity buyouts** permit businesses that are generating revenue but are not yet profitable enough to realize their economic potential with the opportunity to grow their capital bases by expanding into new markets or financing acquisitions
- Private equity generally needs 10 to 15 years to achieve its expected returns
- Tax exemptions present enormous growth and innovation opportunities
- Tax-exempt hospital bond financings provide needed capital for growth
- Tax-exempt hospitals should take advantage of their exemption from taxes as opposed to manipulating this financial incentive

(McCue, 2011; Wharton, 2015).

Their great advantage, or so it is commonly thought, is that the rules signal, in a clear and distinct language, precisely what the financial obligations are for health care businesses and how health care systems may take care of their interests (Pauly et al., 2015).

Moving forward, the health care industry is increasingly in need of customized health care systems and innovative approaches that will enable the insurance and hospital industries to be more responsive to the needs and wishes of their customers (Minvielle et al., 2014). The U.S. health care industry is in for an era of innovative medicine if it puts finances at the service of scientific advances and not vice versa (Wharton, 2015).

MANAGEMENT AND LAW ISSUES

3. Should bankruptcy courts consider the health needs of medically underserved communities in bankruptcy reorganizations?
4. Should bankruptcy courts ever approve the reorganization of a health care system that chooses to divest all of its hospitals in medically underserved communities while it reallocates the funds from their closures and sales to a flagship hospital in a higher income community?
5. Should the legal privilege of bankruptcy be available to health care systems that abuse the tax-exempt hospital bond system and/or other standard financial controls, or should such systems be forced to go out of business and simply close their doors?

LAW FACT

Voluntary Closure of Insolvent Hospitals in Medically Underserved Communities

Are states required to consider the needs of individual patients before approving the closure of insolvent hospitals in medically underserved communities?

No. Public needs analysis or community input is not required before states approve the voluntary closure of insolvent hospitals as opposed to involuntary, **state-mandated closures**. Hospitals need only provide information to patients regarding their ability to obtain future medical services and establish a plan for the storage and safekeeping of patient medical records. *See* 11 U.S.C.A. § 351 (2005) (describing procedure to dispose of patient records in health provider's bankruptcy).

— *In re: St. Vincent's Catholic Medical Centers*, 449 B.R. 209 (U.S. District Court for the Southern District of New York 2011), *affirmed*, *In re St. Vincent's Catholic Medical Centers of New York*, 581 Fed. Appx. 41 (U.S. Court of Appeals for the 2nd Circuit 2014).

CHAPTER SUMMARY

- One of the consequences of the Affordable Care Act is that hospitals are increasingly facing restructurings and/or bankruptcies.
- The managed care framework failed to solve high costs and poor quality-of-care problems; restructuring is the next step being taken in hopes of improving the delivery of U.S. health care.
- One popular method of restructuring involves not-for-profit hospitals converting into for-profit hospitals.
- Other methods involve private equity buyouts of for-profit hospitals and bankruptcy restructurings.
- Very few hospitals are consistently profitable, have excellent credit ratings, or claim a substantial share of their market.
- Beyond patients' failure to pay medical bills and lack of full payment from third-party payers, hospitals are also faced with overcapacity and competition from other forms of health care delivery (such as freestanding surgical facilities), all contributing to hospitals' financial viability problems.
- One of the most shocking health care bankruptcies was AHERF, the nation's largest not-for-profit health care provider, which had been rapidly expanding just prior to filing for bankruptcy.
- Among the problems that contributed to AHERF's financial failure were a breakdown in accountability, flawed corporate strategy, overloaded debt, faulty integration of primary care practices, lack of bargaining power as compared to third-party payers, faulty financing mechanisms, improperly rated bonds, hidden cash transfers, inadequate corporate governance, and excess system capacity.
- Results of AHERF's bankruptcy included wealth destruction and unfunded pension funds.
- Despite AHERF's failure, other academic medical centers continue to engage in and suffer from some of the same behaviors that led to AHERF's downfall.
- Hospital bankruptcies are likely to continue because, although health care is viewed slightly differently than other service industries, it is subject to the same financial constraints as all service industries.

LAW NOTES

1. The aggressive mergers and acquisitions of Norwell Health have turned this not-for-profit health care system into the largest employer in New York, encompassing 21 hospitals and over 450 facilities and physician practices, including skilled nursing facilities, rehabilitation centers, a medical research institute, homecare services, and hospice facilities. With its own medical school (Hofstra Northwell School of Medicine), Norwell Health employs more than 2,300 physicians. Norwell Health recently began offering medical coverage through its own insurance company, CareConnect. *See generally* Jarrett, 2016.

2. Of the 8 hospitals with close to 2,500 licensed beds acquired by Tenet Healthcare during the AHERF bankruptcy, only 2 facilities remain as acute-care hospitals:

   - City Avenue Osteopathic Hospital: 228 beds (closed)
   - Elkins Park Hospital: 280 beds (sold to the Albert Einstein Medical Network and converted to a rehabilitation center)
   - Graduate Hospital: 330 beds (sold to the University of Pennsylvania Health Care System and converted to a rehabilitation and hospice center)
   - Hahnemann University Hospital: 618 beds
   - Medical College of Pennsylvania Hospital: 465 beds (closed and sold to for-profit Solis Healthcare and now in bankruptcy)
   - Parkview Hospital: 200 beds (closed and then sold to for-profit Cancer Treatment Centers of America and converted into a skilled nursing home)
   - St. Christopher's Hospital for Children: 183 beds
   - Warminster Hospital: 180 beds (sold to Solis Healthcare and then resold to current owners, Abington Memorial Hospital and since converted into an outpatient-care center)

   Pauly, 2015; Wharton, 2015.

3. Full integration under one umbrella gives the insurance and hospital industries the tools to align with the Affordable Care Act's mandates and value-based health care incentives (Stilson et al., 2015). For instance:

   - Ascension Health acquired Michigan-based U.S. Health and Life Insurance (Ascension, 2015).
   - Catholic Health Initiatives acquired a majority interest in Soundpath Health, a Washington-based Medicare Advantage company (CHI, 2012) and then extended its reach into the Georgia insurance sector by acquiring QualChoice (CHI, 2014).
   - HealthPartners and Park Nicollet Health Services merged, creating a 1,500 physician network with hospitals and multispecialty group practices integrated with HealthPartners' insurance plan and its own provider network in Minnesota (HealthPartners, 2012)
   - Highmark, the nation's fourth largest Blue Cross/Blue Shield affiliate, acquired West Penn Allegheny Health System with eight hospitals in Western Pennsylvania (Evans, 2013 and 2015).
   - Insurer Wellpoint acquired CareMore, a health care operator that provides managed care to the Medicare-insured population in Los-Angeles (Lattman, 2011).

4. The quest by integrated health care systems to be like Kaiser Permanente may prove to be an unreachable goal (Town, 2011). Indeed, Kaiser has expanded to six additional states and the District of Columbia, but has not quite found the same success in those places as it did in California. In 2013, Kaiser sold off its faltering Ohio division to Catholic Health Partners. Significant scale is required to be both the insurer and the hospital system (Wharton, 2015). To get there, substantial business has to be taken from existing health providers and high fixed-cost facilities established (Gaynor & Town, 2012b). It is hard to get the scale to make it work.

5. Five major academic medical centers are located in Philadelphia:

   - Jefferson Health System
   - MCP (Medical College of Pennsylvania)-Hahnemann Health System
   - Philadelphia College of Osteopathic Medicine
   - Temple University Health System
   - University of Pennsylvania Health Care System

6. The Pension Benefit Guaranty Corp. currently guarantees payment of pension benefits earned by U.S. workers and retirees participating in private-sector **defined benefit pension plans**. The percentage of defined benefit plans, however, has dropped dramatically in the last two decades (today, most employers have switched their plans to **defined contribution plans** or cash balance plans, such as 401(k) plans, which employees are responsible for funding, often matched by employer contributions but with no guaranteed retirement benefits and subject to market risks) (Greszler, 2015). While the Pension Benefit Guaranty Corp. receives no funds from general tax revenues, it faces a current retiree shortfall of over $62 billion in pension benefits (PBGC, 2015). Operations are financed by:

   - Assets from pension plans trusted by the Pension Benefit Guaranty Corp.
   - Insurance premiums set by Congress and paid by sponsors of defined benefit pension plans

- Investment income
- Recoveries from the corporations formerly responsible for the pension plans (if there are still ongoing concerns and their pension obligations have not been discharged in bankruptcy proceedings)

The maximum monthly guarantee for failed multiemployer plans is capped at $12,900 per year, while beneficiaries in single-employer programs can receive up to $60,136 per year, depending on work history. Financial problems arise for retirees of bankrupt corporations when they expected to receive significantly higher annual retirement incomes. Unfortunately, most retirement plans are not insured by the Pension Benefit Guaranty Corp., including:

- Employers with fewer than 26 employees
- Federal, state, or local governments
- Profit-sharing and 401(k) pension plans
- Religious organizations
- Retirement plans offered by professional service employers (such as physician practices)

REFERENCES

Acquaviva, G. L. (2010). The certification of unsettled questions of state law to state high courts: The Third Circuit's experience. *Penn State Law Review, 115*, 377–406.

Argue, D. A., & Stein, S. D. (2015). Cross-market health care provider mergers: The next enforcement frontier. *American Bar Association Antitrust, 30*, 25–36.

Ascension Health Alliance. (2015, March 31). *Management's discussion and analysis of financial condition and results of operations for Ascension: As of and for the nine months ended March 31, 2015 and 2014.* St Louis, MO: Ascension Health Alliance.

Bentham, J. (1789). *Introduction to principles of morals and legislation.* London, England: W. Pickering.

CHI (Catholic Health Initiatives). (2014, May 1). *Press release: Catholic Health Initiatives, QualChoice Agreement Finalized.* Englewood, CO: CHI.

____. (2012, October/November). Press release: CHI acquires majority interest in Medicare Advantage plan.

CHS (Community Health Systems). (2015). *Annual report.* Franklin, TN: CHS.

Cobb, A. L., & Hotchkiss, H. G. (2004). AHERF: It may have started with a bang, but did it end in a whimper? *American Bankruptcy Institute, 13*(8), 30–31.

Cogan, J. F., et al. (2012). *Working paper: Cost shifting from the uninsured: Assessing the evidence.* Philadelphia, PA: Wharton School of the University of Pennsylvania.

DeMott, D. A. (2012). Further perspectives on corporate wrongdoing, *in pari delicto*, and auditor malpractice. *Washington and Lee Law Review, 69*, 339–354.

Eason, J. K. (2010). Motive, duty, and the management of restricted charitable gifts. *Wake Forest Law Review, 45*, 123–180.

Evans, C. (2012). What makes you so special?: Ending the credit rating agencies' special status and access to confidential information. *Valparaiso University Law Review, 46*, 1091–1138.

Evans, M. (2015, April 1). Highmark Health reports larger operating loss for 2014. *Modern Healthcare*, p. 7.

____. (2013, April 29). Highmark completes West Penn deal, announces new system. *Modern Healthcare*, p. 5.

Fishman, J. J., & Schwartz, S. (2015). *Nonprofit organizations: Cases and materials* (University Casebook Series: 5th ed.). Eagan, MN: Foundation Press.

Fox, D. M. (2014). Policy commercializing nonprofits in health: The history of a paradox from the 19th century to the Affordable Care Act. *The Milbank Quarterly, 93*(1), 179–210.

Francis, T. (2007, February 6). Hospitals look healthy for now: After Triad deal, buyout players may find new gems. *Wall Street Journal*, p. C3.

FTC (Federal Trade Commission) & DOJ (U.S. Department of Justice). (2015, February 24–25). *Joint public workshop on examining health care competition.* Washington, DC: FTC and DOJ, Antitrust Division.

Gaynor, M., & Town, R. J. (2015). The industrial organization of health care markets. *Journal of Economic Literature, 53*(2), 235–284.

____. (2012a). Provider competition. In M. V. Pauly, et al. (Eds.), *Handbook of health economics* (Vol.2, pp. 499–637). Amsterdam, NL: North Holland Publishing Co.

____. (2012b). The impact of hospital consolidation; update. *Robert Wood Johnson Synthesis Report, Policy Brief No. 9*, 1–8.

Goldsmith, J., et al. (2015). *Panel on addressing pricing power in health care markets: Integrated delivery networks: In search of benefits and market effects.* Washington, DC: National Academy of Social Insurance.

Gowrisankaran, G., et al. (2016, in progress). Government policy and the dynamics of market structure: Evidence from critical access hospitals.

Greaney, T. L. (2014). The tangled web: Integration, exclusivity, and market power in provider contracting. *Houston Journal of Health Law and Policy, 14*, 59–93.

Greszler, R. (2015). *Bankrupt pensions and insolvent pension insurance: The case of multiemployer pensions and the PBGC's multiemployer program.* Washington, DC: The Heritage Foundation.

Grusin, S. L. (2015). Holding health insurance marketplaces accountable: The unheralded rise and imminent demise of structural reform litigation in health care. *Annals of Health Law, 24*, 337–401.

Hall, M. A., & Conover, C. J. (2006). For-profit conversion of Blue Cross plans: Public benefit or public harm? *Annual Review of Public Health, 27*, 443–463.

Hazen, T. L., & Hazen, L. L. (2012). Punctilios and nonprofit corporate governance; A comprehensive look at nonprofit directors' fiduciary duties. *University of Pennsylvania Journal of Business Law, 14*(2), 348–416.

HCA (Hospital Corporation of America). (2015). *Annual report.* Nashville, TN: HCA.

Health-Partners. (2012, August 30). *Press release: Health-Partners, Park Nicollet sign agreement to combine organizations.* Bloomington, MN: HealthPartners.

Houle, D., & Fleece, J. (2011). *The new health age: The future of health care in America*. Naperville, IL: Sourcebooks.

Jarrett, M., Senior Vice President, Clinical Excellence and Chief Quality Officer, Northwell Health (2016, November 3). Keynote Speaker at the 2015 U.S. News and World Report Best Hospitals Conference on the Healthcare of Tomorrow, Washington, DC.

Joynt, K., et al. (2013). Impact of hospital conversion to for-profit status on acute myocardial infarction care. *Journal American College of Cardiology, 61*(10S), 17–37.

Kallenberger, M. B. (2015). Policing charitable organizations: Whose responsibility is it? *Louisiana Law Review, 76*, 661–689.

Kimberly, J. R. (2013). Globalization and the business of health care. *European Journal of International Management, 7*(2), 159–170.

Komesar, N. K. (2001). *Law's limits: Rule of law and the supply and demand of rights*. New York, NY: Cambridge University Press.

Lattman, P. (2011, June 8). WellPoint to buy CareMore for $800 million. *New York Times*, p. A1.

Maizel, S. R., & Lane, M. D. (2011). The sale of nonprofit hospitals through bankruptcy: What BAPCPA (The Bankruptcy Abuse Prevention and Consumer Protection Act) wrought. *American Bankruptcy Institute Journal, 30*(5), 12–75.

MedPAC (Medicare Payment Advisory Commission). (2015). *Hospital inpatient and outpatient services*. Washington, DC: MedPAC.

McCue, M. J. (2011). Association of market, organizational and financial factors with the number and types of capital expenditures. *Health Care Management Review, 36*(1), 67–77.

McPherson, B. (2014). Time for a new test on hospitals' tax exemptions. *Modern Healthcare, 4*(14), 27.

Pauly, M. V., et al. (2015). *Handbook of health economics*. Amsterdam, Netherlands: North Holland Publishing Co.

PBGC (Pension Benefit Guaranty Corp.). (2015). *PBGC annual report*. Washington, DC: PBGC.

Reiser, D. B. (2011). Charity law's essentials. *Notre Dame Law Review, 86*, 1–27.

Rizk, E., President and Chief Executive Officer, Accretive Health. (2015, February 20). Keynote Speaker at the 2015 Wharton Health Care Business Conference on Disruption Amidst Uncertainty: Adapting and Innovating for the Future, Philadelphia, PA.

Sather, S. W. (2010). Resolving conflicts between bankruptcy and administrative law. *Texas Tech Administrative Law Journal, 11*, 267–304.

SEC (Securities and Exchange Commission). (2000, June 30). *In the Matter of Allegheny Health, Education and Research Foundation: Order Instituting Cease-and-Desist Proceedings, Making Findings, and Imposing Cease-And-Desist Order*. Accounting and Auditing Enforcement Release No. 1283; Administrative Proceeding File No. 3-10245. Washington, DC: SEC.

Stilson, J., et al. (2015). Reading the tea leaves: Evaluating potential antitrust concerns in vertical mergers between insurers and health care providers. *Antitrust American Bar Association, 30*, 11–12.

Town, R. J. (2011). The effects of consolidations on hospital quality. *International Journal of the Economics of Business, 18*(1), 127–131.

Weinstein, S. W., Attorney, Office of Municipal Securities, U.S. Securities and Exchange Commission. (2000, August 1). Speech on Understanding AHERF: Observations on the Recent Settlements Involving Allegheny Health, Education and Research Foundation at the American Institute of Certified Public Accountants National Healthcare Industry Conference, Washington, DC.

Wharton School at the University of Pennsylvania. (2015). Hospital consolidation: Can it work this time? *Knowledge@Wharton*.

CHAPTER 14

© Andy Dean Photography/ShutterStock, Inc.

Antitrust Regulation of Health Care Providers

"If a firm has been 'attempting to exclude rivals on some basis other than efficiency,' it is fair to characterize its behavior as predatory."

— **Robert H. Bork** (1927-2012), former U.S. Solicitor General and former Circuit Judge of the U.S. Court of Appeals for the District of Columbia Circuit

IN BRIEF

This chapter addresses how antitrust regulations influence hospitals in their transition from managed care to consumer-driven health care. Often what makes good business sense conflicts with antitrust ideals. Antitrust rules and regulations can be difficult to understand and comply with, as the law only sanctions certain kinds of anticompetitive behavior and can be fairly nuanced as far as who is protected and who has standing to sue when wronged by monopolies and conspiracies in restraint of trade. Ideally, antitrust laws should be based upon concrete wrongful conduct, and should not force the health care industry to adopt defensive, cumbersome business practices that actually impede their ability to compete.

LEARNING OBJECTIVES

Upon competition of this chapter readers should be able to:

1. Understand the two major types of anticompetitive conduct that are prohibited: monopolization and conspiracies in restraint of trade.
2. Outline the elements of monopolization.
3. Outline the elements of a conspiracy in restraint of trade.
4. Explain what an innocent monopoly is and why it is legal.
5. Detail why mergers or acquisitions that result in higher costs are subject to antitrust suspicion.
6. List steps a provider may take to protect against the potential for antitrust violation.

KEY TERMS

American Board of Medical Specialties	Divesture	Market share discounts
Anticompetitive effects	Drug reformulation	Mergers and acquisitions
Antitrust	Emergency medicine	Monopoly
Barrier to entry	Exclusive dealing	Non-certified physicians
Bundled rebates	Free enterprise	Not-for-profit status
Charitable care	Geographic market	Patent
Community ratings	Invisible hand	*Per se* violations in restraint of trade
Competition	Integrated health care systems	Physician-owners
Conspiracies	Market power	Plan formularies
Distribution chain	Market share	Preventive

Price discrimination   Referral requirement   System specialization
Price-fixing   Resale prices   Third-party payers
Price inflation   Restraint of trade   U.S. Patent and Trademark Office
Prisoner's dilemma   Specialty hospitals   Wealth creation

FACT OR FICTION

Price-Fixing by Pharmacy Benefit Managers

Are the purchases of pharmacy benefits managers a restraint of trade?

North Jackson, an independent community pharmacy, sued Caremark, a pharmacy benefits manager (PBM), for violating antitrust laws in its efforts to negotiate reduced prices on behalf of its employers, health insurers, and other third-party payers of prescription drugs, as well as for price-fixing. Independent pharmacies are forced into a choice between being included in pharmacy networks and accepting low payment rates or leaving the network and losing access to the large volume of business that such inclusion brings.

Caremark administers prescription drug benefit plans and helps control the cost of prescription drugs by creating a network of community pharmacies where subscribers can purchase discounted drugs. Caremark also lowers costs by processing claims, maintaining patient records, creating and managing formularies (lists of drugs preferred by a given plan), and negotiating discounts or rebates with drug manufacturers that want their drugs included on **plan formularies**. North Jackson entered into an agreement with Caremark to dispense prescription drugs to subscribers; in return for inclusion in Caremark's network, North Jackson must agree to dispense drugs to Caremark subscribers at a discount from prices charged to its cash-paying customers. Such discounted prices are usually determined using a formula based on a drug's average wholesale price plus a dispensing fee. North Jackson objects to Caremark's creation of community pharmacy networks and its negotiation of payment rates. This lawsuit maintained Caremark's negotiation of low payment rates was not a negotiation, but was instead a form of coercion that resulted from an illegal conspiracy to fix drug prices between and among Caremark and the **third-party payers** they represented.

— *See* Law Fact at the end of this chapter for the answer.

Principles and Applications

The increasingly complex U.S. **antitrust** laws are commonly referred to as **competition** laws (Bork, 2009). Competition in the health care industry is the process by which one provider in the marketplace strives to gain something by establishing superiority over other providers who are trying to do the same. In theory, in a **free enterprise**, the health care industry would direct its limited resources to the uses that would best satisfy patients with minimum intervention by the government. Of course, when the government pays for more than 36% of the health care provided in the United States (CMS, 2015), with the remaining care regulated by government, it is clear why the concept of free enterprise is totally theoretical in today's marketplace. Free enterprise in health care exists only in theory; it does not exist in reality.

When competition is stifled, the long arm of government antitrust enforcement replaces the **invisible hand** of the market as the regulator of dealings among health care providers and between providers and patients (Alessi, 2014). The court decisions described in this chapter contain some of the rules of the competitive game in which health care providers are the players, courts are the referees, and patients are the beneficiaries. In theory, in a competitive market, the health care system that provides the best quality care for particular diseases would treat all the patients in a specific region diagnosed with certain diseases because no one else could obtain the treatment outcomes that this given health care system could (Christensen, 2011). All the top specialists in the region treating these diseases would be affiliated with this health care system because of its stellar patient care and reputation. Increased **system specialization** would encourage efficiencies and drive health care costs downward (*See* Christensen, 2016).

All the employers, health insurers, and other third-party payers would encourage patients in the region with certain diseases to use this health care system because of its:

- Innovative care
- Prices for health care
- Treatment outcomes

(Christensen, 2016 and 2009).

None of this would violate any antitrust laws because no one else would be treating patients as well as this particular health care system. After this health care system became the only provider in the region for treating specified diseases, antitrust law would prevent this system from artificially raising its prices for health care once it monopolized treatment for particular disease states. In other words, an innocent health care **monopoly** obtained by merit, by providing the best quality patient care, is perfectly legal (Bork, 2009). Actions to create a coercive monopoly or dealings to artificially preserve the system's status as a monopoly would be illegal (Alessi, 2014).

The purpose of antitrust law is to balance potential pro-competitive benefits against potential **anticompetitive effects** (Areeda & Hovenkamp, 2015). Antitrust law does not penalize health care providers who dominate their markets on their own merit, only those that intentionally dominate the market through wrongful conduct (Bork, 2009). Whenever antitrust violations are claimed to have arisen (except for *per se* **violations in restraint of trade**), the government analyzes this competitive balancing on a case-by-case basis. Often it comes down to the government and the courts weighing what constitutes competition in today's health care markets and then deciding how best to maximize social welfare, or in other words, answering the question of how high-quality, affordable health care can be made most accessible to all members of society.

Defensible Theories of Wrongful Conduct

Antitrust cases brought against health care providers should be tightly tied to defensible theories of wrongful conduct (Epstein, 2014). Antitrust laws justifiably:

- Ban wrongful conduct by health care systems dominating a **geographic market**, such as hospitals paying nurses below-market wages and benefits while artificially holding down staffing levels as the need for more nurses increases, as opposed to legitimate staffing levels based on patient needs with clinically accepted nurse-patient ratios
- Observe the mergers and acquisitions of dominant health care systems, including joint ventures and strategic alliances that may threaten the competitive delivery of health care and prohibit such actions altogether, or approve them subject to remedies such as an obligation to divest part of the merged health care delivery business
- Prevent anticompetitive practices that tend to lead to dominant positions in health care markets, including refusal to grant hospital privileges to physicians who refer patients to competing health care providers (as opposed to refusing hospital privileges to physicians who own interests in competing facilities, which is a legitimate competitive action by a competing hospital)
- Prohibit actions restricting competition, including unwinding the domination of multi-hospital health care systems in geographic regions of the country that have come to control health care in their markets and then have come to abuse their **market power** by setting artificially high prices for health care, accompanied by overly aggressive billing and collection procedures

(Brown, 2014; DOJ & FTC, 2010).

Antitrust remedies should not force the health care industry to adopt business practices and structural reorganizations that substantially impede the ability of providers to compete effectively (Epstein, 2014 and 2011). For instance:

- Mandating over 850 codes for angioplasty will not ensure the medical products industry is not overcharging hospitals for their advanced surgical stent products.
- Prohibiting health insurers from practicing individual **price discrimination** in establishing premium prices (thereby encouraging preventable diseases and illnesses), while requiring **community ratings**, is not the same as regulating health insurance.

- Requiring all health care providers to provide government health insurance programs the lowest market price is not regulating the provision of health care.
- Requiring brand pharmaceuticals to allow their generic competitors access to its patented molecules is not the same as regulating the pharmaceutical industry.

(Epstein, 2014; Issar, 2015).

Analysis of Competition

Antitrust law should direct itself only against conduct that unfairly tends to weaken or reduce competition (Allensworth, 2016; Epstein, 2014). Essentially, antitrust law applies to any anticompetitive activity, such as pricing agreements between competitors, mergers that result in providers owning an unfair share of the market, and exclusive dealing contracts that restrain competition. Consumers of health care are entitled to services and medical products priced at competitive levels and to the opportunity to obtain care that a competitive market would offer.

Defining Market Share

The first step in any analysis of competition involves defining the relevant market. This definition determines whether the business conduct actually harms competition and includes:

- Describing the medical products or services
- Identifying other health care providers that supply the same medical products or services or that easily could do so
- Locating appropriate geographic boundaries in which the competitive battle occurs

(Areeda & Hovenkamp, 2015).

The next step determines how much of all the business done by the providers in the relevant market is controlled by those allegedly involved in wrongful conduct. Only then can **market share** begin to be defined.

Analyzing Wrongful Conduct

The purpose of antitrust laws is not to protect health care providers from competition in relevant markets; it is to protect the public from the failure of providers being able to effectively compete (Hovenkamp, 2015). There are only two basic types of anticompetitive conduct that are prohibited by antitrust laws:

- Monopolization
- Conspiracies in restraint of trade

Monopolization

While economists generally view monopoly power as an economic inequity, dominance of a market is not in itself illegal. In fact, the paradox of antitrust is that a merger of monopolists often makes consumers better off (Bork, 2009). Nowhere is this more evident than in the nation's vertically integrated academic medical centers. Antitrust laws do not prohibit strong, honest competition. It is only when unfair business tactics are used to attain or maintain monopoly status that conduct becomes illegal.

To prove an attempt to monopolize, there must be evidence of specific intent to destroy competition. Intent is determined by evaluating competitive tactics within the context of a health care provider's general business behavior. Individual acts and practices, when viewed in isolation, may not be indicative of anything harmful. However, a pattern of actions, each one taken alone, may reflect intent to monopolize (Areeda & Hovenkamp, 2015), such as seeking enforcement of fraudulent drug **patent** claims or price discrimination.

Arguments about predatory litigation are staples in antitrust law. For instance, this strategy is rampant in the pharmaceutical industry, where generic drug manufacturers often pursue private advantage by seeking to mislead administrative agencies and the courts about the scope of the drug patents they invoke, arguing that brand-name drugs bar more competition than they do, or they may litigate to raise branded manufacturers' costs of doing business, not caring whether they prevail (Posner, 2014).

Conspiracies in Restraint of Trade

Conspiracies require a different antitrust approach. Because relationships among competitors in the health care industry can so easily evolve into conspiracies that threaten the competitive integrity of the marketplace, such relationships are subject to close scrutiny (Areeda & Hovenkamp, 2015). Of course, most contacts among industry competitors, such as the following, elicit little antitrust concern:

- Industry-wide lobbying and petition of politicians for favorable legislation or regulation
- Purely social contacts
- Trade and professional association memberships

(Wilcox & Yan, 2014).

However, any agreements among competing health care providers to control prices, or divide territory, customers, patients, or markets, are inherently illegal by themselves. The prohibition of contracts, combinations, and conspiracies in **restraint of trade** also applies to agreements between manufacturers and distributors of medical products and health care providers. Of course, on numerous occasions the interests of manufacturers, distributors, and providers diverge. As a practical matter, manufacturers can certainly provide price lists or promotional materials that specify a desired price, as long as the distributor remains free to set its own price. Setting minimum or maximum **resale prices** may well trigger antitrust enforcement (Areeda & Hovenkamp, 2015).

Medical Mergers and Acquisitions

Antitrust law is aimed at regulating competition. The Federal Trade Commission, an independent federal agency, shares responsibility with the U.S. Justice Department's Antitrust Division for enforcing antitrust laws in the health arena, with the Justice Department handling most insurance matters and the Federal Trade Commission handling hospital and medical products issues. The Federal Trade Commission sees its antitrust efforts as a potentially powerful force in reining in health care costs (DOJ & FTC, 2010).

While the American Hospital Association reports hospital costs in the United States exceeded $892 billion in 2015 (AHA, 2016), these costs have slowed in recent years (Fox, 2016). Government health insurance costs have also declined as a result of the federal government demanding that health care systems provide better care at lower cost. Still, the growth in health care costs will rise without continued cost control actions (Emanuel & Spiro, 2015). One result of these cost concerns is that the federal government is targeting mergers and acquisitions that result in higher hospital costs. While the consolidation of **integrated health care systems** should make the health care industry more competitive and antitrust policy less important, instead it appears to be producing an increase in antitrust actions. It remains to be seen whether the government will seek to block or undo mergers in the hospital field to preserve independent hospital competitors after years of concentration in the industry (AHA, 2016).

Moreover, state attorneys general are increasingly bringing lawsuits under the federal antitrust laws, in addition to enforcing state antitrust laws. Private parties are also suing in federal courts for injunctions to prohibit violations of the antitrust laws and, importantly, for triple the damages they claim to have suffered (Areeda & Hovenkamp, 2015). Clearly, after years of tax-exempt hospitals engaging in **price inflation** and misreporting **charitable care**, new hospital mergers are now being heavily scrutinized (Groebe, 2015).

COURT DECISION

Hospital Mergers

In the Matter of Evanston Northwestern Healthcare Corporation
Docket No. 9315 Opinion of the Federal Trade Commission (2007),
related proceeding at In re Evanston Northwestern Corp. Antitrust Litigation,
2013 U.S. Dist. LEXIS 173794 (U.S. District Court for the Northern District of Illinois, Eastern Division 2013)

Facts: Evanston Northwestern Hospital, affiliated with Northwestern University, is a major not-for-profit teaching facility in suburban Chicago, with almost 900 beds in three hospitals, about 7,600 employees, and annual revenue of $1.8 billion. After merging 239-bed Highland Park into its hospital system (Evanston and Glenbrook Heights), the Federal Trade Commission alleges, Evanston moved to impose significant price increases on insurers well beyond those at comparable hospitals at the time. For instance, the hospital system raised its health management organization rates by more than 50% and its preferred provider organization rates by almost 200% at Evanston, while significantly increasing rates at its two other affiliated hospitals. Evanston is also accused of **price-fixing** physician fees, after combining two large groups of physicians following the merger.

Issue: Did Evanston, which already operated two hospitals in suburban Chicago (Evanston and Glenbrook Heights), use its post-merger market power with the acquisition of a third hospital (Highland Park) to impose anticompetitive price increases on insurers and employers?

Holding and Decision: Yes, Evanston lessened hospital competition in suburban Chicago through its merger with a third hospital (Highland Park Hospital) and therefore violated antitrust law.

Analysis: After Evanston acquired Highland Park, it operated the three hospitals as a single, integrated entity (Evanston, Glenbrook Heights, and Highland Park Hospitals). The Federal Trade Commission sought a **divestiture** of the takeover of the Highland Park Hospital by Evanston four years post-acquisition. Evanston was found to have acted in an anticompetitive manner by making price increases that ultimately hurt patients. Price increases were far beyond those achieved by comparable hospitals during the same period of time.

An important factor to the Federal Trade Commission was the **not-for-profit status** of Evanston. In some previous mergers, courts pointed to hospitals' not-for-profit status as a reason to let mergers go through. The Federal Trade Commission argued tax-exempt hospitals have an incentive to maintain a surplus of revenue over expenses, and while they do not distribute these profits to shareholders, they should use them for salaries, equipment, or expansion.

The Federal Trade Commission had to prove its case by a process of elimination; it had to rule out other explanations, such as catch-up price increases, leaving market power as the only explanation. The Federal Trade Commission also found itself arguing over the proper definition of the market to determine how much concentration existed in the immediate Chicago region. Evanston did not simply enable the Highland Park Hospital to compete more effectively with Evanston and Glenbrook Hospitals, by merging two financially healthy hospitals with a struggling hospital; rather, the merger lessened hospital competition in suburban Chicago. Patient alternatives for hospital care disappeared with the merger.

After a trial before an administrative law judge from the Federal Trade Commission, Evanston was ordered to divest the acquired assets of Highland Park. On appeal to the full Commission, the finding of anticompetitive actions by Evanston was affirmed, but the Commission reversed the divestiture order. Instead, the Commission found that a conduct remedy, as opposed to a structural remedy such as divestiture, was appropriate. The

Commission ordered Evanston to establish two separate and independent teams for negotiating contracts with insurers and employers: one team for Evanston and Glenbrook Hospital, and another for Highland Park. The remedy was to be in effect for 20 years.

Rule of Law: The merger strategies of multiple hospital systems that grow by acquiring neighboring hospitals will be judged and monitored for anticompetitive activities. The related class action proceedings are adjudicating five private causes of action against Evanston for its anticompetitive behavior and are ongoing.

References discussing this court decision: Ashenfelter et al., 2014; Cotter, 2014; Gaynor & Town, 2012; Groebe, 2015.

Pre-Merger Economics

This case against Evanston Northwestern Hospital was a major Federal Trade Commission antitrust enforcement initiative (Bacallao, 2012). The 20-year remedy sends a signal to large hospital systems that Evanston-type mergers are likely to face stiffer challenges and could even be blocked. Recently, a merger involving Inova Health System Foundation in Northern Virginia was blocked by the Federal Trade Commission as Inova sought to acquire a third hospital (Cooper et al., 2015; Koopman & Stratmann, 2015).

For more than a decade, the number of hospitals involved in **mergers and acquisitions** has risen sharply with approximately 200 hospitals being acquired or merged in the United States each year in transactions valued at more than $9 billion annually (Gowrisankaran et al., 2013). In recent years, hospital and health systems have consolidated in Boston, Cleveland, Philadelphia, Pittsburgh, Salt Lake City, and northern California, among other places (Howard, 2015; Sargent, 2015). For instance, Sacramento, California-based Sutter Health System, which has grown quickly by acquisition, has come under fire for its pricing policies. Recently, the California Health Facilities Financing Authority required Sutter to contribute $8.5 million to clinics and rural hospitals before approving its million-dollar bond application. The Financing Authority was clear in stating that this bond restriction should send a message to Sutter and other tax-exempt hospital borrowers that they have to take seriously their obligations to hold down the cost of patient care and also to provide some form of charitable care, as tax-exempt entities. *See* Webster, 2013.

Post-Merger Hospital Pricing

The issue of post-merger hospital pricing is a controversial topic. The Evanston Northwestern Hospital case presented a rare opportunity to examine the actual effects of a merger on pricing in the hospital industry. Many analyses conclude hospital mergers either result in higher prices or have no effect on pricing (Posner, 2014).

Before Evanston, most antitrust cases were brought pre-merger and therefore involved projections based upon economic theory. When hospitals are not-for-profit members of the community, one side of the debate views them as institutions with a strong humanitarian bent. The other side does not view the hospitals as existing on philanthropy; rather they are seen as existing based on their sales revenue and, therefore, they will exercise market power if they have the opportunity. *See generally* Cooper et al., 2015.

This antitrust assault on tax-exempt hospital systems occurs at a time when the hospital industry is under intensified scrutiny for misuse of its tax-exempt status and failure to provide charitable care (CBO, 2014). Hospitals are being criticized for charging uninsured patients the highest rates and aggressively pursuing patients for unpaid debts (Brown, 2014). *See* Chapter on Affordable Care and Tax-Exempt Hospitals.

MANAGEMENT AND LAW ISSUES

6. Is there a social mortgage on tax-exempt hospitals, in that the very existence of tax exemption is to ensure that the basic medical needs of everyone are met?

Specialty Hospitals

According to the American Hospital Association, Texas and California are the states with the most **specialty hospitals**, followed by Louisiana and Oklahoma. While general hospitals are concerned the number of specialty hospitals could grow rapidly, growth has been moderate and gradual. Within their market niche, specialty hospitals are significant competitors to general acute-care hospitals.

A controversial topic is the effect on general hospitals when specialty hospitals enter a market and target the most profitable patients, leaving less profitable patients to be served by general hospitals (AHA, 2015). To retaliate for loss of referrals, some general hospitals have terminated the privileges of physicians who have an ownership interest in specialty hospitals. Some **physician-owners** have consequently challenged such terminations in court. Stark and the anti-kickback laws generally prevent physicians from referring patients covered by government insurance to hospitals in which the referring physicians have a financial relationship, unless an exception or safe harbor applies (*See* 42 U.S.C.A. § 1395nn).

Most cases that terminate hospital privileges by physician-owners of specialty hospitals, like the *Arnett Physician Group*, have been won by general hospitals on the basis that the markets at issue were competitive. The courts do not find it relevant whether or not physician-owners of specialty hospitals are excluded from privileges at particular general hospitals (Hethcoat, 2015). General hospitals are viewed as simply protecting their viability in the face of specialty hospital competition (Hovenkamp, 2015).

COURT DECISION
Termination of Hospital Privileges by Physician-Owners of Specialty Hospitals

Arnett Physician Group, P.C. v. Greater Lafayette Health Services, Inc.
[Physicians Group v. General Hospital]
382 F.Supp.2d 1092 (U.S. District Court for the Northern District of Indiana 2005);
followed by Mercatus Group, LLC v. Lake Forest Hospital, 695 F.Supp.2d 811 (U.S. District Court for the Northern District of Indiana 2010), *affirmed by Mercatus Group, LLC v. Lake Forest Hospital*, 641 F.3d 834 (U.S. Court of Appeals for the 7th Circuit 2011)

Facts: The case involved contract disputes and negotiations between the Arnett Physician Group and its affiliated clinic, health plan, and HMO against the only existing general acute care hospital in the Indiana community of Lafayette. The general hospital terminated Arnett's exclusive service contract and HMO agreement in response to the physicians' attempt to open their own specialty hospital. Twenty-one physicians subsequently left the Arnett Physician Group and became affiliated with the existing general hospital.

Issue: Did the general hospital unlawfully conspire with the physicians who left the Arnett Physician Group to join the hospital, and did the hospital violate antitrust law in denying the physicians who remained with Arnett access to the hospital's services?

Holding and Decision: No, staffing decisions at a single hospital cannot violate antitrust law.

Analysis: The court held Arnett did not have antitrust standing resulting from a contract dispute with a single hospital. The hospital was found to have simply decided to substitute one exclusive radiology services provider for another. The hiring of physicians by the hospital did not amount to anticompetitive activity or confer antitrust standing. Further, there was no evidence connecting the hospital's termination of staff privileges by the Arnett Physician Group to their efforts to set up a competing acute care hospital. In addition, in an earlier stage of the proceedings, the court held that a publicity campaign by the hospital against construction of a new hospital did not cause antitrust injury. Public expressions of opinion about competitors' plans cannot provide the basis for an antitrust claim, and such conduct is clearly lawful.

Rule of Law: Antitrust laws protect competition, not competitors.

References discussing this court decision: N/A.

Physician Privileges and Credentialing

In the health care industry, private antitrust causes of action often involve physician privileges and credentialing.

COURT DECISION

Physician Credentialing

Daniel v. American Board of Emergency Medicine
[Emergency Medicine Physicians v. Physician-Certification Organization]
428 F.3d 408 (U.S. Court of Appeals for the 2nd Circuit 2005);
followed by Hessein v. American Board of Anesthesiology, Inc., 628 Fed.Appx. 116
(U.S. Court of Appeals for the 3rd Circuit 2015)

Facts: This is a class action composed of approximately 14,000 uncertified, licensed physicians who practice emergency medicine throughout the United States, but who did not complete formal residency training programs in **emergency medicine**. The **non-certified physicians** allege that the physician-certification organizations colluded to hire only certified physicians, including the:

- American Board of Emergency Medicine, a not-for-profit corporation that certifies physicians in emergency medicine who pass its examination
- Council of Emergency Medicine Residency Directors, a national association that facilitates communication among the directors of emergency residency training programs
- Hospitals operating residency programs in emergency medicine

The non-certified physicians maintained the certification requirement restrained trade and competition in the practice of emergency medicine in violation of antitrust laws. The American Board of Emergency Medicine is 1 of 24 medical certification boards who are members of the **American Board of Medical Specialties**.

Issue: Did the physician-certification organizations manipulate the residency training requirement for emergency medicine certification to limit the number of physicians certified in order to guarantee super-competitive compensation for such physicians?

Holding and Decision: The compensation issue was never answered; the non-certified emergency medicine physicians lacked standing to bring an antitrust action against physician-certification organizations.

Analysis: When the American Board of Emergency Medicine became a specialty board in the mid-1970s, only 30 emergency medicine residency programs existed in the United States. In order to increase recognition of the specialty, the American Board of Emergency Medicine proposed two eligibility tracks for physicians:

- The *practice track*, requiring 7,000 hours and 5 years of practicing or teaching emergency medicine
- The *residency track*, requiring completion of an approved residency training program

The American Board of Emergency Medicine limited the practice track as an eligibility alternative to the first eight years after the Board became a specialty board. Thereafter, the residency track was the only option.

Non-certified physicians, who would be eligible to take the American Board of Emergency Medicine exam if the practice track still existed, maintained that by closing the practice track and placing a premium on certification, the physician-certification organizations unlawfully restrained trade and monopolized the market for certified physicians. Specifically, the non-certified physicians argued there was an attempt to limit the pool of eligible certification applicants, thus creating an artificial shortage of certified physicians, with the end goal of demanding super-competitive pay. While certification is not required to practice emergency medicine in any state, the non-certified physicians asserted:

- Leading hospitals only hire certified physicians
- Most hospitals base compensation and promotion decisions on certification
- Non- certified physicians receive lower salaries than certified physicians

Furthermore, non-certified physicians claimed they were denied positions solely by reason of not being certified and some were discharged, demoted, and assigned to undesirable work situations due to the lack of certification. Finally, it was asserted that the Council of Emergency Medicine Residency Directors had an unfair interest in keeping the formal residency training as the only required path to certification. In finding the non-certified physicians lacked standing, the court noted that even if private parties are injured by violations of antitrust laws, the party must still have standing to bring an antitrust claim. The court focused on two relevant factors for determining standing:

- Efficient enforcement of the antitrust claims
- The claimed antitrust injury

First, the non-certified physicians claimed financial injury due to restrictions on the number of eligible physicians that can take the certification exam, which in turn limits the number of such physicians and allows the certified physicians to charge higher costs. However, the non-physicians' injury was not that certified physicians commanded super-competitive salaries; their injury was their inability to do likewise. They never claimed they would have received the same pay but for domination of the market by the physician-certification organizations. Rather, the non-certified physicians sued to restore the practice track as an alternative to residency training so they could qualify for the certification examination. The court ruled the non-certified physicians could not state an antitrust injury when their purpose was to join the cartel as opposed to disband it.

Second, the non-certified physicians were not the best enforcers for an antitrust violation. They had no interest in reducing the cost of emergency care. The relief they sought was to gain entry into an exclusive arrangement in order to share in the super-competitive salaries made possible by certification exclusivity.

Rule of Law: The inability of uncertified emergency medicine physicians, or would-be competitors, to command the same competitive salaries as certified physicians did not constitute an antitrust injury because, by requesting an injunction to temporarily restore the practice track so that they could qualify for certification, they sought to join the cartel.

While the court did not determine whether closing the practice track was an antitrust violation, the court noted that the government or the health insurance industry, and not physicians, would be the best enforcers of any certification actions. Health insurers, who compensate hospitals for most emergency care, have a direct and undivided economic interest in reducing the costs of emergency care.

References discussing this court decision: *E.g.*, Moore, 2013.

Exclusive Dealing

One way monopolists can wield their power unlawfully is through **exclusive dealing** (Szostak, 2015). Exclusive dealing, also known as tying or vertical integration, of contracting has received considerable attention in the health care industry with regard to competitive pricing of medical products or services (Hovenkamp, 2011). In its simplest form, exclusive dealing is a contract restricting health care providers from acquiring products from any other manufacturer. The related practice of **market share discounts** (Moore & Wright, 2015), which reward health care systems for purchasing relatively more of a particular brand product, and **bundled rebates** also have the effect of impeding health care efficiency.

MANAGEMENT AND LAW ISSUES

7. Is charging super-competitive prices for medical products and services ethically wrong?

While it is not illegal for manufacturers to agree to minimum prices, such agreements must be examined case by case for possible antitrust violations (Stucke, 2012; Wright, 2012).

COURT DECISION

Exclusive Dealing

United States v. Dentsply International, Inc.
[Government v. Manufacturer of Dental Products]
399 F.3d 181 (U.S. Court of Appeals for the 3rd Circuit 2005),
cert. denied (U.S. Supreme Court 2006)

Facts: Dentsply manufactured and sold artificial teeth for use in dentures and other restorative appliances to dental products dealers. The dealers, in turn, supplied the teeth and various other materials to dental laboratories, which fabricated dentures for sale to dentists. Dentsply excluded competitors from the artificial teeth market by prohibiting its authorized dealers from handling competitors' teeth, a policy designed to exclude its rivals from access to dealers. At the time of the antitrust action, the manufacturer controlled approximately 75 to 80% of the prefabricated teeth market in the United States.

Issue: Can manufacturers of medical products prevent independent dealers from selling the products of other manufacturers?

Holding and Decision: No, manufacturers of medical products cannot lawfully maintain a monopoly over their products through exclusive dealing policies that prevent independent dealers from selling other manufacturers' products.

Analysis: The court found Dentsply had monopoly power in the relevant market of both sales to the laboratories and dental dealers. This was more than adequate to establish a prima facie case of market power. In addition, Dentsply's actions demonstrated its intent to exclude competitors and maintain monopolistic power by successfully prohibiting dealers from handling competitors' teeth. Another indication of Dentsply's market power was its control of prices, which it was able to set without consideration of its competitors' prices, something that a firm without monopoly power would not be able to do.

In addition, Dentsply used its market power to adversely affect competition in the market by preventing dealers from carrying competitors' teeth. The ultimate users, the laboratories that buy the teeth at the point in the **distribution chain** where they are incorporated into other dental products, also could not purchase teeth of other manufacturers, and thus could not fulfill customer requests for alternative teeth lines. These requests were denied by dealers because of fear of being cut off by Dentsply. Although not illegal in itself, exclusive dealing can be an improper means of maintaining a monopoly and creating a **barrier to entry** to competitors in the market.

Dentsply also maintained resale prices by laboratories. Dental laboratories purchased artificial teeth through a network of authorized dealers. If a dealer did not have the requested teeth in stock, Dentsply would drop ship teeth directly to the laboratories, but billing and collection services were still handled by the dealers. Although Dentsply provided a suggested price list to dealers, which ordinarily is permissible, Dentsply went a step further by requiring any deviation from the suggested prices to be cleared with Dentsply; such deviations from the suggested price were permitted only when a laboratory was considering buying a competitor's teeth for reasons of price. In these instances, Dentsply, not the dealers, negotiated with the laboratories to determine a price at which the dealer would sell the teeth to the laboratory. Dentsply's control of the dealer network was the crucial point in the distribution chain where monopoly power over the market was established. This monopoly resulted in teeth being purchased at artificially high prices.

Rule of Law: A manufacturer of medical products has prima facie monopoly power to exclude competitors when it controls 75 to 80% of its product market for more than 10 years.

References discussing this court decision: Hovenkamp, 2011; Hylton, 2014; Moore & Wright, 2015; Rodgers, 2013; Stucke, 2012; Szostak, 2015; Wright, 2012.

Using Antitrust Laws to Thwart Competition

Health insurers, including government insurance programs, can be used to grant, limit, and condition payments to providers (Yong, 2010). While these limitations are essentially turf wars for health care dollars, they are often challenged on antitrust grounds. The American Medical, Osteopathic, and Chiropractic Associations have each attempted to restrict competition by restricting the care of the others.

COURT DECISION
Competitive Managed Care Restrictions

American Chiropractic Association, Inc. v. Leavitt
[Professional Association v. Federal Government]
431 F.3d 812 (U.S. Court of Appeals for the District of Columbia 2005);
followed by Health v. Burwell, 126 F.Supp.3d 28 (District Court for the District of Columbia, 2015)

Facts: The Medicare program subsidizes medical insurance for the disabled and people 65 years of age and over. An enrollee selects a physician or obtains health care through a managed care provider. Medicare insurance then pays for covered care, such as a chiropractor's manual manipulation of the spine. The American Chiropractic Association, representing its chiropractic physicians, maintained that Medicare insurance only provides health care coverage when such services are performed by a chiropractor. The Association also challenged the requirement that Medicare enrollees must obtain referrals from non-chiropractors for chiropractic corrections.

Issue: Does Medicare insurance only provide health care coverage for spinal manipulation by chiropractors?

Holding and Decision: No, allopathic physicians and osteopathic physicians can receive Medicare payments for performing spinal manipulation.

Analysis: The key question is whether the American Chiropractic Association could have its claims heard at the administrative level or if the claims could receive judicial review after channeling through the administrative system. Despite the fact that Medicare is federal legislation, claimants are prohibited from bringing claims grounded in the Medicare insurance law directly in federal court, with limited exceptions. This bar limits judicial review to claims already channeled through the administrative system; all administrative remedies must be exhausted before a claim can be brought in federal court. The only exceptions are when administrative regulations foreclose judicial review and when severe roadblocks cut off any avenue to federal courts as a practical matter.

The court determined the issue of non-chiropractor referrals could be brought at the administrative level. First, an enrollee must have the spinal manipulation performed by a chiropractor without a referral from a non-chiropractor. If health insurers then refuse to cover the service, enrollees could file a grievance, claiming that the **referral requirement** was illegal. This would then begin the administrative process, leading to judicial review. A second route could be for chiropractors to waive all rights to payment from enrollees and become their assignees, allowing chiropractors to bring the administrative challenge. The court said the minimum amount in controversy for judicial review was not a roadblock, since the amount could be met by aggregating claims. The court then analyzed standing as to whether chiropractors were the only physicians who could perform spinal manipulations. The court's analysis was the same as the question of the necessity of referrals from non-chiropractors.

Rule of Law: Federal courts are prohibited from interpreting the Medicare law until all administrative options are exhausted.

References discussing this court decision: *E.g.*, Mank, 2013.

Following this case, states now mandate health insurance coverage for spinal manipulation by chiropractors (Abbott & Stevens, 2014). Most managed care plans, however, still require referrals from a non-chiropractor for chiropractic correction (Stanley, 2015). While Medicare fee-for-service plans do not require referrals, most Medicare Advantage plans do under the guise of medical necessity.

Life-Cycle Management of Drugs

Drug reformulation is one of the largest issues in antitrust and health care (Royall et al., 2013). It involves the use and misuse of intellectual property in the complex system of patents. Brand-name drugs are generally reformulated by pharmaceutical firms to extend their patent protection. This reformulation requires a careful balance, as altering the drugs too much could result in requiring new clinical trials through the Food and Drug Administration, while altering the drugs too little results in no additional patent protection. Between these two competing forces are the Food and Drug Administration and the **U.S. Patent and Trademark Office**, two federal agencies that do not often work together and whose regulations overlap and contradict one another. *See generally* Bork, 1993/1978.

Brand-name pharmaceuticals and generic manufacturers face the **prisoner's dilemma**: as long as any one of them can play the rigged patent game, they all have to play it. Usually there is a payment by brand-name pharmaceuticals to generic manufacturers to stay off the market. That is a major antitrust concern and there are no explicit laws against this. Congress thought this would be an antitrust matter, and indeed, the Federal Trade Commission has accused a number of brand-name pharmaceutical manufacturers of paying off generic manufacturers to delay competition from generics (*See* Cotter, 2014).

Certainly, both the branded and generic industries maintain this is not collusion at all, but a normal hedging of bets during litigation. While it is perfectly rational for parties in litigation to reach agreement on what the outer limits of liability would be, it is suspect. Anytime a patent holder is paying a claimed infringer, the money is flowing the wrong way and it raises flags. Of course, there are scenarios where all of this is a sophisticated way of dealing with risk. Without more, this policy is not a per se antitrust violation, but it is disconcerting, and will likely continue to attract antitrust scrutiny (Areeda & Hovenkamp, 2015).

Antitrust Compliance

Almost everyone in the health care industry agrees on the need for antitrust compliance programs. Since imprisonment and multimillion-dollar fines can accompany slip-ups, it is best never to face antitrust investigations or litigation. Written policy statements, accompanied by recognized independent reference sources, should be kept at employees' desks and work sites to give comprehensive compliance programs a permanence that compliance training alone cannot always claim, as well as continuous access to up-to-date online antitrust information (*See* Moore & Wright, 2015).

There are no straightforward rules for the health care industry to follow when specific problems or questionable activities arise, since antitrust law is highly fact-specific and based on the detailed facts unique to each situation. Some basic antitrust guidelines, however, are standard:

- Aggressively and uncompromisingly compete for all business; antitrust laws do not penalize market success achieved by merit and lawful means.
- Charge all patients and customers the same price, unless the cost of serving them varies, but freely cut prices to meet the lower prices of competitors.
- Do not price medical products or services below some meaningful measure of cost with the intention of driving out the competition or discouraging new entrants, particularly if providers enjoy dominant market power and it is likely to seriously hurt the competition; consider the effect on competitors of any planned pricing actions and be sure that such harm is a consequence of supportable cost strategies with reliable business justifications.
- Do not tie the sale of one product or service to another; exclusive dealing or vertical integration might be allowed in a few exceptional instances, but generally exclusive dealing runs afoul of antitrust laws if it economically harms competitors in the tied market.
- Impose restrictions on distributors and dealers that contribute to competition with rivals; cancel nonperformers, but keep credible records documenting their poor performance in case disputes arise about the circumstances.
- Join trade associations and participate in professional activities not affecting competition with fellow competitors, but never discuss business strategies, costs or service charges, or product pricing with competitors; this could result in charges of price-fixing (*See Drug Mart Pharmacy Corp. v. American Home Products. Corp.*, 472 F.Supp.2d 385 (U.S. District Court for the Eastern District of New York 2007),

affirmed by Cash & Henderson Drugs, Inc. v. Johnson & Johnson, 799 F.3d 202 (U.S. Court of Appeals for the 2nd Circuit 2015).

- Never enter into agreements with competitors to stay out of each other's markets.
- Never join forces with some competitors to the disadvantage and exclusion of other competitors; while some forms of cooperation, such as joint education and training activities are permissible if their main purpose is to improve competencies and industry effectiveness, other activities, especially those that deny excluded competitors access to essential information or facilities are problematic.
- Pay meaningful living wages with affordable health care benefits, particularly if providers enjoy significant market power in a high cost-of-living market or have sizable profits with a considerable disparity between high wage and low income workers, unless there is a credible business justification to do otherwise and the corresponding rationalization carries great weight with the public and government regulators (*See Fleischman v. Albany Medical Center*, 639 F.3d 28 (U.S. Court of Appeals for the 2nd Circuit 2011).
- Suggest retail prices with distributors and dealers, but never coerce them to accept such prices on a take-it-or-leave-it basis; guide and persuade with aggressively bargained binding agreements, but do not refuse to negotiate, or intimidate or threaten (*See North Shore Home Medical Supply, Inc. Catamaran PBM of Illinois, Inc.* 2015 U.S.Dist.LEXIS 95571 (U.S. District Court for the District of Massachusetts 2015).
- Use exclusive dealing if business necessity justifies such deals, but the higher the market share and the longer the term of the agreement, the more imperative the need for a business justification

(Areeda & Hovenkamp, 2015; Bork, 2009; Hovenkamp, 2015).

Differences in Antitrust Philosophy

Differences in antitrust philosophy[LN1] shape the different kinds of comprehensive settlements the government seeks and the courts grant when antitrust investigations arise (Epstein, 2014; Hylton, 2014). These differences reflect the philosophical differences of two of the nation's founding fathers: Thomas Jefferson and Alexander Hamilton. Jefferson believed in a very weak central government; Hamilton believed in a strong central government. These opposing ideologies were a major factor in shaping American government and remain a major factor in shaping today's politics.

The evolving democracy of the United States is based on reconciling the relationship between these two apparently different views of government. American politics has always been the art of making these apparent conflicting beliefs consistent. In the end, Americans have always championed Hamiltonian practicality to achieve Jeffersonian ideals (Rawls, 2005). Success always centers on ideals and does not confuse methods of achievement with ideals (James, 2015).

While not overly simplifying the differences in political philosophies, it can be said that one extreme wants strong federal antitrust enforcement and wants courts to loosely construct antitrust laws to best serve social welfare goals (health and general welfare of the public at large); the other extreme opposes centralized control of competition (Hovenkamp, 2015). Rarely is either opposite played at its limits; most U.S. antitrust policies champion strong federal enforcement methods to achieve competitive ideals.

Today, rather aggressive enforcement strategies are being used to foster competition (Posner, 2014). Government power is fundamentally altering industry structures and the business practices of the health care industry, as found in the recent spate of consent decrees in the medical products industry. Health care firms are increasingly entering voluntary agreements to cease activities claimed by the government to be illegal in return for an end to charges of anticompetitive behavior (Hovenkamp, 2015).

Almost every major pharmaceutical firm and all of the leading medical devices firms (including Biomet, Johnson & Johnson's DePuy Orthopaedics, Smith & Nephew, Stryker, and Zimmer) are operating under consent decrees with the federal government (Garrett, 2011). More than 500 hospitals are under investigation (OIG, 2015). Government-imposed regulations and remedies that are not tightly tied to defensible theories of wrongful conduct often prove counterproductive; such measures typically force health care providers to adopt business practices and structural reorganizations that substantially impede their ability to compete effectively in the global medical marketplace (Epstein, 2014).

Price-Fixing by Pharmacy Benefit Managers

Are the purchases of pharmacy benefit managers a restraint of trade?
   No. Caremark's purchases are not a restraint of trade; rather, they create pro-competitive efficiencies resulting in substantial benefits and cost savings to patients.

— *North Jackson Pharmacy, Inc. v. Caremark RX, Inc.*, 385 F.Supp.2d 740 (U.S. District Court for the Northern District of Illinois, Eastern Division 2005). *Followed by Mueller v. Wellmark*, 861 N.W. 563 (Iowa Supreme Court 2015).

See Alexander, 2007 (discussing the Caremark decision).

CHAPTER SUMMARY

- Innocent monopolies obtained by meritorious competition are perfectly legal; actions to create a coercive monopoly or dealings to artificially preserve one's status as a monopoly are illegal.
- Antitrust law directs itself only against conduct that unfairly tends to destroy competition; it does not prohibit strong, honest competition.
- The purpose of antitrust laws is not to protect health care providers from competition in relevant markets; it is to protect the public from the failure of providers being able to effectively compete.
- Antitrust law does not penalize health care providers who dominate their market on their own merit, only those that intentionally dominate their market through wrongful conduct, or who use their market strength to promote abusive practices, such as paying subpar wages or charging inflated prices.
- The two basic types of anticompetitive conduct that are prohibited are monopolization and conspiracies to restrain trade.
- To prove a prohibited attempt at monopolization, there must be evidence of intent to improperly destroy competition; this can be obtained by reviewing a pattern of individual acts and practices that alone are innocent, but when taken together are collusive.
- Conspiracies in restraint of trade are tricky to prove, as many contacts between competitors are not inherently unlawful; however, any agreement between competitors to control prices or to divide territory, customers, patients, or markets is inherently illegal.
- Medical mergers and acquisitions are generally intended to improve efficiency and lower costs; therefore, the Federal Trade Commission views mergers and/or acquisitions that result in higher costs with a suspicious eye, especially because the number of them has risen so sharply in recent years.
- Another recent area of concern for the Federal Trade Commission is the relationship between brand-name pharmaceuticals and generic manufacturers regarding artificial methods of protecting patents and keeping generic drugs off the market.
- Antitrust cases and sanctions should be tightly tied to defensible theories of wrongful conduct in order to properly reflect what society thinks is wrong and clarify what is punishable conduct.
- Ideally, antitrust regulations would not force health care entities to adopt business practices that impede their ability to compete effectively.
- Health care entities can take steps to ensure that their conduct is not viewed as anticompetitive; some steps include refraining from making improper agreements with competitors, engaging in sustainable, justifiable forms of competition, keeping good records, and negotiating with as opposed to coercing competitors.

LAW NOTES

1. The classical economic philosophies of the 17th and 18th centuries would restrain business to preserve liberty and competition (Mill, 2008/1859; Smith, 2012/1776). In the 20th century there was a shift in economic theory

with an emphasis on precise models of competition; this neoclassical model of free markets held that competitive free markets maximize social welfare (Samuelson, 2004). At the dawn of the 21st century, the Chicago school of economic philosophy, largely associated with the University of Chicago, is the theory most recently used by the U.S. Supreme Court (Bork, 2009 and 1993/1978; Posner, 2014). This school of thought allows vertical agreements (integrated health care systems) and price discrimination (consumer-driven health care) if they do not harm society and prohibits only a few acts, namely:

- Business alliances that fix prices and divide markets
- Dominant pricing that destroys other businesses for financial gain
- Mergers that create monopolies

REFERENCES

Abbott, R., & Stevens, C. (2014). Redefining medical necessity: A consumer-driven solution to the U.S. health care crisis. *Loyola of Los Angeles Law Review, 47,* 943–965.

AHA (American Hospital Association). (2016). *AHA hospital statistics.* Chicago, IL: AHA.

___. (2015). *Preserve existing restrictions on physician self-referral to physician-owned hospitals.*

Alessi, S. A. (2014). Making the competition for health care dollars a fair fight: The role of antitrust law in improving efficiency in the U.S. health care market. *DePaul Journal of Health Care Law, 16,* 107–140.

Allensworth, R. H. (2016). The commensurability myth in antitrust. *Vanderbilt Law Review, 69,* 1–69.

Alexander, L. (2007). Monopsony and the consumer harm standard. *Georgetown Law Journal, 95,* 1611–1643.

Areeda, P. E., & Hovenkamp, H. (2015). *Antitrust law: An analysis of antitrust principles and their application.* (4th ed.). New York, NY: Aspen Law and Business.

Ashenfelter, O. C., et al. (2014). Did Robert Bork understate the competitive impact of mergers? Evidence from consummated mergers. *The Journal of Law and Economics, 57,* 67–94.

Bacallao, J. (2012). *Messner's* effect on hospital consolidation and anticompetitive behavior. *The Seventh Circuit Review, 8,* 1–35.

Bork, R. H. (2009). *A time to speak: Selected writings and arguments.* Wilmington, DE: Intercollegiate Studies Institute.

___. (1993). *The antitrust paradox: A policy at war with itself.* New York, NY: Basic Books (Original work published 1978).

Brown, E. C. F. (2014). Irrational hospital pricing. *Houston Journal of Health Law and Policy, 14,* 11–58.

CBO (Congressional Budget Office). (2014). *Updated estimates of the effects of the insurance coverage provisions of the Affordable Care Act.* Washington, DC: CBO.

Christensen, C. M., et al. (2016). *Competing against luck: The story of innovation and customer choice.* New York, NY: Harper Business.

Christensen, C. M. (2011). *The innovator's dilemma: The revolutionary book that will change the way you do business.* New York, NY: Harper Business.

Christensen, C. M., et al. (2009). *The innovator's prescription: A disruptive solution for health care.* New York, NY: McGraw Hill.

CMS (Centers for Medicare and Medicaid Services). (2015). *National health care expenditure reports.* Baltimore, MD: CMS.

Cooper, Z., et al. (2015). *The price ain't right? Hospital prices and health spending on the privately insured.* Cambridge, MA: National Bureau of Economic Research.

Cotter, T. F. (2014). Patents, antitrust, and the high cost of health care. *American Bar Association: Antitrust Source, 13*(4), 2–20.

DOJ (U.S. Department of Justice) & FTC (Federal Trade Commission). (2010). *Horizontal merger guidelines.* Washington, DC: DOJ-FTC.

Emanuel, E., & Spiro, T. (2015, July 7). The coming shock in health-care cost increases. *Wall Street Journal,* p. A1.

Epstein, R. A. (2014). *The classical liberal constitution. The uncertain quest for limited government.* Cambridge, MA: Harvard University Press.

___. (2011). *Design for liberty: Private property, public administration, and the rule of law.*

Fox, J. (2016). Reforming healthcare reform. *University of Richmond Law Review, 50,* 557–609.

Garrett, B. L. (2011). Globalized corporate prosecutions. *Virginia Law Review, 97,* 1775–1870.

Gaynor, M., & Town, R. (2012). *The impact of hospital consolidation.* Princeton, NJ: Robert Wood Johnson Foundation–The Synthesis Project.

Gowrisankaran, G., et al. (2013). Mergers when prices are negotiated: Evidence from the hospital industry. *American Economic Review, 105*(1), 172–203.

Groebe, C. Z. (2015). The evolution of federal courts' healthcare antitrust analysis: Does the PPACA [Patient Protection and Affordable Care Act] spell the end to hospital mergers? *Washington University Law Review, 92,* 1617–1645.

Hethcoat II,, G. O. (2015). Terminating the hospital–physician employment relationship: Navigating conflicts arising from the physician's dual roles as employee and medical staff member. *University of Miami Business Law Review, 23,* 425–448.

Hovenkamp, H. (2015). *Federal antitrust policy: The law of competition and its practice (Hornbook)* (5th ed.). St. Paul, MN: West Academic Publishing.

___. (2011). Post-sale restraints and competitive harm: The first sale doctrine in perspective. *New York University Annual Survey of American Law, 66,* 487–546.

Howard, C. H. (2015). The Federal Trade Commission and federal courts' scrutiny of healthcare mergers: Do inflexible standards and increased scrutiny stifle the legislative intent of the Patient Protection and Affordable Care Act? *Quinnipiac Health Law Journal, 18,* 67–97.

Hylton, K. N. (2014). A unified framework for competition policy and innovation policy. *Texas Intellectual Property Law Journal, 22,* 163–179.

Issar, N. (2015). More data mining for medical misrepresentation? Admissibility of statistical proof derived from predictive methods of detecting medical reimbursement fraud. *Northern Kentucky Law Review, 42,* 341–374.

James, A. (2015). How to construct global justice. *San Diego Law Review, 52,* 1013–1033.

Koopman, C., & Stratmann, T. (2015). *Certificate-of-need laws: Implications for Virginia.* Arlington, VA: Mercatus Center at George Mason University.

Mank, B. C. (2013). Is Prudential standing jurisdictional? *Case Western Reserve Law Review, 64,* 413–454.

Mill, J. S. (2008). *On liberty*. New York, NY: Oxford University Press. (Original work published 1859).

Moore, D. W., & Wright, J. D. (2015). Conditional discounts and the law of exclusive dealing. *George Mason Law Review, 22*, 1205–1246.

Moore, R. (2013). A sight for sore eyes: The Seventh Circuit correctly interprets section 12 of the Clayton Act. *The Seventh Circuit Review, 9*, 1–20.

OIG (Office of the Inspector General). (2015). *Health care fraud and abuse control program report*. Washington, DC: U.S. Department of Health and Human Services, OIG.

Posner, R. A. (2014). *Economic analysis of law* (9th ed.). New York, NY: Wolters Kluwer Law and Business.

Rawls, J. (2005). *A theory of justice*. Cambridge, MA: Harvard University Press, Belknap Press.

Rodgers, III, C. P. (2013). The incredible shrinking antitrust law and the antitrust gap. *University of Louisville Law Review, 52*, 67–103.

Royall, M. S., et al. (2013). Antitrust scrutiny of pharmaceutical product hopping. *Antitrust: American Bar Association, 28*, 71–86.

Samuelson, P. (2004). *Economics: An introductory analysis*. (18th ed.). New York, NY: McGraw-Hill.

Sargent, N. D. (2015). The national imperative for health care system transformation: Why certain mergers and acquisitions are appropriate despite section 7 of the Clayton Act. *Cleveland State Law Review, 64*, 83–106.

Smith, A. (2012). *The wealth of nations*. New York, NY: Bantam Classics-Random House. (Original work published 1776).

Stanley, C. (2015). The Patient Protection and Affordable Care Act: The latest obstacle in the path to receiving complementary and alternative health care? *Indiana Law Journal, 90*, 879–900.

Stucke, M. E. (2012). Is intent relevant? *Journal of Law, Economics and Policy, 8*(4), 801–858.

Szostak, D. C. (2015). Vertical integration in health care: The regulatory landscape. *DePaul Journal of Health Care Law, 17*, 65–119.

Webster, K. (2013, April 2). California Health Facilities Financing Authority approves issuing $450m in bonds for Sutter Health. *The Bond Buyer, 122*, 62.

Wilcox, M., & Yan, J. (2014). Antitrust violations. *American Criminal Law Review, 51*, 837–873.

Wright, J. D. (2012). Moving beyond naïve foreclosure analysis. *George Mason Law Review, 19*, 1163–1198.

Yong, P. L., et al. (2010). *The healthcare imperative: Lowering costs and improving outcomes*. Washington, DC: Institute of Medicine, the National Academies Press.

© Andy Dean Photography/ShutterStock, Inc.

CHAPTER 15

Global Supply Chain Management[1]

"I cannot say whether things will get better if we change; what I can say is they must change if they are to get better."

— **Georg Christoph Lichtenberg** (1742–1799), German scientist

In Brief

This chapter addresses supply chain management and the rapidly expanding integration and outsourcing industry surrounding the health care market. Outsourcing of business processes by the health care industry, from general administrative services to clinical data analysis, is proliferating. Outsourcing of knowledge processes, from telemedicine to cybersurgery to drug development and manufacturing of medical products, continues to increase with innovations in health information technologies. This chapter provides an overview of outsourcing principles applicable to a variety of health care settings.

LEARNING OBJECTIVES

Upon completion of this chapter readers should be able to:

1. Describe the high costs of health care overhead and management.
2. Explain the elements that favor using business process outsourcing services to reduce costs.
3. Describe why much outsourcing deals with the evaluation of images and medical data.
4. List how the medical products industry uses contract research organizations to contract for offshore services.
5. Explain how fiduciary duty may be avoided by use of outsourcing.
6. Detail the importance of metrics in outsourcing.
7. Describe why India leads in outsourced health care services.
8. Explain why captive organizations are less efficient than business process outsourcing in-house.
9. Describe the need for restriction of tacit residual knowledge.

KEY TERMS

Active ingredient
Bioinformatics
Business process outsourcing
Captives
Clinical support functions
Codifiability
Computerized provider order entry systems
Connectivity

Consumer-directed health care
Contract research organizations
Core competencies
Corporate epistemology
Cybersurgery
Data protection laws
E-health
Economies of scale
Electronic medical records

Food and Drug Administration Safety and Innovation Act of 2012
Generic
Information infrastructure
Inshoring
Integration
Internet of things
IT-enabled services
Joint ventures

---

[1]Contributor: Melissa Ertl, MBA in Biotechnology and Health Industry Management, Global Director of Quality and Compliance, Sodexo for SmithKlineBeecham.

Knowledge management	Provider's value package	Telemedicine
Near-shoring	Reshoring	Teleradiology
Nomenclature integration	Residual knowledge	Telesurgery
Non-core job functions	Sole source	Two-pronged cost escalation
Offshoring	Supply chains	Virtual captives
Pricing traps	System integration	Wage arbitrage
Program offices	Tacit knowledge	

FACT OR FICTION

Global Drug Outsourcing

Are imported drug ingredients inspected by the U.S. Food and Drug Administration?

Baxter International, of Deerfield, Illinois, procures the active pharmaceutical ingredient for the anticlotting, generic drug heparin from Scientific Protein Laboratories of Waunakee, Wisconsin. Scientific Protein is owned by a buyout and financing firm called American Capital Strategies, based in Bethesda, Maryland. American Capital Strategies receives the **active ingredient**, which mainly originates from the mucus of pig intestines and other animal tissues, from a majority-owned U.S. joint venture called Changzhou SPL located in Changzhou, China. The **generic** heparin active ingredient, which is used primarily for kidney dialysis, heart surgery, and a procedure called apheresis in immune disorder patients, has been tied to at least 80 deaths in the United States and several hundred extreme allergic reactions resulting in vomiting, diarrhea, low blood pressure, speeding heartbeats, and fainting.

— *See* Law Fact at the end of this chapter for the answer.

Principles and Applications

Leveraging network connectivity, also referred to as the **internet of things**, is the next frontier for the health care industry (Deichmann et al., 2016). More remarkably, the internet of things could revolutionize global supply chain management (Poudel, 2016). The biggest impact may be realized in optimization of supply chain logistics, making the outsourcing of business processes more efficient (Fischer, 2015). Efficient **supply chains** can create value for health care providers by:

- Cutting costs
- Deploying new delivery system models
- Offering new medical products and services

(Wharton, 2014).

The global supply chain for medical products is being reshaped by the **Food and Drug Administration Safety and Innovation Act of 2012**. This legislation strengthens the Food and Drug Administration's (FDA) ability to safeguard and advance public health by enhancing the safety of global supply chains. The FDA's expansion of authority over supply chains occurs as the medical products industry struggles with decisions on how much to outsource in a fast-changing and competitive industry.

Choosing where and who to source from to create the greatest value is not always easy. Too little outsourcing means a health provider may lose the pricing and payment advantages that can come with using outside vendors globally; too much or the wrong kind of outsourcing, and quality and **knowledge management** can suffer (Wharton, 2013).[2] The

---

[2]In this text, for purposes of simplicity, *outsourcing* stands for business process outsourcing, as well as **inshoring**, **near-shoring**, and offshoring. Outsourcing is the practice of running the business functions of health care providers by their own captives or by outsourcing job functions to outside vendors offshore and inshore locations, as well as in-house.

architecture of supply chains in health care delivery can vary widely depending on the medical services and products involved; the cheapest solution is not always the best value for patients (Cohen, 2013).

Business Process Outsourcing

Business process outsourcing, the use of outside vendors for the performance of general administrative services, is a critical issue for the health care industry, in:

- Accounting
- Claims processing
- Customer relationship management
- Finance
- Human resources
- Procurement

The need for outsourcing is intensifying as the demand to create value in health care continues to multiply. The effective use of outsourcing is commonsensical given that over one-third of U.S. health care costs are attributed to overhead and management expenses (Himmelstein, 2014; IOM, 2010).

The value of the **integration** and outsourcing market for the health care industry worldwide is expected to reach $36 billion (Deloitte, 2015). Clearly, outsourcing remains a legitimate strategic option for health care systems operating at margins of 3 to 5%, when somewhere between a third and half of the nation's hospitals are losing money (Maizel et al., 2015). As discretionary patient spending expands due to the growth of **consumer-directed health care**, the demands for cost-effective care and medical products will only increase. To the extent that acceptance of outsourcing accelerates, the health care industry is continually seeking to outsource non-strategic services that can be accomplished more cost efficiently by outsourcing (Jain, 2011). Outsourcing transfers responsibility for ongoing management tasks and execution of business activities, processes, or functional areas in order to improve efficiency and performance (Kable, 2015). Outsourcing arrangements are often exceedingly complex because they involve the transfer of one or more complete business processes or entire business functions to an external contractor who will perform them.

Offshoring of Health Care Outsourcing

The use of offshore outsourcing has increased dramatically in recent years due to the increased flexibility in services offered by new health information technologies (AMA, 2014). As illustrated in **TABLE 15-1**, the leading outside vendors serving the U.S. health care industry are in India.

The following specialized medical services are outsourced and sent offshore with growing frequency as hospitals and health plans come under heightened pressure to cut costs and enhance value:

- Billing
- Collation
- Insurance claims processing
- Technical information support
- Transcription
- X-ray analysis

(GAO, 2016).

TABLE 15-1 Profile of the Outsourcing Industry

Firms Headquartered in India	Sales	1-Year Sales Change	Employees
Tata Consultancy Services	$1.09 trillion	14.8%	353,900
Wipro	$512.4 billion	9.1%	150,000
Infosys	$624.4 billion	17.1%	194,000

Data retrieved from the 2015 Annual Report filings with the U.S. Securities and Exchange Commission.

As the cost of telecommunications time falls and cloud technologies and robotic process automation expands, the volume of medicine practiced in cyberspace is steadily increasing (Kable, 2015). It has been estimated that the $20 billion industry that transcribes physicians' dictated notes into written form outsources as much as half of its work offshore (Kshetri & Dholakia, 2011; Schutzbank, 2016). Similarly, almost half of the claims processing for Medicare insurance is outsourced offshore (GAO, 2005; Pegnato, 2011).

Flattening of the U.S. Health Care System

While the boundaries of health care providers are being flattened at the same time that they are being expanded, outsourcing is not a straightforward proposition, and it is very difficult to generalize about its virtues (Friedman, 2007). The U.S. health care industry is only flat in some places; if the industry were entirely flat, it would always make sense to outsource where wages and other costs are lower, but that is not the case (Wharton, 2011). What makes sense for some medical services just does not make sense for others. Nevertheless, it is possible to do business nearly instantaneously worldwide with:

- **Connectivity**
- Globalization
- Technology

(George et al., 2014).

When a health care provider has an outsourcing firm handle certain medical services in exchange for a fee, what was once handled inside a hospital or physician's office becomes a market transaction handled outside the hospital or physician's office. As a result, the boundaries of the health care provider are flattened or connected to the outsourcing firm; the playing field becomes level as the provider and contractor are linked together in a logical and intelligible way (Fund et al., 2007). Meanwhile, a different game is starting. An extended organization in which health care providers relinquish control in return for monitoring knowledge is developing.

Since the purpose of outsourcing is to delegate one or more functions to an external contractor, the decision to outsource the function allows health care providers to focus their resources on their **core competencies**, which are:

- Clinical care
- Medical education
- Research, from epidemiology to genetics
- Strategic treatment procedures

(Wharton, 2011).

Core competencies consist of the fundamental parts of a **provider's value package**, or the medical functions that constitute the provider's competitive advantage (Border, 2012). Most academic medical centers do not engage in business functions unrelated to their core functions, such as:

- Food services
- Insurance claim processing
- Maintenance
- Patient billing
- Security staffing

(Wharton, 2011).

They focus instead on clinical care, medical education, and research. With this flattening, the outsourcing industry has now achieved critical mass in its quest for providing knowledge process services, where skills, judgment, and discretion are the tools (Wharton, 2012).

The outsourcing of American medical jobs will only surge with technological innovations in the fields of **telemedicine** and **cybersurgery** (Allain, 2013; Barlow & Hodge, 2015). As used in this text, *telemedicine* is the diagnostic practice of medicine over distance using telecommunications and interactive video technologies (AMA, 2014). Telemedicine is distinguished from **e-health**, which is broader in scope as it includes not only health care delivery but also health information technologies. Digitalization of medical data in virtually every medical discipline, coupled with recent advancements in telecommunications, means that physicians and their clinical support staff are no longer required to reside on the same continents as their patients (Gilman, 2011).

Supplying Hospital Staff Versus Medical Expertise

When examining outsourcing, there is a difference between the supply of staff and the supply of medical expertise (Browne et al., 2013). Health information technology enables the establishment of deep, information-based linkages between a health care provider and its outsourcing firm. For instance, with radiology services, each sees the same patient X-rays; the provider takes the X-rays (records the medical data), and the outsourcing firm interprets the X-rays (explains the meaning of the medical data). At one level, a hospital and the outsourcing firm engage in a market transaction, but at another level, the outsourcing firm is an extension of the hospital (Wharton, 2014).

Today most U.S. hospitals are part of vast, complex networks.[LN1] The issue for many hospitals is how multifaceted they need to be: how many different functions does a hospital need to perform by itself as opposed to having an outsourcing firm perform those functions for the hospital? U.S. auto manufacturers realized in the early part of the 19th century that there was no reason for them to own rubber plantations in the Amazon so that they could make their own tires; another entity could make the tires while they could focus on assembling automobiles. In the same way, hospitals are beginning to recognize that they do not need to do everything to support their organizations. Some levels of better quality medical expertise and **clinical support functions**, as well as business functions, can be acquired far less expensively from outside their organizations by outside vendors (*See* DeHondt & Nezlek, 2010). There are outsourcing specialists for almost every business process who are better at providing the service for many health care providers than any one provider on their own (Narman et al., 2014; Oberle et al., 2013), from health care standards for health care **system integration**, **bioinformatics**, and regulatory compliance, to telemedicine. For instance,

- In health care systems integration, outside vendors can integrate data standards for use in **electronic medical records**, **computerized provider order entry systems**, and genetic databases, within technical frameworks to clean and integrate quality medical data.
- In **nomenclature integration**, outside vendors can integrate Systematized Nomenclature of Medicine, developed by the College of American Pathologists and used in electronic medical records, computerized provider order entry systems, and genetic databases.
- In bioinformatics, outside vendors can provide high-performance computing technology to enhance the storage and analysis of molecular information in areas ranging from protein structure production to machine learning techniques for target identification to molecular modeling to lead identification and optimization of drug ingredients.
- In regulatory compliance, outside vendors can provide comprehensive solutions to resolve compliance issues as opposed to isolated applications for managing quality guidelines (*See* 21 C.F.R. §§ 1271.1–1271.85), Sarbanes-Oxley, and privacy regulations, while improving validation processes across teams and aligning compliance strategies with broader business goals.
- In telemedicine, when health care providers face high patient volume in remote locations, outside vendors can provide leading-edge technology and strategies for the transfer of medical information online and in real time for use in diagnosis, treatment, and education across distances.

(HHS, 2016; NSB, 2016).

There is a need for access to complete and accurate medical data; however, most health care providers have multiple, patchwork applications running on disparate platforms that cannot provide rapid and integrated patient information at the point of service. In addition, different health care providers and health care networks use different clinical terms that mean the same thing. For instance, the terms *myocardial infarction, heart attack*, and *MI* may mean the same thing to a cardiologist but, to a computer, they are different. There is a need for access to consistent medical data between different health care providers and, because patient information is recorded differently from place to place, a comprehensive medical terminology system is needed as part of any **information infrastructure.**

Teleradiology

As discussed, the traditional system of providing health care is in the process of being flattened. Statistics show radiological outsourcing growing with a significant number of hospitals currently engaging in such a practice. However, reliable estimates as to the size of this offshore market do not exist since **teleradiology** is currently provided primarily by a number of private firms that are not obligated to file public reports (Pratt, 2015).

Teleradiology is the largest component of international telemedicine today in terms of complexity, and hence cost; it is roughly midway between teleconsultations and cybersurgery (Barlow & Hodge, 2015). For instance, when X-ray analysis is moved from a U.S. hospital to an offshore outsourcing firm, the hospital stops exercising control over medical personnel analyzing patient X-rays. The hospital looks at the number of errors per number of X-rays processed and controls the level of quality; the hospital also randomly samples X-rays to monitor the quality of the analysis. The hospital no longer tells the physicians and technicians how to analyze patient X-rays; now the hospital and outsourcing firm agree on the outcomes of the analysis and the hospital pays the outsourcing firm depending on the number of X-rays analyzed (Wharton, 2012). Thus, the extended health care organization is one in which the hospital relinquishes local control. The outsourcing firm actually hires the physicians and technicians who analyze patient X-rays while the hospital monitors their analyses and attempts to control overall quality.

Telecardiology, Teledermatology, Telepharmacy, Telepathology, Telepsychiatry, and Telesurgery

The points raised concerning the practice of radiology apply equally to any branch of medicine that is primarily concerned with the evaluation of images or medical data that can be reduced to an image format. Most branches of medicine are ripe for business process outsourcing, including cardiology (Zilis, 2012), dermatology (Davis et al., 2015; Hoffmann & Rowthorn, 2011; Siegal, 2013), pathology (Pratt, 2015), pharmacy (Gilman & Stensland, 2013), and psychiatry (Little, 2015). Some endoscopy procedures, such as virtual colonoscopies, are already being replaced by innovative radiology techniques that render endoscopy obsolete (NIH, 2013).

Teledermatology, telecardiology, telepathology, and telepsychiatry simply involve videoconferencing, whereas **telesurgery** occurs either when a remotely located physician provides video assistance to physicians performing a surgery or when a physician uses a remote robotic arm during surgery. Telepharmacy works by having a pharmacist-staffed central order entry site that provides supervisory oversight to pharmacy technicians in remote sites.

Outsourcing Centers of Excellence

In a world of telemedicine it is possible to concentrate expertise in centers of excellence that receive health data from multiple health care systems. For instance, it is not hard to imagine centers of excellence where radiologists would work around the clock to perform all of the data interpretations for images generated in several states in the United States (Bennie, 2014). With health data concentrated into centers of excellence where the best skill sets exist, the **economies of scale** would cause the net unit cost for radiographic interpretation to fall below the costs currently generated by radiologists interpreting films under exclusive contracts in hospitals.

Other centers of excellence could be staffed by cardiologists and still others by pathologists and trauma physicians (Sorondo, 2011; Trupp & Sieck, 2012). Additionally, nothing would prevent such centers of excellence from competing to provide services on the third shifts in hospitals in countries eight time zones ahead or behind. Such centers of excellence could be located in U.S. health care facilities where patient care is offered at an exemplary level on a wide range of measures or in emerging economies in health care facilities with exemplary patient care in Eastern Europe, India, China, or South Africa; centers of excellence would have the labor resources to compete with radiologists, cardiologists, or pathologists on a global basis.

Medical Products Outsourcing

The number of medical products made outside of the United States has significantly expanded in the past two decades. Nearly 80% of the active ingredients and almost 40% of the finished drugs and medical devices used by U.S. consumers are manufactured abroad (FDA, 2015a). The United States increasingly imports pharmaceutical materials from emerging economies such as India and China, yet the FDA lacks the resources to conduct sufficient oversight visits to foreign sites to ensure compliance with U.S. law (Buckler & Jackson, 2014). Inspections are critical because good manufacturing practices are costly and thus prone to circumvention, as compliance with internal quality systems and regulations can represent up to one-fourth of a finished drug manufacturer's operating costs (Pew, 2011). To offer more competitive pricing and gain market share, at the expense of compliant pharmaceutical firms, some overseas plants that manufacture generics have forgone good manufacturing practices and thereby caused adulteration of the U.S. drug supply (*e.g.*, Darrow, 2014; GAO, 2010). It is imperative that the U.S. marketplace be protected against unfairness to the domestic medical products industries following the law and incurring the attendant expenses, where overseas operations skirt the law at a considerable cost savings and produce mislabeled generics that are imported into the United States to the detriment of U.S. consumers (Moss, 2011).

In the majority of areas of medical products outsourcing, most of the concerns boil down to audit of standardized procedures, including:

- Business data analytics
- Clinical trials
- Cost and price analyses
- Early-stage drug development
- Enterprise resource planning systems
- Environmental health and safety
- Manufacturing
- Production planning
- Quality assurance and quality oversight

(FDA, 2015a; Liu, 2012).

The FDA regulations that standardize procedures and verification work make it easy for the non-core functions of clinical research and development and commercialization to be outsourced.[LN2] Producers of medical products must document what their systems do and prove that the systems function consistently within a certain margin of error; producers must also perform audits whenever called upon to do so by the FDA (Rodwin, 2015). Global pharmaceuticals have between 500 and 800 environmental health and safety workers, from regulation statisticians to analysts and other back-office function workers, to monitor outsourcing (FDA, 2015a; GAO, 2010).

FDA guidelines provide a system of business processes to assure that the medical products produced by manufacturers have what they are represented to possess in terms of:

- Composition
- Identity
- Purity
- Quality
- Strength

(FDA, 2015a).

Good manufacturing practice guidelines address operating procedures and documentation requirements for:

- Distribution
- In-house testing
- Production and process controls
- Qualifications of manufacturing personnel
- Raw materials quality assurance
- Record-keeping of substances throughout the manufacturing process
- Standards for cleanliness and safety
- Warehousing

(FDA, 2015b).

From this perspective, it is advantageous for producers of medical products to use outside vendors for outsourced work. If the procedures are in writing and are auditable, the producers of medical products and the outside vendors will each be familiar with them and know how to evaluate them. The leading contract research organizations that provide support to the medical products industry are illustrated in **TABLE 15-2**.

Risk Management of Outsourcing Relationships

Understanding and defining acceptable risk levels is one of the first hurdles for outsourcing (*See* Caruso et al., 2014). Firms involved in outsourcing offshore are incorporating detailed clauses into their outsourcing contracts. They are setting up integrated metrics within the outsourcing relationship with:

- Clear deadlines
- Database locks that prevent reopening the data after it is finalized
- Standards for accuracy

(European Commission, 2016).

TABLE 15-2   Profile of the Contract Research Organization Sector

Firms and State Headquarters	Sales	1-Year Sales Change	Number of Employees
Quintiles (NC)	$5.7 billion	5.3%	36,100
IMS Health (CN)	$2.9 billion	10.6%	15,000
Covance (NJ)	$2.6 billion	N/A	12,500
Parexel (MA)	$2.3 billion	3.0%	18,700
ICON (Ireland)	$1.6 billion	4.8%	11,900
Charles River Laboratories (MA)	$1.4 billion	5.1%	8,600

Note: IMS Health and Quintiles announced their merger in May 2016.

Data from the 2015 Annual Report filings with the U.S. Securities and Exchange Commission (Fiscal Year Ends December 31).

Definition: Contract research organizations provide support to the medical products industry in the form of research services outsourced on a contract basis.

There are hundreds of line items that are agreed upon in industry-wide, standardized master agreements and statements of work. The key point is that information transferred offshore is only protected insofar as the terms of the outsourcing contract provide and as the destination country permits. Thus, a U.S. health care provider's ability to safeguard the personal medical data it transfers to outside vendors in countries with weaker **data protection laws** is largely limited to the ability to enforce any data protection clauses in its outsourcing contract (Border, 2012). U.S. providers also have to weigh:

- Operational risks, such as natural disasters and technology failures
- Performance risks, such as **pricing traps** and non-delivery on service-level agreements

(Sao & Gupta, 2013).

All of these risks can be managed by the right:

- Acceptable service-level agreements
- Outsourcing delivery model
- Clear-cut price negotiations
- Proper contractor selection

U.S. providers should also check the geopolitical stability and infrastructure capabilities, among the other factors, in the outsourcing firm's country. Above all, U.S. health care providers should consider a risk mitigation approach by spreading their operational risks over multiple locations (Wharton, 2012).

Protection of Tacit Knowledge

The health care industry is often concerned about the misuse of **residual knowledge** about strategy when considering outsourcing (Vitasek & Ledyard, 2010). Such concerns, however, can be mitigated by requiring outside vendors to be quarantined after sensitive projects, which means they cannot work with competitors for a limited period of time. This loss of **tacit knowledge**, of how things are done, is constantly a concern with outside vendors. Nonetheless, outsourcing is so cost-effective that health care providers and producers of medical products are often tempted to outsource without worrying about tacit knowledge. This unstated oversight, however, could lead to real problems with execution.

MANAGEMENT AND LAW ISSUES

1. Does the FDA have a moral responsibility to protect the U.S. population by becoming more accountable for inspecting and monitoring overseas outside vendors?
2. Is the U.S. health care industry relinquishing too much control to developing countries by outsourcing processes overseas?

There is no easy way to pass along tacit knowledge to outside vendors unless firms are very good at formalizing their business processes and documenting everything that is done. **Corporate epistemology** must be documented before outsourcing can be successful (Polanyi, 2007/1958). Epistemology is the branch of philosophy that explains how a person gains and verifies knowledge. The intuitive process of how knowledge is acquired without any explicit direction must be converted into detailed requirements that can be given to outside vendors for proper implementation. Alternatives to thorough documentation of tacit knowledge could include running captive centers or adopting other business relationships that are at an arm's length with respect to outsourcing as opposed to using outside vendors. The less tangible the work, though, the more closely strategic activities should be held and not outsourced (Wharton, 2012).

Global Drug Manufacturing in China

China occupies center stage for outsourcing of raw materials for the pharmaceutical industry. The manufacturers, in turn, are responsible for sourcing raw materials and appropriately processing the material (Banister, 2014). The quality of exported chemicals from China is the responsibility of importers and importing countries (FDA, 2015b). The Chinese State Food and Drug Administration (Chinese State FDA) works with its foreign regulatory counterparts to monitor drug-ingredient production to ensure that raw materials are:

- Clean
- Consistent
- Traceable

(Zettler, 2015).

Based on international practice, however, safeguarding the legality, quality, and safety of active pharmaceutical ingredients is the ultimate responsibility of the global pharmaceutical and generic manufacturers and the importing countries, not the exporting countries (FDA, 2015b). While approximately 80% of the active pharmaceutical ingredients in U.S. drugs originate from foreign manufacturers, the FDA currently only inspects about 6% of foreign drug producers due to insufficient field-force funding (*See* IOM, 2012).

The generic heparin case that started this chapter highlights regulatory gaps that have opened as generic manufacturers globalize their purchase of active ingredients (*See In re: Heparin Products Liability Litigation*, 2011 U.S.Dist.LEXIS 36299 (U.S. District Court for the Northern District of Ohio 2011)). While suppliers in China that export to the pharmaceutical industry in the United States are licensed and inspected by the Chinese State FDA or the U.S. FDA; the same cannot be said for the generic manufacturers who have been found to use unlicensed and uninspected suppliers in China (*e.g.*, Darrow, 2014). More than 700 Chinese facilities are involved in making drugs or drug ingredients for the U.S. market (FDA, 2015a; Zettler, 2015). In China, few raw material suppliers are certified by Chinese drug regulators as drug producers; most are registered as chemical makers or agricultural byproducts firms and are not checked by state drug authorities (*See* Brennan, 2015).

Early-Stage Medical Products Research in India

Instead of routine data work, outsourcing is moving toward information extraction, which involves interpretation and inference (Bennie, 2014). More and more of this trend is occurring with medical products research. Instead of data entry, outside vendors are now offering high-end research services. The most popular service for outsourcing is performing clinical trials. As medical products pass through the clinical trial process, data regarding their safety and

MANAGEMENT AND LAW ISSUES

3. Should labor, human rights, and environmental standards be considered in outsourcing contracts and costs?
4. Does offshore contracting of outsourcing services decrease U.S. employment opportunities, and in turn hurt the U.S. economy?

efficacy must be gathered to support an application to the FDA because it is only through FDA approval that a company can capitalize on its products. Outside vendors supply the necessary staff to appropriately collect, store, question, report, and analyze that data to provide justification for FDA approval to market a medical product.

Patent Protection

Producers of medical products have become much more efficient by outsourcing to vendors (WHO, 2016). Earlier concerns about protection of intellectual property in India diminished significantly after the Indian government introduced patent legislation allowing medical product companies to obtain patent protection on almost every aspect of product development, from molecules and microorganisms to processes (Shaffer et al., 2015).

Ready Access to Clinical Trial Participants

There is also a growing desire among producers of medical products to conduct their clinical research in India due to the relatively easy access to participants in clinical trials (Levinson, 2010; Schuster, 2015). Research indicates that conducting clinical trials in India can lower early-stage drug discovery costs by $35 to $50 million per new drug due to:

- Rapid enrollment of participants in trials
- Shortened enrollment timelines for clinical trials
- Producer's avoidance of fiduciary status with participants in trials
- Shifting of liability claims to the clinical research organizations in India that are conducting the clinical trials

(Wilson, 2013).

While the cost of creating a new drug can be as high as $1.7 billion, it takes $2.6 billion to take a new chemical entity through all the stages of clinical trials and reach the market (DiMasi et al., 2014).

Avoidance of Fiduciary Status

More important than the cost efficiencies, producers of medical products can avoid fiduciary status and some liability claims by designing protocols to comply with FDA regulations and outsourcing their clinical research (Janssen, 2014). Court decisions on fiduciary duty of outside vendors have led to discussion of federal legislation to address the liabilities of offshore vendors, but there is no groundswell of public demand for any legislative change (Miller & Weijer, 2006; *See* Lázaro-Muñoz, 2014).

Wage Arbitrage of Educated Workforce

India occupies center stage for outsourcing in health care because of the country's large educated labor force, especially its reservoir of high-quality research and engineering graduates. The sheer numbers of India's talent force make a compelling case for outsourcing to India. India has some 22 million university graduates, including:

- 6 million science graduates
- 1.2 million with engineering degrees
- 600,000 physicians

(NASSCOM, 2015).[LN3]

India's educated population is growing rapidly, with nearly 2.5 million graduates added every year, including 25,000 new physicians and nearly 600,000 science and engineering graduates annually (NASSCOM, 2016). **Wage arbitrage** is another reason. Health care providers in the United States must pay a 40 to 80% cost premium in direct wages alone to obtain the quality of labor they can obtain more cheaply from vendors in India (Blair et al., 2011). It is estimated that the cost of conducting clinical drug trials in India is only one-seventh of that in the United States or Europe (Strakosch, 2015). Even with all these advantages, India is still facing intense competition from outside vendors in other emerging markets in China, Eastern Europe, and South Africa (Gereffi, 2014).

Captives and Business Process Organizations

Back offices (or **captives**, as they are referred to in the information technology and outsourcing industries) are generally less efficient than outside vendors that specialize in integration and outsourcing. For some types of back-office work, captives' costs were 30% higher (Chandok et al., 2013). At the same time, higher captive costs did not lead to lower staff turnover or better-quality work (Lacity & Wilcocks, 2013).

Outsourcing of health care service functions began with setting up domestic captive service centers. These centers began by executing enterprise-wide operations that involved the conversion of medical records from patient charts to electronic medical records. Today, these domestic captive centers are starting to move their information extraction and reporting tasks offshore.

Two factors are making this possible. They include:

- The convergence in health care computing platforms
- The rapid advances in communications technology

As enterprise-wide platforms, such as relational databases and networking standards, become standardized and software tools that facilitate porting large medical data sets between dispersed information technology systems become available, the flow of medical data and personal health information within health care systems should become more practical and cost less.

As the flow of medical data between computers swells, so will the extent of human intervention and the degree of expertise required to transform data into information. As a result, the costs of providing accurate and timely personal health information to support clinical decision-making will begin mounting by orders of magnitude (Siegal, 2013). As this happens, the U.S. health care industry will be faced with a **two-pronged cost escalation**. Providers will need to:

- Hire more staff
- Increase the expertise levels of existing staff

(Bales et al., 2014).

The move to centralize non-strategic functions in lower cost labor regimes is an obvious response to the cost frontier faced by the U.S. health care industry (Wolf, 2013). Initial reports suggest that some health care providers benefit by up to 60% in cost savings in lower wage markets (Wharton, 2011).

Hybrid Program Offices

Outside vendors have developed businesses for the delivery of higher end health care services that are a hybrid between captive organizations doing business in house and traditional work outsourced by contractors (WHO, 2016). The outsourcing captive work model executed by traditional managerial authority has been merged with the outside work model facilitated by price and contract, to create what are known as **program offices** (also known as program management offices, project offices, project management offices, and project control centers). Program offices are actually centralized centers that monitor, influence, and control projects to make them more efficient. What makes program offices unique is that they have no responsibility for the activities of projects; they are uninvolved in project management. With the development of health information technology, program offices can work very closely with U.S. health care providers to the point where the outsourcing firm's employees become almost like the U.S. provider's employees (Manyika, et al., 2015).

Virtual Captives

Virtual captives are the latest outsourcing model to evolve in the U.S. health care industry (Wharton, 2014)[LN4]; they are like health care providers having their own captive. But it is the outsourcing firm that sets up its virtual development center in a particular city, which could be in the domestic United States or in a low-cost foreign city. The captive obtains the following resources required to do the work:

- Human resources
- Management
- Administration

Virtual captives satisfy:

- Cost benefits
- Obtaining the right skill sets
- Protecting intellectual property

(Aron et al., 2011).

Also, to some extent, the culture of the health provider is incorporated into the development center that is being run by the outsourcing firm. Predictions are that in-house outsourcing and virtual captives will be the future outsourcing models apart from **reshoring**, which is happening because of the U.S. job situation and political protectionism (Wharton, 2014).

In-House Outsourcing and Reshoring Versus Offshoring

Even though there is a long-term trend toward outsourcing and **offshoring**, especially to places like China and India, a reversal is also occurring. A significant number of outsourced functions are actually coming back to the United States. Many health care providers are talking about in-house outsourcing and reshoring as opposed to offshoring (Wharton, 2013).

As a whole, the health care industry is seeking to create employment opportunities in the United States itself. Health providers, unlike many other industry sectors, also want to participate in outsourcing decisions as opposed to turning over their employees and asking the outside vendors to do specific functions for them (Merk, 2014). The health care industry generally wants to ensure that employment opportunities in the United States are secure, and they want to ensure they get the right people (Wharton, 2013).

Management of Multiple Supply Chains

Another evolution is that health care providers generally refuse to **sole source**; they will no longer deal with only one outsourcing firm. The tradition was always to get one large outsourcing firm and outsource everything to that firm. Today supply chain management is more dependent upon the kind of specific skills an outsourcing firm brings. Health providers will go to multiple outside vendors to get their **non-core job functions** done. Outside vendors must show good:

- Business processes, which they already have
- Domain expertise in the business functions in which they participate

(Wharton, 2013).

Moreover, contracting with multiple outside vendors helps keep everybody very honest because the U.S. health care industry is not looking for cost arbitrage anymore (Wharton, 2014). They are looking for ways in which outsourcing can increase:

- Their revenue or their patient base
- The satisfaction of their customers, the patients

(Deichmann et al., 2016; Manyika et al., 2015).

The change in delivery of health care is thinking in terms of the patients as their customers as opposed to in terms of the disease states and the health care system itself.

Privacy Concerns

Isolated data security and privacy violations have become high-visibility issues disproportionate to the ground realities of outside vendors (Briskin et al., 2014). Many can recall headlines about the disgruntled medical transcriptionist in Pakistan who threatened to disclose the University of California–San Francisco Medical Center's patient records if she was not given her back pay (Smith, 2015). At the same time, few people remember that most privacy violations of personal health information occur in the United States and are the result of individuals not protecting their own medical data (ITA, 2015); many voluntarily relinquish their privacy online via social media and through participation in Internet surveys.

Even so, with outsourcing, there has been a rise in the privacy concerns of patients with regard to improper disclosures of personal medical data and fraud such as medical identity theft (Szerejko, 2015). As the health care industry moves toward greater use of health information technology, particularly in the transition to electronic medical record systems, this concern will need to be addressed (Terry, 2014). With the movement toward electronic health records, the health care industry will face many of the same privacy concerns and risks that have confronted financial institutions.

Thus, the recommendations of the Federal Deposit Insurance Corporation (FDIC) with regard to consumer privacy risks can serve as a model for health care entities. The FDIC recommends that three general areas be considered when outsourcing offshore:

- Privacy risks in the offshore outsourcing firm's country
- Ongoing oversight of all third party contractors, including the:

  ○ Contractor's activities
  ○ Status of data protection in the contractor's country
  ○ Use of independent audit reports

- Contract provisions that protect the privacy of patients and their medical data, including:

  ○ Choice of law
  ○ Local legal review of the outsourcing firm's contract to determine enforceability of all aspects of the contract
  ○ Prohibition on use or disclosure of offshore data except to carry out the contracted services

(FDIC, 2010 and 2004).

What Lies Ahead for Outsourcing?

The health care industry must realize that once the door to collaboration or outsourcing is opened, it can never be closed. Given the huge risks of failure for medical services and products, health care providers must think about not only the benefit for tomorrow but also about whether they can sustain it (Wharton, 2013). To keep a competitive edge requires constant innovation; health care providers must innovate more than providers in other industries (Cohen, 2013). There is also the requirement that intellectual property be protected; it does not take a genius to dismantle a medical product and reverse engineer it. The only way to maintain preeminence is innovation (Cobee, 2013). Overlaid on all this are the mandates for patient privacy and confidentiality.

At present, most outsourcing of medical services in the United States is done to provide medical coverage at community hospitals on the third shift (11:00 PM to 7:00 AM) when it is hard to find physicians and other professionals who can work those hours. Yet because outside vendors allow hospitals to tap into low-income labor pools in resource limited nations, the U.S. health care system could potentially lower costs by outsourcing even more medical services (Burghard et al., 2016). Independent of the potential for system-wide efficiencies, increased use of outside vendors could:

- Create economies of scale
- Improve access to care
- Improve competition among providers
- Reduce medical errors

(Concentrix, 2016; IBM, 2016).

MANAGEMENT AND LAW ISSUES

5. Do the cost efficiencies of utilizing outside vendors outweigh the risks of contaminated supply chains?
6. Should consumers have a more active say in whether U.S. medical product firms outsource processes to developing countries?

If such efficiencies can be documented, it is likely that more services will be outsourced on the first and second shifts, not necessarily because physicians cannot be found but because it will cut costs and improve efficiency. As the U.S. health care industry struggles with restructuring the delivery of existing medical services, new opportunities will emerge to improve efficiencies and medical treatments that do not yet exist. This will lead to the next wave of integration and outsourcing.[LN5]

For instance, over the years health care providers and the insurance industry have collected mountains of personal medical data on their patients; outside vendors could offer to interpret that data (Kotlik et al., 2015). If analyzed, that medical data could provide valuable insights into new ways to effectively restructure the strategic functions of the U.S. health care system. While waiting for that to unfold, no outsourcing industry observers have placed bets on what other unprecedented products and services await discovery (Wharton, 2012).

LAW FACT

Global Drug Outsourcing

Are imported drug ingredients inspected by the U.S. Food and Drug Administration?

No. The legal requirement for drug manufacturers to get inspected every two years applies only to domestic plants, not offshore facilities. Indeed, the U.S. FDA inspects less than 6% of the entire foreign drug manufacturing sites.

— *In re: Heparin Products Liability Litigation*, 2011 U.S.Dist.LEXIS 36299 (U.S. District Court for the Northern District of Ohio 2011).

See Buckler & Jackson, 2014; Liu, 2012; Moss, 2011 (discussing this decision); *See also* Mundy, 2010; Pew, 2011.

CHAPTER SUMMARY

- It is estimated that at least one-third of U.S. health care costs are a result of overhead and management expenses, or otherwise non-strategic services that can be accomplished more cost-efficiently by collaborative outsourcing.
- Technical information support, transcription, collation, billing, insurance claims processing, and X-ray analysis are sent offshore with increasing frequency as health care systems come under greater pressure to reduce costs.
- When examining health care industry outsourcing, there is a difference between the supply of staff and the supply of expertise.
- Any branch of medicine that is primarily concerned with the evaluation of images or the evaluation of medical data that can be reduced to an image format is suitable for collaborative outsourcing.
- The FDA's regulations that standardize manufacturing, clinical trials, drug development procedures, and verification work make it easy to outsource the non-core functions of research and development and commercialization.
- India's patent legislation allows medical product firms to obtain patent protection on almost every aspect of product development, from materials to processes.
- There is a growing desire among producers of medical products to conduct their clinical research in India due to the relatively easy access to clinical trial participants, which can lower early-stage drug discovery costs by $35 to $50 million per new drug.
- As important as the cost efficiencies are for the U.S. health care industry, producers of medical products can avoid fiduciary status and some liability claims by designing protocols to comply with FDA regulations and then outsourcing their clinical research.
- The FDA's regulations charge hospital institutional review boards, not producers of medical products, with protecting the human rights of clinical trial volunteers in the United States.
- When outsourcing offshore, detailed clauses should be incorporated into outsourcing contracts that define the integrated metrics that will be used to monitor the outsourcing relationship with clear deadlines for performance as well as the standards to be used for informational accuracy and database locks.

- Information transferred offshore is only protected insofar as the terms of the outsourcing contract provide and as the destination country permits, in terms of enforcement and recognition of a right to legal action.
- India possesses the largest advantage for outsourcing health care because of the wage arbitrage of its large educated labor force which has the potential to save about 80% in direct wages alone.
- Captive organizations are significantly less efficient than firms that specialize in integration and outsourcing.
- Even though there is a long-term trend toward offshoring, due to political protectionism, a significant number of outsourced functions are coming back to the United States, particularly in the medical products industry where outsourcing is performed in-house.
- The misuse of residual knowledge about strategy and best practices can be mitigated by restricting outsourcing organizations from working with competitors for a limited period of time.
- The less tangible the work, the more closely health care providers and producers of medical products should hold strategic activities inside their organizations as opposed to outsourcing.
- As the U.S. health care industry struggles to restructure the delivery of existing medical services, new opportunities to improve efficiencies and medical treatments that do not yet exist will be revealed. This will likely result in another round of integration and outsourcing.

LAW NOTES

1. The Children's Hospital of Philadelphia (CHOP) is a 430-bed hospital receiving over one million outpatient and inpatient visits per year. Founded in 1855, CHOP is now the largest integrated pediatric health care network in the United States, with:

   - primary care (Kids First) practices in Pennsylvania, New Jersey, and Delaware
   - primary care centers
   - off-site inpatient and intensive care units for neonatal and pediatric care
   - outpatient specialty centers
   - poison control center

   It is the pediatric teaching site for the University of Pennsylvania School of Medicine, although it operates autonomously medically, administratively, and financially.

2. National centers of excellence for comprehensive health care were first established in the United States in 1996 by the U.S. Department of Health and Human Services to improve the health status of women. Located in academic medical centers, they bring together the work of their schools and departments to address women's health. Centers of excellence on Women's Health unites:

   - Community linkages
   - Education and training
   - Gender-based research
   - Leadership positions for women in academic medicine
   - State-of-the-art health care services addressing all of women's needs

3. Two key variables that determine whether it makes sense to outsource the non-core functions of clinical research and development and commercialization are:

   - Their **codifiability**
   - The nature of the metrics involved

   (Wharton, 2014).

   If the process can be codified, then the function should be outsourced. As for metrics, outsource firms need to have precise, well-defined metrics so they know exactly how to measure their performance (Aron et al., 2011). If the performance metrics are precise or objective, outsourcing makes sense (Wharton, 2014). In this instance, regulations relating to the following practices can be outsourced:

   - Good clinical practices (GCPs) and clinical trials (*See* 21 C.F.R. §§ 11, 50, 54, 56, 312, 314, 601, 812, and 814)
   - Current good manufacturing practices (CGMPs) (*See* 21 C.F.R. §§ 210 and 211)

- Good automated manufacturing practices (GAMPs) (*See* ICH-Q, 2016), including guides from the International Society for Pharmaceutical Engineering that provide interpretation of regulatory standards (e.g., ISPE, 2014, 2012a, and 2012b).

(*See* Baciu et al., 2007).

4. NASSCOM (National Association of Software and Service Companies—India), the Indian technology and outsourcing industry trade group, represents information technology firms and outside business process outsourcing vendors, which are also known as **IT-enabled services** (ITES) providers.

5. Outsourcing has evolved into six models:

- Offshore development centers, which are outsourcing centers in low-cost cities (most common)
- Domestically owned captives in low-cost countries or cities in India or China
- Build-operate-transfer models (limited success)
- **Joint ventures**
- In-house business process outsourcing
- Virtual captives, which are the most transparent of the models

(Merk et al., 2014; Wharton, 2013).

REFERENCES

Allain, J. S. (2013). From jeopardy! to jaundice: The medical liability implications of Dr. Watson and other artificial intelligence systems. *Louisiana Law Review, 73*, 1049–1079.

AMA (American Medical Association). (2014). *Telemedicine to improve access to care for patients*. Washington, DC: AMA.

Aron, R., et al. (2011). The impact of automation of systems on medical errors: Evidence from field research. *Information Systems Research, 22*(3), 429–446.

Baciu, A., et al. (2007). *Institute of Medicine: The future of drug safety; promoting and protecting the health of the public*. Washington, DC: The National Academies Press.

Bales, R., et al. (2014). A comparative analysis of labor outsourcing. *Arizona Journal of International and Comparative Law, 31*(3), 579–622.

Banister, J. B. (2014). New technology and increased globalization: Addressing difficulties presented in the current FDA inspection process. *Indiana Health Law Review, 11*, 753–792.

Barlow, C. L., & Hodge, Jr., S.D.(2015). Teleradiology: The perks, pitfalls and patients who ultimately pay. *Rutgers Computer and Technology Law Journal, 41*, 1–30.

Bennie, R. (2014). Medical tourism: A look at how medical outsourcing can reshape health care. *Texas International Law Journal, 49*, 583–600.

Blair, M. M., et al. *(2011)*. Outsourcing, modularity, and the theory of the firm. *Brigham Young University Law Review, 2011*(2), 263–314.

Border, A. C. (2012). Untangling the web: An argument for comprehensive data privacy legislation in the United States. *Suffolk Transnational Law Review, 35*, 363–392.

Brennan, H. (2015). The cost of confusion: The paradox of trademarked pharmaceuticals. *Michigan Telecommunications and Technology Law Review, 22*, 1–52.

Briskin, A., et al. (2014). Offshoring health information: Issues and lingering concerns. *Journal of Health and Life Sciences Law, 8*(1), 100–110.

Browne, M. N., et al. (2013). American medical tourism: Regulating a cure that can damage consumer health. *Loyola Consumer Law Review, 25*, 319–362.

Buckler, M., & Jackson, B. (2014). Section 337 as a force for "good"? Exploring the breadth of unfair methods of competition and unfair acts under § 337 of the Tariff Act of 1930. *The Federal Circuit Bar Journal, 23*, 513–560.

Burghard, C., et al. (2016). *IDC FutureScape: Worldwide healthcare 2016 predictions*. Framingham, MA: International Data Corp (IDC).

Caruso, D., et al. (2014). *Institute of Medicine: Characterizing and communicating uncertainty in the assessment of benefits and risks of pharmaceutical products: Workshop summary*. Washington, DC: The National Academies Press.

Chandok, P., et al. (2013). Taking captive offshoring to the next level. *McKinsey on Business Technology, 32*, 14–20.

Chui, M., et al. (2010). *The Internet of Things*. New York, NY: McKinsey & Company.

Cobee, V., Corporate Vice President, Datsun, at The Wharton School, University of Pennsylvania. (2013, May 25).Remarks at the panel discussion on Global Supply Chain Management: Outsourcing, Re-Shoring, and Near-Shoring at the Wharton Global Alumni Forum, Tokyo, Japan.

Cohen, M. A., Professor of Manufacturing and Logistics and Co-Director, Fishman-Davidson Center for Service and Operations Management at The Wharton School, University of Pennsylvania. (2013, May 25). Remarks at the panel discussion on Global Supply Chain Management: Outsourcing, Re-Shoring, and Near-Shoring at the Wharton Global Alumni Forum, Tokyo, Japan.

Concentrix. (2016). *Listening to America's health plan operations executives: Our top 9 innovation prescriptions*. Fremont, CA: Concentrix.

Darrow, J. J. (2014). Pharmaceutical gatekeepers. *Indiana Law Review, 47*, 363–420.

Davis, A., et al. (2015). Access and innovation in a time of rapid change: Physician assistant scope of practice. *Annals of Health Law, 24*, 286–335.

DeHondt, II, G., & Nezlek, G. (2010). Risk effect on offshore systems development project cost. *Journal of Computing and Information Technology, 18*(2), 11–120.

Deichmann, J., et al. (2016). *Creating a successful Internet of Things data marketplace*. New York, NY: McKinsey & Company.

Deloitte. (2015). *Global health care outlook: Common goals, competing priorities*. Philadelphia, PA: Deloitte, Global Health Care Sector.

DiMasi, J., et al. (2014). *Tufts CSDD cost study*. Boston, MA: Tufts University, Tufts Center for the Study of Drug Development (CSDD).

European Commission. (2016). *Protection of personal data*. Brussels, Belgium: European Commission.

FDA (U.S. Food and Drug Administration). (2015a). *Regulatory information: Food and Drug Administration Safety and Innovation Act (FDASIA)*. Silver Spring, MD: FDA.

___. (2015b).*Regulatory procedures manual: Import operations and actions (Chapter 9)*.

FDIC (Federal Deposit Insurance Corporation). (2010). *Guidance for financial institutions on the use of foreign-based third-party service providers*. Washington, DC: FDIC.

___. (2004). *Offshore outsourcing of data services by insured institutions and associated privacy risks*.

Fischer, E. A. (2015). *The internet of things: Frequently asked questions*. Washington, DC: Congressional Research Service.

Friedman, T. L. (2007). *The world is flat: A brief history of the twenty-first century: Further updated and expanded*. New York, NY: Picador.

Fund, V. K., et al. (2007). *Competing in a flat world: Building enterprises for a borderless world*. Upper Saddle Hill, NJ: Pearson Prentice Hall.

GAO (U.S. Government Accountability Office). (2016). *Claim review programs could be improved with additional prepayment reviews and better data*. Washington, DC: GAO.

___. (2010). *Drug safety:* FDA has conducted more foreign inspections and begun to improve its information on foreign establishments, but more progress is needed.

___. (2005). *Privacy: Domestic and offshore outsourcing of personal information in Medicare*, Medicaid, and Tricare.

George, K., et al. (2014). *Next-shoring: A CEO's guide*. New York, NY: McKinsey & Company.

Gereffi, G. (2014). A global value chain perspective on industrial policy and development in emerging markets. *Duke Journal of Comparative and International Law, 24*, 433–457.

Gilman, D. J. (2011). Physician licensure and telemedicine: Some competitive issues raised by the prospect of practicing globally while regulating locally. *Journal of Health Care Law and Policy, 14*, 87–117.

Gilman, M., & Stensland, J. (2013). Telehealth and Medicare: Payment policy, current use, and prospects for growth. *Medicare and Medicaid Resource Review, 3*(4), E1–E17.

HHS (U.S. Department Health and Human Services). (2016).*Patient privacy: A guide for providers. Washington, DC: HHS, Office of Civil Rights*.

Himmelstein, D. U., et al. (2014). A comparison of hospital administrative costs in eight nations: U.S. costs exceed all others by far. *Health Affairs, 33*(9), 1586–1594.

Hoffman, D., & Rowthorn, V. (2011). Roundtable on legal impediments to telemedicine: Legal impediments to the diffusion of telemedicine. *Journal of Health Care Law and Policy, 14*, 1–53.

IBM. (2016). *IBM global process services: Business process re-invention; life sciences and healthcare*. White Plains, NY: IBM.

ICH-Q (International Council on Harmonisation-Quality). (2016). *Quality guidance documents*. Silver Spring, MD: U.S. Food and Drug Administration.

IOM (Institute of Medicine). (2012). *Ethical and scientific issues in studying the safety of approved drugs*. Washington, DC: The National Academies Press.

___. (2010). *The healthcare imperative: Lowering costs and improving outcomes*.

ISPE (International Society of Pharmaceutical Engineers). (2014). *GAMP® Good Practice Guide: A Risk-Based Approach to Regulated Mobile Applications*. Bethesda, MD: ISPE.

___. (2012a). GAMP® Good Practice Guide: A Risk-Based Approach to GxP Compliant Laboratory Computerized Systems (2nd ed.).

___. (2012b). *GAMP® Good Practice Guide: A Risk-Based Approach to Testing of GxP Systems* (2nd ed.).

ITA (International Trade Administration). (2015*). Health information technology: Top markets report*. Washington, DC: U.S. Department of Commerce, ITA.

Jain, A. (2011). Mitigating vendor silence in offshore outsourcing: An empirical investigation. *Journal of Management Information Systems, 27*(4), 261–298.

Janssen, W. M. (2014). A "duty" to continue selling medicines. *American Journal of Law and Medicine, 40*, 330–392.

Kable. (2015). *Strategic focus report: Business process outsourcing; Technology and market trends*. London, England: Kable Business Intelligence.

Kotlik, L., et al. (2015). *Making big data work: Supply chain management*. Boston, MA: Boston Consulting Group.

Kshetri, N., & Dholakia, N. (2011). Offshoring of healthcare services: The case of US-India trade in medical transcription services. *Journal of Health Organization and Management, 25*(1), 94–107.

Lacity, M. C., & Wilcocks, L. P. (2013). Outsourcing business processes for innovation. MIT *Sloan Management Review, 54*(3), 63–69.

Lázaro-Muñoz, G. (2014). The fiduciary relationship model for managing clinical genomic "incidental" findings. *Journal of Law, Medicine and Ethics, 42*, 576–586.

Levinson, D. R. (2010). *Challenges to FDA's ability to monitor and inspect foreign clinical trials. Washington, DC: U.S. Department of Health and Human Services, Office of Inspector General*.

Lichtenberg, G. C. (2013). *Georg Christoph Lichtenberg: Philosophical writings*. (A. Tester, Trans.). Albany, NY: SUNY (State University of New York) Press (Original work published 1778).

Little, J. M. (2015). Into the future: The statutory implications of North Carolina's telepsychiatry program. *North Carolina Law Review, 93*, 864–910.

Liu, C. (2012). Leaving the FDA behind: Pharmaceutical outsourcing and drug safety. *Texas International Law Journal, 48*, 1–32.

Maizel, S., et al. (2015). The healthcare industry post-Affordable Care Act: A bankruptcy perspective. *Emory Bankruptcy Developments Journal, 31*, 249–273.

Manyika, J., et al. (2015). *Unlocking the potential of the Internet of Things*. New York, NY: McKinsey & Company.

Merk, C., et al. (2014). *Rebalancing your sourcing strategy*. New York, NY: McKinsey & Company.

Miller, P. B., & Weijer, C. (2006). Fiduciary obligation in clinical research. *Journal of Law, Medicine and Ethics, 34*, 424–437.

Moss, J. (2011). Patients at risk: The need to amend the Food, Drug, and Cosmetic Act to ensure the safety of imported prescription drugs. *Thomas Jefferson Law Review, 33*, 297–323.

Mundy, A. (2010, July 22). China never investigated tainted heparin. *Wall Street Journal*, p. A1.

Narman, P., et al. (2014). An enterprise architecture framework for multi-attribute information systems analysis. *Software Systems Model, 13*, 1085–1116.

NASSCOM (National Association of Software and Service Companies-India). (2016). *Domestic BPM market 2016: On the cusp of transformation.* New Delhi, India: NASSCOM.

___. (2015). *Application, innovation and maturity of Indian analytics.*

NIH (National Institute of Health). (2013). *Virtual colonoscopy.* Bethesda, MD: NIH, The National Institute of Diabetes and Digestive and Kidney Diseases.

NSB (National Science Board). (2016). *Science and engineering indicators: A broad base of quantitative information on the U.S. and international science and engineering enterprise.* Arlington, VA: National Science Foundation, NSB.

Oberle, D., et al. (2013). A unified description language for human to automated services. *Information Systems, 38*(1), 155–181.

Pegnato, J. A. (2011). What is the right balance between outsourcing government work to the private sector versus performing the work in-house? A look at outsourcing trends in government outsourcing, their implications, and suggestions for finding the right balance. *Journal of Contract Management, 9*, 91–102.

Pew Health Group. (2011). *After heparin: Protecting consumers from the risks of substandard and counterfeit drugs.* Philadelphia, PA: Pew Charitable Trusts.

Pew Research Center. (2014). *The Internet of things will thrive by 2025.* Washington, DC: Pew Research Center.

Polanyi, M. (2007). *Personal knowledge towards a post-critical philosophy.* London, England: Taylor and Francis (Original work published 1958).

Poudel, S. (2016). Internet of things: Underlying technologies, interoperability, and threats to privacy and security. *Berkeley Technology Law Journal, 31*, 997–1030.Pratt, D. (2015). Telehealth and telemedicine. *Albany Law Journal of Science and Technology, 25*, 495–545.

Rodwin, M. A. (2015). Independent drug testing to ensure drug safety and efficacy. *Journal of Health Care Law and Policy, 18*, 45–84.

Sao, D., & Gupta, A. (2013). Threats to the international trade regime: Economic and legal challenges arising from anti-offshoring measures across the globe. *The International Lawyer, 47*(3), 407–439.

Schuster, B. M. (2015). For the love of drugs: Using pharmaceutical clinical trials abroad to profit off the poor. *Seattle Journal for Social Justice, 13*, 1015–1067.

Schutzbank, A., Vice President, Clinical Development, Iora Health. (2016, February 19). Remarks at the panel discussion on Putting Patients at the Center: The Race to Re-engineer How Care Is Delivered at the Wharton Health Care Business Conference on the Innovation Game: The Race Between Entrants+Incumbents, Philadelphia, PA.

Shaffer, G., et al. (2015). State transformation and the role of lawyers: The WTO, India, and transnational legal ordering. *Law and Society Review, 49*, 595–626.

Siegal, G. (2013). Enabling globalization of health care in the information technology era: Telemedicine and the medical worldwide web. *Virginia Journal of Law and Technology, 17*(1), 1–34.

Smith, Z. W. (2015). Privacy and security post-Snowden: Surveillance law and policy in the United States and India. *Intercultural Human Rights Law Review, 9*, 137–227.

Sorondo, R. J., et al. (2011). Telemedicine consultation for emergency trauma: The 130 million square foot trauma room. *Bulletin of the American College of Surgeons, 96*(6), 12–19.

Strakosch, R. (2015). From pirate to plaintiff: Accelerating development through the strategic evolution of intellectual property doctrine. *Journal of High Technology Law, 16*, 29–95.

Szerejko, J. D. (2015). Reading between the lines of electronic health records: The Health Information Technology for Economic and Clinical Health Act and its implications for health care fraud and information security. *Connecticut Law Review, 47*, 1103–1152.

Terry, N. P., et al. (2015). Google glass and health care: Initial legal and ethical questions. *Journal of Health and Life Sciences Law, 8*(2), 93–103.

Terry, N. P. (2014). Big data proxies and health privacy exceptionalism. *Health Matrix, 24*, 65–108.

Trupp, R. J., & Sieck, S. G. (2012). Society of chest pain centers: Building better value into health care. *Critical Pathways in Cardiology, 11*(3), 160–162.

Vitasek, K., & Ledyard, M. (2010). *Vested outsourcing: A better practice for better results.* New York, NY: National Contract Management Association.

Wharton School of the University of Pennsylvania. (2014). Outsourcing is going to become more collaborative. *Knowledge@Wharton.*

___. (2013). To be made here, or elsewhere; A look inside outsourcing decisions.

___. (2012). Research roundup: The "flip side" of open innovation, productivity losses from bad weather and assessing the risks of outsourcing.

___. (2011). Outsourcing: New pressures to stay home, old reasons to go abroad.

WHO (World Health Organization). (2016). *Trade, foreign policy, diplomacy and health: Pharmaceutical industry.* Geneva, Switzerland: WHO.

Wilson, B. (2013). Clinical studies conducted outside of the United States and their role in the Food and Drug Administration's drug marketing approval process. *University of Pennsylvania Journal of International Law, 34*(3), 641–685.

Wolf, C. (2013). Delusions of adequacy? Examining the case for finding the United States adequate for cross-border EU-U.S. data transfers. *Washington University Journal of Law and Policy, 43*, 227–256.

Zettler, P. J. (2015). Toward coherent federal oversight of medicine. *San Diego Law Review, 52*, 427–500.

Zilis, A. E. (2012). The doctor will Skype you now: How changing physician licensure requirements would clear the way for telemedicine to achieve the goals of the Affordable Care Act. *University of Illinois Journal of Law, Technology and Policy, 2012*(1), 193–217.

PART VI

PRODUCERS OF MEDICAL PRODUCTS

Part VI reviews the producers of medical products

CHAPTER 16

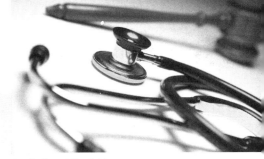

Pharmaceuticals

"A society without any objective legal scale is a terrible one indeed. But a society with no other scale but the legal one is not quite worthy of man either."

— **Alexander Isayevich Solzhenitsyn** (1918-2008), winner of Nobel Prize in Literature

IN BRIEF

While the pharmaceutical industry is frequently criticized by patients, consumer groups, and others for charging high prices, a realistic view of the industry involves the interplay of high risk and long timelines for product development. This chapter focuses on drug pricing and the impact of managed care on regulating drug prices. Particular attention is directed to unapproved (off-label) drug uses, the latent effects of drugs, and the effect of generic competition on the innovative pharmaceutical industry. No pharmaceutical overview would be complete without looking at the vaccine industry as it gains new interest in response to flu-shot shortages, concerns about global pandemics, and the development of potential vaccines targeted at new markets, including cancer. Vaccines are an important part of our normal health care system; the rationale as to why vaccines should be covered by health insurance and how they effectively reduce costs is explained.

LEARNING OBJECTIVES

Upon completion of this chapter readers should be able to:

1. Describe why the pharmaceutical industry is moving away from developing blockbuster drugs and toward acquiring and merging with the biotechnology and medical device industries.
2. Explain the reason for pricing drugs based on their economic value.
3. List the costs of research by the pharmaceutical industry.
4. Explain the complexity of global drug pricing.
5. Describe why the Food and Drug Administration struggles to regulate imported drugs.
6. Talk about how pharmacy benefit managers exercise market power over the pharmaceutical industry and drug pricing.
7. Describe how the learned intermediary doctrine works with unapproved (off-label) drug uses.
8. List the four elements of product liability lawsuits.
9. Explain why the pharmaceutical industry does not conduct comprehensive research.
10. Explain how litigation forces the pharmaceutical industry to protect consumers.
11. Outline the difficulties of balancing patent and antitrust laws with the pharmaceutical industry and generic manufacturers of medical products.
12. Explain the use of no-compete agreements made with generic manufacturers.
13. Clarify why vaccines make good economic sense.

KEY TERMS

30-month moratorium	180-day exclusivity period	Antitrust
95% degree of certainty	Abbreviated new drug application	Antitrust immunity

Bet-the-firm risks
Blockbuster drugs
Brand-name drugs
Breach of duty
Burden of proof
Causation
Childhood vaccines
Clinical trials
Commodity business
Computational power
Cost-effectiveness
Cost per life-year gained
Cost per quality-adjusted life-year
Counterfeiting
Current good manufacturing
   practices
Damages
Daubert principle
Differential pricing
Doctrine of *res ipsa loquitor*
Drug Price Competition and Patent
   Term Restoration Act of 1984
Duty
Duty to warn
Emerging Infections Program
Encode
Equity
Failure-to-warn
Fairness
First Amendment
Food and Drug Administration
Food, Drug and Cosmetic Act of
   1938

Formularies
Forseeable risks
Fraud
General causation
Generic manufacturers
Genes
Genomics
Global drug pricing
Global spillover
Global supply chains
Gross domestic product purchasing
   power parity per capita
Hatch-Waxman
Health-neutral
Hybrid pricing
Importation
Independent advisory committees
Investigational new drug (IND)
Large molecule business
Latent effects
Learned intermediary doctrine
Legal standard for admissibility of
   scientific evidence
Legal standard of certainty
Litigation risks
Malpractice
National Vaccine Injury
   Compensation Program
New drug application (NDA)
New Vaccine Surveillance
   Network
Noerr-Pennington doctrine
Off-label use

One-price policy
Opiate analgesics
Outsourcing
Patent infringement
Patents
Per se violation of the Sherman
   Act
Personal autonomy
Pharmacoeconomics
Pharmacy benefit manager
Phase II studies
Phase IV studies
Polypharmacy
Population health management
Prospective, randomized, placebo-
   controlled clinical trial
Proteomics
Reasonable degree of certainty
Recall
Regulation by litigation
Safe and effective
Segmented market pricing
Seizure
Shortages
Small molecule business
Specific causation
Stakeholder
Standards of conduct
Suboptimal prescribing
Supplemental FDA application
Universities Allied for Essential
   Medicines
Unlawful gains

FACT OR FICTION

State Preemption of Drug Labeling

Should drug-labeling judgments of the FDA preempt state law product liability claims?

Vermont guitarist Diana Levine lost an arm to gangrene after Wyeth's anti-nausea drug Phenergan was inadvertently injected into one of her arteries during an IV-push injection. Levine had gone to a clinic for treatment of a migraine headache. Levine argued Phenergan's labeling was defective because although it was approved by the **Food and Drug Administration (FDA)**, it did not provide proper warnings of the risk of administering the drug through an IV-push injection instead of using an IV-drip. A Vermont jury awarded Levine $6.7 million in damages.

The Vermont Supreme Court upheld the award; FDA drug regulations do not prevent a firm from being sued under state law over drug labeling. Wyeth maintained Levine's **failure-to-warn** claim, which was based on Vermont law, should be preempted by federal drug labeling regulations. Wyeth claimed it fully complied with federal labeling law. The FDA knew of the drug's risks and benefits and instructed the firm to use labeling that encompassed both. Wyeth maintained federal law prohibited the firm from revising the warnings on its product label as the Vermont court required.

— *See* Law Fact at the end of this chapter for the answer.

Principles and Applications

The U.S. pharmaceutical industry is maturing and moving away from the growth strategy perfected in the 1990s, a strategy based on **blockbuster drugs** that generated over $1 billion in revenue per drug each year. The pace of drug discovery has since slowed amid tougher regulatory scrutiny. At the same time, revenue has declined as **patents** for blockbuster drugs have expired and competition from **generic manufacturers** has expanded. Together these forces have resulted in an increased urgency to add new lines of business to offset the weak core drug business. *See generally* Hugin, 2014; Vagelos, 2014.

Today, the pharmaceutical industry is rapidly consolidating into more diversified firms, as illustrated in **TABLE 16-1**, becoming less reliant on traditional pharmaceutical research and the attendant unpredictability of drug development. The historical divide between the pharmaceutical and biotechnology sectors is quickly closing. For instance, Pfizer's acquisition of Wyeth added biotechnology drugs, vaccines, and consumer health products to its lineup. Merck's takeover of Schering-Plough brought biotechnology, consumer health, and animal health care to its ledger. These two multibillion-dollar mergers, along with Roche's purchase of Genentech, a biotechnology stand-alone company, are uniting pharmaceuticals with biotechnology.

While the growing convergence of pharmaceutical and biotechnology firms was expected, how the intersection of **small molecule businesses** (pharmaceutical companies) and **large molecule businesses** (biotechnology firms) will play out is still debated within the health care industry (*See* Burstein, 2012). In the trade, pharmaceutical drugs are generally referred to as small molecules and drugs from the biotechnology industry as large molecules. Drug molecule proteins manufactured in living cells are much larger and more complex than small molecule drugs produced by synthesizing chemicals. Pharmaceutical firms are looking outside their own laboratories for new drugs, and there is significant **outsourcing** to smaller life science firms to develop medical products. Global pharmaceutical firms are competing intensely for new ideas as a new global paradigm slowly emerges (Vagelos. 2014).

Health care investors are pulling back from early-stage investments to focus on compounds that have been proven safe in the short term and are already in **Phase II studies** to determine whether they actually work against targeted diseases. While there is a higher chance of giving up a blockbuster drug, there is greater certainty of the drug in a Phase II study being approved and actually making it to market (Wharton, 2006).

Overview of the Pharmaceutical Market

The U.S. pharmaceutical industry has traditionally been research driven; it is one of the most research-intensive industries in the United States, investing five times as much in research and development relative to sales than the average U.S. manufacturing firm (CBO, 2014). Domestic research and development spending by both pharmaceutical and biotechnology firms exceeds $130,000 per employee, or about 12 times the published estimates of research and development spending per employee in all manufacturing industries (Pham, 2015). The key segments in

TABLE 16-1   Profile of the Global Pharmaceutical Industry

Firms	Market Value	Sales	Number of Employees
Johnson & Johnson (United States)	$279.0 billion	$70.2 billion	121,700
Novartis (Switzerland)	$240.8 billion	$47.6 billion	118,700
Pfizer (United States)	$211.6 billion	$48.9 billion	97,900
Roche (Switzerland)	$222.2 billion	$48.2 billion	91,700
Merck (United States)	$163.9 billion	$38.8 billion	68,000
Sanofi (France)	$130.7 billion	$34.5 billion	115,600
GlaxoSmithKline (Great Britain)	$113.1 billion	$23.9 billion	101,200
Abbott Laboratories (United States)	$91.9 billion	$20.5 billion	74,000
Eli Lilly (United States)	$78.0 billion	$20.0 billion	41,300
AstraZeneca (Great Britain)	$88.5 billion	$16.2 billion	61,500

Data from: Income and Revenue Statements in the 2015 Annual Report filings with the U.S. Securities and Exchange Commission.

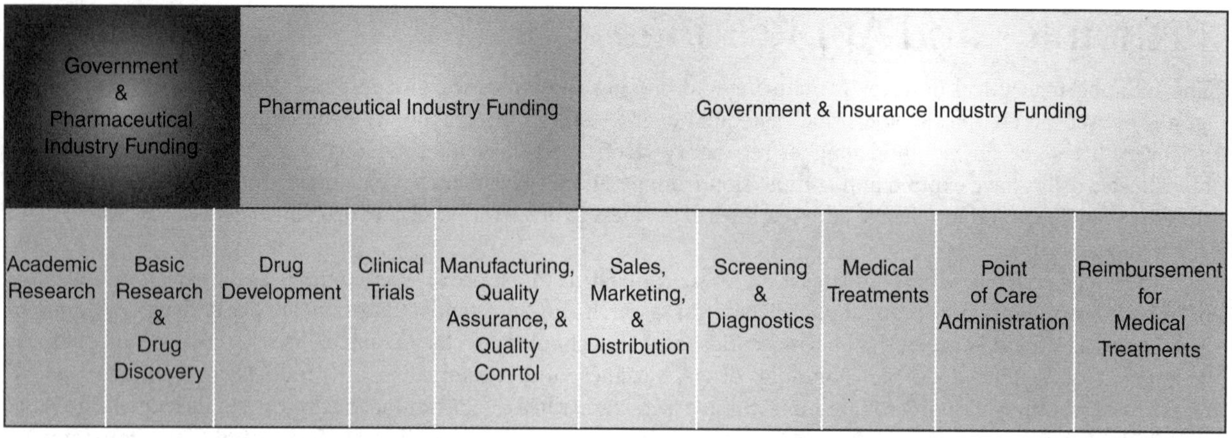

FIGURE 16-1 View of the Pharmaceutical Market

the pharmaceutical industry's landscape are often misunderstood—from the basic academic research that builds understanding of human biological processes to treat diseases and illnesses through drug discovery, development, clinical trials, manufacturing, sales and marketing, and distribution (CBO, 2014). **FIGURE 16-1** provides an overview of the global pharmaceutical market.

Academic and Basic Research (3 to 6 Years)

Drug discovery is the result of laboratory collaboration between the pharmaceutical industry, small drug firms, the nations' academic research groups, and the National Institutes of Health. Scientists work to understand the disease to be treated and the underlying cause of the condition. They try to understand:

- How **genes** are altered
- How alterations affect the proteins they **encode**
- How those proteins interact with each other in the cells
- How those cells affect the specific tissue they are in
- How the tissue affects individual patients

(PhRMA, 2016).

The National Institutes of Health and the pharmaceutical industry are the major sources of funding for this basic research. The pharmaceutical industry's funding of $37.3 billion was the source of nearly one-third of the biomedical research funding in the United States, accounting for the largest share of government or private funding (Moses, 2015).

Drug Discovery and Development (10 to 15 Years)

For the first time in history, scientists are beginning to understand the inner workings of human disease at the molecular level. Recent advances in **genomics, proteomics**, and **computational power** present new ways to understand illness. The task of discovering and developing safe, effective drugs is even more promising as knowledge of disease increases (PhRMA, 2016).

As illustrated in **FIGURE 16-2**, it can take 15 years to develop one new drug from the time of the initial drug discovery to the point of care where it is administered to patients. Hundreds of people are engaged in this process; depending on the complexity of the drug, as many as 2,000 can be involved. Many of the new drugs now coming to market were in the early stages of discovery in 2000. The average cost to discover and develop each successful new drug now exceeds $2.6 billion (PhRMA, 2016). This number includes the costs of thousands of failures. One new drug product receives FDA approval for every 5,000 to 10,000 chemical compounds entering the drug discovery pipeline (PhRMA, 2016).

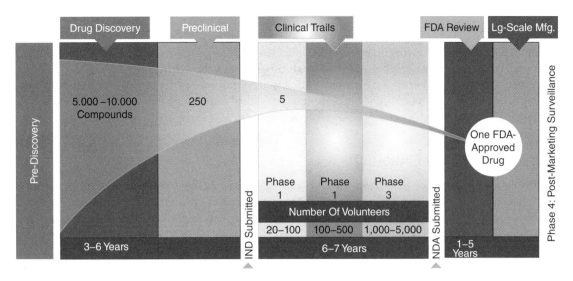

FIGURE 16-2 Drug Discovery and Development

Data from: DiMasi, J. A., et al. (2016). Innovation in the pharmaceutical industry: New estimates of R&D costs. *Journal of Health Economics*, 47, 20–33; DiMasi, J. A., et al. (2014). *Briefing: Cost of developing a new drug. Boston.* MA: Tufts Center for the Study of Drug Development; FDA (Food and Drug Administration). (2016b). *Drug approval process.* U.S. Bethesda, MD: FDA; PhRMA (Pharmaceutical Research and Manufacturers Association). (2016). *Biopharmaceuticals in perspective.* Washington, DC: PhRMA.

Clinical Trials (6 to 7 Years)

After discovery and development, the drug candidate then goes into **clinical trials** in humans, where the drug must be proven to be **safe and effective** before the FDA will approve it. This process involves a series of trials, each with its own clinical goals and regulatory requirements. Physicians carry out each trial with patients in hospitals, offices, and clinics, in coordination with the sponsoring pharmaceutical firm.

Before any clinical trials can begin, an **investigational new drug (IND)** application must be filed with the FDA. The IND includes the:

- Results of the pre-clinical work
- Drug candidate's chemical structure
- Explanation of how it is thought to work in the body
- Listing of any anticipated side effects
- Description of how it is to be manufactured

(FDA, 2016c; *See* 21 U.S.C.A. § 312).

The IND also provides a detailed clinical trial plan outlining how, where, and by whom the clinical trial will be performed. The approved IND grants authority for the medication's sponsor to ship this unapproved medicine in interstate commerce for clinical testing. In addition to the IND, all clinical trials must be reviewed by the institutional review board at a teaching institution where the trials are to take place. Throughout the clinical trial process, the sponsoring pharmaceutical firm must provide information to the FDA and the institutional review boards about how the trials are progressing. *See generally* FDA, 2016c.

New Drug Application and Approval (2 Years)

Once the clinical trials are complete, the sponsoring pharmaceutical firm reviews all the data. If the firm decides the drug candidate is both safe and effective, it prepares and files a **new drug application (NDA)** requesting FDA approval to market the drug. The NDA describes the decade of testing and generally runs 100,000 pages or more. The NDA is reviewed by the FDA and **independent advisory committees** of experts appointed by the FDA, who then decide under what market conditions the drug should be approved. The FDA is not required to accept the recommendations of the advisory committee, but it generally does. *See generally* FDA, 2016d; 21 U.S.C.A. § 314.

Drug Manufacturing

Going from small-scale manufacturing of supplies for clinical testing to large-scale manufacturing for the public market is a major undertaking. In many cases, a new manufacturing site must be constructed because the manufacturing process is different from drug to drug. Each manufacturing facility must meet strict **current good manufacturing practices (GMPs)**. Drug manufacturing is not only one of the most highly skilled forms of manufacturing, but it is also one of the most regulated (PhRMA, 2016).

Ongoing Research and Monitoring

Even after a drug is approved for marketing, research and monitoring of the drug continues. Pharmaceutical firms must continuously monitor the usage of their drugs and report adverse events to the FDA (FDA, 2016e). In addition, the FDA may require the firm to conduct **Phase IV studies** to determine long-term safety or how the drug affects specific subpopulations (FDA, 2016f).

Global Pricing of Drugs

Global drug pricing is a complex process lacking a clear, simple explanation (DiMasi et al., 2016). In most discussions about the cost of drugs, three parts of the cost equation are often overlooked:

- Cost of disease and illness
- Economic benefits of improved health
- Global complexity of drug pricing

(DiMasi et al., 2016).

Cost of Disease and Illness

The cost of disease and illness includes the cost of:

- Drugs
- Hospitalizations
- Physical therapies
- Physician visits
- Surgeries

(PhRMA, 2016).

When a drug can significantly reduce or eliminate these other costs, that reduction is a factor in determining the price of the drug, especially when the drug can permanently cure or alleviate previously fatal or debilitating conditions. If patients adhered to their recommended drug regimens, the savings to the health care system could be dramatic. For instance:

- For the $100 billion that is spent on cholesterol drugs, there is over $510 billion in savings to the health care system
- For the $44 billion spent on diabetes drugs, over $310 billion is saved on health care costs

(IMS Institute, 2016).

It is important to note that the cost of ingredients on production can be a very minor contribution to the total product cost (akin to women's high-fashion shoes).

As illustrated in **FIGURE 16-3**, better use of prescribed drugs could eliminate up to $213 billion in the nation's health care costs annually, which represents 8% of the nation's health care spending (IMS Institute, 2016). The most avoidable cost is **suboptimal prescribing**, which includes:

- $12 billion in suboptimal generic use
- $35 billion in inappropriate antibiotic use
- $40 billion in untimely use of prescribed drugs

(IMS Institute, 2016).

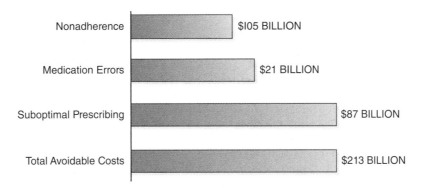

FIGURE 16-3 Avoidable Health Care Costs

Data from: IMS Institute for Healthcare Informatics. (2016). *Avoidable costs in U.S. healthcare: The $200 billion opportunity from using drugs more responsibly*. Plymouth Meeting, PA: IMS Health; PhRMA (Pharmaceutical Research and Manufacturers Association). (2016). *Biopharmaceuticals in perspective*. Washington, DC: PhRMA;

Medication errors account for another $20 billion in avoidable health care costs, while mismanaged **polypharmacy** or the practice of prescribing too many drugs to patients (also referred to as drug cocktails) accounts for another avoidable cost of $1 billion (IMS Institute, 2016).

Economic Benefits of Improved Health

Drugs are increasingly priced to reflect economic benefits to individual patients. This includes making economic calculations as to how much money a drug saves when it prevents a patient from having surgery, or the economic benefit of allowing a patient to continue working when, without the drug, employment would not have been possible. The key measure used to assess the marginal value of a drug for different patient groups is generally the additional **cost per quality-adjusted life-year (QALY)** gained (Babaian, 2014). If appropriate data on quality of life is unavailable, **cost-effectiveness** is estimated using alternatives such as **cost per life-year gained** (Furrow, 2013). When determining the economic benefits of a drug, the pharmaceutical industry considers:

- The innovative nature of the drug
- The particular features of the health condition
- The degree of uncertainty surrounding these price estimates
- The wider societal costs and benefits, where appropriate

(*See* Kesselheim & Darrow, 2015).

Global Complexity of Drug Pricing

It seems everyone wants lowered drug prices, but no one (including the health care industry) knows how to deliver them while maintaining resources for future innovative research and development. This quandary is due to the multitude of factors influencing global pricing decisions:

- Competing **stakeholders**' interests between developed and developing nations
- Complex regulatory policies that differ by country and have contradictory pricing goals
- Costs of global research and development
- Desire to donate drugs for the uninsured and low-income patients, both in the United States and globally
- Economic objectives behind drug pricing in negotiation and management of price decisions by **pharmacy benefit managers**, the health insurance industry, and governments worldwide
- Social welfare differences between higher income and lower income patient communities

(Brennan et al., 2016; Kirkwood, 2016).

Facing a situation where costs to market drugs to physicians and the public are increasing enormously while pharmaceutical laboratories are having trouble developing new blockbuster drugs to drive revenue, something will have to give. Many within the health care industry, including most members of the Pharmaceutical Research and Manufacturers Association, agree that the blockbuster model of drug development has to go, as its costs have become astronomical (*e.g.*, Tironi, 2010; Vagelos, 2014). While some pharmaceutical firms operate as if they are still in a growth industry, delivering 10 or 12% growth per year, pharmaceuticals is now a mature global industry focused on product quality and innovative product improvement (Vagelos, 2014).

Correlation Between Global Drug Prices and International Per Capita Incomes

In general, global drug price differences correlate with per capita income differences among countries. This is a critical fact to consider when high drug prices in the United States are criticized. Pricing occurs on a global basis, and the **gross domestic product (GDP) purchasing power parity per capita** of the United States in relationship to the rest of the world is generally higher, as compared to other developed economies like most of Europe or Japan (CIA, 2016; IMF, 2016;).

While the ability to pay higher drug prices is greater for Americans compared to most other citizens in the world, drug prices in the United States are generally 6 to 33% higher than in other countries (Hugin, 2014). In terms of global **fairness** and **equity**, it could be argued Americans should be paying higher prices for their drugs, given their comparable wealth. For instance, the average income for Americans is $48,000 according to the International Monetary Fund, compared to $10,500 for most non-Americans. Therefore, by way of illustration, a $10.00 drug in the United States should cost $2.00 in the rest of the world, or one-fifth as much.

At the same time, the use of generic drugs is higher in the United States with 9 out of every 10 prescriptions filled with generics, and generic prices are lower (OECD, 2015). Further, the differences in drug pricing are not as significant when exchange rates and gross domestic product rates are being considered. Even if per capita income is used as the basis for comparison, price differences as they relate to income are relatively proportionate globally (IMS Institute, 2016). In summary, drug pricing is complex, in part because of the need to balance the interests of industry innovation with public need and entitlement (Epstein, 2008).

Differential Pricing System

One possible solution to high drug prices in the United States is to adopt the European **differential pricing** system. Under this system, developed countries help underwrite the cost of drug research and development, and resource-limited countries help pay for the costs associated with manufacturing the drugs. This system also supports global patent protection so **brand-name drugs** can receive premium pricing in order to help fund innovative drug development. Lastly, this system aims to control **global spillover** that occurs when low-priced drugs gain entry back into high-priced markets, thereby reducing demand and prices in those markets. Advantages of a differential pricing system include:

- Marginal cost of drug consumption
- Efficient use of existing drugs by market forces
- No harm to consumers of health care in developed, high-income markets

Further, this system opens markets; resource-limited countries are better off, while developed countries are no worse off. This is not a cost-shifting scheme since the cost of research and development would be a joint cost not attributable to a single country. If resource-limited countries pay any portion of the manufacturing costs, then it is possible that drug prices will be lower in the United States (Danzon & Furukawa, 2008).

One-Price Policy

The other policy proposal is for the pharmaceutical industry to adopt a **one-price policy** when selling drugs in different countries, a strategy that would neutralize the debate over drug imports and also would spread out the costs of research more evenly across consumers in different countries (Kirkwood, 2016). Achieving a one-price policy would be difficult (Gregg, 2015). With firms bringing similar drugs to market, the pharmaceutical industry would have to compete on price, something it has not done traditionally; as a result, prices could decrease.

Re-Importation and Secure Global Supply Chains

In an effort to work with the pharmaceutical industry in systematically improving global production and distribution efficiencies, the FDA recently initiated a voluntary pilot program to promote the safety of drugs and active pharmaceutical ingredients produced outside the United States. To qualify, firms need to maintain control over their drug products from the time of manufacture through entry into the United States. The goal is to develop secure **global supply chains** (*See* Chapter on Global Supply Chain Management). Such a program would assist the agency in its efforts to prevent the **importation** of drugs not in compliance with applicable FDA requirements; this would allow the agency to focus its resources on foreign-produced drugs that may not be compliant. A secure global supply chain will also help mitigate crises such as contamination and **counterfeiting** (Foote, 2015).

Market Changes: Cost Management

Managed care (or more accurately, cost management) has affected the pharmaceutical industry in several ways, some but not all of which improve the quality of health care. The focus on cost management exacerbates three issues relating to FDA regulation of the industry:

- Managed care forces focus on reducing industry costs while seeking improvements in the effectiveness of drugs.
- Pharmacy benefit managers have come to function as the intermediary between physicians who actually prescribe drugs and the pharmaceutical industry by screening drugs for placement on drug formularies.
- Managed care increases cost pressures that impact a maturing industry.

(Comanor & Needleman, 2016).

It has been argued that cost management has induced the pharmaceutical industry to curtail its research and development of new drugs. Regardless of the merits of this contention, managed care has considerable leverage to negotiate drug prices and pharmaceutical firms now directly market their drug products to pharmacy benefit managers. The two areas most affected by managed care are the use of:

- Cost-effectiveness data
- **Off-label use** promotion

(Abbott & Ayres, 2014).

New Targets of Promotional Information

Unlike physicians who seek information in order to prescribe specific drugs, pharmacy benefit managers and the government seek information in order to make cost-benefit tradeoffs among different drugs. The pharmaceutical industry caters to this need for information, creating at least two issues for the FDA:

- **Pharmacoeconomics** as a tool to manage drug costs
- Information provided to the pharmacy benefit managers about unapproved (off-label) uses

Pharmacoeconomics

Pharmacoeconomics is the study of the relative cost-effectiveness of treatments. Managed care uses such studies to create their **formularies** or list of covered drugs. The primary benefit is economic; pharmacoeconomics helps lower health care costs by helping to select the least expensive but still effective drugs for placement on formularies. The pharmaceutical industry may provide pharmacoeconomic information about drug products to formulary committees, pharmacy benefit managers, and similar large-scale buyers of medical products. The law, however, does not permit the dissemination of pharmacoeconomic information that could affect prescribing choices to individual prescribers (Darrow, 2014).

While the law is intended to provide the health insurance industry with dependable facts about the economic consequences of their procurement decisions, the pharmaceutical industry uses pharmacoeconomic studies as marketing devices to promote specific drugs (Kesselheim & Darrow, 2015). Because the FDA has the power to regulate advertising and marketing, it needs to determine whether it is wise to review these cost-effectiveness claims with the same rigorous validation procedures it uses for claims of safety and effectiveness in drug marketing, labeling, and advertising (*See* 21 U.S.C.A. §§ 351 *et seq.*).

Unapproved (Off-Label) Drug Use

The FDA has taken the position that if unapproved (off-label) use must occur, then it should be limited to the confines of individualized treatments requested by a physician. Managed care has an interest in off-label uses in order to create formularies and guidelines that:

- Constrain costs
- Limit physicians' treatment decisions

(Comanor & Needleman, 2016).

However, formulary decisions are usually made in advance, creating a problem when a potential use is unapproved and managed care organizations cannot gain access to information to evaluate that use. Information to create formularies is requested one to two years in advance for a formulary listing, yet the pharmaceutical industry cannot provide unapproved (off-label) information ahead of actual availability about unapproved drugs. This creates a difficult dilemma from which there is no escape because of mutually dependent conditions (Kesselheim & Darrow, 2015).

The **learned intermediary doctrine** imposes an obligation on pharmaceutical firms to warn physicians of **foreseeable risks** associated with the use of its drugs (Restatement, 2013, § 6(d)(1)). The justification for this doctrine is that physicians are in a better position to supply patients with information about the drugs and to warn them of the risks appropriate for the patient's individual circumstances so the patient is in the best position to make an informed decision regarding treatment. In prescription drug cases involving the learned intermediary doctrine, when a warning specifically mentions the circumstances complained of, the warning is generally considered adequate as a matter of law (Bi, 2015).

While any advertising of unapproved (off-label) uses directed to patients is prohibited, peer-reviewed journal articles about an off-label use of drugs may be disseminated by a pharmaceutical firm provided the firm commits itself to file, within a specified time frame, a **supplemental FDA application** based on appropriate research to establish the safety and effectiveness of the unapproved use. The primary assumption is managed care organizations and physicians can view such information critically, but this does not hold true for patients. How the FDA should protect consumers in off-label use of drugs is an issue of continued debate (Kesselheim & Darrow, 2015).

COURT DECISION
Products Liability for Unapproved (Off-Label) Drug Use

McNeil v. Wyeth
[Patient v. Pharmaceutical Firm]
462 F.3d 364 (U.S. Court of Appeals for the 5th Circuit 2006),
settled following mediation, 2007 U.S.Dist.LEXIS 97604 (U.S. District Court for the Northern District of Texas, Dallas Division 2007);
followed by Brinkley v. Pfizer, Inc., 772 F.3d 1133 (U.S. Court of Appeals for the 8th Circuit 2014), *rehearing denied*, 2015 U.S.App.LEXIS 157 (U.S. Court of Appeals for the 8th Circuit 2015)

Facts: Sue McNeil claimed Wyeth did not adequately warn physicians of the increased risk of neurological disorders associated with long-term use of Reglan, a drug manufactured by Wyeth to treat gastroesophageal reflux disease (GERD). Dr. Eduardo Wilkinson, McNeil's primary physician, prescribed Reglan to treat symptoms related to McNeil's gastroesophageal reflux disease. Reglan's labeling warned the drug could produce drug-induced movement disorders.[LN1]

Dr. Wilkinson gave McNeil a six-month prescription of Reglan even though the FDA only approved Reglan's use for three months. Two additional physicians renewed McNeil's prescription for Reglan for eight additional months. After taking Reglan for 14 months, McNeil went to an emergency room complaining of shortness of breath and an involuntary chewing motion of her mouth. The emergency room physician diagnosed her with tardive dyskinesia, which he believed was likely caused by her long-term exposure to Reglan. Dr. Wilkinson confirmed the diagnosis and discontinued her use of Reglan. When her symptoms failed to improve, she consulted a neurologist and two physicians specializing in movement disorders. All three specialists diagnosed McNeil with tardive dyskinesia, a Reglan-induced neurological disorder characterized by involuntary movements of the face and jaw, confirming that Reglan was the cause of her condition. McNeil sued Wyeth in state court claiming Wyeth failed to provide adequate warnings to physicians and consumers of the increased risk of neurological disorders associated with the long-term use of Reglan. Wyeth maintained Reglan's labeling sufficiently warned of the dangers of Reglan.

Issue: Does understating the risk of side effects render drug labels misleading and ineffective?

Holding and Decision: Yes. When there is a warning of a much lower risk than the actual risk, the warning label is misleading and ineffective. Drug labels should explain the higher risks of developing side effects from long-term use of a drug.

Analysis: The court distinguished this case from other cases based on the learned intermediary doctrine. McNeil did not claim the warning was inadequate because her condition was not mentioned, but rather that the warning was misleading as to the level of risk associated with developing the condition. The court found that warning a learned intermediary, such as Dr. Wilkinson, of a much lower risk than the actual risk of developing a condition renders a warning both misleading and ineffective.

Wyeth maintained it did not have a **duty to warn** about risks related to using Reglan beyond a period of three months because the labeling stated it was not intended for use over longer periods. The court, however, disagreed with Wyeth's argument, finding Reglan was routinely prescribed for long-term use. Wyeth's own marketing data indicated most patients were using Reglan for periods beyond the recommended three months. In addition, medical journals drew attention to the common use of Reglan as a long-term treatment. Because of the widespread use of Reglan for more than three months, a jury could infer the warning was ineffective and inadequate.

Wyeth claimed it was not required to update its label because studies indicating the risk of developing tardive dyskinesia due to long-term use of Reglan merely demonstrated an association between the two without actually showing **causation**. However, FDA regulations require drug labels to be revised to include a warning as soon as there is reasonable evidence of an association of a serious hazard with a drug; a causal relationship need not be proved. Furthermore, Wyeth was not relieved of this duty to warn solely because no clinical trials proved actual causation. The pharmaceutical industry frequently warns physicians certain drug use is not recommended, even if clinical trials do not confirm risk or causation.

The court further found it was a question of fact for the jury to determine whether Wyeth should have warned physicians of the risks of the long-term use of Reglan. The side effects of neurological disorders are highly predictable for drugs, such as Reglan, that block dopamine receptors. Thus, the court found there was a genuine issue of fact concerning whether Reglan's labeling was adequate. Wyeth failed to warn physicians and patients that the risk of developing neurological disorders increased significantly with long-term use.

Finally, the court found there was a genuine issue of material fact as to whether the label's inadequate information caused Dr. Wilkinson to prescribe the drug to McNeil. If an adequately informed learned intermediary would have adequately informed a patient of the risks of a disease had a label been sufficient, but failed to do so because of the lack of information provided on the label, and if the patient would have rejected the drug if informed, then an inadequate label could be considered to have produced the injury. The rationale for this rule is that the ineffective label essentially defeats the purpose behind the learned intermediary doctrine.

On the issue of whether the label was clearly misleading, the court held there were enough arguments on either side that the issue should be decided by a trial court. Furthermore, there was a genuine issue concerning whether, had the warning label accurately conveyed the level of risk involved, McNeil's physician would have nevertheless prescribed the drug.

Rule of Law: Drug labels may be misleading, even without evidence proving a causal relationship connecting long-term use with a serious side effect; all that needs to be shown is some association between long-term use and increased risk for the claimed side effect.

References (discussing this court decision): Miller, 2013. *See also, Pliva, Inc. v. Mensing*, 564 U.S. 604 (U.S. Supreme Court 2011) (issue of off-label drug use is ongoing in litigation against generic manufacturers).

The *Wyeth* case suggests the pharmaceutical industry may be held liable for warnings of a much lower risk than the actual risk of developing side effects from their drugs if:

- Use beyond the package insert is widespread
- Pharmaceutical firms know, or should know, of the common unapproved (off-label) use of their drugs

In light of this decision, the pharmaceutical industry may need to update its warnings to address these risks, even if the risks are only merely associated with the drug and causation has not been definitively proven (Miller, 2013).

MANAGEMENT AND LAW ISSUES

1. Should the FDA regulate cost-effectiveness claims made by the pharmaceutical industry? If so, should the same validation procedures used for safety and effectiveness claims be used to rigorously validate claims of cost-effectiveness?
2. Should the FDA more thoroughly protect consumers from unapproved (off-label) use of drugs?

Pharmaceutical Benefit Managers

Pharmaceutical benefit managers directly affect the provision of health care. They administer and process drug benefits claims and are often electronically linked to the community pharmacies participating in their programs. Pharmacy benefit managers also seek to lower drug costs by restricting patient choices of drugs to cheaper generics or to preferred brands (Grabowski et al., 2016). More often than not, substitutions rely on formularies chosen by the managed care organizations to reduce drug costs as opposed to therapeutic effectiveness (Hall, 2014).

Pharmacy benefit managers also actively encourage physicians to alter prescription patterns within the same therapeutic class to reduce drug costs. Many managed care organizations use pharmacy benefit managers to educate individual professionals and patients about drugs. Thus, in some instances, a pharmacy benefit manager may offer services that fall within a traditional definition of health care provision rather than just cost management. **Population health management** programs deepen these concerns because they provide information on dosage and choices available to patients. Although substitutions based on price may seem **health-neutral,** consider the effect pharmacoeconomic data could have: instead of merely trading price, if the pharmacy benefit manager trades price for quality, then more than just the cost of health care is being affected (Callam, 2014).

Exposure Game

For years the traditional requirements needed to prove consumers were injured by drugs created insurmountable obstacles to recovery from the pharmaceutical industry. Generally, four elements must be proven in any **malpractice** case:

- *Duty:* the firms owed consumers a duty
- *Breach of duty:* the firms breached that duty
- *Causation:* the breach of duty caused personal injury to consumers
- *Damages:* proven with a **reasonable degree of certainty**

As between injured consumers and the pharmaceutical industry, the task of the law is to determine who should bear the loss. The law protects **personal autonomy** by compensating victims for intrusions of their bodily integrity (Calabresi, 2014). The law also enforces **standards of conduct**. When pharmaceutical firms market drugs that unreasonably endanger the safety of consumers, they must pay for the harms they inflict. However, the goal of the law extends beyond compensation; optimal drug safety does not mean perfect drug safety, but instead seeks to balance the risks and benefits of drugs against consumers' interest in being effectively treated for a health condition (Sheley, 2015).

Causation Requirement

The **burden of proof** required to prove **causation** is fourfold:

- *Exposure:* consumers were exposed to the drug.
- *General causation:* the drug was capable of causing the injury complained of.
- *Specific causation:* the drug actually caused the injury.
- *Responsibility:* the pharmaceutical firm being sued was responsible for manufacturing the drug that caused the injury.

(Restatement, 2013).

General Versus Specific Causation

Proving general causation involves introducing statistical evidence comparing the incidence of an injury in the general population and the incidence of the injury in the patient population exposed to the drug. Proving specific causation involves testimony that the drug in question was produced by the pharmaceutical firm and probably caused the injury. Both of these proof requirements involve scientific and statistical evidence, the admissibility of which can be controversial (Green & Sanders, 2015).

Admissibility of Scientific Evidence

The standard for admitting scientific evidence in courts is a two-part test, known as the **Daubert principle**:

- Whether testimony conveys scientific knowledge grounded in the methods and procedures of science and is more than subjective belief or unsupported speculation
- Whether it is relevant

(*See Daubert v. Merrell Dow Pharmaceuticals, Inc.*, 509 U.S. 579 (U.S. Supreme Court 1993).[LN2]

The **legal standard for admissibility of scientific evidence** remains high because of the high standards the scientific community imposes on itself. In science, a hypothesis is never proven. It is either rejected or not rejected with a certain degree of reliability. The **legal standard of certainty** for scientific evidence to be considered by the courts is generally 95%. This is a difficult standard to meet because of scientific uncertainty and often because of the limited data available. Because the burden of proof is on the injured consumer, these difficulties work in favor, in theory at least, of the pharmaceutical industry (Chlistunoff, 2016).

The $7 Billion Recall

Vioxx was a $2.5 billion **blockbuster drug** for Merck, before its **recall**.[LN3] The litigation that followed the recall is a classic example of how courts view the causation requirement. The Ernst case is a landmark decision highlighting what Merck faced after it voluntarily took Vioxx off the market.

COURT DECISION

Evidence of Causation

Merck & Co. v. Ernst
[Widow v. Pharmaceutical Company]
296 S.W.3d 81 (Court of Appeals of Texas, 14th District, Houston 2008),
cert. denied, 132 S.Ct. 1980 (U.S. Supreme Court 2012)

Facts: Robert Ernst, a marathon runner, fitness trainer, and manager for a Texas Wal-Mart, died of a cardiac arrhythmia and atherosclerosis after taking Vioxx for seven months. In her lawsuit against Merck, his widow, Carol Ernst, claimed negligent failure to warn of the dangers associated with the drug and civil conspiracy to conceal the danger. By the time the case went to trial, it was one of about 4,200 Vioxx lawsuits nationwide.

Right before the Ernst trial was scheduled to begin, Texas filed widely publicized charges against Merck for falsely advertising the safety of Vioxx and defrauding the state Medicaid program. *See Texas v. Merck & Co., Inc.*, 385 F.Supp.2d 604 (U.S. District Court for the Western District of Texas, Austin Division 2005). Although Merck filed for a continuance, claiming the publicity prejudiced any possible jury member and prevented a fair trial, the Ernst trial proceeded in an untraditional way.

The jurors awarded Ernst $253.4 million, $229 million of which was punitive damages. Ernst had asked for $40 million. This appeal followed, in which Merck claimed the causation requirement was not met.

Issue: Was Ernst's death caused by a blood clot triggered by Vioxx?

Holding and Decision: No. There was no competent and legally sufficient evidence on the issue of causation and the existence of a blood clot, and therefore, Ernst could not collect any damages.

Analysis: The Ernst trial was not a causation case about heart attacks and strokes being increased by the use of Vioxx; it evolved around corporate accountability. While Ernst had to establish to a reasonable degree of medical certainty that Vioxx probably (not possibly) caused her husband's fatal cardiac arrhythmia, causation was not an issue for this Texas jury. Following this overturned trial verdict, Merck attempted to refute evidence it knew Vioxx to be dangerous. In doing so, Merck acknowledged the battleground was the morality of Merck's actions, not the legal validity of the injury claims.

The issue shifted toward whether Merck knowingly marketed a dangerous drug and away from the evidence of causation. No reliable scientific evidence demonstrated Vioxx caused cardiac arrhythmias, and no epidemiological study with a placebo demonstrated a statistically significant effect from Vioxx taken for less than 18 months.

Rule of Law: Legally sufficient evidence of causation must be presented in order for damages to be awarded in a personal injury and wrongful death lawsuit against a pharmaceutical firm; testifying experts may not simply speculate as to whether a drug caused an injury.

References discussing this court decision: *E.g.*, Brown, 2014.

Doctrine of *Res Ipsa Loquitor*

In most pharmaceutical cases, the central issue is proof of causation because the standard for admissibility of scientific evidence can be very high and such evidence is expensive and often unavailable (Restatement, 2013, § 6). In some lawsuits against members of the pharmaceutical industry, however, the requirements of causation can be relaxed such as when an injury is of a type that does not occur except as a result of negligence, using the **doctrine of** *res ipsa loquitor* (Restatement, 2013, § 328D comment (a)). *Res ipsa loquitor* is a Latin phrase that translates to "the thing speaks for itself." In these situations, the occurrence of an injury is enough to infer both negligence and causation as a matter of fact.

Latent Effects from Approved Drugs

The number of successful lawsuits over **latent effects** from approved drugs might indicate the research required by FDA regulation is often not enough to assess all of the harmful effects of a drug (*See* Laakmann, 2015).

COURT DECISION
Restitution Under the Food, Drug and Cosmetic Act

United States v. Rx Depot, Inc.
[Federal Government v. Re-Importer]
438 F.3d 1052 (U.S. Court of Appeals for the 10th Circuit 2006),
cert. denied, 549 U.S. 817 (U.S. Supreme Court 2006);
followed by United States v. Zen Magnets, LLC, 2016 U.S.Dist.LEXIS 36888 (U.S. District Court for the District of Colorado 2016)

Facts: Rx Depot helped patients in the United States obtain reduced-priced pharmaceutical medicines from Canada by acting as the middleman in a reimportation scheme. Customers gave Rx Depot information about their prescriptions from U.S. physicians. Rx Depot then transmitted this information to cooperating Canadian physicians and pharmacies. Once Canadian physicians rewrote the prescriptions from the United States, Canadian pharmacies dispensed these prescriptions and sent them directly to patients in the United States.

The federal government filed a lawsuit against Rx Depot, claiming the firm violated the federal **Food, Drug and Cosmetic Act of 1938** (FDCA) by reimporting pharmaceutical medicines originally manufactured in the United States and introducing new drugs into interstate commerce without approval (*See* 21 U.S.C.A. §§ 301 *et seq.*). The parties subsequently agreed to a consent decree, which confirmed Rx Depot violated federal law and prevented the firm from resuming business operations. The consent decree, however, left it to the courts to determine what equitable relief to award the federal government.

Issue: Can courts order restitution to the federal government for violations of federal law?

Holding and Decision: Yes. Courts may order violators of federal law to pay restitution to the federal government.

Analysis: The court analyzed whether restitution is available when a federal law invokes equity jurisdiction, and it determined that the courts may use all equitable powers available to them to exercise jurisdiction unless the law restricts the form of equitable relief by clear and valid legislative command or necessary and inescapable inference. Because restitution is a traditional equitable remedy, courts are permitted to grant restitution unless the:

- FDCA contains clear legislative language preventing courts from ordering restitution
- Purposes of the FDCA are inconsistent with granting restitution

Additionally, cases involving the public interest provide courts with broader and more flexible equitable powers. Since the United States brought this case to protect public health and safety, the court has broader and more flexible equitable powers.

Rx Depot maintained language within the FDCA implies only forward-looking remedies are available (21 U.S.C.A. § 332(a)). The U.S. Supreme Court has, however, declined to determine whether laws similar to the FDCA's language permit courts to order restitution. The court therefore found the FDCA's language does not prohibit courts from ordering restitution.

Rx Depot also asserted that since the FDCA expressly authorizes certain remedies, a court should be reluctant to infer additional remedies. Congress, however, authorized courts to provide all traditional equitable remedies when it granted courts general equity jurisdiction under the FDCA. Additionally, express remedies do not limit courts to providing only those remedies listed in the FDCA. The FDCA's express authorization of certain remedies does not prohibit courts from ordering equitable remedies not listed in the FDCA.

Additionally, Rx Depot claimed that since the FDCA specifically authorizes restitution for certain medical devices, Congress did not intend to allow restitution under other FDCA provisions. Restitution refers to the return of **unlawful gains**, in this case whatever profits Rx Depot obtained as a result of its reimportation activities, also referred to as disgorgement. The restitution the FDCA specifies refers to powers the FDA has to order restitution payments, powers that are not limited to the equitable powers the FDCA grants to courts.

Finally, Rx Depot argued the FDCA's legislative history prohibits courts from ordering restitution because Congress intended for **seizure** to be the harshest remedy available. This argument fails, however, because seizures can be harsher than restitution. For instance, the FDCA permits seizures based on the FDA's request to a court upon a showing of reasonable belief that a party is in violation of the FDCA, without hearing from the party, while a court can only order restitution after a party is found to be in violation of the FDCA. In addition, seizures under the FDCA deprive a pharmaceutical firm of its capital investment and potential profit, while restitution only deprives a firm of its profits. Therefore, the court held the FDCA permits restitution when it furthers the purposes of the FDCA because the FDCA does not contain a clear legislative command or compel a necessary and inescapable inference precluding restitution.

Rule of Law: Courts can order restitution because the FDCA invokes general equity jurisdiction and does not contain a clear legislative command prohibiting restitution.

References discussing this court decision: *E.g.* Horvath, 2015; Noah, 2014; Phillips et al., 2015; Rodwin, 2015.

Pain Management

Pain management drugs can be used for legitimate medical purposes to relieve pain and suffering and allow management of medical and surgical conditions, whether acute or chronic in duration. However, because **opiate analgesics** to treat chronic pains are addictive, diversion from the prescribed use by physicians and pharmacists can lead to serious health problems (Fry-Revere & Do, 2013). Consequently, the public has a vested interest in protecting the medical uses of pain management drugs while reducing the morbidity and mortality from their misuse. Of concern are the increased federal and state criminal investigations and prosecutions of physicians for their prescribing practices. At the same time,

MANAGEMENT AND LAW ISSUES

3. Is the clinical research required by the FDA rigorous enough to assess all of the harmful effects of new drugs?

there has been substantial regulatory policy development to address pain management issues, with medical boards adopting regulations, guidelines, and policy statements to provide guidance to licensees about using opioids to treat pain (Goldberg, 2013).

Regulation by Litigation

Federal regulators, state attorneys general, and attorneys for consumers increasingly rely upon litigation to impose regulatory constraints on the pharmaceutical industry. Through such **regulation by litigation**, government officials and private attorneys bypass traditional processes and reorient regulatory priorities (Wharton, 2011). Some claim regulation by litigation is attractive to regulators because it provides a shortcut to imposing regulatory burdens on private pharmaceutical firms and needs to be curbed. Others argue regulation by litigation is an important regulatory tool that can help control corporate abuses and encourage the adoption of needed consumer protections. The issue to be addressed is why regulation by litigation is on the rise (Northhaft, 2011; Shell, 2004).

There is little to distinguish regulation by litigation from taxation or tort law as a form of regulation on malpractice disputes.

No-Compete Agreements with Generic Manufacturers

There is a controversial debate concerning the validity of no-compete agreements between the innovative pharmaceutical firms and generic manufacturers. More broadly, the issue is defining the appropriate balance between the seemingly competing interests of patent and **antitrust** laws (Wharton, 2011). Today 9 out of 10 drug prescriptions in the United States are dispensed using generics, much higher than other developed nations in the world (Danzon & Furukawa, 2008; PhRMA, 2016).

Federal antitrust law finds contracts that restrain trade are illegal (*See* Sherman Antitrust Act, 15 U.S.C.A. §§ 1-7). The ban on contracts that restrain trade has been interpreted to include only unreasonable restraints on trade— that is, those that impair competition. A **per se violation of the Sherman Act** occurs when an agreement is obviously anticompetitive and the court can predict with confidence the rule of reason will condemn it (*See In re Cardizem CD Antitrust Litigation*, 332 F.3d 896 (U.S. Court of Appeals for the 6th Circuit 2003), *cert. denied*, 544 U.S. 1049 (U.S. Supreme Court 2005)).

The U.S. Supreme Court has articulated an **antitrust immunity**, referred to as the **Noerr-Pennington doctrine**, under which the **First Amendment** protects firms actively seeking to protect their economic and business interests from infringing competitors (*See Eastern Railroad Presidents Conference v. Noerr Motor Freight, Inc.*, 365 U.S. 127 (U.S. Supreme Court 1961)). However, this protection does not extend to lawsuits without a sufficient basis or that are simply seeking to harm competitors.

Generic Substitution

Approval for new drugs to enter the U.S. market must be granted by the FDA. In 1984, Congress passed the **Drug Price Competition and Patent Term Restoration Act of 1984**, also known as **Hatch-Waxman**, to accelerate the development and introduction of generic drugs in the United States. Hatch-Waxman was intended to encourage generic manufacturers to challenge invalid or unenforceable branded drug patents. The law:

- Allows generic manufacturers to rely on the safety and efficacy tests of the original brand-name drug, which results in an expedited process of filing an **abbreviated new drug application (ANDA)**, rather than the previously required NDA

MANAGEMENT AND LAW ISSUES

4. Is regulation of the pharmaceutical industry by litigation a problem, and, if so, how should it be controlled?

- Gives the first mover a **180-day exclusivity period** to market a generic drug
- Requires a generic manufacturer filing an ANDA to show the patent for the branded drug:
  - Was never filed with the FDA
  - Has expired or will expire
  - Is invalid or will not be impinged by the generic drug

(*See* 21 U.S.C.A. § 355(b)(2)(A)).

If the generic manufacturer attempts to demonstrate the last of these three options, then the filer of the ANDA must inform the holder of the patent, and the patent holder has 45 days to sue for **patent infringement**.

A lawsuit results in a **30-month moratorium**, preventing the filer of the ANDA from bringing the product to market. The *Valley Drug* case illustrates the competitive nature of the pharmaceutical industry and how the low barriers to generic entry under Hatch-Waxman make patent protection crucial to the survival of the nation's pharmaceutical industry (Nothhaft, 2011). With the influx of cases at the federal appellate level and congressional discussion of further amendments to Hatch-Waxman, the debate about no-compete agreements is warming up as the judicial and legislative branches attempt to balance the incentives for innovation with the incentives to lower drug costs (Epstein, 2008).[LN4] A number of debates, however, fail to put the multimillion-dollar payments by pharmaceutical patent owners into appropriate perspective (Laakmann, 2014). The issue is really about how the regulatory system can assist the pharmaceutical industry to make its drugs affordable while balancing the industry's need to recoup its research and development investments (Wharton, 2011).

Patent Challenges

Pharmaceutical firms are often forced to defend their patents in order to recoup their investments. Under Hatch-Waxman, as early as four years after a brand-name drug is approved by the FDA, a generic manufacturer may challenge patents associated with the branded drug (PhRMA, 2016). As illustrated in **FIGURE 16-4**, patent challenges are occurring earlier and more frequently. Patent challenges are generally occurring as early as five years after a brand-name drug product launch (Nothhaft, 2011). Generic manufacturers can obtain windfalls when they prevail in patent lawsuits, but, if they lose, they incur only insignificant economic risks. The high profitability potential coupled with low **litigation risks** makes generic manufacturers willing to invest millions of dollars in these patent challenges (Wharton, 2011).

At the same time, the pharmaceutical industry is struggling to fill the financial holes resulting from patent expirations or early generic entry in the U.S. market. Faced with patent challenges from generic manufacturers at increasingly early stages of their patent terms, the pharmaceutical industry has been trying to protect the exclusive rights for their patented drugs, while being forced to compromise in negotiating patent settlement terms with generic manufacturers. The no-compete agreements are just one form of these compromises (Nothhaft, 2011).

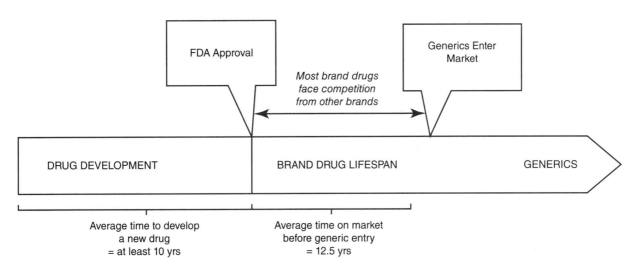

FIGURE 16-4 Patent Challenges by Generic Manufacturers

Data from: Grabowksi H., et al. (2016). Updated trends in U.S. brand–name and generic drug competition. *Journal of Medical Economics, 2016*, 1-9; PhRMA (Pharmaceutical Research and Manufacturers Association). (2016). *Biopharmaceuticals in perspective.* Washington, DC: PhRMA.

For several years, Congress has proposed legislation to penalize generic manufacturers for entering into agreements with pharmaceutical firms that pay the generics not to compete. Both the House and Senate passed Medicare bills with provisions stating that if a generic manufacturer signs an agreement not to market its generic drug in exchange for a payment from a pharmaceutical firm, it forfeits its right to the 180-day exclusivity period under Hatch-Waxman. In addition to this provision, the bills provide for only one moratorium, as opposed to multiple, 30-month moratoriums when a pharmaceutical firm sues for patent infringement (the FDA amended its rules governing patent submissions to include this provision). The bills also allow generic manufacturers to file counterclaims when sued for patent infringement. These efforts are targeted to eliminate loopholes that allow the pharmaceutical industry to repeatedly extend patents and keep generics off the market. By making it more difficult for the pharmaceutical industry to stop generics from entering the market, drug costs could be reduced by $3.5 billion per year (Hugin, 2014).

However, some argue these provisions give too much benefit to generic manufacturers, a result that will provide a disincentive to pharmaceutical innovation. Proponents of this view point out the average effective patent life of approved drugs is far below that of other non-drug patented products. Reducing the patent life further could result in the pharmaceutical industry being less willing to incur the costs of research and development to stimulate innovation. In short, the current regulatory scheme appears to favor generic manufacturers while increasing litigation costs. The intensified patent challenges and early entry of generics have adversely affected the financial stability of the pharmaceutical industry (Grabowski et al., 2016).

Challenging a $1.3 Billion Investment

One of the most contentious issues facing the pharmaceutical industry is how to best protect their multibillion-dollar investments when faced with generic challenges 4 to 5 years into their 20-year market exclusivity period (PhRMA, 2016). It makes economic sense for Abbott Laboratories (the world's eighth-largest pharmaceutical firm in terms of global revenue), to pay two generic manufacturers $78 million a year to protect $540 million in annual revenue.

COURT DECISION
No-Compete Agreements

> *Valley Drug Co. v. Geneva Pharmaceuticals, Inc.*
> [Drug Wholesaler v. Generic Manufacturer]
> 350 F.3d 1181 (U.S. Court of Appeals for the 11th Circuit 2003),
> *rehearing, en banc, denied, Valley Drug Co. v. Abbott Labs.*, 92 Fed.Appx. 783
> (U.S. Court of Appeals for the 11th Circuit 2004),
> *cert. denied*, 549 U.S. 1156 (U.S. Supreme Court 2007)

Facts: In this litigation, a consolidated group of health insurance firms, pharmacy benefit managers, and pharmacy chains claimed they were injured by the antitrust activities of innovative pharmaceutical firm, Abbott Laboratories, and by generic manufacturers, Geneva Pharmaceuticals and Zenith Goldline Pharmaceuticals when they entered into agreements not to compete.

Abbott invested $1.3 billion to develop Hytrin to treat hypertension and enlarged prostate over a 10-year period by the time its patent was filed. Abbott was entitled to exclusive marketing of its patented brand-name drug for 20 years. Zenith and Geneva, two generic manufacturers, however, challenged the Hytrin patent when Abbott had over 13 years remaining on its market exclusivity patent. At the time of the generic challenge, Hytrin resulted in $540 million a year in revenues, and it made up 20% of Abbott's sales.

Geneva subsequently filed four ANDAs in pursuit of FDA approval for its generic version of Hytrin, claiming its generic did not infringe any valid patent by Abbott. Zenith also filed an ANDA for a generic. Abbott sued each firm within the 45-day window set by the FDA, thereby delaying FDA approval for the generic drugs for at least 30 months.

Although the litigation remained unresolved, the 30-month moratoriums were nearing expiration when Abbott struck agreements with Geneva and Zenith to prevent introduction of their generics. The generic drugs cost 60 cents less per tablet than Abbott's brand-name drug. Abbott paid Zenith $3 million up front and promised an additional $6 million per quarter if Zenith did not produce its generic. Geneva received $4.5 million per month in exchange for not marketing its generic until a final, unappealable judgment that Abbott's patent was invalid was handed down. At the time the Abbott-Geneva and Abbott-Zenith agreements were struck, the FDA had a successful defense requirement for generic manufacturers that required them to successfully defend their applications before they could begin exclusively marketing their generics.

Issue: Are the agreements in which pharmaceutical firms pay generic manufacturers not to compete valid?

Holding and Decision: Agreements in which pharmaceutical firms pay generic manufacturers not to compete are valid if they merely confirm the exclusivity of a patented drug.

Analysis: The court focused on the existence of a patent. If Abbott had made payments to Geneva and Zenith in return for their exiting and refraining from entering the market, this would have violated antitrust laws. However, this is not what Abbott did because it owned a patent with the lawful right to exclude the generics from the market. This exclusionary right is granted to allow patent holders to exploit whatever degree of market power they might gain as an incentive to induce investment in drug innovations. The anticompetitive and exclusionary nature of patents does not necessarily lead to antitrust violations. If the Abbott agreements only provided for payments before the patent expired or were declared invalid, then they did not prolong the exclusionary effect of the patent.

The court further addressed the invalidity of one of Abbott's patents and the impropriety of paying potentially infringing competitors. First, Abbott's patent rights were declared nonexistent after the agreements were entered into; therefore, their subsequent invalidity is irrelevant. Only patents procured by **fraud** are relevant to antitrust claims. Second, payments alone from Abbott to the generic manufacturers do not demonstrate the exclusionary effect was beyond that allowed by the patent.

Rule of Law: Agreements between pharmaceutical firms and generic manufacturers not to compete are not *per se* unlawful if the agreements do not expand the existing exclusionary right of patents.

References discussing this court decision: *E.g.*, Levy, 2014.

Vaccines

Many pharmaceutical firms are increasing their stake in the vaccine market:

- GlaxoSmithKline acquired both the Pennsylvania vaccine plant where Wyeth once made flu vaccine and the Canadian flu-vaccine producer ID Biomedical.
- Novartis has taken a controlling stake in Chiron, a California vaccine maker.
- Pfizer-Wyeth, on the strength of its childhood vaccine Prevnar, opened a research and manufacturing plant in Ireland.
- Sanofi, the world's largest vaccine maker, has secured millions in U.S. government contracts to boost flu-vaccine production and test new technology to produce vaccines more efficiently.

(IOM, 2008; Kalorama, 2014).

This new interest in vaccines represents a significant uptick for the industry. For years, vaccines were on pharmaceutical firms' back burners as they pulled out of what had come to be viewed as a high-risk **commodity business**.

MANAGEMENT AND LAW ISSUES

5. Has the entire regulatory system broken down when innovative pharmaceutical firms are forced to pay generic manufacturers to ensure the exclusivity of their patented drugs?

In the late 1960s, there were 26 vaccine manufacturers in the U.S. market; today, four firms produce almost all routine childhood vaccines and many of the recommended pediatric vaccines have a single supplier:

- GlaxoSmithKline
- Novartis
- Pfizer
- Sanofi

(Kalorama, 2014; Noah, 2016).

Now, after decades of decline, vaccines are gaining new interest from:

- Concerns about public emergencies from bioterrorist attacks
- Development of potential vaccines targeted at new therapeutic markets (including diabetes, cancer, and smoking cessation)
- Fears about pandemics from the avian and/or swine influenzas
- The pharmaceutical industry and the federal government in response to flu-shot shortages

(Reiss, 2015).

Despite this growing interest and the emergence of new vaccine technologies, vaccines remain a small piece of the overall health care industry market. With sales of over $16 billion, vaccines make up less than 5% of the global pharmaceutical industry (IMS Health, 2016). While vaccines do not face significant generic competition due to their high entry and manufacturing costs, vaccine firms continue to face lengthy and expensive research and development costs.

Anti-Vaccine Movement

The strength of the vaccine sector of the pharmaceutical industry is that vaccines work: they effectively create induced immunity for many infectious diseases. With the historic success of vaccines in virtually eliminating many life-threatening and debilitating diseases, their obvious benefit is preventing disease before it occurs. As listed in **FEATURE BOX 16-1**, vaccines currently prevent 21 diseases and illnesses. Despite this success, the vaccine industry faces an active anti-vaccine movement, which includes:

- Campaigns against cervical cancer vaccines (Gardasil)
- Controversy surrounding mercury-containing vaccines
- Misinformation about the side effects of vaccines

(Kalorama, 2016)

Vaccinations for Children

The United States has a patchwork system of paying for childhood immunizations. One anomaly of this system is that for children whose health insurance does not cover newly recommended vaccines, it is better to have no insurance at all since free vaccines are available to children who are uninsured or qualify for Medicaid insurance (Noah, 2016). Many states do not help children with inadequate private insurance (Hansen & Newman, 2015). One estimate is that current policy puts more than a million children at risk for diseases such as chickenpox, pneumonia, and hepatitis A (Fox, 2016).

Unfortunately, health insurance plans are not keeping up with new vaccines for children; the private-sector cost for all recommended childhood immunizations averages $300 per child every year for the first six years of each child's life (CDC, 2016a). The average annual per-child cost was $26 a decade ago, meaning there has been a 13-fold increase over the course of a decade for recommended vaccines. About 55 million employees and their dependents get health care coverage through self-insured plans that are exempt from state immunization mandates; these employees' children are the most likely to be underinsured for vaccines (Reiss, 2015). While other employer-provided plans provide vaccine coverage, co-payments and deductibles apply that often leads to lack of immunizations (CDC, 2016a).

Childhood vaccines have become a $1-billion-a-year endeavor since the development of polio vaccine in the 1950s. Yet, while much of the responsibility for immunizations is falling to the government, the Centers for Disease Control opposes prioritizing vaccines and instead favors better health care coverage by insurers and more government funding

FEATURE BOX 16-1

Vaccine-Preventable Diseases and Illnesses

- Cervical cancer/human papillomavirus (HPV)
- Chickenpox and shingles
- Cholera
- Diphtheria
- *Haemophilus influenzae* type b (Hib) diseases
- Hepatitis A and hepatitis B
- Influenza
- Japanese encephalitis
- Measles
- Meningococcal diseases
- Mumps
- Pertussis
- Polio
- Rotavirus diseases
- Rubella
- *Streptococcus pneumoniae* infections
- Tetanus
- Tick-borne encephalitis
- Tuberculosis
- Typhoid
- Yellow fever

Data from: Kalorama, 2016.

(Landro, 2008). With costs rising, a debate is emerging concerning whether it may be time to decide at a national level which vaccines are most important:

- Sixteen states require health insurers to cover all recommended vaccines, but this policy does not cover employees covered by self-insured health insurance plans.
- Seventeen states did not give meningitis vaccines to children with inadequate private insurance.
- Eight states do not give pneumococcal shots to underinsured infants and toddlers.
- A handful of states do not provide shots for chickenpox and hepatitis A to the underinsured.
- Two states do not provide Tdap, the combined booster shot for tetanus, diphtheria, and pertussis (whooping cough), for 11- to 12-year-olds.
- More than 1 million insured children are unable to get the meningococcal vaccine, leaving them vulnerable to potentially deadly infections.

(Noah, 2016; Reiss, 2015).

Adult Vaccinations

Six vaccines are recommended for adults. Although immunization rates for children are high, and young people rarely die from diseases vaccines can prevent, that is not the case for adults. For instance, pediatric hospitalizations associated with laboratory-confirmed influenza infections are monitored by two population-based surveillance networks: the **Emerging Infections Program** (EIP) and the **New Vaccine Surveillance Network** (NVSN). As many as 70,000 American adults die each year from vaccine-preventable diseases like influenza, pneumonia, and complications of hepatitis; such diseases also sicken hundreds of thousands of adults at a cost of treatment exceeding $10 billion annually (CDC, 2015; Williams et al., 2014).

One problem is a lack of any national system to promote and monitor adult vaccinations (Landro, 2008). Only about 60% of adults aged 65 and over have ever had a pneumonia vaccine (CDC, 2016c). While the federal Vaccines for Children Program provides vaccines at no cost to children who cannot afford them, and carefully monitors supply and demand, the infrastructure to ensure the adult vaccination pipeline is inadequate (Temte, 2009). There is currently little coordination between federal public health agencies, private medical providers, and the private firms that make adult vaccines (Landro, 2008).

Targeted Medicines with Hybrid Pricing

The traditional view of vaccines as a bulk-order commodity is changing. In fact, it is almost a misnomer to call some of the new products vaccines. They are patented, targeted treatments and can command **hybrid pricing** (Wharton, 2005). For instance, the childhood MMR vaccine (for measles, mumps, and rubella), Prevnar, has proven itself as such a superior product that it commands $84 per dose from insurers, compared to generic competitors' average price at $47 per dose (CDC, 2016a).

Insurers are increasingly willing to support new, high-priced vaccines that are proven to keep immunity long term and are a very efficient way to prevent illness. Prevention of disease has significant economic advantages (Wharton, 2005). The pharmaceutical industry is at a point in the market where developing vaccines are attractive, which has not been true in the recent past. The role the government and the health insurance industry increasingly plays in determining what is valuable in the pharmaceutical market cannot be underestimated.

GlaxoSmithKline has more than 20 new vaccines under development, including products to combat strep, meningitis, and rotavirus. Attention was formerly directed to childhood vaccines, but more and more research and development is focusing on vaccines for adolescents and young adults, and on adult vaccines for diseases such as cancer (Danzon & Furukawa, 2008; DiMasi et al., 2016). The U.S. health care system approach to vaccines must adapt to accommodate these new products by focusing on disease prevention through vaccines versus treatment of disease (Wharton, 2005). Prevention is much more cost-effective than treatment of diseases.

Vaccine Shortages

The U.S. vaccine market is prone to **shortages**. This is an industry with a relatively small market where prices are set, so it tends to gravitate to the best producer in a sole-supplier situation (Danzon, 2005; Engstrom, 2013). When a supplier experiences a problem or cuts back production, shortages arise. For instance, a severe influenza vaccine shortage occurred during the mid-2000 influenza season because of the loss of all vaccines made by Chiron for U.S. distribution when the firm faced contamination issues at its manufacturing site (Parmet, 2010).

The United States must find a better way to finance vaccines and expand insurance coverage, while facing single or few suppliers. National mechanisms to stockpile vaccines are needed as well as a backup system to bring vaccines back into the system quickly when they are needed (Danzon, 2005; Engstrom, 2013). Some of the vaccine shortages in recent years have come as a result of stepped-up FDA review of vaccine manufacturing. The more serious the FDA became about manufacturing site inspections, the more shortages arose (Engstrom, 2013).

Over-Regulated Market

The role of government in the vaccine market cannot be overlooked. Assertions that a market-driven system for vaccines has failed are wrong. While the pharmaceutical industry provides vaccines, this market sector has never had a chance to be a free market (Monahan, 2012). Vaccine production is among the most heavily regulated sectors in the medical products industry, since vaccines are derived from living organisms (Wharton, 2005).

An Institute of Medicine report found that the federal government often mandates vaccine protection, but then it does not provide enough money to encourage vaccine manufacturers to develop new products or maintain production (IOM, 2008). Some argue that if government is going to require vaccination protection, then it should pay for it. Essentially these vaccines are thought of as a public good and thus they are an obligation for the government to finance (Levin, 2015). Vaccines should be thought of as an important part of the nation's normal health care system and should be covered by insurance because they are so effective in reducing health care costs (Danzon, 2005). For instance, a recent analysis showed that routine childhood immunization among U.S. children prevent 42,000 early deaths and 20 million cases of disease, with net savings of $13.5 billion in direct health care costs annually (Zhou, 2014). Yet, the Institute of Medicine report on vaccines has been met with stunning silence.

The insurance industry is disinterested in receiving government subsidies for mandated vaccine programs because it fears it might ultimately be left with the mandate but not the subsidy (Hoffman, 2010). At the moment, there is a total lack of trust among these three parties: government, insurers, and the vaccine industry. The government generates additional mistrust when it threatens to step in and cut pharmaceutical prices when demand is high, as it did with the antibiotic Cipro during the anthrax attacks on U.S. postal facilities. There is talk about better planning, but no movement yet (Levin, 2015; Pauly, 2005).

One proposal is a system that provides some government pricing guarantees to encourage vaccine manufacturers, especially for flu vaccines, to remain in business. The flu vaccine market is particularly complicated because vaccines are formulated each year based on strains expected to be most prevalent. They cannot be stockpiled if they go unused. Governments could:

- Make concessions to compensate for the price cap, such as extended patent life, to avoid temporary spikes
- Set a trigger price above which vaccine manufacturers could not raise prices if shortages develop

(*See generally* Wharton, 2005).

Commodification of Mandatory Vaccines

Increasing the relative prices paid for new vaccines to levels more closely reflective of their social value compared to other new drugs is essential to achieving appropriate incentives for allocation of research and development (Danzon & Pereira, 2005). The biggest obstacle vaccine manufacturers face is little payback for their risk because many of their products are purchased in bulk by governments and other public health authorities, including humanitarian agencies. These large buyers are able to negotiate low prices. In the United States, the government is paying for over half of all vaccines for children, and the vaccine industry is more or less forced to take low prices (Wharton, 2005). It is difficult to pursue innovative vaccine research and development with negotiated low prices.

National Vaccine Injury Compensation Program

The **National Vaccine Injury Compensation Program** is one example of some meeting of the minds when it comes to differing perceptions of health risk (Levin, 2015). In 1986, Congress established a no-fault system for compensating those who may have been injured by routine childhood vaccines (Wharton, 2005). This program arose in part because different groups had very different views on the health risks posed by pediatric vaccines. Some people believed there was a high health risk of side effects; others believed it was low.

The strategy was to levy an excise tax on vaccine sales, use the proceeds to set up a trust fund, and pay claims for actual damages on a no-fault basis. After an initial flurry of payments for previous injuries, the level of payments fell dramatically, and the trust fund balance grew. Those who thought adverse effects would be common turned out to be wrong. The point is, those who thought side effects were unlikely did not expect to get money back, and those who thought side effects were likely felt they were protected; both groups could agree with the compensation proposal. Nevertheless, while the National Vaccine Injury Compensation Program was designed to streamline and limit the liability of vaccine manufacturers, lawsuits continue to be brought against vaccine manufacturers by using opt-out provisions in the federal legislation (Wharton, 2005).

Demand Side of the Vaccine Market

The demand side of the vaccine market is crucial to keeping the vaccine industry vibrant. Even with successful development of safe vaccines:

- Health care professionals must be willing to administer vaccines.
- People must be willing to pay for vaccines.
- People need to know about vaccines and believe they are beneficial.

(Wharton, 2005).

Vaccine Litigation

Lawsuits filed against the vaccine industry alleging its products have harmed patients are another reason the pharmaceutical industry has become wary of vaccine production. Because vaccines have the potential to reach millions of patients, a bad outcome has the potential to bankrupt a manufacturer. In the case of widely distributed vaccines, a firm is engaging in a **bet-the-firm risk** if things go badly (Monahan. 2012). This discourages research and development on certain types of vaccines and discourages production and marketing (Wharton, 2005).

Few areas of pharmaceuticals have seen the fast-moving developments in the marketplace that the vaccine market has recently had (Kalorama, 2014). The new interest in vaccines comes at a time when the pharmaceutical industry is struggling with few new products coming to market. While there are challenges on the revenue side of the business, the process of developing vaccines is more predictable, cheaper, and faster than it is for other drugs (Wharton, 2005).

If insurers increase interest, vaccine manufacturers will invest in manufacturing plants in the United States (Danzon & Furukawa, 2006; DiMasi et al., 2016). Today, there is a tremendous amount of research activity in vaccines by both the pharmaceutical and biotechnology industries. With adequate payment, the problem of innovation may take care of itself (Wharton, 2005).

Future Challenges Facing the Vaccine Sector

The most important issue in the debate over vaccines is how to finance new vaccine research and development. Right now, the best route to development of novel vaccines is continued investment in basic pharmaceutical research that might lead to wide-ranging discoveries that could be applied to vaccine development (McClellan, 2014). The real need is a way to fund basic research. Only a few global firms have taken upon themselves the risk of developing and testing vaccine products (Kalorama, 2016).

Value of Pharmaceutical Innovation

The pharmaceutical industry has made significant advances in helping consumers live longer and better lives. Today, pharmaceutical medicines treat health care conditions once thought to be untreatable. Both mortality and disability rates have fallen consistently over the years as a result of new drugs being brought to market (DiMasi et al., 2016). Drugs prevent the need for hospital, emergency, and long-term care for heart attacks, strokes, HIV/AIDS, and many cancers that at one time debilitated individuals. Today, even without full cures, drugs greatly delay the onset and severity of major diseases and illnesses and reduce expensive and unproductive time spent in hospitals, nursing homes, and under the care of family members (PhRMA, 2016). All too often, however, discussions center on the increase in spending on health care as opposed to the benefits of improved health care the spending brought. The pressure to control drug prices is targeted well beyond their contribution to overall health care cost increases (Epstein, 2008).

A focus on drug prices alone often overlooks the value consumers and society derive from improved health. While high drug prices must be part of any debate on health care, the cost of drugs should be considered in the context of the total benefits received from increased longevity without disabilities, as well as total savings achieved from not having to use hospitals and nursing homes. The basic question is whether Americans find the increase in health care spending for new life-saving pharmaceutical medicines and disease-eradicating vaccines is worth it. Perhaps an unexpected health emergency will unfortunately answer this question sooner than anticipated.

LAW FACT

State Preemption of Drug Labeling

Should drug-labeling judgments of the FDA preempt state law product liability claims?

No. When the risk of gangrene from IV-push injection of the drug became apparent, Wyeth had a duty to provide a warning adequately describing that risk. While the warnings on the drug's label were deemed sufficient by the FDA, Wyeth failed to demonstrate it was impossible for it to comply with both federal and state requirements. FDA regulations permitted Wyeth to unilaterally strengthen its warning, and the mere fact the FDA approved the drug's label did not establish it would have prohibited such a change.

—*Wyeth v. Levine*, 555 U.S. 555 (U.S. Supreme Court 2009).

See also Pliva v. Mensing, 564 U.S. 604 (U.S. Supreme Court 2011) (emerging issue for generic manufacturers). *See E.g.*, Ausness, 2014; Laakmann, 2015; Maher, 2014; Paradise, 2015; Sawyer, 2013 (discussing this decision).

CHAPTER SUMMARY

- The global pharmaceutical industry is moving away from a growth strategy based on blockbuster drugs and toward a growth strategy based on acquiring and merging with biotechnology firm ties in order to have a more diverse product base.
- High prices for drugs without significant health care value are increasingly unjustified, so the pharmaceutical industry is moving toward pricing drugs based on the economic value they provide to patients.
- The pharmaceutical industry is one of the most research-intensive industries in the United States; pharmaceutical firms invest five times as much in research and development relative to sales than the average U.S. manufacturing firm.
- The stages of research and development include academic and basic research, drug discovery and development, clinical trials, new drug applications and approval, drug manufacturing, and ongoing research and monitoring.
- Global drug pricing is very complex and does not have one methodology that can satisfy everyone.
- The FDA struggles to efficiently and effectively regulate drugs imported into the United States.
- Pharmacy benefit managers exercise great power over the pharmaceutical industry in terms of determining drug prices and perhaps hindering the development of new drugs in the process.
- The learned intermediary doctrine imposes an ethical obligation on the pharmaceutical industry to warn physicians of foreseeable risks associated with the use of their drugs, including potential unapproved (off-label) uses.
- Of the four elements consumers must prove to win a products liability lawsuit against a pharmaceutical firm (duty, breach, causation, and damages), causation is the hardest element to prove because of the high standard of scientific evidence required.
- The number of successful lawsuits over latent effects from regulated and approved pharmaceuticals is an indication the research required by regulation is often not enough to assess all of the harmful effects of a drug; however, there is little regulatory incentive for the pharmaceutical industry to do more comprehensive research.
- Because federal drug regulations are incomplete, litigation is increasingly used to force the pharmaceutical industry to better protect consumers.
- Balancing the competing interests of patent and antitrust laws in the pharmaceutical and generic industries is difficult because it is easier for generics to gain FDA approval, and branded drug firms often seek to discourage generic competition through no-compete agreements under which they pay the generic manufacturers not to compete.
- After decades of declining focus in the vaccine market, the pharmaceutical industry is increasing its interest in this market sector due to the potential value of vaccine products and the decline in profitability of the blockbuster drug model of business; focus is increasing on vaccines for adults and on how to surge vaccine production, if necessary.
- Vaccine laws and funding for them vary immensely between the states; a higher emphasis is placed on vaccinating children than adults, and much more funding is available for childhood immunizations.
- The federal government highly regulates and monitors vaccines and has set up a fund to reimburse those who were likely injured by routine childhood vaccines.
- The attention given to vaccinations as opposed to other health care concerns is due in part to the fact vaccinations make good economic sense in terms of the costs they save by preventing illness in the first place.

LAW NOTES

1. In most instances, gastroesophageal reflux disease (GERD) can be addressed by lifestyle changes (weight loss and dietary restrictions), if not, over-the-counter antacids and surgery are options. In instance of acute GERD, Reglan aids in controlling the disease by blocking dopamine receptors in the brain and throughout the body, enhancing movement or contractions of the esophagus, stomach, and intestines. By blocking these receptors, Reglan can, however, cause irreversible extrapyramidal symptoms, which are adverse drug reactions involving the extrapyramidal nervous system. Tardive dyskinesia is a particularly severe form of extrapyramidal symptoms causing grotesque involuntary movements of the mouth, tongue, lips, and extremities, involuntary chewing movements, and a general sense of agitation.

2. *Daubert v. Merrell Dow Pharmaceuticals, Inc.*, 509 U.S. 579 (U.S. Supreme Court 1993) involved children with serious birth defects, in which scientific experts testified that in vitro and in vivo testing (test tube and animal studies) showed the drug Bendectin, used during pregnancy for antinausea, could cause limb-reduction birth defects. The lower court ruled testimony was inadmissible because it was not generally accepted by the scientific community, and Merrell was granted summary judgment. The U.S. Supreme Court vacated the judgment and remanded so the expert testimony could be reevaluated in keeping with the new standard for admission of scientific evidence; heretofore, scientific evidence had to be generally accepted by the scientific community. On remand, the 9th Circuit applied the two-part Daubert standard and found that none of the children's experts based their testimony on preexisting or independent research, published their work in scientific journals, or adequately explained their methodology. The court concluded the proffered scientific testimony was not derived by scientific method. *See Daubert v. Merrell Dow Pharmaceuticals, Inc.*, 43 F.3d 1311 (U.S. Court of Appeals for the 9th Circuit 1995), *cert. denied*, 516 U.S. 869 (U.S. Supreme Court 1995).

3. The Vioxx downfall is a classic example of the collapse of a blockbuster drug due to possible complications (Brown, 2014). Vioxx was part of a new class of antiarthritis drugs called COX-2 blockers. Unlike traditional antiarthritis drugs (nonsteroidal anti-inflammatory drugs), COX-2 blockers selectively targeted the COX-2 enzyme (bad enzyme) without affecting the function of the COX-1 enzyme (good enzyme) (Kim, 2014). As a result, COX-2 blockers reduced symptoms of arthritis with minimal side effects. When a Merck-sponsored **prospective, randomized, placebo-controlled clinical trial** (the gold standard in clinical research) revealed an increased risk of heart attacks and strokes, five years after the drug was approved, Merck immediately recalled Vioxx. The litigation ensued.

    In the first Vioxx jury trial in Texas, the lack of scientific evidence of causation was not an obstacle to a multimillion-dollar damage award. The case turned on juror impressions of Merck's corporate behavior. Jurors reportedly believed Merck had marketed a drug it knew to be dangerous, and this belief overcame the causation requirement. (Brown, 2014). This jury decision was, nevertheless, subsequently overturned by the *Ernst* decision analyzed in this chapter *Ernst v. Merck & Co., Inc.*, 296 S.W.3d 81 (Court of Appeals of Texas, 14th District, Houston 2008) *cert. denied*, 132 S.Ct. 1980 (U.S. Supreme Court 2012)

4. An issue not addressed in this chapter is pharmaceutical patents held by research universities and public sector research institutes in developed nations. **Universities Allied for Essential Medicines**, an international student group with over 46 campus chapters (with the slogan: *Our Labs, Our Drugs, Our Responsibility*), is advocating **segmented market pricing** where universities and public research institutes in developed nations open access to their patented drugs to resource-limited countries (*E.g.*, Collinsworth & Crager, 2014; Kiddell-Monroe, 2013; Treasure et al., 2014).

REFERENCES

Abbott, R., & Ayres, I. (2014). Evidence and extrapolation: Mechanisms for regulating off-label uses of drugs and devices. *Duke Law Journal, 64*, 377–435.

Ausness, R. C. (2014). Danger is my business: The right to manufacture unsafe products. *Arkansas Law Review, 67*, 827–872.

Babaian, D. C. (2014). Adopting pharmacogenomics and parenting repurposed molecules under the Orphan Drug Act: A cost dilemma? *John Marshall Law School Review of Intellectual Property Law, 13*, 667–718.

Bi, K. (2015). What is "false or misleading" unapproved (off-label) promotion? *University of Chicago Law Review, 82*, 975–1020.

Brennan, H., et al. (2016). A prescription for excessive drug pricing: Leveraging government patent use for health. *Yale Journal of Law and Technology, 18*, 275–354.

Brown, H. (2014). Eight gates for expert witnesses: Fifteen years later. *Houston Law Review, 52*, 1–297.

Burstein, M. J. (2012). Exchanging information without intellectual property. *Texas Law Review, 91*, 227–257.

Calabresi, S. G. (2014). The classical liberal constitution: On liberty, equality, and the constitution: A review of Richard A. Epstein's *The Classical Liberal Constitution. New York University Journal of Law and Liberty, 8*, 839–960.

Callam, M. (2014). Who can afford it? The Patient Protection and Affordable Care Act's failure to regulate excessive cost-sharing of prescription biologic drugs. *Journal of Law and Health, 27*, 99–129.

CBO (Congressional Budget Office). (2014). *Federal policies and innovation.* Washington, DC: CBO.

CDC (Centers for Disease Control and Prevention). (2016a). *CDC vaccine price list.* Atlanta, GA: CDC.

___. (2016b). *Births and natality.*

___. (2016c). *Pneumococcal vaccines.*

___. (2015). *Vaccine-preventable adult diseases.*

Chlistunoff, M. M. (2016). Expert testimony and the quest for reliability: The case for a methodology questionnaire. *Texas Law Review, 94*, 1055–1078.

CIA (Central Intelligence Agency). (2016). *The world factbook.* Washington, DC: CIA.

Collinsworth, B., & Crager, S. (2014). Should academic therapeutic patents go to the highest bidder? *Expert Opinion on Therapeutic Patents, 24*(5), 481–484.

Comanor, W. S., & Needleman, J. (2016). The law, economics, and medicine of off-label prescribing. *Washington Law Review, 91*, 119–146.

Danzon, P. M. (2005). Vaccine supply: A cross-national perspective. How do the economics of vaccines differ in the U.S. from other countries, both industrialized and developing? *Health Affairs, 24*(3), 706–717.

Danzon, P. M., & Furukawa, M. F. (2008). International prices and availability of pharmaceuticals. *Health Affairs, 27*(1), 221–233.

___. (2006). Prices and availability of biopharmaceuticals: An international comparison. *Health Affairs, 25*(5), 1353–1362.

Danzon, P. M., & Pereira, N. S. (2005). Why sole-supplier vaccine markets may be here to stay: Vaccine markets tend to evolve toward a single dominant supplier, which has advantages as well as disadvantages. *Health Affairs, 24*(3), 694–696.

Darrow, J. J. (2014). Pharmaceutical gatekeepers. *Indiana Law Review, 47*, 363–420.

DiMasi, J. A., et al. (2016). Innovation in the pharmaceutical industry: New estimates of R&D costs. *Journal of Health Economics, 47*, 20–33.

___. (2014). *Briefing: Cost of developing a new drug*. Boston. MA: Tufts Center for the Study of Drug Development.

Engstrom, N. F. (2013). A dose of reality for specialized courts: Lessons from the VICP. *University of Pennsylvania Law Review, 163*, 1631–1717.

Epstein, R. A. (2008). *Overdose: How excessive government regulation stifles pharmaceutical innovation*. New Haven, CT: Yale University Press.

FDA (Food and Drug Administration). (2016a). *FDA approved drug products*. Bethesda, MD: FDA.

___. (2016b). *Drug approval process*.

___ (2016c). *Investigational new drug (IND) application*.

___. (2016d). *New drug application (NDA)*.

___. (2016e). *MedWatch: The FDA safety information and adverse event reporting program*.

___ (2016f). *Postmarket drug and biologic safety evaluations*.

___. (2009, January 14). *Press release: FDA launches pilot program to improve the safety of drugs and active drug ingredients produced outside the United States*.

Foote, E. A. (2015). Prescription drug importation: An expanded FDA personal use exemption and qualified regulators for foreign-produced pharmaceuticals. *Loyola Consumer Law Review, 27*, 369–398.

Fox, J. (2016). Reforming healthcare reform. *University of Richmond Law Review, 50*, 557–608.

Fry-Revere, S., & Do, E. K. (2013). A chronic problem: Pain management of non–cancer pain in America. *Journal of Health Care Law and Policy, 16*, 193–213.

Furrow, B. (2013). Under the knife: Health law, health care reform, and beyond; Cost control and the Affordable Care Act: CRAMPing our health care appetite. *Nevada Law Journal, 13*, 822–871.

Goldberg, D. S. (2013). Intervening at the right point in the causal pathways: Law, policy, and the devastating impact of pain across the globe. *Annals of Health Law, 22*, 198–223.

Grabowski, H., et al. (2016). Updated trends in U.S. brand-name and generic drug competition. *Journal of Medical Economics, 19*(9) 1–9.

Gregg, J. (2015). The implications, negative health effects, legal issues, and potential solutions associated with the shortage of essential drugs in the U.S. medical care market. *Albany Law Journal of Science and Technology, 25*, 381–454.

Green, M. D., & Sanders, J. (2015). Admissibility versus sufficiency: Controlling the quality of expert witness testimony. *Wake Forest Law Review, 50*, 1057–1094.

Hall, M. A. (2014). Valuating the Affordable Care Act: The eye of the beholder. *Houston Law Review, 51*, 1029–1056.

Hansen, R., & Newman, R. (2015). Health care: Access after health care reform. *Georgetown Journal of Gender and the Law, 16*, 191–226.

Hoffman, A. K. (2010). Oil and water: Mixing individual mandates, fragmented markets, and health reform. *American Journal of Law and Medicine, 36*, 7–77.

Horvath, G. (2015). Recovery and preemption: The collision of the Medicare Secondary Payer Act and the Medical Device Amendments. *California Law Review, 103*, 1353–1402.

Hugin, R. J., Chairman and Chief Executive Officer of Celgene Corporation (2014, February 21). *Keynote Speaker at the Wharton Health Care Business Conference: Reimagining Healthcare; Driving Change in a Patient-Centered World*, Philadelphia, PA.

IMF (International Monetary Fund). (2016). *World economic outlook*. Washington, DC: IMF.

IMS Health. (2016). *Top 20 global therapy areas*. Plymouth Meeting, PA: IMS.

IMS Institute for Healthcare Informatics. (2016). *Avoidable costs in U.S. healthcare: The $200 billion opportunity from using drugs more responsibly*. Plymouth Meeting, PA: IMS Health.

___. (2015). *Medicines use and spending in the U.S.—A review of 2015 and outlook to 2020*.

IOM (Institute of Medicine) Committee on Review of Priorities in the National Vaccine Plan. (2008). *Initial guidance for an update of the national vaccine plan: A letter report to the National Vaccine Program Office*. Washington, DC: IOM.

Kalorama International. (2016). *Global human vaccine*. Rockville, MD: Kalorama.

___. (2014). *Vaccines: World market analysis, key players, and critical trends in a fast-changing industry*.

Kesselheim, A. S., & Darrow, J. J. (2015). Hatch-Waxman turns 30: Do we need a re-designed approach for the modern era? *Yale Journal of Health Policy, Law and Ethics, 15*, 293–347.

Kiddell-Monroe, R. (2013). *A non-state centric governance framework for global health*. Barcelona, Spain: Universities Allied for Essential Medicine and ISGlobal Barcelona Institute for Global Health.

Kim, M. (2014). Pharmacogenomics and pharmacologic class effect in drug safety management. *Food and Drug Law Journal, 69*, 603–634.

Kirkwood, J. B. (2016). Buyer power and healthcare prices. *Washington Law Review, 91*, 253–293.

Laakmann, A. B. (2015). When should physicians be liable for innovation? *Cardozo Law Review, 36*, 913–968.

___. (2014). The Hatch-Waxman Act's side effects: Precautions for biosimilars. *Loyola of Los Angeles Law Review, 47*, 917–941.

Landro, L. (2008, July 9). The informed patient: Get your shots: Adults need vaccines, too; Public-health experts push for national inoculation plan; a rise in whooping cough. *Wall Street Journal*, p. D1.

Levin, A. (2015). Closing the door to lost earnings under the National Childhood Vaccine Injury Act of 1986. *Food and Drug Law Journal, 70*, 593–616.

Levy, J. (2014). When the stars align: Narrowing the scope of appellate reversals of judicially approved class action settlements. *Seton Hall Law Review, 44*, 631–657.

Maher, B.S. (2014). The Affordable Care Act, remedy, and litigation reform. *American University Law Review, 63,* 649–714.

McClellan, M. B., Senior Fellow and Director of the Initiative on Value and Innovation in Health Care, Brookings Institution (2014, February 21). *Remarks at the Panel Discussion on Health Care Policy: Untangling Today's Regulatory Environment and Preparing for the Future at the Wharton Health Care Business Conference: Reimagining Healthcare: Driving Change in a Patient-Centered World,* Philadelphia, PA.

Miller, R. K. (2013). Sacrificial lambs: Compensating first subscribers to FDA-approved medications for post-marketing injuries resulting from unlabeled adverse events. *Catholic University Law Review, 62,* 429–472.

Monahan, A. B. (2012). Fairness versus welfare in health insurance content regulation. *University of Illinois Law Review, 2012(1),* 139–223.

Moses, III, H., et al. (2015). The anatomy of medical research: US and international comparisons. *Journal of the American Medical Association, 313(2),* 174–189.

Noah, L. (2016). State affronts to federal primacy in the licensure of pharmaceutical products. *Michigan State Law Review, 2016,* 1–54.

___. (2014). Governance by the backdoor: Administrative law (lessness?) at the FDA. *Nebraska Law Review, 93,* 89–138.

Nothhaft, H. R. (2011). *Great again: Revitalizing America's entrepreneurial leadership.* Cambridge, MA: Harvard Business Review Press.

OECD (Organisation for Economic Co-operation and Development). (2015). *Health at a glance 2015: OECD indicators.* Paris, France: OECD.

Paradise, J. (2015). The legal and regulatory status of biosimilars: How product naming and state substitution laws may impact the U.S. healthcare system. *American Journal of Law and Medicine, 41,* 49–84.

Parmet, W. E. (2010). Pandemics, populism and the role of law in the H1N1 vaccine campaign. *Saint Louis University Journal of Health Law and Policy, 4,* 113–153.

Pauly, M. V. (2005). Improving vaccine supply and development: Who needs what? *Health Affairs, 24(3),* 680–690.

Pham, N. D. (2015). *IP-intensive manufacturing industries: Driving U.S. economic growth.* Washington, DC: NDP Analytics.

Phillips, E. T., et al. (2015). Racketeer influenced and corrupt organizations. *American Criminal Law Review, 52,* 1507–1566.

PhRMA (Pharmaceutical Research and Manufacturers Association). (2016). *Biopharmaceuticals in perspective.* Washington, DC: PhRMA.

Reiss, D. R. (2015). Herd immunity and immunization policy: The importance of accuracy. *Oregon Law Review, 94,* 1–21.

Restatement (third) of torts: Products liability. (2013). Philadelphia, PA: American Law Institute.

Rodwin, M. A. (2015). Do we need stronger sanctions to ensure legal compliance by pharmaceutical firms? *Food and Drug Law Journal, 70,* 435–452.

Sawyer, C. (2013). Duty of sameness? Bartlett preserves generic drug consumers' design defect claims. *Boston College Law Review E. Supp., 54,* 1–13.

Sheley, E. (2015). Rethinking injury: The case of informed consent. *Brigham Young University Law Review, 2015,* 63–117.

Shell, G. R. (2004). *Make the rules or your rivals will.* New York, NY: Crown Business, Random House.

Sokol, M. C., et al. (2005). Impact of medication adherence on hospitalization risk and healthcare costs. *Medical Care, 43(6),* 523–530.

Temte, J. L. (2009). ACIP (Advisory Committee on Immunization Practices) releases 2009 adult immunization schedule. *American Family Physician, 79(2),* 152–156.

Tironi, P. (2010). Pharmaceutical pricing: A review of proposals to improve access and affordability of pharmaceutical medicines. *Annals of Health Law, 19,* 311–364.

Treasure, C., et al. (2014). What is the public's right to access medical discoveries based on federally funded research? *Journal of the American Medical Association, 311(9),* 907–908.

Vagelos, P. R., Retired Chairman and CEO of Merck & Co., Chairman of Regeneron Pharmaceuticals, Inc. (2014, February 21). *Keynote Speaker at the Wharton Health Care Business Conference: Reimagining Healthcare: Driving Change in a Patient-Centered World,* Philadelphia, PA.

Wharton (Wharton School at the University of Pennsylvania). (2011). What poor patent protection costs us. *Knowledge@Wharton.*

___. (2006). Will it pay off, or become a write off? *Managing risk in venture capital investing.*

___. (2005). After decades of malaise, the vaccine industry is getting an injection.

Williams, W. W., et al. (2014, February 7). Noninfluenza vaccination coverage among adults. *Morbidity and Mortality Weekly Report, 63(5),* 95–102.

World Bank (2016). *World development indicators.* Washington, DC: World Bank.

Zhou, F., et al. (2014). Economic evaluation of the routine childhood immunization program in the United States. *Pediatrics, 133(4).*

CHAPTER 17

Biopharmaceuticals

"Since the 1980s, biotechnology has moved us, literally or figuratively, from the classroom to the boardroom and from the New England Journal of Medicine *to the* Wall Street Journal.

— **Leon Rosenberg**, former dean of Yale University School of Medicine

IN BRIEF

This chapter explains the laws affecting gene and protein therapy and other biotechnology fields such as genomics, bioinformatics, and proteomics, which hold the potential to transform health care delivery. There are almost 200 marketed biopharmaceuticals worldwide, many of which have substantially impacted patients' lives. The U.S. health care industry will only be able to capitalize on these opportunities if it understands this research and the legal restraints affecting these producers of medical products. The two U.S. Supreme Court decisions presented in this chapter's *Fact or Fiction* section represent two sides of the same biotechnology patent coin. One side of the coin involves patent disputes pursuant to licensing agreements; the other side of the coin involves patent disputes where there are no licensing agreements.

LEARNING OBJECTIVES

Upon completion of this chapter readers should be able to:

1. Explain the challenges facing the biotechnology industry from regulatory structures.
2. List the issues in global drug pricing.
3. Describe the drivers of bioscience.
4. Discuss the emerging areas of biotechnology research.
5. Differentiate between pharmaceutical drugs and biopharmaceuticals.
6. Explain why the full potential of biotechnology has yet to be realized.
7. Discuss the possibility of personalized medical products and the potential to live forever.
8. Explain the convergent technology represented by the intersection of nanotechnology, biotechnology, information technology, and cognitive science.

KEY TERMS

Active ingredient	Biologics	Convergent technology
American Medical Association	Biopharmaceuticals	Cooperative research and
Biobanking	Bioprospecting research laws	development agreements
Biocomparables	Biosimilars	Coordinated care programs
Bioequivalence	Biotechnology Industry Organization	Cosmeceutical products
Biogenerics	Coexpression technology	Credible placebo drugs
Bioinformatics	Computational biology	Daltons

Declaratory relief
DNA technology
Drug delivery mechanisms
Drug formulation
Drug patent
Drug pipelines
Drug pricing standards
Early stage upstream research
Enzyme
Enzyme replacement therapy
Esthetician products
Excessive pricing
Follow-on protein biologics
Full price or free strategy
Gene-guided drug development
Gene therapies
Genetic age
Genetic diagnostics
Genome
Genomics
Government agencies
Gross domestic product

Harmonized standards
Human-to-machine interferences
Industry-university cooperation
Innovator biopharmaceuticals
Invisible hand
Late-stage clinical trials
License agreement
Market exclusivity
Microfluids
Nanomedicine
Neglected diseases
Net exporters
Orphan diseases
Orphan Drug Act of 1983
Outsourced
Per capita
Pharmaceuticals
Pharmacoeconomics
Placebo effects
Precision medicine
Price controls
Product portfolios

Proteomics
Recombinant DNA technology
Regulatory procedure and marketing
Repositioning of chemical
    compounds
Reprogenics
Ribonucleic acid interference
Silicon chips
Small molecule drugs
Specialty pharmaceuticals
Synthesizing chemicals
Synthetic biology
Targeted therapy
Telomerase technology
Telomere biology
Therapeutic equivalence
Therapeutic vaccines
Top-down effect
Trade deficits
Ultra-high-throughput screening
Value chain
Venture capital

FACT OR FICTION

Bioscience Research

Are the interests of patent holders and the users of patented inventions being balanced by the courts in patent disputes?

The patented invention in this case was a tripeptide. Integra Lifesciences used the tripeptide to test its tumor-suppressing function without obtaining the patent holder's approval or first entering into a **license agreement** with Merck, the patent holder. Merck sued Integra Lifesciences for patent infringement.

The patented invention in another case was an experimental process called **coexpression technology**, a research tool used to produce immunoglobulin chains in a recombinant host cell. MedImmune was assigned the right to use the coexpression technology to manufacture a drug under a license agreement with Genentech, the patent holder. MedImmune paid the demanded royalties under protest, but sought **declaratory relief** claiming that the patent at issue was invalid and unenforceable.

— *See* Law Fact at the end of this chapter for the answer.

Principles and Applications

Over the past 30 years, biotechnology has come to represent an American success story, as illustrated in **TABLE 17-1**. With 1,500 public and private firms employing tens of thousands of people, the United States is universally considered to be the global biotechnology leader. U.S. biotechnology firms capture almost half of the global revenue in biotechnology sales (Deloitte, 2015). While several global European pharmaceutical firms outsource bioscience research and development operations to the United States, it should be noted that although the revenue may be captured in the United States, much of the work associated with bringing **biopharmaceuticals** to market (research and development, manufacturing, fill finish, packaging, and labeling) is **outsourced** beyond the United States to take advantage of specific tax strategies (*See* Chapter on Supply Chain Management). The availability of **venture capital**, combined with the willingness of investors

TABLE 17-1 Profile of the Global Biotechnology Industry

Firms and State or Country Headquarters	Market Value	Sales	1-Year Sales Change	Number of Employees
Amgen (CA)	$113.9 billion	$21.3 billion	+6.5%	17,900
Gilead Sciences (CA)	$110.4 billion	$32.4 billion	+16.5%	8,000
Celgene (NJ)	$78.3 billion	$8.9 billion	+28.7%	7,000
Biogen (MA)	$57.9 billion	$9.3 billion	-3.9%	7,400
Regeneron Pharmaceuticals (NY)	$40.3 billion	$2.6 billion	+45.6%	4,300
CSL (Australia)	$37.9 billion	$6.6 billion	+12.8%	14,000
Alexion Pharmaceuticals (CN)	$31.9 billion	$2.5 billion	+12.3%	2,900
Shire (Ireland)	$28.0 billion	$6.0 billion	+14.8%	5,500
Illumina (CA)	$20.6 billion	$2.2 billion	+19.3%	4,600
Vertex Pharmaceuticals (MA)	$20.2 billion	$1.1 billion	+77.9%	2,000

Data from: Income and Revenue Statements in the 2015 Annual Report filings with the U.S. Securities and Exchange Commission.

to support the development of the nation's biotechnology firms with initial public offerings, has put the United States as much as 5 to 10 years ahead of Europe and Japan in developing a biotechnology industry (Brillis, 2015).

The most important metric, however, is the biotechnology industry's impact on combating diseases and illnesses, including cancer, multiple sclerosis, rheumatoid arthritis, and rare genetic disorders, as illustrated in **FIGURE 17-1**. With over 900 drugs under development for over 100 diseases (PhRMA, 2016), the biotechnology sector has been at the forefront of scientific medical innovations. Biotechnology firms have also assumed leadership roles in developing vaccines for pandemic influenzas.

Biotechnology will be one of the major wealth creators in the next two decades and, even more importantly, a new science that will significantly improve the lives of consumers of health care (Wicks & Keevil, 2014). Although there is considerable social and political debate about how to best use this emerging technology, the stakes are too high for health care providers to be on the sidelines of biotechnology (Starr, 2013).

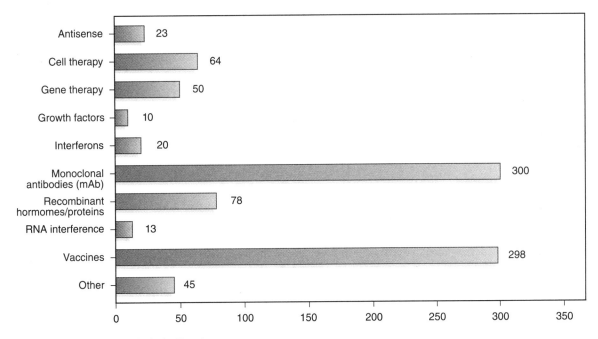

FIGURE 17-1 Biopharmaceuticals in Development

Bonifant, B., Partner at Triangle Insight Group & Thomas, D., Senior Director of Industry Research, Biotechnology Industry Organization (2016, June 9). Remarks at the panel discussion on State of the Innovation Industry and Drivers of Forecasting Success at the 2016 International Biotechnology Industry Organization Conference, San Francisco, CA; PhRMA (Pharmaceutical Research and Manufacturing Association). (2016). Biotechnology medicines in development. Washington, DC: PhRMA.

Challenges Facing the Biotechnology Industry

Many of the same challenges facing the pharmaceutical industry in bringing new medical products and services to the market are also faced by the biotechnology sector. The challenges of getting to the market are magnified in the biotechnology sector, where the:

- Need for the health insurance industry to be involved in biopharmaceuticals pricing to treat rare **orphan diseases** (defined as those diseases that affect fewer than 200,000 people) is just being worked out
- Roles of **government agencies** in regulation of biotechnology products are unclear

Regardless of the market challenges, the potential for scientific breakthroughs is enormous and the marketplace is responding with a willingness to continue investing in new opportunities (PwC, 2015). While the complex patterns of regulatory and scientific change in biotechnology leads to more surprises than in traditional pharmaceutical firms,[LN1] investors in the biotechnology industry must recognize that biotechnology firms are partners with the market in developing new biosciences.

Unclear Regulatory Structure

While the U.S. Food and Drug Administration (FDA) has the mandate to regulate the biotechnology industry, federal regulations have not kept pace with the rapidly developing biosciences. Some newly emerging areas of the biotechnology industry, such as **reprogenics** (genetic engineering) and **synthetic biology**, have largely escaped regulation, while other areas face regulations that appear contradictory on their face (*See* Chapter on Cellular Therapeutics and Precision Medicine). For instance, chemically synthesized gene therapy products meet the current drug definition but not the biologic product definition for regulation by the FDA (21 C.F.R. pts. 20, 312, and 601); nor does **RNA interference** therapy meet the definition of human gene therapy (Dolin, 2013). Given the rate of change in the biotechnology industry, the issue is whether the current regulatory definitions should be brought up to date. A more accurate definition of **biologics** certainly can be provided today than was the case in 1993.

Defining and Understanding Biopharmaceuticals

The dynamic nature and complexity of biotechnology makes it difficult to understand, much less differentiate between biopharmaceuticals and pharmaceuticals. This confusion is a potential danger that can lead to less than optimal policy and political decisions about issues involving the biotechnology industry (Havighurst & Richman, 2011). There are no better examples of this confusion than references to:

- Biopharmaceutical therapies compared to non-treatment of orphan diseases
- Global pricing of biopharmaceutical drugs
- **Pharmacoeconomics** and the cost-effectiveness of biopharmaceutical therapies
- Similarities and clinical differences between brand-name biopharmaceuticals and **biosimilars** (copies of off-patent biologics)

(Djokovich, 2016; Jackson, 2016).

There is no consensus on these issues and, in reality, debate participants often fail to appreciate that they are using words in a variety of conflicting and imprecise ways. For instance, orphan drug status can be given to older biopharmaceuticals if they are being used in new ways to treat rare diseases, which is a policy allowing biotechnology firms that did not pay development costs to receive protection from competition in small markets that affect less than 200,000 people in the United States at any given time (such as treatments for cystic fibrosis, Lou Gehrig's disease, and Tourette's syndrome).[LN2]

Definition of Pharmaceutical Drugs

Traditional pharmaceutical firms make **small molecule drugs** usually in the form of tablets and capsules. Most drugs are produced by **synthesizing chemicals** in a series of well-defined steps through the processes of chemistry with a predictable outcome. The chemicals have well-defined molecular structures that result from, or take part in, chemical

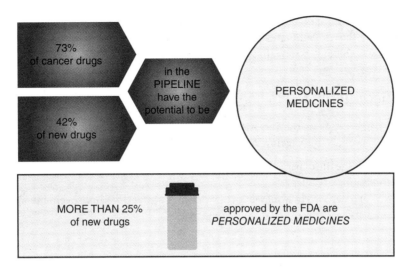

FIGURE 17-2 Precision Medicine

Reproduced from PhRMA (Pharmaceutical Research and Manufacturing Association). (2016). *Biotechnology medicines in development.* Washington, DC: PhRMA. Data from: Personalized Medicine Coalition. (2015). *Progress report: Personalized medicine at FDA.* Washington, DC: Personalized Medicine Coalition; Tufts Center for the Study of Drug Development (CSDD). (2015). Personalized medicine gains traction but still faces multiple challenges. *Tufts CSDD Impact Report. 17* (3).

reactions during manufacturing; the chemical reactions change the properties of the small molecule drugs as they are manufactured into pills. *See gene*rally Kesselheim & Darrow, 2015.

Definition of Biopharmaceuticals

While biopharmaceuticals are also known as bioengineered drugs, biotechnology drugs, and **specialty pharmaceuticals** (the term health insurance providers use), this chapter consistently uses the term *biopharmaceutical* to refer to drug molecule proteins manufactured in living cells, as distinguished from the term **pharmaceuticals**, which refers to small molecule drugs produced by synthesizing chemicals. In other words, biopharmaceuticals are engineered from living cells instead of from chemical molecules like most pharmaceuticals (*See* Ho, 2013).

Biopharmaceuticals are a new class of drugs derived from proteins manufactured in living cells. Bioscientists usually use **DNA technology** to splice genetic material into bacterial, yeast, or mammalian cells, which then produce proteins. A single molecule of these proteins may weigh 100 times as much as a single molecule of the active ingredient in Lipitor (atorvastatin), the world's best-selling brand-name cholesterol-lowering drug manufactured by Pfizer. However, biopharmaceuticals are not made by chemical synthesis. Biopharmaceuticals are often made from Chinese hamster ovary cells or an *Escherichia coli* bacterium through a very complex manufacturing route (Ho, 2013). It is the complexity of the production process, of coaxing live cells in a sterile, temperature-controlled environment to make biological matter that makes biopharmaceuticals so expensive to produce.

Since biopharmaceuticals interfere with the way a disease causes damage as opposed to treating the consequences of a disease, the risks of taking biopharmaceuticals are significant and often unpredictable. As illustrated in **FIGURE 17-2**, there have been remarkable advances in **targeted therapy**, and the research and development pipeline has never been more promising (Grabowski, 2016). Individually tailored to the person taking the drug, the benefits of **precision medicine** will generally outweigh the risks. At the same time, however, it must be said that precision medicine is still out on the horizon for most patients in all but a few instances.

Global Pricing

Significant biopharmaceutical advances in treatments for Alzheimer's disease, cancer, diabetes, and other diseases are all but inevitable in the coming years. The biotechnology industry, however, is courting disaster with pricing policies that appear divorced from the economic benefits its drugs provide (Vagelos, 2015). While **per capita** spending on biopharmaceuticals is at least twice as high in the United States as in the other countries, this price difference reflects primarily greater availability and use of new, relatively high-priced molecules and formulations (Jackson, 2016).

Although pricing new drugs is currently the most controversial issue in the biotechnology industry, prices for identical formulations of biopharmaceuticals are not higher on average in the United States (Vagelos, 2015). The broader price indexes, which do not control formulation, are also not higher in the United States after adjusting for income. In summary, while the United States might spend more on biopharmaceuticals, prices are not noticeably higher (Danzon & Furukawa, 2006; Jackson, 2016).

Problem: Drug Prices Unrelated to Value

Price controls on brand-name drugs or the introduction of biosimilars are regulatory possibilities where economic standards are breached (Jackson, 2016; Vagelos, 2015). For instance, **drug pricing standards** are breached whenever:

- A cancer drug extends the life of patients by a few months but does not treat the underlying cancer, and is priced at hundreds of thousands of dollars
- **Drug formulation** of two separately available drugs delivers a marginal improvement in effectiveness, but one drug is twice as expensive as the other at double the price

(Jackson, 2016).

High prices for such drugs without profound medical value cannot be justified. Regardless of these economic breaches, the biotechnology industry continues to have vast potential to improve the health of individuals and society.

Biopharmaceuticals Compared to Non-Treatment of Rare Orphan Diseases

Orphan diseases are so called because no one was treating them before Congress enacted the **Orphan Drug Act of 1983** (*See* 21 U.S.C.A. §§ 360aa-ee (2006); *see also* 26 U.S.C.A. § 45(C) (2008); 35 U.S.C.A. § 155 (2002); 42 U.S.C.A. § 236 (1992), 255 (1984)). Congress originally envisioned the development of drugs for rare orphan diseases as a sideline for the pharmaceutical industry to treat **neglected diseases** affecting small numbers of people; however, it has become a multibillion-dollar business for biotechnology firms.

Once the FDA certifies a drug with orphan status, firms have seven years of **market exclusivity**; in effect, firms are granted the same market protection as a **drug patent** would provide. Orphan drug protection compares to pharmaceutical drug patents that are only effective for an average of 11 years due to generic competition (Ackland, 2016). While the law provides that drug patents have 17 years of market exclusivity from the date of issue to 20 years from the date of application, with the longer of the two terms allowed for some drugs already on the market, the effective market exclusivity of drugs with sales over $100 million has been reduced to 11 years due to generic competition (Miller, 2016). Another difference is that, unlike patents for new drug discoveries, a drug that has been on the market for other diseases or used in other countries can be given orphan drug status. While competing patent claims often face lengthy court battles, orphan drugs are protected by the FDA, which is barred by law from approving another drug with the same **active ingredient** unless the new drug is proven clinically superior. The law also grants firms a 50% subsidy for research and development, grant money to defray the costs of clinical testing, and assistance in obtaining regulatory approval. *See generally* FDA, 2016.

Similarities and Clinical Differences Between Innovator Biopharmaceuticals and Biosimilars

There is no federal process for gaining approval of biosimilar versions of innovator biopharmaceuticals. The term *biosimilars* is used in this text to refer to **biogenerics, follow-on protein biologics, biocomparables**, off-patent or multi-source biopharmaceuticals, or other terms for generic versions of biopharmaceuticals. FDA regulations for industrial laboratory manufacturing are distinct from regulations for production of therapeutic compounds produced by cellular processes. *See generally* Shepherd, 2015.

MANAGEMENT AND LAW ISSUES

1. Should the free market dictate biopharmaceutical price points, or is it the government's fiduciary responsibility to ensure adequate patient access to these therapies?

Generic Versions of Traditional Pharmaceutical Drugs

For traditional pharmaceutical drugs, a generics manufacturer must merely show that its product has the same characteristics as the brand-name drug:

- Active ingredient
- Dosage form and strength
- Proposed labeling
- Route of administration

(*See* 21 U.S.C.A. § 355(j)).

A generics manufacturer must also show **bioequivalence** to the original brand-name drug to win FDA approval. Bioequivalence is defined as:

The absence of a significant difference in the rate and extent to which the active ingredient or active moiety in pharmaceutical equivalents or pharmaceutical alternatives becomes available at the site of drug action when administered at the same molar dose under similar conditions in an appropriately designed study. (See 21 C.F.R. §320.1(e)).

Bioequivalence is very different from **therapeutic equivalence** or equivalence in how the human body metabolizes a drug. For instance, the active molecule in a generic drug may be a bioequivalent to the brand-name drug's active ingredients, but their absorption rates may vary by as much as 40% under provisions of the Hatch-Waxman law. This means that their bioequivalency may be 20% more or 20% less than the brand-name drug. The critical distinction is that brand-name drugs also have this 20% range of bioequivalence, which means a brand-name drug may be 20% more effective in some patients and 20% less effective in other patients. So, in effect, a bioequivalent generic drug may be 40% less effective than a brand-name drug if it is manufactured at the lower end of the bioequivalent curve, and the generic will still be termed equivalent. Similarly, the generic could be toxic or have adverse side effects if it is manufactured at the upper end of the bioequivalent curve, and the generic will still be termed equivalent.

There is no requirement that generics be exactly the same as brand-name drugs in controlling symptoms or illnesses; meaning there is no mandated actual therapeutic equivalence requiring generics to have the same clinical effect or safety as brand-name drugs (*See* Chao, 2014). Nor is there any requirement for bioequivalency in **drug delivery mechanisms**, which means some generics may come with side effects not found in the brand-name drugs, such as:

- Headaches from dyes that make generics look similar to brand-name drugs
- Heartburn, acid indigestion, or upset stomach related to ingestion of lower quality capsule and tablet fillers
- Hives or other skin irritations from less expensive raw materials used in the formulation of generics
- Other physical discomforts or illnesses from contamination during the production and manufacturing of generics

(Chao, 2014; *See* Davis, 2014; Favole, 2008 for information on deaths from use of generic heparin).

Moreover, the therapeutic effectiveness of generic drug delivery mechanisms varies from manufacturer to manufacturer. The manufacturing sites of U.S. manufacturers are significantly different when compared to many foreign-based manufacturers in developing nations where quality control standards are inferior. Moreover, the pharmaceutical industry closely monitors its foreign-based manufacturing sites to ensure compliance with good manufacturing practices, whereas the generic industry does not always do so (*e.g.,* IOM, 2012; Pew, 2011). *See* Chapter on Global Supply Chain Management; *See also In re: Heparin Products Liability Litigation*, 2011 U.S.Dist.LEXIS 36299 (U.S. District Court for the Northern District of Ohio 2011).

Credible Placebos

Some lower-grade generic drugs could be compared to **credible placebo drugs**. Both types of drugs have a role in medical treatments. Credible placebos can help relieve and sometimes even cure physical and mental ailments, cardiovascular disease, and depression (Ariely, 2010).

Placebo effects are now detectable with functional magnetic resonance imaging where placebo effects account for both lower reported pain and reduced activity in pain-processing areas of the brain (Chandler et al., 2015). Placebo effects are even detectable on the price of drugs. Consumers of health care who buy cold medicine at discount prices report significantly worse medical outcomes than those who pay list price (Ariely, 2010). While placebo effects have long been shown to be pervasive, findings of pricing effects on physical ailments are relatively new. It should be understood, nevertheless, that the placebo effect is normally a short-term effect and only curative in rare examples.

With increasing evidence about the robustness of placebo effects, the **American Medical Association** issued an opinion against the use of placebos for clinical purposes (Kolber, 2011). More generally, a series of studies demonstrates a strong **top-down effect** of expectation on experience; if there is an expectation something will taste bad, the actual experience is worse than if there had been no biased expectation (Ariely, 2010). Recently, the connection between expectations and experience has been demonstrated at the neural level as well (Chandler et al., 2015). The short-term nature of this placebo effect could confound the data derived from placebo-controlled clinical trials. Clearly, the placebo effect makes it difficult to use studies that test a new treatment side by side against an existing one and determine whether the new treatment works (Lietzan, 2016; *See* Miglani, 2016). The question remains, can the therapeutic equivalence of generic and brand-name drugs be accurately tested?

Complexity of the Biotechnology Sector

While bioscientists struggle to understand the workings of the human body, biotechnology managers and investors are searching for ways to gain a greater understanding of the complexity in the biotechnology sector. The founding of Genentech in 1976 launched the biotechnology industry.[LN3] Genentech was the first company to successfully engineer drugs from living cells instead of engineering drugs from chemicals in test tubes, which is the same process the pharmaceutical industry has used for more than 250 years.

Compared to other industries where few founders are academics, more than half of those founding biotechnology firms are academics, primarily from MIT and Stanford University (Lee, 2013, 2012). This movement of people has proved to be an important means for translating **early stage upstream research**, characteristic of university-based bioscience, to product development and commercialization (Karshtedt, 2015). Moreover, while this degree of movement of people from the academic to the corporate sector is unique to the biotechnology industry, it is consistent with the tendency for biotechnology firms to cluster around universities (Lee, 2013). Academics are founders in firms mainly in the fields of biotechnology, pharmaceuticals, fine organic chemistry, and information and communications technology; however, the biotechnology industry is unique in the absolute number of academics that have founded biotechnology firms, as well as the percentage of the total industry that comprises former academics (Sammut, 2016). A similar trend in England highlights the success of Cambridge Enterprise, the University of Cambridge's knowledge and technology transfer services company.

With nearly 2,800 biotechnology firms, total sales revenue for the U.S. biotechnology industry is expected to exceed $110 billion in 2016 (Brillis, 2015). Despite advances in biotechnology, production of biopharmaceuticals via synthesis, tissue culture, or genetic manipulation often remains uneconomical for most firms (Hugin, 2015). While biotechnology may have the distinction of being the biggest money-losing sector of the health care industry (Sammut, 2016), and while the biotechnology sector is often described as an industry that hemorrhages money, biotechnology still attracts investors. **Industry-university cooperation** in biotechnology research and development is still advancing.

The nation's leading research universities have research and development departments, or knowledge transfer offices, as well as firms that provide commercialization services to the universities. The creation of research-owning firms provides medical research departments with the requisite legal capacity to enter into contracts for the development of medical products. With Genentech being the exception to characterizations of this medical products sector, a sector more often than not characterized as having a steady flow of financial losses and a stream of high-profile failures, investors still hope to be a part of the "next" Genentech (Wharton, 2010).

Inexplicable Future Possibilities

Bioscience differs from other medical technologies that have reconfigured the business landscape for the last two centuries in that the research underlying product development is far less easily understood (PwC, 2015). For instance, while the basic concept of coronary stents can be understood, what is happening in bioscience is more complex:

- **Bioinformatics**: using computers to create information databases that permit analyses of genomes, protein sequences, biomolecules, and other organic matter
- **Genomics**: the study of genomes, including gene mapping, which involves figuring out the positions of genes on a DNA molecule
- **Proteomics**: the cataloguing and analyzing of proteins in cells and tissue

(PwC, 2015; Deloitte, 2015).

Even scientists in the research and development areas of biotechnology firms are not completely certain what the future possibilities are for bioinformatics, genomics, and proteomics. The uncertainty factor is much greater in bioscience than with other medical technologies because there is much still to understand and developments are occurring at a rapid pace (Taylor, 2013).

Also affected will be chemicals, agriculture (plant genetics), consumer products, information technology, and life and health insurers, where the potential use of genetic profiles to decide who gets health care coverage and at what cost has already generated debate. It is difficult to keep up with the stories about advances in biotechnology without feeling lost. Genomics, reprogenics, synthetic biology, and the rest of the biotechnology arsenal seem like something out of science fiction, but they are very real and potentially highly profitable (Starr, 2013).

Valued-Added Medical Treatments

Most health care professionals, including physicians, are not trained in genomics, so they must also learn about the rapid advances in biopharmaceuticals for medical treatments. One way to look at genomics and the other biosciences is from the perspective of the **value chain**. A value chain is a set of activities that directly add value to a product or process.

In health care, bioscience research holds significant promise for patients facing serious illnesses, rare diseases, or life-threatening conditions. The biotechnology industry, however, must understand and overcome the barriers to seeing that promise realized by rank-and-file health care professionals and the consumers of health care. Overcoming those barriers is how the biotechnology sector can add value to the health care industry and move forward within it.

In fact, today's biotechnology industry can be compared to the far-reaching changes ushered in by **silicon chips** or, to go farther back in time, petrochemicals (chemical products obtained from petroleum) and plastic. Fifty years ago, the microchip revolutionized the way the world computes, calculates, and communicates, ushering in the information age. These component materials remade society in pervasive and sometimes unexpected ways, forcing legal institutions to adapt old strategies to meet the new challenges. For instance, biotechnology did away with the traditional distinction between drugs and biologics; **nanomedicine** may do the same to the line separating devices and biologics. No one now could reasonably deny that regulatory agencies or courts have failed to appreciate these forces and design uniform responses (*See generally* Noah, 2016).

Drivers of Bioscience

With about 300 biopharmaceuticals in **late-stage clinical trials**, the long view of the biotechnology industry actually looks very promising (Brillis, 2015). Advancements in biology and chemistry have increased the volume and quality of potential drugs undergoing research, especially as the number of young biotechnology firms is growing (Sammut, 2016). Seven key forces are driving this change in bioscience and in the biotechnology industry, in particular:

- Capital availability
- Market conditions, such as an aging population

- Maturing pharmaceutical sector
- Movement toward precision medicine
- Ongoing consolidation and shakeout in the biotechnology industry
- Pricing pressure
- Value-creating innovations, such as predictive medicine and **gene-guided drug development**

(Brillis, 2015; Day & Schoemaker, 2004; Hugin, 2015).

One ongoing challenge is that of being able to unlock the human genome, the genetic material in the chromosomes of an organism, using very large-scale computers greater than anything currently on the market, to analyze gene structures and the flaws in them. When this technological challenge is met, genomics will allow for the advancement of precision medicine with the ability to custom tailor medicine to a patient's particular combination of genes and defects (*See* Hiller, 2016).

Precision Medicine as a Major Wealth Creator

As the scientific breakthrough of precision medicine occurs and the world's medical community moves away from the trial-and-error approach to medical diagnostics and treatment, the biotechnology industry should become one of the major wealth creators in the United States. Biopharmaceutical care is currently seeing greater customization to the unique needs of individual patients in targeted cancer treatments and the expansion of **coordinated care programs** for patients with specialized medical needs (Hiller, 2016).

The importance of maintaining this leadership role is critical as the nation seeks to control health care costs and expand health insurance coverage. Advances in genetic testing will help physicians and other health care professionals predict the benefits and risks of drugs for each patient, so that decisions about drug selection and dosing can be more accurate and cost-effective (Kim, 2014).

The biotechnology industry is a key component of stability and future growth for the U.S. economy. U.S. biotechnology firms:

- Are **net exporters** in foreign trade, at a time when the United States is facing severe declines in its exportable products
- Conduct most of their research, development, and manufacturing in the United States, at a time when the nation is facing one of the highest trade deficits in the nation's history
- Have a highly educated, well-paid workforce, at a time of high unemployment of all economic classes

(Bagley & Tvarno, 2015).

While declining exports, massive **trade deficits**, and unemployment are national concerns, the immediate focus must be on the economic stimulus of U.S. industries that will contribute to future U.S. prosperity. Closely related to this stimulus is reform of the regulatory regime of the U.S. health care system and supervision of large medical products firms by the various federal authorities (Dolin, 2015).

Effects of a Stumble or Fumble

If the United States stumbles in its support of the biotechnology sector or fumbles regulatory overhaul of its health care system, China, India, Singapore, and other emerging countries will gladly seize the leadership role in biotechnology and medicine. These countries are already actively courting global biotechnology firms and offering a persuasive blend of financial incentives with lower corporate taxes, improving intellectual property laws, and a vast pool of scientific talent and expertise (Jurata & Owens, 2015).

American "Can-Do-Ism"

While helping to maintain the economic leadership of the United States, the biotechnology industry and new biosciences could significantly improve the lives of consumers of health care; oft characterized as American "can-do-ism," they can do it. The biotechnology industry should quickly mature as it gives birth to new biosciences and innovative medical technologies. Innovations beyond anyone's imaginations will be developed and become reality. Further, the potential opportunity for real health care reform will present itself to innovative health care firms that are able to attract individuals trained to think outside their traditional roles (Wharton, 2010).

There are those who think this sounds promising, yet overly idealistic, considering the lack of equal access to health care in the United States at this time. They ask whether biotechnology will somehow help overcome this disparity in delivery of health care and whether the medical advances arising from the new biosciences will be affordable and accessible to the masses. Above all, they cannot envision how what is still a rather uneconomic enterprise could possibly transform health care (Vagelos, 2015).

The Renaissance, the Industrial Revolution, and the information age each represented great leaps forward in human potential; the **genetic age** promises another exponential increase in human knowledge and potential (Rifkin, 2013). Expanding on this prediction, many believe that once biotechnology has achieved this promise, all that must be done is to make U.S. biotechnology products and biopharmaceuticals accessible and affordable and provide them to the rest of the world.

Emerging Bioscience Technologies

Today, advances in health information technology have led to industrialized methods of research where tens of thousands of experiments can be done simultaneously, such as:

- **Computational biology**, which applies the techniques of computer science, applied mathematics, and statistics to address phenomena in biology
- **Microfluidics**, which makes it possible to perform tasks such as analyzing DNA sequences by taking advantage of the chemical properties of liquids and gases with the electrical properties of semiconductors by combining them on a single microchip
- **Ultra-high-throughput screening** that screens and analyzes thousands of genes or molecules at a time versus conventional methods that screen one gene or molecule at a time to see which items are active in particular conditions

(*See* Jones, 2014).

Bioscience has a confluence of multiple streams of technology, from gene sequencing to traditional molecular biology to information technology. Other medical technologies are just emerging into their own fields, such as:

- Reprogenics
- Stem cell research
- Synthetic biology

The 2000 announcement regarding mapping of the human **genome** made worldwide news. Whether more than a handful of bioscience scientists really understood, what this meant at the time is unclear. For even though scientists have successfully sequenced the human genome, they still lack a clear picture of exactly how coding and non-coding DNA sequences function together, or how genomes evolve over time (Vagelos, 2015).

Ribonucleic Acid Interference

At least three large global pharmaceutical firms have product development deals with biotechnology firms that support **ribonucleic acid interference (RNAi)**, the emerging area of bioscience research that involves blocking disease-causing proteins using technology in RNAi. Such technology is used in developing treatments for diseases such as HIV/AIDS, hepatitis C, cancer, and autoimmune diseases (Hugin, 2015). In cancer treatments, therapeutic RNA pairs up with cancer cell RNA, triggering an immune response that both destroys RNA strands and starves the cancer cell of necessary proteins (Brillis, 2015).

AstraZeneca, Merck, and Pfizer have records of accomplishment of making the right calls at the right time when acquiring and striking deals with smaller biotechnology firms, so this bioscience technology should be monitored for opportunities. The fact that RNAi technology is also used to produce decaffeinated coffee plants is simply another business opportunity that helps pharmaceutical firms offset the cyclicality and risks of the drug industry (Tran, 2016).

Telomerase Technology

Another emerging science, **telomere biology**, hints at the prospect of enhancing life spans. Parts of the human chromosomes called telomeres serve as a genetic clock for cellular aging. Telomeres shorten with each division of the cell and, at a certain length, they turn off the division process, which seems to lead to destructive effects. On the other hand, an **enzyme** called telomerase is capable of restoring telomere length, or resetting the clock, thereby increasing the life span of cells. *See generally, e.g.*, Ram, 2015.

Geron, a California biotechnology company, has focused its **telomerase technology** on goals such as improved wound healing and cancer treatments. While Geron has never suggested its products will allow people to live forever, the National Science Foundation sees science quickly turning fiction into factual possibilities (National Science Board, 2009). A private, start-up company based out of San Francisco, Twist Bioscience Corporation, licensed the single molecule that activates the telomerase gene from Geron and developed a nutraceutical to help manage aging. The downside is that the pill must be taken on an ongoing basis and costs about $23,000 a year, unless you are over 40 and an employee of TA Biosciences. The company is also developing **cosmeceutical products** which are new **esthetician products** emerging from the convergence of the cosmetic and pharmaceutical industries and directed at the high-end consumer market that purchases antiaging skin treatments, body creams, and lotions. *See generally* Leproust, 2016.

Convergent Technology

The National Science Foundation has taken a leadership role in determining how nanotechnology, biotechnology, information technology, and cognitive science can combine in what has been termed **convergent technology**. The driver in convergent technology is the life biosciences where the focus is on enhancing both human performance and productivity (Fateh & Haw, 2015). While some envision a time in the 21st century when death may become postponed indefinitely, the immediate focus is on what is possible with regard to ability-enhancing technologies (Wharton, 2010).[LN4] Many see the health care industry at the threshold of a renaissance in knowledge, based on the structure and behavior of matter from the nanoscale up to the complex system of the human brain (Starr, 2013).

Examples of the revolutionary changes in health care might include:

- Advancing human capabilities for reproductive purposes
- Ameliorating the physical and cognitive decline common to the aging mind
- Early disease detection
- Enhancing individual sensory and cognitive capabilities
- Improving both individual and group efficiency
- Perfecting **human-to-machine interfaces**

(National Science Board, 2009; Sammut, 2016).

Emerging Areas of Bioscience Research

Biopharmaceuticals have become some of the most important, and expensive, medical treatments in health care. Annual spending on biopharmaceuticals that treat small patient populations with chronic or life-threatening diseases represents a growing component of pharmacy spending. For instance, Genzyme, a Cambridge, Massachusetts-based biotechnology company, posts sales in excess of $1 billion annually on its drug for Gaucher disease, a rare, sometimes fatal disease that causes certain organs to swell and bones to deteriorate. Treating the average patient costs $200,000 annually, but the price of the drug at the highest dose levels (for patients who have used the drug for prolonged periods and developed a tolerance for its usual response) can run as high as $600,000 a year (*See generally*, Gross, 2016; Sammut, 2016).

The philosophy of the biotechnology industry has always been to create medicines to fill unmet needs and to recoup its research and development investment by obtaining patents and charging premium prices for its products and services.

The National Science Board, however, is concerned with declining public support for expensive biopharmaceuticals. Over the past decade, there has been a decline in basic research funds from the federal government for biosciences research and development as biosciences ran into political windstorms of ideology questioning the merits of advanced science (Djokovich2016; National Science Board, 2009).

Biotechnology innovation in the United States historically has benefited from relatively free pricing. For instance, Genzyme follows an extremely disciplined **full price or free strategy**; it locates patients, donates its drug at first, and then pressures the government and private insurers to be paid the full retail price. This **invisible hand** has allowed the biotechnology industry to attract investors to fund research projects that take approximately 10 to 15 years and cost more than $2.6 billion apiece to bring their biopharmaceuticals to market (PhRMA, 2016).

COURT DECISION
Pricing of Biopharmaceuticals

Biotechnology Industry Organization v. District of Columbia
[Biotechnology's Trade Association v. District]
496 F.3d 1362 (U.S. Court of Appeals for the Federal Circuit 2007),
rehearing denied, 505 F.3d 1343 (U.S. Court of Appeals for the Federal Circuit 2007);[LN5]
followed by Auto Body Parts Association v. Ford Global Technologies, LLC., 2014
U.S.Dist.LEXIS 131101 (U.S. District Court for the Eastern District of Texas, Sherman Division 2014)

Facts: The District of Columbia City Council adopted the local drug price control law which prohibited any drug from being sold in the District for an excessive price. The operative section of the local drug price control law reads:

It shall be unlawful for any drug manufacturer or licensee thereof, excluding a point of sale retail seller, to sell or supply for sale or impose minimum resale requirements for a patented prescription drug that results in the prescription drug being sold in the District for an excessive price. D.C. Code § 28-4553

The City Council determined that since excessive drug prices were threatening the health of the District's residents as well as the District government's ability to ensure its residents received basic health care, it was incumbent upon the District to restrain the prices.

Evidence of **excessive pricing** was to be established where the wholesale price of a drug was over 30% higher than comparable prices in other high income countries (like England, Germany, Canada, or Australia, where governments negotiate drug prices with the pharmaceutical and biotechnology firms). Once excessive pricing was shown, the burden shifted to the firms to prove that a given drug was not excessively priced given the following:

- Consideration of any public research that supported development of the drug
- Global sales
- Impact of price on access to the drug by District residents
- Production costs
- Profits
- Research and development costs

The local drug price control law provided for an array of remedies, including injunctions, fines, treble damages, attorney's fees, and litigation costs.

Issue: Was the local drug price control law preempted by federal patent law?

Holding and Decision: Yes. The local drug price control law impermissibly attempted to regulate an area of law Congress intended to control.

Analysis: The biotechnology industry sought to show that federal patent laws preempted the local drug price control law in order to have the law declared unenforceable. The court determined that whether the local drug price control law was actually enforced or not, its existence was likely to cause the biotechnology industry to incur expenses in an effort to comply with it. While the local drug price control law did not directly regulate prices, it regulated the industry's activities, which could have resulted in more excessive drug prices.

Although there is no express provision in federal patent law to prevent regulation of drug prices, a local drug price control law must yield to federal law if it obstructs the purpose of a federal law. This is the purpose of the Supremacy Clause in the U.S. Constitution. The biotechnology industry claimed the local drug price control law offended Congress's intention to provide patent holders with the opportunity to secure the financial rewards that follow from the exclusive rights granted by patents.

The court found the biotechnology industry undertakes research efforts with the expectation it will be able to obtain a patent to protect the forthcoming financial rewards of its development efforts. A patent grants exclusivity over its products, meaning other firms are prohibited from copying products or selling them for a certain length of time. Encouragement of research and development is the fundamental purpose of patents. The court specifically recognized the importance of providing financial incentives to the biotechnology industry to innovate and continue its costly development efforts. The court endorsed competition by determining that financial rewards during the period of patent exclusivity were the carrot to encourage the investment, and that the marketplace should be the only limitation on the size of the carrot as opposed to government regulation or judicial feats.

The court went on to explain why drug patents are granted for a limited time; once that time expires, prices will be lowered by competition. In this way, innovator products first benefit the patent-holder with profit exclusivity, and then benefit the public through liberated use, resulting in competition and lower prices. In this way Congress intended to resolve the tension between the interests of the biotechnology industry and the public's interests. The local drug price control law was an attempt to shift the benefit away from the industry and toward the public earlier in the product patent's lifetime than Congress intended and was thus void. The District impermissibly attempted to change federal patent policy within its borders.

Rule of Law: The local drug price control law violated the Supremacy Clause of the U.S. Constitution by seeking to control an area of law that Congress intended to control and was therefore preempted by federal patent law.

References discussing this court decision: *E.g.*, Djokovich, 2016; Gugliuzza, 2013; Landers, 2015; Noah, 2016.

Genomics and Reprogenics

In the field of genomics, a great deal of attention is focused on the emergence of new therapeutic drugs. However, advances in genomics also hold promise for other health care businesses as the source of future treatments is being developed. The firms that will make significant money in the short run are diagnostics firms and computer manufacturers serving the health information technology sector (Wicks & Keevil, 2014). As more individuals consent to **genetic diagnostics** and participate in **biobanking**, there will be a need to process and data-mine this information for use by the medical products industry. Therefore, while new personalized therapeutic drugs are promising in the long term, diagnostics firms and computer manufacturers will bring in the revenue and profits in the short term.

Genomic Esthetics: Nutraceuticals and Cosmeceuticals

Several consumer products firms, many of which are subsidiaries of global pharmaceutical firms, have changed the way they develop products because of their new knowledge in genomics. New aesthetic products in areas such as hair care, skin care, nutrition, and weight management are being introduced. In the future, product design will be based on looking at consumers' genomes (Deloitte, 2014).

For instance, a person's genes will determine the design of skin care products. To address wrinkling, bioscience research is seeking to define what proteins can be managed within and between cells to cause certain effects that eliminate wrinkles. Some of the new wrinkle filler concentrates on the market are produced using nanotechnology and, while very expensive, are well-regarded in the high-end medical esthetician market. It is a matter of getting product development worked down to the level of impacting the cells as opposed to relying on more surface-oriented changes. *See generally* Watnick, 2014.

Pharmaceutical and Biotechnology Repositioning and Restructuring

Three to four hundred biotechnology firms are public corporations. Most of the remaining 1,100 to 1,200 biotechnology firms are positioning themselves to survive until the day they go public or are acquired by a larger pharmaceutical or biotechnology company (Jackson, 2016).

Mergers of Pharmaceutical and Biotechnology Firms

There is a convergence of pharmaceutical and biotechnology companies. Growing numbers of pharmaceutical firms are depending on biotechnology for:

- New products
- New technologies
- Scientific innovation

Biotechnology is also poised to reap the benefits of new medical technologies, including:

- Gene therapy
- Products from genomics and proteomics

(Ackland, 2016).

While there has been some economic reward for the creation and use of biotechnology tools, the anticipated cash streams from the sale of drugs based on genomic and/or proteomics discoveries may take a decade or two longer than first anticipated (Wicks & Keevil, 2014). There is considerable debate about what direction the medical products industry will take in the next decade as it awaits these discoveries to come to fruition.

Some maintain that the recent trend toward consolidation of the biotechnology industry will continue as larger biotechnology firms seek to enhance their own pipelines and smaller firms hope to leverage a partner's expertise in **regulatory procedure and marketing** (Day & Schoemaker, 2004; Wharton, 2010). Others suggest the consolidations in the medical products industry will only go so far; historically, waves of consolidation end when larger, healthier firms grow reluctant to take on troubled smaller firms (Jackson, 2016). In past cycles, the consolidation process never fully played out; each time a wave of consolidation neared, the financing window opened up and saved all the biotechnology firms from the pain of merging with another company (Day & Schoemaker, 2004).

Strategic Alliances

Biotechnology firms are increasingly turning to global pharmaceutical firms that have a need for new drugs to fill their vast marketing channels, particularly now that the biotechnology firms face a dearth of new products coming out of their own laboratories (Starr, 2013). It has been noted that the:

- Biotechnology industry is opportunity long and capital short
- Pharmaceutical industry is capital long and opportunity short

(Deloitte 2014; Starr, 2013).

The biotechnology industry has a promising pipeline of products but insufficient capital to commercialize all their ideas, while the pharmaceutical industry has a dearth of products in its pipeline but sufficient capital to invest in commercializing promising products it does have.

Licensing

The pace of biotechnology-pharmaceutical licensing deals is slowing because many of the most promising projects have already been acquired. Some products will continue to become available as global pharmaceuticals merge and spin out compounds that do not fit with their larger corporate strategies. Moreover, smaller biotechnology firms can use partnerships with their larger corporate brethren or global pharmaceuticals as validation that their science is valuable (Wharton, 2010).

GlaxoSmithKline, the world's seventh-largest pharmaceutical company, has made licensing a critical part of its research and development strategy. The firm licenses about 10 potential drugs from other firms each year, preferring to buy late-stage products because of the lower risk. The corporate resources and its global sales force give GlaxoSmithKline an advantage in competing for promising drugs since size is very important in the medical products industry; success in final clinical development requires a worldwide infrastructure (Vagelos. 2015).

Need for Capital Investments

One thing is certain: the nation's public and private biotechnology firms need vast amounts of funds (Moses et al., 2015). With combined assets of $43 billion in the nation's biotechnology industry, if all of the biotechnology firms were to push a product through the clinical development pipeline, they would need more than $3.2 trillion in capital investment funding (Bonifant & Thomas, 2016). This is:

- Nearly equivalent to Germany's **gross domestic product**
- Less than the $3.9 trillion in total federal expenditures for all government activities in the United States
- Significantly less than the $9 trillion and counting for the bailout of the U.S. financial industry (only this would not be a bailout investment)

(CBO, 2016).

At this point, perhaps American taxpayers should be willing to loan trillions of dollars to the biotechnology industry (Carrier, 2013; National Science Board, 2009); at least the global population would have the possibility of better health. The investment might even ensure the United States retains its competitive standing as a global leader in biotechnology while acting as an economic engine of growth.

Venture Capital Investments

Global pharmaceutical firms have also acted as venture capitalists in the biotechnology industry to varying degrees over the past two decades (Bonifant & Thomas, 2016). A few pharmaceutical firms, like Johnson & Johnson, have been long-term players, while others step in and out of the role of venture backer. Pharmaceutical firms often begin by investing in venture capital funds. They then gain enough knowledge and confidence to make their own direct investments in biotechnology. Next, a management change determines it is not strategic, so they merge the biotechnology firm into their own research and development division, where interest in biotechnology flags, and the pharmaceutical firm exits the venture business (Starr, 2013). The venture process then repeats itself in 10 years (Day & Schoemaker, 2004).

Repositioning of Chemical Compounds

Another major trend bolstering the convergence of the pharmaceutical and biotechnology industries is the **repositioning of chemical compounds** by pharmaceutical companies. Pharmaceutical firms eager to fill weak **drug pipelines** are going back into **product portfolios** to test old drugs for new uses (Starr, 2013). Since the products have already been proven safe, development time and costs are reduced. Firms are also looking abroad for successful compounds that could be introduced in the U.S. market. Then there are always the serendipitous medical discoveries like Viagra, a drug originally

MANAGEMENT AND LAW ISSUES

5. What will it take for developments in biotechnology to filter into everyday medical practice, and who is going to pay for it?

developed to treat angina; while the clinical study participants showed little success with treating their angina, they did report an unexpected pleasant side effect (*See* Mann, 2015).

Management of New Scientific Developments

Technological revolutions do not come in neat packages, and they defy attempts at simple management (Noah, 2016). The success of the biotechnology industry depends on many things, including the ability to be objective about what is possible and what remains as science fiction. Overall, scientists still do not recognize the full potential of the bioscience research surrounding genomics (Wicks & Keevil, 2014).

In fact, the FDA, accustomed to receiving data from large clinical trials designed to test drugs with significant market potential using a diverse subject population, along with centralized manufacturing facilities and uniform labeling, must learn to deal with a radically altered model of drug development and use for biopharmaceuticals (Noah, 2016). Biopharmaceutical manufacturers rely on cutting-edge medical technologies that target similar subject populations, as illustrated in **FEATURE BOX 17-1**. The aggregate instincts of the biotechnology industry about how best to manage these new and emerging scientific developments may be erroneous. With the level of uncertainty so high in biotechnology, the normal reaction is to try to manage and control things, but this may be the wrong approach (Taylor, 2013; *See* Day & Schoemaker, 2004).

With bioscience, the leading biotechnology firms continue to be flexible, riding the waves of entrepreneurship and developing corporate strategies for succeeding, no matter what their future brings.

FEATURE BOX 17-1

Cutting-Edge Medical Technologies

Medical research is developing cutting-edge technologies, like:

- Protein drugs produced by splicing genes into bacteria, including:

  - Clotting factor for hemophilia patients
  - Erythropoietin to stimulate the production of red blood cells
  - Human growth hormone
  - Recombinant insulin

- Monoclonal antibodies (laboratory-made version of the naturally occurring protein that binds to and neutralizes foreign invaders) and interferons (proteins that interfere with the cell's ability to reproduce) are the basis of drugs for:

  - Chronic granulomatous disease
  - Genital warts
  - Hairy cell leukemia
  - Multiple sclerosis
  - Osteoporosis

- **Gene therapies** that augment normal gene functions or replace or inactivate disease-causing genes are being tested for:

  - Cancers
  - Heart disease

- **Therapeutic vaccines** designed to jump-start the immune system to fight disease are in development to treat:

  - Cancers
  - HIV/AIDS

Data from: Bonifant, B., Partner at Triangle Insight Group & Thomas, D., Senior Director of Industry Research, Biotechnology Industry Organization (2016, June 9). Remarks at the panel discussion on State of the Innovation Industry and Drivers of Forecasting Success at the 2016 International Biotechnology Industry Organization Conference, San Francisco, CA; Gross, D., Chief Executive Officer, Pennsylvania Drug Discovery Institute at The Pennsylvania Biotechnology Center (2016, June 9). Remarks at the Biotechnology Entrepreneurship Boot Camp at the 2016 International Biotechnology Industry Organization Conference, San Francisco, CA.

LAW FACT

Bioscience Research

Are the interests of patent holders and the users of patented inventions being balanced by the courts in patent disputes?

Yes. Biotechnology patent disputes are like a coin: patent holders are on one side and users of patented inventions are on the other side. Both sides of the coin favor the users of patented biopharmaceuticals. Users are not required to break or terminate license agreements before seeking declaratory relief in federal court that the underlying patents are invalid, unenforceable, or not infringed. On the one side, where patent disputes do not involve license agreements, patented biopharmaceuticals may be used in preclinical studies as long as there is a reasonable basis for believing that the experiments will produce the type of information that is relevant to bringing a new drug to market.

— *Merck KGaA v. Integra Lifesciences I, Ltd.*, 545 U.S. 193 (U.S. Supreme Court 2005) *on remand*, 496 F.3d1334 (U.S. Court of Appeals for the Federal Circuit 2007). *Followed by Classen Immunotherapies Inc. v. King Pharmaceuticals, Inc.*, 466 F.Supp.2d 621 (U.S. District Court for the District of Maryland, Northern Division). *See, e.g.*, Chao, 2014; Flynn, 2015; Hubbard, 2013; Jones, 2014; Karshtedt, 2015; Khatibifar, 2013; Lu, 2015; Newman, 2013; Parchomovsky & Stein, 2013; Taylor, 2013; Varadarajan, 2014 (discussing this decision).

On the other side, where patent disputes involve license agreements to research tools, courts must first determine whether the users of the patented invention are being coerced, either by the patent holder or the fear of losing business, to pay royalties under the licensing agreements. If coercion is found, the users of the patented research tool, the licensees, will be allowed to challenge the validity of the patented invention in court without being required to breach the licensing agreements first.

— *MedImmune, Inc. v. Genentech, Inc.*, 549 U.S. 118 (U.S. Supreme Court 2007). *Followed by Medtronic, Inc. v. Mirowski Family Ventures, LLC*, 134 S.Ct. 843 (U.S. Supreme Court 2014).

See, e.g. Dolin, 2015; Hessick, 2016; Schwartz, 2013; Wang, 2016 (discussing this decision).

Patent disputes where there are no licensing agreements will be controlled by the *Merck* decision; patent disputes involving license agreements will be controlled by the *MedImmune* decision.

CHAPTER SUMMARY

- The United States is the world's biotechnology leader, with about half of the industry's revenues.
- The biotechnology industry faces many of the same challenges as the pharmaceutical industry, but on a larger scale because the regulatory roles of the FDA and provider payers are unclear.
- Pharmaceutical drugs are made by synthesizing chemicals, while biopharmaceuticals are proteins made by living organisms.
- Although biotechnology continues to lose money through uneconomical production and failure to bring products to market, investors remain extremely interested in the industry.
- The full potential of the biotechnology industry, including that of bioinformatics, genomics, and proteomics, has yet to be realized; even scientists are unsure of its possibilities.
- Once the human genome is completely unlocked and understood, the field will advance tremendously and scientists will be able to create personalized medical and cosmetic products; the science fiction possibility of living forever may even become a reality.
- The life biosciences are the driver of convergent technology, which is the intersection of nanotechnology, biotechnology, information technology, and cognitive science.
- Although biotechnology has incredible medical technology possibilities, it is losing public support and funding; it currently relies on private investors to continue progressing, and because of this, many biotechnology firms are either merging with each other or merging into the bigger pharmaceutical firms, where they risk falling by the wayside.
- Besides funding, one of the biggest challenges biotechnology faces, as an industry founded and run by academics, is developing corporate strategies to ensure sustainability and success.

LAW NOTES

1. One such surprise was BioMarin Pharmaceutical, a California biotechnology company. BioMarin raised $67 million in an initial public offering based on the promise of a single orphan drug still in clinical trials for mucopolysaccharidosis I, a rare genetic disease affecting fewer than 4,000 people and caused by a deficiency in an enzyme that leads to delayed mental development and impaired vision, among other symptoms. Within months of going public, BioMarin had a market capitalization of more than $1 billion. In a joint venture with Genyzme, BioMarin brought Aldurazyme (laronidase), an **enzyme replacement therapy**, to market in 2003 at an average cost of $175,000 per patient each year. In 2015, global net sales exceeded $130 million (Sanofi, 2015). *See generally, Genzyme Therapeutic Products LP v. BioMarin Pharmaceutical, Inc.*, 2016 U.S.App.LEXIS 10711 (U.S. Court of Appeals for the Federal Circuit 2016).

2. Celegene Corporation, a New Jersey biotechnology company, licensed thalidomide in 1992. Thalidomide is a drug that had been around for decades but had been off the market since the 1960s for causing birth defects. Orphan drug status was obtained for thalidomide's use in treating a side effect of leprosy in 1998, then later for multiple myeloma, a kind of cancer. Today, thalidomide is marketed under a tight distribution system under the trade name Thalomid. Celegene raised the price of a Thalomid pill from $6 in 1992 to about $53 today, in line with the price of other cancer drugs. The drug is so inexpensive to make that it is sold by other firms in Brazil for seven cents a pill (*See generally* Hugin, 2015).

3. Genentech, based in South San Francisco, California, developed the first genetically engineered human therapeutic to win FDA approval in 1977. Trading on the New York Stock Exchange as DNA, Genentech began when venture capitalist Robert Swanson, in his mid-20s, and biochemist Dr. Herbert Boyer agreed to invest $500 apiece to start a pharmaceutical company. Working with bioscientists from the Beckman Research Institute, a research facility affiliated with the City of Hope National Medical Center in Duarte, California, Genentech was the first to successfully express a human gene in bacteria to produce synthetic human insulin. In 2009, Roche Pharmaceutical acquired full ownership of Genentech for $47 billion (Roche, 2015; Wharton, 2010).

4. Memory improvement is a target of several biotechnology firms. Axonyx, for instance, has the rights to a compound called Gilatide that is based on the saliva of the Gila monster, a venomous lizard found in parts of the United States and Mexico. Other firms racing after memory improvement include Memory Pharmaceuticals and Helicon Therapeutics. While Genentech's recombinant human growth hormone was developed to treat growth hormone deficiency, athletes are suspected of using the hormone to boost their athletic performance. The International Olympic Committee has launched an effort to develop ways to detect biosynthetic growth hormones in athletes (*e.g.*, Gallman, 2012). Viagra also raises the therapy versus enhancement issue. Regularly providing sexual potency to 80-year-olds may fix a malady, but it also endows them with unprecedented abilities, including geriatric paternity (Wieland & Ferrucci, 2008).

5. Several states are following the District of Columbia's lead in passing **bioprospecting research laws** requiring that the biotechnology industry enter into **cooperative research and development agreements** providing for benefits sharing of any biopharmaceutical compounds are derived from natural products taken from lands in their state (*See* Utah Bioprospecting Act of 2010, Utah Code Ann.§§ 65A-14-101 *et seq.*). Moving forward, this could impact both pharmaceutical and biopharmaceutical manufacturers since more than half of the most prescribed medicines in the United States contain compounds derived from natural products (Fischer, 2012).

REFERENCES

Ackland, J., Managing Director of Global BioSolutions (in Australia). (2016, June 9). Remarks at the Biotechnology Entrepreneurship Boot Camp at the 2016 International Biotechnology Industry Organization Conference, San Francisco, CA.

Ariely, D. (2010). *Predictably irrational: The hidden forces that shape our decisions (revised expanded ed.)*. New York, NY: Harpers.

Bagley, C. E., & Tvarno, C. D. (2015). Promoting "academic entrepreneurship" in Europe and the United States: Creating an intellectual property regime to facilitate the efficient transfer of knowledge from the lab to the patient. *Duke Journal of Comparative and International Law, 26*, 1–78.

Bonifant, B., Partner at Triangle Insight Group & Thomas, D., Senior Director of Industry Research, Biotechnology Industry Organization (2016, June 9). Remarks at the panel discussion on State of the Innovation Industry and Drivers of Forecasting Success at the 2016 International Biotechnology Industry Organization Conference, San Francisco, CA.

Brillis, D., Corporate Strategy Director, Novartis. (2015, February 20). Remarks at the panel discussion on The Future of Innovation in Pharma and Biotech at the 2015 Wharton Health Care Business Conference on Disruption Amidst Uncertainty: Adapting and Innovating for the Future, Philadelphia, PA.

Carrier, M. A. (2013). Increasing innovation through copyright common sense and better government policy. *Emory Law Journal, 62*, 983–997.

CBO (Congressional Budget Office). (2016). *The budget and economic outlook*. Washington, DC: CBO.

Chandler, J., et al. (2015). Chronic pain, "psychogenic" pain, and emotion. *Journal of Health Care Law and Policy, 18*, 275–293.

Chao, J. (2014). Examining the §271(e)(1) safe harbor of the Hatch-Waxman Act: A legislative proposal granting mandatory post-marketing exceptions. *Cardozo Arts and Entertainment Law Journal. 32*, 651–682.

Danzon, P. M., & Furukawa, M. F. (2006). Prices and availability of biopharmaceuticals: An international comparison: The U.S. might spend more on biologics, but prices are not noticeably higher than in nine other countries. *Health Affairs, 25*(5), 1353–1362.

Davis, C. O. (2014). Red tape tightrope: Regulating financial conflicts of interest in FDA advisory committees. *Washington University Law Review, 91*, 1591–1632.

Day, G. S., & Schoemaker, P. (2004). *Wharton on managing emerging technologies*. New York, NY: Wiley.

Deloitte (2015). *Global life sciences outlook: Adapting in an era of transformation*. New York, NY: Deloitte.

Djokovich, C. (2016). License to pill: Compulsory licensing as a solution to drug over-pricing. *Chapman's Journal of Law and Policy, 21*, 47–66.

Dolin, G. (2015). Dubious patent reform. *Boston College Law Review, 56*, 881–947.

____. (2013). Exclusivity without patents: The new frontier of FDA regulation for genetic materials. *Iowa Law Review, 98*, 1399–1465.

Fateh, L., & Haw, R. F. (2015). Synthetic Biology in the FDA realm: Toward productive oversight assessment. *Food and Drug Law Journal. 70*, 339–377.

Favole, J. A. (2008, November 8). FDA seizes contaminated heparin. *Wall Street Journal*, p. A2.

FDA (Food and Drug Administration). (2016). *Developing products for rare diseases and conditions*. Bethesda, MD: FDA.

Fischer, W. M. (2012). The Utah Bioprospecting Act of 2010: (Unintentional) state-level implementation of the United Nations Convention on Biodiversity. *Journal on Telecommunications and High Technology Law, 10*, 197–226.

Flynn, C. T. (2015). Here today, gone tomorrow? Post-grant review and PTAB interpretation of § 101 subject matter after Myriad. *Buffalo Intellectual Property Law Journal, 11*, 1–27.

Gallman, R. M. (2012). Enhancement or recovery? The scientific and legal paradox of performance-enhancing substances. *SMU Science and Technology Law Review, 15*, 495–524.

Grabowksi, H. (2016). Updated trends in US brand-name and generic drug competition. *Journal of Medical Economics, 4*, 1–9.

Gross, D., Chief Executive Officer, Pennsylvania Drug Discovery Institute at The Pennsylvania Biotechnology Center (2016, June 9). Remarks at the Biotechnology Entrepreneurship Boot Camp at the 2016 International Biotechnology Industry Organization Conference, San Francisco, CA.

Gugliuzza, P. R. (2013). The federal circuit as a federal court. *William and Mary Law Review, 54*, 1791–1864.

Havighurst, C. C., & Richman, B. D. (2011). The provider monopoly problem in health care. *Oregon Law Review, 89*, 847–882.

Hessick, F. A. (2016). Doctrinal redundancies. *Alabama Law Review, 67*, 635–673.

Hiller, J. S. (2016). Healthy predictions? Questions for data analytics in health care. *American Business Law Journal, 53*, 251–314.

Ho, R. J. Y. (2013). *Biotechnology and biopharmaceuticals: Transforming proteins and genes into drugs* (2nd ed.). New York, NY: Wiley-Blackwell.

Hubbard, W. (2013). The competitive advantage of weak patents. *Boston College Law Review. 54*, 1909–1965.

Hugin, R. J., Chairman and Chief Executive Officer, Celgene Corporation. (2015, February 21). Wharton Health Care Business Conference on Disruption Amidst Uncertainty: Adapting and Innovating for the Future, Philadelphia, PA.

IOM (Institute of Medicine). (2012). *Ethical and scientific issues in studying the safety of approved drugs*. Washington, DC: The National Academies Press.

Jackson, A., Executive Vice President, Spectrum Science Communications. (2016, June 10). Remarks at the panel discussion on Pharmacoeconomics: Research and Development Strategies in an Era of Drug Pricing Controversy (Fierce Biotech) at the 2016 International Biotechnology Industry Organization Conference, San Francisco, CA.

Jones, R. A. (2014). Sparse patent protection for research tools: Expansion of the safe harbor has changed the rules. *Emory Law Journal, 63*, 749–779.

Jurata, J. J. A., & Owens, I. M. (2015). A new trade war: Applying domestic antitrust laws to foreign patents. *George Mason Law Review, 22*, 1127–1155.

Karshtedt, D. (2015). The completeness requirement in patent law. *Boston College Law Review, 56*, 949–1029.

Kesselheim, A. S., & Darrow, J. D. (2015). Hatch-Waxman turns 30: Do we need a re-designed approach for the modern era? *Yale Journal of Health Policy, Law and Ethics, 15*, 293–347.

Khatibifar, T. (2013). The need for a patent-centric standard of antitrust review to evaluate reverse payment settlements. *Fordham Intellectual Property, Media and Entertainment Law Journal, 23*, 1351–1394.

Kim, M. (2014). Pharmacogenomics and pharmacologic class effect in drug safety management. *Food and Drug Law Journal, 69*, 603–635.

Kolber, A. J. (2011). The experiential future of the law. *Emory Law Journal, 60*, 585–673.

____. (2007). A limited defense of placebo deception. *Yale Law and Policy Review, 26*, 75–134.

Landers, A. L. (2015). Patentable subject matter as a policy driver. *Houston Law Review, 53*, 505–547.

Lee, P. (2013). Patents and the university. *Duke Law Journal, 63*, 1–87.

____. (2012). Transcending the tacit dimension: Patents, relationships, and organizational integration in technology transfer. *California Law Review, 100*, 1503–1572.

Leproust, E. M., Chief Executive Officer, President, and Director, Twist Bioscience Corporation. (2016, August 11). UBS Genomics 2.0 Summit, Park City, Utah.

Lietzan, E. (2016). The myths of data exclusivity. *Lewis and Clark Law Review, 20*, 91–164.

Lu, D. (2015). In the face of strong patent rights: Using the foreign trade antitrust improvements act to combat patent abuse in international commerce. *Boston University Journal of Science and Technology Law, 21*, 136–166.

Mann, J. M. (2015). FDA adverse event reporting system: Recruiting doctors to make surveillance a little less passive. *Food and Drug Law Journal, 70*, 371–394.

Miglani, S. (2016). Reference pricing: A small and mighty solution to bend the health care cost curve. *Connecticut Insurance Law Journal, 22*, 47–84.

Miller, B. M. (2016). Product hopping: Monopolization or innovation? *Boston University Journal of Science and Technology Law, 22*, 89–120.

Moses, H., et al. (2015). The anatomy of medical research: U.S. and international comparisons. *Journal of the American Medical Association, 313*(2), 174–189.

National Science Board. (2009). *Research and development: Essential foundation for U.S. competitiveness in a global economy.* Washington, DC: National Science Board.

Noah, L. *(2016).* State affronts to federal primacy in the licensure of pharmaceutical products. *Michigan State Law Review, 2016,* 1–54.

Parchomovsky, G., & Stein, A. (2013). Intellectual property defenses. *Columbia Law Review, 113,* 1483–1536.

Pew Health Group. (2011). *After heparin: Protecting consumers from the risks of substandard and counterfeit drugs.* Philadelphia, PA: Pew Charitable Trusts.

PhRMA (Pharmaceutical Research and Manufacturing Association). (2016). *Biotechnology medicines in development.* Washington, DC: PhRMA.

PwC (PricewaterhouseCoopers). (2015). *Biotech funding surges.* New York, NY: PwC.

Ram, N. (2015). DNA by the entirety. *Columbia Law Review, 115,* 873–939.

Rifkin, J. (2013). *The third industrial revolution: How lateral power is transforming energy, the economy, and the world.* New York, NY: Macmillan, St. Martin's Press.

Roche. (2015). *Annual report.* Basel, Switzerland.

Sammut, S., Senior Fellow, Wharton School, University of Pennsylvania. (2016, June 9). Remarks at the Biotechnology Entrepreneurship Boot Camp at the 2016 International Biotechnology Industry Organization Conference, San Francisco, CA.

Sanofi. (2015). *Consolidated net sales by geographic region and product.* Paris, France: Sanofi.

Schwartz, D. L. (2013). The rise of contingent fee representation in patent litigation. *Alabama Law Review, 64,* 335–388.

Shepherd, J. M. (2015). Biologic drugs, biosimilars, and barriers to entry. *Health Matrix, 25,* 139–161.

Starr, P. (2013). *Remedy and reaction.* New Haven, CT: Yale University Press.

Tran, H. T., et al. (2016). Advances in genomics for the improvement of quality in coffee. *Journal of the Science of Food and Agriculture, 96*(10), 3300–3312.

Taylor, D. O. (2013). Formalism and antiformalism in patent law adjudication: Rules and standards. *Connecticut Law Review, 46,* 415–496.

Vagelos, P. R., Retired Chairman and Chief Executive Officer, Merck, and Chairman of the Board, Regeneron Pharmaceuticals. (2015, February 21). Wharton Health Care Business Conference on Disruption Amidst Uncertainty: Adapting and Innovating for the Future, Philadelphia, PA.

Varadarajan, D. (2014). Trade secret fair use. *Fordham Law Review, 83,* 1401–1454.

Wang, D. Z. N. (2016). End of the parallel between patent law's § 284 willfulness and § 285 exceptional case analysis. *Washington Journal of Law, Technology and Arts, 11,* 311–330.

Watnick, V. J. (2014). The missing link: U.S. regulation of consumer cosmetic products to protect human health and the environment. *Pace Environmental Law Review, 31,* 595–650.

Wharton (Wharton School at the University of Pennsylvania). (2010). Anatomy of a merger: Hostile deals become friendly in the end, right? *Knowledge@Wharton.*

Wicks, A. C., & Keevil, A. C. (2014). The buying and selling of health care: When worlds collide; Medicine, business, the Affordable Care Act and the future of health care in the U.S. *Journal of Law, Medicine and Ethics, 42,* 420–430.

Wieland, D., & Ferrucci, L. (2008). Multidimensional geriatric assessment: Back to the future. *The Journals of Gerontology. Series A, Biological Sciences and Medical Sciences, 63*(3), 272–274.

CHAPTER 18

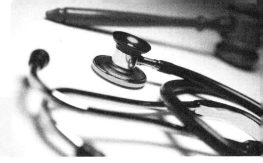

© Andy Dean Photography/ShutterStock, Inc.

Medical Devices

"Every man is the builder of a temple called his body."

— **Henry David Thoreau** (1817–1862), American philosopher, author, and poet

IN BRIEF

This chapter describes how the use of implanted medical devices to treat heart disease, orthopedic and ophthalmologic complaints, and other health conditions is growing rapidly via advancing technology. It focuses on the rationing of health care products and the increasing demand created by and for new device technologies. The difficulties in regulating the medical devices industry are also explained.

LEARNING OBJECTIVES

Upon completion of this chapter readers should be able to:

1. Explain why drug prescriptions are almost always chosen over surgery.
2. Discuss market growth in the medical device industry.
3. List major areas for the use of medical devices.
4. Discuss problems with pediatric device use.
5. Detail issues of inspections for medical device manufacturing facilities.
6. Explain problems of postmarket surveillance.
7. Describe concerns over reprocessed medical devices.
8. List issues with malpractice claims against medical device manufacturers.
9. Describe entertainment purposes for medical devices and their possible risks.
10. Project the future of the medical device industry.

KEY TERMS

Anti-kickback law
Biologic
Biologic/device products
Biologic drugs
Blockbuster status
Branded medical devices
Burden of proof
Carbon nanosensors
Cardiac resynchronization therapy
Class action lawsuit
Clinical studies
Cochrane Collaboration

Combination drug/device
Comparative effectiveness research
Computer-assisted artificial limbs
Concept of preemption
Conflicts of interest
Counterfeit devices
Deferred prosecution agreement
Device consultants
Drug-coated stents
Drug/device hybrid
Early device replacement

Foreign Corrupt Practices Act of 1977
Generally accepted medical practices
Health care fraud
High-risk patients
Implanted defibrillators
Implanted medical device
Implied warranty
Informed consent
Kickbacks
Luer fittings

FACT OR FICTION

Medical Monitoring

Do healthy patients have standing to sue device manufacturers if they face increased risks of harm from defective medical devices compared to those undergoing traditional surgery?

Michael Sutton sought to bring a **class action lawsuit** on behalf of about 50,000 patients who underwent cardiac bypass surgery using a medical device manufactured by St. Jude Medical, called the Symmetry Bypass System Connector device. Surgeons used this device during cardiac bypass surgery to attach vein grafts to the aortic surface of the heart without sutures. Sutton was implanted with the device during treatment for his heart condition. The device, however, led to severe and disabling health conditions resulting from collapse and scarring of the graft in numerous patients, necessitating removal of the device and/or monitoring for further harm, including possible death. Sutton alleges St. Jude failed to use reasonable care, was negligent in designing the device, that the device was defective and unreasonably dangerous, and was sold and marketed without proper warnings. Although St. Jude had been informed of the adverse consequences associated with the device through incident reports from surgeons before Sutton had the defective device implanted in him, St. Jude continued to market and distribute the device without warnings. Sutton maintains he suffered economic losses and medical expenses when he had the defective device implanted and he now has a device in his body that increases his risk for cardiac occlusion and death. While future injuries are hypothetical, Sutton maintains his increased risk necessitates both current and future medical testing and monitoring.

— *See* Law Fact at the end of this chapter for the answer.

Principles and Applications

Generally, a medical device is any medical product that does not achieve its principal intended purpose(s) by chemical action in or upon the human body. **Medical devices** include instruments, apparatuses, machines, and implants that are intended for diagnosis or treatment of diseases or injuries, or that affect the structures or any function of the human body (*See* 21 U.S.C.A. § 321(h)). With an estimated 86 million Americans suffering from conditions that can be treated by medical devices, and only some 2.5 million actually using them, there is an enormous capacity for incorporating medical device technology within the practice of medicine (Pew, 2013). The medical device market is expected to reach $155 billion per year and has grown by 8% over the last 5 to 7 years (Freedonia, 2012; TMR, 2016a).

As illustrated in **TABLE 18-1**, the device industry is by all measures one of the most productive and profitable sectors in health care. Average operating profit margins refers to earnings before taxes and interest relative to sales. The average operating profit margins for the larger device manufacturers have consistently been over 10%; three manufacturers are Fortune 500 firms: Johnson & Johnson, GE Healthcare, and Abbott Laboratories.

TABLE 18-1 Global Profile of the Medical Device Industry

Firms and State Headquarters	Sales	1-Year Sales Change	Number of Employees
Medtronic (Ireland)	$30.2 billion	49.4%	88,000
Johnson & Johnson (NJ)	$25.1 billion	–8.7%	60,000
Abbott Laboratories (IL)	$20.4 billion	0.7%	74,000
GE Healthcare (WI)	$17.7 billion	–4.0%	N/A
Baxter (IL)	$10.0 billion	–40.2%	50,000
Stryker (MI)	$10.0 billion	2.8%	27,000
Boston Scientific (MA)	$7.4 billion	1.3%	25,000
Zimmer Biomet (IN)	$6.0 billion	28.3%	17,500

Data from: Income and Revenue Statements in the 2015 Annual Report filings with the U.S. Securities and Exchange Commission.

The economic principle that demand falls as the price of goods rises does not seem to hold true for medical devices. In the medical device products industry, growth is sustainable because it is driven by:

- Demographic trends of age and obesity and the corresponding increasing demands from an aging and overweight population
- Continued prevalence of diseases
- Near infinite capacity for absorbing advanced medical technology within the practice of medicine
- Greater acceptance by physicians and patients of implantation as an alternative or a complement to medication

(Gardner & Hathaway, 2016; Wallenfelt. 2014).

The use of **implanted medical devices** to treat heart disease, orthopedic problems, and other conditions is growing strongly. Consider the use of implantable defibrillators, which monitor the heartbeat and give a potentially lifesaving shock when needed. About 100,000 of these medical devices, costing approximately between $30,000 and $50,000 each, are implanted in patients in the United States each year (Al-Khatib et al., 2011).

Stents are another example. About 1.2 million bare-metal stents were implanted in the United States each year after they were approved for use (Wharton, 2006b). Soon after, drug-coated stents were designed and approved to prevent the reclogging of arteries (FDA, 2008). They are considered a **drug/device hybrid**. Over 7 million people worldwide have a drug-coated stent placed inside of a previously clogged artery to prop it open, and approximately 130,000 stents are implanted each month in the United States (Evans, 2016). They cost about $1,700 to $2,000 more each, which is triple the cost of plain stents, but neither patients nor their physicians object (Schafer et al, 2011).

Medication over Surgery

Lifestyle choices seem to point to increased demand for medical devices. The increasing obesity of the U.S. population, notably among young people, suggests an enduring need for artificial measures such as coronary stents to keep clogged arteries from closing up altogether. The upbeat prospects have led stocks of leading device manufacturers to outperform the stock market as a whole. However, growth is restrained by physicians' reluctance to use the technology until they see clear evidence of the benefits of medical device therapy, and by resistance from some patients who avoid implantation because it involves surgery. Until all parties are convinced, medication is likely to remain the first choice overall. Implants are almost always the therapy of last resort because they are invasive, involve surgical risk, and usually require monitoring for the remainder of the patient's life (Abbott & Ayres, 2014).

The device market is also prevented from reaching its potential by diagnoses that do not make a clear case for implantation. Hip replacements, for instance, could in theory be performed on the estimated 20 million Americans with osteoarthritis (CDC, 2016a). In some cases, the disease may not have progressed sufficiently to warrant hip replacement; in others, the patient may choose to defer the operation for as long as possible for personal reasons (*See generally* U.S. Bone and Joint Initiative, 2015).

Physicians are understandably cautious about adopting new medical device technology. It sometimes takes a number of years to show how safe the latest innovative device technology is (Laakmann, 2015). The first cardiac pacemaker was developed in 1959 for just a few patients and has now become a multibillion-dollar device. Implantable defibrillators were initially seen as having a limited market and are now used for about half a million patients a year (Bradley & Taylor, 2015). Together, pacemakers and implantable defibrillators now make up a $13 billion market (MarketandMarket, 2015).

Market Growth

While cardiac stents can save lives if implanted during or shortly after a heart attack, heart disease is still the leading cause of death in the United States and the number one reason for hospitalization among people over 65 (CDC, 2016a, b). Five million people a year suffer from heart failure, half of whom will die within five years, and the incidence of heart disease is expected to double within the next five years because of increasing obesity rates and sedentary lifestyles (NCHS, 2008).

Growth in the market for implantable technology is also driven by an aging population, which requires more medical devices like pacemakers, defibrillators, artificial hips, and neurological medical devices (Jackson & Howe, 2008). The device industry is responding with smaller, more reliable, and less power-consuming equipment. More intelligent medical devices are constantly being developed, allowing medical problems to be better identified and dealt with in an appropriate and timely way (Robinson, 2015).

Cardiology

A developing field is **cardiac resynchronization therapy**, in which an implanted electronic medical device corrects the widespread tendency in heart failure patients for the heart chambers to contract at the wrong time, forcing the heart to work harder and increasing the risk of a heart attack (Russom et al., 2013). By achieving a resynchronization of the chambers, patients experience a remarkable improvement in quality of life. The patient not only has fewer symptoms, but tissue that has declined in efficiency then regains its effectiveness (Kramer et al., 2014).

Among other sectors of the cardiac market, HealthCare Capital Advisors expects pacemakers to grow by 5% a year from the current $3 billion market. Medical devices designed to counter congestive heart failure are projected to surge 50% per year from a modest $1 billion base. Biodegradable stents, which treat blockages in coronary arteries and then degrade, are getting increased attention from the medical and investment communities.

Drug-Coated Coronary Stents

The Food and Drug Administration (FDA) approved **drug-coated stents** for use in 2003; since then, the U.S. market has grown to roughly $2.4 billion (Waldman, 2013). While standard stents are permanently inserted in a diseased coronary artery to keep it open, the new device builds on this platform by delivering a controlled flow of medication into the patient's bloodstream for a limited period to prevent the passageways from becoming reclogged by tissue buildup. Cardiologists quickly embraced the tiny mesh scaffolds, even when other physicians may have recommended more expensive bypass surgery (Beck, 2015). Today, drug-coated stents are used in almost all coronary interventions in the United States; about 700,000 stents are implanted each year (Waldman, 2013). Some are questioning what to do with device technologies that could be used in virtually everybody, even though they have only been studied in a minority of patients (Beck, 2015).

MANAGEMENT AND LAW ISSUES

1. Before a new medical device has the potential to reach **blockbuster status** and before introduction into the marketplace, should it be subject to higher standards of safety and effectiveness?
2. Alternatively, should blockbuster devices be subject to closer post-marketing surveillance studies?

The safety of drug-coated stents has not been established for relatively **high-risk patients,** a group that accounts for the majority of stenting procedures and for whom the new stents are not approved (Beck, 2015). Some studies suggest the newer medical devices increase the risk of blood clots in high-risk patients compared with bare-metal stents (Waldman, 2013). Drug-coated stents are approved for use in patients with simple artery blockages, but more than half the procedures involving the medical devices are performed in patients with more complex conditions when many physicians generally recommend bypass surgery, such as for:

- Heart attacks
- Multiple blockages requiring more than one stent
- Blockages in more than one branch of an artery

(Beck, 2015).

There is no conclusive evidence drug-coated stents increase the risk of blood clots, heart attack, or death, compared with bare-metal stents when used within the scope of their FDA approval (Douglas & Sedrakyan, 2009). While off-label use of drug-coated stents appears to raise risks, it is unclear whether the increased risk is caused by the drug-coated stents or if it is a result of the poorer health of the higher-risk patients (Winslow & Mathews, 2006).

Implantable Cardiovascular Devices

The market for **implanted defibrillators**, medical devices about the size of a pager that shock the heart back to a normal rhythm when necessary, is expected to see sharp growth, with some 900,000 patients eligible to receive them (Lennox, 2014). The value of the market could be as much as $73 billion a year (Bradley & Taylor, 2015). The device industry's prospects are enhanced by the fact that implant technology saves the U.S. health care system money (Lennox, 2014). The potential of medical devices such as implantable defibrillators to save money will likely be the key to whether the health insurance industry is willing to continue paying for them. If they are proven to prevent heart attacks, or give early warning signs of problems that would otherwise be more expensive to treat if not detected until later, they will arguably be more attractive to insurers (Lennox, 2014).

While implanted defibrillators are underutilized worldwide (Horvath, 2015), it is estimated as many as one-third of U.S. patients have defibrillators implanted into their chests needlessly (Buck, 2015). The overuse or inappropriate use of medical devices is a familiar theme, but defibrillators pose unique issues because they are increasingly used as a standard piece of safety equipment, like an air bag in an automobile, in an ever-growing number of heart patients whose individual need for the device is not clear (Horvath, 2015). Medical experts agree that many, if not the majority, of defibrillator candidates are at a low risk of cardiac arrest (Lennox, 2014). The dilemma reflects a growing medical conundrum: groups at risk can be identified for use of advanced device technologies, but individual patients in those groups who are at higher risk cannot be identified.

Given their overuse in the United States, it is difficult to determine whether implanted defibrillators actually reduce health care costs. However, if Medicare insurance is willing to pay for a device, private health insurers often follow (Horvath, 2015). The commercial potential of medical devices also depends on whether patients are willing to pay for them over and above their regular health insurance premiums (Buck, 2015).

Ophthalmology

Technology's advance has also reached into ophthalmology, where work is under way at Harvard Medical School to create an artificial retina with a chip inserted in the back of the eye (Rojahn, 2013). Medical device researchers are hoping to develop a camera the size of a pea that can be implanted within the eyeball, replacing natural tissue with artificial technology (Bagheri et al., 2015).

MANAGEMENT AND LAW ISSUES

3. Should a patient who would have died or suffered greatly without a medical device and who had no alternative treatment options be permitted to sue for damages if the medical device does not perform as expected?

Neurology

In neuroscience, Medtronic has developed a technique known as Activa tremor control therapy. Activa can control trembling, such as occurs in advanced Parkinson's disease, by using an implanted medical device that can deliver electrical stimulation to certain areas of the brain (MedtronicNeuro, 2016). Individual results vary, however, and the specific benefit for individual patients cannot be predicted.

Orthopedics

In orthopedics, the focus is on minimally invasive procedures in which physicians operate through ports into the body, particularly for hip and knee operations. At the same time, integrated medical products are increasingly used in orthopedic surgery. One such medical device used in spinal surgery involves a metal cage prepacked with **biologic drugs** to promote bone growth (Hsu, 2016).

Mandated Prosthesis Coverage

Amputees and device manufacturers of prosthetic limbs are urging states to introduce legislation that would require the health insurance industry to provide prosthesis coverage. Eight states currently have laws mandating prosthesis coverage similar to Medicare insurance, and most states are considering similar legislation (Simshaw et al., 2016). The Amputee Coalition is lobbying to introduce federal legislation. Medicare insurance covers at least 80% of the cost of prostheses and allows regular replacement, generally every five years (Avalere, 2015). Medicare insurance also covers **computer-assisted artificial limbs**. As technological advancements have caused manufacturing and sales costs of the medical devices to rise, many health insurers have placed medical coverage limits of $2,500 or $5,000 annually on prosthetic medical devices, or restricted coverage to just one device per recipient in a lifetime (Porter, 2014). The cost for regular prosthetic limbs can range between $5,000 and $15,000, and costs can reach as high as $50,000 for more technologically advanced or computer-aided medical devices (Amputee Coalition, 2016).

Prosthetic medical devices, among the most expensive implants on the market, are the medical items most affected by efforts to contain rising health care costs (Simshaw et al., 2016). It is not that there has been an increase in need for prosthesis, rather it is the cost of acquiring the most advanced prosthetic technology that is being met with resistance by health insurers (Porter, 2014). Supporters of mandates maintain the additional medical coverage for prostheses would cost just pennies in monthly premium increases. Health insurers believe mandates collectively affect the affordability of health insurance.

Telemedicine and Remote Monitoring Technologies

Despite technological feasibility, leading-edge patient monitoring systems fall short on providing a comprehensive picture of chronic diseases to aid physicians. Moreover, there is fear among health care providers that with **remote monitoring**, they could incur legal liability for failure to recognize warning signals. Others predict the careful use of monitoring technologies could actually reduce liability (Choi, 2016). In addition to the technological and legal challenges, health care providers face a pragmatic financial concern about gathering and reviewing remote data. Most health insurers are providing little or no payment for such work. Payment rates are in the range of $25 to $100 for each review of remote monitoring data.

Although most health insurance plans pay for physicians and nurses to check on patients in person from a distance, many physicians currently rely on data collection services run by the device manufacturers and independent monitoring services to warn them of anomalies requiring prompt attention (Pratt, 2015). For instance, there is an implantable electrocardiogram monitoring system composed of a wireless medical device about the size of a dollar coin, or the size of the smallest pacemakers, that can continuously gather data and then automatically and regularly forward it to a monitoring center operated by the manufacturer (Sage, 2016). There, certified cardiac technicians review the patient's information and send cardiac event data to the patient's physician. A significant advantage of remote monitoring technology is technicians at monitoring centers can automatically receive patient data, thereby allowing them to frequently review patient information for clinical irregularities.

Implant Devices

Implanted under the skin, the electrocardiogram loop recorder device monitors and records heart activity, allowing a physician to interrogate it noninvasively to check a patient's health condition and detect any danger signs. The medical device is also used to treat epilepsy, following the discovery that a large number of epileptics actually have cardiac arrhythmia, or an irregular heartbeat, indicating they need a pacemaker as opposed to anti-seizure medicine (Brook & Irle, 2016). Another implanted medical device, a hemodynamic monitoring system, measures vital signs including blood pressure, pulmonary artery diastolic pressure, and heart rate. Its data can be downloaded to a physician's computer from the patient's phone line, facilitating timely decisions on treatment (Pratt, 2015).

New device technologies could allow tens of millions of Americans with chronic diseases, such as heart failure, diabetes, and mental illnesses, to have their conditions constantly monitored, remotely and virtually, as they go about their daily lives (Schumacher, 2015). The advanced technologies developed by Medtronic and Abbott Laboratories allow:

- Alerts to lung and/or circulatory problems
- Blood pressure, glucose, and weight monitoring
- Regulation of heart rate and delivery of shocks when necessary
- Wireless Internet communication between patients and physicians

(Brook & Irle, 2016; Pratt, 2015).

Although data gathered by the newest devices reconstruct events that send patients to emergency rooms, the payoff for patients could be:

- Fewer and shorter hospital stays
- Longer stretches between routine visits to physicians' offices
- More effective use of drugs

(Schumacher, 2015).

According to a Department of Veteran Affairs study that followed 70 patients over three months, remote monitoring of their heart implants significantly reduced the time their physicians would have spent on office visits (Stachura & Khasanshina, 2016).

Telehealth Monitors

An increased number of device manufacturers are competing in the market for telehealth monitors, which allow physicians and nurses to track the health of patients from remote locations. Use of **telehealth monitors** can keep patients comfortably at home and allow physicians and nurses to focus on the most serious cases, as well as save the expense and disruption hospital visits cause by catching signs of trouble before patients need an ambulance.

The Department of Veteran Affairs spent $20 million to install about 50,000 telehealth monitors in homes of veterans (Stachura & Khasanshina, 2016). In addition, some home health care device manufacturers have begun to offer telehealth monitors to patients. Patients who require home health care, however, are unlikely to be able to navigate most systems and interfaces currently available in the market. Telehealth monitor manufacturers are beginning to address this concern (Pratt, 2015). The cost is about $200 monthly to purchase and operate a telehealth monitor, compared with about $78 for a single nurse visit (Lewis, 2015). In addition, telehealth monitors decrease health care costs through a reduction in hospitalizations. Predictions are the technology could reduce health care costs by one-third for patients who require home health care (Stachura & Khasanshina, 2016).

Integrated Medical Products

Adapting existing regulations to fit novel technologies and medical products is not a new challenge for U.S. regulatory agencies or for the FDA specifically. There is, however, typically a lag between the development of innovative technologies, their adoption by the medical community, and the laws to oversee it. Nevertheless, the century-old definitions for classifying medical products as drugs, devices, or **biologics** may be unsuitable for the convergence of devices combined with drug or biologics properties. Looking ahead, the trend toward integration is bound to increase as science and technologies advance (Gardner & Hathaway, 2016).

Combination Devices

Combination drug/device and **biologic/device products**, which contain more than one regulated product, are rapidly advancing and may pose technological challenges for current FDA regulatory schemes (FDA, 2016a). While devices and drugs such as drug-coated stents, antimicrobial catheters, and cell-matrix cartilage implants have coexisted for decades, devices and biologics, such as orthopedic repair using morphogenetic protein, are rapidly increasing.

Nanodevices

The area with the most potential to produce revolutionary scientific changes to health care is **nanomedicine**, particularly **nanodevices** (Hall et al., 2016). Nanodevices are extremely small; a nanometer, one billionth of a meter, is about the size of a few atoms put together. By comparison, a human hair is about 80,000 nanometers wide. Most medical product firms are now following the example of nanodevice manufacturers and building from the molecular level downwards (Thompson, 2012). The typical approach of device manufacturers has generally been top-down by taking existing medical devices and making them smaller.

The technology is moving forward and the global market for nano-formulated devices is estimated to be $64 billion by 2019 (BBC Research, 2015). Scientists are using silica spheres coated with gold to attack cancerous tumors; infrared light heats the gold, and the heat kills the cancer. Likewise, nanofilters are used to purify blood (Hall et al., 2016). Other medical device nanoproducts that have entered the market include Vitoss bone graft substitute, TiMesh tissue reinforcement and hernia repair, EnSeal tissue sealing, and hemostatis systems for laparoscopic and open surgery. **Carbon nanosensors**, made of tiny cylinders of graphite, with walls the width of a single carbon atom and a diameter of one to two nanometers, about the same size as a strand of DNA, help emergency medical technicians monitor patients' breathing (Theodore & Stander, 2013).

Perhaps the most recognized nanotech product is sunscreen. People no longer look like they are smeared with white paint because their sunblock has been replaced by nanocrystalline sunscreens. Sunscreens formerly contained particles that reflected light; now the same particle compounds are nanosize and do not reflect light (*See* Hall et al., 2012).

With the rising interest in nanodevices, a field with neither a single scientific definition nor a formal regulatory or statutory definition, attention is being drawn to the need for examining existing regulatory systems in terms of their applicability to nanoproducts (FDA, 2015a). This is especially the case when nanodevices are regulated on the assumption that the toxicological profiles of nanoparticulate versions of compounds, like carbon or titanium, are the same as their larger chemically identical counterparts, for instance, molecules (Snir, 2014). This regulatory assumption, however, is not necessarily true. One research study found fish swimming in water containing nanoparticles called buckyballs (soccer-ball shaped synthetic carbon molecules comprised of sixty atoms each) ended up with brain damage (Hall et al., 2012).

Direct Marketing to Physicians

Medical devices are marketed to a defined group of physicians who select the products for their patients (Abbott & Ayres, 2014). Millions of stents are placed annually, yet only 6,200 interventional cardiologists do the brand selection. Hip implants are installed in hundreds of thousands of patients in the United States annually, but only 17,000 orthopedic surgeons do the procedures. Device manufacturers aim their marketing efforts directly at physicians, avoiding the expense of convincing patients one product is better than another.

Potential Conflicts of Interest

While some health care providers, such as the University of Pennsylvania Health Care System, require physicians to tell patients about any financial relationship with device firms, not all health systems have this professional restriction. Many physicians have financial ties to device manufacturers that are often not revealed to their patients or to hospitals. For instance, 40 surgical groups each receive at least $1 million in payments from medical device manufacturers every year (Abbott & Ayres, 2014; Bi, 2015). There is certainly the appearance of **conflicts of interest** when physicians use certain **branded medical devices** and also receive royalty payments or consulting fees from that brand firm (Bi, 2015).

While there is a myriad of reasons why device use has soared, questions arise as to whether financial ties between physicians and device manufacturers could be a factor in driving up spending on medical devices. An important FDA reform has been full disclosure by surgeon-consultants of their contracts with medical device firms. Another concern is the practice of sales representatives of device manufacturers often being present in operating rooms during surgical procedures and helping physicians select medical devices (Brougham, 2016). This custom increases the potential for conflicts of interest, because firm representatives usually work on commission and can make as much from an operation incorporating the device as the surgeon does.

Kickbacks

In addition to conflicts of interest, the federal government is also focusing on **kickbacks** by the device industry. While kickbacks to physicians who recommend the manufactuer's products do not necessarily lead to higher Medicare insurance spending since the government pays the same rate for a device regardless of the make, the **anti-kickback law** can be violated if a single bill is submitted for a procedure linked to a kickback (Halabi, 2016).

Although illegitimate payments to physicians have led to increased use of lower quality medical devices in the spinal-implant market (Brougham, 2016), the elimination of all such payments likely will prove difficult because they have become commonplace. Moreover, the anti-kickback law itself is insufficient to address the influence of money in the device industry because of the high **burden of proof**; prosecutors must generally meet a high specific intent standard, requiring proof defendants knew their conduct was unlawful and nevertheless engaged in the prohibited conduct (Brougham, 2016). This requirement makes criminal convictions more difficult to obtain because of the need to prove intent to disobey the law (Reilly, 2015). Supporters of the consulting arrangements say they allow physicians and device manufacturers to collaborate, resulting in important advances in technology.

Truthfully, most arrangements are quite legitimate compensation packages for research or product development, or royalties for products (Halabi, 2016). The concern, however, is kickbacks might result in physicians opting for more expensive, lower quality, or medically unnecessary medical devices for patients, which drives up health care costs, especially for Medicare insurance (Avalere, 2015). According to the Centers for Medicare and Medicaid Services, more than half of the nation's 700,000 hip and knee replacements are performed on Medicare insurance beneficiaries. In theory, physicians use their best judgment about what is best for their patients, but to the extent they are given consulting arrangements, it could distort their intentions.

Artificial Joint Firms

Before 2007, **pretrial diversion** had been used in the **health care fraud** context in only two cases (Spivack & Raman, 2008). The first case was against the University of Medicine and Dentistry of New Jersey. The university accepted a **deferred prosecution agreement**, which included the placement of a federal monitor to supervise all of its finances, or face indictment for federal fraud charges for overbilling, double-billing, and **upcoding practices**. In the second case, the U.S. Department of Justice entered into a **non-prosecution agreement** with Micrus Corp., a medical device firm, in connection with its disclosure of $340,000 in bribes to physicians in France, Austria, Turkey, and elsewhere. Micrus agreed to pay a $450,000 fine, cooperate fully with the government's investigation, adopt a compliance program to monitor activities prohibited by the **Foreign Corrupt Practices Act of 1977** (15 U.S.C.A. §§ 78dd-1, *et seq.*), and retain an independent compliance expert (DOJ, 2005).

In the past decade since 2007, there has been a notable increase of pretrial diversions in health care fraud involving violations of the:

- Anti-kickback law (42 U.S.C.A. § 1320a-7b)
- Federal Food, Drug, and Cosmetic Act of 1938 (FDCA) (21 U.S.C.A. §§ 301 *et seq.*)
- Health care fraud law (18 U.S.C.A. § 1347)

(Lennox, 2014).

This marked increase in the use of deferred prosecution and non-prosecution agreements, also known as pretrial diversion agreements, is arguably the most profound development in corporate white-collar criminal practice (Brougham, 2016; Spivack & Raman, 2008). The federal government reached settlements with the leading five artificial joint firms over kickbacks on hundreds of agreements under which physicians across the country received vacations and lavish meals. Some individual physicians accepted consulting fees as high as $200,000 from the firms in return for recommending their products. Biomet, Johnson & Johnson's DePuy Orthopaedics, Smith & Nephew, and Zimmer entered into deferred prosecution agreements and agreed to pay a combined $311 million to settle a federal investigation over allegations they paid about $800 million in kickbacks to physicians over a four-year period. A fifth device firm, Stryker, which cooperated early in the investigation, entered into a non-prosecution agreement and paid no fines. As part of the settlement, all five device manufacturers were required to make their consulting arrangements with physicians public and agreed to federal monitoring.

Stryker's non-prosecution agreement did not require the device firm to admit to any facts or acknowledge any responsibility for its behavior. The other four device manufacturers did acknowledge responsibility and had criminal complaints filed against them generally outlining some of the relevant facts. In their civil settlements with the government, however, each of the four firms denied engaging in any wrongdoing and specifically denied any of the payments were illegal or resulted in any fraudulent claims. No physicians were identified or charged (Ridge & Baird, 2008; *See also* DOJ, 2005).

These diversion agreements were the first time firms were able to negotiate language affirmatively denying any wrongdoing. This major development is now commonly used in health care fraud contexts. This change reflects the belief that the principal role of the federal government in corporate criminal prosecution is to reform corporate cultures and affect widespread structural reform as opposed to indicting, prosecuting, and punishing (Spivack & Raman, 2008). Federal prosecutors, for instance, declared the diversion agreements they negotiated with the orthopedic device sector were the new compliance standards for the device industry (DOJ, 2005).

Spinal Surgery

There is similar concern about device manufacturers in the $5.0 billion spinal-implant and spinal device market (MarketsandMarkets, 2016). In orthopedics in general, it has become almost commonplace for surgeons to get money as **device consultants** and owners of device distributorships, according to the Association for Ethics in Spine Surgery (Brougham, 2016). Yet, the federal Agency for Healthcare Research and Quality has little clinical evidence showing back surgery works for most patients, whether they get traditional fusion surgery or have a disk replaced (Abbott & Stevens, 2014).

Synthes, the third largest manufacturer of spinal implant devices, behind Medtronic and Johnson & Johnson, is facing conflict-of-interest claims regarding surgeon investigators who conducted a clinical trial of its artificial spinal disk, which the FDA approved in 2006. The surgeon investigators claimed, in submissions to the FDA, the Synthes spinal disk worked much better than conventional surgery in which patients' vertebrae were fused (Breen & Retzinger, 2013). This claim, however, became tainted when it was discovered the **surgeon investigators** making the claims had hundreds of thousands of dollars invested with the New York investment firm behind the device (Abbott & Stevens, 2014). Additional lawsuits across the country are being filed against Synthes, as a growing number of patients experience problems with their spinal implants.

Device manufacturers have a legal obligation to inform the FDA of the financial interests of surgeon investigators before they use a study's results for approval of their medical devices (Brougham, 2016). While the FDA permits surgeons to have financial ties with manufacturers of the device they are studying, such relationships must be fully disclosed. When the FDA is aware of potential conflicts, it tends to subject the studies to a higher level of scrutiny. In addition, the FDA conducts on-site audits of clinical research study sites to detect chicanery; other times, simple data analysis reveals abnormalities requiring scrutiny of investigators. In the submissions by Synthes, the surgeons were found to have excluded an unusually high number of study participants with adverse outcomes from their study report to the FDA (Brougham, 2016).

Surgeon investigators play a critical role in the FDA approval process for new medical devices. These surgeons are expected to act objectively in testing the safety and effectiveness of medical devices coming to market; however, when they stand to profit from FDA approval of the device they are testing, their professional objectivity is called into question. The investment interests of surgeons raise serious conflict of interest concerns about the integrity of **clinical studies**. Even though fusion surgery (surgically implanting an artificial vertebrae device onto the spine) continues to be the treatment of choice, there is substantial debate over how many patients actually benefit from it according to the **Cochrane Collaboration**, an international organization providing evidence-based research about the effects of medical treatments. Artificial spinal disks are now drawing the same skepticism from Medicare insurance and most health insurers, who generally refuse to pay for artificial spinal disk surgeries. Meanwhile, thousands of patients worldwide have received the spinal-implant devices manufactured by Synthes, which sell for $2,300 to $8,400 in the United States (Smith, 2015). The surgeon investigators involved in the Synthes research, in the meantime, have moved on to study other medical devices by other device firms (Greenwood, 2014).

MANAGEMENT AND LAW ISSUES

4.   How could neutral, unbiased, thorough testing of new medical devices be ensured?

Pediatric Devices

The Institute of Medicine found **pediatric devices** are an example of how the FDA regulatory system does not work well for medical products where there are small numbers of widely varying patients. As defined by the FDA in connection with medical devices, a child is between the ages of 2 and 11. Physicians frequently jury-rig adult medical devices to fit in children's bodies, sometimes causing unexpected side effects. Yet the FDA lacks data on how medical devices affect children's growth and development or how the functioning of devices can be affected by the lifestyles and hormonal changes of children (Hilton, 2015).

While the FDA is required to track **postmarket study commitments** from the device industry involving children (21 U.S.C.A. § 360j(m)(8)), such commitments are generally not forthcoming (IOM, 2011). Agency regulators want extensive data before approving pediatric medical devices, yet there are few patients to acquire the data from because it is not feasible to conduct traditional regulated clinical trials on children. Moreover, when only a few children have a health condition in need of a pediatric device, clinical trials and FDA approval of each device are impractical (Noah, 2014).

Pediatric Coronary Stents

There was little regulatory focus on the needs of children before the criminal investigation and misdemeanor conviction of pediatric device firm NuMED (Field & Tilson, 2005). Since 1982, NuMED manufactured custom-made catheters, therapeutic balloons, and stents for children. NuMED's founder, president, and chief executive officer pleaded guilty in federal court in Delaware on charges the firm marketed unapproved stents for use in children, which resulted in a multimillion-dollar fine. The FDA and the U.S. attorney's office in Wilmington, Delaware, took the position NuMED was using exceptions under FDA law to sell pediatric stents widely as opposed to supplying individual devices in cases of special need (Burton, 2007).

The FDA found NuMED had delivered more than 30 stents to pediatric surgeons at the DuPont Hospital for Children in Wilmington, Delaware, and concluded the hospital was using the medical devices too often for them to be considered custom medical devices, approved for use in emergencies. The FDA told NuMED it needed to obtain specific approvals each time it sold a device, which NuMED admits it did not do (*See generally* FDA, 2016f).

Currently, few U.S. firms make custom pediatric devices. The FDA has approved some pediatric devices for sale; it has not approved most. Some devices are used **off label**, meaning for a use the FDA has not specified; others are adult devices used off label for children. Still others are allowed by federal loopholes, including the custom device exemption, in which otherwise unapproved devices can be employed in emergency situations (Burton, 2007).

The case against NuMED offers a window into a crucial dilemma involving pediatric heart medical devices. While the FDA is not questioning the safety of NuMED's medical devices, pediatric surgeons worry the pediatric medical devices will become even harder to get with the new restrictions placed on NuMED. Pediatricians say treating infants and children with medical devices approved for use in adults is less safe than using the unapproved medical devices manufactured by NuMED (Burton, 2007).

Without device manufacturers such as NuMED, children will need to go to Europe to receive pediatric cardiac medical devices. During the past two decades a number of pediatric catheterization devices, like the NuMED stents in question, have been developed in the United States, approved and used extensively and safely outside the United States, but never approved for use inside the United States. Many health care professionals blame cumbersome FDA policies and procedures that place children's safety over access to new pediatric devices that are needed by American children (Burton, 2007).

Inspections of Medical Device Manufacturing Facilities

The reauthorized **Medical Device User Fee Act of 2007** provides almost $50 million for the FDA each fiscal year (*See* 21 U.S.C.A. § 379j). Yet, the resources and technology of the FDA are not enough to meet its regulatory responsibilities to oversee the device industry. For instance, the General Accounting Office found the FDA cannot meet requirements for inspections of **medical device manufacturing facilities** in the United States or abroad. The FDA inspects U.S. facilities that manufacture the highest-risk medical devices once every three years and facilities that manufacture moderate-risk medical devices once every five years; both are supposed to be visited every two years (GAO, 2011).

COURT DECISION
Negligence Per Se

In re: Sulzer Hip Prosthesis and Knee Prosthesis Liability Litigation
[Patients v. Medical Device Manufacturer]
455 F.Supp.2d 709 (U.S. District Court for the Northern District of Ohio,
Eastern Division 2006); *motion granted by* 2011 U.S. Dist. LEXIS 3441(U.S. District Court for the Northern
District of Ohio, Eastern Division 2011);
related proceeding Howard v. Zimmer, Inc., 718 F.3d 1209 (U.S. Court of Appeals for the 10th Circuit 2013)

Facts: While the FDA granted approval of Sulzer hip and knee implants, it soon turned out unsanitary conditions at the manufacturing facility kept the implants from bonding properly with patients' bones. The implants were coated with a lubricant during the manufacturing process, and the lubricant was not completely removed before the implants were distributed for surgical placement in human bodies. Sulzer subsequently notified the FDA it was recalling about 40,000 defective hip implants, 26,000 of which had already been implanted in patients. Among the failed implants were approximately 6,100 implants that Sulzer, with the FDA's permission, reprocessed and sold. Many of the patients had to undergo multiple additional replacement surgeries to remove the faulty devices and replace them with more effective ones. To help compensate victims, Sulzer entered into a settlement agreement and established a research and monitoring fund for close to $1.0 billion. *See In re: Sulzer Hip Prosthesis & Knee Prosthesis Liability Litigation*, 2006 U.S. Dist. LEXIS 76009 (U.S. District Court for the Northern District of Ohio, Eastern Division 2006).

Issue: Are **state claims** premised on violation of FDA premarket approval requirements automatically preempted by the FDCA?

Holding and Decision: No, the FDCA automatically preempts state law claims for approved medical devices unless the device failed to conform to FDA premarket approval requirements.

Analysis: The federal trial court began its analysis by affirming that FDA provisions preempt almost every type of state law claim that seeks to hold medical products firms liable for approved medical devices. *See* 21 U.S.C.A. § 360k(a) (1976). The only exception to this federal provision is a claim that a medical device failed to conform to the FDA requirements prescribed by the premarket approval process.

To determine whether a particular state law claim is preempted involves a three-part inquiry: first, courts examine the general duties imposed by the state law causes of action; next, they consider the effect a successful lawsuit, asserting those state causes of action, would have on the FDCA; and third, they determine whether the state claims threaten the federal premarket approval process requirements. Under this inquiry, state law claims of design defect are preempted. State law claims for failure to warn are also preempted, since the premarket approval process includes FDA scrutiny of the medical device's warning labels.

Implied warranty claims are based on the accepted standards of design and manufacture of medical devices. In the case of approved devices that have gone through the premarket approval process, these criteria are set by the FDA. Allowing breach of implied warranty claims would therefore create an irreconcilable conflict: a judgment for breach of implied warranty that rested on allegations about standards other than those permitted by the FDA would necessarily interfere with the premarket approval process and, indeed, would supplant FDA requirements. Accordingly, state claims for breach of implied warranty are also preempted by the FDCA.

Rule of Law: Approved medical devices that conform to FDA premarket approval requirements are not subject to state negligence per se, design defect, failure to warn, or breach of warranty claims.

References discussing this court decision: *E.g.*, Reiss et al., 2007.

While Sulzer lost its independence as a result of its failure to comply with **generally accepted manufacturing practices** (GAMP) and was purchased by Zimmer, this case demonstrates the lack of FDA regulatory enforcement of medical device manufacturers. Air emissions from medical device manufacturing facilities are routinely and arduously regulated by the federal Environmental Protection Agency, less any volatile organic compounds foul the nation's atmosphere. (Approval and promulgation of air quality implementation plans; Control of volatile organic compounds from medical device manufacturing, 72 F.R. 1289 (2007)), whereas the FDA inspects high-risk domestic facilities about once a year, medium-risk facilities are inspected on average once every two years, and low-risk sites are seldom inspected unless problems arise, such as leakage in surgical gloves.

FDA enforcement has been practically nonexistent for foreign medical device manufacturers with only about 11% of all foreign establishments being inspected each year (Liu, 2012). Perhaps this inspection activity can be attributed to the fact that the FDA cannot determine the number of medical device manufacturing facilities abroad that export products to the United States. Nevertheless, even without knowledge of the number of foreign facilities exporting medical devices into the United States, the FDA has estimated inspections of all medical device manufacturing facilities abroad would take 27 years (Kramer et al., 2014).

Post-Marketing Surveillance

The FDA has suffered a string of regulatory failures with respect to medical devices, which is not necessarily unexpected, because it is difficult to test medical devices for safety and effectiveness (IOM, 2011). This difficulty explains why the statutory standard requiring a reasonable assurance of safety and effectiveness before approving medical devices is lower than the standard for drugs, which may receive approval only if shown to be safe and effective for their intended use. *Compare* 21 U.S.C.A. §§ 360c(a)(1) and 360d(a)(2)(A) (providing the standard for medical devices), *with* 21 U.S.C.A. § 355(d) (providing the standard for new drugs). Moreover, the device industry is limited in its clinical testing of medical devices on healthy patients; thus, devices often receive approval on the basis of a single clinical trial. (*See* 21 C.F.R. § 814.20(b) (2015)). For this key reason, it is not uncommon for unforeseen risks to emerge after medical devices are approved for general marketing (Fry, 2014).

Furthermore, unless **medical innovations** are discontinued and medical devices are held to the status quo, it is a given that patients will be subject to some unforeseen risks in new treatments that come with the potential of improved care. Nevertheless, any serious failures are cause for concern. There have been massive recalls of pacemakers, heart valves, heart pumps, defibrillators, and hip and knee prostheses over the past two decades, all of which have exacted a serious toll on the patients who faced removal and replacement surgeries (IOM, 2011).

While the FDA posts information about the status of medical device studies online to improve its procedures for regulating the studies, the agency still faces challenges in monitoring medical devices after they have been approved. The FDA has been challenged by:

- Competing interests of patient safety and approving new technology that could benefit patients
- Complexity of medical devices
- Growth in the device industry
- Increasing popularity of medical devices

(FDA, 2015b; Lennox, 2014).

As a growing number of medical devices with more and more technological complexities are approved by the FDA, there is less and less room for error. Yet, the FDA is confronted by administrative difficulties due to:

- Conflicting patient privacy and legal concerns
- Ongoing regulatory and/or criminal investigations of device manufacturers
- Inconsistent requirements for preserving trade secrets covering medical devices

(Alao, 2015; IOM, 2011).

MANAGEMENT AND LAW ISSUES

5.   Does quickly approving new medical devices do more harm than good?

Inadequate tracking and enforcement within the FDA has allowed several device manufacturers to avoid completing follow-up studies required as part of the approval of their products (FDA, 2015b).

Internal Analysis of Follow-Up Studies

When an internal FDA task force examined approved medical devices where device manufacturers were required to complete follow-up studies, they found poor communication, a flawed safety reporting system, and inadequate enforcement within the agency. In addition, the task force found problems with medical devices are vastly underreported, and most data submitted to the agency included incomplete and unreliable information (FDA, 2015b). Specifically:

- More than half the device manufacturers' annual reports to the FDA lacked required post-marketing data.
- Final results of **post-marketing surveillance** were overdue from most of the device manufacturers.
- Follow-up results were unavailable for about one-fourth of the medical devices.
- Information from reports to the FDA, or from FDA reviews of device manufacturers, were unavailable on approximately one-fifth of the medical devices.
- The progress and results of follow-up surveillance studies by device manufacturers were not being monitored by the FDA.
- Required follow-up studies for completion were not being tracked by the FDA, even though they were considered a condition of approval.
- Device manufacturers were not being sanctioned for poor regulatory compliance.

(FDA, 2015b).

One in four of the FDA researchers, as well as an increasing number of outside experts (Field & Tilson, 2005), believe the agency lacks an effective system for monitoring the safety of approved medical devices. After shortfalls in the FDA's monitoring of medical devices were identified, several specific recommendations were made (Fry, 2014). FDA researchers recommended the agency:

- Improve its tracking of studies done by device manufacturers after products are on the market
- Work with the private sector to improve device tracking methods, including the use of digital medical records
- Engage in less secrecy and more openness in the sharing of information about the benefits and risks of medical devices
- Collaborate with the National Institutes of Health to prioritize research on medical devices used on children, despite a lack of firms' studies in the pediatric field
- Collaborate with patients, health care organizations, and the device industry to increase the reporting of safety concerns
- Create a public database indicating the status and findings of post-marketing surveillance studies
- Develop a unique tracking number for each medical device to serve as an identifier in the event of postmarket concerns about a device
- Improve the way the FDA communicates with the public about recalled medical devices
- Integrate the medical device data maintained by other federal agencies including the Department of Veteran Affairs and the Department of Defense
- Expand **MedSun**, a pilot program that collects safety reports from 350 hospitals in real time, and disseminate its findings to more medical professionals outside the network

(FDA, 2015a, 2014; *See* Bi, 2015; Fry, 2014).

Sentinel Initiative

The FDA always used voluntary self-reporting to discover adverse reactions from devices. However, self-reporting from health care providers revealed only an estimated 1 in 10 problems (Kramer et al., 2014). Health care providers are required to report deaths or serious injuries resulting from the use of medical devices within 10 business days to the FDA, and, if the manufacturer's identity is known, to the manufacturer as well; the device manufacturer must, in turn, investigate the event and provide additional information to the FDA within 30 calendar days (Medical device reporting: Manufacturer reporting, importer reporting, user facility reporting, distributor reporting, 65 F.R. 4112 (2000)). *Serious injury* is defined as any injury or illness that is life-threatening, results in permanent impairment to body function or permanent damage to body structure, or requires medical or surgical intervention to prevent such impairment or damage (*See* 21 U.S.C.A. § 803.3).

A program called the **Sentinel Initiative** allows the FDA and state regulatory agencies to mine electronic health records and claims data to identify patterns for possible problems with medical devices. Mining of this data helps ensure medical devices are safe for consumers after they enter the marketplace. Sentinel accesses data from more than 100 million Americans (Price, 2016). Sentinel could help reduce the $900 million spent on treating outcomes of adverse events each year.

Data collected by Sentinel is also used for **comparative effectiveness research** to compare the cost and effectiveness of different medical products (Kramer et al., 2014). Patient privacy is preserved because the data stays with Medicare insurance and the private insurers (Avalere, 2015). Personal information is not used for Sentinel. What the FDA needs to know is what is going on in the population being treated by all these different medical devices. While the device industry is concerned that Sentinel's analysis of data is not as rigorous as clinical trials, the analysis allows the FDA to move from reliance on voluntary reporting of adverse events to proactive monitoring of medical devices (Mann, 2015).

Reprocessed Medical Devices

There is increasing concern about **reprocessed medical devices** designated for single use as the practice has developed into a $3 billion market (TMR, 2016b). Currently, the FDA requires reprocessors to register and obtain approval for each medical device they seek to reprocess. In addition, the FDA relies on physicians to report malfunctions of used medical devices, but this reporting is voluntary. While the FDA requires health care facilities to report patient deaths involving medical devices, there is no requirement to report device malfunctions.

Some U.S. hospitals reduce costs by recycling medical devices labeled for single use. Among the devices being reused are biopsy forceps (including those used for stomach and bowel surgery), membrane scrapers (often used in eye surgery), breast pump kits, surgical blades, and drill bits used to bore through bone (FDA, 2015e). The FDA has approved the following reprocessed medical devices:

- Cardiovascular devices (angiography catheters, blood pressure cuffs, cardiac guide wires, compressible limb sleeves, angiographic needles, intra-aortic balloon systems, trocars, and percutaneous transluminal coronary angioplasty catheters)
- Gastro/urology devices (endoscopic needles and urological catheters)
- General hospital devices (nonpowered floatation therapy mattresses, mattress covers, surgical gowns, and irrigating syringes)
- Obstetrics and gynecological devices (laparoscopic dissectors, scissors, endoscopic electrocautery devices and accessories, and episiotomy scissors)
- Respiratory devices (short-term spinal needles, gas masks, breathing mouthpieces, tracheal tubes, and oral and nasal catheters)
- Surgical devices (endoscopic blades, guide wires, blood lancets, disposable vein strippers, forceps, scalpel blades, and pneumatically powered saws)

(FDA, 2015c, d; *See* Persad, 2015).

The practice is legal and well established as long as hospitals follow FDA regulations for reprocessing medical devices (*See* FDA, 2015c). The policy rationale for permitting this practice is the belief that medical device manufacturers routinely designate devices for single use for economic, not safety reasons. Whether medical device firms would always escape liability if their single-use devices are recycled and lead to serious injuries remains to be determined.

While the practice of reprocessing devices in-house is fraught with risk and the difficulty of infection control, the process of shipping medical devices to reprocessing facilities to be cleansed, sterilized, and tested for reuse also raises safety concerns. Firms of the single-use medical devices say their medical products are not designed to withstand the strong chemicals and sterilization methods used at reprocessing plants. In addition, used medical devices with porous surfaces or small gaps may still contain traces of blood, tissue, or other bodily fluids that could transmit viral and bacterial infections (GAO, 2015).

Hospitals and reprocessing firms say reprocessed medical devices are just as safe as new single-use medical devices because of modern sterilization methods (Klein, 2005b). Supporters of the practice also say used medical devices cost 40 to 60% less. Estimates are the Department of Veteran Affairs could save as much as $30 million a year by using reprocessed medical devices. A GAO analysis of eight years of FDA data concluded there was no evidence reprocessed single-use medical devices increased health risks for patients. As many as 100 single-use medical devices, or 2% of all single-use medical devices, are currently reprocessed for further use (GAO, 2011). The question arises whether this reprocessing industry could resemble the body parts industry addressed in a subsequent chapter. What actually happens to those ocular implant devices in the deceased?

Informed Consent for Use of Reprocessed Medical Devices

Device manufacturers are lobbying several states for legislation that would require hospitals and other health care providers to obtain **informed consent** from patients before reprocessed medical devices are used in medical procedures (Hall & Mercer, 2012). Currently, informed consent is not required for the use of reprocessed medical devices; patients are unaware used devices are being used by hospitals in their treatment (Persad, 2015). Theoretically, physicians know whether they are using reprocessed devices because of an FDA regulation requiring medical products to be marked as reprocessed.

Unregulated Internet Transactions

Auction websites are selling reprocessed medical devices designated for one-time use (Klein, 2005a; Persad, 2015). Where the websites are getting their devices is unclear; are there established systems for collecting discarded devices from hospitals and medical clinics, or are there other sources? With the Internet sale of reprocessed medical devices unregulated, there is no reliable way of knowing:

- Where sellers obtained such used medical devices
- Who is authorized to purchase the used devices
- Whether the devices were first used by physicians or veterinarians (in human or animal patients)
- How used medical devices were handled and re-sterilized before being sold online
- What quality controls were utilized before the used medical devices are invasively used on patients

(Klein, 2005a, b).

For instance, eBay only requires sellers of regulated medical devices to add a disclaimer that no one should bid on the medical products unless they are authorized purchasers. One eBay seller offers laparoscopic medical devices used in abdominal surgery, circumcision trays, catheters, and biopsy instruments, which are purchased by physicians, veterinarians, and hospitals. For its part, eBay claims no responsibility for items sold on its site; it views the site as a marketplace (Klein, 2005a). Alliance Medical, the largest U.S. reprocessor of medical devices, neither condones nor supports auction websites for the sale of reprocessed medical devices. ClearMedical, one of the five largest U.S. reprocessors, operates an eBay virtual storefront that sells non-invasive reprocessed medical devices, which do not enter the bloodstream when used on patients, such as pulse oximeter sensors and compression sleeves. Although ClearMedical does not confirm the identity of authorized purchasers, it is not concerned with who could buy its used medical devices (Persad, 2015).

Joint Device Registry

The FDA lags behind other countries' similar agencies when it comes to monitoring how people are faring with joint devices such as the metal hip socket from Zimmer (Lennox, 2014). Zimmer suspended sales of the socket after physicians noticed patients who had received them were experiencing severe pain and needed another round of surgery to replace them. Problems with the medical device could have been detected sooner if the United States, like most other countries, had a registry of patients who receive joint devices. The risk in the United States that a patient will need a replacement procedure because of a flawed product or technique can be up to double the risk in countries with such databases (Lennox, 2014; Scheetz, 2011).

The federal Agency for Healthcare Research and Quality says the United States wastes billions of dollars annually on medical treatments that may not work; the financial and human consequences are also large when evidence exists but is not collected. The toll of **early device replacement** is magnified in the United States because of the sheer number of procedures that take place[LN1] (Lennox, 2014). Nearly 1 million hip and knee joint devices are used each year (Nunley, 2016).

The FDA does have a registry for some medical products, for instance, for patients on the acne drug Accutane (isotretinoin), which can cause birth defects, but various hurdles block most product registries, including:

- Conflicting legal and privacy concerns
- A decentralized health care system where physicians often do not report problems with medical devices

- Lack of funding
- Irreconcilable differences regarding whether participation should be mandatory
- Overwhelming number of medical devices to monitor
- Refusal by the Centers for Medicare and Medicaid Services to gather registry data like private insurers

(Avalere, 2015; Gardner & Hathaway, 2016).

Two months after Congress introduced legislation to create a government-backed **national device registry**, the American Academy of Orthopaedic Surgeons formed the American Joint Replacement Registry, a not-for profit organization dedicated to collecting and reporting on hip and knee joint replacement procedures (Avalere, 2015). Today, 72 hospitals collect data on more than 30,000 total joint arthroplasty procedures and the registry continues to grow (Etkin & Hobson, 2016). The need for federal legislation has faded.

Counterfeit Medical Device Transactions

Sophisticated, technologically savvy, and organized counterfeiters have entered the medical device market, especially the surgical supply sector (McIntyre, 2014). The process for **counterfeit devices** is virtually identical to problematic counterfeit pharmaceutical transactions with detection very much lacking due to underdeveloped and impractical technology by federal regulatory and law enforcement agencies. The FDA and international government authorities have warned counterfeit sales are linked to funding international criminal operations and terrorist activities, including those of Hezbollah and Al Qaeda (IACC, 2005; King, 2013). The World Health Organization estimates 10 to 15% of all medical devices in the world are counterfeit. In one case, a U.S. firm was convicted for introducing counterfeit surgical mesh, which it had purchased overseas and then resold to domestic distributors. The counterfeit surgical mesh was not only misbranded by virtue of being counterfeit, but was also adulterated as a result of unsanitary contamination. The firm claimed it bought the product from an unnamed seller, mistakenly believing it was authentic (Jammal, 2014).

Counterfeiters sell tainted, fake, and ineffective medical devices to unsuspecting health care providers, and they make a lot of money in the process. Passing off counterfeit devices is surprisingly easy because there is a general lack of suspicion in the medical community about fakes. Several interacting factors contribute to this reality:

- Poor clinical responses are often attributed to human variation.
- Providers rarely ask where medical devices were purchased to identify potentially problematic sources such as certain foreign countries or the Internet.
- Penalties for counterfeiting are low.

(Jammal, 2014; Shapiro, 2014).

Medical Errors from Tube Misconnections to Devices

A small but steady number of tubes and catheters are being inadvertently connected to the wrong medical devices. Hospital errors each year involve **misconnections**, including:

- Intravenous lines connected to epidural lines
- Bladder irrigation solutions connected to central IV catheters
- Intravenous solutions sent through urinary tract, epidural, and kidney dialysis catheters

(FDA, 2016b, e; Scott, 2011).

The Joint Commission says misconnections generally are unreported and there is no accurate way to compare errors on a year-to-year basis, but they are a persistent and potentially deadly occurrence (Scott, 2011). The main cause of misconnections is the universal connection system known as **Luer fittings**, which connect a broad range of medical devices (FDA, 2016c). Several hospital alliances and device manufacturers are working to address the problem (FDA, 2016d). Premier, the purchasing alliance of 1,500 U.S. hospitals, is leading the most significant initiative by educating hospital staff about the errors and working with device manufacturers to redesign equipment so tube connectors are not compatible with each other (*See* FDA, 2016e). A system designed by Viasys Healthcare uses new connectors that are compatible with Luer connectors and other tubes that have received FDA approval. Other groups are working to develop technical standards for use in designing safer tubing and connection systems (FDA, 2015f).

Product Recalls

Not all problems with medical devices are discovered before distribution. One of the most important sources of authority the FDA can exercise is the ability to force entities in the chain of distribution to notify the medical community that there is a problem with a medical device and to take other action (FDA, 2014). Historically, device manufacturers and the FDA have failed to provide patients and physicians with adequate information about potential safety concerns in medical devices.

Malpractice Claims Against Device Manufacturers

Federal law makes no provision for damage suits against device manufacturers, and, as a result, injured patients have turned to state law and have won substantial awards. For years, the device industry maintained the FDA's authority preempted tougher state regulation. In 2004, longstanding federal policy on preemption was reversed; the FDA maintained that approved medical devices should override most claims for damages under state law, such as claims for defective design of devices, failure to warn, and negligence.

COURT DECISION
Federal Preemption

Riegel v. Medtronic, Inc.
[Patient v. Medical Device Manufacturer]
552 U.S. 312 (U.S. Supreme Court 2008);
followed by Cornett v. Johnson & Johnson, 48 A.3d 1041 (Supreme Court of New Jersey 2012)

Facts: Charles Riegel experienced serious complications when a balloon in a catheter manufactured by Medtronic burst in his severely blocked right coronary artery. Riegel and his wife filed a lawsuit against Medtronic, alleging the catheter had design flaws and a misleading label. Riegel died of unrelated causes, but his wife pursued the lawsuit. Medtronic had received FDA approval to market the catheter in 1994. Two lower federal courts dismissed the lawsuit, based on the argument that firms who manufacture medical devices approved by the FDA are protected from product liability lawsuits filed in state courts.

Issue: Does FDA approval of medical devices protect firms from product liability lawsuits filed in state courts?

Holding and Decision: Yes, because product liability lawsuits filed against device manufacturers in state courts could undermine the balance between the benefits and risks of medical technologies as determined by the FDA.

Analysis: The Court reaffirmed what most federal courts have regarded as settled law since the 1976 Medical Device Amendments were enacted; the FDA, as opposed to differing state regulations and multiple conflicting jury verdicts, should determine the safety and effectiveness of medical technology. Congress gave the FDA preemptive authority for device approvals in 1976, and further review by state courts will not improve patient safety but will result in needless delays in patient access to essential medical technologies, more lawsuits, and ultimately higher health care costs. The preempted claims only address design and labeling; device manufacturers still could be held liable for other issues such as faulty manufacturing if something goes wrong.

Rule of Law: States cannot implement safety requirements for medical devices that differ from federal requirements.

References discussing this court decision: *E.g.*, Chasnow & Levitt, 2016; Fekete, 2016; Gable & Meier, 2013; Goldberg & Zipursky, 2016; Horvath, 2015; Lindenfeld & Tran, 2016; Peterson, 2015; Schulke, 2013; Schwartz & Appel, 2014; Smith, 2015.

The **concept of preemption** has its foundation in the U.S. Constitution, which provides that whenever there is a substantial conflict, federal law is superior to state law. Article VI of the Constitution provides that the laws of the United States "shall be the supreme Law of the Land;… any Thing in the Constitution or Laws of any state to the Contrary notwithstanding." Legislation has been introduced to overturn *Riegel v. Medtronic* whereby FDA approval of certain medical devices protects firms from product liability lawsuits filed in state courts. Opponents of *Riegel* are concerned that if device manufacturers are not held liable, financial incentives will lead them away from ensuring the safety of their medical devices. Supporters of *Riegel* argue deferring scientific judgment from the FDA to the states would create a system where each state would have its own requirements, which would be cost prohibitive for device manufacturers (Goldberg & Zipursky, 2016). The medical products industries have contended for years the legal environment around their products has grown too restrictive and is stymieing innovation.

Riegel applies only to medical devices that have undergone the FDA premarket approval process, the most thorough process used by the agency. In 1996, the Supreme Court ruled that FDA approval of medical devices through other processes does not protect firms from product liability lawsuits filed in state courts. *See Medtronic, Inc. v. Lohr*, 518 U.S. 470 (U.S. Supreme Court 1996) (holding that the Medical Devices Act does not preempt state law claims that are equal to those imposed under federal law, or state law defective design claims); *See also Hillsborough County, Florida v. Automated Medical Laboratories, Inc.*, 471 U.S. 707 (U.S. Supreme Court 1985) (holding that the FDA's authority in regulating blood banks was not sufficient to preempt local regulation). Most medical devices currently on the market underwent a process in which the FDA found them substantially equivalent to those marketed before the enactment of the 1976 Medical Device laws. Some legal experts are recommending a government-run compensation fund be established for patients harmed by medical devices, similar to the fund for vaccines.

Use of Medical Devices for Nonmedical or Entertainment Purposes

There is debate over the ethics and safety of using medical devices, such as ultrasound machines, for **nonmedical entertainment purposes**. In most states, there are gaping holes between federal and local oversight of ultrasound machine use. Pregnant women can pay $160 to $295 at fetal imaging centers to receive high-resolution videos of moving images of their fetuses. The centers, which have operated in nonmedical settings across the United States for several years, have caused concern because they are not regulated and because anyone with an ultrasound machine can open such a studio. While some believe the service is safe, the FDA and the American Institute of Ultrasound Medicine frown upon the practice. The FDA warns pregnant women against the fetal videos, saying it is an unapproved use of a medical device and people who perform ultrasounds for this purpose without physician oversight might be violating state or local laws (Nabili, 2016). In addition, the agency says while there is no evidence of ultrasound scanning harming a fetus, casual exposure should be avoided because it can produce vibrations and increases the temperature of tissues (Rebouché, 2015). At the same time, device manufacturers maintain extra scans done purely for entertainment are not harmful, if the equipment is used properly.

Future of the Device Industry

Pharmaceutical firm interest in acquiring medical device firms runs in cycles. The device industry goes through boom and bust cycles (Cooper, 2014). During each boom, most new entrants are not device manufacturers in the traditional sense; they have one product and probably should not go public. However, investors get caught up in the hype. During bust cycles, all but a few such one-product device manufacturers trade well below their offering price. Today, pharmaceuticals are starting to acquire device manufacturers to make them more diverse (Llewellyn et al., 2015).

While the device industry does not have a tradition of spinning out or licensing products, there have been cases where larger device manufacturers bought entire firms for their products. An attractive option for venture capitalists and entrepreneurs is a sale to a large pharmaceutical or device firm. Even though the public markets are currently shaky, device manufacturers with significant medical advancements have attractive valuations (Gardner & Hathaway, 2016).

While prospects for the device industry are positive, the industry may be challenged in the long term by the ability and willingness of the U.S. health care systems to pay for medical devices (Bradley & Taylor, 2015). With higher federal budget deficits, government spending on health care is unlikely to keep up with the demand created by and for new technologies. Unless the budget increases dramatically, the United States will have to start rationing medical technology.

LAW FACT

Medical Monitoring

Do healthy patients have standing to sue device manufacturers if they face increased risks of harm from defective medical devices compared to those undergoing traditional surgery?

Yes. An increased risk of future harm requiring ongoing medical monitoring due to an implanted cardiac medical device was sufficient to qualify as injury-in-fact to fulfill the first element of the standing to sue requirement. Standing may be conferred even though the device had not yet malfunctioned or caused any demonstrable physical injuries.

— *Sutton v. St. Jude Medical S.C., Inc.*, 419 F.3d 568 (U.S. Court of Appeals for the 6th Circuit 2005), *rehearing denied, en banc*, 2006 U.S. App. LEXIS 1881 (U.S. Court of Appeals for the 6th Circuit 2006). *Followed by McIntosh v. Data Rx Management, Inc.*, 2014 U.S. Dist. LEXIS 23566 (U.S. District Court of the Western District Of Kentucky, Paducah Division 2014).

See, e g. Davis et al., 2014; Isaacs, 2015; Winters, 2012 and 2013 (discussing this decision).

CHAPTER SUMMARY

- The potential market for medical devices is enormous, as up to 35 million Americans have conditions that could be treated by them.
- The market is helped by the federal government, which quickly approves new medical devices and helps facilitate patient payment.
- Physicians and patients, however, are slow to accept new medical device technology before it is proven safe and effective, especially as it usually requires invasive surgery to implant.
- It is difficult to test new medical devices for safety as there is often not a large pool of patients to test upon and patients' unique characteristics may affect the device's success or lack thereof; furthermore, the FDA lacks the resources to closely monitor testing, manufacturing, or results after approval, meaning problems are often largely undiscovered or unreported.
- Many medical devices require constant monitoring, and often insurance plans will not pay for remote monitoring, creating financial difficulties for both patients and health care providers; however, such devices can actually save insurers money, as they often allow the patient to receive treatment at the first sign of a problem, which usually costs less than receiving treatment after a problem has fully developed and sometimes even saves the patient's life.
- The FDA's regulations require updating in order to account for new hybrid devices that incorporate drugs and/or biologics.
- Nanodevices are the newest form of medical device technology and offer great promise; some are only the size of a few atoms.
- Children's medical devices are another area of the industry's market with the potential for further development.
- The medical device industry is wrought with conflict of interest problems, as physicians sometimes receive substantial kickbacks for utilizing certain brands and sometimes have financial ties to the investment firms funding device research and development.
- Reprocessed medical devices are another cause for concern as FDA standards are not always strictly adhered to, patients are not necessarily informed they are receiving a reprocessed device, and such devices are often obtained from unregulated sources, such as the Internet.
- Counterfeit medical devices also find their way into the market somewhat easily, as they are difficult to detect, the medical community does not have a high level of awareness of counterfeits, and the sanctions for counterfeiting are low.

- Debate over whether patients should be allowed to sue device manufacturers under product liability theories is ongoing; on one hand, it would encourage manufacturers to make their products safer; on the other, it would allow the FDA less control over product standards, possibly resulting in varying or conflicting standards between the states.
- As technology continues to allow for more advanced, and more expensive, medical devices, at some point, insurers may not be able to afford to reimburse every patient for every device.

LAW NOTES

1. During the life of the Swedish Hip and Knee Registries, the revision burden was reduced from 17% to 7%. In one year, the Australian National Joint Replacement Registry reported a 0.6% decrease in revision knee surgery at a savings value of $8.7 million. One estimate is that the American Joint Replacement Registry could result in a one-year savings of $30 million by simply reducing the number of revision surgeries and using more suitable medical products (*See generally* Fry, 2014; Scott, 2011).

REFERENCES

Abbott, R., & Ayres, I. (2014). Evidence and extrapolation: Mechanisms for regulating off-label uses of drugs and devices. *Duke Law Journal, 64,* 377–435.

Abbott, R., & Stevens, C. (2014). Redefining medical necessity: A consumer-driven solution to the U.S. health care crisis. *Loyola of Los Angeles Law Review, 47,* 943–964.

Alao, M. B. (2015). Thirty-eight years and counting: The FDA's misuse of the 510(k) notification process and consequent under-regulation of implantable medical devices. *Saint Louis University Journal of Health Law and Policy, 8,* 347–373.

Al-Khatib, S. M., et al. (2011). Non-evidence-based ICD implantations in the United States. *Journal of the American Medical Association, 305*(1), 43–49.

Amputee Coalition. (2016). *Prosthetic FAQs for the new amputee.* Manassas, VA: Department of Veteran Affairs, Amputee Coalition.

Avalere Health. (2015). *The impact of medical technology on Medicare spending.* Washington, DC: Advanced Medical Technology Association.

Bagheri, Z., et al. (2015). Properties of neuronal facilitation that improve target tracking in natural pursuit simulations. *Journal of the Royal Society Interface, 12*(108), 201–214.

BBC Research. (2015). *Nanotechnology: A realistic market assessment.* Wellesley, MA: BBC Research.

Bi, K. (2015). What is "false or misleading" off-label promotion? *University of Chicago Law Review, 82,* 975–1021.

Bradley, E. H., & Taylor, L. A. (2015). *The American health care paradox: Why spending more is getting us less.* New York, NY: Public Affairs.

Breen, G. B., & Retzinger, J. D. (2013). The resurgence of the Park Doctrine and the collateral consequences of exclusion. *Journal of Health and Life Sciences Law, 6*(3), 90–108.

Brook, M., & Irle, K. (2016). Litigating intraoperative neuromonitoring. *University of Baltimore Law Review, 45,* 443–481.

Brougham, J. (2016). Physician-owned distributorships. *Notre Dame Journal of Law, Ethics and Public Policy, 30,* 369–401.

Buck, I. D. (2015). Breaking the fever: A new construct for regulating overtreatment. *UC Davis Law Review, 48,* 1261–1318.

Burton, T. M. (2007, July 31). NuMED is guilty in FDA case. *Wall Street Journal,* p. B8.

CDC (Centers for Disease Control and Prevention). (2016a). *Arthritis-related statistics.* Atlanta, GA: CDC.

___. (2016b). *Heart disease.*

Chasnow, J., & Levitt, G. (2016). Preemption of non-federal restraints on off-label product communications. *Food and Drug Law Journal, 71,* 249–270.

Choi, J. S. (2016). Mental health services via skype: Meeting the mental health needs of community college students through telemedicine. *Southern California Review of Law and Social Justice, 25,* 331–354.

Cooper, L. D. (2014). The business of nation-building: Value-add: An empirical study of idiosyncratic value in the biotech IPO market. *Columbia Business Law Review, 2014,* 512–547.

Davis, J. P., et al. (2014). The puzzle of class actions with uninjured members. *The George Washington Law Review, 82,* 858–889.

DOJ (U.S. Department of Justice). (2005). *Press release: Micrus Corporation enters into agreement to resolve potential Foreign Corrupt Practices Act liability.* Washington, DC: DOJ.

Douglas, P. S., & Sedrakyan, A., Professors of Medicine at Duke University. (2009, March 28). Clinical effectiveness of coronary stents in the elderly: Results from 262,700 Medicare patients in ACC-NCDR, American College of Cardiology's 58th Annual Scientific Session, Orlando, FL.

Espicom Healthcare Intelligence. (2009). *The medical device market: USA.* Rockville, MD: Espicom.

Etkin, C. D., & Hobson, S. E. (2016). *American joint replacement registry continues to grow.* Rosemont, IL: American Academy of Orthopaedic Surgeons.

Evans, C., Vice President, Global Innovation, West Pharmaceutical Services, Inc. (2016, October 19). Parenteral Drug Association Drug Delivery Combination Products Workshop: Providing Approaches and Solutions to Help Navigate the Evolving Combination Product Environment. Huntington Beach, CA.

FDA (U.S. Food and Drug Administration). (2016a). *Frequently asked questions about combination products.* Silver Spring, MD: FDA.

___. (2016b). *Examples of medical device misconnections.*

___. (2016c). *Reducing risks associated with medical device misconnections.*

___. (2016d). *Reducing risks through standards development for medical device connectors.*

___. (2016e). *Tips for health care providers to reduce medical device misconnections.*

___. (2016f). Letter from Bram D. Zuckerman, M.D., Director, Division of Cardiovascular Devices Office of Device Evaluation, Center for Devices and Radiological Health, to Michelle LaFlesh, Regulatory Affairs Manager, Compliance Officer, NuMED (2016, March 25).

___. (2015a). *Nanotechnology fact sheet.*

___. (2015b). *FDA pharmaceutical quality oversight: One quality voice.*

___. (2015c). *Reprocessing of reusable medical devices: Information for manufacturers.*

___. (2015d). *Reprocessing medical devices in health care settings: Validation methods and labeling guidance for industry and Food and Drug administration staff.*

___. (2015e). *Devices for which a 510(k) should contain validation data (Reprocessing final guidance appendix E.)*

___. (2015f). *Safety considerations to mitigate the risks of misconnections with small-bore connectors intended for enteral applications guidance for industry and Food and Drug administration staff.*

___. (2014). *Guidance for industry: Product recalls, including removals and corrections.*

___. (2008). *Guidance for industry: Coronary drug-eluting stents.*

Fekete, S. P. (2016). Litigating medical device premarket classification decisions for small businesses: Have the courts given the FDA too much deference? The case for taking the focus off of efficacy. *Catholic University Law Review, 65,* 605–633.

Field, M. J., & Tilson, H. (eds.). (2005). *Safe medical devices for children.* Washington, DC: Institute of Medicine.

Freedonia. (2012). *Implantable medical devices.* Cleveland, OH: Freedonia.

Fry, B. M. (2014). A reasoned proposition to a perilous problem: Creating a government agency to remedy the emphatic failure of notified bodies in the medical device industry. *Willamette Journal of International Law and Dispute Resolution, 22,* 161–197.

Gable, L., & Meier, B. M. (2013). Complementarity in public health systems: Using redundancy as a tool of public health governance. *Annals of Health Law, 22,* 224–245.

GAO (General Accountability Office). (2015). *Medical devices: FDA ordered postmarket studies to better understand safety issues, and many studies are ongoing.*

___. (2011). *Medical devices: FDA's premarket review and postmarket safety efforts.*

Gardner, M., & Hathaway, I. (2016). *A future at risk: Economic performance, entrepreneurship, and venture capital in the U.S. medical technology sector.* Washington, DC: Advanced Medical Technology Association.

Goldberg, J. C. P., & Zipursky, B. C. (2016). The Supreme Court's stealth return to the common law of torts. *DePaul Law Review, 65,* 433–456.

Greenwood, K. (2014). Physician conflicts of interest in court: Beyond the "independent physician" litigation heuristic. *Georgia State University Law Review, 30,* 759–822.

Halabi, S. F. (2016). Collective corporate knowledge and the Federal False Claims Act. *Baylor Law Review, 68,* 265–334.

Hall, R. F., & Mercer, M. (2012). Rethinking *Lohr*: Does "SE" mean safe and effective, substantially equivalent, or both? *Minnesota Journal of Law, Science and Technology, 14,* 737–792.

Hall, R. F., et al. (2016). A portrait of nanomedicine and its bioethical implications. *Journal of Law, Medicine and Ethics, 40,* 763–793.

Hilton, K. (2015). Off-label prescribing in a vulnerable pediatric marketplace. *Health and Biomedical Law Society, 10,* 403–439.

Horvath, G. (2015). Recovery and preemption: The collision of the Medicare Secondary Payer Act and the Medical Device Amendments. *California Law Review, 103,* 1353–1402.

Hsu, W. K., Professor of Orthopaedic Surgery, Northwestern University Feinberg School of Medicine. (2016, April 14). Session on Bone Healing through Synthetic Scaffolds at the World Forum for Spine Research. Dubai, United Arab Emirates.

IACC (International Anti-Counterfeiting Coalition). (2005). *White paper: The negative consequences of international intellectual property theft: Economic harm, threats to the public health and safety, and links to organized crime and terrorist organizations,* Washington, DC: IACC.

IOM (Institute of Medicine) Committee on the Public Health Effectiveness of the FDA 510(k) Clearance Process, Board on Population Health and Public Health Practice. (2011). *Medical devices and the public health: The FDA 510(k) clearance process at 35 years.* Washington, DC: National Academies Press.

Isaacs, E. T. (2015). Exposure without redress: A proposed remedial tool for the victims who were set aside. *Oklahoma Law Review, 67,* 519–558.

Jackson, R., & Howe, N. (2008). *The graying of the great powers: Demography and geopolitics in the 21st century.* Washington, DC: Center for Strategic and International Studies.

Jammal, J. (2014). The gray market infiltration of a vulnerable United States health care. *Health and Biomedical Law Society, 9,* 553–576.

King, Z. J. (2013). Knock-off my mark, get set, go to jail? The improprieties of criminalizing post-sale confusion. *New York University Law Review, 88,* 2220–2253.

Klein, A. (2005a, December 22). Used medical devices being sold on eBay; Refurbished items have little oversight. *Washington Post,* p. D1.

___. (2005b, December 11). Hospitals save money, but safety is questioned. *Washington Post,* p. A1.

Kramer, D. B. (2014). Ensuring medical device effectiveness and safety: A cross-national comparison of approaches to regulation. *Food and Drug Law Journal, 69,* 1–33.

Laakmann, A. B. (2015). When should physicians be liable for innovation? *Cardozo Law Review, 36,* 913–968.

Lennox, K. (2014). Substantially unequivalent: Reforming FDA regulation of medical devices. *University of Illinois Law Review, 2014,* 1363–1400.

Lewis, C. B. (2015). A private payer parity in telemedicine reimbursement: How state-mandated coverage can be the catalyst for telemedicine expansion. *University of Memphis Law Review, 46,* 471–502.

Lindenfeld, E., & Tran, J. L. (2016). Prescription drugs and design defect liability: Blanket immunity approach to the increased costs and unavailability of prescription medication. *Drake Law Review, 64,* 111–139.

Liu, C. (2012). Leaving the FDA behind: Pharmaceutical outsourcing and drug safety. *Texas International Law Journal, 48,* 1–43.

Llewellyn, C., et al. (2015). *Capturing the new "value" segment in medical devices.* New York, NY: McKinsey & Company.

Mann, J. M. (2015). FDA adverse event reporting system: Recruiting doctors to make surveillance a little less passive. *Food and Drug Law Journal, 70,* 371–394.

MarketsandMarkets. (2016). Spinal implants and spinal devices market by product. Maharashtra, India: MarketsandMarkets.

___. (2015). *Defibrillators market by product (implantable cardioverter defibrillator by end user.)*

McIntyre, S. (2014). Game over for first sale. *Berkeley Technology Law Journal, 29*, 1–59.

MedtronicNeuro. (2016, October 25). *Press release: Clinical trial; deep brain stimulation (DBS) for Parkinson's disease international study*. Minneapolis, MN: MedtronicNeuro.

Nabili, M. (2016). *Technical electronic product radiation safety standards committee meeting on medical and nonmedical ultrasound*. Rockville, MD: FDA, Center for Devices and Radiological Health.

Noah, L. (2014). Governance by the backdoor: Administrative law(lessness?) at the FDA. *Nebraska Law Review, 93*, 89–137.

Nunley, R. M., Associate Professor of Orthopaedic Surgery, Washington University School of Medicine. (2016, November 10). Industry Symposia on Collaboration and outcomes in the era of bundled payments at the 2016 American Association of Hip and Knee Surgeons Annual Meeting, Dallas, TX.

Persad, G. (2015). The medical cost pandemic: Why limiting access to cost-effective treatments hurts the global poor. *Chicago Journal of International Law, 15*, 559–611.

Peterson, L. K. (2015). Evading preemption: The state's search for recovery for the masses. *Charleston Law Review, 9*, 403–445.

Pew Research Center. (2013). *Health fact sheet*. Washington, DC: Pew.

Porter, N. B. (2014). The new ADA backlash. *Tennessee Law Review, 82*, 1–82.

Pratt, D. (2015). Telehealth and telemedicine. *Albany Law Journal of Science and Technology, 25*, 495–544.

Price, W. N. (2016). Big data, patents, and the future of medicine. *Cardozo Law Review, 37*, 1401–1453.

Rebouché, R. (2015). Intersections in reproduction: Perspectives on abortion and assisted reproductive technologies: Non-invasive testing, non-invasive counseling. *Journal of Law, Medicine and Ethics, 43*, 228–237.

Reilly, P. R. (2015). Justice deferred is justice denied: We must end our failed experiment in deferring corporate criminal prosecutions. *Brigham Young University Law Review, 15*, 307–357.

Reiss, J. B., et al. (2007). Your business in court. *Food and Drug Law Journal, 62*, 305–353.

Ridge, R. J., & Baird, M. A. (2008). Unearthing corporate wrongdoing: Detecting and dealing with ethical breaches in the business world: The pendulum swings back: Revisiting corporate criminality and the rise of deferred prosecution agreements. *University of Dayton Law Review, 33*, 187–204.

Robinson, W. K. (2015). Patent law challenges for the internet of things. *Wake Forest Journal of Business and Intellectual Property Law, 15*, 655–670.

Rojahn, S. Y. (2013). What it's like to see again with an artificial retina. *MIT Technology Review, 5*, 9–11.

Russom A. M., et al. (2013). Appropriate use criteria for implantable cardioverter-defibrillators and cardiac resynchronization therapy, *Heart Rhythm, 10*, 11–17.

Sage, W. M. (2016). Assembled products: The key to more effective competition and antitrust oversight in health care. *Cornell Law Review, 101*, 609–700.

Schafer, P. E., et al. (2011). Cost-effectiveness of drug-eluting stents versus bare metal stents in clinical practice. Circulation: Cardiovascular Quality and Outcomes, 4, 408–415.

Scheetz, T. K. (2011). Say what you mean: The discoverability of medical device adverse event reports. *University of Illinois Law Review, 11*, 1095–1124.

Schulke, D. F. (2013). The regulatory arms race: Mobile-health applications and agency posturing. *Boston University Law Review, 93*, 1699–1752.

Schumacher, A. (2015). Telehealth: Current barriers, potential progress. *Ohio State Law Journal, 76*, 409–438.

Schwartz, V. E., & Appel, C. E. (2014). Government regulation and private litigation: The law should enhance harmony, not war. *The Boston University Public Interest Law Journal, 23*, 185–218.

Scott, B. (2011). Oversight overhaul: Eliminating the premarket review of medical devices and implementing a provider-centered postmarket surveillance strategy. *Food and Drug Law Journal, 66*, 377–421.

Shapiro, J. K. (2014). Substantial equivalence premarket review: The right approach for most medical devices. *Food and Drug Law Journal, 69*, 365–394.

Simshaw, D., et al. (2016). Regulating healthcare robots: Maximizing opportunities while minimizing risks. *Richmond Journal of Law and Technology, 22*, 3–60.

Smith, C. (2015). Scouting for approval: Lessons on medical device regulation in an era of crowdfunding from Scanadu's "scout." *Food and Drug Law Journal, 70*, 209–237.

Smith, L. (2015). See how prices change for spinal implants. *Healthcare Finance, 3*, 7–9.

Snir, R. (2014). Trends in global nanotechnology regulation: The public-private interplay. *Vanderbilt Journal of Entertainment and Technology Law, 17*, 107–173.

Spivack, P., & Raman, S. (2008). Regulating the new regulators: Current trends in deferred prosecution agreements. *American Criminal Law Review, 45*, 159–190.

Stachura, M. E., & Khasanshina, E. V. (2016). *Telehomecare and remote monitoring: An outcomes overview*. Washington, DC: Advanced Medical Technology Association.

Theodore, L., & Stander, L. H. (2013). Regulatory concerns and health/hazard risks associated with nanotechnology. *Pace Environmental Law Review, 30*, 469–485.

Thompson, D. K. (2012). Small size, big dilemma: The challenge of regulating nanotechnology. *Tennessee Law Review, 79*, 621–668.

TMR (Transparency Market Research). (2016a). *U.S. implantable medical devices market*. Albany, NY: TMR.

___. (2016b). Reprocessed Medical Devices Market: Global Industry Analysis, Size, Share, Growth, Trends and Forecast.

U.S. Bone and Joint Initiative. (2015). *What is the impact of burden of musculoskeletal disorders and why is the U.S. bone and joint initiative important?* Rosemont, IL: U.S. Bone and Joint Initiative.

Waldman, P. (2013, October 30). Doctors use euphemism for $2.4 billion in needless stents. *Bloomberg News*, p. 3.

Wallenfelt, B. O. (2014). The 30th anniversary of the Hatch-Waxman Act: Hatch-Waxman and medical devices. *William Mitchell Law Review, 40,* 1407–1426.

Wharton School at the University of Pennsylvania. (2006a). The business of healthcare innovation: How new products come to market. *Knowledge@ Wharton.*

___. (2006b). Personalized medicine and nanotechnology: Trying to bring dreams to market.

Winslow, R., & Mathews, A. W. (2006, December 9). How doctors are rethinking drug-coated stents; safety concerns are altering treatment, narrowing use; FDA panel divisions emerge. *Wall Street Journal,* p. A1.

Winters, D. R. H. (2013). False certainty: Judicial forcing of the quantification of risk. *Temple Law Review, 85,* 315–384.

___. (2012). Not sick yet: Food-safety-impact litigation and barriers to justiciability. *Brooklyn Law Review, 77,* 905–957.

CHAPTER 19

© Andy Dean Photography/ShutterStock, Inc.

Clinical Trials

"The history of the last 20 years is one of crises with drugs and medical devices, many approved despite the objections of the FDA's own scientists."

— **Sidney M. Wolfe**, physician; member, Drug Safety and Risk Management Committee, U.S. Food and Drug Administration; co-founder and director of Public Citizen's Health Research Group; editor of the book and website, *Worst Pills, Best Pills* (2005)

IN BRIEF

This chapter provides an overview of the complex multistage pathways of medical product research and development. The laws and regulations governing clinical trials are examined, including access to experimental drugs and devices, transparency and full disclosure in clinical testing, informed consent of participation of children in human subject research, conflicts of interest, and informed consent in general. The statistics involved in clinical trials and observational studies are generally outlined. In this chapter, the generic term *drugs* includes pharmaceuticals and biopharmaceuticals.

LEARNING OBJECTIVES

Upon completion of this chapter readers should be able to:

1. Discuss the differences between clinical trials for new drugs and those for generics.
2. List the main elements and number of clinical trial participants in each phase of drug testing.
3. Explain the difference between bioequivalent and biotherapeutic.
4. Distinguish between branded generics and generics.
5. Understand the concepts involved in health risk assessments.
6. Describe expanded access protocols in the context of investigational new drug applications and patients' rights to lifesaving experimental drugs.
7. Outline the problems involved with termination of clinical trials especially with respect to statistical measures and the desires of clinical trial participants.
8. Explain why observational studies without control groups can lead to erroneous conclusions.
9. Provide the advantages and disadvantages of international drug trials.
10. Discuss the problems of informed consent and the role of institutional review boards.
11. Explain financial conflicts of interest in drug research.

KEY TERMS

Abigail Alliance's proposal	Bioequivalent	Citizen petition
Active ingredient	Bonferroni adjustment	Clinical trials
Affirmative case	Brand formulation	Control groups
Asserted right	Branded generics	Cost recovery
Battery claim	Child advocates	Declaration of Helsinki

Disease development
Doctrine of informed consent
Double-blind, placebo controlled
    study
Drug discovery
Due Process Clause
Drug-naive patients
Emergency Research Rule
En banc
European model
Evidence-based medicine
Experimental drug
False association
Federal Trade Commission
Fiduciary duty
Fifth Amendment
Full disclosure requirement
Fundamental right
Gene-environment interactions
Generic formulation
Generics

Good clinical practices
Health risk assessments
Industry interests
Informed consent
Informed consent claim
Institutional review boards
International Conference on
    Harmonisation
Investigational new drug application
Latency periods
Liberty interest
Material risk
Monitoring boards
Multistage pathways
Narrow use
New drug application
New drugs
Newborn screening programs
Nontrivial chance
Observational studies
Off-patent drugs

Open label studies
p-value
Patient preferences
Phase I clinical trials
Phase II clinical trials
Placebo
Post-Phase I clinical trials
Post-marketing surveillance
Preclinical testing
Relative risk
Right to personal autonomy
Rule of seven
Statistical boundary
Statistical significance
Strict scrutiny standard
Substantive due process analysis
Termination of a clinical trial
Therapeutic equivalence
Validation
Vulnerable populations
Vulnerable research subjects

FACT OR FICTION

Clinical Trials in Developing Nations

Should the medical products industry be liable in U.S. courts for violation of good clinical practice standards in international clinical trials?

   A 10-year-old girl was suffering from bacterial meningitis, a serious infectious disease that was sweeping through West Africa. Meningitis attacks the protective membranes covering the brain and spinal cord and can cause serious neurologic damage or even death. An effective treatment for this disease is intravenous antibiotics. Once the family arrived at the clinic in Kano, Nigeria, they met physicians who were offering free drugs. However, three days later, the girl died; she had not received the proven antibiotic therapy, but only an **experimental drug** called Trovan. The girl's family, along with many others, claimed that instead of receiving health care, they were unwittingly participating in clinical trials sponsored by Pfizer that led to the serious impairment or death of many children. After several weeks of injuries and fatalities to some 200 children resulting from the experimental drug treatment, Pfizer concluded its clinical trial and left without administering follow-up care.

—*See* Law Fact at the end of this chapter for the answer.

Principles and Applications

Clinical trials are essential to understanding the efficacy of medical interventions. The biopharmaceutical, medical device, and pharmaceutical industries invest over $68.5 billion in researching and developing **new drugs** every year (PhRMA, 2016). This represents almost 19% of the total U.S. sales for the combined industries. This 19% commitment by the biopharmaceutical, medical device, and pharmaceutical industries is almost 5 times the investment level of other U.S. manufacturers who invest on average about 4% of their sales into research and development (PhRMA, 2016). As illustrated in **FIGURE 19-1**, an additional $31.4 billion in basic research funding for development of drugs was provided by the National Institutes of Health (Moses et al., 2015). The result of this billion-dollar investment is that more than 7,000 products are in development (PhRMA, 2016).

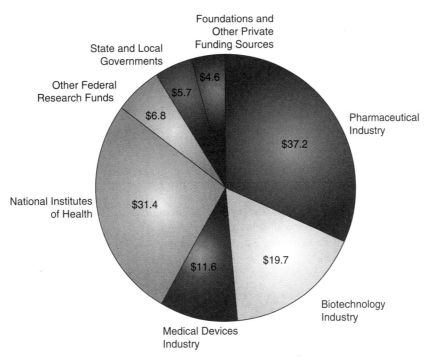

FIGURE 19-1 $117 Billion Investment in Biomedical Research

Data from: Moses III, H., et al. (2015). The anatomy of medical research: U.S. and international comparisons. Journal American Medical Association, 313 (2), 174–189.

Research and Development Investments Fund a Complex Multistage Pathway

Research and development funding for innovative medical products (not generic products) covers a complex, **multistage pathway** from discovery through approval of drugs. Although clinical testing represents the greatest share of costs, as illustrated in **FEATURE BOX 19-1**, the entire process is expensive, risky, and time consuming.

Some major expenses are research materials, advanced computers, and other highly sophisticated machines that support research activities, and salaries of scientists. Stage-specific activities include:

- **Drug discovery**
- **Preclinical testing**
- Clinical trials
- Approval by the FDA
- **Post-marketing surveillance**

FEATURE BOX 19-1

The Research and Development Process

- *Expensive*: $2.6 billion to bring a new drug to market
- *Risky*: fewer than 12% of products that make it into **Phase I clinical trials** approved by the U.S. Food and Drug Administration (FDA)
- *Time-consuming*: 10 to 15 years

DiMasi et al., 2016 and 2014; Moses et al., 2015.

Drug Discovery

Researchers first identify a target for a new drug, such as a molecule believed to affect a particular disease. Then they use computers to screen or biotechnology to create thousands of compounds, identifying hundreds of potential drugs. While most compounds will never be approved for use, each one is evaluated to determine its potential value compared to existing therapies, complexity of large-scale manufacturing, and other factors (PhRMA, 2016).

Preclinical Testing

Candidate drugs from the discovery stage then receive one to three years of extensive testing in the laboratory and in animals to assess safety and show biological activity against a disease. In addition:

- Chemical tests establish a compound's purity, stability, and shelf life.
- Manufacturing tests determine what will be involved in mass producing the drug.
- Pharmaceutical development studies explore dosing, packaging, and formulation of the drug (capsule, inhaler, injection, tablet, etc.).

(PhRMA, 2016)

Clinical Trials

In the three phases of clinical trials, which can take anywhere from 2 to 10 years, teams of research investigators test a new drug in clinical trial participants to learn if it is safe and effective. For drugs in various stages of development, the odds for reaching the market are well known (PhRMA, 2016). There is a significant drop-off during each of the three phases of clinical trials before submission of a **new drug application** (NDA).

These trials compare the experiences of randomly selected groups of clinical trial participants with similar characteristics, some of whom take the new drug being tested while others take a **placebo** (PhRMA, 2016). By taking part in a clinical trial, participants who have the disease can try a new treatment that may or may not be better than those that already exist. In addition, clinical trial participants are generally paid $100 to $200 per day; if travel to a trial site is required, travel expenses are covered, including international travel. In comparison, egg donors receive $5,000 to $8,000 per cycle and sperm donors receive $50 to $100 per contribution; prices vary by site.

While Phase I, II, and III studies are taking place, research investigators are also:

- Conducting toxicity tests and other long-term safety evaluations
- Evaluating dosage forms
- Planning for mass production
- Designing packaging
- Preparing the extensive application required for FDA approval

Even with this complex process, only one out of five drugs that enter clinical testing is ever approved by the FDA (PhRMA, 2016). Specifically,

- *20% of the drugs that enter Phase I are approved to enter Phase II*: 20 to 80 healthy clinical trial participants are generally tested at low dosage levels, if the FDA approves human testing to determine safety, safe dose range, and mechanism of action (*See* 21 C.F.R. § 312.21(a))
- *30% of the drugs that enter Phase II are approved to enter Phase III*: 100 to 300 participants who have the disease are tested to look for efficacy and side effects, and to determine optimal dose strength and schedule (*See* 21 C.F.R. § 312.21(b))
- *60% of the drugs that enter Phase III are approved for a new drug application*: 1,000 to 5,000 participants are tested to determine effectiveness and monitor adverse reactions to long-term use (*See* 21 C.F.R. § 312.21(c))
- *80% of the new drug applications are approved by the FDA for market entry*

In Phase I clinical trials, researchers find the best way to administer a new treatment and how much they can safely give. Healthy humans are used, if the FDA allows it, especially if there are no animal models for the disease or condition. All testing is done first in animals to determine if it is likely to be safe to be tested in humans (*See* 21 C.F.R. § 312.82).

Approval by the U.S. Food and Drug Administration

The new drug application is the vehicle through which the pharmaceutical and biopharmaceutical industries formally propose that the FDA approve a new drug for sale and marketing in the United States. The data gathered during the animal studies and human clinical trials become part of the new drug applications. The FDA's goal is to review 90% of new drug applications within 10 months. FDA scientists and sometimes advisory committees review all clinical trial results and decide whether the data justifies approval for patient use (PhRMA, 2016).

According to the FDA, the documentation required in a new drug application is supposed to tell the drug's whole story as illustrated in **FIGURE 19-2**, including:

- What happened during the clinical trial tests
- What the ingredients of the drug are
- Results of the preclinical animal studies
- How the drug behaves in the human body
- How the drug is manufactured, processed, and packaged

(FDA, 2015a, b)

Post-Marketing Surveillance

Phase IV studies are generally ongoing for years. These studies continue to evaluate safety and generate more data about how the drug affects particular groups of clinical trial participants, such as children or the elderly (Shah, 2013). In addition to these targeted post-marketing surveillance studies, firms are meant to continue to monitor all approved drugs for long-term safety and regularly report results to the FDA (PhRMA, 2016).

It is important to note that clinical trials cannot always detect risks that are relatively rare, have long **latency periods**, or affect **vulnerable populations**. In addition, clinical trials cannot detect risks involved in patients who take multiple prescribed drugs, over-the-counter drugs, vitamins, and nutritional supplements at the same time. For these reasons, most serious adverse effects do not become evident until a drug is used in larger population groups for periods in

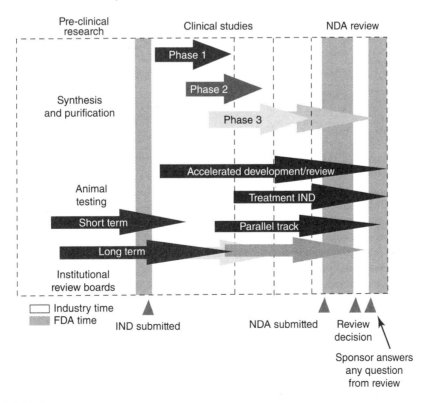

FIGURE 19-2 Clinical Trial Process

Data from: Moses III, H., et al. (2015). The anatomy of medical research: U.S. and international comparisons. Journal American Medical Association, 313 (2), 174–189.

excess of one year (Radis, 2015). Many industry insiders and researchers advocate the ultraconservative **rule of seven**: they themselves will only take approved drugs that have been on the market for at least seven years without serious adverse effects (Wolfe et al., 2005).

Clinical Trials of Generic Drugs

In contrast to the $2.6 billion-dollar, 10- to 15-year investment that branded, innovative drugs undergo, approval for **generics** only requires clinical trials of 100 patients at an average cost of $100,000. Congress lessened the standards for generic drug product market entry, favoring economic advantages over detailed scientific evaluation of drugs (*See* Drug Price Competition and Patent Term Restoration Act of 1984, 21 U.S.C.A. § 355(j)) (allowing the filing of, and stating the requirements for, an abbreviated application for the approval of a new drug).

Branded generics are an important part of the pharmaceutical industry (*E.g.*, Murphy, 2016). They enable very large, underserved population segments to access important drugs. In addition, branded generics ensure that innovation truly takes place in the marketplace (Wharton, 2006). With truly innovative pharmaceutical firms that are continually producing new and innovative products, when generics enter the market following patent expiration, it frees up resources to license **off-patent drugs** and invest in new breakthrough products. More innovative approaches are starting to appear in the larger pharmaceutical firms with the expanded use of branded generics. The line between brand name and branded generics is beginning to blur within the industry, just as the line between the pharmaceutical and biotechnology industries is blurring. Branded generics are evolving both as an opportunity to get access to drugs as well as an emerging business model for the pharmaceutical industry (Wharton, 2006). The biopharmaceutical firms of the future may have a breadth of businesses across biotechnology, the pharmaceutical industry, and branded generics.

Distinction Between Bioequivalent and Biotherapeutic

Generic versions of branded drugs need not demonstrate their scientific merits by controlled human clinical trials or other testing the brand pharmaceutical firms conducted (*See* 21 U.S.C.A. § 355(j)(2)(A)(ii)-(iv); *See also* 21 U.S.C.A. § 355(j)(8)(B)). Moreover, while generics may be more or less efficacious in delivering the **active ingredient** to the target condition in the human body, generics are labeled **bioequivalent** as long as the active ingredient's rate of absorption is similar (or bioequivalent) to the delivery of the active ingredient in the branded drug (*See* 21 C.F.R. § 320.23).

By definition, generics may be up to 45% less or 25% more efficacious than branded drugs, yet still meet the legal definition of being bioequivalent. This is because of how the term *bioequivalent* is defined (*e.g.*, Eban, 2013). The relative mean of the **generic formulation** should be within 80 to 125% of the **brand formulation**, which is the basis for stating generics may be more or less efficacious than branded drugs.

For instance, the response that a drug elicits in individual patients can be significantly different for generics that are deemed bioequivalent; slight changes in the chemical composition can affect the molecular degradability of the generic and be responsible for widely varying responses (*e.g.*, Blessy et al., 2014). A critical distinction between generics and branded drugs is the difference between being bioequivalent and having **therapeutic equivalence**. Bioequivalence concerns the dose and rate of absorption. A generic is considered a bioequivalent to the branded drug if the rate and extent of absorption of the drug is not significantly different than that of the branded drug at the same dosage when taken in the prescribed amount (*See* 21 U.S.C.A. § 355(j)(2)(A)). Therapeutic equivalence, on the other hand, means the generic controls the symptoms or illness "exactly the same" as the branded drug controls the symptoms or illness. In reality, the generic components may be similar but how generics are manufactured is different. Generics are reverse engineered from the branded drug, and the result is an approximation rather than a duplicate of the original. While the active ingredient in generics is required to be therapeutically the same as branded drugs, generics do not have to treat symptoms or the disease in the same way as branded drugs as long as they are absorbed by the body in a similar manner, up to 20% less metabolism of the active ingredient to 20% more is still deemed bioequivalent (FDA, 2013). Generics may have side effects, may be absorbed differently by the human body, or simply have no therapeutic effect, and yet still be defined as bioequivalent to the branded drug.

Most important, and this cannot be emphasized enough, generics are not required to provide independent proof of their safety or efficacy to be labeled bioequivalent (*See* 21 U.S.C.A. § 355(j)(2)(A)). Generics may be safe or efficacious, but no evidence is required that they are, or that they are not; they may produce the desired result of treating a disease or illness or they may not. Perhaps this is why many generics are less expensive than branded drugs. Other reasons for generics being less expensive include the use of lower quality fillers/coatings, and the fact that generic manufacturers do not need to incur significant research and development costs to bring a generic to market.

Distinction Between Branded Generics and Generics

The pharmaceutical industry also markets authorized branded generics, which are branded drugs that have lost their patent status but are labeled and marketed as generics (Feldman & Frondorf, 2016). The difference between a branded generic and a non-brand generic can be best understood by looking at the distinction between the two products. A branded generic is the result of a $2.6 billion product-level investment that has been clinically tested on 1,000 to 5,000 patients over 10 to 15 years; this compares to a $100,000 investment to reverse engineer a branded drug and clinically test the generic product on 100 patients in a matter of months. Off-patent branded drugs are available as authorized generics; sometimes the same drug is sold as a branded drug and an authorized generic drug at the same time by the same firm, off the same production line. Since the early 1990s, numerous authorized generics have been marketed by pharmaceutical firms holding the original patent or their licensee.

As the practice of branded generics has grown in recent years, the generic industry has met the competition by turning to the FTC and Congress about the competitive effects of this practice. The pharmaceutical industry has challenged the generic industry's argument against it by maintaining branded generics are simply bringing competition to the generic industry. Both empirical and theoretical studies evince that generic entry is inversely related to price (Stoddart, 2012). The greater the number of generics, the lower the price becomes. So far, the pharmaceutical industry appears to be winning the battle against the generic industry; no court has found branded generics to be unlawful, and the FDA and the **Federal Trade Commission** have expressed favorable opinions on the practice. Moreover, no government regulator or enforcement agency has publicly condemned or challenged the practice of introducing branded generics to the market (*See, e.g.*, Avery & Nguyen, 2013).

Health Risk Assessments

The ethical foundation of clinical trials involving human subjects is codified in the Belmont Report and the Declaration of Helsinki (FDA, 1979; WMA, 2006). These documents require that the results of trials be publicly available to inform medical practice as well as future research. In addition, basic principles of **evidence-based medicine** require the analysis of all data on a given topic (Choi, 2015). Recent debate has evolved around the practice of publishing only some results of clinical trials, but not others. Industry critics claim this undermines the health care industry's collective ability to make rational decisions about health care.

Information on Post-Phase I Clinical Trials

Congress expanded the requirements for all sponsors and research investigators to share information about **post-Phase I clinical trials**, including selected aspects of trial results, on the U.S. government website, ClinicalTrials.gov. This site has more than 67,000 registered trials for drugs, devices, surgical interventions, and procedural interventions from about 160 countries (Choi, 2015). These expanded requirements apply no matter what the source of funding is for the clinical trials and include, for the first time, penalties for noncompliance, including the loss of funding from the National Institutes of Health and civil penalties of up to $10,000 per day. *See* Food and Drug Administration Amendments Act of 2007, 21 U.S.C.A. §§ 321 *et seq.*

Balancing Risks and Benefits

Proper **health risk assessment** is critical for new drug product treatments. Patients and physicians often weigh the pros and cons of one treatment versus another; the FDA also wrestles with the trade-offs between health risks and benefits (Wharton, 2007). There are 11,000 FDA-regulated drug products on the market (including both prescription and over-the-counter drug products), with nearly 100 more approved each year (FDA, 2015b). The reality is that the FDA does not have the resources to perform the Herculean task of monitoring comprehensively the performance of every drug product on the market (Croom, 2014). An ongoing issue is whether the FDA should do more to ensure the safety of new drug products and expose potential side effects before a drug product comes into widespread use (FDA, 2016c). Patients who have life-threatening illnesses for which there are no effective treatments, however, are generally willing to assume the health risk of taking a drug product that has not been studied for very long if it offers them the possibility of a cure or at least less suffering (Wharton, 2007).

MANAGEMENT AND LAW ISSUES

1. Has patient protectionism translated into ever-longer clinical trials and administrative delays, with the real risk being that too few drugs now reach the market?

There is a tug of war between the two mind-sets. In the **European model**, decisions cannot be based only on clinical or medical knowledge, but also depend in part on **patient preferences**. The question is which, or whose, preferences should dominate. Virtually any drug will be too risky for the most risk-averse patients, but virtually any delay is too long for many more patients willing to take a chance for much better outcomes. Also in the equation are **industry interests**, which want the FDA to approve new drugs as quickly as possible so they will begin getting a return on the money they spent on research and development (Wharton, 2007).

Clinical trial participants with advanced cancer are now arguing for something closer to the European model when it comes to approval of new drug products. They are willing to accept the health risk of side effects from investigational treatments because they attach more value to the possibility of good outcomes and less value to the possibility of side effects. The FDA and its expert panels, on the other hand, place more weight on the health risk of side effects (Wharton, 2007).

Expanded Access Protocols

Human use of investigational new drugs takes place in controlled clinical trials. Data from the trials serve as the basis for the new drug application. Sometimes, however, patients do not qualify for these carefully controlled trials because of other health problems, age, or other factors. For patients who may benefit from the drug use but do not qualify for the clinical trials, FDA regulations enable manufacturers to provide for expanded access to the drug during the trial stage before being approved to market.

An **investigational new drug application**, or treatment protocol, is a relatively unrestricted study. The primary intent of an investigational new drug application is to authorize shipment of an unapproved drug product into interstate commerce. A much less common purpose is to provide for access to the new drug for patients with a life-threatening or serious disease for which there is no alternative treatment, which includes about 2% of the investigational new drug shipments. Another secondary purpose, which is about 1% of the purpose for an investigational new drug application, is to generate additional information about the drug, especially its safety. Investigational new drug applications can be undertaken only if clinical research investigators are actively studying the experimental treatment in clinical trials, or all trials have been completed. In addition, there must be evidence the drug may be an effective treatment in patients like those to be treated by the investigational new drug application. Furthermore, the drug cannot expose patients to unreasonable risks given the severity of the disease to be treated (NLM, 2008).

COURT DECISION
Right to Lifesaving Experimental Drugs

Abigail Alliance v. Von Eschenbach
[Patients v. FDA]
495 F.3d 695 (U.S. Court of Appeals for the D.C. Circuit 2007),
cert. denied, 552 U.S. 1159 (U.S. Supreme Court 2008)

Facts: The Abigail Alliance for Better Access to Developmental Drugs appeared to have a victory when a divided panel of the Court of Appeals for the District of Columbia Circuit ruled that terminally ill, mentally competent adult patients had a constitutionally protected right to access experimental drugs that have not reached **Phase II clinical trials** (*See Abigail Alliance v. Von Eschenbach*, 445 F.3d 470 (Court of Appeals for the DC Circuit 2006)). This victory was short lived, however. In 2007, the D.C. Circuit sitting *en banc* reversed this earlier decision, marking a setback in the campaign for removal of the regulatory barriers that currently prevent terminally ill patients from gaining early access to experimental drugs.

The *en banc* reversal represents the latest act in a drama that began in June of 2003, when Abigail filed a **citizen petition** with the FDA (*see* 21 C.F.R. § 10.30 (2000)). Abigail's petition proposed adding an early approval regimen for experimental drugs, a scheme Abigail called "Tier 1 Initial Approval" that would allow terminally ill patients to gain earlier access to those experimental drugs. Although many other advocacy groups and advisory committees wrote to the FDA either in support of or in opposition to Abigail's Tier 1 Initial Approval concept, the FDA failed to respond to Abigail's proposal, thus prompting the Alliance to proceed to judicial challenge.

Issue: Does a fundamental right exist under the **Fifth Amendment**, which contains the **Due Process Clause**, provide terminally ill patients access to potentially lifesaving experimental drugs?

Holding and Decision: No, terminally ill patients do not have a fundamental right to access experimental drugs under the Due Process Clause of the Fifth Amendment. Thus, there was no constitutional deficiency in the existing FDA regulations regarding experimental drugs, and because those regulations had a rational basis, the court could not disturb them. The dissent argued that terminally ill patients do have a fundamental right to access potentially lifesaving experimental drugs.

Analysis: Whether an **asserted right** in a particular case constitutes a **fundamental right** and **liberty interest** is extremely important in constitutional litigation. If the government wishes to restrict a fundamental right, then the government must prove that it has a compelling governmental interest justifying the restriction, and that the restriction is narrowly tailored to serve that interest. The restriction is subject to this **strict scrutiny standard** (*See Skinner v. Oklahoma ex rel. Williamson*, 316 U.S. 535 (U.S. Supreme Court 1942)). If the restricted right is not a fundamental right, however, then the government can justify its intervention by showing that there is a rational basis for the restriction, an easier standard to meet than strict scrutiny for fundamental rights. What, then, are the fundamental rights and liberty interests protected by the Due Process Clause? Since such human rights are not explicitly enumerated in the U.S. Constitution, the U.S. Supreme Court has established a two-pronged analysis, known as the **substantive due process analysis**, to determine if the asserted right is a fundamental one (*See Washington v. Glucksberg*, 521 U.S. 702 (U.S. Supreme Court 1997)). This analysis requires proponents of a proposed fundamental right to do the following:

* Provide a careful description of the asserted fundamental liberty interest
* Show that the asserted right is deeply rooted in the nation's history and tradition and implicit in the concept of ordered liberty, such that neither liberty nor justice would exist if it were sacrificed

The first prong of the substantive due process analysis, the description of the asserted right, is very important: too broad and a right becomes all-encompassing and impossible to evaluate; too narrow and a right appears trivial.

Rule of Law: The majority opinion described Abigail's asserted right as terminally ill patients' right to access experimental drugs and found it not to be a fundamental right. The dissenting opinion cast it as the right to attempt to preserve one's life and found it to be a fundamental right.

References discussing this court decision: *E.g.*, Fultz, 2013; Janssen, 2014; Kumar, 2013; Lamkin, 2016; Orentlicher, 2014; Pivarnik, 2014; Smith, 2016; Wiley, 2014, 2016a, b.

The key question, if the U.S. Supreme Court had heard this case, would have been how the rights asserted by Abigail would have been described. Given that the majority and dissent in this decision each came up with substantially different rights, it will be interesting to see if future cases provide a more principled manner of extracting the fundamental rights to be analyzed. If future cases choose to define Abigail's asserted right narrowly, whether courts will infer a narrow right from a broader, established fundamental right will be noteworthy. This has been done in the past. For instance, the specific rights to:

* Determine extended family living arrangements has been inferred from broader constitutional protections for the sanctity of the family (*See Moore v. City of East Cleveland*, 431 U.S. 494 (U.S. Supreme Court 1977))
* Terminate a pregnancy from a broader right to privacy (*See Roe v. Wade*, 410 U.S. 113 (U.S. Supreme Court 1973), *rehearing denied*, 410 U.S. 959 (U.S. Supreme Court 1973))
* Use contraception from a general right to be free from intrusion into the sacred precincts of marital bedrooms (*See Griswold v. State of Connecticut*, 381 U.S. 479 (U.S. Supreme Court 1965))

Abigail Alliance's Two-Tier Approval Proposal

The issue of access to lifesaving experimental treatments and medical products continues to present itself. If Congress were to permit terminally ill patients to access experimental medical products, then the FDA would have to create a system to allow that access. The Abigail Alliance's Tier 1 Approval proposal represents one legislative possibility for addressing this problem for drug products. The proposal would involve:

- Granting terminally ill patients who have exhausted all FDA-approved therapies the autonomy of selecting post-Phase I experimental medical products with their physicians
- Lifting the current prohibition of charging any price higher than the cost for experimental products

The second feature of the **Abigail Alliance's proposal**, allowing commercialization, or charging a price higher than the cost of experimental products, would safeguard clinical trials. The intention of this feature is to create incentives for the medical products industry to actively distribute its experimental products, as opposed to merely impose **cost recovery** under the current FDA regulation. Sufficiently high price may act as a barrier to some patients seeking access to experimental products, thus forcing them to participate in free clinical trials, while creating disparities in access based on economics (Janssen, 2014).

Balancing Patient Rights: Access Versus Personal Autonomy

Determining the safeguards for access to clinical trials is an economic decision, as opposed to the question of patient autonomy. In a sense, the **right to personal autonomy** affects individual interests in obtaining investigational medical treatments and medical products, while the right to access pertains to the public's interests in filtering safe and efficacious products through clinical trials.

It will be more difficult to find a rational basis in preventing investigational access if an alternative regulation like the Abigail Alliance's proposal can manage to preserve the public's interests while also promoting individuals' interests (Janssen, 2014). Congress may be better suited to decide the proper balance between the risks and benefits of medical technology. The individual autonomy of terminally ill individuals, if not a constitutional right, is still a policy issue that Congress can endorse.

Termination of Clinical Trials

Regardless of the reason for **termination of a clinical trial**, the high cost of bringing a medical product to market presents a valid reason for halting a clinical investigation (Dresser, 2015); for instance, the legal guidelines for regulation of a product may be unresolved. Clinical trials usually get halted for one of two reasons:

- New drug shows overwhelming promise and it would not be fair to delay its release
- Results suggest great risk

(Wiley, 2016b).

COURT DECISION

Obligations to Provide Experimental Drugs to Clinical Trial Participants

Abney v. Amgen, Inc.
[Clinical Trial Participants v. Pharmaceutical Firm]
443 F.3d 540 (U.S. Court of Appeals for the 6th Circuit 2006)

Facts: Amgen sought to evaluate a method of delivering a potential breakthrough drug for Parkinson's disease, glial-cell-line-derived neurotropic factor (GDNF), to dopamine-producing neurons in the brain. Two **open label studies** where all clinical trial participants received GDNF, and a Phase II trial that later converted to a third open label study, were conducted by Amgen. The delivery method required research investigators to implant into a participant's abdomen a drug reservoir and pump, drill a hole in the participant's skull, and run an attached catheter from the pump through the participant's neck, cheek, and skull, and into the brain, where the GDNF from the reservoir was delivered by the pump via the catheter.

Amgen supported its first open label trial involving five clinical trial participants suffering from Parkinson's disease in the United Kingdom, which yielded favorable results. Desiring further support, Amgen sponsored a second open label trial that showed improvement in 10 clinical trial participants at the University of Kentucky Medical Center. Lacking **control groups** to validate these positive results in the open label studies, Amgen next sponsored a multicenter, Phase II, randomized, **double-blind**, **placebo controlled study** of GDNF's efficacy. Amgen selected eight sites to carry out the Phase II clinical trials. A protocol is a study plan on which a clinical trial is based. The plan is designed to safeguard the health of clinical trial participants as well as answer specific research questions. A protocol describes:

• Who may participate in a clinical trial
• Schedule of tests, procedures, and investigational drugs
• Length of the study

While in a clinical trial, clinical trial participants following a protocol are seen regularly by the clinical trial research investigators to monitor their health and to determine the safety and effectiveness of their experimental treatment.

Amgen's protocol, approved by the **institutional review boards** at the study centers agreeing to follow it, provided that after an initial study period, clinical trial participants could elect to continue treatment for up to an additional two years. Amgen and the research investigators signed a clinical trial agreement, but Amgen did not sign the consent forms signed by the clinical trial participants that explained the risks of the trial. The consent forms provided the option to continue receiving GDNF for two years after the trial and further reserved the right to end the trial if investigators found that its risks outweighed its benefits, or if Amgen decided to prematurely terminate the trial. Amgen hoped to see increases in the motor scores of clinical trial participants receiving GDNF 25% greater than those of the placebo, or control group.

Research investigators observed that motor scores increased by only 10% in the GDNF group and 5% in the placebo group. Seven of the 34 Phase II trial participants demonstrated dramatic improvement, but 4 of the 7 were receiving the placebo. Amgen responded by continuing the trial, but converted it into an open label study, providing all clinical trial participants with GDNF. After receiving the FDA's authorization, Amgen decided to terminate all clinical use of GDNF once several participants developed neutralizing antibodies, which could neutralize the drug's effect and could attack GDNF occurring naturally in the body, and primates receiving GDNF during a long-term toxicology study developed cerebella lesions. Cerebella lesions could affect cognitive functions in humans and lead to muscular weakness.

The clinical trial participants claimed Amgen stopped providing GDNF regardless of markedly improved physical, cognitive, and emotional states among all participants. They maintained Amgen terminated the trial for financial reasons. Despite the FDA's permission to permit compassionate use of GDNF after the termination, Amgen denied such use. The clinical trial participants responded by filing this lawsuit against Amgen.

Issue: Are pharmaceutical firms obligated to continue providing experimental drugs to clinical trial participants after the trials are terminated?

Holding and Decision: No, sponsoring pharmaceutical firms are not obligated to continue providing experimental drugs to clinical trial participants after termination of clinical trials.

Analysis: After filing the lawsuit, the clinical trial participants moved for a preliminary injunction, which would have required Amgen to provide GDNF to research investigators and to allow them to fill the participants' pumps with the drug. The court denied the motion, finding no contract bound Amgen to continue supplying GDNF to the clinical trial participants. The consent form signed by the clinical trial participants and the principal investigators did not directly bind Amgen because neither Amgen nor any agent of Amgen signed the consent forms.

Although the principal investigators promised to act in the clinical trial participants' best interests, and to continue administering GDNF if it proved safe and effective, no such promises were ever made by Amgen. While acts of the research investigators participating in the clinical trials might have bound Amgen, there was nothing that led the clinical trial participants to believe the principal investigators were agents of Amgen. The court found the clinical trial participants could probably not prove Amgen undertook a **fiduciary duty**, through the principal investigators, to treat their disease with the best drug available. No evidence suggested a fiduciary relationship was established. Neither Amgen nor the clinical trial participants understood that benefiting the participants would be the primary reason for Amgen's sponsorship of the clinical trials. While a special relationship between investigators and clinical trial participants normally creates duties enforceable in negligence actions, this duty was never characterized as fiduciary. Furthermore, Amgen designed its protocol to comply with FDA regulations. While the clinical sites and investigators conducted the GDNF trial, recruited the clinical trial participants, and obtained their consent, Amgen did not. Thus, there was no breach of fiduciary duty by Amgen.

The court suggested the clinical trial participants might be more likely to succeed in establishing a contract between them and either the institutional review boards or the research investigators involved in the clinical trial, noting that the consent forms constituted a contract that obligated the clinical sites to continue providing GDNF. The FDA's regulations charge institutional review boards, not the medical products industry, with ensuring the rights and welfare of clinical trial participants in clinical trials. The court also noted that institutional review boards could possibly avoid similar suits by clearly disclosing in consent forms the terms for terminating access to investigational drugs and experimental treatments.

The court next held that the desired injunction would not serve the public interest. While the clinical trial participants claimed research investigators, not Amgen, should decide whether to administer experimental drugs, and that denying the injunction would cause unnecessary suffering and deter others from participating in clinical trials, the court found that granting the injunction could deter Amgen from sponsoring future clinical trials. In addition, the claim that the investigators should be the sole arbiter of patient care wholly undermines the purpose and value of the FDA. The public has a strong interest in ensuring the FDA decides what drugs are safe and efficacious.

Rule of Law: Amgen was not required to continue supplying an experimental drug because:

- Amgen undertook no fiduciary duties with respect to the clinical trial participants
- The research investigators lacked agency status or apparent authority to bind Amgen and the clinical trial participants to a contract or quasi-contract
- There was no contract between Amgen and the clinical trial participants

References discussing this court decision: *E.g.* Janssen, 2014; Laakmann, 2015; Shah, 2013.

The court decision may leave injured clinical trial participants, who have had invasive procedures to participate in clinical trials (like the abdominal implants with internal catheters into the brain in the Amgen trials), with limited recourse for damages from the medical products industry when participating in clinical trials that are terminated. The trial protocol that clinical trial participants sign at the onset of their participation in any clinical trial defines participant rights to recovery, if any, with regard to termination of a trial in which they chose to participate. There is an obligation to clinical trial participants injured in a clinical trial, but causality of injuries is legally difficult to determine, and often impossible.

The necessary relationship between participation in a clinical trial (the claimed cause of an injury) and the claimed injury (the effect) must be the direct consequence of participation. Institutional review boards fearing liability may respond by more clearly explaining the risks and consequences of participating in clinical trials. The medical products industry will likely avoid fiduciary status and binding agreements with respect to clinical trial participants by:

- Designing sponsor protocols to comply with FDA regulations
- Forgoing control over clinical studies
- Outsourcing clinical trial design and administration

Clinical trial sponsors as a rule usually reimburse clinical trial participants for the necessary medical expenses incurred for the treatment of any injuries. The exceptions to this general rule are if the trial research investigator failed to follow the trial protocol, was negligent, or there was willful misconduct. Recovery generally survives termination of a clinical trial.

Monitoring Board Decisions

This section on the statistical analysis of clinical trials draws on the "Numbers Guy" column by Carl Biliak of the *Wall Street Journal* (Biliak, 2006). Pfizer rattled the health care industry when it abandoned a potential blockbuster cholesterol drug, Lipitor-plus, called torcetrapib, after some clinical trial participants died during clinical trials. While each clinical trial is different, for many trials, **monitoring boards** set numerical thresholds for bad outcomes before the trial begins. When the thresholds are crossed, the trials are stopped.

Often, the decisions seem hasty. In this instance, the Pfizer clinical trial involved over 15,000 clinical trial participants at high risk for cardiovascular disease. Some 82 clinical trial participants taking the new drug died, while 51 participants in a control group also died. The issue is why such a small difference was enough to justify a decision to walk away from a drug Pfizer had spent over $1 billion developing. A closer look at the numbers and an understanding of the roles statistics plays in clinical trials shows why this small difference had such an impact at Pfizer.

Participant pools are generally divided down the middle in clinical trials. In this clinical trial, half the control group took the cholesterol-lowering drug Lipitor and the other half took Lipitor-plus. On a straight percentage basis, about 0.7% of those in the Lipitor group died, while 1.1% of people taking Lipitor-plus died. This is a difference of only 0.4 of a percentage point.

Relative Risks

What is important is the **relative risk** facing the two groups. The relative risk is that clinical trial participants taking the Lipitor-plus were 60% more likely to die. This statistic suggests why Pfizer might have wanted to stop the trial. To understand why Pfizer chose to stop the testing when it did, statistical boundaries have to be examined. As in most clinical trials, the difference between stopping and proceeding comes down to just a few deaths.

Statistical Boundaries

When an imbalance in deaths crosses the **statistical boundary** set before the trial begins, clinical trials are automatically halted. This statistical boundary is not some arbitrary figure, but rather a single number that is calculated as part of the trial protocol. The magic number is called a ***p*-value**.

Generally, p measures the probability that a particular result, in this case, the difference in the rates of death between the two drug groups, can be a statistical anomaly. In simple terms, a p-value of 0.01 means that there is a 1 in 100 chance that the results are due to chance alone. Put another way: if a different 15,000 clinical trial participants had been selected to participate in the Pfizer clinical trial, would the outcome have been the same? The lower the p-value, the more certain it is that the deaths are not due to some anomaly, or chance alone.

Calculating p in this case is complex, and takes into account several factors, including the number of clinical trial participants in the clinical trial. The threshold for the Pfizer study was set at 0.01, meaning that once research investigators computed a p that fell below that number, they would know that the results were significant, and not something that would be likely to change by evaluating a different pool of clinical trial participants. Investigators calculated p monthly; given the deaths, any number below 0.01 would mean immediately halting the trial. Indeed, the study was halted when new data produced a p that crossed the threshold.

Statistical Significance

Thresholds are usually set at 0.05 for **statistical significance**. Using such a value, the Pfizer study could have been halted even sooner. However, thresholds are set higher when there are frequent measurements of p, to make sure that too much weight is not given to any single reading (Biliak, 2006). While one anecdote does not drive the decision to halt a clinical trial, subjective clinical expertise does determine these thresholds before the clinical trial starts.

If a new drug could cure cancer or another incurable disease when there is no other investigational treatment, more risk is tolerated before a trial is terminated. Where the new drug is a lifestyle drug or one where there are other safe drugs available, less risk is tolerated. In this instance, the purpose of the drug was to reduce the chance of death, and since Lipitor-plus increased the death rate, there was no reason to pursue it further. This Pfizer analysis shows how sensitive outcomes are to small numbers.

Just 2 fewer deaths among those taking Lipitor-plus, or 80 instead of 82 deaths, would have led to a p-value just above the threshold (Biliak, 2006). With Lipitor coming off patent and accounting for about one-quarter of Pfizer's sales, this decision to terminate the clinical trial for Lipitor-plus received little attention outside the health care industry. While it was the right clinical decision ethically speaking, industry critics ignored the merits of the decision! With a different drug approval strategy, Pfizer could have sought initial approval for a **narrow use** by adjusting inclusion and exclusion criteria in a clinical trial so that clinical trial participants included only those patients most likely to benefit from Lipitor-plus without adverse events. Once the narrow use was approved by the FDA and Pfizer had more definitive data on Lipitor-plus, Pfizer could have adjusted its inclusion and exclusion criteria before running a subsequent trial for general use.

Observational Studies

Can eating breakfast cereal determine the sex of a baby (Mathews et al., 2008)? A debate over this question shows why **observational studies**, which are not experiments with control groups, should be considered with a grain of salt. In this instance, researchers found breakfast cereals eaten before conception were the most significant food linked with baby boys. Researchers asked 740 pregnant women to record what they ate just before their pregnancy; 56% of women who consumed the most Calories before conception gave birth to boys, compared with 45% of those who consumed the least. Of 132 individual foods tracked, breakfast cereal was the most significantly linked with baby boys (*See generally* Beck, 2009).

Statisticians claim these findings were simply a **false association** that can occur by chance in a large set of data. In observational studies, it is impossible to prove that some other underlying factor is not causing what has been observed (Beck, 2009). Some myths have been observed for generations: meat and other high-protein foods, as well as foods rich in potassium, vitamins, and salt, produce baby boys; for other families, it is beans and peas.

A bewildering number of hormones and growth factors are involved in sex determinations beyond the traditional sex chromosomes (*See* Gilbert, 2013). Regardless, following health news reporting observational studies is like watching a ping-pong match: reports linking eggs or coffee or alcohol with various illnesses one week often get contradicted the next. Such findings come from observational studies that are not as precise as randomized, controlled trials. Many experts think they should not be published at all until they have been confirmed with repeat studies (Beck, 2009).

Nature of Nontrivial Chance

Behind the cereal debate is the divide between statisticians and epidemiologists about the nature of **nontrivial chance** in observational studies where research investigators track clinical trial participants' habits and look for associations with their health, but do not intervene at all. Statisticians say random associations are widespread in observational studies, which is why so many have contradictory findings. To prove the point, research investigators in Ontario studied the astrological signs of hospital patients and found that Sagittarians are susceptible to fractures and Pisces are prone to heart failure (Austin et al., 2006). The links met the traditional mathematical standard for statistical significance, but the association was completely random and disappeared when the study was repeated with a different sample (*See* Beck, 2009).

Validation

Some statisticians argue for **validation**, that a tougher standard of proof should be required when research investigators are fishing in large data sets. One method, a **Bonferroni adjustment**, requires multiplying the usual mathematical formula by the number of variables; if 100 foods are studied, the link must be 100 times as strong as usual to be considered significant. Otherwise, statisticians say only strict clinical trials with a control group and a test group and one variable can truly prove a cause-and-effect association.

Epidemiologists argue that a Bonferroni adjustment throws out many legitimate findings, and that it is irrelevant how many other factors are studied simultaneously. They also note that controlled clinical trials are costly, time consuming, and sometimes unethical. So does breakfast cereal affect a baby's gender? A good rule is to wait and see if an observation association appears when the study is repeated several times using different participants.

MANAGEMENT AND LAW ISSUES

2. What are the merits, if any, of seeking a narrow use for new medical products until a sponsor has definitive clinical data on a product and then adjusting the inclusion and exclusion criteria before running a clinical trial for general use?

International Clinical Trials

Most clinical late-stage human trials are now done at sites outside the United States, where results can be obtained cheaper and faster. Researchers at Duke University found that more than half the sites being used for trials sponsored by the largest U.S. pharmaceutical firms (Amgen, AstraZeneca, Bayer, Boehringer Ingelhelm, Bristol-Myers Squibb, Eli Lilly, GlaxoSmithKline, Johnson & Johnson, Merck, Novartis, Pfizer, and Roche) were in low- and middle-income countries (Nichols, 2016). This change has raised concerns about the treatment of clinical trial participants and the integrity of the research data produced in today's studies (Schuster, 2015).

Fifty Percent Cost Savings

Late-stage clinical trials in lower income countries cost less than half as much as they do in the United States and Europe because of lower salaries for physicians and clinical research personnel (Nichols, 2016). While clinical trial standards and the treatment of trial participants are the same as in higher income countries, patient recruitment is faster in countries such as India, China, and in Eastern Europe, where:

- Competition for patients is less intense.
- Clinical trial participants are far less likely to be taking other medicines, a factor that is important for trials requiring **drug-naive patients**; drug-naive patients are sought because it is easier to show that experimental treatments are better than placebos, as opposed to trying to show an improvement over currently available drugs.
- Patient populations are larger.
- Patients are more willing to enroll in studies because of lack of alternative treatment options.

(FDA, 2015a; Nichols, 2016).

Good Clinical Practices

The FDA has adopted standards used by many countries and organizations known as **good clinical practices** that:

- Encourage postmarket drug access to be discussed during protocol design
- Mandate that studies be reviewed by international ethics committees
- Permit placebo-controlled trials only under certain circumstances
- Require **informed consent** from all clinical trial participants

(FDA, 2016a; Raper, 2016).[LN1]

Good clinical practices are meant to assure quality clinical trials worldwide. The regulatory hurdles and administrative requirements in the United States are partly responsible for making going abroad so attractive (Schuster, 2015). In the United States, each site seeking to conduct a study must have its ethics board approve it. However, many present day studies are considered multisite, where one sponsor runs the same trial at different centers and pools the data. The U.S. review process means redundant effort and costs for multisite studies. If a trial sponsor, research investigator, or monitor fails to follow the standards on how clinical trials should be conducted, approval of the investigational drug will be delayed or may never obtain FDA approval. Documentation of adherence to the good clinical practices is part of every new drug application (*See* FDA, 2016b).

Inconsistent Oversight and Informed Consent

Research suggests oversight and adequate informed consent for clinical trial participants in clinical trials is inconsistent in resource-limited countries (OIG, 2007; Schuster, 2015). In one clinical trial, only half of the sites had been approved by ethics boards or health officials. In another clinical trial, less than one out five clinical trial participants was informed about the study before being enrolled (Nichols, 2016). While the medical products industry generally uses the same protocol regardless of where its clinical trials occur, international sites are not routinely monitored and not all research investigators have experience conducting clinical trials (Bizarro, 2015; OIG, 2007). Regulatory approval is not always sought in each nation in which clinical trials are conducted, and clinical trial participants do not always have access to the products or a suitable alternative after the trials end (Bizarro, 2015).

Informed Consent in General

At the beginning of the 20th century, Justice Benjamin N. Cardozo, former Associate Justice of the U.S. Supreme Court, stated that "Every human being of adult years and sound mind has a right to determine what shall be done with his own body." *Schloendorff v. Society of New York Hospital*, 105 N.E. 92 (Court of Appeals of New York 1914), *abrogated on other grounds, Bing v. Thunig*, 143 N.E.2d 3 (Court of Appeals of New York 1957). The **doctrine of informed consent** has evolved from simply telling clinical trial participants how they were going to be treated, to disclosing alternatives and risks, to letting participants make the decision. Informed consent protects individual autonomy and the participant's status as a human being. It also helps:

- Avoid charges of fraud or duress against clinical trial sites
- Encourage research investigators to carefully consider their clinical decisions
- Foster rational decision-making by the clinical trial participants
- Involve the public generally in medicine

(Wiley, 2016b).

Clinical trial participants have the right to consent based on all of the information available. A physician must disclose all **material risks** and major acceptable alternatives. A material risk is one that would cause someone to change their minds about participation in a study or procedure. A risk that is too small to be material need not be disclosed. In other words, the physician should disclose what a reasonable participant would need to know in order to make an informed decision. Medical custom dictates that a reasonable physician should disclose what would be reasonable under the circumstances (Laakmann, 2015). Disclosure may include:

- Diagnosis
- Nature and purpose of the proposed treatment
- Risks of the treatment
- Legitimate treatment alternatives, including doing nothing

(Koch, 2015).

Federal regulations govern clinical research protocols and define what information is required to obtain informed consent, including:

- Circumstances under which the study might be terminated
- Compensation
- Details of the research
- Foreseeable benefits to the subjects
- Major legitimate and acceptable alternative courses of treatment
- Material risks of the treatment
- No penalty to withdraw
- Voluntary participation

(45 C.F.R. Part 46).

Placebos

Placebos may be used in order to test the rate of success. Institutional review boards must continually review the research and determine that:

- Confidentiality is maintained
- Data collected is monitored
- Informed consent was obtained
- Risks are minimized and reasonable in relation to the anticipated benefits
- Selection of volunteer subjects is equitable

(Koch, 2015).

Institutional review boards have the authority to suspend or terminate approval of research and have an obligation to satisfy federal requirements in order to use federal funds for research. Informed consent is not a one-time procedure; it should be ongoing as the conditions of the study change and if new information comes to light, such as increased risks or decreased benefits.

Declaration of Helsinki

The **Declaration of Helsinki** sets forth the international ethical principles for medical research involving human subjects (*E.g.*, Raper, 2016). Research on human subjects who cannot give consent is only permissible if the condition that prevents consent from being given is what is being tested or researched (Bizarro, 2015). Other forms of consent may still be required, however, and placebos may not be used if there is a treatment available (Koch, 2015; Schuster, 2015).

Battery Claims

If there was no consent given at all, clinical trial participants may have a **battery claim**, which simply requires a showing that there was unconsented-to contact (Koch, 2015). Clinical trial participants need not prove the contact caused injury and expert testimony is not required. There are few defenses against a battery claim.

Informed Consent Claims

If there was insufficient consent, clinical trial participants may have an **informed consent claim**, which is pursued under a theory of negligence (Koch, 2015). It is very difficult to win a negligence-based informed consent case because it is almost impossible to show that clinical trial participants would have chosen otherwise if fully informed of all the details and risks (Janssen, 2014), or that the patient did not fully comprehend the information disclosed during the risk discussion. Consent forms are presumptively valid consent to the treatment, with the burden to rebut such consent being on the patient. The researcher is responsible to obtain informed consent for the record when the therapy is experimental. However, informed consent forms are not generally an important part in a patient's decision-making process because they are treated as a formality (Koch, 2015).

Newborn Screening Programs

The *Bearder v. State of Minnesota* decision highlights the issues of informed consent in the debates surrounding the genetic privacy of newborn blood samples. **Newborn screening programs** provide enormous public health benefits, and their repositories of collected blood samples provide an invaluable resource to research institutions studying **disease development** and **gene-environment interactions**. A blood sample is capable of being used for clinical trials for up to 20 years. Most states, however, do not inform parents of the retention and additional uses of newborn blood samples after testing is complete (Pike, 2016).

COURT DECISION
Genetic Privacy in Newborn Screening Programs

Bearder v. State of Minnesota
[Families with Newborn Children v. State]
806 N.W.2d 766 (Supreme Court of Minnesota 2011)

Facts: The newborn screening program requires health care providers to collect blood samples from newborn children by the fifth day after birth. A sample consists of a few blood drops collected on a specimen card, which is sent to the state within 24 hours of collection. Nine families with 25 children sued the state for violating the genetic privacy law by collecting, storing, using, and disseminating newborn blood samples without obtaining written informed parental consent.

As part of the newborn screening program, blood samples of these 25 children were collected and tested for inheritable and congenital disorders. Without early diagnosis, many of the disorders tested by the newborn screening program can lead to brain damage, mental retardation, or death. The controversy arose over the prohibition to collect, store, use, or disseminate genetic information without written informed consent. Unless a request is received to destroy a collected blood sample, portions of samples that remain after the screening tests are completed are retained indefinitely. Further, a state contract allows laboratories to use excess blood samples for clinical trials unrelated to the newborn screening program if the samples have been deidentified or if written parental consent has been received.

Issue: Should states enhance protections for the genetic privacy of newborn blood samples?

Holding and Decision: Yes, the genetic information contained in DNA brings newborn blood samples within the protection of the genetic privacy law.

Analysis: The court accepted the parents' contention that blood samples collected by the newborn screening program constitute genetic information protected by the genetic privacy law. The newborn screening laws provide an exception, however, to the genetic privacy law to the extent that the state is authorized to test newborn blood samples for inheritable and congenital disorders, record and report test results, maintain its registry of positive cases for the purpose of follow-up services, and store test results in strict compliance with federal law.

States are required to obtain parental consent for the collection, storage, use, and dissemination of newborn blood samples beyond the initial screening tests. It is not enough to give new parents a pamphlet informing them that any bit of leftover blood (without their newborn's personal information) may be used for public health research and clinical trials to improve screening and protect babies. The court clarified that the genetic privacy law restricts state authority to use genetic information obtained under the newborn screening program, even for public health research to improve newborn screening tests or to refine the newborn screening program. Without a federal standard governing the disposition of samples after screening is complete, however, states will pursue various approaches.

Rule of Law: Newborn blood samples are genetic information subject to the right to privacy.

References discussing this court decision: *E.g.*, Abrams & Garrett, 2015; Barraza & Burkhart, 2014; Leeb, 2014; McFerrin, 2013; Pike, 2016; Sawicki, 2016; Strand, 2013; Whelan, 2013.

There are three views on whether researchers should acquire informed parental consent for the use of newborn blood samples (Barraza & Burkhart, 2014). One view is that infants are human research subjects whose blood samples are collected for an identified research project; therefore, parental consent is required to permit subsequent use. Others maintain that additional clinical trials are an extension of the newborn screening program, and thus, the state health departments and laboratories do not need to inform parents or obtain their consent. Lastly, some distinguish newborn screening from clinical trials but recommend allowing laboratories to use collected samples unless parents choose to opt out. While some states have specific legislation authorizing the retention of newborn blood samples for clinical trials, others do not allow subsequent use without parental consent, and many contain ambiguous or conflicting laws governing screening, clinical trials, and genetic privacy (McFerrin, 2013).

Advances in technology have led to parental concern regarding the privacy of their children's genetic information. While most studies performed by outside laboratories use deidentified blood samples, technological advances have eroded the anonymity of deidentified genetic data. For instance, the National Human Genome Research Institute removed free access to pooled genomics data that it had posted on the Internet after researchers at Arizona's Translational Genomics Research Institute demonstrated how to detect individual genetic profiles in pools of DNA donors (Abrams & Garrett, 2015).

Emergency Research Rule

Something few Americans realize is that they may receive experimental drugs, devices, or surgical and procedural interventions in emergency situations. Clinical trial research may be conducted on unconscious people or shock patients experiencing life-threatening conditions, such as cardiac arrest, stroke, or traumatic injury, without obtaining informed consent. In 2006, draft guidelines on exceptions from informed consent requirements were issued (FDA,

2011). Since then, there has been a substantial increase in the use of the **Emergency Research Rule**, with most of this increase related to studies supported by the National Institutes of Health. *See* Informed Consent and Waiver of Informed Consent Requirements in Certain Emergency Research, 21 C.F.R. § 50.24.

Currently, NIH is funding emergency research studies, which consider consent waived after institutional review boards sign off on each clinical trial, if:

- A physician and an institutional review board agree that a patient's life is in danger
- Proven treatments will not work
- Clinical research is necessary to determine what intervention is best
- Research could not be done otherwise

The procedural interventions must also be related to the emergency. Emergency situations are predefined in clinical trial protocols approved by institutional review boards. For instance, unconscious trauma patients may be transfused with experimental artificial blood products; they will not, however, receive new artificial breast implants. Patients will not be transfused with experimental artificial blood products in nonemergency situations without their informed consent. The studies seek to enroll non-consenting patients with life-threatening conditions, with an unspecified additional number of patients to be enrolled in studies currently in planning stages.

With the increasing frequency of research studies entailing waived informed consent, it is important to understand this aspect of clinical trial research. It is widely argued that the benefits and burdens of clinical trial research must be fairly distributed (FDA, 1979). One criticism is that NIH emergency research is occurring primarily in poor urban areas of the United States (Raper, 2016). One such instance is the patient study involving over 700 trauma patients by Northfield Laboratories of Chicago (Burton, 2006a; Eckstein, 2011). Thirty-one inner city hospitals in 18 states participated in a clinical trial for the blood substitute PolyHeme. Half the patients got PolyHeme both in the ambulance and the hospital, while the other half got saline solution in the ambulance followed by donor blood in the hospital. The study was conducted under the Emergency Research Rule based on the belief that a blood substitute could potentially be a lifesaving therapy, especially for the military.[LN2] While participating hospitals received $10,000 for each patient who participated in the clinical trial, most patients never learned of their participation (Burton, 2006g). A concern raised by many ethicists with this clinical trial protocol was that the Emergency Research Rule requires that standard treatment (in this case, the use of donor blood) be unproven or unsatisfactory; giving blood to trauma patients was neither unproven nor unsatisfactory (Eckstein, 2011; *See generally* Burton, 2006a-g).

Informed Consent and Participation of Children in Human Subject Research

Children in general are considered **vulnerable research subjects** (HHS, 2008; Shah, 2013). Minors cannot provide informed consent because they are considered incapacitated under the law, meaning that they lack the ability to acquire the knowledge necessary to make a truly informed, voluntary decision. Federal regulations establish specific protections for clinical trials involving children and limit the level of risk permitted. Institutional review boards can approve pediatric research only in three risk-benefit categories:

- Greater than minimal risk but with a prospect of direct benefit
- Minimal risk
- Minor increase over minimal risk without a prospect of direct benefit

(*See* 45 C.F.R. §§ 46.404-407).

Research that exceeds these risk levels can in some cases be approved by special review (Shah, 2013).

MANAGEMENT AND LAW ISSUES

3. What standards should regulate clinical trials conducted on clinical trial participants experiencing life-threatening conditions without informed consent?

Approximately half of the children in the United States known to have HIV/AIDS are in foster care. New York City's Administration for Children's Services made the controversial decision to enroll foster children in HIV/AIDS clinical trials sponsored by NIH, beginning in the 1990s. At least seven states (Illinois, Louisiana, Maryland, New York, North Carolina, Colorado, and Texas) followed New York City's lead and are involved in almost 50 different NIH clinical trials. North Carolina does not have policies of any kind regarding the enrollment of foster children in clinical trials. Thirteen additional states lack policies: Alaska, Georgia, Kansas, Minnesota, Missouri, Nevada, New Hampshire, New Jersey, North Dakota, Pennsylvania, South Carolina, West Virginia, and Wisconsin (HHS, 2008). The foster children range from infants to teenagers. The NIH trials were most widespread through the 1990s as foster care agencies sought treatments that were not yet available in the marketplace for HIV-infected children.

While the practice ensures that foster children, mostly poor, receive care from researchers at government expense, it also exposes a vulnerable population to the risks of experimental drugs that are known to have serious side effects in adults and for which the safety for children is completely unknown (FDA, 2015b). For foster children, access to health care without sufficient protections is, perhaps, worse than no access at all (Buske, 2007; Camp, 2011). For instance, the Vera Institute, an independent research organization commissioned by New York City to independently monitor this situation, finds continuing violations of clinical trial review, enrollment policies, and federal regulations for human subjects for foster children in the City:

- One in five foster children is enrolled in clinical trials without informed consent.
- Foster children are enrolled in unapproved clinical trials.
- Medical records are unavailable or incomplete for almost one-third of the children.
- Foster children are being enrolled in Phase I clinical trials.
- Foster children receive unapproved experimental drugs for HIV/AIDS.

(Camp, 2011; Ross & Lifflander, 2009; Shah, 2013).

In addition, child advocates express concerns that not all foster children receiving HIV/AIDS drugs and vaccines in clinical trials have been properly diagnosed with the disease (Ross & Lifflander, 2009).

While foster children are covered by the same regulations as other children and while foster children should arguably have the same access to clinical trials as other children, current federal regulations are not always strictly enforced to adequately protect foster children in trials (AAP, 2005). Foster children generally have no real advocate to protect their interests and assure that regulations designed to protect children are enforced for them, especially when the government agencies charged with protecting the interests of foster children are seeking to enroll them in trials for free drugs or compensation is paid to the agency responsible for their care as opposed to the child research subjects.

Child advocates should be appointed for all foster children participating in pediatric clinical trials, and children should be afforded additional protections if they are wards of the state. For instance, additional regulations could require that significant compensation for participation in clinical trials be held in trust for foster children, a mandate that could be easily implemented through the regulations of individual child protection agencies. Furthermore, oversight of pediatric clinical trials is particularly weak when government agencies seek enrollment of foster children; few institutional review boards have child welfare experts reviewing pediatric trials (HHS, 2008; Shah, 2013).

Transparency and Full Disclosure in Clinical Testing

A major shortcoming of the **full disclosure requirement**, also referred to as the § 801 requirement, is that the results of older clinical trials of drugs that were approved before the disclosure requirement became law in 2007 do not need to be made public, and such drugs constitute the vast majority of the drugs currently used by patients (*See* Food and Drug Administration Amendments Act of 2007, 21 U.S.C.A. §§ 321 *et seq.*). Likewise, there is no requirement for posting the results of trials of drugs that were never approved (Upadhye, 2014; *See also* Choi, 2015).

Financial Conflicts of Interest

It is tempting to think of the lack of transparency and full disclosure in clinical testing in terms of unethical people doing unethical things. The conflicts of interest problem is, however, more complex than that. The increase in financial conflicts of interest is likely a result of the change in federal policy that was designed to expedite the progress of research results from the laboratory to patients. This occurred primarily as a result of the Bayh-Dole Act, which transferred the property rights in the products of federally funded research to the research investigators and their institutions, thereby relieving the federal government of the task of patenting results (Sandrik, 2016). Confidence in clinical trials has been undermined by the conflicts of interest on the part of the research investigators and the medical products industry. The concern mainly centers on financial conflicts of interest, particularly regarding the relationship between academic and industry interests (Wiley, 2016b).

While research organizations are in the best position resource-wise to assess and manage conflicts of interest, they should also make use of independent, external methods of evaluating potential conflicts. Perhaps more important than instituting or reforming legal mechanisms of governing conflicts of interest is that the health care industry cultivate an ethical research culture (Morain et al., 2015). The Institute of Medicine suggests that institutional review boards review the ethics of clinical trials. While financial interests should not affect the scientific foundation of clinical trials, the potential for conflicts is expanding, both in terms of frequency and complexity, as the convergence of many health care sectors is rapidly changing the laws governing provider competition and regulation (Vertinsky, 2015).

A process for analyzing such potential conflicts of interest is critical to public confidence in the health care industry. For instance, during the 1970s, 80% of the public had confidence in the FDA; in 2000, 61% reported confidence in the FDA; by 2015, the percentage of the public having confidence in the FDA dropped to 36% (FDA, 2015b). So, the issue is how the health care industry and the FDA, as well as other regulatory agencies, should help restore public confidence in the U.S. health care system.

Commitment to the Life Sciences

First and foremost, the health care industry and the government must renew their commitment to science. The ability to reach this goal depends heavily upon strict adherence to scientifically motivated decision-making (Lemmens & Telfer, 2012). Scientists should be insulated from financial and political pressures when making decisions about which medical treatments and products warrant approval to enter the marketplace and about which measures are appropriate when addressing unforeseen risks to patients (Rodwin, 2012). In short, financial and political decisions by the industry and government agencies should be separate from science.

LAW FACT

Clinical Trials in Developing Nations

Is the medical products industry liable in U.S. courts for violation of good clinical practice standards in international clinical trials?

Yes, the prohibition in customary international law against nonconsensual human medical experimentation can be enforced through the Alien Tort Statute.[LN3]

— *Abdullahi v. Pfizer, Inc.*, 562 F.3d 163 (U.S. Court of Appeals for the 2nd Circuit 2009), *cert. denied*, 561 U.S. 1041 (U.S. Supreme Court 2010).

See, e.g., Coyle, 2015; Grimmelmann, 2015; Kenney, 2015; Meyer, 2014; Nersessian, 2015 (discussing this decision).

CHAPTER SUMMARY

- The pharmaceutical and biopharmaceutical industries spend billions of dollars on clinical trials each year.
- Research and development of new medical products is complex, time-consuming, expensive, and risky.
- The stages of research and development include drug discovery, preclinical testing, clinical trials, FDA approval, and post-marketing surveillance; the clinical trial stage alone involves three phases.

- Even the most thorough clinical trial cannot detect all negatives, such as rare risks, risks that take an exceedingly long time to manifest, risks that only affect vulnerable subpopulations, and risks for patients who take other drugs and supplements.
- In contrast to the requirements for new medical products to obtain FDA approval, the standards for generic versions are much lower, reflecting Congress' decision to prioritize financial advantages over therapeutic advantages.
- There is ongoing debate over how much influence patients' preferences should have in drug approval; some patients, especially the terminally ill, are willing to accept a much higher risk than others.
- Clinical trials may be halted if a new drug shows such promise that it would be unethical to delay its release or if the new drug presents great risks not outweighing the potential benefits.
- Before a clinical trial begins, a numerical threshold is determined for bad outcomes that, if crossed, will halt the trial; although the threshold may seem arbitrarily low in some cases, the statistic it represents is significant because it represents whether the bad outcomes are simply an anomaly due to chance or whether they represent a real risk to clinical trial participants.
- Clinical trial research may be conducted without obtaining informed consent on people who are experiencing a life-threatening condition.
- An ongoing controversy in clinical trials involves research conducted outside the boundaries of the United States; the integrity of the research is called into question because it is more difficult to regulate, good clinical practices may not be observed, and informed consent may not be obtained.
- Observational studies and results that have not been validated may not be as reliable as other studies.
- Many argue that the results of all clinical trials, including older clinical trials and unsuccessful clinical trials, should be fully disclosed.
- Informed consent allows clinical trial participants to protect their personal autonomy and make an informed decision as to whether or not to participate in the research based upon its predicted nature, purpose, risks, benefits, and alternatives, including doing nothing; obtaining informed consent from children, and particularly foster children, is replete with problems.
- Conflicts of interest, especially financial, call the integrity of clinical trials into question and do not necessarily result from intentional unethical conduct.

LAW NOTES

1. ICH is the **International Conference on Harmonisation**, a joint initiative involving both regulators and research-based industry representatives of the European Union, Japan, and the United States. They engage in scientific and technical discussions of the clinical testing procedures required to assess and ensure the safety, quality, and efficacy of drugs. The European Free Trade Association is represented by Swissmedic (Swiss Agency for Therapeutic Products), Health Canada, and the World Health Organization.

2. The military dictatorship that was in power during the Trovan clinical trial at the start of this chapter was subsequently replaced by a democratically elected civilian government. The *Washington Post* ran an exposé about Pfizer's clinical trial that prompted Abdullahi's lawsuit and a Nigerian government investigation into what happened to children at the clinic in Kano, Nigeria (Stephens, 2006). The government report concluded that Pfizer conducted an illegal drug trial that exploited those who did not clearly know that their children were participating in a clinical trial and that the government never gave authorization for this trial. However, for unidentified reasons, the Nigerian government suppressed this report for over five years. One of the authors of the report allegedly received death threats in connection with producing the document. It was only through an anonymous leak to the *Washington Post* that this report became public after five years. As a result of the leaked report, Nigeria filed criminal charges against Pfizer and sought almost $7 billion in a separate civil lawsuit for the children injured in Pfizer's clinical trial (Khan, 2008). Pfizer eventually settled the multibillion-dollar damages case with 200 claimed victims in Kano, Nigeria (*See* Bray & Wang, 2009).

REFERENCES

AAP (American Academy of Pediatrics) Task Force on Health Care for Children in Foster Care. (2005). *Fostering health: Health care for children and adolescents in foster care.* New York, NY: AAP.

Abrams, K., & Garrett, B. L. (2015). DNA and distrust. *Notre Dame Law Review, 91*, 757–812.

Austin, P. C., et al. (2006). Testing multiple statistical hypotheses resulted in spurious associations: A study of astrological signs and health. *Journal of Clinical Epidemiology, 59,* 964–969.

Avery, M., & Nguyen, M. (2013). The roadblock for generic drugs: Declaratory judgment jurisdiction for later generic challengers. North Carolina Journal of Law and Technology, 15, 1–47.

Barraza, L., & Burkhart, L. (2014). The expansion of newborn screening: Implications for public health and policy. *Annals of Health Law, 23,* 183–199.

Beck, M. (2009, January 27). Does bran make the man? What statistics really tell us. *Wall Street Journal,* p. D1.

Biliak, C. (2006, December 6). Relatively small numbers of deaths have big impact in Pfizer drug trial. *Wall Street Journal,* p. B1.

Bizarro, B. (2015). "Vigilant doorkeeping": Post-*Kiobel* corporate accountability under the alien tort statute for negligence and violations of the international prohibition on nonconsensual medical experimentation. *Boston University International Law Journal, 33,* 493–526.

Blessy, M., et al. (2014). Development of forced degradation and stability indicating studies of drugs—A review. *Journal of Pharmaceutical Analysis, 4*(3), 159–165.

Bray, C., & Wang, S. S. (2009, January 30). Court revives cases against Pfizer. *Wall Street Journal,* p. B1.

Burton, T. M. (2006a, July 11). FDA to weigh test of blood substitute out of public view. *Wall Street Journal,* p. D3.

___. (2006b, July 6). FDA to weigh using fake blood in trauma trial. *Wall Street Journal,* p. B1.

___. (2006c, March 20). Use of substitution for blood draws ethics challenge. *Wall Street Journal,* p. A2.

___. (2006d, March 17). SEC begins probe of Northfield Labs over blood studies. *Wall Street Journal,* p. A2.

___. (2006e, March 14). Grassley accuses FDA of laxity in study of blood substitute. *Wall Street Journal,* p. D5.

___. (2006f, March 10). Blood-substitute study is criticized by U.S. agency. *Wall Street Journal,* p. A3.

___. (2006g, February 22). Red flags: Amid alarm bells, a blood substitute keeps pumping: Ten in trial have heart attacks, but data aren't published; FDA allows a new study; Doctors' pleas are ignored. *Wall Street Journal,* p. A1.

Buske, S. L. (2007). Foster children and pediatric clinical trials: Access without protection is not enough. *Virginia Journal of Social Policy & Law, 14,* 253–307.

Camp, A. R. (2011). A mistreated epidemic: State and federal failure to adequately regulate psychotropic medications prescribed to children in foster care. *Temple Law Review, 83,* 369–404.

Choi, R. (2015). Increasing transparency of clinical trial data in the United States and the European Union. *Washington University Global Studies Law Review, 14,* 521–548.

Coyle, J. F. (2015). The case for writing international law into the U.S. Code. *Boston College Law Review, 56,* 433–492.

Croom, B. (2014). Buyer beware: *Mutual Pharmaceutical Co. v. Bartlett* continues to alter the true costs and risks of generic drugs. *North Carolina Journal of Law and Technology, 15,* 1–31.

DiMasi, J. A., et al. (2016). Innovation in the pharmaceutical industry: New estimates of R&D costs. *Journal of Health Economics, 47,* 20–33.

___. (2014). *Briefing: Cost of developing a new drug: Innovation in the pharmaceutical industry: New estimates of research and development costs.* Boston, MA: Tufts Center for the Study of Drug Development.

Dresser, R. (2015). Science challenges for law and policy: The "right to try" investigational drugs: Science and stories in the access debate. *Texas Law Review, 93,* 1631–1657.

Eban, K. (2013, January 10). Are generics really the same as branded drugs? *Fortune,* pp. 3–7.

FDA (U.S. Food and Drug Administration). (2016a). *Clinical trials and human subject protection.* Bethesda, MD: FDA.

___. (2016b). *Selected FDA Good Clinical Practice/Clinical Trial Guidance Documents.*

___. (2016c). *FDA seeks $5.1 billion total for FY 2017, including funds to implement food safety law, improve medical product safety and quality.*

___. (2015a). *Acceptance of medical device clinical data from studies conducted outside the United States: Draft guidance for industry and Food and Drug administration staff.*

___. (2015b). *Report of the Science Looking Forward Subcommittee for the FDA Science Board: Mission possible: How FDA can move at the speed of science.*

___. (2014). *New drug application (NDA).*

___. (2013). *Guidance for industry: Bioequivalence studies with pharmacokinetic endpoints for drugs submitted under an Abbreviated New Drug Application (ANDA).*

___. (2011). *Guidance for institutional review boards, clinical research investigators, and sponsors: Exception from informed consent requirements for emergency research.*

___. (1979). *Belmont report: Ethical principles and guidelines for the protection of human subjects of research.*

Feldman, R., & Frondorf, E. (2016). Drug wars: A new generation of generic pharmaceutical delay. *Harvard Journal on Legislation, 53,* 499–561.

Fields, G. (2013). Parallel problems: Applying institutional corruption analysis of Congress to big pharma. *Journal of Law, Medicine and Ethics, 41,* 556–560.

Fultz, S. L. (2013). If it quacks like a duck: Reviewing health care providers' speech restrictions under the first prong of *Central Hudson. American University Law Review, 65,* 567–606.

Gilbert, S. F. (2013). *Developmental biology* (10th ed.). Sunderland, MA: Sinauer Associates Inc.

Grimmelmann, J. (2015). The law and ethics of experiments on social media users. *Colorado Technology Law Journal, 13,* 219–274.

HHS (U.S. Department of Health and Human Services). (2008). *Survey of states on the participation of foster children in clinical drug trials.* Washington, DC: HHS.

Janssen, W. M. (2014). A "duty" to continue selling medicines, *American Journal of Law and Medicine, 40,* 330–392.

Kenney, C. C. (2015). Measuring transnational human rights. *Fordham Law Review, 84,* 1053–1115.

Khan, F. (2008). The human factor: Globalizing ethical standards in drug trials through market exclusion. *DePaul Law Review, 57,* 877–915.

Koch, V. G. (2015). A private right of action for informed consent in research. *Seton Hall Law Review, 45,* 173–213.

Kumar, S. (2013). Life, liberty, and the pursuit of genetic information. *Alabama Law Review, 54,* 625–681.

Laakmann, A. B. (2015). When should physicians be liable for innovation? *Cardozo Law Review, 36,* 913–968.

Lamkin, M. (2016). Regulating identity: Medical regulation as social control. *Brigham Young University Law Review, 16,* 501–573.

Leeb, M. D. (2014). Newborn screening programs and privacy: Shifting responsibility from the parent to the laboratory. *University of Baltimore Law Review, 44,* 105–125.

Lemmens, T., & Telfer, C. (2012). Access to information and the right to health: The human rights case for clinical trials transparency. *American Journal of Law and Medicine, 38*, 63–112.

Mathews, F., et al. (2008). You are what your mother eats: Evidence for maternal preconception diet influencing fetal sex in humans. *Proceedings of the Royal Society of Biological Sciences, 275*(1643), 1661–1668.

McFerrin, C. (2013). DNA, genetic material, and a look at property rights: Why you may be your brother's keeper. *Texas Wesleyan Law Review, 19*, 967–998.

Meyer, J. A. (2014). Extraterritorial common law: Does the common law apply abroad? *Georgetown Law Journal, 102*, 301–350.

Morain, S. R., et al. (2015). Institutional oversight of faculty-industry consulting relationships in U.S. medical schools: Adelphi study. *Journal of Law, Medicine and Ethics, 43*, 383–413.

Moses, III, H., et al. (2015). The anatomy of medical research: U.S. and international comparisons. *Journal of the American Medical Association, 313*(2), 174–189.

Murphy, B. (2016). Getting high on profits: An analysis of current state and federal proposals to rein in soaring drug prices. *Journal of Health and Biomedical Law, 12*, 37–88.

Nersessian, D. (2015). Business lawyers as worldwide moral gatekeepers? Legal ethics and human rights in global corporate practice. *Georgetown Journal of Legal Ethics, 28*, 1135–1187.

NIH (National Institutes of Health). (2007). *Understanding clinical trials.* Washington, DC: NIH.

NLM (National Library of Medicine). (2008). *Clinical research FAQ.* Washington, DC: NLM.

OIG (Office of Inspector General). (2007). *The Food and Drug Administration's oversight of clinical trials.* Washington, DC: U.S. Department of Health and Human Services, OIG.

Orentlicher, D. (2014). A restatement of health care law. *Brooklyn Law Review, 79*, 435–456.

PhRMA (Pharmaceutical Research and Manufacturing Association). (2016). *Biopharmaceuticals in perspective.* Washington, DC: PhRMA.

Pike, E. R. (2016). Securing sequences: Ensuring adequate protections for genetic samples in the age of big data. *Cardozo Law Review, 37*, 1977–2036.

Pivarnik, G. (2014). Cells as drugs?: Regulating the future of medicine. *American Journal of Law and Medicine, 40*, 298–321.

Radis. J. T. (2015). The Lanham Act's wonderful complement to the FDCA: *POM Wonderful v. Coca-Cola* enhances protection against misleading labeling through integrated regulation. *Loyola University Chicago Law Journal, 47*, 369–434.

Raper, S. (2016). An artless tale: Challenges faced in clinical research. *Food and Drug Law Journal, 71*, 59–104.

Rodwin, M. A. (2012). Independent clinical trials to test drugs: The neglected reform. *Saint Louis University Journal of Health Law and Policy, 6*, 113–165.

Ross, T., & Lifflander, A. (2009). *The experiences of New York City foster children in HIV/AIDS clinical trials.* New York, NY: Vera Institute.

Sandrik, K. E. (2016). Innovative contracting for better material transfers. *Texas Intellectual Property Law Journal, 24*, 49–101.

Sawicki, N. N. (2016). Modernizing informed consent: expanding the boundaries of materiality. *University of Illinois Law Review, 2016*(1), 821–871.

Schuster, B. M. (2015). For the love of drugs: Using pharmaceutical clinical trials abroad to profit off the poor. *Seattle Journal for Social Justice, 13*, 105–1067.

Shah, S. (2013). Does research with children violate the best interests standard? An empirical and conceptual analysis. *Northwestern Journal of Law and Social Policy, 8*(2), 121–173.

Smith, K. A. (2016). "Transplanting" organ donors with printers: The legal and ethical implications of manufacturing organs. *Akron Law Review, 49*, 739–769.

Stephens, J. (2006, May 7). Panel faults Pfizer in '96 clinical trials in Nigeria. *Washington Post*, p. A1.

Stoddart, A. (2012). Missing after *Mensing*: A remedy for generic drug consumers. *Boston College Law Review, 53*, 1967–2001.

Strand, N. (2013). A constitutional right to know: Are research participants entitled to results of genetic tests? *University of Pennsylvania Journal of Constitutional Law, 15*, 1299–1322.

Tufts Center for the Study of Drug Development. (2014). *Innovation in the pharmaceutical industry: New estimates of R&D costs. In Briefing: Cost of Developing a New Drug.* Boston, MA: Tufts University.

Upadhye, S. (2014). The 30-year anniversary of the Hatch-Waxman Act: Resolved and unresolved gaps and court-driven policy gap filling. *William Mitchell Law Review, 40*, 1307–1367.

Vertinsky, L. S. (2015). Patents, partnerships, and the pre-competitive collaboration myth in pharmaceutical innovation. *UC Davis Law Review, 48*, 1509–1580.

Wharton (Wharton School at the University of Pennsylvania). (2007). A prescription for healthier medical care decisions: Begin by defining health risk. *Knowledge@Wharton.*

____. (2006). Novartis' Alex Gorsky: Ensuring that patients get access to the medicines they need.

Whelan. A. M. (2013). That's my baby: Why the state's interest in promoting public health does not justify residual newborn blood spot research without parental consent. *Minnesota Law Review, 98*, 419–453.

Wiley, L. F. (2016a). Deregulation, distrust, and democracy: State and local action to ensure equitable access to healthy, sustainably produced food. *American Journal of Law and Medicine, 41*, 284–314.

____. (2016b). From patient rights to health justice: Securing the public's interest in affordable, high-quality health care. *Cardozo Law Review, 37*, 833–888.

____. (2014). Sugary drinks, happy meals, social norms, and the law: The normative impact of product configuration bans. *Connecticut Law Review, 46*, 1877–1888.

WMA (World Medical Association). (2006). *Declaration of Helsinki: Ethical principles for medical research involving human subjects, as amended by the 48th World Medical Assembly, Somerset West, Republic of South Africa.* Ferney-Voltaire, France: WMA.

Wolf, S. M. (2005). *Worst pills, best pills: A consumer's guide to avoiding drug-induced death or illness.* New York, NY: Simon and Schuster, Pocket Books.

Health Information and Telehealth Technologies

"Privacy is not simply an absence of information about us in the minds of others; rather it is the control we have over information about ourselves."

— **Charles Fried**, Harvard Law School professor and former U.S. Solicitor General

IN BRIEF

Health information technology is reshaping how hospitals, physicians, patients, and the health insurance industry interact with one another. E-health, electronic health records, information security, and privacy issues in this product sector are evolving and complex. Telehealth technology and telemedicine are diverse and rapidly changing, and are altering the practice of medicine.

LEARNING OBJECTIVES

Upon completion of this chapter readers should be able to:

1. Describe issues surrounding electronic health record systems.
2. Outline solutions for online control and management of medical information.
3. Discuss methods of remote monitoring and management of patients.
4. Explain how electronic medicine works in general.
5. List issues with the emergence of health space on the Internet.
6. Talk about potentials for information privacy.
7. Consider why identifiable prescription data cannot be restricted.
8. Understand that whoever gathers an individual's health information owns it.
9. Discuss the dilemmas of mature adolescents in the medical system.
10. Distinguish between websites legally covered by the Health Insurance Portability and Accountability Act (HIPAA) and those not covered.

KEY TERMS

Accountable care organizations
Anonymizer technology
Assumption of risk
At-risk populations
At-risk variables
Biosensors
Clickstream data
Clinical decision support systems

Computerized physician order entry
Content-based burdens on speech
Cyberspace
Data brokers
Data-mining laws
Defamation
Detailing
Drug contraindications

E-health
Electronic cookies
Electronic health records
Harris Interactive
Health care proxy
Health information technology
Health Insurance Portability
   Accountability Act of 1996

FACT OR FICTION

Internet Prescribing

Can online questionnaires be substituted for face-to-face examinations or one-on-one conversations before approved drugs can be prescribed?

Thomas Hanny, a licensed physician for 30 years, began working for a health information company that sold prescription drugs over the Internet after his retirement as a surgeon. Hanny approved prescription requests based on a questionnaire completed by customers but never reviewed the customers' health records. The Missouri Board of Medicine contacted Hanny and informed him that his actions constituted the illegal practice of medicine. When Hanny ignored this communication, the United States charged him with conspiring to distribute controlled substances outside the course of normal medical practice.

— *See* Law Fact at the end of this chapter for the answer.

Principles and Applications

Health care is one of the nation's most formidable economic challenges with the world's most unaffordable fixed-cost infrastructure (Blatt, 2012). Yet the U.S. health care system may not need, and probably cannot afford, physicians as the front line of defense anymore. So physicians take note: "There are not 10 million nerdy-looking Ph.D.s reading search requests at Google. Instead search expertise is embedded in Google's algorithms on servers in cool dry places; this is scale, so beware" (Khan, 2016 quoting Kessler, 2006, p. 110).

The geeks are at the gate of the U.S. health care industry. The geeks know that the United States needs a **Moore's law** for health care: double the number of patients seen and cut the costs in half (Wharton, 2006). To achieve this takes a new workflow approach that merges nearly all of the trends in **health information technology** (HIT) and **telehealth technology** to create coordinated communications and control matrices that connect patients, physicians, and health care systems (Levins, 2012).[LN1]

Digital Revolution

The HIT industry envisions a future with **integrated networks sharing records** that are completely electronic and accessible from anywhere. The goal is one of improving health care and reducing human errors and omissions. Over the next decade, of all the medical technologies that affect the health care experience, **telehealth technology** holds one of the greatest potentials for positive change:

- Greater price and quality transparency
- Improved access

- Less duplicative and more effective health care through better management of chronic diseases, shared health professional staffing, reduced travel times for patients, and fewer or shorter hospital stays
- More rapid and accurate diagnoses, particularly in mental health and intensive care
- Reduction in the rise of health care costs

(ATA, 2016).

It is estimated that a nationwide integrated health care network would save the U.S. health care system $78 billion a year (Walker, 2005; *See* Porter & Lee, 2013).

Electronic Health Records Systems

The most important application of HIT is arguably the **electronic health record**. Since the 1970s, paper medical charts have been replicated in electronic form. Digitizing medical charts and creating mechanisms for making them usable at different points in the patient care process, from physician offices to diagnostic laboratories to operating suites to hospital rooms, has been a challenging technical aspiration for several decades. Yet today only 14% of the nation's physicians have interoperable electronic health records that share data beyond their own organization, a firewall delay that:

- Impedes diagnosis
- Jeopardizes treatment
- Puts patients' lives on the line from medical error

(Lieber, 2015).

Electronic Health Records Interoperability

Congress passed legislation in 2015 mandating electronic health records' **interoperability** by 2020, a decade after making billions of dollars in funding available to link electronic health records and make all patient histories, laboratory results, and prescriptions interoperable in hospitals and physician offices (Lieber, 2016). Interoperability is to be established nationwide so that systems can exchange and use electronic health information without special effort on the part of the user (ONC, 2014). Medical errors will not disappear with interoperability, but this reform could help ensure physicians do no harm. While some electronic health records progress has been made, medical errors still kill between 210,000 and 440,000 Americans each year, an occurrence that is much too common (Leapfrog Group, 2013).

Defining Electronic Health Record Transactions

Today, there are two forms of electronic health records transactions:

- Web-based **personal health records** that are individually controlled and potentially portable
- **Institutional health records** that are used by hospitals to share lab results, X-rays, MRIs, CAT scans, medication history, and other information internally

In this chapter, the term personal health records include continuity of care records. **Computerized physician order entry** facilitates real-time information sharing by embedding medication orders and diagnostic procedures in electronic health records, enabling physicians to respond directly to changes in a patient's status. This clinical process is further enhanced by **clinical decision support systems** that audit medical orders and flag decisions that might place patients at risk for adverse events.

Potential Privacy Costs

These technologies come with a potential cost in **privacy** and their own set of legal risks (Nambisan et al., 2013). This chapter will review the health law issues surrounding the adoption and use of these important health information technologies with a focus on privacy of information. Privacy lacks a uniform definition and is not defined in the U.S. Constitution. Indeed, some scholars debate whether the Constitution actually confers a right to privacy, as that right is not explicitly set forth within its language. In this chapter, privacy is defined as the management and control of health information about identifiable patients and Internet users and its communication to third parties.

Nationwide Interoperable Health Care Network

One principle of law is clear: privacy rights should be addressed before **intelligent record patterns** are established and built into any technology infrastructure (Habib, 2010). Computerized physician order entry and clinical decision support systems will inevitably change both the clinical process and the division of administrative responsibilities within health care systems (Swisher, 2014). With these changes, distinct HIT systems across the nation's clinical and administrative departments are combining into a single patient care process such as **accountable care organizations** and **medical homes**. As disjointed health information domains are integrated, the patient care process itself is changing its inherent fragmentation, from a clinical system with tremendous variation in responses to diagnostic uncertainty, to a system with improved clinical performance and efficiency. The inconsistency in treatment, from patient to patient and hospital to hospital, is disappearing as HIT grows in sophistication and better assists physicians in remaining current with the evolving state of medical knowledge as well as new medical product uses (Greaney, 2014).

Whether the United States has the proper legal framework in place to proceed with building the nation's clinical information systems into one integrated nationwide network is a challenging question (Swisher, 2014). Health laws are changing as health care systems move from supporting batch processing of health care transactions to adopting sophisticated, artificial intelligence-assisted, real-time control of patient care processes. Clinical services and administration will be reshaped as technologies increasingly expand, including:

- Customized consumer-directed health insurance plans
- Diagnostic radiology picture archiving and communication systems
- Electronic health records
- Real-time claims management and payment systems
- Remote clinical management systems

(Hayden, 2014; Johnson, 2015; Simer & Schoeffel, 2015).

While the need is without dispute, the road to building this nationwide integrated health care network is politically complex, and it could cost upwards of $400 billion (ONC, 2014).

Constraints on Adoption of Information Technologies

The United States is approximately a decade behind other industrialized countries in terms of adoption of health information technologies. These other countries' governments have played major roles in establishing their national integrated health care networks, and health insurers there have paid most of the costs. Nevertheless, U.S. health spending per capita is almost two and a half times the median per capita health spending rate of other economically similar countries, such as Australia, Canada, Europe, and Japan (Yong et al., 2010).

Adoption of electronic health records and other related information technologies has been minimal in the United States. It is estimated that only one in four physicians use electronic health records, while the use of computerized physician order entry and clinical decision support systems is even lower among hospitals (Abraham et al., 2011). Moreover, while electronic health records have been deployed by many major health care systems, a single national standard still does not exist for sharing information between different neworks.[LN2]

Still, experts agree that the only way to reduce the number of medical errors along with duplicative and ineffective treatment services is widespread adoption of standardized HIT (Lieber, 2016, 2015). Electronic health records that can collect and share essential health information about patients and their care should ideally be linked to computerized physician order entry and clinical decision support systems in a national network accessible by all health care organizations (Agarwal et al., 2011). Two of the main reasons for hesitancy to adopt HIT are cost and privacy concerns (Yan et al., 2012).

Online Control and Management of Health Information

The need for patients to have more control over their personal medical records and access to more relevant health information is largely driving this anticipated change. Hospitals, health insurance plans, and the government are all seeking to be part of this push to use HIT to give patients more control over their online health records and access to their health information. HIT could in turn lower health care costs if access to more information helps physicians and patients make better choices.

Among the firms involved in the online health market are Aetna and WellPoint, which have built personal health records from billing and claims data, and newcomers like Google[LN3] and Microsoft,[LN4] which have developed their own **cyberspace** ventures. Web-based personal genetic analysis company, 23andMe, allows patients to pay about $200 for the opportunity to explore their own genomes. Some employers (including Intel, Pitney Bowes, British Petroleum, and Applied Materials) are also promoting personal health records in conjunction with group-sponsored health insurance plans. These developments, and dozens of similar initiatives, are pushing the online sharing of **identifiable information** into the mainstream (Ohm, 2015).

Personal Health Records

In theory, **personal health records** could be a link among the various electronic records. Many institutional electronic health records systems provide a patient portal that provides records and interactions with physicians in their health care networks. The ideal would be a shared global repository under patient control with records stored on the Internet or a portable device. For instance, a patient could take a record from one health care network, store it on a Web-based service, and then share that information with other physicians or specialists of a different network anywhere in the world.

However, the issue is that there is no agreement within the health care industry on where personal health records fit relative to other electronic records (Fox, 2014). Another issue is how personal health records work with institutional electronic health records systems and how this information could be shared with other health care networks in an emergency. For instance, if patients were incapacitated, how would they provide access to their Web-based records in a different network? It is logical to expect personal health records to complement existing electronic health records systems; however, there is no standard norm for Web-based health information.

A partnership between the private sector and the government would be ideal. To achieve uniformity, it might help if there were tools endorsed by the federal government and professional associations. For complete accessibility, the government and the many firms in the HIT industry must cooperate in building a nationwide integrated health care network. There is also a concern regarding quality of electronic records. Patients are probably not the best judge of what should be in their personal health records. Moreover, it is difficult to know how useful electronic health records will be to physicians and other health professionals if they are not standardized and complete. Patients could record popular test results such as a cholesterol score, but omit a lesser known detail such as the triglyceride level. Personal health records are only as complete as the information entered. Selective disclosure could be a common problem and would hinder physicians' ability to render appropriate care using personal health records.

Online Sharing of Personal Health Records

Privacy issues are yet another major concern. Individuals' health records are personal and sensitive, but online personal health records are not yet covered by federal privacy laws (*See* **Health Insurance Portability and Accountability Act of 1996 (HIPAA), 42 U.S.C.A. § 300gg, 29 U.S.C.A. §§ 1181** *et seq.*, and 42 U.S.C. §§ 1320d *et seq.*). HIPAA addressed security and privacy issues and created minimum standards for:

- Access to health information
- Correction of erroneous information
- Disclosure of **individually identifiable health information**
- Other elements of fair information practices

Under HIPAA, a patient's medical records and payment history cannot be linked together by an unauthorized person. These rules, however, apply only to covered entities, including:

- Health care clearinghouses, such as billing services and information providers
- Health care networks
- Health care providers
- Health insurance plans

HIPAA does not apply to the records themselves (*See* Standards for Privacy of Individually Identifiable Information, 65 FR 82462-01).

No HIPAA Protection

Although HIPAA covers health care systems installing electronic health records, regulations do not cover independent Web services that store personal health records online (Foster, 2010). For instance, Microsoft's HealthVault records are individually controlled. In its *frequently asked questions* document, Microsoft outlines that individuals decide what information is stored in HealthVault, access is granted on a case-by-case basis, and health records are not used for commercial purposes unless authorized by opting in. Genetic testing firms, like 23andMe, deCODE genetics, Navigenics, and other Internet-based firms make similar promises stating that it simply links patients to their genetic data and then stores and helps interpret the information (Kaplan, 2015). Moreover, HIPAA does not prevent patients from uploading their personal health records and accepting terms of questionable online privacy agreements.

Still, there is the potential to restrict health plan benefits and employment from **at-risk populations** based on the information in online personal health records (Gantt, 2014). At-risk could be defined by any number of factors from familial history to laboratory results to environmental exposures. Benefit coverage could be restricted unfairly or employment could be negatively affected by medical history and **at-risk variables** with the online availability of individually identifiable health information (Zarsky, 2013). This is important since not all states have privacy laws that apply to online personal health records, and most privacy laws regarding individually identifiable health information have yet to be tested in courts (Gantt, 2014).

Moreover, any rights to privacy could vanish at any time because most websites reserve the right to change their privacy policies without providing notice to their Internet users (Balkin, 2016). There is a significant difference between websites legally covered by HIPAA versus sites that simply voluntarily comply with HIPAA. **Voluntarily compliant websites** can subject their users to this sudden change. While this is increasingly recognized as a privacy issue, legislation is required to regulate websites containing individually identifiable health information that currently only voluntarily comply with HIPAA (Ohm, 2015).

Although it may be idealistic to trust patients to maintain their own complete personal health records, and to maintain their own confidentiality in the age of social media, third party providers also present risks. Other parties, including the government, may have access to identifiable information from third party providers under subpoena power. Websites can promise privacy, but in reality, they may not be able to keep personal health records posted online completely private from other parties, including the government.

While health information is typically considered more sensitive than financial data, there are similarities. Initially, financial data was largely paper-based and consumers were reluctant to share information electronically. Today, Web-based banking and financial transactions are commonplace. Personal health records may soon follow the same path with privacy safeguards in place.[LN5]

Public Health Monitoring of Chronic Diseases

One particular challenge facing health care providers is applying personal health records to those who may need them the most: patients with chronic diseases. This is a new role for most health care providers. Though this role has traditionally been filled by public health agencies, the monitoring and management of patients with chronic health conditions, such as diabetes, will eventually require integration of personal health records with care continuum applications managed by hospitals or large physician clinics.

The New York City Department of Health and Mental Hygiene, for instance, maintains a public health registry on diabetics. Laboratories are required to submit electronic reports of blood sugar levels for diabetics by name and without patient consent (*See* New York City Health Code art. 13, § 13.07). The City Health Department then intervenes and contacts patients at risk who are not controlling their blood sugar to encourage them to:

- Increase exercise
- Make better diet choices
- Take prescription drugs properly

(Hoppin, 2012).

The hope is that these earlier interventions will help stave off more costly medical care by helping the patient to avoid suffering a medical emergency or requiring more intensive treatment. With appropriate HIT adaptations, public health laws authorizing this type of preventive health program could be expanded to include other chronic disease interventions. Public health agencies could monitor diseases until medical intervention is needed for:

- Alzheimer's disease and related dementia
- Asthma
- Cardiac instability
- Chronic obstructive pulmonary diseases
- Congestive heart failure

More than a quarter century ago, a U.S. Supreme Court case established the foundation for this newly emerging type of public health monitoring (*See Planned Parenthood of Southeastern Pennsylvania v. Casey*, 505 U.S. 833 (U.S. Supreme Court 1992 (upholding a Pennsylvania law that required all abortions to be reported without the patient's name)).

Interventions with Information Technologies

If patients with unstable health due to chronic diseases have implantable medical devices, advanced HIT can monitor their health conditions continuously. This remote HIT monitoring and management is, in principle, no different than the HIT applications used in telemetry units at hospitals or the observation units attached to emergency rooms. Rather than waiting to intervene until a catastrophic medical event occurs, HIT interventions like this can take place and potentially avert the crisis. The earlier point of intervention might make the difference in the outcome of the situation (Hoppin, 2012).

For instance, insulin pump devices developed by Medtronic can be implanted to alter insulin dosages continuously. Through wireless HIT, pump devices store and send information about an individual diabetic's status to a monitoring station as well as respond to external signals that can alter the insulin dosage. Pacemakers are being implanted in the same manner to monitor heart rhythms for cardiac patients and alert caregivers to the need for medical intervention when necessary (Noah, 2013). Biometric sensor arrays are increasingly affordable. Sensor arrays can also be integrated with real-time, two-way voice communications, so that patients with implantable medical devices can be monitored with wireless connections, almost like a human OnStar safety system. Guidant and Boston Scientific have developed devices that are compatible with electronic health records through wireless HIT.

Patients being monitored can span the health spectrum. Chronic diseases can be managed at home in the same way as critically ill patients are monitored in hospital intensive care units. For years, hospitals with 24-hour cardiology coverage have monitored critically ill patients in remote locations at smaller hospitals and clinics through electrocardiograph signals transmitted through telephone lines. Today, with biometric and HIT advances, the physiological characteristics of patients in unstable health with a wide range of chronic clinical conditions can be monitored continuously from remote wireless locations (*See* Kramer et al., 2014).

Public Health Registries

The law on **public health registries** has involved two different kinds of privacy interests:

- The individual interest in avoiding disclosure of individually identifiable health information
- The public health interest in having the independence to make certain kinds of important decisions for the community at large

(*Whalen v. Roe*, 429 U.S. 589 (U.S. Supreme Court 1977)).

Like all individual interests, though, the two interests are constrained and compete with the needs of the public.

When the federal agency that administers Medicare/Medicaid insurance estimates that government spending on health care could increase exponentially, questions arise in communities nationwide as to why this spending is surging and what can be done to control the surge. Driven by the rising costs of new drugs and medical technologies, overall health care spending is projected to increase to almost $5 trillion by 2024 (Keehan et al., 2015). Given this dire warning, individual privacy interests may not prohibit public health agencies from taking action and making sure that chronic diseases are monitored and managed in their local communities.

The New York City public registry law merely reflects the current public health policy of collecting individually identifiable health information about chronic diseases, as opposed to infectious diseases (New York City Health

Code art. 13, § 13.07; *See* Ray, 2014). Whether this policy shift is consistent with the personal autonomy to decide whether to accept medical care is uncertain and has not been addressed by the courts (Leonard et al., 2016). The U.S. Supreme Court has, however, found that this public health policy is consistent with making sure that the abuse of pharmaceutical drugs is monitored and managed, and that unlawful diversion and use of legal drugs is minimized. *See Whalen v. Roe*, 429 U.S. 589 (U.S. Supreme Court 1977). Whether this public health policy on drug abuse will be extended to other health conditions, without informed consent, is a Machiavellian decision that consumers will have to soon decide upon.

The tradition of personal autonomy and privacy in the United States can still be respected and is not mutually exclusive with the concept of identifying, monitoring, and managing patients with chronic diseases. At issue is not whether there is a right to individual privacy; rather, the issue is whether that right should be subverted to the importance of monitoring and managing chronic diseases, which may minimize health care costs. This is the focus of policy debates and the emerging changes in the future of public health (Ray, 2014).

Computerized Physician Order Entry Systems

Experts agree that **computerized physician order entry** systems, along with the addition of **clinical decision support systems**, lie at the core of medicine's future (Bates, 2012). Physician order entry systems allow health care providers to electronically enter medication orders as well as orders for:

- Admissions
- Laboratory tests
- Radiology diagnostic tests and procedures
- Referrals
- Treatment procedures

Decision support provides real-time information on a range of diagnosis- and treatment-related data as well as tools aimed at improving patient care and reducing medical errors and costs. Rules check for:

- Allergies
- **Drug contraindications** in which two or more drugs are being prescribed together (**polypharmacy**)
- Overdoses
- Renal- and weight-based dosing

(Leapfrog Group, 2016).

The significance of these systems was validated by England's action to devote nearly $6 billion to implement computerized physician order entry for its National Health Service (Burns, 2005). Computerized physician order entry with decision support can:

- Assure compliance with guidelines
- Enhance efficiency of workflow
- Improve medication safety and quality of care
- Reduce the cost of care

(AHRQ, 2016; Nuckols et al., 2015).

Computerized physician order entry alone has the potential to eliminate 200,000 adverse drug events and medication errors in U.S. hospitals, saving the U.S. health care system more than $1 billion a year (Shekelle et al., 2006; *See* Jones et al., 2010). The federal Agency for Healthcare Research and Quality (AHRQ), like England's National Health Service a decade prior, supports research to help build the technical and operational foundation of HIT in U.S. clinical settings.

Despite projected cost-savings, the investment in computerized physician order entry is often difficult to justify given the short-term cost pressures facing most hospitals (Kruse et al., 2014). The Leapfrog Group, a national coalition of major U.S. employers, advocates computerized physician order entry but notes that adoption has been dismally slow (Martin, 2011). Few hospitals have computerized physician order entry, in part because the HIT can cost $500,000 to $14 million depending on hospital size (Saxena, 2016), and in part because of some unplanned consequences of computerized physician order entry such as resistance by physicians and hospital staff to adopt HIT (AHRQ, 2016; McKay et al., 2015; *See* Ash et al., 2007).

Remote Monitoring and Management of Patients

Further advances in HIT can resolve the concerns with controlling and managing electronic records. When personal health records are automatically shared between medical devices (that test for chronic conditions), and electronic health records systems, there will be one integrated delivery system (Kaelber et al., 2012). For chronic diseases, implantable devices could be linked to health care providers, and patients could be continuously monitored and managed. With identifiable information from continuously monitored patients, there would be:

- Ability to define health populations and subpopulations where medical care could be targeted, accessed, refocused, and improved
- Possibility to study health trends and hypotheses
- Potential to study the natural history of health conditions and the health impact of different environmental or social circumstances, and then to identify at-risk populations
- Research opportunities to prospectively analyze the effectiveness of different treatments and diagnostic tests, from:
  - Screening programs and prevention strategies
  - Prognosis and the potential survival statistics associated with different conditions or different treatments

(AHRQ, 2013; Silow-Carroll et al., 2012).

Biosensors could conceivably transmit identifiable information into information systems that would populate personal health records. As HIT advances, biosensors could eventually enable physicians to monitor patients on a continuous basis. Medical device firms are already developing intelligent implantable devices for virtually every organ system in the body. These can continuously monitor and intervene to stabilize patients as necessary as well as alert caregivers and monitoring centers if additional stabilization is required.

Remote monitoring of patients with chronic diseases has the potential to improve care and reduce hospitalizations but it has been slow to catch on (Fried, 2016). It is fair to wonder why. One reason is that the health insurance industry has not adapted to this changing patient treatment approach. Most insurers still only reimburse for traditional patient care where patients are taken into physical custody for hands-on monitoring of their conditions. Without health insurers' acceptance of these new technological advances, health care providers are not reimbursed for care provided remotely.

Telemedicine

Telemedicine is closely allied with HIT. HIT refers to electronic medical records and related information systems while telemedicine refers to the actual delivery of remote clinical services using technology. Just as the remote monitoring and management of patients is advancing through developments in HIT, telemedicine or electronic medicine is also pushing into the mainstream. Telemedicine is dividing along two lines:

- Free general medical advice, such as the MedlinePlus program found on the Library of Medicine's patient website
- More time-consuming and personalized online and telephone consultations for which health care providers charge

Increasingly, health insurance plans are reimbursing for online and telephone consultations, and the pressure is mounting for all payers to do so (Schumacher, 2015) Patients are increasingly demanding electronic medical services beyond general medical advice and recommendations found on websites. Although three out of four patients go online for health information, many actually want more online interaction with their physicians (Pew, 2013). While most physicians recommend websites to patients, few health care systems use e-mail to communicate with patients (Pratt, 2015). Again it is fair to question why. The answer is because the following questions remain unaddressed:

- Are there justifiable concerns that physicians will be inundated with patient e-mails?
- Is it more efficient to have support staff screen patient issues as opposed to taking time for physicians to individually respond when they are not rendering direct clinical care?
- What assurance would patients have that they are actually communicating with their physician as opposed to support staff?

Payment remains another stumbling block to telemedicine. Professionals expect to be paid for their time. Medical groups have called on the federal Centers for Medicare and Medicaid Services and all other payers to work with providers to develop guidelines for payment of online and telephone consultations (Johnson, 2015). Information benefits are just as important as drug benefits and would cost far less if provided electronically or by telephone (Berg, 2014). Online and telephone consultations can more efficiently address non-urgent care, such as:

- Continued personal counseling after an office visit
- Diagnosing common symptoms
- Follow-up care for problems that have not worsened
- Prescription refills
- Reporting certain test results

For insured consumers facing higher out-of-pocket costs from their health insurance plans, the idea of being able to get health information and advice from physicians without expensive, time-consuming, and sometimes unnecessary office visits is an attractive alternative, even if there is still a fee. Many health care systems let patients search online for physicians who use online and telephone consultations. As costs are increasingly shifted to patients, patients are looking for more efficient ways of obtaining quality care at an affordable price (Terry, 2014).

E-Health

Related to telemedicine, and one of the more diverse segments of HIT, is the rapidly changing **e-health** or Internet space dedicated to health care. For anyone with access to the Internet, an array of drug and therapeutic offerings is easily found. The intricate global network of chemical and drug manufacturers, distributors, and buyers behind telemedicine and e-health is challenging the ability of the U.S. Food and Drug Administration to provide its traditional public health safety net for consumers (Smith, 2015).

Health Websites

The proliferation of health information on the Web has the ability to positively affect health care. However, it is difficult to know if information on the Internet is updated and accurate. Fully three-quarters of online health information seekers say they check the source and date *only sometimes, hardly ever,* or *never,* which translates to about 85 million consumers gathering health advice online without consistently examining the quality indicators of the information they find (Fox, 2014).

As might be expected, there are gaps in the integrity of online information. Information about physician credentials, training, and experience is available, but there is not much available regarding outcomes or quality (Terry, 2014). The fact that information is available in some form, however, means Internet users are becoming more involved in their own health care. The Pew Internet and American Life Project surveys Internet use in the United States and paints a picture of consumers who are:

- Considering entering clinical trials in greater numbers
- Paying attention to warnings about obesity and poor nutrition
- Researching physicians
- Taking steps to better manage their health care costs

(Goetz, 2010; Pew Internet, 2016).

The fastest growing topics of interest for Internet users include:

- Diet, nutrition, and vitamins
- Experimental treatments
- Health insurance coverage
- Information on physicians and hospitals
- Prescription and over-the-counter drugs

(Fox, 2014).

By reflecting consumers' shifting priorities in health care, the Pew findings may help provide a road map for employers, health insurance plans, and patient advocates looking to provide better health information for patients in the future.

Importantly, the survey also raises concerns about a new digital divide between more educated and affluent Internet users with high-speed broadband access, which is about half of all Internet users at home, and less educated or older users with dial-up connections who are less likely to have sought various kinds of health information online (Pew, 2016). Health insurance plans probably view this as a mixed blessing because it is likely to increase demand for new medical services and treatment procedures. At the same time, it helps disseminate information on evidence-based medicine, which can then be used by patients and physicians to better understand the outcomes of certain treatments (Schumacher, 2015).

It is estimated that 1 million new websites go up each month (Fox, 2014). Some of the most frequented ones are health-related. Eighty percent of Internet users, including some 113 million consumers, access health care information online each year; conducting searches for health care information is one of the most common reasons patients use the Internet (Fox, 2015). Online tools to evaluate and choose health care only scratch the surface, and websites:

- Educate Internet users about their health
- Help change unhealthy behaviors
- Help Internet users communicate with disease- and care-management professionals

(Caulfield, 2015; Schumacher, 2015).

The value of these thousands of websites varies. Reputable websites, such as those of the National Institutes of Health and the Clinical Trials Database, are a public service. Many commercial websites mix accurate information with advertising, making it difficult to distinguish meaningful information from misleading and potentially harmful information. Many health websites advertise heavily but lack substance or are even fraudulent (Szerejko, 2015). Some actually promote therapies that do not have a scintilla of truth behind them.

Social Networking Technologies

The health care industry has embraced the advanced HIT that is part of the social networking revolution. Timely personalized health information is readily available online. Patients who once connected mainly through e-mail discussion groups and chat rooms[LN6] have now built virtual communities to share information about their treatments with a network of online friends. The American Cancer Society and the Centers for Disease Control and Prevention have space on social media to assist with publicizing issues such as nutrition awareness, cancer screening, and infectious disease prevention.

Online support groups offer the most promise for patients with uncommon diseases or hard-to-diagnose conditions. Frequently, the Internet has the broadest approach to issues arising from rare and orphaned diseases. The combined wisdom of these patients and caregivers is frequently deeper than single physicians can possibly develop in the time available unless their entire careers have been devoted to the disease (Terry, 2014).

At the same time, traditional websites that once offered cumbersome pages of static data have developed blogs on Facebook or other social networking pages, podcasts, and customized search engines like WebMD and NBC Universal's iVillage to deliver the most relevant information on health topics. Johnson & Johnson was one of the first pharmaceutical firms in the blogosphere. Patients are constantly updated on relevant health news with personalized health awareness messages, reminders, and alerts delivered to their e-mail accounts, wireless devices, and mobile phones. **Wikis** allow patients to collaborate online on websites with photo albums and contact lists. Wikis are websites full of information that users build together. Communities even have websites to plan for public health emergencies such as flu pandemics.

Unprotected Communications Networks

Very little is known about these complex communications networks. One thing is certain, however: the HIT industry is actively monitoring all of this (Francis, 2012). What Internet users say online in discussion groups, chat rooms, health blogs, podcasts, virtual communities, and wikis is generally not protected information. To the extent that a private and confidential infrastructure is absent, these communications networks call for further study.

While remedies exist in the form of civil lawsuits if health advocacy groups, government agencies, and health care providers fail to adhere to their posted privacy policies, most courts maintain that if Internet users object to privacy violations, they can simply not use those websites whose policies they do not like. Some firms, however, have been sued for tracking Internet users without their permission. For instance, for several years many companies within the pharmaceutical industry contracted with Pharmatrak, a data-mining company that collected personal and identifying data on Internet users visiting pharmaceutical websites to learn about their drugs and to obtain rebates. When the tracking practice became public, the pharmaceutical companies terminated their relationships with Pharmatrak and litigation ensued. In no time at all, Pharmatrak went out of business. *See Blumofe v. Pharmatrak, Inc.* (*In re Pharmatrak, Inc. Privacy Litigation*), 329 F.3d 9 (U.S. Court of Appeals for the 1st Circuit 2003).

Most websites do not disclose the use of **Web bugs** in their online privacy policies, even as it gets more and more difficult to block the bugs. Web bugs (also referred to as Web beacons, clear gifs, and pixel tags):

- Intercept personal information
- Obtain and collect the IP address, type of browser, and operating system of users
- Track Internet users' browsing patterns

(Ard, 2015; Zarsky, 2015).

Moreover, most websites do not strictly comply with their own privacy policies, and many regularly modify their policies without alerting users to the changes (Bagley & Brown, 2015). In another example involving a pharmaceutical company, Eli Lilly promised in its privacy policy to maintain the confidentiality of information provided on its Prozac. com website. Yet, it inadvertently sent website subscribers an e-mail with over 670 subscribers' addresses visible at the top of a drug alert (Solove & Hartzog, 2014). This meant that the Medicaid-insured could potentially infer that all of the other Medicaid-insured were:

- Being advised to watch for suicidal thoughts
- Being treated for depression
- Had an interest in Prozac
- Taking antidepressants

While some states have mandatory regulations covering websites, they do not require any specific privacy policy terms. The question is whether Internet users have an enforceable right, and therefore a legal remedy, when their privacy is violated. Eli Lilly paid several states $160,000 to cover the costs of investigating its website policies; however, none of the 670 individual subscribers who had their e-mail addresses made public received compensation for violation of their privacy (Clearwater & Hughes, 2013); *See In re Eli Lilly & Co.*, 133 F.T.C. 763 (Federal Trade Commission 2002). Eli Lilly's response to violation of its privacy policy is in line with the fact that no one has been willing to subject themselves to appropriate penalties when they violate their own privacy rules (Schwartz & Solove, 2011). In addition, few websites have transparent privacy practices or offer users choices about how the sites may use posted identifiable information (Fuelleman, 2011; Hoppin, 2012).

Protected Communications Networks

Sermo, the nation's largest online physician community, is designed to redefine the way physicians in the United States and the health care industry work together to improve patient care. In collaboration with Pfizer and the American Medical Association, Sermo (the Latin word for *conversation*), is a Web-based community where more than 31,000 physicians:

- Discuss emerging trends
- Provide new insights into medical products and treatment procedures
- Share observations from daily practice

(Terry, 2012).

As a **protected communications network**, Sermo protects and highly regulates the personal information on its social network. Access to Sermo is restricted to physicians and acquisition of the online information on the network site (for instance by the health insurance industry) or particular uses of such data (for instance, employment-related decisions) is walled-off and actively controlled (Terry, 2010).

Internet Pharmacies

The traditional way in which drugs are dispensed in the United States by state-licensed health care practitioners encompasses an important risk management system. Internet pharmacies are challenging long-established regulatory schemes and selling pharmaceuticals in confusingly diverse ways. The U.S. Food and Drug Administration (FDA) classifies Internet pharmacies into five categories requiring different levels of scrutiny:

- Reputable, regulated websites that simply dispense approved drugs (state-licensed online pharmacies that require valid prescriptions for orders filled online)
- Sites offering other drug products and making unproven claims, such as miracle weight-loss drugs
- Sites that provide drugs never approved anywhere, which are of questionable safety and effectiveness
- Sites that provide drugs off label in the United States but approved in other countries (which may not necessarily be safe or effective for their intended use)
- Unregulated websites that actually prescribe approved drugs but circumvent traditional pharmacy safeguards

(FDA, 2016; Schultz, 2015).

The difference between regulated websites that dispense and unregulated websites that prescribe is noteworthy. **Internet dispensing** involves the delivery of prescription drugs by an Internet pharmacy. **Internet prescribing** arises when the Internet pharmacy prescribes the drug to patients without a physical examination.

The **Ryan Haight Online Pharmacy Consumer Protection Act of 2008** prohibits substituting online medical questionnaires for live interaction with a health care professional (*See* 21 U.S.C.A. §§ 802(50)-(56), 829(e), 841(h)). This substitution constitutes the unlawful practice of pharmacy and the FDA is shutting down such Internet pharmacies. Besides constituting unlawful, substandard health care, such questionnaires might jeopardize the confidentiality of health records. Nevertheless, there continue to be online transactions in which physicians are completely absent. Patients self-diagnose and treat themselves with the risk of:

- Improper dosing
- Misdiagnosis and thus the failure to properly diagnose and treat the actual problem
- Negative outcomes such as harmful drug interactions or allergic reactions

(Schultz, 2015).

Regardless, over 36 million Americans purchase drugs online without a prescription every year (Lipman, 2013). It is important to note that in instances in which patients go online to order prescribed drugs without a lawful prescription, they are breaking the law; their acts are the same as purchasing illegal drugs from a street drug dealer. More important is the national security threats funded by drug products sold over the Internet. Among the organizations using funds from drug sales are:

- Al Qaeda
- Chinese triads
- Columbian drug cartels
- Hezbollah
- Russian mafia

(Finley, 2011).

The receipt of unlawful drugs is subject to prosecution, no matter how the drugs are obtained. One example of this is the unlawful obtaining of steroids by sports participants. Lifestyle drugs are another example of a $28 billion market that is very popular on the Internet:

- Meridia, Xenical, and Reductil for obesity
- Propecia and Revivogen for hair loss
- Viagra, Levitra, and Cialis for erectile dysfunction

(DOJ, 2011; White House, 2011).

All these lifestyle drugs have dangerous side effects for certain patients, making their use without a prescription risky. Antihistamines and painkillers are also frequently ordered Internet pharmaceuticals. It appears some patients turn to the Internet when their physicians refuse to write additional prescriptions. Beyond simply wishing to circumvent physicians, many consumers shop for medical products online simply for the:

- Accessibility to product information
- Convenience
- Privacy as far as avoiding meeting face-to-face with a medical professional

Others use the Internet in hopes of finding better prices, but cost savings are generally a myth. Once all the charges are considered, the costs even out and sometimes increase, especially if patients cause further health troubles because of what they did or did not order (Lipman, 2013; Schultz, 2015). *See also* Haight, 2006 (mother's account of her 17-year-old son's death from prescription drugs dispensed over the Internet).

The Internet's ability to allow users to cross state and international lines with anonymity and speed presents another regulatory issue for the FDA and law enforcement. Historically, states have had the authority to regulate both the practice of pharmacy and of medicine. However, most websites selling drug products are made up of multiple related sites and links that often cross state and country borders (Lipman, 2013). Moreover, there are no international laws or treaties that regulate Internet drug sales from outside the United States to individuals located within the United States (Finley, 2011). Through the World Health Organization, countries can share their regulations and monitor what is going on in other countries, but that is the only formal mechanism currently in place (*See* Darrow, 2014).

Information Privacy

Privacy is a significant issue for the HIT industry. An estimated 150 different individuals (from physicians and nurses to technicians and billing clerks) have access to at least part of a patient's health records during a typical hospitalization (*See* Huntington, 2014). Self-regulation proposals from the HIT industry, patient-advocacy groups intent on curbing online profiling, and various new health information firms aimed at helping patients protect their privacy have legitimate concerns.

At the same time, the HIT industry has a genuine commercial interest in individually identifiable health information because it allows patients to receive information targeted to their personal health conditions (Pasquale, 2014). Health information firms offer patients free access to information that would otherwise cost money, in return for allowing the company to track the patient's personal health. Clearly, the boundaries of privacy are uncertain.

Data Mining

Should health websites be permitted to track internal data from browsers if they guarantee they will not give identifiable information to anyone else? Unfortunately, there are many instances of identifiable information being sold to **data brokers**, drug and medical device manufacturers, or to private data collection agencies without the patients' knowledge or permission (Crawford & Schultz, 2014). Consent is often given for data mining when hypothetically the request states that identifiable information will be used to identify medical products and services that will better fit one's needs. At this moment, secondary use of identifiable information is a multibillion-dollar business, including some uses that have not yet been imagined (Pasquale, 2014; Tomain, 2014).

Put another way, most patients probably do not object to the practice of health insurance plans and pharmacy benefit managers suggesting lab tests and drugs to them based on their health history (Hoffman, 2014). What they probably would object to, if they knew it was happening, is the way in which their identifiable information is used for things other than their own individual health care. Some of these secondary uses include:

- Certification and accreditation of facilities
- Clinical audits
- Clinical research
- Marketing of medical products and services

(Abbott, 2013; Hoffman, 2014; Hoffman & Podgurski, 2012; Price, 2015).

Identifiable information could certainly be used by predatory marketers to sell to populations using scare tactics. Information could be targeted to patients who are most likely to be susceptible to sales pitches for bogus products. While it is important that patients' needs are met, marketing and its use in health care commercial purposes are places where the law is unclear (Terry, 2012).

Commercial Use of Individual Identifiable Health Information

At the time of its passage, New Hampshire's **data-mining law** was the first of its kind in the United States. Now both Vermont and Maine have similar laws and numerous other states have proposed prescription information laws that are narrowly drawn around the states' interest in improving public health and mitigating health care costs. Vermont's prescription monitoring system restricts the sale of prescriber-identifiable data unless the prescriber (physician, nurse practitioner, physician assistant, mental health professional, or other health care professional authorized by state law to prescribe drugs) opts in to a program authorizing use of their prescribing records (*See* Protection and Disclosure of Information, 18 V.S.A. § 4284). Maine has an opt-out law that prohibits the sale of prescriber-identifiable data from prescribers who have filed for confidentiality protection (*See* Confidentiality of Prescription Drug Information, 22 M.R.S. § 1711-E). Patients are entitled to inspect the prescriber-identifiable data collected on them but have no control over who has access to their identifiable information (Terry, 2012).

Beneficial Uses of Individually Identifiable Health Information

The issues of privacy, confidentiality, and security must be viewed within the context of the very important and beneficial uses that go along with data mining. When considering this issue it is important to remember that data mining is the analysis of health information for relationships that have not previously been discovered. Data could be used to look at:

- Cost-effectiveness of different medical products
- Government policy proposals
- Regional performance and quality improvement strategies

National research studies could be done in ways that have never been done before (Price, 2015).

Few patients understand how easy it is to mine data, how much information is readily available, or how information that is collected can be saved forever. The reality is that as a result of HIT, private space is shrinking and public space is increasing. Data mining uses specialized software tools based on advanced electronic search and pattern recognition algorithms, multiprocessor computers, and comprehensive databases to develop measures that can investigate risk-related results and outcome comparisons, such as[LN7]:

- Infections, including viruses with the potential to become pandemics
- Medical errors and omissions
- Unnecessary diagnostic procedures
- Unwarranted medical treatments

(Altman et al., 2015).

Detrimental Uses of Individually Identifiable Health Information

What worries privacy advocates are the increasingly sophisticated methods, such as electronic tracking tags known as **electronic cookies** and information transmitting devices known as Web bugs that are used to secretly track down information on individuals. Indeed, many Internet business models are based on the ability to aggregate and analyze identifiable information for a variety of profit-generating purposes. For instance, data brokers collect **clickstream data** to help construct computer profiles that are sold to Fortune 500 firms that regularly review this health information before making hiring and advancement decisions (Solove & Schwartz, 2014).

While everyone realizes that on one level it is acceptable to sell information, the question now is whether this has gone too far in terms of the amount of processing going on and the correlation of health information back to one's physical identity (Fuelleman, 2011). Even more disturbing is that individuals do not know how their identifiable information is being used and so have no way of tracking it, much less stopping it. One of the most notorious examples of violation of privacy policies involves ChoicePoint (*See United States v. ChoicePoint Inc.*, Federal Trade Commission Matter/File Number: 052-3069 (2010) ($15 million settlement)). ChoicePoint originally specialized in providing credit

MANAGEMENT AND LAW ISSUES

1. If data-mining prohibitions increase the safe use of generics and result in substantial cost savings, should data-mining laws be drawn for the purpose of mitigating health care costs?

data to the insurance industry but it soon evolved into an all-purpose information broker by data mining public records and then augmenting this information with:

- Conviction records
- Credit histories
- Employment histories
- Insurance claims
- Media reports
- Private investigations
- Social Security numbers

Its database now contains information about nearly every American. Employers often hire ChoicePoint and other commercial data brokers to conduct background checks (including health information) on potential employees (*E.g.*, Hartzog & Stutzman, 2013; Weiss, 2012). Government agencies (including law enforcement) routinely use its database (Leary, 2013).

Prescriber-Identifiable Data

The use of **prescriber-identifiable data** was examined, and the U.S. Supreme Court decided that state laws cannot bar the data-mining industry from using prescriber-identifiable data for commercial purposes. The *IMS Health* litigation draws attention to this controversy as the facts of the data-mining industry were revealed in open courts of law.

COURT DECISION
Permissible Data Mining

Sorrell v. IMS Health Inc.
[State of Vermont v. Health Information Technology Firm]
564 U.S. 552 (U.S. Supreme Court 2011)

Facts: The FDA requires pharmacies to record patient prescription data including the identity of prescribers. This patient-prescriber data is then sold to third parties who use the data to produce prescribing reports that are sold to the pharmaceutical industry for use in their marketing. Pharmaceutical sales representatives, in turn, use the data in the prescribing reports to tailor their face-to-face conversations with individual prescribers, known in the industry as **detailing.**

The Vermont State legislature enacted its Prescription Confidentiality Law to address the use of prescriber-identifying data to enhance prescriber detailing. Vermont was concerned that industry sales tactics were influencing prescribers to promote newer brand-name drugs over generics. Vermont was also concerned that industry sales tactics were contributing to rising Medicaid insurance costs. Vermont additionally expressed concern about the protection of patient privacy. The Vermont law mandated the collection of prescriber data and provided state funding for counterdetailing to educate physicians on the use of generics.

The Vermont law:

- Applied only to pharmacies, health insurers, and the pharmaceutical industry
- Was limited only pharmaceutical marketing
- Was designed to impact detailers whose speech conflicted with the goals of the government in reducing health care costs

Vermont prohibited the sale of prescriber-identifying data and the use of that information for industry marketing. In so doing Vermont sought to foster more neutral and scientific detailing discussions centered on the safety, effectiveness, and costs of drugs. IMS Health,[1] the medical products industry's leading data miner, challenged the Vermont law as an affront to free speech under the First Amendment.

---

[1]Hammaker, the coauthor of this text, was a former employee of IMS Health.

Issue: Should the government be able to limit the use of patient-prescriber data that was gathered in accordance with state regulations, if this data was subsequently used by the pharmaceutical industry in a way that violated patient privacy or failed to serve the government's interests in controlling health care costs?

Court's Holding and Decision: No. The Vermont law was a violation of the First Amendment. Although the government may place incidental burdens on commercial speech, for instance to protect patient privacy and control costs, the Vermont law was more than a mere incidental burden and thus was subject to the strict scrutiny test of a law's constitutionality, which the law did not survive.

Analysis: The Court held that the Vermont law contained both content- and speaker-based restrictions that were designed to restrict the effectiveness of marketing tactics by the pharmaceutical industry. The legislative findings acknowledged that the law's express purpose was to lessen the effectiveness with which detailers could market their brand-name drugs. The Court saw Vermont's opposition to the industry's targeted marketing as nothing less than viewpoint discrimination aimed at suppressing the industry's commercial messages in favor of Vermont's message of cost effectiveness.

By restricting the use of the patient-prescriber identifying data, Vermont tried to indirectly influence the pharmaceutical industry's promotion of more expensive brand-name drugs over less expensive generics. The effect of detailing on physician prescribing, however, cannot justify restrictions on commercial speech. The fear that patients might make bad decisions if given data about using brand-name drugs as opposed to generics cannot justify **content-based burdens on speech**. First Amendment jurisprudence is especially skeptical of regulations that appear to keep patients in the dark for what the government perceives to be their own good, such as using less expensive generics. Persuasive information alone does not permit the government to quiet the speech or to burden its messengers.

The Court concluded that the debate over detailing and the prescription of brand-name drugs must be settled by free and uninhibited speech, not by restricting the pharmaceutical industry's ability to promote its pro-brand messages. Accordingly, the Vermont law was struck down. The Court was not persuaded by Vermont's cost justifications for the law.

Rule of Law: Although the First Amendment right to free speech restricts the government's ability to limit the use of patient-prescriber data, commercial speech may be restricted to protect patient privacy and serve a state's interest of reducing health care costs.

References discussing this court decision: *E.g.*, Blackman, 2014; Dhooge, 2014; Gooch et al., 2013; Jacobs, 2014; Janssen, 2014; Mermin & Graff, 2013; Pasquale & Ragone, 2014; Schindler & Brame, 2013; Shinar, 2013; Spacapan & Hutchison, 2013; Spears et al., 2015; Thomson, 2013; Wolf, 2013.

Opting In or Out

The opting system is another controversy facing the HIT industry (Peters, 2014). One issue under debate is whether health websites must obtain opt-in permission from Internet users before using any identifiable information (Ford, 2016). This approach is favored by many patient-advocacy groups.

The other option is whether users should be required to take steps to opt out of any data-collection process, an approach generally favored by the HIT industry. One consistent barrier to the reliability of any opting system is that websites frequently revise their terms. These changes mean that the privacy permission Internet users initially granted could gradually become obsolete over time.

Numerous health information firms have chief privacy officers apparently to articulate and enforce privacy policies. A combination of government regulation and industry self-regulation are necessary to move forward (Gratton, 2014). The HIT industry alone cannot completely address privacy concerns, although it is certainly the preferred choice. Government can establish incentives for the HIT industry to self-regulate, but at the same time it should set minimum standards to ensure fair dealing for all involved.

MANAGEMENT AND LAW ISSUES

2. Does self-regulation alone adequately protect the privacy of online health information, or is federal legislation needed to supplement self-regulatory efforts and guarantee basic protections?

Protection of Privacy Space

While patient advocacy groups are challenging the HIT industry, new firms are emerging to offer protection against the growing variety of Web bugs that collect identifiable information in ever more sophisticated ways (Terry, 2014).[LN8] In this manner, as HIT provides business opportunities to violate privacy, it also provides opportunities to protect identifiable information. Numerous fee-based services prevent tracking of identifiable information, which is an example of the market providing a solution to privacy concerns. Users of social networks might ask themselves whether it is worth paying to try to stop the HIT industry from doing what they are doing or whether resistance is futile.

The core questions raised by misuse of identifiable information are not new. They are related to the general way that HIT uses identifiable information that they can collect to advance their interests. The difference is the ease with which electronic information can be collected and shared, and the ease with which it can be maintained for indefinite periods of time. In general, there has never been so much long-term readily accessible identifiable information as there is today on the Internet (Bernstein, 2014).

Nonetheless, there is a difference between putting identifiable information on a purely public website and putting information on controlled, private sites available only to members. The question of who owns the identifiable information on these private websites is unclear. Most have policies declaring ownership of anything posted there, but clearly that does not grant the site's owners leeway to freely use the information as they see fit. These sites claim to have privacy policies that impose limits on how they can use that identifiable information, but it is simply unclear under current law whether the posted information actually belongs to the Internet users or the website owners. With so much identifiable information available, it may all be considered part of the public domain (Terry, 2014). It may not be legally public, but there is so much widely disseminated information and there are so many ways to access and collect it, that the issue of ownership may be a moot question.

The real question is whether it is feasible to provide some privacy protection in order to prevent all information about patients from being accessed by anyone and everyone. If that is not possible, how can individual privacy be protected? There are several critical questions with regard to the privacy of identifiable information:

- Are patients aware of how high their expectations of privacy probably are and that they might be impossible to meet?
- Do patients expect their identifiable information to be private and, if so, are these expectations valid?

Property or Privacy Rights

It is debatable whether it is more appropriate to view health records information as a form of property that is owned and therefore subject to property protections or whether it is appropriate to consider identifiable information protected by privacy rights (Gratton, 2014). The debate centers on whether the Internet and advances in HIT over the last 30 years, from the time when the U.S. Supreme Court recognized a constitutional right to privacy, have made the property model more suitable for protecting electronic health records and online identifiable information. *See Whalen v. Roe*, 429 U.S. 589, 599-600 (U.S. Supreme Court 1977).

If the right to privacy of health records was similar to personal **property rights**, privacy could be exchanged for other rights. Under the property model, privacy belongs to individuals and it may be traded away in exchange for something of commensurate value, such as:

- Access to health information
- Cash payments
- Health care

(Price, 2015).

Internet users surfing the Web would be allowed to determine whether to submit requested pieces of identifiable information in return for free access to website content, or pay to access a website containing similar information without having to submit any identifiable information. If the identifiable information requests are too intrusive, Internet users may always withhold their valuable information and move to a competitor's website that is less privacy intrusive.

Under the privacy model, consent to medical care cannot be considered to include consent to any and all uses of identifiable information. The right to have health records information kept confidential includes the right to make certain kinds of important health care decisions. In this situation, HIPAA requires health care providers to state the intended use of any information collected for purposes other than personal health care, such as medical research and training (*See* 45 C.F.R. § 164.520(b)(1)(i)). Patients have a right to know how their information may be used and disclosed and how they can get access to this information before they decide to accept services from a particular health care provider. This includes the right to request restrictions on certain uses and disclosures of information (*See* 45 C.F.R. § 164.520(b)(1)(iv)(A-F)) (HIPAA-covered entities are not required to honor such requests because access is already restricted)).

Over time, the concept of property rights, as opposed to privacy rights, has emerged as the prism through which courts view rights to identifiable information. Under the privacy model, individuals have a fundamental right to maintain a sphere of privacy that should be protected from major invasions. However, with the growth of HIT, this privacy model may not be as useful. The property model may be better suited to protect basic information rights given the ever-expanding Internet. It could be argued that identifiable information, like all other forms of information, should be treated as property (Posner, 2007).

It can be argued that identifiable information should be part of the protected sphere of privacy and should not be freely exchanged in an economic marketplace with information inequalities and differing power relationships stacked against the individual. Some websites advise users to check their privacy policy periodically for changes. Under this scenario, the party with the best knowledge that the changes have occurred and the extent of such changes requires the less informed party to take the initiative to discover any modifications. The property model might be preferable because transaction costs are extremely low; individuals can reach bargains that reflect their actual preferences for different levels of privacy.

Ownership of Personal Health Information

The property ownership model has not yet succeeded in health law. Essentially, whoever gathers the health information owns it whether it is the individual or not. For instance, courts have generally rejected arguments by patients who have challenged the ability of health care providers to use identifiable information collected from them. The notion that patients own their health records has been rejected by the courts; health records are the property of health care providers, not patients.

Records taken by physicians in their examination and treatment of patients become property belonging to the hospital or treating physicians. Nevertheless, while health care providers own the actual health records and have primary custodial rights to the records of patients, patients have a property right in the information contained in the records. This property right is sufficient to give patients reasonable access to their records (Jefferson, 2015).

Public Disclosure of Private Facts

There are limits to what one can say or post on the Internet without running the risk of being successfully sued. One limit is making money off the fame of someone else, such as a celebrity. Another is **identity theft**. However, for **defamation** by website postings, truth is an absolute defense, meaning one cannot necessarily sue another solely for publicizing truthful information.

While an individual can sue someone for **public disclosure of private facts**, this is difficult in the HIT industry. For one thing, the websites generally disclaim any liability for postings. For another, it is hard for patients to convince a court that they were harmed by information that they themselves posted or by true information about them posted by others. Nevertheless, for those wishing to go down this road, the **tort** of public disclosure of private facts consists of four elements:

- Not of legitimate public concern
- Objectionable and offensive to a reasonable person
- Private fact
- Public disclosure

Most courts have found that to support this theory of liability, widespread dissemination of information to the public must be proven (*See* Standards for information transactions and data elements, 42 U.S.C.A. § 1320d-2). This tort theory works mostly for cases involving publication through the media. In the context of HIPAA violations, however, health information will generally be delivered to interested parties (such as health care providers) as opposed to the general public, and thus the tort of public disclosure of private facts will generally be inapplicable (Chang, 2013).

Assumption of Risk

E-mail also poses privacy problems, especially due to the notion of **assumption of risk**. The risk that an e-mail might be forwarded is a risk assumed whenever an e-mail is sent, regardless of whether the information therein is considered private or confidential. If an e-mail is sent, the law considers that risk accepted.

When it comes to online consultations and e-mail messages between patients and physicians, patients tend to think of it as private correspondence similar to a letter in a sealed envelope. However, e-mails are more like postcards. The administrators of e-mail servers are like the post office; e-mails are just files on the server. Most administrators have no reason to look at them, but they are there nonetheless. Are deleted e-mails gone? They may be gone from some places, but they could be backed up by the Internet service provider.

It is nearly impossible to determine when, if ever, deleted e-mails are fully eradicated. One overarching concern is that patients are growing increasingly insensitive to their own privacy interests. Many patients are indiscreet when it comes to identifiable information. It might be argued that if such personal indiscretion becomes the norm, then the need for privacy protection might be lost. This is likely an outcome that not all patients would willingly accept.

Rethinking Social Norms on Privacy

Privacy is only one issue regarding the amount of identifiable information available on the Internet in an age of increasingly universal connectivity. Health laws are gradually evolving to accommodate:

- Biosensors that can track individual activity
- Internet
- Mobile devices
- Wireless radio frequency identification tags

(Francis, 2012).

The reality is that a great deal of identifiable information is on the Internet. The reasons for this often have nothing to do with intentional efforts to convey identifiable information. Nevertheless, privacy is probably not the best lens through which to examine HIT management. Instead, there is a need to rethink what the health care industry considers the norm to be for identifiable information in a digital age. Privacy is certainly important. There is personal health records data that should not be disclosed. However, privacy laws and policies tend to impose formalistic rules that may not be conducive to the Internet or other advanced HIT (Trubek, 2006). The focus is slowly moving away from privacy and toward industry norms. In a way, the **small-town model** is returning where everyone knows about everyone else by virtue of the ever-expanding global information superhighway (McLaughlin, 2007).

Balancing Individual versus Community Needs

The privacy issues with public health registries remain. Do patients have a right to expect that their health information will remain confidential? In this ongoing debate, privacy is sometimes defended as an individual right. Patients, however, can and often must give up their individual right to privacy for the **public good**. For instance, when children come into a hospital with signs of abuse, physicians set in motion investigations that violate the privacy of the family to protect the safety and welfare of children.

Most patients want their privacy to be protected, but the other half of the equation is the need to give up privacy for the benefit of the community. The threat to privacy is implicit in the accumulation of vast amounts of identifiable information in computerized data banks or other massive files, including:

- Distribution of welfare and social security benefits
- Enforcement of criminal laws
- Management of the military
- Supervision of public health
- The collection of taxes

All require the orderly maintenance of identifiable information, much of which is potentially harmful if improperly disclosed. Traditionally, the privacy battle was between individual interests and government intrusion. Currently there is a third factor: electronic cookies and other data-mining technologies that silently sweep up information and shuttle it from server to server. This is perhaps the broadest challenge to privacy on the Internet (Orts & Sepinwall, 2015).

It is difficult to determine the weight that the right to privacy ought to be given. In the case of drug store chains and the pharmaceutical industry buying and selling identifiable information, privacy may be eroded without benefiting the community, which is the traditional reason given to justify the invasion of privacy (Terry, 2014). Millions of health records are systematically mined for purposes that have nothing to do with the public good (Angwin & Stecklow, 2010). On the other hand, a decision by most states to use blood taken from the heels of newborn children to test them for HIV may be a case in which privacy is weighed too highly, thereby sacrificing the human rights of the newborn (*See* Hale-Kupiec, 2016). Should states require that newborns undergo HIV tests without parental consent if newborns could benefit from immediate treatment, even though information about the family may be revealed? The debate surrounding the family's right to privacy is again manifest when it comes to medical care for adolescents between the ages of 10 and 19 years (Brobst, 2015).

Adolescent Health Records

Electronic health records confront legal and technical challenges when balancing the rights of parents and adolescents in access to health records. Many adolescents depend substantially on the public sector as opposed to parents to help support their healthy sexual development and to protect them from:

- Disease
- Pregnancy
- Sexual violence

(Francis, 2012).

Laws setting the age of consent vary from state to state and are even different within the states themselves depending on the medical concern at issue (Perlmutter, 2011). Various federal and state laws allow adolescents, between 13 and 17 years of age, to seek confidential family planning and mental health services without their parents' consent (Cullitan, 2011; *See* Dudley, 2013). Such laws keep certain aspects of adolescents' health records private from parents.

However, electronic health records cannot always flag all confidential material and hide it from parents in the same way as paper records generally allow for. A further complication in most states is the inability of minors to enter into the security agreements required to grant access to their online personal health records, as most states only allow minors to enter into contractual agreements under very limited circumstances. Until providers can figure out how to give parents access to basic health care information for adolescents without breaking confidentiality or other rules, many are leaving adolescents out of new electronic medical records systems altogether (Francis, 2012). Other providers are revoking parental access to adolescent records as soon as a child turns 13 (Demleitner, 2014).

Parents still have access to paper versions of an adolescent's nonconfidential records, including:

- General medical care
- Immunizations
- Treatment for chronic conditions, such as diabetes

Meanwhile, the health insurance industry routinely modifies adolescent online health records so parents can view standard nonconfidential health information while letting adolescents confidentially refill prescriptions online and e-mail their physicians without parental access to either activity.

Adolescent Assent and Disclosure Rules

Who should have access to adolescents' health information is a difficult question. The laws are subtle and do not always provide clear direction. Some states have laws regarding parental notification based on age and the specific medical problem (Drobac & Goodenough, 2015). Other states leave many decisions about whether to notify parents up to the physicians.

Adolescents have wide confidentiality protection as part of an effort to reduce adolescent pregnancy rates and sexually transmitted diseases. Title X of the Public Health Service Act and the federal Medicaid insurance law both require all family planning clinics to offer confidential services to adolescents. Federal privacy laws, including HIPAA, extend additional protections to adolescents including confidentiality of their medical records and health Most states allow minors to consent to treatments involving:

- Mental health counseling
- Sexually transmitted diseases
- Substance abuse

Minors in most states can seek treatment for chemical dependency at age 13 and seek contraception and reproductive health care at age 14 without parental consent or notification.

Health insurance plans generally have parental access services, but parents lose access to an adolescent's online health records and services once the adolescent is 13 years old. One of the nation's largest health insurance plans, Kaiser Permanente, has a **health care proxy** agreement that allows adults to access health records of adult family members for whom they are caregivers such as a sick spouse or elderly parent or minor children.

Efforts to come up with clear policies for adolescent health records are only likely to become more complicated. Examples of this are birth control and abortion, with most states mandating some sort of parental involvement (either consent or notice) before a minor can obtain abortion services. Advocates of more parental control continue to lobby to restore parental rights. Some states have already considered repealing or modifying laws that allow minors control over reproductive health care decisions. In other states adolescents must give explicit permission for their parents to review their health records, while still other states require assent for treatment from the adolescent combined with parental informed permission.

Eventually HIT will make it possible for physicians to create health records that can automatically determine by age and state laws what information can be accessed by a parent. The guiding principle of privacy for adolescents is that certain areas of care require that an adolescent be treated more as an adult than a child. Importantly, the goal is to not deter adolescents from seeking treatment for fear of disclosure of private information to their parents.

Need for Clarification in an Age of Rapid Technological Change

Although the right to privacy is not absolute, there are ways to achieve common goals with little sacrifice of individual privacy. One way Congress and state legislatures have come to assess common goals is to use empirical studies, like **Harris Interactive**, to determine how consumers actually perceive issues. It is not an absolute trade-off between individual rights and the public good. While the concept of the public good is often used to justify intrusions on individual rights, trade-offs are rarely simple. Moreover, the assertion of an absolute right to privacy may fade as privacy expectations continue to erode.

A public that is captivated by HIT may have already desensitized itself to the need for privacy. Facing rapid technological change, the need exists for consumers to further clarify privacy issues. Historically, it is worth remembering that technological developments continually outpace social and moral developments (Wharton, 2006).

Balancing Power with Responsibility

It was not until the latter half of the 19th century to the early 20th century that the following medical transformations arose:

- Antiseptic protocols
- Hospitals as a place for curing disease as opposed to segregating the hopelessly ill and impoverished
- Laboratory testing
- Professional training for physicians and nurses
- Radiology
- Standardized scientific techniques

(Starr, 1994/1984).

Health care information and telehealth technologies fit into this narrative, not only as medical transformations but also as disruptive transformation in how patients and physicians will relate to one another within society's modern health care systems (Khan, 2016). As a society, we need to balance this technological power that will alter our health care with responsible choices as opposed to simply accepting the inevitability of such transformations.

LAW FACT

Internet Prescribing

Can online questionnaires be substituted for face-to-face examinations or one-on-one conversations before approved drugs can be prescribed?

No. Licensed physicians cannot substitute online medical questionnaires for live consultations before prescribing approved drugs over Internet pharmacy websites. An Internet pharmacy cannot actively prescribe controlled substances online.

— *United States v. Hanny*, 509 F.3d 916 (U.S. Court of Appeals for the Eighth Circuit 2007) (addressing the use of a website to solicit customers for an illegal scheme, such as purchasing illegal products). *Followed by United States v. Executive Recycling, Inc.*, 953 F.Supp.2d 1138 (U.S. District Court for the District of Colorado 2013). *See* Hodge & Kilcourse, 2014 (for discussion of this case).

CHAPTER SUMMARY

- Telehealth technology holds great potential for positive change of the U.S. health care system by allowing for more rapid and accurate diagnoses, fewer human errors and omissions, and reduction in the rise of health care costs.
- A single global standard does not exist for sharing information among different electronic health records, and there is no agreement within the health care industry on how personal health records work with other electronic records.
- A standard norm for Web-based health information is ideal so that personal health records can be compatible with institutional electronic health records.
- Personal online health records are not currently covered by HIPAA.
- There is a significant difference between websites legally covered by HIPAA and websites that voluntarily comply with HIPAA; voluntarily compliant sites could change their policies quickly and without notice.
- Disclosure of identifiable information to public health officials does not automatically amount to an impermissible invasion of privacy.

- There are gaps in the integrity of online information; data about the credentials, training, and experience of physicians is available, but information about outcomes or quality of care is limited.
- There are no international laws or treaties that regulate Internet drug sales from entities outside the United States to individuals located within the United States.
- The issues of privacy, confidentiality, security, and performance incentives must be viewed within the context of the very important and beneficial uses that go along with data mining.
- Restrictions on identifiable prescription data are unconstitutional under the First Amendment because they stifle constitutionally protected commercial speech, which is not permissible unless the restriction directly serves a strong enough state interest.
- One consistent barrier to the reliability of any opt-in or opt-out system is that health websites frequently revise their policies, meaning that any permission Internet users initially grant regarding their privacy might gradually become obsolete over time.
- What is posted on Internet discussion groups, chat rooms, health blogs, podcasts, virtual communities, and wikis is not protected information because it is in the public domain.
- Most health websites do not disclose the use of Web bugs in their privacy policies or fully comply with their own privacy policies, and they regularly modify their policies without alerting Internet users to the change.
- Whoever gathers an individual's health information owns it, whether it is the individual or not.
- The small-town model has returned to the HIT industry; everyone has access to everyone else's information by virtue of the continually expanding World Wide Web.
- Physicians must figure out how to give parents basic health information about their adolescent children without breaking confidentiality or other rules.

LAW NOTES

1. General Electric and Intel offer hospitals large-scale remote health management systems for regional populations. Intel and the Mayo Clinic have launched a telehealth home-monitoring system for chronically ill patients. Telemedicine pilots are focused on refining high volume routine care systems that largely eliminate the need for face-to-face visits between physicians and patients (Blatt, 2012; Levins, 2012).
2. The University of Pennsylvania Health System (UPHS) uses an electronic health records system by Epic Systems, one of the leaders in the HIT field.[2] While UPHS's system yields benefits among its five Philadelphia regional hospitals (Hospital of the University of Pennsylvania, Penn Presbyterian Medical Center, Pennsylvania Hospital, Chester County Hospital, and Lancaster General Hospital), nine outlying facilities, and the PennCare primary care network, the electronic record ends if a patient goes to another health care network. For instance, if patients at UPHS go to the Thomas Jefferson University Hospital in Center City Philadelphia or the Main Line Health System in suburban Philadelphia, these hospital systems have no information about them without phone calls, time, and faxing. This means that diagnostic procedures are often repeated with a consequent rise in duplicative costs, even though these hospitals use the same Epic system.
3. Google entered the online health care space with the Cleveland Clinic, a globally renowned academic medical center. Patients who already use the clinic's personal health records can share prescriptions, conditions, and allergies between the clinic and a Google Health online profile, with patients controlling the information in their profile. The venture frees identifiable information from electronic health records so that patients can share identifiable information with health care providers and professionals and pharmacies outside the clinic's network. Since identifiable information is generally stored in institutional electronic health records instead of in the hands of patients, this is a step in giving patients more control over their identifiable information. This is especially useful for Cleveland Clinic patients who are retirees and spend about five months elsewhere, typically in Florida or Arizona.
4. Microsoft's HealthVault, a competing service to Google's venture with the Cleveland Clinic, is a free, Web-based service that allows Internet users to store their health records online and eventually share them with their physicians. One distinctive aspect of Microsoft's HealthVault is its number of project partners, including Allscripts (which provides electronic health records systems), the American Heart Association, Healthways (which provides wellness and disease prevention services), and various health care networks such as the Mayo

---

[2] Thomas Knadig, coauthor of this text, is an employee of UPHS.

Clinic and New York Presbyterian Hospital. Other partners include medical device makers for monitoring various health conditions (Johnson and Johnson LifeScan for blood glucose, Microlife and Omron for blood pressure, and Polar for heart rate). Many smaller firms, in addition to Google and Microsoft, are engaged in providing devices that monitor health vitals and upload them to the cloud (Ohm 2015).

5. The average victim of identity theft becomes aware only after about 14 months have passed, but in some cases discovering the crime takes 10 years or more (*See* Ball, 2011). This chapter does not specifically address the theft of personal health information, which could be harder to discover than financial theft from credit cards or banks.

6. While not social networking sites per se, many websites take advantage of the phenomenon of connecting online to reach out to special audiences. The Cancer Support Community, a not-for-profit group that provides free support and education to cancer patients and families, has a site called Group Loop that claims to reach more than 15% of the approximately 50,000 adolescent cancer survivors in the United States. With scheduled professionally moderated support groups, adolescents have access to message boards in a password-protected site. A comprehensive search engine allows adolescents to search for other adolescents with cancer by such criteria as age, location, or diagnosis.

7. SPSS's data-mining software, IBM's DB2 Intelligent Miner, and ACS's MIDAS+Data Vision full spectrum data management services (a Xerox company) are being used to identify hidden problems, trends, and patterns that are fixable in health care systems.

8. **Anonymizer technology** firms such as Hushmail, IDcide, and ZL Technologies have emerged to protect *privacy space* by making activity on the Internet untraceable. **Proxy server computers** and **onion routers** act as an intermediary between the user and the rest of the Internet; onion routers randomly bounce communications through a network of relays run by volunteers around the globe (Kozinski, 2015). Meritus Intelytics and Security Space have anonymizer programs that Internet users can use to spy on the spies. Their home pages promise Internet users that their software platforms can provide the protection to safely navigate through the increasingly unsafe channels of the connected cyber world (*See generally* Cortes, 2015).

REFERENCES

Abbott, R. (2013). Big data and pharmacovigilance: Using health information exchanges to revolutionize drug safety. *Iowa Law Review, 99,* 225–292.

Abraham, J. M., et al. (2011). Prevalence of electronic health records in U.S. hospitals. *Journal of Healthcare Engineering, 2*(2), 121–142.

Agarwal, R., et al. (2011). *Understanding development methods from other industries to improve the design of consumer health IT.* Rockville, MD: Agency for Healthcare Research and Quality.

AHRQ (Agency for Healthcare Research and Quality). (2016). *Health information technology: Computerized provider order entry.* Rockville, MD: AHRQ.

_____. (2013). *Practice facilitation handbook: Electronic health records and meaningful use.*

Altman, M., et al. (2015). Towards a modern approach to privacy-aware government data releases. *Berkeley Technology Law Journal, 30,* 1967–2071.

Angwin, J., & Stecklow, S. (2010, October 12). "Scrapers" dig deep for data on web. *Wall Street Journal,* p. A1.

Ard, B. J. (2015). The limits of industry-specific privacy law. *Idaho Law Review, 52,* 607–619.

Ash, J. S., et al. (2007). The extent and importance of unintended consequences related to computerized provider order entry. *Journal of the American Medical Informatics Association, 14*(4), 415–423.

ATA (American Telemedicine Association). (2016). *What is telemedicine?* Washington, DC: ATA.

Bagley, A. W., & Brown, J. S. (2015). Limited consumer privacy protections against the layers of big data. *Santa Clara High Technology Law Journal, 31,* 483–526.

Balkin, J. M. (2016). Information fiduciaries and the First Amendment. *University of California Davis Law Review, 49,* 1183–1234.

Ball, S. C. (2011). Ohio's aggressive attack on medical identity theft. *Journal of Law and Health, 24,* 111–149.

Bates, D. W. (2012). Clinical decision support and the law: The big picture. *Saint Louis University Journal of Health Law and Policy 5,* 319–324.

Berg, J. (2014). The e-health revolution and the necessary evolution of informed consent. *Indiana Health Law Review, 11,* 591–609.

Blatt, M., Global Medical Director, Intel. (2012, October 27). Remarks at the panel discussion on Physician Restructuring at the 2012 Wharton Alumni Healthcare Conference, Philadelphia, PA.

Brobst, J. A. (2015). Reverse sunshine in the digital wild frontier: Protecting individual privacy against public records requests for government databases. *Northern Kentucky Law Review, 42,* 191–283.

Burns, L. R. (Ed.). (2005). *The business of healthcare innovation.* New York, NY: Cambridge University Press.

Caulfield, T. (2015). The obesity gene and the (misplaced) search for a personalized approach to our weight gain problems. *Wake Forest Journal of Law and Policy, 5,* 125–143.

Chang, J. L. T. (2013). The dark cloud of convenience: How the new HIPAA omnibus rules fail to protect electronic personal health information. *Loyola of Los Angeles Entertainment Law Review, 34,* 119–154.

Clearwater, A., & Hughes, T. (2013). The second wave of global privacy protection: In the beginning… an early history of the privacy profession. *Ohio State Law Journal, 74,* 897–921.

Cortes, S. (2015). MLAT jiu-jitsu and tor: Mutual legal assistance treaties in surveillance. *Richmond Journal of Law and Technology, 22,* 1–99.

Crawford, K., & Schultz, J. (2014). Big data and due process: Toward a framework to redress predictive privacy harms. *Boston College Law Review, 55,* 93–128.

Cullitan, C. M. (2011). Please don't tell my mom! A minor's right to informational privacy. *Journal of Law and Education, 40,* 417–460.

Darrow, J. J. (2014). Pharmaceutical gatekeepers. *Indiana Law Review, 47,* 363–420.

Demleitner, N. V. (2014). The state, parents, schools, culture wars, and modern technologies: Challenges under the U.N. Convention on the Rights of the Child. *The American Journal of Comparative Law, 62,* 491–514.

DOJ (U.S. Department of Justice, National Drug Intelligence Center). (2011). *The economic impact of illicit drug use on American society.* Washington, DC: DOJ.

Drobac, J. A., & Goodenough, O. R. (2015). Exposing the myth of consent. *Indiana Health Law Review, 12,* 471–531.

Dudley, T. I. (2013). Bearing injustice: Foster care, pregnancy prevention, and the law. *Berkeley Journal of Gender, Law and Justice, 28,* 77–115.

FDA (U.S. Food and Drug Administration). (2016). *BeSafeRx: For health professionals.* Silver Spring, MD: FDA.

Finley, B. D. (2011). *Counterfeit drugs and national security.* Washington, DC: The Stimson Center.

Ford, R. A. (2016). Unilateral invasions of privacy. *Notre Dame Law Review, 91,* 1075–1115.

Foster, A. (2010). Critical dilemmas in genetic testing: Why regulations to protect the confidentiality of genetic information should be expanded. *Baylor Law Review, 62,* 537–572.

Fox, B. (2014). Mobile medical apps: Where health and Internet privacy law meet. *Houston Journal of Health Law and Policy, 14,* 193–221.

Fox, S., Associate Director of Digital Strategy at the Pew Research Center's Internet and American Life Project. (2015, February 13). Remarks at the panel discussion on What Information Do Patients Want and Need? At the National Quality Forum's 2014 Annual Conference on Making Sense of Quality Data for Patients, Providers, and Payers, Washington, DC.

Francis, L. P. (2012). When patients interact with electronic health records: Problems of privacy and confidentiality. *Houston Journal of Health Law and Policy, 12,* 171–199.

Fried, A. J. (2016). Behavioral health and population health management: Is it time for real progress? *Journal of Health and Life Sciences Law, 9*(2), 57–80.

Fuelleman, A. S. (2011). Right of publicity: Is behavioral marketing violating the right to control your identity online? *The John Marshall Law School Review of Intellectual Property Law, 10,* 810–831.

Gantt, Jr., G. (2014). Hacking health care: Authentication security in the age of meaningful use. *Journal of Law and Health, 27,* 232–257.

Goetz, T. (2010). *The decision tree: Taking control of your health in the new era of personalized medicine.* Emmaus, PA: Rodale Books.

Gratton, E. (2014). If personal information is privacy's gatekeeper, then risk of harm is the key: A proposed method for determining what counts as personal information. *Albany Law Journal of Science and Technology, 24,* 105–209.

Greaney, T. L. (2014). The tangled web: Integration, exclusivity, and market power in provider contracting. *Houston Journal of Health Law and Policy, 14,* 59–92.

Habib, J. L. (2010). Electronic health records, meaningful use, and a model electronic medical record. *Drug Benefit Trends, 22*(4), 99–101.

Haight, F. (2006). Illegal sales of pharmaceuticals on the Internet. *Albany Law Journal of Science and Technology, 16,* 565–570.

Hale-Kupiec, T. (2016). Immortal invasive initiatives? The need for a genetic right to be forgotten. *Minnesota Journal of Law, Science and Technology, 17,* 441–487.

Hartzog, W., & Stutzman, F. (2013). The case for online obscurity. *California Law Review, 101,* 1–49.

Hayden, T. P. (2014). Using the medical loss ratio to incentivize the adoption of innovative medical technology. *Vanderbilt Journal of Entertainment and Technology Law, 17,* 239–265.

Hodge, S. D., & Kilcourse, A. (2014). Gauging the heartbeat of e-prescriptions? A retrospective analysis. *Michigan State University Journal of Medicine and Law, 18,* 1–27.

Hoffman, S. (2014). Medical big data and big data quality problems. *Connecticut Insurance Law Journal, 21,* 289–316.

Hoffman, S., & Podgurski, A. (2012). Balancing privacy, autonomy, and scientific needs in electronic health records research. *Southern Methodist University Law Review, 65,* 85–144.

Hoppin, M. B. (2012). Overly intimate surveillance: Why emergent public health surveillance programs deserve strict scrutiny under the Fourteenth Amendment. *New York University Law Review, 87,* 1950–1994.

Huntington, A. R. (2014). Ready or not, here they come: A discussion of the legal and ethical considerations for the implementation of electronic medical records. *Annals of Health Law, 23,* 153–198.

Jefferson, D. J. (2015). Biosociality, reimagined: A global distributive justice framework for ownership of human genetic material. *Chicago–Kent Journal of Intellectual Property, 14,* 357–378.

Johnson, C. (2015). Crossroads: How the intersection of technology, medicine, and the law impact the administration of healthcare in Florida and Puerto Rico. *University of Miami Inter-American Law Review, 46,* 209–240.

Jones, S. S., et al. (2010). Electronic health record adoption and quality improvement in U.S. hospitals. *American Journal of Managed Care, 16*(12), 64–71.

Kaelber, D. C., et al. (2012). *The value of personal health records.* Charlestown, MA: Center for Information Technology Leadership.

Kaplan, B. (2015). Selling health data: De-identification, privacy, and speech. *Cambridge Quarterly of Healthcare Ethics, 24*(3), 256–271.

Keehan, S. P., et al. (2015). National health expenditure projections, 2014–24: Spending growth faster than recent trends. *Health Affairs, 34*(8), 1407–1417.

Kessler, A. (2006). *The end of medicine: How Silicon Valley (and naked mice) will reboot your doctor.* New York, NY: HarperCollins.

Khan, F. (2015). The "uberization" of healthcare: The forthcoming legal storm over mobile health technology's impact on the medical profession. *Health Matrix, 26,* 123–172.

Kozinski, A. (2015). The two faces of anonymity. *Capital University Law Review, 43,* 1–17.

Kramer, D. B., et al. (2014). Ensuring medical device effectiveness and safety: A cross-national comparison of approaches to regulation. *Food and Drug Law Journal, 69,* 1–23.

Kruse, C. S., et al. (2014). Factors associated with adoption of health information technology: A conceptual model based on a systematic review. *Journal of Medical Internet Research: Medical Informatics, 2*(1), 9–19.

Leapfrog Group. (2016). *Leapfrog hospital survey. Factsheet: Computerized physician order entry.* Washington, DC: Leapfrog Group.

___. (2013). *Hospital errors are the third leading cause of death in United States, and new hospital safety scores show improvements are too slow.*

Leary, M. G. (2013). *Katz* on a hot tin roof: Saving the Fourth Amendment from commercial conditioning by reviving voluntariness in disclosures to third parties. *American Criminal Law Review, 50*, 341–386.

Leonard, E. W., et al. (2016). Best practices for establishing Georgia's Alzheimer's disease registry. *Minnesota Journal of Law, Science and Technology, 17*, 221–275.

Levins, H. (2012, December). *The end of face-to-face doctor visits? Intel medical director calls for disruptive change.* Penn Leonard Davis Institute of Health Economics.

Lieber, J. B. (2016, May 18). How to make hospitals less deadly. *Wall Street Journal*, p. A13.

___. (2015). *Killer care: How medical error became America's third largest cause of death and what can be done about it.* Amazon Digital.

Lipman, B. (2013). Prescribing medicine for online pharmacies: An assessment of the law and a proposal to combat illegal drug outlets. *American Criminal Law Review, 50*, 545–573.

Martin, T. D. (2011). The impact of healthcare reform on revenue-cycle management and claim coding. *Journal of Health and Life Sciences Law, 4*(3), 159–206.

McKay, M., et al. (2015). Frequency and severity of parenteral nutrition medication errors at a large children's hospital after implementation of electronic ordering and compounding. *Nutrition in Clinical Practice, 31*, 195–206.

McLaughlin, S. T. (2007). Pandora's box: Can HIPAA still protect patient privacy under a national health care information network? *Gonzaga Law Review, 42*, 29–60.

Nambisan, P., et al. (2013). Understanding electronic medical record adoption in the United States: Communication and sociocultural perspectives. *Interactive Journal of Medical Research, 2*(1), 1–11.

Noah, L. (2013). Medical device law: Turn the beat around? Deactivating implanted cardiac-assist devices. *William Mitchell Law Review, 39*, 1229–1286.

Nuckols, T., et al. (2015). Implementing computerized provider order entry in acute care hospitals in the United States could generate substantial savings to society. *Joint Commission Journal on Quality and Patient Safety, 41*(8), 341–351.

Ohm, P. (2015). Sensitive information. *Southern California Law Review, 88*, 1125–1196.

ONC (Office of the National Coordinator for Health information Technology). (2014). *Connecting health and care for the nation: A shared nationwide interoperability roadmap.* Washington, DC: U.S. Department of Health and Human Services, ONC.

Orts, E. W., & Sepinwall, A. (2015). Privacy and organizational persons. *Minnesota Law Review, 99*, 2275–2323.

Pasquale, F. (2014). Redescribing health privacy: The importance of information policy. *Houston Journal of Health Law and Policy, 14*, 95–128.

Perlmutter, B. P. (2011). More therapeutic, less collaborative? Asserting the psychotherapist–patient privilege on behalf of mature minors. *Barry Law Review, 17*, 45–87.

Peters, R. M. (2014). So you've been notified, now what? The problem with current data-breach notification laws. *Arizona Law Review, 56*, 1171–1202.

Pew Internet and American Life Project. (2016). *Shared, collaborative and on demand: The new digital economy.* Washington, DC: Pew Research Center.

___. (2013). *Health fact sheet.*

Porter, M. E., & Lee, T. H. (2013). The strategy that will fix health care. *Harvard Business Review, 91*(10), 50–70.

Posner, R. A. (2007). *Economic analysis of the law* (7th ed.). Amsterdam, Netherlands: Wolters Kluwer Law and Business.

Pratt, D. (2015). Telehealth and telemedicine. *Albany Law Journal of Science and Technology, 25*, 495–545.

Price, II, W. N. (2015). Black-box medicine. *Harvard Journal of Law and Technology, 28*(2), 420–467.

Ray, A. (2014). Bye-bye Big Gulp? New York City's attempt to limit the sale of soda. *Stetson Law Review, 44*, 265–287.

Saxena, S., Associate Partner, IBM Global Business Services. (2016, February 19). *Remarks at the panel discussion on Clinical Data Analytics: Getting Personal: Harnessing Analytics for New Patient Insights at the Wharton Health Business Conference on The Innovation Game: The Race Between Entrants+Incumbents*, Philadelphia, PA.

Schultz, B. (2015). Online pharmacy regulation: How the Ryan Haight Online Pharmacy Consumer Protection Act can help solve an international problem. *San Diego International Law Journal, 16*, 381–415.

Schumacher, A. (2015). Telehealth: Current barriers, potential progress. *Ohio State Law Journal, 76*, 409–439.

Schwartz, P. M., & Solove, D. J. (2011). The personally identifiable information problem: Privacy and a new concept of personally identifiable information. *New York University Law Review, 86*, 1814–1894.

Shekelle, S. P., et al. (2006). *Costs and benefits of health information technology.* Rockville, MD: AHRQ.

Silow-Carroll, S., et al. (2012). *Using electronic health records to improve quality and efficiency: The experience of leading hospitals.* New York, NY: The Commonwealth Fund.

Simer, J. A., & Schoeffel, S. (2015). The wide world of narrow networks: How health care providers can adapt and succeed. *Journal of Health and Life Sciences Law, 9*(1), 9–23.

Smith, M., Global Risk Management Officer Global Patient Safety Amgen, Inc. (2015, October 5). Remarks on Integrating Risk Evaluation and Mitigation Strategies (REMS) into the Health Care Delivery System at the Food and Drug Administration Public Meeting on REMS: Understanding and Evaluating Their Impact on the Health Care Delivery System and Patient Access, Bethesda, MD.

Solove, D. J., & Hartzog, W. (2014). The FTC and the new common law of privacy. *Columbia Law Review, 114*, 583–676.

Solove, D. J., Hartzog, W., & Schwartz, P. (2014). *Information privacy law* (5th ed.). Amsterdam, Netherlands: Wolters Kluwer Law and Business.

Starr, P. (1994). *The social transformation of American medicine* (4th ed.). New York, NY: Perseus Book Group, Basic Books. (Original work published 1984.)

Swisher, A. W. (2014). The importance of clinical integration to provider networks under the Affordable Care Act. *Journal of Health and Life Sciences Law, 8*(1), 1–19.

Szerejko, J. D. (2015). Reading between the lines of electronic health records: The Health Information Technology for Economic and Clinical Health Act and its implications for health care fraud and information security. *Connecticut Law Review, 47*, 1103–1152.

Terry, N. P. (2014). Pit crews with computers: Can health information technology fix fragmented care? *Houston Journal of Health Law and Policy, 14*, 129–189.

___. (2012). Fear of Facebook: Private ordering of social media risks incurred by healthcare providers. *Nebraska Law Review, 90*, 703–751.

___. (2010). Physicians and patients who "friend" or "tweet": Constructing a legal framework for social networking in a highly regulated domain. *Indiana Law Review, 43*, 285–341.

Tomain, J. A. (2014). Online privacy and the First Amendment: An opt-in approach to data processing. *University of Cincinnati Law Review, 83*, 1–70.

Trubek, L. G. (2006). New governance and soft law in health care reform. *Indiana Health Law Review, 3*, 137–169.

Walker, J., et al. (2005). The value of healthcare information exchange and interoperability. *Health Affairs*, W10–W18.

Weiss, N. (2012). Combating inaccuracies in criminal background checks by giving meaning to the Fair Credit Reporting Act. *Brooklyn Law Review, 78*, 271–303.

Wharton School at the University of Pennsylvania. (2006). Lawton Burns on the critical, and costly, role of companies that make healthcare-related products. *Knowledge@Wharton.*

White House, The. (2011). *Counterfeit pharmaceutical inter-agency working group report to the Vice President of the United States and to Congress.* Washington. DC: Office of the Intellectual Property Enforcement Coordinator, U.S. Food and Drug Administration, U.S. Customs and Border Protection, U.S. Immigration and Customs, U.S. Departments of Justice, State, and Commerce, and the Agency for International Development.

Yan, H., et al. (2012). Beyond the focus group: Understanding physicians' barriers to electronic medical records. *Joint Commission Journal on Quality and Patient Safety, 38*(4), 184–191.

Yong, P. L., et al. (2010). *The healthcare imperative: Lowering costs and improving outcomes: Institute of Medicine roundtable on evidence-based medicine.* Washington, DC: National Academies Press.

Zarsky, T. Z. (2015). The privacy-innovation conundrum. *Lewis and Clark Law Review, 19*, 115–168.

___. (2013). Transparent predictions. *University of Illinois Law Review, 2013*, 1503–1569.

PART VII

IMPROVING THE QUALITY OF HEALTH CARE

Part VII explores areas that could combat rising health care costs and improve the quality of health care.

© Andy Dean Photography/ShutterStock, Inc.

CHAPTER 21

Population Health Management

"Moving into the next century, the most important breakthroughs will be in the form of clinical process innovation rather than clinical product improvement."

— **J. D. Kleinke**, Health care economist and author of *Bleeding Edge: The Business of Health Care in the New Century (1998)*

IN BRIEF

This chapter describes the demand for greater transparency regarding how hospitals and physicians effectively treat patients and the concomitant drive to develop clinical databases and other processes to assist health care systems in making responsible medical treatment decisions.

LEARNING OBJECTIVES

Upon completion of this chapter readers should be able to:

1. Explain why management of population health is critical to containing health care costs.
2. List the key elements in population health management.
3. Explain how and why employers are shifting health care costs to employees.
4. Describe how the Leapfrog Group achieves its mission of reducing preventable medical mistakes.
5. Distinguish the approach of Bridges to Excellence from that of the Leapfrog Group.
6. Outline ideas of incentive-based programs.
7. Describe the evidence of effectiveness of incentive-based programs.
8. Discuss why the American Medical Association thinks population health management programs violate physician privacy and encounter problems.

KEY TERMS

Accountability
Acute episodes
Bridges to Excellence
Budget neutrality
Bundled payments
Care continuum programs
Chronic disease
Chronic health care initiatives
Clinical guidelines
Clinical outcome targets
Clinical outcomes
Collaborative practice
  models

Computerized physician order entry
  systems
Consumer-driven cost-sharing
  programs
Cost-sharing
Cost-shifting
Employer-based initiatives
Evidence-based medicine
Fee-for-service
Government-based initiatives
Health information technology
Health insurance designs
Health insurer-based initiatives

Health maintenance organization
Health outcomes
Incentive-based programs
Leapfrog Group
Medical errors
Medical home
National Committee for Quality
  Assurance
Nationally standardized rewards
  program
Outcome-oriented
Physician Voluntary Reporting
  Program

443

FACT OR FICTION

Transparency of Physician Effectiveness

Are the privacy interests of individual physicians more important than the public's need to monitor the cost and quality of health care provided under the Medicare insurance program?

A lawsuit, explained in an earlier chapter on patient rights and responsibilities, is a key battle in the effort to reshape the U.S. health care system. Consumer advocates, employers, and the health insurance industry maintain access to Medicare insurance claims filed by physicians' offices could help independent groups monitor quality and wasteful health care; patients would not be identified. Physicians are worried such disclosures would violate their privacy, and that resulting ratings could portray some physicians' offices inaccurately. The not-for-profit ratings group, Consumers' Checkbook, won a lower court ruling directing the government to release the records under the federal Freedom of Information Act. The U.S. Department of Health and Human Services, joined by the American Medical Association, appealed over the issue of who should be allowed to see Medicare data on individual physicians.

— *See* Law Fact at the end of this chapter for the answer.

Principles and Applications

Population health management for common, preventable health conditions, such as hypertension and diabetes, is critical to containing health care costs. Seven of the top 10 causes of death each year are because of **chronic disease**. Estimates indicate that about half of all adults in the United States live with a chronic disease, the ongoing care for which amounts to 86% of the annual $2.6 trillion health care budget (CDC, 2016). The disconnect between reimbursing for **chronic health care initiatives** and poor **health outcomes** has become an issue, not only for physicians and health care professionals, but for employers and **third-party payers** that ultimately play a major role in financing health care costs related to chronic diseases (Wolff & Boult, 2005).

Population health management is one of the reform strategies proposed to moderate health care spending growth and improve quality. Six key elements of population health management programs are:

- **Collaborative practice models**
- **Evidence-based medicine** guidelines
- Patient self-management education
- **Population identification processes**
- Process and outcomes measurement, evaluation, and management
- Routine reporting/feedback

(NCQA, 2015).

Although each of these components individually helps to achieve quality in health care, the impact of each is much more significant when combined. The extent to which a specific population health management program incorporates each component varies, but the most successful programs fully incorporate all six components (NCQA, 2015). An example of care continuum initiatives at Merck and Dow Chemical, two corporate members of the highly successful Leapfrog Group, follows.

Health Care Quality

Many U.S. employers are investing in new population health management programs to improve the quality of health care for chronic health conditions (NCQA, 2015). Simultaneously, these employers are shifting more of the health care costs to their employees without understanding the implications on the amount and type of care employees will seek or receive (Satz, 2015). **Cost-shifting** to individuals with chronic health conditions, who need extensive care, does not constrain costs; in fact, it increases costs if employees cannot afford to pay for the cost shift and forgo monitoring and preventive health care (Miglani, 2016). These seemingly contradictory actions reflect the employer's inability to make an accurate assessment regarding how their decisions about providing health insurance to their employees affect their profits.

Like the cycle of poverty, the cycle of chronic health conditions continues indefinitely. Examples include employees with uncontrolled cholesterol who develop atherosclerosis, which leads to heart disease and strokes, and overweight employees who develop diabetes, which leads to kidney disease and renal failure, and eventually may result in the need for dialysis. Uncontrolled diabetes is the number one reason adults need dialysis (NIDDK, 2014).

When employees fail to monitor their chronic health conditions, they risk developing **acute episodes**; acute episodes often require emergency care and/or hospitalization. The cost of health care delivered in an emergency setting, as well as hospital care, almost always exceeds whatever it would have cost to monitor and take preventive measures in the first place (Dean & Grabowski, 2014). The end result, cost-shifting for chronic health conditions, is not cost-effective unless people can afford the shift in costs. Employers must:

- Determine how much should be invested in employee health
- Encourage appropriate use of health care by their employees
- Identify the best benefit designs to encourage appropriate delivery of health care

(NCQA, 2015; Underhill, 2016).

One method, developed by Merck and Dow Chemical, improves employee health using estimates of the benefits of reducing absences and improving productivity. Employers benefit from:

- Decreased health care costs
- Improved on-the-job productivity
- Lower turnover
- Reduced absences

(Hickox & Guzman, 2014).

An employee who takes a sick day affects the entire workplace, with far-reaching financial consequences that go beyond the employee's individual duties, especially when the employee's team performs time-sensitive work. It is difficult, however, to measure the impact of employee absenteeism.

Job-by-Job Assessments

There are broad implications for job-by-job assessments. For instance, when the cumulative cost of productivity losses is calculated, estimates of the overall cost of health-related workforce absences increase by one-third (IOM, 2003; Standard Insurance, 2012). More importantly, the assessment can help justify spending more money to improve the quality of employer-provided health insurance. Population health management programs that help employees manage chronic health conditions, for instance, could pay for themselves by reducing absences and improving productivity, yet hard numbers are required to justify making these up-front expenditures. Relative to healthy employees, employees in poor health are more likely to be absent from work and less productive when they are at work. These indirect costs of poor health may actually exceed direct health care costs (IOM, 2003). The question is how employers can quantify the benefits of investing in employee health.

Costs of Health-Related Absences from Work

The cost of health-related work absences often goes beyond salaries paid to absent employees. When perfect replacement employees are not available to substitute for an ill colleague, there are broader implications for productivity. As mentioned, this is especially true where employees work in teams and where team output is time sensitive. For instance, many nurses serve as the physician's memory by tracking patients and ensuring diagnostic tests and treatments are delivered in a timely fashion. When a nurse is absent, the loss in productivity can be large, as replacements struggle to learn about the absent nurse's workload. That is not as true, however, with the office phlebotomist trained to draw blood from patients. Because the phlebotomist tends to perform discrete, measurable tasks and works individually, medical practices do not face the same struggles in replacing a phlebotomist.

Salary Multipliers

Researchers at the Wharton School at the University of Pennsylvania put numbers to this concept of costs and identified 35 jobs in 12 industries involving different types of **production functions**. They then interviewed more than 800 managers to determine the financial consequences of employee absences. Based on the interviews, they estimated **salary multipliers** for each of the jobs. The multiplier reflects the costs of health-related absences from work as a proportion of the absent employee's daily salary. The median multiplier was 1.28, which means that for the median job, the cost of an absence was 28% higher than the employee's salary because of the impact on overall productivity (NCQA, 2015). For instance, maintenance workers in hospitals and health care clinics were on the low end of the scale, with multipliers less than 1.1. Physicians were at the high end, with multipliers greater than 1.5.

Employers with employees that have high multipliers would be more likely to invest in their employees' health, because the productivity impact of absenteeism is relatively high (NCQA, 2015). While most employers believe management of chronic disease programs are effective in containing health insurance costs, employers who account for salary multipliers when evaluating potential expenditures on employer-sponsored health insurance plans make very different decisions (Business Roundtable, 2009).

Population Health Management Programs

The extended hospital stay or major health complication for just one employee can be a huge financial burden for a small employer. To prevent such expenses, some small businesses are installing **care continuum programs** staffed by nurses who work with employees to better manage and treat their chronic illnesses. Multinational corporations have used such programs for some time. Smaller employers are now finding the programs help employees reduce health complications, which leads to lower long-term health care costs (Morrell & Krouse, 2014).

For instance, with population health management programs, nurses monitor employees with chronic health conditions to ensure they receive appropriate, timely health care. The programs do not generate enough of a return on investment simply in terms of health care costs they help employees avoid. Nor are the programs' net present values overwhelmingly positive when considering the **salary value** of the absences they help reduce. However, when employee salary values are weighted by salary multipliers, the scenario is different. The net present value of population health management programs over the first five years jumps nearly fourfold, making them a much easier sell (NCQA, 2015).

Presenteeism

Research at Dow Chemical took the salary multiplier concept one step further by looking at **presenteeism**, or the impact of sickness on the productivity of those who come to work while ill (Wharton, 2005). When Dow asked about presenteeism (working with reduced productivity) issues in a survey on employee health (as opposed to absenteeism, missing work), the survey found more than half of its employees reported having one or more chronic conditions (Johns, 2010). This generated a startling finding: while chronic ailments, such as diabetes, arthritis, and circulatory disorders, were responsible for the most direct health care costs, the costliest condition per employee overall, after factoring the costs of presenteeism, was depression (Polaris, 2016). Such data helped Dow develop focused intervention strategies on specific conditions it would not have known about without the survey. Dow's strategy is now focusing more on:

- Prevention
- Quality of health care
- Value, with more sophisticated purchasing of health care, such as incentive-based programs that incorporate population health management

(Anderson et al., 2016).

Employer Ambivalence About Health Insurance

Theoretically, like Dow Chemical, employers could serve as catalysts for improving health care if they mobilized their purchasing power to compel the health care industry to focus on safety and quality. In theory, U.S. employers have the power to drive change because they provide health insurance coverage for over 160 million people at a cost of nearly $2 trillion (Kaiser & HRET, 2016). Indeed, employers spent an average of $12,700 for family health insurance premiums above the employee's contribution (an additional $4,800) (Long et al., 2016a). Collectively, employers have the market power to demand transparency and easy access to health care information. Ambivalence on what strategy to pursue to change the U.S. health care system appears to be thwarting this market force. Three current and seemingly contradictory trends in employer-provided health insurance suggests the American public is still ambivalent about the direction health care reform should take (Sides et al., 2016).

Consumer-Driven Health Insurance

More employers are shifting the costs of their health insurance plans to employees, partly because costs have ballooned (Kaiser & HRET, 2016). The highest profile example of this trend has been the move to higher deductible plans combined with health savings accounts, championed as a way to combat health care inflation by giving consumers of health care incentives to shop more astutely for care. The accounts also represent a way for employers to make employees more responsible for their own health care (NCQA, 2015).

Higher Employee Cost-Sharing

High-profile health savings accounts aside, **cost-sharing** can also be something as simple as increasing co-payments. Taken together, the expansion of consumer-driven health plans with higher employee cost-sharing illustrate that employers are struggling to make an accurate assessment about how health insurance decisions affect the bottom line. The cost-sharing trend, in particular, comes at a time when information is lacking about whether:

- Short-term savings will lead to long-term health problems and costs because employees avoid primary care for financial reasons
- Employees will try harder to stay healthy in order to avoid paying more if they get sick

(NCQA, 2015).

Tighter Managed Care Networks

At the same time that employers are implementing **consumer-driven cost-sharing programs**, many are investing in population health management. Some employers are investing in **incentive-based programs**, which are particularly controversial as a means of paying individual physicians based on quality of care (Underhill, 2016). In an attempt to control costs, employers more tightly manage the care networks employees can use so as to improve health care quality. The rationale is that if the quality of care improves by use of health care systems with less medical errors, less system defects, and a reduced level of unnecessary treatments, health care costs can be better controlled by the reduction in waste and inefficiencies caused by errors, misuse, and overuse of health care. While disease management is a system of coordinated interventions for populations with health conditions in which self-care is significant, another managed care intervention movement that involves adding an incentive component to population health management has emerged: incentive-based payments to health care providers based on meeting specific agreed-upon outcomes targets for each individual patient (Anderson et al., 2016).

Leapfrog Group

The **Leapfrog Group** was formed when a group of large employers expressed an interest in influencing the quality and affordability of health care. They recognized the dysfunction in the health care marketplace: they were spending billions of dollars on health care for their employees with no way of assessing its quality or comparing health care providers. The initial focus of the Leapfrog Group was reducing preventable medical mistakes (Dine, 2016).

Health care in the United States is not as safe as it should be and can be. Hospital safety breakdowns, including patient injuries, accidents, and infections, kill over 200,000 Americans each year, making these **medical errors** the third-leading cause of death in the United States (Leapfrog, 2016). In fact, more deaths occur in hospitals each year from medical errors than from vehicle accidents, breast cancer, and AIDS combined.

To address this problem, the Leapfrog Group is providing market reinforcement for the quality and safety of health care. The Leapfrog Group decided it could take 'leaps' forward with its employees, retirees, and families by rewarding hospitals that implemented significant improvements in quality and safety (Moss, 2005). Funding to set up Leapfrog came from the Business Roundtable and the Johnson & Johnson Foundation, as well as member employers.[LN1]

Leapfrog members agreed to base their purchase of health care on principles that encouraged quality improvement among providers and consumer involvement. One of the Leapfrog Group's stated missions is to promote high-value health care through incentives and rewards. In response to this mission, it initiated a **nationally standardized rewards program** for participating hospitals and encouraged hospitals to adopt three practices to prevent medical errors:

- **Computerized physician order entry** systems for prescribing drugs
- Evidence-based hospital referrals
- Intensive care unit staffing by physicians experienced in critical care medicine

(Moriates et al., 2015).

Rewards in the form of bonus payments and higher payment rates are given to hospitals that demonstrate excellence or show improvement.

The Leapfrog Group has documented that:

- By referring patients needing certain complex medical procedures to hospitals offering the best survival odds based on scientifically valid criteria (such as the number of times a hospital performs these procedures each year), a patient's risk of dying can be reduced by 40%.
- Computerized physician order entry systems reduce serious prescribing errors in hospitals by more than 50%.
- Staffing ICUs with physicians who have special training in critical care medicine (intensivists) reduces the risk of patients dying in the ICU by 40%.

(Leapfrog, 2016; Moriates et al., 2015).

The Leapfrog Group also focuses on measuring effectiveness and affordability in five clinical areas by having hospitals voluntarily establish system and process standards for:

- Acute myocardial infarction
- Coronary artery bypass graft
- Obstetrical deliveries
- Percutaneous coronary intervention
- Pneumonia

Currently, more than 1,800 hospitals participate in this Leapfrog Group program and agree to adhere to the evidence-based standards (Leapfrog, 2016). Participating hospitals, covering six out of 10 hospital beds in the United States, are surveyed on a regular basis, and the results of the survey are made public.

Bridges to Excellence

Bridges to Excellence is a national program initiated by employers with health insurers and individual physicians in response to the Institute of Medicine's report, *Crossing the Quality Chasm: A New Health System for the 21st Century*, and, in particular, the report's recommendation to redesign payment in order to effectuate **quality improvement**. General Electric worked for at least five years on this insurer-focused program to identify the higher quality physicians used by its employees, thereby setting the stage for providing financial incentives for those employees who use better health care providers (NCQA, 2015).

The Leapfrog Group is involved in this insurer-focused effort as well, along with the **National Committee for Quality Assurance**. The three key principles guiding Bridges to Excellence are:

- Reengineering health care processes to reduce mistakes will require investments, for which employers and health insurers should create financial incentives.
- Significant reductions in **system defects** (misuse, underuse, overuse) will help reduce waste and inefficiencies in U.S. health care.
- Increased **accountability** and quality improvements will be encouraged by the release of comparative performance data on individual physicians, delivered to consumers of health care.

(Moriates et al., 2015; *See* NCQA, 2016).

In general, participating health insurers pay bonuses to individual physicians for program compliance. Currently, Bridges to Excellence consists of **health information technology** programs that encourage physicians to become less reactive and more proactive in five areas:

- Cardiac care focused on hypertension, hyperlipidemia, coronary artery disease, and cardiovascular disease
- Depression care management
- Diabetes care
- Physician office management with development of medical homes for patients where specialist health care is coordinated, instead of patients receiving fragmented care from numerous unrelated health care providers
- Spine care

(Moriates et al., 2015).

Patient-Centered Medical Homes

Some patients have multiple chronic conditions, such as advanced diabetes or heart disease, that require population health management across many different specialties and one **medical home**, or one physician coordinating the patient's plan of care. Currently, when patients seek care for multiple problems, they often receive health care with little or no coordination between health care providers (NCQA, 2015). Specialty and primary care providers often administer parallel treatments with minimal ability to share information regarding a common patient. For instance, one patient may see a specialist, and then see their primary care physician, for the same condition. The primary care physician may be unaware of treatments, diagnostic tests, or drugs prescribed by the specialist. This lack of coordination can lead to:

- Complication of ongoing treatment plans
- Jeopardizing patient safety, often resulting in conflicting medicines
- Loss of critical patient information
- Repeat of needless treatment procedures
- Treatment delays
- Unnecessary expenditures and administrative waste

(Moriates et al., 2015).

Numerous factors drive this disjointed care:

- Health insurance coverage
- Institutional and practice boundaries
- Professional behavior and staffing
- Technology availability to gather and exchange data

(Dine, 2016).

Successful and efficient patient outcomes require increased efforts to share patient information among health care providers, linked by health information technology programs. These coordinated efforts must be tied to best practices and clinical outcomes that can be measured and shared across clinic sites as standard treatment plans that define the acceptable level or type of care the patient should receive.

Employer Payoffs from Improving Employee Health

What is missing in this debate about health insurance, with both the Leapfrog Group and Bridges to Excellence approaches, is:

- An accurate method to determine how much employers should invest in the health care of their employees
- Identification of the best **health insurance designs** to encourage appropriate health care delivery and use, such as:
  - Adjusting employers' contribution rates
  - Cost-sharing adjustments (coinsurance and out-of-pocket expenses)
  - Elimination of coverage for particular conditions

(Moriates et al., 2015).

When measuring the true cost of employee absences, employers should also accurately measure the payoffs that come from improving the health of their employees. Health care system improvements aside, how does this translate into lower health insurance premiums? Or does it?

Incentive-Based Programs

The number of incentive-based programs has increased from the Leapfrog Group and Bridges to Excellence initiatives to about 160 different programs (Baker & Delbanco, 2007). While all these various programs attempt to link health care spending to **quality care**, not all population health management is the same. The most important distinctions include:

- How individual physicians and hospitals are compensated for quality or performance
- How performance is measured
- The level of involvement by physicians and other health care professionals
- Who sponsors the program

(Shah, 2016).

Clinical and Nonclinical Performance Measures

Most incentive-based programs measure performance in both clinical and non-clinical areas. Patient satisfaction and the use of information technology constitute common performance measures outside of the clinical realm (Van Tassel, 2013). Whereas clinical practice guidelines, fashioned from properly conducted systematic reviews, are used to implement most incentive-based programs in the clinical area (Rosoff, 2012).

Information Technology

Many incentive-based programs use information technology as the primary non-clinical measure. An adequate information technology structure is required for efficient collection and reporting of relevant measurement criteria. Incentive-based programs may evaluate whether physicians have adequate information technology and whether physicians are using the technology. Since information technology is an integral component of incentive-based programs, the cost of information technology may be one of the major obstacles to widespread implementation of these programs (Van Tassel, 2013).

Process of Care Targets

Clinical measurements can be categorized as **process-oriented** or **outcome-oriented**. Incentive-based programs may measure several aspects of the **process of care**. For instance, the programs may review whether a physician uses a tracking system to remind patients to follow up on treatments, tests, or medication reviews. A program may also measure whether a physician uses any tools, such as education or resources, to assist patients in managing their own conditions. Programs typically measure whether the physician provides specific brand-name drugs or diagnostic screenings to all patients with a certain disease. Finally, a major part of the process measures whether physicians follow **clinical guidelines** or evidence-based medicine for certain conditions (Rosoff, 2012).

Clinical Outcome Targets

Most incentive-based programs also measure **clinical outcomes** (Rosoff, 2012). For instance, a program may measure whether hypertension patients are within a range of acceptable blood pressure levels or diabetes patients are controlling their glucose levels. This is probably the most controversial aspect of performance measurement because outcomes are not entirely within the physician's control (Underhill, 2016).

A patient's clinical outcome depends on many factors unrelated to a physician's performance, and some argue this measurement fails to consider those factors (Rosoff, 2012). Basic population health management standards are being jointly developed by the federal government, the health insurance industry, and professional physician groups as illustrated in **FEATURE BOX 21-1**. All health care providers should seek to meet certain **clinical outcome targets**, meaning their patient population should fall within certain percentage ranges, with outlier providers requiring further examination of their performance. For instance, one standard is that patients should be receiving an annual influenza vaccine; another standard is that patients with coronary artery disease should be prescribed lipid-lowering therapy. This is not to say that every patient should be vaccinated for influenza or that every patient with coronary artery disease should be prescribed lipid-lowering medicines; rather, there should be a clinical justification for patients not to be vaccinated, or for patients not to be prescribed lipid-lowering medicines (Underhill, 2016).

FEATURE BOX 21-1

Basic Set of Population Health Management Standards

General Preventive Measures

- All female patients should receive breast cancer screenings, beginning between ages 40 to 44
- All female patients, ages 21 to 65, should receive cervical cancer screenings
- All patients should receive regular colorectal cancer screenings, beginning at age 50
- All patients should receive an influenza vaccine annually
- All patients should receive a pneumonia vaccine at 65 years and older
- All patients who smoke should be offered smoking cessation advice
- All patients should receive a tobacco use inquiry

Asthma

- Percentage of patients identified as having persistent asthma who were prescribed drugs
- Percentage of patients prescribed preferred, long-term control drugs or acceptable alternatives

Coronary Artery Disease

- Beta-blocker treatment immediately after myocardial infarction
- Percentage of patients with coronary artery disease prescribed lipid-lowering therapy
- Persistent beta-blocker treatment months after discharge

Depression

- Percentage of adults diagnosed with a new episode of depression treated with an antidepressant and who remained on medication during 84-day acute treatment phase
- Percentage of adults who remained on antidepressant for six months

Diabetes

- Percentage of patients who received retinal or dilated eye exam by specialist
- Percentage of patients with at least one LDL test
- Percentage of patients with blood pressure below 140/90
- Perform one or more A_{1c} tests (for glucose control or blood sugar)
- Percentage of patients with most recent A_{1c} level greater than 9% (poor control)
- Percentage of patients with most recent LDL less than 100 mg/dL or 130 mg/dL

Heart Failure

- Certain patients prescribed ACE inhibitor (pharmaceutical used primarily in treatment of hypertension and congestive heart failure) or ARB therapy (pharmaceutical given in combination with ACE inhibitors)
- Left ventricular failure assessment (classic site of myocardial infarction or heart attacks)

AAFP, 2016; ACP, 2016; AHIP, 2016; AHRQ, 2014; NCQA, 2015.

Program Sponsorship by Health Insurers and the Government

Even though incentive-based programs vary, most can be categorized into a few common models:

- **Employer-based initiatives**: Employers coordinate bonuses to individual physicians for each patient for achieving performance measures or improving performance; payments are usually true bonuses with the potential to change behavior.
- **Health insurer-based initiatives**: Insurers coordinate bonus payments to individual physicians for improved performance measures.

Health Insurer-Based Initiatives

Other than the Bridges to Excellence program, numerous health insurers implemented their own individualized incentive programs to compel physicians' better use of evidence-based medicine and to cut down on over-treating and under-treating of chronic conditions. Most have been judged failures (Marmor & Sullivan, 2015; Sage, 2016). Health care cost, quality, and access remain perennial problems no matter how physicians work to lower health care costs while simultaneously improving health care quality and patient outcomes (Hermer, 2014).

Harvard Pilgrim Health Care   Harvard Pilgrim Health Care, a not-for-profit health care management organization serving Massachusetts, New Hampshire, and Maine, implemented an incentive program during negotiations for rate increases. The subsequently enacted rate increase included a portion that evaluated performance in specific areas, including:

- Adult diabetes
- Inpatient utilization
- Pediatric asthma

(Chorney, 2014).

In this program, health care providers receive the full amount of withheld funds if they demonstrate improved performance. Additionally, the Harvard Pilgrim Health Care plan withholds funds as opposed to giving physicians a true bonus. If physicians do not meet performance measures, they do not receive their negotiated rate increase (*See generally* Mantel, 2015).

Integrated Healthcare Association   In California, six health insurers (Aetna, Blue Cross of California, Blue Shield of California, CIGNA, Health Net, and Pacific Care Health Systems) collaborated with a statewide initiative known as the Integrated Healthcare Association to establish an incentive-based program. The pilot was judged a failure by its evaluators, largely because it did not achieve the desired scale (Marmor & Sullivan, 2015). However, the experience is important in distinguishing **bundled payments** from the wholesale transfer of insurance risk to providers. These lessons include:

- Paying for the health care after it is delivered rather than projecting use in advance
- Redesigning how the health care is going to be delivered when the payment bundles are created
- Targeting patient markets that currently pay providers using fee-for-service insurance plans rather than capitation

(Sage, 2016).

Empirical Evidence of Effectiveness

While incentive-based programs have become standard features of health insurance design, there is thin evidence concerning their effectiveness (Shah, 2016).[LN2] Two systematic literature reviews found few empirical studies assessing the effect of explicit financial incentives for improved performance on measures of health care quality (CBO, 2004; Moriates et al., 2015).

Critics maintain the programs are nothing more than disguised withholding programs that consumer-driven health care previously implemented to limit care, especially when bonuses are based on **referral limitations** and on physician productivity (Madison, 2016).[LN3] Humana was brought to task for this very criticism as described in the only lower **state trial case** cited in this text; this case demonstrates one way attorneys are attempting to hold the health insurance industry accountable in the administration of its population health management programs.

COURT DECISION

Mismanagement of an Incentive-Based Program

In re Humana Health Plan of Texas, Inc.
[Incentive-based Program v. Patient's Widowed Husband]
2005 Tex.App.LEXIS 5389 (Court of Appeals of Texas, Fourth District, San Antonio 2006),
vacated upon settlement of the parties, 2006 Tex.App.LEXIS 1576 (Court of Appeals of Texas, Fourth District, San Antonio 2006)

Facts: John Smelik sued his wife's physicians and Humana, a **health maintenance organization**, after she died from problems associated with kidney failure. Smelik claimed Humana breached its duty to supervise the quality of care provided to his wife. More specifically, Smelik claimed Humana did not:

- Furnish access to appropriate tests
- Properly inform his wife of her diagnosis and treatment options
- Provide a physician who specialized in kidney disease
- Supply the proper chronic care continuum programs her condition warranted

The Texas Court of Appeals vacated the trial court's opinion at the parties' request once the parties reached a settlement. The case was dismissed with prejudice, meaning the parties are not permitted to later sue on the same claims again.

Issue: Did Humana mismanage its incentive-based program?

Holding and Decision: Yes, Humana was negligent in the coordination and supervision of its enrollee's health care.

Analysis: Smelik reached a confidential settlement with his wife's physicians prior to trial, but the suit against Humana proceeded to jury trial. The jury awarded $9 million in total damages to Smelik, of which Humana was responsible for $4.2 million. The jury determined Humana was 35% negligent, placing the remaining 65% of liability on the physicians and physicians' group. Following appeal of its $4.2 million judgment, Humana reached a confidential settlement with Smelik. This was a mismanagement-of-managed-care case, not a denial-of-benefits case. Smelik did not claim Humana failed to pay for his wife's medical treatment, but instead argued Humana was negligent in the coordination and supervision of her care.

Rule of Law: The trial court found that health maintenance organizations must ensure that health care services are provided to enrollees under reasonable standards of quality of care that are consistent with prevailing standards of medical practice.

References discussing this court decision: *See, e.g.*, Roth, 2015.

Government-Based Initiatives

The federal government has implemented different demonstration efforts to evaluate incentive-based programs. Involving some 300,000 Medicare beneficiaries, each of the programs has tied payment to quality of care and other evidence-based outcomes (Reschovsky & Hadley, 2007). While the programs include provider-based, third party, and

MANAGEMENT AND LAW ISSUES

1. Should population health management programs be supported if they have potentially become merely a disguised framework for rationing care and addressing rising health care costs?

hybrid models, reducing costs sufficient to cover the costs of the population health management programs has proved particularly challenging. Final evaluations found quality improvement at or near **budget neutrality**, meaning the changes in delivery of health care covered the costs of the program. Interim monitoring on the remaining 15 programs suggests 4 are close to covering their fees (Moriates et al., 2015).

Physician Group Practice Demonstration Program   Ten large physician groups, each with over 200 physicians from different communities across the United States, are participating in the Physician Group Practice project. Payment in that program is based on improving the quality and cost efficiency of health care delivered to Medicare **fee-for-service** beneficiaries (Madison, 2016; Trisolin et al., 2008). Unfortunately, the limited empirical work on the program suggests mixed results (Wilensky, 2011).

Premier Hospital Quality Incentive Demonstration Program   Another project, the **Premier Hospital Quality Incentive Demonstration**, helps to determine whether providing financial incentives to hospitals will improve patient outcomes and reduce costs. Participation is voluntary, and hospitals receive bonuses in Medicare payments based upon performance of certain quality measures. Conversely, hospitals that do not perform well receive their standard Medicare fees without any incentive bonuses. Premier collects a set of more than 30 evidence-based clinical quality measures from hospitals across the United States. The quality measures track process and outcome measures in five clinical areas:

- Acute myocardial infarction
- Heart failure
- Coronary artery bypass graft
- Pneumonia
- Hip/knee replacement

(*See* El-Said, 2016).

Physician Voluntary Reporting Program   The federal government also implemented a **Physician Voluntary Reporting Program**. This is a simple performance program without the payment incentive. Under this program, physicians report 16 performance measures of care data. That data is then analyzed to measure physician performance. Currently, neither participation nor the physician's performance results affects payments (*See generally* Afemeister & Spinos, 2009).

Push-Back from the American Medical Association   The stated purpose of the government initiatives is to pay less for substandard health care. In order to do this, the government will differentiate among physicians by attempting to address an inequity in the current Medicare system: paying physicians equally, regardless of who provides better care and who does not. The plan is to implement its incentive-based program without any additional costs, which means payments to higher-performing physicians will come out of the pockets of lower-performing physicians. Some are concerned that the real goal is not to encourage physicians to achieve higher goals, but to eliminate lower performing physicians. The concern is that "lower performing physicians" are actually highly skilled physicians seeing and treating sicker patients, especially those in underserved areas of the country (GAO, 2007). The fear is that this initiative may result in some physicians refusing to treat the sickest patients with multiple disease conditions.

To address physicians' concerns, the American Medical Association developed five guiding principles in implementing incentive-based programs:

- Ensure quality of care: Programs should use evidence-based measures created by physicians and allow for variations based on sound clinical judgment.
- Foster the patient-physician relationship: Fair programs should support the relationship and recognize some obstacles, such as the patient's financial circumstances and compliance with treatment regimens.
- Incentives should be fair: New funds should be provided for positive incentives.
- Participation should be voluntary: The programs should not adversely affect physicians who choose not to participate.
- Use accurate data and fair reporting: Physicians should be allowed to review, comment, and appeal the results.

(AMA, 2016).

2. Does the need for population health management programs indicate that physicians are not always motivated to achieve certain performance standards or strive for quality improvement, without financial incentives?
3. Is the public's interest in health care quality data and physician performance justified?

The American Medical Association remains critical of incentive-based initiatives and is prepared to oppose Medicare programs that do not comport with American Medical Association principles and guidelines. Additionally, the American Medical Association opposed the physician voluntary reporting program prior to its implementation. One of the American Medical Association's main concerns is the manner in which physicians are required to report data with a new additional coding system that does not correlate to Medicare treatment codes. The American Medical Association is also concerned the program will become mandatory, with a correlation between performance data and future payment rates. Physicians cannot always control medical outcomes despite doing everything humanly possible; not every bad outcome is the result of poor health care (*See generally* Mantel, 2013).

Transparency and Access to Health Information

The tussle between the federal government and the American Medical Association is a reminder of the relentless push and push-back highlighted at the start of this chapter in the Fact or Fiction case regarding patients' access to previously unavailable health information. While the American Medical Association backs the ratings of physicians by the health insurance industry, the fear is Medicare data could be misinterpreted or oversimplified by **ratings agencies** without oversight by physicians and other health care professionals. However justified this concern, such interests are unlikely to stop the tide of groups seeking to tie data monitoring the costs and quality of health care to performance incentives, especially if such programs have the potential to reduce health care costs long-term.

LAW FACT

Transparency of Physician Effectiveness

Are the privacy interests of individual physicians more important than the public's need to monitor the cost and quality of health care provided under the Medicare insurance program?

No. The court refused to allow the public's need to monitor health care costs and quality of health care to outweigh the physicians' privacy interests, thereby rejecting a consumer group's bid to use Medicare insurance records to rate the effectiveness of individual physicians.

— *Consumers' Checkbook v. U.S. Department of Health and Human Services*, 554 F.3d 1046 (U.S. Court of Appeals for the D.C. Circuit 2009), *cert. denied*, 559 U.S. 1067 (U.S. Supreme Court 2010). *See, e.g.*, Candeub, 2011 (for discussion of this case). *Contra*, CMS, 2014 (four years after this court decision, the federal government released the requested Medicare data on physicians with the express goal of making the U.S. health care system more transparent and accountable; hospital data for Medicare insurance were released to the public three years after this decision; however, information was only released to the public for the year 2014 and the litigation over the release of future years' data has continued (*See Consumers' Checkbook v. U.S. Department of Health and Human Services*, 130 F.Supp.3d 1 (U.S. District Court for the District of Columbia 2015)).

CHAPTER SUMMARY

- Population health management for common, chronic, and preventable health conditions is critical to containing health care costs because such diseases consume 75% of the nation's health care budget.
- Population health management standards encompass general preventive measures, as well as standards for treating coronary artery disease, heart failure, diabetes, asthma, depression, and prenatal concerns.
- The key elements of population health management include evidence-based medicine, population identification, patient self-management education, collaborative practice models, routine reporting/feedback, process and outcomes measurement, evaluation, management.
- Population health management is important to employers because it helps reduce health care costs and improve the quality of health care; when an employee is out sick, the financial impact on the employer goes beyond just the job that the sick employee performs, but it is difficult to concretely measure.
- Although chronic ailments, such as diabetes, are responsible for most direct health care costs incurred by employers, depression is actually the most costly condition overall when other costs, such as lower employee productivity, are taken into account.
- Employers are increasingly shifting health care costs onto employees. This is being done without knowing whether short-term cost cutting might result in long-term increased costs due to health problems from employees choosing to avoid paying their own health care costs. Also not known is whether this will motivate employees to try harder to stay healthy in order to avoid paying their own health care costs.
- The Leapfrog Group was formed with the mission of reducing preventable medical mistakes, and its overall aim is to improve health care quality and safety, which it does through financial incentives.
- The Bridges to Excellence program has goals similar to those of the Leapfrog Group, and it aims to accomplish these goals through encouraging investment in reengineering health care processes, reducing system defects, and increasing accountability and quality improvements; it also uses financial incentives.
- There are approximately 160 different incentive-based programs, with varying ways of measuring performance, methods of sponsorship (employer or government), levels of health care provider involvement, and compensation for quality or performance.
- Employer participation in incentive-based programs for their employees are voluntary because the costs to participate in this reform effort, especially with regard to improving information technology, are significant.
- Incentive-based programs are increasingly common, but there is still little evidence regarding their effectiveness; critics argue they are actually ill-disguised withholding programs, modeled after managed care programs.
- The American Medical Association is concerned that population health management programs will violate physician privacy and that performance data may come to determine payment rates; it is also a concern that data may be misinterpreted or oversimplified if there is no appropriate oversight of its analysis.

LAW NOTES

1. Employers who are members of the Leapfrog Group provide health insurance to more than 37 million employees in all 50 states, including Alabama Power Company, Board of Pensions of the Presbyterian Church, Boeing, Chrysler, EMC, Federal Express, General Motors Corporation, Goodwill Industries, IBM, Intel, Marriott, Motorola, Qwest, Sprint, Toyota, UPS, United Technologies, and municipal and state retirement plans in California, Ohio, and Maine.
2. The Commonwealth Fund sponsored the first study to assess the effects of quality incentives in a large health insurance plan. Researchers examined population health management in an incentive-based program implemented by PacifiCare Health Systems (one of the nation's largest health plans) and found that a physician network that offered bonus payments outperformed another network that did not (Rosenthal et al., 2005). However, a year later, PacifiCare dropped out of the program, citing rising costs (Benko, 2006).
3. Other insured-based programs have been disguised as incentive-based programs (Thompson, 2011). The most infamous is likely the UnitedHealth program, implemented in the St. Louis area. UnitedHealth identified health care providers who had achieved quality and cost control and designated them as star providers. Enrollees who sought health care from non-star providers had to pay significant out-of-pocket expenses. Physicians and health systems had no input in the program and no warning prior to its implementation. Some quality measurements existed, but the star rating was largely based on costs. Originally, only about

one of four physicians in the St. Louis area received a star rating. Shortly after the program began, the area's largest employer gave notice that it would terminate its contract with United Health, and the program was subsequently modified (Stilson et al., 2015).

REFERENCES

AAFP (American Academy of Family Physicians). (2016). *Clinical practice guidelines*. Leawood, KS: AAFP.

ACP (American College of Physicians). (2016). *Clinical guidelines and recommendations from the American College of Physicians*. Philadelphia, PA: ACP.

Afemeister, T. L., & Spinos, S. (2009). Lean on me: A physician's fiduciary duty to disclose an emergent medical risk to the patient. *Washington University Law Review, 86*, 1167–1210.

AHIP (America's Health Insurance Plans). (2016). *Ensuring access to quality behavioral health care: Health plan examples*. Washington, DC: AHIP.

AHRQ (Agency for Healthcare Research and Quality). (2014). *Evaluation of the U.S. Preventive Services Task Force recommendations*. Rockville, MD: AHRQ.

AMA (American Medical Association). (2016). *Medicare payment and delivery changes: Increase understanding of MACRA's components and the effects they have on improving Medicare payments*. Chicago, IL: AMA.

Anderson, G. F., et al. (2016). *Medicare payment reform: Aligning incentives for better care*. New York, NY: The Commonwealth Fund.

Baker, G., & Delbanco, S. (2007). *Pay for performance: National perspective*. Leapfrog Group and Med-Vantage.

Benko, L. B. (2006). Disease management strikes out; Pacific-Care ends program early, CMS cites rising costs. *Modern Healthcare, 36*(4), 8–10.

Birkemeyer, J. D., & Dimick, J. B. (2004). *The Leapfrog Group's patient safety practices: The potential benefits of universal application*. Ann Arbor, MI: University of Michigan and Hanover, NH: Dartmouth Medical School.

Business Roundtable. (2009). *Health care reform: Creating a sustainable health care marketplace*. Washington, DC: Business Roundtable.

CBO (Congressional Budget Office). (2004). *An analysis of the literature on disease management programs*. Washington, DC: CBO.

CDC (Centers for Disease Control and Prevention). (2016). *Chronic disease overview*. Atlanta, GA: CDC.

Chorney, D. (2014). A mental health system in crisis and innovative laws to assuage the problem. *Health and Biomedical Law Society, 10*, 215–249.

Conrad, D. A., & Gardner, M. (2005). *Updated economic implications of the Leapfrog Group patient safety standards*. Seattle, WA: University of Washington.

Covel, S., & Spors, K. K. (2008, June 26). Providing health insurance on a budget: Wellness programs, screenings and other services can help small firms rein in the rising cost of care. *Wall Street Journal*, p. B6.

Dean, K. M., & Grabowski, D. C. (2014). Care coordination for dually eligible beneficiaries. *Saint Louis University Journal of Health Law and Policy, 8*, 35–46.

Dine, E. E. (2016). Money will likely be the carrot, but what stick will keep ACOs accountable? *Loyola University Chicago Law Journal, 47*, 1377–1436.

El-Said, M. K. (2016). TRIPS-plus, public health and performance-based rewards schemes options and supplements for policy formation in developing and least developed countries. *American University International Law Review, 31*, 373–443.

GAO (General Accountability Office). (2007). *Focus on physician practice patterns can lead to greater program efficiency*. Washington, DC: GAO.

Hermer, L. D. (2014). Aligning incentives in accountable care organizations: The role of medical malpractice reform. *Journal of Health Care Law and Policy, 17*, 271–302.

Hickox, S.A., & Guzman, J. M. (2014). Leave as an accommodation: When is enough, enough? *Cleveland State Law Review, 62*, 437–488.

IOM (Institute of Medicine) Committee on the Consequences of Uninsurance. (2003). *Hidden costs, values lost: uninsurance in America*. Washington, DC: National Academies Press.

Johns, G. (2010). Presenteeism in the workplace: A review and research agenda. *Journal of Organization Behavior, 31*(10), 519–542.

Kaiser Family Foundation & HRET (Health Research and Educational Trust). (2016). *Employer health benefits survey*. Menlo Park, CA: Kaiser and Chicago, IL: HRET.

Kleinke, J. D. (1998). *Bleeding edge: The business of health care in the new century*. Gaithersburg, MD: Aspen.

Leapfrog Group. (2016). *Leapfrog hospital survey*. Washington, DC: Leapfrog Group.

___. (2013). *Hospital safety score: Hospital errors are the third leading cause of death in U.S., and new hospital safety scores show improvements are too slow*.

Long, M., et al. (2016a). Kaiser Family Foundation: Recent trends in employer-based health insurance premiums. *Journal of the American Medical Association, 315*(1), 18–20.

Madison, K. (2016). Health care quality reporting: A failed form of mandated disclosure? *Indiana Health Law Review, 13*, 310–347.

Mantel, J. (2015). Ethical integrity in health care organizations: Currents in contemporary bioethics. *Journal of Law, Medicine and Ethics, 43*, 661–664.

___. (2013). The myth of the independent physician: Implications for health law, policy, and ethics. *Case Western Reserve Law Review, 64*, 455–520.

Marmor, T. R., & Sullivan, K. (2015). Medicare at 50: Why Medicare-for-all did not take place. *Yale Journal of Health Policy, Law and Ethics, 15*, 41–183.

Miglani, S. (2016). Reference pricing: A small and mighty solution to bend the health care cost curve. *Connecticut Insurance Law Journal, 22*, 47–84.

Moriates, C., et al. (2015). *Understanding value-based healthcare*. New York, NY: McGraw-Hill.

Morrell, M. T., & Krouse, A. T. (2014). Accountability partners: Legislated collaboration for health reform. *Indiana Health Law Review, 11*, 225–301.

Moss, R. (2005). *The future of learning: Building a bridge between competency and patient safety*. Denver, CO: Competency and Credentialing Institute.

NCQA (National Committee for Quality Assurance). (2016). *Bridges to excellence: Rewarding quality across the healthcare system*. Washington, DC: NCQA.

___. (2015). *State of health care quality report*.

NIDDK (National Institute of Diabetes and Digestive and Kidney Diseases). (2014). *Kidney disease of diabetes*. Bethesda, MD: NIDDK.

Polaris, J. J. Z. (2016). Personal networks: Health coverage status and the invisible burden on family and friends. *Harvard Journal of Law and Gender, 39*, 115–187.

Reschovsky, J., & Hadley, J. (2007). Physician financial incentives: Use of quality incentives inches up, but productivity still dominates. *Issue brief: Center for Studying Health System Change, 108,* 1–4.

Rosenthal, M. B., et al. (2005). Early experience with pay-for-performance: From concept to practice. *Journal of the American Medical Association, 294*(14), 1788–1793.

Rosoff, A. J. (2012). The role of clinical practice guidelines in healthcare reform: An update. *Annals of Health Law, 21,* 21–33.

Roth, L. R. (2015). Overvaluing employer-sponsored health insurance. *Kansas Law Review, 63,* 633–667.

Sage, W. M. (2016). Assembled products: The key to more effective competition and antitrust oversight in health care. *Cornell Law Review, 101,* 609–700.

Satz, A. B. (2015). Fragmentation after health care reform. *Houston Journal of Health Law and Policy, 15,* 171–228.

Shah, N., Assistant Professor at Harvard Medical School and Associate Faculty at the Ariadne Labs for Health Systems Innovation. (2016, December 6). Keynote Speaker at the Leapfrog Annual Meeting: Passing the Baton, Transparency and Value-Based Care in a Post-Election World, Washington, DC.

Sides, J., et al. (2016). The electoral landscape of 2016. *The Annals of the American Academy of Political and Social Science, 667,* 50–69.

Standard Insurance Company. (2012). *Health-related lost productivity: The full cost of absence.* Portland, OR: Standard Insurance Co.

Stilson, J., et al. (2015). Reading the tea leaves: Evaluating potential antitrust concerns in vertical mergers between insurers and health care providers. *Antitrust: American Bar Association, 30,* 11–16.

Thompson, D. B. (2011). The next stage of health care reform: Controlling costs by paying health plans based on health outcomes. *Akron Law Review, 44,* 727–768.

Trisolin, M., et al. (2008). *The Medicare physician group practice demonstration: Lessons learned on improving quality and efficiency in health care.* New York, NY: Commonwealth Fund.

Underhill, K. (2016). When extrinsic incentives displace intrinsic motivation: Designing legal carrots and sticks to confront the challenge of motivational crowding-out. *Yale Journal on Regulation, 33,* 213–279.

Van Tassel, K. (2013). Harmonizing the Affordable Care Act with the three main national systems for healthcare quality improvement: The tort, licensure, and hospital peer review hearing systems. *Brooklyn Law Review, 78,* 883–928.

Wilensky, G. R. (2011). Lessons from the physician group practice demonstration: a sobering reflection. *New England Journal of Medicine, 365,* 1659–1667.

Wolff, J. L., & Boult, C. (2005). Moving beyond round pegs and square holes: Restructuring Medicare to improve chronic care. *Annals of Internal Medicine, 493,* 439–445.

CHAPTER 22

© Andy Dean Photography/ShutterStock, Inc.

Evidence-Based Medicine

"The bottom line: all adults are at risk for receiving poor health care, no matter where they live; why, where, and from whom they seek care; or what their race, gender, or financial status is."

— **RAND Corp.** (2006), The First National Report Card on Quality of Health Care in America

IN BRIEF

Evidence-based medicine, a philosophy of medicine that has been around in force since the early 1990s, is at the top of the list of industry improvements in the United States to help rein in health care costs and provide more reliable medical treatment. This chapter provides an introduction to use of the best scientific evidence (current, valid, unbiased, clinically significant medical research) to make decisions about the care individual patients should receive.

LEARNING OBJECTIVES

Upon completion of this chapter students should be able to:

1. Describe the basis of evidence-based medicine.
2. Distinguish the traditional practice of medicine and practice of evidence-based medicine.
3. Explain the relation between epidemiological principles and evidence-based medicine.
4. List the criticisms of evidence-based medicine and how they have slowed its acceptance in the United States.
5. Discuss evidence-based medicine studies and organizations undertaking them.
6. Explain how evidence-based medicine helps identify which courses of care are overused, underused, and misused.

KEY TERMS

Actimmune
Agency for Healthcare Research and Quality
Antihypertensive and Lipid-Lowering Treatment to Prevent Heart Attack Trial
Authority-based medical opinions
Beta-blocker
Black box warning
Care continuum programs
Clinical Antipsychotic Trials in Intervention Effectiveness
Clinical guidelines
Comparative research
Compulsory vaccination

Computed tomography (CT) scans
Computerized decision support system
Content aggregators
Deferred prosecution agreement
Differential diagnosis
Do no harm
Drug Effectiveness Review Project
Epidemiological principles
Evidence-based medicine
Experimental treatments
Federal health programs
First Amendment
Formulary restrictions
Futile medical care

General causation
Health Care Common Procedure Coding System
Health outcomes
Heightened scrutiny
Hormone replacement therapy
Investigational treatments and medical products
Malpractice
Mental model
Meta-analysis
National Childhood Vaccine Injury Act of 1986
National Guidelines Clearinghouse
National Lung Screening Trial

Off-label	Primary care	Specialty medical groups
Off-label prescriptions	Product liability damages	Standards of care
Off-label promotion	Proven care	Statins
Off-label uses	Purchasers of care	Survival rates
Overuse of antibiotics	Quality of care organizations	Traditional medical paradigm
Pathophysiology	Randomized clinical trials	Transparency initiatives
Patient-Oriented Evidence That Matters System	Rates of use	U.S. Preventive Services Task Force
Patient registries	Recommended health care	Vaccine manufacturer
Placebo	Scientific literature	Vaccines
	Shared decision-making	Women's Health Initiative

FACT OR FICTION

Hormone Replacement Therapy

Is there any reliable evidence-based scientific research that combination hormone replacement therapy can cause breast cancer, heart disease, or dementia?

It is said that no other drugs in the history of medicine have been as consistently controversial as **hormone replacement therapy**. The debate began in the late 1800s, when physicians first began to feed pulverized cow ovaries to women, and it continues to this day. At the start of the 21st century, the National Institutes of Health warned women there was no safe hormone replacement therapy. In 2003, some 3,000 women in 29 states claimed Wyeth's combination hormone therapy, estrogen-plus-progestin, had increased their risk of developing serious latent diseases and conditions. Women sued Wyeth, claiming it failed to adequately test and sufficiently warn of the drug's dangers and that their breast cancer, heart disease, or dementia were caused by the failure to adequately test Prempro.

— *See* Law Fact at the end of this chapter for the answer.

Principles and Applications

One of the professional norms imposed on physicians by state licensing boards, **quality of care organizations**, medical associations, and health insurance plans is the use of **evidence-based medicine**. Evidence-based medicine is among the professional norms physicians must adhere to, along with:

- Doing no harm
- Erring on the side of safety
- Referring patients to specialists when appropriate
- Staying current

(Kukura, 2016a).

Definition of Evidence-Based Medicine

Best defined as an attempt to apply **epidemiological principles** to clinical care, evidence-based medicine promotes reliance on research data, particularly randomized controlled trials, in the practice of medicine (Kukura, 2016a). Evidence-based medicine, which began in the early 1990s in Canada and the United Kingdom and developed later in the United States, is a key component of **care continuum programs** (Corbett, 2015). Now, medical schools, government agencies, and the health care industry are participating in the development of clinical guidelines, not only on how to treat common ailments such as asthma and upper respiratory infections, but also on how to perform surgeries and tackle serious diseases such as cancer.

With physicians unable to keep abreast of hundreds of clinical studies, make sense of conflicting scientific findings, and sift through available medical research for the most reliable and useful treatment conclusions, it is difficult to ensure they provide the best care to patients. Evidence-based medicine, which entails incorporating key scientific findings into medical practice and measuring the associated outcomes, provides a counterweight to this situation (Gould, 2014). In order to evaluate the limitations and criticisms of evidence-based medicine, it is useful to provide a specific definition on which to base this analysis. The 1995 editorial in the *British Medical Journal*, announcing the creation of the *Evidence-Based Medicine Journal*, gave this definition of evidence-based medicine:

- Clinical decisions should be based on the best available scientific evidence.
- The clinical problem, as opposed to habits or protocols, should determine the type of evidence to be sought.
- Identifying the best evidence means using epidemiological and biostatistical ways of thinking.
- Conclusions derived from identifying and critically appraising evidence are useful only if put into action in managing patients or making health care decisions.
- Performance should be constantly evaluated.

(Davidoff et al., 1995).

While none of the later definitions are in disagreement with this definition, none of them are as complete. Most important, this definition contains the core set of issues historically and currently surrounding evidence-based medicine (Kukura, 2016a).

Paradigm Shift in Medicine

Consumers of health care are ambivalent about evidence-based medicine in terms of medical coverage. In spite of this public ambivalence, evidence-based medicine has been characterized as a paradigm shift in medicine (Friedland, 2009). Today, a new **mental model** has evolved in the health care industry that is changing clinical decisions from one point of view to a new one. The change is from a model of clinical decision-making based on traditional experience and authority-based clinical training to a model based on scientific evidence. This paradigm shift, with results from clinical trials as opposed to anecdotes, occurred when it was discovered that one-third of the nation's health care costs is devoted to health care services that do not improve health or the quality of care (*See* Johnson & Stukel, 2016). There are undeniable outcome anomalies in traditional medical assumptions when one-third of the spending on health care may actually make things worse (Johnson & Stukel, 2016). Dr. David Sackett, a pioneer of evidence-based medicine, famously said,

> Half of what you will learn in medical school will be shown to be either dead wrong or out of date within five years of your graduation; the trouble is nobody can tell you which half, so the most important thing to learn is how to learn on your own.

(Groopman & Hartzband, 2009, p. A13).

This is why medicine is referred to as a 'practice.' This responsibility to learn on one's own, along with making an effort to know what is going on with regards to one's health conditions, applies to the American consumer of health care, as well.

Traditional (Authority-Based) Assumptions

The **traditional medical paradigm** comprises four assumptions:

- Clinical experience and expertise in a given subject area is a sufficient foundation to enable physicians to understand and apply clinical guidelines.
- Individual clinical experience provides the foundation for diagnosis, treatment, and prognosis.
- Knowledge of pathophysiology, or changes and disturbances in human organs caused by disease, provides the foundation for clinical practice.
- Traditional medical training and common sense are sufficient to enable physicians to evaluate new tests and treatments.

(Friedland, 2009; Sackett, 1996; *See* Friedland, 2016).

Evidence-Based Assumptions

Evidence-based medicine helps physicians make medical decisions with their patients systematically. The new evidence-based medicine paradigm comprises a different set of assumptions:

- Knowledge of **pathophysiology** is necessary but is insufficient for the practice of clinical medicine.
- Understanding of certain rules of research and evidence is necessary to evaluate and apply the medical literature effectively.
- When possible, physicians use information derived from systematic, reproducible, and unbiased studies to increase their confidence in the true prognosis, efficacy of therapy, and usefulness of diagnostic tests.

(Friedland, 2009; Sackett, 1996; *See* Friedland, 2016).

Failure to Use Evidence-Based Medicine

Over the last few years, focus has been directed to costs and reliability in the U.S. health care system as a result of three forces:

- The number of reports about how well the U.S. health care system distributes medical technology
- Research about how the health care system is functioning
- Rising premiums for health insurance

(IOM, 2015, 2001; Grout et al., 2013)

U.S. physicians and hospitals too often do not use the best scientific evidence available for treating even the most common health conditions. There is a tremendous gap between what treatment is known to work and what treatment patients actually get, because some physicians simply are not aware of what the most effective treatments are, or else have their own reasons for not using them. Examples of failures to use evidence-based medicine include:

- Almost one-third of the surgeries performed on Medicare-insured patients are unnecessary.
- Less than one-fourth of the people with hypertension have it under control with recommended blood pressure drugs.
- One-third of health care costs are devoted to services that do not improve health or the quality of care and may make things worse.
- More than three-fourths of diabetics are not getting routine hemoglobin screening, which is essential to detect complications such as kidney failure.
- Adhering to clinical guidelines for treating hypertension alone could save at least $1.2 billion annually.
- Less than half of heart attack patients are on beta-blockers, which cut the risk of premature death.
- Brain cancer in adults is a dreaded diagnosis with few established clinical guidelines, resulting in wide variations in care that can make things worse for some patients.
- Nearly half of patients with brain cancer receive no chemotherapy, despite evidence that it can boost survival; antiseizure drugs are widely used even though most patients do not have seizures.
- While depression is common in people with brain cancer, more than 90% are never given antidepressants.

E.g., Deshpande & DeMello, 2011; Grout et al., 2013; Johnson & Stukel, 2016; Milstein et al., 2010; Preusser et al., 2011. *See* Tanner, 2005.

These statistics highlight a major shortcoming of the decentralized U.S. health care system: physicians treat common illnesses in a variety of ways, even though only one treatment has shown the most success.

Breakdown in Efficiency

The Commonwealth Fund publishes a scorecard on American medicine that establishes benchmarks for health care quality, access, equity, and outcomes. According to these measures of reasonably attainable levels of performance, an optimal score of 100 in each of these areas was actually being achieved, for international comparisons, by the average of the three best countries, or, for comparisons within the United States, the best 10% of states. Overall, American health care earns a score of 66, otherwise commonly known in academia as a D. Some comparisons reinforce this point include:

- Infant mortality rate in the United States is 7 per 100,000 births, while the international benchmark is 2.7.
- Sixty-year-old American men live 2.1 years less than the international benchmark.
- Sixty-year-old American women live 2.9 years less than the international benchmark.

(Radley et al., 2014).

The efficiency of U.S. health care, or how much health Americans get for the money spent, earned a 51, otherwise commonly known in academia as an F. In other words, the United States wastes significant resources on suboptimal health care.

Halftime Estimates of Unnecessary Care

Do no harm is a bedrock principle of medicine. While needless tests and procedures provide no real benefit to patients and often cannot do anything but harm, they do enrich the health care industry. Estimates are that patients get the care they need, and only the care they need, less than half of the time (Grout et al., 2013; *See* RAND, 2006). This halftime estimate is supported by studies that indicate as much as half of the care provided to Americans is unnecessary, including:

- Diagnostic tests that are repeated
- Drugs and medical treatments for which there is no evidence of benefit
- Medical products and services that do not do any good

(IOM, 2015, 2001).

Research also supports the degree to which there are high variations in health care spending between specific regions of the country (Johnson & Stukel, 2016).[LN1] There is accumulating evidence that excess quantity of care in the United States is actually overdosing Americans with respect to their **health outcomes**. More health care does not result in better health outcomes or higher satisfaction with care (Johnson & Stukel, 2016).

RAND Corp. also released results from 12 major metropolitan areas supporting the Dartmouth research (described in Law Note 1), saying all Americans are at risk for receiving poor health care, even from hospitals or physicians considered top notch (*E.g.* Suthar & Patel, 2014; *See* Kerr et al., 2004). The 12 metropolitan areas in this research included, Boston, Massachusetts; Cleveland, Ohio; Greenville, South Carolina; Indianapolis, Indiana; Lansing, Michigan; Little Rock, Arkansas, Miami, Florida; Newark, New Jersey; Orange County, California; Phoenix, Arizona; Seattle, Washington; and Syracuse, New York. Substantial gaps between what physicians know works and the health care actually provided were revealed; these deficits persist despite initiatives by both the federal government and private health care delivery systems to improve care (RAND, 2005).

- On average, residents received 50 to 60% of the recommended care for cardiac conditions and pulmonary problems; specifically, care for the following chronic conditions was unsatisfactory half the time: asthma, atrial fibrillation, chronic obstructive pulmonary disease, congestive heart failure, coronary artery disease, and hypertension.
- Preventive care for sexually transmitted diseases, including human immunodeficiency virus (HIV), the virus that causes acquired immune deficiency syndrome (AIDS), and substance abuse was consistently low.
- The quality of preventive care for diabetes was consistently the worst in all 12 communities.

(*E.g.*, Fu et al., 2012; Hysong et al., 2011; Miller, 2013; See RAND, 2005).

Evidence-Based Medical Principles Widespread

The principles of evidence-based medicine are already widespread among hospitals, medical groups, and health insurers in the United States (Kukura, 2016a). In most cases, clinical guidelines are implemented as a **computerized decision support system** that provides physicians, nurses, and health plan case managers with a wide variety of information on accepted best practices for treating similar patients. Clinical guidelines (such as those in **FEATURE BOX 22-1**) from the federal **Agency for Healthcare Research and Quality** (AHRQ) are authored by reputable and authoritative medical groups and often linked to financial incentives by health insurance plans.

FEATURE BOX 22-1

Clinical Guidelines for Selected Medical Conditions

National guidelines exist for the following medical conditions:

- Acute low back problems in adults
- Acute pain management
- Benign prostatic hyperplasia
- Cardiac rehabilitation
- Cataracts in adults
- Depression
- Early Alzheimer's disease
- Early HIV infection
- Heart failure
- Management of cancer pain
- Otitis media with effusion
- Post-stroke rehabilitation
- Pressure ulcer prevention
- Pressure ulcer treatment
- Quality mammography
- Sickle-cell disease
- Smoking cessation
- Unstable angina
- Urinary incontinence in adults

National Guideline Clearinghouse, an initiative of the Agency for Healthcare Research and Quality, U.S. Department of Health and Human Services, in partnership with the American Medical Association and America's Health Insurance Plans.

The National Guideline Clearinghouse gives providers an additional set of tools to analyze and evaluate potential care plans while maintaining the flexibility to deal with an individual patient's unique circumstances. The final medical decisions are still made by physicians and nurses consulting with their patients.

Point, Counterpoint on Evidence-Based Medicine

While over the last 50 years, **randomized clinical trials** have produced relatively solid evidence, and their legitimacy and usefulness keeps growing, critics still claim evidence-based medicine is not what it purports to be. The chief criticism is that many clinical guidelines are based on small trials with insufficient statistical power and nonrandomized studies. A second claim is that while clinical guidelines are indisputable in some areas, such as controlling diabetics' blood sugar levels, for many conditions, few reliable clinical guidelines exist, or the evidence is contradictory, or new studies quickly emerge that undermine the original evidence (Preusser et al., 2011).

Traditional Medical Culture

Patients typically trust their physicians are relying on experience and research when they are diagnosed and fail to ask about the cost-effectiveness of their treatment options. The option of simple surgical procedures over long-term drug use and its consequent side effects are seldom fully explained, so many patients never have the opportunity to make an informed individual choice. For instance, women experiencing stress incontinence seldom are offered the option of a retropubic suspension or suburethral sling; instead they are offered lifetime prescriptions for Pfizer's Detrol with the side effects of weight gain and mental confusion. Or, it is simply recommended they use pelvic floor exercises and adult diapers, as opposed to any surgical procedure. In this instance, even though one-third of women experience this condition as they age, reliable evidence on which to judge whether or not slings are better or worse than other surgical or conservative management is currently not available (Scott, 2011).

Why the resistance to evidence-based medicine? Physicians simply do not want anyone advising them what is best for their patients when they believe a particular treatment works (Kukura, 2016b). Some physicians claim that results of clinical trials do not apply to their patients. Other physicians take a "show me" attitude, waiting to see if treating patients according to clinical guidelines produces better outcomes. But treatment effects are often small—for instance, reducing future risk of heart attack by 25%—individual physicians typically have too few patients with any one illness or do not follow them long enough to detect such effects (Madison, 2016).

Time Commitment

Another obstacle to treating patients according to clinical guidelines is it takes time physicians claim they do not have. Proper treatment of diabetes, for instance, means blood tests, eye exams, meal plans, and more, much of which is poorly reimbursed by insurers. It also requires a team approach some group practices, let alone solo physicians, cannot manage. Moreover, outside of the academic medical centers, hospitals often lack the information technology to let physicians electronically record information about patients and match it to clinical guidelines (Madison, 2016).

Spinal Fusion Controversy

One controversy, however, makes proponents of evidence-based medicine question how many physicians believe in science-based care. When the AHRQ issued a clinical guideline for lower back pain, which concluded that spinal fusion surgery usually does no good, and suggested there were too many unnecessary back surgeries, orthopedic surgeons responded by lobbying Congress to punish the agency (Francis, 2012). Congress cut the group's budget and stripped its authority to make Medicare insurance payment recommendations, crippling for years the very idea of evidence-based medicine.

Today, studies continue to challenge the overuse of spinal fusion surgery. There are:

- Excessive rates of complications
- High rates of reoperation
- Rapidly rising rates of surgery
- Wide variations in the **rates of use**

(ASNM, 2016; Brook & Irle, 2016).

All this indicates spinal fusion continues to be overused, with inpatient hospital patient care costs exceeding $12 billion per year (Brook & Irle, 2016). All the while, surgical effectiveness for degenerative disk disease, the most common indication, still remains unclear (Yue & Long, 2017). The AHRQ and the Robert Wood Johnson Foundation are calling for a shift from examining how to perform fusion to examining who should undergo spinal fusion surgery (Wang et al., 2009).

Best Practice Guidelines for Treatment

Clinical guidelines are one embodiment of evidence-based medicine; in practice, the two terms are often used interchangeably. The complex history of clinical guidelines can be traced back to the fourth century B.C. and has included repeated calls for protocols by such luminaries as Florence Nightingale (1920-1910), founder of modern nursing, and Abraham Flexner (1886-1959), 20th century reformer of medical education (Gilman & Fairman, 2014).

With studies showing Americans get only half of the **recommended health care**, health insurers are increasingly using clinical guidelines drawn from evidence-based medicine to make health care coverage decisions about drugs and treatments and to reward physicians who follow the guidelines (*E.g.*, Brook & Irle, 2016; Lee, 2014). The National Business Group on Health, for instance, which represents large employers covering more than 45 million workers, retirees, and their families, is developing recommendations for employers to use in designing health insurance plans that promote greater use of treatments and procedures supported by evidence-based medicine. It is important for patients to understand the personal autonomy of their physicians is being very closely scrutinized (Preusser et al., 2011).

Most clinical guidelines have been developed by medical schools, **specialty medical groups**, government agencies, or health care firms, and range from how to treat common ailments such as asthma and hypertension, to how to perform surgeries and tackle serious diseases such as cancer. But how good is the evidence behind the clinical guidelines? Proponents of clinical guidelines based on scientific studies are the best way to fix the health care system and ensure treatments are backed up by solid scientific proof they are effective from both a cost and quality standpoint (Preusser et al., 2011). Consider clinical guideline resources from the:

- National Guidelines Clearinghouse
- U.S. Preventive Services Task Force
- Medical specialty organizations such as the American Association of Clinical Endocrinologists and the American College of Cardiology

Each of these groups explains and grades the quality of the research their recommendations are based upon.

National Guidelines Clearinghouse

The **National Guidelines Clearinghouse** was created by the AHRQ in partnership with the American Medical Association and America's Health Insurance Plans. Summaries of current recommendations about a wide range of medical treatments are available based on AHRQ data. At present, the National Guidelines Clearinghouse contains nearly 2,700 clinical guidelines with comparisons and syntheses of competing guidelines (Frakes, 2015). Though primarily used by physicians and health care providers, patients can view the clinical guidelines and updates on new evidence that should be considered in medical treatment. For instance, as soon as a drug or other medical product is withdrawn from the market, all references to the product in the National Guidelines Clearinghouse covering the medical diseases and conditions it treated are flagged, with a note explaining the reasons behind the withdrawal.

U.S. Preventive Services Task Force

The **U.S. Preventive Services Task Force** is an independent panel of experts in **primary care** and prevention that systematically reviews the evidence of effectiveness and develops recommendations for clinical preventive services. Sponsored by the AHRQ, the Task Force makes recommendations about which preventive services should be incorporated routinely into primary medical care in the United States and for which populations. It also identifies a national research agenda for clinical preventive care (*See generally* AHRQ, 2014).

Content Aggregators Such as MedExact

Given the amount of health care information in today's marketplace, there is a role for **content aggregators**, such as search engines, that summarize clinical content from reputable sources (O'Connor, 2013). MedExact offers centralized treatment information, on over 600 health conditions and disease states, from the National Cancer Institute, the National Institutes of Health, the American Diabetes Association, and other leading medical associations and institutions.

Many leading academic health care systems offer portal-like blogs that tend to serve as content aggregators for health consumers by offering links to personal blogs, news stories, discussion threads, and other electronic content. Law and management text publishers are also having their authors develop personal blogs to provide updated headlines and news articles to sites that are of interest to their readers, including commentaries and recommendations compiled by the authors of their leading texts on health care.

Patient Registries

Diabetes registries have become prevalent in the past decade (Mariner, 2016). The most renowned active diabetes registry in the United States is the Vermont Diabetes Information System, sponsored by the National Institutes of Health. The Vermont system is primarily intended to improve adult diabetes treatment by monitoring patients and testing, but a secondary role is discovering new information for advancing diabetes management by providing researchers with access to collected data (Candeub, 2015).

There is a call for better evidence gathering to identify adverse effects and new risks, including the use of **patient registries** to track drug side effects once drugs or treatments are approved, and new information technology systems to synthesize data from clinical trials (Preusser et al., 2011). There is also a need to track off-label use of drugs for clinical effectiveness. Similar to the diabetes registries, the Food and Drug Administration (FDA) can require pharmaceutical and biotechnology firms to submit a risk evaluation and mitigation strategy for their medical products based on the FDA's determination that a registry is necessary to ensure that the benefits outweigh the risks (OIG, 2006; *see* 21 U.S.C.A. § 355-1).

Off-Label Prescribing

While the courts have been limiting the FDA's ability to regulate the pharmaceutical industry by restricting promotional speech, in recent years the federal government has collected billions of dollars from the industry in criminal and civil penalties for off-label promotion of their products (*E.g.*, Buck, 2015). **Off-label** means that the therapeutic claims or other information that the pharmaceutical industry disseminates about their products has not been authorized by the FDA, although the products themselves have been approved for marketing by the FDA. This off-label practice invokes the same concerns as health care fraud:

- Information asymmetry between patients and providers regarding the quality and necessity of care
- Overuse
- Waste

(Herbst, 2015; Laakmann, 2015).

COURT DECISION
Off-Label Promotion of Prescription Drugs

United States v. Caronia
[Federal Government v. Sales Representative for the Pharmaceutical Industry]
703 F.3d 149 (U.S. Court of Appeals for the 2nd Circuit 2012)

Facts: Alfred Caronia was a specialty sales consultant employed by Orphan Medical, Inc., to promote Xyrem, a drug approved by the FDA to treat a very specific subset of narcoleptic patients with a sudden temporary inability to move and excessive daytime sleepiness. The FDA required Xyrem to have a **black box warning**, the most serious warning placed on prescription labels. Caronia was recorded promoting Xyrem for **off-label uses** for unapproved purposes, including the treatment of excessive pain associated with fibromyalgia. Because Xyrem was approved to treat only a narrow set of narcolepsy patients, the government charged Caronia with two misdemeanors, and he was convicted of misbranding. Caronia appealed the trial decision, and his conviction was vacated.

Issue: Should the pharmaceutical industry be permitted to promote off-label use of its approved products?

Holding and Decision: Yes, it should. A pharmaceutical sales representative did not violate federal misbranding laws by promoting off-label uses of a prescription drug approved by the FDA.

Analysis: The U.S. Supreme Court has all but collapsed the distinction between **First Amendment** protection accorded to commercial and noncommercial speech. Caronia was prosecuted for off-label promotion of an FDA-approved drug outside the clinical trial context; the government prosecuted Caronia not for his conduct but for his speech. His prosecution was for promoting the use of an approved drug for unapproved purposes. Yet, his conviction was vacated when speech in the aid of pharmaceutical marketing was found to be protected by the First Amendment.

Second, the court, relying on a recent U.S. Supreme Court decision, *Sorrell v. IMS Health, Inc.*, 564 U.S. 552 (U.S. Supreme Court 2011) found interpretation of the federal misbranding law warranted application of the legal standard of **heightened scrutiny**. This interpretation was both content-based and speaker-based. By construing the misbranding law to prohibit and criminalize off-label drug promotion by the pharmaceutical industry, the FDA was regulating based on content. In other words, the FDA was attempting to prohibit speech regarding the off-label use of an FDA-approved product. The FDA's interpretation of the misbranding law was found to be speaker-based; it attempted to prevent the pharmaceutical industry from marketing off-label uses while allowing physicians and academics to discuss such uses.

Third, the court determined that the FDA's speech restrictions on off-label use could not withstand heightened scrutiny. The FDA misbranding regulations were found to be too broad to support the FDA's objective of promoting drug safety and public health. The prohibition on off-label promotion did not directly advance the goals of preserving the integrity of the FDA's drug approval process and reducing patient exposure to unsafe drugs. Since only the *promotion* of off-label use, but not the off-label use itself, is prohibited, a ban on promotion may interfere with the ability of physicians and patients to receive potentially relevant treatment information.

Lastly, FDA interests can be served through more limited and targeted restrictions on speech. The ban on off-label promotion was not narrow enough for its purported intent of maintaining drug safety and public health. Prohibiting off-label promotion was more extensive than necessary because alternative schemes could be implemented to achieve the same goals without excessively constraining First Amendment free speech rights. Legitimate alternatives include issuing guidance to help physicians and patients differentiate between misleading and truthful promotional information and placing limits on **off-label prescriptions**.

Rule of Law: **Off-label promotion** is protected by the First Amendment; when misbranding laws are content- and speaker-based, heightened scrutiny is warranted.

References discussing this court decision: *E.g.*, Buck, 2015; Calvert & Bunker, 2013; Coleman, 2014; Copeland, 2014; Ho, 2015; LaMontagne, 2015; Massaro, 2014; Mermin & Graff, 2013; Neyarapally, 2013; Philip, 2014; Riley, 2015; Scheineson & Cuevas, 2013; Shik, 2015; Spacapan & Hutchison, 2013; Spears et al., 2015; Thomson, 2013.

Physicians' freedom to prescribe drugs off-label stems from the refusal to permit direct regulation of the practice of medicine; however, without direct regulation, the FDA has been unable to prevent abuse of this practice (Buck, 2015). While the *Caronia* court correctly avoided punishing truthful speech with a criminal sanction, this decision undermines the fundamental purpose of the FDA to ensure the safety and effectiveness of prescription drugs through a rigorous premarket approval process. If the pharmaceutical industry can freely market its products for off-label uses, its incentive to seek further approval for non-approved uses are eliminated (Riley, 2015). The FDA's ability to weigh the full benefits and risks of prescription drugs becomes near impossible to exercise.

Moreover, prohibiting the restriction of off-label promotion is a barrier to the ability of physicians and patients to receive relevant treatment information. Unless this decision is interpreted narrowly, it opens a path for the pharmaceutical industry to retain a First Amendment right to distribute prescription drugs for almost any use (LaMontagne, 2015). Moving forward, the FDA may, therefore, begin to assert that particular off-label promotion, besides being evidence of misbranding, is also false or misleading (Buck, 2015).

Off-Label Use of Actimmune

One instance of ineffective off-label drug use is **Actimmune** (interferon gamma-1b), manufactured by InterMune and prescribed off-label to patients with a potentially fatal lung condition, idiopathic pulmonary fibrosis (IPF). Actimmune was approved by the FDA to treat two other extremely rare diseases, but substantially all its sales (over $107 million annually) came from the off-label use for IPF, which costs each patient about $50,000 per year. There was, however, no reliable evidence Actimmune was an effective treatment for IPF (Comanor & Needleman, 2016). InterMune abandoned its efforts to develop Actimmune as a treatment for IPF because clinical trials showed it failed to prolong lives and was no more effective than a **placebo** (Lewellen, 2015).

InterMune entered into a **deferred prosecution agreement** and paid nearly $37 million to resolve criminal charges and civil liability in connection with the illegal promotion and marketing of Actimmune. InterMune also entered into a five-year corporate integrity agreement with the Office of the Inspector General for the U.S. Department of Health and Human Services. Although a clinical trial in fact failed, InterMune issued a press release claiming the results of the trial established Actimmune helped IPF patients live longer. The former chief executive officer of InterMune was subsequently indicted on wire fraud and felony charges for his role in the creation and dissemination of false and misleading information about the efficacy of Actimmune. Following its off-label prosecutions, InterMune merged with specialty biopharmaceutical firm, Horizon Pharma, headquartered in Ireland.

Federal Agency for Healthcare Research and Quality

The AHRQ, which conducts research for **federal health programs**, has developed state-of-the-art information about the effectiveness of treatments, including prescription drugs, for the top conditions affecting Medicare insurance beneficiaries, including:

- Arthritis
- Asthma
- Depression
- Diabetes

- Heart disease
- Pneumonia
- Stroke

The aim is to get better information on side effects and risks faster and make it easier for physicians and patients to make informed decisions about health care. While there is a great deal of evidence and innovation in medicine, there is no effective way for patients to determine what medical treatments are right for them (Preusser et al., 2011). The AHRQ says the new studies of specific health conditions will make it easier to speed up the adoption of treatments once they are proven effective. The good news about having clinical guidelines is they synthesize all of the information about scientific evidence and tell physicians what they need to do. The next step is to make sure physicians have information at hand exactly when they need it. The Centers for Medicare and Medicaid Services and the AHRQ are sponsoring several pilot projects encouraging hospitals and physicians to use information technology, such as handheld prescribing devices and computerized decision support systems for quick access to clinical guidelines at the point of care where they need it most.

Overused, Underused, and Misused Health Care

Longstanding physician resistance to using clinical guidelines is often cited as a reason health care quality in the United States is not up to par with similar countries, especially considering how much is spent. Wide variations in how physicians treat patients with similar ailments are epidemic in American medicine, reflecting a large gap between medical knowledge and clinical practice. Many researchers and large **purchasers of care** consider evidence-based medicine a critical factor in both cost and quality woes infecting the health care system. For instance, research shows health care is often overused, underused, or misused (Johnson & Stukel, 2016).

Where there are more cardiac surgeons, for instance, there is greater utilization of their services; whether this is an overuse problem or simply the appropriate use of available resources is unclear. There is also an underuse problem in which physicians do not treat medical ailments as aggressively as best practices recommend. Individuals suffering myocardial infarctions are reportedly put on beta-blockers only half the time (Deshpande & DeMello, 2011). The use of evidence-based medicine can help reduce this variation on the supply side.

In addition, numerous customary care practices have no benefit but are still affirmatively used on a daily basis (Van Tassel, 2015). These misused practices are a waste. In a national initiative, 60 major medical specialty groups issued recommendations that physicians stop using over 300 different unnecessary, but frequently used, tests and procedures that can actually be harmful for patients (Van Tassel, 2013b).

Pay for Quality

Linking financial incentives with evidence-based medicine is controversial. Some question why physicians should be paid or incentivized to follow clinical guidelines they should be adhering to already. Others say the financial incentive tactic is simply cost-containment disguised as evidence-based medicine. Apart from the controversy, employers, health insurers, and government payers are experimenting with programs that reward adherence to clinical guidelines.

While few would argue against using scientific evidence to treat patients, others worry going strictly by clinical guidelines is akin to cookbook medicine and may interfere with physicians' intuition and experience when it comes to treating individual cases. A set-in-stone practice guideline for a specific disease or condition, they argue, does not allow physicians to use their medical experience and diagnostic skills fully. They also fear it could allow insurers to refuse to cover care that medical professionals might deem necessary for a patient if it does not follow exact clinical guidelines.

Defenders insist, however, the clinical guidelines do not exclude alternative treatments. They also stress that clinical trials of **experimental treatments** and procedures will always be important methods of gathering new evidence for the ever-evolving clinical guidelines and they ask that all therapies be proven effective. Moreover, clinical guidelines help physicians stay on top of the explosion in new data from clinical trials and medical research.

An instance of the tension between evidence-based medicine and traditional medical intuitions is the medical basis for routine male genital alteration of newborns. In the 1970s, the American Academy of Pediatrics stated there was no medical need for circumcision. Then in 1989 it referred to potential medical benefits, and in 1999, it released a policy statement stating the practice does not have health benefits strong enough to warrant recommendation as a routine procedure (Laufer-Ukeles, 2016). Regardless of the evidence, some physicians still perform circumcisions because of religious and cultural-based demands (Schuz, 2015).

Treatment Effectiveness

Sound scientific evidence now exists for about half of the most prevalent health conditions, but the gap between knowing what works best and the day-to- day provision of treatment services is wide and continually expanding (Laakmann, 2015). One way to close this gap between knowledge and clinical practice is by insisting physicians' choice of treatment be backed by current evidence of a treatment's effectiveness. To budget billions for basic medical research by the National Institutes of Health and not get the benefits to patients is a huge, unnecessary waste (Straus et al., 2010).

Not all studies have speckled histories. Many uncover significant advances. Problems arise when studies are pursued to achieve economic goals; where political motivations seem to intrude on the design and conduct of the trials and bias not only how results are interpreted, but especially, how they are reported. For instance:

- Antibiotics are overused.
- Statins and beta-blockers are underused.
- Antidepressants are misused in the treatment of depressed children and adolescents.

Antibiotics: Overused

Another opportunity to save money is to eliminate the **overuse of antibiotics,** which account for 15 to 20% of the average hospital's drug budget (Mantel, 2015). Overuse has caused microbe resistance to many antibiotics, leading to more medical complications and costs. A study of 11 hospitals by the Veterans Health Administration found three common antibiotics used in patients with kidney failure or urinary tract infections were overused or unnecessarily used, based on clinical guidelines for their conditions (Milstein et al., 2010). By using lower doses or less expensive drugs, the average 250-bed hospital found savings of $100,000 annually, which indicates more than $1 billion could be saved nationwide in all hospitals.

Statins and Beta-Blockers: Underused

Clinical guidelines call for most patients with established heart disease to take aspirin as well as prescription drugs to lower cholesterol and blood pressure, yet only about 25% of such patients are consistently taking the recommended regimen (Resnick, 2014). Money saved from the overuse of antibiotics could be redirected into **proven care**. For instance, the money spent on excess drugs used after surgery could give everyone a **beta-blocker** to help control blood pressure after a heart attack (AHRQ, 2010, 2005).

After using its electronic records to identify people at risk for heart attacks, Group Health (a member-governed, nonprofit health care system that coordinates care and coverage in Seattle, Washington), started 11,000 previously untreated patients on cholesterol-lowering drugs called **statins**. It based the move on evidence of the effectiveness of statins in the Heart Protection study, a five-year trial of more than 20,000 patients. The decision cost Group Health $700,000 per year, but the expectation is it will save $5.0 million (Resnick, 2014). Six years later, one-fourth of the outpatients at high cardiovascular risk continue to be undertreated as a result of a combination of physician underestimation of cardiovascular risk and barriers to implementation of evidence-based medicine; the good news is three-fourths of the patients are now being successfully treated (Group Health, 2016).

Antidepressants in the Treatment of Depressed Children and Adolescents: Misused

The criterion of reliability of scientific evidence is whether study results are published, and therefore available to physicians, purchasers of health care, and policy makers. The classic instance here is the safety and efficacy of antidepressants in the treatment of depressed children and adolescents. In the **scientific literature** there were six articles, all showing these drugs to be safe and effective. Physicians had good reason to believe treatment of depressed children and adolescents with the new antidepressants was proper, evidence-based care. What they did not know is that not six, but 15 studies of the safety and efficacy of these drugs in children and adolescents were completed. The other nine unpublished studies had shown the drugs were neither effective nor safe, and that they doubled the rate of suicidal thoughts and behaviors. In fact, even among the six positive studies, the published claims in three were not confirmed after independent analysis (Abramson, 2006).

After the nine unpublished studies became public knowledge, the FDA issued warnings that use of antidepressants posed a small but significantly increased risk of suicidal thoughts and behavior ideation for children and adolescents (Brausch & Gutierrez, 2010). Review of 27 subsequent published studies found the benefits of antidepressants to be much greater than the risks, but called for continued clinical caution (Pickar & Kaufman, 2015). A study at the University of Pittsburgh Medical Center validated the scientific literature and confirmed that the rate of suicidal thoughts and behaviors increases with antidepressants in the treatment of depressed children and adolescents and called for continued study and reiterated the call for clinical caution (Brent et al., 2009). Nevertheless, the damage was done by misuse of scientific evidence: the reliability of antidepressants is now questioned, treatment with antidepressants has significantly dropped by 30%, and the annual suicide rate in children and adolescents has increased by 10%, or 3,000 more suicides are predicted as a direct result of this debacle (Pickar & Kaufman, 2015).

Elimination of Geographic Variations

Another benefit of evidence-based medicine would be to eliminate geographical variations in health care. Research shows physicians are not uniformly following clinical guidelines. If they were, there would not be six times as many angioplasties in Ohio per 1,000 Medicare-insured patients as there are in Pennsylvania. Nor would there be the national variability in breast cancer screening that exists.

Even when there is a strong body of scientific evidence about new drugs and devices, it can take 15 to 20 years for physicians and hospitals to incorporate them (IOM, 2015, 2001) Between the health care we have and the care we could have lies not just a gap, but a chasm (IOM, 2001). Evidence-based medicine could close it. The AHRQ is funding research at 12 medical centers in the United States and Canada with the aim of developing evidence reports on a wide variety of diseases and conditions.

Access to Government Databases

Information sharing is an imperative of evidence-based medicine. Uniform sets of performance measures provide benchmarks and promote the development of independent **standards of care**, which are the recognized degrees of care expected and required of health care professionals who have an obligation to conduct themselves accordingly under like circumstances. Independent standards of care, as opposed to professional standards, could define the appropriate conduct of physicians, nurses, and other health care professionals in comparison to what reasonable professionals either do, or should do, in similar situations. In turn, this data could provide a limited but important set of measures of differences in the rates at which patients use key health care services.

Shared Decision-Making with Patients

The concern of evidence-based medicine proponents is that patients waste valuable time and money on treatments that do not work. Patients also need to be made aware of the pros and cons of treatments so they can be involved in **shared decision-making** with their physicians. Moreover, giving patients clinical guidelines will encourage them to follow treatment regimens and comply with physicians' orders, proponents say. Compliance is increasingly important to health insurers and employers eager to eliminate unnecessary tests and ineffective procedures and to push patients to adopt healthier lifestyles, all of which help reduce medical bills in the long run.

Medical Technology Decisions

Increasingly, medical technology decisions are being used in every aspect of hospital operations, including questions such as whether it is necessary to use a high-priced medical device when a less expensive one is available. At the same time, while evidence-based medicine will offer guidance on a wide range of medical technologies, clinical evidence

MANAGEMENT AND LAW ISSUES

1. Should government funds be spent on researching the best evidence-based medicine available to treat preventable, self-inflicted ailments, such as those resulting from smoking or lack of healthy diet and exercise?

must be distinguished from the financial components of such decisions. The financial aspects of making a decision are important, as long as they are not disguised as science (Straus et al., 2010), in other words, as long as the science is not bent in order to justify financial considerations.

End-of-Life Care

One area where medical technology decisions are increasingly arising is in end-of-life treatment of terminal disease and illness. What factors define **futile medical care** for patients with terminal prognosis, and should there be an expectation that insurers, including Medicare insurance, will pay for it? Courts are increasingly faced with the struggles of families to compel the termination or to not stop the termination of an incompetent person's life-sustaining treatment. *See, e.g., Schiavo ex rel. Schindler v. Schiavo,* 403 F.3d 1289 (U.S. Court of Appeals for the 11th Circuit 2005), *stay denied,* 544 U.S. 957 (U.S. Supreme Court 2005).

Investigational Treatments and Medical Products

Another area where debate arises is the right to access **investigational treatments and medical products**. Should terminally ill patients be able to access experimental treatments and medical technologies that have not completed the FDA approval process? Are there instances where individual rights should override scientific process and standards in determining the safety, efficacy, medical necessity, and medical appropriateness of medical technologies?

Evolving Medical Advancements and Medical Efficacy

By definition, clinical guidelines are developed in good faith based on the best available scientific evidence, whose performance is constantly evaluated. Unfortunately this is not always the case, and this shortcoming must be acknowledged in any criticism of the medical profession's resistance to following clinical guidelines. The history of bias in development of clinical guidelines is a real problem, from insurers as well as from government-sponsored medical research.

While the trend is to independently commission and evaluate medical research as opposed to relying solely on information presented by providers of medical products and services, federally funded drug trials show it is unwise to develop clinical guidelines in advance of or contrary to existing epidemiological and biostatistical evidence. Trials that did this include:

- **Women's Health Initiative**
- **Antihypertensive and Lipid-Lowering Treatment to Prevent Heart Attack Trial**
- **Clinical Antipsychotic Trials in Intervention Effectiveness**
- Macular Degeneration Trial
- **National Lung Screening Trial**

Most importantly, government research must be transparent. Sometimes, public outcome data is subject to secrecy for years following the comparative studies, as was the case with hormone replacement therapy research (Parker-Pope, 2007). Then, when the government data is finally released, often the results cannot be replicated and the government's initial conclusions are directly contradicted by independent studies. Such scenarios are not uncommon, however, with respect to pharmaceutical products or, indeed, any product or medical service that may implicate evolving scientific developments. The historical lack of scientific transparency in recent years, however, does make physician resistance to so-called evidence-based medicine entirely understandable and valid. While the concept of evidence-based medicine cannot be refuted, its implementation over the years raises serious concerns for the health care industry.

Women's Health Initiative

Prescriptions for hormone replacement therapy to treat the symptoms of menopause fell dramatically after interim results from a government study of the drugs showed they were causing heart attacks. However, follow-up studies based on the government data found many of the initial conclusions were:

- Clearly incorrect
- Not clear and not precisely defined
- Premature and without any link to the research data

(Parker-Pope, 2007).

While the $725 million Women's Health Initiative was well intended, it was surrounded by fiscal and political disputes over the efficacy and cost of hormone replacement therapy. Unfortunately, this influenced not only how the findings were computed but also how they were received. When initial results appeared to confirm hormone replacement therapy was overused, the data were widely disseminated, while subsequent efforts to test the initial conclusions were given little notice.

In the case of the Women's Health Initiative, although the government initially said the findings applied to *all* women, regardless of age or health status, subsequent **meta-analysis** by the Mayo Clinic using the same data showed the age of a woman and the timing of hormone use dramatically changed the risk and benefits (Neyarapally, 2013). In fact, the findings of these later studies directly contradicted some of the government's initial conclusions. For instance, women in their 50s who took a combination of estrogen and progestin or estrogen alone had a 30% lower risk of dying from cancer than women who did not take hormones. At the same time, women in their 50s who regularly used estrogen alone showed a 60% lower risk for severe coronary artery calcium, a risk factor for heart attack (*See generally* Parker-Pope, 2007).

Antihypertensive and Lipid-Lowering Treatment to Prevent Heart Attack Trial

More than 60% of Americans 65 years of age and older have hypertension, while estimates of the cost of its treatment have ranged from $7 billion to $15.5 billion per year (Johnson & Stukel, 2016). The Antihypertensive and Lipid-Lowering Treatment to Prevent Heart Attack Trial was the largest clinical study of blood pressure treatments ever conducted in the United States. With more than 42,000 patients ages 55 and older participating and followed over an eight-year period, the trial was designed to test:

- How calcium channel blockers compared to angiotensin-converting enzyme inhibitors
- Whether diuretics were as good as newer blood pressure drugs

Federal researchers questioned the degree to which the newer pharmaceuticals improved upon older treatment options. The initial reports found older, inexpensive diuretic drugs were just as good or better than costlier new drugs for treating high blood pressure. The older diuretics cost around $40 compared to $700 for the newer drugs (Ho, 2014).

The results have been corroborated by smaller scale trials undertaken in Europe, as well as in a follow-up heart attack study (Kapczynski & Syed, 2013). Nevertheless, the interpretation of the heart attack trial results has been called into question by many leading experts. Medical researchers, physicians, and patients are discussing and debating the meaning of head-to-head studies (Taylor et al., 2013). For one thing, as the heart attack trial proved, detecting small clinical differences between two active drugs, such as whether one pill lowers blood pressure more than another, requires very large studies that often fail to capture all of the patient preferences and characteristics that go into real-world medical decisions (Ho, 2014). Determining whether small differences are clinically meaningful can take years of follow-up, and the statistics can be argued in favor of multiple conclusions.

Clinical Antipsychotic Trials in Intervention Effectiveness

The federally funded Clinical Antipsychotic Trials in Intervention Effectiveness (CATIE) research found older and less expensive schizophrenia brand-name drugs were just as good as newer, more expensive (and many believe far more tolerable) atypical antipsychotic drugs with fewer side effects (Bennion, 2013). CATIE followed nearly 1,500 schizophrenic patients in 57 cities across the country for 18 months. It compared the efficacy of an older antipsychotic drug, perphenazine, with four newer atypical antipsychotics:

- Olanzapine
- Quetiapine
- Risperidone
- Ziprasidone

(*E.g.*, Stroup et al., 2011).

Its result, however, has made little impact on real-world medical practice because few physicians believe the study was credible (Bennion, 2013). Incredibly, CATIE's complete safety data was not released until almost four years after the study was completed; an unbelievable delay. Moreover, the drugs involved in these studies were for conditions where there is a great deal of individual variation in how people respond. Critics claim the government studies did not take measure of that (Jakubovski et al., 2015).

Macular Degeneration Trial

Now the government is sponsoring a trial to test whether Avastin, a drug meant for injection into the veins to treat breast, colon, and rectal cancer, can also treat age-related macular degeneration, in which one loses central vision, and which is a leading cause of blindness in people over age 50 (*See* Todd, 2011). Medicare insurance reimburses providers for off-label use of Avastin for treatment of age-related macular degeneration, but most health insurers do not. Because of this reimbursement problem, Avastin's manufacturer, Genentech, developed a completely new drug called Lucentis, which is specifically designed to be injected into the eye and is better adapted to treat retinal degenerative diseases and blindness (Herbst, 2015).

Since a single cancer infusion of Avastin contains a large volume of the drug, breaking the dose down into the small aliquots needed for the eye injections costs literally pennies on the dollar, making the government's study of it, when it was clearly not designed for eye treatments, a matter of cost containment. Surely if Avastin ends up harming those eyes, a plausible consequence of this off-label, if not illegally compounded use, it will not be the government on the hook with **product liability damages**, but Genentech. Genentech is directly or indirectly accepting funds from Medicare insurance for off-label use and it is not providing a specific warning on the Avastin label warning of the dangers of periocular injections (Buck, 2016).[LN2]

National Lung Screening Trial

In a dispute with broad implications for cancer treatment, controversy surrounds the objectivity of the National Lung Screening Trial, a nine-year study that tracked 50,000 smokers at a cost of $200 million. The federal study was supposed to determine whether annual **computed tomography (CT) scans** of smokers' lungs can save lives. Funded by the National Cancer Institute, the study has had a major impact on whether regular CT scans for smokers can be considered a justifiable standard of care. For instance, the U.S. Preventive Services Task Force recently recommended CT screening for lung cancer in heavy smokers between the ages of 55 and 80 (Abbott & Stevens, 2014). The 90 million current and former smokers in the United States are all potential screening candidates, as are the millions exposed to secondhand smoke (family, workplace, and social) (Surgeon General, 2015). It seems virtually everyone could be a screening candidate (Wasserman, 2014). The economic justification, if any, of this medical monitoring is unclear.

The question under consideration in the study was a complex one. CT scanning is adept at detecting abnormalities that might be cancerous. Once they are detected, potentially risky lung biopsies are usually needed to confirm the presence of cancer in the lung. Often, the biopsies turn up no cancer. Skeptics say patients may suffer health problems as a result of universal screening, such as complications from biopsies or needless surgery, offsetting any gains from enhanced detection (Surgeon General, 2015). Critics also say 50,000 patients are too few to detect a benefit.

Other Lung Screening Initiatives

A study of asymptomatic smokers found that while annual CT scans increased the rate of lung cancer diagnoses, there was no evidence CT screening reduced the risk of death due to lung cancer(Wasserman, 2014). The increase in diagnoses failed to reduce the death rate because the annual CT scans detected cancers that would not have grown sufficiently during the patient's lifetime to cause any harm. Yet the tenfold increase in the number of thoracic surgeries resulting from the additional diagnoses may well have caused harm because of the postoperative mortality rate of 5% and the frequency of serious complications, 20 to 44%. While another study found screening for lung cancer might be beneficial (Surgeon General, 2015), this study met with heavy criticism because it was based on **survival rates** as opposed to mortality rates and incorrectly assumed everyone with lung cancer would die of it without treatment, when the 5-year survival rate for lung cancer is 18% after diagnosis or the start of treatment. More than half the people with lung cancer die within one year of being diagnosed (National Cancer Institute, 2016).

As a result, the position held by leading medical organizations that the costs of universal screening for lung cancer outweigh its benefits is unlikely to change. Unless the National Cancer Institute study releases significantly different information, there appears to be no pressing need to adopt a medical monitoring claim for asymptomatic smokers. Although medical monitoring is useful in some cases, the medical community has cast significant doubt on the monitoring regimen for lung cancer (*See generally* Abbott & Stevens, 2014; Surgeon General, 2015).

2. Is it possible to conduct an entirely objective, accurate clinical study?

Drug Effectiveness Review Project

The **Drug Effectiveness Review Project** is a collaboration of 15 states that commissions and uses systematic reviews of global research to inform drug purchasing decisions in an effort to compare the effectiveness of popular drugs (Gooch et al., 2013). The logic behind this effort is clear: to win FDA approval, a pharmaceutical firm generally has to demonstrate a new drug is safe and more effective than a placebo. It does not, however, have to show how the new drug compares with other drugs already on the market. That is useful information, however, particularly when the new drug might cost significantly more than an over-the-counter alternative (Darrow, 2014).

Formulary Restrictions

The Drug Effectiveness Review Project has resulted in **formulary restrictions** that have reduced patients' access to medicines, according to a Kaiser Family Foundation report. The program distorts evidence-based medicine to create a veil behind which the health care industry justifies restrictions on patients' access to health care in order to reduce short-term drug costs. The project fails to adequately take into account individual patients' medical needs and ways to contain health care costs overall in the long and short term (Darrow, 2014).

Independent Comparative Effectiveness Research

Better information about the effectiveness of drugs as well as their safety ought to be a starting point. Supporters of the Drug Effectiveness Review Project challenge the pharmaceutical industry to take the lead in coming up with alternatives to their efforts. At issue is whether the pharmaceutical industry should be expected to do **comparative research** itself. Others ask whether the United States needs a respected, independent organization, perhaps funded jointly by the health care industry and government, to study the available evidence and, when necessary, commission further research, including studies of alternative and complementary medicine and other non-drug treatments like diet and exercise (*See generally, e.g.*, Buck, 2016; Hiller, 2016; Kukura, 2016a).

Hierarchy of Scientific Research

The gold standard of evidence in scientific research is a combination of double-blind, randomized controlled trials and a systematic review of medical studies called meta-analysis (Beales & Muris, 2015). Evidence-based medicine suggests that when a clinical problem arises, physicians should, in descending order of preference, look for guidance in:

- Systematic reviews of randomized controlled trials
- Results of individual controlled clinical trials
- Observational (uncontrolled) studies
- Anecdotal reports of clinical observations

(Straus et al., 2010).

This hierarchy implies a clear course of action for physicians addressing patient problems: they should look for the highest value available evidence.

Confusion Between Epidemiology and General Causation

The comparative effectiveness debate is clouded by epidemiological studies that can only go to prove a drug could have caused, but not that it actually did cause, a health condition in a particular individual (Sackett, 1985). There is often confusion in this regard; the incidence of disease in populations does not address the question of the cause of an individual's disease, and neither does the identification of factors that are correlated with whether or not a disease develops. This question, sometimes referred to as specific causation, is beyond the science of epidemiology. Indeed, it can be argued that disease causation can never be definitively proven; it can only ever be argued in terms of 'more likely than not,' or a statistical likelihood better than that of chance alone.

Epidemiology has its limits, located at the points where an inference can reasonably be made that the relationship between a drug and a disease is causal (**general causation** – a legal standard, not a scientific one) and where the risk attributed to the drug has been determined. That is, epidemiology can only address whether a drug *can* cause a disease or condition, not whether a drug really did cause a specific individual's ailment (*See generally* Federal Judicial Center, 2015). One case clarified the issue of general causation in drug liability lawsuits.

COURT DECISION

General Causation in Drug Products Liability Actions: Differential Diagnosis

Ruggiero v. Warner-Lambert Co.
[Patient's Widow v. Pharmaceutical Firm]
424 F.3d 249 (U.S. Court of Appeals for the 2nd Circuit 2005),
summary judgment granted and case dismissed,
524 F.Supp.2d 436 (U.S. District Court for the Southern District of New York 2007);
followed by Best v. Lowe's Home Centers, Inc., 563 F.3d 171 (U.S. Court of Appeals for the 6th Circuit 2009)

Facts: Anne Ruggiero is the widow of Albert Ruggiero who was diagnosed with type 2 diabetes. Albert Ruggiero died of liver failure caused by cirrhosis 15 months after he had started taking the diabetes drug Rezulin. Two years later, manufacturers and distributors of Rezulin halted its distribution in response to concerns Rezulin caused increased liver toxicity.

Anne Ruggiero filed a federal product liability lawsuit against Warner-Lambert Co. and Parke Davis, who manufactured and sold Rezulin. She claimed Rezulin caused her husband's death. The federal trial court dismissed the claim, holding Ruggiero produced insufficient evidence to show Rezulin was indeed capable of causing or exacerbating cirrhosis of the liver. Specifically, the court found the medical expert's **differential diagnosis** that Rezulin led to Mr. Ruggiero's death was insufficient to support general causation without a scientifically valid methodology for establishing the drug as a possible cause.

Issue: Can a differential diagnosis be used to show the use of Rezulin, an antidiabetes drug, caused the death of Mr. Ruggiero by liver failure?

Holding and Decision: No, medical experts may not rely on differential diagnosis alone to corroborate that Rezulin was the cause of Mr. Ruggiero's liver failure; positive evidence from a scientifically valid methodology is required to support general causation, which is a necessary component of a products liability lawsuit.

Analysis: General causation is the concept that a particular factor had the potential, or capability, of causing the alleged injury, while specific causation is the concept that the particular factor did indeed cause the alleged injury. The district court excluded the expert testimony of Dr. Douglas Dietrich, the sole evidence of general causation submitted by Mrs. Ruggiero, because Dr. Dietrich's testimony failed to meet the standards required by the U.S. Supreme Court, the so-called *Daubert* principles, which suggest courts might consider:

- Whether a theory or technique has been and could be tested
- What its error rate was
- Whether scientific standards exist to govern the theory or technique's application

    In addition, the rules of evidence require expert witnesses to:

- Base their testimony upon sufficient facts or data
- Use reliable principles and methods
- Apply the principles and methods reliably to the facts of the case

See Daubert v. Merrell Dow Pharmaceuticals, 509 U.S. 579 (U.S. Supreme Court 1993).

The court concluded Dr. Dietrich lacked a reliable basis for his opinion because he failed to reference any studies or anything else to suggest Rezulin could cause or exacerbate cirrhosis.

Dr. Dietrich employed a methodology known as differential diagnosis, which is a patient-specific process of elimination physicians use to identify the most likely cause of symptoms from a list of possible causes. In other words, physicians using differential diagnosis provide testimony countering other possible causes of the injuries at issue. The court found this technique insufficient to support general causation. Differential diagnosis does not necessarily support an opinion on general causation because, as with any process of elimination, it assumes the final, suspected cause remaining after this process of elimination must actually have caused the injury. Furthermore, when an expert employs differential diagnosis to eliminate potential causes for a specific injury, he also must prove the suspected cause using scientifically valid methodology.

In *Daubert*, the U.S. Supreme Court held a court may refuse to admit evidence if it concludes there is simply too great an analytical gap between the data and the opinion proffered. When expert testimony is based on data, a methodology, or studies that are inadequate to support the conclusions reached, *Daubert* mandates the exclusion of such unreliable opinion testimony because it does not rise to the level of being considered "expert." Although differential diagnosis was not accepted as a valid methodology to support expert testimony on general causation in this case, the court cautioned that its ruling did not mean a differential diagnosis could never provide a sufficient basis for an opinion as to general causation. The court stated there may be instances where, because of the rigor of differential diagnosis performed, the expert's training and experience, the type of illness or injury at issue, or some other case-specific circumstance, a differential diagnosis is sufficient to support an expert's opinion on both general and specific causation. In other words, medical experts may not rely on differential diagnosis alone as a methodology to corroborate a particular drug is the cause of a specific illness in a patient. Instead, experts should be positive that evidence derived from a scientifically valid method supports general causation.

Rule of Law: Expert witnesses must produce positive evidence to establish general causation in drug products liability actions.

References discussing this court decision: *E.g.*, Bernstein & Lasker, 2015.

Problems with Authority-Based Medical Opinions

Uncritical acceptance of **authority-based medical opinions** is pervasive in U.S. medicine, even though top authorities unsuccessfully predict what scientific knowledge will be preserved as fact (Straus et al., 2010). Reliance on expert medical opinions, which is not based upon an objective methodology, gives the status of knowledge to uncertainties (*See* Perez, 2016). For instance, with infrequent medical complications, such as a patient who develops pneumonia following a heart-lung transplant, recommendations are sought, accepted, and applied from authorities in the relevant branch of medicine. When this health care is objectively appraised, some of it is effective, harmful, or useless, but in the traditional medical paradigm, there is no way to be sure which is which.

Vaccines and Childhood Autism

There is probably no better medical controversy to support the need for evidence-based medicine than the dispute surrounding childhood autism, a neurodevelopment disorder marked by impaired social interactions, deficits in verbal and nonverbal communication, and restricted and repetitive patterns of behavior that persist throughout a person's lifetime. The debate over whether **vaccines** cause autism ignited in 1998, when an NIH-sponsored study posited a connection (Hardee, 2016). At the same time, the incidence of autism started increasing, with some figures estimating roughly 1 in 45 children suffers from autism (CDC, 2016). One side of this controversy relies on anecdotal evidence to link the rising prevalence of autism to mercury-laden vaccines; the other side claims autism is simply better diagnosed and treatment services are better funded.

The courts are strictly construing federal law in vaccine litigation. No statutory protections are being extended to manufacturers of vaccine preservatives, such as thimerosal. Therefore, if victims are able to trace their injury to manufacturers of a vaccine preservative, there is nothing to prevent them from litigating their claims. This decision was the first time a federal appellate court found that parents of an injured child could sue vaccine manufacturers.[LN3] Considering the number of vaccine-related lawsuits brought against vaccine manufacturers, the implications of this decision are far-reaching. *See Aventis Pasteur, Inc. v. Skevofilax*, 914 A.2d 113 (Court of Appeals of Maryland 2007) (case dismissed due to inability of the Skevofilax family to obtain a medical expert to testify that their son's autism was caused by thimerosal used in pediatric vaccines).

Side Effects of Vaccines

In rare cases, vaccines can cause shock, brain inflammation, and death, especially in children with allergies or compromised immune systems. The **National Childhood Vaccine Injury Act of 1986** recognizes specified side effects for each vaccine; autism is not among them. It allows parents to make claims for other side effects, but sets specific criteria they must meet to show blame. For instance, two recognized side effects of the rubella virus-containing vaccine are chronic arthritis, which is said to manifest in seven to 42 days, and encephalopathy, which is said to manifest within 5 to 15 days after administration of the vaccine (*See* 42 C.F.R. § 100.3(a)).

In a settlement reached in the U.S. Vaccine Court, the federal government did concede that a young girl with autism had been damaged by vaccines (*See Poling v. Secretary of HHS*, 2008 U.S. Claims LEXIS 167 (U.S. Court of Federal Claims 2008)). The case was not a precedent, however, because the child had rare genetic mitochondrial disorders that likely contributed to her autism. Mitochondria, the energy factories of cells, have their own genetic material that is passed directly from mother to child. Flaws in this material are relatively common. As those flaws multiply, they interfere with mitochondrial function. According to the Centers for Disease Control and Prevention, as many as 700,000 people in the United States have flawed mitochondria, and in roughly 30,000 of them, the genetic flaws are expansive enough to cause disease.

COURT DECISION
Remedies Available to Parents of Children with Vaccine-Related Injuries Under the National Childhood Vaccine Injury Act

Moss v. Merck & Co.
[Parents of Injured Child v. Pharmaceutical Firm]
381 F.3d 501 (U.S. Court of Appeals for the 5th Circuit 2004);
followed by Reilly v. Wyeth, 876 N.E.2d 740 (Appellate Court of Illinois, First District, Third Division 2007),
appeal denied, 882 N.E.2d 83 (Supreme Court of Illinois 2008)

Facts: Scott and Janice Moss, the parents of a young child who was diagnosed with autism after receiving vaccines containing mercury, pursued a **malpractice** claim for injuries they suffered as a result of their child's health condition. The Mosses filed a lawsuit against Merck, Aventis, Wyeth, and Eli Lilly. The federal trial court dismissed their claims on the grounds that the National Childhood Vaccine Injury Act precluded a malpractice remedy for a vaccine-related injury (*See* 42 U.S.C.A. §§ 218 *et seq.*).

Federal law bars victims of a vaccine-related injury or death from seeking redress in court against a vaccine manufacturer unless the victims have first filed a claim for recovery in the specialized U.S. Vaccine Court. The term *vaccine-related injury or death* means an illness, injury, condition, or death associated with one or more of the vaccines set forth in the Vaccine Injury Table, except that the term does not include an illness, injury, condition, or death associated with an adulterant or contaminant intentionally added to such a vaccine (*See* 42 U.S.C.A. § 300aa-33(5)). Congress designed the federal law to provide compensation to children injured by vaccines, while ensuring the nation's supply of vaccines was not unduly threatened by malpractice litigation.

To file a petition for compensation, there must be a vaccine-related injury. Legal representatives may file petitions for compensation on behalf of disabled or deceased children. If they are successful, acceptance of a compensatory award from the government causes the vaccine-injured children to waive any further malpractice rights. If a child declines the award, traditional malpractice relief may be available, but punitive damages are prohibited.

Issue: Can the parents of a child injured by a vaccine sue in federal court for their own injuries suffered as a result of their child's health condition?

Holding and Decision: Yes, while the injured child may be precluded from suing for a vaccine-related injury, the parents are not.

Analysis: Eli Lilly argued federal law barred the Mosses' claims because Eli Lilly was a vaccine manufacturer. The court held thimerosal was not a vaccine and Eli Lilly was not a **vaccine manufacturer** as defined in federal law. According to the court, thimerosal, when used as a preservative, is merely a component of a vaccine and, therefore, not the finished product itself. Federal health officials recommended that thimerosal be removed from vaccines in 1999. Since 2001, thimerosal has not been used in routinely recommended childhood vaccines, with the exception of some flu shots, yet autism rates seem unaffected.

Multiple studies have failed to find any relationship between thimerosal exposure and autism. On its face, the National Childhood Vaccine Injury Act only governs lawsuits filed against manufacturers of a completed vaccine shipped under its own label. Thimerosal is not sold as a vaccine; therefore, Eli Lilly is not a vaccine manufacturer, and is not entitled to federal protection.

In concluding federal law does not protect Eli Lilly from suit, the court rejected Eli Lilly's argument that any injury arising from thimerosal is encompassed within the statutory definition of vaccine-related injury, and that those alleging an injury or death from the thimerosal preservative in vaccines are obligated to file their claim against a manufacturer of the vaccine in the U.S. Vaccine Court. Eli Lilly claimed victims of thimerosal-related injuries were obligated to pursue relief in the U.S. Vaccine Court. The court disagreed with Eli Lilly, stating that while a thimerosal-related injury is a vaccine-related injury, the inquiry does not end there. A claim is not barred unless the vaccine-related injury is filed against a vaccine manufacturer, which Eli Lilly is not.

Additionally, Eli Lilly argued federal law expressly barred the Mosses' claims of vaccine-related injury. The court determined federal law does not protect non-manufacturers of vaccines, and it does not apply to all malpractice claims having some connection to the administration of a vaccine. Rather, federal restrictions apply only to the claims of those who have sustained a vaccine-related injury or death.

Because Scott and Janice Moss never received a vaccine and did not personally sustain a vaccine-related injury or death, federal restrictions did not apply to them. Eli Lilly also claimed literal application of federal provisions would impede the statutory goal of reducing the costs and risks of malpractice litigation. Relying on basic strict construction of federal law, the court rejected Eli Lilly's argument, stating that because federal law neither provides a remedy nor openly bars the right of parents of vaccine-injured children to pursue remedies afforded by state malpractice law, the Mosses may pursue their claims.

Rule of Law: Because thimerosal, a mercury-containing preservative used in several childhood vaccines, is not a vaccine under the plain meaning of the law, Eli Lilly is not entitled to the protections of the National Childhood Vaccine Injury Act.

References discussing this court decision: *E.g.*, Crawford & Axelrad, 2012; Engstrom, 2015; Greenleaf, 2012.

Implications of Not Vaccinating

The availability of exemptions from **compulsory vaccination** is a growing concern with 10% of the nation's children not being vaccinated with recommended pediatric vaccines (Hill et al., 2016). This represents about 7.4 million children. Outbreaks of diphtheria, mumps (including a 2009 outbreak at Northeastern University), pertussis (whooping cough), polio, and rubella (measles) have confirmed the continued threat of vaccine-preventable diseases.[LN4]

When people decide to forgo vaccination, they threaten the entire public health care system. They increase their own risk and the risk of everyone else, including infants too young to be vaccinated and people with immune systems impaired by disease, other medical treatments including chemotherapy, or age. Of course, it is the very success of modern vaccines that makes exemptions possible. In previous generations, when epidemic diseases swept through communities, it was easy to persuade everyone that the small risks associated with vaccination were worth it. Now that infectious disease epidemics have stopped, because of widespread vaccinations, it is easy to forget the world of microbes is still dangerous.

The Future of Evidence-Based Medicine

As the debate on evidence-based medicine continues, many agree the current health care system covers too few, costs too much, and does not deliver consistently high-quality health care. The question is how to ensure patients receive quality, affordable health care. Without ensuring quality, access to health care may be meaningless. Without addressing costs, health care becomes inaccessible. By building evidence-based medicine into reform measures, Americans might get the right health care at the right time for the right price.

LAW FACT

Hormone Replacement Therapy

Is there any reliable evidence-based scientific research that combination hormone replacement therapy can cause breast cancer, heart disease, or dementia?

No. However, "patient safety" is a relative term in the medical products industry. Nevertheless, 50 years after the introduction of hormone replacement therapy by the pharmaceutical industry, enough convincing information has been found that juries have awarded millions of dollars in punitive damages, indicating reckless disregard for women's health in selling the drug without warnings or ethical research. More than 9,000 women have sued.

Class action status was denied in *Reeves v. Wyeth (In re Prempro Products Liability Litigation)*; each individual case has to be tried separately. Women could not overcome the problems with individual issues of law and fact as to what caused each woman's health condition. In one of the latest trials, *Fraser v. Wyeth*, the jury awarded $1.7 million in punitive damages against Wyeth Pharmaceuticals (which was acquired by Pfizer in 2009) for failure to warn about the full risks associated with hormone replacement therapy.

— *Reeves v. Wyeth (In re Prempro Products Liability Litigation)*, 2006 U.S.Dist.LEXIS 59049 (U.S. District Court for the Eastern District of Arkansas, Western Division 2006).

CHAPTER SUMMARY

- Evidence-based medicine is the application of epidemiological principles to clinical health care; it entails incorporating key scientific findings into medical practice and measuring the associated outcomes.
- The traditional way of practicing medicine focused more on the physician's individual experience, familiarity with and observation of the patient, and common sense.
- Evidence-based medicine encourages the use of reliable studies based upon scientifically sound rules of research and evidence.
- Although evidence-based medicine can help pinpoint which treatments are best for which conditions, patients often still do not receive the best available treatment because health care professionals are not aware of the best treatment or have their own reasons for not using the recommended treatment.
- The fact that evidence-based medicine has not been thoroughly implemented in U.S. health care is likely one reason why American health care falls short of international benchmarks despite its high cost.

- A chief criticism of evidence-based medicine is it is extremely difficult to design a study that accurately determines exactly what the best course of care is or what the cause of a medical problem is; related to this problem is the criticism that studies often emerge contradicting other studies.
- Another chief criticism of evidence-based medicine is studies are too easily tainted by any number of causes, including bias, financial concerns, lack of transparency, and failure to consider all factors affecting the outcome; the gold standard of study design in evidence-based medicine is a combination of double-blind, randomized, controlled trials and a systematic review of medical studies called meta-analysis.
- Some physicians are resistant to implementing evidence-based medicine because they want to be sure it will work for their patients and that it is better than the treatments they currently offer; also, to fully implement evidence-based medicine is cost- and time-prohibitive for many conditions.
- Physicians are also resistant to relying solely upon evidence-based medicine because they feel it interferes with their personal autonomy and intuition.
- There are several organizations attempting to collect and condense the most reliable evidence-based medicine studies for both health care insurers' and providers' use.
- Evidence-based medicine can help identify which courses of care are overused, underused, and misused, which could help allocate health care dollars more efficiently.

LAW NOTES

1. Dartmouth Medical School's Center for the Evaluative Clinical Sciences analyzed variations in health care costs in all 306 Medicare insurance regions in the United States. Each state has 10 to 50 Medicare insurance regions to maximize Medicare insurance plan participation and the availability of plans to Medicare insurance beneficiaries. The description of the 306 regions is complex, confusing, and impossible to understand, let alone use to implement insurance plans without violating some other regulations (Van Tassel, 2013a). The study found patients living in the highest spending regions received 60% more care than patients living in the lowest spending regions, and these differences were not explained by age, sex, or disease burden (Van Tassel, 2015; *See, e.g.,* Fischer et al., 2008). Researchers then looked at how patients with three distinct disease entities were treated according to the level of spending in their Medicare insurance region:

   - First broken hip
   - First heart attack
   - Initial diagnosis of colon cancer

   (Van Tassel, 2013b; *See, e.g.,* Fischer et al., 2008).

   Patients in the higher spending regions had no:

   - Better access to health care
   - Greater patient satisfaction with care
   - Higher quality of care

   (Van Tassel, 2015; *See* Fischer et al., 2008).

   Based on this data, the Commonwealth Fund subsequently determined that if all Medicare-insured patients with these three health conditions had received the quality of care provided in the best performing Medicare insurance regions, better health outcomes would have been achieved for significantly less money:

   - 8,400 lives could be saved each year
   - $900 million in unnecessary health care costs could be saved annually

   (Radley et al., 2014; Van Tassel, 2015).

2. Specifically, the off-label use is one that is not provided for on Avastin's FDA-approved labeling (Robertson, 2015). In this instance, the off-label use involves using an injectable drug for treatment to a patient group other than those for whom the FDA approved it. Even though Genentech developed Lucentis expressly for this patient group, it still has a continuing duty to warn of related risks from Avastin since it knows it is being used as substitute for Lucentis based on the price differential. Genentech has a duty to warn patients and physicians of the possible dangers and must share this information with them by means of warnings. In this situation, Genentech is aware of the risks associated with periocular injection of Avastin and is also aware the drug is being

administered in this fashion as an off-label use. Consequently, Genentech has a legal obligation to warn about the risks of periocular injection of Avastin (Herbst, 2015). *Compare Proctor v. Davis*, 682 N.E.2d 1203 (Appellate Court of Illinois, 1st District, 5th Division 1997) (involving periocular injections of Depo-Medro manufactured by Upjohn Pharmaceutical), *appeal denied*, 689 N.E.2d 1146 (Supreme Court of Illinois 1997).

3. A special master in the U.S. Court of Federal Claims ruled that routine childhood immunizations are not linked to autism, handing down the first decision from the U.S. Vaccine Court since hearings began in the controversy over whether vaccines can cause autism. The court denied damages to three families who claimed the thimerosal found in the measles, mumps, and rubella vaccine (the MMR vaccine) made in the United States by Merck led to their children's autism. *See Cedillo v. Secretary of HHS*, 89 Fed. Cl. 158 (U.S. Court of Federal Claims 2009); *See also* Greenleaf, 2012 and Meyers, 2011 (discussing *Cedillo*). The U.S. Vaccine Court found the anecdotal evidence did not support a connection between vaccines and autism, noting that numerous evidence-based medicine studies performed by scientists worldwide have agreed. Some 5,000 families are seeking damages from the federal Vaccine Injury Compensation Fund program to compensate children allegedly harmed by vaccines. *See* 26 U.S.C.A. § 9510 (establishing a Vaccine Injury Compensation Trust Fund in the Treasury of the U.S. States); *See also* 26 U.S.C.A. § 4131 (imposing a tax of 75 cents per dose of vaccine). Each of the test cases represents different theories for how vaccines could cause autism:

   - Measles vaccine causes a low-level measles infection that affects children's brains.
   - Mercury-containing vaccine preservative, thimerosal, poisons the brain, causing autism.
   - Vaccines may cause or contribute to an underlying mitochondrial disorder, which in turn causes autism.

   (Deisher & Doan, 2015; Engstrom, 2015).

   New hypotheses rapidly replace those that are scientifically refuted (Laskowski, 2016). Evidence-based medicine studies have discredited the connection between vaccines and autism, but parents have continued to argue for a link, with some accusing the government and medical communities of a cover-up (Tolsma, 2015).

4. The symptoms of these vaccine-preventable diseases are noteworthy because many people have forgotten how horrible these diseases are:

   - *Diphtheria*: This is a highly contagious upper respiratory tract illness characterized by sore throat and fever; it causes the progressive deterioration of myelin sheaths in the central and peripheral nervous system, leading to degenerating motor control and loss of sensation.
   - *Mumps*: This is characterized by a painful swelling of the salivary glands and sometimes a rash; in teenage males, testicular swelling often results in infertility.
   - *Whooping cough*: People experience spasms of coughing involving up to a dozen coughs before they can catch their breath. Such coughing spasms may occur up to 50 times a day. The cough produces large amounts of mucus, and vomiting of mucus and food is common during the coughing spasms. Complications include choking, which may lead to convulsions, cerebral hemorrhage, brain damage, and death. Hernias of the rectum or abdomen also occur and bleeding from small ruptured blood vessels of the eye, face, and neck are common. Inhaled secretions into the lungs during the coughing spasms can cause lung complications including pneumonia and collapse of the lungs.
   - *Polio*: Polio is an acute viral infection where most people develop nonparalytic meningitis; headaches and pain in the neck, back, abdomen, and extremities; fever; vomiting; and lethargy. Some cases progress to paralytic disease, in which the muscles become weak and finally completely paralyzed.
   - *Measles*: Measles is characterized by a mild pinpoint rash, swollen and tender glands, and fever with joint pains that can last up to a month. Complications may include infection of the brain tissues (encephalitis). Almost all fetuses exposed to measles (also known as rubeola) develop syndromes that generally result in serious, incurable birth defects, including hearing impairment, cataracts, glaucoma, and other eye problems, heart defects, brain problems, stunted growth, and bone disease (*See generally* Hamborsky et al., 2015).

REFERENCES

Abbott, R., & Stevens, C. (2014). Redefining medical necessity: A consumer-driven solution to the U.S. health care crisis. *Loyola of Los Angeles Law Review, 47*, 943–965.

Abramson, J. (2006). The reliability of our medical knowledge as a product of industry relationships. *Hofstra Law Review, 35*(69), 691–704.

AHRQ (Agency for Healthcare Research and Quality). (2014). *Guide to clinical preventive services: Recommendations of the U.S. Preventive Services Task Force*. Rockville, MD: AHRQ.

___. (2010). *Beta blockers are underused in patients receiving implantable cardioverter defibrillators.*

___. (2007). *Hospital stays involving musculoskeletal procedures: Healthcare cost and utilization project (HCUP) statistical brief.*

___. (2005). *Fact sheet: Beta-blockers for acute myocardial infarction.*

Asch, S. M., et al. (2006). Who is at greatest risk for receiving poor-quality health care? *New England Journal of Medicine, 354*(11), 1147–1156.

ASNM (American Society of Neurophysiological Monitoring). (2016). *Position statement.* Elmhurst, IL: ASNM.

Beales, J. H., & Muris, T. J. (2015). FTC consumer protection at 100: 1970s redux or protecting markets to protect consumers? *The George Washington Law Review, 83*, 2157–2228.

Bennion, E. (2013). A right to remain psychotic? A new standard for involuntary treatment in light of current science. *Loyola of Los Angeles Law Review, 47*, 251–317.

Bernstein, D. E., & Lasker, E. G. (2015). Defending *Daubert*: It's time to amend federal rule of evidence 702. *William and Mary Law Review, 57*, 1–48.

Brausch, A. M., & Gutierrez, P. M. (2010). Differences in non-suicidal self-injury and suicide attempts in adolescents. *Journal of Youth and Adolescence, 39*, 233-242.

Brent, D. A., et al. (2009). Predictors of spontaneous and systemically assessed suicidal averse events in the treatment of SSRI-resistant depression in adolescents (TORDIA) study. *American Journal of Psychiatry, 166*, 418–426.

Buck, I. D. (2016). Furthering the fiduciary metaphor: The duty of providers to the payers of Medicare. *California Law Review, 104*, 1043–1093.

___. (2015). Side effects: State anti-fraud statutes, off-label marketing, and the solvable challenge of causation. *Cardozo Law Review, 36*, 2129–2181.

Calvert, C., & Bunker, M. D. (2013). An "actual problem" in First Amendment jurisprudence? Examining the immediate impact of *Brown's* proof-of-causation doctrine on free speech and its compatibility with the marketplace theory. *Hastings Communications and Entertainment Law Journal, 35*, 391–428.

Candeub, A. (2015). Digital medicine, the FDA, and the First Amendment. *Georgia Law Review, 49*, 933–993.

CDC (Centers for Disease Control and Prevention). (2009). *National health interview survey.* Atlanta, GA: CDC, National Center for Health Statistics.

CMS (Centers for Medicare and Medicaid Services). (2014). *Press release: Historic release of data gives consumers unprecedented transparency on the medical services physicians provide and how much they are paid.* Washington, DC: CMS.

Coleman, T. S. (2014). Origins of the prohibition against off-label promotion. *Food and Drug Law Journal, 69*, 161–236.

Comanor, W. S., & Needleman, J. (2016). The law, economics, and medicine of off-label prescribing. *Washington Law Review, 91*, 119–146.

Copeland, K. B. (2014). The crime of being in charge: Executive culpability and collateral consequences. *American Criminal Law Review, 51*, 799–836.

Corbett, T. L. (2015). Healthcare corporate structure and the ACA: A need for mission primacy through a new organizational paradigm? *Indiana Health Law Review, 12*, 103–181.

Crawford, K. S., & Axelrad, J. (2012). Legislative modifications to tort liability: The unintended consequence of public health and bioterrorism threats. *Creighton Law Review, 45*, 337–360.

Darrow, J. J. (2014). Pharmaceutical gatekeepers. *Indiana Law Review, 47*, 363–420.

Davidoff, F., et al. (1995). Editorial: Evidence-based medicine. *British Medical Journal, 310*, 1085.

Deshpande, S. P., & DeMello, A. (2011). Comparative analysis of factors that hinder primary care physicians' and specialist physicians' ability to provide high-quality care. *Health Care Manager, 30*(2), 172–178.

Deisher, T. A., & Doan, N. V. (2015). Sociological environmental causes are insufficient to explain autism changepoints of incidence. *Issues In Law and Medicine, 30*, 25–44.

Engstrom, N. F. (2015). A dose of reality for specialized courts: Lessons from the VICP. *University of Pennsylvania Law Review, 163*, 1631–1717.

Federal Judicial Center. (2015). *Reference manual on scientific evidence.* Washington, DC: Federal Judicial Center.

Fischer, E. S., et al. (2008). *Regional and racial variation in health care among Medicare beneficiaries: A brief report of the Dartmouth Atlas Project.* Hanover, NH: Dartmouth Medical School.

Frakes, M. D. (2015). The surprising relevance of medical malpractice law. *University of Chicago Law Review, 82*, 317–391.

Francis, M. H. (2012). Beyond safe and effective: The role of the federal government in supporting and disseminating comparative-effectiveness research. *Annals of Health Law, 21*, 329–381.

Friedland, D. J. (2016). Leading well from within: A neuroscience and mindfulness-based framework for conscious leadership. San Diego, CA: SuperSmartHealth.

___. (2009). *Evidence based medicine: A framework for clinical practice.* New York, NY: Prentice-Hall.

Fu, P. C., et al. (2012). The impact of emerging standards adoption on automated quality reporting. *Journal Biomedical Informatics, 45*(4), 772–781.

Gilman, D. J., & Fairman, J. (2014). Antitrust and the future of nursing: Federal competition policy and the scope of practice. *Health Matrix, 24*, 143–207.

Gooch, G. R., et al. (2013). The moral from *Sorrell*: Educate, don't legislate. *Health Matrix, 23*, 237–277.

Gould. B. (2014). How the countervailing power of insurers can resolve the tradeoff between market power and health care integration in accountable care organizations. *George Mason Law Review, 22*, 159–200.

Greenleaf, R. A. (2012). Why plaintiffs shouldn't have it their way: Revisiting concurrent jurisdiction of autism claims against thimerosal manufacturers. *Federal Circuit Bar Journal, 21*, 299–329.

Groopman, J., & Hartzband, P. (2009, April 8). Why "quality" care is dangerous. *Wall Street Journal*, p. A13.

Group Health. (2016). Atherosclerotic cardiovascular disease (ASCVD): Secondary prevention guideline. Seattle, WA: Group Health.

Grout, J. R., et al. (2013). Mistake-proofing medicine: Legal considerations and healthcare quality implications. *Minnesota Journal of Law, Science and Technology, 14*, 387–438.

Hamborsky, J., et al. (Eds.). (2015). *Centers for Disease Control and Prevention: Epidemiology and prevention of vaccine-preventable diseases* (12th ed.). Washington, DC: Public Health Foundation.

Hardee, C. A. (2016). Considering consequences: Autonomy's missing half. *Pepperdine Law Review, 43*, 785–835.

Herbst, J. L. (2015). Off-label "promotion" may not be merely commercial speech. *Temple Law Review, 88*, 43–89.

Hill, H. A., et al. (2016). Vaccination coverage among children aged 19–35 months. *MMWR Morbidity Mortal Weekly Report, 65*, 1065–1071.

Hiller, J. S. (2016). Healthy predictions? Questions for data analytics in health care. *American Business Law Journal, 53*, 251–314.

Ho, C. S. (2015). Exceptions meet absolutism: Outlawing governmental underreach in health law. *Denver University Law Review, 93*, 109–171.

___. (2014). Drugged out: How cognitive bias hurts drug innovation. *San Diego Law Review, 51*, 419–507.

Howlader, N., et al. (2016). *Surveillance, epidemiology, and end results program (SEER) cancer statistics review.* Bethesda, MD: National Cancer Institute.

Hysong, S. J., et al. (2011). Passive monitoring versus active assessment of clinical performance: Impact on measured quality of care. *Medical Care, 49*(10), 883–890.

IOM (Institute of Medicine). (2015). *Improving diagnosis in health care.* Washington, DC: National Academy of Medicine.

___. (2001). *Crossing the quality chasm: A new health system for the 21st century.*

Jakubovski, E., et al. (2015). Prognostic subgroups for remission, response, and treatment continuation in the Clinical Antipsychotic Trials of Intervention Effectiveness (CATIE) trial. *Journal of Clinical Psychiatry, 76*(11), 1535–1545.

Johnson, A., & Stukel, T. A. (2016). *Medical practice variations.* New York, NY: Springer.

Kapczynski, A., & Syed, T. (2013). The continuum of excludability and the limits of patents. *Tulane Law Review, 122*, 1900–1963.

Kerr, E., et al. (2004). Profiling the quality of care in twelve communities: Results from the Community Quality Index, *Health Affairs, 23*(3), 247–256.

Kukura, E. (2016a). Contested care: The limitations of evidence-based maternity care reform. *Berkeley Journal of Gender, Law and Justice, 31*, 241–297.

___. (2016b). Giving birth under the ACA: Analyzing the use of law as a tool to improve health care. *Nebraska Law Review, 94*, 799–861.

Laakmann, A. B. (2015). When should physicians be liable for innovation? *Cardozo Law Review, 36*, 913–968.

LaMontagne, E. (2015). Off-label promotion, the First Amendment, and practically addressing antibiotic resistance. *California Western Law Review, 51*, 293–326.

Laskowski. M. (2016). Nudging towards vaccination: A behavioral law and economics approach to childhood immunization policy. *Texas Law Review, 94*, 601–628.

Laufer-Ukeles, P. (2016). The relational rights of children. *Connecticut Law Review, 48*, 741–816.

Lee, W. B. (2014). Recalibrating "experimental treatment exclusion": An empirical analysis. *University of Cincinnati Law Review, 83*, 171–201.

Lewellen, N. (2015). Beating the odds: The public policy of drug efficacy and safety. *Minnesota Law Review, 99*, 1541–1570.

Madison, K. (2016). Health care quality reporting: A failed form of mandated disclosure? *Indiana Health Law Review, 13*, 310–347.

Mantel, J. (2015). A defense of physicians' gatekeeping role: Balancing patients' needs with society's interests. *Pepperdine Law Review, 42*, 633–725.

Mariner, W. K. (2016). Reconsidering constitutional protection for health information privacy. *University of Pennsylvania Journal of Constitutional Law, 18*, 975–1054.

Massaro, T. M. (2014). Tread on me! *University of Pennsylvania Journal of Constitutional Law, 17*, 365–436.

Mermin, S. E., & Graff, S. K. (2013). The First Amendment and public health, at odds. *American Journal of Law and Medicine, 39*, 298–307.

Meyers, S. J. (2011). Denying the obvious: Why the special masters should have found for petitioners in the autism omnibus test cases. *The Federal Circuit Bar Journal, 20*, 633–664.

Miller, G. (2013). "The best health care system in the world"? *Social Work, 58*(2), 181–183.

Milstein, B., et al. (2010). Analyzing national health reform strategies with a dynamic simulation model. *American Journal of Public Health, 100*(5), 811–819.

Neyarapally, G. A. (2013). A review of recent federal legislative and policy initiatives to enhance the development and evaluation of high value drugs in the United States. *DePaul Journal of Health Care Law, 14*, 503–556.

O'Connor, D. (2013). The apomediated world: Regulating research when social media has changed research. *Journal of Law, Medicine and Ethics, 41*, 470–481.

OIG (Office of Inspector General) & HHS (U.S. Department of Health and Human Services). (2006). *FDA's monitoring of postmarketing study commitments.* Washington, DC: OIG & HHS.

Parker-Pope, T. (2007). *The hormone decision: Untangle the controversy—understand your options—make your own choices.* Emmaus, PA: Rodale.

Perez, O. (2016). Judicial strategies for reviewing conflicting expert evidence: Biases, heuristics, and higher-order evidence. *American Journal of Comparative Law, 64*, 75–120.

Philip, E. (2014). *United States v. Caronia*: How true does "truthful" have to be? *Vanderbilt Law Review En Banc, 67*, 157–170.

Pickar, D. B., & Kaufman, R. L. (2015). Parenting plans for special needs children: Applying a risk-assessment model. *Family Court Review, 53*, 113–131.

Preusser, M., et al. (2011). Current concepts and management of glioblastoma. *Annals of Neurology, 70*(1), 9–21.

Radley, D., et al. (2014). *Aiming higher: Results from a scorecard on state health system performance.* New York, NY: Commonwealth Fund.

RAND Corp. (2006). *First national report card on quality of health care in America.* Santa Monica, CA: RAND.

___. (2005). *Consumer use of information when making treatment decisions.*

Resnick, A. (2014). *Statins and ACE inhibitors to manage heart disease.* Seattle, WA: Group Health Research Institute.

Riley, M. F. (2015). An unfulfilled promise: Changes needed to the drug approval process to make personalized medicine a reality. *Food and Drug Law Journal, 70*, 289–314.

Robertson, C. (2015). Should patient responsibility for costs change the doctor-patient relationship? *Wake Forest Law Review, 50*, 363–380.

Sackett, D. L. (1996). Evidence based medicine: What it is and what it isn't. *British Medical Journal, 312*, 71–72.

___. (1985). *Clinical epidemiology: A basic science for clinical medicine.* Boston, MA: Little Brown.

Scheineson, M. J., & Cuevas, G. (2013). *United States v. Caronia*: The increasing strength of commercial free speech and potential new emphasis on classifying off-label promotion as "false and misleading." *Food and Drug Law Journal, 68*, 201–216.

Schuz, R. (2015). The dangers of children's rights' discourse in the political arena: The issue of religious male circumcision as a test case. *Cardozo Journal of Law and Gender, 21*, 347–391.

Scott, B. (2011). Oversight overhaul: Eliminating the premarket review of medical devices and implementing a provider-centered post-market surveillance strategy. *Food and Drug Law Journal, 66*, 377–405.

Shik, O. (2015). The *Central Hudson* zombie: For better or worse, intermediate tier review survives *Sorrell v. IMS Health. Fordham Intellectual Property, Media and Entertainment Law Journal, 25*, 561–588.

Spacapan, L. T., & Hutchison, J. M. (2013). Prosecutions of pharmaceutical companies for off-label marketing: Fueled by government's desire to modify corporate conduct or pursuit of a lucrative revenue stream? *Annals of Health Law, 22*, 407–444.

Spears, J. M., et al. (2015). Embracing 21st century information sharing: Defining a new paradigm for the Food and Drug Administration's regulation of biopharmaceutical firm communications with healthcare professionals. *Food and Drug Law Journal, 70,* 143–160.

Straus, S. E., et al. (2010). *Evidence-based medicine: How to practice and teach it* (4th ed.). Oxford, England: Elsevier, Churchill Livingstone.

Stroup, T. S., et al. (2011). A randomized trial examining the effectiveness of switching from olanzapine, quetiapine, or risperidone to aripiprazole to reduce metabolic risk: Comparison of antipsychotics for metabolic problems (CAMP). *American Journal of Psychiatry, 168*(9), 947–956.

Surgeon General, U. S. (2015). *Surgeon General's report: The health consequences of smoking—50 years of progress.* Atlanta, GA: Centers for Disease Control and Prevention.

Suthar, J. V., & Patel, V. J. (2014). Prescribing quality in patients with chronic diseases at primary and secondary health care facilities using prescription quality index tool. *Journal of Basic and Clinical Pharmacology, 3*(3), 553–559.

Tanner, L. (2005, February 1). Study says brain cancers vary. *Wall Street Journal,* p. A1.

Taylor, F., et al. (2013). Statins for the primary prevention of cardiovascular disease. *Cochrane Database of Systematic Reviews, 1,* 1–96.

Thomson, H. B. (2013). Whither *Central Hudson*? Commercial speech in the wake of *Sorrell v. IMS Health. Columbia Journal of Law and Social Problems, 47,* 171–207.

Todd, A. E. (2011). No need for more regulation: Payors and their role in balancing the cost and safety considerations of off-label prescriptions. *American Journal of Law and Medicine, 37,* 422–443.

Tolsma, E. C. (2015). Protecting our herd: How a national mandatory vaccination policy protects public health by ensuring herd immunity. *The Journal of Gender Race and Justice, 18,* 313–339.

Van Tassel, K. V. (2015). Modernizing the Emergency Medical Treatment and Labor Act to harmonize with the Affordable Care Act to improve equality of emergency care. *Houston Journal of Health Law and Policy, 15,* 131–168.

___. (2013a). Harmonizing the Affordable Care Act with the three main national systems for healthcare quality improvement: The tort, licensure, and hospital peer review hearing systems. *Brooklyn Law Review, 78,* 883–927.

___. (2013b). Using clinical practice guidelines and knowledge translation theory to cure the negative impact of the national hospital peer review hearing system on healthcare quality, cost, and access. *Pepperdine Law Review, 40,* 911–974.

Wang, M. C., et al. (2009). *Trends and variations in cervical spine surgery in the United States.* Princeton, NJ: Robert Wood Johnson Foundation.

Wasserman, R. (2014). American dispute resolution in 2020: The death of group vindication and the law: Future claimants and the quest for global peace. *Emory Law Journal, 64,* 531–590.

Yue, J. J., & Long, W. (2017). Full endoscopic spinal surgery techniques: Advancements, indications, and outcomes. *International Journal of Spine Surgery, 9*(17), 1–11.

CHAPTER 23

© Andy Dean Photography/ShutterStock, Inc.

Improving Patient Safety and Quality of Health Care

"These are complicated issues... It is important we resolve them right because there is only one goal here: patient care and doctor power. That's what has made America's health care system great. And that's where we have to end up. And if it takes a day or two longer, if it takes a week or two longer, if it takes a month longer, that is not the issue."

— **Rep. Nancy Johnson**, Former member of the U.S. House of Representatives from Connecticut's 5th District

IN BRIEF

This chapter reviews programs targeting patient safety that are meant to prevent dangerous lapses in quality care, such as when health care professionals fail to explain and monitor medical product use, deliver test results, or schedule follow-up care.

LEARNING OBJECTIVES

Upon completion of this chapter readers should be able to:

1. Describe the alarming statistics of U.S. medical errors and quality of care in comparison to other countries.
2. Explain why the tendency of the health care industry to apportion blame for patient safety problems rather than address root causes is the wrong approach.
3. Talk about patient safety being best served by improving health care systems.
4. Explain why patients cannot choose better health care systems due to lack of comprehensive relevant data.
5. Discuss the increasing tendency of insurers to deny payments for health care providers for costs resulting from medical errors.
6. Explain the benefits evidence-based guidelines can provide for patient safety.
7. Describe why some patients are willing to undertake higher risks than others due to their particular health condition.
8. List the issues of Food and Drug Administration reforms in industry user fees and post-marketing drug surveillance.

KEY TERMS

Adverse event
Adverse Events Reporting System
Age-adjusted mortality
Agency for Healthcare Research and
　Quality

Antitrust
Catastrophic outcomes
Clinical privileges
Competition
Defamation

Direct-to-consumer marketing
Disability-adjusted life
　expectancy
Drug-by-drug regulation
Drug review time

FACT OR FICTION

Patient Safety

Can a hospital suspend a physician's clinical privileges without a pre-suspension hearing, where there are reasonable grounds for assuming that patient safety is at risk?

When the chairman of the Department of Radiology informed the Medical Executive Committee at Midland Memorial Hospital and Medical Center that Dr. P. V. Patel, a board-certified cardiologist, had an unusually high rate of **catastrophic outcomes** among his recent interventions, the Medical Executive Committee conducted a **peer review** of his cases. The internal peer review prompted Midland to revoke Dr. Patel's clinical privileges. A subsequent outside peer review found evidence that suggested poor medical judgment and Dr. Patel was suspended from the practice of medicine at Midland. Dr. Patel requested a full hearing, at the conclusion of which the hearing committee found that while Dr. Patel was not a danger to his patients, his inadequate documentation had contributed to the questionable appearance of his cases. The hearing committee also held that there were reasonable grounds for the action taken by the physicians who had reviewed Dr. Patel's cases prior to the suspension.

After his **clinical privileges** were restored, Dr. Patel filed suit against Midland and its physicians, claiming they violated his **due process rights** by failing to provide him with a **pre-suspension hearing**. Dr. Patel also filed **antitrust** and **defamation** claims against Midland and the physicians. Midland and the physicians claimed they were immune from due process, antitrust, and defamation claims under the **Health Care Quality Improvement Act of 1986** (*See* 42 U.S.C.A. §§ 11101 *et seq.*). They maintained they had **immunity** from damages to Dr. Patel because they were participating in a professional review action that met statutory requirements.

— *See* Law Fact at the end of this chapter for the answer.

Principles and Applications

An important development in health law over the last decade has been the growing emphasis on **patient safety**, quality of health care, and the availability of information about provider safety and quality for consumers. After decades of inattention to the problem of **medical injuries**, patient safety is now occupying a prominent place on the health policy agenda and garnering renewed regulatory interest (Liang, 2015). When people think of patient safety, they might think of the Institute of Medicine landmark reports that estimate the numbers of deaths due to **medical errors**:

- Improving Diagnosis in Health Care (IOM, 2015a)
- To Err Is Human (IOM, 1999)
- Crossing the Quality Chasm (IOM, 2001)

New research estimates up to 440,000 patients die each year because of medical errors (Leapfrog, 2013). This puts medical errors as the third leading cause of death in the United States (CDC, 2016). The estimated annual cost of medical errors, including the expense of additional care, lost income, and disability, could be at least $265 billion annually (*See* IOM, 2015a and 1999).[LN1] While the financial pressures in the U.S. health care system are very real, an arguably more important issue is patient safety and the quality of health care services.

Most Americans will experience at least one diagnostic error in their lifetime, sometimes with devastating consequences (IOM, 2015b). In addition, evidence suggests that Americans receive lower quality care than the residents of other developed nations:

- Out of 13 comparably developed countries, the United States ranks an average of 12th on 16 **health indicators** such as years of potential life lost and **age-adjusted mortality**.
- The United States ranks 72nd in the world on the World Health Organization's index of how efficiently health systems translate expenditures into health as measured by **disability-adjusted life expectancy**.
- The United States spends more per capita on health care than all other countries, yet Americans' health status lags far behind that of other nations.

(WHO, 2016, 2013).

Malpractice Framework

Today, when a hospital's **quality management committee** learns that a medical error or **adverse event** has occurred, they question:

- What are the implications for payment?
- What is the appropriate course of action?
- Who needs to know?

(IOM, 2015b).

Trend Toward Enterprise Liability

The **malpractice** framework, which is primarily designed to apportion blame to individual health care providers, has failed to adequately address patient safety problems (IOM, 2015a, 1999). For instance, malpractice lawsuits allow patients to recover only if they can prove a causal connection between a health care professional's lapse in applying treatment protocols and their resulting injury. Some have suggested moving toward an **enterprise liability model**, in which financial liability is imposed on hospitals as opposed to individuals, although a breach of duty would remain a predicate for liability (Baker, 2005).

Poorly Designed Systems

There is widespread agreement that the root cause of most medical errors is poorly designed systems (IOM, 2015a, 1999). The tremendous complexity of **health care delivery systems** makes hospitals highly susceptible to both technological and human error. Hospitals must strive to create a culture of safety in which systems are designed to cooperatively keep patients safe from harm, rather than blaming individual health care professionals for adverse outcomes. Faulting individuals for errors generated by systems only discourages health care professionals from candidly identifying and addressing medical errors (IOM, 2015a, 1999). The rough consensus is that bad systems, not careless health care professionals, are responsible for most medical errors (IOM, 2015b).

Market Competition

The federal government sought to determine how to reconfigure the multiple levels of the health care system so as to improve patient care (IOM, 2001). In response, Congress appropriated $50 million annually for patient safety research to be conducted by the federal **Agency for Healthcare Research and Quality**. Subsequently, a joint report by the U.S. Federal Trade Commission and the U.S. Department of Justice called for **competition** in the health care market as a way to push patients to choose better health care systems as their providers of choice (*See* FTC & DOJ, 2004). Theoretically, if patients are free to pursue their individual preferences in choosing their health insurance plans (with access to their providers of choice), they will secure the optimal allocation of health resources, as opposed to having government prescribed insurance plans.

National Database for Patient Safety Research

The Agency for Healthcare Research and Quality grants funding for research on:

- Health information technology
- Patient safety
- Pharmaceutical outcomes
- Prevention and care management

Just as the National Institutes of Health steers national research on the best ways to treat specific health conditions, the Agency for Healthcare Research and Quality's role is to identify prescriptions for health care processes.

Health Information Technology

Health information technology initiatives are the only health care reform proposals to gain bipartisan support in recent years (Russo & Rishikof, 2016). The Agency for Healthcare Research and Quality has prioritized digitized personal health data as a means for improving patient safety and reducing bureaucratic costs (Hiller, 2016). *See* Chapter on Health Information and Telehealth Technologies.

The Joint Commission

The **Joint Commission** could implement a system for reporting medical errors. The Joint Commission currently requires reporting of **sentinel events**, which are not the same as **preventable medical errors**. A sentinel event is defined as an unexpected incident or risk of an unforeseen occurrence that involves death or serious physical or psychological injury to an individual patient (Joint Commission, 2016).

Hospitals that do not comply with accreditation requirements risk losing Medicare insurance funding, so The Joint Commission could therefore enforce mandatory, confidential reporting as a condition of accreditation. However, The Joint Commission is generally reluctant to actually withdraw accreditation, making any requirements somewhat ineffective (*See* Ho, 2014). The Joint Commission's existing policy on sentinel events is widely regarded as futile; it has not resulted in the aggregation of national patient safety data (Price, 2012).

Disclosure of Medical Errors

Today, more than half the states have some form of **mandatory disclosure law** for medical errors (NCSL, 2011). For instance, in Pennsylvania, the State Health Care Cost Containment Council:

- Imposes penalties for failures to report medical errors
- Publishes each hospital's rate of infection
- Requires hospitals to disclose specific hospital-acquired infections
- Requires reporting of serious events to both the state and to patients directly affected by the medical error

(*See* Medical Care Availability and Reduction of Error Act of 2002, 40 P.S. §§ 1303.101 *et seq.*).

Pennsylvania also protects whistleblowers by allowing health care employees to anonymously report events, as well as immunizes documents provided to the state from discovery in most litigation (Young, 2012). With a few exceptions, patient safety work product is not subject to discovery or **subpoena** in state, federal, civil, or criminal proceedings, nor is it admissible in disciplinary proceedings conducted by state professional bodies (Lahav, 2016).

The federal government also encourages voluntary reporting by shielding providers from legal liability related to patient safety data. *See* **Patient Safety and Quality Improvement Act of 2005** (*See* 42 U.S.C.A. §§ 299b-21 *et seq.*). A national public-private partnership aimed at increasing voluntary hospital reporting of quality data is premised on consumer use of health care data to select high-quality providers. When the Healthcare Infection Control Practices Advisory

Committee (which advises the U.S. Department of Health and Human Services and the Centers for Disease Control and Prevention on infection control), recently evaluated mandatory reporting laws, however, it found no evidence that public disclosure of infection rates was effective in reducing hospital-acquired infections (Brass, 2010). The health insurance industry is, nonetheless, selecting health care providers that will be included in **managed care networks** based on this quality data.

While there are no nationwide standards applicable to patient safety reporting regarding mandatory versus voluntary reporting and disclosure issues, the consensus appears to support the states in mandating reporting. Mandated reporting of quality data is both a way to provide information to consumers of health care and a means designed to collect information for analysis to prevent medical errors from occurring in the first place.

Patient Safety Organizations

In an effort to minimize medical errors and prevent adverse events from occurring in the first place, Congress has proposed that health care providers use independent third parties to monitor and evaluate their provision of care in terms of patient safety. Consequently, **patient safety organizations** have arisen to contract with health care providers to review and analyze patient safety reports and make recommendations for improving the quality of health care, which includes:

- Collecting and analyzing patient safety work product
- Developing and disseminating information to improve patient safety (recommendations for system improvements, protocols, and best practices)
- Maintaining procedures to preserve the confidentiality and security of patient safety work product
- Providing feedback and assistance to minimize patient risks and medical errors
- Utilizing patient safety work product to encourage a culture of safety by health care providers

(*See* 42 U.S.C.A. § 299b-21(5)).

Payment Incentives

Medicare, as well as several private health insurers, such as Aetna and WellPoint, have moved to end payments to hospitals for treatment that results from serious medical errors. Similarly, the insurers also will not allow their members to be billed for hospital errors. Medicare insurance will no longer reimburse hospitals for the treatment of bedsores, falls, and other preventable conditions that occur in the facilities. Nor will hospital-acquired infections, blood clots in legs and lungs, and pneumonia contracted from a ventilator be reimbursed (AHRQ, 2016).

In hospital contracts, Aetna includes a provision that ends payments for 28 **never events** outlined by the National Quality Forum. In Virginia, WellPoint tested a policy that ends payments for four never events before expanding the policy to eight states (Connecticut, Georgia, Maine, Massachusetts, New Hampshire, New York, Rhode Island, and Vermont). UnitedHealth Group and Cigna have similar policies. Providers of other private health insurance are now banning payments for only the gravest of mistakes, such as:

- Administration of incompatible blood
- Infants discharged to the wrong person
- Medication errors that result in death or disability
- Surgeries on the wrong limbs

(AHRQ, 2016).

It is most likely only a matter of time before the health insurance industry also stops paying for some of the more common and less clear problems that Medicare insurance is tackling. Medicare insurance is refusing to make payments for:

- Air embolisms
- Blood poisoning arising from incompatibility
- Hospital-acquired injuries
- Hospital-acquired urinary tract infections associated with catheters
- Objects left behind in surgery
- Pressure ulcers

Pharmaceutical Outcomes

Every 5 to 10 years, major legislation addresses pressing issues concerning the federal Food and Drug Administration (FDA). Sometimes, reform is motivated by the perception that the FDA is not getting new drugs to market as efficiently as possible. Other times, the leading concern is that the FDA is not protecting the public from the risks of drugs as effectively as it might.

Vioxx started the drive for tougher **drug safety laws** and an overhaul of FDA oversight. An exhaustive analysis of drug safety data recently conducted by researchers at the Massachusetts Institute of Technology and the University of Chicago concluded, among other things, that congressional efforts in the 1990s to speed up FDA review times did not fuel a drug safety crisis; rather, the data indicates that about 2 to 3% of approved drugs continue to be withdrawn, which is the same rate as before passage of these reforms (Wachter, 2007; *See* Tabler, 2016).

A very careful balance exists at the FDA, which looks at the benefits and risks of potential treatments to determine if they should be approved. It is not a perfect system. Then again, in the real world, patients' tolerance for risk depends in large measure on the disease from which they suffer. In fact, every day, patients make this **risk-risk assessment**. They decide whether the potential risk of a therapeutic option outweighs the risk of a given disorder. Thus, cancer patients are willing to tolerate chemotherapy in an attempt to rid themselves of their disease.

Risk-Risk Calculus

This risk-risk proposition was evident when Elan Pharmaceutical withdrew Tysabri, a multiple sclerosis therapy, from the market because of a rare and serious potential side effect. Multiple sclerosis patients with limited therapeutic options organized, made their voices heard, and demanded a return of Tysabri to the market. Today, Tysabri is back on the market in no small measure because of the efforts of patients with multiple sclerosis. While patients want to be warned of known risks, they also understand their disease and want, even demand, the right to choose their own therapies (Garg, 2012).

Although not every negative care outcome is a result of negligence, or even an entirely preventable error, providers of health insurance maintain that the **no-pay policies** will help improve patient safety and reduce health care costs (Sugarman, 2014). Some hospitals have raised concerns that the new strategy could drive up health care costs in other ways as hospitals absorb or pass on the expense of introducing the safety and screening procedures needed to help avoid mistakes (Garg, 2012).

Evidence-Based Guidelines

The lack of standardized, universally accepted treatment guidelines, firmly supported by scientific evidence, is a significant obstacle to the prevention of medical errors (McNeill et al., 2005). Since 2000, it has been recognized that physicians' expertise should be applied in a manner consistent with information from scientific research. Processes that support more accurate identification of what treatment is appropriate for each patient can have profound implications for decreasing adverse events and containing the escalating costs of health care (Lamkin & Elliott, 2014).

Moreover, nearly all of these adverse events could be prevented with simple clinical processes in place. Evidence suggests that using chlorhexidine to clean the skin prior to placing a central venous catheter can cut the risk of catheter-related bloodstream infections in half with minimal, if any, increase in costs. Yet it is infrequently used (Welsh, 2013; *See* Pronovost et al., 2006). Many commentators ask why patient safety procedures such as this are not mandated by states and accreditation organizations.[LN2]

A key incident in raising such concern was the withdrawal by Merck of Vioxx, because of an apparent increased risk of serious cardiovascular events. The withdrawal came amid questions about the FDA's handling of a possible

---

MANAGEMENT AND LAW ISSUES

1. Should the federal government support the states and begin mandating the use of generally accepted clinical procedures approved by the Agency for Healthcare Research and Quality in all acute-care hospitals, not just those receiving Medicare insurance funding, in an effort to decrease health care costs?

association between selective serotonin-reuptake inhibitors and suicidal ideation in adolescents. Further concerns were raised about the agency's handling of staff disagreements about these and other drugs. In this context, the FDA sought a review from the Institute of Medicine.

The Institute of Medicine report included a broad range of recommendations (IOM, 2007), and the FDA has issued an action plan (FDA, 2007). Based on these documents, Congress developed a more systematic approach to improving drug safety and effective use (*See* Food and Drug Administration Amendments Act of 2007, 21 U.S.C.A. §§ 321 *et seq.*; 42 U.S.C.A. §§ 247d-3b *et seq.*). However, the steps intended to enhance safety also increase costs and reduce access to beneficial drugs. **Over-warning**, just like under-warning, can similarly have a negative effect on patient safety (*See* 21 C.F.R. Parts 201, 314, and 601).

The tools available for learning about drugs and their effectiveness include:

- Drug coverage, including **tiered benefits** by the health care industry based on proven effectiveness (i.e., patients may have access to prescribed drugs that their physicians believe are more efficacious in treating their particular health conditions, but if therapies are not supported by evidence-based studies as the most cost-effective means of treatment, patients will be required to pay more out of pocket for selecting such drugs)
- **Drug utilization management programs** that influence prescribing (alerting to under- and overprescribing, as well as patient adherence to drug therapies)
- Electronic data on prescription use and patient outcomes (controlling for adverse reactions to incompatible drugs, as well as attempting to minimize **polypharmacy**, where patients are taking dozens of medicines that counteract one another)
- Internet resources for consumers of health care to understand their use of prescription drugs

(*E.g.,* Callam, 2014; Lamkin & Elliott, 2014; Platt, 2007).

Institute of Medicine and Food and Drug Administration Reforms

The reforms recommended by the Institute of Medicine and proposed by the FDA fall into four main categories:

- Balancing drug safety against access to innovative treatments
- More effective use of prescribed drugs
- Need to balance **industry user fees** and **federal appropriations**
- **Post-marketing drug surveillance**

(*See* The **Prescription Drug User Fee Act of 1992**, 21 U.S.C.A. §§ 379g, 379h, providing for user fees to be paid by the pharmaceutical and biotechnology industries for review of new drugs).

Need to Balance Industry User Fees and Federal Appropriations

Total user fees exceed $2.2 billion per year, accounting for more than half of the FDA resources for drug regulation (FDA, 2016). While FDA critics claim this has affected drug safety, the rate at which drugs have been withdrawn from the market has not increased since user fees were implemented (Fain et al., 2014). In addition, the increase in FDA resources has resulted in important public health benefits, including a reduction in **drug review time**, which is estimated to save 180,000 to 210,000 lives year (Philipson et al., 2006). While critics claim this level of industry user fees fuels a perception that the FDA is beholden to the industry it regulates, others assert that regulated industries should cover the costs required to help regulate and monitor their conduct in the marketplace.

Balancing Drug Safety with Access to Innovative Treatments

The FDA has authority to help assure drug safety, including the ability to:

- Impose special requirements for prescribers, such as documentation of laboratory testing that would be monitored by the FDA
- Limit **direct-to-consumer marketing**
- Mandate post-marketing drug surveillance

- Require special medication guides for patients
- Restrict which physicians can prescribe a drug, for instance, restricting certain therapeutic classes to oncologist or cardiologist prescribers

Critics believe such steps strengthen the FDA's enforcement authority. Although the agency can already remove drugs from the market for noncompliance with marketing or labeling recommendations, it rarely takes this extreme step. However, others counter that the liability and adverse publicity facing firms that fail to act on FDA drug safety findings already compel compliance. Some also argue that increased reliance on special, drug-by-drug regulatory steps is burdensome and confusing, leading to access problems, the substitution of less safe or effective treatments, and medical errors (*See* Sasinowski & Varond, 2016).

Post-Marketing Drug Surveillance

A fundamentally better system for post-marketing drug surveillance could help avoid increased costs and reduced access due to **drug-by-drug regulation**, with the development of better risk information based on actual experience with every new drug. Many high-profile safety problems have resulted not from the FDA's inadequate authority to regulate drugs on the basis of known risks, but from post-marketing delays in determining whether suspected adverse events were causally related to drug use (Mann, 2015).

One reason drugs may be used for years by millions of Americans before risks become evident is that the United States has no active drug surveillance system. While the United States obtains innovative drugs two to three years ahead of its European counterparts, Europe has a compulsory drug surveillance system. The FDA relies on its **Adverse Event Reporting System**, which involves the investigation of voluntary adverse event reports from health care providers, pharmaceutical firms, and consumers of health care.

While the FDA Adverse Event Reporting System is important, unfortunately it captures only a fraction of adverse events (Mann, 2015). With almost all prescriptions now processed electronically, and with the availability of increasingly detailed data on health care utilization and outcomes for insured Americans, a routine, systematic approach to active population-based drug surveillance could be implemented that could identify potential safety problems much more effectively and relatively inexpensively (AHRQ, 2016). For instance, with a (now feasible) data network, including information on 100 million patients, a statistically significant signal of serious cardiovascular risk could have been detected after less than three months of experience with Vioxx (Platt, 2007). Such an electronic surveillance network could also help in targeting **follow-up clinical studies** to determine:

- Causality, or the causal relationship between drug use and adverse events, when necessary
- Follow-up actions on adverse events causally related to drug use, to influence future prescribing

(Mann, 2015).

More Effective Use of Prescribed Drugs

While it has been proposed that a regulatory entity be formed that is separate from the FDA pre-marketing review process, this possibility has generally been rejected (IOM, 2007). Achieving a balanced approach to the assessment of risks and benefits would be greatly complicated, or even compromised, if two separate agencies were working in isolation from one another. Ideally, a more systematic approach to post-market monitoring of drugs needs to be implemented. More effective use of drugs could be promoted by augmenting FDA resources with the rapidly growing array of electronic resources related to drug use. Such an approach could help to minimize the safety problems and scientific disagreements that accompany drug use when evidence is limited, without pushing the pendulum toward excessive restrictions on access to valuable drugs (Hoffman, 2014).

Prevention of Medical Errors and Adverse Events

While some still claim adverse events are an inherent risk in receiving health care, the consensus is that medical errors should not be tolerated. States are increasingly requiring health care professionals to report adverse events, with harsh penalties for non-reporting; transparency and public disclosure of medical errors are gradually becoming mandatory. The financial disincentives for medical errors also are becoming more significant, as Medicare insurance and the health insurance industry refuse to compensate care associated with adverse events. It is becoming imperative that health care providers develop health information systems for tracking adverse events so they are prepared to make mandatory reports, are able to track the costs of care associated with medical errors and adverse events, and, ultimately, take action to prevent medical errors from happening in the first place (Forrest, 2016).

LAW FACT

Patient Safety

Can a hospital suspend a physician's clinical privileges without a pre-suspension hearing, where there are reasonable grounds for assuming that patient safety is at risk?

Yes or no. The court agreed that Dr. Patel should be suspended from Midland for placing patient safety at risk, but avoided deciding the issue of Midland's immunity under the Health Care Quality Improvement Act. Until courts are willing to enforce the Health Care Quality Improvement Act, hospitals and other health care providers will remain reluctant to rely solely on its protections when suspending or denying clinical privileges to physicians who are perceived to be a danger to patients' safety. In *Patel*, the court passed up the opportunity to provide such an incentive by avoiding the issue of immunity altogether, thus frustrating Congress' intent to reduce this type of litigation.

— *Patel v. Midland Memorial Hospital and Medical Center*, 298 F.3d 333 (U.S. Court of Appeals for the 5th Circuit 2002), *cert. denied*, 537 U.S. 1108 (U.S. Supreme Court 2003). Followed by *Kinnison v. City of San Antonio*, 480 Fed. Appx. 271 (U.S. Court of Appeals for the 5th Circuit 2012).

See, e.g., Stone, 2011 (discussing this decision).

CHAPTER SUMMARY

- Several thousand patients die each year because of medical errors; medical errors result in billions of dollars in costs annually.
- Evidence suggests Americans are likely to receive lower quality care than residents of other developed countries.
- One shortcoming of the health care industry is that it tends to apportion blame for patient safety problems rather than address their root causes, which are often poorly designed systems.
- Competition within the health care industry is meant to encourage patients to choose better health care systems, but it is often difficult for consumers to do this due to the lack of a comprehensive set of relevant data, such as treatment success or failure for a particular condition.
- At least half of the states have laws mandating disclosure of medical errors; there are no nationwide standards for disclosure.
- Patient safety organizations are third parties that contract with health care providers to monitor patient safety and recommend ways to improve the quality of health care.
- Many private health insurers, as well as Medicare insurance, will no longer reimburse health care providers for costs resulting from medical errors, even though not all such errors result from negligence or are necessarily entirely preventable.
- Many adverse medical events could be prevented with the implementation and use of evidence-based guidelines; many question why they are not mandated.
- Although some patients are willing to tolerate higher risks than other patients due to their particular health conditions, there is still substantial concern over whether the FDA is effectively protecting the public from the risks of prescription drugs, particularly after drugs are approved for marketing.
- Proposed FDA reforms include balancing industry user fees and federal appropriations, balancing drug safety against innovation, better post-marketing drug surveillance, and more effective use of prescribed drugs.

LAW NOTES

1. This cost estimate for 440,000 patient deaths is based on a future value projection from the experiences of hospital patients in the 1990s (*See* IOM, 2015a, 1999). At that time, the Institute of Medicine estimated that the economic cost of 44,000 to 98,000 patient deaths was between $17 and $29 billion (IOM, 1999).

2. Five procedures in the Keystone intervention developed by John Hopkins Health System for use in intensive care units are:

   - Avoiding the femoral vein
   - Cleaning the skin with chlorhexidine, a topical antiseptic
   - Hand washing
   - Removing catheters as soon as they became clinically unnecessary
   - Using full barrier precautions when inserting catheters into central lines

   (Johns Hopkins, 2016).

   Intensive care units in other health care systems eliminated catheter-related bloodstream infections in their intensive care units with these straightforward, simple procedures.

REFERENCES

AHRQ (Agency for Healthcare Research and Quality). (2016). *Never events.* Rockville, MD: U.S. Department of Health and Human Services, AHRQ.

Baker, T. (2005). *The medical malpractice myth.* Chicago, IL: University of Chicago Press.

Brass, C. (2010). A proposed evidentiary privilege for medical checklists. *Columbia Business Law Review, 2010,* 835–894.

Callam, M. (2014). Who can afford it? The Patient Protection and Affordable Care Act's failure to regulate excessive cost-sharing of prescription biologic drugs. *Journal of Law and Health, 27,* 99–129.

CDC (Centers for Disease Control and Prevention). (2016). *Leading causes of death.* Atlanta, GA: CDC.

Fain, K. M., et al. (2014). An analysis of FDA's drug safety authorities: Challenges and opportunities under a new regulatory framework. *New York University Journal of Legislation and Public Policy, 17,* 1–36.

FDA (U.S. Food and Drug Administration). (2016). *Food and Drug Administration Congressional Justification.* Rockville, MD: FDA.

___. (2007). *The future of drug safety: Promoting and protecting the health of the public: FDA's response to the Institute of Medicine's 2006 report.*

Forrest, M. H. (2016). Why reporting is not enough: Improving the Patient Safety and Quality Improvement Act of 2005. *University of Toledo Law Review, 47,* 475–494.

Garg, N. (2012). Hospital value based purchasing and the bundled payment initiative under the Affordable Care Act: A good start, but is it good enough? *Annals of Health Law, 22,* 171–197.

FTC (U.S. Federal Trade Commission) & DOJ (U.S. Department of Justice). (2004). *Improving health care: A dose of competition.* Washington, DC: FTC & DOJ.

Hiller, J. S. (2016). Healthy predictions? Questions for data analytics in health care. *American Business Law Journal, 53,* 251–314.

Ho, P. L. (2014). HCQIA does not provide adequate due process protection, improve healthcare quality and is outdated under "Obama Care." *Indiana Health Law Review, 11,* 303–346.

Hoffman, S. (2014). Medical big data and big data quality problems. *Connecticut Insurance Law Journal, 21,* 289–316.

IOM (Institute of Medicine). (2015a). *Protecting patients: Advances and future directions in patient safety.* Washington, DC: National Academy of Medicine.

___. (2015b). *Improving diagnosis in health care.*

___. (2007). *Challenges for the FDA: The future of drug safety.*

___. (2001). *Crossing the quality chasm: A new health system for the 21st century.*

___. (1999). *To err is human: Building a safer health system.*

Johns Hopkins Health System. (2016). *Delivering the promise of medicine: Johns Hopkins Medicine biennial report.* Baltimore, MD: Johns Hopkins Health System.

Joint Commission, The. (2016). *Sentinel event policy and procedures.* Chicago, IL: The Joint Commission.

Lahav, A. D. (2016). The roles of litigation in American democracy. *Emory Law Journal, 65,* 1657–1704.

Lamkin, M., & Elliott, C. (2014). The buying and selling of health care: Curing the disobedient patient: Medication adherence programs as pharmaceutical marketing tools. *Journal of Law, Medicine and Ethics, 42,* 492–499.

Leapfrog Group, The. (2013). *Hospital safety score: Hospital errors are the third leading cause of death in U.S., and new hospital safety scores show improvements are too slow.* Washington, DC: The Leapfrog Group.

Liang, C.-M. (2015). Rethinking the tort liability system and patient safety: From the conventional wisdom to learning from litigation. *Indiana Health Law Review, 12,* 327–381.

Mann, J. M. (2015). FDA adverse event reporting system: Recruiting doctors to make surveillance a little less passive. *Food and Drug Law Journal, 70,* 371–394.

McNeill, D., et al. (2005). Beyond the dusty shelf: Shifting paradigms and effecting change. In *Advances in patient safety: From research to implementation.* Rockville, MD: AHRQ.

NCSL (National Conference of State Legislatures). (2011). *Medical liability/medical malpractice laws.* Washington, DC: NCSL.

Philipson, T. J., et al. (2006). *Assessing the safety and the efficacy of the FDA: The case of the Prescription Drug User Fee Act*. Cambridge, MA: National Bureau of Economic Research.

Platt, R. (2007). *The future of drug safety: Challenges for FDA*. Washington, DC: Institute of Medicine Forum.

Price, III, J. F. (2012). The new frontier of healthcare: Accountable care organizations and the changing interplay among quality, cost, and peer review. *University of Detroit Mercy Law Review, 90*, 121–140.

Pronovost, P., et al. (2006). An intervention to decrease catheter-related bloodstream infections in the ICU. *New England Journal of Medicine, 355*, 2725–2727.

Russo, K., & Rishikof, H. (2016). Cyberwars: Navigating responsibilities for the public and private sector: Cybersecurity: Executive orders, legislation, cyberattacks, and hot topics. *Chapman Law Review, 19*, 421–444.

Sasinowski, F. J., & Varond, A. J. (2016). FDA's flexibility in subpart H approvals: Assessing quantum of effectiveness evidence. *Food and Drug Law Journal, 71*, 138–199.

Stone, K. L. (2011). Shortcuts in employment discrimination law. *Saint Louis University Law Journal, 56*, 111–169.

Sugarman, S. D. (2014). New approaches for a safer and healthier society: Outcome-based regulatory strategies for promoting greater patient safety. *Theoretical Inquiries in Law, 15*, 573–603.

Tabler, N. G. (2016). Sixteen myths of medicine and medical malpractice. *Indiana Health Law Review, 13*, 363–383.

Wachter, R. (2007). *Understanding patient safety*. New York, NY: McGraw-Hill.

Welsh, B. C. (2013). Regulatory overlap and the common rule: Redefining research on human subjects and quality improvement. *University of Memphis Law Review, 43*, 847–888.

WHO (World Health Organization). (2016). *World health statistics: Monitoring health for the (health-related) sustainable development goals*. Geneva, Switzerland: WHO.

___. (2013). *The world health report: Research for universal health coverage*.

Young, D. (2012). Curing what ails us: How the lessons of behavioral economics can improve health care markets. *Yale Law and Policy Review, 30*, 461–501.

PART VIII

OUR HEALTH CARE SYSTEM'S RESPONSE TO ILLNESS

Part VIII takes a systematic look at mortality and other dimensions of ill health in the United States, with a focus on the costs of living with a disease or disability.

CHAPTER 24

Human Body Parts Industry

"You are a little soul carrying around a corpse."

— **Epictetus** (55–135 A.D.), Greek philosopher

IN BRIEF

This chapter describes the procurement side of the billion-dollar human body parts industry and how it is intertwined with the U.S. health care system. Willed body programs, the marketing and commoditization of human cadavers, property rights, and the implications of publicized scandals involving the illicit sale and resale of donated human body parts are examined.

LEARNING OBJECTIVES

Upon completion of this chapter readers should be able to:

1. Describe how human body parts are used in medical research, training, treatment, consumer product testing, and military research.
2. Explain the concepts of the National Organ Transplant Act.
3. Explain the concepts of the Uniform Anatomical Gift Act.
4. List what costs are legal to receive for human body parts.
5. Describe the two forms of misconduct in the human body parts industry.
6. Explain the problems that arise when the ultimate purchaser is far removed from the original acquirer of the body.
7. Describe how traffic in body parts may be prosecuted under the federal Racketeer Influenced and Corrupt Organizations Act.
8. Explain why a legalized market for body parts and products may minimize the underground trade, and what ethical concerns would be involved.

KEY TERMS

Affirmative evidence
Body broker
Breach of duty
Cadaver donation
Class-action lawsuit
Commodities
Criminal liability
Enterprise corruption
Euthanasia underground
Fraud
Grand theft
Human body parts industry

Informed consent
International black market
Interred bodies
Limited property interest
Multidistrict litigation
National Anatomical Service
National Organ Transplant Act of 1984
Necessary medical treatment
Negligence *per se*
Patent
Principle of *caveat emptor*

Principle of good faith
Racketeer Influenced and Corrupt Organizations Act of 1961
Racketeering
Theft
Tissue banks
Tissue processing firms
Tissue processing market
Uniform Anatomical Gift Act of 2006
Willed body programs

FACT OR FICTION

Willed Body Programs

Can human body parts lawfully obtained from cadavers that are donated to universities for medical research be subsequently sold to third parties?

Henry Reid, director of the **willed body program** at the University of California Los Angeles (UCLA) Medical School, was arrested and charged with **grand theft** for allegedly selling hundreds of cadavers donated to UCLA. Reid charged Ernest Nelson more than $1 million over a five-year period for the sale of 496 cadavers that had been donated to the university. Nelson, a **body broker** and former mortuary worker associated with Empire Anatomical Services in Los Angeles, was arrested and charged with receipt of stolen property.

About twice a week, Nelson entered the UCLA Medical Center with a saw and collected tissue, organs, tendons, bones, joints, limbs, hands, feet, torsos, and heads culled from the dead; he then sold the human body parts to a number of firms in the medical products industry, including a Johnson & Johnson subsidiary, DePuy Mitek. Massachusetts-based Mitek manufactures medical devices that treat soft tissue injuries. The UCLA program, the oldest willed body program in the country, receives donated cadavers for use by its researchers and medical students.

Reid, hired after claims that the UCLA program had mishandled and improperly disposed of donated remains, allegedly drew from and sold the program's surplus materials for about $1,400 per body. Nelson maintains that his role in the reselling of cadavers and human body parts received from Reid was legal because he had no reason to believe that he was in receipt of stolen goods, and because he did not sell the remains for a profit. Johnson & Johnson admitted that Mitek purchased dismembered human remains from Nelson but claimed ignorance as to their stolen origin. A **class-action lawsuit** alleges that Johnson & Johnson, Mitek, Empire, and other associates violated the federal **Racketeer Influenced and Corrupt Organizations Act of 1961 (RICO)** by buying, selling, and reselling whole and dismembered human remains (*See* 18 U.S.C.A. §§ 1961-1968). They are also claimed to have engaged in **fraud** and **negligence** *per se* by improperly obtaining human body parts. At issue is whether the parties lawfully obtained human body parts from cadavers donated to UCLA.

— See *Law Fact* at the end of this chapter for the answer.

Principles and Applications

Human material is used to develop medical devices and cosmetic products as well as in most surgeries.[LN1] Multinational corporations, such as Johnson & Johnson, Bristol-Myers Squibb, Stryker, and Medtronic, rely on human remains to guide them in developing medical products. Multinational consumer product corporations use body tissues to develop cosmetics. Physicians and dentists use human body parts to:

- Plump up lips and eliminate wrinkles
- Repair bones
- Replace heart valves
- Treat burn victims

(Goodwin, 2015).

It is estimated that the **human body parts industry** in the United States generates $500 million annually in the not-for-profit organ procurement side of the industry alone; some attribute a significantly higher dollar figure to the entire domestic industry given the cash transfers involved in many of the sales transactions (Williams et al., 2015). By some estimates, more than 8,000 donated cadavers are sold annually in the United States, some of which are closely tied to major medical research organizations (Goodwin, 2015).

Misconduct in the Human Remains Market

American medicine has always struggled to procure enough cadavers for research and education. Since the late 18th century, when dissection became an essential component of medical training, the demand for cadavers has far exceeded the supply. Back then, the solution was the robbing of graves. Entrepreneurs could make a tidy profit digging up freshly

interred bodies and delivering them, under cover of night, to medical men willing to pay handsomely for them. People also obtained bodies from orphanages, poor houses, and insane asylums. These were good sources of bodies since disease was often rampant there and society never questioned what happened to orphans, the indigent, or the insane (Capron, 2014).

Today body brokers are not robbing graves; they are violating corpses. There are two distinct forms of misconduct in the human remains market (Goodwin, 2013). The first is the procurement, harvesting, and sale of human body parts taken from the dead who never consented to be donors. The second, more complicated form of misconduct involves the illicit trade in the bodies of people who have donated themselves to science.

COURT DECISION
Medical Products Litigation

In Re: Human Tissue Products Liability Litigation
[Decedents' Relatives v. Human Material Processing Corporations]
582 F.Supp.2d 644 (U.S. District Court for the District of New Jersey 2008);
related proceeding at Commonwealth v. Garzone, 131 A.3d 104 (Pennsylvania Superior Court 2015)

Facts: This is a class action comprising 42 lawsuits in 16 states (Alabama, California, Florida, Georgia, Indiana, Iowa, Kentucky, Louisiana, Minnesota, New Jersey, New York, Ohio, Pennsylvania, South Carolina, Tennessee, and West Virginia) against firms that harvested human tissue from corpses without obtaining proper consent and without following proper procedures. The scheme by Medical Tissue Services and its ringleader, former oral surgeon Dr. Michael Mastromarino, involved procuring human tissues from funeral homes and crematoria without the proper consents and then selling the tissue to **tissue banks, tissue processing firms**, and the medical products industry which bought the tissue without checking or following procedures to determine the origin, nature, or suitability of the tissue for human transplantation. Moreover, it is claimed that the tissue processors engaged in flawed procedures that did not properly cleanse the received tissue before distributing it.

Dr. Mastromarino made between $6 million and $12 million over a four-year period selling tissue and bone illicitly carved from corpses. Following almost three years of legal proceedings and a criminal investigation by the Brooklyn District Attorney, Mastromarino had his dental license revoked and agreed to a prison sentence of 18 to 54 years after pleading guilty to charges of body stealing, forgery, grand larceny, and **enterprise corruption**.

More than a thousand civil suits from tissue recipients have been filed against Mastromarino, his tissue harvesting company, Medical Tissue Services Ltd., and three tissue-processing firms that sold Mastromarino's human material to hospitals and other health facilities. First headquartered in Brooklyn, New York, and then Fort Lee, New Jersey, Mastromarino paid funeral directors $1,000 per corpse. He then divided each corpse and sold the bone and tissue for at least $13,000 per corpse to tissue-processing firms, who then resold the human body parts to hospitals for many times that amount. Human body parts included sheets of skin for burn victims and cosmetic operations, bone for dental implants, tendons and ligaments for orthopedic replacement procedures, and cardiac valves for those with heart problems.

With a crew of cutters, including several nurses, Mastromarino harvested more than 1,600 bodies from funeral homes without consent. Mastromarino and his assistants forged consent forms and death certificates to conceal the fact that many of the corpses died from hepatitis, cancer, AIDS, or other dangerous ailments. Under federal regulations, transplants from such corpses are prohibited. They falsely lowered the ages of the deceased to make the stolen specimens appear more desirable.

Issue: Are organs and tissue from human corpses being harvested without obtaining proper consents?

Holding and Decision: Yes. While litigation is ongoing, this case demonstrates one way the courts are attempting to hold the human body parts industry accountable for the administration of its illegitimate body harvesting programs.

Analysis: This RICO case is pending resolution before the 3rd Circuit Court of Appeals and the New York Court of Appeals. Separate criminal proceedings related to the harvesting of human body parts are ongoing in state courts.

Rule of Law: This medical products litigation will likely result in changes to regulation of the human body parts industry as new rules of law emerge to address this controversy.

References discussing this court decision: None.

Billion-Dollar Global Industry

The true prevalence of the illicit sale of discarded human body parts is anyone's guess. Legitimate sales of human body parts are a billion-dollar global industry. The answer to the question about the level of corruption is in the details; with one harvested corpse worth $200,000 on the black market, the temptations are great and the oversight almost nonexistent (Williams et al., 2015). To further complicate the issue, there are legitimate sales arising out of illegitimate means, such as lack of consent.

As **multidistrict litigation** proceeds in the federal courts on an international human body parts operation involving Medical Tissue Services and Mastromarino, the global pervasiveness of the illegal harvesting of human body parts may be brought to light. Criminal proceedings related to this operation are also ongoing in state courts nationwide. Some commentators think about 15% of the multibillion-dollar global human body parts industry could be illegitimate or as high as $1.2 billion (Capron, 2014; Goodwin, 2013). This estimate is extrapolated from a comparative analysis of the $4.5 trillion retail industry, where an estimated $30 billion is illegitimate due to organized crime, exclusive of shoplifting. Keep in mind that just one body broker, Dr. Mastromarino, harvested more than 1,600 bodies in the United States before he was caught. From the body broker scandals that have been uncovered, prosecutors cannot assign an accurate sales figure to the clandestine operations they investigated for years. Sales are speculated to be in multimillion-dollar ranges for each case. What we do know is there appears to be no shortage of reportable cases and scandals for this scarce commodity of human materials.

The Underground Market in Human Body Parts

As the host of Public Broadcasting Services' long-running *Masterpiece Theater*, Alistair Cooke represented American taste and refinement at its best. Since his death, Cooke has also become the symbol of America's underground market that illegally sells corpses and human body parts. Unbeknownst to his family, Cooke's bones were cut out of his body before he was cremated and his bones were sold for $7,000 by Regenerative Processing Plant, a Florida-based tissue processor with over $20 million in revenue, and by Tutogen Medical, a manufacturer of biological implant products with over $30 million in revenue (Goodwin, 2009; Oberman, 2006). While Cooke's fate was gruesome, what is perhaps most disturbing is that it was not unusual. The Cooke scandal raised concerns about the marketing and commoditization of human bodies, property rights, and the implications for medical research that are arising from publicizing this illicit sale and resale of human body parts (Williams et al., 2015).

Fraud and Negligence in the Illicit Sale of Human Body Parts

Fraud and negligence issues surround both the sale of human corpses and human body parts as well as the medical research industry. Liability for the fraudulent receipt of stolen goods is a factual issue determined by the courts after considering all relevant evidence. In the case of Cooke, the difficulty with holding anyone liable is proving a buyer's knowledge that the human body parts were stolen. The **Uniform Anatomical Gift Act of 2006** (UAGA) prohibits the sale of human body parts and was adopted by the states in order to protect corpses. Congress subsequently set a minimum standard of care for the procurement of organs and transplantable tissue when it passed the **National Organ Transplant Act of 1984** (NOTA), but it does not regulate human remains (*See* 42 U.S.C.A. § 274(e)).

Negligence may arise when either of these laws is violated, resulting in injury to a corpse. Corpses are a statutorily protected group. Negligence *per se* arises as a matter of law. Courts are not free to decide what a reasonable person would have done under the circumstances, and a **breach of duty** owed the victim is not required, unlike in a regular negligence action. For instance, the UCLA scandal at the start of this chapter involved the negligent sale and receipt of cadavers. A reasonable person might have accepted the cadavers and human body parts believing that they were not stolen and sold, but that is irrelevant.

Federal laws were violated, and whoever accepts the stolen human body parts may be liable. In other words, when Johnson & Johnson admitted that Mitek purchased dismembered human remains from Nelson, it could not claim ignorance as to their stolen origin and subsequent sale. Their error in judgment in dealing with suspect body brokers is irrelevant; they may be determined to have been negligent *per se*. The same rationale applies to Regeneration Technologies and Tutogen Medical, two firms intertwined in the class action products liability litigation described in this chapter on this very issue. *See In Re Human Tissue Products Liability Litigation.*

General Unawareness of Corruption

There is general unawareness and lack of knowledge about how pivotally positioned health care professionals may exploit the dead and endanger the living. Given that the demand for human cadavers consistently exceeds supply, the allocation of scarce human body parts is an issue of great value with no easy solutions. Moreover, there is no political consensus on whether:

- A legalized market for buying and selling cadavers would decrease illicit transactions
- More explicit rules and regulations should be adopted for the sale of human body parts
- Society is so opposed to the commoditization of the human body that such a market would be incomprehensible

As seen in the UCLA willed body program at the start of this chapter, although cadavers were stolen, then bought and sold and resold, the dismembered human body parts were ultimately used in medical research. While the lack of an open market for human body parts may be stifling medical research and challenging the potential lifesaving ability of the human body parts industry, perhaps the societal value of assuring funeral rights for the families of loved ones is a more important value until a political consensus can be reached about the value of human materials (Eisenberg, 2015).

COURT DECISION
Illegal Harvesting of Human Body Parts

Graves v. Biomedical Tissue Services, Ltd
(In Re Human Tissue Products Liability Litigation)
[Decedents' Relatives v. Human Material Processing Corporations]
2009 U.S.Dist.LEXIS 66619 (U.S. District Court for the District of New Jersey 2009),
summary judgment granted in part, 2010 U.S.Dist.LEXIS 17667 (U.S. District Court
for the District of New Jersey 2010)

Facts: This lawsuit was brought by the immediate family of Graves, who died from complications arising from cancer. Following the death of Graves, his family contracted with a funeral home for funeral arrangements and cremation services. After the funeral home took possession of Graves's body for cremation, it allowed a tissue bank to remove bones and tissue from Graves's body for medical research and implantation. Neither Graves nor his family consented to the harvesting of the human body parts and the funeral home never disclosed that such harvesting would occur.

Issue: Did the tissue banks fail in their legal duty to obtain proper consents, and did they willfully disregard regulations regarding the procedures for harvesting human organs?

Holding and Decision: The issue of consent was never addressed in this part of the lawsuit. Summary judgment was granted and the complaint was dismissed without prejudice against one of the five tissue banks that had no records of receiving any human organs or tissue from the funeral home that handled Graves's cremation; the remaining four tissue banks remain involved in this ongoing class-action litigation. Plaintiffs failed to meet their burden to provide **affirmative evidence** of the particular tissue bank's involvement in the harvesting or processing of Graves's body or human body parts.

Analysis: Separate criminal proceedings related to the harvesting of human body parts are ongoing in state courts.

Rule of Law: There must be records indicating that a tissue bank received or processed organs and tissue from the specific funeral home that handled Graves's cremation; the remaining four tissue banks did have such records.

References discussing this court decision: Struve, 2008.

Commodification of Human Materials

Dead human bodies are the cornerstone of the lucrative and important business of advancing scientific knowledge and improving medical techniques. Human body parts underwrite both cutting-edge research and everyday medical procedures. Medical researchers rely on human cadavers to hone surgical techniques. Yet, there is no consensus about the possibility of commodifying human body parts.

MANAGEMENT AND LAW ISSUES

2. How much independence should universities have in determining the uses of donated cadavers?
3. Should donors begin to explicitly define the roles regarding the future use of their bodies?
4. If so, what rights should donors have in this regard, if any?

The human body parts industry could thrive if cadaveric human body parts could be permitted to enter an open marketplace and the sale of cadavers could be properly regulated (Goodwin, 2013). A regulated trade would be preferable to existing black market organ dealings, which can be exploitative and unsafe (Williams et al., 2015). The case of an inmate on death row selling his human body parts through an eBay auction is just one bizarre example of the current system (Morris, 2009). See **FEATURE BOX 24-1** for the story of an international body broker.

COURT DECISION
Medical Research

Washington University v. Catalona
[Medical Research Institution v. Medical Researcher]
490 F.3d 667 (U.S. Court of Appeals for the 8th Circuit 2007),
cert. denied, 552 U.S. 1166 (U.S. Supreme Court 2008)

Facts: This case involved a dispute between Washington University and Dr. William Catalona, a medical researcher, who left his position at Washington University and took a position at a new institution. Catalona wanted to take with him the tissue samples he had collected from his patients for his prostate cancer research. He maintained the samples belonged to his patients and that they had consented to let him take their parts with him to his new institution. Washington University maintained that because it had developed, paid for, and maintained a substantial repository of tissue samples for prostate cancer research, and that because the initial consent forms were made out in the name of Washington University, not Dr. Catalona personally, the University owned the tissue samples.

Issue: Once patients sign an **informed consent** form donating their tissue, blood, DNA, or other human body parts for research purposes to a university, who has the right of ownership?

Holding and Decision: Patients surrender all rights of ownership to direct the use and transfer of their human body parts once they consent to donate; they cannot come back later and direct a new use or ownership.

Analysis: The court was ambiguous as to whether the patients ever had a property interest in their tissue samples. On the one hand, they potentially had such an interest but lost it when they donated their tissue for research. On the other hand, they never had such an interest.

The court equated the University's possession and control over the tissue samples with ownership under state law and concluded that the University owned and controlled the removed samples. In reaching its conclusion, the court relied on the case, *Moore v. Regents of the University of California,* and one subsequent case, *Greenberg v. Miami Children's Hospital Research Institute* (see 793 P.2d 479 (Supreme Court of California 1990), and 264 F.Supp.2d 1064 (U.S. District Court for the Southern District of Florida, Miami Division 2003), respectively).

In the *Moore* case, Moore underwent supposedly **necessary medical treatment** at a university medical center where his physician and others used human body material extracted from him for medical research without his permission. In *Greenberg,* families with a rare genetic disorder believed they had an agreement with researchers that, in return for their donation of tissue and other samples with genetic materials, the researchers would develop a genetic test that would be made widely available to the families. The researchers, however, gained a **patent** over the genetic test and disagreements arose between the patent holders and the families as to the manner in which the tests would be made broadly available and affordable. The families sued, claiming that their property had been unjustly used to enrich the researchers and claimed conversion of property. The lower court, citing *Moore,* found that the families had no property rights in their donated tissue and DNA.

Rule of Law: Once a patient donates human body parts for research, regardless of what relationship or legal interest the individual had prior to the donation, the human body parts become an object, similar to equipment, brick and mortar, or intellectual property, in which title and ownership vests with the institution conducting the research.

References discussing this court decision: Ghosh, 2014; Horton, 2014; Pike, 2016; Ram, 2015; Townsley, 2015.

FEATURE BOX 24-1

International Body Broker

Anyone could have found James Cohan of Sun Valley, California, on the Internet selling organ transplant brokering services. His stated fee was $140,000 for a kidney and $290,000 for a heart, liver, or lung. These fees included hospital and surgeon charges, and flights and accommodations to a network of 15 or so transplant hospitals in China, India, the Philippines, South Africa, Singapore, Pakistan, and South America. Cohan's sales pitch was that the quality of the organs was more important than the choice of the physician performing the transplant surgery, and he claimed that he knew how to get fresh organs quickly from healthy, young donors.

Cohan spent several months in an Italian jail in the late 1990s on ultimately unsubstantiated allegations that he was buying and selling organs from South Africa, following articles published in *The New York Times* and the *Washington Post*, that were similar to articles in the *Sunday Times* (London), and *The Globe and Mail* (Canada). In all the interviews Cohan claimed that his body brokering service, in existence for more than 20 years, was entirely legal; he was simply pairing customers facing certain death if they did not procure organ transplants with hospitals that were equipped to provide organ transplants in the developing world. Cohen claimed that his customers came in at the rate of one a week from all over the Western world.

All information about his international business quickly disappeared as soon as the light of day exposed his operation. For a decade after the U.S. Federal Bureau of Investigations searched his home and suggested Cohan was nothing more than a scam artist who never delivered on the promised transplants and that his body broker scheme was a fantasy, Cohen's international body brokerage operation was repeatedly described in news reports in the United States, Canada, and England, before all information about him disappeared.

E.g., Harlow & Bagenal, 2007; Jones, 2007; Macaskill, 2007; Morais, 2007.

Limited Property Interest in Human Material

Corpses and human material have characteristics similar to property in the law. Most courts refuse to overturn traditional notions of a **limited property interest** in the human body. Sometimes, the U.S. health care system fails to carry out donors' wishes and puts patients at risk because health care providers are complacent about what actually happens to corpses and discarded human body parts or products. Few ask the body brokers where the human material that sustains this enormous industry comes from. Johnson & Johnson never asked, nor did the U.S. Army, in a situation to be discussed later in this chapter.

Through ongoing lawsuits, questions are proliferating about the entire human body parts industry. Unanswered are questions about the liability and benefits of the various willed body programs in the medical schools running such programs and about the legal status of the medical research community itself. While it is legal to gift human body parts to a specific person or entity in private through one's last will and testament, people generally cannot place restrictions on the gift. As the courts review the human body parts industry and the need for cadavers in medical research and education, the rationale behind the criminality of human body parts sales may come under scrutiny and undermine the ideals behind willed body programs and medical research on cadavers in general.

The growth in the **tissue processing market** has raised concerns about the transfer of disease during orthopedic and neurosurgical operations. Dr. Mastromarino contributed to those concerns by acknowledging that he sold several tissue samples that were cancerous or infected with the human immunodeficiency virus (HIV) and/or hepatitis, but disguised those facts through fake documentation. The human body parts were used in disk replacements, knee operations, dental implants, and other surgical procedures performed by unsuspecting physicians across the United States.

More than 10,000 people received tissue supplied by Medical Tissue Services; the Food and Drug Administration (FDA) recalled 13,000 pieces of tissue. According to the Uniform Anatomical Gift Act, it is illegal to buy and sell the dead. The law provides that a *person may not knowingly, for valuable consideration, purchase or sell an organ for transplantation or therapy, if removal of the organ is intended to occur after the death of the decedent (See § 10(a), 8A U.L.A. 62 (2014)).* However, according to National Organ Transplant Act, it is legal to recuperate *costs* involved in securing, transporting, storing, and harvesting human body parts. The law excludes *reasonable payments associated with... the expenses of travel, housing, and lost wages incurred by the donor of a human organ in connection with the donation of the organ* from the definition of *valuable consideration (See 42 U.S.C.A. § 274e(c)(2) (2007)). Cost* is an expansive term; it can mean whatever the body brokers want it to represent.

In practice, the loopholes in the Uniform Anatomical Gift Act and National Organ Transplant Act mean that bones, tissue, organs, joints, limbs, heads, and even entire torsos are scarce commodities in an international marketplace where the demands of medical researchers, product developers, and physicians far exceed the supply.[LN2] Heads currently sell for upwards of $900, legs for close to $1,000, and hands, feet, and arms for several hundred dollars each (Carney, 2011; Goodwin, 2015).[LN3] According to Organs Watch, a live donor kidney typically trades for:

- $1,500 in the Philippines
- $2,700 in Moldova and Romania
- $7,500 in Turkey
- $10,000 in Peru
- $30,000 in the United States

For the body brokers who supply materials to corporations, research centers, tissue banks, and other health care clients, the profit motive is strong and government oversight is weak.

Many families now wonder whether their loved ones may have been sold and resold into the hands of large multinational corporations or used gruesomely by the U.S. military. The cremation and burial in which they participated may have only been an illusory gesture. At this point in time, the human body parts scandals may discourage donation of cadavers or cause contracts to be rescinded by those who have willed their corpses to medical research. How all this

MANAGEMENT AND LAW ISSUES

5. What legal and ethical distinctions are there between selling human body parts versus human tissue, blood plasma, ova, or sperm?

will affect the manner in which willed body programs function and how medical research firms go about obtaining research subjects in the future cannot be determined. One thing is certain: the issues highlighted in this chapter are what keep many people from signing up to become organ donors, and thus many lives are lost while waiting for a transplant.

Illegal Procurement and Sale of Human Body Parts

The first form of misconduct in this arena is the illegal procurement and sale of human body parts. The lawful as well as the unlawful procurement and sale of human body parts is a complex and confusing interplay of:

- Economic opportunity
- Legal loopholes
- Moral limits
- Scientific innovation

In the absence of medical and moral clarity about the interchange of human biological material, people are left with the corrupting promise of unlimited economic opportunity in exchanging superfluous human body parts, and a legal system that is ill equipped to cope with the kind of ethical dilemmas being raised by scientific innovation. The disposition of a decedent's remains is a largely unregulated area. While there are federal regulations concerning the funeral industry, there are none dealing with the disposition of remains in particular (*See* Farmer, 2015). Sometimes human body parts are illicitly taken from corpses during autopsies or in morgues and funeral homes before burial in the ground, internment in a vault, or cremation.

Few states inspect crematoria or require crematorium workers to be certified. Regulation in some parts of the country is weak; some states have no regulations at all, and except for Environmental Protection Agency regulations governing emissions from the amalgam fillings in teeth of the corpses (McGrath, 2013), many crematoria are unregulated. Cremation services, another thinly regulated business intertwined with the U.S. health care system, are of vital importance to those working in the **euthanasia underground** or in those states where physician-assisted dying is banned. When corpses are cremated, it eliminates the possibility of police, coroners, or other investigatory agencies finding out what drugs were in the patient's body at the time of death (Shah & Miller, 2010).

One California crematorium owner made hundreds of thousands of dollars illicitly dismembering cadavers meant for cremation and then selling the human body parts to the highest corporate bidders; he was convicted for mutilation of human remains and embezzlement (Goodwin, 2015). The assistants who help pathologists with autopsies and manage morgues are also well positioned to covertly sell human body parts. So are undertakers.

Often morticians replace the stolen human body parts with pieces of plastic or metal pipe as was done to Alistair Cooke's body, mentioned at the start of this chapter, in order to cover the damage for open casket funerals. The sale of caskets is more heavily regulated than the state licensing of morticians and funeral home owners (Kingsmill, 2015). Some states even limit who may sell a casket, which can preclude families from purchasing caskets through entities such as Costco.

Illegal Sale of Cadavers Through University Willed Body Programs

The second, more complicated, form of misconduct involves the trade in corpses from university willed body programs. Donors will their corpses to science, expecting that their cadavers will be delivered to the anatomy laboratories of medical schools, and that, in being dissected, they will help train the next generation of physicians. Most do go this route, but not all.

Louisiana State University, Tulane University, and the University of California at Los Angeles (UCLA) were all implicated in the underground traffic of cadavers. They were caught selling human body parts to brokers and suppliers who then resold them to independent buyers. All three universities are now involved in ongoing class-action lawsuits with regards to their willed body programs.

For years, military researchers bought corpses through this market to use in research involving explosive devices. The U.S. Army has used cadavers to determine safe standoff distances from explosives in tests to determine how to build the best blast shelters and to improve combat helmets. Along the way these cadavers make a lot of money for the brokers, suppliers, and vendors who handled them. Needless to say, donors' families are neither informed of that profit nor invited to share in it.

COURT DECISION
Unauthorized Mutilation of Cadavers

Gudo v. Administrators of the Tulane Education Fund
[Family Members of Donated Cadavers v. University]
966 So.2d 1069 (Court of Appeal of Louisiana, 4th Circuit 2007),
writ denied, 972 So.2d 1170 (Supreme Court of Louisiana 2008)

Facts: The cadavers in question had been sent to the willed body programs at Tulane University's Health Sciences Center for the purpose of medical research and training. Because more bodies were collected than were needed, they were sold to other entities without informing the family members. The University acknowledged that the U.S. Army acquired cadavers donated to them. Cadavers were allegedly given to New York–based **National Anatomical Service**, a national distributor of donated cadavers, which then sold them to the Army for between $3,600 and $4,300 per body, according to the Army's Medical Research and Materiel Command in Fort Detrick, Maryland. The cadavers were then blown up in land mine experiments at Fort Sam Houston in San Antonio, Texas. Family members contended that their loved ones' donated cadavers had not been used properly.

Issue: Can donated cadavers be used in a manner not authorized by the surviving family members?

Holding and Decision: Yes. The statutory definition of what encompasses an action for the unauthorized desecration and mutilation of a cadaver is broad enough to cover cadavers being blown up in land mind experiments.

Analysis: This case was settled and is under seal; the decision is without a published opinion. The public will never know whether the U.S. Army believed surviving family members donated their family members' corpses for this kind of research or whether this constituted medical research or training.

Rule of Law: In order to maintain an action for the unauthorized mutilation of cadavers, the unauthorized mutilation must be negligent or wanton and the surviving family members must have suffered emotional distress as a direct result upon becoming aware of the unauthorized mutilation.

References discussing this court decision: Ling, 2004; Snyder, 2005.

Sale and Transplantation of Contaminated Body Tissue

These two types of misconduct, the illegal procurement and sale of corpses and human body parts and the improper use of corpses donated for medical research and training, blur together in another health care problem of systemic proportions: the harvesting of contaminated ligaments, tendons, bones, and other valuable body tissues. Cases of contaminated tissue are rare, but they are making headlines more often. Tissue from one contaminated donor can go to dozens of patients.

The UAGA bans the sale of transplant tissue and the FDA forbids the transplanting of cancerous tissue. The FDA Center for Biologics Evaluation and Research has a regulatory framework for human tissue and cellular and tissue

MANAGEMENT AND LAW ISSUES

6.   What legal and ethical considerations underlie willed body programs and the human body parts industry itself?

based products that is designed to prevent the introduction, transmission, or spread of communicable diseases by tissue products.

Commercial human tissue recovery firms are required to screen and test donors for relevant communicable disease agents and diseases and to ensure that tissues are processed in a way that prevents communicable disease contamination and cross contamination. However, the reality is that the regulations governing donor screening and record-keeping practices are seldom enforced (Williams et al., 2014):

- Death certificates maintained by human tissue recovery firms often do not match state death certificates regarding the cause of death
- Donors are not always screened for risk factors or clinical evidence of disease agents and diseases
- Human tissues are often recovered in a manner that causes contamination

The FDA does not have the investigation or enforcement staff to stop corrupt body brokers who simply change the cause of death on the certificate in order to circumvent the one restriction on transplant tissue, while simply ignoring the other restriction forbidding commercial sales. One untrustworthy operator using one set of sources to get tissues can skew the whole regulatory system.

Today medical technology can transform tissue from cadavers into a variety of skin graft or bone chip implants. Surgeons use implants to repair a wide variety of bone and other tissue defects, including spinal vertebrae repair, musculoskeletal reconstruction, fracture repair, joint repair, and reconstruction for sports medicine injuries. More than a million Americans every year undergo medical procedures that use skin tissue or bone harvested from cadavers (Wharton, 2006). Contaminated and cancerous tissue transplants, however, can injure, infect, and even kill. The corrupt world of global body brokering threatens the health of everyone who receives such transplants.

Laundering of Corpses

When corpses have been sold and resold, it is unclear when the charge of receipt of stolen human body parts may be dropped, or if such charges should ever be dropped. When the purchase of human body parts is highly separated from the act of **theft** (for instance, when a large medical research corporation purchases stolen human body parts that have already been sold and resold numerous times), can the purchasing entity be absolved of the earlier crimes, or would this simply encourage a longer chain of transfers before stolen human body parts would ever reach the medical research corporation? The legal **principle of *caveat emptor*** states that buyers must be aware that what they purchase may be accompanied with legal baggage, but the **principle of good faith** also excuses those who, even with due diligence, claim ignorance to the stolen nature of their purchase. It is unclear how far each of these legal principles can or should be extended to purchasers of stolen human body parts, particularly when many of the middlemen in the procurement chain are linked to the U.S. medical products industry and the U.S. military. We are challenged to consider the ethics of the industry (**FEATURE BOX 24-2**).

Criminal and Civil RICO Liabilities

The RICO legislation, originally passed to control organized crime, may create both criminal and civil liabilities against individual health care providers and medical research corporations involved in the underground human body parts industry. RICO does not specifically prohibit the sale of human materials but rather prohibits the means used to achieve fraudulent ends. Fraud refers to the deception of another for the purpose of obtaining money or property from

MANAGEMENT AND LAW ISSUES

7. What legal and ethical considerations are behind the criminality of human body parts sales?
8. Is the trading of human body parts different from slavery and prostitution? If so, what is the distinction?

FEATURE BOX 24-2

The Challenge to Think About the Societal Costs of Ignoring This Human Body Parts Industry

In Claire Denis' film *L'Intrus*, the protagonist is an active man who has lived an isolated existence on the French-Swiss border. As he ages and becomes ill with a weak heart, he begins to recognize his own physical vulnerability and decides to purchase a new heart (and transplant surgery) from the **international black market** in organs and organ transplants. He travels to Geneva, Switzerland, to pay for the transplant, where he meets a woman in a hotel room to whom he gives his order for a young heart. Scenes of him moving effortlessly through a number of countries in order to accomplish his project are intercut with scenes of attempts at illicit border crossings both by individuals engaged in illegal imports smuggling and by undocumented immigrants. The film, however, does not operate only at the level of the story of the purchase of a heart; the heart transplant is a symbol of the effects of the human body parts industry. It highlights the inequalities that exist in an open market through which the privileged can move with ease and can benefit. The film challenges everyone to think about what it means to take from others for their own personal benefit. This challenge is presented in the film through two images. First, Claire Denis presents the image of the heart as an intruder in the host body, as she forces viewers of the film to ask:

- Does the new heart, as such a dominant organ, change the old person?
- Is identity, the sense of self, changed?
- Will the new heart be willing to operate as part of the old body?
- Will the old body refuse the new heart?

Second, Claire Denis presents the cost of such a transaction through the image of the contract for the new heart. Having paid the full price demanded for the heart, the protagonist in the film is thrown off balance when he realizes the woman to whom he paid the money keeps reappearing at different locations: it seems that she is following him. When he confronts her, reminding her that he has already paid the price for the heart, she tells him that he will never finish paying. When he bought her heart, he took on her liabilities for where she came from both ethically and in terms of her previous biological and genetic history; it is a transaction that will never really end. She has become not only a continual reminder of his heart transplant but also his own memory of that which he can never escape; she is now as much a part of him as his transplanted heart. In the final moments of the film, when the credits roll on the screen, her role is named as 'the angel of death.' The film was inspired by Jean-Luc Nancy's meditation on his own heart transplant, also entitled *L'Intrus*.

—*L'Intrus* (Claire Denis, Director, 2005).

---

them. The UCLA scandal involved the fraudulent sale and receipt of stolen human body parts. In other words, at the start of this chapter, Reid sold Nelson cadavers that had been donated to UCLA for medical research and training; Nelson sold the stolen dismembered human body parts to Empire for harvesting; Empire then resold the remains to Mitek for medical research. This chain of business transactions constitutes fraud. While RICO does not deal with the specific business transactions in the human body parts industry and does not address the legal and medical questions confronting the sale of human materials, prosecutors are beginning to use this law in an attempt to address some of the scandals in the human body parts industry.

If the government proves **criminal liability**, all parties may be compelled to forfeit any property or money used in the criminal acts or derived from them. This could potentially include all revenue derived from the sale of medical products developed from improperly obtained cadavers. Forfeitures from the sale of medical products could easily exceed the value of this billion-dollar human body parts industry. This has never occurred, but theoretically, a prosecutor might be able to convince a court that this is what should happen.

RICO also creates civil liability. Hypothetically, donors' families could seek treble damages from both individuals and corporations for violating RICO. In other words, a judgment could conceivably be rendered for three times the harm actually suffered, plus legal fees. This is the part that frightens the middlemen and makes them turn over information on the medical products industry to law enforcement. One might ask what could constitute a RICO violation in the human body parts industry. Hypothetically, it could be argued that RICO prohibits using two or more **racketeering** acts to accomplish:

- Acquiring legitimate human body parts that were stolen from donated cadavers
- Maintaining human tissue processing organizations and medical research organizations through acceptance of stolen human body parts
- Operating a human body parts business with resold human body parts that never should have been commoditized

A two-step process could be used to prove that individuals and corporations violated RICO, whether it would be a criminal prosecution or a civil lawsuit. First, it would have to be shown that two or more racketeering acts were committed, which would be any of a list of specified criminal acts, including:

- Fraud
- Sale and receipt of stolen property
- Theft

Thus, if stolen human body parts were accepted from one donated cadaver, and later additional human body parts are sold from another donated cadaver, that commercial exchange would constitute two racketeering acts. Second, it must be shown that the racketeering acts were used to accomplish one or more of the aforementioned three purposes. If stolen corpses were sold to a body broker, who brokered a sale for harvesting of the human body parts, who then resold the remains for medical research, this would violate RICO.

Medical Research and Development of Medical Products

This chapter is more than an inquiry into criminal law and the resale of stolen property for medical research and development of medical products. It raises concerns about the purpose and value behind organ procurement and transplantation and the role of the U.S. health care system. Though the idea of placing a price on corpses and human body parts as products may be objectionable to some people, this commoditized value must be weighed against the intangible value of human lives. Although cadavers are bought and sold as **commodities**, this commodity market is used for the benefit of the living.

Cadavers and human body parts, though they may be illegally bought and sold, are often ultimately used in medical research. However, as new medical products are continually developed, more and more human tissues such as skin, bones, heart valves, embryos, and stem cell lines are being stored and distributed for therapeutic and research purposes in a hidden market with few regulations and great opportunities for financial gain. The reality of the multibillion-dollar human body parts industry is not well understood due to a paucity of data and also a lack of effort to integrate the available information. It is arguably unfair that neither the decedents' estates nor their families are receiving any of the industry's profit.

The health law issue that must be addressed is whether the lack of an open, free market for cadavers and human body parts affects medical research and its potential lifesaving ability (Williams et al., 2015). Right now, several class action lawsuits are focusing on those that deal in cadavers and human body parts:

- Body brokers who supply human materials to the medical products industry
- Medical research centers that accept the human body parts from the brokers
- Tissue banks and other health care providers who act as middlemen
- Tissue processing industry that processes tissue and body parts for sale
- Hospitals that do business with all these players

There is no oversight of hospitals involved in the human body parts industry; it remains to be seen what, if any, sanctions will be imposed on hospitals involved in the *Human Tissue Products Liability Litigation* case. It should be remembered that physicians and dentists treat patients frequently with medical products made from these cadavers and dismembered human body parts. As medical researchers continue to push the frontiers of science, it will become even more critical to strike a balance between stronger legal scrutiny of transactions involving corpses on the one hand and, on the other hand, allowing the medical products industry the freedom to develop lifesaving technologies without the burden and cost resulting from excessive regulation.

LAW FACT

Willed Body Programs

Can human body parts lawfully obtained from cadavers that are donated to universities for medical research be subsequently sold to third parties?

Yes. It is an open secret that university-willed body programs dispose of human materials, without calling the transactions 'sales,' and then collect procurement, transportation, and storage costs. The legal and financial repercussions of designating human body parts as medical waste and then recycling the human material for medical research is a subject that is just beginning to come under investigation, in what has come to be known as the human body parts scandal. The problems at the University of California, Los Angeles (UCLA) willed body program are drawing attention to complex issues surrounding **cadaver donation** and the sale of human body parts, as well as the medical products industry generally. Indications are that this incident is part of a larger problem in the procurement sector of the human body parts industry, which is certainly not limited to the United States. The *Human Tissue Products Liability Litigation* case outlined in this chapter will draw attention to this emerging controversy as the facts of the underground human body parts trade are revealed in open courts of law.

— *Regents of the University of California v. Superior Court of Los Angeles County*, 183 Cal. App 4th 755 (Court of Appeal of California, Second Appellate District, Division Three 2010), *review denied*, 2010 Cal.LEXIS 5826 (Supreme Court of California 2010).

See, e.g., Goodwin, 2015 and 2013 (discussing this decision).

CHAPTER SUMMARY

- Human body parts and products are used for medical research, medical teaching, medical treatment, consumer product testing, and for military purposes.
- There is a legitimate multibillion-dollar human body parts and products industry; in addition, some experts estimate that the underground market is worth at least $1.2 billion.
- The NOTA regulates the procurement of human organs and transplantable tissue, but it does not regulate human remains used for research and education.
- The UAGA prohibits the buying and selling of corpses and bans the sale of human transplant tissue.
- While people can donate their bodies or body parts to a specific person or entity, they cannot place restrictions on the gift's uses.
- It is legal to recuperate costs involved in securing, transporting, storing, and harvesting human body parts.
- There are two distinct forms of misconduct in the human body parts industry: the procurement, harvesting, and sale of human body parts from the dead who never consented to be willed donors, and the trade in corpses of willed donors who did consent but not to that particular purpose.
- Recently, several scandals have come to light involving harvesting human body parts from the dead without consent, either from the deceased's last will and testament or the surviving family members, and then sold for profit; all of the pieces of a corpse combined can generate up to $200,000.
- The other kind of scandal that has recently emerged involves universities selling corpses or human body parts and products that were donated with the intent of being used for research or teaching purposes as opposed to being sold for profit.
- The FDA forbids the transplanting of human tissue contaminated with cancer or communicable diseases; one major problem with the underground trade of such products is that they are often contaminated.
- The theory of *caveat emptor* states that buyers must be aware that what they purchase may be accompanied by legal problems.
- When the ultimate purchase is highly separated from the initial acts of fraud and theft, purchasers may be absolved of procurers' earlier crimes.
- In commercial sales, the principle of good faith excuses buyers who, even with due diligence, can claim ignorance to the stolen nature of their purchase.

- RICO creates both criminal and civil liabilities, with the potential of being assessed treble damages.
- In theory, if the government proves criminal liability under RICO, all parties involved may be compelled to forfeit any property or money used in the racketeering acts or derived from them.
- The lack of an open free market for human cadavers and human body parts hinders medical research and its potential lifesaving ability.
- A legalized market for human body parts and products may minimize the underground trade, but ethical concerns surrounding the commoditization of the human body have hindered progress toward such a market.

LAW NOTES

1. Human material in this chapter only includes body parts and tissues; the active markets for blood and blood products, sperm, ova, bone marrow stem cells, hair, breast milk, and urine are not addressed. It is interesting, however, that the global marketplace for human hair, known as black gold, is about $900 million alone; about half of that hair is sold for human extensions (Carney, 2011).

2. Despite the regulatory schemes under the UAGA and NOTA, organs are bought and sold on black markets. Traffic in organs from executed Chinese prisoners or the poor in Brazil, Russia, India, and other less developed, poor nations is well documented. The Institute of Medicine's report on organ donation discusses a study of individuals in Chennai, India, who sold kidneys to pay off debt. Ultimately these organ transplants resulted in poor outcomes for all involved. There were complications, including sepsis, hepatitis B, and liver cirrhosis, as well as other complications in those who received the organs; and there were no long-term benefits to the donors as their health deteriorated without adequate follow-up care. *See, e.g.,* Goodwin, 2015 and 2013.

3. Renowned German anatomist Professor Gunther von Hagens is the brain behind Body Works, a museum exhibition dedicated to showcasing the human body at each layer from all different perspectives. When he began constructing the exhibition, von Hagens reportedly spent $1,500 on a sliver of a human head, $3,600 on a pair of smoker's lungs, and $185 for a slice of a human hand.

REFERENCES

Capron, A. M. (2014). Organs and inducements: Six decades of organ donation and the challenges that shifting the United States to a market system would create around the world. *Law and Contemporary Problems, 77*, 25–69.

Carney, S. (2011). *The red market: On the trail of the world's organ brokers, bone thieves, blood farmers, and child traffickers.* New York, NY: HarperCollins, William Morrow.

Eisenberg, A. K. (2015). Criminal infliction of emotional distress. *Michigan Law Review, 113*, 607–661.

Epictetus & Lebell, S. (2014). *Art of living: The classical manual on virtue, happiness, and effectiveness.* New York, NY: Harper and Row.

Farmer, T. J. (2015). Don't die in Iowa: Restoring Iowans' right to direct final disposition of their bodily remains. *Iowa Law Review, 100*, 1813–1838.

Ghosh, S. (2014). The taking of human biological products. *California Law Review, 102*, 511–541.

Goodwin, M. B. (2015). *The global body market: Altruism's limits.* New York, NY: Cambridge University Press.

____. (2013). *Black markets: The supply and demand of human body parts* (reprint). New York, NY: Cambridge University Press.

____. (2009). Lecture series on empires: Empires of the flesh; Tissue and organ taboos. *Alabama Law Review, 60*, 1219–1248.

Harlow, J., & Bagenal, F. (2007, January 28). NHS patients buy organs from Third World. *The Sunday Times* (London), p. 27.

Horton, D. (2014). Indescendibility. *California Law Review, 102*, 541–600.

Jones, D. (2007, March 25). Exclusive: People revealed true extent of the cash crisis facing our organ failure. *The People: Sunday Star Edition* (London), p. 16.

Kingsmill, A. B. (2015). Of butchers, bakers, and casket makers: *St. Joseph Abbey v. Castille* and the Fifth Circuit's rejection of pure economic protectionism as a legitimate state interest. *Louisiana Law Review, 75*, 933–971.

Ling, A. (2004). UCLA willed body program comes under scrutiny as companies sued for the purchase of human body parts. *Journal of Law, Medicine and Ethics, 32*, 532–534.

Macaskill, M. (2007, May 20). Twenty patients buy organs in Pakistan. *The Sunday Times* (London), p. 16.

McGrath, K. (2013). A toxic mouthful: The misalignment of dental mercury regulations. *Boston College Journal of Law and Social Justice, 33*, 347–382.

Morais, R. C. (2007, January 29). Desperate arrangements. *Forbes, 179*(2), 72.

Morris, B. (2009). You've got to be kidneying me! The fatal problem of severing rights and remedies from the body of organ donation law. *Brooklyn Law Review, 74*, 543–578.

Oberman, M. (2006). Precious commodities: The supply and demand of body parts; When the truth is not enough: Tissue donation, altruism, and the market. *DePaul Law Review, 55*, 903–941.

Pike, E. R. (2016). Securing Sequences: Ensuring adequate protections for genetic samples in the age of big data. *Cardozo Law Review, 37*, 1977–2038.

Ram, N. (2015). DNA by the entirety. *Columbia Law Review, 115*, 873–939.

Shah, S. K., & Miller, F. G. (2010). Can we handle the truth? Legal fictions in the determination of death. *American Journal of Law and Medicine, 36*, 540–585.

Snyder, D. (2005, June 30). A dispute over brain donations: Families allege improper consent in lawsuits against Bethesda Institute (Stanley Medical Research Institute). *Washington Post*, p. B1.

Struve, C. T. (2008). Greater and lesser powers of tort reform: The primary jurisdiction doctrine and state-law claims concerning FDA-approved products. *Cornell Law Review, 93*(5), 1039–1073.

Townsley, M. L. (2015). Is there any body out there? A call for a new body of law to protect individual ownership interests in tissue samples used in medical research. *Washburn Law Journal, 54*, 683–740.

Wharton School at the University of Pennsylvania. (2006). The billion-dollar human body parts industry: Medical research alongside greed and corruption. *Knowledge@Wharton*.

Williams, K. L., et al. (2015). Just say no to NOTA: Why the prohibition of compensation for human transplant organs in NOTA should be repealed and a regulated market for cadaver organs instituted. *American Journal of Law and Medicine, 40*, 275–329.

CHAPTER 25

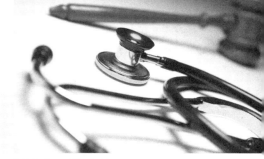

© Andy Dean Photography/ShutterStock, Inc.

Organ and Tissue Procurement and Transplantation

"Our bodies are our gardens to which our wills are gardeners."

— **William Shakespeare** (1564–1616), English poet and playwright, from *Othello*

IN BRIEF

This chapter describes the process of organ and tissue procurement and transplantation as it relates to donors and recipients. Organs represent one of the most highly regulated and cumbersome of the fields involving human biological materials as well as one of the more publicly visible uses of body parts. Regulation of the tissues industry lacks this public visibility and consistent oversight. This chapter explains the principles and flaws of organ and tissue transplants. Proposals to increase the number of patients receiving organ transplants are also reviewed. The legal process itself and its accompanying ethical arguments for and against the sale of donated organs and tissue are discussed.

Presumed consent, directed donations, commoditization, and xenotransplants (the transplant of cells, tissues, and whole organs across species) offer future alternatives for enhancement of the supply of body parts. Xenotransplantation poses greater risks to human health and it is far too premature to guarantee success. None of these alternatives is without controversy.

LEARNING OBJECTIVES

Upon completion of this chapter readers should be able to:

1. Explain why the demand for transplantable organs exceeds supply.
2. List the methods of allocating organs.
3. Discuss the system for allocation of organs using points.
4. Describe the means of obtaining permission for organ donation.
5. Distinguish the methods of declaring a person dead.
6. Discuss the potential for providing financial incentives for organ donations.
7. Distinguish organ transplantation from tissue transplantation regarding the economics involved.
8. Explain issues with xenotransplantation.

KEY TERMS

Acquired Immunodeficiency Syndrome	Anencephalic neonates	Black market drugs
Allogenic grafts	Aplastic anemia	Brain death
Allotransplants	Assistive reproductive techniques	Campaign for Responsible Transplantation
Alternate heart programs	Autografts	Cardiac death
American Association of Tissue Banks	Autotransplants	Cofinity Institute of Excellence
	Biosynthetic tissues	

Cognitively impaired
Cold ischemic times
Commoditized
Compelled living donations
Desecration of the body
Equity
Fairness
Fanconi anemia
Good faith immunity provision
HIV Organ Policy Equity Act of 2013
HIV-positive organs
Human Immunodeficiency Virus
Human tissue
Hurler syndrome
Immunologically incompatible
In vitro fertilization
Incompetency

Kidney-paired donation
Kidney swaps
Leukemia
LifeSharers
Living donors
Mandated choice
Maple syrup urine disease
National Organ Donor Registry
National Organ Transplantation of 1984
Net benefit
No-sale policies
Norwood Living Donation Act of 2007
Opt-out plan
Organ procurement agencies
Organ Procurement and
   Transplantation Network
Paired kidney transplants

Paired organ donation
Partially humanized organs
Pluripotent stem cells
Postmortem donations
Preimplantation genetic diagnosis
Presumed consent
Stem cells
Thalassemia
Tissue bank industry
Tissue processors
Tissue type
Uniform Anatomical Gift Act of 2006
Utility
Xenotransplants
Xenozoonosis
Zero antigen mismatch
Zoonoses

FACT OR FICTION

Medicaid Insurance Coverage for a Liver Transplant

Must a state's taxpayers pay for a liver transplant to cure a hereditary disease if the disease can be treated by dietary management?

Physicians at the Children's Hospital of Pittsburgh determined an eight-year-old child with a severe genetic disorder known as **maple syrup urine disease** could only be cured with a liver transplant. The Missouri Medicaid insurance program declined to cover the liver transplant and maintained the child's disease had been well managed by diet. Children with maple syrup urine disease are unable to metabolize essential amino acids used by the body to build proteins. As a result, children with the disease must restrict their intake of natural proteins, replacing them with daily intake of a special amino acid formula. When affected children become ill with a routine viral or bacterial illness or are unable to maintain their special diet, they are at risk for severe metabolic decomposition with neurological deterioration, brain swelling, coma, permanent brain injury, and death. Even with dietary management, metabolic decomposition can occur. The medical community was split over the medical necessity of a liver transplant when a child's condition was otherwise managed by diet. Given the risks associated with a liver transplant, there was disagreement over the possible outcomes of the child's treatment.

— *See* Law Fact at the end of this chapter for the answer.

Principles and Applications[LN1]

The primary need for human body parts is for the transplantation of organs, tissues, and cells into humans. A secondary need for human body parts is for medical research in regenerative medicine, especially in stem cell and gene-based therapy (Terzic & Nelson, 2010). Human organ transplantation can be used to treat diseases of the heart, lungs, liver, kidneys, and pancreas, which are some of the most common causes of infirmity and death. Organ failure and tissue loss account for almost $400 billion in U.S. health care costs today, particularly among older adults. This cost covers approximately eight million surgical procedures to treat these disorders as well as recurring treatments for related chronic diseases and their subsequent complications (Terzic & Nelson, 2010). Treatment needs for organ failure and tissue loss are expected to increase as the average age of the population increases, including the need for:

- Mechanical devices (mechanical kidneys as opposed to dialysis machines)
- Surgical reconstructions
- Transplants

While each of these treatments has its own limitations, of the three treatments, transplantation of organs and tissues has the greatest potential to treat:

- Acquired conditions such as cancer (by replacing the removed cancerous tissue with externally grown healthy tissue)
- Chronic conditions like diabetes (through regeneration of islets) and Parkinson's disease
- Congenital conditions such as hemophilia
- Gross organ failure, such as renal failure

(Bluhm, 2016).

Organ transplantation is often the only treatment for end-stage organ failure, such as liver and heart failure.

Types of Transplants and Limitations

There are three types of transplants:

- **Autotransplants**
- **Allotransplants**
- **Xenotransplants**

The first two are used extensively; the third is developing amidst rigid regulations.

Autotransplants

Autotransplants involve a process through which human material is harvested and subsequently transplanted from one part of a patient's body to another. The limitations associated with **autografts** (the material used in autotransplants) include the availability of human material as well as donor site diseases. The most litigated issue in this type of transplant involved insurance coverage for bone marrow autotransplants (Lee, 2014). For more than a decade, the medical community generally thought bone marrow transplants produced remissions in advanced breast cancer patients unresponsive to conventional therapy. While some states mandated coverage, insurers often excluded coverage of the bone marrow transplant procedure as experimental treatment or as medically unnecessary. After a decade of controversy, medical studies concluded the procedure was in fact ineffective and even potentially harmful (Wiley, 2016).

Allotransplants

Allotransplants occur where human material is harvested from one individual and subsequently transplanted to another individual. The challenges associated with **allogeneic grafts** (cells, tissues, or organs involved in allotransplants) include:

- Damage to donor organs and tissue during the transport process
- Donor-recipient blood type compatibility
- Donor-recipient physical compatibility (organ size, capacity, and lifespan)
- Rejection of **immunologically incompatible** organs and tissues
- Shortage of organs and tissue
- Transmission of donor site diseases to recipients, such as **Human Immunodeficiency Virus** (HIV), as well as hepatitis B and C viruses
- Use and long-term cost of immunosuppressive drugs to circumvent transplant immunorejection

(Parent, 2015).

Xenotransplants

Xenotransplantation is the use of animal materials to replace human cells, tissues, or organs. A central limitation is the risk of transmission of novel viral and microbial pathogens from donor xenografts to human recipients, known as **xenozoonosis**. For instance, diseases that began in animals, but that now affect humans include:

- Avian flu (from chickens, ducks, and geese)
- Ebola (from baboons, bats, chimpanzees, duikers, monkeys, and gorillas)

- Hantavirus pulmonary syndrome (from mice)
- Hepatitis B and C (from horses)
- Herpes (from chimpanzees)
- HIV (from monkeys)
- Influenza virus of 1918 (from birds)
- Mad cow disease
- Rabies (from bats, dogs, jackals, mongooses, raccoons, and wolves)

(Pippin, 2013; President's Council on Bioethics, 2004).

Not surprisingly, rejection is a more significant issue with interspecies transplants. While litigation is just beginning to emerge for these transplants, the **Campaign for Responsible Transplantation** has been engaged in the federal courts since the late1990s for freedom-of-information demands for proprietary information about the FDA's regulation of xenotransplants (Crepelle, 2016).

Organ Transplants

The law addressing organ transplants is vast, contradictory, and complex. How to treat organ transplants is far from obvious as case law and statutory regulations are to a large extent conflicted over the best approach to apply in allocating a scarce resource (Williams et al., 2014). Each potential framework for organ transplants offers appealing aspects, but each also has difficulty in meeting all of the concerns and interests surrounding the use of human biological material.

Organ transplants are not a new scientific concept, although several important medical advances have occurred recently, allowing for more successful transplants in terms of recipient survival and improved quality of life. Eighteenth-century experimentation with animal organ transplants led to the early human organ transplants. The first actual documented human organ transplants began to occur in the 1950s and 1960s. Other transplant developments are shown in **FEATURE BOX 25-1**.

Tissue typing dramatically improved the survival odds for transplant patients. Organs that can be transplanted from corpses include:

- Bone marrow
- Connective tissue
- Corneas
- Heart valves
- Hearts
- Intestines
- Kidneys
- Livers
- Lungs
- Pancreata
- Skin

(Doty, 2015; Williams et al., 2014).

Living donors can donate:

- Bone marrow
- Kidney
- Part of the liver
- Part of the lung

(Meckler, 2007d).

Over three-quarters of transplants come from patients who indicate their desire to be organ donors after death by either signing a directive or directing their personal representative to allow for donation (Capron, 2014).

Current Context

The remarkable potential for saving lives with organ transplants is severely constrained by the failure of regulatory policy to keep pace with technological advances in medicine (Kessler & Roth, 2012; Wharton, 2011). Cadaveric

FEATURE BOX 25-1

Important Transplant Developments

- 1869—The first tissue transplant was performed.
- 1911—The first human-to-human organ transplant was conducted in the United States.
- 1954—The first *successful* human-to-human organ transplant was performed in the United States (a living donor donated his kidney to his identical twin).
- 1968—The first heart transplant took place.
- 1968—The **Uniform Anatomical Gift Act of 2006** legalized donating tissues and organs (*See* 8A U.L.A. §§ 1-27) (every state has adopted its own version of this model legislation).
- 1983—The FDA granted approval of the first antirejection drug (cyclosporine) that helps stop transplant organ or tissue rejection from the recipient's body and thus improves the recipient's chance of survival.
- 1984—The **National Organ Transplantation Act**, which rendered it unlawful to "knowingly acquire, receive, or otherwise transfer any human organ for valuable consideration for use in human transplants if the transfer affects interstate commerce" was passed (*See* 42 U.S.C.A. § 274e (2007)) (§ 274e is named for Charlie W. Norwood, the late congressman from Georgia (1941-2007), who underwent a lung transplant and who was an avid advocate of patients' rights).
- 1986—Congress established the **Organ Procurement and Transplantation Network**, which sets standards and regulates organ transplant centers across the country; the Network establishes the process and policies for allocating organs (*See* 42 U.S.C.A. § 274 (2008)).
- 1988—The Joint Commission set donor standards and required hospital policies and procedures for organ and tissue procurement.
- 1996—Congress authorized the dissemination of organ donation information along with income tax refunds to approximately 70 million households to increase awareness and encourage organ donation; state tax agencies followed the federal example soon after.
- 1999—The Organ Procurement and Transplantation Network Final Rule was enacted (*See* 42 C.F.R. §§ 121.1-121.13) (13 years after the Network was established).
- 2000—The Children's Health Act established the National Center on Birth Defects and Developmental Disabilities (42 U.S.C.A. § 247b-4).
- 2004—The Organ Donation and Recovery Improvement Act was enacted to provide funding for transplant centers and qualified **organ procurement agencies** to increase the rate of organ donations (*See* 42 U.S.C.A. §§ 273a, 274f-1-274f-4).
- 2006—The Uniform Anatomical Gift Act, a model law for adoption by the states that bars others from revoking the consent of a donor after death who legally registered as a donor during their lifetime, was passed (8A U.L.A. §10).
- 2007—The **Norwood Living Organ Donation Act of 2007** codified a U.S. Justice Department ruling intended to increase the number of patients receiving **paired kidney transplants** by ensuring that criminal penalties do not apply (42 U.S.C.A. § 274e (2007)).
- 2013—The **HIV Organ Policy Equity Act of 2013** directing the Organ Procurement and Transplantation Network to establish standards for transplant of **HIV-positive organs** was passed (127 Stat. 579 (2013)).
- 2014—Skin, bone, muscles, blood vessels, nerves, and connective tissue are added to the definition of organs covered by the National Organ Transplant Act.

HHS, 2016; NKF, 2016.

organ procurement policies in the United States and other countries have failed to effectively respond to the growing demand for transplantable organs that has resulted from significant strides achieved in immunosuppressive therapy (Capron, 2014).

The result of this regulatory policy failure has been a chronic and growing shortage of human organs available for transplants (Kessler & Roth, 2012). At any one time there are over 120,000 patients awaiting organ donations (Mayo Clinic, 2016). Competing ideals surround the entire process of organ procurement and transplants. Current legislation regulating the process is unable to reconcile practical necessities with ethical considerations, resulting in a demand for transplantable organs that far exceeds the available supply.

Critical Shortage of Kidneys

Of all transplantable organs, the shortage of kidneys is most critical (Kessler & Roth, 2012). More than three-quarters of the wait list population on the **National Organ Donor Registry** comprises patients suffering from renal failure, also called end-stage renal disease. Over 84,000 patients are waiting for kidneys. Presumably a central financial authority could pay for these kidney transplants from tax revenues, such as Medicare's end-stage renal disease program for dialysis and transplant services (Bluhm, 2016). Taxpayers could save money with this approach so long as the cost was less than $90,000 (Bluhm, 2016; Kessler & Roth, 2012).

Other Organ Shortages

Although more than 450,000 transplants have been performed in the United States, the number of patients who need transplants is growing at about five times faster than the rate of donations (OPTN & STRT, 2016b). Another 16,500 patients or so are waiting for livers. The rest are waiting for pancreata, intestine, heart, or lung transplants. Many patients are waiting for more than one kind of organ (*See generally* OPTN & STRT, 2016b).

Demand Exceeds Supply

About 7,700 Americans unnecessarily die waiting for transplant operations each year (Mayo Clinic, 2016). While only about 15,000 patients a year die under circumstances that would make them suitable donors for lifesaving transplants, these deaths could help more than 15,000 patients live because each person can donate multiple needed organs. Patients generally wait 5 years for donated organs, and on average, 22 of them die each day. Although most Americans claim to approve of organ donation and transplants, only about one in four expressly declare themselves organ donors (*See generally* OPTN & STRT, 2016b). Clearly the demand for organs far exceeds the supply, and much could be done to alleviate the shortage, such as:

- Relaxing the restrictions on who can donate
- Clarifying the misunderstandings surrounding organ donation
- Compensating donors or their families

(Kessler & Roth, 2012).

Whatever approach is chosen, it is worth keeping in mind that the United States is among 11 countries listed by the World Health Organization as organ importers, meaning that a relatively high number of citizens get organs from another nation (Crepelle, 2016; Krawiec & Rees, 2014).

In Theory: How Organ Procurement and Transplants Occur

The federal government oversees the transplantation of human organs. To address the nation's critical organ donation shortage and improve the organ matching and placement process, Congress passed the National Organ Transplantation Act. This law makes it illegal to sell human organs and tissues and imposes fines and imprisonment for doing so. Congress went on to institutionalize a complex system of not-for-profit organizations solely responsible for collecting and allocating all transplantable organs.

Organ Procurement and Transplantation Network

The National Organ Transplantation Act provided for the establishment of the Organ Procurement and Transplantation Network, which administers the retrieval, distribution, and transplantation of organs. All U.S. transplant centers

---

MANAGEMENT AND LAW ISSUES

1. Can we confine our arguments about health care efficiency to organ transplants, or can one argue that other types of medical treatments and health care services are also scarce?
2. Is the shortage of organs available for transplant one health care problem that could be solved by unlimited funding of the health care system?

and organ procurement agencies must be members of this network in order to receive any funds through Medicare insurance (OPTN & STRT, 2016b). Currently, there are about:

- 100 transplant centers for liver transplants
- 150 for heart transplants
- 200 for kidney transplants

(NKF, 2016).

The network also standardizes the criteria for placement on distribution lists and maintains a National Organ Donor Registry for organ matching. A Web-based computer system stores the nation's organ transplant waiting list and matches recipient and donated organ characteristics. The organ matching and placement process is facilitated by a fully staffed organ center that operates 24 hours a day (*See generally* NKF, 2016). Despite all this legislation and accompanying regulatory oversight, there are still many problems with organ procurement (O'Brien, 2015). Some of the criticisms are that the network fails to detect or fix problems at some transplant centers, and when there is a problem, the investigation is slow and its findings are kept secret. Transplant centers with problems are almost never sanctioned, or very weak sanctions are imposed (Capron, 2014).

Furthermore, the Organ Procurement and Transplantation Network is unable to police itself because it is essentially a membership association with no overarching supervision. Transplant centers are able to find ways around transplant rules, and patients are often not informed about a particular center's transplant policies or outcomes. The federal government has previously sued the Network and has threatened to become more involved in its oversight.

Procurement Violations   Several studies have revealed that nearly every organ procurement agency is in violation of at least one government policy on the distribution of organs (Childress & Liverman, 2006; Truog, 2015). In response, more federal regulations were adopted allowing the government additional control and further limitations over how organs are allocated. The problem is that it often takes a decade or more for policy changes to become effective. The 1999 regulations that became effective 15 years after National Organ Transplantation Act was adopted by Congress sought to establish a standardized method of distributing donated organs to patients on transplant waiting lists and also made organ transplant data more available to the public (OPTN & STRT, 2016b).

Prior to 1999, organs were retained in the geographic area where they were obtained if a transplant patient was also waiting in that area. This meant the waiting time for organs varied wildly between geographic regions and patients with a more urgent need or with a better chance of survival often were denied organs. For instance, the waiting time for a liver in one region may be as low as 20 days, while in another region it may be as high as 443 days. The thinking behind this policy was that organs could be better preserved and patient costs could be kept to a minimum if transplants remained localized. The 1999 regulations allocated organs based on medical urgency and patient appropriateness, with the goal of making wait times more even across the country (*See generally* Capron, 2014).

Multidisciplinary Approach   There are many different health care professionals on a patient's transplant team. Clinical transplant coordinators oversee patient evaluation, treatment, and follow-up care. Transplant physicians manage patient health care. Transplant surgeons perform the actual transplant surgery and follow-up. Financial coordinators organize and clarify the financial aspects of patient care before, during, and after the transplant. Finally, social workers help patients and their families cope with the issues associated with the transplant, including any illness or side effects (*See generally* OPTN & STRT, 2016b).

MANAGEMENT AND LAW ISSUES

3. What is the justification underlying laws restricting accepting or offering payment for transplant organs?
4. What legal distinction is there between selling human organs versus human tissues, blood plasma, ova, and sperm?
5. What practical considerations support or detract from legally regulating organ procurement and transplants?
6. Would it be permissible to remove the organs of healthy, deceased prisoners to save the lives of five to eight others who need organ transplants?
7. Under what circumstances might palliative sedation facilitate organ transplants?

United Network for Organ Sharing

The first step in the transplant process is that the physician and transplant center decide whether and when to place a patient on the National Organ Donor Registry's wait list. Age is by far the biggest factor predicting how long someone will live after a transplant (DeVito, 2014). Organs are currently allocated based on a point system that considers how long the patient has been on the donor list and how urgent the patient's medical status is.

Allocation of Donated Kidneys

For kidneys, it is proposed that time on the donor list be substituted with time on dialysis; time on the donor list would be a secondary factor, particularly for the best-quality kidneys. This regulatory change would favor healthier patients over those who may be too ill to benefit from a transplant. This change has already been adopted for livers, hearts, and lungs. Under the proposed scenario, the healthiest kidneys would be distributed through a formula relying largely on **net benefit**, while the formula for kidneys coming from older or sicker donors would give greater weight to time on dialysis. Already, kidneys from donors under age 35 are automatically offered first to children under 18 if any are on a waiting list (Meckler, 2007c).

Basis of Allocation Decisions

Many factors affect how long a patient may be on the National Organ Donor Registry's wait list, such as the:

- Number of organs available for donation
- Patient's blood type, **tissue type**, height, and weight
- Size of available organs
- Transplant center's criteria for accepting donated organs

(Cook & Krawiec, 2014; DeVito, 2014; OPTN & STRT, 2016b).

Factors that do not affect the waiting time are gender, religion, financial status, and the willingness of recipients to someday donate their own organs. The patient's physician has a considerable amount of discretion in deciding how to list the patient on the registry (Frank, 2014). The federal government has previously investigated listing practices at major hospitals, such as the University of Chicago and the University of Illinois, where physicians were accused of exaggerating their patients' medical urgency status (*See* Cook & Krawiec, 2014). The hospitals denied the allegations and settled with the government.

There are no uniform criteria for deciding when to list patients for a transplant or for identifying patients' medical urgency status. Moreover, medical criteria differ with each organ; certain organs require extensive prescreening to find a positive match for a patient while different organs remain viable before transplant for different periods of time (Capron, 2014). In addition, United Network for Organ Sharing encourages physicians to consider nonmedical factors such as whether patients have:

- Caused their organ failure by their own behavior (diseases tied to smoking, drinking, or unhealthy diet and exercise patterns, among other lifestyle factors)
- Complied with and adhered to their treatment regimen
- Had or might have success with treatment other than a transplant (such as adults with maple syrup urine disease)
- Received prior organ transplants

The United Network for Organ Sharing suggests nonmedical factors used to evaluate transplant candidates should be monitored and updated to reflect changes in technology and medicine, and to minimize subjectivity. For instance, African Americans are much more likely than Caucasians to have blood type B, but there are not as many type B organ donors, which is a major obstacle for African Americans waiting for kidney transplants (NKF, 2016). To resolve this disparity, it is proposed that certain blood type A kidneys, which work effectively in both A and B patients, be made available to patients with blood type B (*See* Saitta-Gill & Hodge, 2015).

Donor Reforms

While potential donors who die in a hospital have the best chance of donating viable organs (because organs have to be harvested almost immediately after death), alternatives are arising to address this issue. Most major cities, including New York City and Philadelphia, have special organ recovery ambulances that travel to the homes of patients who die suddenly. With improved medical technologies, **cold ischemic times** have been extended to allow for truly national allocations. Cold ischemic time is the time interval that begins when an organ is cooled with a solution after organ procurement surgery and ends when the organ is implanted (O'Brien, 2015).

Nongovernmental Networks

There is an ideological and practical divide between the United Network for Organ Sharing and the medical community concerning the procedures and criteria for allocating organs as well as the procedures for reviewing the organ allocation system. The root of this disagreement appears to be how to deal with scarcity. Regulatory policy decisions determining who receives the limited number of organs have crucial consequences for patients.

These are medical decisions that might better be made by the medical community as opposed to the government. It should be noted this does not imply that the United Network for Organ Sharing is ineffective, but it only suggests that commercial networks may better allocate scarce organs on a competitive basis (*See* Parish, 2015). For instance, Aetna developed the national **Cofinity Institute of Excellence** network comprising facilities that manage heart, lung, simultaneous heart/lung, kidney, liver, pancreas, simultaneous kidney/pancreas, small bowel/intestinal, bone marrow, and stem cell transplants. All of the transplant centers in the Aetna network have met quality, volume, and outcomes standards through Aetna's credentialing process and external quality guidelines like those established by organizations such as Medicare and the United Network for Organ Sharing. Similar commercial developments may produce a change in how organ procurement and transplants occur, and will more closely parallel the rapid advances occurring with tissue transplants.

Donation Criteria

Nondirected donations, or donations by strangers, account for less than 1% of live kidney donations in the United States (NKF, 2016). Donors themselves must usually be 18 years of age or older unless a parent or guardian of a deceased minor consents to donation (OPTN, 2016a). Donors must also have written documentation of their wish to donate, such as a signed donor card or indication on their driver's license (Capron, 2014). If a deceased person did not consent to donation prior to their death, a spouse, adult child, parent, adult sibling, grandparent, or legal guardian can consent to donation (Satel et al., 2014).

Even when patients did consent to donation prior to death, their relatives may still be asked for permission, and in some cases, the relatives may deny permission (Iltis, 2015). This is one example of the many factors resulting in a shortage of organs available for donation. Less than half the families give permission to donate a relative's organs after death even when the decedent previously consented (Tenenbaum, 2016). One reason for this is because some cultures and religions forbid donating organs after death (Foos, 2012). Even if a culture or religion does not expressly forbid organ donation, some are under the false impression that their culture or religion does forbid it.

This falsehood seems to be particularly rampant among the Jewish community, many of whom believe organ donation is a **desecration of the body**; Jewish religious law is more nuanced than that. All four branches of Judaism (Orthodox, Conservative, Reform, and Reconstructionist) support and encourage donation. The Rabbinical Council of America (Orthodox) even approves organ donations from brain-dead patients (*See generally* Foos, 2012).

Zero Antigen Mismatch Rule

The question of how to distribute scarce organs presents a classic conflict between **utility**, which seeks to provide the greatest good for the greatest number, and **equity**, which seeks **fairness** for all individuals. The changes now under way are the most significant since a national allocation policy was first developed. A new allocation policy scraps rules automatically sending organs to anyone who is a perfect match on six antigens relevant to transplants (OPTN, 2016a).

One factor consistently overriding all other factors was whether there was a **zero antigen mismatch** between the transplant patient and the donated organ. A zero antigen mismatch meant the antigens all matched up, meaning the transplant patient's body was much less likely to reject the organ; in short, it was akin to a perfect match between organ and patient. If there was a patient who had a zero antigen mismatch to an available organ, that patient automatically had top priority in receiving the available organ (Richards, 2013). If there were no patients with zero antigen mismatches to the available organ, the organ went to a patient with a partial antigen match. All these zero antigen mismatches have been eliminated (OPTN, 2016a).

This so-called zero antigen mismatch rule accounted for how almost one-fifth of the donated kidneys were distributed in the United States (NKF, 2016). Because more Caucasians donate organs than any other race, this resulted in more Caucasians receiving organs because there are more likely to be zero antigen mismatches when the donor and transplant patients are of the same race. Because of this disparity, the zero antigen mismatch rule has been relaxed, which allowed more minorities to receive donated organs. In reality, the rule did little to improve kidney transplant outcomes because of advanced antirejection drugs (NKF, 2016). This is a classic example of regulatory policy failing to rapidly adapt to technological advances in medicine.

COURT DECISION
Harvesting of Body Parts

Carey v. New England Organ Bank
(Parents of Tissue Donor v. Organ Bank)
843 N.E.2d 1070 (Supreme Court of Massachusetts 2006)

Facts: A 16-year-old boy was mortally injured in a vehicle accident. About two hours after his death, his parents consented to tissue donation; however, their son's cornea and blood vessels were harvested and his tissues were unusable following saline infusions in the hospital emergency room before his death.

Issue: Were the boy's organs improperly harvested when his parents only consented to donate the tissues of their deceased son for transplant?

Holding and Decision: No. Organ and tissue banks are not required to harvest and allocate body parts according to the donor's wishes.

Analysis: The court reviewed the Uniform Anatomical Gift Act and acknowledged time is always very limited for obtaining consent and procuring body parts. Once consent for a postmortem gift is received, organ and tissue banks are not required to disclose that the donation may be unusable for specified purposes. While a cause of action may arise when organs are harvested beyond the scope of consent, the law's **good faith immunity provision** often protects organ banks. Moreover, improper harvesting claims address the right to prevent the harvesting of corpses without consent; there is no requirement that banks harvest and allocate body parts according to the donor's wishes.

Rule of Law: The Uniform Anatomical Gift Act may provide grounds for a donor's family to sue when donated body parts are used for a purpose other than their specified purpose of transplant, although organ and tissue banks may be excused from liability by good faith protections.

References discussing this court decision: Bonnie et al., 2008.

Limited Property Interest in Human Biological Material

Regardless of all these regulatory changes, and even as scientific advances lead to increased use of and demand for human organs, the body continues to take on the functional characteristics of property in the law. Most courts refuse to overturn traditional notions of a limited property interest in the human body as demonstrated by the landmark *Colavito* case.

COURT DECISION
Property Right in Donated, Cadaveric Organs

Colavito v. New York Organ Donor Network, Inc.
(Recipient of a Designated Kidney v. State Network for Organ Sharing)
486 F.3d 78 (U.S. Court of Appeals for the 2nd Circuit 2007)

Facts: A widow made a directed donation of her husband's kidney to Colavito. While awaiting implantation of the first kidney, the attending surgeon discovered the kidney had been damaged by aneurysms. Therefore, a staff member called to request the second kidney be airlifted for transplant. However, the New York Organ Donor Network informed the party that the second kidney had already been implanted in another recipient; as it turned out, the kidney was not transplanted until three days later. Instead of Colavito receiving both kidneys, one kidney was successfully transplanted in another donee. Colavito brought suit, alleging fraud and conversion in the kidney donation, and alleging the New York Organ Donor Network violated organ donor laws. As it turned out, the donated kidneys were incompatible with Colavito's immune system, although Colavito refused to concede that he could not have derived a medical benefit from the transplant.

Issue: Does either the donor or next of kin have a property right in regards to a cadaveric organ donated for transplant?

Holding and Decision: No. Neither the donor nor next-of-kin has any property rights to a donated incompatible organ.

Analysis: The court found that corpses are not recognized as property in common law. Property interests only extend to preserving and burying the corpse. Therefore, it would be against regulatory policy to recognize broad property rights in the body of a corpse.

The court reasoned there was no consensus that body parts are excluded from conversion actions, noting that the existence of property rights in body parts is a new question with very little authority and commentary. The court concluded Colavito may have been able to maintain a cause of action had the organ been compatible because, as a human organ recipient, the suit was not brought for control of the corpse and its parts but rather for the deprivation of a working organ.

In short, the court argued Colavito may have had a legal claim based on the loss of a functioning organ if the organ would have otherwise medically benefited him. The court adhered to the common law rule and refused to identify or forecast the circumstances in which someone might have actionable rights in the corpse or organ of a deceased person.

Rule of Law: No one can have a property right in a corpse; next of kin only have a common law right to possess the corpse for the purposes of burying it and a corresponding duty to do so.

References discussing this court decision: *E.g.*, Hain, 2015; Terrell, 2014.

In Reality: How Organ Procurement and Transplants Occur

Historically, organs were recovered from patients who suffered **cardiac death** (meaning the victim was no longer breathing, had no pulse, and the heart could not be revived). This often meant that by the time their organs could be transplanted, they could no longer be used because they had been without a blood and oxygen supply for so long that they would be unlikely to function in the recipients (Saitta-Gill & Hodge, 2015). In 1968, the medical community redefined death to include **brain death** which occurs when the brain is no longer functioning, despite the body being sustained by drugs and machines (Williams et al., 2014). This means organs can be transplanted earlier, or before they suffer blood and oxygen deprivation, making them much more likely to be viable.

The concept of brain death has been described as *at once well settled and persistently unresolved* (*E.g.*, Dolgin, 2016). Use of brain death has, however, led to the rampant misunderstanding that patients who might otherwise survive might be *killed* for their organs, something unconditionally prohibited. Although organs transplanted from a brain-dead patient are more likely to be useful, only 1 to 2% of patients who die in hospital are declared brain dead (Capron, 2014).

Deaths occurring outside of a hospital setting generally do not result in usable transplant organs because organs need a continuous supply of blood and oxygen in order to be transplantable. Some transplant centers still do not consider transplanting organs from patients who are older than 65 or who have high blood pressure, even though studies have shown organs from these "less than perfect" patients can be successfully transplanted. This factor further contributes to the short supply of usable transplant organs.

This is also why the transplant community wants to do more for living donors such as providing health insurance and reimbursing them for their time. At the same time, there is significant disagreement about how far medicine should go in encouraging patients to donate organs. Disagreements extend to living and **postmortem donations**.

Access to Organs

As illustrated in **TABLE 25-1**, organ transplants are expensive procedures, available only to those who have health insurance and private funds. Many health insurance policies do not cover the full cost of a transplant, which then must be paid out of pocket.

Kidney Transplants

Kidney transplants are the most frequently performed organ transplant and the least expensive transplant procedures (OPTN & STRT, 2016b). This can be expected since the diseases with a high predisposition to end-stage renal disease are diabetes and hypertension, which are tied to the nation's obesity epidemic (Tenenbaum, 2016). It is debatable whether

TABLE 25-1 Estimated Average First-Year Billed Charges per Transplant

Transplant	Procurement	Hospital	Physician	Evaluation	Follow-Up	Immunosuppressants	Total
Double lung only	$133,100	$419,500	$85,700	$51,500	$169,600	$48,600	$907,900
Heart only	$146,400	$624,400	$65,500	$37,300	$151,500	$47,900	$1,073,000
Heart-lung	$249,100	$819,200	$92,500	$43,000	$171,700	$50,000	$1,425,000
Intestine only	$122,900	$981,300	$141,900	$67,900	$128,000	$38,100	$1,480,000
Kidney only	$95,000	$121,400	$35,000	$23,800	$78,200	$48,100	$401,400
Kidney-heart	$241,400	$682,800	$65,500	$37,300	$151,500	$57,200	$1,235,800
Kidney-pancreas	$202,800	$196,000	$40,100	$24,000	$78,700	$59,900	$600,400
Liver only	$96,000	$404,100	$109,900	$42,200	$144,200	$50,700	$846,400
Liver-intestine	$219,200	$1,098,800	$141,900	$67,900	$144,200	$57,500	$1,723,500
Liver-kidney	$278,700	$523,000	$109,900	$42,200	$144,200	$60,600	$1,070,200
Liver-pancreas-intestine	$327,000	$957,400	$141,900	$67,900	$144,200	$57,200	$1,695,500
Pancreas only	$107,800	$175,400	$40,100	$23,900	$78,700	$59,300	$484,300
Pancreas-intestine	$230,700	$955,800	$141,900	$67,900	$128,000	$57,700	$1,581,800
Single lung only	$65,800	$341,000	$54,100	$32,600	$106,900	$49,700	$651,700

Note: Where the itemized charges were inconsistent from the data sources, the billed charges were averaged. The total billed charges were generally consistent across the data sources. All charges were calculated to future values for 2016.

Data from Analogous Blood and Marrow Treatment Registry, International Bone Marrow Transplant Registry, National Marrow Donor Program, Organ Procurement and Transplantation Network, Scientific Registry of Transplant Recipients, United Network for Organ Sharing, U.S. Renal Data System.

the comparatively high number of kidney-only transplants is a factor in driving down the charges per transplant. A typical 25-year-old diabetic will gain an extra 8.7 years of life from a transplant, while a typical 55-year-old diabetic will gain 3.6 extra years (NKF, 2016).

Regardless of age, most individuals with end-stage renal disease are covered under Medicare's end-stage renal disease program. The cost of lifetime dialysis or, for individuals who receive kidney transplants, the costs of the transplants and three years of follow-up care including immunosuppressive drugs needed to sustain the transplants are covered by Medicare insurance. Although end-stage renal disease can be treated through other renal replacement therapies, kidney transplants are generally accepted as the best treatment both for quality of life and cost-effectiveness (NKF, 2016).

Medicare insurance has been paying in excess of $32 billion in end-stage renal disease-related costs each year, or about $65,000 per person (NKF, 2016). A debatable issue is whether Medicare insurance should continue paying for most adult kidney transplants in the United States when the underlying diseases leading to the need for transplants are usually caused by lifestyle choices. This question is directly related to the high incidence in transplant failures from one year to three years due to treatment noncompliance and continued unhealthy habits (Tenenbaum, 2016). As discussed, the new United Network for Organ Sharing policy relies significantly, though not exclusively, on net benefit, which seeks to give kidneys first to those who will benefit most from them (Beard & Leitzel, 2014). This would favor recipients who have more years to gain from a new organ, meaning individuals with healthier lifestyles and who have demonstrated compliance with their treatments plans (Fleck, 2014).

Heart Transplants

Every year about 500 patients on the National Organ Donor Registry's wait list die before a heart is made available. Thousands more die because they are considered too old or sick to get on the list. Many of these patients could be saved if transplant centers were less particular about the quality of donor hearts. In response to this need, more hospitals are starting **alternate heart programs** that provide lower quality hearts to older and sicker patients. While about 2,000 hearts are transplanted each year, an additional 3,000 are offered by families of the deceased and are rejected (OPTN & STRT, 2016b). These 3,000 hearts are often rejected because they are not top quality, and the hearts were consequently buried or cremated with their original owners. Estimates are that half the rejected hearts are suitable for transplanting (O'Brien, 2015).

One limitation to establishing alternate heart programs is that insurers scrutinize success rates at each transplant center to decide whether they will cover transplant operations performed there. If a transplant center accepts too many sick recipients or individuals over the age of 65, its success rate will go down and health insurers may refuse to pay for its treatment procedures. Heart transplants, which cost patients upwards of $600,000, are a profit generator at many hospitals (OPTN & STRT, 2016b). This is one reason alternate heart programs are usually only found at major teaching hospitals like the UCLA Medical Center, which can afford to accept donor hearts that either require bypass surgery prior to transplant or originate from older donors.

While UCLA was the nation's first alternate heart program to offer transplants to seniors with end-stage heart failure, other teaching hospitals have developed similar programs (Satel & Hippen, 2007). Alternate heart recipients do somewhat worse than top-quality heart recipients, but still do fairly well in comparison to how they would have done with no heart transplant at all. The United Network for Organ Sharing will often find no takers for alternate hearts, and that is where UCLA and other transplant centers with alternate donor lists come in. After everyone else says no, the United Network will call an alternate heart program and look for a patient to accept the lower quality heart (Noah, 2013). Patients on the alternate list must agree they will not ordinarily be eligible for a heart from the regular list. This leaves another dilemma for the medical community: how far should transplant centers go in using lower quality organs?

Anencephalic Neonates

One of the earliest controversies surrounding organ donation involved **anencephalic neonates**.[LN2] Anencephalic neonates are babies who are born nearly brain dead, with the exception of minor electrical activity. They have no possibility of living a life beyond the vegetative state within which they are born and are permanently unconscious. They do not feel pain due to the lack of cerebral function. Most, in fact, die within days of birth (*See generally* CDC, 2015; Gilman, 2012).

In order to donate organs, there must be either total brain death or cardiac death (Shuster, 2014). An anencephalic neonate cannot be declared dead either way (Gilman, 2012). If their life support machines are turned off and death occurs naturally, their organs are no longer usable because of the time it takes death to occur and the damage to their fragile organs in the meantime (CDC, 2015). The American Medical Association was originally of the opinion that it was ethically acceptable to transplant the organs of such infants even before they were technically dead as long as there was parental consent and certain other safeguards were followed, but they withdrew that opinion due to controversy (Gilman, 2012).

HIV-Positive Transplant Candidates

There is public controversy over whether HIV-positive transplant candidates should receive organs, even if they have no symptoms and are not in the end stage of the disease. While positive HIV status was once thought to be a relative or even absolute contraindication to receiving a transplant, the United Network for Organ Sharing does not bar HIV-positive patients from receiving organs. HIV-positive patients argue their status is at least equal to other transplant patients who previously received transplants but whose bodies rejected the organs, or to transplant patients with other diseases such as hepatitis or diabetes, or to elderly transplant patients (White, 2016). With the advent of antiretroviral drugs, those infected with HIV are now living longer and dying from illnesses other than **Acquired Immunodeficiency Syndrome (AIDS)**.

Recent transplant studies have demonstrated results comparable to those of recipients without HIV infection (*See* Saitta-Gill & Hodge, 2015). Still, a number of issues persist regarding ethics, patient selection, postoperative management, and drug interactions between antiretroviral and immunosuppressant agents. Some transplant centers often refuse to list HIV-positive patients in the National Organ Donor Registry's wait list; this is so even though some HIV-positive patients have the disease through no fault of their own, such as those who were born with the disease or who contracted it through violence or medical error. Since 2013, when the federal HIV Organ Policy Equity Act was enacted, only HIV-positive patients are eligible to receive HIV-positive organs (*See* 42 U.S.C.A. § 274(b)(3)(A)).

These and other controversies over the way organs are allocated have led to the suggestion that potential survivability should be the only criteria for selecting transplant recipients. Some states have gone as far as to reject the federal regulations. These states have enacted their own state legislation in an attempt to maintain local geographic preferences for organ transplants by restricting organ donors from donating their organs out of state (*See generally* White, 2016).

Alternative Procurement of Organs

Several alternatives to xenotransplants are immediately available to enhance organ procurement and increase organ supply. Federal and state governments are considering alternatives such as **mandated choice**, which would force everyone to choose whether or not they want to be a donor, or **presumed consent**, which would assume everyone wants to be a donor unless they indicate otherwise.

While stem cell therapies and xenotransplants offer future alternatives for organ enhancement or supply, neither is without controversy (Crepelle, 2016). Both alternatives pose greater risk to human health since they are both emerging medical procedures without guaranteed success. Further controversy surrounds how organs for transplant are sometimes obtained. Many states have laws allowing any organ to be removed from a cadaver without consent as long as an attempt was made to contact the family. California and Idaho are two such states. Other states allow for the removal of specified items as long as no objection is actually known, whether or not an attempt to notify the family was made. Missouri, Arkansas, and Colorado are three such states. The Uniform Anatomical Gift Act allows a donor to specify a recipient, a regulatory policy adopted to encourage more donations (OPTN, 2016a).

Presumed Consent or Opt-Out

Presumed consent systems, common in Europe and Eastern Asia, provide that organs will be automatically donated at death, unless stated otherwise (Kessler & Roth, 2012). This method is often called an **opt-out plan** because persons who do not wish to donate their organs upon death must opt out during life. The advantage of this system is an increase in the available supply of organs (Wharton, 2011). However, there is some opposition to the practice of silence as consent.

Mandated Choice

Mandated choice is very similar to presumed consent except that under mandated choice individuals must either opt in or opt out; there is no presumption of opting in (Orenstein & Bettini, 2014). The advantage of this system is greater personal autonomy, the lack of which is the main criticism of presumed consent. Similar to the presumed consent method, it places the burden on individuals to think about organ donations. The largest criticism of mandated choice is the cost of coordinating a national system, since everyone's organ donation preference would have to be recorded and followed (Beard & Leitzel, 2014).

Internet Solicitation

Another approach to organ procurement involves communication between potential donors and recipients through Internet-based chat rooms and websites (Saitta-Gill & Hodge, 2015). The website MatchingDonors.com and a free message board at livingdonorsonline.org have allowed individuals in need of organs to meet and chat with others who are willing to be living organ donors. The idea remains controversial because it raises questions about potential commercialism and donor compensation.

MatchingDonors.com, created in 2004, is a for-profit Internet business with over 5,100 organ recipients registered. Several hundred recipients are from the United States. Potential donors determine who the most deserving person is for their organ based on information provided by potential recipients.

Live Organ Swaps and Paired Living Donations

There are also organizations, such as **LifeSharers**, designed to improve transplant candidates' chances of receiving an organ by requiring members to agree to donate organs to other members before the general public. LifeSharers has over 9,000 members. These organizations argue it is not fair to give organs to patients who have not also agreed to donate their own organs should the opportunity arise. LifeSharers points out organ donors themselves receive only about 30% of donated organs, whereas the remaining 70% go to non-donors.

Kidney swaps are one newly popular but complex method for doing so. Also known as **kidney-paired donation**, the process connects an incompatible donor-recipient pair such as a husband and wife or a parent and child with another incompatible donor-recipient pair. The healthy member of each pair donates a kidney to the person who is the medical match in the other pair, and the surgeries are performed simultaneously so one healthy donor cannot back out after their loved one receives a kidney. Sometimes the swaps involve as many as five pairs. The first swap of this kind actually occurred in 2000 and several hundred have occurred since then. At least three paired kidney organizations foster this method of allocating kidneys:

- Alliance for Paired Donation
- New England Organ Bank
- North American Paired Donation Network

(Meckler, 2007b).

Regulatory Changes

The slow initial growth of **paired organ donations** reflected concerns that trades might violate a federal ban on selling organs. However, Congress passed Norwood in 2007 clarifying that such arrangements are legal. It is estimated there are as many as 4,000 kidney exchanges per year (NKF, 2016), a big addition to the kidney transplants performed every year involving living donors. Still, this is not nearly enough organs to satisfy the need for kidney transplants. As interest in kidney swaps grows, logistical, medical, ethical, and legal questions are emerging.

One of the fundamental issues is who should get priority on a match (Tenenbaum, 2016). A donor with blood type O, for instance, can give to patients of any blood type and might match with hundreds of pairs. In the early days of kidney swaps, transplant surgeons matched pairs using a pen and paper or by moving magnetic pieces around on a board. Today, computer experts, working with economists and clinical researchers, are optimizing matches to enable the greatest number of organ transplants (Wharton, 2011). Mathematical techniques from major league baseball schedules, airline departures, and online driving directions are being used. The days when federal regulations allocated scarce organs based on a list of evolving technical criteria are over. The goal of many is to develop a national paired kidney network (White, 2016).

Federal and State Innovations

The federal government established a program to reimburse living donors for expenses including travel, lodging, and meals (OPTN & STRT, 2016b). States are also experimenting with how to increase cadaveric and live donor rates with more than a dozen states offering tax deductions to help defray expenses (Underhill, 2016). Wisconsin gives state tax breaks of up to $10,000 to benefit organ donors for expenses such as travel, hotel bills, and lost wages. Pennsylvania has a fund from voluntary donations when state residents apply for driver's licenses or vehicle registration; the fund provides up to $3,000 per cadaveric donor to help with hospital, medical, and funeral expenses. In both instances, the expenses are paid directly to providers to avoid conflicting with the ban on payment for organs.

Some states propose mandates requiring all organ donors to have lifetime insurance coverage; others propose that Medicare insurance cover all organ donors. Both proposals could serve as an inducement (Capron, 2014). Most recently, South Carolina introduced legislation that would shorten the term of prisoners' sentences if they chose to donate an organ. Other ideas include tax credits, tuition vouchers, deposits in retirement accounts, and recognition of tax deductions for charitable contributions. All these could be offered in a regulated environment overseen by tax authorities. The savings from dialysis could be used to underwrite the various types of compensation. According to the Congressional Budget Office, Norwood alone will save almost $500 million in Medicare insurance costs over 10 years (Williams, 2014).

Compelled Donations

Advances in immunology and the growing ability to circumvent rejection of transplanted organs are slowly replacing the need for compelled donations (AMA, 2011). The focus has turned to anonymous donations, which again brings to the fore the place where strangers go to transact business: the market. Still, every year, organs are harvested from minors and mentally incompetent adults who neither voluntarily donate their organs nor consent to the surgical procedure (Longo, 2011). **Compelled living donations** from children and incompetent persons are the least desired forms of organ donation (Coleman, 2014). Since living donations generally involve kidneys, part of a liver, or bone marrow, donation does not involve serious physical harm to donors. However, the physical pain or risks to the donor should not be minimized, especially in the case of kidney or liver donations, which are major surgeries involving general anesthesia. Also, in the case of kidney donation, donors are left with only one kidney, which puts them at a greater risk for kidney complications in the future. Siblings are usually the best donors for reasons including matching blood types and relative ages of the donor and recipient. Sometimes the best possible match, and maybe the only possible match, will be the recipient's incompetent sibling (Ouellette, 2010).

Incompetency is defined as a lack of legal ability in some respect. Looking to a variety of factors, courts determine whether a person is legally incompetent. Generally, organ donations from living minors are only permitted if the donor is above the age of 12 or 13 (Coleman, 2014). Children under the age of 18 are generally considered legally incompetent and cannot independently provide consent to donate their organs or tissues.

Cognitively impaired children are considered legally incompetent if born severely cognitively impaired or if born healthy but become severely cognitively impaired before age 18. Legal competency is disputable if a child is close to 18 before becoming severely cognitively impaired. Incompetence can vary among persons from severe and profoundly impaired, to mild and less impaired. When incompetence is severe, individuals will have limited awareness of their surroundings and will often have serious medical conditions. The severity of incompetence can therefore vary significantly and should be considered (Coleman, 2014).

Generally courts use substituted judgment reasoning to determine whether the best interests of potential donors are being met (Sabatello, 2014). Most family requests are resolved at the lower court level in favor of donation with few decisions appealed, thus there is a paucity of reported cases. In an attempt to address donor coercion, organ transplant teams have long allowed potential donors to opt out of donation by providing faux medical excuses that are intended to shield donors from external pressures, real or perceived, to donate (Coleman, 2014).

Creation of Child Donors Through Assisted Reproductive Technologies

Parents sometimes conceive another child for the purpose of donating bone marrow to an older sibling in need of a human leukocyte antigen match. Whether this is a legally or ethically sound practice remains unclear. It is clear that there is no legal obligation for siblings to donate. The practice of procuring tissue and organs from children drastically changed when it became possible to use **assistive reproductive techniques** primarily for the purpose of a child becoming an organ donor. **Preimplantation genetic diagnosis** and **in vitro fertilization** (IVF) can be used to conceive a child who is a perfect antigen match for an older sibling. **Stem cells** from the child's umbilical cord blood can be harvested from the newborn at birth and transplanted into the older sibling. This controversial technique has been used in only about 2,000 children because:

- Cord blood is in short supply.
- The process is time consuming.
- The procedure is expensive.
- There are only about 50 reproductive centers worldwide offering the technique.

(McClean, 2016).

Despite the limited use of this procedure, it is likely to be used extensively in the near future to conceive child donors as the costs decrease, as technological advances in assistive reproductive techniques are made, and as the number of reproductive centers offering the procedure increases. Just as the history of organ donation has rapidly evolved, so likely will the use of assistive reproductive techniques to create child donors. Healthy cord blood donors hold great promise to treat those with **Fanconi anemia, leukemia, thalassemia, Hurler syndrome**, and other diseases causing the immune system and bone marrow to fail.[LN3]

What is perhaps more worrisome than using assistive reproductive techniques more extensively in the future to create perfectly human leukocyte antigen-matched child donors is the fact that younger siblings might be asked to donate their bone marrow if the stem cell transplants are unsuccessful. If a bone marrow transplant fails for any reason, they may be asked to donate other tissues and organs. In fact, children conceived via assistive reproductive techniques combined with in vitro fertilization and preimplantation genetic diagnosis for human leukocyte antigen-matching could be asked to serve as donors for their ailing siblings throughout their entire lives.

Procurement Protections for Compelled Donors

The current legal framework under which compelled donations occur may not adequately protect children and the cognitively impaired unless several standards are followed. Most important, a guardian *ad litem* should always be appointed to look out for the interests of compelled donors. Many courts require family and independent counseling to ensure parents understand the dynamics and depth of their actions and the potential long-term consequences. Often, independent physicians are appointed for the prospective compelled donors to avoid conflicts of interest. Ideally, a statement should be issued to the court from the donor as to why they desire to participate as an organ or tissue donor. Restricting compelled donations may reduce the pool of viable organs, and other solutions may have to be sought. However, limiting the pool of incompetent donors will necessitate and hopefully force a reconsideration of the altruistically based procurement regimen (Goodwin, 2007).

Lengthening Post-Transplant Organ Survival

A variety of techniques prevent injury that results from temporary arterial blockage and restoration of blood flow to transplanted organs. Rejection of the donor organ or tissue is also preventable through the use of a variety of tissue and molecular manipulations before the transplant occurs. Medicare provides insurance coverage for most organ transplants; however, coverage of immunosuppressant drugs ends 36 to 44 months after transplant surgery or when the patient reaches adulthood (OPTN & STRT, 2016b). Many patients, especially young adults, cannot afford to pay for these maintenance drugs without health insurance (Tenenbaum, 2016). Transplant patients who lose their insurance coverage are more likely to stop taking necessary antirejection drugs, and not taking the drugs increases the risk of losing the transplanted organs due to organ failure or other complications (Frank, 2014).

Immunosuppressive drugs that prevent organ rejection can be as high as $60,000 for the first year following a transplant. This represents a significant financial burden for families, even if insured, because of co-payment obligations. If families cannot afford the drugs, it can mean losing the transplanted organ or even death. Outcomes for children whose families are uninsured are very poor (Strong, 2014). The cost of failed organ transplants is also high. Functioning transplants are 10 times less expensive to maintain than the costs involved in the years following a failure; the cost of returning to dialysis after a transplant failure averages $89,000 annually (USRDS, 2015). This is one reason proposals are emerging to provide lifetime medical coverage for organ transplant recipients; it would be cost-effective and would prolong patients' longevity and their productivity.

There are **black market drugs** available through an underground network run by transplant patients with the cooperation of sympathetic health care workers and overlooked by law enforcement. They simply give drugs away to patients who cannot afford immunosuppressant drugs. Their sources include patients who have changed drug regimens and contribute their old medicines, some drug manufacturers, and drugs scavenged and unused from the dead and passed on to the underground. There is probably an illicit underground in every major metropolitan area (Weinstock, 2014).

Tissue Transplantation

Human tissue is anything donated from the human body that is not a vital organ. Blood vessels, bone, bone marrow, connective tissues such as tendons and cartilage, corneas, heart valves, and skin are common types of tissues used for transplants to help patients in many different types of surgeries (OPTN & STRT, 2016b). Transplantation of musculoskeletal tissues is the most common medical procedure, including skin tissue replacements to treat burns, bone to facilitate spinal fusions, and tendons to reconstruct knee ligaments and repair joint and limb injuries (Saitta-Gill & Hodge, 2015). It also includes implantation of brain matter, hematopoietic stem/progenitor cells derived from peripheral and cord blood, oocytes, and semen (McClean, 2016).

U.S. Navy Tissue Bank

The first tissue bank was established by the U.S. Navy in 1949 to deal with war injuries and remained the primary tissue bank in the United States for almost 30 years. Scientists at the Navy Tissue Bank pioneered many of the commercial standards followed today:

- Cryopreservation, freeze drying, and irradiation sterilization of tissue
- Documentation and clinical evaluation of tissues
- Establishment of a graph register
- Identification of appropriate donor criteria for tissue donation
- Immunological principles of tissue transplants, including cadaveric bone marrow recovery and immunosuppressive protocols
- Procurement and processing methods

The Navy was also instrumental in establishing the National Marrow Donor Program and the American Association of Tissue Banks. Although the Navy Tissue Bank ceased operations after 50 years, it pioneered the establishment of regional tissue banks. Similar to blood banks, they provided the human tissue necessary to meet the demands of their local communities.

Current Context

The practice of tissue transplantation has grown quickly; its visibility and ability to escape government overregulation has allowed it to separate itself from organ transplants. This new visibility has come with the rise of for-profit tissue banks that process, transform, package, and store tissue for years before distribution for transplants, unlike organs that are transported quickly and rarely change form before getting to a recipient (Williams, 2015). With the growth of tissue transplants, it has been easy for human tissue to be **commoditized** and turned into valuable medical products. As the market expanded, the regional tissue banks began to distribute outside of their local communities. The 1990s saw an expansion and consolidation in the tissue industry as the large for-profit tissue banks moved to control more than half of the tissue bank business (Townsley, 2015). Today, the typical tissue donation chain is as follows:

- Organ procurement agencies meet with the donor's family in order to get consent for tissue removal and then procure the tissue at a hospital (most of the recoveries occur in hospital operating rooms) or morgue; recoveries are often made at multiple sites.
- Organ procurement agencies then give the recovered tissue to a processor and collect recovery fees.
- **Tissue processors** process the transplantable tissue into marketable tissue products and then distribute the processed tissue products to marketing agencies and collect processing fees.
- Marketing agencies sell the processed tissue products to hospitals and physicians for transplantation and collect distribution fees.
- Hospitals and physicians then transplant the processed tissue products into patients and collect medical fees.

(*See* Townsley, 2015; Williams, 2015).

Some of the most important technological advances in the tissue industry have occurred because of for-profit tissue processors. Over the course of two decades, the tissue industry has evolved from a $20 million industry to a multibillion-dollar industry with double-digit growth.

Regulatory Oversight of Human Tissue

When the **tissue bank industry** emerged, federal regulations were nonexistent. Even though tissue transplantations are similar to organ transplantations, the two entities are treated completely differently. Traditionally, organs have been thoroughly regulated by the federal government and individual state governments. The same cannot be said for human tissue (Williams et al., 2014). Until 1993, the idea of regulating the tissue industry was foreign. The government did not have regulations for tissue banks until the 1990s, when it was discovered there was a need to protect the public from the possibility of transmitting disease through tissue transplants. Even with this pressing need, it still took years to enact regulations.

Today, human tissue is regulated by the Center for Biologics Evaluation and Research (*See* 21 C.F.R. §§ 1270-1271). The federal regulations act as a base for the state regulations to stand on. The regulations created by the states require that tissue banks comply with federal regulations, but often the state regulations appear more specific and better enforced. The states appear to give additional protection and instructions to tissue banks than the federal regulations do. Florida, New York, Maryland, and California have enacted their own state regulations and standards for tissue banks that operate in their states. In addition, the **American Association of Tissue Banks** has its own voluntary regulations and accreditation guidelines for all tissue banks. In order to legally comply with federal regulations, tissue banks must register with the U.S. Food and Drug Administration. Many do not register, and thus exist under the radar of government supervision (Williams et al., 2014).

American Association of Tissue Banks

The American Association of Tissue Banks accredits tissue banks with higher standards than the FDA or state laws require. Created in 1976, the Association works through regional and local tissue banks to ensure the availability of a safe, adequate, and economical supply of tissues and cells for medical procedures and research, as it seeks to:

- Create a forum for scientific exchange
- Encourage human tissue donation
- Ensure quality standards
- Promote ethical standards throughout the tissue industry
- Secure an adequate supply of transplantable human tissue

(American Association of Tissue Banks, 2012; Neal, 2012).

While most of the major U.S. tissue banks are accredited, fewer than 100 of the 2,000 tissue banks registered with the FDA are actually accredited (Williams, 2015). When a tissue bank is in the process of accreditation, inspectors visit the bank and review its on-site operations and procedures. Tissue banks that do not meet the Association standards are denied accreditation. Tissue banks are accredited for three years.

The Association also develops technical standards for recovery and preservation of human tissues. Specific areas cover screening for communicable diseases, tissue labeling, qualification of tissue bank personnel, safety practices, equipment testing, and facilities for tissue storage. The FDA and the Association work together to address tissue bank donor selection criteria, quality processing, and record-keeping in an attempt to keep infectious tissue out of circulation (FDA, 2014). Neither the FDA nor the Association concerns itself with distribution issues in the tissue industry; allocations are market driven.

Biosynthetic Tissues

Biosynthetic tissues, including synthetic skin and bone substitutes, are viable alternatives to traditional human transplant materials. Numerous restrictions, however, such as the technical limitations associated with engineering complex tissues so as to duplicate their innate function in vivo, currently limit their use outside major teaching hospitals (Weinstock, 2014). As a result, the leading potential solution to this shortage for the foreseeable future is xenotransplantation (*See generally* Hagen & Gittens, 2008).

Xenotransplants

Fewer than 5% of the human organs needed are actually made accessible for transplant. This disparity between need and availability has led medical researchers to consider the possibility of animal-to-human transplants, or xenotransplants. Strictly regulated by the FDA, xenotransplantation involves any procedure that transplants, implants, or infuses into a human one of the following:

- Live cells, tissues, or organs from a nonhuman animal source
- Human body fluids, cells, tissues, or organs that have had ex vivo contact with live nonhuman animal cells, tissues, or organs

A medical practice endorsed by the President's Council on Bioethics, xenotransplants are used to treat certain diseases such as neurodegenerative disorders, liver failure, and diabetes where human body parts are not usually available (President's Council, 2004). While the transplant, implantation, or infusion into a human recipient of cells, tissues, or organs from an animal source has been occurring in some fashion for over 100 years, it often results in rejection by the body's immune system (Crepelle, 2016).

In order to minimize the rejection of xenotransplants, the possibility of using part-human organs, tissues, and cells, such as pig hearts containing human DNA, for transplantation is actively being explored. Xenotransplants, developed in the late 20th century simultaneously with the use of artificial organs, calls into question the once clear distinction between human and animal life (Westphal, 2006). As human genes are introduced into mammals such as pigs to make the animals' organs more acceptable to the human body for the purposes of organ transplants, this scientific development blurs distinctions. These technologies are expensive and have lower success rates than human organ donation, so they are unlikely to comprise many organ transplants in the near future.

Oversight of Safety and Effectiveness

For over 20 years, the National Institutes of Health publicly disclosed summary safety and effectiveness data for studies related to xenotransplants (Crepelle, 2016). In 2001, proposed rules were made to extend this same level of disclosure to the FDA's regulation of xenotransplants, given the concerns about protecting animals and humans from cross-species diseases, known as **zoonoses**. However, the rules were never finalized. The concern is that communicable diseases, or the infectious agents that cause them, might move from animals to humans through xenotransplants (Spillman & Sade, 2007). An edifice of exemptions has protected confidential commercial information about xenotransplants from disclosure to the public. At the same time, the larger question of whether commercial interests should automatically take priority over public health concerns is strongly debated (Lurie & Zieve, 2006).

Most current xenotransplant research focuses on the pig as an organ donor because of its size and commonalities with humans in some physiological pathways. New strategies are being examined for their ability to prevent rejection of organ allograft. The goal of preventing rejection of donor tissue is to selectively suppress the immune response to the organ while retaining normal immune response to pathogens.

Techniques to accomplish this selective immune suppression are expected to improve in the future as medical researchers gain and apply new knowledge about immune function from the results of the Human Genome Project (Pippin, 2013). A number of potential methods are under consideration and are being pursued. These include:

- Modification of the donor to increase its compatibility with the recipient
- Organ and clonal T-cell deletion
- Transplant of bone marrow (as a source of precursor donor T cells)

(*See* Brody, 2015; Pippin, 2013).

The latter is considered the most successful medical treatment, with transgenic techniques used to introduce genes for recipient surface antigens. Efforts to produce transgenic animals such as pigs altered with human DNA are under way in the hopes of tricking the human body into accepting the animal organ (Brody, 2015). The goal is to create **partially humanized organs** to use as spare parts for humans. A number of additional issues must be overcome before xenotransplantation becomes widespread. For instance, organs and tissues from animal sources may carry endogenous retroviruses, which must be identified and removed (Macintosh, 2015). Additionally, the ethics surrounding the use of animals for human benefit must be explored and resolved. Nevertheless, xenotransplants of nerve tissue are currently used to treat patients with Parkinson's disease.

Xenotransplant Tourism

One resulting problem is xenotransplants occurring in countries with no regulatory oversight. Patients seeking xenotransplant procedures visit countries like Mexico, Cambodia, Laos, and Myanmar for controversial treatments that can be exceedingly dangerous (Cortez, 2008). Moreover, xenotransplant tourism by patients willing to pay for unproven interventions in countries without adequate controls risks global dissemination of new pathogens and may undermine this fledgling field just as it is emerging (Delmonico, 2011).

Alternative Strategies for Developing Organ and Tissue Replacements

Current research efforts can be divided into four areas:

- Development of new organs, taking advantage of advances in stem cell biology, genetic engineering, and tissue engineering
- Improvement in medical devices to replace organ functions
- Methods for improving organ and tissue preservation during transport from donor to recipient
- Procedures for lengthening postimplantation survival of the organ and the recipient

While engineering of replacement tissues now uses large-scale tissue cultures, research is extending relatively crude current cell and tissue culture techniques to better determine the conditions required to create organ systems in vitro. Matrices and factors controlling tissue architecture outside the human body are continuously enhanced. Research laboratories and the medical products industry are actively trying to create skin, blood vessels, cartilage, bone, and corneas through similar tissue engineering techniques (Strong, 2014). Other efforts in less-advanced stages include windpipe, kidney, pancreas, liver, and heart tissue (Weinstock, 2014). Tissue engineering has seen a number of ups and downs in the 20 years since its inception.

Initial success at growing tissues in labs and in small animals led researchers to declare success too early. As soon as the same tissues were tested in larger animal models, it became clear that size is one of the significant limiting factors in tissue engineering; the thicker the tissue one aims to grow, the harder it is to create. Use of undifferentiated **pluripotent stem cells** and other undifferentiated cells is extending the possibilities for tissue culture. Further research is occurring on stem cell isolation and culture, while identification of cell surface markers allows for easier isolation of stem cells. In addition, the conditions required for stem cell differentiation are being identified, including signaling pathways, transcription factors, and gene activation sequences (*See generally* Morad, 2012).

Moving Altruism Forward

Competing legal and social interests surround the transplant of human organs in the United States. As medical advances have made organ transplants easier and more successful, questions arise:

- Are living donations ethical?
- Should organ donors be compensated similarly to those who donate plasma or reproductive material?
- Which patient should be the priority when an organ becomes available: the sickest and the one suffering the most, or the healthiest and the most likely to survive, or the one who has been waiting the longest?
- Who should receive the limited supply of transplantable organs?

Equal and fair access to the few other goods or services (if any) there is is as highly controversial as access to health care, particularly access to transplantable organs. Health care is perhaps the only service Americans view as something beyond a commodity. Rather, health care is viewed as something everyone should have access to. The question becomes, then, if basic economic concepts are not an appropriate way to distribute scarce transplantable organs, what is the best way to do so?

Now that Congress has clarified the National Organ Transplantation Act through Norwood, the next move might be to change the prohibition against rewarding those who decide to donate their organs or families who donate the deceased member's organs. The current procurement system demands altruism as the sole legitimate motivation for donation of human biological material. However, altruism is not producing the number of organ donors necessary to keep pace with the ever-increasing number of wait-listed patients, many of whom die while waiting. The current altruistic system of organ procurement, which relies primarily on cadaveric donors, does not take into account today's technological advances.

Organ procurement policies based on a transplant system relying exclusively on living related donors has evolved into a system that now relies heavily on cadaveric organs and living unrelated donors. **No-sale policies** are now one of the principal causes of the ongoing organ shortage (Meckler, 2007a). Transplant policies have not kept pace with medical technology or the realities of the marketplace. While altruistic procurement of organs is not meeting the growing demand for transplantable organs, there is not sufficient moral certainty to warrant allowing marketplace approaches to organ transplants (Wharton, 2011).[LN4] The idea of combining organ donation with material gain can make some patients uneasy, yet the mix of financial and altruistic motives is common. Few object to tax credits for charitable contributions. An increase in the supply of organs could prevent needless suffering and death. It could be argued this is more important than whether an organ has been given freely or for material gain.

LAW FACT

Medicaid Insurance Coverage for a Liver Transplant

Must a state's taxpayers pay for a liver transplant to cure a hereditary disease if the disease can be treated by dietary management?

Yes. The harm to an individual life and health clearly outweighs any fiscal harm a state may suffer. Notwithstanding the fact that lifelong dietary management is an option for maple syrup urine disease sufferers, the United Network for Organ Sharing ranks children with classical symptoms as high-priority liver transplant candidates because of the neurological burden and risks of the disease.

— *J. D. v. Sherman*, 2006 U.S.Dist.LEXIS 78446 (U.S. District Court for the Western District of Missouri, Central Division 2006).

CHAPTER SUMMARY

- Organ transplants date back to the late 1800s, although more recent scientific advances have made the process much more likely to be successful and have expanded the kinds of transplantations that can be accomplished, leading to a higher demand for transplantable organs across the board.
- The demand for transplantable organs far exceeds the supply. Of the nearly 120,000 patients awaiting organ donations, approximately 70% are awaiting kidneys. This is leading the federal and state governments to consider incentivizing donations.
- Patients wait an average of 5 years for a transplant, and every day 21 patients die waiting. Despite the fact that most Americans approve of organ donation, only about 25% expressly declare themselves donors.
- The National Organ Transplantation Act makes it illegal to sell human organs and established the Organ Procurement and Transplantation Network, which administers the organ transplant process. However, other methods of allocating organs have appeared such as LifeSharers, paired-kidney swaps, and making use of lower quality donor organs.
- Although the Organ Procurement and Transplantation Network makes the recipient patient selection process more fair and equitable through the establishment of standardized criteria, it has been criticized for not regulating transplant centers more closely in order to ensure they adhere to the regulations.
- Organs are allocated based upon a point system that considers how long the patient has been on the list and the urgency of the patient's medical status, as well as criteria matching an available organ to a patient on the list, such as blood types.
- Organ donations come from those with written documentation prior to death of their wish to donate, or those whose family members consent to donation after death. Even when there is written documentation of a desire to donate, in some states family members may withdraw permission after death and prevent donation. In other states, donation will proceed as long as there is no known objection. New methods of procurement are under consideration, including presumed consent, opting out, and mandated choice.
- Before organs can be removed from a body, the person must be declared dead—whether the death is cardiopulmonary death or brain death. This regulation excludes some potential donors such as anencephalic infants.

- There are many ethical controversies over how organs are allocated, such as whether HIV-positive patients should receive organs, or whether patients who have not declared themselves donors should receive organs.
- The Uniform Anatomical Gift Act prohibits the sale of human organs, but there are loopholes allowing practically everyone involved in the trade of human organs, except for the donors and their families, to profit. This has led to support for financial incentives for donation, as has the argument that financial incentives would increase the number of donors.
- Those against financial incentives argue it demeans the human body and may exploit the poor to the advantage of the rich.
- Demand for organs is so high that Americans have resorted to visiting other countries in order to receive transplanted organs, and sometimes organs transplanted from animals, because the wait time is too long in the United States.
- Tissue transplants appear much less controversial than organ transplants and are treated entirely differently. The tissue industry is composed of for-profit tissue banks and is run according to basic market principles of supply and demand. Further, it appears to be more highly regulated by states and other organizations, as opposed to the federal government.
- Xenotransplants are emerging as one possible solution to the shortage of human organs. However, much research must be done in order to ensure safety and effectiveness before it can become widely accepted or supported by the health insurance industry.

LAW NOTES

1. The data reported in this chapter were prepared by the Scientific Registry of Transplant Recipients, a national database of transplant statistics at the University of Michigan, unless otherwise stated. Data in the National Organ Donor Registry are collected by the Organ Procurement Transplantation Network from hospitals and organ procurement agencies across the country. The National Organ Donor Registry contains current and past information about the full continuum of transplant activity, from organ donation and waiting list candidates, to transplant recipients and survival statistics.
2. In a high-profile case, parents of an anencephalic newborn sought a Florida Supreme Court declaration stating their child was legally dead so they could donate its organs (*See In re: T.A.C.P.*, 609 So.2d 588 (Supreme Court of Florida 1992)). The newborn had a fatal birth defect in which the child was born with only a brain stem but otherwise lacked a brain. In this case, the back of the skull was entirely missing. Anencephalic newborns can sometimes survive several days after birth because their brain stem has a limited capacity to maintain autonomic bodily functions such as breathing and heartbeat; this ability soon ceases, however, in the absence of regulation from the missing brain. The parents found out about the child's condition during the mother's eighth month of pregnancy, but on the advice of physicians expressly continued the pregnancy in the hopes they could donate the child's organs and save the lives of other children. After the child's birth, however, health care providers refused to declare the child dead for donation purposes out of fear they would incur civil or even criminal liability. The child died while court proceedings were ongoing, thereby preventing the donation of any organs, as child organs are too fragile to be sustained after cardiopulmonary death. The court denied the parents' request to declare their newborn legally dead for several reasons:
   - It was uncertain whether anencephalic newborns could provide viable organs to be successfully transplanted to other children in need.
   - The medical community's opinions on the ethical considerations were in flux.
   - The court was reluctant to possibly create further legal or constitutional issues without any consensus on the merits of using anencephalic newborns as organ donors.
3. Cord blood transplants are being used as an alternative to transplants of bone marrow to treat diseases such as:
   - **Aplastic anemia**, a serious blood disorder where the bone marrow does not make enough new blood cells and that leads to heart failure (*E.g.*, Hosokawa et al., 2016)
   - Hurler syndrome, in which the body is missing an enzyme that builds bones and tissues and leads to organ and tissue damage with death by 5-10 years of age
   - Leukemia, which is cancer of the white blood cells
   - Thalassemia, in which the body makes an abnormal form of hemoglobin that leads to anemia and body shrinking (*E.g.*, Amid et al., 2015; Goss et al., 2014)

4. Until recently, outright sales of human organs have remained a largely unpopular subject. However, the American Society of Transplant Surgeons is now in favor of studying incentives for living donors and the fastest growing source of transplantable organs is now living donors. The American Medical Association is also calling for pilot studies of incentives for organs (AMA, 2011).

REFERENCES

AMA (American Medical Association). (2011). *AMA Code of Medical Ethics: Transplantation of organs from living donors* (Opinion 2.15). Washington, DC: AMA.

American Association of Tissue Banks. (2012). *Code of ethics.* McLean. VA: American Association of Tissue Banks.

Amid, A., et al. (2015). Thalassaemia in children: From quality of care to quality of life. *Archives of Disease in Childhood, 100*(11), 1051–1057.

Beard, T. R., & Leitzel, J. (2014). Organs and inducements: Designing a compensated-kidney donation system. *Law and Contemporary Problems, 77,* 253–287.

Bluhm, N., Director of Strategy and Government Policy at Remedy. (2016, February 19). Remarks at the panel discussion on Payer-Provider Convergence: From Volume to Value: New Frontiers in Payer/Provider Collaboration at the Wharton Health Care Business Conference, Philadelphia, PA.

Bonnie, R. J., et al. (2008). Organ donation and death from unexpected circulatory arrest: Engaging the recommendations of the Institute of Medicine: Legal authority to preserve organs in cases of uncontrolled cardiac death: Preserving family choice. *Journal of Law, Medicine and Ethics, 36,* 741–749.

Brody, T. (2015). Enabling clinical-treatment patent method claims with culture and animal model data. *Journal of the Patent and Trademark Office Society, 97,* 328–414.

Capron, A. M. (2014). Organs and inducements: Six decades of organ donation and the challenges that shifting the United States to a market system would create around the world. *Law and Contemporary Problems, 77,* 25–69.

CDC (Centers for Disease Control and Prevention). (2015). *Anencephaly.* Atlanta, GA: CDC.

Childress, J. F., & Liverman, C. T. (Eds.). (2006). *Organ donation: Opportunities for action.* Washington, DC: Institute of Medicine Committee on Increasing Rates of Organ Donation.

Coleman, D. L. (2014). Testing the boundaries of family privacy: The special case of pediatric sibling transplants. *Cardozo Law Review, 35,* 1289–1358.

Cook, P. J., & Krawiec, K. D. (2014). Organs and inducements: A primer on kidney transplantation: anatomy of the shortage. *Law and Contemporary Problems, 77,* 1–23.

Cortez, N. (2008). Patients without borders: The emerging global market for patients and the evolution of modern health care. *Indiana Law Journal, 83,* 71–132.

Crepelle, A. (2016). A market for human organs: An ethical solution to the organ shortage. *Indiana Health Law Review, 13,* 17–81.

Delmonico, F. L., et al. (2011). Organ transplantation: A call for government accountability to achieve national self-sufficiency in organ donation and transplantation. *Lancet, 378,* 1414–1418.

DeVito, M. (2014). The judge put me on the list: Judicial review and organ allocation decisions. *Case Western Reserve Law Review, 65,* 181–207.

Dolgin, J. L. (2016). Dying discourse: Contextualizing advance care planning. *Quinnipiac Law Review, 34,* 235–298.

Doty, A. (2015). Organ transplants from executed prisoners. *Syracuse Science and Technology Law Reporter, 32,* 179–203.

FDA (U.S. Food and Drug Administration). (2014). *U.S. Public Health Service guideline on infectious disease issues in National Organ Donor Registry.* Bethesda, MD: FDA.

Fleck, L. M. (2014). Just caring: Do the indolent, the inebriated and the irresponsible deserve equal access to needed health care? *Indiana Health Law Review, 11,* 555–589.

Foos, D. (2012). State ready-to-embalm laws and the modern funeral market: The need for change and suggested alternatives. *Michigan State Law Review, 2012,* 1375–1418.

Frank, S. (2014). Eligibility discrimination of the intellectually disabled in pediatric organ transplantation. *Health and Biomedical Law Society, 10,* 101–136.

Gilman, S. J. (2012). The use of anencephalic infants as an organ source: An on-going question. *Elon Law Review, 4,* 71–92.

Goodwin, M. (2007). The body market: Race politics and private ordering. *Arizona Law Review 49,* 599–636.

Goss, C., et al. (2014). Red blood cell transfusions for thalassemia: Results of a survey assessing current practice and proposal of evidence-based guidelines. *Transfusion, 54*(7), 1773–1781.

Hagen, G. R., & Gittens, S. A. (2008). Patenting part-human chimeras, transgenics and stem cells for transplantation in the United States, Canada, and Europe. *Richmond Journal of Law and Technology, 14,* 11–74.

Hain, E. R. (2015). I want YOU to have MY heart: How using a will may better protect a donor's intent in insuring successful directed donation of organs. *The Quinnipiac Probate Law Journal, 28,* 304–322.

HHS (U.S. Department of Health and Human Services). (2016). *Timeline of historical events and significant milestones in organ donation and transplantation.* Washington, DC: HHS.

Hosokawa, K., et al. (2016). Memory stem T cells in autoimmune disease: High frequency of circulating CD8+ memory stem cells in acquired aplastic anemia. *Journal of Immunology, 196*(4), 1568–1578.

Iltis, A. S. (2015). Organ donation, brain death and the family: Valid informed consent. *Journal of Law, Medicine and Ethics, 43,* 369–378.

Kessler, J. B., & Roth, A. E. (2012). Organ allocation policy and the decision to donate. *The American Economic Review, 102*(5), 2018–2047.

Krawiec, K. D., & Rees, M. A. (2014). Organs and inducements: Reverse transplant tourism. *Law and Contemporary Problems, 77,* 145–173.

Lee, W. B. (2014). Recalibrating experimental treatment exclusion: An empirical analysis. *University of Cincinnati Law Review, 83,* 171–201.

Longo, D. O. (2011). Are we bad Samaritans? A comparative analysis of duty to rescue legislation and cadaveric organ donation systems in Spain and the United States. *Syracuse Journal of International Law and Commerce, 39,* 55–88.

Lurie, P., & Zieve, A. (2006). Sequestered science: The consequences of undisclosed knowledge; Sometimes the silence can be like the thunder: Access to pharmaceutical data at the FDA. *Law and Contemporary Problems, 69*, 85–97.

Macintosh, K. L. (2015). Chimeras, hybrids, and cybrids: How essentialism distorts the law and stymies scientific research. *Arizona State Law Journal, 47*, 183–233.

Mayo Clinic Staff. (2016). *Organ donation: Don't let these myths confuse you.* Rochester, MN: Mayo Clinic.

McClean, M. (2016). Children's anatomy v. children's autonomy: A precarious balancing act with preimplantation genetic diagnosis and the creation of "savior siblings". *Pepperdine Law Review, 43*, 837–878.

Meckler, L. (2007a, November 13). Kidney shortages inspires a radical idea: Organ sales; As waiting list grows, some seek to lift ban; Exploiting the poor? *Wall Street Journal*, p. A1.

___. (2007b, October 15). Kidney swaps seen as way to ease donor shortage. *Wall Street Journal*, p. A1.

___. (2007c, March 10). Picking winners, more kidneys for transplants may go to young: Policy to stress benefit to patient over length of time on wait list. *Wall Street Journal*, p. A1.

___. (2007d, January 30). What living organ donors need to know: Even as transplants surge, data on long-term impact on givers remain scant. *Wall Street Journal*, p. A1.

Morad, L. (2012). Stemming the tide: On the patentability of stem cells and differentiation processes. *New York University Law Review, 87*, 551–590.

Neal, L. (2012). Organ donation, therapeutic cloning, and laws of the states. *Syracuse Science and Technology Law Reporter, 2012*, 146–170.

NKF (National Kidney Foundation). (2016). *Transplantation.* New York, NY: NKF.

Noah, L. (2013). Medical device law: turn the beat around?: Deactivating implanted cardiac-assist devices. *William Mitchell Law Review, 39*, 1229–1286.

O'Brien, S. (2015). The impact and implications of Sarah Murnaghan on the Organ Procurement and Transplantation Network's lung allocation policy and a proposal for further change. *Quinnipiac Health Law Journal, 18*, 99–156.

OPTN (Organ Procurement and Transplantation Network). (2016a). *Policies.* Richmond, VA: OPTN.

___, & SRTR (Scientific Registry of Transplant Recipients). (2016b). OPTN/SRTR annual report. *American Journal of Transplantation, 16*(S2), 4–215.

Orenstein, D. G., & Bettini, L. M. (2014). Flipping the light switch: New perspectives on default to donation for organs and tissues. *Annals of Health Law, 23*, 141–159.

Ouellette, A. (2010). Shaping parental authority over children's bodies. *Indiana Law Journal, 85*, 955–1002.

Parent, B. (2015). Informing donors about hand and face transplants: Time to update the Uniform Anatomical Gift Act. *Health and Biomedical Law Society, 10*, 309–326.

Parish, C. (2015). Rules are meant to be broken: The Organ Procurement and Transplantation Network should allow pediatric transplantation of adult lungs. *Journal of Law and Health, 28*, 319–354.

Pippin, J. J. (2013). Animal research in medical sciences: Seeking a convergence of science, medicine, and animal law. *South Texas Law Review, 54*, 469–511.

President's Council on Bioethics. (2004). *Reproduction and responsibility: The regulation of new technologies.* Washington, DC: President's Council on Bioethics.

Richards, D. (2013). The defibrillation of NOTA: How establishing federal regulation of waitlist eligibility may save organ transplant patients with disabilities from flat-lining. *Southern California Law Review, 87*, 151–194.

Sabatello, M. (2014). Posthumously conceived children: An international and human rights perspective. *Journal of Law and Health, 27*, 29–67.

Saitta-Gill, N., & Hodge, S. D. (2015). Solving the problem of organ donation shortage. *University of Baltimore Law Review, 45*, 29–55.

Satel, S. L., et al. (2014). Organs and inducements: State organ-donation incentives under the National Organ Transplant Act. *Law and Contemporary Problems, 77*, 217–252.

___, & Hippen, B. E. (2007). When altruism is not enough: The worsening organ shortage and what it means for the elderly. *Elder Law Journal, 15*, 153–204.

Shakespeare, W. (2009). *Othello (Oxford school Shakespeare series).* New York, NY: Oxford University Press. (Original work published 1603.)

Shuster, K. (2014). "When has the grim reaper finished reaping?" How embracing one religion's view of death can influence acceptance of The Uniform Determination of Death Act. *Touro Law Review, 30*, 655–674.

Spillman, M. A., & Sade, R. M. (2007). Clinical trials of National Organ Donor Registry: Waiver of the right to withdraw from a clinical trial should be required. *Journal of Law, Medicine and Ethics, 35*, 265–272.

Strong, C., Counsel for New Jersey Sharing Network. (2014, April 9). Remarks at the panel discussion on Health Law and Organ Donation at the Rutgers-Camden Health Law Society Symposium, Camden, NJ.

Tenenbaum, E. M. (2016). Bartering for a compatible kidney using your incompatible, live kidney donor: Legal and ethical issues related to kidney chains. *American Journal of Law and Medicine, 42*, 129–169.

Terrell, T. P. (2014). Right to shop: An essay on normative, social, and legal fundamentals. *Georgetown Journal of Law and Public Policy, 12*(1), 1–56.

Terzic, A., & Nelson, T. J. (2010). Regenerative medicine: Advancing health care 2020. *Journal of the American College of Cardiology, 55*(20), 2254–2257.

Townsley, M. L. (2015). Is there any body out there? A call for a new body of law to protect individual ownership interests in tissue samples used in medical research. *Washburn Law Journal, 54*, 683–740.

Truog, R. D. (2015). Science challenges for law and policy: Defining death: Getting it wrong for all the right reasons. *Texas Law Review, 93*, 1885–1913.

Underhill, K. (2016). When extrinsic incentives displace intrinsic motivation: Designing legal carrots and sticks to confront the challenge of motivational crowding-out. *Yale Journal on Regulation, 33*, 213–279.

USRDS (U.S. Renal Data System). (2015). *Annual data report: Atlas of end-stage renal disease in the United States.* Bethesda, MD: National Institutes of Health, National Institute of Diabetes and Digestive and Kidney Diseases.

Weinstock, L., Vice President, Administration and General Counsel of Gift of Life Donor Program. (2014, April 9). Remarks at the panel discussion on Health Law and Organ Donation at the Rutgers-Camden Health Law Society Symposium, Camden, NJ.

Westphal, S. P. (2006, April 4). Bladders built in the lab: Cells, plastic shell combine to make the nearest thing yet to a fully man-made organ. *Wall Street Journal*, p. D1.

Wharton School at the University of Pennsylvania. (2011). How to encourage people to become organ donors: An incentive system with heart. *Knowledge@Wharton*.

White, E. K. (2016). A reason for hope? A legal and ethical implementation of the HIV Organ Policy Equity Act. *Boston University Law Review, 96*, 609–654.

Wiley, L. F. (2016). From patient rights to health justice: Securing the public's interest in affordable, high-quality health care. *Cardozo Law Review, 37*, 833–889.

Williams, K. L. (2015). The hidden economy of HSC transplantation is inconsistent with prohibiting the compensation of HSC donors. *Minnesota Journal of Law, Science and Technology, 16*, 215–267.

Williams, K. L., et al. (2014). Just say no to NOTA: Why the prohibition of compensation for human transplant organs in NOTA should be repealed and a regulated market for cadaver organs instituted. *American Journal of Law and Medicine, 40*, 275–318.

CHAPTER 26

© Andy Dean Photography/ShutterStock, Inc.

AIDS Pandemic

"No State, no matter how powerful, can by its own efforts alone make itself invulnerable to today's threats."

— **Kofi Annan**, Former United Nations Secretary-General

IN BRIEF

This chapter describes the global human immunodeficiency virus (HIV)/acquired immune deficiency syndrome (AIDS) pandemic and examines the efforts of the United States to deal with this disease within its own borders. Attention is increasingly focused on drug patents and how the pharmaceutical industry controls prices for HIV/AIDS drugs. Bowing to a variety of forces, the pharmaceutical industry now offers key drugs to resource-limited countries and low-income Americans at prices far below market value. Rather than ending debate about the role and responsibility of the pharmaceutical industry in addressing the AIDS pandemic, however, the industry's humanitarian moves have spurred further demands to address additional threats to global public health.

The AIDS pandemic has led to a critical examination of the U.S. Food and Drug Administration's system for oversight of the development and marketing of new drugs in the United States. The pandemic has also intensified the call to address the long-term health needs of the chronically ill, including Americans living with HIV/AIDS. One policy issue under debate is whether a profit-oriented economic scheme is the most effective system for dealing with public health issues like the AIDS pandemic. The effort of the United States to deal with the AIDS pandemic is described in this chapter within the context of the global fight against HIV/AIDS. This chapter focuses on three economically vulnerable populations: low-income citizens in the United States who do not have affordable access to comprehensive medical treatment until they are disabled and become eligible for Medicaid insurance; newborns in the United States; and resource-limited countries that do not have the manufacturing resources to supply their citizens with essential antiretroviral and AIDS drugs or the resources to import them.

LEARNING OBJECTIVES

Upon completion of this chapter readers should be able to:

1. Describe the serious threat that HIV, the virus that causes AIDS, poses for the U.S. health care system.
2. List the two-pronged approach to health care as illustrated by the AIDS pandemic.
3. Understand the effects of successive waves of the AIDS pandemic.
4. Discuss the effect stigma and discrimination has on HIV/AIDS victims, research, and health care in general.
5. Explain problems from HIV in the blood supply and the differences that appear among countries.
6. Outline the issues of pharmaceutical pricing for antiretroviral drugs (ARVs) and AIDS drugs.
7. Contrast differential pricing compared to compulsory licensing of HIV/AIDS drugs.

KEY TERMS

Acquired immune deficiency virus	Americans with Disabilities Act of 1990	Antiretroviral
Affordable Care Act of 2010	AMEX Pharmaceutical Index	Barebacking
AIDS pandemic	Antidiscrimination	Bargain rates

Blood-borne pathogens
Blood solids
Case of first impression
Children
Common good
Communicable disease
Compounding access
Compulsory licensing
Concessionary price reductions
Co-payments
Duty-to-warn laws
Epidemic
Essential health care
First Amendment
Fractation firms
Gay blood ban
Generic
Health Insurance Portability and
    Accountability Act of 1996

Heightened duty of care
High-risk groups
HIV Past-Exposure Registry
HIV-related infections
HIV testing
Human immunodeficiency
    virus (HIV)
Impairment
Individual entitlement to
    health
International Partnership for
    Microbicides
Knowing transmission of HIV
Market prices
Medicaid insurance
Microbicides
Minimum obligations
Moral imperative
Multidrug-resistant tuberculosis

Need-to-know
Opportunistic infections
Parallel importing
Patents
Preventable behavior
Preventable condition
Resource-limited countries
Right to health care
State confidentiality laws
Tuberculosis
Universal infection control
    precautions
Universal rights
Values
Wave of AIDS illnesses
Wave of HIV infections
Wave of opportunistic diseases
Wave of preventable deaths

FACT OR FICTION

Early Detection of HIV

Is there a heightened duty of care to routinely test high-risk patients for HIV infection?

Armando Lopes, a gay man in Philadelphia, began treatment at Thomas Jefferson University Hospital for regular checkups and sick visits, including at least three routine blood screenings over a seven-year period. Lopes never requested a test for **human immunodeficiency virus (HIV)**, the virus that causes **acquired immune deficiency syndrome (AIDS)**, at any time during the eight times he presented himself to the Department of Internal Medicine complaining of fatigue, anxiety, weight loss, memory loss, and dizziness. It was not until referral to a neurology resident after his eighth visit that Lopes underwent an HIV test, which came back positive. Lopes filed a malpractice suit claiming his referring physician knew or should have known of his sexual orientation and that since he was at high risk for HIV, an HIV test should have been performed before his HIV infection progressed to symptomatic AIDS. Lopes maintained that if his HIV status had been detected earlier, his HIV infection could have been managed with **antiretroviral (ARV)** treatment, which could have slowed the disease's progression.

— *See* Law Fact at the end of this chapter for the answer.

Principles and Applications

HIV/AIDS is the foremost preventable disease worldwide (WHO, 2016). Despite this, the **AIDS pandemic** is one of the most pressing threats to global public health in the present day. This chapter refers to AIDS as a pandemic, as opposed to an **epidemic**, because it more accurately describes the widespread destructiveness of the incidence of this **communicable disease**. Epidemics are defined as communicable disease outbreaks that infect at least 1% of the general population and then spread more quickly and extensively among groups of people than expected (CDC, 2015a). Epidemics become categorized as pandemics when, like HIV, the virus that causes AIDS, the disease occurs over a wide geographic area and affects large numbers of people (Kaiser, 2014a). Often, the terms *pandemic* and *epidemic* are used interchangeably; this chapter, however, only uses the term *pandemic* in reference to HIV/AIDS and **tuberculosis**.

Leading Communicable Disease Killer Worldwide

The global impact of HIV/AIDS has been described as no less destructive than war (UNF, 2012). AIDS is the second leading communicable disease killer worldwide, with tuberculosis being the number one killer (WHO, 2016). Although the highest number of deaths from the AIDS pandemic occurred in the early 1990s, the pandemic is not in decline in the United States (CDC, 2015a-c). In fact, the incidence of HIV infections is higher than ever before, with more than 1.3 million Americans living with the infection (CDC, 2015b).

By definition, HIV and AIDS are simply two different stages of the same disease, hence the frequent use of the term *HIV/AIDS* throughout this chapter. HIV basically destroys certain white blood cells that are critical to the normal functioning of the human immune system. When HIV weakens the immune system, a person becomes more susceptible to developing a variety of cancers and infections from viruses, bacteria, and parasites that might not otherwise have developed (CDC, 2014c). People who test positive for HIV are diagnosed with AIDS when laboratory tests show their immune system is severely weakened by the virus or when **opportunistic infections** develop, which are diseases that might not affect people with normal immune systems but that take advantage of damaged immune systems (CDC, 2014b).

There is no cure for HIV/AIDS at this time, and a widely disseminated preventive vaccine or curative medicine is likely years away (HHS, 2014). Once people are infected with HIV, they either control the damaging progression of the virus with ARV treatment before infections appear, or they become symptomatic with AIDS and face imminent death from multiple cancers and infections. ARVs can slow down the rate at which HIV weakens the immune system to the point of being diagnosed with full-blown AIDS, but they cannot stop the progression of HIV completely (IOM, 2013).

There are medical treatments that can prevent or cure some of the infections associated with AIDS, but nothing can cure HIV/AIDS itself. The simple but essential fact is that most of the deaths due to the disease could be prevented if people everywhere had access to information and medical treatment for preventing and treating HIV infection (Cohen et al., 2011). It is important to understand that HIV can be managed as a chronic lifelong disease *if* the HIV infection is detected early enough and *if* the infected person has access to medical treatment to treat the opportunistic infections. It is these two '*ifs*' that make the AIDS pandemic such a tragedy. Once a person is infected with HIV, they remain infected for life. HIV infections, however, do not have to lead to AIDS if infected people have access to ARVs (Goldfein & Schalman-Bergen, 2010).

With global access to **essential health care**, AIDS deaths need not occur: 4,400 adults need not die every day from AIDS and 800 children need not die every single day because they lack access to the necessary health care (UNAIDS, 2013). This chapter uses the internationally accepted definition of **children** as those under the age of 15, which is also the definition used by most global health organizations. This is the primary reason why so much attention is being directed to AIDS: millions of people, including children, are dying from this preventable disease.

Key Public Health Statistics

Over 37 million people worldwide are infected with HIV (WHO, 2016). If it is difficult to imagine this number of people living with HIV/AIDS worldwide, imagine all the college and university students in the United States and then double this number; this statistic represents about 37 million people. Statistics like this are important, but they can also be numbing and desensitizing. As illustrated in **FEATURE BOX 26-1**, statistics can make one forget an important fact: each of these numbers represents a person, not just a faceless, anonymous statistic.

The question is: who should fund the staggering cost of treating this pandemic? Who is responsible for addressing a disease process that is still not completely understood and a pandemic with no known cure? What is the role of individual responsibility in preventing communicable infections in the first place? The answer to these questions really depends upon how much the health care industry and the American public choose to engage this issue.

FEATURE BOX 26-1

Key U.S. Public Health Statistics

- Almost 1 in 7 Americans infected with HIV are unaware of their infection.
- About 1.3 million Americans are living with HIV.
- There are more than 50,000 new HIV infections annually.
- One out of four new HIV infections occurs among adolescents 13-24 years old.
- Casual hookups by people diagnosed as HIV-positive are widespread.
- There are 13,500 deaths from AIDS and related illnesses each year (over 658,000 have died from AIDS since the pandemic reached the United States).

CDC, 2015a-c, 2014a; Kaiser, 2015; White House, 2015.

MANAGEMENT AND LAW ISSUES

2. Is HIV/AIDS generally a **preventable condition**?
3. Are casual hookups without prophylactics a **preventable behavior**?

Successive Waves of the AIDS Pandemic

One thing is certain: the impact of HIV/AIDS is still not fully understood, particularly when the long term is considered. The AIDS pandemic appears to come in successive, overlapping waves in different geographic areas. The first wave is HIV infection. This is followed several years later by a **wave of opportunistic diseases**, and then a **wave of AIDS illnesses**. Last, there is a **wave of preventable deaths**.

Africa is just entering the second wave of the AIDS pandemic (UNAIDS & WHO, 2016b):[LN1]

- Africa has about 22.5 million people living with HIV/AIDS, almost 70% of the total HIV/AIDS cases worldwide.
- Nearly 90% of all HIV-positive children live in sub-Saharan Africa, one of the poorest places in the world.[LN2]
- Almost all of these HIV-positive children were born with the virus.
- Botswana is said to have not yet been hit by the peak of the third wave, and has not advanced very far into the fourth wave.

(UN Secretary-General, 2016; UNAIDS & WHO, 2016b).

The United States has not successfully quarantined itself from Africa's first **wave of HIV infections**, as tuberculosis, the oldest disease of mankind rises one more time (Novogrodsky, 2014). Today, the second wave of opportunistic diseases is rising with **multidrug-resistant tuberculosis** infections from Africa and India (WHO, 2016). In the mid-1970s, HIV crossed the shorelines of the United States, followed by the crossing of multidrug-resistant tuberculosis in late 1979 (CDC, 2013a). Clearly, public health contagion is no longer restricted by country boundaries—if infectious disease waves ever were constrained by geographic boundaries. Today, no nation exists in isolation; AIDS and tuberculosis are global phenomena (Novogrodsky, 2014).

Global Interdependence

Beyond doubt, the AIDS pandemic has made the world more globally interdependent. While this trend is not new, the United States has reached a degree of more personal interdependence that Americans have never experienced before;

what happens on one continent today affects those on another continent tomorrow. In this instance, a subspecies of chimpanzees native to West Equatorial Africa was the original source of HIV (Gao et al., 1999). HIV most likely was introduced into the human population when hunters were exposed to the infected blood of nonhuman primates (Weis & Wrangham, 1999).

The HIV/AIDS infection crisis is just the latest instance of the global phenomenon facing leaders in the health care industry. Virus infections in Africa infect people in the United States, and vice versa. Interdependencies in public health are the direct consequence of globalization; it is also the recognition that we all live in a continually shrinking global village (Wharton, 2011).

The Second Wave of the HIV/AIDS Pandemic: Tuberculosis

There is no need to look further than the airborne infectious disease of tuberculosis to fully grasp the global nature of public health today. The connectivity of communicable diseases is most evident with the AIDS pandemic, with HIV/AIDS being largely responsible for the growing number of tuberculosis cases in Asia and Africa (WHO, 2014). One-third of the world's population is infected with tuberculosis, with more latent than active infections as must be acknowledged; nevertheless almost 13 million are infected with active and latent tuberculosis in the United States (CDC 2014a), compared to the 1.3 million living with HIV/AIDS in the United States. HIV weakens the cells in the immune system needed to fight tuberculosis; up to half of all those living with AIDS eventually develop tuberculosis, and it is the leading killer among patients who are HIV-positive (WHO, 2014).

Coinfections of HIV and Tuberculosis

The seriousness of this emerging epidemic becomes obvious when the epidemiological data of this disease is analyzed in **FEATURE BOX 26-2**. Worldwide, more than 9.2 million new tuberculosis cases are appearing each year, with about 1.7 million deaths, of which about 700,000 cases and 200,000 deaths are AIDS-related (WHO, 2014). At the same time, the United States continues to see a significant increase in the number of tuberculosis infections (CDC, 2014a).

Multidrug-Resistant Tuberculosis

Most significant is the fact that multidrug-resistant tuberculosis appeared in the United States in the 1990s (CDC, 2013a). Public officials knew then and know now that this strain of tuberculosis is virtually incurable. The fear is that

---

FEATURE BOX 26-2

Connectivity of HIV/Tuberculosis Coinfections in the United States

- Currently: People who have both HIV and latent tuberculosis infections are 20 to 30 times as likely to develop active tuberculosis disease as those who do not have an HIV infection.
- 2024 Prediction: About 250,000 to 400,000 active tuberculosis cases will most likely be multidrug-resistant.
- 2024 Prediction: There could be 75,000 to 120,000 multidrug-resistant tuberculosis deaths each year compared to 13,500 AIDS deaths.

CDC, 2014b-c; Saleem & Asher, 2013.

the present global caseload of tuberculosis infections may eventually be replaced by patients with multidrug-resistant tuberculosis.

Roughly half the multidrug-resistant cases are currently in India and China (Anand, 2012). Yet, the extent of global resistant tuberculosis is largely unknown to epidemiologists. Data on drug resistance were available in only six countries in Africa where tuberculosis has tripled in the past 15 years along with the rise of AIDS (WHO, 2014). What is known is that the biggest single factor driving up resistance of tuberculosis to drugs is irregular use of antibiotics, often a result of infrastructure breakdowns in the delivery of antibiotics to patients (Tracey & Lange, 2012). It is also known that HIV/AIDS is aggravating and contributing to the spread of multidrug-resistant tuberculosis (CDC, 2014c; WHO, 2014).

By contrast, although ARVs can treat HIV infections as a chronic disease, treatment for multidrug-resistant tuberculosis works for only about 30% of those infected, even when the highest quality health care is available. With communicable diseases like tuberculosis, bacteria is spread from person to person through the air; someone in Africa or India can cough at an airport, the bacteria contaminates a plane, and the plane heads to the United States filled with people who have been exposed to the bacteria. Clearly, it really does matter what happens outside the United States.

The Dual Role of Governments and the Global Pharmaceutical Industry

While critics claim the global pharmaceutical industry is excessively profitable, there is no compelling evidence one way or the other. The **AMEX Pharmaceutical Index**, composed of the 15 largest pharmaceutical firms, has given investors returns below the Standard and Poor's 500 Index, a gauge of the broad market. All of the major HIV/AIDS drug manufacturers are in the AMEX Index, which has seen a decline in growth over the past decade. Still, there are suggestions the AIDS pandemic is a special disease state, one so serious the pharmaceutical industry has an ethical obligation to provide essential ARVs and AIDS drugs to ameliorate this preventable disease, an ethical obligation that should come before profits.

Calls for the global pharmaceutical industry to do more to meet the needs of people living with HIV/AIDS, however, are not limited to HIV/AIDS activists. The World Health Organization, along with almost every advocate of world economic reform, is demanding more action from the global pharmaceutical industry (Gostin et al., 2011).

At the same time, it should not be forgotten that governments worldwide have responsibility for providing essential health care, including lifesaving ARVs and AIDS drugs, to their citizens. The United States and Europe, in particular, greatly benefit from their immense pharmaceutical resources. The AIDS pandemic obliges both the global pharmaceutical industry and governments worldwide, but especially governments in the high-income nations that benefit the most from the pharmaceutical industry, to ask how they can help correct things for those infected by HIV/AIDS (Gregg, 2011).

Individual Entitlement to Health

The dual responsibility of the global pharmaceutical industry and governments worldwide to take action arises from the **universal rights** founded in international law and the principle of **moral imperative**. The **individual entitlement to health** is emphasized in customary international laws (ICASO, 2015). For instance, the International Covenant on Economic, Social, and Cultural Rights acknowledges the universal right to enjoyment of the highest attainable standard of health. The Academy of European Law goes so far as to argue that this means those infected with HIV are entitled to ARVs to prevent their disease from progressing to full-blown AIDS.

Access to Essential Health Care

Closely related to this individual entitlement to health are a government's **minimum obligations** to its citizens, one obligation of which is the provision of access to essential health care. The debate over what constitutes access (who has the right to make use of what medical innovations) and what essential health care comprises is unclear. What is clear is there is no consensus on either question.

One argument is that lack of early access to ARVs to slow down the rate at which HIV weakens the immune system is the difference between life and death for some people. Therefore, there is a right of mutually affordable access to ARVs (Winslow, 2010). In this instance, the universal right to benefit from medical progress applies to medical treatment and the provision of ARVs as well as other essential AIDS drugs. How these dual obligations to individual citizens, the entitlement to health and the **right to health care**, are being met in the United States is the topic of the next part of this chapter. The focus is on the role of government and the global pharmaceutical industry in their fight against HIV/AIDS.

The Fight Against HIV/AIDS in the United States

This section focuses on the fight against the AIDS pandemic in the United States. Since the first case of AIDS was documented in the United States in 1981 (it was an additional two years before HIV was identified), the pandemic has changed dramatically. At the same time, some attitudes have remained unchanged. The onset of the AIDS pandemic set the tone for blatant stigma and discrimination in the United States. People with HIV/AIDS were:

- Evicted from their homes
- Excluded from schools
- Routinely fired from their jobs
- Shunned by family members
- Threatened with or subjected to violence

(Gregg, 2011; NASTAD, 2016).

Without existing treatment, people with HIV had little hope of survival in the 1980s and much of the 1990s. A positive HIV test result meant social isolation along with an inevitably painful death. At the onset of the AIDS pandemic, HIV infection was primarily limited to three risk groups:

- Hemophiliacs
- Gay men
- Injection drug users[LN3]

Accordingly, public health policies and laws were targeted to those specific **high-risk groups**. HIV testing was offered only to people who engaged in specific risk behaviors (IOM, 2010). Counseling and testing were available only for high-risk groups and for those in health care settings with high HIV prevalence (CDC, 2013b). This approach lasted until the late 1990s, as more than 40,000 Americans became newly infected with HIV each year.

A significant number of Americans still regard the high-risk groups of HIV/AIDS victims as evidence the disease is a curse; others seek to shun and even punish anyone who becomes HIV-infected (Fishman, 2013; *cf.* Langner, 2015 (explaining **barebacking**)). Opinions about the AIDS pandemic are highly charged and will become more charged as the second wave of opportunistic diseases hits the United States. The debate is emotional, opinionated, and thorny because it elicits reactions that are often religiously based about:

- Abortion by HIV-positive women
- Pandemic deaths from multidrug-resistant tuberculosis
- Responsibility of government in delivery of essential health care
- Rights to freedom of speech versus rights of confidentiality about HIV infections
- Rights to self-determination and human dignity by sexual minorities
- Role of criminal law in public health
- Sexual morality

(Perone, 2013).

Two-Pronged Approach

In the late 1990s, when ARVs first became widely available, the law and health care policies began to change. Today there are two prongs of the approach to the AIDS pandemic in the United States. The first prong is early detection and treatment of HIV; the second prong is containment (IOM, 2011). In an effort to contain the spread of HIV, the United States has:

- Criminal sanctions in place for the knowing transmission of HIV
- Mandatory reporting requirements of HIV/AIDS infections

(White House, 2015).

Changing Demographics of the Disease

Both approaches to the AIDS pandemic are influenced by the changing demographics of the disease. While one-third of the new HIV infections are still among injection drug users, a trend that appears to have remained constant since the early 1980s (CDC, 2014a), the remaining two-thirds of those newly infected with HIV fall into groups not traditionally associated with HIV/AIDS:

- Blacks
- Heterosexual men and women
- People living outside of urban areas, many of whom do not believe they are at risk for HIV
- People under the age of 20

(CDC, 2015b and 2015d; White House, 2015).

Disparate Impact of the Disease

Blacks make up about 47% of the total HIV-positive population and more than half of new HIV cases in the United States, despite making up only 12% of the population (CDC, 2015b).

- Black teenagers account for most of the new HIV cases reported.
- AIDS is one of the top causes of death for Blacks.
- Black women are 19 times more likely to contract HIV than other groups of women.
- The rates of perinatal-acquired HIV infections in Black newborns are 9 to 15 times higher than all other newborn groups.

(CDC, 2016, 2014a and 2014c; Kaiser, 2014a).

This racial disparity is attributed primarily to high risk heterosexual contact between Blacks who are unaware of their HIV status. Other contributing explanations are barriers to early diagnosis of HIV and poor access to quality health care (Winslow & McKay, 2010).

Late Testers

Unfortunately, most people in the United States are tested only after HIV/AIDS symptoms appear, which may be 10 years or more after being infected (Corey, 2011). These late testers are more likely to be Black and are more likely to have contracted HIV through heterosexual contact (Kaiser, 2014c). A debate is emerging in the United States over whether the concentrated attention upon the AIDS pandemic in **resource-limited countries** may inadvertently have caused the decline of HIV/AIDS detection in the United States (*See* Tramont & Boyajian, 2010).

One of the most important factors linking poverty to HIV/AIDS in the United States is the lack of affordable access to health care. More than one-quarter of the unemployed and most low-income earners in the United States lack health insurance. Over 15% of full-time workers and 20% of part-time workers are uninsured. The incomes of many low-income earners make them ineligible for **Medicaid insurance**, and those who have employer-provided health insurance often delay accessing health care due to high deductibles and other cost-sharing mechanisms in their insurance plans (NCHHSTP, 2016).

In part because of barriers to access, economically vulnerable populations often postpone treatment until they have full-blown AIDS (Fagan et al., 2010; *See* Greene, 2016). Even when they are aware of their HIV status during the early stages of infection, their lives are so disorganized they do not access ARVs or comprehensive treatment to manage and monitor medical complications associated with HIV (Burris et al., 2010). This lack of access inevitably fuels a downward cycle of poverty, especially once they become so sick they cannot work.

Individuals with HIV/AIDS who are unable to obtain treatment are forced to abandon the labor force due to illness and infection and are pushed further down the economic ladder as they seek to attend to their most basic needs

(NCHHSTP, 2016). Over one-third of Americans living with HIV/AIDS delayed or did not obtain needed health care because of food and housing needs (CSDH, 2015), while one-third to one-half are either homeless or in imminent danger of losing their homes (HUD, 2015). Homelessness and loss of homes are due to compounding factors such as increased health care costs and limited incomes or reduced ability to keep working due to HIV/AIDS and related illnesses (HIV Justice Network & Global Network for People Living with HIV, 2016).

First Prong: Detection and Treatment of HIV/AIDS

Angered by apparent intolerant reactions to individuals with HIV/AIDS, activists have demanded greater confidentiality and **antidiscrimination** protections for this vulnerable population (UCSF & National HIV/AIDS Clinicians' Consultation Center, 2008). Federal legislation protects individuals with serious disabilities and a few states afford protection against discrimination for individuals with HIV who are not disabled. The lack of comprehensive protection before serious disability occurs, however, may be related to concerns regarding the potential costs of accommodating the 1.3 million people living with HIV in the United States, especially if such accommodation occurs from the time of their infection.

Current restrictions on discrimination against individuals with HIV-positive status mirror existing social **values** (Mendonsa, 2010). While enactment of the **Americans with Disabilities Act of 1990** represented a consensus in the United States that there should be a comprehensive national mandate for the elimination of discrimination against individuals with serious disabilities (*See* 42 U.S.C.A. §§ 12101 *et seq.*), there is little support for extending antidiscrimination laws to those who appear undeserving of protection. Thus, there is generally broad support for protecting individuals with serious disabilities at the end stage of AIDS, but there is little support for extending protections to asymptomatic HIV-infected individuals (Kaiser, 2011).

Routine HIV Testing and Detection in the United States

The good news is with improvements in treatment and the advent of some confidentiality protection, **HIV testing** is slowly becoming a more constructive tool in the fight against HIV/AIDS (CDC, 2014b). The federal government revised its guidelines for HIV testing and detection and routine testing of everyone between the ages of 13 and 64 is now recommended, regardless of individual risk factors. While HIV testing remains voluntary, it is usually offered on an opt-out basis (Mariner, 2016). Separate, written informed consent is no longer needed (CDC, 2014b). Consent is part of the general informed consent for health care.

In addition, counseling is no longer required with HIV testing. Routine HIV screenings should identify people with unrecognized infections in the same way as screening and diagnostic tests for high cholesterol or some sexually transmitted diseases do. Today, HIV tests are increasingly treated the same as cholesterol tests and Pap smears, similar standard diagnostic tests routinely administered.

Early HIV diagnosis is crucial because early intervention leads to slower disease progression. When ARVs are taken early and consistently, HIV is a chronic, manageable disease that usually does not develop into full-blown AIDS because of the low maintained level of virus in the bloodstream (Kaiser, 2014a). Opportunistic diseases arising from the HIV infection can generally be individually treated with other curative drugs. ARVs also significantly reduce the transmissibility of HIV by lowering the amount of virus in the bloodstream of those infected (CDC, 2014a).

HIV Testing Among Pregnant Women

Approximately 8,500 women living with HIV give birth annually (CDC, 2016). Federal guidelines recommend HIV testing for all pregnant women since perinatal transmission of HIV is substantially reduced by the administration of ARVs to HIV-infected pregnant women and their newborns (CDC, 2014a). Transmission of HIV can be managed during the period surrounding childbirth, which is around week 28 of an HIV-infected mother's pregnancy to around one month after the birth (Helmink, 2010).

The development of ARVs means an HIV-positive diagnosis no longer a reason women cannot carry a child to term. Nonetheless, and in spite of this available health care, HIV testing is not routinely offered to pregnant women on a standard basis in the United States (Khan, 2015). Yet, with proper prenatal treatment, the risk of an HIV-positive pregnant woman passing HIV to her newborn child is less than 1% (CDC, 2015c).

Repeat HIV screening in the third trimester is recommended for high-risk women and for women in areas with elevated rates of HIV infection among pregnant women (Pierce et al., 2011). High-risk women are most likely to be under 30 years of age and have:

- A partner who has HIV
- A partner who may have had sex with other men
- Shared needles or other equipment with injection partners
- Unprotected intercourse with multiple sex partners (male or female)
- Used, or have a partner who has used, injection drugs in the past 10 years

(CDC, 2015d; Spindelman, 2013 and 2011).

It is recommended that pregnant women receive preventive information including a description of interventions that can reduce HIV transmission from mother to infant, such as not breastfeeding and the meanings of positive and negative HIV test results. Pregnant women need to understand that test results may not appear positive until three months after infection (CDC, 2015c). As is, it is simply a matter of time before HIV-positive mothers are prosecuted for exposure of the virus to their fetuses or children using the HIV criminal transmission laws (Khan, 2015). Given the positive medical advancements in HIV prevention and treatment, the stakes are too high for HIV-positive women who might become pregnant to risk ignoring preventive interventions.

Newborn HIV Testing

It is said that "a mother's love for her child is like nothing else in the world; it knows no law, no pity; it dares all things and crushes down remorselessly all that stands in its path" (Christie, 2003/1933, p. 137). Yet, over 5,000 children diagnosed with AIDS have died since the beginning of the epidemic. Clearly much work remains regarding testing pregnant women (Khan, 2015).

Between 180 and 200 infants are infected with HIV each year (CDC, 2016). Many of these newborn infections involve women who were not treated early enough in pregnancy or who did not receive detection services or information on preventing transmission (CDC, 2015a). Perinatal HIV transmission is the most common route of HIV infection in children and is now the source of almost all HIV/AIDS cases in children in the United States (CDC, 2016). Children born HIV-positive who go without treatment usually develop **HIV-related infections** within the first year of life (Khan, 2015). Without treatment, children infected with HIV progress very rapidly towards AIDS and die within a few years (DuBois et al., 2015). With treatment, ARVs can prevent children with HIV from developing AIDS (Bitnun et al., 2014).

Newborn testing is generally mandatory if a mother's HIV status is unknown or test results are not available (CDC, 2014b). If the mother's HIV status is unknown prior to the onset of labor and rapid HIV testing is not done during labor, rapid HIV testing of the infant immediately postpartum is routinely done with or without the mother's consent (CDC, 2016). However, postpartum monitoring is not routine in children with HIV-positive mothers (Khan, 2015).

Minors' Right to Consent to HIV Testing and Treatment

Since the first HIV/AIDS case was reported in the United States, states have expanded minors' authority to consent to health care without parents taking part in the decisions, including care related to sexual activity. The age of majority is generally accepted as 18 years in this chapter, as distinguished from the international definition of children as those under the age of 15. All states allow most minors, generally beginning at 12 to 14 years of age, to consent to HIV testing (AGI, 2015). While all states permit minors to consent to HIV/AIDS treatment, some states allow physicians to inform parents if a minor is seeking or receiving treatment (Manian, 2016). Iowa is the only state that requires parental notification in the case of a minor's positive HIV test; in Colorado, physicians may inform parents of a minor's decision to consent to HIV/AIDS medical services if the minor is younger than 16 (AGI, 2015).

Access to Medical Treatment

HIV testing should ideally be coordinated with treatment, which raises the issue of affordable access to essential health care in the United States (CDC, 2013b). Early medical treatment significantly improves the health of HIV-positive patients while also greatly reducing transmissibility of the disease. Therefore, early access to ARV treatment is crucial to the success of widespread HIV testing. Unfortunately, early access in the United States is unobtainable for many people with HIV, especially those without private health insurance (Fagan et al., 2010) or anyone living in a state that refused to expand Medicaid insurance under the **Affordable Care Act**. Medicaid insurance coverage for ARV treatment was a flashpoint in states declining to expand Medicaid insurance and will continue to be a source of health insurance controversy over the next decade of the nation's response to HIV (Underhill, 2012).

Medicaid insurance represents the largest source of medical coverage for Americans living with HIV/AIDS. Almost half of the individuals living with HIV/AIDS are enrolled in Medicaid insurance programs; 20% are uninsured or underinsured (NASTAD, 2016). In order to qualify for Medicaid insurance, most HIV-positive people must be both low income and disabled. While all states are required to provide Medicaid insurance to the disabled, people with HIV do not qualify as disabled without an AIDS diagnosis in most states (Kaiser, 2014a and 2014b). The cruel irony is Medicaid insurance requires patients to manifest symptoms of the disease before providing the ARV treatment that would have prevented the symptoms. This means treatment is withheld for many low-income Americans until it is too late for preventive care (Dodd et al., 2010).

Second Prong: Containment of HIV Infections

The second prong of the United States' approach to containment is reporting and contact notification of HIV infections. Numerous health laws come into conflict on this debate, including:

- Duty to warn
- Entitlement to know of risks
- Obligation to protect the public health
- Protection against discrimination
- Right of confidentiality and privacy

Coupled with these conflicts is the tension between public health agencies with their duty to the greater good of the community and physicians with their duty towards their individual patients.

Protection of Public Health

Government has an interest in controlling the HIV/AIDS pandemic and the potential second wave of tuberculosis infections. Yet, the only **case of first impression** associated with the AIDS pandemic in the past decade addressed tattooing and its purported association with the transmission of HIV. In *Anderson v. City of Hermosa Beach*, a court found that the restriction of First Amendment expression was too broad as compared to the public health interests in containing HIV infections that were at stake.

COURT DECISION
Containment of HIV Infections

Anderson v. City of Hermosa Beach
[Tattoo Parlor Owner v. Local Municipality]
621 F.3d 1051 (U.S. Court of Appeals for the 9th Circuit 2010);
followed by Coleman v. City of Mesa, 284 P.3d 863 (Supreme Court of Arizona 2012)

Facts: Johnny Anderson ran Yer Cheat'n Heart tattoo parlor in Redondo Beach, within the City of Los Angeles. He wanted to open another parlor in the City of Hermosa Beach, within the County of Los Angeles. The City of Los Angeles generally permits tattoo establishments; Hermosa Beach does not. Anderson filed a civil rights action alleging that the local zoning ordinance in the City of Hermosa Beach was unconstitutional when he was denied permission to open a second tattoo parlor. While Anderson sought to strike down the local zoning ordinance, the municipality feared the risk for acquiring and transmitting communicable diseases like HIV, hepatitis, and tuberculosis in local tattoo parlors.

Issue: Is the **First Amendment** protection of tattoos going too far when it invalidates a municipal ban on tattoo parlors as being unreasonable?

Holding and Decision: Although an outright municipal ban on tattoo parlors violates the First Amendment, tattoo parlors can be regulated under proper time, place, or manner restrictions.

Analysis: This case is considered by many to be a landmark decision in its recognition of tattoos as a protected form of pure speech. Tattoos can mark rites of passage, express feelings about others, show religious devotion, or symbolize a collection of significant moments in one's life. By articulating tattoos as a protected form of communication, public health and safety disputes about regulation of tattoo parlors are effectively restricted. The court found that tattooing can be conducted safely and that the failure of a municipality to have appropriate health and safety regulations cannot be a means to restrict free speech.

With regard to the First Amendment, the court decided it was better to err on the side of permission than prohibition. The municipal ban on tattoo parlors was found to be not narrowly tailored, and it did not leave open alternative channels of communication. Specifically, the court focused on the general principle that absolute bans are disfavored in First Amendment cases.

Rule of Law: Tattoos are forms of pure expression fully protected by the First Amendment; local time, place, and manner restrictions are permissible only if they are narrowly tailored to serve the concern of protecting the public's health while allowing for freedom of expression.

References discussing this court decision: *E.g.*, Calvert, 2013; Nickow, 2013.

Although health inspections may enforce the use of sterile tattooing equipment, there are potential safety risks of communicable diseases being transferred through the inks or through the needles used to transmit those inks if proper precautions and procedures are not followed (Nickow, 2013). The *Anderson* case is more remarkable for the public health protections it did not address than what it did address; the court was so concerned about the impropriety of tattoo prohibitions as a restriction on free speech that it did not substantively recognize the public health realities of tattooing as involving a potential risk of HIV disease transmission (Calvert, 2013).

Partner Notification Requirements

Both physicians and laboratories are required to report the names of newly diagnosed HIV patients to state communicable disease registries. A controversial issue is whether physicians should also disclose the HIV status of their patients to known sexual partners, such as spouses, to whom HIV is likely to be transmitted. The failure to warn does not give rise to liability if the known sexual partner simply fears becoming infected, but physician liability could arise if the known sexual partner subsequently becomes HIV-positive (Avraham & Meyer, 2016). At the same time, physicians of HIV-infected patients are not required to investigate and notify third parties about their risk of contracting HIV.

The confidentiality requirements of the **Health Insurance Portability and Accountability Act of 1996** (HIPAA) and various confidentiality laws that vary by state, all add to the confusion (*See* 45 C.F.R. parts 160 and 164). Most states have **duty-to-warn laws** requiring sexual partners to be informed of their HIV exposure; other states require that if a newly diagnosed HIV patient refuses to report a partner who may have been exposed, physicians must report any partner of whom they are aware (Burke, 2014). Some states also have laws mandating a duty to warn and requiring disclosure by physicians to third parties known to be at risk for future HIV transmission from patients known to be infected (Klemm, 2010). In general, states have one of three types of partner notification laws:

- Physicians are mandated to report the partner's name and the state then notifies the partner.
- Physicians may either report the partner's name or notify the partner directly.
- Reporting is optional.

Obviously, all information regarding HIV status must be reported on a **need-to-know** basis; otherwise, health care providers may face liability for publicly and needlessly disseminating personal information. The Americans with

Disabilities Act and a number of court decisions treat HIV status as a private fact whose disclosure is highly offensive (Avraham & Meyer, 2016). Health care providers may be assessed punitive damages for wrongful disclosure of HIV status in violation of HIPAA and **state confidentiality laws** if such information is disclosed to anyone without the need to know.

Wrongful Disclosure of HIV Status

Individuals with HIV, whose status was made public to someone without the need to know, have found limited relief in attempts to protect the privacy of their HIV status (Fishman, 2013). One obstacle to finding liability for wrongful disclosure is that the definition of publicity in many states is disclosure and release of information to a large group of people. Communication of facts, such as HIV status, to a single person or even to a small group of people is not wrong under many state confidentiality laws unless a special relationship exists, such as the relationship between a patient and health care professional or between employee and employer.

Criminal Laws

Many states have criminal laws that in effect discourage HIV testing (Langley & Nardi, 2010). For instance, most states will prosecute people with HIV who engage in various sexual activities without first disclosing their HIV-positive status to prospective sex partners (DOJ & CDC, 2014). Almost all states have criminal laws that punish HIV-positive individuals for sexual behaviors posing some risk of HIV transmission, even if no transmission occurs, with the exceptions listed below. Most states have laws criminalizing sexual contact by people with HIV unless they:

- Abstain from unsafe sex
- Disclose their HIV status to their partners
- Obtain consent from their partners

(Lee, 2014; *See* Dean, 2013).

Most states find the **knowing transmission of HIV** to be a felony (Strangio, 2015). Alabama, Kansas, Montana, and New York are the only four states to recognize transmission as a misdemeanor crime (ACLU, 2008; Frost, 2016). Whether these contrasting laws influence high-risk sexual behaviors is debatable, since most of these laws were passed before research showed that ARV treatment reduces HIV transmission risk (Lehman et al., 2014). In addition, all states have general criminal laws that can and have been used to prosecute individuals for HIV transmission:

- Assault and battery
- Attempted murder
- Reckless endangerment

(CDC, 2015e).

Mandatory Testing of Sexual Offenders

HIV testing is generally required for anyone arrested for a crime involving sexual intercourse or sexual contact (Baskin et al., 2016). Most states require accused sex offenders to submit, in response to a court order or a request by a victim, to HIV testing and follow-up testing if the initial test is negative. Some states require that an indication of potential viral transmission take place, such as the exchange of bodily fluids, before testing is required (Lozoya, 2016).

HIV as Another Communicable Disease

In the United States, HIV is technically treated no differently from other communicable diseases. There are two sides to this policy. One side maintains the current privacy and antidiscrimination laws at the federal and state levels sufficiently protect people living with HIV/AIDS. Advocates of this view accept routine HIV testing and do not see any significant existing stigma associated with HIV/AIDS (CDC, 2014b).

The other side maintains there is ongoing discrimination and distrust of the health care system in many high-risk communities in the United States. Advocates of this view are concerned with civil rights and privacy protections of those in society at the greatest risk of discrimination. They want to treat HIV/AIDS differently from other afflictions. Both sides of this debate agree on the need for a national, coordinated public health response to the AIDS pandemic in the United States (UNAIDS, 2016b).

Adequacy of Protection from Stigma and Discrimination

One central disagreement over routine HIV detection, testing, and reporting is whether current antidiscrimination laws adequately protect against the stigma of HIV/AIDS. Though confidentiality and antidiscrimination protections exist, state laws vary widely, many without fully protecting people living with HIV/AIDS (*See* Gerwint, 2011).

HIV Discrimination Under the Americans with Disabilities Act

At the federal level, people with HIV do not enjoy guaranteed protection against discrimination. Courts, including the U.S. Supreme Court, insist that only a narrow set of deserving individuals with HIV-positive status qualify for protection from discrimination. For the first time, in *Bragdon v. Abbott*, the U.S. Supreme Court had the opportunity to address the issue of whether HIV infection itself constituted a disability. This landmark decision is still relied upon as precedential almost two decades after it was decided.

COURT DECISION
HIV Infection as a Disability

Bragdon v. Abbott
[Dentist v. HIV Patient]
524 U.S. 624 (U.S. Supreme Court 1998);
followed by United States v. Hayes, 555 U.S. 415 (U.S. Supreme Court 2009)

Facts: Sidney Abbott, after being refused in-office treatment by her dentist due to her HIV-positive status, sued under the Americans with Disabilities Act. Abbott refused to pay $185 for a hospital procedure that would cost only $35 at her dentist's office.

Issue: Did a dentist's refusal to treat an HIV-infected patient constitute disability discrimination?

Holding and Decision: Yes. HIV-positive status, from the moment of infection, constitutes a disability if the HIV infection substantially limits a major life activity.

Analysis: The U.S. Supreme Court applied a three-part test to determine whether Abbott was disabled and found that her HIV-positive status constituted a disability under the Americans with Disabilities Act. The Court held Abbott was disabled because of reproduction concerns. Abbott's decision not to have children was motivated by her HIV diagnosis. Therefore, her HIV infection was an impairment that substantially limited the major life activity of reproduction.

First, the Court decided that HIV-positive status constituted an **impairment**. The Court was influenced by the fact that HIV followed a predictable and unalterable course. It was assumed HIV was nontreatable; HIV-positive status was characterized as being constant and permanent.

Second, the Court determined HIV-positive status affected the major life activity of reproduction. The possibility that an individual's HIV status might affect other major life activities was left open. Finally, the Court found Abbott's HIV-positive status substantially limited her ability to reproduce; the risks of HIV transmission to a male sexual partner, and the risks of perinatal transmission of HIV to a newborn constituted substantial limitations on reproduction. While the use of ARV treatment to lower the risk of perinatal transmission was considered, the Court did not find the reduction in risk affected the limitations on reproduction. HIV-positive status was characterized as a dreadful and fatal disease.

The Court conceded reproduction may be possible for women infected with HIV, but found the danger to public health resulting from such reproduction constituted a substantial limitation on procreation. To support this conclusion, the Court considered the negative economic and legal consequences of the decision of HIV-infected women to have children, including the costs of treating a newborn with HIV and the criminality of sexual activity for individuals with HIV/AIDS in most states.

Rule of Law: The Court held that an individual's HIV infection must substantially limit a major life activity to be considered a disability and declined to decide whether HIV/AIDS infection was a per se disability.

References discussing this court decision: *E.g.*, Benge, 2016; Gordon, 2015; Heindel, 2013; Hickox & Guzman, 2014; Newman, 2013; Noonan, 2014.

The U.S. Supreme Court remanded the case to determine whether filling the dental cavity of an asymptomatic HIV patient posed a direct threat to a dentist. The lower court subsequently ruled that universal precautions sufficiently reduced the risk of infection in a dentist's office. The *Bragdon* decision that HIV infection is not by itself a per se disability remains controversial to this day (Christie, 2007). The Supreme Court still remains very hesitant to open the door to nontraditional disabilities such as a communicable disease.

COURT DECISION
HIV Infection as a Disability

Waddell v. Valley Forge Dental Associates
[Dental Hygienist v. Dental Clinic]
276 F.3d 1275 (U.S. Court of Appeals for the 11th Circuit 2001),
cert. denied, 535 U.S. 1096 (U.S. Supreme Court 2002)

Facts: Spencer Waddell, an HIV-positive dental hygienist, sued Valley Forge Dental Associates, his employer, alleging *inter alia* that he was discriminated against in violation of the Americans with Disabilities Act when his employer refused to allow him to continue treating patients due to his HIV-positive status.

Issue: Was an HIV-positive dental hygienist discriminated against in violation of federal disabilities law?

Holding and Decision: No. Because the hygienist posed a significant risk of transmitting his disease to patients, he was not an individual qualified for protection under federal disabilities law.

Analysis: The court concluded that several factors, when taken together, indicated the hygienist posed a significant risk to others in the workplace:

- Possibility of an inadvertent bite or other accident during a dental cleaning
- Risk that hygienists will be stuck or pricked while using an instrument
- Routine patient bleeding during dental work
- Statements of the hygienist and his medical experts acknowledging there was some risk, even if theoretical and small, that blood-to-blood contact between hygienist and patient can occur

The court noted that the U.S. Supreme Court declined to address whether asymptomatic HIV is a per se disability. This suggests that the preferred method is to address whether an impairment causes a substantial limitation upon a major life activity on a case-by-case, individualized basis.

Rule of Law: The hygienist, because he was infected with HIV, was a direct threat to his workplace and, therefore, was not a qualified individual entitled to protection from discrimination under federal disabilities law.

References discussing this court decision: *E.g.*, Kaplan, 2015; Mendonsa, 2010.

Review of subsequent court decisions finds individuals with HIV-positive status are continually failing to present the necessary evidence to obtain protection from discrimination.[LN4] Any further restriction in the U.S. Supreme Court's interpretation of the Americans with Disabilities Act law could have significant repercussions for HIV-infected people (Metnick, 2003).

Confidentiality of HIV Status

Virtually every state collects the names of individuals who test positive for HIV. Many states also require physicians to report private information, such as drug use and sexual history about anyone who tests positive (Burda, 2016). While public health reporting actions are a valid exercise of the state's police powers and are not viewed as an impermissible intrusion into personal privacy, the collection of identifiable HIV test results is still strongly debated. Despite the U.S. Supreme Court's ruling on medical privacy issues, the privacy arguments in *Whalen* are being repeated in battles over HIV reporting (Mariner, 2016; *See Whalen v. Roe*, 429 U.S. 589 (U.S. Supreme Court 1977) (examining the constitutionality of mandatory reporting requirements as they pertain to the physician-patient relationship and prescription drugs)). The debate over whether states are required to report new cases of HIV infection by full names as opposed to by codes is another aspect of the argument over whether to treat HIV as a routine communicable disease in the United States. One side of the debate claims name-based reporting is essential for epidemiological purposes, while the other side claims the practice is unnecessary and dissuades some people from being tested out of concern for their confidentiality (Frost, 2016).

Preventing Occupational HIV Transmission

The **HIV Post-Exposure Registry** documents about 60 cases of occupational exposure among health care professionals since AIDS first appeared in the United States in 1981. This means one to two health care professionals become infected with HIV each year. To prevent HIV transmissions, health care professionals should assume the blood and other body fluids from all patients are potentially infectious. They should therefore follow **universal infection control precautions** at all times (CDC, 2015c). These precautions include:

- Careful handling and disposing of sharp instruments during and after use
- Routine use of barriers such as gloves and/or goggles when anticipating contact with blood or body fluids
- Washing hands and other skin surfaces immediately after contact with blood or body fluids

(CDC, 2001).

While safety devices have been developed to help prevent needle-stick injuries, they must be used properly to reduce the risk of exposure to HIV. Most infections are related to sharps disposal. Although the most important strategy for reducing the risk of occupational HIV transmission is to prevent occupational exposures to **blood-borne pathogens**, risk plans for post-exposure prophylaxis should be in place in all health care settings (CDC, 2001; Underhill, 2012).

The Global Blood Supply

HIV tests currently in use are highly accurate, but still cannot detect HIV 100% of the time in donated blood (CDC, 2015f). This is especially true as HIV sometimes cannot be detected until three months after infection took place.

Blood Safety in the United States

Today, the blood supply in the United States is one of the safest in the world, with stringent donor selection practices and numerous diagnostic screenings. For over two decades, gay and bisexual men were banned from the donation of blood because HIV/AIDS was thought to predominantly, if not exclusively, affect gay and bisexual men (Nelson, 2014). Today, there is a one-year deferral in place where gay and bisexual men who have had sex with other men are prohibited from donating blood (CDC, 2015f).

This so-called **gay blood ban** is one of the few government policies that makes any differentiation based on sexual orientation, despite the thorough testing of blood for blood-borne diseases and despite the reality that HIV-tainted blood can come from a donor of any sex and sexual orientation (Nelson, 2014). The improvement of collection and processing methods for blood products has reduced the number of HIV infections resulting from the use of these products. Currently, the risk of infection with HIV through receiving a blood transfusion or blood products is extremely rare in the United States. This risk has become progressively lower even in geographic areas with high HIV rates (CDC, 2015f).

Nearly everyone infected with HIV through blood transfusions received those transfusions before 1985, the year HIV testing began for all donated blood. The Institute of Medicine found many organizations shared blame for the compromised U.S. blood safety at the onset of the AIDS pandemic in the 1980s:

- American Red Cross
- Blood and plasma collection agencies
- Blood product manufacturers
- Centers for Disease Control and Prevention
- Community blood banks
- National Hemophilia Foundation
- National Institutes of Health
- U.S. Food and Drug Administration

(Leveton et al., 1995).

Blood banks and **fractionation firms** were criticized for not initiating surrogate laboratory testing and for accepting blood donations from gay and bisexual men (Leveton et al., 1995). As a result of the contaminated blood supply in the 1980s, HIV-infected transfusion recipients received compensation awards and financial settlements. The federal Ricky Ray Hemophilia Relief Fund Act authorized $750 million in taxpayer payments to more than 6,200 hemophiliacs who had received HIV-infected clotting concentrate (*See* 42 U.S.C.A. § 300c-22 note). Four pharmaceutical firms subsequently completed a financial settlement with the Committee of Ten Thousand, a group of 10,000 HIV-infected hemophiliacs. It authorized individual payments of $100,000 to about 8,700 HIV-infected hemophiliacs and to individuals they had infected (Pulver, 2008).

This settlement involved a nationwide group of HIV-positive hemophiliacs who sued the pharmaceutical firms that manufactured **blood solids**, claiming that their negligence caused the plaintiffs' infections. First identified in 1981, AIDS was diagnosed in hemophiliacs beginning in 1982, and by 1984 the medical community agreed that the virus was transmitted by blood as well as by semen and vaginal fluids. That year it was demonstrated that treatment with heat could kill HIV in the blood supply and in the following year a reliable test for the presence of the virus in blood was developed. By this time, however, a large number of hemophiliacs had become infected. HIV-positive hemophiliacs who could prove they had not engaged in high-risk behaviors received compensation from the settlement since it was more likely than not that contaminated blood caused their HIV infections.

Blood Safety in Resource-Limited Countries

It is estimated that up to 10% of the global HIV infections result from transfusion of blood or blood products (UNAIDS, 2016a). Blood safety continues to be a global concern, as almost half the donations in resource-limited countries are not screened for HIV (UNAIDS, 2016b). Clearly, the need to ensure the safety of the global blood supply must remain a matter of interest.

Lack of Access to Health Care

The fight against the AIDS pandemic still continues, with the rates of infections in young men on the rise (UNAIDS, 2016a). AIDS remains a death sentence for many low income adults in the United States and for those in resource-limited countries (Jones, 2014). While HIV has become a serious, but manageable, chronic condition for those with the resources to gain access to health care, lack of early access to care is the difference between life and death from AIDS (UNAIDS, 2016a and 2016b).

The Global HIV/AIDS Crisis and Pharmaceuticals

The search for new health care models to help the world's poorest populations is perhaps most evident in sub-Saharan Africa where the HIV/AIDS crisis has drawn international attention to the suffering of millions who live without essential health care. Although the AIDS pandemic has focused largely on the development of drugs, it has raised awareness about the lack of essential health care systems to deliver health care in poverty-ridden, resource-limited countries. Coupled with the debate about global responsibility for the AIDS pandemic is the question of how to address the pandemic in the United States. While recognizing the nature of the global pandemic, HIV/AIDS has enabled broader health care development in the United States (Mukherjee, 2007). All the money and attention being directed to this particular disease helped build a foundation for universal primary care (Wharton, 2006a).

Access to ARVs and AIDS Drugs

The public perception of the AIDS pandemic and pharmaceuticals situation is that there needs to be an immediate procurement of drugs. However, the problem with access to medical treatment is not necessarily the cost of drugs like it was in the earlier years of the outbreak. Instead, it is now the multifaceted difficulty of finding the workers to provide health care in resource-limited countries and the struggle of obtaining early access to medical treatment (UN Secretary-General, 2016).

These difficulties are intertwined with the willingness of those infected to accept responsibility for adherence to their drug regimen (Tsai, 2007) as well as the responsibility to not knowingly infect others. HIV treatment requires a high degree of adherence to taking ARVs. With the advent of combination drug therapies, regimen compliance for HIV/AIDS patients is particularly complex. In the past, some of the ARVs were unpleasant, debilitating, and lifestyle limiting, but this is no longer the case for most brand drugs. Nevertheless, ARV therapy should be part of an integrated package of interventions that includes care and support activities, all of which complement and reinforce adherence to ARV drug regimens.

People living with HIV who take fewer than 95% of their drugs run the serious risk of developing resistance and failing therapy. Additionally, there is the very real danger noncompliance will lead to transmission of resistant viruses to others, a phenomenon that is already emerging. On the other hand, the virulence of HIV decreases if ARVs are taken as prescribed. Transmission of HIV is always possible with someone who is HIV-positive, but with safe sex practices such as condom use, transmission of the disease is less likely. Nevertheless, it is bears repeating that once infected with HIV, individuals are infected for life; there is no cure for HIV infections (IAVI, 2006).

Humanitarian Tradition of the Pharmaceutical Industry

The global pharmaceutical industry does, contrary to widespread belief, have a humanitarian tradition. Pharmaceutical employees believe their corporations are different from other multinational corporations. While there is a long-standing norm in the United States for industry to engage in philanthropic activities, the most effective and appropriate contributions are those that draw on core business expertise. At the same time, discounting ARVs and AIDS drugs in resource-limited countries is not entirely altruistic. For one thing, the pharmaceutical industry is not giving up many sales at higher prices, since these countries are too poor to pay otherwise. The industry also needed a public relations boost in the United States, as it became clear the HIV/AIDS crisis was reaching catastrophic proportions worldwide, partly because of the industry's early failure to supply needed drugs to resource-limited countries (Vagelos, 2014).

Pricing of ARVs and AIDS Drugs

The publicly traded firms that make up the pharmaceutical industry are obligated to seek profits for shareholders. Like any profit-seeking firm, they are free to charge the highest prices the market will bear. Consider though, is the pharmaceutical industry really like other for-profit businesses when it comes to the AIDS pandemic? ARVs and AIDS drugs are not like most consumer products. For instance, Apple may have a monopoly on iPhone technology, but if it charges too much, customers can choose Samsung or Google Nexus instead. Pharmaceuticals, on the other hand, can charge patients $10,000 to $15,000 a year for drugs costing only a few hundred dollars to make, but there are often no other options for patients to choose from. Thus, most patients do not have the option of not buying most lifesaving drugs; they either pay the retail price or go without the drug treatment (Gregg, 2015). Where a **generic** is available, patients may have the option of choosing a cheaper drug. But this is another misnomer when it comes to the pharmaceutical industry because not all generics are cheaper (Brennan et al., 2016). In countries where drug prices are regulated, there is no substantive difference in the price of generics. However, any debate about profit margins is an unsuitable way to describe how drugs are priced because it is based on an incomplete picture of the industry (Rosebush & Holmes, 2016).

Manufacturing costs alone do not reflect the hundreds of millions of dollars that have gone into discovering, testing, and marketing new ARV and AIDS drugs (Brennan et al., 2016). Three pharmaceutical firms, Merck, Bristol-Myers Squibb, and Gilead Science, stepped up research to produce a new combination drug AIDS patients can take in one daily dose. The goal is to make treatment for the disease easier and less costly, which are crucial elements in the effort to help millions of AIDS victims in Africa and other regions of the world (Sevilla, 2016). This needed innovation would probably never have happened if the pharmaceutical industry was in a price-regulated market worldwide.

The United States is the only country that does not regulate drug prices, and there is much debate on whether price regulation would affect pharmaceutical innovation (Brennan et al., 2016). The pharmaceutical industry maintains most ARVs and AIDS drugs under study since 1981 never made it to market. They turned out to be ineffective, burdened by side effects, and/or too expensive to produce and disseminate. A few successful drugs must recoup the research and development costs of all the failures under the current global regulatory scheme for drugs (Sevilla, 2016). The HIV/AIDS pandemic has forced examination of the entire regulatory scheme and how to best price drugs (Rosebush & Holmes, 2016).

Price Discrimination

At present, the global pharmaceutical system relies on its relatively wealthy markets to subsidize the research and development costs of both its successful and unsuccessful ARVs and AIDS drugs (Sevilla, 2016). Wealthy markets subsidize poorer ones, just as the affluent in theory pay more taxes. The best way to get ARVs and AIDS drugs to resource-limited countries is to have wealthier countries pay more for them (Azgad-Trome, 2014). This kind of price discrimination is what the pharmaceutical industry already does and with regard to ARVs and AIDS drugs, it is probably best for everyone it does this (Brennan et al., 2016). Not only are ARVs and AIDS drugs cheaper in resource-limited countries, they are cheaper in many developed ones as well, frequently because of price regulation. **Bargain rates** come at a cost, though, because they result in less money spent on researching and developing new ARVs and AIDS drugs (Sevilla, 2016).

Some argue Americans pay for most of the new drugs coming out all over the world, not just ARVs and AIDS drugs. Even within the United States, different HIV/AIDS patients are charged different prices for the same drug (Sevilla, 2016). HIV/AIDS patients who purchase health insurance are likely to pay less than if they are uninsured or otherwise pay out of pocket. Other industries do this too. An airline passenger forced to fly on short notice may pay significantly more than one who reserved an identical seat weeks in advance. Price discrimination is both equitable and efficient; without it, seizing **patents** might be a justified action for resource-limited countries (Vagelos, 2014). The pharmaceutical industry has research and development costs that, as a whole, are worth incurring and that have to be dispersed. Somebody has to pay them. Many economists would argue these costs should be paid by those who are most able and willing to pay them (Azgad-Trome, 2014).

Access as an Insurance Problem, Not Simply a Drug Pricing Problem

In recent years, the pharmaceutical industry's long-standing price discrimination system has come under pressure. The uninsured and those with inadequate prescription benefit plans have discovered they are paying much more for ARVs and AIDS drugs than HIV/AIDS patients in the rest of the world. Low income patients in the United States complain about being denied access to ARVs that can prevent their immune systems from being weakened to the point where they are disabled by full-blown AIDS (Fagan et al., 2010). However, this may not be simply price discrimination.

The problem of obtaining access to ARVs is also an insurance problem, not simply a problem due to drug prices. Individuals who are HIV-positive need health insurance with reasonable prescription coverage, meaning **co-payments** that are at an affordable level and plans that provide medical coverage for needed drugs without unnecessary restrictions and barriers to access. The pharmaceutical industry is reluctant to sell large quantities of drugs at low prices in resource-limited countries for fear some will flow back to the United States, known as **compounding access**. Underground drug markets will undermine the high prices being charged in high-price markets (Yu, 2007). Still one must ask why patients living with HIV/AIDS in resource-limited countries are being provided access to ARVs at three times the rate of infected Americans (WHO, 2016). HIV/AIDS statistics can, however, be misleading. Are some HIV/AIDS patients in the United States being denied access to care due to price, or is there another explanation for this disparity in rates of access?

Pricing Incentives

Few issues are as controversial as drug pricing (Sevilla, 2016). At the onset of the AIDS pandemic, the pharmaceutical industry erred by not quickly reaching an agreement to provide lifesaving ARVs and AIDS drugs cheaply to African nations. It did so only after massive public pressure and as the number of people who have been, or are, directly affected by this pandemic approached 100 million worldwide (WHO, 2010).

A radical change occurred as more than 73 million people contracted HIV over time since 1981 (UNAIDS, 2016b). In 2006, the pharmaceutical industry looked at risks in isolation. More and more the industry now recognizes the risks' interdependencies when mapping their vulnerabilities. More than 34 million people have died of AIDS since 1981 (HHS, 2016); many of these deaths were due to the lack of access to drugs in sub-Saharan Africa in the early years of the pandemic (WHO, 2016). This fact alone significantly damaged the reputation of the global pharmaceutical industry and made governments worldwide scrutinize the industry in all other respects.

To critics of the pharmaceutical industry, any effort to keep the prices of ARVs and AIDS drugs high seems immoral in the face of the seriousness of the pandemic. It was not difficult for activists to argue the industry has a debt to society (Azgad-Tromer, 2014). At issue was whether the pharmaceutical industry was meeting its corporate obligations in return for the government benefits it was receiving (Sevilla, 2016). What was society obtaining for the billions of dollars in government-financed biomedical research from agencies such as the National Institutes of Health? Also, what was society receiving in return for governments providing patent protection with up to 20 years of monopoly?

When tens of millions of people died as a direct result of lack of access to available ARVs and AIDS drugs, the pharmaceutical industry suddenly faced different pressures than other industries enjoying similar government benefits. While parallels can be made to demands placed on the oil industry whenever Americans face the rising costs of energy, there is a stark difference between pricing lifesaving drugs and pricing a gallon of gasoline. Both examples, however, go to show whenever the balance between public expectations of a fair price for a product and the price set by an industry dramatically differ, the vulnerabilities of industry players come into play. Be it the price of drugs or the price of a gallon of gasoline, the value dynamics are the same. While incentive policies are meant to encourage drug development, HIV/AIDS activists question whether the rewards for the pharmaceutical industry are higher than they should be. Similar questions are being directed to research universities and their commercialization activities. Ideally society would find the exact point at which the financial incentives are just strong enough to cause needed drugs to be developed, and no stronger (Sevilla, 2016). It is very difficult to know when an incentive is too much, or at what point it generates windfall profits or benefits (Rosebush & Holmes, 2016). The calls to the pharmaceutical industry for assistance are widespread and come from both activists and advocates of world economic reform (Azgad-Trome, 2014). As an example, the pharmaceutical industry has been asked for:

- Guarantees for an uninterrupted supply of donations to all resource-limited countries without arbitrary time limitations
- Permission for governments to employ **compulsory licensing**, **parallel importing**, and other mechanisms to protect public health
- Reduction in the price of ARVs and AIDS drugs to levels affordable for populations of resource-limited countries
- Removal of all conditions from **concessionary price reductions**

(*E.g.*, Fagan et al., 2010; George, 2011).

It is not possible to gauge the right level of incentive with mathematical precision (Rosebush & Holmes, 2016). It is, however, obvious that as the AIDS pandemic tears through the world, new incentive policies need to be developed to overcome the failure of the pharmaceutical industry and governments worldwide to help the millions of people suffering from HIV/AIDS and lack of access to essential health care (Sevilla, 2016).

Price Discounting

It is clear the pharmaceutical industry is under siege by political forces that are threatening to revoke intellectual property rights, which are the foundation of the pharmaceutical industry's profit structure (Anderson, 2010). The issues surrounding patents, licensing, and knowledge management are not unique to pharmaceuticals, however; the same intellectual property questions face many industries worldwide. The focus in this chapter is simply on how intellectual property affects the prices of ARVs and AIDS drugs.

Intellectual property threats are based on concerns the pharmaceutical industry is using its patent protections to prevent generics from offering ARVs and AIDS drugs to the global marketplace (UNAIDS, 2013). This is not to say the current 20-year protection length is exactly right for these drugs, but any judgment about the system's effectiveness would necessarily involve opinions on whether the world is getting the ARVs and AIDS drugs it needs.[LN5]

Compulsory Licensing

How can the pharmaceutical industry be encouraged to produce new drugs? Merck sells its ARVs and AIDS drugs at a discounted price to resource-limited countries and is involved in a joint project with the Gates Foundation and the government of Botswana to provide detection, education, and ARVs in the country, which has an HIV infection rate of over 40% of its population. Taking such steps in Botswana muted calls for compulsory licensing and an overthrow of Merck's patents on its drugs. Botswana was prepared to authorize a generic firm to produce Merck's patented products without Merck's consent before Merck finally agreed to significantly discount its prices for ARVs and AIDS drugs (Guzik, 2007).

The economic fact is: if financial incentives are too strong, the world gets more drugs than it needs and prices are too high; if incentives are too weak, the world gets cheaper drug prices but misses out on valuable innovations. This is a concern for current and future HIV/AIDS patients and for the global population at large. There are many small firms looking for new ARVs and AIDS drugs, and much research and drug development by established pharmaceutical firms in response to the effectiveness of the current incentives (Lazo, 2007). Whether there is too much or too little research and development is difficult to tell. Even when a new HIV/AIDS drug comes to market, it is often impossible to precisely gauge its value.

International Partnership for Microbicides

Significant progress has been made in recent decades to reduce drug prices and increase access to ARV treatments in low- and middle-income countries in response to the AIDS pandemic (Ulrich, 2015). The question remains: when is a new HIV/AIDS drug worth the research and development costs if it is provided royalty-free? For instance, in sub-Saharan Africa, where the AIDS pandemic has hit hardest, women and girls are particularly vulnerable to infection due to a combination of biology and gender inequities, yet they lack the tools they urgently need to protect themselves (IPM, 2016). In response, Bristol-Myers Squibb and Merck agreed to license to the **International Partnership for Microbicides** experimental ARV treatments that were formulated and tested as **microbicides** (like a monthly ring or a single-use film or tablet), to help prevent infection among women by preventing HIV from entering the immune system cells it normally invades.

The microbicide licenses, which are royalty free, provide the Partnership with the rights to distribute the compounds in resource-limited countries. This is the first time the pharmaceutical industry helped develop gels, sponges, and other products to help prevent the sexual transmission of HIV and other sexually transmitted diseases in women (IPM, 2016). Notwithstanding, AIDS remains the leading cause of death for women ages 15-44 worldwide (UN, 2016).

MANAGEMENT AND LAW ISSUES

8. What factors should be considered when encouraging pharmaceutical corporations to develop needed ARVs and AIDS drugs without generating windfall profits?
9. Is the AIDS pandemic so catastrophic and overwhelming that the ordinary rules of doing business should be set aside?
10. If so, do pharmaceutical corporations have a moral obligation that should override best business practices?

The Unrelenting Stigma of AIDS

The paradox of our time is that although AIDS causes more than 4,400 deaths each day worldwide, in many ways the AIDS pandemic remains hidden (UNAIDS, 2016b). With 38 deaths per day in the United States, the AIDS pandemic is not seen as a devastating issue to most Americans. There is no simple solution for eliminating HIV/AIDS. A complex set of intertwined factors presents significant challenges, including:

- Denial
- Discrimination
- Fear
- Homophobia
- Limited access to high-quality health care
- Misinformation
- Poverty
- Racism
- Stigma

(*E.g.,* Fagan et al., 2010).

Each of the factors further complicates efforts to comprehensively address the AIDS pandemic (CDC, 2014a).

In many parts of the United States, the stigma from testing HIV-positive today is not substantially different from testing positive in the 1980s:

- Antidiscrimination protections in many states are inadequate.
- No laws can address the stigma that alienates HIV-positive people from their families and communities.
- Medicaid insurance is structured as a disability care system as opposed to a health care system that helps prevent diseases and illness.

What should be accomplished before the AIDS pandemic could possibly devastate the health of communities worldwide? What can the global community do, in addition to everything already being done? Suggestions include:

- Comprehensively contain communicable diseases acquired from birth, accidents, violence, or lifestyle choices
- Continue funding comprehensive public health programs to address communicable diseases worldwide
- Find a way to weigh and then balance civil liberties protections with routine HIV testing
- Provide palliative care to people experiencing AIDS-related end-stage illnesses

(Mikkonen & Raphael, 2010; UNAIDS, 2013).

Acceptance of Individual Responsibility

Controversy over the role of individual responsibility for preventing HIV infections by preventive drug and sex practices is hard to address in a society like the United States (Gordon, 2015). The very idea of mandating routine testing for HIV for the **common good** of society is even harder to deal with given the nation's differences in values and what constitutes right and wrong lifestyles. It is almost impossible, but not out of the question, to agree on incentives for individuals who are HIV infected to take responsibility for adherence to their treatment regimens (*See* Jordan, 2015). When the second wave of the AIDS pandemic hits the United States, the nation might then insist that everyone accept individual responsibility for preventable behaviors related to this communicable disease.

The Second Wave of HIV/AIDS

Almost 700,000 Americans have died from AIDS since the first case was documented in the United States in 1981 and 1.3 million people are currently living with the disease in the United States (CDC 2015a). The world has begun to accept responsibility. Worldwide, about 350,000 deaths are averted every year as a result of increased treatment access (UNAIDS, 2016a).

All the same, almost 200 nations agree HIV/AIDS is both a local and worldwide issue of the highest priority (White House, 2015). As the second wave of the AIDS pandemic begins to hit Africa and India with a wave of opportunistic infections, the question is whether we are taking too long to learn from the lessons of the recent past. To paraphrase a question put forth by Archbishop Desmond Tutu, former President of South Africa, at the University of Washington: "When will we come to learn we are not our brother or sister's keeper? We are our brother's brother, and our sister's sister" (Tutu, 2002, p. 73).

LAW FACT

Early Detection of HIV

Is there a heightened duty of care to routinely test high-risk patients for HIV infection?

No. High-risk patients themselves make conscious decisions to knowingly subject themselves to a lifestyle that carries fatal risks affecting their health. It is this participation alone that places them at higher risk for contracting HIV, not any delay in detection and treatment for HIV/AIDS infections. There is no **heightened duty of care** to test high-risk patients for HIV simply because of their sexual preference.

— *Lopes v. Shpigel*, 965 A.2d 311 (Superior Court of Pennsylvania 2008) (affirming Philadelphia Court of Common Pleas' decision without opinion).

CHAPTER SUMMARY

- An HIV infection is a serious, but manageable, chronic condition if detected and treated early and if patients have access to comprehensive, lifelong medical treatments that treat opportunistic infections associated with a weakened immune system.
- HIV infection remains a fatal illness for those in resource-limited countries and for most low-income adults in the United States without early access to medical treatment.
- Almost half of all new adult HIV infections in the United States occur among young people 15 to 24 years of age.
- Perinatal HIV transmission is the source of almost all HIV/AIDS cases in children under 15 year of age in the United States.
- HIV/AIDS treatment requires a very high degree of adherence to drug regimens; noncompliance leads to the serious risk of developing resistance, which may lead to transmission of resistant HIV strains to others.
- The current problem with access to medical treatment is not necessarily the cost of ARVs and AIDS drugs as it was in earlier years of the outbreak; instead, it is the multifaceted difficulty of finding health care in resource-limited countries and of obtaining early access to high-quality care in the United States.
- Manufacturing costs alone do not reflect the hundreds of millions of research and development dollars that go into discovering, testing, and marketing new ARVs and AIDS drugs.
- Drug price discrimination enables the pharmaceutical industry to provide low-priced, high-quality innovative ARVs and AIDS drugs to resource-limited countries.
- The global pharmaceutical system relies on its relatively wealthy markets to subsidize poorer ones; the most efficient way to get ARVs and AIDS drugs to resource-limited countries is to have more wealthy countries like the United States pay more for them.
- Intellectual property rights are the foundation of the pharmaceutical industry's current profit structure.
- There are two prongs of the approach to the AIDS pandemic in the United States: early detection and treatment of the HIV infection, and containment of the disease.
- The government recommends everyone in the United States between the ages of 13 and 64 be routinely tested for HIV, regardless of individual risk factors; at this time, HIV testing remains voluntary on an opt-out basis.
- The government recommends all pregnant women be tested for HIV because perinatal transmission of HIV can be reduced to less than 1% by the administration of ARVs to infected mothers and their newborns.
- Most minors can consent to testing and treatment of HIV/AIDS.

- In states where Medicaid insurance has not been expanded under provisions of the Affordable Care Act, HIV-positive individuals cannot access Medicaid insurance before they are certified disabled; symptoms that would have prevented the symptoms in the first place must be manifest before medical treatment is provided.
- Both physicians and laboratories are required to report the names of newly diagnosed HIV patients to government communicable disease registries, along with personally identifiable information about drug use and the sexual history of people infected.
- In the absence of state duty-to-warn laws, a physician's failure to warn the known partners of a newly diagnosed HIV patient does not generally give rise to liability.
- All states have criminal laws punishing HIV-positive individuals for sexual behaviors that pose a risk of HIV transmission, even if no transmission occurs; such behavior is usually a felony.
- HIV-infected individuals do not enjoy guaranteed protection against discrimination under the Americans with Disabilities Act.
- Health care professionals should follow universal infection control precautions at all times to prevent exposure to blood-borne pathogens.
- Federal policy bans gay and bisexual men from donating blood if they have had sex with other men in the prior 12 months; however, blood establishments may voluntarily elect to totally ban all gay and bisexual men from donating.
- Almost half the blood donations in resource-limited countries are unscreened for HIV; therefore, 1 in 10 HIV infections is the result of tainted blood or blood product transfusions.

LAW NOTES

1. This measure is from the Joint U.N. Programme on HIV/AIDS (UNAIDS), comprised of 10 U.N. system organizations: The Office of the U.N. High Commissioner for Refugees; the U.N. Children's Fund; the World Food Programme; the U.N. Development Programme; the U.N. Population Fund; the U.N. Office on Drugs and Crime; the International Labour Organization; the U.N. Educational, Scientific and Cultural Organization; the World Health Organization; and the World Bank.
2. Sub-Saharan Africa comprises the eight countries of Botswana, Lesotho, Mozambique, Namibia, South Africa, Swaziland, Zambia, and Zimbabwe.
3. Injection drug use is a disturbing transmitter of HIV infections (Lee, 2015). At the start of every injection, blood is introduced into the needle and syringe. Therefore, a needle and syringe that someone who is HIV-positive uses can contain blood that contains the virus. The reuse of a contaminated needle or syringe by another drug injector carries a high risk of HIV transmission because infected blood can be injected directly into the bloodstream. Sharing other drug equipment also can be a risk for spreading HIV. Infected blood can be introduced into drug solutions through using blood-contaminated syringes to prepare drugs; reusing water; reusing bottle caps, spoons, or other containers used to dissolve drugs in water and to heat drug solutions; or reusing small pieces of cotton or cigarette filters used to filter out particles that could block the needle.
4. The U.S. Supreme Court held Bragdon was disabled because her HIV substantially limited her major life activity of reproduction. The Court found Bragdon's decision not to have children was motivated by her HIV diagnosis. Given that many HIV-infected people have never considered having children, and given that current therapies make the risk of mother-to-child transmission negligible today, the protections extended in *Bragdon* are far from comprehensive. Further, because personal choice is almost always a factor in a decision to reproduce, the Court set the standard of what constitutes a disability excessively high, requiring specific evidence HIV status is the sole reason for a decision not to procreate. *See Blanks v. Southwestern Bell Communications, Inc.*, 310 F.3d 398, 401 (U.S. Court of Appeals for the 5th Circuit 2002) (declining to classify an HIV-positive man as disabled because his wife had undergone a tubal ligation and he had no plans to have more children; therefore, the activity of reproduction was not considered a major life activity for him).
5. In South Africa, a low-cost, generic, three-drug ARV treatment costs $2,000 per person each year at private-sector wholesale prices and $750 per person per year for the public sector. However, the median yearly household income in South Africa is only $1,000, much too little to afford complete ARV treatment (Collins-Chase, 2008). Without treatment, HIV-positive individuals develop AIDS and die within 10 years.

   With partial ARV treatment, HIV-positive individuals frequently develop resistance to existing ARVs and AIDS drugs, and the virulence of HIV is enhanced more often than not. Highly virulent strains of HIV more rapidly weaken the immune system of individuals, eventually leading to full-blown AIDS. The higher the viral load, the shorter the time to develop AIDS, and the shorter the survival rate.

REFERENCES

ACLU (American Civil Liberties Union). (2008). *State criminal laws on HIV transmission*. New York, NY: ACLU.

AGI (Alan Guttmacher Institute). (2015). *Minors' access to STI services: State policies in brief*. New York, NY: AGI.

Anand, G. (2012, June 19). India in race to contain untreatable tuberculosis. *Wall Street Journal*, p. A1.

Anderson, Jr., H. E. (2010). We can work it out: Co-op compulsory licensing as the way forward in improving access to anti-retroviral drugs. *Boston University Journal of Science and Technology Law, 16*, 167–193.

Avraham, R., & Meyer, J. (2016). The optimal scope of physicians' duty to protect patients' privacy. *Minnesota Law Review Headnotes, 100*, 30–60.

Azgad-Trome, S. (2014). The case for consumer-oriented corporate governance, accountability and disclosure. *University of Pennsylvania Journal of Business Law, 17*, 227–291.

Baskin, S., et al. (2016). Criminal laws on sex work and HIV transmission: Mapping the laws, considering the consequences. *Denver University Law Review, 93*, 355–388.

Benge, S. G. (2016). Section 1557 of the Affordable Care Act: An effective means of combating health insurers' discrimination against individuals with HIV/AIDS? *Indiana Health Law Review, 13*(1), 194–232.

Bitnun, A., et al. (2014). Early initiation of combination antiretroviral therapy in HIV-1-infected newborns can achieve sustained virologic suppression with low frequency of CD4+ T cells carrying HIV in peripheral blood. *Clinical Infectious Diseases, 59*, 1012–1014.

Brennan, H., et al. (2016). A prescription for excessive drug pricing: Leveraging government patent use for health. *Yale Journal of Law and Technology, 18*, 275–354.

Burda, J. P. (2016). PrEP and our youth: Implications in law and policy. *Columbia Journal of Gender and Law, 30*, 295–363.

Burke, J. (2014). Discretion to warn: Balancing privacy rights with the need to warn unaware partners of likely HIV/AIDS exposure. *Boston College Journal of Law and Social Justice, 35*, 89–115.

Burris, S., et al. (2010). Racial disparities in injection-related HIV: A case study of toxic law. *Temple Law Review, 82*, 1263–1302.

Calvert, C. (2013). Fringes of free expression: Testing the meaning of "speech" amid shifting cultural mores and changing technologies. *Southern California Interdisciplinary Law Journal, 22*, 545–590.

CDC (Centers for Disease Control and Prevention). (2016). *HIV among pregnant women, infants, and children*. Atlanta, GA: U.S. Department of Health and Human Services, CDC.

___. (2015a). *HIV surveillance report: Diagnoses of HIV infection in the United States and dependent areas*.

___. (2015b). *HIV in the United States: At a glance*.

___. (2015c). *About HIV*.

___. (2015d). *HIV among youth*.

___. (2015e). *HIV-specific criminal laws*.

___. (2015f). *Revised recommendations for reducing the risk of human immunodeficiency virus transmission by blood and blood products; questions and answers*.

___. (2014a). *CDC fact sheet: HIV in the United States: The stages of care*.

___. (2014b). *CDC fact sheet: HIV testing in the United States*.

___. (2014c). *Tuberculosis and HIV coinfection*.

___. (2013a). *Extensively drug-resistant tuberculosis (XDR tuberculosis)*.

___. (2013b). *Background brief on the prevention benefits of HIV treatment*.

___. (2001). *Updated U.S. Public Health Service guidelines for the management of occupational exposures to HBV, HCV, and HIV and recommendations for post-exposure prophylaxis*.

Christie, A. (2013). *The hound of death (Agatha Christie collection)*. New York, NY: HarperCollins Publishers. (Original work published 1933.)

Christie, S. R. (2007, October). AIDS, employment, and the direct threat defense: The burden of proof and the circuit court split. *Fordham Law Review, 76*, 235–282.

Cohen, M. S., et al. (2011). Prevention of HIV-1 infection with early antiretroviral therapy. *New England Journal of Medicine, 365*(6), 493–505.

Collins-Chase, C. T. (2008, Spring). The case against TRIPS PLUS protection in resource-limited countries facing AIDS epidemics. *University of Pennsylvania Journal on International Law, 29*, 763–802.

Corey, L. (2011, June 18). Thirty years of fighting AIDS: A progress report. *Wall Street Journal*, p. A15.

CSDH (Commission on the Social Determinants of Health). (2015). *Health in the Americas*. Geneva, Switzerland: World Health Organization.

Dean, T. (2013, November 28). In barebacking culture, HIV is embraced, not avoided. *New York Times*, p. D1.

Dodd, P. J., et al. (2010). Examining the promise of HIV elimination by 'test and treat' in hyper-endemic settings. *AIDS, 24*(5), 729–735.

DOJ (U.S. Department of Justice) & CDC (Centers for Disease Control and Prevention). (2014). *Prevalence and public health implications of state laws that criminalize potential HIV exposure in the United States, AIDS and behavior*. Washington, DC: DOJ and Atlanta, GA: CDC.

DuBois, J. M., et al. (2015). Overcoming barriers to effective legislative and regulatory changes in health care: Anticipating HIV vaccines: Sketching an agenda for public health ethics and policy in the United States. *Saint Louis University Journal of Health Law and Policy, 8*, 225–257.

Fagan, J. L., et al. (2010). Understanding people who have never received HIV care: A population-based approach. *Public Health Reports, 125*, 520–527.

Fishman, H. R. (2013). HIV confidentiality and stigma: A way forward. *University of Pennsylvania Journal of Constitutional Law, 16*, 199–231.

Frost, S. (2016). HIV criminalization laws: A poor public policy choice in the new era of PreEP. *Wake Forest Journal of Law and Policy, 6*, 319–347.

Gao, F., et al. (1999). Origin of HIV-1 in the chimpanzee: *Pan troglodytes troglodytes*. *Nature, 397*, 436–441.

George, E. (2011). The human right to health and HIV/AIDS: South Africa and South-South cooperation to reframe global intellectual property principles and promote access to essential medications. *Indiana Journal of Global Legal Studies, 18*, 167–197.

Gerwint, L. E. (2011). Planning for pandemic: A new model for governing public health emergencies. *American Journal of Law and Medicine, 37*, 128–171.

Goldfein, R. B., & Schalman-Bergen, S. R. (2010). From the streets of Philadelphia: The AIDS law project of Pennsylvania's how-to primer on mitigating health disparities. *Temple Law Review, 82*, 1205–1230.

Gordon, A. J. (2015). End around: HIV discrimination in the post-amendments ADA workplace. *Berkeley Journal of Employment and Labor Law, 36,* 215–260.

Gostin, L. O., et al. (2011). Restoring health to health reform: Integrating medicine and public health to advance the population's well-being. *University of Pennsylvania Law Review, 159,* 1777–1822.

Greene, S. S. (2016). Race, class, and access to civil justice. *Iowa Law Review, 101,* 1263–1320.

Gregg, J. (2015). The implications, negative health effects, legal issues, and potential solutions associated with the shortage of essential drugs in the U.S. medical care market. *Albany Law Journal of Science and Technology, 25,* 381–454.

Gregg, S. (2011). Health, health care, and rights: A new natural law theory perspective. *Notre Dame Journal of Law, Ethics and Public Policy, 25,* 463–478.

Guzik, B. (2007). Botswana's success in balancing the economics of HIV/AIDS with TRIPS obligations and human rights. *Loyola University of Chicago International Law Review, 4*(2), 4–271.

Heindel, C. (2013). Medical advances, criminal disadvantages: The tension between contemporary antiretroviral therapy and criminal HIV exposure laws in the workplace. *Washington Journal of Law, Technology and Arts, 9,* 35–51.

Helmink, J. M. (2010). Sexually transmitted identification. *Information Society Journal of Law and Policy, 5,* 569–601.

HHS (U.S. Department of Health and Human Services). (2016). *Global statistics.* Rockville, MD: HHS, Health Resources and Services Administration.

____. (2014). *Guide for HIV/AIDS clinical care.*

Hickox, S. A., & Guzman, J. M. (2014). Leave as an accommodation: When is enough, enough? *Cleveland State Law Review, 62,* 437–490.

HIV Justice Network & Global Network of People Living with HIV. (2016). *Advancing HIV justice: Building momentum in global advocacy against HIV criminalisation.* Brighton and Amsterdam, Holland: HIV Justice Network and Global Network of People Living with HIV.

HUD (U.S. Department of Housing and Urban Development). (2015). *The annual homeless assessment report to Congress.* Washington, DC: HUD.

IAVI (International AIDS Vaccine Initiative). (2006). *Imagining a world without AIDS: A history of the International AIDS Vaccine Initiative.* New York, NY: IAVI.

ICASO (International Council of AIDS Service Organizations). (2015). *Working together: A community-driven guide to meaningful involvement in national responses to HIV.* Toronto, Ontario, Canada: ICASO.

IOM (Institute of Medicine). (2013). *Evaluation of the President's Emergency Plan for AIDS Relief (PEPFAR).* Washington, DC: National Academies Press.

____. (2011). *HIV screening and access to care: System capacity for increased HIV testing and provision of care.*

____. (2010). *HIV screening and access to care: Exploring barriers and facilitators to expanded HIV testing.*

IPM (International Partnership for Microbicides). (2016). *New technologies for women's HIV prevention: The payoff for sustainable development.* Silver Spring, MD: IPM.

Jones, A. (2014). The more things change, the more they stay the same: A section 504 examination of the Social Security Administration's use of 1993 medical criteria to determine disability in 2014. *American University Journal of Gender, Social Policy and the Law, 22,* 651–692.

Jordan, K. A. (2015). The contraceptive mandate: Compelling interest or ideology? *Journal of Legislation, 41,* 1–64.

Kaiser Family Foundation. (2015). *Estimated number of adults and adolescents living with an HIV diagnosis.* Menlo Park, CA: Kaiser.

____. (2014a). *The HIV/AIDS epidemic in the United States.*

____. (2014b). *State Medicaid coverage of routine HIV screening.*

____. (2014c). *HIV testing in the United States.*

____. (2011). *HIV/AIDS at 30: A public opinion perspective.*

Kaplan, M. (2015). Taking pedophilia seriously. *Washington and Lee Law Review, 72,* 75–169.

Khan, S. K. (2015). The threat lives on: How to exclude expectant mothers from prosecution for mere exposure of HIV to their fetuses and infants. *Cleveland State Law Review, 63,* 429–457.

Klemm, S. (2010). Keeping prevention in the crosshairs: A better HIV exposure law for Maryland. *Journal of Health Care Law and Policy, 13,* 495–524.

Langley, E. E., & Nardi, Jr., D. J. (2010). The irony of outlawing AIDS: A human rights argument against the criminalization of HIV transmission. *Georgetown Journal of Gender and Law, 11,* 743–794.

Langner, B. J. (2015). Unprotected: Condoms, bareback porn, and the First Amendment. *Berkeley Journal of Gender, Law and Justice, 30,* 199–224.

Lazo, J. A. (2007). The Life-Saving Medicines Export Act: Why the proposed U.S. compulsory licensing scheme will fail to export any medicines or save any lives. *Brooklyn Journal of International Law, 33,* 237–276.

Lee, D. J. (2015). Injections, infections, condoms, and care: Thoughts on negligence and HIV exposure. *Cornell Journal of Law and Public Policy, 25,* 245–267.

Lee, S. G. (2014). Criminal law and HIV testing: Empirical analysis of how at-risk individuals respond to the law. *Yale Journal of Health Policy Law and Ethics, 14,* 194–238.

Lehman, J. S., et al. (2014). Prevalence and public health implications of state laws that criminalize potential HIV exposure in the United States. *AIDS and Behavior, 18*(6), 997–1006.

Leveton, L. B., et al. (1995). *HIV and the blood supply: An analysis of crisis decision-making: U.S. Institute of Medicine Committee to study HIV transmission through blood and blood products.* Washington, DC: IOM.

Lozoya, A. (2016). Mandatory HIV testing of pregnant women: Public health or privacy violation? *Houston Journal of Health Law and Policy, 16,* 77–111.

Manian, M. (2016). Minors, parents, and minor parents. *Missouri Law Review, 81,* 127–203.

Mariner, W. K. (2016). Reconsidering constitutional protection for health information privacy. *University of Pennsylvania Journal of Constitutional Law, 18,* 975–1054.

Mendonsa, L. R. S. (2010). Dualing causation and the rights of employees with HIV under 504 of the Rehabilitation Act. *The Scholar: St. Mary's Law Review on Minority Issues, 13,* 273–316.

Metnick, J. M. (2003). Evolving to asymptomatic HIV as a disability per se: Closing the loophole in judicial precedent. *DePaul Journal of Health Care Law*, *7*, 69–104.

Mikkonen, J., & Raphael, D. (2010). *Social determinants of health: The Canadian facts.* Toronto, Canada: York University School of Health Policy and Management.

Mukherjee, G. N. (2007). Improving the pharmaceutical industry: Optimality inside the framework of the current legal system provides access to medicines for HIV/AIDS patients in sub-Saharan Africa. *Journal of Transnational Law & Policy*, *17*, 121–150.

NASTAD (National Alliance of State and Territorial AIDS Directors). (2016). *National ADAP monitoring project annual report.* Washington, DC: NASTAD & Menlo Park, CA: Kaiser Family Foundation.

NCHHSTP (National Center for HIV/AIDS, Viral Hepatitis, STD, and Tuberculosis Prevention). (2016). Health disparities in HIV/AIDS, viral hepatitis, sexually transmitted diseases and tuberculosis in the U.S.: Issues, burden and response. In *Update: NCHHSTP health disparities report.* Washington, DC: U.S. Department of Health and Human Services.

Nelson, R. H. (2014). An indirect challenge to the FDA's gay blood ban. *Tulane Journal of Law and Sexuality*, *23*, 1–15.

Newman, S. J. (2013). Prevention, not prejudice: The role of federal guidelines in HIV-criminalization reform. *Northwestern University Law Review*, *107*, 1403–1436.

Nickow, A. L. (2013). Getting down to (tattoo) business: Copyright norms and speech protections for tattooing. *Michigan Telecommunications and Technology Law Review*, *20*, 183–214.

Noonan, C. A. (2014). Art expressed on a living canvas: Proposing a balance between the protection of free expression and the governmental interest in regulating the tattoo industry. *Loyola Law Review*, *60*, 137–170.

Novogrodsky, N. (2014). After AIDS. *Melbourne Journal of International Law*, *14*, 643–669.

Perone, A. (2013). From punitive to proactive: An alternative approach for responding to HIV criminalization that departs from penalizing marginalized communities. *Hastings Women's Law Journal*, *24*(2), 363–406.

Pierce, M. W., et al. (2011). Testing public health ethics: Why the CDC's HIV screening recommendations may violate the least infringement principle. *Journal of Law, Medicine and Ethics*, *39*, 263–270.

Pulver, A. R. (2008). Gay blood revisionism: A critical analysis of advocacy and the gay blood ban. *Law & Sexuality*, *17*, 107–130.

Rosebush, L. H., & Holmes, L. P. (2016). Select issues in negotiating drug pricing and reimbursement contracts. *Journal of Health and Life Sciences Law*, *10*(1) 59–77.

Saleem, A., & Asher, M. (2013). The next pandemic - tuberculosis: The oldest disease of mankind rising one more time. *British Journal of Medical Practitioners*, *6*(2), 1–8.

Sevilla, J. P. (2016). On the potential impact of value pricing by developing countries on allocative and dynamic efficiency in the global pharmaceutical industry. *Journal of Law, Economics and Policy*, *12*, 147–176.

Spindelman, M. (2013). Sexuality's law. *Columbia Journal of Gender and the Law*, *24*, 87–252.

___. (2011). Sexual freedom's shadows, unlimited intimacy: Reflections on the subculture of barebacking in response to Jim Dean. *Yale Journal of Law and Feminism*, *23*, 179–253 (*See supra* Dean).

Strangio, C. (2015). *HIV is not a crime.* New York, NY: American Civil Liberties Union.

Tracey, E., & Lange, R. (2012). *A medical news roundup from Johns Hopkins: One in three patients had some drug resistance.* Baltimore, MD: Johns Hopkins Medicine.

Tramont, E. C., & Boyajian, S. S. (2010). Learning from history: What the public health response to syphilis teaches us about HIV/AIDS. *Journal of Contemporary Health Law and Policy*, *26*, 253–299.

Tsai, J. T. (2007). Not tripping over the pebbles: Focusing on overlooked TRIPS article 66 for technology transfer to solve Africa's aids crisis. *Michigan State University College of Law Journal of Medicine and Law*, *11*, 447–476.

Tutu, D. M. (2002). HIV/AIDS and the global community: We can be human only together. *Seattle Journal of Social Justice*, *1*, 253–254.

UCSF (University of California-San Francisco) & National HIV/AIDS Clinicians' Consultation Center. (2008). *State HIV testing laws compendium.* San Francisco, CA: UCSF.

Ulrich, L. (2015). TRIPS and compulsory licensing: Increasing participation in the medicines patent pool in the wake of an HIV/AIDS treatment timebomb. *Emory International Law Review, 30,* 51–84.

UN (United Nations). (2016). *World mortality report.* New York, NY: UN, Department of Economic and Social Affairs, Population Division.

UN Secretary-General. (2016). *A more secure world: Our shared responsibility: Report of the high-level panel on threats, challenges and change.* New York, NY: United Nations General Assembly.

UNAIDS (United Nations Programme on HIV/AIDS) & WHO (World Health Organization). (2016a). *AIDS Pandemic Update.* New York. NY: UNAIDS.

___. (2016b). *Global AIDS update.*

UNAIDS (United Nations Programme on HIV/AIDS). (2013). *Report on the global AIDS epidemic.* Geneva, Switzerland: World Health Organization.

___. (2013). *Report on the global AIDS epidemic.*

Underhill, K. (2012). Paying for prevention: Challenges to health insurance coverage for biomedical HIV prevention in the United States. *American Journal of Law and Medicine*, *38*, 607–666.

UNF (United Nations Foundation). (2012). *Global reach, global connections, global change.* Washington, DC: UNF.

Vagelos, P. R., Chairman of the Board, Regeneron Pharmaceuticals and Retired Chairman and Chief Executive Officer of Merck & Co. (2014, February 21). Keynote Speaker at the 2014 Wharton Health Care Business Conference on Reimagining Health Care: Driving Change in a Patient-Centered World, Philadelphia, PA.

Weis, R. A., & Wrangham, R. W. (1999). From *Pan* to pandemic. *Nature*, *397*, 385–386.

Wharton (Wharton School at the University of Pennsylvania). (2011). What's behind U.S. pharmaceutical companies' response to the AIDS crisis abroad? Knowledge@Wharton.

___. (2006a). Raising money to treat the world's sickest people isn't the problem: Spending it is. *Knowledge@Wharton*.

White House, The. (2015). *National HIV/AIDS strategy for the United States: Update of 2020 federal actions to achieve national goals and improve outcomes along the HIV care continuum.* Washington, DC: The White House, Office of National AIDS Policy.

Winslow, R. (2010, July 23). Crucial window to beat back HIV. *Wall Street Journal*, p. A5.

Winslow, R., & McKay, B. (2010, July 19). Study links HIV to urban poverty. *Wall Street Journal*, p. A2.

World Health Organization (WHO). (2016). *World health statistics.* Geneva, Switzerland: WHO.

___. (2014). *Global tuberculosis report.*

___. (2010). *Report on the global AIDS epidemic.*

Yu, P. K. (2007). The international enclosure movement. *Indiana Law Journal, 82,* 827–909.

CHAPTER 27

© Andy Dean Photography/ShutterStock, Inc.

Mental Heath

"It must be remembered that for the person with severe mental illness who has no treatment the most dreaded of confinements can be the imprisonment inflicted by [their] own mind, which shuts reality out and subjects [them] to the torment of voices and images beyond our own powers to describe."

— **Justice Anthony Kennedy**, Associate Justice of the U.S. Supreme Court in *Olmstead v. L.C. ex rel. Zimring*, 527 U.S. 581, 609–610 (U.S. Supreme Court 1999)

IN BRIEF

This chapter focuses on the health care system's response to mental illness. This epidemiological approach reveals the magnitude of mental illness and ranks depression as more of a burden to the U.S. health care system than any other illness. A significant number of new mental health issues were recently judicially addressed by the highest federal legal authorities; therefore, five case decisions are presented in this chapter.

LEARNING OBJECTIVES

Upon completion of this chapter, readers should be able to:

1. Distinguish between mental illness and intellectual disability.
2. Describe the problems of stigma attached to mental illness.
3. Understand the relationship between mental illness and homelessness.
4. Discuss involuntary civil commitments and the requisite quantum of proof involved.
5. List the particular populations especially prone to mental illness.
6. Distinguish between the issues surrounding dangerous and not dangerous mental illnesses.
7. Explain the problems of advocacy for individuals with mental illness.
8. Describe the magnitude of the impact of sex addition on society.

KEY TERMS

Affirmative duty to intervene
Borderline personality disorder
Burden of disease
Clear and convincing evidence
Co-occurring substance abuse
Cognitive-behavioral therapy
Communicable diseases
Conditional releases
Dangerous mental disorder
Dangerousness
Delusional disorder
Depressive disorder
Diminished capacity

Disability-adjusted life-year
Disease burdens
DSM-5
Due process of law
Electroconvulsive treatment
Emergency court order
Evidence-based care
Failure-to-warn
Family Educational Rights and
   Privacy Act of 1974
Fourteenth Amendment
Global Burden of Disease Study
Gross negligence

Imminent risk
Inappropriate incarceration
Intellectually disabled
Involuntary civil commitment
Known wishes
Liberty
Lower standard of proof
Major depressive disorders
Medical comorbidities
Medical necessity
Mental capacity
Mental disorder
Mental health

Mental Health Parity and Addiction Equity Act of 2008	Protection and Advocacy for Individuals with Mental Illness Act of 2000	Standard of care
Mental illness	Punitive damages	Sub-average intellectual functioning
Negligence	Qualified immunity	Supportive housing
Non-treatment-related conditions	Quality of life offenses	Temporary detention order
Not responsible by reason of mental disorder or defect of insanity	Residential/day treatment	Tort Claims Act
Patient advocates	Severe mental disorder	Traffickers
	Sex addiction	Transitional residence program
		Treatment slots
		Unnecessary disability

FACT OR FICTION

Medical Coverage for Acute Mental Health Treatment

Following a precertification approval, can an insurer retrospectively deny coverage for ensuing treatment of a severe mental disorder when the patient is completely dysfunctional and suicidal?

The State of Vermont contracted with Merit to provide mental health care benefits to state employees under the state's medical benefit plan. By providing these benefits, Merit functioned as a review agent. For its part, Merit contracted with Austen Riggs, a mental health care facility, to be one of its mental health care service providers under the state plan. Austen Riggs specialized in the care of severely ill, treatment-resistant patients. Under its contract with Merit, Austen Riggs agreed to cooperate with precertification and concurrent review procedures and policies.

Jane Doe, a state employee covered under the state's plan, was referred to Austen Riggs for treatment of a long-term **mental disorder**. Doe was in the midst of a major depressive episode of the illness, which had proven resistant to various attempts at treatment over the years, including short-term hospitalization, **residential/day treatment**, aggressive medication therapy, **cognitive-behavioral therapy**, and **electroconvulsive treatment**. After Doe's pre-certified admission to Austen Riggs, a dispute arose between Merit and Austen Riggs over Doe's treatment plan. The conflict centered around inconsistencies between Austen Riggs's policy of having patients stay a minimum of 30 days once they were found to be appropriate candidates for treatment and Merit's policy of requiring daily review to ensure continued residential mental health care services were medically necessary.

Shortly after Doe was admitted to Austen Riggs, Merit's medical director informed Austin Riggs he could not conduct concurrent review of Doe's treatment because Austen Riggs's treatment plan did not fit Merit's method of managing inpatient treatment. Merit's medical director noted Austen Riggs did not share Merit's assumptions that each day needed to be reviewed and a patient should be released or at least stepped down to a lesser level of care as soon as clinically appropriate. Merit claimed it had been misled about Austen Riggs's willingness to work with its system of review and length of stay for admitted patients, while Austen Riggs claimed Merit knew of its policies, including its minimum stay policy, when Merit contracted with it to be one of its mental health care providers.

In the end, Merit informed Austen Riggs it would approve Doe's initial six-day stay and consider her claim for further treatment after retrospective review of her medical record. Several days later, Merit informed Doe it had authorized payment for her initial stay at Austen Riggs but would determine the medical necessity of Doe's treatment after her release. Austen Riggs also sent Doe a letter stating that because Merit had declined its request for approval of a further medically necessary stay, she would have to guarantee payment for treatment herself if she decided to stay at Austen Riggs. She agreed to do so and remained at Austen Riggs for the next several months.

After her release, Doe sought payment from Merit for her treatment at Austen Riggs. Merit denied Doe's claim because available documentation did not support the **medical necessity** of her level of care. Doe appealed to the Independent Panel of Mental Health Care Providers, an agency established to consider adverse decisions made by review agents. Following a hearing, the independent panel concluded Doe's treatment at Austen Riggs was medically necessary and therefore covered under the state's plan. Merit appealed the Independent Panel's coverage decision.

— *See* Law Fact at the end of this chapter for the answer.

Principles and Applications

The population of those with **severe mental disorders** has less access to treatment and receives poorer quality of treatment than people without mental illness (Ezell et al., 2013; Lawrence & Kisely, 2010). Even though **mental illness** is one of the leading **disease burdens** on the U.S. health care system (WHO, 2014), it takes tragedies such as the shootings at Sandy Hook Elementary School that killed 26 people, to focus attention on the nation's response to the most overlooked disease in the United States (Roach, 2016). While only a small percentage of the 44 million Americans suffering from mental illness has a severe mental disorder, it is the mentally ill population at **imminent risk** of causing substantial harm to themselves or others that should concern everyone (Hedden et al., 2015; *See* 18 U.S.C.A. § 4246(f)). Unfortunately, even less attention is paid to **depressive disorders** upon everyday life; how this illness affects U.S. productivity in the workspace is generally ignored (Wharton, 2015).

Continuum of Mental Health and Mental Illness

The law has rarely doubted the existence of mental illness but has struggled with its definition and its disposition. Although **mental health** and mental illness are points on a continuum, the first Surgeon General's report ever issued on the topic set forth the most accepted definition of mental health as a condition of successful performance of mental function, resulting in:

- Ability to adapt to change and cope with adversity
- Fulfilling relationships with other people
- Productive activities

(U.S. Surgeon General, 2011).

Mental illness, in contrast to mental health, was broadly defined as all diagnosable mental disorders, as defined by the American Psychiatric Association, which developed the *Diagnostic and Statistical Manual of Mental Disorders*, currently in its fifth edition and known by mental health professionals as **DSM-5**. *DSM-5* contains diagnostic codes and detailed descriptions for all recognized iterations of mental illness. Although there may not be biological tests to diagnose different mental disorders, standard methods of diagnosis do exist (APA, 2013). Mental disorders, in turn, may be defined as biologically based health conditions characterized by:

- Alterations in thinking, mood, or behavior
- Distress, defined as mental anguish and misery characterized by feelings of grief, anxiety, and unhappiness
- Impaired mental functioning, characterized by a heightened risk of death, pain, disability, or loss of freedom

(APA, 2013).

Contrary to how public stigma would frame it, mental disorders are not character flaws but legitimate illnesses that respond to specific treatments, just as other physical health conditions respond to medical interventions (Wharton, 2015). The shame and disgrace attached to mental disorders indicates that in the 21st century, mental illness is still regarded by many as a socially unacceptable health condition.

While most definitions of what constitutes mental illness are expansive, various mental disorders range in severity and treatment. Some of the more severe mental disorders include:

- Alzheimer's disease, a mental disorder marked by alterations in thinking, especially forgetting
- Bipolar disorder
- **Borderline personality disorder**
- Major depression, a mental disorder largely marked by alterations in mood
- Obsessive compulsive disorder
- Panic disorder
- Posttraumatic stress disorder
- Schizophrenia

(APA, 2013).

Although less severe, attention-deficit disorder and attention-deficit/hyperactivity disorder, often diagnosed in children (mental disorders largely marked by alterations in behavior (over activity) and/or thinking (inability to concentrate), are considered to be within the definition of mental illness (APA, 2013).

Epidemiology of Mental Illness

Even though mental illness is widespread in the population, the main burden of severe mental disorders is concentrated in a much smaller proportion:

- About 6%, or 1in 17 Americans, suffers from a severe mental disorder
- At any one time, as many as 2 million and up to 6 million Americans with a severe mental disorder are at risk of causing harm to themselves or others
- Mental illness affects one in five families in the United States

(NAMI, 2016a; WHO 2014).

Treatments for severe mental disorders are highly effective; between 70 and 90% of individuals have significant reduction of symptoms and improved quality of life with a combination of pharmacological and psychosocial treatments and support (WHO, 2014). Without treatment, the consequences of mental illness for the individual and society are staggering:

- **Co-occurring substance abuse**
- Homelessness
- **Inappropriate incarceration**
- Suicide
- Unemployment
- **Unnecessary disability**
- Wasted lives

(U.S. Surgeon General, 2011).

Individuals with co-occurring substance abuse suffer from both mental illness and substance abuse. This chapter does not address substance abuse alone or the abuse of alcohol and drugs in the absence of mental illness. While spending on hospitalization, drugs, and therapy for mental illness and co-occurring substance abuse treatment is about $150 billion year, this spending is falling as a share of all health care costs, as coverage for health care of this nature is decreasing (Wharton, 2015).

Although the federal **Mental Health Parity and Addiction Equity Act of 2008** mandates that health insurers treat mental illness in the same manner as physical illness (*See* 29 U.S.C.A. §1185a), government funds to treat mental illness are declining and in many instances, simply disappearing. The United States is increasingly facing a shortage of **treatment slots**; publicly funded and private treatment facilities are generally running at full capacity with growing wait lists (Chorney, 2014). The result of this treatment shortage is that while costs of mental health and co-occurring substance abuse treatment are increasing, the number of individuals being treated remains the same; only the most serious cases are being accepted to receive treatment (NAMI, 2016b). Non-serious cases are dealt with by the general health care system, including by physicians not trained to treat either mental health illnesses or co-occurring substance abuse, and by the nation's emergency rooms.

Global Burden of Disease Study

The **Global Burden of Disease Study** originated in the early 1990s by the World Health Organization in collaboration with the World Bank and Harvard University. This study was the first systematic effort to look at mortality and other dimensions of ill health. The overall **burden of disease** was assessed using the **disability-adjusted life-year** (also referred to as the DALY metric), a time-based measure that combines years of life lost due to premature mortality and years of life lost due to time lived in states of less than full health (WHO, 2014). By focusing not just on causes of death but also charting the costs of living with a disease or disability, the study reveals the magnitude of health issues such as mental illness:

- Four of the 10 leading causes of disability in the United States are mental disorders.
- Mental disorders collectively account for more than 15% of the overall burden of disease from *all* causes and slightly more than the burden associated with all forms of cancer.
- Mental illness is the second leading cause of premature mortality.
- Workers with mental illness can expect to earn less than others; about $16,000/year less for each worker, or, as a group, about $193 billion annually in unrealized earnings.

(Wharton, 2015; WHO, 2014).

Major depressive disorders are more common in people who have a history of trauma, sexual or physical abuse, bereavement at a young age, alcoholism, or insufficient family structure. These are common psychosocial and environmental factors in many parts of the United States and descriptive of the largest parts of America's inner cities:

- By 2020, major depressive illness will be the leading cause of disability for women and children as the rate of this disease state continues to grow.
- The cost to the economy of major depressive disorders exceeds $210 billion every year.

(Wharton, 2015; WHO, 2014).

Homelessness and Mental Illness

There is a high incidence of mental illness among the homeless with approximately one-third of the estimated 600,000 homeless suffering from a severe and persistent mental disorder (USICH, 2012). This number of people without shelter is a major health care problem in need of attention (HUD, 2015). What these numbers would be but for the $1.5 billion in federal assistance to address homelessness every year is debatable (*See* Stewart B. McKinney Homeless Assistance Act, 42 U.S.C.A. § 11301(b)(2)-(3) (also establishing the Interagency Council on Homelessness)).

While there is no definitive estimate of the percentage of homeless who suffer from mental illness, estimates vary from 10% to 90%; the government estimates that one in three is a reliable number of mentally ill individuals among the homeless, or 78,000 to 145,000 people (HUD, 2015). Most homeless people with mental illness do not need to be institutionalized, but can live in the community with appropriate supportive housing options. However, many mentally ill homeless people are unable to obtain access to **supportive housing** or other treatment services. Consequently, they are over 10 times more likely to be incarcerated than the general population (Peterson & Heinz, 2016).

Incarceration and Mental Illness

Involuntary civil commitments by the courts and a safety conscious society have left the prisons and jails in the United States unable to control their inflow and outflow (Simon & Rosenbaum, 2015). For the first time in U.S. history, 1 out of every 100 Americans is imprisoned on any given day (Vera, 2013). Government acquires obligations when it imprisons people, even when it does so for good reason; significant obligations are acquired when it decides to imprison over 2.2 million Americans (Glaze & Kaeble, 2013), a higher percentage of the general population than any other country in the world (Walmsley, 2014).

More than one-fifth of the world's prison population is held in the United States, followed by China (1.7 million sentenced prisoners), then Russia (0.6 million), three countries that account for just over a quarter of the world's population. As illustrated in **TABLE 27-1**, the United States has the world's highest prison population rates, incarcerating 7 people out of 1,000, which is higher than Russia and China combined (Walmsley, 2014). By comparison, other industrialized nations have universal medical coverage with better mental health care options and significantly lower rates of incarceration (Huxter, 2013).

TABLE 27-1   Prison Population Rate per 100,000 National Population

United States	698
Russia	445
Australia	151
England	148
China	119
Canada	106
France	96
Japan	48

Data from: Walmsley, R. (2014). *World prison population list* (11th ed.) London: King's College International Centre for Prison Studies.

When most incarcerated people in the United States have a severe mental disorder (NAMI, 2016b), a grave health care problem is being ignored (Osher et al., 2012). The surge in imprisonment of people with mental illness appears to be a phenomenon caused by the failure of the nation's community mental health sector, combined with criminal sentencing processes that increase penalties for drug and **quality of life offenses,**[LN1] while reducing the exculpatory effects of mental illness (Wilson, 2012). Today, it seems that the nation's largest mental health facilities are in urban jails:

- About two out of every three prisoners have a severe mental disorder.
- An estimated 700,000 people with severe mental disorders are placed in American jails each year, about three-quarters of who also have co-occurring substance abuse disorders.
- Fewer than half of the prisoners who have a mental disorder have ever received treatment for their problem; less than a third received mental health treatment after their incarceration.
- The incidence of schizophrenia in state prisons is three to five times higher than in the general population, and two to three times higher in local jails than in the general population likely to suffer from severe mental disorders and psychosis.

(Glaze & Kaeble, 2013; NIC, 2012; Osher et al., 2012; Torrey et al., 2014).

While this data on the prevalence of mental illness among prisoners may be contested in their specifics, it is clear that severe mental disorders among the incarcerated are a significant health problem that defies explanation and resolution.

Self-Defeating Cycle of Delusion

Prisoners commonly suffer from a **delusional disorder**, a psychiatric diagnosis denoting a psychotic mental illness that involves holding the fanciful delusion that they are unfairly imprisoned or that if a judge or someone in the criminal justice system would simply understand what happened to them, they would no longer need to be incarcerated. Though these false beliefs are pathological, many prisoners hold these extremely unreasonable beliefs with absolute conviction of their certainty. Moreover, many prisoners are incorrigible; no compelling counterargument or proof to the contrary could ever convince them to accept responsibility for the actions that led to their incarceration. While these prisoners think that the more appeals they file, the more likely they will be released the judiciary becomes convinced the prisoners are precisely where they should be and sees their endless appeals as a failure to accept responsibility for their criminal behavior. The judiciary considers them just another instance of a vicious self-perpetuating cycle of severe mental disorders and depravity (Hafemeister et al., 2013a).

Constitutional Rights of Prisoners with Severe Mental Disorders

While the constitutional rights of prisoners with severe mental disorders may be violated by the nation's systemic failure to provide adequate treatment before, during, and after their imprisonment, the courts have repeatedly indicated that government has an affirmative duty to act. It is an obligation state and local governments have largely ignored, however, notwithstanding constant arguments and court orders to the contrary. States facing limited financial resources for social programs prefer to allocate taxpayer funds to the community's economic development, education, or other health care rather than to its criminal justice system (Smith, 2012).

Even when the criminal justice system does receive government funding, when a choice has to be made between allocating funds for law enforcement or corrections, funds generally go the police rather than to jails or prisons (Kopel & Cramer, 2015). Without federal mandates and oversight, the nation's correctional system may continue to deteriorate (Johnston, 2013). While the human rights of prisoners with severe mental disorders will continue to be recognized by the judiciary, remedies for violation of prisoner rights will be denied without federal funds to meet the affirmative duty of state and local governments to act (Huxter, 2013).

Perhaps treatment of the incarcerated population with severe mental disorders should be advanced pursuant to selfish interests based on the potentially devastating effects on the public health of the general population flowing from poor prison care. Most of the mentally ill prisoners incarcerated today will eventually be released to their communities (Johnston, 2013). The failure of prisons to provide adequate treatment for mental illnesses, not to mention the variety of sexually transmitted and **communicable diseases**, including those acquired while in prison, threatens those communities to which prisoners are released with physical and financial harm, infection, and illness. Such public health arguments might have the potential to move society to pay the costs for mental health care in prisons out of clear self-interest, where heretofore the public has been unwilling to do so (Peterson & Heinz, 2016).

Mental Illness Within Specific Populations

Three particular populations are addressed in terms of mental illness:

- College-age adults
- Health care professionals
- Returning combat veterans

College-Age Adults

Mental illness usually strikes during adolescence and young adulthood. All ages are susceptible, but college-age adults are especially vulnerable because their lives are generally characterized by rapid intellectual and social development (Botello, 2016). The National Institute on Alcohol Abuse and Alcoholism recently released the National Epidemiologic Survey on Alcohol and Related Conditions, a nationwide longitudinal survey of alcohol and drug use and associated psychiatric and **medical comorbidities**. The survey looked at the 19- to 25-year-old college-age adult population in the United States and found:

- 1 in 5 has a severe mental disorder that disrupts their daily lives
- Less than 1 in 4 with severe mental disorders actually seeks treatment (5% of the total college-age adult population seeks treatment)
- The most common disorder is alcohol abuse

(Bibelhausen et al., 2015; Kern, 2015).

While these incidence numbers may be increasing, the increase may be partly because:

- The stigma attached to mental illness is fading, and therefore mental illness is diagnosed more often
- New drugs are allowing college-age adults to function better while acknowledging that they are having difficulty adjusting to life on their own

(Wharton, 2015).

These findings underscore the importance of treatment and prevention interventions by health care professionals serving this population cohort (Botello, 2016). The overall rate of mental disorders is not different between college-attending individuals and their non-college-attending peers (Jones, 2015). At the same time, college-attending individuals cannot be forced to obtain mental health treatment.

While schools often decline to reach out to parents or share information about students' behavior, citing the federal **Family Educational Rights and Privacy Act of 1974** (*See* 20 U.S.C.A. § 1232g), this law only protects student health and academic records. Moreover, students can sign a waiver allowing information to be shared with their parents, something more schools are offering (Waldman, 2015). The federal privacy law also has loopholes whereby schools may alert parents and authorities (Riggs, 2014).

While federal privacy law protects the academic records of students of any age, it allows schools to break confidentiality and notify parents or authorities in the case of a health or safety emergency, or a drug or alcohol violation involving students under age 21. Schools can also share information with parents who claim students as dependents on their tax returns. Further, if a potential danger stems from behavior that is not part of academic records, schools need not apply the privacy law at all. While state laws protect the privacy of medical records, including mental health counseling records, these laws allow mental health professionals to share information with police or other authorities, or even call for forced hospitalization if there is an imminent risk that someone will cause substantial harm to themselves or others (Kopel & Cramer, 2015).

MANAGEMENT AND LAW ISSUES

1. How much access and influence should parents have when it comes to college-age students, particularly if parents are paying the student's tuition and living expenses?
2. Should colleges and universities offer student privacy waivers to their students so parents can have more oversight of their behavior, or should schools encourage parents to take a hands-off approach?

Health Care Professionals

Given the health care community's access to and ability to prescribe drugs, it has always been assumed health care professionals have higher rates of drug abuse than other similar professionals (Halat, 2016). There is no credible research, however, to support this assumption. While the health care industry continues to be accused of not prioritizing mental health within its four walls, health care professionals seem to have rates of substance abuse similar to the general population, no higher and no lower:

- About 10 to 15% of all health care professionals misuse drugs during their career.
- Roughly, 6 to 8% of physicians have substance use disorders.
- About 15% of physicians have alcohol use disorders.

(Haston, 2014; Monroe et al., 2013; Schmitter & Bernstein, 2014).

Although the use of drugs and alcohol is slightly higher for some medical specialties, such as emergency medicine, psychiatry, anesthesiology, and high-stress nursing specialties, the rate of recovery is also significantly higher (Halat, 2016).

Returning Combat Veterans

More than 2.2 million U.S. troops have returned from being deployed in Afghanistan and Iraq and other conflict zones. Early evidence suggests the mental toll of these deployments, many involving prolonged exposure to combat-related stress over multiple deployments, may be disproportionately high compared with the physical injuries of combat (SAMHSA, 2012). Increasing problems for returning veterans include preventing suicides and treating:

- Depression
- Posttraumatic stress disorder
- Traumatic brain injury

(Bilmes, 2011; Meadows et al., 2016).

One issue that must be addressed is the denial of medical and disability benefits to veterans of the wars in Afghanistan and Iraq who were diagnosed with posttraumatic stress disorder (SAMHSA. 2012). Individuals are being released from duty after military review boards conclude they had experienced posttraumatic stress disorder and are unable to continue serving. However, following their release, the Veterans Administration often rules that these same veterans do not qualify for medical coverage to treat their posttraumatic stress disorder because their disorders are not severe enough (Roach, 2016).

With personnel from the armed services deployed around the world as part of the U.S. efforts to combat global terrorism, countless thousands have been exposed to traumatic events during combat and many have returned home with a variety of psychological and mental injuries (Farmer et al., 2016b). A decision needs to be made whether veterans who are released from service for posttraumatic stress disorder are entitled to medical coverage for treatment of the disorder that led to their release (Hepner et al., 2016). The magnitude of severe mental disorders in returning veterans from conflict zones also needs to be addressed:

- About 1 in 3, or about 300,000, returning veterans have severe mental disorders, generally posttraumatic stress disorder or major depression.
- More than one in five returning veterans has traumatic brain injury.
- Roughly half of the returning veterans who need treatment for posttraumatic stress disorder, traumatic brain injury, or depression seek it.
- Only slightly more than half of the returning veterans who seek treatment actually obtain quality, **evidence-based care** (meaning that less than one in four who need quality evidence-based care, in fact receive it).
- The number of returning veterans diagnosed with posttraumatic stress disorder is growing by about 8,000 per year.

(Brown et al., 2015; Farmer et al., 2016a; Meadows et al., 2016).

Veterans Administration specialty mental health services serve an average of 37,000 veterans per year, including more than 22,000 per year with posttraumatic stress disorder from prior wars and conflicts, as well as those returning from Afghanistan and Iraq (Bilmes, 2011; SAMHSA, 2012).

COURT DECISION
Liability for Deaths Caused by a Mentally Ill Veteran After Release from Treatment

DeJesus v. U.S. Department of Veterans Affairs
[Parents of Murder Victims v. Veterans Administration]
479 F.3d 271 (U.S. Court of Appeals for the 3rd Circuit 2007);
followed by Squeo v. Norwalk Hospital Association, 113 A.3d 932 (Supreme Court of Connecticut 2015)

Facts: Alejandro DeJesus, an unemployed, homeless Vietnam veteran with substance abuse disorder and a history of domestic violence, voluntarily entered a Veterans Administration inpatient program where he was diagnosed with intermittent explosive disorder, a condition characterized by repeated violent outbursts. He was prescribed drugs to control his condition. Later, DeJesus was diagnosed with only mild depression. In response to this depression diagnosis, the Veterans Administration assigned DeJesus to psychotherapy and substance abuse counseling. After a few months of inpatient treatment, the Veterans Administration recommended DeJesus for a transitional residence program that provided mental and physical health care to homeless veterans.

The Veterans Administration failed to inform the program about his intermittent explosive disorder and did not release his inpatient records even though the records would have alerted the program that DeJesus suffered from violent outbursts and suicidal ideations. While in the program, DeJesus threatened another resident with a knife, leading the Veterans Administration to recommend his release from the transitional residence program. The transitional residence program acknowledged it dismissed DeJesus because of this recommendation.

Before DeJesus left the **transitional residence program**, he gave away all his possessions and shredded his clothing. Despite the fact that this behavior indicated suicidal intentions, none of the staff who participated in DeJesus' release followed involuntary civil commitment procedures or internal emergency psychiatric intervention procedures. Eighteen hours after leaving the transitional residence program, DeJesus charged into his estranged wife's apartment, and shot and killed two of their children and two other children before turning the gun on himself.

His wife and the mother of the other deceased children filed a federal claim against the Veterans Administration. They claimed that by negligently discharging and subsequently failing to recommit DeJesus, even when he overtly posed an imminent threat, the Veterans Administration caused the wrongful deaths of their children. Further, they claimed the Veterans Administration negligently failed to warn them about DeJesus' mental state.

Issue: Is the Veterans Administration liable for the wrongful death of four children who were killed after DeJesus was released from a transitional residence program for homeless veterans while severely mentally ill?

Holding and Decision: Yes. The Veterans Administration is liable for the wrongful death of the four children; it breached the standard of care established by state law in deciding DeJesus should be released from a transitional residence program; it was grossly negligent in its failure to recommit DeJesus involuntarily.

Analysis: The court looked to Pennsylvania law and common law to determine the **standard of care** for federal agencies under the federal **Tort Claims Act** (*See* 28 U.S.C.A. 171 §§ 2671–2680). First, the court addressed the **failure-to-warn** claim and analyzed whether the Veterans Administration had a duty to warn third parties about DeJesus's mental health status. Mental health workers have an affirmative duty to warn an intended victim if a patient poses a severe danger of violence. However, this duty does not extend to a situation involving nonspecific threats of immediate harm to a readily identifiable victim.

The court then considered whether the Veterans Administration was grossly negligent. Here, a state mental health law provided the source of state law necessary to hold the government liable under the federal Tort Claims Act. The state mental health law provided immunity to health care providers for treating and discharging mentally ill patients in the absence of willful misconduct or gross negligence. While this state law generally protects providers from liability, it also imposes an affirmative duty to refrain from **gross negligence** in the treatment and release of mentally ill patients. In the present case, DeJesus received inpatient treatment at a Veterans Administration facility, and the Veterans Administration participated in the decision to release him from a transitional residence program for homeless veterans, thus imposing on the Veterans Administration a duty to refrain from gross negligence in DeJesus' treatment and release. In evaluating the gross negligence standard, the court looked at the definition of *gross negligence*, which is a form of **negligence** where the facts support substantially more than ordinary carelessness, inadvertence, laxity, or indifference.

It essentially borders on criminal conduct. Here, several actions demonstrated the Veterans Administration's gross negligence:

- DeJesus' complete medical history, including his diagnosis as having an intermittent explosive disorder, was never transmitted to his treatment providers, either while he was receiving inpatient or outpatient treatment at Veterans Administration facilities.
- The Veterans Administration failed to recognize DeJesus' violent outbursts leading up to the shootings as consistent with his particular mental illness.
- The Veterans Administration failed at both preventing DeJesus' release and effecting his recommitment, despite his suicidal tendencies.

Simple negligence involves significantly less egregious breaches of the standard of care. Finding the Veterans Administration's actions met the standard for gross negligence, the Veterans Administration was liable for breaching its duty under the state mental health law, and thus was liable for DeJesus' post-release actions.

Rule of Law: The federal Tort Claims Act overcomes sovereign immunity and makes the federal government liable for tort claims in the same manner and to the same extent as private parties under like circumstances. A federal agency's duty under the federal Tort Claims Act stems from state law, which the Veterans Administration violated by discharging and failing to recommit DeJesus after his release from a transitional residence program for veterans.

References discussing this court decision: None.

The *DeJesus* decision has influenced the mental health sector of the U.S. health care system by reinforcing the fact that health care providers must be familiar with the mental health laws in the states in which they practice. While the duty owed to mentally ill patients differs by state, state laws written to protect mental health providers from liability can be broadly read as imposing an affirmative duty to refrain from negligence in the treatment and release of such patients. Accordingly, providers may be liable for the actions of mentally ill patients they release. Discharging a severely mentally ill patient from treatment is a potential danger not only to the patient but to others. Given this heightened standard, providers should exercise due care in treating and discharging patients (Hafemeister et al., 2013b).

Intellectually Disabled

Intellectually disabled people are one of the most socially stigmatized groups health care providers encounter when dealing with mental illness (Smith, 2015). This is so because their disability renders them less able either to assert their human rights or to protect themselves with regard to medical decisions (Kamin & Marceau, 2015).

Medical Decision-Making

There is a critical shift occurring in the perspective of what is referred to as intellectual disability (Buechele, 2015; Wong, 2016). During this transition, courts are struggling with providing medical care for intellectually disabled people. One recent case to tackle this issue was a lawsuit in the District of Columbia.

COURT DECISION
Medical Decisions on Behalf of the Intellectually Disabled

Doe ex rel. Tarlow v. District of Columbia
[Intellectually Disabled People v. District Mental Health Agency]
489 F.3d 376 (U.S. Court of Appeals for the D.C. Circuit 2007),
reconsideration denied, 2007 U.S.App.LEXIS 26150 (U.S. Court of Appeals for the D.C. Circuit 2007)

Facts: This is a class action; the class is comprised of intellectually disabled people who live in District of Columbia facilities and receive medical services from the District. They have never had the **mental capacity** to make medical decisions for themselves. The policy at issue was adopted to regulate the medical care of intellectually disabled people in the District. For intellectually disabled people who have always lacked the mental capacity to make informed medical decisions, the policy authorized the District mental health agency to make medical decisions on their behalf if:

- Attempts were made to provide an explanation of the proposed treatment to the intellectually disabled person
- No guardian, family member, or other close friend or associate is available to consent or withhold consent
- Two licensed physicians have certified in writing that the proposed treatment is in the best interests of the intellectually disabled person

The Health Care Decisions Act is the District of Columbia law claimed to be inconsistent with the policy on medical care of intellectually disabled people. This law provides that in making a medical decision on behalf of an incompetent person, the decision must be based on the **known wishes** of the incompetent person; or, if the wishes of the person are unknown and cannot be ascertained, on a good faith belief as to the best interests of the incompetent person.

Issue: Do the wishes of incompetent, intellectually disabled people, who have never had the mental capacity to make medical decisions for themselves, need to be considered?

Holding and Decision: No. The policy was consistent with the Health Care Decisions Act.

Analysis: The court began its statutory analysis by observing that the Health Care Decisions Act implicitly distinguishes between two categories of people who lack mental capacity, those who:

- Have always lacked the mental capacity to make medical decisions
- Once possessed the mental capacity to make medical decisions (such as those in a coma)

For people who once had the mental capacity to make medical decisions, medical decisions must be based on the known wishes of the person if those wishes can be ascertained. For patients who have never had the mental capacity to make medical decisions, medical decisions must be based on the best interests of the patient.

The court then held that the policy regulating the medical care of intellectually disabled people did not infringe upon either procedural or substantive due process rights. While acknowledging the policy did not consider the wishes of people who have never possessed the mental capacity to make a medical decision, the court held that this does not violate procedural due process because acting on the wishes of such people could result in erroneous medical decisions with harmful or even deadly consequences. People who have always lacked the mental capacity to make medical decisions do not have a constitutional right to have their wishes considered.

Rule of Law: The human rights of incompetent people who once possessed the mental capacity to make medical decisions are distinct from the rights of intellectually disabled people who never had such capacity.

References discussing this court decision: None.

While the known wishes and the best interests standards are almost ways guaranteed to result in the same outcome for competent adults, this is not always the case for incompetent people. Incompetent people may wish to make decisions that have harmful consequences or that are even deadly; they lack the ability to know what is in their best interests. Therefore, the courts have logically determined that people who never met a competency standard are incapable of knowing which decisions are in their best interests (*See* Buechele, 2015).

Defining Intellectual Disability

The term *intellectually disabled* does not define a distinct class of people; in fact, individual abilities may differ widely and there is no recognized assessment method firmly grounded in scientific evidence (Saviello, 2015). The term *intellectually disabled* focuses on intellectual capabilities instead of mental functions and properly categorizes the condition as a disability. Current clinical definitions of the intellectually disabled, as recognized by the U.S. Supreme Court, require not only **sub-average intellectual functioning** but also significant limitations in adaptive skills to care for themselves and a **diminished capacity** to:

- Abstract from mistakes and learn from experience
- Communicate
- Control impulses and act pursuant to a premeditated plan
- Engage in logical reasoning
- Self-direct themselves (in group settings they are followers)
- Understand and process information
- Understand the reactions of others

(*See Atkins v. Virginia*, 536 U.S. 304 (U.S. Supreme Court 2002) (holding death is an inappropriate criminal sentence for intellectually disabled people but leaving it to the states to determine who is intellectually disabled)).

Today, most Americans could quickly identify people who fit the clinical definition recognized by the U.S. Supreme Court; at least one commentator has suggested justifying Congressional term limits based on this list of adaptive limitations.

Significant sub-average intellectual functioning is defined by an IQ standard score of approximately 70 to 75 or below. Although such intellectual deficiencies diminish the personal culpability of intellectually disabled people for their actions while they are undergoing treatment, it also leads to confusion as to what constitutes a disability when health care providers are facing questions such as:

- End-of-life care
- Informed consent for life-threatening medical treatments
- Involuntary civil commitments and hospitalizations

(Carroll, 2016; Frank, 2014).

The consensus is that a person is intellectually disabled when they fail to achieve minimal functional capability levels (Buechele, 2015).

Involuntary Civil Commitments

There are at least two divisive issues confronting health care providers as they provide treatment to mentally ill people with severe mental disorders:

- **Conditional releases** of mentally ill people from involuntary civil commitment
- Involuntary civil commitment procedures for the mentally ill, especially for people suffering from dangerous mental disorders

Involuntary civil commitment is a process governed by state law that allows mentally ill people to be committed to a hospital on an involuntary basis. The two major phases of the process are the petition and prehearing detention period, and the involuntary civil commitment hearing. Mentally ill people enter the process through an **emergency court order** requiring they be taken into custody and examined. Following the evaluation, they are either released or detained for additional evaluation and treatment under a **temporary detention order**. Courts may order involuntary civil commitments only if there is **clear and convincing evidence** that individuals:

- Have no less restrictive alternative treatment available
- Are largely incapable of caring for themselves
- Pose a danger to themselves or others

(Saviello, 2015).

Dangerous Mental Disorders

While the insanity defense dates back at least to the days after the Norman conquest of 1066 when the English common law began developing, the law continues to struggle with involuntary civil commitment procedures for people who are dangerous to themselves and to society. The U.S. Supreme Court has addressed this double-edged issue in at least five decisions.[LN2] Though the *Ernst v. Stone* case allows New York to continue recommitting people **not responsible by reason of mental disorder or defect** at a lower evidentiary standard, it is not clear this policy will remain in place indefinitely. Because the *Ernst* court does not foreclose the possibility that other people may raise a constitutional objection to New

York's recommitment procedure or seek relief through other legal means, it appears likely this issue is not settled, and other cases may have the opportunity to challenge the New York law (Gordon, 2016).

COURT DECISION
Involuntary Civil Commitment of Mentally Ill People

Ernst J. v. Stone
[Mentally Ill Patient v. State Commissioner of Mental Health]
452 F.3d 186 (U.S. Court of Appeals for the 2nd Circuit 2006)

Facts: Ernst suffered from chronic schizophrenia. During a psychotic episode when he heard voices and thought an elderly man was the devil, Ernst attacked the man, leaving him with severe bite wounds to his hand and genitalia. Ernst was charged with assault in the first degree, assault in the second degree, and burglary in the second degree. Ernst pleaded not responsible because of mental disorder or defect to assault in the second degree.

In accordance with criminal procedure, psychiatrists examined Ernst and determined that although he suffered from schizophrenia, at the time of the examination he was not suffering from a **dangerous mental disorder**, nor was he mentally ill. The psychiatrists recommended that Ernst be required to obtain psychiatric treatment in an outpatient setting. The court agreed with the psychiatrists' recommendation and ordered Ernst to be conditionally released, subject to a five-year order of conditions. One of the conditions was that Ernst was required to remain in outpatient treatment five days per week for his ongoing mental illness.

Two years later Ernst was arrested for criminal trespass and harassment. He pleaded guilty to harassment in the second degree and sentenced to conditional release. The following year Ernst was arrested again for criminal trespass although he was not prosecuted for this offense. As time passed Ernst's behavior became increasingly violent. A year later and within days of the expiration of his five-year order of conditions, Ernst, while living in a residential treatment center, took a female social worker hostage and threatened to assault her sexually. After this incident, he was transferred to the custody of Interfaith Hospital on an emergency basis. Soon after, Ernst's order of conditions was extended and his involuntary civil commitment was extended.

A month later Ernst was transferred to Kingsboro Psychiatric Center, where he continued his violent behavior. Kingsboro requested a three-month period of retention upon clear and convincing evidence Ernst was mentally ill and posed a substantial threat of physical harm to himself and others. Additionally, his order of conditions was extended for the second time, this time for an additional period of three years. After three months of treatment, Kingsboro determined Ernst had developed a dangerous mental disorder and sought a court order for him to be committed to a secure psychiatric facility.

Ernst moved to dismiss the application for recommitment. He argued that the **Fourteenth Amendment**'s protection against state action depriving an individual of life or **liberty** without **due process of law** prohibited New York from recommitting him under the lower evidentiary standard of a preponderance of the evidence as opposed to the higher clear and convincing evidence standard required for an original determination of involuntary civil commitment. Ernst claimed that because at the initial commitment hearing the court found him mentally ill but not afflicted with a dangerous mental disorder, there was no basis to subject him to a lower standard of proof for the recommitment proceedings.

Issue: Can New York law have one set of administrative procedures for the involuntary civil commitment of people suffering from mental illness who are not dangerous and a different set of procedures for mentally ill people determined to be dangerous?

Holding and Decision: Yes. A **lower standard of proof** may be used to involuntarily hospitalize people suffering from a dangerous mental disorder who are determined to be not responsible by reason of mental disorder or defect, as opposed to the higher standard required for mentally ill people who are not dangerous.

Analysis: Certain protections exist for involuntary civil commitment such as requiring clear and convincing evidence that a mentally ill person poses a danger to themselves or others. Extensive evidence must be presented to show the mentally ill person is substantially more likely than not to engage in dangerous behavior. Mentally ill means:

- The person is currently suffering from a mental disorder or defect
- The person's judgment is so impaired they are unable to understand the need for such treatment
- Treatment in an inpatient psychiatric center is essential to the person's welfare

Courts must first order a psychiatric examination to determine the person's current mental condition, followed by a hearing as to their appropriate treatment. The person is placed in one of three tracks according to the preponderance of the evidence based on the findings at the hearing. The tracking decision requires a lower standard of proof than the commitment decision. The 'preponderance of the evidence' standard means that the evidence is merely required to show that a mentally ill person is more likely than not to demonstrate one of three behaviors:

- People on track one are determined to suffer from a dangerous mental disorder and must be committed to a secure psychiatric facility
- People on track two are determined not to be suffering from a dangerous mental disorder, but are nonetheless mentally ill
- People on track three are neither mentally ill nor suffering from a dangerous mental disorder

People assigned to track two are remanded to the custody of the state mental health agency subject to an order of conditions. An order of conditions means a court order directing a mentally ill person to adhere to their treatment regimens or any other conditions the court determines to be reasonably necessary or appropriate. Orders of conditions are valid for five years except for good cause shown; the court may extend the period for an additional five years. The person's commitment is then governed by the civil commitment provisions of the state mental hygiene law.

People assigned to track three are either released unconditionally or released subject to an order of conditions; this generally requires them to enroll in outpatient psychiatric treatment. State law recognizes the possibility a person on track two or track three may, during the course of outpatient care, develop a dangerous mental disorder and require commitment in a secure psychiatric facility. For a court to order recommitment, the person must have a dangerous mental disorder. 'Dangerous mental disorder' means:

- A person currently suffers from a mental disorder
- A person currently constitutes a physical danger to themselves or others because of the mental disorder

In civil commitment proceedings, states must prove the elements of mental illness and **dangerousness** by no less than clear and convincing evidence (*See Addington v. Texas*, 441 U.S. 418 (U.S. Supreme Court 1979)). This evidentiary standard concerns only the initial confinement of mentally ill people and does not specifically address the legal standard of proof applicable to recommitment or release proceedings (*See Jones v. U.S.*, 463 U.S. 354 (U.S. Supreme Court 1983)). States may not, consistent with the Fourteenth Amendment, continue to confine in a psychiatric facility people who may remain dangerous but who no longer suffer from any mental illness (*See Foucha v. Louisiana*, 504 U.S. 71 (U.S. Supreme Court 1992)).

Rule of Law: It is reasonable for New York to provide for the recommitment of mentally ill people who pleaded not responsible due to mental disorder or defect under the low preponderance of the evidence standard. This mental health policy does not violate either the due process or the **equal protection** clauses of the Fourteenth Amendment.

References discussing this court decision: *E.g.*, Halbrook, 2015.

Conditional Releases

Involuntary confinement cannot be justified absent:

- Need for mental health treatment
- Public safety concerns

Mental illness alone cannot justify involuntary confinement of a person indefinitely against their will (*See O'Connor v. Donaldson*, 422 U.S. 563 (U.S. Supreme Court 1975)). For instance, a person cannot be confined because of an antisocial personality absent a showing of dangerousness because the behavior is not a recognized mental disorder (*See Foucha v. Louisiana*, 504 U.S. 71 (U.S. Supreme Court 1992)).

Other courts have added nonmedical conditions to the conditional release of mentally ill patients from involuntary civil commitment, if the patients have been found **not responsible due to mental disorder or defect of insanity**, also referred to as *not guilty by reason of insanity*. This chapter uses the former term. Some courts have extended this policy with respect to people in federal custody for other mental health-related reasons and then went one-step further by providing for recommitment as a permissible mechanism for enforcing such conditions.

COURT DECISION
Conditional Release from Involuntary Civil Commitment

U.S. v. Franklin
[Federal Government v. Involuntarily Committed Patient]
435 F.3d 885 (U.S. Court of Appeals for the 8th Circuit 2006),
rehearing denied, 2006 U.S.App.LEXIS 7760 (U.S. Court of Appeals for the 8th Circuit 2006);
followed by U.S. v. Conrad, 2010 U.S.Dist.LEXIS 66523 (U.S. District Court for
the Western District of Virginia, Abingdon Division 2010)

Facts: Gordon Franklin was involuntarily committed for 12 years due to mental illness. When he was released due to improvement in his mental condition, his release was subject to seven conditions requiring him to comply with prescribed treatment regimens. In addition, he was required to comply with the standard conditions of probation.

A year following his release, Franklin called the probation office and first spoke to a receptionist, and then to his probation officer, Mark Davy. Davy told Franklin he should discuss his issues with Davy or Davy's supervisor rather than with the receptionist. In response, Franklin became agitated and upset with Davy and made death threats directed toward Davy, Davy's supervisor, and the judge who had ordered his commitment, such as "I will blow your brains out" and "the judge who messed me up needs to be killed."

Franklin's conditional release was immediately revoked on the grounds that he violated the required conditions of his release and he was recommitted. Franklin then filed a motion for his release and requested a mental examination. A clinical psychologist examined him and concluded he continued to suffer from bipolar disorder and met the criteria for involuntary civil commitment.

A risk assessment report compiled by a panel of mental health experts found that despite Franklin's compliance with his treatment regimen, his mental condition had deteriorated to a point where his prescribed drugs were no longer adequate. The report concluded that because Franklin had resisted increasing the dosage level of his drugs, his release would pose a significant risk of causing substantial harm to himself or others. Franklin's conditional release was revoked and he was involuntarily committed.

Issue: May the release of a mentally ill patient from hospitalization be conditioned upon fulfilling requirements, other than the requirement to comply with a prescribed treatment regimen?

Holding and Decision: Yes. The conditional release of a mentally ill patient from hospitalization may be revoked and the patient may be involuntarily recommitted for failure to comply with requirements other than the requirement to adhere to treatment regimens.

Analysis: Franklin claimed there was insufficient evidence to conclude he violated the requirements of his release by failing to adhere to his treatment regimens. The government maintained Franklin violated his probation by breaking the law when he threatened Davy, Davy's supervisor, and the judge who had ordered his commitment. Franklin countered he could not be recommitted on these grounds because federal law only allows the revocation of a conditional release when a person fails to comply with their adherence to treatment regimens.

The court held that when a person suffering from a mental disorder is released from hospitalization, additional conditions may be imposed that are ancillary to the adherence to treatment regimens, such as probation, as long as the additional conditions are:

- Reasonably necessary to protect the safety of others
- Related to the person's mental illness

In addition, a conditional release may be revoked for violation of a non-treatment-related condition, at least when the violation flows from the person's mental disorder and demonstrates that the release would present a risk of causing harm to others. Although federal law does not specifically mention what recourse is available when a released person violates a non-treatment-related condition, the court reasoned that Congress must have contemplated a mechanism for enforcing violations of **non-treatment-related conditions**.

Otherwise, the released person could blatantly violate such conditions and courts would be powerless to revoke their release, even if the violations demonstrated the person posed a danger to the public. Applying these principles to this situation, the court found the condition of probation was related to Franklin's illness. His probation was reasonably necessary to ensure his safety and the safety of others, as least as far as it required Franklin to refrain from violating probation standards by threatening the lives of his probation officers and the judge who had ordered his commitment. The court revoked Franklin's conditional release, finding his violation of probation flowed directly from his mental disorder and demonstrated a threat to himself and others.

Rule of Law: When mentally ill people are released from an involuntary civil commitment, additional conditions may be imposed on their release that are unrelated to compliance with their adherence to treatment regimens; their release may be subsequently revoked and they may be recommitted for violating such nonmedical conditions.

References discussing this court decision: None.

This decision raises the issue of patient confidentiality for the mentally ill. For instance, mentally ill people are often required to waive their right to confidentiality regarding their mental health treatment to allow sharing of information with their probation officers. This waiver is a condition of their release from hospitalization and is considered reasonably necessary to protect the community's safety. Health care providers serving mentally ill people should be aware of this court's holding and its potentially broad reach.

Expanding Definitions of Dangerousness

The definition of dangerousness is being expanded under the rubric of public safety. Involuntary civil commitment procedures are being extended to:

- Convicted pedophiles who have served their criminal sentences
- Pregnant women who smoke or abuse alcohol or drugs (including prescription drugs that are teratogenic) to safeguard the health of their fetuses

(Kaplan, 2015; Stutz, 2013).

Both civil commitment areas are currently being debated by Congress, state legislatures, and lower trial courts (Borgmann, 2014). To date, neither issue has been satisfactorily dealt with by the highest federal or state appellate courts, or the U.S. Supreme Court.

MANAGEMENT AND LAW ISSUES

3. While clear and convincing evidence is required for involuntary civil commitment of mentally ill people, what standard of proof should be used for recommitment or release proceedings?
4. What standard of proof should be used to determine whether a mentally ill person has in fact developed a dangerous mental disorder?
5. Should courts be permitted to force antipsychotic drugs on a mentally ill person so they can stand trial for a criminal offense or should the person always be committed involuntarily?
6. Like the commitment of the mentally ill, should pregnant women who smoke or misuse alcohol or drugs retain their independence or face incarceration, detention, or hospital confinement so as to protect the health of their fetuses?
7. Can involuntary civil commitment of pregnant women be justified because a woman's refusal to safeguard the health of her fetus will result in a lifetime of preventable health care costs that will be incurred by her children (and possibly grandchildren)?

Protection and Advocacy for Individuals with Mental Illness

Congress adopted the federal **Protection and Advocacy for Individuals with Mental Illness Act of 2000** to curb abuse and neglect of the mentally ill, primarily in institutions (*See* 42 U.S.C.A. §§ 10801–10851). Beginning in the 1960s and 1970s, many abuses were uncovered at state hospitals for the mentally ill where patients were inappropriately physically restrained, neglected, overmedicated, and abused. Today many physicians, hospital administrators, and mental health workers claim patient advocates endanger the mentally ill by fighting for their right to refuse treatment when the mentally ill actually present a risk of causing harm to themselves or others. Proponents of **patient advocates** say refusals to accept treatment are essential to protecting the human rights of the mentally ill from inappropriate incarceration and homelessness, as well as unnecessary seclusion and restraint (Zdanowicz, 2015).

COURT DECISION
Violation of Patient Rights

Davis v. Rennie
[Mentally Ill Patient v. Mental Health Staff]
264 F.3d 86 (U.S. Court of Appeals for the 1st Circuit 2001),
cert. denied, 535 U.S. 1053 (U.S. Supreme Court 2002);
followed by Clifford v. Maine General Medical Center, 91 A.3d 567 (Supreme Court of Maine 2014)

Facts: Jason Davis, a mentally ill patient involuntarily committed at Westborough State Hospital, suffered from schizoaffective and bipolar disorders. Davis and another patient violated hospital rules by leaving the grounds without permission. Greg Plesh, a police officer from the hospital, found the patients consuming alcohol behind a local liquor store and brought them back to the hospital. The hospital staff found both patients to be loud and demanding, and the unit's head nurse, Joyce Wiegers, decided to place Davis in an isolation room.

According to Davis, two mental health staff workers, Michael Hanlon and Paul Rennie, remained outside the isolation room and taunted him. Davis tried to do a double drop kick; it is disputed as to whether Davis intended to kick one of the guards or just aimed toward the wall. According to Davis, Rennie then entered the room, choked Davis, and threw him to the ground with deadly force. Rennie disputes this account and contends he merely physically restrained Davis and did not injure him.

At this point, Wiegers summoned several more staff and Plesh to lead Davis out of the room. Davis alleges Rennie continued to taunt him, and Davis kicked Rennie in the stomach. The staff wrestled Davis to the ground, with one person on each limb. Davis testified another staff member, Phillip Bragg, punched him repeatedly in the head. Plesh testified that since no one intervened, he pushed Bragg away while the others rolled Davis onto his stomach. Bragg denied punching Davis and the other mental health staff denied seeing Bragg punch Davis. Davis also testified Wiegers taunted him while Plesh handcuffed him for transport to another room. After Plesh secured Davis in another room, he arrested Bragg for assault and battery.

Scientific evidence introduced at trial showed Davis suffered serious physical injuries from the assault. Davis sued eight mental health staff workers involved for the use of excessive force during the two instances of physical restraint. Davis also sued the staff for failing to intervene to prevent Bragg's use of excessive force during the second restraint and for violating Davis' right to freedom from unreasonable bodily restraint. The jury returned a verdict against the staff.

Issue: Were an involuntarily committed mentally ill patient's rights violated when a staff member punched him repeatedly while he was physically restrained?

Holding and Decision: Yes. The mental health staff used excessive force, violated Davis' right of freedom from unreasonable bodily restraint, and failed to intervene when a staff member repeatedly punched him.

Analysis: Davis' constitutional rights were violated; therefore, he was entitled to $100,000 in compensatory damages and $1.5 million in punitive damages. The damage award was based on a fourfold analysis:

- Evil motives, lying, and attempts to cover up wrongdoing justify punitive damages.
- The staff failed to intervene when Davis was attacked while restrained.
- Mental health staff violated the Massachusetts Civil Rights Act by coercively abusing Davis with the use of excessive force to restrain him and then threatening more abuse after the restraint.
- Qualified immunity is negated when an **affirmative duty to intervene** is disregarded.

Davis' claim is based on the Fourteenth Amendment's protection against state action depriving an individual of life or liberty without due process of law. There is a duty to protect those who are involuntarily committed for mental disorder or defect. Failures to act may create a due process violation because the confinement of mentally ill patients prevents them from being able to help themselves. Although Davis was drunk and potentially threatening, once he was restrained, the situation no longer required the use of force. Moreover, patients who are involuntarily committed are entitled to more considerate treatment than criminals; the conduct of mental health staff is held to a higher standard than prison guards or police officers.

The mental health staff maintained there was no evidence Bragg punched Davis. The court noted there was sufficient evidence to infer the staff witnessed the attack. In addition, the court found there was time and opportunity to intervene based on testimony, which created a possible inference the staff was nearer to Davis than Plesh when Plesh intervened. Thus, the court found the staff failed to intervene to protect Davis as he was repeatedly punched while restrained.

The court next held the actions of the mental health staff in continuing to hold Davis down was a form of acquiescence to Bragg who clearly intended to violate Davis' rights, and the restraint was coercion under the Massachusetts Civil Rights Act. Furthermore, the court found Rennie's use of excessive force in the first physical encounter was intimidating and coercive in itself. Finally, the court found Wiegers threatened Davis with more abuse after the restraint. Therefore, the court found liability against all of the staff under the Massachusetts Civil Rights Act.

In addition, the court defined **qualified immunity** as a protection for state actors from liability for civil damages arising from their conduct as long as the actors did not violate some clearly established right a reasonable person would have known. With regard to this situation, the court held that the mental health staff should have known they had a legal duty to intervene when Bragg used excessive force against Davis. Specifically, the court found Wiegers had a duty to stop Bragg, or at least to attempt to stop Bragg by calling out rather than physically interfering. The qualified immunity defense of the mental health staff failed because they were reasonably expected to know Bragg's attack created an affirmative duty to intervene.

Finally, while the mental health staff denied harboring any ill will toward Davis, the court found there was sufficient evidence to support a finding of evil motive toward Davis. Rennie taunted and provoked Davis and then used excessive force to restrain him, the staff held Davis down knowing Bragg was punching him, and Wiegers did nothing to protect Davis. Furthermore, the court found the staff attempted to cover up their wrongdoing by filing inaccurate reports and lying when they testified. Thus, the court held **punitive damages** were appropriate due to the reprehensible conduct of the staff.

Rules of Law: Patients who have been involuntarily committed must be given extra protections from abuse because they may be unable to help or control themselves; mental health staffs, therefore, have an affirmative duty to intervene and prevent any excessive force from being applied to patients to restore order. This affirmative duty also applies to observers, such as supervisory nurses, to prevent excessive force, even if the observers do not directly participate in any of the physical restraining. Furthermore, mental health staffs do not have the same freedoms police officers or prison guards have to use force to restore order.

References discussing this court decision: *E.g.*, Bambauer & Massaro, 2015; Levinson, 2013.

In recent years, there has been a wave of legislative efforts, many inspired by violent crimes, to make it easier to mandate treatment for the mentally ill who pose a risk of causing harm to themselves or others. Patient advocates have blunted those efforts in California, New Mexico, and Michigan. Nevertheless, the mental health sectors are being given greater leeway to disclose patient information to those who may be affected by the conduct of the mentally ill. Further, it is becoming easier to medicate involuntarily committed patients (*See* Stone, 2013).

Sex Addictions

When does a pattern of behavior become a mental disorder? In the case of **sex addiction**, this question has been debated for decades (Tovino, 2015a). Sex addiction was added to the *DSM-3* in 1980, dropped from *DSM-4* in 1994, and was not restored in the *DSM-5*. The official position is that sexual behavior becomes a disorder when it adversely affects a person's life and the lives of others (APA, 2013). The blend of humor and pathos in the fictional portrayal of sex addiction in the United States, as well as the nation's acceptance of pornography, implies a collective ambivalence of Americans toward sex addiction (Harrison, 2015).

Human Trafficking for the Purpose of Sexual Exploitation

Yet, societal ambivalence aside, the magnitude of human trafficking for sex by people with sex addictions has exploded in the United States in the past decade:

- The government estimates that 4,500 to 17,500 victims (including men) are trafficked into the United States every year.
- The number of women and children involved in the sex trade is as high as 50,000 to 100,000.

(Berger, 2012; U.S. Department of State, 2015).

Trafficking for sex is a sophisticated underground industry that generates billions of dollars in profit every year, yet destroys the lives of innocent victims (U.S. Department of State, 2015). Many of the trafficked victims are impoverished children and young women from economically depressed countries who are forced to work as prostitutes under brutal conditions in the United States (DeVolld, 2014). Sometimes they are tricked into the trade. One example is when a victim applies for what they think is an au pair position, only to be enslaved upon arrival in the United States (Berger, 2012).

To date, the legislative and law enforcement attention has focused on the supply side of the sex trafficking equation in the United States, namely, the **traffickers** and the victims (DeVolld, 2014). Little focus has been directed to the demand side of the problem, namely the sex addicted patrons of the prostitutes (Berger, 2012). The demand for commercial sexual services sustains and grows the sex trafficking industry. If sexual addiction was recognized as a mental disorder, the United States could possibly take a more demand-oriented approach to fighting sex trafficking. The issue under debate is whether offenders who participate in sex trafficking should be involuntarily committed like pedophiles or face extreme penalties more befitting their behavior.

Sex Addiction or Mental Distractions and Internet Pornography

The number of Americans who are active users of Internet pornography is having a devastating effect on marriages and relationships. In addition, there is a huge problem with Internet pornography in the workplace (Harrison, 2015). While the research continues to grow and demonstrates a serious mental health issue, whether Internet pornography is a mental disorder or an excuse to behave badly remains to be determined.

One thing is certain, Internet pornography is a growing industry, generating over $12 billion a year in revenue (*See* Sbardellati, 2013; Vardaman & Raino, 2013). Moreover, while many believe that viewing online pornography is a harmless expression of sexual curiosity, its effects are often more profound. For 15% of the online porn habitués, viewing pornography develops into compulsive behavior that disrupts their lives (Harrison, 2015; Love et al., 2015).

MANAGEMENT AND LAW ISSUES

8. If pedophilia is a recognized mental disorder for purposes of involuntary civil commitment, should the *DSM-5* also add sexual addictions that harm others?

Uncertain but Changing Stigma About Mental Illness

There is a significant stigma around mental illness. Most Americans still believe mental disorders are character flaws as opposed to something physiological; they believe that if someone wants to change their thinking, mood, or behavior, they could just do it (Wharton, 2015). These beliefs are a reflection of the current values of American society and are reflected in the treatment of people with a mental disorder at any given time. The mentally ill are the most misunderstood patient group of our time (Tovino, 2015b).

LAW FACT

Medical Coverage for Acute Mental Health Treatment

Following a precertification approval, can an insurer retrospectively deny coverage for ensuing treatment of a severe mental disorder when the patient is completely dysfunctional and suicidal?

No. Insured people are entitled to the assurance of timely notification concerning approval and reimbursement; reviewing agents and mental health care providers are required to make timely decisions, thereby giving the insured the security of focusing on their true task: rehabilitation.

— *Merit Behavioral Care Corp. v. State of Vermont Independent Panel of Mental Health Providers*, 845 A.2d 359 (Supreme Court of Vermont 2004).

CHAPTER SUMMARY

- Mental illness is the leading disease burden on the United States, with 44 million sufferers, but it receives very little public attention.
- A healthy psyche is indicated by engaging in productive activities, fulfilling relationships with other people, and an ability to adapt to change and cope with adversity.
- Mental disorders are characterized by alterations in thinking, mood, or behavior, distress, and impaired mental functioning.
- Mental disorders are legitimate illnesses that respond to specific treatments, just as other physical health conditions respond to medical treatment.
- About 6% of Americans suffer from severe mental disorders.
- There is a risk of two to six million Americans with severe mental disorders causing harm to themselves or others at any one time.
- There is a particularly high incidence of mental disorders among the homeless, the incarcerated, college-age adults, and returning combat veterans.
- State laws written to protect mental health providers from liability can be broadly read as also imposing an affirmative duty to refrain from negligence in the treatment and release of mentally ill patients.
- The intellectually disabled are a subset of people with mental illness; they are characterized by sub-average intellectual functioning and significant limitations in the ability to care for themselves.
- Involuntary civil commitments require future dangerousness coupled with a mental disorder as the basis for the imposition of commitment and mental health treatment.
- Absent public safety concerns or the need for mental health treatment, involuntary civil commitment is not permitted for a mental illness alone.
- When mentally ill people are released from an involuntary civil commitment, various conditions may be imposed upon their release and they may be recommitted for violating such conditions.
- Although patient advocates may play a critical role in overseeing the treatment of the mentally ill, some argue that the human rights of the mentally ill to refuse treatment should not take precedence over the patient's or others' safety.
- Mental health care workers are subject to a higher standard of care than police officers or prison guards when using force to maintain or restore order.
- One subset of mental disorders currently receiving much public attention is sexual disorders, particularly because they result in pedophilia and fuel widespread human trafficking for sexual exploitation purposes.

LAW NOTES

1. Quality of life offenses include public nuisance offenses such as:

    - Disorderly conduct
    - Noise violations
    - Urinating in public

2. (Wilson, 2012).Civil commitments regard future dangerousness when coupled with a mental disorder as a legitimate basis for the imposition of involuntary civil commitment and mandatory treatment for violent offenders:

    - *Kansas v. Crane,* 534 U.S. 407 (U.S. Supreme Court 2002) (requiring proof of a serious difficulty in controlling behavior in order to involuntarily commit a sexual offender)
    - *Kansas v. Hendricks,* 521 U.S. 346, 358 (U.S. Supreme Court 1997) (finding of dangerousness alone is ordinarily not a sufficient ground upon which to justify indefinite involuntary civil commitment; civil commitment laws may be sustained when proof of dangerousness is coupled with proof of some additional factor, such as a mental disorder or abnormality)
    - *Heller v. Doe,* 509 U.S. 312, 314–15 (U.S. Supreme Court 1993) (sustaining Kentucky law permitting commitment of dangerous individual who is intellectually disabled or mentally ill)
    - *Allen v. Illinois,* 478 U.S. 364, 366 (U.S. Supreme Court 1986) (sustaining Illinois law permitting commitment of mentally ill and sexually dangerous individual)
    - *Minnesota ex rel. Pearson v. Probate Court of Ramsey County*, 309 U.S. 270 (U.S. Supreme Court 1940) (upholding Minnesota law permitting commitment of dangerous individual with psychopathic personality)

REFERENCES

APA (American Psychiatric Association). (2013). *American Psychiatric Association: Diagnostic and statistical manual of mental disorders* (5th ed.). Arlington, Virginia: American Psychiatric Publishing, Inc.

Bambauer, J. R., & Massaro, T. M. (2015). Outrageous and irrational. *Minnesota Law Review, 100,* 281–354.

Berger, S. M. (2012). No end in sight: Why the 'end demand' movement is the wrong focus for efforts to eliminate human trafficking. *Harvard Journal of Law and Gender, 35,* 523–570.

Bibelhausen, J., et al. (2015). Mental health: Reducing the stigma: The deadly effect of untreated mental illness and new strategies for changing outcomes in law students. *William Mitchell Law Review, 41,* 918–947.

Bilmes, L. (2011). *Current and projected future costs of caring for veterans of the Iraq and Afghanistan wars.* Cambridge, MA: John F. Kennedy School of Government, Harvard University, Faculty Research Working Paper Series.

Borgmann, C. E. (2014). The constitutionality of government-imposed bodily intrusions. *University of Illinois Law Review, 2014,* 1059–1127.

Botello, L. (2016). The Affordable Care Act's opportunities and challenges to improve college student mental health. *Quinnipiac Health Law Journal, 18,* 335–368.

Brown, R. A., et al. (2015). *Access to behavioral health care for geographically remote service members and dependents in the United States.* Santa Monica, CA: RAND Center for Health Policy Research.

Buechele, B. (2015). Psychology's role in law: A discussion of how the Supreme Court views the role of the DSM-V in *Hall v.* Florida. *Southern Methodist University Law Review, 68,* 275–282.

Carroll, J. E. (2016). Brain science and the theory of juvenile mens rea. *North Carolina Law Review, 94,* 539–599.

Chorney, D. (2014). A mental health system in crisis and innovative laws to assuage the problem. *Health and Biomedical Law Society, 10,* 215–249.

DeVolld, A. (2014). Refugee roulette: Wagering on morality, sexuality, and normalcy in U.S. asylum law. *Nebraska Law Review, 92,* 627–654.

Ezell, J. M., et al. (2013). Contours of usual care: Meeting the medical needs of diverse people with serious mental illness. *Journal of Health Care for the Poor and Underserved, 24*(4), 1552–1573.

Farmer, C. M., et al. (2016). *Understanding treatment of mild traumatic brain injury in the military health system.* Santa Monica, CA: RAND Corporation.

Farmer, M. M., et al. (2016). Depression quality of care: Measuring quality over time using VA electronic medical record data. *Journal of General Internal Medicine, 31*(1), 36–45.

Frank, S. (2014). Eligibility discrimination of the intellectually disabled in pediatric organ transplantation. *Journal of Health and Biomedical Law, 10,* 101–136.

Freedman, A. (2014). Mental retardation and the death penalty: The need for an international standard defining mental retardation. *Northwestern University Journal of International Human Rights, 12,* 1–21.

Glaze, L. E., & Kaeble, D. (2013). *Correctional populations in the United States.* Washington, DC: U.S. Department of Justice, Bureau of Justice Statistics.

Gordon, S. (2016). The danger zone: How the dangerousness standard in civil commitment proceedings harms people with serious mental illness. *Case Western Reserve Law Review, 66,* 657–700.

Hafemeister, T. L., et al. (2013a). Forging links and renewing ties: Applying the principles of restorative and procedural justice to better respond to criminal offenders with a mental disorder. *Buffalo Law Review, 60,* 147–222.

___. (2013b). Parity at a price: The emerging professional liability of mental health providers. *San Diego Law Review, 50,* 29–88.

Halat, A. (2016). An anesthesiologist, a brain surgeon, and a nurse walk into a bar: A call for change in how America handles health care worker substance abuse. *Seton Hall Law Review, 46*, 939–990.

Halbrook, W. P. (2015). New York's not so "SAFE" Act: The Second Amendment in an Alice-in-Wonderland world where words have no meaning. *Albany Law Review, 78*, 789–817.

Harrison, A. (2015). Nudge, don't thrust: The application of behavioral law and economics to America's porn addiction. *Texas Review of Law and Politics, 19*, 337–339.

Haston, S. (2014). Impaired physicians and the scope of informed consent: Balancing patient safety with physician privacy. *Florida State University Law Review, 41*, 1125–1145.

Hedden, S. L., et al. (2015). *Behavioral health trends in the United States: Results from the national survey on drug use and health.* Bethesda, MD: National Institute of Mental Health.

Hepner, K. A., et al. (2016). *Quality of care for PTSD and depression in the military health system: Phase I report.* Santa Monica, CA: RAND Corporation.

HUD (U.S. Department of Housing and Urban Development). (2015). *The annual homeless assessment report to Congress.* Washington, DC: HUD.

Huxter, M. J. (2013). Prisons: The psychiatric institution of last resort? *Journal of Psychiatric and Mental Health Nursing, 20*(8), 735–743.

Johnston, E. L. (2013). Vulnerability and just desert: A theory of sentencing and mental illness. *Journal of Criminal Law and Criminology, 103*, 147–229.

Jones, J. T. R. (2015). High functioning: Successful professionals with severe mental disorders. *Duke Forum for Law and Social Change, 7*, 1–35.

Kamin, S., & Marceau, J. (2015). Waking the Furman giant. *University of California Davis Law Review, 48*, 981–1042.

Kaplan, M. (2015). Taking pedophilia seriously. *Washington and Lee Law Review, 72*, 75–170.

Kern, B. (2015). Balancing prevention and liability: The use of waivers to limit university liability for student suicide. *Brigham Young University Education and Law Journal, 15*, 227–270.

Kopel, D. B., & Cramer, C. E. (2015). Reforming mental health law to protect public safety and help the severely mentally ill. *Howard Law Journal, 58*, 715–778.

Lawrence, D., & Kisely, S. (2010). Inequalities in healthcare provision for people with severe mental disorders. *Journal of Psychopharmacology, 24*(4), 61–68.

Levinson, R. B. (2013). Wherefore art thou *Romeo*: Revitalizing *Youngberg's* protection of liberty for the civilly committed. *Boston College Law Review, 54*, 535–575.

Love, T., et al. (2015). Neuroscience of internet pornography addiction: A review and update. *Behavioral Sciences, 5*(3), 388–433.

Meadows, T., et al. (2016). *How military families respond before, during and after deployment: findings from the RAND deployment life study.* Santa Monica, CA: RAND Corporation.

Monroe, T. B., et al. (2013). The prevalence of employed nurses identified or enrolled in substance use monitoring programs. *Nursing Research, 62*(1), 10–15.

Musgrave, S. (1994). *Musgrave landing: Musings on the writing life.* Toronto, Canada: Stoddart Publishing Co. (quoting Rita May Brown).

NAMI (National Alliance on Mental Illness). (2016a). *Mental health conditions.* Arlington, VA: NAMI.

___. (2016b). *Grading the states: A report on America's health care system for severe mental disorders.*

NIC (National Institute of Corrections). (2012). *Adults with behavioral health needs under correctional supervision: A shared framework for reducing recidivism and promoting recovery.* Washington, DC: NIC.

Osher, F., et al. (2012). *Adults with behavioral health needs under correctional supervision: A shared framework for reducing recidivism and promoting recovery.* New York, NY: Council of State Governments Justice Center.

Peterson, J., & Heinz, K. (2016). Understanding offenders with serious mental illness in the criminal justice system. *William Mitchell Law Review, 42*, 537–563.

Riggs, G. (2014). Taking HIPAA to school: Why the privacy rule has eviscerated FERPA's privacy protections. *John Marshall Law Review, 47*, 1–31.

Roach, J. (2016). Discrimination and mental illness: Codified in federal law and continued by agency interpretation. *Michigan State Law Review, 2016*, 269–310.

SAMHSA (Substance Abuse and Mental Health Administration). (2012). *Behavioral health issues among Afghanistan and Iraq U.S. war veterans.* Rockville, MD: SAMHSA.

Saviello, T. R. (2015). The appropriate standard of proof for determining intellectual disability in capital cases: How high is too high? *Berkeley Journal of Criminal Law, 20*, 163–226.

Sbardellati, E. (2013). Skin flicks without the skin: Why government mandated condom use in adult films is a violation of the First Amendment. *Northwestern Journal of Law and Social Policy, 9*, 138–162.

Schmitter, C., & Bernstein, J. A. (2014). Priorities in public health law: A practice-based analysis of trends in the legal needs of public health professionals. *Annals of Health Law, 23*, 228–251.

Simon, J., & Rosenbaum, S. A. (2015). Dignifying madness: Rethinking commitment law in an age of mass incarceration. *University of Miami Law Review, 70*, 1–52.

Smith, K. L. (2012). Lost souls: Constitutional implications for the deficiencies in treatment for persons with mental illness in custody. *Golden Gate University Law Review, 42*, 497–523.

Smith, R. J. (2015). Forgetting *Furman. Iowa Law Review, 100*, 1149–1207.

Stone, D. H. (2013). The dangers of psychotropic medication for mentally ill children: Where is the child's voice in consenting to medication? An empirical study. *Temple Political and Civil Rights Law Review, 23*, 121–164.

Stutz, L. (2013). Myth of protection: Florida courts permitting involuntary medical treatment of pregnant women. *University of Miami Law Review, 67*, 1039–1069.

Torrey, E. F., et al. (2014). *The treatment of persons with mental illness in prisons and jails: A state survey.* Arlington, VA: Treatment Advocacy Center and Alexandria, VA: National Sheriffs Association.

Tovino, S. A. (2015a). The DSM-5: Implications for health law. *Utah Law Review, 2015*(4), 767–802.

___. (2015b). Will neuroscience redefine mental injury? Disability benefit law, mental health parity law, and disability discrimination law. *Indiana Health Law Review, 12*, 695–728.

U.S. Department of State. (2015). *Trafficking in persons report*. Washington, DC: Department of State.

U.S. Surgeon General. (2011). *Mental health: A report of the Surgeon General*. Rockville, MD: U.S. Department of Health and Human Services, Office of the Surgeon General.

USICH (U.S. Interagency Council on Homelessness). (2012). *Searching out solutions: Constructive alternatives to criminalization*. Washington, DC: USICH.

Vardaman, S. H., & Raino, C. (2013). Prosecuting demand as a crime of human trafficking: The Eighth Circuit decision in *United States v.*Jungers. *University of Memphis Law Review, 43*, 917–967.

Vera Institute of Justice. (2013). *The potential of community corrections to improve communities and reduce incarceration*. New York, NY: Vera Institute of Justice, Center for Sentencing and Corrections.

Waldman, E. G. (2015). Show and tell? Students' personal lives, schools, and parents. *Connecticut Law Review, 47*, 699–740.

Walmsley, R. (2014). *World prison population list* (11th ed.). London, England: King's College, International Centre for Prison Studies.

Wharton, University of Pennsylvania. (2015). Mental health in the workplace: How we can move beyond the stigma. *Knowledge@Wharton*.

WHO (World Health Organization). (2014). *The global burden of disease*. Geneva, Switzerland.

Wilson, W. J. (2012). *The truly disadvantaged: The inner city, the underclass, and public policy* (2nd ed.). Chicago, IL: University of Chicago Press.

Wong, A. S. (2016). Aligning the criminal justice system with the mental health profession in response to *Hall v.* Florida. *Oregon Law Review, 94*, 425–452.

Zdanowicz, M. T. (2015). Keeping the mentally ill out of jail: Sheriffs as litigants. *Albany Government Law Review, 8*, 536–562.

PART IX

End-of-Life Health Care

© Andy Dean Photography/ShutterStock, Inc.

CHAPTER 28

Hospice Care

"Now, death is not the worst that can happen to men...."

— **Plato** 423–347 (B.C.), Greek philosopher

IN BRIEF

Hospice occupies a specialized and growing niche in the health care economy. With more than two out of every five of the nation's deaths occurring in Medicare-certified hospice programs, it has been demonstrated that hospice care improves quality of life for patients and families. Hospice is that rare situation in the U.S. health care system through which quality of life is improved while costs may be reduced. This chapter focuses first and foremost on hospice care as it relates to elder care. Many children and young adults, however, also qualify for hospice care, including accident victims and those who have acquired immune deficiency syndrome (AIDS), fatal birth defects, muscular degeneration, spinal cord injuries, strokes, and other debilitating medical conditions. Additionally, perinatal hospice is available for families where the fetus has a lethal condition.

LEARNING OBJECTIVES

Upon completion of this chapter readers should be able to:

1. Outline the major elements of hospice care.
2. Detail the Medicare coverage and requirements for hospice care.
3. Explain the dilemma physicians face in providing the justification for hospice care required by Medicare insurance.
4. List and describe the various legal instruments people should prepare to be sure their wishes are carried out at the end of their lives.
5. Describe the problems of surrounding a patient in a permanent or persistent vegetative state.
6. Discuss the potential that for-profit businesses will enter to consolidate hospice care organizations.
7. Detail the potential cost savings brought about by hospice care.
8. Discuss the concept of medical futility.

KEY TERMS

Advanced health care directive	Co-payments	End-of-life care
Americans with Disabilities Act of 1990	Cruel and unusual punishment	Fetal demise
	Death	Fourteenth Amendment
Artificial nutrition and hydration	Deductibles	Freestanding centers
Best interests standard	Do-not-resuscitate protocols	Health care proxy
Brink-of-death care	Due Process Clause	Hospice
Budgetary scorekeeping	Dying process	Hospice-licensing regulations
Clear and convincing evidence	Economic pyramid	Informed consent

Joint Commission	Neonatal death	Preponderance of evidence
Legal competency	Noncurative treatments	Private equity
Mandated choice	Overtreatment	Prognosis
Marginalization	Palliative care	Proof beyond a reasonable doubt
Medicaid insurance	Per diem rate	Rehabilitation Act of 1973
Medicare insurance	Perinatal hospice	State surrogate laws
Medicare hospice benefit	Persistent vegetative state	Surrogates
Medicare's hospice eligibility requirements	Physician orders for life-sustaining treatment	Systemic cost savings Terminal
Mental capacity	Premiums	Uniform Anatomical Gift Act

FACT OR FICTION

Acceptance of Patients into Hospice Care

Should hospice be required to provide artificial nutrition and hydration to a patient who is transferred to their care by a valid court order?

Terri Schiavo, age 27, suffered cardiac arrest as a result of a potassium imbalance brought about by the eating disorder of bulimia. Her husband, Michael Schiavo, called 911 and Terri was immediately rushed to a hospital, but she never regained consciousness. For 10 years, Terri lived in nursing homes with constant care where she was fed and hydrated by tubes. She had numerous health problems, but none were life threatening. The evidence was overwhelming that Terri was in a permanent or **persistent vegetative state**.

After 10 years of futile health care, Michael sought judicial authorization to terminate Terri's life-prolonging procedures and permit her entry into **hospice**. Following a five-day trial, the trial court ordered that Terri's **artificial nutrition and hydration** be removed and that she be transferred to a hospice where her natural **death** process could take its course. Four years of litigation followed Terri's transfer to hospice care, beginning in the Florida state courts and ending in the Eleventh Circuit U.S. Court of Appeals five years later. All the while, Terri's artificial nutrition and hydration were maintained in hospice.

— *See* Law Fact at the end of this chapter for the answer.

Principles and Applications

The pattern of life and death has shifted dramatically in the last century in developed economies and for the billion people in the top 15% of the economic pyramid. The average life span of Americans has nearly doubled, from just 49 years in 1900 to nearly 80 years today (CDC, 2016a). Lifetimes have increased by about three months every year since the mid-19th century as a direct result of improved health care (CDC, 2011).

At the same time, the pattern of life and death in developing economies and for people in the bottom 85% of the **economic pyramid** (the remaining 5.8 billion people in the world) is what it was in North America and Western Europe in the mid-17th century (Prahalad, 2009). For most of the world's population, health care has not improved in the last century. Half the people in the world die by the age of 20 from severe diseases that quickly result in death (WHO, 2014).

Demographics of Life and Death

While people at the top of the economic pyramid live longer, healthier lives, most of them will spend their last few years living with disabilities or chronic illnesses. Relatively few Americans die of acute causes or accidents anymore. Instead, most Americans die from lingering and often complex or combined illnesses that eventually prove fatal. Dementia and frailty shape the last years of life for a large part of the population in developed economies (WHO, 2016a). By 2030, the baby boom generation born after World War II will begin to turn 85, an age when most people are showing evidence of frailty. In 2000, approximately 4 million Americans were 85 or older; in 2030, this number is projected to be over 9 million (Werner, 2011).

Overview of Hospice Care

The term *hospice* is derived from the Latin *hospes*, referring to both *guest and host* and in honor of the hospices that sheltered members of the early Christian church and pilgrims of the Middle Ages (Barger, 2016). Hospice is not a place; rather, it is a philosophy of palliative care that provides pain management, symptom control, psychosocial support, and spiritual care to patients and their families (NHPCO, 2015). In most cases, care is provided in the hospice patient's home, but care can also be given in **freestanding centers**, hospitals, nursing homes, and other long-term care facilities.

With roughly one in three older Americans using hospice services to cope with the dying process, hospice has evolved from a purely not-for-profit mission into a growing health care business (CDC, 2016a; NHPCO, 2015). Four out of five hospice patients are 65 years of age or older, and over 40% are 85 years of age or older. As the baby boom generation of some 76 million ages, the number of people aged 65 and older is also expected to grow (NHPCO, 2015). The hospice industry in turn expects considerable future growth in both the number of hospice patients and the type of care expected by hospice patients (Misichko, 2014).

The death-with-dignity movement and its accompanying hospice philosophy started in England and came to the United States in the early 1970s.[LN1] The movement did not gain widespread recognition until Medicare insurance began to pay for hospice services and the Joint Commission on Accreditation of Healthcare Organizations (now known as **The Joint Commission**) initiated hospice accreditation criteria. While The Joint Commission is not an official governmental regulatory agency, it is instrumental in developing and maintaining standards of quality in hospice care, and accreditation is an indication that a hospice program maintains a certain standard of care. Today, about 1.7 million Americans receive hospice care (NHPCO, 2015). This represents a steady increase of about 100,000 new patients using hospice in each of the past several years, a growing trend that is expected to continue as an aging generation of baby boomers born in 1946-1964 faces end-of-life care situations (Misichko, 2014).[LN2]

A handful of publicly held firms provide hospice care along with hundreds of smaller private firms and well-established not-for-profit ventures. Medicare insurance currently funds more than three-quarters of the cost of hospice care (NHPCO, 2015). From the late 1980s to the mid-1990s, hospital managers believed the health care industry's future would expand to include offering integrated services to hospice patients. They began buying physician practices and other health service organizations, including hospices, thereby spurring interest in the hospice business. For-profit programs now provide care for 68% of hospice patients; not-for-profit groups provide care for 28%, while government and other types of organizations help the remaining 4% (CMS, 2015; NHPCO, 2015).

State Licensing Regulations

Reducing **overtreatment** requires aligning physicians' interests with the goal of using hospice for end-of-life care. Toward that end, recent payment reforms establish a range of financial incentives that encourage continuum of care practices among physicians. Physicians, however, do not practice medicine in a vacuum; they are profoundly influenced by the organizational culture of the U.S. health care system (Mantel, 2015). Far too often the nation's culture of new high technologies and treatments leads physicians to provide patients care of questionable medical value for terminal illness and disease. If the United States is to successfully contain health care costs, hospitals must move away from cultures of overtreatment to continuum of care cultures that focus on care and respect for patients (Misichko, 2014). Current licensing regulations, however, do too little to address hospitals' cultures of overtreatment to successfully integrate care both inside and outside the hospital setting. Under current state laws, most hospice facilities must be licensed as one of the following:

- Assisted living facilities
- Hospitals
- In-home services agencies
- Nursing facilities

(*See* 42 C.F.R. §§ 418.1-418.405).

Hospices are distinctly licensed as opposed to being certified as an integral part of one health care system where payments would be tied to the system's success of continuously treating patients both inside and outside the hospital setting.

While most states do not have detailed **hospice-licensing regulations**, several states apply the federal regulations for certification of hospices. Some have raised concern about the integration of assisted living facility and in-home services regulations to hospices. To address this concern, states have adopted regulations specific to hospice facilities that are not inpatient facilities and are currently licensed as assisted living facilities or in-home services agencies. For instance, there are regulations particularly unique to hospice care for nutrition services and treatments for infections.

Nutrition Services

Artificial nutrition and hydration through intravenous administration or by putting a tube in the stomach is available for patients who are very sick and receiving curative treatments or recovering from surgery. However, the service is rarely used for hospice patients whose bodies are beginning to stop functioning and instead require comfort treatments (Shepherd, 2014). When hospice patients with a serious, life-limiting illness are no longer able to eat or drink, it usually means that their bodies are beginning to stop functioning. Artificial nutrition and hydration will not bring them back to a healthy state. Most physicians agree that artificial nutrition and hydration can increase suffering in patients who are dying and no longer have the ability or interest to eat food and drink liquids themselves (Dolgin, 2016). Artificial nutrition and hydration can add more discomfort to a dying patient's physical symptoms such as:

- Bloating
- Cramps
- Diarrhea
- Shortness of breath
- Swelling

(*See* Cavallaro, 2015; O'Neill, 2014).

It is important to remember that the body is beginning to shut down because of disease and the **dying process**, not because of the absence of foods and liquids (Santoro, 2015). Allowing a natural death means that only comfort measures are provided (Jennison, 2015). There are ways to ensure comfort at the end of life; hospice and palliative care professionals are experts in providing comfort treatments that allow the dying process to occur with as little discomfort as possible (Brown, 2015).

Treatments for Infections

Infections are generally treated for hospice patients who are receiving other curative treatments. With hospice patients at the very end stage or active phase of dying, however, where treatment for an infection would not be effective, it is generally declined or withheld as part of good health care (Mantel, 2015). Dying should not be prolonged simply because it can be (Dolgin, 2016). Treatments for infections, similar to artificial nutrition and hydration, can also increase discomfort in dying patients.

Hospice's Financing Structure

A measure of the increased acceptance of hospice as a viable treatment option is the fact that many third-party payers (Medicare insurance, Medicaid insurance, and most private insurance plans) extend medical coverage for hospice care.[LN3] Medicare insurance initiated the hospice benefit in response to the finding that most Americans preferred to die at home devoid of pain and surrounded by loved ones (Federal Interagency Forum on Aging-Related Statistics, 2012). Since then, more people are dying in hospice and fewer are dying in hospitals. Yet, knowing where someone dies does not say much about the care they receive at the end of their life. The nuanced reality of most **end-of-life care** is very different between patients:

- Americans are also being hospitalized more frequently in the last three months of their lives.
- Americans are more likely to spend time in intensive care units.
- Americans often receive hospice care for just a few days before they die.

(Dolgin, 2016; Teno et al., 2013).

The Medicare consideration of the site of death as a quality measure for end-of-life care is misleading. While hospice use is increasing, about a third of hospice patients are enrolled for three days or less. Clearly, there is still a lot more to learn about how to deliver care at the end of life. The **Medicare hospice benefit**, however, is the dominant source of payment to hospice providers and is very different from other health care programs.

Medicare's Six-Month Restriction

Given mounting national attention to poor-quality, protracted, and futile end-of-life procedures, it is essential to understand whether the quality of end-of-life care and the failure to use hospice care is affected by government policy (Carr, 2016). One barrier to hospice referral arises from **Medicare's hospice eligibility requirements**, which are instances of health care delivery being driven by **budgetary scorekeeping**. Congress, concerned that large numbers might choose the Medicare hospice benefit as an alternative to home care, added the six-months-to-live requirement to address this cost concern. This has resulted in one major problem in hospice care: the fact that hospice providers are not reaching hospice patients in a timely manner (NHPCO, 2015).

This barrier to hospice care will be difficult to eliminate without major changes to hospice organization and financing, yet it's a barrier that should no longer dictate end-of-life care (Kaplan, 2015). To enter hospice, a patient's physician must certify that they believe their patient could die within six months if their illness runs its normal course, which is a criterion for admission that has much more to do with how long hospice patients have to live than with what hospice patients need (Misichko, 2014). The Medicare hospice benefit is available only to hospice patients who:

- Are eligible for insurance coverage under Medicare Part A
- Have been certified by their physicians that their expected mortality is less than six months
- Understand the nature and purpose of palliative care
- Agree that by selecting hospice, they waive their right to certain other Medicare services

(CMS, 2015; *See* 42 C.F.R. § 418).

Hospice care was at first controversial because of the waiver requiring hospice patients and their physicians to forgo further efforts at finding a cure. Today, hospice is controversial because hospice providers are doing **brink-of-death care** as opposed to end-of-life care (Misichko, 2014). While Medicare legislation clearly structured hospice as an alternative to conventional care, hospice care is at odds with the training and mindset of most attending physicians whose end goal is always the same: do everything possible to prolong life. It is this medical philosophy that renders many physicians unable to refer their patients to hospice care.

This philosophy is not limited to individual physicians; the U.S. health care *system* is a death-denying system that advocates for as much treatment as possible (IOM, 2014). Regulations require explicit and careful consent from hospice patients, acknowledging that they are giving up curative treatment (Smith, G., 2014). Sometimes, this requirement delays hospice care because a family member is unwilling to accept that someone is dying (Misichko, 2014). Other reasons include misconceptions that hospice refers to a place for end-of-life treatment. The hospice philosophy, however, neither hastens nor postpones death; it simply focuses on compassion and care in acceptance of death (IOM, 2014).

Medicare's Per Diem Payment Schedules

Most hospice payments are based on an all-inclusive **per diem rate**, except for physician services, which are mostly paid for in the conventional manner.[LN4] When hospices were first established, Medicare insurance covered virtually every service required, with the possible exception of long-term assistance by an aide. Today, the Medicare hospice benefit is paid at one of five rates for custodial care:

- Continuous attendance at home
- Inpatient respite care and general inpatient care
- Inpatient symptom management care
- Spiritual care
- Routine home care

(CMS, 2015).

For qualified hospice patients, hospice benefits include:

- Durable medical equipment and supplies
- Home health aide and homemaker services
- Nursing care
- Nutrition and dietary counseling
- Physical therapy, occupational therapy, and speech/language pathology services
- Physician services (if that physician is part of the hospice team)
- Prescription drugs related to the terminal illness
- Short respite care in an inpatient facility
- Social services, including bereavement counseling

(CMS, 2015).

Additional covered hospice services are defined as any other item or service covered by Medicare insurance, which is indicated as necessary for the treatment of the terminal illness or related conditions. Medicare Part A insurance will reimburse a hospice for two 90-day periods and then repeated 60-day periods during a hospice patient's lifetime. Hospice coverage is unlimited so long as the patient remains eligible, meaning that the expected prognosis of the hospice patient's health condition if it took its standard course would be a mortality of less than six months. Services must be provided through an interdisciplinary team that assesses the needs of each patient and the hospice patient's family and then develops and implements an appropriate care plan (*See generally* CMS, 2015).

Medicaid Insurance Restrictions

In recognition of the fact that Medicaid insures the poorest Americans, Medicaid insurance protects hospice patients from the out-of-pocket costs typically imposed by private health plans. While Medicare insurance has always imposed substantial **premiums**, **deductibles**, and **co-payments**, Medicaid prohibits states from imposing any enrollment fees or cost sharing on the Medicaid-insured for hospice services (*See* 42 U.S.C.A. § 1396o; 42 C.F.R. § 447.53). States are specifically prohibited from imposing enrollment fees for hospice services (*See* 42 U.S.C.A. § 1396o(a)(1)).

Growth Industry

Since the first hospice program opened in 1974, approximately 4,500 hospice programs are now operating in the United States. Medicare payment for hospice care has grown from around $68 million in 1986 to almost $14 billion (NHPCO, 2015). By 2030, as baby boomers enter their 80s and beyond, hospice spending is expected to climb to almost $46 billion (CMS, 2015). In addition to the aging of the population, hospice programs are accommodating health conditions beyond cancer, traditionally the illness that has been most often associated with hospice care. Hospice is increasingly caring for hospice patients in the final stages of chronic diseases, such as:

- AIDS
- Alzheimer's disease
- Amyotrophic lateral sclerosis, often referred to as Lou Gehrig's disease
- Diabetes
- Emphysema
- Heart disease and strokes
- Neuromuscular, kidney, and liver diseases
- Other life-limiting conditions

(NHPCO, 2015).

Growth is also likely to occur by geographic region. In 10 states, including Arizona, Texas, and Florida, more than half the deaths occurring in the population over age 65 were under hospice care. By contrast, in 13 states, including Massachusetts, New York, and also Washington, DC, hospice deaths occur in only 20% of the same population group (*See generally* NHPCO, 2015).

MANAGEMENT AND LAW ISSUES

1. Does the large number of hospice patients with terminal prognoses, such as cancer or multiorgan system failure, dying in intensive care settings as opposed to hospice care, indicate that there is a systemic failure in meeting patients' needs and expectations?
2. Considering medical technology's ability to prolong near-death life longer and longer, should economic reasoning ever be used to stop treatment?
3. Should the compassionate administration of life-shortening analgesia in hospices be unlawful?

Advocates for hospice argue it is primarily a compassionate way to not prolong the suffering of patients. While hospice makes it easier for people to die quietly at home, hospice can also reduce costs for Medicare insurance. The routine Medicare hospice benefit costs are in the range of $150 for routine care to $900 for continuous care and supervision, compared to daily inpatient payments of more than $2,000 (CMS, 2015). Regardless of these potential cost savings, more than half of all hospice service ends before 30 days, with about a third of those hospice patients having hospice care for less than a week (NHPCO, 2015). The hospice industry should close the gap between the average length of days a hospice patient receives care (20 days) and the eligible amount of time a hospice patient can continue receiving hospice care (180 days minimum) (Misichko, 2014).

Conflicting Perspectives

America avoids death (Smith & Himmel, 2014). The largest portion of hospital expenses is incurred during the last few weeks of a patient's life. One could argue that if it were possible to make relatively accurate judgments about when an illness is **terminal**, and if legitimate hospice services can be provided to the patient, cost savings would result. If a patient is terminally ill, why spend money to prolong life for one week or three weeks? Why spend money on increasingly desperate attempts at curative treatment? While this arguably does not appear to be money well spent, some hospice patients and their families want to do everything possible to prolong life. So there is a potential conflict on the surface of hospice between cost-containment and potential legal disputes with the family.

There is no conflict, however, if hospice patients and their families want to pay for medically futile care for hospice patients with terminal prognosis and there is no expectation that insurers, including Medicare insurance, will pay for ineffective health care. The problem with all this is that there is no legal or ethical consensus as to what futile health care means. Nevertheless, hospice patients are distinctly less likely to have surgery, hospitalization, resuscitation, or other technological interventions, although these services are not explicitly precluded by Medicare insurance regulations (CMS, 2015). Perhaps, the growing interest in hospice care versus high-technology curative care for an additional few weeks of living with a terminal illness may demonstrate a growing recognition that death is part of life and should not to be resisted at every turn (Dolgin, 2016).

Informed Consent

Hospice care brings various legal issues to the forefront. From a health law perspective, **informed consent** for hospice treatment is one of the most important concerns (Brown, 2015). If the patient is competent or has signed an advance directive and/or a power of attorney giving someone else the authority to make their medical decisions, the patient's wishes should be determined prior to admission to hospice care. Hospices that are Medicare/Medicaid insurance providers are required to give hospice patients, at the time of their enrollment, information about their rights under state laws, including their rights to:

*   Accept or refuse treatment
*   Direct their own health care decisions
*   Get information on the hospice's policies that govern rights
*   Prepare an advance directive

(*See* 42 U.S.C.A. §§ 1395cc).

While the law of informed consent favors a hospice patient's rights, the potential for serious legal issues arises when hospice patients are not legally competent and have no advance directive. Every hospice struggles with what to do with patients who at the time of potential entry to hospice lack the capacity to make end-of-life medical decisions.

Legal Competency

The question of when a patient is determined to be competent to make end-of-life decisions is very different from competency in general. **Legal competency** is often defined as the ability to make clear and definite decisions (LeCluyse, 2015). In this instance, it is the ability to choose and make up one's mind about stopping curative treatments for a terminal illness without too much wavering, after considering the other possible choices of **palliative care** and entry to hospice. Where mature minors have been determined to be competent to make their own medical decisions, the criteria should be the same for determining whether a child is competent to accept entry to hospice (Laskin et al., 2014). Most likely this will be a court determination if the parents disagree with the child's decision about hospice care.

Best Interests Standard

When making decisions about entry to hospice for those adults who lack decision-making capacity and have no discernible preferences, the **best interests standard** is generally used (Shepherd, 2014). The same standard for entry into hospice care is recommended for minors (Laskin et al., 2014). This standard means the best available care will be administered to the patient. This care is not necessarily for the purpose of extending biological life for the longest time, but to offer comfort and pain control (Rosoff & Leong, 2015).

Legal problems arise with hospice patients who are in a persistent vegetative state; they also arise where hospice patients suffer from various forms of dementia, in cases of severe mental illness, and in situations where curative treatment itself interferes with **mental capacity**. Each state has had to resolve what to do in such situations; there is no overriding federal legislation. The result has been an array of state laws and regulations dictating how hospice decisions are to be made, and how the wishes of hospice patients are to be determined in such uncertain situations (Smith, C., 2014).

One Hospice's Debacle

This chapter opened with the Terri Schiavo case to illustrate what hospices face when they accept patients who cannot make their own end-of-life decisions. This case was one of the most bitter and protracted civil actions regarding end-of- life medical treatment ever in U.S. jurisprudence, with hospice care at the center of the debate (Caplan et al., 2006). There was a disagreement within the family that presented legal difficulties resulting in litigation. The debate centered on the right to die in accordance with the true wishes of a patient on life support. Family members simply disagreed about what the wishes of the patient were and had differing levels of understanding relative to the health condition and **prognosis** of someone in a persistent vegetative state (Shah, 2015). Consequently, one side was not allowed to make a decision to disconnect her life support, while the other side was not allowed to make a decision to maintain life support.

This family dispute could have been avoided if an advance directive (popularly known as a living will) and a health care proxy had been in place. As it turned out, after Schiavo's cardiac arrest stopped her heart and killed her brain in 1990; she received artificial nutrition and hydration for 15 years before she died (Ouellette, 2014). The following federal decision from the Eleventh Circuit U.S. Court of Appeals finally resolved this controversy.

MANAGEMENT AND LAW ISSUES

4. Does inappropriate use of curative treatment deprive hospice patients of their fundamental right to dignity and humane treatment?

COURT DECISION

Discontinuance of Life Support

Schiavo ex rel. Schindler v. Schiavo
[Parents of Daughter v. Hospice and Husband/Son-in-Law]
403 F.3d 1289 (U.S. Court of Appeals for the 11th Circuit 2005)

Facts: This is the highly publicized court battle between Terri Schiavo's parents and Michael Schiavo, her husband and legal guardian, regarding the removal of her artificial life-prolonging measures. Terri was a persistent vegetative state patient in a hospice center in Florida and her parents were seeking an injunction to require that she be transported to a hospital for restoration of nutrition and hydration and for medical treatment. In a persistent vegetative state, Terri was not in a coma; she had cycles of apparent wakefulness and sleep, but was without any cognition or awareness. As she breathed, she often moaned; her hands, elbows, knees, and feet were severely contracted. Over the span of 10 years, her brain deteriorated from the lack of oxygen it suffered at the time of her heart attack. By mid-1996, CAT scans of her brain showed that most of her cerebral cortex was gone and had been replaced by cerebral spinal fluid.

Issues: Do hospices violate the Americans with Disabilities Act and the **Rehabilitation Act of 1973** when they withhold artificial nutrition and hydration from persistent vegetative state hospice patients? (*See* Rehabilitation Act, 29 U.S.C.A. § 701 (protects the right of the disabled to be free from Discrimination); **Americans with Disabilities Act**, 42 U.S.C.A. § 12101 *Et seq.* and 47 U.S.C.A. § 225 (provides additional protections to the disabled)). If so, must an incapacitated patient's wishes be proven by clear and convincing evidence prior to hospice care in order to comport with the Due Process Clause, and does hospice care constitute cruel and unusual punishment under the Eighth Amendment?

Holding and Decision: No. The court rejected all claims based on statutory and constitutional arguments holding that denial of a temporary restraining order was proper where the parents of a severely brain-damaged patient sought to restore life support that had been removed in compliance with a state court order following eight years of litigation.

Analysis: The court addressed each of the five counts of the parents' complaint. The first count alleged that Michael Schiavo and the hospice were acting in violation of the ADA. The court found that Michael was neither a public entity nor a public accommodation, nor was he acting under color of state law, as required for a claim under the ADA to proceed. Turning to the claim against the hospice, the court noted that if the hospice was a place of public accommodation, the withholding of nutrition and hydration was not done on the basis of Terri's disability but in compliance with a valid court order. The court further observed that the ADA was never intended to provide an avenue for challenging judicial orders in termination of care cases.

The next count alleged that the hospice violated the **Rehabilitation Act** by refusing treatment to Terri on the basis of her disability. The court found that the case was not within the scope of the Rehabilitation Act because Terri would not have had any need for a feeding tube to deliver nutrition and hydration but for her health condition. The court noted that, like the ADA, the Rehabilitation Act was not meant to deal with end-of-life medical treatment.

The third count alleged that an incapacitated patient's wishes must be proven by clear and convincing evidence prior to admission to hospice and termination of curative care in order to comport with the Due Process Clause. There are three standards of proof used in different legal contexts in U.S. courts to prove that something is true:

* *Lowest standard*: **Preponderance of evidence** is a finding that more than half the people would find something to be true.
* *Middle standard*: **Clear and convincing evidence** is a finding that more than half the people would find something to be true, but still not everyone would find to be true.
* *Highest standard*: **Proof beyond a reasonable doubt** is a finding that any reasonable or rational person would find something to be true.

The court found this argument to be without merit for two reasons. First, the court noted that states may apply a clear and convincing standard of review in termination of care proceedings, but they are not required to do so. Second, the state courts in this case had already chosen to apply the clear and convincing standard of review as opposed to the higher standard.[LN5]

Fourth, the court held that the count of **cruel and unusual punishment** under the Eighth Amendment was without merit. This constitutional provision applies only to punishments inflicted after conviction for crimes, not to life support or medical treatment decisions.

The fifth and final count was that the **Due Process Clause** of the **Fourteenth Amendment** was violated when the hospice deprived Terri of nutrition and hydration against her wishes. However, the court noted that eight years of litigation was procedural due process in abundance. Turning to substantive due process, the court noted that it does not require a state to protect its citizens against injury by non-state actors; therefore, since neither the husband nor the hospice were state actors, the claim of violation of substantive due process was without merit.

Rule of Law: Hospice care does not violate the ADA or the Rehabilitation Act, nor is it considered cruel and unusual punishment under the Eighth Amendment. In termination of care proceedings, a clear and convincing standard of review may be used by states, but is not required, and lastly, Terri's Due Process rights were not violated.

References discussing this court decision: *E.g.*, Persad, 2015; Shepherd, 2014.

The *Schiavo* case galvanized millions to think about end-of-life decision-making and question when life ends and how to define a good death. The attorney for Nancy Cruzan, whose case pre-dated *Schiavo* and was one of the first to raise such questions, reminds us that the right to die is a relatively new subject because the modern day technology that allows us to keep hospice patients alive has only been more recently developed (Colby, 2007).

In the wake of the *Schiavo* case, the American Medical Association adopted a policy opposing state legislation that presumes incapacitated hospice patients want life-sustaining treatment unless they have clearly stated otherwise (Truog, 2015). This policy was in response to proposed model legislation from the National Right to Life Committee requiring physicians and hospitals to presume that all hospice patients unable to speak for themselves would want to continue to receive hydration and nutrition, unless the hospice patients had clear living wills stating otherwise (Dolgin, 2016). Looking beyond *Schiavo*, policy proposals are beginning to emerge in several states that would create a presumption mandating life-sustaining treatment (Cavallaro, 2015). Against this trend, current case law supports self-determination at the end-of-life decision-making stage (Ouellette, 2014). Every competent adult has liberty interests over their person, notwithstanding attempts to restrict and limit these natural rights inherent to death with dignity (Lim, 2015), including the accepted rights of:

- Choosing a **health care proxy**
- Executing an **advanced health care directive**
- Refusing medical intervention
- Using hospice to ease pain and increase comfort level at the end of life

(Dolgin, 2016; Truog, 2015).

Health Care Decision Laws

Decision-making of patients in hospice care is affected by:

- Advanced health care directives
- Health care proxies
- State surrogate laws
- **Do-not-resuscitate protocols** (DNRs)
- **Physician orders for life-sustaining treatment** (POLSTs)
- Anatomical gifts

MANAGEMENT AND LAW ISSUES

5. What human rights do family members have to weigh in on decisions about hospice care?
6. How should hospice programs balance the liberty interests of persistent vegetative state hospice patients to refuse life-saving hydration and nutrition alongside the right to self-determination at the end of life with the state's interest in preserving life?

Advanced Health Care Directives

Survey after survey documents that most Americans emphatically agree they should have the power to make their own health care decisions, but they do not take the necessary steps to ensure their wishes are known or honored (Cavallaro, 2015). There are approximately 2.6 million deaths annually in the United States, and **advanced health care directives** were executed less than half the time (CDC, 2016b; Dolgin, 2016). An advanced health care directive, also commonly known as an advance decision or living will, provides instructions about what health care actions should be taken in the event of an individual's illness or incapacity and they are no longer able to make decisions. A health care proxy, another part of the advanced health care directive, allows individuals to appoint someone to make health care decisions on their behalf if they cannot speak for themselves.

Health Care Proxies

Health care proxies (or durable powers of attorney for health care, medical powers of attorney, health care agents, or authorized surrogates) grant authority to give substituted consent for decisions regarding another person's health care (Rosoff & Leong, 2015). All states permit pre-identified proxies to make decisions about life-sustaining treatment if a person is incapacitated. Some states limit the proxy's authority to medical precondition requirements. For instance, the proxy could make decisions about medical complications arising from pre-existing Parkinson's disease but would not be authorized to make decisions if the same person were involved in a life-threatening auto accident. Iowa is the only state to require that a witness be present when a proxy consents to forgo life-sustaining treatment (Shepherd, 2014).

State Surrogate Laws

Without a health care power of attorney, **state surrogate laws** will determine who will make decisions on behalf of a person when they are incapacitated. Laws vary by state, but generally have a priority list that begins with family members. **Surrogates** can make decisions based on the expressed preferences of the patient first, then on the patient's values through a substituted judgment process, and in some states on the basis of the patient's best interests (Shepherd, 2014).

Do-Not-Resuscitate Protocols

DNRs prohibit physicians and other health care professionals from performing cardiopulmonary resuscitation on patients when resuscitation would otherwise be required (LaBruzza, 2015). Such orders exist by law in all but four states: Minnesota, Mississippi, Missouri, and North Dakota (Gordy, 2011). Hospice patients, along with their attending physician, must sign most DNRs; some states also require one or two witnesses.

Physician Orders for Life-Sustaining Treatment

Increasingly, states are adopting POLSTs (or medical orders for life-sustaining treatment) as an alternative to DNRs (Cavallaro, 2015). POLSTs are similar to DNRs in that they outline an individual's wishes regarding health care as an illness or disease advances, with regards to forms of treatment, such as:

- Antibiotics
- Hospitalization
- Nutrition and hydration
- Resuscitation
- Ventilation

While similar to advance health care directives, POLSTs do not replace them (Shepherd, 2014). Rather, POLSTs combine an advance health care directive and surrogate decision-making into a single document (Dolgin, 2016)

Anatomical Gifts

A source of confusion arises when hospice patients execute organ donation documents and advance health care directives (Cavallaro, 2015). Which document controls? **Mandated choice**, which ensures that organs are actually donated, has been adopted by all but four states under the **Uniform Anatomical Gift Act** (Hain, 2015). When individuals are incapacitated, their health care proxies make decisions about organ donation (*See* Revised Uniform Anatomical Gift Act § 21). Three states, Arkansas, Idaho, and Montana, still require affirmative donations (opt-in rules) by individual donors (*See* Arkansas Code Ann. § 20-17-1221; Idaho Code Ann. § 39-3422; Montana Code Ann. § 72-17-216). Donor procurement agencies in Indiana face a six-hour time restriction on finding evidence of individual donor intent, after being notified of a potential organ donation, to determine the eligibility of donors on life support (*See* Indiana Code Ann. § 29-2-16.1-20(b)).

Industry Consolidation

The U.S. hospice market has consolidated the top five publicly held hospice firms collectively controlling most of the market (CMS, 2015):

- Beverly Enterprises of Ft. Smith, Arkansas, was recently acquired by a private equity firm and subsequently delisted in 2006.
- ManorCare of Cleveland, Ohio, operates hospice divisions as part of their larger health care operations.
- Odyssey HealthCare of Dallas, Texas, is publicly traded.
- VistaCare of Scottsdale, Arizona, is publicly traded.
- Vitas of Miami, Florida, the nation's largest hospice company, serves more than 12,000 hospice patients per day.

While there are a number of hospice start-ups still occurring, like in other growth industries, a natural consolidation is occurring. **Private equity** has moved into the hospice sector with an array of mergers, takeovers, acquisitions, buy-outs, and injections of investment capital into the taxpayer-funded hospice business, primarily through purchase and consolidation of small hospices but also a handful of large transactions, including:

- 2004—Chemed purchased Vitas for $406 million.
- 2008—VistaCare Hospice was acquired by Odyssey HealthCare for $147 million.
- 2010—Odyssey HealthCare was acquired by Gentiva Healthcare for approximately $1 billion.
- 2015—Gentiva was acquired by Kindred Healthcare for $1.8 billion.

(Barger, 2016; Smith & Himmel, 2014).

Unique Challenges of For-Profit Hospices

Hospice is heavily reliant on Medicare funding, and Congress seems intent on keeping hospice well-funded. Medicare spending on hospice services has increased more than 400% over the past decade, the majority of which has gone to firms owned by investors seeking a profitable return on their capital (Barger, 2016; Smith & Himmel, 2014). While Medicare mandates much of what the hospice industry must provide and what they will be paid, there are ways for providers to run profitably. It is really about the ability to get a toehold in local markets. The for-profit providers point to well-run not-for-profit organizations as their major competitors in many markets because they have been there longer and have better name recognition. For-profit providers with better access to funding and economies of scale, however, are competing effectively against local not-for-profit organizations for the largest patient enrollment possible (Misichko, 2014). The questions that must remain in the forefront are what is the for-profit hospice industry competing to provide and how can for-profit competition be vigorous and successful for its customers, the hospice patients (Sage, 2016)?

Profit margins for the major for-profit hospices range from 6% to nearly 15% (Barger, 2016). Meanwhile, personal and home care aides earn less than $10 per hour, without health benefits (Kennedy, 2016). All the same, running a for-profit hospice offers some unique challenges. Hospice care is a highly regulated industry in which federal oversight over the quality of care and payment rates is a major part of the business model. As in so many other industries, the hospice business is likely to be transformed as the baby boom generation ages and confronts death.

A constant challenge for the hospice industry is finding good direct care workers. While the labor shortage and turnover for nurses has improved over the past several years, there remains a shortage of home care workers (Misichko, 2014). The shortage and high turnover rates are crucial, since most hospice care is provided by home care workers, variously known as home health aides, personal care aides, and personal care attendants. Home care workers number over 2 million; most face continued **marginalization** in the United States because of laws that do not always regulate their wages, hours, health, or safety (Kennedy, 2016).

COURT DECISION
Regulation of Home Care Workers' Wages and Hours

Long Island Care at Home, Ltd. v. Coke
[Hospice Worker v. Hospice Provider]
551 U.S. 158 (U.S. Supreme Court 2007)

Facts: Evelyn Coke, a home care worker who provided companionship services, sued Long Island Care at Home, alleging that she had not been paid the minimum wages and overtime wages to which she was entitled under the Fair Labor Standards Act (*See* 29 U.S.C.A. §§ 201-204, 206, 207, 209-219).

Issue: Are home care workers entitled to federal minimum wages and overtime wages?

Holding and Decision: No. Home health care workers are not entitled to federal minimum wages and overtime.

Analysis: A unanimous Supreme Court rejected Coke's claim for wage protection, upholding a U.S. Department of Labor regulation exempting home care workers from federal minimum wage and overtime rules. While the Fair Labor Standards Act clearly exempted home care workers hired directly by hospice patients, it was unclear whether home care workers hired by an agency were also meant to be exempt from the minimum wage and overtime provisions. The federal regulation exempted such workers from the wage protections, and the question in this case was whether that regulation was consistent with the Fair Labor Standards Act. The Court found the federal regulation was entitled to deference because Congress had left a definitional gap in the statute, and the Department of Labor's interpretation was reasonable.

Rule of Law: Direct health care workers employed by hospice agencies to work in hospice patients' homes are exempt from federal minimum wage and overtime protections.

References discussing this court decision: *E.g.*, Dioguardi & Lamba, 2014; Kennedy, 2016; Klein & Boris, 2013; Smith, 2013.
 This holding was overruled by 29 C.F.R. § 552, effective November 13, 2015, which extended the Fair Labor Standards Act's minimum wage and overtime protections to most direct care workers (*See* DOL, 2016).

This U.S. Supreme Court decision was severely criticized by labor unions and women's groups that pointed to the fact that home care workers, the majority of whom are low-income African American women, provide indispensable services to the terminally ill. Without a doubt, the wage protections that became effective in late 2015 will erode operating margins of the for-profit hospice industry. This wage issue bears scrutiny to see if the for-profit organizations continue to seek additional revenue growth where they can find it by:

- Increasing hospice patient census regardless of the prognosis of the patient
- Manipulating the aggregate cap by lengthy stays
- Seeking those patients who require little, if any, care

(Barger, 2016).

In addition to these unique challenges, Medicare insurance states that hospice operators must include volunteer workers in their operations, an unusual requirement for any industry. Today, the U.S. hospice industry has about 500,000 volunteers, although most contribute only a few hours overall (NHPCO, 2015). It would be beneficial to everyone if one-time volunteers could be persuaded to continue their charitable involvement with the hospice industry as opposed to simply being used as a government mandated statistic.

Cost Analysis

Medicare insurance has not done a cost-benefit study of hospice but recognizes that this would require taking into account many variables, including the cost of treating conditions not related to the underlying terminal illness (Carr, 2016). However, if costly hospitalizations are relinquished in return for palliative care at home, it is reasonable to expect cost savings. Hospices have been expected to reduce health expenditures since their addition to the Medicare benefit package in the early 1980s, but the literature on their ability to do so has been conflicting (Barger, 2016). In the early days of the Medicare benefit, hospice benefits were designed around the disease trajectory for cancer, in which hospice patients followed a fairly predictable course. At that time, in-home hospice care appeared to be a major cost savings, but more recent reports have shown mixed results in overall **systemic cost savings**.

Likewise, the cost savings proposition is contrary to the parallel increase in Medicare spending generally and hospice spending in particular over the last decade (MedPAC, 2016). As previously stated, while more patients are dying with hospice care, they are increasingly doing so for only a very few days that follow expensive treatment in an intensive care unit (Dolgin, 2016). For many hospice patients, hospice care happens only as an afterthought (Teno et al., 2013). Moreover, it bears repeating that the corruption of hospice perverts any cost savings design, particularly the schemes of:

- Admitting and billing for nonterminal patients who would not otherwise incur daily costs
- Revoking patients from hospice into the hospital to be paid directly by insurers after the hospice has already billed for *per diem* payments, essentially causing insurers to pay twice

(Barger, 2016; Misichko, 2014).

Hospice care reduces the costs of care for many terminally ill hospice patients with various forms of cancer due to a reduction in expensive aggressive treatments (MedPAC, 2016). The savings, however, are not as clear for other diagnoses, including dementia and advanced stage organ system failures such as chronic congestive heart failure and chronic obstructive pulmonary disease, which are increasingly part of the hospice treatment mix (*See* Levinson, 2015). Among the patient populations studied in assisted living facilities, the mean survival was about a month longer for hospice patients than for non-hospice patients. In other words, hospice patients who chose hospice care lived an average of one month longer than similar patients who did not choose hospice care. While hospice use beyond these periods cost Medicare more than conventional care, more effort needs to be put into increasing short stays as opposed to focusing on shortening long ones (MedPAC, 2016).

Prevention Versus Add-On Costs

Hospice programs offer unique benefits for hospice patients nearing the end of life and for their families, and growing evidence indicates that hospice can provide high-quality care. Despite these benefits, many hospice patients do not enroll in hospice, and those who do enroll generally do so very late in the course of their illness (Dolgin, 2016). This delay is often attributable to the fact that physicians, while doing their best to predict a disease's course or the length of time someone has until their death, are often inaccurate (Teno et al., 2013). The higher health costs for hospice patients are a result of delays in hospice patients entering the program. For years, the average length of stay has held steady at about two months; but a third of those who die under hospice care are in the program seven days or less, especially inpatient hospice (NHPCO, 2015). Medicare insurance costs would be reduced for most hospice patients if hospice were used for a longer period of time, in contrast to having hospice patients use futile intermittent hospitalizations at the end of life. In other words, given the length of hospice use, increasing the length of the hospice stay for most patients earlier in their terminal disease states would increase savings (Teno et al., 2013). Clearly, the biggest problem is the patients that receive inpatient hospice care for too short a time; too many patients are being transferred from hospitals to inpatient hospice and dying within days of their admission. Hospice adds value by providing quality care. If the patient is transferred from a hospital to inpatient hospice and lives seven days or less, it is already too late to have prevented that final hospitalization and hospice care just becomes an add-on cost (Dolgin, 2016).

While hospitals do earn substantial revenue providing services to patients in their dying days, treating those patients also results in high costs that can exceed what Medicare insurance and other insurers cover. In addition, Medicare regulations prevent payment for providers that attempt to push unnecessary services to generate profits

(Barger, 2016). While Medicare insurance tries hard to set payment rates to avoid unusually high profits, its payment system does not reward health providers who find ways to keep hospice patients out of the hospital (Levinson, 2015).

Perinatal Hospice

An estimated 23,000 of all live-born babies each year are afflicted with defects severe enough to cause **neonatal death** within the first month of life, and there are also significant numbers with conditions severe enough to cause **fetal demise** (CDC, 2016a). Thus, there are a significant number of children who are candidates for **perinatal hospice**, a compassionate intervention for cases where there is diagnosis of a terminally ill fetus *in utero* (AAPLOG, 2015; WHO, 2016b). Yet, there is an unmet demand for perinatal hospice (Coleman, 2015). This apparent need for hospice care appears to exist even though 9 out of 10 parents with a fetus with known severe chromosomal or anatomic anomalies chose to terminate their pregnancy (Coleman, 2015; ISPD, 2015; *See* Hern, 2014). At the same time, experience with perinatal hospice finds that more than 90% choose hospice when it is offered in a supportive environment (*E.g.*, Asplin et al., 2013; Benute et al., 2012; ISPD, 2015).

Medical Futility

Mounting national attention is being given to poor-quality, protracted, and futile end-of-life care in hospital intensive care units in which the dying process is marked by:

- Acquiescence in end-of-life decision-making versus personal control
- Medical care that departs from rather than accords with one's wishes
- Pain versus comfort and denial versus awareness and acceptance

(Carr, 2016).

Hospice might be most valuable for families who want extra assurance that physicians will not use heroic measures to prolong a patient's life for only a short, and often painful, period of time. Given the hospital culture of trying to save patients no matter what, hospice is a way to signal to the health care system, more strongly than a living will, that a patient is ready to let go as opposed to continue treatments that have a small probability of success, are costly, and can seem inhumane. The advent of new lifesaving medical technology has made it more difficult for physicians to resist attempting to save a terminally ill patient (Mischko, 2014). Because the technology for heroic measures now exists, the technology tends to be used, not from a financial point of view, but from a cultural point of view (IOM, 2014).

Consequently, hospices often face a double-edged sword when treating terminally ill hospice patients (Pope, 2013). The law requires that hospices provide treatment to the best of their ability or potentially face heavy fines. At the same time, physicians do not want to be investigated for overprescribing drugs to terminally ill hospice patients. It is claimed that recent federal regulatory oversight hinders effective palliative care to terminally ill hospice patients (Brown, 2015), at a time when most pain associated with severe illness can be relieved if well-established palliative care guidelines are followed (Edwards, 2012; Smith, G., 2014).

For once, the law is clearer than the cultural views in this regard. The courts have accepted determinations of physiological medical futility as a legitimate reason for withdrawing care; physicians have no duty to continue life-sustaining treatment once it becomes futile (Smith, C., 2014). Despite the popular misconception that people try

9. What kind of new end-of-life or curative technology developments do you envision occurring during your lifetime that might present additional ethical challenges?

everything when finally faced with death, hospice patients generally accept death when the time actually arrives (Casarett & Quill, 2007; Dansicker, 2015).

Pre-Hospice Palliative Care

Patients who are terminally ill and seeking palliative care often choose hospice care (IOM, 2014). While palliative care may be offered to any seriously ill patient, hospice care is offered only to a patient with a life expectancy of months as opposed to years. When the U.S. hospice community was established in the 1970s, cancer patients made up the largest percentage of hospice admissions, but today cancer diagnoses account for about a third of all hospice admissions (NHPCO, 2015). In fact, less than one in 10 U.S. deaths are now caused by cancer, with the majority of deaths due to other chronic conditions (CDC, 2016c). The top four chronic conditions served by hospice include heart disease, unspecified debility, dementia, and lung disease (NHPCO, 2015).

Hospitals are increasingly adding pain management and other **noncurative treatments** to their business models. Some hospitals are developing innovative programs for palliative care that serve as pre-hospice care for patients in need of pain and symptom management, but who are not quite ready for hospice care, thereby eliminating the terrible choice between curative treatment and hospice services (Walsh, 2013). There is a synergy developing between hospice and hospitals that may yet improve quality of care while reducing health care costs (IOM, 2014). Hospice is finally being viewed as a way to live, not a medical failure; it is an inevitable passage and an acknowledgement that dying is not an *if* but a *when* event (Smith & Himmel, 2014).

LAW FACT

Acceptance of Patients into Hospice Care

Should hospice be required to provide artificial nutrition and hydration to a patient who is transferred to their care by a valid court order?

Yes. The hospice faced years of litigation when it accepted into its care the transfer of a persistent vegetative state patient. Interested parties may challenge decisions of a proxy or surrogate concerning discontinuance of life support to a hospice patient. In Florida, if the evidence of the hospice patient's wishes is conflicting, it must be assumed that the patient would choose to defend life.

—State court proceedings: *In re Guardianship of Schiavo*, 780 So.2d 176 (District Court of Appeal of Florida, Second District 2001), *review denied*, 789 So.2d 348 (Supreme Court of Florida 2001) and *Bush v. Schiavo*, 885 So.2d 321 (Supreme Court of Florida 2004), *cert. denied*, *Bush v. Schiavo*, 543 U.S. 1121 (U.S. Supreme Court 2005).
—Federal court proceedings: *In re Guardianship of Schiavo*, 932 So.2d 264 (Court of Appeal of Florida, Second District 2005).

See, e.g., Dioguardi & Lamba, 2014; Kennedy, 2016; Klein & Boris, 2013; Smith, 2013; Colby, 2007.

CHAPTER SUMMARY

- Hospice is a philosophy of palliative care that provides pain management and symptom control at the end of life.
- The Medicare hospice benefit is available only to hospice patients eligible for Medicare Part A and who are expected to live less than six months.
- Medicare hospice benefits cover all-inclusive per diem rates for routine home care, continuous attendance at home, inpatient respite care, or general inpatient symptom management care.
- Covered hospice services must be necessary for the treatment of terminal illnesses and related conditions provided in the patient's home, freestanding centers, hospitals, nursing homes, or other long-term care facilities.
- Medicare insurance will reimburse a hospice for two 90-day periods and then repeated, unlimited 60-day periods during a patient's lifetime.
- The largest portion of hospital expenses is incurred in the last few weeks of life.
- The law of informed consent favors a competent adult's right to choose between forms of end-of-life care, but an advanced directive or a living will, and a health care proxy should be in place before entry to hospice care.
- When making decisions about entry to hospice for adults lacking decision-making capacity and having no discernible preferences, the "best interests" standard prevails, meaning the best available care that will control pain will be provided to the patient.
- A collection of state laws protect hospice patients with limited mental capacity, such as those in a permanent vegetative state and those suffering from dementia or mental illness.
- Hospice care does not violate the Americans with Disabilities Act or the Rehabilitation Act, nor is it considered cruel and unusual punishment under the Eighth Amendment, despite the fact that it does not include curative care.
- Current laws support self-determination at the end of life, with the right to refuse medical intervention.
- Hospice care is a highly regulated industry in which the federal Centers for Medicare and Medicaid Services and corresponding state agencies oversee the quality of care and payment rates.

LAW NOTES

1. Dr. Cicely Saunders started the death-with-dignity movement in 1967 when she founded St. Christopher's Hospice in London. Hospice in the United States was cultivated by the influences of Dr. Saunders, Florence Wald, former dean of the Yale School of Nursing, and Dr. Elisabeth Kubler-Ross, a psychiatrist who studied and wrote extensively on the psychology of end-of-life issues. The first congressional legislation for hospice care failed in 1974; however, Congress took the program more seriously after the U.S. Department of Health, Education and Welfare reported that hospice might reduce overall health care costs. By 1983, hospice became a valid health care option in the United States when Congress approved the Medicare hospice benefit. (*See generally* Kubler-Ross, 2007/1969 and Kubler-Ross & Kessler, 2006).

2. In the late 1960s, as hospice was first appearing in the United States, early versions of the mechanical respirator called "the Bird" were being used. This respirator was invented by a California physician named Forrest Bird; it looked like a glass lunch box on a metal stand. Lacking an automatic switch, nurse's aides (like Hammaker, the author of this text when she was a premedical student) would sit with the patient and the machine in shifts, flipping the switch on the Bird every couple of seconds to shoot air into the patient's body. No one thought about whether extended use of this medical technology was appropriate; either patients breathed on their own after a few days, or they died. Thirty years later, an article in the journal *Nature* appeared about a physician in New York City doing robotic gallbladder surgery on a patient in France. The so-called Lindbergh operation (named after the first transatlantic plane flight by Charles Lindbergh, who contributed to the invention of the artificial heart), manipulated a robot's arms with signals that went under the ocean on transatlantic cable (Goldberg, 2012). If the U.S. health care system has moved from the Bird respirator to the Lindbergh operation in 30 years, what kind of end-of-life choices are going to be available in the next 30 years?

3. Individuals may be eligible for both Medicare and Medicaid insurance to cover their hospice costs. **Medicare** is a federal insurance program available primarily for individuals age 65 or older, but is also available to anyone with disabilities or end stage renal disease (permanent kidney failure requiring dialysis or a transplant). **Medicaid insurance**, on the other hand, is a federal-state medical assistance program available to:

   - Low-income individuals
   - Those who fit into eligibility groups recognized by federal and state law (pregnant, disabled, blind, or aged)
   - Those with excessive medical expenses

   Each state sets its own eligibility guidelines for Medicaid services. States are entitled to receive federal matching funds for optional services such as hospice (*See generally* CMS, 2015).

4. The attending physicians of hospice patients bill Part B of Medicare insurance (covering outpatient health care expenses including physician fees). The hospice physicians who meet the general medical needs of hospice patients to the extent that they are not met by the attending physicians may not bill Part B for what would normally be Part B services. Rather, the hospice bills Part A (covering inpatient hospital expenses) and reimburses the hospice physician (*See* 42 C.F.R. §418.304). However, if the attending physician is unable to continue rendering services to a hospice patient, then the hospice physician must provide direct care and is brought in as a consultant, and physician visits are covered under Part B. (*See* 42 C.F.R. §418.58).

5. The third appellate trial court opinion summarized the evidence of Terri Schiavo's wishes in *In re Guardianship of Schiavo*, 800 So.2d 640 (District Court of Appeal of Florida, Second District 2001) as follows:

   - Her prognosis was the type of end-stage health condition that permits the withdrawal of life-prolonging procedures (the trial court determined on the basis of expert testimony that Terri was in a persistent vegetative state; the only disputed issue was whether she had a small amount of isolated living tissue or no living tissue in her cerebral cortex).
   - She did not have a reasonable medical probability of recovery so that she could make her own decision to maintain or withdraw life-prolonging procedures.
   - The trial court had the authority to make such a decision when a conflict within the family prevented a qualified person from effectively exercising the responsibilities of a proxy (Terri's husband sought the removal of her feeding tube many years after her initial collapse, while Terri's parents fought against the removal).
   - Clear and convincing evidence at the time of trial supported a determination that Terri would have chosen in February 2000 to withdraw the life-prolonging procedures.

REFERENCES

AAPLOG (American Association of Pro-Life Obstetricians and Gynecologists). (2015). AAPLOG Practice bulletin no. 1: Perinatal hospice; care with compassion for families with an adverse prenatal diagnosis. *Issues in Law and Medicine, 30*, 89–97.

Asplin, N., et al. (2013). Pregnant women's perspectives on decision-making when a fetal malformation is detected by ultrasound examination. *Sexual and Reproductive HealthCare, 4*, 79–84.

Barger, J. F. (2016). Life, death, and Medicare fraud: The corruption of hospice and what the private public partnership under the federal False Claims Act is doing about it. *American Criminal Law Review, 53*, 1–64.

Benute, G. R., et al. (2012). Feelings of women regarding end-of-life decision making after ultrasound diagnosis of a lethal fetal malformation. *Midwifery, 28*, 472–475.

Brown, T. R. (2015). Denying death. *Arizona Law Review, 57*, 977–1040.

Caplan, A., et al. (Eds.). (2006). *The case of Terri Schiavo: Ethics at the end of life*. Amherst, NY: Prometheus Books.

Carr, D. (2016). Is death "the great equalizer"? The social stratification of death quality in the United States. *The Annals of the American Academy of Political and Social Science, 663*, 331–352.

Casarett, D. J., et al. (2008). The terrible choice: Re-evaluating hospice eligibility criteria for cancer. *Journal of Clinical Oncology, 27*, 953.

___. (2006). How should nations measure the quality of end-of-life care for older adults? Recommendations for an international minimum data set. *Journal of American Geriatrics Society, 554*, 1765–1771.

___. (2003). Identifying ambulatory cancer patients at risk of impaired capacity to consent to research. *Pain and Symptom Management, 26*, 619–620.

Casarett, D. J., & Quill, T. E. (2007). I'm not ready for hospice: Strategies for timely and effective hospice discussions. *Annals of Internal Medicine, 146*, 443–449.

Cavallaro, V. (2015). Advance directive accessibility: Unlocking the toolbox containing our end-of-life decisions. *Touro Law Review, 31*, 555–587.

CDC (Centers for Disease Control and Prevention). (2016a). *Life expectancy*. Atlanta, GA: CDC, National Center for Health Statistics.

___. (2016b). *Deaths and mortality*.

___. (2016c). *Leading causes of death.*

___. (2011, May 20). Top great public health achievements; United States. *Morbidity and Mortality Weekly Report (MMWR), 60*(19), 619–623.

CMS (Centers for Medicare and Medicaid Services). (2015). Coverage of hospice services under hospital insurance in *Medicare benefit policy manual* (Ch. 9). Baltimore, MD: CMS.

Colby, W. H. (2007). *Unplugged: Reclaiming our right to die in America.* New York, NY: American Management Association.

Coleman, P. K. (2015). Diagnosis of fetal anomaly and the increased maternal psychological toll associated with pregnancy termination. *Issues in Law and Medicine, 30,* 3–20.

Dansicker, A. (2015). Paying docs for end-of-life discussions: Can monetary incentives change the failures inherent with physician-patient communication? *Saint Louis University Journal of Health Law and Policy, 9,* 149–178.

Dioguardi, C., & Lamba, A. (2014). Employment-related crimes. *American Criminal Law Review, 51,* 1009–1050.

DOL (U.S. Department of Labor). (2016). *We count on home care.* Washington, DC: DOL, Wage and Hour Division.

Dolgin, J. L. (2016). Dying discourse: Contextualizing advance care planning. *Quinnipiac Law Review, 34,* 235–298.

Edwards, H. (2012). Risky business: How the FDA overstepped its bounds by limiting patient access to experimental drugs. *George Mason University Civil Rights Law Journal, 22,* 389–425.

Federal Interagency Forum on Aging-Related Statistics. (2012). *Older Americans: Key indicators of well-being.* Washington, DC: Federal Interagency Forum on Aging-Related Statistics.

Goldberg, M. (2012). The robotic arm went crazy! The problem of establishing liability in a monopolized field. *Rutgers Computer and Technology Law Journal, 38,* 225–253.

Gordy, K. (2011). Adding life to the adolescent's years, not simply years to the adolescent's life: The integration of the individualized care planning and coordination model and a statutory fallback provision. *Yale Journal of Health Policy, Law, and Ethics, 11,* 169–221.

Hain, E. R. (2015). I want you to have my heart: How using a will may better protect a donor's intent in insuring successful directed donation of organs. *The Quinnipiac Probate Law Journal, 28,* 304–321.

Hern, W. M. (2014). Fetal diagnostic indications for second and third trimester outpatient pregnancy termination. *Prenatal Diagnosis, 34,* 438–444.

IOM (Institute of Medicine). (2014). *Dying in America: Improving quality and honoring individual preferences near the end of life.* Washington, DC: The National Academies.

ISPD (International Society for Prenatal Diagnosis). (2015, July 12). Panel discussion on Pregnancy Outcomes, Placenta Markers and Screening; An Update at the 2015 International Conference on Prenatal Diagnosis and Therapy on Building Global Partnerships in Genetics and Fetal Care, Washington, DC.

Jennison, B. P. (2015). Reflections on the graying of America: Implications of physician orders for life-sustaining treatment. *Rutgers Journal of Law and Public Policy, 12,* 295–327.

Kaplan, R. L. (2015). Reflections on Medicare at 50: Breaking the chains of path dependency for a new era. *Elder Law Journal, 23,* 1–38.

Kennedy, E. J. (2016). Wage theft as public larceny. *Brooklyn Law Review, 81,* 517–561.

Klein, J., & Boris, E. (2013). We have to take it to the top! Workers, state policy, and the making of home care. *Buffalo Law Review, 61,* 293–319.

Kubler-Ross, E. (2007). *On death & dying.* London, England: Taylor & Francis. (Original work published 1969.)

Kubler-Ross, E., & Kessler, D. (2006). *On grief and grieving: Finding the meaning of grief through the five stages of loss.* New York, NY: Simon & Schuster: Scribner.

LaBruzza, A. R. (2015). In case of emergency, please comply: Louisiana's outmoded advance directive legislation and the patient's need for reform. *Loyola Law Review, 61,* 705–751.

Laskin, A., et al. (2014). Beyond autonomy? A transnational comparison of end-of-life decision making by mature minors. *Michigan State University Journal of Medicine and Law, 18,* 139–159.

LeCluyse, E. (2015). The spectrum of competency: Determining a standard of competence for pro se representation. *Case Western Reserve Law Review, 65,* 1239–1267.

Levinson, D. R. (2015). *Medicare hospices have financial incentives to provide care in assisted living facilities.* U.S. Department of Health and Human Services, Office of Inspector General.

Lim, M. (2015). A new approach to the ethics of life: The will to live in lieu of inherent dignity or autonomy-based approaches. *Southern California Interdisciplinary Law Journal, 24,* 27–144.

Mantel, J. (2015). Spending Medicare's dollars wisely: Taking aim at hospitals' cultures of overtreatment. *University of Michigan Journal of Law Reform, 49,* 121–177.

MedPAC (Medicare Payment Advisory Commission). (2016). *Report to the Congress: Medicare payment policy.* Washington, DC: MedPAC.

Misichko, M. E. (2014). A HELP-ing hand: How legislation can reform the Affordable Care Act and hospice care to prioritize comfort and prepare for the baby boomer generation. *Elder Law Journal, 21,* 419–464.

NHPCO (National Hospice and Palliative Care Organization). (2015). *Facts and figures: Hospice care.* Arlington, VA: NHPCO.

O'Neill, E. A. (2014). End-of-life care in Connecticut: Whose decision is it and when does the conversation begin? *The Quinnipiac Probate Law Journal, 27,* 317–343.

Ouellette, A. (2014). Freedom of choice at the end of life: Patients' rights in a shifting legal and political landscape: Context matters: Disability, the end of life, and why the conversation is still so difficult. *New York Law School Law Review, 58,* 371–389.

Persad, G. (2015). Priority setting, cost-effectiveness, and the Affordable Care Act. *American Journal of Law and Medicine, 41,* 119–166.

Plato. (2016). *Laws* (Cambridge Texts in the History of Political Thought). (M. Schofield, Ed. and T. Griffith, Trans.). New York, NY: Cambridge University Press. (Original work published 360 B.C.)

Pope, T. M. (2013). Freedom of choice at the end of life: Patients' rights in a shifting legal and political landscape: Dispute resolution mechanisms for intractable medical futility disputes. *New York Law School Law Review, 58,* 347–368.

Prahalad, C. K. (2009). *The fortune at the bottom of the pyramid: Eradicating poverty through profits.* Saddlebrook, NJ: Pearson Financial Times Press.

Rosoff, P. M., & Leong, K. M. (2015). An ethical and legal framework for physicians as surrogate decision-makers for their patients. *Journal of Law, Medicine and Ethics, 43,* 857–876.

Sage, W. M. (2016). Assembled products: The key to more effective competition and antitrust oversight in health care. *Cornell Law Review, 101*, 609–700.

Santoro, R. J. (2015). Giving POLST a pink slip: Why Connecticut was right to reject the national POLST paradigm. *The Quinnipiac Probate Law Journal, 28*, 411–434.

Shah, S. K. (2015). Piercing the veil: The limits of brain death as a legal fiction. *University of Michigan Journal of Law Reform, 48*, 301–346.

Shepherd, L. (2014). Health care decisions in the new era of health care reform: The end of end-of-life law. *North Carolina Law Review, 92*, 1693–1748.

Smith, C. W. (2014). Elder law and disability rights: Advising clients on Medicare. *Michigan Bar Journal, 93*, 34–39.

Smith, F., & Himmel, S. (2014). *Changing the way we die: Compassionate end of life care and the hospice movement.* Waterville, ME: Gale Cengage Learning: Thorndike Press.

Smith II, G. P. (2014). *Cura personalis*; A healthcare delivery quandary at the end of life. *Saint Louis University Journal of Health Law and Policy: The future of health law: Exemplary insight into trending topics, 7*, 311–329.

Smith, P. R. (2013). Who will care for elderly? The future of home care. *Buffalo Law Review, 61*, 323–342.

Teno, J. M., et al. (2013). Change in end-of-life care for Medicare beneficiaries: Site of death, place of care, and health care transitions in 2000, 2005, and 2009. *Journal of the American Medical Association, 309*(5), 470–477.

Truog, R. D. (2015). Science challenges for law and policy: Defining death: Getting it wrong for all the right reasons. *Texas Law Review, 93*, 1885–1914.

Walsh, R. A. (2013). Matter of life, death, and children: The Patient Protection and Affordable Care Act section 2302 and a shifting legal paradigm. *Southern California Law Review, 86*, 1119–1163.

Werner, C. (2011). *The older population: 2010 census briefs.* Washington, DC: U.S. Census Bureau.

WHO (World Health Organization). (2016a). *Dementia.* Geneva, Switzerland, WHO.

___. (2016b). *Global health observatory data: Neonatal mortality.*

___. (2014). *The top 10 causes of death.*

CHAPTER 29

© Andy Dean Photography/ShutterStock, Inc.

Mature Minor Rights to Refuse Life-Sustaining Treatment

"Neither youth nor childhood is folly nor incapacity. Some children are fools and so are some old men."

— **William Blake** (1757–1827), British poet and artist

IN BRIEF

This chapter is focused on the question of whether mature minors have the right to refuse life-sustaining treatment. Herein, a *mature minor* is defined as a child, generally an adolescent, who has decision-making capacity. The state's interest in preserving life and in protecting the health and welfare of children is greatest when a child desires to refuse life-sustaining treatment. Depending on one's view of life support, as well as the circumstances, the term *death-prolonging* could be substituted for *life-sustaining*.

LEARNING OBJECTIVES

Upon completion of this chapter readers should be able to:

1. Provide criteria for determining the maturity of minors.
2. Explain the concept of parental autonomy.
3. Describe the common law principle of self-determination.
4. Talk about the right to refuse life-sustaining treatment.
5. Differentiate between the "best interests of the child" and the "substituted judgment" standards.
6. Explain when a minor may refuse life-sustaining treatment.

KEY TERMS

Adolescents
Artificial life support
Best interests of the child
Clear and convincing evidence
Common law
Competence
Condition of consent
Confidentiality
Do-not-resuscitate orders
Emancipated minors

Good faith determination
Informed consent
Juvenile Justice and Delinquency
   Prevention Act of 1974
Legal capacity
Legal competency
Life-sustaining treatment
Manslaughter
Mature minor doctrine
Mature minors

Medical ethics committee
Neglect
Personal autonomy
Preservation of life
Rule of sevens
Self-determination
Substituted judgment standard
Temporary guardian
Wrongful death

FACT OR FICTION

Withdrawal of Life-Sustaining Treatment

Should life-sustaining treatment ever be withdrawn from a stable and completely alert minor with a progressive terminal disease?

H is a 14-year-old boy who suffers from Hunter syndrome, a rare but progressive and ultimately fatal genetic disorder for which there is no known cure. The buildup of complex carbohydrates that occurs from Hunter syndrome eventually causes permanent damage affecting appearance, mental development, organ function, and physical abilities. Patients suffer from various defects in bone, cartilage, and connective tissue, as well as seizure disorders and congenital heart disease. The defects in their aortic and mitral valves are eventually fatal. Patients also suffer from enlarged livers and spleens as well as characteristic body features, including a short stature with an enlarged head. The disease affects the airways, trachea, and large bronchial tubes because their structural support disappears and they collapse.

H was admitted to University Medical Center with breathing difficulties; within a day, he was placed on a ventilator to enable him to breathe, had a tracheostomy performed in order to stop aspiration, and had a feeding tube inserted into his stomach. H's condition is now stable, and he is completely alert. Generally, H is not in pain although he experiences pain whenever he is moved, washed, or suctioned, since water fills his connective tissues. H is slowly but progressively becoming more rigid and anatomically malformed as his disease progresses.

He is generally not on any pain medication due to the fleeting nature of his pain when he moves. H has requested removal of the ventilator and palliative care while his dying process occurs; he clearly understands this action will bring about his death. H is informed of his health condition and rationally acknowledges he is aware he is becoming deaf and losing his sight. At the court hearing to determine H's level of maturity to make this decision, H's parents testified they agreed to the withdrawal of H's life-sustaining treatment; they felt it was in their son's best interests to be weaned from the ventilator in an effort to end his discomfort and suffering. The hospital **medical ethics committee** supported the parents' decision. However, the director of pediatric critical care and H's pediatrician testified they would feel very uncomfortable removing the ventilator from H because he was an awake and alert minor who was not immediately terminal. Both testified they were involved in removing ventilators from other minors, but they were always comatose with no quality of life.

H is to be transferred to a nursing home where his parents cannot visit and care for him every day. While H's parents have provided care for H in their home since his diagnosis of Hunter syndrome at the age of three, they can no longer care for him on **artificial life support**. Everyone agrees H could be kept alive another two to three years through artificial means without any hope of recovery or cure as his disease progresses and his heart fails from the progressive thickening of its valves. H's parents are concerned their son will not receive the monitoring and care during his final years of his life that they have provided to him at their home.

— *See* Law Fact at the end of this chapter for the answer.

Principles and Applications

In order to understand precisely what this chapter is about, it is crucial to define **life-sustaining treatment**, a term that refers to advanced medical technologies, such as:

- Dialysis
- Feeding tubes to provide artificial hydration and nutrition
- Intravenous medicines that maintain blood pressure
- Mechanical ventilators and respirators

Although life-sustaining treatment forestalls the moment of death, by definition life-sustaining treatment can only sustain life. It cannot save life or improve a patient's condition. This is a crucial distinction, because medical treatment at the end of life at best merely prolongs the inevitable slow deterioration and predictable death of patients. *See In the Matter of Karen Quinlan,* 355 A.2d 647, 663 (Supreme Court of New Jersey 1976), *cert. denied,* 429 U.S. 922 (U.S. Supreme Court 1976).

The potential benefit of life-sustaining treatment can only be measured in relation to the patient's personal values.

The right to be free from unwanted medical attention is a right to evaluate the potential benefit of treatment and its possible consequences according to one's own values and to make a personal decision whether to subject oneself to the intrusion. *See Cruzan v. Director, Missouri Department of Health*, 497 U.S. 261, 309 (U.S. Supreme Court 1990) (Brennan, J., dissenting).

The decision to accept or refuse life-sustaining treatment determines not only the time of one's death, but also the manner in which death occurs. Thus, a denial of a mature minor's **personal autonomy** to refuse life-sustaining treatment is a denial of the right to decide whether the medical prolongation of life, as it transforms into a prolongation of death, is worth the high physical and psychological burdens that will have to be endured, including:

- Embarrassment and humiliation
- Emotional suffering
- Intractable pain
- Invasive and/or inhumane interventions designed to sustain life
- Irremediable disability or helplessness
- Other activities that severely detract from the quality of life as viewed by the patient

(AAP, 2012).

Parental Autonomy

As a rule, only parents can grant or decline permission for medical treatment of their children. The exception is that a state may seek to override parental choices that jeopardize a child's welfare. The power of parents to make decisions regarding medical treatment of their children does not require any assessment of the child's level of maturity, nor does it allow for any degree of personal autonomy for the child. *See Troxel v. Granville*, 530 U.S. 57 (U.S. Supreme Court 2000) (explaining that because of the presumption that fit parents will act in the **best interests of the child**, there is usually no reason for a state to become involved in the private realm of the family to decide what is in the best interests of the child). The emerging exception, however, is that for **mature minors** (AAP, 2012; Mutcherson, 2006).

In the United States, **adolescents** (10 to 19 years old) and preadolescents constitute the largest class of patients of questionable or borderline **competence** for the health care decisions they commonly face (Hartman, 2012). The consensus is that some minors have sufficient maturity to understand and appreciate the benefits and risks of proposed medical treatment of all kinds, and thus those mature minors should have the right to give or decline to give **informed consent** regarding all health care decisions (Wilson, 2015). Since the 1960s, states have recognized mature minors as enjoying adult rights of medical consent. States have passed laws allowing minors to bypass the parental consent tradition and to consent to a narrow range of medical treatments:

- Care related to a sexual assault
- Contraceptive services
- Drug and alcohol abuse and dependency treatment
- Emergency treatment where parents are not immediately available
- Mental health care
- Pregnancy-related care
- Treatment for sexually transmitted diseases

(Benson, 2016; Hill, 2015).

Adolescents can give independent consent for reproductive health services if their capacities for understanding have sufficiently evolved.

Although not every state has laws covering minors in each of the health status categories listed above, every state has provisions for at least some of them (Drobac & Hulvershorn, 2014). Courts have recognized the mature minor doctrine as one of at least seven exceptions to the requirement for parental consent in medical treatment of minors. These state laws recognize some measure of personal autonomy for certain types of treatment and allow minors to give informed consent on their own. Such consent is to be:

- Informed, with the ability to understand conflicting advice
- Rational, showing evidence of clear thinking and sensible judgment based on reason rather than emotion

- Voluntary, free of any coercion or duress
- Intentional, not arbitrary or capricious

(Tennison & Pustilnik, 2015).

Criteria for Determining Maturity of Minors

Whether a minor has the capacity to consent to medical treatment depends upon the totality of their circumstances and the facts of their case. There are no bright line rules applicable across the board. Criteria to be considered include:

- Age
- Conduct and demeanor of the minor at the time of the incident involved
- Degree of maturity or judgment
- Education and training (whether the minor is a high school graduate)
- Life experiences (such as whether the minor is emancipated, married, pregnant, a parent, or is living apart from the parents)
- Minor's ability to appreciate risks and consequences
- Nature of the treatment

(Hill, 2015).

Adoption of the mature minor exception to the **common law** is not a general license to treat minors without parental consent. There is always the problem of deciding whether minors are in fact mature enough to make their own medical decisions, which is determined strictly on a case-by-case basis.[LN1]

In other contexts, states have developed standards for determining whether minors have the capacity to formulate the necessary intent to commit crimes so as to be tried as adults. For instance, most state Juvenile Court Acts and the federal **Juvenile Justice and Delinquency Prevention Act of 1974** presupposes a sliding scale of maturity in which minors can be mature enough to be tried and convicted as adults (*See* 18 U.S.C.A. §§ 4351 *et seq.*). When a minor is mature enough to have the capacity to formulate criminal intent, minors are generally treated as adults. The concept of **legal competency**, used in criminal law and in determining the capacity of minors to testify as witnesses, applies the common law **rule of sevens**, under which minors:

- Under the age of 7 are presumed not to be competent or mature
- Between 7 and 14 are presumed not to be competent or mature, but may be proved otherwise
- From 14 to 21 are presumed to be competent and mature

(Wilson, 2015).

Clear and Convincing Standard of Maturity

There are so many factors to be considered when determining if a minor is mature that a well-reasoned uniform standard has failed to emerge (Silva, 2014). **Clear and convincing evidence** must demonstrate that a minor is mature enough to:

- Appreciate the consequences of their choices and actions
- Exercise the judgment of a competent adult
- Make personal health choices

Is it more likely than not that a mature minor can make the decision to refuse life-sustaining treatment? If the evidence is clear and convincing, then the mature minor doctrine affords mature minors the common law right to consent to or refuse medical treatment. While judicial proceedings are generally necessary to assess the minor's maturity in order for a minor's medical choices to be valid (when a temporary guardian is not appointed), in some situations a minor is so seriously ill or injured, recourse to the courts is impractical. In these situations, considerable emphasis is generally placed on whether the parents agree with their child's decision.

Interesting questions emerge. For instance, a 14-year-old minor, presumed to be mature under common law, has a baby. The baby is on life support with no chance of recovering from some terminal illness. Would anyone question the 14-year-old mother's right to make decisions for her baby? Would it not be strange if she were allowed to make that kind of decision for her own baby but not for herself, assuming she lives in a state that would not consider her a mature minor regardless of her life experience of being a parent? What if a minor was determined competent to stand trial as an adult for some terrible crime, but then fell ill with a terminal illness and was not allowed to make the decision to terminate life-sustaining measures?

Common Law Principle of Self-Determination

The international Convention on the Rights of the Child, almost universally ratified, limits parental powers and duties by a minor's evolving capacities for **self-determination** (Acharya, 2014). While the U.S. Supreme Court recognized the right of adults to refuse life-sustaining treatment, this right was never extended to mature minors. In the United States, the **mature minor doctrine** is generally a creature of case law that extends the common law principle of self-determination to minors (Wilson, 2015). The doctrine recognizes that decision-making capacity increases with age. There is usually no chronological age for giving consent for health care, but rather a **condition of consent**, meaning does the child have the capacity for understanding (*See* Ikuta, 2016)? This capacity is best assessed on a case-by-case basis.

Even though parents may authorize **do-not-resuscitate orders** for their children, health care professionals should obtain the consent of mature minors before administering or withholding treatment to avoid the possibility of **wrongful death** or other malpractice suits when a child dies (Hartman, 2012). Health care professionals have an affirmative duty to find out whether their patients are mature enough to consent to do-not-resuscitate orders and, by implication, to other kinds of protocols before authorizing them. If health care professionals conclude a minor is mature, then the minor's choices must be followed notwithstanding the objections of the parents. While this places a professional in the difficult position of determining the minor's maturity, and while a professional's decision on the maturity level of a minor will often be second-guessed, nonetheless the decision should be made using the professional's best medical judgment (Ikuta, 2016). Professionals who make **good-faith determinations** about the maturity of a minor are not generally liable for failing to obtain parental consent if the parents disagree with the minor's decision (Burda, 2016).

States have enacted legislation codifying these principles and reflecting policy judgments that certain minors have attained a level of maturity or personal autonomy that makes it appropriate for them to make their own medical decisions (Hill, 2015). For instance, West Virginia's legislation provides:

> If the minor is between the ages of 16 and 18 and, in the opinion of the attending physician, the minor is of sufficient maturity to understand the nature and effect of a do-not-resuscitate order, then no such order shall be valid without the consent of such minor. In the event of a conflict between the wishes of the parents or guardians and the wishes of the mature minor, the wishes of the mature minor shall prevail. For purposes of this section, no minor less than 16 years of age shall be considered mature. (West Virginia Code §16-30C-6(d)).

In other states minors, regardless of their maturity, may not refuse unwanted health care. *See, e.g.*, Code of Laws of South Carolina § 44-78-50(b); Tennessee Code Annotated § 68-11-224(a). This policy approach, in limiting the rights of mature minors, is opposed by the Society for Adolescent Medicine (*See* Burda, 2016).

Right to Refuse Life-Sustaining Treatment

At issue is whether and when, if ever, mature minors have the right to refuse life-sustaining treatment. This is particularly controversial when treatment is refused based on religious beliefs and when treatment would most likely achieve remission of a disease or illness (Laskin et al., 2015). Generally, hospitals seek to have the courts appoint a **temporary guardian** with authority to consent or refuse consent of all medical treatment required (Wilson, 2015).

MANAGEMENT AND LAW ISSUES

1. Could there ever be justification for a medical team to withhold individualized prognosis or adherence to treatment regimens information from a mature minor?
2. What is the proper balance between a parent's right to choose or refuse life-sustaining treatment for their child over a mature minor's rights?

3. Should the First Amendment's Free Exercise Clause entitle a mature minor to decline health care because it contravenes sincerely held religious beliefs?
4. At what point, if ever, should a state intervene when the failure of parents to accept and begin life-sustaining treatment endangers a child's life?
5. What should determine the proper balance between the human rights of mature minors and parental rights when the minor requests protection of the state to begin or end life-sustaining treatment?
6. Does a state have the fiscal ability or responsibility to pay for a child's medical treatment of a life-threatening condition when a parent refuses traditional medicine?

State interests may be greater than the interests of mature minors or their parents in refusing to consent to medical treatments if the treatment options and their risks, side effects, and benefits are negligible (such as is often the case for refusing blood transfusions for religious reasons). In these situations, parents who support their child's right to refuse life-sustaining treatment risk being charged with **neglect** or even **manslaughter** if death results from the minor's refusal of treatment.

Common Law Right to Refuse Medical Treatment

Still, mature minors have a common law right to consent to or refuse medical treatment. Like adults, mature minors enjoy **confidentiality** and the right to treatment according to their wishes as opposed to their best interests. Minors capable of self-determination may grant or deny assent to treatment regardless of whether parents or guardians provide consent (Hill, 2015).

Emancipated minors' self-determination may also be recognized in some contexts, such as upon marriage or default of adults' guardianship. Since most states do not have absolute 18-year-old age barriers prohibiting minors from consenting to medical treatment, age is not a barrier that necessarily precludes minors from exercising medical rights normally associated with adulthood. Thus, unless expressly prohibited by state law, mature minors may refuse medical treatment, even if this refusal results in their death.

Common law rights are not, however, absolute, and as with adults they must be balanced against state interests, such as:

- Maintaining the ethical integrity of the medical profession
- Preserving human life
- Preventing suicides
- Protecting the interests of third parties

(*See generally Vacco v. Quill*, 521 U.S. 793 (U.S. Supreme Court 1997)).

The most significant of the four interests is the **preservation of life**, which is particularly compelling when dealing with minors. If parents oppose a mature minor's refusal to consent to life-sustaining treatment, this opposition weighs heavily against the minor's right to refuse (Burda, 2016).

Withdrawal of Life-Sustaining Treatment

When deciding whether to withdraw life-sustaining treatment, the best interests of the child as opposed to a **substituted judgment standard** applies. A substituted judgment standard permits a surrogate to make decisions regarding health care based on what a person would have chosen had they been competent (Wilson, 2015). As for clear and convincing evidence of a child's best interests, courts generally consider such factors as:

- Benefits from treatment versus the burdens to the child
- Degree of humiliation, dependence, and loss of human dignity resulting from the condition and treatment
- Likelihood pain or suffering from withholding or withdrawal of treatment could be avoided or minimized
- Motivations of the family in advocating a particular course of treatment
- Nature and degree of physical pain or suffering resulting from the health condition
- Opinions of the family
- Pain, suffering, or serious complications caused or that may be caused by the treatment
- Physical, sensory, emotional, and cognitive capacities of the child

7. Who should determine what is in the best interests of mature minors regarding the value of their life and the end of their life?

- Preferences of the child, if they can be ascertained
- Quality of life, life expectancy, and prognosis for recovery with and without treatment
- Suffering to the child if treatment is withdrawn
- Treatment options and their risks, side effects, and benefits

(*See generally In re Christopher I,* 131 Cal.Rptr.2d 122 (Court of Appeal, Fourth District, Division 3, California 2003); Benson, 2016).

This modified approach, while often problematic, appears to provide the best solution for making medical decisions for mature minors regarding life-sustaining decisions.

Words of Caution for Health Care Providers

Health care providers face complicated issues with regard to life-sustaining treatment for minors. Since legitimate public concerns underlie this evolving controversy over the right to refuse health care, providers should obtain and document informed consent from all appropriate, authorized legal representatives including the parents, the mature minor, and any other authorized persons. To be valid, any consent must be informed and must be given by a person with the requisite **legal capacity**. Thus, a physician who proceeds with a treatment in conformity with a mature minor's request and a signed agreement still might be proceeding without legal consent because the minor may lack capacity due to age. On the other hand, if a physician proceeds at the parents' request in conformity with the best interests of a mature minor, the physician might be proceeding without legal consent because the minor may have legal capacity due to maturity. Providers should be particularly attentive when treating mature minors; mature minors need to understand the nature of their medical treatment, its risks, benefits, and alternatives, so their decisions along with their parents' decisions are truly informed (*See* Burda, 2016). Determining the maturity of minors is essential to legal compliance, protecting against liability, and ensuring children receive the best end-of-life care possible (Burda, 2016).

Withdrawal of Life-Sustaining Treatment

Should life-sustaining treatment ever be withdrawn from a stable and completely alert minor with a progressive terminal disease?

Yes. Since the 1960s, the technological innovations of science and medicine have had a significant impact on life and death and blurred the line between the two. Members of our society now enjoy healthier and longer lives. The symptoms of some rare diseases that at one time would have resulted in certain early death in children are now treatable, but the child's discomfort and suffering become indescribable. Medical treatment can keep children with progressive terminal diseases alive without any hope of recovery, cure, or even improvement in their condition. The ability of the medical community to artificially keep bodies alive has given rise to many ethical issues and arguments, with no clear answers.

The court found that the minor lacked the capacity to make reasoned decisions concerning his treatment and that his parents' request to discontinue his treatment was premature and not in the minor's best interests. However, the court recognized the parents' right to work with the medical community to reach a medically appropriate decision concerning their son. The court found no reason for the government to become involved in the private realm of this family; the parents could decide, with their son's treating physician, what was in the best interests of their son.

— Case synopsis based on *In re Gianelli*, 834 N.Y.S.2d 623 (Supreme Court of New York, Nassau County 2007).

See Tuthill, 2010; *See also* Garrison, 2014.

CHAPTER SUMMARY

- Generally, parents have the responsibility of deciding upon medical treatment for their children; the government may only intervene when the parents' choice may jeopardize the child's welfare.
- An exception to parents' complete control of medical decision-making regarding their children is emerging for mature minors; the consensus is that mature minors should be able to consent to or decline treatment.
- In many states, minors can now make medical treatment decisions without their parents' input regarding mental health, drug and/or alcohol dependency, sexually transmitted diseases, pregnancy, contraception, sexual assault, and emergency treatment.
- The criteria for minors to give informed consent are generally the same as for anyone else; the consent must be based on the ability to understand conflicting advice, it must be voluntary and intentional, and it must be based upon rationality as opposed to emotion.
- Criteria for determining whether a minor is mature include the minor's age, life experiences, education, demeanor, and the minor's ability to appreciate the risks and consequences of consenting to or declining treatment; the standard of evidence required for determining whether a minor is mature is clear and convincing.
- If health care professionals determine that a minor is mature, then the minor's choices take precedence over the parents' choices; in some states, minors may not refuse medical treatment regardless of their maturity.
- In some states, parents may be charged with neglect or even manslaughter if death results from the minor's refusal of treatment, especially if the refusal was made for religious reasons and the treatment's risks or side effects would have been negligible compared to the treatment's benefit.
- Unless expressly prohibited by state law, mature minors may refuse life-sustaining medical treatment.
- The reason states get involved in minors' health care is to protect the states' interest in preserving human life, preventing suicides, protecting third parties, and maintaining the ethical integrity of the medical profession, the strongest of which is the interest in preservation of human life.
- When deciding whether to withdraw life-sustaining treatment from a minor, a "best interests of the child" standard is applied, taking into account many factors, such as the child's quality of life, treatment options, degree of pain and suffering, and family opinions.
- Determining and documenting a minor's maturity is essential for health care providers to protect themselves from liability and to ensure the minor receives the best care possible.

LAW NOTES

1. While developmental psychologists define maturity as anyone who responds to circumstances in a socially appropriate manner, determining the maturity of minors has proven to be complicated. Medical literature questions the validity of the concept of legal competency and the rule of sevens in minors (Wilson, 2015). While developmental theorist Jean Piaget's four-stage model of development proposes that most minors begin to employ mature thinking processes between the ages of 11 and 15, critics question whether Piaget's developmental stages take into account the social and environmental pressures affecting the decision-making capability of minors when faced with the intense stress of life-threatening health conditions (Preston & Crowther, 2014). Some studies show 14-year-olds possess the same maturity and decision-making capability as adults (Carroll, 2016). Other developmental research claims minors and adults have very different perspectives on the world. Minors generally:

   - Are more susceptible to peer pressure
   - Have impaired judgment when facing the possibility of death regardless of their age
   - Make riskier choices
   - Tend to focus on immediate as opposed to long-term consequences

   (Schad, 2011).

   Modern cognitive theory has not yet defined the interaction between personal characteristics and maturity; while narrowly focused research has not identified the personality traits or individual behaviors that could be used to define the maturity of minors (*See* House, 2013). In recognition of the fact that some minors are more mature than some adults will ever be, the concept of maturity in general requires better definition in the social and legal contexts of life-sustaining treatment.

REFERENCES

AAP (American Academy of Pediatrics) Committee on Bioethics. (2012). Guidelines on forgoing life-sustaining medical treatment. *Pediatrics, 123*(5), 1421.

Acharya, U. (2014). The future of human development: The right to survive as a fundamental element of the right to development. *Denver Journal of International Law and Policy, 42,* 345–372.

Benson, S. (2016). Not of minor consequence? Medical decision-making autonomy and the mature minor doctrine. *Indiana Health Law Review, 13,* 1–16.

Blake, W. (1997). *The complete poetry and prose of William Blake.* (D. V. Erdman et al., Eds.). New York, NY: Penguin Random House, Anchor.

Burda, J. P. (2016). PrEP (HIV pre-exposure prophylaxis) and our youth: Implications in law and policy. *Columbia Journal of Gender and Law, 30,* 295–363.

Carroll, J. E. (2016). Brain science and the theory of juvenile mens rea. *North Carolina Law Review, 94,* 539–598.

Drobac, J. A., & Hulvershorn, L. A. (2014). The neurobiology of decision making in high-risk youth and the law of consent to sex. *New Criminal Law Review, 17,* 502–527.

Garrison, A. H. (2014). The traditions and history of the meaning of the rule of law. *Georgetown Journal of Law and Public Policy, 12,* 565–619.

Hartman, R. G. (2012). Noblesse oblige: States' obligations to minors living with life-limiting conditions. *Duquesne Law Review, 50,* 333–409.

Hill, B. J. (2015). Constituting children's bodily integrity. *Duke Law Journal, 64,* 1295–1362.

House, R. (2013). Seen but not heard: Using judicial waiver to save the juvenile justice system and our kids. *The University of Toledo Law Review, 45,* 149–179.

Ikuta, E. (2016). Overcoming the parental veto: How transgender adolescents can access puberty-suppressing hormone treatment in the absence of parental consent under the mature minor doctrine. *Southern California Interdisciplinary Law Journal, 25,* 179–228.

Laskin, A., et al. (2015). Beyond autonomy? A transnational comparison of end-of-life decision making by mature minors. *Michigan State University Journal of Medicine and Law, 18,* 139–159.

Mutcherson, K. M. (2006). Minor discrepancies: Forging a common understanding of adolescent competence in healthcare decision-making and criminal responsibility. *Nevada Law Journal, 6,* 927–965.

Preston, C. B., & Crowther, B. T. (2014). Legal osmosis: The role of brain science in protecting adolescents. *Hofstra Law Review, 43,* 447–480.

Schad, S. (2011). Adolescent decision making: Reduced culpability in the criminal justice system and recognition of capability in other legal contexts. *Journal of Health Care Law and Policy, 14,* 375–403.

Silva, L. R. (2014). The best interest is the child: A historical philosophy for modern issues. *Brigham Young University Journal of Public Law, 28,* 415–470.

Tennison, M. N., & Pustilnik, A. C. (2015). And if your friends jumped off a bridge, would you do it too? How developmental neuroscience can inform legal regimes governing adolescents. *Indiana Health Law Review, 12,* 533–590.

Tuthill, B. (2010). Want to terminate life support? Not in New York: Time to give New Yorkers a choice. *Touro Law Review, 26,* 675–707.

Wilson, M. J. (2015). Legal and psychological considerations in adolescents' end-of-life choices. *Northwestern University Law Review, 109,* 203–251.

CHAPTER 30

© Andy Dean Photography/ShutterStock, Inc.

Care of the Critically Ill and Dying

"It is impossible that man should not be a part of nature or that man should not follow nature's general order."

— **Benedict De Spinoza** (1632–1677), Portuguese philosopher

IN BRIEF

This chapter deals with the question of whether we have a right to die in peace, at a time and place of our own choosing. Answers to this question and the implications of palliative sedation and physician-assisted dying are explained, as well as the distinction between the two acts.

LEARNING OBJECTIVES

Upon completion of this chapter readers should be able to:

1. Explain the right to die in the context of personal dignity.
2. Describe palliative sedation usage in near-death circumstances.
3. Outline the double effect principle.
4. Describe the issues surrounding palliative sedation in contrast to those surrounding refusal of nutrition and hydration.
5. Explain why the term *assisted dying* is preferable to the term *physician-assisted suicide*.
6. Contrast the intent to cause death with the intent to alleviate suffering.

KEY TERMS

Ashcroft rule
Battery
Bodily integrity
Compassionate intent
Controlled Substances Act of 1976
Human dignity
Double effect principle
Euthanasia
Futile medical care
Informed consent

Intractable symptoms
Involuntary euthanasia
Legitimate medical purpose
Liberty interest
Life-sustaining treatment
Longevity
Palliative care
Palliative sedation
Persistent vegetative state
Personal autonomy

Physician-assisted dying
Reasonable person standard
Referendum
Right not to consent
Right to die
Right to privacy
Terminal prognosis
Terminal sedation

End-of-Life Care

Should you and your family plan for end-of-life care even though everyone is relatively young and healthy?

Imagine that you are a college student with cancer. You undergo a year of chemotherapy and after a brief return to normal life you relapse. Your physician says chemotherapy and radiation therapy could be tried, but a bone marrow transplant is your only chance for a real cure. He tells you and your parents complications from the transplant could cause your death but, without it, you may only live one year. You and your family discuss the alternatives and decide to have the transplant. You ask what will happen if the transplant fails, but your physician and family tell you to concentrate on getting better and avoid negative thoughts. You do not ask any more questions.

The physician provides you with the consent form to read over. You briefly look at it and sign it. The transplant preparation is worse than you had imagined and you experience painful side effects. You are fearful because you overheard through the hospital grapevine that some bone marrow transplant patients went to the intensive care unit and never came back. Still, you do not ask your family if these patients died and neither your family nor your physician ever inquires about your wishes in the event of your own need for intensive care. One week after the bone marrow transplant, before the new marrow has even taken hold in your body, you begin experiencing breathing difficulties. Over the next 24 hours, it becomes harder to breathe and difficult to speak more than a few words at a time. You are frightened because you feel so hungry for air. As your family watches you struggle to breathe, they become frightened as well.

A physician explains how you may soon need a ventilator, which requires a transfer to intensive care. You fear you will die there. You and your parents look to your physician, who is obviously worried. Your parents ask the physician to save you; he says the ventilator is your only chance. You are transferred to intensive care and are put into a deep sleep as the physician promised. You wake up enough to realize your fingers cannot move, your eyelids will not open, you cannot speak, and even a grimace is impossible. You are groggy most of the time. The voices of family members, of certain nurses that you have come to recognize, occasional music, a light stroking on your arm: these become the highlights of your existence. Time passes slowly and you lose track of the days. After some weeks, you notice you are more awake than before, yet you still cannot move. Nobody prepared you for the fact that you might be awake but unable to move a muscle. They had promised you would be asleep. The air goes into your lungs with so much force you feel like your lungs will burst. You choke on the tube in your windpipe. The ulcerations in your mouth and throat hurt continuously. Even worse than the pain and discomfort is the dawning realization that you are dying.

You want to ask for more medicine to keep your discomfort and anxiety under better control. You want to say goodbye to your family and go home to die, but you cannot move or speak at all. You hear your family members whispering to each other. They tell you how much they love you, but you cannot respond to them. You die alone in the middle of the night; your last fleeting thought is that you wish you could have died surrounded by your family. They said you sighed before dying, but you were just trying to tell them not to die alone and totally helpless like you were given no choice but to do. You know your death could have been different.

— *See* Law Fact at the end of this chapter for the answer.

Principles and Applications

The personal decision regarding how and when to die is one of the most intimate choices a person may make in a lifetime (*See Planned Parenthood of S.E. Pa. v. Casey*, 505 U.S. 833, 851 (U.S. Supreme Court 1992)). During the past century, advances in health care have led to dramatic changes in the life expectancy and death processes of Americans. Social and legal conventions from earlier times have struggled to effectively respond to today's unprecedented and unforeseen medical advancements. Since 1900, the average life span of Americans has increased by more than 30 years, to 79 years (CDC, 2016).

This increase in **longevity** is accompanied by the emergence of more complicated deaths (NIH, 2013). At the beginning of the 20th century, death was typically a relatively rapid process and could occur at any age; now, three out of four deaths in the United States result from progressive or chronic, critical illness (CDC, 2015). Unlike earlier times, most Americans will die slowly in the last year of life (IOM, 2014). Society and the legal system have struggled to respond to this shifting paradigm of dying. That we die is certain, while how we die is anything but.

Right to Die

The U.S. Supreme Court speaks in terms of the **right to die** and the meaning of **human dignity** in extremely individualized terms, analyzing both sides of the coin of death in individual and societal contexts. That human dignity is individual suggests each individual may have their own definition of human dignity, thus recognizing that human dignity requires recognition of each person's uniqueness (White, 2015). The right to die is broadly defined in this chapter to include all the rights that patients with advanced serious illness may have in controlling the circumstances of their death. Thus, the right to die includes the right of competent individuals who are nearing the end of life to refuse **life-sustaining treatment** as well as the right to hasten, or at least stop prolonging, their death.

Challenges to the right to die have generally focused on the concept of **bodily integrity**. The legal notion of bodily integrity, which includes the right to be free from **battery**, has its origin in the requirement that **informed consent** is generally required for medical treatment (*See Cruzan v. Director, Missouri Department of Health*, 497 U.S. 261 (U.S. Supreme Court 1990)). This principle leads to the corollary that patients generally possess the **right not to consent**, that is, to refuse treatment, even if it is lifesaving or life-sustaining. The informed consent principle and its corollary often lead to conflicts between patients asserting their right to be free from unwanted medical treatment, and a health care system and families who want to provide treatment (Parker, 2015). See **FEATURE BOX 30-1** for examples of laws and court cases addressing patients' rights.

FEATURE BOX 30-1

Important Legal Decisions and Legislation

1828—The earliest American law explicitly outlawing **physician-assisted dying** is enacted in New York (Act of Dec. 10, 1828, ch. 20, § 4, 1828 N. Y. Laws 19).

1969—The first living will is written by attorney Louis Kutner, and his arguments for it appear in the *Indiana Law Journal* (Kutner, 1969).

1969—Daniel Callahan founds the Hastings Center and launches the discipline of bioethics.

1972—The U.S. Senate Special Commission on Aging, chaired by attorney and Senator Frank Church, holds the first national hearings on death with dignity.

1973—The American Medical Association adopts a Patient's Bill of Rights recognizing the right of patients to refuse medical treatment.

1974—The first American hospice opens in New Haven, Connecticut.

1974—The Society for the Right to Die is founded.

1974—Federal funding is provided for hospice programs.

1976—The New Jersey Supreme Court allows the parents of a young woman in a persistent vegetative state to remove her from a life-sustaining ventilator; the Court authorized removal on a basis of a **right to privacy**[LN1] (*See Matter of Quinlan*, 355 A.2d 647 (New Jersey State Supreme Court 1976), *cert. denied, Garger v. New Jersey*, 429 U.S. 922 (U.S. Supreme Court 1976)).

1976—The California Natural Death Act is passed; it is the nation's first aid-in-dying law, giving legal standing to living wills and protecting physicians from being sued for declining to treat incurable illnesses (*See* California Probate Code § 4670; California Probate Code § 4740).

1976—Eight states (Arkansas, California, Idaho, Nevada, New Mexico, North Carolina, Oregon, and Texas) enact right-to-die laws recognizing the right to refuse life-sustaining treatment.

1980—The World Federation of Right to Die Societies is formed, numbering 27 organizations from 18 different countries.

1983—The Medicare hospice benefit providing payment for hospice programs caring for patients with progressive or chronic, critical illness begins.

1986—The California Court of Appeals finds that a 27-year-old competent woman with severe cerebral palsy has the right to forgo life-sustaining treatment (*See Bouvia v. Superior Court of Los Angeles*, 179 Cal. App.3d 1127 (Court of Appeal of California, Second Appellate District, Division 2 1986)).

FEATURE BOX 30-1 (CONTINUED)

1987—The California State Bar Conference passes a resolution to become the first public body to approve of physician aid in dying.

1990—The U.S. Supreme Court decides that states are free to adopt evidentiary standards to indicate when a family member can make end-of-life decisions for one unable to do so; five Justices recognize a constitutional right of competent people to refuse life-sustaining treatment[LN2] (*See Cruzan*, 497 U.S. 261).

1990—The American Medical Association adopts the formal position that, with informed consent, a physician can withhold or withdraw treatment from a patient who is close to death, and may also discontinue life support of a patient in a permanent coma.

1991—The Patient Self Determination Act mandates that health care institutions receiving Medicare or Medicaid insurance funding give patients written information about their right to participate in medical decision-making and write advance directives (*incorporated into* 42 U.S.C.A. 1395cc(f)).

1993—Compassion in Dying is founded in the state of Washington to counsel patients with progressive or chronic, critical illness and provide information about how to die without suffering.

1997—The U.S. Supreme Court finds there is no constitutional right to physician-assisted dying; the Court indicates the issue is one state legislatures should determine; several Justices' opinions establish that Americans have a right to palliative sedation (*See Washington v. Glucksberg*, 521 U.S. 702 (U.S. Supreme Court 1997) (holding there is no constitutionally protected interest in the right to die that prohibits states from enacting laws against physician-assisted dying); *Vacco v. Quill*, 521 U.S. 793 (U.S. Supreme Court 1997) (holding state laws may distinguish between the withdrawal of life-sustaining treatment and physician-assisted dying without violating the U.S. Constitution)).

1997—Oregon becomes the first state in the nation where physician-assisted dying is legal (*See* Oregon Death with Dignity Act of 1997, Oregon Rev. Stat. §§ 127.800-127.897).

1997—The Institute of Medicine finds widespread dissatisfaction with end-of-life care; most Americans with serious, advanced illnesses prefer to die at home and receive a more conservative pattern of end-of-life care, yet the majority died in hospitals and received more aggressive care than was desired.

2001—The Netherlands officially legalizes euthanasia.

2005—The U.S. Court of Appeals for the 11th Circuit upholds the trial court's decision finding that a clear and convincing standard of evidence was met and that termination of Terri Schiavo's life-sustaining treatment was appropriate (*See Schiavo ex rel. Schindler v. Schiavo*, 403 F.3d 1289 (U.S. Court of Appeals for the 11th Circuit 2005)).

2006—The U.S. Supreme Court holds that the **Controlled Substances Act of 1976** does not authorize the U.S. Attorney General to ban the use of controlled substances for physician-assisted dying; Oregon's Death with Dignity Law is upheld (*See Gonzales v. Oregon*, 546 U.S. 243 (U.S. Supreme Court 2006)).

2008—The State of Washington voters passed a physician-assisted dying **referendum** closely patterned after the Oregon Death with Dignity Act.

2009—The Montana Supreme Court rules that physicians may prescribe lethal drugs to the competent patients with progressive or chronic, critical illness.

2014—The Institute of Medicine issues a second report echoing 1997's findings and showing continued widespread dissatisfaction with end-of-life care (IOM, 2014).

2015—California becomes the fifth state to legalize physician-assisted dying.

Data derived from E.g., NHPCO, 2016a.

Palliative Sedation

The term **palliative sedation** is used in this chapter, but the process is also called:

- Continuous deep sedation
- Palliative sedation to unconsciousness
- Pharmacological oblivion in end-of-life care
- Primary deep continuous sedation
- **Terminal sedation**

When the U.S. Supreme Court endorsed palliative sedation as an alternative to physician-assisted dying, it set the stage for another battle in the right-to-die controversy (*See Cruzan*, 497 U.S. 261; *Glucksberg*, 521 U.S. 702; *Vacco*, 521 U.S. 793)).

Most patients reach a point where the goals of health care change from an emphasis on prolonging life and optimizing function to maximizing the quality of remaining life, and **palliative care** becomes a priority (Leven, 2013). Palliative care focuses on easing symptoms such as pain and shortness of breath that are often overlooked amid aggressive efforts to save seriously ill patients (Beck, 2016). Palliative sedation is a routine continuation of palliative care enabling patients to maintain a sense of self-control and strength in their final days and hours. Continued intimate involvement in each of the final stages of death is essential in palliative care. When palliative sedation is viewed as a continuum of effective health care, it grants control to patients and their families under the principle of respect for **personal autonomy** (Smith, 2014).

Definition of Palliative Sedation

Palliative sedation is defined as the induction of an unconscious state to relieve otherwise intractable distress and pain, and is frequently accompanied by the withdrawal of any life-sustaining treatments (Parker, 2015). When less aggressive means fail for patients suffering from severe pain, dyspnea (difficulty in breathing), or other symptoms resistant to treatment, palliative sedation becomes a clinical option of last resort (Quill, 2012). Palliative sedation was an end-of-life care option long before the U.S. Supreme Court considered the constitutional implications of physician-assisted dying. Physicians have always used palliative sedation to:

- Alleviate physical discomfort and pain
- Produce an unconscious state before the withdrawal of nutrition and hydration
- Relieve nonphysical suffering

(IOM, 2011).

There is currently no comprehensive data regarding the use of sedation for pain control among palliative care patients who, faced with the prospect of a prolonged and painful death from a progressive or chronic, critical illness, choose to end their lives instead in a peaceful and dignified manner (*E.g.*, Bohnert et al., 2011; Klothen, 2013). Various hospice and other patient studies have reported that sedation, with or without medical intervention or the withdrawal of nutrition and hydration, is generally used for symptom control among patients with advanced critical illness. The average time from sedation to death appears to be less than two weeks (Quill, 2012). Palliative sedation changes the timing of death in only a minor way, but adds control in a major and socially approved way (Tucker, 2012).

Doctrines Supporting Palliative Sedation

Palliative sedation is typically the combination of two distinct actions. These include the

- Induction of unconsciousness
- Withholding or withdrawal of life-sustaining treatment, such as nutrition and hydration

The implications of palliative sedation depend upon whether individuals view these acts separately or as a single action (Tucker, 2011).

Double Effect Principle

Palliative sedation is justified by the **double effect principle** as an alternative to what otherwise could be a prolonged and painful death (Tucker, 2012). According to this principle, consequences that would be wrong if caused intentionally become acceptable, even when foreseen, if the actions creating those consequences are intended for a morally permissible purpose. Generally, reliance on the principle of double effect requires the presence of four conditions:

- Act creating the risk of adverse consequences should be good, or at least morally neutral
- Actor should intend the good effect and not the bad effect, although the bad effect may be foreseen
- Bad effect should not be a means to the good effect
- Good effect should outweigh the bad effect

(Quill, 2012).

Under this principle, prescription drugs that may hasten death may be administered so long as the intent is solely to relieve suffering. In this scenario, the good effect of relief from suffering is intended, while death is merely foreseen. Criticism of the role of the double effect principle occurs on various grounds, including an overemphasis on forbidding actions.

Overemphasis on Forbidding Actions

Emphasis against intentionally causing death may encourage some health care professionals to be overly apprehensive in providing appropriate end-of-life care (Parker, 2015). This apprehension might lead to conflicts when patients wish to withdraw nutrition and hydration. Another risk is that prescription pain drugs may be underprescribed (ASA & ASRAPM, 2010). Unfortunately, the likelihood of these situations arising is probably unavoidable, given the current state of the law.

Complexity of Determining Compassionate Intent

Although ascertaining intent is generally complex, the legal system regularly relies upon its ability to perform this function, particularly in the criminal justice context. While intent is difficult to judge, the law has developed a presumption in favor of **compassionate intent** in the context of end-of-life decisions as opposed to intent to kill (Pope & Anderson, 2011). Although the concept of compassionate intent is still undeveloped, the law will eventually take the complexity of this issue into account.

Lack of Unanimous Acceptability

Though the absolute prohibition on intentionally causing death does not comport with all religious and cultural principles, it is consistent with the current state of the law (Noah, 2013a). No state permits voluntary **euthanasia**, and only five states (California, Montana, Oregon, Vermont, and Washington) allow physician-assisted dying (Klothen, 2013). Voluntary euthanasia, where someone other than the patient administers a lethal drug, is generally prohibited in the United States, but is legal in:

- Belgium
- Columbia
- Luxembourg
- The Netherlands

(*E.g.*, Reynolds, 2014; *See* Blumenson, 2015).

Thus, the double effect principle represents a sound policy in the United States to the extent that it allows palliative sedation without engaging in illegal conduct. The alternatives to the double effect principle are to:

- Accept the intent to cause death, or
- Forbid conduct with the foreseeable effect of hastening death

The former alternative directly contradicts the law of almost every state, and the latter alternative leaves some patients (those who are incapacitated before sedation, yet who have previously clearly stated their desire to hasten their death at some point) without the ability to obtain palliative sedation. Even with excellent pain and symptom management, a fraction of dying patients will still confront a dying process so prolonged and marked by such extreme suffering and deterioration, that palliative sedation is the least-bad alternative (Tucker, 2012). Thus, as a matter of public policy, the double effect principle is arguably the most practical option.

COURT DECISION

Physician-Assisted Dying

Baxter v. State of Montana
[Physicians v. State Government]
224 P.3d 1211 (Montana State Supreme Court 2009)

Facts: Robert Baxter was a truck driver with a progressive critical illness, debilitated from both his lymphocytic leukemia and attendant chemotherapy. Baxter suffered from a variety of debilitating symptoms, including infections, chronic fatigue and weakness, anemia, night sweats, nausea, massively swollen glands, significant ongoing digestive problems and generalized pain and discomfort. The symptoms were expected to increase in frequency and intensity as the chemotherapy lost its effectiveness. He challenged the constitutionality of applying Montana's homicide laws to his physicians who sought to assist him and others in dying with dignity. Baxter had no chance of recovery and could expect, at best, only a small degree of symptomatic relief. In his case, even symptomatic relief was impossible to achieve without the use of terminal sedation, a pharmacological technique that would render him unconscious prior to his death. The professional opinion of his physicians was that physician-assisted dying would be a medically and ethically appropriate option for him.

Baxter's physicians asked that they be allowed to engage in physician-assisted dying. Specifically, they asked the court to order the state not to prosecute them, or any other physician, if they provided assistance in dying by prescribing lethal drugs to this competent patient with a progressive critical illness. The criminal law at issue states a person is guilty of manslaughter when they intentionally cause or aid another person to commit suicide; the law also prohibits murder, which is defined to include intentionally causing a suicide. Taken together, these laws prohibit all physician-assisted dying.

Issue: Should physicians be allowed to engage in physician-assisted dying?

Holding and Decision: Dismissed because this is a claim that must be decided by the legislature and not by the judiciary.

Analysis: The physicians asked the court to issue a judgment declaring that the law does not provide a valid basis to prosecute licensed physicians for providing assistance in dying because the choice of a mentally competent patient with a progressive critical illness for a peaceful death, as an alternative to enduring a dying process the patient finds unbearable, does not constitute suicide. In response, the court stated that the law in question and the commentary to and legislative history of the law make it quite clear that physician-assisted dying, even for humanitarian reasons, is a crime. In almost every state—indeed, in almost every Western democracy—it is a crime for physicians to assist patients in dying. Legislative determination is particularly important given the significant medical, legal, and ethical concerns about legalized physician-assisted dying that have been raised across the country.

The court found that the legislature should evaluate difficult and important policy concerns because they are uniquely positioned in our system of government to evaluate whether physician-assisted dying:

- Opens the door to the possibility of **involuntary euthanasia**, as has occurred in the Netherlands, because a limited right to physician-assisted dying could effect a much broader license which could prove extremely difficult to police and contain; and, if so, how best to design effective legal and regulatory controls to avoid involuntary euthanasia
- Shifts the focus of physicians and insurers away from vitally important measures such as identifying and treating depression and providing end-of-life pain control and palliative care; and, how best to ensure that all appropriate treatment and care options are considered and made available to patients who may be considering physician-assisted dying
- Threatens the most vulnerable in society, including the poor, the elderly, and the disabled, who are at risk of being coerced or influenced to end their lives to spare their families the financial costs and emotional strain of caring for them; and, if so, who should protect vulnerable individuals from undue influence, pressure, or coercion
- Undermines the physician-patient relationship and the integrity of the medical profession by eroding patient trust in the physician's role as healer; and how best to avoid or limit such harms

The court acknowledged numerous public concerns about permitting physician-assisted dying:

- Is this the kind of choice, assuming it can be made in a fixed and rational manner, that we wish to offer patients with progressive or chronic, critical illness?
- Will some feel an obligation to have themselves eliminated in order that the funds allocated for their illness might be better used by their families; or financial worries aside, in order to relieve their families of the emotional strain involved?
- Will some who are not really tired of life, but think others are tired of them, and others who do not really want to die, but who feel that they should not live on because to do so when there exists an alternative is selfish and cowardly, be swept into accepting physician-assisted dying?

The court held that legislatures and the legislative process are the most appropriate body to evaluate these important questions as well as a host of other complex issues, such as:

- How competency should be determined
- How progressive or chronic critical illness should be defined
- How the decision to end life will be limited to the competent patient when existing laws allow conservators, next of kin, and others to make decisions for the patient
- Whether disinterested witnesses are required
- Whether patients must be competent when they take lethal drugs or only when they request them

Rule of Law: Legislatures are the most appropriate body to evaluate important policy questions and public concerns on a host of complex issues regarding physician-assisted dying.

References discussing this court decision: Busscher, 2015; Franklin, 2015; Klothen, 2013; Noah, 2013a; Orentlicher, 2014; Reynolds, 2014; Rountree, 2015; White, 2015.

Misplaced Emphasis on Personal Autonomy

Personal autonomy in medical decision-making, regardless of its merits, is of little value in end-of-life legal issues, since there is no constitutional right to state-sanctioned physician-assisted dying. If more states begin to permit physician-assisted dying, then personal autonomy will become a more viable public policy to guide palliative sedation. Similarly, civil liability is based upon the objective, **reasonable person standard**. In the context of professional medical liability, the fact that palliative sedation is part of the standard continuum of palliative care should preclude liability. Thus, the fact that a patient's death is a foreseeable consequence to palliative sedation would only be one element for determining civil liability.

Foreseen and Unintended Consequences

The fact that both foreseen and unintended consequences are taken into account by the law does not necessarily mean that actions undertaken pursuant to the double effect principle are a basis for civil or criminal liability (Parker, 2015). None of the modern laws treat attempted suicide as a crime; moreover, even long ago when attempted suicide was a crime in the United States, prosecutors only rarely filed charges for a suicide attempt that harmed no one but the attempter (Rountree, 2015). The reason for this suicide policy is perhaps obvious: criminal liability for foreseen consequences arises only upon unjustified actions.

Voluntary Refusal of Nutrition and Hydration

The voluntary refusal of nutrition and hydration takes two forms. Patients:

- Refuse artificial nutrition and hydration
- Refuse to eat and drink

Clinically, at the time of palliative sedation, most patients have generally already stopped eating and drinking. For patients who require artificial nutrition and hydration, the right to refuse is the same right as being free from other unwanted medical intervention. The act of refusing artificial nutrition and hydration is like a medical

MANAGEMENT AND LAW ISSUES

1. If personal autonomy extends to the time and manner of one's death in states that have adopted physician-assisted dying laws, should this principle not also apply whenever people believe their death is better than continued life regardless of the state in which they reside?
2. If it is no longer criminal to attempt suicide, can it logically be criminal to assist someone in committing suicide?

intervention and, thus, the legal right to forgo this treatment is more clearly established than the voluntary cessation of eating and drinking.

Voluntarily refusing to eat or drink has been likened to suicide by opponents of palliative sedation. Despite the lack of judicial authority on this issue, courts are unlikely to intervene when competent dying patients voluntarily stop eating and drinking (Pope & Anderson, 2011). A desire to die does not decide the final outcome of a refusal of medical intervention. As long as death is approached passively, palliative sedation is the same as withdrawal of life-sustaining treatment (Schwarz, 2011). Personal autonomy supports the refusal or withdrawal of life-sustaining health care; it is not contingent upon whether the refusal is of artificial nutrition and hydration or whether the patient voluntarily elects to discontinue eating and drinking (Noah, 2013a).

The Debate over Palliative Sedation

Focusing on whether palliative care constitutes euthanasia often obfuscates the palliative sedation debate. There is a range of opinions, from those inflexibly opposed to palliative sedation to advocates of the practice (Smith, 2014). Some critics of palliative sedation compare it to euthanasia, viewing the induction of unconsciousness and the withdrawal or refusal of life-sustaining intervention as continuous acts that actively cause death (Parker, 2015).

Combining the induction of unconsciousness with the withdrawal of life-sustaining treatment, however, confuses the legal issues raised by palliative sedation (Tucker, 2012). Although the two acts together constitute palliative sedation, the induction of unconsciousness and the withdrawal of life-sustaining medical interventions are separate acts supported by different legal and ethical doctrines. The induction of unconsciousness relies upon long-standing and accepted palliative care (Parker, 2015); the withdrawal of life-sustaining treatments relies upon the principle of personal autonomy (Smith, 2014). Despite the U.S. Supreme Court's endorsement of palliative sedation as a whole, the debate continues. While many issues center on the principle of double effect, three general positions have emerged on palliative sedation:

- Approval
- Conditional support
- Criticism

Approval of Palliative Sedation

Most Americans and physicians support palliative sedation based upon the principles of informed consent and double effect (Parker, 2015). The American Medical Association views palliative sedation as a medically proper way to assure a modicum of human dignity at the time of death (AMA, 2016, 2008). It is a form of patient affirmation and empowerment when properly understood (Tucker, 2012). Proponents of palliative sedation maintain the practice is best understood as a continuum of proper treatment to which every patient should be entitled; it validates personal autonomy and self-determination (Smith, 2014). Indeed, it can even be viewed as respecting life.

Conditional Support for Palliative Sedation

Others conditionally support palliative sedation, depending upon the form it takes. While palliative sedation is clearly lawful, some people find the withholding of artificial nutrition and hydration to be problematic, particularly when it takes place at an earlier point in the dying process than the sedation. This viewpoint distinguishes three forms of palliative sedation:

- Accompanying the withdrawal of artificial nutrition and hydration
- At the end stage of a dying process, where a patient has not been dependent upon artificial nutrition and hydration
- In a patient not dependent upon artificial nutrition and hydration and accompanied by palliative sedation

(Parker, 2015; Smith, 2014).

The first two forms of palliative sedation are justified under general principles of palliative care. The patient or patient's surrogate consents to the process and no less risky means of relief are available (Parker, 2015).

Simultaneous Request for Palliative Sedation and Refusal of Nutrition and Hydration

The troublesome scenario for conditional supporters of palliative sedation involves patients whose dependence on nutrition and hydration accompanies the sedation administered to relieve **intractable symptoms** during the dying process. There is resistance to scenarios in which patients address palliative sedation and the withholding of nutrition and hydration simultaneously. Awareness that the alternative is forcing patients to eat and drink against their will alters this calculus for some people. Others remain concerned that unlike patients who first elect to forgo artificial nutrition and hydration, patients who simultaneously choose palliative sedation and the withdrawal of nutrition and hydration have no opportunity to reflect upon their decision and change course prior to the induction of unconsciousness (Parker, 2015).

Inconsequence of Timing

There is no legal distinction between palliative sedation administered following the withdrawal of nutrition and hydration and simultaneous sedation. Although a state's interests in the preservation of life may be implicated, palliative sedation has not relied upon the degree to which the patient's decision is irreversible (*Cruzan*, 497 U.S. 261). The focus has always been on the need for and right to relief from pain and suffering when patients seek such relief (*See* ASA & ASRAPM, 2010). Assuming a state's procedural requirements with respect to the withdrawal of life-sustaining medical intervention are established, supporters of the process claim that patient decisions to forgo artificial nutrition and hydration should not be subject to additional legal scrutiny based solely upon the timing of when this occurs. To do so would undermine the personal autonomy principle that grants patients this right in the first place (Noah, 2013b).

Criticism of Palliative Sedation

Criticism of palliative sedation often centers on its comparison to physician-assisted dying. Unfortunately, empirical and anecdotal evidence indicates health care professionals are not always informing patients with progressive or chronic, critical illness of all legal medical options (Suter, 2013). As a result, patients are not always given the opportunity to make fully informed decisions about palliative care at the end of their lives.

In imposing their view on unsuspecting patients, critics refuse to distinguish between withdrawal of medical treatment and euthanasia. Critics argue that the process of withholding nutrition and hydration to induce unconsciousness actively and intentionally causes death. This refusal to distinguish underlying compassionate intent in end-of-life care can be likened to the example U.S. Supreme Court Justice Oliver Wendell Holmes gave when he wrote about the need to distinguish between intentional conduct and unintentional conduct. Over a hundred years ago, Holmes noted that even a dog distinguishes between being stumbled over and being kicked (Holmes, 1881).

Underlying Disease Distinctions

In rejecting all arguments that palliative sedation is an alternative to physician-assisted dying, critics distinguish between death from palliative sedation and death resulting from the withdrawal of nutrition and hydration without the induction of unconsciousness. Critics claim that with palliative sedation, the induced state of unconsciousness is responsible for the inability to eat and drink, not the natural progression of the underlying disease (Giest, 2012). On the other hand, proponents claim the inability to eat and drink is a result of the underlying disease (AMA, 2016).

Validity of the Double Effect Doctrine

Critics of palliative sedation reject the doctrine of double effect. They maintain that because the doctrine of double effect justifies hastened death, it justifies only sedation; the withdrawal of nutrition and hydration does nothing to relieve pain but serves only to bring about death (Parker, 2015). In contrast, proponents claim the withdrawing of life-sustaining treatment is premised on the doctrine of informed consent, and note that artificial nutrition and hydration can actually increase patients' discomfort at the end of life (Tucker, 2014, 2012). Thus, the double effect principle should not be rejected simply because it offers only a partial justification (Noah, 2013a). Although viewing palliative sedation as a single act is not unreasonable, critics would reverse decades of case law related to personal autonomy (Smith, 2014). Whether palliative sedation is a superior medical alternative to physician-assisted dying is a separate issue from whether it is a legal and appropriate continuation of palliative care.

Palliative Sedation Compared to Physician-Assisted Dying and Euthanasia

Critics often compare palliative sedation to physician-assisted dying and euthanasia, concluding palliative sedation has become more problematic than physician-assisted dying or euthanasia. Specifically, critics contend palliative sedation poses the same risks of abuse as euthanasia, and greater risks of abuse than physician-assisted dying, while serving fewer purposes of the right to die than either alternative. The only right-to-die issues addressed by palliative sedation are those relating to pain and suffering. In contrast, physician-assisted dying and euthanasia address concerns related to:

- Avoiding a death that compromises human dignity
- Controlling the timing of one's death
- Pain and suffering

Similarly, all of the concerns related to physician-assisted dying and euthanasia exist with palliative sedation:

- Danger that the lives of patients with progressive or chronic, critical illness and the disabled may be undervalued
- Erosion of trust in the health care system as a result of health care professionals causing (euthanasia) or hastening death (physician-assisted dying)

Critics contend that palliative sedation has more in common with euthanasia than with physician-assisted dying because the death-causing act is more under the control of someone other than the patient (Franklin, 2015). Finally, critics maintain palliative sedation offers no advantage over physician-assisted dying. Blaming the underlying disease for creating the need for palliative sedation is equally applicable to physician-assisted dying (Blumenson, 2015). Proponents dismiss all these contentions and maintain palliative sedation is not euthanasia; death results from the withdrawal of artificial nutrition and hydration, not the introduction of an analgesic agent to relieve pain (Federation of State Medical Boards, 2013).

Intent to Cause Death, or Alleviate Suffering?

Critics claim that relying upon compassionate intent as a basis to justify palliative sedation fails because unlike the withdrawal of an unwanted medical treatment, the intent of palliative sedation is to induce death. Proponents who argue this characterization of palliative sedation is similar to euthanasia, however, do not take into account the legal distinction between the withdrawal of unwanted medical treatment and euthanasia. The withdrawal of unwanted treatment and the refusal of nutrition and hydration are related to the patient's **liberty interest** to act without constraint, not to intent. Regardless of whether clinical realities support personal autonomy, the law places this decision ultimately with the patient. Patients may elect to forgo treatment or nutrition and hydration because of their:

- Liberty interest resulting from the principle of personal autonomy
- Right to be free from battery

Intent is irrelevant with respect to the refusal of or request for the withdrawal of a life-sustaining medical intervention. Intent is a legal factor only when there is an intervention to cause death (*See Vacco*, 521 U.S. at 802 (painkilling drugs may hasten death, but the intent is, or may be, only to ease pain and suffering)). As a practical matter, intent is hard to discern when the same prescription drugs used in both treatment of symptoms and in palliative sedation both end in the death of the patient (Tucker, 2014).

Justification for Palliative Sedation

Palliative sedation is justifiable palliative care, supported by established jurisprudence. The U.S. Supreme Court bases its reliance on the existence of palliative sedation upon long-standing principles arising from law and standards of health care. However, this conclusion does rely upon the double effect principle. Assuming the double effect principle is ethically sound, the legal justification is clear. As long as the compassionate intent is not to cause death, the risk of death

MANAGEMENT AND LAW ISSUES

3. Can anyone prove palliative care actually hastens death if there is no way of knowing whether the patient would have died naturally within the same time frame?

is justifiable in end-of-life care. For instance, the double effect could be compared to ordering dinner at a restaurant: when diners do not intend to order the most expensive item on the menu, but when they order surf and turf, their selection is one and the same thing. Selecting the most expensive item on the menu is unacceptable; ordering one's favorite meal is an acceptable choice. Under the double effect principle, one may not justify an intended harm with good consequences, but may justify with such consequences, a harm that is only foreseen (Parker, 2015).

The principle of double effect guides the provision of palliative care and is not some fabrication to shield the truth; rather, it is a highly useful ethical construct to guiding care at the bedside and reducing, but not eliminating, uncomfortable ambiguity in end-of-life care. Of course, licensed prescribers know the use of an opioid infusion, morphine drip, or other interventions may shorten life in those imminently dying from a progressive or chronic critical illness. Under Justice Holmes's approach to the law, end-of-life law is not a science founded on abstract principles but a body of practices that responds to particular situations. In other words, the life of the law is not logic: it is experience (Holmes, 1881).

The debate surrounding palliative sedation revolves largely around the validity of the double effect principle as a viable ethical construct. Critics tend to view palliative sedation as one continuous act directed by health care professionals (Parker, 2015). Supporters, on the other hand, view palliative sedation as an extension of sound palliative care, fully justified by the double effect principle and the doctrine of informed consent. Logic and experience need not always be different in end-of-life debates.

End-of-life palliative care is challenging, presenting the potential for clinical ambiguities. Health care professionals should struggle with the conflicting imperatives they face. Nonetheless, struggling with concerns about hastened death is not the same as inaction. Palliative sedation is a topic almost everyone will eventually have to confront. The current alternative is the undertreatment of pain and discomfort and the possibility of facing death alone in the middle of the night.

Physician-Assisted Dying

The term *physician-assisted dying* refers to the end-of-life choice made by a mentally competent, patient with progressive or chronic, critical illness to self-administer a prescribed drug for the purpose of hastening death. The term *physician-assisted suicide* has been rejected as too emotionally charged, and less accurate. Assisted dying, after all, simply permits patients to actively choose to end their lives before their illness ends their lives (Straton, 2006).

Most adults indicate that, if they had a progressive or chronic, critical illness or advanced serious illness, they would seek a hospice program during the last year of life until death occurred naturally (IOM, 2014). Only about one-third indicated that they would ask their physician to assist them to end their life (NHPCO, 2016b). Other studies have shown that hospice care is a meaningful alternative for patients and is effective in reducing the demand for physician-assisted dying. Although the unease about physician-assisted dying has been tempered by a greater focus on palliative care, recent developments regarding end-of-life issues may indicate that closer attention will be paid to hospice care. Society is already actively discussing the intersection between medicine and technology, the issue that captivated the nation in the Terri Schiavo debate (as outlined in the chapter on hospice care in this text).

At the corners of this intersection are the death with dignity discussions, health law, and the important court cases of *Quinlan*, 355 A.2d 647, *Cruzan*, 497 U.S. 261, and *Schiavo*, 403 F.3d 1289. Since Oregon became the first state to enact a physician-assisted dying law, there have been no reported instances of physician abuse and no successful wrongful death lawsuits under the Oregon law, while more than a thousand Oregonians have ended their lives pursuant to procedures approved by the state (Oregon, 2016a). One explanation for this very low number is the high quality of hospice care in Oregon; nine out of 10 people who have used the Oregon Death with Dignity Act were enrolled in hospice (Oregon, 2016b). At the same time, this compares to the Netherlands, where about one in four Dutch deaths are due to physician-assisted dying or euthanasia, which comprises about 5,300 annual requests (*See* CIA, 2016).

COURT DECISION
Assisted Dying

Gonzales v. Oregon
[U.S. Attorney General v. State of Oregon]
546 U.S. 243 (U.S. Supreme Court 2006)

Facts: Voters approved a ballot initiative making Oregon the first state to legalize physician-assisted dying. Three years later, voters affirmed the measure. The Oregon Death with Dignity Act exempts from civil or criminal liability licensed prescribers who, in compliance with specific safeguards, prescribe a lethal dose of drugs upon the request of patients with advanced serious illness. The law requires that patients seeking clinical assistance in dying :

- Receive a diagnosis that they suffer from an incurable and irreversible disease that, within reasonable medical judgment, will cause death within six months
- Have two separate physicians review their request in order to determine it was made voluntarily and the decision was informed

The Oregon law, however, encountered resistance on the federal level from Attorney General John Ashcroft. The drugs used to assist patients with suicide are federally regulated under the federal Controlled Substances Act (*See* 21 U.S.C.A. Ch. 13 §§ 801 *et seq.*). The law's main objectives are combating drug abuse and controlling the legitimate and illegitimate traffic of controlled substances. Drugs used in physician-assisted dying are grouped under Schedule II and require that patients receive a written, non-refillable prescription before gaining access to such drugs.

The federal government grants licensed prescribers a registration subject to regulations from the U.S. Justice Department so Schedule II drugs can be lawfully prescribed. The Controlled Substances Act also provides that the federal government may deny, suspend, or revoke this registration if prescriber registrations are inconsistent with the public interest. One federal regulation requires that prescribers acting in the usual course of their health care issue prescriptions only for a **legitimate medical purpose**. Ashcroft, an opponent of physician-assisted dying, issued an interpretive rule declaring the use of controlled substances in physician-assisted dying was not legitimate health care, thus making such prescriptions under the Oregon law a federal offense.

Accordingly, anyone who prescribed a lethal dose of a controlled substance under the Oregon law would render their prescribing registration inconsistent with the public interest and could have their licenses suspended or revoked. Because prescribers could not prescribe controlled substances without a registration, the **Ashcroft rule** effectively blocked physician-assisted dying. The state of Oregon, along with a physician, a pharmacist, and several patients sought relief to prevent enforcement of the Ashcroft rule.

Issue: Does the federal government have the authority under the Controlled Substances Act to prohibit prescribing prescription drugs under a state law decriminalizing physician-assisted dying?

Holding and Decision: No. The Controlled Substances Act does not authorize the federal government to ban the use of prescription drugs for physician-assisted dying.

Analysis: The Court held that the Ashcroft rule was not entitled to the deference to which administrative rules are generally entitled. Administrative rules may receive substantial deference if they interpret an issuing agency's own ambiguous regulation. Unlike regulations that give specificity to laws and reflect the expertise of the agency interpreting the regulations, the regulation the Ashcroft rule was interpreting merely restated the terms of the Controlled Substances Act. An agency does not acquire special authority to interpret its own words when, instead of using its expertise to formulate a regulation, it merely paraphrases or parrots statutory language.

Moreover, the Court held that the Ashcroft rule was not entitled to deference as an interpretation of an ambiguous law. Rules interpreting an ambiguous law may receive substantial deference when Congress delegated authority to the agency to make rules carrying the force of law, and the agency interpretation was in the exercise of that authority. While the Court held the Controlled Substances Act term *legitimate medical purpose* was ambiguous, the federal government did not have the authority to declare state laws illegitimate; state law authorizes medical standards for patient care and treatment, not federal law.

According to the Court, Congress only delegated authority to the federal government to promulgate rules regarding the registration and control of the dispensing of controlled substances. The Ashcroft rule did not fall within the statutory definition of *control*, a term that was limited to adding prescription drugs and other substances to regulatory schedules. Moreover, the Ashcroft rule did not fall within the registration authority of the U.S. Department of Justice. The Ashcroft rule was an interpretation of the federal requirements for valid prescriptions and went well beyond the federal government's power to register or deregister. Furthermore, the Court held the federal government was not entitled to define the substantive state standards of health care as it did in promulgating the Ashcroft rule. After finding that the Ashcroft rule did not deserve deference, the Court held that the federal government's interpretation of the Controlled Substances Act was not persuasive. From the text of the federal law, the Court found Congress intended to regulate the health care given by physicians insofar as it bars physicians from using their prescription-writing powers as a means to engage in illicit drug dealing and trafficking, but not to regulate medicine generally.

The Controlled Substances Act presumes the regulation of medicine is a function of state police powers. In addition, the federal law specifically included a preemption provision stating the law should not be construed as congressional intent to occupy the medical field to the exclusion of any state law within the authority of a state. In the Court's analysis, the treatment regimen under the Oregon law was precisely the type of state regulation the Controlled Substances Act had presupposed not to regulate. In the face of the federal law's silence on palliative care and recognition of state regulation of the medical profession, the Court found it difficult to defend the federal government's declaration that the Controlled Substances Act criminalized state-sanctioned physician-assisted dying.

The Court went on to address the federal government claim that the Controlled Substances Act requirement to dispense every Schedule II drug pursuant to a prescription necessarily implies the substance is being made available to a patient for a legitimate medical purpose, thus requiring the federal government's judgment about the term *medical*. In turn, the federal government argued that *medical* refers to a healing art and cannot embrace the intentional causing of a patient's death. The Court, however, rejected the argument that the federal prescription requirement allowed the federal government to ban the prescription of controlled substances for state-sanctioned physician-assisted dying on this basis.

While the Court recognized the federal government's interpretation was reasonable, it held the Controlled Substances Act undermined this assertion of an expansive federal authority to regulate medicine. Regarding the remainder of the federal law, the prescription requirement is understood as a provision to ensure patients use controlled substances under the supervision of a physician and to prevent addiction and recreational abuse. This bars physicians from prescribing Schedule II drugs to patients who crave the drugs for prohibited uses. Read this way, the Court held the Controlled Substances Act did not support the federal government's interpretation.

Rule of Law: The regulation of licensed prescribing has traditionally been under the states' police power; it is unlikely the federal government has the authority to prohibit prescribers from prescribing lethal doses of prescription drugs under the Controlled Substances Act.

References discussing this court decision: *E.g.*, Busscher, 2015; Green, 2016; Greve & Parrish, 2015; Orentlicher, 2014; Price & Keck, 2015; Roniger, 2015; Smith, 2016; Su, 2013.

While this decision appears to clear the way for state measures to decriminalize physician-assisted dying, the U.S. Supreme Court may not have settled the issue. Opponents of physician-assisted dying are seeking federal legislation to ban physician-assisted dying or grant the federal government the specific authority the U.S. Supreme Court said it lacked (Ouellette, 2014).

More Compassionate Palliative Care

One of the unexpected, yet undeniable, consequences of states permitting physician-assisted dying is that many improvements in end-of-life care have occurred following implementation of each state's physician-assisted dying legislation (Tucker, 2014). Rather than becoming the brutal abattoir for unfortunate patients as some critics predicted, the states where it is legal have become national leaders in providing compassionate palliative care (White, 2015; *See* Johnson et al., 2015). They have helped the nation create medical environments where end-of-life issues can be openly discussed (Ouellette, 2014).

Prescriptions for Controlled Substances

Specialists in palliative care have developed guidelines for the aggressive pharmacological management of intractable symptoms in dying patients, including sedation for those near death (Tucker, 2014). Nonetheless, licensed prescribers may find their palliative care scrutinized for the prescription of legally controlled substances by opponents of palliative sedation and state-sanctioned physician-assisted dying. There is no evidence, however, of medical boards pursuing physicians for overprescribing pain drugs (Tucker, 2014).

Palliative sedation is more likely to alleviate concerns if safeguards exist to address opponents' concerns (Federation of State Medical Boards, 2013). Where physician-assisted dying is already legal, there is no current evidence for the

---

MANAGEMENT AND LAW ISSUES

4.　Is death always the least desirable option?

---

claim that legalized physician-assisted dying will have a disproportionate impact on patients in vulnerable groups (Shaffer et al., 2016). The most vulnerable patients often share three characteristics. They:

- Fear being a burden and adversely impacting their families
- Have misperceptions of what the last stages of life will be like
- Lack effective symptom control

(Ouellette, 2014).

Safeguards should be responsive to individual patients while being rigorous enough to protect vulnerable groups by:

- Ensuring the availability and effectiveness of palliative care
- Maintaining clarity with respect to the patient's disease state and anticipated life span
- Obtaining fully informed consent from patients
- Reaching a consensus with the immediate family

(Tucker, 2014).

Patients' **terminal prognosis** should be imminent, generally defined as less than six months of life (*See Gonzales v. Oregon*, 546 U.S. 243 (U.S. Supreme Court 2006)). Patients should also be competent and fully informed, or incompetent with irreversible suffering and an ascertainable intent through an advanced health care directive or otherwise. When patients are incompetent but who have unequivocally stated their intent for physician assisted dying through health care directives, and surrogate decision-makers are not available, caregivers should agree that no other acceptable means of palliative care is available before seeking physician-assisted death (Dolgin, 2016). For instance, unconscious congestive heart failure patients with advanced health care directives stating the manner of their death should be given palliative care before physician-assisted death is made available.

Lastly, are perspectives about inclusion of groups considered potentially vulnerable. Numerous groups (such as the chronically ill; the elderly; infants and minors; poor and financially distressed patients; patients with psychiatric illnesses, including depression; the physically disabled) are explicitly labeled as vulnerable to physician-assisted death (Dolgin, 2016; Tucker, 2014). However, this group approach to vulnerability leads to the routine exclusion of these groups from the benefits of physician-assisted death and hence exacerbates end-of-life care (Dolgin, 2016). Moreover, this group approach leads to under-protection because it does not address different ways in which people can be vulnerable (Shaffer et al., 2016); for instance, an elderly unconscious patient with advanced Parkinson's disease in the process of dying, or terminally ill infants and minors receiving life-sustaining treatment who are subject to their parent's control and authority.

Confronting the End of Life

Health care experts often lament that one-quarter of all Medicare spending—$150 billion annually—goes to treating patients in their last year of life (Beck, 2016). Though compassionate end of life care may contribute to a more sustainable health care system (IOM, 2014); identifying patients in their last year of life in advance and cutting back on **futile medical care** has been difficult.[LN3] This chapter and the preceding two chapters have looked at the debate over end-of-life issues, a topic that everyone is eventually forced to confront. As the U.S. Supreme Court has observed, controlling the time and manner of one's own death is the most evident way, the most profound way, to "define one's own concept of existence, of meaning, of the universe, and of the mystery of human life" (*Casey*, 505 U.S. at 851).

End-of-Life Care

Should you and your family plan for end-of-life care even though everyone is relatively young and healthy?

Yes. Everyone should plan for and decide what health care they would like to receive at the end of their lives, who should make decisions on their behalf if they are dying and incapable of deciding when they have the right to die, and when they would consider, if ever, that their lives would not be worth saving because they are beyond their own definition of an acceptable quality of life.

— The scenario at the beginning of this chapter was given to Hammaker by a student nurse at Immaculata University; *See generally* Derish & Heuvel, 2000 (setting forth a similar scenario).

CHAPTER SUMMARY

- The increase in Americans' life expectancies now means chronic disease is a common form of death, necessitating the reconsideration of how individuals approach and cope with death. Most patients reach a point where the goal of health care changes from prolonging life and improving health to maximizing quality and comfort of remaining life.
- The U.S. Supreme Court has repeatedly leaned toward protecting human dignity, bodily integrity, and personal autonomy in the right-to-die debate.
- Palliative sedation, endorsed by the U.S. Supreme Court, is an induced state of unconsciousness usually accompanied by the withdrawal of life-sustaining health care; it is not the same as physician-assisted dying or euthanasia, as the physician does not actively or directly cause death such as by administering a lethal drug cocktail.
- Long-accepted palliative care methods support the induction of unconsciousness, while the withdrawal of life-sustaining medical intervention is supported by the principle of personal autonomy.
- The double effect principle consists of two distinct actions viewed separately: one, the induction of unconsciousness, and two, the withholding or withdrawal of artificial life-sustaining treatment (such as nutrition and hydration).
- Palliative sedation is justified by the double effect principle, which requires that the physician's actions leading to the consequence of death be intended for a morally permissible purpose (to relieve discomfort and pain) rather than the morally impermissible purpose of ending life.
- Those who argue it discourages physicians from palliative care have criticized the double effect principle.
- Intentional death is not necessarily unacceptable in all circumstances.
- A patient's personal autonomy and right to self-determination should have priority in palliative sedation.
- Most Americans and physicians approve of palliative sedation; others conditionally approve of it depending on the form it takes; still others refuse to view it as anything other than euthanasia.
- California, Montana, Oregon, Vermont, and Washington are the first five states to decriminalize physician-assisted dying, and thus far the policy appears to have had a positive effect in terms of providing compassionate end-of-life care.
- States with physician-assisted dying legislation employ safeguards such as ensuring that the patient has a progressive or chronic, critical illness, and obtaining fully informed consent from the patient or at least ascertainable intent such as from an advanced directive.
- Americans can protect their end-of-life wishes by drafting an advance directive and health care power of attorney; yet more than 70% have failed to do so, despite their strong desire to exercise power over their own health care decisions.

LAW NOTES

1. In *Quinlan*, 355 A.2d 647, the New Jersey Supreme Court held that an incompetent patient in a **persistent vegetative state** has a constitutional right to privacy that overrides the state's interest in preserving the patient's

life; the patient's surrogate may dictate that life-sustaining medical interventions be removed. While the states are split as to whether this right to refuse treatment is based solely on the doctrine of informed consent or also in the federal and state constitutions, under either theory, the emphasis is on personal autonomy. Moreover, the right to forgo unwanted medical treatment exists where the patient neither has progressive or chronic critical illness, nor is in a persistent vegetative state.

2. In *Cruzan*, 497 U.S. 261, the U.S. Supreme Court found that although patients may refuse life-sustaining treatment, states may establish rational procedures to ensure the patient's intent is accomplished. Focusing on common law doctrines supporting informed consent and against battery, the Court concluded that the corollary of the doctrine of informed consent is that patients generally possess the right not to consent; that is, they have the right to die instead. The Court inferred a competent person has a constitutionally protected liberty interest in refusing unwanted medical treatment. This inference was based on four prior decisions:

   - *Jacobson v. Massachusetts*, 197 U.S. 11 (U.S. Supreme Court 1905) (balancing an individual's liberty interest in declining an unwanted smallpox vaccine against the state's interest in preventing the disease)
   - *Parham v. J.R.*, 442 U.S. 584 (U.S. Supreme Court 1979) (recognizing a substantial liberty interest in not being confined unnecessarily for medical treatment)
   - *Vitek v. Jones*, 445 U.S. 480 (U.S. Supreme Court 1980) (noting that transferring a patient to a mental hospital coupled with mandatory behavior modification treatment implicates liberty interests)
   - *Washington v. Harper*, 494 U.S. 210 (U.S. Supreme Court 1990) (recognizing a significant liberty interest in avoiding the unwanted administration of antipsychotic drugs under the Due Process Clause of the Fourteenth Amendment)

   Because of the consequences involved in refusal of life-sustaining treatment, the Court was willing to assume the Constitution would grant a competent person a protected right to refuse nutrition and hydration.

3. Aspire Health, a Nashville for-profit startup, successfully predicts which patients are likely to die in the next year and is reducing their medical bills substantially by offering them palliative care at home, keeping them comfortable while avoiding costly emergency room visits and hospital stays. By managing the care of more than 20,000 Medicare Advantage patients in 19 states in exchange for a monthly fee, the company estimates that it is saving health insurance plans $8,000 to $12,000 per patient (Beck, 2016). Hospitals that offer in-house palliative-care programs find that they save an average of $7,000 per patient, according to the National Palliative Care Research Center.

REFERENCES

AMA (American Medical Association). (2016). *AMA code of medical ethics. Opinion 2.201–Sedation to unconsciousness in end-of-life care*. Chicago, IL: AMA.

___. (2008). *Sedation to unconsciousness in end-of-life care*.

ASA (American Society of Anesthesiologists) & ASRAPM (American Society of Regional Anesthesia and Pain Medicine. (2010). *Practice guidelines for chronic pain management: An updated report by the American Society of Anesthesiologists task force on chronic pain management and the American Society of Regional Anesthesia and Pain Medicine*. Washington, DC: ASA & ASRAPM.

Beck, M. (2016, December 2). Can a death-predicting algorithm improve care? A startup says it can tell which patients will die in the next year and lower their medical costs by providing palliative care in their homes. *Wall Street Journal*, p. B1.

Blumenson, E. (2015). Four challenges confronting a moral conception of universal human rights. *George Washington International Law Review, 47*, 327–352.

Bohnert, A. S., et al. (2011). Association between opioid prescribing patterns and opioid overdose-related deaths. *Journal of the American Medical Association, 305*(13), 1315–1321.

Busscher, D. (2015). Linking assisted suicide and abortion: Life, death, and choice. *Elder Law Journal, 23*, 123–149.

CDC (Centers for Disease Control and Prevention). (2016). *Life expectancy*. Atlanta, GA: CDC, National Center for Health Statistics.

___. (2015). *Mortality in the United States*.

CIA (Central Intelligence Assistance Agency). (2016). *World fact book: Europe*. Washington, DC: CIA.

Derish, M. T., & Heuvel, K. V. (2000). Mature minors should have the right to refuse life-sustaining medical treatment. *Journal of Law, Medicine and Ethics, 28*, 109–124.

Dolgin, J. L. (2016). Dying discourse: Contextualizing advance care planning. *Quinnipiac Law Review, 34*, 235–297.

Federation of State Medical Boards (FSMB). (2013). *Model policy on the use of opioid analgesics in the treatment of chronic pain*. Washington, DC: FSMB.

Franklin, K. (2015). Physician-assisted death, dementia, and euthanasia: Using an advanced directive to facilitate the desires of those with impending memory loss. *Idaho Law Review, 51*, 547–573.

Giest, Y. (2012). Are the distinctions drawn in the debate about end-of-life decision making "principled"? If not, how much does it matter? *Journal of Law, Medicine and Ethics, 40*, 66–80.

Green, C. (2016). Turning the kaleidoscope: Toward a theory of interpreting precedents. *North Carolina Law Review, 94*, 379–484.

Greve, M. S., & Parrish, A. C. (2015). Administrative law without Congress. *George Mason Law Review, 22*, 501–545.

Holmes, Jr., O. W. (1881). *The common law*. Boston, MA: Little, Brown, and Co.

IOM (Institute of Medicine). (2014). *Dying in America: Improving quality and honoring individual preferences near the end of life*. Washington, DC: National Academies Press.

____. (2011). *Relieving pain in America: A blue-print for transforming prevention, care, education and research*.

Johnson, S. M., et al. (2015). What patient and psychologist characteristics are important in competency for physician-assisted suicide evaluations? *Psychology, Public Policy and Law, 21*, 420–430.

Klothen, K. (2013). Tinkering with the legal status quo on physician assisted suicide: A minimalist approach. *Rutgers Journal of Law and Religion, 14*, 361–387.

Kutner, L. (1969). Due process of euthanasia: The living will, a proposal. *Indiana Law Journal, 44*, 539–554.

Leven, D. C. (2013). Health justice denied or delayed at the end of life: A crisis needing remedial action. *New York Law School Law Review, 58*, 403–415.

NHPCO (National Hospice and Palliative Care Organization). (2016a). *History of hospice care*. Alexandria, VA: NHPCO.

____. (2016b). *Commentary and resolution on physician assisted suicide*.

NIH (National Institutes of Health). (2013). *End-of-life care*. Bethesda, MD: NIH.

Noah, B. A. (2013a). In denial: The role of law in preparing for death. *Elder Law Journal, 21*, 1–29.

____. (2013b). Medical device law: Turn the beat around? Deactivating implanted cardiac-assist devices. *William Mitchell Law Review, 39*, 1229–1286.

Oregon (Oregon Department of Human Services). (2016a). *Prescription history; Oregon Death with Dignity Act*. Portland, OR: Oregon Office of Disease Prevention and Epidemiology.

____. (2016b). *Oregon Death with Dignity Act. Data report*.

Orentlicher, D. (2014). Aging populations and physician aid in dying: The evolution of state government policy. *Indiana Law Review, 48*, 111–123.

Ouellette, A. (2014). Context matters: Disability, the end of life, and why the conversation is still so difficult. *New York Law School Law Review, 58*, 371–388.

Parker, Jr., F. R. (2015). Law, bioethics, and medical futility: Defining patient rights at the end of life. *University of Arkansas at Little Rock Law Review, 37*, 185–234.

Pope, T. M., & Anderson, L. E. (2011). Voluntarily stopping eating and drinking: A legal treatment option at the end of life. *Widener Law Review, 17*, 363–427.

Price, R. S., & Keck, T. M. (2015). Movement litigation and unilateral disarmament: Abortion and the right to die. *Law and Social Inquiry, 40*, 880–914.

Quill, T. E. (2012). Physicians should assist in suicide when it is appropriate. *Journal of Law, Medicine and Ethics, 40*, 57–65.

Reynolds, L. (2014). Losing the quality of life: The move toward society's understanding and acceptance of physician aid-in-dying and the Death with Dignity Act. *New England Law Review, 48*, 343–370.

Roniger, L. N. (2015). Regulatory dissent and judicial review. *Columbia Business Law Review, 2015*, 390–437.

Rountree, M. M. (2015). Criminals get all the rights: The sociolegal construction of different rights to die. *Journal of Criminal Law and Criminology, 105*, 149–202.

Schwarz, J. K. (2011). Death by voluntary dehydration: Suicide or the right to refuse a life-prolonging measure? *Widener Law Review, 17*, 351–360.

Shaffer, C., et al. (2016). A conceptual framework for thinking about physician-assisted death for persons with a mental disorder. *Psychology, Public Policy and Law, 22*, 141–152.

Smith, F. (2016). Local sovereign immunity. *Columbia Law Review, 116*, 409–485.

Smith, II, G. P. (2014). *Cura personalis*; A healthcare delivery quandary at the end of life. *Saint Louis University Journal of Health Law and Policy, 7*, 311–329.

Spinoza, B. D. (2005). *Ethics*. (E. Curley, Trans.). New York, NY: Random House, Penguin Classics. (Original work published 1677.)

Straton, J. B. (2006). Physician assistance with dying: Reframing the debate; Restricting access. *Temple Political & Civil Rights Law Review, 15*, 475-482.

Su, A. M. (2013). Physician assisted suicide: Debunking the myths surrounding the elderly, poor, and disabled. *Hastings Race and Poverty Law Journal, 10*, 145–190.

Suter, S. M. (2013). The politics of information: Informed consent in abortion and end-of-life decision making. *American Journal of Law and Medicine, 39*, 7–61.

Tucker, K. L. (2014). Give me liberty at my death: Expanding end-of-life choice in Massachusetts. *New York Law School Law Review, 58*, 259-276.

____. (2012). Aid in dying: An end of life-option governed by best practices. *Health and Biomedical Law Society, 8*, 9–26.

____. (2011). When dying takes too long: Activism for social change to protect and expand choice at the end of life. *Whittier Law Review, 33*, 109–159.

White, C. (2015). Physician aid-in-dying. *Houston Law Review, 53*, 595–629.

PART X

OUR HEALTH CARE SYSTEM'S RESPONSE TO BIOMEDICINE

Part X examines emerging discoveries in regenerative and precision medicine, new technologies that have the potential to take health care in a whole new direction.

CHAPTER 31

© Andy Dean Photography/ShutterStock, Inc.

Stem Cell Therapy and Regenerative Medicine*

"I would rather be exposed to the inconveniences attending too much liberty than those attending a too small degree of it."

— **Thomas Jefferson** (1743–1826), Third President of the United States and principal author of the *Declaration of Independence*.

IN BRIEF

This chapter starts with a tutorial, underscoring how the term *stem cell* can have different meanings. It then looks at the potential of stem cell therapy and the controversy surrounding the use of human embryonic stem cells. This is the only topic in this text where an appreciation of the science is essential to understanding the political and ideological agendas dictating the direction of this controversial medical research.

   While attention focuses on human embryonic stem cells, somatic (or adult) stem cells also typically give rise to the type of cells in the tissues in which they are found. With the promise of stem cells, studying the scientific, ethical, and legal aspects of this research will illustrate the possibilities of implementing innovative technologies and the infrastructure needed for such medical breakthroughs to flourish. Fatal diseases that might be alleviated through stem cell research and its resulting applications in regenerative medicine are briefly noted throughout this chapter.

LEARNING OBJECTIVES

Upon completion of this chapter readers should be able to:

1. Describe the fundamental characteristics of stem cells.
2. Distinguish among totipotent, pluripotent, multipotent, and unipotent stem cells.
3. Explain the potential for medical uses of stem cell research.
4. Outline the idea of and potential for regenerative medicine.
5. Describe the basic disagreements between individuals supporting human embryonic stem cell research and those opposing and those who would restrict such research.
6. Explain the sources of funding for stem cell research and the limitations of each.
7. Describe the intellectual rights available for stem cell research.

KEY TERMS

Adrenoleukodystrophy disease	Bayh-Dole Act of 1980	Cell sorting process
Altered nuclear transfer	Biomarkers	Cellular reprogramming
Amyotrophic lateral sclerosis	Blastocyst	Chimera
Apheresis	Blastomere	Chromosomes
Aspiration	Bone marrow transplants	Clone
Autologous organ replacement	Cadaveric fetal tissue	Cloning
Autologous stem cell transplants	Cell-based therapies	Cystic fibrosis

*Contributor: Michael Weber, MBA in Biotechnology and Health Industry Management, MS in Animal Science and Virology, Senior Scientist, Janssen Pharmaceuticals, Inc, of Johnson & Johnson.

Dickey-Wicker Amendment
Differentiation
Downstream product
Ectoderm
Embryonic death
Embryonic germ cells
Embryonic stem cell lines
Embryos
Endoderm
Equal Protection Clause
Fallacy of the beard
Gene expression profiles
Genetic constitution
Genetic disorder
Germ layers
Hematopoietic stem cells
Human embryonic stem cells
Huntington's disease
Implantation
In vitro
In vitro fertilization
In vivo
Induced pluripotent stem cells

Inner cell mass
IVF embryos
Lineages
Lou Gehrig's disease
Marfan syndrome
Mesoderm
Multipotent stem cells
Muscular dystrophy
National cord blood stem cell bank
 network and registry
National Organ Transplant Act of
 1984
Neural stem cells
Neural transplant
Neurofibromatosis
Neurons
Parkinson's disease
Parthenogenesis
Patent
Patient-specific cell lines
Planned Parenthood
Pluripotency
Pluripotent

Precision medicine
Preimplantation
Preimplantation genetic diagnosis
Primitive streak
Prior art
Proprietary and trade secret
 issues
Reasonable expectation of patent
 success
Red herring argument
Regenerative medicine
Retrovirus
Sickle cell anemia
Somatic cell nuclear transfers
Somatic stem cells
Stem cell lines
Stem cells
Tay-Sachs disease
Thalassemia
Totipotent stem cells
Transgenics
Unipotent stem cells
Zygote

FACT OR FICTION

Research on Human Embryonic Stem Cells

Should the federal government provide funding for basic scientific research involving human embryonic stem cells?
    Mary Doe was a frozen human embryo in liquid nitrogen in a state of cryopreservation in which her life was suspended, at an unnamed fertility clinic. Mary's name was given by the National Association for the Advancement of Preborn Children, an organization dedicated to advocating for equal humanity and personhood of so-called preborn children. In response to President Clinton's policy favoring research and permitting funding for stem cells from **cadaveric fetal tissue** and embryos remaining after infertility treatments, a lawsuit was filed on behalf of Mary and all other frozen human embryos similarly situated. The lawsuit sought a permanent injunction against any and all plans to undertake **human embryonic stem cell (hESC)** experimentation in the United States (*Doe v. Shala*, 122 Fed. Appx. 600 (U.S. Court of Appeals for the 4th Circuit), *cert. denied*, 546 U.S. 822 (U.S. Supreme Court, 2005)).
    Legal challenges to funding for hESC research are still prevalent. In the most notable and recent lawsuit, James Sherley, a bioengineer opposed to the use of embryonic stem cells for research representing scientists in the field of somatic stem cells, challenged the National Institutes of Health's Guidelines for federal funding of hESC research. Sherley opposed the use of federal funding for the development of hESCs, contending that human embryos like Mary were threatened once again. The distinction between funding research involving the destruction of human embryos and using hESCs derived from an earlier destruction underlies this ongoing competition between hESC and somatic stem cell scientists. The Sherley lawsuit sought a permanent injunction against funding of all hESC research in which human embryos were destroyed.

— *See* Law Fact at the end of this chapter for the answer.

Principles and Applications

The International Society for Stem Cell Research has called for the U.S. government to join the global community in funding all avenues of stem cell research and to replace politics and ideology with dispassionate scientific investigation. An open letter from the Society noted that, while reprogramming of **somatic stem cells** (adult stem cells) has captured the imagination of scientists everywhere, research on hESCs should not be abandoned (ISSCR, 2015). For nearly two decades, the medical products industry has been using animal and human stem cells in its laboratories to help screen new drug compounds and identify safer and more effective medicines (Pfizer, 2016). Many of the common human virus vaccines, such as measles, rubella, hepatitis A, rabies, and poliovirus, have been produced in stem cells (*See* Pfizer, 2016; Sepper, 2015).

It is estimated that over 100 million Americans are suffering from conditions that might be alleviated or cured through stem cell research (Berjis, 2010). As illustrated in **FIGURE 31-1**, stem cells help the medical products industry better understand:

- Genetic development and control
- Identification of important **biomarkers** (distinctive indicators of disease, disability, or the aging process)
- **Precision medicine**

(Kwon, 2016).

Precision medicine is the use of **gene expression profiles** to tailor health care to meet the health care needs of specific patients, as determined from the patient's medical history and physical profile (derived from laboratory tests, imaging, and other medical tests) (Price, 2015). It also refers to drugs tailored to specific genotypes in terms of dosing, as opposed to drug dosing developed for a general disease population (An, 2016).

The Science of Stem Cells

Stem cells are primal cells that have the potential to develop into many different cell types in the body; they are not yet specialized or differentiated into any of over 200 somatic cell types (NIH, 2015a). Stem cells do not perform the tasks somatic cells do. For instance, stem cells do not deliver oxygen like the red blood cells do (Smith, S., 2015). Rather, stem cells act as the repair system for the body; theoretically they can divide without limit to replenish other cells. When a stem cell divides, each new stem cell has the potential to remain a stem cell or become a more specialized cell, such as a red blood cell or a muscle cell (Harn, 2015). Although stem cells do not offer the ability to change the **genetic constitution** of a person, they are capable of replacing or repairing specific tissues (Torrance, 2010).

There are currently more than 300 clinical trials for stem cells happening worldwide across a variety of diseases. Many of these clinical trials are focused on heart disease, and a few dozen are focused on brain disorders like strokes, **Parkinson's disease**, and **amyotrophic lateral sclerosis** (ALS), also known as **Lou Gehrig's disease**.[LN1] Stem cell research could greatly facilitate the study of disease, drug development, and toxicology testing and may allow the production of therapeutically useful immune-compatible stem cells (Hoxha, 2015).

Categories of Stem Cells

Many of the terms used to define stem cells depend on the behavior of the cells in the living organism, under specific laboratory conditions outside a living organism (**in vitro**), or after transplants into a living organism (**in vivo**) (Smith, S., 2015). In vitro generally refers to stem cells in a laboratory dish or test tube. The four categories of stem cells, based on their ability to transform into different cell types, are:

- Totipotent (able to give rise to all embryonic cell types)
- Pluripotent (potential to give rise to many different cell types)
- Multipotent (able to give rise to multiple types of cell lineages with specific functions, such as blood and skin stem cells)
- Unipotent (able to contribute only one single cell type)

(Sax, 2006).

Another difference between these types of cells is that multipotent and unipotent stem cells persist throughout life, whereas pluripotent and totipotent stem cells exist predominantly in embryos and fetuses (Wakeman & Kordower, 2014).

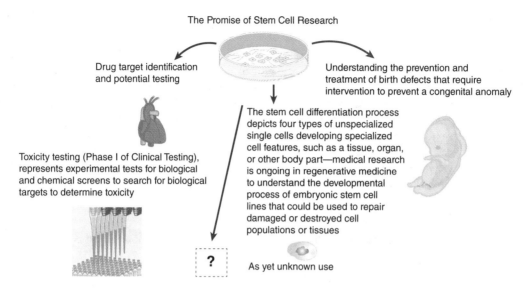

The Promise of Stem Cell Research

Drug target identification and potential testing

Understanding the prevention and treatment of birth defects that require intervention to prevent a congenital anomaly

The stem cell differentiation process depicts four types of unspecialized single cells developing specialized cell features, such as a tissue, organ, or other body part—medical research is ongoing in regenerative medicine to understand the developmental process of embryonic stem cell lines that could be used to repair damaged or destroyed cell populations or tissues

Toxicity testing (Phase I of Clinical Testing), represents experimental tests for biological and chemical screens to search for biological targets to determine toxicity

?

As yet unknown use

FIGURE 31-1 The Promise of Stem Cell Research

Data from: Yu, J., & Thomson, J. A. (2010). *Stem cell information: Embryonic stem cells.* Bethesda, MD: U.S. Department of Health and Human Services, National Institutes of Health.

Totipotent Stem Cells

Totipotent stem cells are able to differentiate into an entire organism if they divide normally (Smith, S., 2015). For this reason, hESCs are considered controversial. A fertilized egg (**zygote**) is considered totipotent.

Distinction Between In Vivo and In Vitro Embryos

A human zygote undergoes cell division after it travels through the oviduct to the uterus where it may implant and may grow to an embryo. In this chapter, human organisms in the early stages of growth, from fertilization to about the beginning of the third month of pregnancy, are defined as **embryos**. Although there is a medical distinction between the viability of an embryo in vivo and its viability in vitro, to simplify understanding of stem cells, no distinction is made between embryos in vivo and in vitro in this chapter. An in vitro embryo is not viable in terms of a living human organism outside the uterus; whereas an in vivo embryo is not viable until at least week 24 or 25 following fertilization.

Plato (424-348 BC), a philosopher in Classical Greece, compared this viability distinction to the **fallacy of the beard** (Plato, 2016/1892). Some argue there is no distinction between a clean-shaven beard and a beard because at every point between the two there is some measure of hair. Others claim there is a discernible difference between being clean shaven and bearded. Plato suggested reasonable judgments may be made to delimit stages within continuous processes.

Continuous Processes

A range of positions are taken about fertilization as a continuous process and the morality, if any, that defines the value accorded to each stage. The moral standing attributed to embryos is therefore likely to determine the level of legal protection granted to them. This is the core of the debate about stem cell research (Steiger, 2010).

In general science terms, about three days after fertilization, the cells are totipotent, or capable of giving rise to an entire organism, including all the cell types in the human body and all the cell types in the extra-embryonic supporting tissues such as the placenta and the umbilical cord (Atala & Lanza, 2010). The process of fertilization begins with the union of the male sperm and female egg cells and ends with the fusion of the maternal and paternal DNA creating a single cell, called a zygote (Steiger, 2010). The zygote travels down the fallopian tube where it becomes a blastocyst once it reaches the uterus. **Implantation** of the blastocyte into the wall of the uterus occurs about five days after conception (NIH, 2015a). Embryos develop from this cluster of blastocyte cells, which are pluripotent embryonic stem cells and give rise to all of the different types of cells of the developing embryo. Implantation connects the embryo to the maternal blood supply, allowing it to continue developing and establishing pregnancy (Garner, 2014). Embryonic stem cells can therefore be either totipotent or pluripotent, depending on the state of the development of the embryo from which they are isolated (Steiger, 2010).

Pluripotent Stem Cells

Embryonic stem cells can be undifferentiated **pluripotent** cells that can indefinitely grow in vitro in a controlled environment (NIH, 2015b). While there is no standardized definition of **pluripotency** (NIH, 2015b), pluripotent stem cells can give rise to any type of body cell (NIH, 2015a). Pluripotent stem cells are able to differentiate into all of the specialized cell types of the body, but cannot generate an entire organism on their own (Harn, 2015; Steiger, 2010). **Differentiation** is the developmental process whereby an unspecialized cell acquires the features of a specialized cell such as those in tissue, organs, or other body parts (NIH, 2015c). Placenta and umbilical cord cells are extra-pluripotent supporting tissues.

Human embryonic stem cells are derived from the **inner cell mass**, the cluster of cells inside the blastocyst. Inner cell mass cells give rise to the embryo and ultimately the fetus (NIH, 2015c). Because of the ability of inner cell mass cells to differentiate into **germ layers**[LN2] and finally into specialized somatic cell types, pluripotent stem cells are thought to have much greater developmental potential than multipotent stem cells (Davis & Grega, 2010).

The first differentiation event occurs in humans at approximately five days, when an outer layer of cells committed to becoming part of the placenta separates from the inner cell mass (King et al., 2011). The inner cell mass cells are pluripotent and have the potential to generate any cell type of the body. After implantation, pluripotent inner cell mass cells are quickly depleted as they differentiate into other specialized somatic cell types with more limited development potential, or multipotent and unipotent stem cells (Atala & Lanza, 2010).

Multipotent Stem Cells

Stem cells that can give rise to a small number of different cell types are generally called multipotent (NIH, 2015b). **Multipotent stem cells** can develop into more than one cell type but are more limited than pluripotent cells (Davis & Grega, 2010). Found in very small numbers throughout the body, multipotent stem cells replenish and repair many of the cells of the body. Somatic stem cells and cord blood stem cells are considered multipotent.

In vivo multipotent stem cells can only differentiate into a particular subset of specialized cell types; they are believed to differentiate only into the types of cells near where they are located (King et al., 2011). Multipotent stem cells are difficult to locate in the organs because there may be only one multipotent stem cell in the millions of cells making up an organ (Atala & Lanza, 2010). In addition, multipotent stem cells are more challenging to culture in the lab than hESCs (Smith, S., 2015).

Unipotent Stem Cells

Unipotent stem cells are usually cells in adult organisms that are capable of differentiating along only one lineage, meaning the cells are only capable of evolving descendants from their immediate predecessor cell line (for instance, skin tissue cells from skin tissue cells). Multipotent stem cells, on the other hand, can produce a small number of different specialized types of unipotent cells. Found in small numbers throughout the body, multipotent stem cells in many differentiated tissues and organs are typically unipotent and give rise to just one cell type under normal conditions (for example, unipotent stem cells can only give rise to a single type of tissue). This differentiation process allows for a steady state of self-renewal and repair for tissues and organs (Torrance, 2010). (*See generally* Wakeman & Kordower, 2014).

Sources of Naturally Occurring Human Stem Cells

The sources of human stem cells that are naturally occurring include:

- hESCs (isolated from the inner cell mass of blastocysts)
- Multipotent stem cells
- Stem cells from amniotic fluid
- Umbilical cord blood cells

Alternative Sources of Human Embryonic Stem Cells

Stem cells isolated from human embryos are a few days old (NIH, 2015a). Initial hESCs are derived by removing the inner cell mass from its normal embryonic environment and culturing the cells under appropriate conditions (Atala & Lanza, 2010). Cells from these embryos can then be used to create **embryonic stem cell lines**, as cell cultures can be grown indefinitely in the laboratory (NIH, 2015c).

These pluripotent inner cell mass-derived cells are hESCs and can continue to proliferate and replicate themselves indefinitely and still maintain the developmental potential to form any cell type of the human body (Atala & Lanza, 2010; Battey et al., 2010). Stem cell lines grown in the lab provide scientists with the opportunity to engineer them for use in transplants or treatment of diseases. For instance, before scientists can use any type of tissue, organ, or cell for transplants, they must overcome attempts by the immune system to reject the transplant. In the future, scientists may be able to modify hESC lines in the laboratory by using gene therapy or other techniques to overcome this immune rejection. Scientists might also be able to replace damaged genes or add new genes to hESCs in order to give them characteristics to prevent, treat, or ultimately even cure diseases (Battey et al., 2010).

Techniques Involving Embryonic Intermediates

As illustrated in **FIGURE 31-2**, hESCs usually come from surplus embryos from **in vitro fertilization** (IVF), where the egg and sperm cells are united in a clinical laboratory instead of inside the female body (NIH, 2015c). Alternatively, hESCs can also be created from:

- Embryonic germ cells
- Dead embryos
- Genetically abnormal embryos
- Single cell blastocyst biopsies
- Parthenogenesis
- Somatic cell nuclear transfers
- Altered nuclear transfers (ANT)

(Battey et al., 2010).

Traditional Techniques from Surplus Embryos

The University of Wisconsin-Madison generated the first hESC lines from embryos obtained from an IVF clinic (Harn, 2015). These embryos were no longer wanted for reproductive purposes and donated with consent for research purposes. **Embryos** no longer wanted for reproductive purposes are generally incinerated as medical waste. The original hESC lines were prepared by removing the inner cell mass from donated blastocysts and placing those cells into a specialized culture medium (Battey et al., 2010). As noted above, a **blastocyst** develops five to six days after fertilization and contains all the material necessary for a complete human being (Kelly, 2014). It is smaller than the period at the end of a sentence (IOM, 2010).

Human embryonic **stem cell lines** are extremely difficult to grow in culture. The cells require a highly specialized growth medium that contains essential ingredients critical to maintain the cell's self-renewing and pluripotent properties (Harn, 2015). Cultures require the support of cells either directly as a feeder cell layer or indirectly as a source of conditioned medium in feeder-free culture systems (Kelly, 2014).

The feeder cells secrete important nutrients and otherwise support stem cell growth but are treated so they cannot divide (Battey et al., 2010). Critically, scientists are only permitted government funding to continue work on a handful of batches of stem cells already extracted from embryos. The number of viable batches has varied, from about 20 to about 60. Many of these embryos were created at IVF clinics and were either in indefinite frozen storage or destined to be discarded (Wharton, 2016). In addition, the culture medium used for the hESC lines approved by the federal government for research contains mouse cells and bovine serum (Diamond, 2013).

This makes these approved lines unacceptable for therapy due to the risk of contamination by rodent viruses or other proteins that may cause immune rejection and cancers. Although scientists first developed a technique for generating hESC lines by culturing embryonic germ cells from five- to seven-week-old embryos, it took a decade of

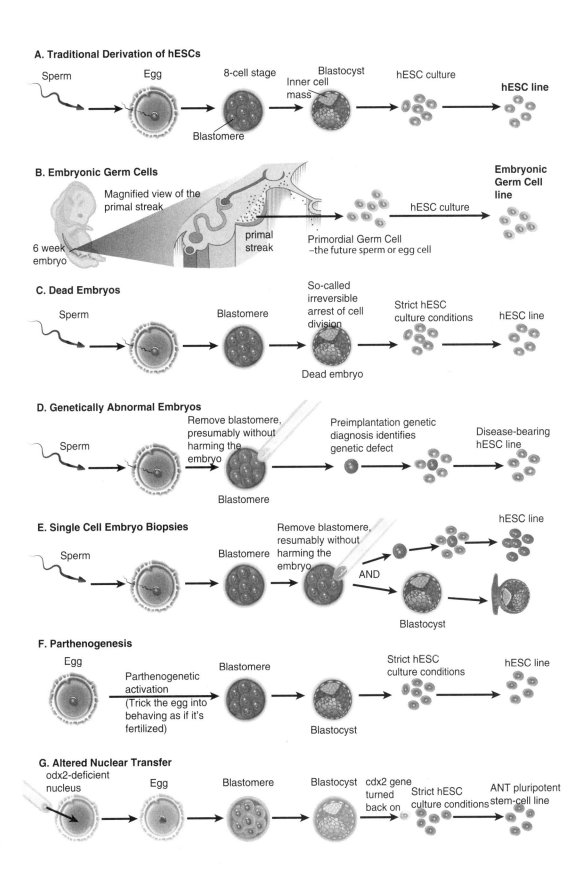

FIGURE 31-2 Alternative Methods of Human Pluripotent Stem Cells

Data from: Battey, J. F., et al. (2010). *The clinical application of pluripotent cells: The promise and the challenges.* Bethesda, MD: NIH (National Institutes of Medicine).

European research to produce human embryonic germ cells in useful numbers (Diamond, 2013). Scientists recently isolated two hESC lines from human embryonic germ cells, which will significantly expand this research avenue (McGuire, 2010).

From Embryonic Germ Cells

Of all the cell types obtained from the differentiation of hESCs, **embryonic germ cells** are arguably the most fascinating, as they represent the in vitro completion of the reproductive cycle of the organism from which the hESC lines are derived (Macintosh, 2015). Some embryonic germ cells are destined to become either egg or sperm cells; other embryonic germ cells migrate to the outer layer of the blastocyst. The resulting cell lines of the blastocyst are called germ cell lines and share many of the same properties as hESCs (Battey et al., 2008).

From Dead Embryos

There is no legal criterion for determining when human embryos are dead. For developed humans, life is considered to end when the criteria for irreversible cessation of either circulatory and respiratory functions or brain death are met (Misna, 2010). In this instance, scientists generate hESC lines from **IVF embryos** that have stopped dividing. They derive hESCs using traditional techniques from surplus blastocysts; the IVF embryo is simply considered dead because it ceases to divide. Embryos that stop dividing are not suitable for implantation; they are considered nonviable because they are not capable of living or developing successfully (King et al., 2011).

The legal framework for justifying the use of this technique for embryos is similar to organ donation from a deceased donor who is declared dead. Embryos that die from natural causes cannot develop into fetuses. Since dead embryos are not preferentially selected for implantation in women undergoing fertility treatment, they can provide a source from which to derive hESCs without destroying a living embryo (King et al., 2011). Therefore, dead embryos should arguably be morally acceptable and consequently legally acceptable to the federal government as a source of hESCs (Misna, 2010).[LN3] To be useful for stem cell therapy, hESC lines derived from dead embryos should be carefully monitored for genetic abnormalities or other defects.

From Genetically Abnormal Embryos

When a couple is concerned about producing a child with a genetic (or chromosomal) disorder, they may choose to conceive via IVF, using a technique known to determine whether the embryo carries the **genetic disorder**. This technique involves the removal of one or two cells from the embryo for testing. If the embryo is found to be positive for the genetic disorder it is generally discarded (Reynolds, 2010). Scientists have derived hESC lines from genetically abnormal embryos to help understand genetically based disorders that are irreversible (Schechter, 2010).[LN4] Unfortunately, genetic diagnosis is still limited for many diseases because scientists are unable to identify the specific mutations causing the abnormalities and therefore, detection prior to fertilization is impossible.

MANAGEMENT AND LAW ISSUES

1. Ethically speaking, is the federal government's justification for freezing a fast-growing area of scientific inquiry acceptable in a democratic capitalist economy, where church is allegedly separated from state?
2. When, if ever, should the Executive Orders of a president influence private/government funding balances and restrict scientists' freedom to conduct their research?
3. Should private/government funding balances be a legislative function rather than a function of the executive branch of government?
4. When, if ever, should government funds be used for hESC research when there is political deadlock about its merits and morality?

From Single Cell Blastocyst Biopsies

Scientists at Advanced Cell Technologies were the first to establish hESC lines from single blastomeres, a type of cell produced by division of the egg immediately after fertilization and prior to implantation (Macintosh, 2013). Biopsy of a single blastomere is similar to the technique used in **preimplantation genetic diagnosis**, which does not interfere with the development potential of the blastocyst, a pre-implantation embryo produced five or six days after fertilization (Sosnow, 2012). In preimplantation genetic diagnosis, after the egg is fertilized, one of its cells is extracted and then cultured and implanted in a woman's uterus. By growing a single blastomere, the resulting cells may be used for both genetic testing and stem cell derivation without affecting the clinical outcome of the procedure.

Nevertheless, there is debate about the ethics of this technique. Proponents of this technique suggest that since it requires only one **blastomere**, the remaining blastomeres may yet be implanted and develop into a blastocycst and eventually an embryo (Macintosh, 2013). The ability to create new stem cell lines and clinical therapies without destroying blastocysts should address any ethical concerns and allow the generation of matched tissue for children and siblings born from transferred blastocysts. Critics maintain the question is unanswered as to whether the single blastomere removed for the purposes of developing a stem cell line is itself totipotent and therefore capable of developing into an embryo. If this is the case, then the destruction of a blastomere is destruction of a potential embryo, which is no different than destruction of the blastocyst from which it was extracted (NIH, 2015b). Any form of genetic manipulation of the reproductive process is objectionable to critics of stem cell research.

Created via Parthenogenesis

Scientists at Kyoto University in Japan first showed that four genes inserted into the mature skin cell of a mouse were enough to return the cell to an embryonic-like state. Several groups of scientists have since achieved the same result with human cells (Colangelo, 2014). Scientists at the University of Wisconsin-Madison and Kyoto University used **parthenogenesis** to derive hESCs (Dolin, 2014). Parthenogenesis is the creation of a human embryo without fertilization. To achieve this feat, scientists trick the egg into believing it is fertilized so it will begin to divide and form a blastocyst (Battey et al., 2010) (perhaps leading to the day females no longer need male organisms).

Essentially, human somatic cells are reprogrammed to become hESCs (Diamond, 2013). This technique may lead to the ability to generate tissue-matched stem cells for transplants (Battey et al., 2010). Such induced hESC lines should also be useful in the production of new disease models and in drug development, as well as for other applications in transplant medicine (Morgan & Sandoval, 2014).

From Somatic Cell Nuclear Transfers

This technique uses a genetically modified somatic cell as the source of a nucleus and genome for transfer into a human egg (NIH, 2015b; Tachibana et al., 2013). With **somatic cell nuclear transfers**, human eggs are collected from a volunteer donor who has taken drugs to stimulate the release of more than one egg during her menstrual cycle. Scientists then remove the nucleus from the donated egg and replace it with the nucleus from a somatic cell, a differentiated multipotent cell from elsewhere in the body. The egg with the newly transferred nucleus is then stimulated to develop through parthenogenesis. The egg may develop only if the transplanted nucleus is returned to the pluripotent state by factors present in the egg cytoplasm. When the parthenogenesis progresses to the blastocyst stage, the inner cell mass is removed and placed into culture (Battey et al., 2010).

While traditional techniques involving embryonic intermediates may trigger the immune response when introduced into the body of another person, somatic cell nuclear transfer has the advantage of being made from a person's own body cells (Trounson & DeWitt, 2013). Most importantly, somatic cell nuclear transfer may be used to create a bank of stem cells from people who have a genetic disease; this will in turn help scientists learn more about genetic diseases and their progression (Heled, 2014). This type of second-generation **cloning** would lend itself to patient-tailored cell therapy in the future, bypassing the need for creating or destroying embryos (Russo, 2014).

From Altered Nuclear Transfer

Altered nuclear transfer can be carried out to produce hESCs (King et al., 2011; Skene, 2010). This method employs the techniques of somatic cell nuclear transfer; the nucleus of the host egg is removed and replaced with the nucleus from a somatic cell, then stimulated to divide. In altered nuclear transfer, scientists turn off a gene needed for implantation in the uterus in the patient cell nucleus before it is transferred into the donor egg (Battey et al., 2010). This alteration precludes the coordinated organization and developmental potential necessary for the resulting biological entity to be an embryo, but it still allows the entity to generate hESCs (Skene, 2010). Abnormal nuclear transfer blastocysts that are inherently unable to implant into the uterus but that are capable of generating customized hESCs are then created (King et al., 2011).

The derivation of hESCs by altered nuclear transfer holds great promise for research and therapy. In contrast to traditional techniques from surplus blastocysts, altered nuclear transfer could produce hESC lines with an unlimited range of specifically selected and controlled genotypes. Altered nuclear transfer could also help define the boundaries that distinguish human organisms from nonhuman organisms and thereby provide moral precedent to guide future progress in developmental biology (Skene, 2010).

Techniques Not Involving Embryonic Intermediates

For the past decade, since the original isolation of hESC lines and the isolation of embryonic germ cell lines, controversy has surrounded pluripotent cell lines. The most basic objection to hESC research is rooted in the fact that cell derivation deprives embryos of any further potential to develop into a complete human being (Skene, 2010). Therefore there is interest in two techniques for deriving stem cell lines that do not result from the controversial use of embryonic intermediates: amniotic fluid-derived stem cells and induced pluripotent stem cells. These new and exciting areas of research have many advantages over the embryonic intermediate techniques, including the potential for **patient-specific cell lines** that could reduce immune rejections prevalent with many transplants. While these latest advances have spurred a rush to improve non-embryonic techniques, they have also given fresh ammunition to those who oppose all research on hESCs (Skene, 2010).

Amniotic Fluid-Derived Stem Cells

Recently, scientists have generated non-embryonic stem cell lines from amniotic fluid. Amniotic fluid-derived stem cells are in between pluripotent and multipotent cells in terms of their ability to permanently change into specialized cells, also referred to as differentiation (Atala & Lanza, 2010). While these self-renewing cells maintain the normal number of **chromosomes** after a prolonged period in culture, like hESCs, undifferentiated amniotic fluid stem cells do not produce all of the proteins expected of pluripotent cells (Battey et al., 2010).

Nerve cells, liver cells, and bone-forming cells can be produced from amniotic fluid stem cells. Further experiments using the nerve, liver, and bone-forming cells have also shown they can produce proteins typical of specialized cells (King et al., 2011). The research opportunities for amniotic fluid stem cells are tremendous (Varkey & Atala, 2015).

Induced Pluripotent Stem Cells

Scientists have **induced pluripotent stem cells** through somatic cell reprogramming without going through an embryonic intermediate (Smith, 2014). Induced pluripotent stem cells have all the defining criteria for pluripotency, with the exception that they are not derived from embryos (Harn, 2015). Although in its infancy, induced pluripotent stem cell research is showing results (Hoxha, 2015). Scientists have produced induced pluripotent stem cell lines for diseases by cultivating skin cells from patients suffering conditions ranging from diabetes to muscular dystrophy (Norris, 2014).

Scientists have also generated induced pluripotent stem cells from human dermal fibroblasts. The resultant cell lines are morphologically indistinguishable from hESCs generated from the inner cell mass of blastocysts or human preimplantation embryos. **Preimplantation** means that the embryo has not yet implanted in the wall of the uterus; hESCs are derived from preimplantation-stage embryos fertilized outside a woman's body (in vivo) (NIH, 2015c). This is another important step toward manipulating somatic human cells to generate an unlimited supply of patient-specific cells (Harbaugh, 2015).

Although the induced pluripotent stem cell technique does not use embryo intermediates, it is not without controversy. One goal of using the induced pluripotent stem cell technique is for scientists to prepare stem cell lines that model diseases with no cures. Scientists must be careful, however, not to take unfair advantage of volunteer donors. Unlike stem cell research using IVF embryos, human-induced pluripotent stem cell research leaves a developed human donor behind who is the genetic source of the stem cell line; these donors are likely suffering from grave medical conditions (Miller, 2015). Those who volunteer to donate somatic human cells for induced pluripotent stem cell research may do so in the hopes of directly benefiting through downstream therapeutic applications of genetically matched stem cell lines, an expectation that may not always be realistic or possible (Lowenthal et al., 2012).

Potential Stem Cell Therapies: Parkinson's Disease

Parkinson's disease is a neurodegenerative disorder of the nervous system in which the nerve cells in the brain that produce dopamine are progressively depleted, affecting movement and speech. The generation of induced pluripotent stem cells from an individual patient could enable the large-scale production of the cell types affected by that patient's disease (Hoxha, 2015). These cells could, in turn, be used for disease modeling, drug discovery, and eventually autologous cell replacement therapies (Smith, S., 2015).

Potential Stem Cell Therapies: ALS

Recent research has demonstrated successful stem cell reprogramming in patients with genetically based ALS (Goldstein, 2010). Patient-specific induced pluripotent stem cells that possess pluripotency properties have been successfully directed to differentiate into motor **neurons**, the nerve cells destroyed in ALS (Skene, 2010).

Cell Replacement Therapy

In **cell-based therapies**, stem cells are induced to differentiate into the specific cell type required to repair damaged or destroyed cells or tissues (NIH, 2015c). The stem cells that are collected from an individual are then transplanted back into that same individual (autologous stem cell transplants). Several challenges, however, must still be resolved before cell replacement therapy using induced pluripotent stem cell technology can become a clinical reality (McGuire, 2010). Because the technique of preparing induced pluripotent stem cells uses a **retrovirus** and a gene known to cause cancer, this technique cannot be used to prepare cells for clinical trials, but can be used to prepare cell lines for developing a better understanding of the mechanisms of diseases and to screen potential cures (Lo & Parham, 2010; Morad, 2012).

Among several safety issues, induced pluripotent stem cell-derived neurons may not be suitable for transplants until the tumor-causing genes and retroviruses are replaced with more controlled techniques of reprogramming (McGuire, 2010). Recently, scientists were able to generate induced pluripotent stem cells using recombinant proteins in mice as opposed to the viral vectors (Ji et al., 2016). It will be necessary to understand and correct any intrinsic defects in the induced pluripotent stem cells before they can be used as a basis for cell therapy (McGuire, 2010; Morad, 2012). Nevertheless, induced pluripotent stem cells will be important tools for further studying mechanisms by which genetic diseases arise (Robertson, 2010).

Transgenics

There are some issues around **transgenics**, or the mixing of animal genes into human genes to study what would happen. This may be too radical for many people and may alienate some to the point of thinking there is a risk of making **chimera** come to life (Wharton, 2016). Moreover, some scientists are using induced pluripotent stem cells in animal trials, including ones where the cells are implanted into animal brains (Smith, 2014). The fear of a chimera-like organism being related to a donor may not be something every stem cell donor is comfortable with, especially if it is done without the donor's knowledge (Macintosh, 2015).

Another controversial issue is that induced pluripotent stem cells might be used to derive human egg and sperm cells (Macintosh, 2015) that could be used in IVF procedures. The result would not be an identical **clone**, but it could be dangerously close (Holman, 2015). Clones are genetically identical to the originating line of cells (NIH, 2015c).

Donation of Human Eggs for Stem Cell Research

One of the drawbacks of the somatic cell nuclear transfer technique is the need for many eggs from donors. The ethical controversy involves having a donor volunteer their eggs in the same manner as women go through IVF: hyperstimulation of their ovaries followed by surgery to remove the eggs with all the risks associated with IVF, but arguably without any of the benefits. Many donors decide against volunteering to donate their eggs for research when they are informed a fertility clinic would better compensate them for the same procedure ($5,000 to $10,000 compensation for research purposes versus $35,000 to more than $100,000 in compensation for reproduction purposes) (Foohey, 2010; Rausch, 2012).

Regulations for donation of human eggs vary from state to state (ASRM, 2013). Some states allow for payment of lost wages, expenses, or child care during the procedure. Other countries, including England, allow compensation in different forms, such as offsetting the costs of fertility treatment in return for research material (Mortazavi, 2012). The National Research Council and the Institute of Medicine advise against indirect compensation (costs for other than payment of expenses), and most states prohibit compensation to egg donors (Williams, 2015). The International Society for Stem Cell Research prohibits undue inducements, leaving open the possibility of modest compensation beyond direct expenses (ISSCR, 2013).

Supporters of the no-compensation rule contend allowing compensation would unduly influence donor decisions to provide their eggs for research and the potentially large sums of money would induce low-income women to subject themselves to unnecessary risks. Critics argue withholding compensation is paternalistic, but concede large sums of money can be coercive (Merjan, 2015). While debate over whether women should be allowed to exploit themselves by choice continues, the current voluntary guideline for IVF clinics is $10,000 if egg donations are for research (Rausch, 2012).

Underlying the debates about the best way to preserve women's personal autonomy is the seriousness of the medical risks to the donors. As in live organ donations, the potential for harm is so severe, any inducements which might cloud the risk evaluation are forbidden. In contrast, when one donates bone marrow or other tissues for research, the risks are not as high and donors are generally reimbursed for their time and discomfort. Nevertheless, payments for time and discomfort are not allowed for egg donors (Williams, 2015).

The risks and demands of egg donation are substantial, requiring significant investments of time, 56 hours by one estimate, plus several weeks of discomfort from the prescribed drugs. It also involves a small but serious risk of ovarian hyperstimulation syndrome. The long-term health risks remain unknown; some research suggests a link between the hormone treatments needed for egg retrieval and some cancers (Merjan, 2015). Finally, there may be detrimental effects on future fertility and future offspring (Margalit, 2016).

On the other hand, these risks are also cited as justification for fair compensation (Neal, 2011). However, if excessive payments exploit donors, so do low payments. Moreover, profit incentives are acceptable for the scientists, universities, biotechnology firms, pharmaceutical firms, state governments, attorneys, and health care providers profiting from stem cell research, while egg donors, without which the research cannot be done and new medical treatments cannot be developed, are singled out for remuneration prohibitions (Conklin, 2013). This is largely similar to organ donation, where everyone except the donor is paid.

As a result of the no-compensation rule, there is a substantial risk of having an insufficient supply of eggs for research. The use of somatic cell nuclear transfer to clone hESCs and create a viable stem cell line requires large numbers of donor eggs. While stem cell lines can and have been created without somatic cell nuclear transfer, the use of eggs is important for basic science research; it is the only technique thought to have the potential ability to create stem cells genetically matched to donors, which may then be used to develop replacement organs.

In European countries with a no-compensation policy for both research and IVF, demand outstrips the supply (ISSCR, 2015). Indeed, IVF compensation practices developed as demand exceeded supply. Further accentuating the potential shortage is that compensation for IVF egg donation remains unregulated. Donors interested in donating their eggs have the choice between donating for no money and uncertain research goals and donating for money. Thus, stem cell scientists not only need donors willing to make their eggs available for free, but donors willing to forgo a substantial amount of money in the bargain (Townsley, 2015).

Pluripotent Stem Cell Therapies

While this research area has been around since the mid-1990s, the only stem-cell based therapy currently in common use is in **bone marrow transplants** (Von Tigerstrom, 2015). In early 2009, the FDA gave Geron Corporation the green light to begin the first human trials of hESC to treat spinal cord injuries (Hoxha, 2015; Wilcoxson, 2015). In 1996, two private biotechnology firms were dedicated to hESC research: Geron Corporation and Advance Cell Technology; today, GlaxoSmithKline, Roche, AstraZeneca, Eli Lilly, Bristol-Myers Squibb, Novartis, and Pfizer all have research divisions to focus on stem cell therapies. Expectations are that a commercial market may develop for transplants of engineered organs (Wharton, 2016). There might also be a day when cell biologists are engineering the human genome (as the pharmaceutical industry currently does in plasmids, yeast, and bacteria genomes) to make anything in the human body from hESCs, including neurons, lung cells, and blood-forming cells (Kelly, 2014).

Meanwhile, Geron, the firm that funded the original derivation of stem cells at the University of Wisconsin-Madison, is developing therapeutic products for cancer and degenerative diseases including spinal cord injury, heart failure, and diabetes. Following regulatory delays to begin the first clinical trial using hESCs, Geron relocated to Europe. As the evidence mounts linking stem cells with cancer treatments, the pharmaceutical industry is showing increasing interest in stem cell research. GlaxoSmithKline formed a $1.4 billion strategic alliance with OncoMed of California to target cancer stem cells. All the while, **patents** covering cancer stem cells are increasing, and the number of firms dedicated to this sector has grown to almost 200 (*See* Bridy, 2015).

Cellular Reprogramming of Multipotent Stem Cells

Although initially believed to be limited in their ability to permanently change into specialized cells, scientists are currently evaluating the ability of multipotent stem cells from one tissue to differentiate into cells of another tissue, also known as **cellular reprogramming** (Hoxha, 2015). Though demonstrated only in animals so far, there are key achievements in the fledgling science of cellular reprogramming of multipotent cells. The hope is to create human, embryonic-like stem cells, which can be turned into all the other tissue types of the body, without using eggs or destroying embryos (Selvaraj et al., 2012). The ability to manufacture stem cells could eventually eliminate the need to harvest stem cells from embryos, thereby rendering the hESC debate irrelevant, at least in its current form (Smith, D., 2015). Freshly derived tissue could then be transplanted into ill or diseased patients to treat various illnesses or diseases in which cells or tissues are damaged.

Cord Blood Therapies

One of the sources of human stem cells now includes blood cells from the umbilical cord. Because it is uncertain whether stem cell processes can be patented, it is not clear whether the bar is being raised for patentability of medical products or whether excessively technical requirements that shield medical patents from invalidation claims are being tightened (Wharton, 2016). Patent questions like this are of critical importance since intellectual property rights are the foundation of the profit structure for the medical products industry involved in stem cells (Wilcoxson, 2015). Private entities will likely not fund stem cell research if they cannot be guaranteed the benefit of exclusive profits from their research (Wharton, 2016).

The federal government is proposing development of a **national cord blood stem cell bank network and registry** to advance research in cord blood clinical therapies. Meanwhile, New Jersey created the nation's first public cord and placental blood bank for research. With higher concentrations of multipotent stem cells in umbilical cord blood from the placenta, many parents are storing their newborn's cord blood for the possibility of use in future medical treatments. Scientists at the University of Florida are conducting pediatric clinical trials to ameliorate and reverse the progression of type 1 diabetes, while researchers successfully reversed type 1 diabetes in adults at Northwestern University in Chicago. Stem cells derived from umbilical cord blood are also showing early potential in fighting Alzheimer's disease, and Yale University is looking at the possibilities of cord blood tissue engineering (Wang, 2015).

COURT DECISION
Transplants of Stem Cells in Umbilical Cord Blood

Pharmastem Therapeutics, Inc. v. Viacell, Inc.
[Inventor v. Competing Regenerative Medicine Companies]
491 F.3d 1342 (U.S. Court of Appeals for the Federal Circuit 2007),
cert. denied 128 S.Ct. 1655 (U.S. Supreme Court 2008)

Facts: Inventors claimed their competitors infringed two patents relating to a procedure for treating persons with compromised blood and immune systems. The two patents recite compositions and techniques relating to a transplants procedure. The treatment is based on the discovery that blood from a newborn infant's umbilical cord is a rich source of stem cells useful for rebuilding an individual's blood and immune system after the system has been compromised by disease or a medical treatment such as chemotherapy.

Stem cells are fundamental, immature cells from which specialized, mature cells derive. **Hematopoietic stem cells** are ultimately responsible for producing the various specialized cells of the blood and immune system. Although hematopoietic stem cells are present in various types of human tissue, they are found in unusually high concentration and potency in umbilical cord blood.

The patents in this case describe a process for collecting a newborn infant's umbilical cord blood at the time of birth, testing it for suitability for later use, and then infusing it into an individual, either the donor or another person, whose hematopoietic stem cells have been destroyed. The object of such transplantations is grafting. A successful graft results when the donor's stem cells migrate into the recipient's bone marrow, resulting in the renewed production of normal, specialized blood cells and ultimately the reconstitution of the recipient's entire blood and immune system.

Issue: Were the inventors' patents for a transplants procedure intended for treating persons with compromised blood and immune systems infringed?

Holding and Decision: No, the inventors' patents for using cryopreserved umbilical cord stem cells for rebuilding a person's compromised blood and immune systems were an obvious transplants procedure, therefore the inventors' patents were invalid and not infringed.

Analysis: The issue of obviousness turns on whether the **prior art**, or public information about stem cells in blood, gave a **reasonable expectation of patent success** that a patent would be valid when using cord blood in transplants for hematopoietic reconstitution. The court found the inventors had demonstrated only the presence of stem cells in cord blood, which was inferred by prior art. While the inventors may have proved conclusively what was strongly suspected before, that umbilical cord blood is capable of hematopoietic reconstitution, and while their work may have significantly advanced the state of the science of transplantations by eliminating any doubt as to the presence of stem cells in cord blood, the conclusions drawn from their work were not inventive in nature. Instead, the inventors merely used routine research techniques to prove what was already believed to be the case. The patent was obvious under these circumstances.

Patenting medical advances occurring in the ordinary course of research, without real innovation, retards progress; verification of new properties through testing does not satisfy the test for patentability because it is derivative from earlier innovative work. The inventors did not invent a new transplants procedure or a new composition; instead, they simply provided experimental proof that umbilical cord blood may be used to effect hematopoietic reconstitution of mice and, by extrapolation, could be expected to work in humans as well. Patenting such derivative innovations would strip earlier innovations of their value.

Rule of Law: Scientific confirmation of what is already believed to be true does not give rise to a patentable medical invention.

References discussing this court decision: Heinrich & Abernethy, 2013; Oswald, 2014; Rose, 2012; Wilensky, 2013.

Regenerative Medicine

Regenerative medicine has long been heralded as the new frontier of medicine (Harn, 2015). The business of regenerative medicine has revenues in excess of $18 billion and is expected to grow at a 23% compound annual growth rate from 2016 to about 2020 (Wharton, 2016). Regenerative medicine involves many facets of medicine:

- Creating good laboratory cultures and scaffolding to grow cells and tissues
- Devising delivery techniques to get the biological products back into patients
- Harvesting stem cells

Scientists hope stem cells will be able to trigger the body to repair itself or alternatively to grow cells, tissues, and organs to replace those damaged or deteriorated due to injury, disease, or the aging process. Stem cell research could have unintended benefits for the field of regenerative medicine; scientists are likely to discover a biomarker or some other diagnostic tool having nothing directly to do with stem cells, but with the potential to revolutionize precision medicine (*See generally* Wharton, 2008).

In addition to repairing or replacing damaged or deteriorating body parts, scientists are trying to understand what factors influence a stem cell to rapidly multiply or become almost immortal. This area of research could lead to:

- Screening potential pharmaceuticals for their potential risks or benefits
- Testing the toxicity or irritation of pharmaceutical products destined for market as opposed to using animal models
- Treatment techniques to control cancer and diabetes

(Naik, 2015).

Hematopoietic Stem Cell Transplants

The most established stem cell therapies use hematopoietic stem cells (the specialized stem cells that give rise to all blood cell types) (Levine & Wolf, 2012; NIH, 2013). Hematopoietic stem cell transplants treat patients with:

- Bone marrow damage
- Immunodeficiency
- Leukemia
- Metabolic disorders
- Sickle cell anemia
- Skin grafts for healing severe burns (skin contains stem cells immediately under its top layer)

(Levine & Wolf, 2012; Mohapatra, 2013; Williams, 2015).

Autologous Stem Cell Transplants

Stem cells offer the potential to treat, cure, and understand the more complicated diseases that have so far eluded cure by simpler science. Autologous stem cells, derived from a patient's own body, are used to treat blood cancers and related diseases, diabetes, and developmental disorders. About 15,000 people have **autologous stem cell transplants** each year for blood cancers (Pivarnik, 2014).[LN5] Stem cell therapies also offer a chance for diagnosis and prevention of early human developmental problems and treatment of infertility, miscarriages, and birth defects (*See* Zettler, 2015).

Recently, researchers have used hematopoietic stem cells to reverse type 1 diabetes (CUMC, 2016; Goldstein, 2010). Diabetics need replacement insulin-secreting beta cells that would not require immune suppressants, or alternatively, the ability to reactivate their own insulin-secreting beta cells. Today, mature human skin cells can be reprogrammed into cells to produce insulin, the hormone used to treat diabetes.

Neural Transplants

Early **neural transplant** research with hESCs shows promising results in alleviating the symptoms of Parkinson's disease and other neurodegenerative disorders (Hyun, 2010). Human **neural stem cells** derived from normal brain tissue extracted from donated corpses are also being targeted. Transplanting the nerve cells into children with Batten disease (a fatal, inherited neurodegenerative disorder), is proving effective (Wharton, 2008). This treatment offers the potential of using normal, non-genetically modified cells in clinical therapies.

Bone Marrow Transplants

In 1956, the first successful bone marrow transplant took place; today, more than 40,000 transplants are performed annually (IOM, 2010). A higher concentration of hematopoietic stem cells can be found in bone marrow, which has led to more than 50 years of stem cell study and clinical use for treating:

- Aplastic and sickle cell anemia
- Leukemia
- Lymphoma
- Patients undergoing high-dose chemotherapy

(Atala & Lanza, 2010).

A leader in bone marrow transplants is Neuronyx, a biopharmaceutical firm in Malvern, Pennsylvania, which works with stem cells from adult human bone marrow to devise treatments for heart disease and other disorders. A sample of cells from a donor can be turned into a batch of cells that can be frozen and then thawed and administered intravenously as needed to target tissue damaged with inflammation (Hunsberger et al., 2016).

The therapy has been characterized as little factories that secrete a potent cocktail of pro-regenerative cells. In animal models, the cells promote repair of damaged heart tissue. Neuronyx has applied to the FDA to begin testing the therapy in heart attack patients. Although the technique may be on the cutting edge, it could also be cost-effective. A sample of cells from a single donor could be turned into 6 billion doses of therapy. It has the potential to keep the cost of regenerative clinical therapies reasonable in the future (*See generally* Wharton, 2008).

COURT DECISION
Compensation of Bone Marrow Donors

Flynn v. Holder
[Parents v. State Regulatory Agency]
684 F.3d 852 (U.S. Court of Appeals for the 9th Circuit 2011)

Facts: A diverse group (parents of children with diseases that can be fatal without bone marrow transplants; a physician specializing in bone marrow transplants; a leukemia patient; and MoreMarrowDonors.org, a California not-for-profit corporation) argued that compensation should not be prohibited for bone marrow donations. At least one in five patients die because no donor can be found, while other patients experience life-threatening complications because the scarcity of donors compels them to receive transplants sourced from imperfectly matched donors.

MoreMarrowDonors.org sought to offer $3,000 in the form of scholarship awards, housing subsidies, and charitable gifts as compensation for bone marrow donations. The not-for-profit claimed that it could not launch this compensation initiative because the **National Organ Transplant Act of 1984** outlaws payments for organs and expressly classifies bone marrow as an organ (42 U.S.C.A. §§ 201 *et seq.*). Together, the groups contended that permitting compensation for blood and sperm cell donation while banning it for bone marrow donations did not evince a rational basis, and thus, the National Organ Transplant Act violated the Equal Protection clause.

Issue: Do the federal restrictions on compensation apply to bone marrow transplantations?

Holding and Decision: No, hematopoietic stem cells are extracted from the blood; they are not a subpart of bone marrow, but are a subpart of blood for which the National Organ Transplant Act permits compensation; the constitutionality of the federal ban on markets for organs expressly covered under the law remains in force.

Analysis: The National Organ Transplant Act makes it a felony to buy or sell any human organ to be used in transplants and defines bone marrow as a human organ. According to this definition, the court held that the law prohibits compensation for bone marrow transplants using an invasive, surgical method of extracting bone marrow tissue, known as **aspiration**. The court found that this prohibition of compensation for bone marrow donations does not violate the Equal Protection Clause of the Constitution, as Congress had a rational basis for prohibiting compensation for donations involving significant risks, while permitting compensation for donations of other bodily material such as blood and sperm cells.

The restrictions on compensation, however, do not apply to bone marrow transplantations using **apheresis** which involves a less invasive process that is similar to blood donations. The court distinguished between transplants performed by apheresis and by the older aspiration method in its analysis, which involves a small risk of death from anesthesia and risk of damage to the nerve, muscle, or bone at the insertion site. The court read the National Organ Transplant Act to expressly prohibit payment for donation of tissue extracted through aspiration. Although Congress intended certain types of regenerable tissue to fall outside the statutory defini- tion of *human organ*, the court noted that the material extracted through aspiration is undoubtedly bone mar- row, which is clearly defined as a human organ. The court read the National Organ Transplant Act to prohibit compensation for bone marrow donations performed using aspiration, as the plain language of the law did not expressly permit compensation for regenerable organs.

To determine whether there was a rational basis for the distinction between the organs for which the National Organ Transplant Act permits and prohibits compensation, the court speculated that Congress could have been concerned that compensation might induce poor individuals to sell their organs in situations involving substantial risks, allow donors to extort large sums of money from sick patients, or damage the quality of the organ supply. Although the court conceded that these reasons are in some respects vague and in some instances arguably misplaced, it concluded that it was the prerogative of Congress to decide such legislative concerns. The court held that the distinction between bodily material that was and was not compensable was sufficiently rational such that a prohibition on compensation for bone marrow donations by aspiration does not violate the Equal Protection Clause.

For bone marrow donations performed by apheresis, the court conducted a separate analysis. Apheresis is a newer method that involves withdrawing the donor's blood to extract hematopoietic blood stem cells (HBSCs) within it. Hematopoietic stem cells are capable of turning into blood cells, and nothing else.

Although donations using this method are referred to as bone marrow donations, apheresis extracts cells from the blood as opposed to the bone marrow cavity. Most hematopoietic stem cells mature into blood cells within the bone marrow cavity, but some peripheral stem cells circulate into the bloodstream prior to maturity. The donor sits in a recliner for several hours while an apheresis machine filters peripheral stem cells from the donor's blood. Apheresis is akin to blood donations as the donated material is rapidly regenerated within the donor; the human body constantly produces hematopoietic stem cells in the bone marrow throughout one's life span. It allows donors to avoid the risks of complications associated with aspiration.

The court avoided an **Equal Protection Clause** inquiry regarding apheresis by finding that National Organ Transplant Act does not contain an express prohibition on compensation for donations of tissue extracted by this method. Neither the National Organ Transplant Act nor related regulations interpret blood to be categorized as a human organ. The court rejected the argument that hematopoietic stem cells should be classified as a subpart of bone marrow and therefore covered under National Organ Transplant Act. The court noted that red and white blood cells drawn in a blood donation originate in the bone marrow like hematopoietic stem cells, but are not classified as subparts of the bone marrow. The court found that the word *subpart* in the National Organ Transplant Act refers to the organ from which the material was taken, not the organ from which it originated.

Rule of Law: The National Organ Transplant Act does not apply to hematopoietic stem cells for bone marrow transplants obtained through apheresis.

References discussing this court decision: Choi et al., 2014; Cohen, 2014; Jefferson-Jones, 2013; Ligotti, 2013; Mattie, 2014; Robertson, 2013; Satel et al., 2014; Williams, 2015; Williams et al. 2014; Zarif, 2015.

Autologous Organ Replacements

Regenerative medicine focuses on repairing and replacing cells, tissues, and organs (Atala & Lanza, 2010). Animals such as starfish and salamanders have the innate ability to regrow limbs; salamanders can also grow back their tails, parts of their hearts, and retinas and lenses in their eyes. Humans can, under some circumstances, regenerate their livers, muscles, skin, and bones, but human regeneration is generally limited to single types of tissues when the damage is not too extreme (Naik, 2015). This regeneration can be achieved by administering stem cells, or specific cells derived from stem cells, or by administering drugs to coax stem cells already present in tissues and organs to more efficiently repair the damaged areas (Wilcoxson, 2016).

Autologous organ replacement research represents progress in the quest to make increasingly complex body parts. Scientists have grown kidney-like organs in a laboratory dish, the latest advance in the effort to bioengineer complex human organs for medical use (Naik, 2015). They have also previously made simple body parts in the lab dish, such as tear ducts, arteries, and windpipes (Naik, 2013a). But recently they have grown more elaborate human organs, including pea-size structures that resemble the developing brain, tiny stomachs, and an "optic cup" with photoreceptors and other retinal cells (Naik, 2013b).

Replacement bladders have also been created using a patient's own stem cells. The technology is aimed at children with spina bifida or people with spinal cord injuries who lose bladder function. The technique involves doing a biopsy of the patient's bladder to collect stem cells, which are capable of regeneration. The cells are placed on a biodegradable scaffold in the shape of a bladder and given time to grow and mature. The neo-bladder is then implanted in the patient and becomes functional (Harbaugh, 2015).

Moral Issues and Public Sensitivities

Stem cells, autologous organs, and other technologies offer great promise, though scientific, business, and political challenges remain (ASRM, 2015). Despite many advances in hESC technology, the destruction of a human embryo is one factor that is limiting the development of stem cell-based clinical therapies (Macintosh, 2015).

Proper ethical safeguards should take into account both the moral issues and public sensitivities. For instance, the pharmaceutical industry and the states that are funding stem cell research adhere to the guidelines developed by the National Academy of Sciences (IOM, 2010). At the same time, the sensitive political issues raised by research must be acknowledged by both sides of the debate:

- How many cells does it take to be a human?
- If an embryo is no longer wanted for reproduction and is considered medical waste, is it acceptable to use that embryo to help find a medical cure?
- What if there is a mixture of human and other animal cells?
- When is the beginning of life? Fertilization? Implantation? Viability? Birth?
- Why is stem cell research so controversial?

Two primary issues of research revolve around the assessment of when human life begins and the use of human embryos as research subjects (Marvin, 2011). It involves a debate over potential people versus actual people (Wharton, 2008).

- If a technique such as somatic cell nuclear transfer is used, would the zygote be considered human?
- Is it when the egg and sperm cell fuse to form a zygote?
- When do organisms become a human?

Pluripotent Versus Multipotent Stem Cells

Those who oppose hESC and somatic cell nuclear transfer argue amniotic fluid and induced pluripotent stem cells show embryos are not needed for regenerative medicine research. Scientists, however, insist hESCs are the gold standard of pluripotency; the newer techniques must be tested against hESCs (Roxland & Caplan, 2015). Scientists also point out that since the induced pluripotent stem cells are made using genes known to promote cancer, the resulting cells can be used to study disease, but may not be used as stem cell therapy because of the risk of inciting cancer (Smith, S., 2015).

Neither scientific assertion assuages critics of hESC research. Multipotent stem cells are viewed as being sufficient for research purposes and the direction the basis for research should take because they offer hope for real clinical applications with no loss or compromising of human life. Phrases such as "just because it is scientifically possible does not make something ethically right to pursue" and "the ends do not justify the means" are cited to justify this position (Hoxha, 2015).

Potential Versus Actual People

Backers of stem cell research believe hESCs hold the promise of someday curing diseases from Alzheimer's to Parkinson's (Wang, 2015). Unlike multipotent stem cells, which generally replicate the tissue of their origin, hESCs have the potential to develop into other cell types, offering the tantalizing possibility of regenerating a variety of diseased or damaged tissues (Wharton, 2008). At this end of the spectrum, supporters of hESC research view the zygote as representing a potential for human life; it is not human until successfully implanted, at the very earliest.

While *Roe v. Wade* granted the embryo some value, it does not have the same value or rights and legal status of a human until it is viable (*See* 410 U.S. 113 (U.S. Supreme Court 1973)). In addition, many people with the potential for genetic disease wish to avoid passing disorders onto the next generation. They use IVF to prepare embryos and have them screened for genetic abnormalities using preimplantation genetic diagnosis. Embryos found to have the genetic code causing the disease are discarded.

The embryos slated to be discarded due to abnormality arguably have no potential for life since they will not be implanted, and may even have fatal defects regardless. Moreover, women generally miscarry when they are carrying an embryo with a chromosomal abnormality. The argument is that these embryos should be used to benefit society by either using the hESCs to study the disease and hopefully provide a cure or by using the discarded embryos and replacing their nucleus with the nucleus of a cell that does not have the disease in order to prepare hESC lines for stem cell therapies for actual living people (Roxland & Caplan, 2015).

Critics maintain the zygote is a human with unique DNA and inherent rights to life; therefore no technique to produce hESCs that uses an embryo is acceptable (Paulk, 2014). They object to hESCs taken from embryos or aborted fetal tissue. This view disallows generating or creating embryos as disposable, destructible cells for research or stem cell therapies. Even though the hESCs come from IVF clinics that would otherwise destroy excess embryos, critics warn the process desecrates life. As an alternative, critics suggest using stem cells taken from adults, umbilical cords, or placentas, though these cells are not as flexible in creating different organs or tissue (Wharton, 2016).

Private Versus Government Funding of Scientific Research

Yet another obstacle is the set of ethical questions raised by the debate over hESCs and whether the stem cell therapies will widen the rift between "haves" and "have-nots." Critics of stem cell research claim venture capitalists and the medical products industry should pay for research and development costs. These cost arguments are used as another reason to limit hESC research.

With many people not able to afford preventive medicine and care, critics argue resources are better distributed by using known cures and treatments for those who are presently suffering and can definitely have their suffering relieved by current medical treatments. Diverting limited resources to research with no proven clinical therapies is a disservice to those who are in need of medical care and could benefit now. Supporters counter these cost arguments by asking critics how known cures were found to begin with (*See generally* Freeland, 2014).

Slippery Slope

Critics also fear regenerative medicine tinkers with the very stuff of life and poses ethical risks. They claim it would be the first step on the slippery slope to human cloning (Wharton, 2008), or even creating designer humans. Critics fearing regenerative medicine will open the door a crack toward allowing human cloning, however, are making a **red herring argument** that distracts attention from one of the most innovative and fast-paced sectors in modern medicine. While one technique for hESC production does involve duplicating embryos, federal and state laws expressly bar efforts at human cloning.

Funding of Stem Cell Research

Even though the U.S. National Institutes of Health provided $76 million for hESC research in 2015, up from about $66 million in 2011, the very process of government sponsorship of scientific research was under siege during the George W. Bush presidency (2001-2009). Politicians' ideological agendas dictated what stem cell research should be government funded. The recent controversy over **Planned Parenthood** allegedly selling fetal tissue has drawn new attention to the use of hESCs for medical research, a decades-old practice that remains common even as alternatives are explored (Radnofsky, 2015).

Forcing controversial areas of research to rely on the marketplace, however, proved to be an unsatisfactory solution to scientific advancement because the market wants quick returns and will only allow for a measurable risk of failure, and the risk of a lot of early scientific research cannot be measured (Wharton, 2008). Unless Congress passes legislation codifying the 2009 rules enacted under the Obama administration, making it harder for a future president to change them, the federal restrictions on basic scientific research could return again (Lempinen, 2011).

Restrictions on Stem Cell Research

For more than seven years (September 2001 to March 2009), restrictions prohibited the use of federal funds for the creation of hESCs for research purposes or research in which human embryos were destroyed, discarded, or knowingly subjected to risk of injury or death greater than that allowed for research on fetuses (over eight weeks in utero development). The National Institutes of Health continued to permit federal funding for research using:

- Animal stem cells
- Cord blood stem cells
- Multipotent stem cells

(Executive Order No. 13435 (2007, June 20). *Expanding approved stem cell lines in ethically responsible ways*).

Now, hESCs derived from IVF embryos no longer needed for reproductive purposes can be used for research. Each embryo can yield one stem cell line, which can continue replicating indefinitely (Berjis, 2010). **FEATURE BOX 31-1** discusses ethically responsible ways of expanding approved stem cell lines.

FEATURE BOX 31-1

Expanding Approved Stem Cell Lines in Ethically Responsible Ways

Important Legal Developments

1973—As a result of *Roe v. Wade*, a fetus acquires legal status as a human when it is viable (*Roe v. Wade*, 410 U.S. 113 (U.S. Supreme Court 1973) (finding normal gestation of a human is 40 weeks; present medical technology can help a child who is born at 24 weeks of gestation live)).

1992—*Planned Parenthood v. Casey* reaffirms but weakens *Roe v. Wade* by giving states leeway to regulate abortions (505 U.S. 833 (U.S. Supreme Court 1992)).

1993—Congress eliminates the need for the National Ethics Advisory Board to approve embryo research.

1993—The National Institutes of Health (NIH) forms the National Embryo Research Panel to review federal funding of embryo research.

1994—The NIH recommends federal funding of embryo research.

1994—President Clinton forbids the use of federal funding for embryo research in which embryos were created or destroyed; this left open the possibility for federal funding of hESC research using embryos created for reproductive purposes that would otherwise be discarded (or excess IVF embryos).

1995—President Clinton orders a review of all research involving human subjects and created the National Bioethics Advisory Commission (Executive Order No. 12975 (42 U.S.C.S. § 6601 note), as amended by Executive Order Nos. 13018, 13046, and 13137, establishing the National Bioethics Advisory Commission).

1996—Congress prohibits federal funding for all embryo research (Dickey Amendment) (appropriations ban on human research on embryos: NOT-OD-07-050: NIH notice of legislative bans in effect).

1997—Dolly the sheep, the world's first cloned animal, is born.

1997—Executive Order forbids the use of federal funding for human cloning.

1997—The President's Council on Bioethics recommends the use of fetal cells or leftover embryos from IVF for research, but not somatic nuclear transfer to create stem cells.

1998—HESCs and germinal cells are isolated.

1999—The Robb memo permits funding of hESCs since a blastocyst is not a human embryo within the statutory definition.

2001—Eighty Nobel laureates urge the federal government to support hESCs.

2001—Presidential policy decision restricts federal funding of hESCs.

2004—New Jersey becomes the first state to fund hESC research.

2005—The President's Council on Bioethics endorses four techniques involving embryonic intermediates as potential sources of hESC lines: dead embryos, altered nuclear transfers, single cell blastocyst biopsies, and cellular reprogramming.

2007—President George W. Bush issues an Executive Order that expands four techniques for expanding hESC lines endorsed by the President's Council on Bioethics (Executive Order No. 13435 (2007, June 20). *Expanding approved stem cell lines in ethically responsible ways*).

2007—*Gonzales v. Carhart* reaffirms but further weakens *Roe v. Wade* by giving federal and state legislators discretion to pass legislation whenever there is medical and scientific uncertainty regarding a medical procedure (550 U.S. 124 (U.S. Supreme Court 2007)).

2009—The FDA approves the first clinical trial using hESCs to treat spinal cord injuries.

2009—President Obama issues an Executive Order allowing federal funding of all stem cell research (Executive Order No. 13505 (2009, March 9). *Removing barriers to responsible scientific research involving human stem cells*).

2011—*Sherley v, Sebelius*, 644 F.3d 388 (U.S. Court of Appeals for the District of Columbia Circuit 2011) backs the 2009 Executive Order easing funding restrictions on stem cell research.

2013—The U.S. Supreme Court declines to hear the *Sherley v. Sebelius* appeal.

2013—A human liver is created from hESCs.

2013—hESCs are derived through somatic cell nuclear transfer.

2014—Transplants of hESCs improve sight in macular degeneration patients.

2016—Kidney, heart, and appendages tissue are being regenerated.

Modified from: ISSCR (International Society for Stem Cell Research). (2015). *Guidelines for stem cell science and clinical translations.* Skokie, IL: ISSCR; Research America (2015). *Timeline of major events in stem cell research policy.* Arlington, VA: Research America.

Researchers must have a stable regulatory framework based on dispassionate science to conduct their long-term research, as opposed to an unpredictable framework influenced by politics (Wharton, 2008). Debate is ongoing about the effect of U.S. scientists not having consistent federal funding for hESC research during the George W. Bush presidency and why it is important they obtain basic research funds for unfettered research. At issue in this debate is how political controversy over federal funding affects scientists and funding of private medical research (ISSCR, 2015).

Dickey-Wicker Amendment

The **Dickey-Wicker Amendment**, initially proposed in response to fears about human cloning, is a rider that Congress has attached to appropriations bills, with no debate, for the past 20 years (Gluck et al., 2015). Per the amendment, federal funds are not available for research that destroys human embryos (from conception to about eight weeks) or subjects them to risk of injury or death greater than permitted under federal regulations that govern research on fetuses (from eight weeks after conception to birth) (Macintosh, 2015). The broad language of this legislation places embryos in the same category as human subjects (Hurlbut, 2015). The Dickey-Wicker Amendment reflects no understanding of the crucial biological differences between embryos and fetuses; it sidesteps addressing the issue of the damage such restrictions can inflict on the progress of regenerative medicine (Dolin, 2014).

Restricted U.S. Competitiveness

Those supporting government funding of hESC research contend stem cell science is so young it needs government funds to get off the ground and attract private capital (Vertinsky, 2015). Typically in the United States, the bulk of basic medical research is funded through the federal government; private funding is generally directed toward taking the government's basic research findings and converting them into commercial medical products. The rationale for government funding of hESC research is that the United States should stay at the competitive forefront in this new frontier of regenerative medicine in the interests of economic stability.

To remain competitive and help reduce its trade deficit, the United States must remain at or near the forefront of innovation and health care technology in the global marketplace. The role of regulatory agencies and their potential impact on U.S. competitiveness in regenerative medicine is therefore of vital importance (Pivarnik, 2014). Political controversy that affects regulatory agencies eventually adversely affects U.S. global competitiveness in any fast-moving area of the health care industry (Von Tigerstrom, 2015). In this instance, the major pharmaceutical firms largely abandoned hESC research in the United States during the George W. Bush presidency and either shut-down their research and development efforts or shifted their research offshore, as Merck and GSK did (*See* ASRM, 2015).

Fostered Uncertainty in the Commercial Sector

A steady, generous source of money is the lifeline for stem cell scientists in a research sector with high capital requirement and long development time. Scientists can accept venture capital and go private with a small firm, but this means leaving the research university, and most scientists do not want to leave academia. Moreover, most academic scientists do not have the infrastructure to leave and continue their research. Also, **proprietary and trade secret issues** begin to intervene and a lot of scientists dedicated to academia are turned off by the trade secrecy required in private models of research (Wharton, 2016).

The federal restrictions made it difficult for scientists to work in the stem cell field, since hESC scientists could not collaborate with other stem cell researchers (Smith, 2014). Such limitations and controversy led many scientists to choose other subject matters on which to expend their efforts. While one major bottleneck for research was funding restrictions, the most devastating one was the perception of the controversial nature of the hESC field (Harn, 2015).

Lack of a specific legal status in a controversial area also led to less private funding since venture capitalists wanted a return on their investment (Wharton, 2016). Controversial areas meant there could be pending laws restricting potential opportunities and therefore the potential return on investment (Briggs, 2014). For instance, bills have been introduced to make therapeutic cloning, such as somatic cell nuclear transfer, a criminal offense (Neal, 2012). Other legislation proposes to protect somatic cell nuclear transfer, but prohibit human cloning.

State Initiatives for Stem Cell Research

State initiatives were intended to replace, in part, the federal NIH funds that had been withheld (Wharton, 2016). Individual states circumvented the lack of federal funding on hESC lines by independently raising monetary support for the research. Forty-one states tried to create bioscience clusters. It was legal to conduct research using blastocysts and to derive new cell lines in most states (IOM, 2010). Many state laws responding to the federal restrictions on research were enacted to address abortion and IVF. Varying laws restrict the use of hESCs from some or all sources, or specifically permit certain activities (NCSL, 2015). While most state laws encourage embryonic research:

- Arkansas, Indiana, Michigan, North Dakota, South Dakota, and Virginia prohibit research on cloned embryos.
- California, Connecticut, Illinois, Iowa, Massachusetts, New Jersey, New York, and Rhode Island prohibit human cloning, but allow for hESC research.
- Illinois and Michigan prohibit research on live embryos.
- Louisiana specifically prohibits research on in vivo fertilized embryos.
- South Dakota strictly forbids research on embryos regardless of the source.

(NCSL, 2015).

States may serve as national laboratories to develop optimal business models for scientific experimentation on hESC research. Former Supreme Court Justice Louis Brandeis believed one of the strengths of a federalist structure is that each state can be a laboratory for social and institutional experimentation. One danger to this state approach, however, is that when hESC therapies become possible, these states might have a problem implementing such advancements (Neal, 2012). Leaving stem cell research to a handful of states also risks fragmentation of the overall stem cell effort and raises the question of whether there will be enough resources to successfully fund stem cells and regenerative medicine long term (Wharton, 2016). Further, it is arguably inequitable for all of the states to benefit from the research funded by a few.

MANAGEMENT AND LAW ISSUES

6. While stem cell research remains legal, should scientists working on this research be regulated by the government?
7. How significant can stem cells actually become?
8. Are stem cells an area where there is more controversy than actual scientific potential?
9. Is hESC research morally different from research on the birth control pill and IVF, both of which developed in the United States without federal funds and in an environment of ambiguous legality?
10. Is the field of stem cells and regenerative medicine merely a collection of clever medical technologies, or does it have the potential for revolutionizing health care?

Intellectual Property Rights

In addition to the laws governing the practice and funding of stem cell research at the state and federal levels, scientists must legally protect their intellectual property (ASRM, 2015).[LN6] Scientists need first-mover profit advantage in this competitive medical sector to obtain venture capital and to protect their ability to do their research. At the same time, issues surrounding the intellectual property rights pertaining to stem cells, such as patent infringement and liability, create great uncertainty in stem cell research (Colangelo, 2014).

The research community is already fractured by ideological agendas dictating the direction of scientific research. This has led to a lack of cooperation among scientists and regenerative medicine firms so concerned about guarding their stem cell patents that they essentially divert funds away from the primary goal of research and development for new therapies and toward legal fees instead (Swanson, 2014). There is not enough money for stem cell research as-is, without diverting money to infringement issues (particularly when most of the activity is exempt anyway); the diversion is puzzling given the limited resources for this medical sector (Sherkow, 2015).

Wisconsin Alumni Research Foundation Patent Controversy

In vivo stem cells are naturally occurring and cannot be patented. The process for obtaining and culturing and the in vitro purified preparation of hESCs, however, can be patented. The Wisconsin Alumni Research Foundation (WARF) obtained three patents on hESCs. In 2006, the Foundation for Taxpayers and Consumer Rights and Public Patent Foundation challenged the patents as overreaching and a barrier to promising stem cell research (Smith, 2014). The Patent and Trademark Office reexamined the patents and in a preliminary ruling found prior literature references to work similar to the material claimed in the patents (Hoxha, 2015). The prior work was not applied in the original examination of the patent application. Therefore, the Patent and Trademark Office rejected the patents on the basis of this previous work, concluding the patented material was not novel and was obvious to a person skilled in the field (Harn, 2015). WARF appealed the ruling.

On appeal, the Patent and Trademark Office upheld the three WARF patents, stating that given the unpredictability associated with both the isolation and long-term sustainability of hESCs, the present claims were not obvious (Hoxha, 2015). During the course of the patent examination, WARF eased up on the proprietary claims and stopped demanding licensing fees from firms doing university-based research with its cells and narrowed its claims to apply only to hESCs derived from fertilized embryos and not hESCs from other sources such as clones or induced pluripotent stem cells (Dreyfuss, 2015).

Bayh-Dole Act

At one time, Congress understood the importance of enabling innovative technologies and medical sector infrastructure. The **Bayh-Dole Act**, or Patent and Trademark Law Amendments Act of 1980, made it much easier for universities to obtain patents from research funded by the federal government (35 U.S.C.A. §§ 200-212). The act provided incentives to universities to reduce basic research, which does not generate licensing fees, and to increase applied research, which does generate patents and licensing fees (Karshtedt, 2015). Industry is therefore more willing to fund university research and development projects because the results are easier to patent. In practice, higher rates of stem cell innovation have consistently been achieved through collaborative research activities between academia and industry as opposed to individual scientific endeavors (Ponchek, 2015).

Unfortunately, due to political controversies, the federal government did not sponsor the basic research to derive human hESCs. The research was paid for by a private firm, Geron Corp. In return, Geron received certain exclusive rights. If the federal government had funded the research, the Bayh-Dole Act would have applied, and the United States might have more competitive stem cell and regenerative medicine sectors (Harn, 2015).

European Patents for Stem Cells

In Europe, the first patents claiming unmodified stem cells were denied based on a European Patent Convention rule excluding inventions involving the use of human embryos for industrial or commercial purposes (Smith, 2014). These denials included the WARF decisions (Atala & Lanza, 2010). The European ruling applies to patenting embryos and any **downstream product** of embryos, but not necessarily to the isolated hESCs, which are available through legal importation in many European countries. One could infer Europe will allow patents on hESCs derived from techniques not involving an embryo, such as induced pluripotent stem cell techniques.

Moving Forward with Innovative Medical Technologies

This chapter tackles management and law issues that are on or just beyond the horizon. An understanding of stem cells provides an appreciation of regenerative medicine and the innovative medical technologies that are rapidly emerging in this medical sector, and the controversy underlying both. Scientists do not yet know what this promising research will yield, and they want all pathways to remain open until it can be determined which are the best leads to pursue (Levine & Wolf, 2012). Regenerative medicine is very much in the early days in terms of stem cell therapies, with the medical products industry essentially still being in a race to the starting line (Munzer, 2012).

Management of Controversial Research

Americans are divided on when human life begins, but agree the zygote is more than just a cluster of cells. The spectrum of beliefs ranges from full human rights from fertilization to rights only once the fetus is viable. The legal ramifications of determining the rights, if any, of a zygote through viability of the fetus have far-reaching implications and are the subject of far-reaching political controversy, including numerous presidential vetoes (Schechter, 2010). Investors are concerned about funding research, given the:

- Political controversy
- Threat of regulatory changes
- Potential upheaval of intellectual property rights

(McEwen et al., 2014; Von Tigerstrom, 2015).

Even more damaging to the controversial stem cell field may be the discouragement of scientists from entering regenerative medicine. To maintain U.S. competitiveness, states are supplementing federal funding of hESC research. Stem cell products have the potential to give patients access to treatments and cures for diseases and conditions that are currently beyond the scope of modern medicine (Munzer, 2012). Citing the expansion of stem cell research in other countries (Levine & Wolf, 2012; Master et al., 2013), states have strong economic motives to fund regenerative medicine.

Emerging Stem Cell Technologies

Multipotent stem cells have already proven their use mainly in blood disorders using cord blood and bone marrow. One source of confusion seems to be the belief multipotent stem cells would not have an immune rejection problem; this is only true in cases where the patient's own stem cells can be used for the therapy (Schechter, 2010). For genetic diseases where patients' stem cells would also carry the disease or are damaged, the use of their own stem cells without modification, which is not presently available, would not render a cure. In this case, patients would need to have a good match and immune suppressants to avoid rejection (Berjis, 2010). As the **cell sorting process** improves, isolation of rare stem cells will open new research opportunities and technologies.

The low turnover numbers in cultivating multipotent stem cells relative to hESCs make them less attractive for research, while the current clinical use and lack of potential for producing noncancerous tumors make them more attractive for fighting disease. Multipotent stem cells cannot, however, further understanding of early embryo development stages that can contribute to birth defects and miscarriage (Berjis, 2010). Many scientists are excited about the recent pluripotency discovery of amniotic fluid and induced pluripotent stem cells, which are easier to prepare and do not have the controversy of an embryo intermediate. Recent work using hESCs resulting in generating glucose-responsive, insulin-secreting cells may lead to a cure for diabetes (Munzer, 2012).

While significant confusion exists over what stem cells, autologous organs, and other cutting-edge technologies may someday offer, there are important roles for entrepreneurs in shaping regenerative medicine into an important health care sector (McEwen et al., 2014). Backers of research believe hESCs hold the promise of curing Alzheimer's disease and Parkinson's disease, as well as the replacement of tissue and organs. In 2015, the U.S. Food and Drug Administration granted investigational new drug approval for the first clinical trial of stem cells to treat Alzheimer's disease in the United States (Hunsberger, 2016).

Unlike multipotent stem cells, which generally replicate the tissue of their origin, hESCs have the potential to develop into other cell types, offering the exciting potential of regenerating a variety of diseased or damaged tissue (Wharton, 2008). Coupled with technologies such as whole genome sequencing, genetic engineering, and synthetic biology, stem cells may provide a reliable platform for replacing tissues and organs, or even altering the genetic constitution of humans (Torrance, 2010).

Stem cell research and regenerative medicine are harbingers of things to come (Munzer, 2012). The key for most scientists and physicians is simply proceeding with hESC research (Hunsberger et al., 2016). Stem cell research and its resulting applications in regenerative medicine will unquestionably have a major impact on the U.S. health care system, unless the U.S. forgoes the opportunity to be at the forefront of this field by constructively forcing such research to go offshore due to regulatory and funding restrictions, as well as unfavorable intellectual property policies. As Hans Keirstead, a University of California physician-scientist was quoted as saying at a legislative hearing on the merits of providing government funding for stem cell research: "Maybe every one hundred years there is one major milestone, like the invention of penicillin. Stem cell research is such a thing" (Wharton, 2004).

LAW FACT

Research on Human Embryonic Stem Cells

Should the federal government provide funding for basic scientific research involving human embryonic stem cells?
Yes. In August 2001, President George W. Bush issued a presidential policy decision restricting federal funding for hESC research. No federal funds could be used to further scientific research involving the derivation of new stem cell lines from intact human embryos like Mary Doe; federal funding was limited to scientific research involving already-existing hESC lines from the University of Wisconsin-Madison. In March 2009, President Obama reversed the Bush policy; the lawsuit involving Mary Doe was subsequently dismissed as moot (*Doe v. Shalala*, 122 Fed. Appx. 600 (U.S. Court of Appeals for the 4th Circuit), *cert. denied*, 546 U.S. 822 (U.S. Supreme Court, 2005)).

Six years later, another lawsuit again sought termination of all hESC research in the United States. In *Sherley v. Sebelius*, the court determined that the NIH reasonably interpreted the congressional ban on funding research in which embryos were destroyed to allow federal funding of hESC research. Federal funding of research that uses already-derived hESCs (which are not themselves embryos) are permitted because no human embryos are destroyed in such projects. This decision will allow U.S. scientists to make strides in stem cell research; it could allow for scientists to begin characterizing genetic abnormalities that predispose humans to develop particular diseases or disabilities.

— *Sherley v. Sebelius*, 689 F.3d 776 (U.S. Court of Appeals for the District of Columbia Circuit, 2012), *cert. denied*, 133 S.Ct. 847 (U.S. Supreme Court, 2013).

See Dharamsi, 2013; Diamond, 2013; Macintosh, 2013; McGuire, 2010; Roxland & Caplan, 2015 (discussing this decision).

CHAPTER SUMMARY

- Pluripotent stem cells are cells that can develop into any of over 200 kinds of specialized cells in the human body other than those needed to create an embryo.
- The main focus of the current research is on pluripotent stem cells and on multipotent stem cells that can develop into a limited number of kinds of specialized cells.
- Stem cells can be obtained from live embryos, embryonic germ cells, dead embryos, genetically abnormal embryos, single cell blastocyst biopsies, parthenogenesis, animals, cord blood, altered nuclear transfer, somatic cell nuclear transfer, amniotic fluid, and inducement.
- Some states allow women to be reimbursed for egg donation, but donation regulations differ between states.

- Stem cell research has the potential to result in organs and tissue engineered for transplants and treatments for diseases such as cancer, diabetes, Alzheimer's, and Parkinson's.
- The ability to patent stem cell research findings is crucial to encourage such research; private firms are unlikely to fund such research if they cannot be guaranteed exclusive profits to recoup the costs of their initial research and development; yet, it is currently difficult to tell whether the federal government will make such patents relatively accessible.
- Perhaps the majority of the controversy surrounding stem cell research centers on the derivation of hESCs that deprives human embryos, in theory but not in practicality, of the potential to become a completely developed human.
- Human cloning is expressly prohibited in the United States.
- Restricted federal funding for stem cell research during the George W. Bush presidency (2001-2009) resulted in the following: a limited number of stem cell lines available for research; the failure of the United States to keep pace with other countries' research developments; additional research expenses caused by the need to build separate facilities for federally funded and privately funded research due to legal concerns; a lack of collaboration between scientists.
- Limited federal funding of stem cell research has resulted in state funding initiatives; this creates the potential for all of the states to benefit from the research funded by a few.
- Stem cell research is the first major scientific endeavor the federal government has attempted to strictly regulate; the effects of this have dramatically altered scientific research in the United States.

LAW NOTES

1. Parkinson's disease is a common and complex neurodegenerative disorder of the nervous system in which dopaminergic neurons, or nerve cells, in the brain stem are progressively depleted, affecting movement, gait, and cognition (Kalia & Lang, 2015). ALS is a neurodegenerative disorder in which motor neuron loss in the spinal cord and motor cortex leads to progressive paralysis and death (Steinbeck & Studer, 2015).

2. After the blastocyst stage of embryonic development, the inner cell mass of the blastocyst goes through a period when the cell mass becomes organized into three distinct germ layers: the ectoderm, endoderm, and mesoderm. The outermost germ layer, the **ectoderm**, gives rise to the nervous system, sensory organs, skin, and related structures. The innermost germ layer derived from the inner cell mass, the **endoderm**, gives rise to the lungs, other respiratory structures, and digestive organs. The **mesoderm**, the middle layer of a group of cells derived from the inner cell mass, gives rise to bone, muscle, connective tissue, kidneys, and related structures. (*See generally* NIH, 2015c).

3. Scientists at Columbia University undertook a natural history study of **embryonic death**. Viable embryos were compared to nonviable embryos created for IVF, but not used for implantation. Many nonviable embryos had fewer cells than normal and lacked compaction. All of the dead embryos did not progress to compacted morula (a four-day-old embryo) or normal blastocyst (a five-day old embryo). No criteria could be discerned for the diagnosis of death on the three-day-old embryo. The scientists therefore concluded that arrested development at the multicellular stage on embryonic day five indicates an irreversible loss of integrated organic function, and hence, the condition of death for the organism. Consequently, they proposed that the ethical framework currently used for obtaining essential organs from deceased persons for transplants could be applied to the harvesting of live cells from dead human embryos for the creation of stem cells (Harris, 2016). Ethically speaking, scientists should therefore be able to harvest cells from dead human embryos in experimental efforts to generate hESC lines (Carvalho & Ramalho-Santos, 2013). (*See generally* Fainstein et al., 2013).

4. Numerous genetic disorders are being researched using preimplantation genetic diagnosis, stem cell transplants, and gene therapy (Battey et al., 2010; Sosnow, 2012). Stem cell trials are currently under way for some irreversible disorders:

   - **Adrenoleukodystrophy disease**, which disrupts the metabolism of certain fats, progressively resulting in nervous system deterioration, paralysis, and coma (Haldeman-Englert, 2013)
   - **Cystic fibrosis**, a disease of the mucous and sweat glands, which affects the lungs, pancreas, liver, intestines, sinuses, and sex organs with chronic infections leading to progressive organ damage (Stoltz et al., 2015)
   - **Huntington's disease**, which wastes away certain nerve cells in the brain with progressive loss of the ability to walk, talk, and swallow (Cefalo et al., 2016)

- **Marfan syndrome**, which affects the connective tissue that supports the skin, bones, blood vessels, and other organs, resulting in weakness in the aorta or heart valves and chronic bone, eye, skin, nervous system, and lung problems (Dietz, 2014)
- **Muscular dystrophy**, which results in progressive muscle loss with eventual inability to walk (Govoni et al., 2013)
- **Neurofibromatosis**, which affects how nerve cells form and grow, resulting in chronic development of benign and cancerous tumor growths within the nervous system (Julian et al., 2014)
- **Sickle cell anemia**, in which abnormally shaped red blood cells get stuck in blood vessels, blocking blood flow, and eventually causing organ damage (Meier et al., 2015)
- **Tay-Sachs disease**, in which a rare fatty substance buildup in the brain destroys nerve cells that cause the progressive decline of mental and physical abilities, generally resulting in death by age four (Brooks et al., 2014)
- **Thalassemia**, in which the body makes an abnormal form of hemoglobin that leads to anemia and body shrinking (Amid et al., 2015; Goss et al, 2014; Grygorczyk & Mohandas, 2015) About 3 to 4% of U.S. children are born with congenital or genetic disorders (Fenwick, 2014), most of whom could have been identified through preconception genetic risk assessment if the United States would provide universal screening to people who are identified as familial carriers of these aforementioned diseases (Hussein et al., 2015).

5. Autologous stem cell transplants are used to successfully treat various blood cancers: leukemia, a cancer of the white blood cells that help the body fight infection; myeloma or Kahler's disease, a cancer that begins in the plasma cells, a type of white blood cell, and spreads to the bone marrow and the bones; myelodysplastic syndrome, a rare cancer of the bone marrow that leads to infections and anemia; non-Hodgkin lymphoma, a cancer of the lymph system characterized by abnormal white blood cells (IOM, 2010; Pivarnik, 2014).

6. A patent for an invention is the grant of a property right to the inventor, issued by the U.S. Patent and Trademark Office. Generally, the term of a new patent is 20 years from the date on which the application for the patent is filed or, in special cases, from the date an earlier related application was filed subject to the payment of maintenance fees. The right conferred by the patent is the right to exclude others from making, using, offering for sale, or selling the invention in the United States, or importing the invention into the United States. What is granted is not the right to make, use, offer for sale, sell, or import, but rather the right to exclude others from making, using, offering for sale, selling, or importing the invention. Once a patent is issued, the patentee must proactively enforce the patent.

REFERENCES

Amid, A., et al. (2015). Thalassaemia in children: From quality of care to quality of life. *Archives of Disease in Childhood, 100*(11), 1051–1057.

An, N. (2016). Decline of dosage regimen patents in light of emerging next-generation DNA sequencing technology and possible strategic responses. *Minnesota Journal of Law, Science and Technology, 17*, 907–940.

ASRM (American Society for Reproductive Medicine). (2015). *Moving innovation to practice: A committee opinion.* Birmingham, Alabama: Ethics Committee of the ASRM.

___. (2013). *Donating embryos for human embryonic stem cell (hESC) research: A committee opinion.*

Atala, A., & Lanza, R. (2010). *Principles of regenerative medicine* (2nd ed.). Cambridge, MA: Elsevier-Academic Press.

Battey, J. F., et al. (2010). *The clinical application of pluripotent cells: The promise and the challenges.* Bethesda, MD: NIH (National Institutes of Medicine).

___. (2008). Alternate methods for preparing pluripotent stem cells. In NIH. *Regenerative medicine* (pp. 77–88).

Berjis, M. (2010). Human embryonic stem cell research and surplus embryos: A moral argument. *Mississippi College Law Review, 29*, 427–445.

Bridy, T. (2015). Enabling clinical-treatment patent method claims with culture and animal model data. *Journal of the Patent and Trademark Office Society, 97*, 328–414.

Briggs, W. K. (2014). Freeing archival research from the accidental and overbearing IRB regulation that costs human lives. *Journal of High Technology Law, 14*, 237–315.

Brooks, P. J., et al. (2014). Expanding rare disease drug trials based on shared molecular etiology. *Nature Biotechnology, 32*(6), 515–518.

Carvalho, A. S., & Ramalho-Santos, J. (2013). How can ethics relate to science? The case of stem cell research. *European Journal of Human Genetics, 21*(6), 591–595.

Cefalo, M. G., et al. (2016). Human induced pluripotent stem cells for therapeutic approaches to the nervous system: Present and future applications. *Stem Cells International, 2016*, 1–11.

Choi, S. J., et al. (2014). Altruism exchanges and the kidney shortage. *Law and Contemporary Problems, 77*, 289–321.

Cohen, I. G. (2014). Regulating the organ market: Normative foundations for market regulation. *Law and Contemporary Problems, 77*, 71–100.

Colangelo, G. (2014). From *Brustle* to *Myriad Genetics*: Legal protection of biotechnological inventions in an EU/US comparative perspective. *The Digest National Italian American Bar Association Law Journal, 22*, 55–70.

Conklin, C. (2013). Simply inconsistent: Surrogacy laws in the United States and the pressing need for regulation. *Women's Rights Law Reporter, 35*, 67–94.

CUMC (Columbia University Medical Center). (2016, May 18). *News release: CUMC celebrates 2015–2016*. New York, NY: CUMC.

Davis, D. D., & Grega, D. (2010). Lines of communication: Advances in stem cell policy. *Journal of Law and Health, 23*, 29–43.

Dharamsi, T. (2013). Human embryonic stem cells: Will *Sherley v. Sebelius* expand the definition of the disabled individual? *North Carolina Journal of Law and Technology, 17*, 239–270.

Diamond, N. J. (2013). The flaws of stem cell legislation: *Sherley, Brustle*, and future policy challenges posed by induced pluripotent stem cells. *Minnesota Journal of Law, Science and Technology, 14*, 259–307.

Dietz, H. (2014). A healthy tension in translational research. *Journal of Clinical Investigation, 124*(4), 1425–1429.

Dolin, G. (2014). Speaking of science: Introducing notice and comment into the legislative process. *Utah Law Review, 2014*, 243–279.

Dreyfuss, R. C. (2015). Giving the federal circuit a run for its money: Challenging patents in the PTAB [Patent Trial and Appeal Board]. *Notre Dame Law Review, 91*, 235–300.

Fainstein, N., et al. (2012). Time limited functional properties of transplanted neural stem cells. *Annals of Neurology, 72*, S33.

Fenwick, S. L., President and Chief Executive Officer, Boston Children's Hospital, (2014, February 21). Remarks at the panel discussion on The Future of Medical Care Delivery: Reimaging Health Care: Driving Change in a Patient-Centered World at the 2014 Wharton Health Care Business Conference, Philadelphia, PA.

Foohey, P. (2010). Paying women for their ovum for use in stem cell research. *Pace Law Review, 30*, 900–926.

Freeland, D. M. H. (2014). Law and science: Toward a unified field. *Connecticut Law Review, 47*, 529–571.

Garner, B. A. (2014). *Black's law dictionary* (10th ed.). New York, NY: West Thomson Reuters.

Gluck, A. R., et al. (2015). Unorthodox lawmaking, unorthodox rulemaking. *Columbia Law Review, 115*, 1789–1865.

Goldstein, L. (2010). Law, science, and innovation: The embryonic stem cell controversy: Why scientific details are important when novel technologies encounter law, politics, and ethics. *Journal of Law, Medicine and Ethics, 38*, 204–210.

Goss, C., et al. (2014). Red blood cell transfusions for thalassemia: Results of a survey assessing current practice and proposal of evidence-based guidelines. *Transfusion, 54*(7), 1773–1781.

Govoni, A., et al. (2013). Ongoing therapeutic trials and outcome measures for Duchenne muscular dystrophy. *Cellular and Molecular Life Sciences, 70*(23), 4585–4602.

Grygorczyk, R., & Mohandas, N. (2015). More than one way to shrink. *Blood, 126*(1), 1263–1264,

Haldeman-Englert, C. (2013). Adrenoleukodystrophy. In NIH (National Institutes of Health), NLM (U.S. National Library of Medicine), *Medical encyclopedia*. Bethesda, MD: NIH-NLM.

Harbaugh, J. T. (2015). Do you own your 3D bioprinted body? Analyzing property issues at the intersection of digital information and biology. *American Journal of Law and Medicine, 41*, 167–189.

Harn, R.-H. (2015). Keeping the gates open for human embryonic stem cell research. *Cardozo Public Law, Policy and Ethics, 13*, 525–558.

Harris, J. (2016). Germline modification and the burden of human existence. *Cambridge Quarterly of Healthcare Ethics, 25*(1), 6–18.

Heinrich, A. J., & Abernethy, C. T. (2013). The Myriad reasons to hit "reset" on patent-eligibility jurisprudence. *Loyola of Los Angeles Law Review, 47*, 117–250.

Heled, Y. (2014). On patenting human organisms or how the abortion wars feed into the ownership fallacy. *Cardozo Law Review, 36*, 241–293.

Holman, C. M. (2015). Developments in synthetic biology are altering the IP imperatives of biotechnology. *Vanderbilt Journal of Entertainment and Technology Law, 17*, 385–462.

Hoxha, E. (2015). Stemming the tide: Stem cell innovation in the *Myriad-Mayo-Roslin* era. *Berkeley Technology Law Journal, 30*, 567–610.

Hunsberger, J. G., et al. (2016). Accelerating stem cell trials for Alzheimer's disease. *The Lancet Neurology, 15*(2), 219–230.

Hurlbut, J. B. (2015). Religion and public reason in the politics of biotechnology. *Notre Dame Journal of Law, Ethics and Public Policy, 29*, 423–452.

Hussein, N., et al. (2015, August 12). Preconception risk assessment for thalassaemia, sickle cell disease, cystic fibrosis and Tay-Sachs disease. *Cochrane Database of Systematic Reviews, 8*, 1–18.

Hyun, I. (2010). Law, science, and innovation: The embryonic stem cell controversy; Allowing innovative stem cell-based therapies outside of clinical trials: Ethical and policy challenges. *Journal of Law, Medicine and Ethics, 38*, 277–285.

IOM (Institute of Medicine). (2010). *Final report of the National Academies' Human Embryonic Stem Cell Research Advisory Committee and 2010 Amendments to the National Academies' Guidelines for Human Embryonic Stem Cell Research*. Washington, DC: National Academies Press.

ISSCR (International Society for Stem Cell Research). (2015). *Guidelines for stem cell science and clinical translations*. Skokie, IL: ISSCR.

____. (2013). *Position statement on the provision and procurement of human ovum for stem cell research.*

Jefferson-Jones, J. (2013). The exchange of inmate organs for liberty: Diminishing the "yuck factor" in the bioethics repugnance debate. *Journal of Gender, Race and Justice, 16*, 105–137.

Ji, P., et al. (2016). Induced pluripotent stem cells: Generation strategy and epigenetic mystery behind reprogramming. *Stem Cells International, 2016*, 1–11.

Julian, N., et al. (2014). Neurofibromatosis: Diagnosis and management. *The Journal for Nurse Practitioners, 10*(1), 30–35.

Kalia, L., & Lang, A. E. (2015). Parkinson's disease. *The Lancet, 386*(9996), 896–912.

Karshtedt, D. (2015). The completeness requirement in patent law. *Boston College Law Review, 56*, 949–1029.

Kelly, G. (2014). Choosing the genetics of our children: Options for framing public policy. *Santa Clara High Technology Law Journal, 30*, 303–344.

King, N. M. P., et al. (2011). Pluripotent stem cells: The search for the "perfect" source. *Minnesota Journal of Law, Science and Technology, 12*, 715–730.

Kwon, S. Y. (2016). Cyberlaw and venture law: Regulating personalized medicine. *Berkeley Technology Law Journal, 31*, 931–960.

Lempinen, E. W. (2011). *AAAS [American Association for the Advancement of Science] welcomes court ruling to allow continued federal funding of embryonic stem cell research*. Washington, DC: AAAS.

Levine, A. D., & Wolf, L. E. (2012). The roles and responsibilities of physicians in patients' decisions about unproven stem cell therapies. *Journal of Law, Medicine and Ethics, 40*, 122–133.

Ligotti, L. (2013). Health law: New method of bone marrow transplants not considered transfer of human organs. *Health and Biomedical Law Society, 8*, 555–559.

Lo, B., & Parham, L. (2010). Resolving management and law issues in stem cell clinical trials: The example of Parkinson's disease. *Journal of Law, Medicine and Ethics, 38*(2), 257–266.

Lowenthal, J., et al. (2012). Specimen collection for induced pluripotent stem cell research: Harmonizing the approach to informed consent. *Stem Cells Translational Medicine, 1*, 409–421.

Macintosh, K. L. (2015). Chimeras, hybrids, and cybrids: How essentialism distorts the law and stymies scientific research. *Arizona State Law Journal, 47*, 183–233.

___. (2013). Psychological essentialism and opposition to human embryonic stem cell research. *Journal of Technology Law and Policy, 18*, 229–264.

Margalit, Y. (2016). Bridging the gap between intent and status: A new framework for modern parentage. *Whittier Journal of Child and Family Advocacy, 15*, 1–48.

Marvin, B. L. (2011). Regulating the procurement of female gametes: Donors' health and safety. *Michigan State Journal of Medicine and Law, 16*, 119–142.

Master, Z., et al. (2013). What's missing? Discussing stem cell translational research in educational information on stem cell tourism. *Journal of Law, Medicine and Ethics, 41*, 254–265.

Mattie, R. A. (2014). Say "no" to NOTA [National Organ Transplant Act]: Modifying Florida's organ donation policy through government regulation of donor incentives. *Barry Law Review, 19*, 361–379.

McEwen, J. E., et al. (2014). The ethical, legal, and social implications program of the National Human Genome Research Institute: Reflections on an ongoing experiment. *Genomics and Human Genetics, 15*, 481–505.

McGuire, S. (2010). Embryonic stem cells: Marrow of the Dickey matter. *Journal of High Technology Law, 11*, 160–190.

Meier, E. R., et al. (2015). Current attitudes of parents and patients toward hematopoietic stem cell transplantation for sickle cell anemia. *Pediatric Blood and Cancer, 62*(7), 1277–1284.

Merjan, M. (2015). Rethinking the "force" behind "forced procreation": The case for giving women exclusive decisional authority over their cryopreserved pre-embryos. *DePaul Law Review, 64*, 737–771.

Miller, J. S. (2015). Can I call you back? A sustained interaction with biospecimen donors to facilitate advances in research. *Richmond Journal of Law and Technology, 22*, 1–67.

Misna, L. (2010). Stem cell based treatments and novel considerations for conscience clause legislation. *Indiana Health Law Review, 8*, 471–496.

Mohapatra, S. (2013). Cutting the cord to private cord blood banking: Encouraging compensation for public cord blood donations after *Flynn v. Holder. University of Colorado Law Review, 84*, 933–982.

Morad, L. (2012). Stemming the tide: On the patentability of stem cells and differentiation processes. *New York University Law Review, 87*, 551–590.

Morgan, J., & Sandoval, V. (2014). Pacific Northwest perspective: The impact of the America Invents Act on nonprofit global health organizations. *Washington Journal of Law, Technology and Arts, 9*, 177–225.

Mortazavi, S. (2012). It takes a village to make a child: Creating guidelines for international surrogacy. *Georgetown Law Journal, 100*, 2249–2290.

Munzer, S. R. (2012). Risk and reward in stem cell products: A new model for stem cell product liability. *Boston University Journal of Science and Technology Law, 18*, 102–149.

Naik, G. (2015, October 7). Researchers grow kidney-like organs in laboratory. A human skin cell has been transformed into a kidney-like structure by a team in Melbourne. *Wall Street Journal*, p. A12.

___. (2013a, August 28). Researchers grow human "mini brains": Scientists use stem cells to help model human brain. *Wall Street Journal*, p. A3.

___. (2013b, March 22). Science fiction comes alive as researchers grow organs in lab. *Wall Street Journal*, p. A3.

NCSL (National Conference of State Legislatures). (2015). *Genetics overview*. Washington, DC: NCSL.

Neal, L. (2012). Organ donation, therapeutic cloning, and laws of the states. *Syracuse Science and Technology Law Reporter, 2012*, 146–170.

Neal, M. E. (2011). Protecting women: Preserving autonomy in the commodification of motherhood. *William and Mary Journal of Women and the Law, 17*, 611–637.

NIH (National Institutes of Health). (2015a). *Stem cell information: Frequently asked questions (FAQs)*: Bethesda, MD: U.S. Department of Health and Human Services, NIH.

___. (2015b). *National Institutes of Health guidelines for human stem cell research.*

___. (2015c). *Stem cell information: Glossary.*

___. (2013). *Blood-forming stem cell transplants.*

Norris, A. (2014). An inevitable conflict: The subordination of contract principles to informed consent in the business of banking umbilical cord blood. *William and Mary Business Law Review, 5*, 621–645.

Oswald, L. J. (2014). Simplifying multiactor patent infringement cases through proper application of common law doctrine. *American Business Law Journal, 51*, 1–69.

Paulk, L. B. (2014). Embryonic personhood: Implications for assisted reproductive technology in international human rights law. *American University Journal of Gender, Social Policy and the Law, 22*, 781–823.

Pfizer. (2016). *Pfizer's stem cell research policy*. New York, NY: Pfizer.

Pivarnik, G. (2014). Cells as drugs? Regulating the future of medicine. *American Journal of Law and Medicine, 40*, 298–321.

Plato. (2016). *The dialogues of Plato translated into English with analyses and introductions by B. Jowett.* (3rd ed.). London, England: Oxford University Press. (Original work published 1892.)

Ponchek, T. (2015). Does the patent system promote scientific innovation? Empirical analysis of patent forward citations. *Albany Law Journal of Science and Technology, 25*, 289–338.

Price, W. N. (2015). Black-box medicine. *Harvard Journal of Law and Technology, 28*, 419–467.

Radnofsky, L. (2015, July 28). New strategies deployed in abortion battle: Videos circulated online by abortion opponents have galvanized those on both sides of the issue. *Wall Street Journal*, p. A4.

Rausch, R. L. (2012). Reframing *Roe*: Property over privacy. *Berkeley Journal of Gender, Law and Justice, 27*, 28–63.

Reynolds, M. (2010). How old is too old? The need for federal regulation imposing a maximum age limit on women seeking infertility treatments. *Indiana Health Law Review, 7*, 277–304.

Robertson, J. A. (2013). Paid organ donations and the constitutionality of the National Organ Transplant Act. *Hastings Constitutional Law Quarterly, 40*, 221–275.

___. (2010). The embryonic stem cell controversy: Law, science, and innovation. *Journal of Law, Medicine and Ethics, 38*, 175–203.

Rose, S. A. (2012). Semiconductor chips, genes, and stem cells: New wine for new bottles? *American Journal of Law and Medicine, 38*, 113–157.

Roxland, B. E., & Caplan, A. (2015). Should unclaimed frozen embryos be considered abandoned property and donated to stem cell research? *Boston University Journal of Science and Technology Law, 21*, 108–135.

Russo, A. H. (2014). *Association for Molecular Pathology v. Myriad Genetics, Inc.* and its impact on the patentability of "designer" genes. *New York University Journal of Intellectual Property and Entertainment Law, 4*, 37–66.

Satel, S., et al. (2014). State organ-donation incentives under the National Organ Transplant Act. *Law and Contemporary Problems, 77*, 217–252.

Sax, J. K. (2006). The states "race" with the federal government for stem cell research. *Annals of Health Law, 15*, 1–35.

Schechter, J. (2010). Promoting human embryonic stem cell research: A comparison of policies in the United States and the United Kingdom and factors encouraging advancement. *Texas International Law Journal, 45*, 603–629.

Selvaraj, V., et al. (2012). Switching cell fate: The remarkable rise of iPS cells and lineage reprogramming technologies. *Trends in Biotechnology, 28*, 214–223.

Sepper, E. (2015). Gendering corporate conscience. *Harvard Journal of Law and Gender, 38*, 193–233.

Sherkow, J. S. (2015). Administrating patent litigation. *Washington Law Review, 90*, 205–269.

Skene, L. (2010). Recent developments in stem cell research: Social, ethical, and legal issues for the future. *Indiana Journal of Global Legal Studies, 17*, 211–244.

Smith, B. (2014). The patentability of human embryonic stem cells in light of *Myriad*. *Journal of the Patent and Trademark Office Society, 96*, 112–139.

Smith, D. G. (2015). The increasing use of challenges to expert evidence under *Daubert* and rule 702 in patent litigation. *Journal of Intellectual Property Law, 22*, 345–373.

Smith, S. (2015). Claiming a cell reset button: Induced pluripotent stem cells and preparation methods as patentable subject matter. *Boston College Law Review, 56*, 1577–1611.

Sosnow, R. E. (2012). Genetic material girl: Embryonic screening, the donor child, and the need for statutory reform. *Health and Biomedical Law Society, 7*, 609–650.

Steiger, E. (2010). Not of woman born: How ectogenesis will change the way we view viability, birth, and the status of the unborn. *Journal of Law and Health, 23*, 143–171.

Steinbeck, J. A., & Studer, L. (2015). Moving stem cells to the clinic: Potential and limitations for brain repair. *Neuron, 86*(1), 187–206.

Stoltz, D. A., et al. (2015). Origins of cystic fibrosis lung disease. *The New England Journal of Medicine, 372*(4), 351–362.

Swanson, K. W. (2014). *Banking on the body: The market in blood, milk, and sperm in modern America.* Cambridge, MA: Harvard University Press.

Tachibana, M., et al. (2013). Human embryonic stem cells derived by somatic cell nuclear transfer. *Cell, 153*, 1228–1238.

Torrance, A. W. (2010). Family law and the genomic revolution. *UMKC [University of Missouri-Kansas City] Law Review, 79*, 271–282.

Townsley, M. L. (2015). Is there any body out there? A call for a new body of law to protect individual ownership interests in tissue samples used in medical research. *Washburn Law Journal, 54*, 683–730.

Trounson, A., & DeWitt, N. D. (2013). Pluripotent stem cells from cloned human embryos: Success at long last. *Cell Stem Cell, 12*(6), 636–638.

Varkey, M., & Atala, A. (2015). Organ bioprinting: A closer look at ethics and policies. *Wake Forest Journal of Law and Policy, 5*, 275–298.

Vertinsky, L. S. (2015). Patents, partnerships, and the pre-competitive collaboration myth in pharmaceutical innovation. *University of California Davis Law Review, 48*, 1509–1580.

Von Tigerstrom, B. (2015). Revising the regulation of stem cell-based therapies: Critical assessment of potential models. *Food and Drug Law Journal, 70*, 315–337.

Wakeman, D. R., & Kordower, J. H. (2014). Special issue on stem cells. *Journal of Comparative Neurology, 522*(12), 2689–2690.

Wang, S. S. (2015, December 28). Stem cells help evaluate experimental Alzheimer's drugs: Researchers evaluate new treatments by observing their effects on neurons derived from stem cells. *Wall Street Journal*, p. D2.

Wharton School at the University of Pennsylvania. (2016, February 9). *The future of regenerative medicine. SIRIUSXM Channel—The Wharton Business Channel.* Philadelphia, PA.

Wharton School at the University of Pennsylvania. (2008). A race to the starting line: Diagnosing what's holding biotechnology back. *Knowledge@Wharton.*

____. (2004). Will Proposition 71 make California the mecca of stem-cell research?

Wilcoxson, M. (2015). A lesson learned from *Myriad*: The Affordable Care Act as both an incentive and an alternative for invalidating stem cell patents. *Indiana Law Review, 48*, 723–752.

Wilensky, M. (2013). The past and future of admitted prior art. *Texas Intellectual Property Law Journal, 21*, 237–254.

Williams, K. L. (2015). The hidden economy of HSC transplants is inconsistent with prohibiting the compensation of HSC donors. *Minnesota Journal of Law, Science and Technology, 16*(1), 219–269.

Williams, K. L., et al. (2014). Just say no to NOTA [National Organ Transplant Act]: Why the prohibition of compensation for human transplant organs in NOTA should be repealed and a regulated market for cadaver organs instituted. *American Journal of Law and Medicine, 40*, 275–318.

Zarif, H. (2015). Distributive injustice and organ transplant waitlists. *Hastings Science and Technology Law Journal, 7*, 75–95.

Zettler, P. J. (2015). Toward coherent federal oversight of medicine. *San Diego Law Review, 52*, 427–500.

Contributor: Michael Weber, MBA, MA; Director of Cell Culture and Project Management Screening and Protein Sciences, Merck.

CHAPTER 32

© Andy Dean Photography/ShutterStock, Inc.

Cellular Therapeutics and Precision Medicine*

"Double, double toil and trouble; Fire burn, and caldron bubble. Fillet of a fenny snake, In the caldron boil and bake; Eye of newt, and toe of frog, Wool of bat, and tongue of dog, Adder's fork, and blind-worm's sting, Lizard's leg, and owlet's wing, For a charm of powerful trouble, Like a hell-broth boil and bubble."

— **William Shakespeare** (1564–1616), English poet and playwright, from *Macbeth* (2016/1606).

IN BRIEF

The technologies at the intersection of reproductive medicine and genetics have been termed *reprogenetics*. Reprogenetic technologies are rapidly evolving into tools not only to customize and enhance children through gene editing, but to develop wholly new genetic recipes derived from modification of the genome. A related emerging field approaching the same goals is synthetic biology, a new area of biological research that combines science and engineering in order to create novel biological functions and systems. Both methods of **genome modification** are approaching the point of taking genetic techniques, ingredients, and diagnostic tools, and engineering precision medicines that have the potential to revolutionize the delivery of health care. Who will own the patent rights to the modified genomes underlying these new medicines is unknown.

LEARNING OBJECTIVES

Upon completion of this chapter readers should be able to:

1. Define *chimera* and distinguish it from *hybrid*.
2. Discuss cloning technology.
3. Explain why cloning does not lead to a creature with human-animal DNA.
4. Define synthetic biology.
5. List the Weldon Amendment prohibitions on issuing patents on human organisms and what biological products of human origin the amendment does not restrict from patenting.
6. Discuss the advantages and disadvantages of allowing patents on forms of life.
7. Explain why CRISPR, the genome-editing tool, has scientists excited about its potential.

KEY TERMS

America Invents Act of 2011
Anticommons
Assisted reproductive technology
Biological products
Biologics
Chimera

Cloning
Coordinated Framework for the
 Regulation of Biotechnology
CRISPR (clustered interspaced
 short palindromic repeats)
Diploid

Embryo
Embryonic chimeras
Embryonic stem cells
Enucleating
Gene editing
Gene sequencing

---

*Contributor: Michael Weber, MBA in Biotechnology and Health Industry Management, MS in Animal Science and Virology, Senior Scientist, Janssen Pharmaceuticals, Inc., of Johnson & Johnson.

Gene therapy

Genetic diagnostic testing

Genetic engineering

Genetic recombination

Genome modification

Germline

Germline gene therapy

Haploid

Hepatitis C virus

Human-human chimera

Humanzee

Hybrid

Inheritable genetic modifications

Interspecies combinations

In vitro fertilization

Patent

Patent and Trademark Office

Patent thickets

Pluripotent stem cells

Precision medicine

Privately funded embryo research

Recombinant DNA technology

Reproductive medicine

Reprogenetics

Somatic cell nuclear transfer

Synthetic biology

Transgenes

Transgenic

Transplantation

Triploid

Unpatentable

Xenotransplantation

FACT OR FICTION

Patenting "Humanzee"

Has the U.S. Patent and Trademark Office decided how many human gene sequences are needed for an organism to be considered human?

Stuart Newman, a developmental biologist at New York Medical College and founding member of the Council for Responsible Genetics, and Jeremy Rifkin, author-economist and president of the Foundation for Economic Trends, filed an application to **patent** a human-chimpanzee (**humanzee**) and the various methods of creating it. The humanzee was purely theoretical in 1997. Newman and Rifkin did not file the application with the intention of creating the humanzee, but rather to secure the exclusive right to the technology after the patent was granted, or, if the patent was denied, to reduce the economic incentive for others to develop chimeras. The application specified the percentage of human DNA in the humanzee to be up to 50%, to force the **Patent and Trademark Office** to grapple not only with whether human beings can be patentable subject matter, but also with how much human genetic material it takes to make a living organism human.

The Patent and Trademark Office initially rejected the application because it claimed the invention embraced a human being. When the office was asked to identify the legal basis for banning their patent, the Patent and Trademark Office stated the patent would violate the Thirteenth Amendment, which forbids slavery and the ownership of human beings. After an appeal, the Patent and Trademark Office issued its last rejection letter. The letter stated that the humanzee would be too closely related to a human to be patentable. The Patent and Trademark Office stated that reaching this decision was not difficult, for the proposed technique was too crude to be able to fine-tune the percentage of human cells in the humanzee and therefore could have easily produced a creature that was more human than chimpanzee. Today, **gene editing** technology makes such fine-tuning more feasible. The Patent and Trademark Office will likely have to face the question of what is human again. Still, no one claims to know how to differentiate between humans and animals.

—See Law Fact at the end of this chapter for the answer.

Principles and Applications

A mathematical parrot, a Dutch-speaking orangutan, and a chimpanzee that can pass for a boy are the characters that anchor Michael Crichton's novel *Next* (Crichton, 2008). Trained as a physician, Crichton's futuristic fiction takes scientific possibilities to their logical extremes. In *Next*, Crichton examines **reproductive medicine** and genetics from the vantage point of the law. *Next* weaves together several storylines in order to trace the complex interplay of scientific innovation, law, ethics, politics, and economic opportunity:

- A biotechnology firm calculating how much money it could make with its patented maturity gene, after a scientist's drug-abusing brother accidently inhales a spray containing a retrovirus used to induce aging in rats and then suddenly matures into a responsible, sober adult

- A parrot whose conversational and mathematical abilities stem from an injection of human **transgenes** received as a chick
- A scientist who discovers he is the father of a **transgenic** humanzee, the product of an embryonic experiment he had assumed was abortive, and adopts the half-human as his son, integrates him into his family, and enrolls him in school
- Bounty hunters pursuing a child who has inherited an unusual cell from a grandfather who signed away the commercial rights to his tissues, acting on behalf of the owners of the rights to the cell, who have court approval to forcibly harvest samples from the child
- The jilted husband who uses the threat of genetic testing to pressure his wife into giving up custody of their children

In *Next*, these fantasy plots take their place alongside published material on **reprogenetics** and **genetic engineering**, which are altering genetic material to produce new organisms. Today, there is not yet a public consensus on completely human subject research, such as cloning and **embryo** research (AAAS, 2015). However, with rapid developments in **gene sequencing**, Crichton's characters in *Next* are no longer solely products of science fiction. Rapid advances in genetics, cloning, and embryology have already resulted in the blurring of species lines (Will, 2013). While, technically, cloning involves one species and chimering involves two or more (DeCoux, 2007), recent advances in the sequencing of the genome and **synthetic biology** have led to the creation of a variety of recipes and ingredients with both human and animal components (Caffarini, 2013). Crichton's incredible plot in *Next* thus poses problems that have a significant basis in reality for the health care industry and society as a whole.

Chimera Technology

The word *chimera* has its origin from a mythological creature that was part lion, part serpent, and part goat, slain by the hero of Greek mythology, Bellerophon, considered the greatest slayer of monsters (Hesiod, 2009/700 BC; Homer, 1998/9 BC). Although scientists have been creating human-animal chimeras for several decades, advances in synthetic biology, embryology, and cloning have pushed this technology in new directions. While unprecedented developments in reproductive medicine and genetics have generated public debate, most research involving early human life is unregulated. There are no federal laws regulating **privately funded embryo research** and no significant restrictions on human cloning or the pursuit of **inheritable genetic modifications**, where the genes passed on to future generations are changed (Cone, 2012; Hurlbut, 2015).

Nonetheless, recent scientific advances have expanded the potential to blend species beyond the limits of traditional **transplantation** and **genetic recombination** techniques (Macintosh, 2015). Organs and tissues are being transferred from one part of the body to another and from one person or animal to another, while genes are being transferred from one species to another. Innovations in embryology and cloning enable the creation of modern chimeras, which increasingly blur the line between human and animal. Despite these scientific developments, no regulations address chimeras.

The Food and Drug Administration (FDA) has not extended its regulatory reach to the different combinations of human and animal eggs and sperm, known as **embryonic chimeras**, although it has claimed jurisdiction over human cloning. Since regulation of new stem cell lines does not encompass chimera technology, chimeras are created with increasing quantities of human tissues and genetic materials without limitation (Heled, 2014).

Definition of Chimera

The definition of **chimera** is an organism with a mixture of cells from at least two different genetically distinct organisms, from the same or different species (Macintosh, 2015). Chimeras are generally created by mixing cells from one species with cells of another species, resulting in a combination of mismatched parts. Because the DNA from each species ordinarily does not combine in this process, any offspring of the chimera contains DNA from just one of the original species (Kaye, 2013).

Human-Human Chimeras

Chimeras are found in nature when fertilized eggs fuse or when a fertilized egg fuses with a sperm cell other than the one that fertilized the egg (as opposed to the normal fusion of a female egg with the male sperm that fertilized the egg). An indeterminate number of people are born as natural human-to-human chimeras (Zylstra, 2012). Usually, a chimeric person was destined to be born a twin, but due to a developmental anomaly, cells from the twin become incorporated in the chimeric person's body in one of two ways: Either the twin was spontaneously aborted, leaving behind embryonic blood cells that became part of the chimeric person's bone marrow, or cells of the twin failed to separate at the embryonic stage, so the chimeric person was born with some cells containing DNA from the twin.

These chimeric people possess two types of cells containing different sets of DNA as a result of a rare genetic anomaly that is seldom detected (Arcabascio, 2007). There is no clear evidence the incidence of natural human-to-human chimeras is increasing as the use of **in vitro fertilization** (IVF) techniques expand, although this would be the expectation as multiple births are becoming more common in the United States. In contrast to animal-animal chimeras, the creation of human-human chimeras in the laboratory has been shunned. An experiment that combined male and female human embryos into a single **human-human chimera** was severely criticized and viewed as an example of the inevitable product of years of underregulation of the reproductive technology industry (Zylstra, 2012).

Scientists have injected human cells into pigs to develop various types of tissues (Macintosh, 2015). The hypothesis was if the cells survived and became pluripotent, they would contribute to the formation of all of the chimera's tissues, including cells that could be used for **germline gene therapy**. This theory was tested when scientists produced human-pig chimeras by injecting human stem cells into developing pig embryos (Ballard, 2008). The developing pigs contained both human and pig cells, and some cells fused spontaneously to incorporate both human and pig DNA (Zylstra, 2012). This human-pig DNA can then be inserted into an individual's cells and tissues to treat a hereditary disease in which defective genes are replaced with functional ones.

On a nonembryonic level, the public generally accepts scientific practices involving the transfer of human material to animals, such as in the creation of transgenic pigs for a routine supply of organs for **xenotransplantation** (Zylstra, 2012). The creation of mice with human neurons in their brains received publicity at the Salk Institute for Biological Studies in California, but did not generate much disapproval (Macintosh, 2015). The mice were injected with a human gene that makes an insulin-like growth hormone that delayed symptoms in mice with a laboratory form of Lou Gehrig's disease; the mice did not otherwise manifest any human traits.

Animal-Animal Chimeras

Scientists have already manipulated embryonic mixing in animals. By combining embryos of two organisms at a very early stage, unnatural yet viable transgenic chimeras can be produced. It is important to note that chimeras are not **hybrid** organisms produced for specific genetic characteristics. Hybrids are created as a result of sexual reproduction across species and contain recombined genes throughout their bodies (Sherringham, 2008). The first successful animal-animal experiment resulted in a goat-sheep chimera, or geep, which exhibited attributes of both animals (Zylstra, 2012).

Traditional Technologies for Crossing Species Boundaries

Species boundaries have been crossed for decades by transferring specific genes and other materials from one species to another. Conventional technologies include:

- Animal breeding to produce hybrids, such as mules (male donkey and female horse), geeps (sheep and goat), ligers (male lion and female tiger), and wolphins (male whale and female dolphin) (Zylstra, 2012)
- Genetic recombination techniques
- Interspecies organ donation (xenotransplantation)

The hope is that, in the future, specially bred animals will provide an abundant supply of organs for human recipients (Macintosh, 2015).

Scientists are also modifying donor animals using genetic engineering techniques to provide resistance to diseases, create new viruses, and produce disease-curing microorganisms. These procedures have already resulted in animals with novel biological makeups, such as cows producing milk enhanced with pharmaceuticals (Russo, 2014). Innovations have also allowed scientists to engineer uniquely human susceptibilities into animals. For instance, **recombinant DNA technology** has been refined (including gene deletion, gene doubling, introduction of foreign genes, and changing the positions of genes) to create mice that express human proteins and mice that contain entire human immune systems (Holman, 2015). These innovations could potentially be used to:

- Raise organs for transplants
- Study embryonic development
- Test new biopharmaceuticals

Cloning to Produce Human-Animal Chimeras

A controversial research area is **interspecies combinations** (human nucleus into a nonhuman egg), such as hybrids. The terms *hybrid* and *chimera* are often used interchangeably and confused; it is important to note that they are in fact distinguishable. **Hybrids** are created when an egg and a sperm from different but closely related species join to form a single zygote (Ballard, 2008). In a hybrid, each species contributes half of the DNA contained within a single cell, resulting in a blending of the two species' characteristics, and every cell has that same genome. Although scientists create hybrids in the laboratory by mixing the cells of two zygotes, they also combine material from different species into a single cell using cloning technology.

Cloning, a common **somatic cell nuclear transfer** procedure, involves enucleating a **haploid** egg cell (which has one copy of the entire set of chromosomes) (AAAS, 2015). **Enucleating** means removing the entire nucleus, which contains all of the genetic material, and inserting the nucleus of a somatic cell from the human body (which are **diploid** with two copies of the entire set of chromosomes) (Macintosh, 2015). The transferred genetic material from the somatic cell, when inserted into the egg cell, then replicates the state of the egg after fertilization, allowing normal development to occur (Timmis, 2015). This also allows a perfect clone of the somatic cell donor to be grown, theoretically to adulthood (Macintosh, 2015). Scientists use chemicals or electricity to stimulate cloned embryos to begin dividing as an egg fertilized by a sperm.

It is important to understand that joining a somatic cell nucleus from one species and an egg cell from another species does not result in an organism containing the DNA of both species. This is because an egg cell is haploid and somatic cells are diploid; all cells in a human being are diploid except sperm and eggs. If the genetic material of both types of cells were combined, a **triploid** cell would be created bearing three copies of each chromosome rather than the standard two, which is not viable (Macintosh, 2015). Opponents of cloning technology do not always understand this science; what they envision occurring is a scientific impossibility: a creature with human-animal DNA.

The FDA regards cloning as a form of **gene therapy** subject to biologics regulations, which govern the medical manipulation and reinsertion of human cells (Timmis, 2015). The FDA suggested that it would regulate cloning for reproductive purposes but not necessarily cloning for biomedical research (FDA, 2014). The FDA further stated that cloning to produce children would require filing an investigational new drug application, but it was not prepared to grant such applications for cloning (Macintosh, 2015).

Pluripotent Stem Cells for Human Transplantation

Cloning techniques may yield **pluripotent stem cells** from animal cells and tissues that could be used for human transplantation. As exciting as this may be, when the National Academy of Sciences published its Guidelines for

Human Embryonic Stem Cell Research, one of the few research prohibitions in the guidelines concerned the creation of certain kinds of human-animal chimeras (Macintosh, 2015). At issue is whether this prohibition will remain in force. The aspects of procurement, derivation, banking, and use of pluripotent stem cell lines were given attention in the Guidelines to ensure that every step of chimera research is done in a highly ethical and transparent manner.

Human-Animal Chimeras

Many non-embryonic cell transfers from animals to humans are widely accepted. For instance, an adult human-animal chimera resulted when humans with Parkinson's disease underwent a research procedure in which cells from the brains of pig embryos were injected into human brains at Boston Medical Center. Autopsies on the human research subjects (whose deaths were unrelated to the experiment) demonstrated viable porcine dopaminergic neuroids at the injection site (DeCoux, 2007). In other words, the pig brain cells had become part of the human brains.

In the area of xenotransplantation, the placing of pig heart valves in human beings caused some initial concern among recipients; however, this transplant procedure is now regulated and accepted. It seems the public does not object to the development of single organ transplants from animals into human beings (Macintosh, 2015). Taking science one step further, creation of human-animal chimeras to produce human organs offers a chimerism-induced tolerance that would make these organs advantageous over xenotransplants in overcoming tissue rejection that currently hinders composite tissue allograft in clinical practice (Parasidis, 2012). Yet, using animal parts as transplant organs has its limits.

If a human were to receive many organs from an animal, or if it were possible to transfer a single vital organ from a similar species (such as a primate brain) into a human, then concern might arise as to whether the resulting organism was really human. Concerns are also raised about chimeras made by moving animal parts into human beings when the transfer is significant enough to cast doubts on the humanity of the recipient, such as implanting human-animal chimera or hybrid embryos into women (Macintosh, 2015).

Earlier genome manipulations were largely confined to moving genes from one organism to another. Now, synthetic biology aims to create wholly new genetic recipes (and ingredients) that the older engineering simply could not cook up (Torrance & Kahl, 2014). Today, synthetic biology uses techniques from:

- Computational biology
- Engineering
- High-throughput molecular biology
- Nanotechnology

Synthetic biology is seen as turning the same corner chemistry rounded about 100 years ago, when chemists began to go beyond merely studying chemicals to designing and building them. Now, instead of just trying to figure out how living organisms work, analytic biologists will learn how to build them, either by making genetic changes to existing organisms or by creating essentially new kinds of organisms from scratch (Mandel & Marchant, 2014). More effective targeted biopharmaceuticals and intelligent tumor-seeking bacteria are just a few of the hoped-for medical applications at the forefront of this revolution in **precision medicine** (Fateh & Haw, 2015).

Ban on Patenting Human Organisms

In response to the public controversy over reprogenetics, the **America Invents Act of 2011** (AIA), the most significant patent legislation in 60 years, appended a provision that prohibited the Patent and Trademark Office from issuing patents on human organisms (35 U.S.C.A. §§ 1-37), including:

- Embryonic human organisms
- Fetal human organisms
- Genetically engineered adult human organisms

(Heled, 2014; *See* America Invents Act of 2011, 35 U.S.C.A. §§ 1-37).

The ban, however, does not affect the patentability of the following **biologics** or **biological products** of human origin:

- Cell lines
- DNA sequences
- Other analogous biological products

- Stem cells
- Tissues

Nor does the ban prevent scientists from seeking patents for processes to create biological products. The ban also allows the Patent and Trademark Office to continue to address new claims, including chimeras. The Patent and Trademark Office already grants patents on animals that have been modified to include a few human genes for the production of a human protein or antibody; however, it remains unclear which chimeras are so humanlike that they cannot be patented, such as the transgenic humanzee described by Crichton in *Next*, along with the chimera.

Synthetic Biology

While many people have never heard of this emerging field of cellular and genetic research, a growing number think synthetic biology represents a significant turning point in the life sciences (Fateh & Haw, 2015). It approaches the goals of genetic engineering from the other end; instead of just modifying existing biological systems (as described in the Newman-Rifkin patent application), synthetic biology seeks to create biological systems with novel functions to address medical needs (Bioethics Commission, 2010). Since patents cannot be granted on claims encompassing human organisms at any stage of development, chimeras created from human stem cells may not qualify for patent protection (Heled, 2014).

Regulation of Genetically Modified Human Organisms

There is currently debate on whether chimera research should be further regulated (Presidential Memorandum, 2015). Multiple federal agencies currently regulate genetically modified animals. The **Coordinated Framework for the Regulation of Biotechnology** formalized this decentralized approach (NSTC & OSTP, 2015). The agencies listed in the Framework are governed by almost a dozen federal statutes, regulations, and guidelines. No single agency, however, provides for the comprehensive regulation of genetically modified human organisms, and none of the federal agencies address modern chimera technology directly (Fateh & Haw, 2015).

Under the Framework, the Food and Drug Administration (FDA), the Environmental Protection Agency, and the U.S. Department of Agriculture regulate the research, development, and approval of biotechnology products. The Framework regulates these products according to their composition and proposed uses, rather than by their method of production. As a result, biotechnology is subject to the same laws and policies that govern conventional medical products (Rucker, 2014).

The Food and Drug Administration's Legal Mandate

The FDA has claimed authority over various forms of **assisted reproductive technology** (ART) used to achieve pregnancy, although it has not added human-animal chimeras specifically to its jurisdiction. Jurisdiction has been claimed over:

- Human cloning
- Stem cell research
- Tissue transplants[FN1]

Chimeras could be regulated as biological or pharmaceutical products (Heled, 2014). Either way, if the FDA decides it has jurisdiction, then it would have to approve the use of any new product, technology, or process in human organisms before research could proceed.

MANAGEMENT AND LAW ISSUES

6. Could a subhuman species be produced to perform tasks humans refuse to do?
7. Is there less of an ethical issue to experiment on or destroy human-animal chimeras than there is to experiment on or destroy human life?

Presidential Commission for the Study of Bioethical Issues

The Presidential Commission for the Study of Bioethical Issues (Bioethics Commission) has incorporated chimeras into its discussions of synthetic biology, as it examines the governance of biotechnologies that touch the beginnings of human life (Macintosh, 2015). Suggesting the need to overhaul existing regulations, the Bioethics Commission admits that it is unable to offer clear recommendations regarding major reforms. The Commission has also examined assisted reproductive technologies and explored whether legislation could be tailored to include new technology such as chimeras. The only federal law currently in place to regulate assisted reproductive technologies is the Fertility Clinic Success Rate and Certification Act, which does not encompass chimeras directly (Durrell, 2011). *See* Fertility Clinic Success Rate and Certification Act of 1992, 42 U.S.C.A. §§ 263a-1 to a-7.

Human and Animal Tissues

Creation of human-animal chimeras raises unique challenges to the character of human reproduction (Loike, 2013). The Bioethics Commission distinguished various contexts in which scientists create chimeras, opining that there is nothing inherently objectionable about mixing human and animal tissues. In the context of therapy and preventive medicine, the Bioethics Commission endorsed:

- Animal-derived pharmaceuticals
- Insertion of animal genes into humans or human fetuses to prevent disease
- Xenotransplantation

The Commission recommended two prohibitions: production of hybrid human-animal embryos by fertilization of a human egg by an animal sperm or fertilization of an animal egg by human sperm, and transfer, for any purpose, of any human embryo into the somatic cell of any member of an animal species, explaining that humans should be placed only in human wombs. Production of embryonic chimeras was not prohibited (Heled, 2014).

Genetic Engineering

Even as cloning and **embryonic stem cells** continue to challenge imaginations, today the focus is on a powerful new technique for engineering or editing DNA, which enables scientists to change, replace, or delete a person's genes with the end goal of correcting mutations, damage, or defects (AAAS, 2015; Travis, 2015). Relatively easy to learn and to use, **CRISPR (clustered interspaced short palindromic repeats)** has forced everyone to reconsider the difference between genetically modifying human somatic cells and engineering the **germline** that will be transmitted to future generations (Moreno, 2011). CRISPR is made up of scissors in the form of an enzyme that cuts DNA strands and an RNA guide that knows where to make the cut, so the traits expressed by the gene are changed.

Already, CRISPR is being used with all the specialized types of differentiated cells found in the human organism. Although genetic engineering is being used to help the human immune system's T cells resist the human immunodeficiency virus (HIV), it appears that CRISPR might do this editing task better. CRISPR trials are also on the horizon for diseases like leukemia. CRISPR holds the key to curing a host of intractable diseases, including cystic fibrosis, HIV, sickle cell anemia, cancer, and cataracts. (*See generally* AAAS, 2015).

Gene Patents

There is ongoing debate over which forms of life are patentable, particularly in the area of intellectual property law. The issue first arose when a genetically engineered bacterium was determined to be a patentable invention. *See Diamond v. Chakrabarty*, 447 U.S. 303 (U.S. Supreme Court 1980) (holding bacteria designed to consume oil is patentable subject matter); *see also* Singh, 2015. Since then, "patentable subject matter" has come to include anything under the sun made by humans, excluding the ideas, laws (such as the law of gravity), and processes of nature (like snow) (Klein, 2011). The current debate involves those who believe no one should possess the exclusive rights to living organisms, and those who hope to secure patents on human and animal combinations for the generation of stem cells and tissues (Smith, 2015).

Patents exist to protect inventions; they permit scientists to publish their findings without suffering financial losses, and as such they are a means to encourage the free flow of scientific information (Greenwood & Cohen, 2016).

They also encourage funding of innovation by protecting the innovators' exclusive right to profit from their innovations beyond simply recouping the costs of research and development (Morton & Shapiro, 2014). Problems arise, however, when patents are granted to things that exist independent of an invention, such as gene patents (Greenwood & Cohen, 2016). The National Center for Biotechnology Information's database shows that more than three-fifths of the patents are assigned to private firms and that, of the top 10 gene patent assignees, 9 were based in the United States. The question is whether basic truths of nature should be owned (Beale, 2015).

If a firm invents a new test, the firm may patent it and sell it for as much as the market will permit, and the firm can certainly own a test they have invented. However, should they own the disease itself, or the gene that causes the disease, or essential underlying facts about the disease? There are no consistent answers to patent questions like this in the United States or elsewhere in the world (Beale, 2015). Moreover, just because something is patentable in one country does not mean it is patentable in another country.

Hepatitis C Genome

What is certain is that gene patents can impair scientific progress, making it prohibitively expensive for scientists to study certain diseases (Upadhye & Lang, 2014). Innogenetics litigation with Abbott Laboratories over genotyping the **hepatitis C virus** illustrates the problem. *See Innogenetics, N.V. v. Abbott Laboratories*, 512 F.3d 1363 (U.S. Federal Circuit Court of Appeals 2008). While Innogenetics sought a permanent injunction against Abbott, its request for equitable relief was denied on the basis that Abbott's use of the genome was not in direct competition with Innogenetics's patent. With the denial of the injunction, the power and therefore the value of the hepatitis C genome patent was diminished. It also impacted Innogenetics' ability, as the patent holder, to share its rights to the genome through a license. As a result of this patent controversy, many patients have not been tested or received timely treatment for hepatitis C, an infectious disease that primarily affects the liver (Andrews, 2014).

Breast Cancer Genome

Gene patents can also price patients out of the health care market. Because of costly patents, a test for a breast cancer gene that should cost about $1,000 now costs up to five times that from Myriad Genetics, a private biotechnology firm that monopolizes genetic testing for breast cancer in the United States. This is not the case in Europe. The European Patent Office revoked Myriad's patent on a breast cancer gene in order to facilitate cheaper and more widespread screening across the continent (Greenwood & Cohen, 2016). Europe objected as a matter of social policy to a single firm essentially controlling breast cancer genetic research and testing for commercial gain.

After a 16-year effort (1974-1990), Mary-Claire King of the University of Washington School of Medicine identified the chromosome where the breast cancer genes were located. This was a breakthrough that induced a classic race to the patent office. King, the international scientific community, and Myriad competed to patent this discovery. Myriad first sequenced the gene and filed for a patent, claiming rights to the mutations of the gene and the nucleic acid probes that specifically hybridize to these mutations (Russo, 2014). *See* Linked Breast and Ovarian Cancer Susceptibility Gene, U.S. Patent No. 5,693,473 (filed June 7, 1995) (issued Dec. 2, 1997). Myriad also claimed a patent on a second breast cancer gene. *See* Genetic Markers for Breast, Ovarian, and Prostatic Cancer, U.S. Patent No. 5,622,829 (filed Apr. 19, 1995) (issued Apr. 22, 1997).

The Myriad patents cover the compounds for diagnostic purposes, including genetic tests for cancer and gene therapy (Andrews, 2014). Although the unearthing of the breast cancer genes was achieved by King, Myriad controls the licensing for cancer screenings with at least eight patents and disallows all other genetic tests based on its inventions, including sequencing, except for those conducted in its own laboratories (Cook-Deegan & Chandrasekharan, 2014). Myriad's restrictive licensing requires scientists to submit their cancer screening samples to its testing facility, where Myriad gains access to clinical information that takes other scientists decades to accumulate. Each sample enriches Myriad's collection of DNA and patient profiles, which allow the firm to take even more control over the breast cancer genome (Price, 2015).

Unfortunately, Myriad's licensing delayed the progress of studies about breast cancer (Harmon, 2014). For instance, when the University of Pennsylvania Health Care System (UPHS) offered breast cancer testing to patients where it was apparently being passed down in families, UPHS received cease and desist letters from Myriad, threatening litigation unless the UPHS licensed the Myriad patents (Bolyard, 2015). In one such case at UPHS, the Myriad test came back positive, but because no other institution in the United States performed advanced research in this field, the family had to go to the Institute Curie in Paris to seek a second opinion. The Institute Curie confirmed the mother and the daughter both suffered from significant breast cancer gene deletions. Missing sections of DNA on these two genes were just coming to scientists' attention in the United States, and thus were not detectable by the Myriad test. The delay for the deletion issue to come up in United States probably would not have happened if more academic laboratories had been able to do this research (McManis & Yagi, 2014).

Myriad does not dominate breast cancer genetic testing in Europe as it does in the United States. In fact, the European Parliament passed a resolution that opposed the issuance of breast cancer genome patents by the European Patent Office (Whitley, 2015). *See* Resolution on the Patenting of BRCA1 and BRCA2 ("Breast Cancer") Genes, Bulletin EU 10-2001 (noting that a monopoly on breast cancer genetic testing "could seriously impede or even completely prevent the further use of existing cheaper and more effective tests for the breast cancer genes"). Congress could create a similar research exemption from infringement for research on genetic sequence information and an infringement exemption for **genetic diagnostic testing** (Wilcoxson, 2015).

DNA Patents

Patents on breast cancer genes implicate the larger issue of patenting DNA, which has been a controversial issue for years. The National Institutes of Health (NIH) recommended careful consideration of where incentives are required and therefore when genomic inventions should be patented; they recommended licensing practices to facilitate full access to DNA sequences (Russo, 2014). Nevertheless, nearly 20% of all protein-coding human genes have been patented, with the majority patented by private biotechnology firms (Allison et al., 2015). Though it is now widely conceded that such patents violate the spirit of the law, the Patent and Trademark Office continues to grant gene patents (Greenwood & Cohen, 2016; Yarbrough, 2014).

Patent Quandaries

The legal system that created and upholds gene patents is Crichton's real prey in *Next*. The law does not realize how fast things are changing, a character observes. The legal system does not:

- Comprehend what scientific procedures are done or not done
- Get the new issues
- Understand that there is already a new world

As science outpaces the law, coherent legal positions are being compromised, as shown by the instances of the hepatitis C and breast cancer gene patents. In *Next*, Crichton crafts a novel around this argument as a way of developing his analysis. From an analytical viewpoint, while it may leave something to be desired, a novel offers Crichton something nonfiction does not: it provides him with a way to help readers use their imaginations to grasp the implications of the law as it now stands (Greenwood & Cohen, 2016).

Genomics poses special problems for those seeking ownership of, or access to, what might become vast arrays of new medical technologies. Both **patent thickets** (the need to receive licenses from multiple patent holders) and the **anticommons** (many patent owners blocking each other) are potential roadblocks to the use and distribution of these technologies. Besides patented genes, scientists also often hit roadblocks with therapeutic targets because a receptor has been patented. *See Merck KGaA v. Integra Lifesciences I, Ltd.*, 545 U.S. 193 (U.S. Supreme Court 2005). In order to work around this, they develop a test using a mutant receptor or a receptor from a different but similar species. This is particularly a problem in pharmaceutical research and discovery when chemical compounds are restricted from use. This is an area that will need significant attention as the fields of reproductive medicine and genetics develop. It is being studied by several groups within the academic legal community, such as the Center for the Study of the Public Domain at Duke Law and the

MANAGEMENT AND LAW ISSUES

8. Who should decide which genes should be kept and which altered in reprogenetics—Congress, state legislatures, or the medical community— and what role should science play in this decision process?

Samuelson Law, Technology and Public Policy Clinic at Berkeley Law. The United States is at the juncture where it has to decide whether its patent practices should be aimed at maximizing profit or at maximizing the social benefit of academic research (Nelson, 2011).

The Future of Genomic Technologies

While there are a myriad of issues fueling the debate about the future of genomics, most would agree there is a need to ensure reproductive medicine and scientific inquiry about genetics is conducted responsibly (Moreno, 2011). The policies under debate include:

- Advantages and disadvantages of patenting genes
- Merits of banning certain biomedical research and experiments, such as human cloning
- Scientific and medical use of human tissue
- Value of the Bayh-Dole Act of 1980, 35 U.S.C.A. 18 §§ 200-212, which allows academic scientists to maximize profit by licensing their scientific discoveries to the commercial sector practices, versus maximizing the social benefit of academic research by granting open access to anyone interested

(AAAS, 2015; Carter et al., 2014; Claiborne, 2016).

Emerging medical technologies beg questions about how we know what we know about our reality; indeed, they force us to wonder whether we know anything at all about it (Greenwood & Cohen, 2016). For Crichton in *Next*, the limits of the real, the parameters of how life is understood, are systematically changed by science, while everyone remains secure in unfounded beliefs, such as:

- Human biology is a settled fact of nature.
- Humanity is not going to be altered or threatened anytime soon.
- Humans are a species separate and distinct from other species.
- Individual autonomy only resides within the human species.

(Carter et al., 2014; Moreno, 2011).

As Crichton's epigraph to *Next* announces: his novel is fiction, except for the parts that are not.

LAW FACT

Patenting "Humanzee"

Has the U.S. Patent and Trademark Office decided how many human gene sequences are needed for an organism to be considered human?

No. While there is no consensus in the scientific community on how many human cells scientists should be permitted to implant into animals (Plvarnik, 2014), the Patent and Trademark Office has maintained it will not grant patents on human life nor for the processes to create human life. In denying the Newman-Rifkin patent, however, the Patent and Trademark Office did not explain why chimeras containing less than 50% human DNA would constitute a human being and therefore be **unpatentable**. Hence, the question remains about the humanness of a chimera (Chapman, 2013). The Patent and Trademark Office's denial of patents on human life is the only case law applicable to chimeras.

— Transaction History, U.S. Patent Application No. 08/993,564 (filed December 18, 1997); the Patent and Trademark Office issued a final notice of abandonment for failure to respond to office action on March 1, 2005.

CHAPTER SUMMARY

- There is little federal regulation in the field of synthetic biology, particularly in regard to human subject research on embryos, cloning, or genetic modifications.
- The FDA has claimed jurisdiction over regulating cloning, stem cell research, and tissue transplants for reproductive purposes, but not necessarily for biomedical research purposes.
- The U.S. National Academy of Sciences published one of the few sets of guidelines to encourage ethical and transparent chimera research.
- The Patent and Trademark Office is prohibited from issuing patents on human organisms, such as genetically engineered adult human organisms, fetal human organisms, and embryonic human organisms; however, biological products of human origin, such as cell lines, DNA sequences, stem cells, and tissues, may be patented, as well as animals that have been modified to include human genes.
- The problem the Patent and Trademark Office faces is how to define when something is too human or too much a basic part of nature to be patented.
- No single federal agency comprehensively regulates genetically modified organisms, and none of the agencies address modern chimera technology.
- Chimeras are organisms with cells from at least two genetically distinct organisms, whether from the same or different species; they can be animal-animal, human-human, or human-animal.
- Because current federal regulations do not encompass chimera technology, chimeras are created with increasing quantities of human tissues and genetic materials without limitation.
- Scientists have crossed species' boundaries for decades, by breeding hybrids, developing genetic recombination techniques, and conducting xenotransplantation.
- Benefits of this kind of technology include raising organs for transplants, studying embryonic development, and testing new biopharmaceuticals.
- The U.S. legal system must decide whether patents should be granted in order to maximize profit, which encourages research and development, or to maximize the social benefit of this research, which may pose problems with encouraging scientific innovation.
- Reprogenetics and synthetic biology forces us to question long-held, but perhaps unfounded beliefs, such as human biology being a settled fact of nature, humans being the only species to possess individual autonomy, humans being distinct from other species, and the lack of any threat to humanity.

LAW NOTE

1. Although the FDA declared jurisdiction over porcine heart valves, used in xenotransplantations as biological materials, the FDA did not extend its jurisdiction to human heart valves until many years later (Macintosh, 2015). The FDA acknowledged human tissues could be regulated as drugs, medical devices, or biotechnology products (Zylstra, 2012); however, it did not regulate tissues until concerns about the transmission of infectious diseases (such as HIV) from donors to transplant recipients compelled it to assert its regulatory authority (Munzer, 2012).

REFERENCES

AAAS (American Association for the Advancement of Science). (2015). *Science selects CRISPR genome-editing tool as 2015 breakthrough of the year: CRISPR's ability to deliver the right gene to the right spot, at a relatively low cost, has scientists excited about its potential.* Washington, DC: AAAS.

Allison, J. R., et al. (2015). Our divided patent system. *University of Chicago Law Review, 82*, 1073–1153.

Andrews, L. B. (2014). The "progress clause": An empirical analysis based on the constitutional foundation of patent law. *North Carolina Journal of Law and Technology, 15*, 537–595.

Arcabascio, C. (2007). Chimeras: Double the DNA–double the fun for crime scene investigators, prosecutors, and defense attorneys? *Akron Law Review, 40*, 435–464.

Ballard, R. A. (2008). Animal/human hybrids and chimeras: What are they? Why are they being created? And what attempts have been made to regulate them? *Journal of Medicine and Law, 12*, 297–319.

Beale, K. (2015). The CRISPR patent battle: Who will be "cut" out of patent rights to one of the greatest scientific discoveries of our generation? *Intellectual Property and Technology Forum at Boston College Law School, 2015*, 1–28.

Bioethics Commission (Presidential Commission for the Study of Bioethical Issues). (2010). *New directions: The ethics of synthetic biology and emerging technologies.* Washington, DC: Bioethics Commission.

Bolyard, E. J. (2015). *Association for Molecular Pathology v. Myriad Genetics, Inc.* : Progress by principles. *Journal of Health Care Law and Policy, 18*, 141–168.

Caffarini, A. (2013). Directed to or encompassing a human organism: How section 33 of the America Invents Act may threaten the future of biotechnology. *The John Marshall Law School Review of Intellectual Property Law, 12*, 768–786.

Carter, S., et al. (2014). *Challenges and options for oversight of organisms engineered using synthetic biology technologies.* La Jolla, CA, and Rockville, MD: J. Craig Venter Institute.

Chapman, A. R. (2013). Religious contributions to the debate on the patenting of human genes. *University of St. Thomas Law Journal: Fides et Iustitia, 10*, 650–682.

Claiborne, A. (2016). *Ethical and social policy considerations of novel techniques for prevention of maternal transmission of mitochondrial DNA diseases.* Washington, DC: Institute of Medicine.

Cone, K. L. (2012). Egg donation and stem cell research-eggs for sale: The scrambled state of legislation in the human egg market. *University of Arkansas at Little Rock Law Review, 35*, 189–215.

Cook-Deegan, R., & Chandrasekharan, S. (2014). Patents and genome-wide DNA sequence analysis; Is it safe to go into the human genome? *Journal of Law, Medicine and Ethics, 42*, 42–49.

Crichton, M. (2008). *Next.* New York, NY: HarperCollins.

DeCoux, E. L. (2007). Pretenders to the throne: A First Amendment analysis of the property status of animals. *Fordham Environmental Law Review, 18*, 185–230.

Durrell, J. (2011). Women's eggs: Exceptional endings. *Hastings Women's Law Journal, 22*, 187–229.

Fateh, L., & Haw, R. F. (2015). Synthetic biology in the FDA realm: Toward productive oversight assessment. *Food and Drug Law Journal, 70*, 339–369.

FDA (Food and Drug Administration). (2014). *Guidance for industry: Guidance for human somatic cell therapy and gene therapy.* Silver Spring, MD: FDA.

Greenwood, J., President, BIO (Biotechnology Innovation Organization) & Cohen, R., Chairman, BIO. (2016, June 5). Keynote remarks at the BIO International Convention in San Francisco, CA.

Harmon, E. P. (2014). Promoting the progress of personalized medicine: Redefining infringement liability for divided performance of patented methods. *Hofstra Law Review, 42*, 967–1005.

Heled, Y. (2014). On patenting human organisms or how the abortion wars feed into the ownership fallacy. *Cardozo Law Review, 36*, 241–293.

Hesiod. (2009). *Theogony and works and days.* (M. L. West, Trans). New York, NY: Oxford University Press. (Original work published 700 BC.)

Holman, C. M. (2015). Developments in synthetic biology are altering the IP imperatives of biotechnology. *Vanderbilt Journal of Entertainment and Technology Law, 17*, 385–462.

Homer. (1998). *The Iliad.* (B. Knox, Trans.) New York, NY: Random House-Penguin. (Original work published 9 BC.)

Hurlbut, J. B. (2015). Religion and public reason in the politics of biotechnology. *Notre Dame Journal of Law, Ethics and Public Policy, 29*, 423–452.

Kaye, D. H. (2013). Chimeric criminals. *Minnesota Journal of Law, Science and Technology, 14*, 1–9.

Klein, D. J. (2011). The integrity of section 101: A "new and useful" test for patentable subject matter. *Journal of the Patent and Trademark Office Society, 93*, 287–329.

Loike, J. (2013). The evolving bioethical landscape of human-animal chimeras. In S. Dilley & N. J. Palpant (Eds.), *Human dignity in bioethics: From worldviews to the public square.* London, England: Taylor & Francis-Routledge.

Macintosh, K. L. (2015). Chimeras, hybrids, and cybrids: How essentialism distorts the law and stymies scientific research. *Arizona State Law Journal, 47*, 183–232.

Mandel, G. N., & Marchant, G. E. (2014). The living regulatory challenges of synthetic biology. *Iowa Law Review, 100*, 155–200.

McManis, C. R., & Yagi, E. (2014). The Bayh-Dole Act and the anticommons hypothesis: Round three. *George Mason Law Review, 21*, 1049–1091.

Moreno, J. D. (2011). *The body politic: The battle over science in America.* New York, NY: Bellevue Literary Press.

Morton, F. M., & Shapiro, C. (2014). Strategic patent acquisitions. *Antitrust Law Journal, 79*, 463–499.

Munzer, S. R. (2012). Risk and reward in stem cell products: A new model for stem cell product liability. *Boston University Journal of Science and Technology Law, 18*, 102–149.

Nelson, J. A. (2011). For love or money? Defining relationships in law and life: Does profit-seeking rule out love? Evidence (or not) from economics and law. *Washington University Journal of Law and Policy, 35*, 69–107.

NSTC (National Science and Technology Council) & OSTP (Office of Science and Technology Policy). (2015, October 6). Clarifying current roles and responsibilities in the coordinated framework for the regulation of biotechnology and developing a long-term strategy for the regulation of the products of biotechnology. *Federal Register, 80*, p. 60414.

Parasidis, E. (2012). Defining the essence of being human. *Minnesota Journal of Law, Science and Technology, 13*, 825–865.

Plvarnik, G. (2014). Cells as drugs? Regulating the future of medicine. *American Journal of Law and Medicine, 40*, 298–321.

Presidential Memorandum for Modernizing the Regulatory System for Biotechnology Products. Executive Office of the President of the United States (2015, July 2).

Price, II, W. N. (2015). Black-box medicine. *Harvard Journal of Law and Technology, 28*, 419–467.

Rucker, D. I. (2014). The new era of biologic regulation and patenting under the America Invents Act. *Marquette Intellectual Property Law Review, 18*, 107–137.

Russo, A. H. (2014). *Association for Molecular Pathology v. Myriad Genetics, Inc.* and its impact on the patentability of "designer" genes. *New York University Journal of Intellectual Property and Entertainment Law, 4*, 37–66.

Shakespeare, W. (2016), *Macbeth.* New York, NY: Penguin Classics. (Original work published 1606.)

Sherringham, T. (2008). Mice, men, and monsters: Opposition to chimera research and the scope of federal regulation. *California Law Review, 96*, 765–800.

Singh, T. (2015). Open source business models and synthetic biology. *Chicago-Kent Journal of Intellectual Property, 14*, 455–484.

Smith, S. (2015). Claiming a cell reset button: Induced pluripotent stem cells and preparation methods as patentable subject matter. *Boston College Law Review, 56*, 1577–1612.

Timmis, R. (2015). The Biologics Price Competition and Innovation Act: Potential problems in the biologic-drug regulatory scheme. *Northwestern Journal of Technology and Intellectual Property, 13*, 215–231.

Torrance, A. W., & Kahl, L. J. (2014). Bringing standards to life: Synthetic biology standards and intellectual property. *Santa Clara High Technology Law Journal, 30,* 199–234.

Travis, J. (2015, December 18). Breakthrough of the Year: CRISPR makes the cut. *Science, 350*(6267), 1456–1457.

Upadhye, S., & Lang, B. (2014). The FDA and patent, antitrust, and property takings laws: Strange bedfellows useful to unblock access to blocked drugs. *Boston University Journal of Science and Technology Law, 20,* 84–131.

Whitley, N. C. (2015). An examination of the United States and European Union patent systems with respect to genetic material. *Arizona Journal of International and Comparative Law, 32,* 463–495.

Wilcoxson, M. (2015). A lesson learned from *Myriad*: The Affordable Care Act as both an incentive and an alternative for invalidating stem cell patents. *Indiana Law Review, 48,* 723–753.

Will, J. F. (2013). Beyond abortion: Why the personhood movement implicates reproductive choice. *American Journal of Law and Medicine, 39,* 573–616.

Yarbrough, D. K. (2014). After *Myriad*: Reconsidering the incentives for innovation in the biotech industry. *Michigan Telecommunications and Technology Law Review, 21,* 141–167.

Zylstra, E. (2012). Presumed sapient: A proposed test for the constitutional personhood and patentability of human-animal chimeras and hybrids. *University of San Francisco Law Review, 46,* 1075–1123.

PART XI

ADDITIONAL PRESSING ISSUES FACING OUR HEALTH CARE SYSTEM

Part XI comprises chapters describing pivotal ethical issues and real-world pitfalls the United States is confronting.

CHAPTER 33

Pandemics and Public Health Emergency Threats

"The pandemic clock is ticking; we just don't know what time it is."

— **Edward Marcuse**, Emeritus Professor of Pediatrics and Adjunct Professor of Epidemiology at the University of Washington; Medical Director for Quality Improvement at Seattle Children's Hospital; and former chairman of the U.S. Department of Health and Human Services National Vaccine Advisory Committee

IN BRIEF

This chapter deals with the increasing focus on global health, specifically addressing community health and safety in the event of a pandemic whether naturally occurring or accidentally or deliberately spread. It is suggested that the U.S. health care industry must put more emphasis on planning how to respond to the appearance of novel or previously controlled or eradicated infectious agents and biological toxins as part of a rethinking of its broader strategic plans for emergency public health threats. New information about emerging and zoonotic infectious diseases ranging from anthrax to Zika virus is discussed. While some now view the avian and swine flu viruses in a lackadaisical manner given the emergence of the Zika and Ebola viruses, as long as the avian and swine flu viruses remain active, they threaten to mutate into something more deadly.

LEARNING OBJECTIVES

Upon completion of this chapter readers should be able to:

1. Explain why communicable (or contagious) diseases are only a part of the broader category of infectious diseases.
2. Describe the chronology of global pandemics.
3. List the potential problems in emergency preparedness plans for health care during times of pandemics.
4. Outline the major non-health system breakdowns that will seriously affect the health care system during a pandemic.
5. Understand the dilemma of planning for and funding low-probability, high-impact events such as a very deadly pandemic.

KEY TERMS

Antimicrobial drugs
Avian flu
Communicable diseases
Draconian laws
H proteins
Health care supply chain
Human immunodeficiency virus

Infectious diseases
Influenza A virus
Just-in-time manufacturing
Mental models
N proteins
Operating margins
Optimistic bias

Pandemic
Pandemic vaccines
Quarantine
Risk management
Safety net
Seasonal influenza
Severe acute respiratory syndrome

Silo thinking
Social distancing
Social infrastructure

Surge capacity
Tuberculosis
Undocumented workers

World Health Organization
Zika virus

FACT OR FICTION

National Strategy for Pandemic Influenza

Would the political, social, and legal fabric holding society together be threatened at the height of a pandemic responsible for over 250,000 deaths per day for a year?

Imagine that in January 2020 sporadic human cases of the **influenza A virus** (H5N1) are detected in the Nile Delta and Nigeria. By March, several family clusters are confirmed in Africa and Iraq, and by May the virus is suspected to have spread to families in scattered areas of China. In June and July, cases of human-to-human transmission of H5N1 appear in Europe and South America, killing 1 in 20 of those infected.

The World Health Organization declares a **pandemic** is under way. Five influenza clusters appear in the United States and, soon after, are traced to illegal cockfights in Louisiana and New Mexico. They are initially controlled. In August, clusters emerge in Southern California. They spread despite control measures, and by the end of August, H5N1 has spread throughout the nation.

By mid-September, the pandemic is very serious and getting worse. The virus has become resistant to oseltamivir (Tamiflu) and zanamivir (Relenza), two antiviral drugs, so although the medicines are of some use, they are not as effective as hoped. By the end of September, 45 million people have been infected or 15% of the U.S. population. Outpatient care is provided to serve the needs of 18 million Americans, and 314,000 are hospitalized. Hospitals and clinical staffs are making decisions as to whom to vaccinate; 84,000 Americans have already died.

The major impact is on young people with strong immune systems and anyone else who also did not receive the **seasonal influenza** vaccinations. The **safety net** for the poor and uninsured is nonexistent, as access to clinicians is invisibly rationed. The United States planned to produce enough vaccine to inoculate all Americans within six months, but the nation runs out of vaccines in early October, before the pandemic peaks. By November, an effective vaccine becomes available, and a national vaccination campaign swings into action as an additional 100,000 die.

The vaccine is not perfectly protective and deaths continue into December with mortality rates of 70%. About 35% of the population (100 million people) is now infected; 735,000 Americans are hospitalized. Many bodies remain in frozen storage, while the survivors of families organize funerals. Fear is paralyzing societal life and beginning to lead to panic and further distrust in governments and institutions. The economic burden is estimated at $167 billion. In January, a congressional commission is set up to investigate the nation's management of the pandemic.

— *See* Law Fact at the end of this chapter for the answer.

Principles and Applications

An infectious agent steadily gaining virulence and making its way around the globe will combine with a highly resistant strain of the **human immunodeficiency virus** (HIV) (scientists' worst nightmare), and develop into a pandemic that will infect and kill millions, create mass chaos, and send the world economy into a tailspin. Or it will not. This uncertainty represents a colossal challenge for the health care industry and governments worldwide. No one knows what will happen regarding highly contagious infectious diseases in the coming years and decades. Will some novel disease mutate into a deadly strain where people readily infect others and that sickens or kills untold numbers? Or will the concern fizzle out?

To plan for what could become a public health calamity, all health care providers must assess how their enterprises could be harmed by a pandemic and take preventive measures to mitigate the damage and keep their enterprises operating (Kim, 2016). Pandemics are like hurricanes and most natural disasters: they are one area of public health where predictions can be made beforehand (Meyer et al., 2014). Indeed, health care systems, hospitals, and the medical products industry should be planning for all sorts of risks and preparing for public health emergencies within their broader strategic plans.

Mental Models That Lead to Poor Pandemic Preparation

For the first time, the World Economic Forum in Davos, Switzerland, has identified pandemics as one of the top risks the world faces that is most likely to occur (Kim, 2016). Pandemics could cost the global economy $6 trillion in the 21st century, or $60 billion a year (GHRF, 2016). Yet the United States spends only a fraction of its resources to prevent and prepare for pandemics. One reason for this disconnect could be the nation's **mental models** (Jones et al., 2011).

We are generally not aware of our mental models when faced with emergency threats, so we process pandemic information poorly (Wharton, 2014a). What we think is going to happen is often very different from what actually happens (Meyer et al., 2014). The issue is how to develop better mental models of a public health emergency, so we are able to understand what is going to happen, and so we can then line up what is going to happen with how we are going to prepare for it. When we as a nation are unsure of how to prepare for a threat and cannot decide which of several actions to take, we often fall back to our default biases—that is, if we do not know what to do, we just do what is easiest, or what has always been done (Wharton, 2014a). In the context of pandemic preparations, the default bias is to do nothing (Shepperd et al., 2013).

Another challenge is getting everyone to appreciate the threat that a public health emergency poses (Michel-Kerjan & Slovic, 2010). After every outbreak of infectious disease, there is a flurry of activity, but interest quickly wanes and other priorities dominate (GHRF, 2016). As such, the nation's pandemic preparedness is subject to four biases:

- There is a tendency to underappreciate future consequences.
- We are quick to forget the past.
- We suffer **optimistic bias**; we recognize the threat but think that when it does occur, the real harm is going to be to somebody else; it is not going to be to us.
- When in doubt, we follow the advice of others who are just as prone to default biases as we are.

(Jones et al., 2011; Shepperd et al., 2013; Wharton, 2014a, 2014b).

Potential Dangers to Public Health

Anyone seeking lessons about the value of emergency preparedness need not look far. A good place to begin is the U.S. Gulf and East Coasts, still reeling from the devastation caused by Hurricanes Katrina and Sandy (Meyer et al., 2014). The possible dangers of a pandemic could be catastrophic, potentially taxing federal and state governments to a higher degree than Katrina or Sandy. While pandemics generally infect from 15% to 40% of a population, the concern is not simply with people getting sick and dying (Barry, 2005; Opdycke, 2014). The overarching concerns are the disruptive forces that could cause a fairly substantial breakdown in the nation's infrastructure, far beyond the ability of any infectious disease to injure or kill. If there is a pandemic, people will be reluctant to leave their homes; this means disruptions in food supplies, supply chains, mass transit systems, and information technology systems (Huff, 2015; Kim, 2016). What happens when infrastructure systems stop is simply indescribable.[LN1]

MANAGEMENT AND LAW ISSUES

1. Why not prevent global outbreaks of infectious disease that threaten U.S. security and economic stability?

Operating in a Context of Turmoil

The question, then, is how to manage in the context of turmoil. Each health care system, hospital, and medical products firm must plan for a substantial breakdown in the physical and **social infrastructure** in the event of a pandemic. A supply chain breakdown could cause the health care industry to go into a tailspin since at the first sign of panic all medical products and supplies would disappear from supplier shelves (Rothstein, 2015). An example of this phenomenon is how Tamiflu (oseltamivir, the drug used to treat seasonal flu) disappeared with the emergence of the swine flu, which has only proven thus far to be as lethal as the seasonal flu (Bollinger, 2015). In a pandemic, essential imported goods, such as raw materials, medicines, and certain foods, would also become suddenly unavailable (Hodge et al., 2015). How to ensure day-to-day health care and treatment is the uncertainty that must be addressed (CDC, 2011A).

Imagine just a few of the effects a pandemic would have on attendance at any number of venues (schools and colleges; workplaces, including manufacturing floors; and mass transit systems) as people stayed home, either because they were already sick or feared becoming ill. Absenteeism at work soared to over 50% during the 1918 Spanish flu pandemic (Opdycke, 2014). Economic disruption would be immense, as it was in 1918 when large portions of the population stayed home and away from public places, known as **social distancing** (Rothstein, 2015).

Another significant problem would be a sharp drop in consumer demand; two-thirds of the U.S. economy is sustained by consumer spending, but buying a lot of items can be postponed indefinitely (Schwarcz & Schwarcz, 2014). Then there are venues for entertainment and tourism. If an infectious disease was highly transmissible from person to person, this could have a massive economic impact, as businesses would grind to a halt with forced quarantine of civilian populations, mandatory masking, and harsh restrictions on travel (Hodge et al., 2015). Foreign investment would be deterred as governments sealed their national borders to prevent spread of the disease, the effects of which could resonate for years after the disease had been contained (Levinson, 2014). A pandemic involving a highly virulent flu strain such as the Spanish flu of 1918 could cost the American economy $700 billion; double the economic cost of World War II (*E.g.*, CBO, 2005; Lee, 2015; Schwarcz & Schwarcz, 2014). See **FEATURE BOX 33-1** for an outline of the effects of previous influenza pandemics.

FEATURE BOX 33-1

20th Century Influenza Pandemics

The 1918-1919 Spanish Flu:

- 40 to 50% of the world's population was infected
- 20 to 50 million people died worldwide
- 500,000 people died in the United States

The 1957-1958 Asian Flu:

- 20 to 40% of the world's population was infected
- 2 million people died worldwide
- 100,000 people died in the United States

The 1968-1969 Hong Kong Flu:

- Unknown percentage of worldwide population infection
- 15% of the U.S. population was infected
- 1 million people died worldwide
- 70,000 people died in the United States

The 2009-2010 Swine Flu:

- 24 to 25% of the world's population was infected
- 203,000 to 575,000 people died worldwide

- 18,300 people died in the United States
- The H1N1 virus that caused this pandemic is now a regular human flu virus and continues to circulate seasonally worldwide

Data from: CDC, 2016; Chan, 2009; Opdycke, 2014; Rothstein, 2015 Schwartz & Schwartz, 2014.

Severe Acute Respiratory Syndrome

One example of how countries react to turmoil is **severe acute respiratory syndrome** (SARS), a contagious and sometimes fatal respiratory illness (CDC, 2013a). SARS suddenly appeared in humans in China in 2002 (Shah, 2016).[LN2] Within days, international air travelers carried SARS from Hong Kong to Singapore, Hanoi, and Toronto. Within months, the disease had infected more than 8,000 people in 30 countries (Wharton, 2014b).

In Singapore, each morning, firms made employees report their body temperatures (an indicator of whether they were infected with SARS) before being allowed into their offices to work; a buddy system was implemented nationwide under which one employee was required to take the temperature of a coworker to certify the buddy was not lying about their thermometer reading (Wharton, 2006). Infrared cameras were placed at airports and public venues to identify people with fevers. If someone had a fever, they were required to notify public health officials, who would screen the individual for symptoms, and if the individual was sick, would **quarantine** the individual at home (Rothstein, 2015).

Toronto imposed two types of quarantines: one confined people to their homes; the other allowed some hospital employees to commute in their own cars from home to work but nowhere else (Rothstein, 2015). With SARS causing such great damage to the economies, there was a national sense in Eastern Asia and Canada that everyone had to work together to quickly control the situation. The global economic damage exceeded $32 billion (Hodge et al., 2015).

Spanish Flu Pandemic

An example of how the United States reacted can be seen in the Spanish flu pandemic of 1918 that affected everyone. **Draconian laws** were instituted that placed the needs of the nation ahead of individual needs. Coughing or sneezing without covering one's face was punishable by a year in jail, since flu viruses are spread from person to person by coughing and sneezing (entering the body through the mucous membranes of the eyes, nose, and mouth) (Barry, 2005; Opdycke, 2014). The world has changed dramatically since 1918, however. With today's sharp rise in air travel and the steady increase in worldwide commerce, economic globalization would make the spread of new virulent influenza viruses much more rapid. Moreover, Americans today are not as willing to accept government authority as a wartime

MANAGEMENT AND LAW ISSUES

2. What U.S. health laws should apply if a pandemic occurs, and what standards should determine who receives limited hospital beds, ventilators, respirators, vaccines, or even the attention of overwhelmed hospital staff?
3. Who will determine why some people will receive medical treatments, as well as the more difficult to understand reason why some will be denied treatments?
4. What are the broader management and law issues defining the responsibility of the United States to, and its relationship with, the global community in a situation of a pandemic risk?

society was in 1918 during the final stages of World War I. In 1918, public health officials could easily step in and implement restrictive prevention, diagnostics, and treatment measures based on science; the same scientific limitations would be relentlessly questioned today.

The risk of a pandemic like the Spanish flu is difficult to predict; there is so much uncertainty. The consequence is that about 300,000 Americans might lose their lives based on a modeling approach used by the Centers for Disease Control and Prevention that mirrors the 1918 Spanish flu pandemic (Greene, 2015). Yet, there is no way to rationally consider the possibilities. Quarantine measures have not been implemented in the United States on a large scale since 1918-1919 (Rothstein, 2015).

The Basics About Public Health Emergency Threats

Public health capabilities are deteriorating in some areas of the United States and virtually nonexistent in many resource-limited nations. Severe budget cuts at the federal, state, and local levels threaten U.S. public health preparedness and the ability to respond to a pandemic (TFAH, 2015). Today, complacency and budget cuts are the biggest threats with nearly 52,000 public health positions eliminated since the nation faced the swine flu pandemic in 2010 (BLS, 2015; NACCHO, 2015).

To analogize, for communities to respond like Boston did during the 2013 Boston Marathon bombings, with bystander responders, emergency medical service, the emergency trauma care system, the public health system, and the mental health system all working together, does not just happen. It has to be in-place with a robust day-to-day emergency response system that is adequately rehearsed and practiced (Wharton, 2013). As is said, if you cannot do it every day, you cannot do it on game day; but this preparedness takes adequate personnel and budget to have the ability to respond.

As existing public health systems deteriorate, many **antimicrobial drugs** are losing their effectiveness in treating infectious diseases (Tomaselli, 2013). At the same time, deeply rooted social, economic, and environmental problems provide infectious diseases with fertile conditions to develop (Wiley, 2014). In the United States, as well as many parts of the world, but especially in Africa, a growing problem is the availability of vaccines, antibiotics, antiviral drugs, and other medical technologies (Persad, 2015).

New and Reemerging Infectious Diseases with Pandemic Potential

A large number of **communicable diseases** (also called contagious diseases) with the potential to turn into public health threats are either directly transmitted from animals to humans or are close ancestors of veterinary strains (Lipman, 2015; WHO, 2016e). The term *communicable* is synonymous with *contagious* when emphasizing person-to-person transmission of infection. **Infectious diseases** include any disease transmitted to a human being from any source, whether human, animal, or environmental.

Communicable diseases are a subcategory of infectious diseases only transmitted from one human to another (Bennett et al., 2014). According to most infectious disease authorities, between 75 and 80% of the new and reemerging infectious diseases affecting humans over the past 25 years have been caused by pathogens originating from an animal or from products of animal origin (*e.g.,* Choi, 2008; Quammen, 2013; WHO, 2016e). In particular, a nightmare scenario would await if fungi, which largely confine themselves to reptiles at present, evolved to tolerate the warm blood of mammals (Shah, 2016).

At this time, about one-third of the world's population is infected with **tuberculosis**, the top infectious disease killer worldwide (WHO, 2015b). Cholera is also becoming distressingly common in the Middle East, several decades after it was assumed the disease had been eradicated (Ali et al., 2012; WHO, 2015c).[LN3] Africa, in particular, has seen

MANAGEMENT AND LAW ISSUES

5. How might the United States go into a potential flu pandemic with 52,000 fewer people on the ground for preparedness and response since the swine flu pandemic in 2010?

an alarming increase in the scale and frequency of infectious disease outbreaks. In the past decade, there have been epidemic outbreaks of:

- Lassa fever
- Rift Valley fever
- Yellow fever

(Ali et al., 2012; CDC, 2015a, 2015b, 2013a; WHO, 2015a).[LN4]

However, it was not until the outbreaks of the SARS, swine flu, and Ebola viruses revived fears of natural epidemics that world complacency began to change (IOM, 2014; *see* Sun & Jones, 2013). The topic of infectious diseases now has some prominence on the global health agenda, especially with the outbreak of **Zika virus** (WHO, 2016d).

Zika Virus

The **World Health Organization** (WHO) declared Zika virus an international public health emergency in 2016 (WHO, 2016b). Zika virus causes microcephaly (in which babies are born with undersized heads and brains) and Guillain-Barré (a rare disorder in which the body's immune system attacks nerve cells and leads to paralysis) (Tang et al., 2016; WHO, 2016c). The virus is spreading explosively throughout the Western hemisphere with cases confirmed in more than 60 countries (PAHO, 2016). WHO anticipates that up to 4 million people will become infected and, with large numbers of travelers in and out of the infectious regions, Zika virus could rapidly become a pandemic (Dhillon et al., 2016; WHO, 2016a).

Ebola Virus

The current epidemic of Ebola virus now affects multiple continents and has become the worst outbreak in history since its discovery in 1976 (IOM, 2014). Ebola virus causes a hemorrhagic fever that is severe and often fatal in humans; victims hemorrhage into their brain, kidneys, liver, and lungs (CDC, 2016). Generally speaking, Ebola virus is transmitted by close contact with infected bodily fluids (blood, saliva, stool, and urine), but there is an outside chance that it could spread by a direct sneeze or cough (WHO, 2016e). Except for a few dedicated scientific teams who worked with the virus in Sudan and Congo, the Ebola virus is a case of out of sight, out of mind, as it is a continent away and does not receive much media attention in the United States (Wharton, 2014b).

Contrary to the U.S. public's acceptance of limitations during the 1918 Spanish Flu pandemic, several American volunteers who worked in high-risk Ebola areas in West Africa in 2014—during the worst Ebola outbreak since the virus was first discovered four decades ago (CDC, 2016)—refused to be quarantined during their return to the United States. They maintained rapid diagnostic assessments was sufficient; even though the average time between contracting the Ebola infection and the start of symptoms is 8 to 10 days, symptoms can occur between 2 and 21 days (WHO, 2016e). This tendency to underestimate the personal risk of the Ebola threat relative to that of the general population was a serious misstep (Wharton, 2014b). If something bad had happened in 2014, the American volunteers would have been at fault.

Swine Influenza (Swine Flu)

The swine flu pandemic originated in Mexico in 2009 and ended a year later. Although the outbreak was brought under control, reports persist of **undocumented workers** from Mexico and Central America entering the United States carrying swine flu, a potentially fatal respiratory illness. As a result, there are controversies about measures to avoid reintroduction of this disease into the United States, as well as questions about whether to label the continued outbreaks of swine flu as a pandemic (Anomaly, 2014). While not all the facts about the presence of swine flu are available, three facts are noteworthy:

- Respiratory deaths are occurring in otherwise healthy adults versus children and those with compromised immune systems (individuals with HIV/AIDS or receiving chemotherapy).
- The current viral strain has mutated from pigs which are more susceptible to novel influenza viruses that are infectious and highly transmissible to other mammalian species as opposed to the feared mutation from the less threatening avian influenza.

- Viral infections appear at the end of normal flu seasons when the chance of the swine flu mutating into a strain easily transmittable to humans is at its highest.

(CDC, 2015c).

Avian Influenza (Avian Bird Flu)

Avian influenza is an infectious disease that has affected animals (usually birds, and less commonly pigs) for over 100 years. The avian viruses have pandemic potential because:

- They cause severe disease and death in humans
- They continue to circulate widely in some poultry populations
- Most humans likely have no immunity to them

(Lipman, 2015; WHO, 2014b).

Pigs are a common reservoir for emerging infectious diseases because they can be infected by both human and bird influenza viruses. The avian virus is particularly dangerous for domestic poultry. While transmission to humans is uncommon, there is cause for concern (Lipman, 2015). Because type A strains can infect both animals and humans, there is a possibility that a novel A strain will develop, either through mutation or the mixing of different viruses from different species. A pandemic is triggered when a novel influenza strain emerges in humans through recombination, or a major change in the virus's composition causing serious illness, and then has sustained transmission from person to person.

In mid-2003, the largest and most severe **avian flu** outbreak in history began in Hong Kong, resulting in widespread transmission to poultry and some documented transmission to humans. Type A influenza viruses are subtyped according to surface proteins. There are 16 different **H proteins** and nine different **N proteins**. All H and N proteins occur in birds. Human disease has traditionally been caused by three H subtypes (H1, H2, and H3). Recently, humans have become infected by three novel subtypes from birds (H5, H7, and H9). The fear is one of these subtypes will emerge as the next influenza pandemic. Transmission to humans is of particular concern because the virus mutates rapidly and may therefore quickly change into a highly infectious form for humans, therefore becoming highly contagious (Lipman, 2015).

Unlike the normal seasonal influenza virus, the avian viruses cause severe disease in humans, and are almost always fatal. Seasonal flu viruses are caused by strains of influenza already circulating in the human population.[LN5] People build up immunity either by having had prior contact with specific viruses or through vaccinations. A pandemic flu, however, is a global outbreak caused by new strains of the influenza virus and, as such, no immunity exists in the population, making every individual highly susceptible to infection and serious illness (CDC, 2014b).

Scientists disagree about the likelihood of an avian flu pandemic. Some public health officials view the data and believe a pandemic will not occur because the avian flu has been around since 1997 without causing serious harm. Other officials view the same data and believe the world is much closer to a pandemic.

While not all virus mutations lead to a pandemic, the more times recombination occurs, the more likely the necessary mutations will occur to cause sustained human-to-human transmission. There is an ongoing debate about where the tipping point is in the number of times recombination occurs that leads to a pandemic, and no one really knows the correct answer (HHS, 2014; Homeland Security, 2012). See **FEATURE BOX 33-2** for known facts about avian flu. Additional knowledge includes the following:

- Another pandemic is overdue based solely on the evolution of influenza viruses.
- Avian viruses mirror the 1918-1919 Spanish flu virus.
- No one knows the origins of SARS, caused by a mutation of the avian flu virus in 2003.

(Baskin & Richardson, 2013; WHO, 2015a; *See* Lee, 2004).

The pharmaceutical industry is engaged in making vaccines to combat the avian flu and are stockpiling global supplies for the World Health Organization, while the National Institutes of Health has ongoing clinical vaccine trials using new tissue-based technologies for quicker vaccine production. However, influenza viruses can rapidly become highly resistant, so available stockpiled vaccines may not always work (GAO, 2011b). Generally, vaccines cannot be produced until a virus has emerged in the population, when it is already too late for prevention (*E.g.*, Gable, 2012).

WHO implemented surveillance around the world in 1947 to detect prevalent and emerging types of the influenza virus, and this information is used annually in producing flu vaccines (*See generally* Kim, 2016). Some scientists suggest

Important Facts About the Avian Flu

- More than 200 million domestic and wild migratory birds in Asia, the Middle East, Europe, and Africa have died of the virus or been killed by authorities in an attempt to halt the virus' spread.
- More worrisome is that the disease in birds is out of control in more locations than ever, including places like the Nile Delta and Nigeria, where public health mechanisms are weak to nonexistent, increasing the chances of a mutation to allow bird-to-human and human-to-human transmission.
- Since 2003, fewer than 600 cases of people dying from avian flu have been laboratory confirmed.
- Since 2006, 80 countries on five continents have reported their first outbreaks of avian flu in birds.
- At least 1,100 people have confirmed avian flu infections.
- Young people with the strongest immune systems have been disproportionately affected by the disease.

Data from: Dawood, 2012; WHO, 2014; WHO, 2016b.

some of the flu medicines approved in the United States for seasonal human influenza should work in treating avian flu infections in humans. The avian viruses, however, are resistant to amantadine and rimantadine (Flumadine), two antiviral drugs commonly used for seasonal influenza. Oseltamivir (Tamiflu) might work to treat the avian virus, but additional studies must be conducted to confirm its effectiveness.

So far, few cases of transmission from one human to another have been documented. During the human seasonal flu outbreaks, the chances of the avian viruses mutating into a strain easily transmittable to humans increases. For a pandemic to occur, the avian viruses would have to mutate into a strain that could efficiently pass from person to person. In other words, to produce a pandemic, there must be efficient human-to-human transmission, and this has not happened yet (Hsu, 2015; WHO, 2007).

Lest anyone think this could not happen, it must be remembered that highly pathogenic influenza pandemics have occurred roughly two to three times per century. In addition, the prerequisites for a pandemic have already emerged during spread of the avian flu in Asia, including:

- Identification of a novel viral subtype in animal populations
- Sporadic human-to-human transmission
- Viral replication causing disease and death in humans

(Lechleiter, 2016; Michaud et al., 2013).

Most importantly, it should be realized that the 1918 influenza virus appears to have jumped directly from birds to humans; the genetic changes that allowed it to do so are already beginning to appear in the avian viruses. Some scientists claim avian influenza has already acquired five of the 10 genetic sequence changes associated with human-to-human transmission of the 1918 virus (CDC, 2008), while other scientists claim we simply do not know how many mutations are required to create pandemic strains (WHO, 2014b).

Cockfighting and the Spread of Avian Diseases

Spread of avian flu has been linked to live birds used for cockfighting (Logan, 2013a), a violent, high-stakes gambling activity where two gamecocks with razor-sharp pick implements strapped to their feet are entrapped in a ring to fight. Victorious gamecocks usually leave the ring with severe injuries, such as missing eyes, punctured lungs, and broken bones. Gamecock handlers often suck the blood out of their birds' wounds to alleviate the pain and pressure. This contact with the birds' blood and other bodily fluids puts the handlers at high risk for contracting avian flu and other infectious diseases. Spectators and children of gamecock handlers are also at risk of contracting the avian flu if sprayed with the gamecocks' blood during the matches or exposed afterward. A disproportionate number of children of gamecock handlers have already died from avian flu. The billion-dollar-a-year American cockfighting industry is a likely avenue for the disease to enter the United States (Pacelle, 2007). (*See generally*, Young, 2014).

Gamecocks are illegally transported long distances both within and across international borders. Cockfighting is only legal in Louisiana and New Mexico, but matches regularly occur in several other states. Bans on cockfighting are routinely disregarded worldwide because the penalties for violations are so weak. Moreover, cockfighting has previously brought devastating diseases into the United States. Recently, California declared a state of emergency when illegally transported gamecocks contaminated the state's poultry population. At the time, there were over 5,000 cockfight operators in Southern California alone. Consequently, the public health threat remains (Logan, 2013a).

Emergency Preparedness Plans

The possibility of a public health emergency, no matter how uncertain, has prompted the health care industry to think about how a pandemic could affect its operations. The key is to identify potential surprises (Wharton, 2006). For instance, major health care systems being called on to rapidly expand infrastructure capacity, or surge, beyond normal services to meet the increased demand for qualified personnel and health care, is a predictable consequence of a pandemic. They need to plan in the event suppliers refuse to deliver medical products or if health care professionals decline to report to work because they are too afraid to leave their own families (Rutkow et al., 2014).

Health Care Supply Chains

The **health care supply chain** is almost certain to break in the event of a pandemic, which could cause manufacturers of medical products to close, leading to shortages of drugs and medical supplies, including shortages of drugs to treat the victims of the pandemic. The very rules of capitalism, which make the United States an efficient marketplace, also make it exceptionally vulnerable in a pandemic (Hodge et al., 2015). For instance, many drugs are manufactured outside of the United States because of lower costs, while warehouses in the United States are generally kept nearly empty for efficiency reasons as well as the pharmaceutical industry's **just-in-time manufacturing** as a preferred production model. Many hospitals stock only 30-day supplies of drugs because of costs and waste associated with stockpiling more (Wysocki & Lueck, 2006). Most, if not all, of the medical products industry, including protective device firms in the United States, are operating almost at full capacity (Forlenza, 2013). Therefore, the reality is the health care supply chain operates with almost no **surge capacity** (Pasquale, 2014). If the nation is to meet surge requirements in the event of a pandemic, clearly, this supply chain issue must be addressed.

Global Supply Chains

The most affected parts of the economy are likely to be those with worldwide operations, global supply chains, and international customers (Lloyd's, 2008). Most large multinational corporations have emergency preparedness planning committees. Some have created task forces combining their strategic planning, human resources, and medical services departments to adopt event-specific measures in anticipation of a public health emergency. Others, particularly those in the food industry, have prepared marketing campaigns aimed at allaying fears about the use of their products, and thus protecting their brands if a pandemic should occur.

The federal government and some local and state governments have established emergency plans to curtail travel, close schools, quarantine individuals and communities, and ban public gatherings (Holloway et al., 2014). Such social distancing steps were taken during the SARS epidemic, especially where the disease was most prevalent (Hodge et al., 2015). Despite the high degree of uncertainty over the future course of any public health emergency, there is little choice but to plan.

Nearly everyone is myopic (Michel-Kerjan & Slovic, 2010). It is difficult to think about the future in the long run. People often lack foresight and have difficulty taking steps today where the benefits occur over a number of years (Wharton, 2014a). This means there is a need to rethink the *not in my term of office* philosophy and the resultant failure to maintain the nation's public health infrastructure at a standard that could cope with a pandemic. This conduct makes it more difficult to undertake long-range planning. For instance, most public health services exist at the state and local level, exactly where government is being hurt the most. Just when substantial numbers of public health officials are being laid off, they may be needed. In most pandemics, more people die from official ineptitude than from the pandemic infections (Gable, 2012; Opdycke, 2014).

Business Continuity Management

Planning for a public health emergency is just one component of **risk management**. The question should not be how to prepare for a pandemic alone, but how to take steps that could have planning benefits for any number of risks (Wharton, 2014b). The focus should be on how planning for a public health emergency can help on many different levels. This means planning for operations outside the silo structures of any one part of a health care system and taking a more comprehensive and sophisticated approach to management of risks. It also means planning for a number of risks that, when added together, appear very threatening, but in actuality are each driven by different factors. The chance of all hazards occurring at once, a perfect storm, would be small. Hence, it may be better not to hedge against all hazards all the time and focus instead on those high-impact risks that would be most catastrophic to the community being served.

While **silo thinking** (managing risks inside one's independent control) is hard to break on a day-to-day basis, this is how to think about planning for any public health emergency. For many regions of the United States, this is the only way to adequately prepare for a pandemic (IOM, 2014). Many hospitals are so overcrowded they can barely handle a multiple car crash, let alone mass admissions from a pandemic (Armour, 2015). These hospitals should prioritize pandemic preparedness efforts based on the type of events they are likely to face that threaten their jurisdiction, rather than relying on all-hazards programs that focus on response and recovery situations that necessitate a federal response.

National Biosurveillance Integration and Electronic Disease Surveillance Systems

Today, almost everyone is subject to public health surveillance for planning and management of infectious disease threats (Ramanathan et al., 2015). Like terrorism surveillance, the scope of government surveillance has significantly expanded beyond its contagious disease origins to include more than 60 infectious diseases (Kaiser, 2014). The federal government's National Strategy for Pandemic Influenza has given the Department of Homeland Security the task of developing a National Biosurveillance Integration System to integrate this data. The Centers for Disease Control and Prevention, however, has already developed the National Electronic Disease Surveillance System, intended to bring all kinds of reporting systems into one national integrated electronic database. It can be assumed that the United States is encouraging information sharing like Britain and Israel, while also ensuring competitive analysis of what the gathered intelligence really means (GHRF, 2016; White House, 2011).

Reactions of the Health Care Industry

The way in which the health care industry reacts to the possibility of a pandemic falls into two camps. Some providers spend little time and money on planning; they believe pandemic fears are misplaced, overhyped phenomena that waste billions in resources planning and preparing for nonevents (Kim, 2016). Other providers take a more holistic approach. They realize there is the possibility of a pandemic, and they look at phenomena in a way that allows them to leverage whatever it is they do for other types of public health emergencies (Zettler, 2015). These providers analyze a landscape of threats. They do not focus only on individual threats. Independent of any specific threat, the outcome of public health emergencies affects four areas:

- People
- Physical environments
- Relationships
- Technology and processing

(GAO, 2011a; GHRF, 2016).

If health care providers understand their current risks and the extent to which their current strategy will protect them, they can model other catastrophic threats (Kim, 2016). For instance, the **operating margins** of hospitals average only 3%. In a pandemic, these hospitals would be forced to close clinics, cancel surgeries, and defer most revenue-making

MANAGEMENT AND LAW ISSUES

6. How does the United States retain public health surveillance for the common good without sacrificing the value of individual privacy?

7.   What should the health care industry do if a pandemic strikes?

services to care for the volume of pandemic victims (Homeland Security, 2012). Without federal strategies in place, many hospitals might be forced to close due to lack of revenue (GAO, 2011a). The question is not whether a pandemic will occur, but when, and the extent of damages it will cause. Economically sound strategies must be in place for managing the risk and consequences of a pandemic to avoid unnecessary loss of lives and economic destruction in the affected regions.

Low-Probability, High-Impact Events

Health care providers who think about potential public health emergency scenarios will be better prepared for a pandemic because they have thought about the scenarios ahead of time. Yet, it is very difficult to get health care systems, hospitals, and the medical products industry to do this. Everyone conducts annual risk assessments to satisfy their auditors, but those risks are relatively routine, boilerplate topics, such as what would happen if the organization failed to keep pace with technology. Rarely do risk assessments go into low-probability events, even though these events can have a significant impact (Kim, 2016). The estimated impact of a low-probability, high-impact pandemic on the United States is outlined in **FEATURE BOX 33-3**.

If a vaccine is developed to prevent people from contracting the avian flu, several thorny issues would arise. It is quite likely that if there is a vaccine, it will not be perfectly protective (GAO, 2011b). It is obvious health professionals, rescue personnel, and so forth will be prioritized for receiving vaccinations. But among the general public, there could be hoarding and misallocations of vaccines (Homeland Security, 2012). To avoid this *I-am-going-to-grab-mine* phenomenon, it is important to put emergency preparedness plans in place (*See generally* Kim, 2016).

If a novel influenza virus does emerge, given modern travel patterns, it will likely spread even more rapidly before detection than it did in 1918. It may infect at least several hundred million, and probably more than a billion, people worldwide (Barry, 2005; Opdycke, 2014). The global impact a pandemic would likely have is outlined in **FEATURE BOX 33-4**. As for the effects on business, a pandemic would likely:

- Cause a reevaluation of risks as investors observed the responses of governments
- Cut the global labor forces to different degrees in different countries due to a rise in mortality and illness
- Increase the cost of doing business

(White House, 2011; *See* McKibbin, 2007).

FEATURE BOX 33-3

Estimated Impact of a High-Impact Pandemic on the United States

Based on the latest public health modeling for a very virulent virus with a very high mortality (like Ebola) from the U.S. Department of Homeland Security:

- About 43 million to 100 million people, or 15 to 35% of the U.S. population, would be infected.
- Approximately 89,000 to 207,000 would die.
- Between 314,000 and 733,000 Americans would be hospitalized.
- Health-related economic burden would be $71 billion to $166 billion.
- Outpatient health care would be needed to serve the needs of 18 million to 42 million Americans.

Data from: GAO, 2011a; Homeland Security, 2012; Levi et al., 2010.

FEATURE BOX 33-4

Global Impact of a Pandemic

Mild Pandemic (Similar in Scale to the 1968 Hong Kong Flu):

- Deaths of 1.4 million people worldwide
- Close to 0.8% of global GDP ($330 billion) in lost economic output globally

Ultra Pandemic (Worse than the 1918 Spanish Flu Catastrophe):

- Deaths of 142 million people worldwide
- GDP loss of $4.4 trillion or 12%
- Some national economies in the developing world could shrink by more than half

Data from: McKibbin, 2007; Michaud et al., 2013.

MANAGEMENT AND LAW ISSUES

8. While U.S. health care professionals and some members of the military seem to be likely candidates to be vaccinated in the event of a pandemic, who should receive the second round of vaccines?
9. Would it be better to prepare and stockpile a vaccine in advance than to try to organize provisions of a vaccine if a pandemic actually breaks out?
10. At what price should the United States be protected against a pandemic? How does the United States accomplish this in such a way that resource-limited nations and those who cannot afford to take protection can be assisted?
11. What new policy outcomes could mitigate the impact of a pandemic?

Integrating Pandemic Threats into Business Strategy

There are very few threats that can compare with infectious diseases in terms of their potential to result in catastrophic loss of life (GHRF, 2016). More than 300 infectious diseases have emerged or reemerged since the mid-1960s, and most epidemiologists expect that one of them will go on to cause a disruptive, deadly pandemic at some point in the next two generations (Shah, 2016). Yet, the biggest challenge presented by a pandemic is one of mobilizing the global community to act, and to act quickly, to help address infectious diseases worldwide. The U.S. health care industry, like almost everyone else, is myopic about threats from health emergencies outside its own back yard. Sufficient short-term returns are often required to justify the upfront costs of protection from a pandemic.

Decisions not to invest in risk-reducing measures in high-risk areas of the world are made because of a failure to understand the expected benefits from these actions. Benefits are likely to extend over many years following a pandemic, especially in the form of reduced impacts to countries' and the global economies. Expenditures to reduce or mitigate pandemic risks outside the United States are regularly justified by expecting to recoup economic and development investments within a two- or three-year period following an actual pandemic. There is also a tendency to procrastinate, waiting to make decisions on whether to incur the costs to prepare for a pandemic (Wharton, 2014b). Crying wolf has always been the enemy of managing pandemics, but if public health officials do not do it, when something bad happens, they will be even more at fault (Michel-Kerjan & Slovic, 2010).

The risk of a pandemic is global. One major feature of a global risk is that the United States cannot address a pandemic alone (Michaud et al., 2013). The world is now so interdependent; actions taken today 5,000 miles away affect the United States tomorrow. Conventional wisdom holds that one health care system or one hospital cannot have the capacity and expertise to manage pandemic risks alone. In an increasingly global, interdependent world, they currently have neither.

National Strategy for Pandemic Influenza

Would the political, social, and legal fabric holding society together be threatened at the height of a pandemic responsible for over 250,000 deaths per day for a year?

Yes. The congressional panel is asking whether it would have been better for the United States to have prepared and stockpiled **pandemic vaccines** and drugs in advance (as has been done in Europe for existing epidemics that have the potential to emerge as global pandemics) rather than to have organized provisions of a vaccine once a pandemic actually broke out. Investigations are also under way to determine why the United States and other developed economies did not help people in advance of a pandemic, which would have required public health subsidies to resource-limited nations for infrastructure development, as opposed to waiting until after the pandemic occurred when the world was forced to provide large amounts of global assistance to developing economies. Indeed, economic globalization has created an environment for the evolution and more rapid spread of new strains of contagious diseases, such as influenza.

— Adaptation of Exercise Cruickshank in New Zealand based on scenario data from the U.S. Department of Defense.

See New Zealand Ministry of Health, 2007 (discussing this scenario).

CHAPTER SUMMARY

- Even though no one is sure when, or if, a pandemic will strike, it is actually possible to predict in advance the effects it might have, and therefore to plan ahead in order to mitigate damage.
- Because a pandemic could infect a huge proportion of the population, the concerns go beyond just the number who fall ill or die; the concerns also include how society would continue to function if people were not available to operate mass transit, information technology systems, and manufacturing facilities, as well as how the global economy would recover from the damage.
- We cannot predict how the United States might be able to handle a modern pandemic, as it has been over 90 years since the United States had to implement quarantine or social distancing measures.
- Environmental, social, and economic problems, such as the shortage of public health care, create ideal conditions for infectious diseases to become pandemics.
- Tuberculosis, cholera, yellow fever, Rift Valley fever, Lassa fever, and SARS are recent examples of epidemics that have helped focus increased global attention on infectious diseases.
- Avian flu is perhaps the most pressing threat, as it easily mutates, is transmissible between humans and animals, is widespread, and is almost always fatal, even to young people with relatively strong immune systems.
- It is difficult to create vaccines because viruses can quickly become resistant and time is needed to manufacture the needed quantities, during which the virus continues spreading and mutating.
- One of the most important potential problems for the United States to address is its health care supply chain; the United States has little ability to surge production if necessary and does not have sufficient stockpiles.
- One reason for procrastinating on emergency preparedness is that it is difficult to justify spending large sums of money now for benefits that may never come later; however, the costs of the damage of a pandemic would likely far outweigh the costs to mitigate it in advance.
- Probably the most difficult thing to plan for in the event of a pandemic would be prioritizing who would receive limited vaccinations or treatments.
- The risk of a pandemic is global due to increased travel and countries' interdependence.

LAW NOTES

1. Following the September 11, 2001 attacks on the World Trade Center and Pentagon, federal and state authorities turned great attention to the nation's health emergency preparedness. Many of the laws passed after that day asserted greater influence by the federal government in matters that affect public health in emergency situations (CDC, 2014a). A pandemic, as a matter of national security, will now be subject to federal jurisdiction (Greene, 2015). Two model acts developed subsequent to the terrorist attacks, the Model State Emergency Health Powers Act (MSEHPA) and the Model State Public Health Act, include provisions that all states have now adopted, either in whole or in part, to deal with health emergency threats like a pandemic (Rutkow et al., 2014). Both acts deal with health emergency powers, such as compulsory medical examinations, vaccinations, treatments, and quarantines combined with surveillance and travel restrictions.

   Despite considerable health emergency planning following September 11, 2001, the devastation caused by Hurricanes Katrina and Sandy provided vivid lessons about the nation's deficiencies in emergency preparedness and business continuity management (Meyer et al., 2014). A pandemic is likely to produce far more serious disruptions, casualties, and deaths than Katrina and Sandy; only during a pandemic, efforts will be directed not to getting people out but to keeping people in. Much additional planning, forethought, and funding needs to be implemented before a pandemic outbreak hits the United States (GHRF, 2016). The immediate medical needs of Americans and adequate resources to both treat pandemic victims and return to normal operations after the pandemic crisis has passed must be secured. The underpinnings of this new theoretical framework are the focus of this chapter.

2. The SARS virus, which sparked a global panic, moved from its reservoir in horseshoe bats through raccoon dogs, ferret badgers, snakes, and palm civets, mutating along the way before it was eventually transmitted to humans (Shah, 2016).

3. Cholera is an extremely violent diarrheal disease that is endemic in over 47 countries in Africa and Asia (due to unsafe water and lack of sanitation). It can kill within hours from severe dehydration if untreated. The World Health Organization estimates that there are 1.4 to 1.5 million cases and 28,000 to 142,000 deaths every year (WHO, 2015c). Up to 80% of the cases can be treated in time with rehydration, but the remaining cases are fatal. Several vaccines are available where there are humanitarian crises, but there is a global shortage of cholera vaccine. (*See generally* Ali et al., 2012).

4. Lassa fever is an acute viral illness with 100,000 to 300,000 infections per year and approximately 5,000 deaths in West Africa; 10 to 15% of the hospitalizations in Sierra Leone and Liberia are with this disease (CDC, 2015a). Lassa fever has begun to migrate to other countries with infected rats carrying the virus. The second fever, Rift Valley fever, is transmitted by mosquitoes; severe symptoms appear in approximately 15% of the infected people, who experience hemorrhagic fever, encephalitis, and blindness (CDC, 2013b). Lastly, yellow fever is a viral hemorrhagic fever that affects the body's ability to regulate itself, resulting in damage to the blood vessels and the failure of multiple organs. Because there are no effective treatments for the fevers, there is concern about their use in bioterrorism, and only yellow fever has a vaccine (CDC, 2013c).

5. Seasonal flu symptoms in fall, winter, and spring are recognizable to most people. Fever, headache, sore throat, cough, muscle aches, and fatigue typically last anywhere from 24 hours to 7 days. Seasonal influenza is attributed to three virus types: influenza A, B, and C. The influenza A virus causes widespread serious infections and affects animals and humans alike, while milder illnesses are attributed to influenza types B and C. Because both virus types A and B go through antigenic drift, or constant but relatively slight mutations, it is difficult to control the illness from one flu season to the next. Additionally, influenza viruses are constructed of ribonucleic acid (RNA). This is significant because when an RNA virus replicates itself from inside a human cell, its copying mechanism makes numerous small mutations in genetic translation. These slight mutations are the reason last year's seasonal flu vaccines do not protect against this year's flu types (CDC, 2008, 2011b).

REFERENCES

Ali, M., et al. (2012). The global burden of cholera. *Bulletin of the World Health Organization, 90*(209), 18A.

Anomaly, J. (2014). What is an epidemic? Currents in contemporary bioethics. *Journal of Law, Medicine and Ethics, 42,* 389–391.

Armour, S. (2015). U.S. emergency-room visits keep climbing. People on Medicaid turn to hospital care when doctor access is limited, new survey suggests. *Wall Street Journal,* p. A1.

Barry, J. M. (2005). *The great influenza: The epic story of the deadliest plague in history.* New York, NY: Penguin Group-Random House.

Baskin, C. R., & Richardson, T. J. (2013). Dual use research policy implementation. *Saint Louis University Journal of Health Law and Policy, 7*, 59–80.

Bennett, J. E., et al. (2014). *Mandell, Douglas, and Bennett's principles and practice of infectious diseases* (8th ed.). Philadelphia, PA: Saunders-Elsevier.

BLS (Bureau of Labor Statistics). (2015). *Occupational outlook handbook.* Washington, DC: U.S. Department of Labor, BLS.

Bollinger, A. E. (2015). E-MERS-gency: An application and evaluation of the pandemic influenza preparedness framework to the outbreak of MERS-CoV. *Temple International and Comparative Law Journal, 29*, 1–24.

CBO (Congressional Budget Office). (2005). *A potential influenza pandemic: Possible macroeconomic effects and policy issues.* Washington, DC: CBO.

CDC (Centers for Disease Control and Prevention). (2016). *Ebola (Ebola virus disease).* Atlanta, GA: CDC, National Center for Emerging and Zoonotic Infectious Diseases.

___. (2015a). *Lassa fever.*

___. (2015b). *Yellow fever.*

___. (2015c). *Information on swine influenza/variant influenza viruses.*

___. (2014a). *U.S. commitment to the global health security agenda.*

___. (2014b). *CDC estimates of H1N1 influenza cases, hospitalizations and deaths in the United States.*

___. (2013a). *Remembering SARS: A deadly puzzle and the efforts to solve it.*

___. (2013b). *Rift valley fever (RVF).*

___. (2013c). *Viral hemorrhagic fevers.*

___. (2011a). *Ethical considerations for decision making regarding allocation of mechanical ventilators during a severe influenza pandemic or other public health emergency.*

___. (2011b). *How does seasonal flu differ from global pandemic flu?*

___. (2008). *Interim pre-pandemic planning guidance: Community strategy for pandemic influenza mitigation in the U.S., early, targeted, layered use of non-pharmaceutical interventions.*

Chan, M., Director-General of the World Health Organization. (2009, July 2). Keynote speech at a high-level meeting on influenza A (H1N1): Lessons Learned and Preparedness in Cancun, Quintana Roo, Mexico.

Choi, K. J. (2008). A journey of a thousand leagues: From quarantine to international health regulations and beyond. *University of Pennsylvania Journal of International Law, 29*, 989–1022.

Dawood, F., et al. (2012). Estimated global mortality associated with the first 12 months of 2009 pandemic influenza A H1N1 virus circulation: A modeling study. *Lancet Infectious Diseases, 12*, 687–695.

Dhillon, R. S., et al. (2016). To fight the Zika pandemic, learn from Ebola. *Harvard Business Review, 2*, 4.

Forlenza, V. A., Chairman of the Board, Chief Executive Officer and President, Becton, Dickinson and Company. (2013, February 15). Keynote at the Wharton Health Care Business Conference: Reshaping Healthcare, Emerging Trends Changing the Face of Our Industry, Philadelphia, PA.

Gable, L. (2012). Evading emergency: Strengthening emergency responses through integrated pluralistic governance. *Oregon Law Review, 91*, 375–456.

GAO (U.S. Government Accountability Office). (2011a). *Influenza pandemic: Lessons from the H1N1 pandemic should be incorporated into future planning.* Washington, DC: GAO.

___. (2011b). Influenza vaccine: Federal investments in alternative technologies and challenges to development and licensure.

GHRF (Commission on a Global Health Risk Framework for the Future). (2016). The neglected dimension of global security: *A Framework to Counter Infectious Disease Crises.* Washington, DC: National Academy of Medicine's GHRF.

Greene, J. T. (2015). Federal enforcement of mass involuntary quarantines: Toward a specialized standing rules for the use of force. *Harvard National Security Journal, 6*, 58–111.

HHS (U.S. Department of Health and Human Services). (2014). *Global health security agenda.* Washington, DC: HHS.

Hodge, Jr., J. G., et al. (2015). Efficacy in emergency legal preparedness underlying the 2014 Ebola outbreak. *Texas Wesleyan law Review, 2*, 353–381.

Holloway, R., et al. (2014). *Updated preparedness and response framework for influenza pandemics.* Washington, DC: U.S. Department of Health and Human Services.

Homeland Security (U.S. Department of Homeland Security). (2012). *Pandemic influenza preparedness, response, and recovery guide for critical infrastructure and key resources.* Washington, DC: Homeland Security.

Hsu, S.-L. (2015). Scale economies, scale externalities: Hog farming and the changing American agricultural industry. *Oregon Law Review, 94*, 23–65.

Huff, A. G., et al. (2015). How resilient is the United States' food system to pandemics? *Journal of Environmental Studies and Science, 5*, 337–347.

IOM (Institute of Medicine). (2014). *Research priorities to inform public health and medical practice for Ebola virus disease.* Washington, DC: National Academy of Sciences.

Jones, N. A., et al. (2011). Mental models: An interdisciplinary synthesis of theory and methods. *Ecology and Society, 16*(1), 45–60.

Kaiser Family Foundation. (2014). *The U.S. government and global emerging infectious disease preparedness and response.* Menlo Park, CA: Kaiser.

Kim, J. Y., President of the World Bank Group. (2016, January 24). Remarks at the panel discussion on The Global Agenda: The need for a new global response to pandemics at the World Economic Forum on Mastering the Fourth Industrial Revolution, Davos, Switzerland.

Lechleiter, J. C., Chairman, President and Chief Executive Officer, Eli Lilly and Company. (2016, February 19). Remarks on The Innovation Game: The Race Between Entrants and Incumbents at the 2016 Wharton Health Care Business Conference, Philadelphia, PA.

Lee, B. A. (2015). Emergency takings. *Michigan Law Review, 114*, 391–453.

Lee, J.-W. (2004, February). *Globalization and disease: The case of SARS.* Washington, DC: Brookings Institution.

Levi, J., et al. (2010). *Shortchanging America's health: A state-by-state look at how federal public health dollars are spent and key state health facts.* Washington, DC: Trust for America's Health and Princeton, NJ: Robert Wood Johnson Foundation.

Levinson, D. J. (2014). Incapacitating the state. *William and Mary Law Review, 56*, 181–225.

Lipman, R. (2015). Zoonotic diseases: Using environmental law to reduce the odds of a future epidemic. *Virginia Environmental Law Journal, 33*, 153–171.

Lloyd's Emerging Risks Team. (2008). *Pandemic: Potential insurance impacts.* London, England: Lloyd's.

Logan, T. E. (2013a). Deconstructing penning: A functional approach to prohibiting coyote and fox penning. *Whittier Law Review, 34*, 365–392.

___. (2013b). Dynamic simulation as an approach to understanding hurricane risk response: Insights from the *Stormview* lab. *Risk Analysis, 33*(8), 1532–1552.

Marcuse, E. K., Clinical Professor of Pediatrics and Epidemiology at the University of Washington School of Medicine, School of Public Health and Community Medicine and Associate Medical Director of Quality improvement at Seattle Children Hospital. (2005, March 17). Panel discussion on Exploring Increased Public Participation in Making Public Health Policy Decisions: The Case of Pandemic Influenza and Our Pending Decision About Who First to Vaccinate. American Epidemiological Society Annual Meeting, Baltimore, MD.

McKibbin, W. J. (2007). The global costs of an influenza pandemic. *The Milken Institute Review, 9*(3), 18–27.

Meyer, R. J., et al. (2014). The dynamics of hurricane risk perception: Real-time evidence from the 2012 Atlantic hurricane season. *Bulletin of the American Meteorological Society*, 1389–1404.

Michaud, J., et al. (2013). *The U.S. Department of Defense and Global Health: Infectious disease efforts.* Menlo Park, CA: Kaiser Family Foundation.

Michel-Kerjan, E., & Slovic, P. (2010). *The irrational economist: Making decisions in a dangerous world.* New York, NY: Public Affairs Press, The Perseus Books Group.

NACCHO (National Association of County and City Health Officials). (2015). *The changing public health landscape: Findings from the 2015 forces of change survey.* Washington, DC: NACCHO.

New Zealand Ministry of Health. (2007). *Report on exercise Cruickshank.* Wellington, New Zealand.

Opdycke, S. (2014). *The flu epidemic of 1918: America's experience in the global health crisis (critical moments in American history).* London, England: Routledge-Taylor and Francis Group.

Pacelle, W., President and Chief Executive Officer, Human Society of the United States. (2007, February 6). *Annual Fighting Prohibition Act of 2007, Hearing Before the U.S. Subcommittee on Crime, Terrorism, and Homeland Security,* 110th Congress. Washington, DC.

PAHO (Pan American Health Organization). (2016). *Zika epidemiological update: Zika virus incidence and trends.* Washington, DC: PAHO.

Pasquale, F. (2014). The hidden costs of health care cost-cutting: Toward a post-neoliberal health reform agenda. *Law and Contemporary Problems, 77,* 171–193.

Persad, G. (2015). The medical cost pandemic: Why limiting access to cost-effective treatments hurts the global poor. *Chicago Journal of International Law, 15,* 559–611.

Quammen, D. (2013). *Spillover: Animal infections and the next human pandemic.* New York, NY: W. W. Norton and Company.

Ramanathan, T., et al. (2015). Intersection of law, policy and prevention: The role of law in supporting secondary uses of electronic health information. *Journal of Law, Medicine and Ethics, 43,* 48–51.

Rothstein, M. A. (2015). From SARS to Ebola: Legal and ethical considerations for modern quarantine. *Indiana Health Law Review, 12,* 227–280.

Rutkow, L., et al. (2014). The public health workforce and willingness to respond to emergencies: A 50-state analysis of potentially influential laws. *Journal of Law, Medicine and Ethics, 42,* 64–70.

Schwarcz, D., & Schwarcz, S. L. (2014). Regulating systemic risk in insurance. *University of Chicago Law Review, 81,* 1569–1640.

Shah, S. (2016). *Pandemic: Tracking contagions, from cholera to Ebola and beyond.* New York, NY: Farrar, Straus and Giroux.

Shepperd, J. A., et al. (2013). Taking stock of unrealistic optimism. *Perspectives in Psychological Science, 8,* 395–411.

Sun, L. G., & Jones, A. (2013). Disaggregating disasters. *UCLA Law Review, 60,* 884–948.

Tang, H., et al. (2016). Zika virus infects human cortical neural progenitors and attenuates their growth. *Cell Stem Cell, 2,* 16.

TFAH (Trust for America's Health). (2015). *Outbreaks: Protecting Americans from infectious diseases.* Washington, DC: Trust for America's Health and Princeton, NJ: Robert Wood Johnson Foundation.

Tomaselli, P. M. (2013). Ethical implications of the commercial use of animals: Paving the way; Are half measures in animal factory farm legislation ethical? *South Texas Law Review, 54,* 513–534.

UNAIDS. (Joint United Nations Programme on HIV and AIDS). (2014). *Global statistics, fact sheet.* New York, NY: UNAIDS.

Wharton School of the University of Pennsylvania. (2014a). The faulty 'mental models' that lead to poor disaster preparation. *Knowledge@Wharton.*

____. (2014b). Weighing the risks in the Ebola battle.

____. (2013). U.S. health emergency response system: Good news and bad.

____. (2006). Avian flu: What to expect and how companies can prepare for it.

White House, The. (2011). Global health security fact sheet. Washington, DC: The White House Homeland Security Council.

WHO (World Health Organization). (2016a). *Zika outbreak: WHO's global emergency response plan.* Geneva, Switzerland: WHO.

____. (2016b). *Zika virus fact sheet.*

____. (2016c). *Zika virus, microcephaly and Guillain-Barré syndrome.*

____. (2016d). *Risk communication and community engagement for Zika virus prevention and control: A guidance and resource package for country offices for coordination, planning, key messages and actions.*

____. (2016e). *Managing zoonotic public health risks at the human–animal–ecosystem interface.*

____. (2015a). *Accelerating progress on HIV, tuberculosis, malaria, hepatitis and neglected tropical diseases. A new agenda for 2016–2030.*

____. (2015b). *Global tuberculosis report* (20th ed.).

____. (2015c). *Cholera fact sheet* (No. 107).

____. (2014a). *Infection prevention and control of epidemic and pandemic prone acute respiratory infections in health care.*

____. (2014b). *Avian influenza: Fact sheet.*

____. (2007). *Summary of the second WHO consultation on clinical aspects of human inflection with avian influenza: A (H5N1) virus.*

Wiley, L. F. (2014). Health law as social justice. *Cornell Journal of Law and Public Policy, 24,* 47–105.

Wysocki, B., & Lueck, S. (2006, January 12). Just-in-time inventories make U.S. vulnerable in a pandemic. Low stockpiles at hospitals boost efficiency but leave no extras for flu outbreak. *Wall Street Journal,* p. A1.

Young, K. M. (2014). Everyone knows the game: Legal consciousness in the Hawaiian cockfight. *Law and Society Review, 48,* 499–527.

Zettler, P. J. (2015). Toward coherent federal oversight of medicine. *San Diego Law Review, 52,* 427–499.

CHAPTER 34

Women's Reproductive Rights[1]

"If access to health care is considered a human right, who is considered human enough to have that right?"

— **Dr. Paul Farmer**, Professor of Social Medicine in the Department of Global Health and Social Medicine at Harvard Medical School and Founding Director of Partners in Health

IN BRIEF

This chapter focuses on the disparate provision of health care surrounding procreation concerns. Reproductive issues are addressed against the backdrop of how the newer forms of contraception and maternity care coverage are falling out of reach for more women in the United States. While abortion is emphasized with a focus on state regulations that attempt to limit access, this chapter will also concentrate on related sexual privacy issues such as conscience clause legislation and emergency contraception.

Although gender disparities affecting health care are a major problem in the United States, the economics of this disparity have not received much attention. Only recently has the health care industry discovered that the same diseases and illnesses have different effects or symptoms in women. Adding to these concerns, prescription drugs often work differently for women (or not at all, or may even be harmful), and yet the pharmaceutical industry has not studied this aspect of most products currently on the market. For too long, it has been assumed that what goes for men also goes for women, and this basic assumption is now being called into question.

LEARNING OBJECTIVES

Upon completion of this chapter readers should be able to:

1. Describe some of the attempts being made to restrict women's civil rights.
2. List major health risks that are unique to women.
3. Quote general statistics demonstrating the poor state of reproductive care in the United States.
4. Outline the controversies over birth control and abortion that have been raging in the United States for more than 50 years.
5. Discuss issues related to insurance coverage of contraceptives.
6. Detail the gaps in women's insurance coverage for maternity care.
7. Distinguish among wrongful birth, wrongful pregnancy, and wrongful life causes of action together with the major issues surrounding each.
8. Explain the history of legalized abortion in the United States and the continuing efforts to limit it.
9. Show how the burden of sexually transmitted infections falls more on women than men.
10. Explain why failing to prioritize women's health needs increases the overall cost of health care.

---

[1]Contributor: Emma Hopkins, student at Vanderbilt University; research intern with the National Institute on Health Care Management and the Law.

KEY TERMS

Abortifacient
Abortion
Acquired Immunodeficiency
    Syndrome
Advisory Committee on
    Immunization Practices
Antidiscrimination
Birth control
Bubble zones
Buffer zones
Cases of first impression
Civil Rights Act of 1964
Clinical trial
Closely held corporations
Compelling government interest
Conception
Conscience legislation
Contraception
Corporate conscience exemptions
Cost-sharing
Dilation and evacuation abortions
Drug registries
Due process
Embryos
Emergency contraceptives
Exercise of religion
Family planning
Fertilization
Fetus
Fifth Amendment

First Amendment
Formulary
Free Exercise Clause
Gender-based discrimination
Gender disparities
Genital herpes
Gestation
Gonorrhea
Health exception
Health risks
Human immunodeficiency virus
Human papillomavirus
Implantation
In vitro
In vitro fertilization
Infant mortality
Informed consent
Institutional review boards
Intact dilation and extraction
Judicial bypass
Large fraction test
Least restrictive means
Maternity coverage
Off-label use
Over-the-counter
Parental consent laws
Partial-Birth Abortion Ban Act of 2003
Patch
Per se requirement
Personal autonomy

Personal liberty
Pharmacist refusals
Pre-embryos
Pregnancy
Pregnancy Discrimination Act of 1978
Prematurity
Preterm
Previability
Privacy rights
Procreative liberty
Public health practices
Rational basis
Religious affiliations
Religious employers
Religious Freedom Restoration Act
    of 1993
Religious liberty
Sexually transmitted infections
Schaff protocol
Sidewalk counselors
Single petition rule
Standards for care
Strict scrutiny
Syphilis
Title VII
Vaginal ring
Viability
Wrongful birth
Wrongful life
Wrongful pregnancy

FACT OR FICTION

In Vitro Fertilization

Does Congress or do state legislatures have the right to decide what to do with embryos created through in vitro fertilization?

The Georgia, Louisiana, and North Dakota legislatures have introduced legislation that would make illegal the **fertilization** procedures used in the high-profile case of a California woman who gave birth to octuplets, the second full set to be born alive in the United States (Will, 2013). The state legislation was introduced in the wake of the case of Nadya Suleman (also known as Octomom); a 33-year-old unemployed single woman who gave birth to eight babies through **in vitro** fertilization and who at the time was already caring for six children.

Nadya had six frozen human **embryos** left from prior in vitro treatments at a clinic in Beverly Hills and asked that they all be implanted because she did not want them to be destroyed (Calandrillo & Deliganis, 2015). Two of the embryos twinned and thus eight babies were born. All 14 of Nadya's children, including the octuplets, were born following **in vitro fertilization**.

To make embryos, a physician injects a woman with hormones to produce eggs. These eggs are then harvested in a surgical procedure. The eggs are mixed with sperm in the laboratory and some of the developing embryos are transferred into the uterus. A single cycle of in vitro fertilization with fresh embryos costs more than $15,000 and is often not covered by health insurance. Subsequent attempts at **pregnancy** are less costly if frozen embryos are on hand, and the supply of extras spares a woman another round of hormones to produce eggs. About half the women who undergo in vitro fertilization end up with one or more frozen embryos since no one can predict how many human embryos will be produced or used in any one round of in vitro fertilization (*See* Strasser, 2014).

The Georgia, Louisiana, and North Dakota laws would generally limit the number of embryos that may be implanted in a woman to a maximum of three for a woman age 40 or older and two for a woman younger than that. The state laws would also limit the number of embryos created in one round of in vitro fertilization to the number to be transferred. Supporters of the legislation oppose **abortion** and seek regulation that would treat embryos as human beings. To supporters, this is a rights issue. Embryos deserve legal protection as living human beings rather than as property. The state laws specifically prohibit the intentional destruction of **pre-embryos** (the human organism in the first 14 days after fertilization before **implantation** in the uterus) for any purpose.

Several in vitro fertilization experts and scientific organizations oppose the state laws. They argue that a successful pregnancy sometimes can only be achieved by implanting more than two or three embryos, and that the laws would effectively prevent would-be mothers from freezing unused embryos for later implantation. Opponents of the state laws maintain that it is the right of the women who have gone through in vitro fertilization to decide what they can do with those embryos, not their physicians and not the government.

— *See* Law Fact at the end of this chapter for the answer.

Principles and Applications

Women's health is jeopardized by **gender-based discrimination** when:

- Their reproductive rights are under concerted attack
- They have limited access to health care
- Their health needs are often overlooked

(NWLC, 2016; Siegel, 2013).

Still facing gender discrimination, the battle to expand or at least maintain the rights women have won since passage of the federal **Civil Rights Act of 1964** has shifted (*See* 42 U.S.C.A. § 2000e *et seq.*). Today, the fight is against attempts to carve-out exceptions to women's rights.

In this chapter, 14 health law **cases of first impression** are presented. There was no prior binding legal authority existing on the matters reviewed by the highest state courts or the federal U.S. Circuit Courts of Appeal in these 14 court decisions. This is more appellate litigation than any other chapter in this text. Most of the increased litigation pressure and most of these appellate cases affecting women's health have involved disputes over attempts to restrict, as opposed to expand, application of **antidiscrimination** laws and the rights of women to health care. During the last three decades, the U.S. Supreme Court has played a crucial role in prohibiting discrimination against women and in protecting women's health, safety, and welfare. Nevertheless, the legal rights that some have come to take for granted are not secure (Siegel, 2013).

Health Risks of Women and Children

Women's **health risks** involve health conditions where the intervention or care might be different than they would be for men (in biologically based as opposed to gender-based contexts). It also includes conditions:

- For which the risk factors might be different in women (HIV/AIDS and heart disease)
- That are more prevalent in women (lupus and other auto-immune disorders)
- That are more serious in women (consequences of sexually transmitted diseases)
- Unique to women (pregnancy and ovarian cancer)

(Heinzerling, 2014; Mendelson, 2010).

More must be learned about the distinctions between men and women: when they exist and do not exist, and where there are material differences and similarities. This knowledge will then help drive more appropriate treatment interventions and medical care.

Infant Mortality

Infant mortality (death of children less than one year of age) is one of the most important indicators of the health of a nation, as it is associated with a variety of factors:

- Maternal health
- **Public health practices**
- Quality of and ability to access health care
- Socioeconomic conditions

(Teufel et al., 2015).

There are more than 23,000 infant deaths each year in the United States (NCHS, 2015). The U.S. rate of infant mortality and morbidity is high compared to other industrialized countries, and research indicates that these rates result because babies are born prematurely due to lack of proper prenatal care (Gregory et al., 2014). Each year in the United States, more than half a million infants (or one in eight) are **preterm**, at less than 37 weeks' **gestation**, due to unintended pregnancies and consequent lack of prenatal care (Callaghan, 2010). Fifty-five nations have lower infant mortality rates than the United States, including virtually all European countries and Japan (CIA, 2013).

Premature Births

This high rate of premature births in the United States constitutes a public health concern that costs society in excess of $26 billion a year (Wisanskoonwong et al., 2011). It costs employers, on average, about $4,400 to provide health care to infants who are carried to term, compared to $54,100 for preterm babies (Gandhi, 2016). Prolonging pregnancy by weeks or even days can dramatically affect both health and cost. Moreover, the health consequences of prematurity can include:

- Cerebral palsy
- Chronic illnesses, such as lung disease
- Intellectual impairments and autism
- Intracranial hemorrhage
- Physical and neurodevelopment disabilities
- Respiratory distress syndrome

(Angela et al., 2014; Guttmacher, 2015a; West, 2016).

Reproductive Health

The state of reproductive health in the United States is poor. The needs of women are not being met. Examples of this include:

- Each year more than 750,000 teens become pregnant; the teen pregnancy rates are higher in the United States than any other developed country in the world, yet over the past decade, more than $1 billion has been spent by the federal government on abstinence programs as opposed to comprehensive sex education programs.
- Many women still lack adequate access to the most effective forms of birth control and family planning methods for their circumstances and medical needs, especially women from low-income families.
- Nearly half of all pregnancies are unintended, and nearly 40% of all unintended pregnancies end in abortion.
- One in three sexually active adolescent girls becomes pregnant before 20 years of age, and over 80% of these pregnancies are unintended.
- Women at the bottom of the economic pyramid are five times more likely to have an unintended pregnancy than more affluent women.

(Bader et al., 2014; Finer & Zolna, 2016; Kaiser, 2014).

Emergency Contraception

Infant mortality and **prematurity** are clearly associated with unintended pregnancies (Gregory et al., 2014). Yet, unintended pregnancies are disassociated from unprotected sexual intercourse; there is a general denial of any connection of a resulting pregnancy with the lack of contraception (Siegel, 2013). Given this distancing of the association between contraception and pregnancy, broad cultural and religious disagreements over sexual morality surround the issues of **emergency contraceptives** (also known as morning-after pills) and family planning (Deboer, 2015). The decade-long recalcitrance of the U.S. Food and Drug Administration (FDA) to switch emergency contraception to over-the-counter status for all women is the latest instance of this contraceptive-pregnancy disassociation. The delay in restricting access to emergency contraceptives provides a framework of what challenges to unpopular agency regulations may entail in the future when morality and religion collide with reproductive rights.

Contraceptive Approval

One in 10 American women has used emergency contraceptives. A concentrated dose of a hormone found in many regular birth control pills, it can prevent pregnancy when taken shortly after unprotected sexual intercourse (most effectively, within 12 to 20 hours, but up to 72 hours later) (NCHS, 2013; Trussell et al., 2016). Emergency contraceptives are estimated to be 81 to 90% effective at preventing pregnancy and were first approved as a form of **contraception** for women in 1999 (Mac Dougall, 2015).

Age Restrictions Imposed

In 2006, the FDA announced it wanted more time to review the safety of emergency contraceptives, despite support for over-the-counter sales by the FDA's scientific experts (Winters, 2015). Opponents of over-the counter sales argued that teenagers are not able to make rational decisions about their reproductive health. Claims were made that expanded access jeopardized teens' health and the ability of parents to care for their daughters' physical and emotional well-being (Case, 2015).

   Over-the-counter use for women over 18 years of age was finally approved, but women younger than 18 still had to obtain a physician's prescription in order to receive emergency contraceptives, except in states that allowed otherwise. In these states, all women (including teens) could obtain emergency contraceptives directly from a pharmacist under a state-approved protocol without obtaining a prescription in advance from a physician (Hrobak & Wilson, 2014). Nine states allowed pharmacists to dispense emergency contraceptives in collaboration with a prescriber: Alaska, California, Hawaii, Maine, Massachusetts, New Hampshire, New Mexico, Vermont, and Washington (Fischer & Kasper, 2014).

Age Restrictions Lifted

Then in 2009, the FDA was directed to allow sales of emergency contraceptives to all women without a prescription, rolling back the age limit imposed in 2006. The federal court ruling came in response to a lawsuit filed in 2005 by the Center for Reproductive Rights, a women's health advocacy group. *See Tummino v. Torti*, 603 F.Supp.2d 519 (U.S. District Court for the Eastern District of New York 2009), *reconsideration denied*, 260 F.R.D. 27 (U.S. District Court for the Eastern District of New York 2009). The court criticized current and former FDA officials for using "political considerations, delays and implausible justifications" to hold up nonprescription sales of emergency contraceptives for several years.

Pharmacists' Conscience Legislation

As Americans increasingly integrate religion into their daily lives, **conscience legislation** is proliferating and influencing the conduct of health care professionals across the United States (Del Negro & Aronson, 2015). *See McCreary County v. ACLU*, 545 U.S. 844, 882 (U.S. Supreme Court 2005) (O'Connor, J., concurring) ("*Americans attend their places of worship more often than do citizens of other developed nations, and describe religion as playing an especially important role in their lives*" (citations omitted)). Pharmacists are one of the latest groups to seek conscience protection. Whether the *Tummino* trial court decision mandating over-the-counter sales of emergency contraceptives puts an end to the controversy as to whether women's need to obtain emergency contraceptives on a timely basis outweighs the purported rights of pharmacists licensed by the states remains to be seen. Most likely, it will result in further federal-state conflicts between the FDA and the states. Some pharmacists, whose religious beliefs prohibit the use of birth control for family planning, claim that dispensing emergency contraceptives to women is an infringement on their free exercise of religion since they view emergency contraception as a form of abortion (Sepper, 2015b).

Pharmacist refusals began when the FDA approved emergency contraceptives in 1999 and intensified in 2006 after proponents for restrictions lost their battle against over-the-counter access. These refusals have occurred, regardless of state law and firm policy, at outlets of large drugstore chains, such as Walgreens, Osco, K-Mart, CVS, and Eckerd, as well as at small, independent pharmacies (Drobac & Wesley, 2014).

State laws restricting prescription access to emergency contraceptives include:

- 12 states where pharmacists are expressly allowed to refuse to fill prescriptions that violate their beliefs, including emergency contraceptives (Arizona, Arkansas, Colorado, Florida, Georgia, Idaho, Illinois, Kansas, Maine, Mississippi, South Dakota, and Tennessee).
- Arizona, Arkansas, Georgia, Idaho, Missouri, and South Dakota, where existing laws have been strengthened so pharmacists can refuse to transfer or refer prescriptions for contraceptives, including emergency contraceptives to other pharmacies.
- Arkansas and North Carolina, where emergency contraceptives can be excluded from the federal contraceptive coverage mandate.
- At least 11 states where conscience clauses or laws that would permit pharmacists to refuse to fill certain prescriptions are currently under consideration.

(Guttmacher Institute, 2016b, 2016c; NWLC, 2015a, 2015b).

Opponents object to conscience laws because they say that pharmacists have an obligation to fill all prescriptions and that refusing to fill them violates women's freedom of conscience (Drobac & Wesley, 2014). While state laws generally mandate that pharmacists dispense all safe, legal prescriptions and put the best interests of their customers ahead of their own (Sepper, 2015a), California, Illinois, New Jersey, Washington, and Wisconsin are the only states that require pharmacies to fill all prescriptions (Guttmacher Institute, 2016a).

Constitutional Arguments

The **Free Exercise Clause** of the **First Amendment** protects an absolute freedom of belief and an individual right to practice religion. One side of the pharmacist debate maintains that their religion prohibits the use of birth control for family planning or the practice of abortion, and therefore they cannot freely exercise their religious beliefs if they are forced to dispense emergency contraceptives. Since the First Amendment protects individual free exercise of religion, pharmacists claim they have a right to exercise their religion in the workplace (Drobac & Wesley, 2014). *See Cutter v. Wilkinson*, 544 U.S. 709, 719 (U.S. Supreme Court 2005) (defining free exercise of religion as government respect for and noninterference with citizens' religious beliefs and practices).

The other side argues that since pharmacists are not required to take the drugs themselves, there is no free exercise issue. In addition to the First Amendment arguments, the **Fifth Amendment** is used in the debate for and against conscience legislation. The Fifth Amendment protects property, and the prescription is the woman's property. The Fifth Amendment prohibits deprivation of **personal liberty** without **due process**. Opponents of conscience laws maintain that passing laws to allow individual pharmacists to refuse to refill prescriptions that offend their personal morals deprives women of their liberty without due process (Sepper, 2015a).

MANAGEMENT AND LAW ISSUES

1. Should pharmacists who refuse to fill prescriptions for contraceptives or emergency contraceptives also refuse to fill prescriptions for Viagra or other male sexual enhancement drugs?
2. What considerations underlie the conflict between the rights of health care professionals to not provide certain health care services to women, such as filling of contraceptive prescriptions, and the rights of women to receive these legal medical services?
3. How are Congress, state legislatures, and the courts dealing with competing interests involving the sale of emergency contraceptives?
4. Should the federal government and states consider conscience clause legislation to balance competing interests for health care services to women? Is this the way this conflict should be resolved, and, if so, will it not result in denial of needed health care for women?

Medical Coverage for Contraceptives

Having won the right to health insurance coverage for birth control and family planning for the most part under the Affordable Care Act, the debate has shifted to attempts to carve out exceptions to the mandate that health insurance plans must provide medical coverage for contraceptives. Health insurance plans and employers continue to face increased litigation pressure as new legal theories based on the application of antidiscrimination laws continue to be unleashed. One consequence of this ongoing litigation is that many health insurers are failing to comply with the Affordable Care Act's contraceptive coverage requirements (NWLC, 2015a, 2015c).

Mandated Pelvic Exams as a Condition of Access to Contraceptives

Federally funded family planning programs require women to undergo pelvic exams as a condition of access to oral contraceptives and sometimes other hormonal methods of birth control and family planning (*See* Title X (42 U.S.C.A. §§ 300 *et seq.* and 42 C.F.R. Part 59); Title XIX, Medicaid (42 U.S.C.A. § 1396); and block grants under Titles V (42 U.S.C.A. §§ 701-709) and XX (42 U.S.C.A. § 1397)). There is vigorous debate on whether this invasive procedure infringes upon women's bodily **privacy rights**, especially since women seeking the same birth control from private providers are not subject to this mandate. Moreover, men seeking contraception or sexual-performance-enhancing drugs from federally funded health clinics are not required to undergo invasive prostate exams, despite presenting the same opportunity for preventive health care as women seeking oral contraceptives (Richters, 2013).

In areas of health care services other than women's reproductive care, it is not appropriate to withhold a prescription from someone who has been informed of the risks involved and chooses to forgo screening for an unrelated condition. Yet for the past 50 years, annual pelvic exams have been required of women seeking birth control at health clinics receiving federal funding, which incidentally are not required to screen for contraindications to the pill. The justification for the government mandate is the FDA-approved package inserts accompanying oral contraceptives that recommend pelvic exams if women are using the pill (Mac Dougall, 2015). Interestingly, oral contraceptives are dispensed over the counter without a prescription in Europe, Asia, South America, and much of the rest of the world (Grindlay et al., 2013).

Exclusion of Contraception Coverage Before the Affordable Care Act

Before the passage of the Affordable Care Act, the Equal Employment Opportunity Commission and several federal courts had indicated that denying contraceptive coverage in a comprehensive employer insurance plan discriminates against female employees in violation of **Title VII** of the Civil Rights Act (*See* 42 U.S.C.A. § 2000e *et seq.*) Some states with mandated contraception coverage included exemptions for firms with **religious affiliations** that were opposed to **birth control** (commonly referred to as family planning by physicians and public health officials). These exempted firms were not required to contribute additional taxes or assessments to state health and welfare funds due to the additional social and economic costs that states incur from unwanted or unplanned pregnancies arising from women's lack of access to contraceptives. With the *Standridge* decision, the U.S. Supreme Court left consideration of the social consequences of unplanned pregnancies on women, children, and society for discussion by Congress and the state legislatures (Siegel, 2013).

COURT DECISION
Exclusion of Contraception Coverage

Standridge v. Union Pacific Railroad Company
[Employee v. Employer]
479 F.3d 936 (U.S. Court of Appeals for the Eighth Circuit 2007)

Facts: Union Pacific Railroad Company provided health insurance to its employees through several differ-ent health insurance plans. These plans provided medical coverage for services such as routine physician visits, tetanus shots, and drug and alcohol addiction treatments. The plans excluded, for men and women, prescription and nonprescription contraception unless the contraception was medically necessary for a non-contraceptive purpose, such as treating skin problems. Two female Union Pacific employees, Brandi Standridge and Kenya Phillips, brought suit against Union Pacific for gender discrimination under the federal Civil Rights Act. Standridge and Phillips claimed Union Pacific discriminated against its female employees by failing to cover prescription contraception.

Title VII provides that employers cannot discriminate against any person regarding their compensation, terms, conditions, or privileges of employment because of their gender (*See* 42 U.S.C.A. § 2000e-2(a)(1)). After the U.S. Supreme Court held that denial of pregnancy benefits did not violate Title VII (*General Electric Company v. Gilbert*, 429 U.S. 125 (U.S. Supreme Court 1976), *superseded by statute*), Congress enacted the **Pregnancy Discrimination Act of 1978** that mandates that women affected by pregnancy, childbirth, or related health conditions must be treated the same, including receipt of health insurance plan benefits (*See* 42 U.S.C.A. § 2000e(k)).

Issue: May employers exclude contraception coverage from their health insurance plans?

Holding and Decision: Yes. Employers may exclude all types of contraception coverage (whether prescription, nonprescription, or surgical, and whether for men or women) from their health insurance plans.

Analysis: The court distinguished between preventing **conception** and health conditions that occur only after conception. Applying this distinction, the court held the Pregnancy Discrimination Act does not apply to contraception because contraception is a treatment used prior to pregnancy. Moreover, since contraception is a gender-neutral term that applies to men and women equally, health insurance plans that deny medical coverage for contraception do not violate Title VII.

The court also considered whether the health insurance plan discriminated on the basis of gender. Under a claim of disparate treatment under Title VII, female employees have to establish they were treated less favorably than similarly situated male employees. If pregnancy is considered a medical disease that only adversely affects women, then the issue is whether the medical coverage provided to male employees poses a lesser threat to employees' health than pregnancy does. The court declined to decide whether pregnancy was a disease. Instead, the court held that the comparative of medical coverage between female and male employees provided by the health plan was too broad. The proper comparative was the medical benefit of contraception. Because the health plan did not cover men's contraception (condoms and vasectomies), the court held the plan did not treat men more favorably than women. Thus, the denial of contraception coverage did not discriminate against women.

Rule of Law: Since the Pregnancy Discrimination Act does not require employers to cover contraception as part of their health insurance plans, employers do not violate federal civil rights law by excluding contraception as a benefit.

References discussing this court decision: *E.g.*, Hale, 2015; Hill, 2012; Jordan, 2015; Melling, 2015; Melone, 2015; Morse, 2013; Norris & Turk, 2013; Oleske, 2014; Rudary, 2013; Rutledge, 2014; Sepper, 2015a; Siegel, 2013.

Union Pacific did not drop medical coverage for prescription contraception for non-contraceptive purposes, despite the *Standridge* ruling; the company simply removed any prescription restrictions. While *Standridge* allowed employers to drop medical coverage for prescription contraception, the ruling did not have such an effect for a number of reasons:

- Contraceptive coverage had become standard practice for most employers
- It is less costly for employers to cover prescription contraceptives than to cover a pregnancy
- Most states already had mandated contraception coverage in health insurance plans acquired from commercial insurers

(Rutledge, 2014; Sepper, 2015a).

Exceptions for Religious Employers

More and more, religious restrictions are limiting women's access to reproductive health care (Sepper, 2015a). This has become a divisive issue for many states where women are still treated as inferior to men (*See* Ziegler, 2015). Today, some **religious employers** claim that their religious convictions forbid them from subsidizing health insurance through which their employees might commit a moral wrong by using contraception for family planning (Sepinwall, 2014).

Corporate Conscience Exemptions

Hobby Lobby is the first case to recognize that corporations have rights of religious freedom (Sepinwall, 2015 and 2014). Many believe this U.S. Supreme Court decision opens the courtroom door to corporations and hands them the weapon of "corporate conscience" to fight off regulations that protect the full and equal rights of women (Sepper, 2015b). Although the Court emphasized that its decision applied only to **closely held corporations** (those with only a very few shareholders, such as family-owned corporations), these for-profit corporations, such as the J.W. Marriott Corporation, Cargill, and Koch Industries, employ thousands of employees; these are in addition to all the small and medium-size enterprises that tend not to be publicly traded (Wharton, 2015).

The worry is that *Hobby Lobby* is not just going to be about employers who object to contraception but also about employers who object to other kinds of medical treatments. There is similar fear that corporate conscience exemptions are going to extend beyond health insurance to other kinds of benefits and employment practices (Sepinwall, 2015). For instance, Congress and state legislatures across the country are considering legislation to permit employers to fire women if they have had abortions (Fram, 2015). The question is: What future burdens are women going to be made to bear with this corporate conscience exemption?

COURT DECISION
Health Insurance Exemption for Contraceptives

Burwell v. Hobby Lobby Stores, Inc.
[Federal Government v. For-Profit Closely Held Corporation]
134 S.Ct. 2751 (U.S. Supreme Court 2014);
followed by Holt v. Hobbs, 135 S.Ct. 853 (U.S. Supreme Court 2015)

Facts: Hobby Lobby, a for-profit chain of arts-and-crafts stores and Christian bookstores, has corporate policies and practices that reflect its owners' evangelical Christian faith. The chain provided group health insurance plans to its employees, including medical coverage for most contraceptives, but sought to exclude medical coverage for certain contraceptives, which they believe work as **abortifacients** (causing an abortion). Hobby Lobby objected to two kinds of emergency contraceptives and two kinds of intrauterine devices, all of which can prevent the development of fertilized eggs, but can also prevent an egg from ever being fertilized in the first place. The Affordable Care Act compels employers who provide group health plans to cover all 20 FDA-approved contraceptives at no cost to women. Hobby Lobby opposes, based upon moral grounds, four contraceptives that can interfere with a fertilized egg attaching (implanting) in the uterus, which is essential for a viable pregnancy.

Corporations that qualify as religious employers are exempt from the medical coverage mandate altogether; not-for-profit religious institutions (such as religiously affiliated charities, hospitals, and universities), though exempt from providing insurance that includes contraception, must provide medical coverage for contraception that comes directly from insurance firms. This assures that free preventive care includes access to contraceptive care, while not-for-profit organizations with religious objections do not have to provide these services directly or to pay for them. No such provisions existed for for-profit enterprises prior to this decision.

Issue: Should closely held for-profit corporations who provide health insurance coverage for contraception be required to provide contraceptives that violate the sincerely held religious beliefs of the firms' owners?

Holding and Decision: No. Closely held corporations are not required to fund all approved forms of contraception mandated by the Affordable Care Act.

Analysis: This decision breaks new ground and allows closely held for-profit corporations to avoid complying with laws based on the religious beliefs of their owners. The Court held that the federal government cannot take any action that substantially burdens the **exercise of religion** unless it constitutes the least restrictive means of serving a compelling government interest. The Court rejected the argument that the owners of firms forfeit all protections under the **Religious Freedom Restoration Act of 1993** when they organize their businesses as for-profit corporations (*See* 42 U.S.C.A. §§ 2000bb *et seq.*). The Court concluded that the challenged federal regulations substantially burdened the exercise of religion because compliance was contrary to the owners' religious objections to what they perceived to be abortion and there was a heavy financial penalty for noncompliance. Assuming that the regulations served a **compelling government interest**, the Court found that they were not the **least restrictive means** of serving that interest because there were other ways to ensure that women had cost-free access to contraceptives.

Rule of Law: Closely held for-profit corporations, like individuals, have the right to free exercise of religion.

References discussing this court decision: *E.g.*, Corbin, 2015; Deboer, 2015; Duke, 2015; Greendorfer, 2015; Griffin, 2015; Hale, 2015; Hansen & Newman, 2015; Johnsen, 2015; Melone, 2015; New, 2015; Oleske, 2014; Oman, 2015; Sawyer, 2015; Taub, 2015.

Protection of Religious Liberty

The federal requirement already contained a work-around so that Hobby Lobby did not have to subsidize all FDA-approved contraceptives, and women would not have to pay out of pocket to get contraception. With this compromise, women do not have to bear the costs of their employer's religious observance. The federal government continues to update its stance on the contraceptive mandate in response to **corporate conscience exemptions** and **religious liberty** objections, expanding exceptions to encompass not-for-profit organizations like Wheaton College and Belmont Abbey College.

COURT DECISION
Contraceptive Coverage Mandate

Wheaton College v. Sebelius
2013 U.S.App.LEXIS 23327 (U.S. Court of Appeals for the D.C. Circuit 2013), *consolidated with Belmont Abbey College v. Sebelius*, 878 F.Supp.2d 25 (U.S. District Court for the District of Columbia 2012)

Facts: Belmont Abbey College, a private Benedictine Catholic college in North Carolina, and Wheaton College, a private Christian liberal arts college in Illinois, objected on religious and moral grounds to being forced to offer contraceptives to their employees through their health plans without **cost-sharing**. The colleges joined more than 30 others challenging the federal regulation that requires most group health plans to cover women's preventive care, including all FDA-approved contraceptives, without cost-sharing. Both religious employers and religiously affiliated organizations would be in violation of the regulation if they refused to cover contraceptive services.

Issue: What effect, if any, does the contraceptive mandate have on employers' religious liberty?

Holding and Decision: The challenges to the contraceptive mandate were not ripe for review until the federal government issued its Final Rule.

Analysis: The Belmont and Wheaton decisions bring with them new and somewhat contradictory challenges to the Affordable Care Act, contraception, and **procreative liberty**. Many religious colleges and other religious institutions view the contraception mandate as a violation of their religious liberty. Other courts point out the indirect effect these regulations have on an employer's religious liberty: the contraception mandate is no different than paying employees' wages that the employees themselves could use on anything, including contraception.

The contraception coverage cases have the potential for far-reaching effects for religious-affiliated employers and health care providers in the United States. Some predict an exodus of religious providers that are unwilling to comply with the law if the regulations hold, similar to the closing of religious adoption agencies after same sex marriage and antidiscrimination laws were passed. In fact, Belmont Abbey College says it would close rather than comply with the medical coverage mandate.

Rule of Law: The government's promise made during oral argument to never enforce the regulation in its current form against the colleges or those similarly situated regarding contraceptive services was binding on the government and would be reviewed by the court when the Final Rule was issued.

References discussing this court decision: Ouellette, 2013.

MANAGEMENT AND LAW ISSUES

5. Are for-profit corporations an appropriate platform or venue for individuals to be seeking to express their religious beliefs?
6. Should religious beliefs be private, or should for-profit corporations be free to impose their beliefs on their employees? In other words, should corporate management be able to use their individual religious beliefs to guide for-profit corporations that are first and foremost, entities aimed at making profits?

Wheaton College and Belmont Abbey College note that the federal government's accommodations do not affect their litigation, emphasizing that they want to make a point about religious freedom (Armstrong et al., 2012). No matter the outcome of this ongoing litigation, individual liberty is harmed. Employees will be forced to bear the cost of their employers' religious objections if the federal regulations fall, or the religious liberty of the colleges will be curtailed if they are not fully exempted (Gedicks & Van Tassel, 2014).

Substantial Burden to Religious Employers

For the past decade, courts have found that there is no substantial burden to religious employers seeking exemption from contraception coverage mandates because the determination to access contraceptive services is being made by individual employees whose relationship to the business's religious exercise is weak (Tenenbaum, 2013). The Catholic Charities decision is a case of first impression that continues to be followed a decade after the Supreme Court of California addressed a State contraception mandate.

COURT DECISION
Coverage for Contraceptives by Religious Employers

Catholic Charities of Sacramento, Inc. v. Superior Court of Sacramento County
[Religious-Affiliated Charities v. Local Municipality]
85 P.3d 67 (Supreme Court of California 2004),
cert. denied, 543 U.S. 816 (U.S. Supreme Court 2004)

Facts: The California legislature enacted the Women's Contraception Equity Act to eliminate gender discrimination in health care benefits (*See* California Health & Safety Code § 1367.25(b)(1)(A-D)). Evidence had shown that women spent a great deal more on health care costs during their reproductive years than did their male counterparts. The Equity Act requires that certain health care plans that include prescription drugs must cover prescription contraceptives. At the time, about 10% of California's commercially insured did not have coverage for prescription contraceptives.

Catholic Charities of Sacramento, a church affiliated charity, challenged the constitutionality of the Equity Act. In particular, Catholic Charities took issue with the law's exception for religious employers. In order for a church-affiliated charity to meet the definition of a religious employer under California law, it must meet four criteria. The entity must:

*   Be a not-for-profit organization
*   Have as its primary purpose, the inculcation of religious values
*   Primarily employ persons who share the religious tenets of the entity
*   Serve primarily persons who share the religious tenets of the entity

While acknowledging it did not meet any of the criteria for exemption as a religious employer, Catholic Charities maintained the Equity Act was unconstitutional because it:

*   Burdened the right to free exercise of religion
*   Interfered with the **personal autonomy** of a church-affiliated charity
*   Would fail both **strict scrutiny** and **rational basis** tests

Although the religious employer exemption does not apply to all charities affiliated with the Catholic Church, the lower trial court did not agree that this amounted to discrimination against the Church.

Issue: Must church-affiliated charities provide state-mandated medical coverage for contraceptives?

Holding and Decision: Yes. Church-affiliated charities that are not exempt as religious employers must provide state-mandated medical coverage for contraceptives.

Analysis: The court first analyzed whether the Equity Act interfered with the religious autonomy of Catholic Charities. Courts must accept decisions made by the highest church judicatories regarding questions of discipline, faith, ecclesiastical rule, custom, or law (*See, e.g., Watson v. Jones*, 80 U.S. 679, 727 (U.S. Supreme Court 1872)). Catholic Charities claimed that the Equity Act interfered with matters of internal church governance. The court, however, determined that the legislature had not decided any religious question in enacting the law.

Catholic Charities also made the argument that the Equity Act burdened the right to free exercise of religion. Specifically, Catholic Charities argued that the law effectively coerced a violation of religious beliefs. Regarding this argument, the general rule is that religious beliefs do not excuse compliance with otherwise valid laws regulating matters the government is free to regulate. *See Reynolds v. United States*, 98 U.S. 145, 166-167 (U.S. Supreme Court 1878). This standard removes the need for a law to be justified by compelling governmental interests if it is neutral and of general applicability, even when the law has the incidental effect of burdening a particular religious practice. The court found the Equity Act applies to religious and nonreligious employers equally, except for those employers that fall under the religious employer exemption. The religious employer exemption does not impose a burden on any employer; rather, it removes a possible burden from employers that meet the exemption criteria.

Catholic Charities additionally contended that the Equity Act discriminated against the Catholic Church and other charities affiliated with the church. The court did not agree with this contention since the church had requested the religious employer exemption; the exemption was justified as an accommodation to the exercise of religion. Although the exemption does not apply to all charities affiliated with the church, the court did not agree that this amounted to discrimination against the church itself.

Finally, Catholic Charities argued that strict scrutiny should be applied to the Equity Act and that it would fail such a test. The court again disagreed. While a decision was not made regarding whether strict scrutiny should apply, the court found that the law would nevertheless pass under strict scrutiny standards. In reaching this conclusion, the court explained that the California legislature had shown that the law was meant to achieve a compelling interest and it was narrowly tailored to that purpose: the elimination of gender discrimination. Any narrowing of the law would decrease the positive intended effect on female employees. Furthermore, because the law does not require any church-affiliated charity to offer prescription benefit coverage, Catholic Charities is not compelled to offer medical coverage for contraceptives.

Rule of Law: The Equity Act does not violate the Establishment or Free Exercise Clauses of the U.S. or California Constitutions.

References discussing this court decision: *E.g.*, Epstein, 2013; Laycock, 2014; Lepard, 2013.

Medical Coverage for Newer, More Expensive Birth Control and Family Planning Alternatives

There is a new front in the continuing battle to have the health insurance industry pay for women's birth control and **family planning**. A number of contraceptive alternatives have arrived on the market (from hormone patches, rings, and injections, to new-generation IUDs and noninvasive sterilization techniques), offering women a broad range of choices beyond condoms and the birth control pill. However, many insurers and employer-provided health insurance plans question the need to cover the newer methods. Women's health advocates believe most state-mandate laws apply to all forms of contraception approved by the FDA (NWLC, 2015c).

Prior to the Affordable Care Act's contraception provisions taking effect, many employer-provided health insurance plans were already covering most methods of prescription contraception approved by the FDA (Goldsmith, 2014). In recent years, most employers and health insurers moved to cover birth control pills, but this still left out large numbers of women who preferred other methods of contraception (Fischer & Kasper, 2014). The recent wave of birth control and family planning innovations offers women alternatives that have fewer side effects and can be both more effective and simpler to manage. Under the Affordable Care Act, all health insurance plans must cover contraception without copayments from patients.

The newer methods, however, often are far more expensive for the health insurance industry, which can negotiate discounted bulk rates for birth control pills from the many manufacturers competing for business. Because insurers can pay at least 10 times as much for some forms of contraception over others (NWLC, 2015c), the need to cover all forms of contraception is being questioned. Moreover, if alternative methods are less popular, limiting access to them is a way to curtail health care costs without affecting large numbers of women. However, it may be that these alternative methods are only "less popular" because, until recently, they have been so much more expensive for women to access, constructively forcing them to choose the pill instead.

Many health insurers will not cover a new, less invasive form of permanent sterilization called Essure, an alternative to tubal ligation (Stopler, 2015). Although insurers cover birth control pills, the patch, and the vaginal ring without question, they question universal coverage for IUDs or injectable forms of contraception, such as Depo-Provera (Fischer & Kasper, 2014; NWLC, 2015c). Many insurers would like to only cover birth control pills (NWLC, 2015c). Yet, employers find it costs far less to cover contraceptives than to cover a pregnancy (Sepper, 2015a).

To keep health care costs down, the health insurance industry actively steers women toward specific forms of birth control and family planning (Brown, 2015). For instance, the **patch** and the **vaginal ring** are often excluded from the **formulary** lists of preferred medical products provided to physicians, making it more difficult for women to obtain these more expensive options (Guttmacher, 2015b). Physicians may still prescribe contraceptive methods not on formularies but they must explain their reasons. The insurers hope the additional hassle will encourage physicians to work with less expensive products before they try others (Bagley, 2015). Physicians maintain there has always been coercion that goes on in medical practice (Kapp, 2011).

Gender Discrimination

Much of the effort to have health insurance coverage for alternative methods of birth control and family planning has centered on the issue of gender discrimination: if health insurance plans cover men's reproductive drugs, then they should cover contraception for women as well (Fischer & Kasper, 2014). Among the reasons insurers give for denying benefits is that the new contraception methods do not have enough safety and efficacy data behind them (Mac Dougall, 2015). Most new drugs, however, gain medical coverage shortly after they are approved by the FDA. Viagra and Cialis were added to most health insurance plans very quickly, yet FDA-approved contraceptive methods for women appear to be treated differently.

When the U.S. Supreme Court first evaluated gender discrimination by the insurance industry, the Court held that there was no discrimination when plans denied benefits for pregnancy-related health issues. The primary rationale was that pregnancy exclusions did not adversely impact all women, just those who became pregnant. A secondary rationale was that the pregnancy exclusion was the same for men and women (*See General Electric Co. v. Gilbert*, 429 U.S. 125 (U.S. Supreme Court 1976)). Shortly after *Gilbert*, the federal Pregnancy Discrimination Act was enacted, making pregnancy-related discrimination impermissible in employment situations (*See* 42 U.S.C.A. § 2000e(k)). Subsequent court decisions that have followed have upheld women's right to contraceptive coverage; this area of law, however, is by no means settled, as only a few courts have addressed the issue and this right continues to come under attack (Mattingly, 2013).

Abortions

Now that women have the right to an abortion, the debate is over defining that right and permissible abortion regulations. The number of abortions in the United States has dropped steadily over the past two decades and now stands at about 700,000 a year (CDC, 2015). The use of emergency contraception after unprotected sex or a contraceptive failure accounted for almost half of the total decline in abortions (Smith, 2015). Another reason for this decline is the state restrictions placed on access to abortions; more than two-fifths of American women live in counties with no medical professional who performs abortions (Jones & Jerman, 2014). In other words, women are carrying pregnancies to term because they cannot access abortion services, not because they have expressly decided against having an abortion.

Women's Access to Abortions

States are not responsible for propping up the abortion market or fixing challenges to the abortion market (Quast, 2014). Thus, courts distinguish between impermissibly placing obstacles in the path of women's exercise of their freedom of choice to access abortions and validly opting not to remove obstacles. This distinction provides states with an effective tool to place burdens on the exercise of a constitutionally protected choice to obtain an abortion; then the issue becomes when, if ever, are these burdens too burdensome?

COURT DECISION
Providers' Access to a Patient Compensation Fund

K.P. v. LeBlanc
[Abortion Providers v. State of Louisiana]
729 F.3d 427 (U.S. Court of Appeals for the Fifth Circuit 2013)

Facts: The Louisiana Patient Compensation Fund was created to compensate victims of medical malpractice and protect providers. All health care providers in the state are eligible to participate in the patient compensation fund, the benefits of which include a cap on medical malpractice liability and access to an advisory panel for malpractice prelitigation consults. The law limits compensation fund participation for any damage occasioned by an abortion. In addition, the limits on medical malpractice liability do not apply to abortion providers. Thus, abortions are expressly excluded from medical coverage and abortion providers are denied the benefits of the compensation fund.

This lawsuit arose when the state refused to allow review of an abortion patient's medical malpractice claim, stating that neither abortion providers nor women who had an abortion were eligible to benefit from the compensation fund. A group of abortion providers sued to enjoin the state from preventing abortions from being covered by the compensation fund. They claimed that by precluding abortion claims from medical coverage, the law violated the equal protection and due process protections of the Fourteenth Amendment for both abortion providers and women.

Issue: Can states make it difficult for abortion providers to obtain medical malpractice insurance, if this inflicts an undue burden on women's right to choose to have an abortion?

Holding and Decision: Yes. Applying the rational basis and undue burden tests to state abortion laws that deny abortion providers access to a patient compensation fund does not place an undue burden on women's right to choose to have abortions; nor does it violate the equal protection and due process protections of the Fourteenth Amendment.

Analysis: The court held that the law does not violate the equal protection clause of the Fourteenth Amendment, noting that the classification the patient compensation fund uses is rationally related to a legitimate governmental goal of **informed consent**. The court found that the abortion providers failed to demonstrate that hostility to abortions is not a legitimate goal of the government or that the inapplicability of the compensation fund to them was not rationally related to the promotion of informed consent. In addition, the court found if the liability of abortion providers were capped, it would limit their incentive to disclose low-probability, high-severity risks. The court also noted that abortion providers are not wholly disqualified from participating in the compensation fund; they are only disqualified as it relates to abortions.

The court went on to find that the law does not unduly burden a woman's right to choose. The limitation is merely a means of unequal subsidy of abortions. The court reasoned that while the government may not place obstacles in the path of women's exercise of their freedom to choose abortions, it need not remove those obstacles. The lack of affordable medical malpractice insurance for abortion providers is an obstacle for which the government is not responsible.

Rule of Law: While government may not place obstacles in the path of women's exercise of their freedom of choice, it need not remove those obstacles.

References discussing this court decision: Pruitt & Vanegas, 2015; Quast, 2014.

While this decision does not address the law's impact on women's access to abortions, the exclusion of abortions from the patient compensation fund may chill the inclination of physicians to provide abortions. This exclusion will thus inflict an undue burden on women's right to choose to have an abortion. This allows a state to effectively place an obstacle in women's paths by causing access to abortions to be severely diminished while technically falling on the side of failing to remove an obstacle.

Partial-Birth Abortions (Intact Dilation and Extraction)

While 19 states have made it a crime to perform partial-birth abortions, or **intact dilation and extraction** procedures, the *Carhart* decision is the first time the U.S. Supreme Court has ever held that physicians can be prohibited from using a medical procedure deemed necessary by the physician to benefit a patient's health (Moreno, 2015). It is important to note that the term *partial-birth abortion* is not a term recognized or used by the medical community; it is a term devised by pro-life activists to foster opposition to abortion.

COURT DECISION

Intact Dilation and Extraction

Gonzales v. Carhart
[Federal Government v. Physician]
550 U.S. 124 (U.S. Supreme Court 2007);
followed by Whole Woman's Health v. Hellerstedt, 2016 U.S.LEXIS 4063
(U.S. Supreme Court 2016)

Facts: States are prohibited from restricting abortion in any way before the **fetus** develops to the point where it could live independently of the mother, a period known as **previability** (*See Planned Parenthood of Southeastern Pennsylvania v. Casey,* 550 U.S. 833 (U.S. Supreme Court 1992)). During previability, states cannot impose an undue burden on women seeking to exercise their right to abortion. In the period after **viability**, known as postviability, states may regulate abortion as long as the restrictions do not endanger the life or health of the mother.

After the U.S. Supreme Court struck down Nebraska's so-called partial-birth abortion ban in 2000 (*See Stenberg v. Carhart,* 530 U.S. 914 (U.S. Supreme Court 2000)), Congress enacted a federal version of the Nebraska law. Congress had previously attempted to enact federal legislation banning partial-birth abortions, but President Clinton vetoed both efforts. Congress specifically banned intact dilation and extraction procedures that are used in the second trimester of pregnancy. Most dilation and extractions involve delivering the fetus intact until part of it passes through the vagina, where it is then aborted, a procedure that Congress maintained is never medically necessary. The federal law includes an exception when the woman's life is in danger, but not an exception if the woman's health is merely at risk. Several courts upheld permanent injunctions that facially challenged the federal **Partial-Birth Abortion Ban Act of 2003** and enjoined the federal government from enforcing the law (*See* 18 U.S.C.A. § 1531).

Issue: Does the lack of a **health exception** in the federal Partial-Birth Abortion Ban Act prohibiting intact dilation and extraction withstand constitutional scrutiny?

Holding and Decision: Yes. Intact dilation and extraction are never medically necessary and women have alternatives to the banned procedure.

Analysis: The majority found that in intact dilation and extraction, a health exception was unnecessary based on congressional findings that the procedure was never medically necessary. Additionally, because medical alternatives to the banned procedure that do not violate federal law exist, the Court found that there was no undue burden on pregnant women.

The Court also stated that facial challenges to the federal Partial-Birth Abortion Ban Act require a showing that the law would be unconstitutional in a large fraction of relevant cases. The Court held that relevant cases consist of situations in which physicians want to perform intact dilation and extraction for medically necessary reasons, and not when women are merely suffering from medical complications.

It held that the burden to prove the unconstitutionality of the ban in a large fraction of relevant cases had not been met. While a challenge to the federal law as applied to a particular individual case might lead to a different result, the Court noted that such a review was not needed when a woman's life was threatened because of the law's exception to protect the life of the mother.

The dissent emphasized the necessity of a health exception for the federal law to be constitutional. Since *Roe v. Wade*, the U.S. Supreme Court had never upheld a restriction on abortion that did not have a health exception (410 U.S. 113 (U.S. Supreme Court 1973), *rehearing denied*, 410 U.S. 959 (U.S. Supreme Court 1973)). The dissent recalled the holding in *Stenberg v. Carhart*, that a health exception is required whenever there is substantial medical authority supporting the proposition that banning a particular abortion procedure could endanger women's health. Lower court findings were reviewed in detail by the dissent, and it was noted that substantial medical authority existed indicating that, in some cases, an intact dilation and extraction is the safest procedure.

The dissent also stated that the majority did not respect the difference between previability and postviability, a distinction that is crucial for determining the state's interest in the fetus. The majority stated that the federal law applies during both previability and postviability because the law uses the term *fetus*, which does not specify viability, and the issue was not discussed further.

Examining further inconsistencies with precedent, the dissent declared that the majority abandoned the heightened constitutional scrutiny of *Planned Parenthood of Southeastern Pennsylvania v. Casey*, and instead applied a lower level rational basis test to uphold the federal law. Finally, the dissent took issue with the majority's definition of the relevant group that ought to be examined under *Casey* for determining whether the restriction creates an undue burden in a large fraction of cases. Under *Casey*, when examining whether an undue burden exists, the Court must consider the women who need the procedure to preserve their health as the relevant group and not a large fraction of women overall, whether or not they are pregnant, as the majority maintained.

Rule of Law: Physicians are prohibited from performing intact dilation and extraction abortion procedures.

References discussing this court decision: Abrams, 2013; Anderson, 2015; Bakelaar, 2014; Benedict, 2013; Bonner & Sheriff, 2013; Cahill, 2013; Donley, 2013; Duane, 2013; Forsythe, 2014; Franzonello, 2013; Friedman, 2013; Gray & Holden, 2014; Huberfeld, 2013; Jayadevan, 2015; Johnsen, 2015; Koss, 2014; Lang, 2014; Madeira, 2014; Melling, 2014; Pergament, 2013; Prior, 2014; Samuels, 2014; Scaldo, 2013; Shainwald, 2013; Siegel & Siegel, 2013; Suter, 2013; Toscano & Reiter, 2014; Wardle, 2013; Will, 2013; Young, 2014.

Following this decision is the concern that it will prevent physicians from performing legal intact dilation and extraction procedures out of fear that they might be investigated for criminal wrongdoing (Abrams, 2015). Additionally, *Carhart* creates uncertainty for physicians because it resurrects many states' partial-birth abortion bans, which are now in the process of being modified with constitutionally ambiguous language (Moreno, 2015). The ambiguity of the intent requirement will cause physicians to avoid similar legal medical procedures, such as **dilation and evacuation abortions**, even when the mother's life is in jeopardy (Forte, 2013).

The impact of *Carhart* expands beyond the issue of abortion and intrudes into the practice of medicine. Legislative judgment was allowed to trump medical judgment by preventing physicians from performing a medical procedure they believe to be in the best interests of their patients (Moreno, 2015). *Carhart* marks a significant change in the U.S. Supreme Court's abortion jurisprudence. Future cases will have to further define the state's power to restrict the right to abortion and the rights of physicians to treat their patients.

Parental Notification Prior to Abortions

Many states have parental notification requirements that must be met before abortions may be performed on unemancipated minors that generally require young women to wait at least 48 hours after written notice of the pending abortion has been delivered to their parent or guardian. There are often exceptions where a physician may perform an abortion on a minor child without parental notification.

COURT DECISION
Parental Notification for Abortions

Ayotte v. Planned Parenthood of Northern New England
[New Hampshire v. Reproductive Clinic]
546 U.S. 320 (U.S. Supreme Court 2006);
followed by Toghill v. Commonwealth of Virginia,
768 S.E.2d 674 (Supreme Court of Virginia 2015)

Facts: New Hampshire enacted a parental notification law that required that abortions could not be performed upon an unemancipated minor until at least 48 hours after written notice of the pending abortion had been delivered to the minor's parents or guardian (*See* Parental Notification Prior to Abortion Act, N.H. Rev. Stat. Ann. §§ 132:24-132:28). The law allowed for two exceptions where a physician could perform an abortion on a minor child without parental or guardian notification:

- Abortion is necessary to prevent the minor's death and there is insufficient time to provide the required notice.
- The minor petitions a judge to authorize an abortion, and the judge finds that the minor is mature and capable of giving her informed consent, or that an abortion without parental notification serves the minor's best interests.

This **judicial bypass** measure is confidential and given precedence over other pending matters so that the court may reach a prompt decision. Additionally, the trial and appellate courts must rule on bypass petitions within seven days. Though the exceptions to parental notification are acknowledged prior to a minor's abortion, the law did not expressly allow a physician to perform an abortion in an emergency without parental notification.

Dr. Wayne Goldner, obstetrician and gynecologist, and three clinics including Planned Parenthood of Northern New England that offer reproductive health services and abortions for pregnant minors, brought this lawsuit claiming that New Hampshire's parental notification law was unconstitutional because it did not include an exception allowing a physician to perform an abortion on a minor in a medical emergency. The U.S. District Court declared the law unconstitutional because:

- It failed to meet the constitutional requirement that any law that restricts a woman's access to an abortion must provide an emergency health exception
- It forced physicians to certify with impossible precision when abortion was medically necessary to avoid death
- The judicial bypass provision would not operate quickly enough in medical emergencies

On appeal, the U.S. Court of Appeals for the First Circuit concluded that the law was unconstitutional notwithstanding the judicial bypass measure because the judicial bypass was not an adequate substitute for an emergency health exception. The First Circuit affirmed the District Court's decision, declaring the law unconstitutional and permanently enjoining the law's enforcement and thereby invalidating it entirely.

Issue: What should the appropriate judicial relief be when a court is faced with a law that, in restricting access to abortion, may be applied in a manner that unconstitutionally harms a woman's health?

Holding and Decision: Remanded to determine whether the First Circuit could, consistent with New Hampshire's legislative intent, formulate a more narrow remedy than a permanent injunction against enforcement of the parental notification law in its entirety.

Analysis: The opinion began by stating that the U.S. Supreme Court was not revisiting its abortion precedents, but rather addressing a question of remedy. The Court carefully sidestepped the opportunity to confront its controversial abortion precedents by phrasing the question around the issue of whether the lower courts erred by invalidating the New Hampshire parental notification law in its entirety because it failed to provide an emergency health exception. When confronted with a constitutional flaw in any law, the Court noted that the remedial preference would be to enjoin only the unconstitutional applications of a law while leaving other applications in force or to sever its problematic portions while leaving the remainder intact. The Court enumerated three principles that should inform a court's approach to remedies:

- Courts must not invalidate any more of a legislature's work than is necessary because invalidating an entire law as unconstitutional frustrates the intent of the people's elected representatives (*See Regan v. Time, Inc.*, 468 U.S. 641 (U.S. Supreme Court 1984)); a partial invalidation of the portions of the law that are unconstitutional is the correct response, while the rest of the law is left otherwise intact (*See Brockett v. Spokane Arcades, Inc.*, 472 U.S. 491 (U.S. Supreme Court 1985)).
- Courts must avoid rewriting state law to conform to federal constitutional requirements, even while the courts attempt to salvage the law; making distinctions in murky constitutional contexts may involve an invasion of the legislature's field, and therefore courts should be hesitant to enter that domain (*See Virginia v. American Booksellers Association, Inc.*, 484 U.S. 383 (U.S. Supreme Court 1988)).
- Courts cannot use their remedial powers to skirt the legislature's intent; once a court finds an application or portion of a law unconstitutional, the court must ask whether the legislature would prefer what is left of its law to no law at all (*See Califano v. Westcott*, 443 U.S. 76, 94 (U.S. Supreme Court 1979)).

In *Ayotte*, the Court found that the lower courts had chosen the most blunt remedy by invalidating the parental notification law in its entirety. The Court agreed with New Hampshire's position that such a wholesale invalidation of the parental notification law was unnecessary. Therefore, the Court concluded, as long as the lower courts remain faithful to legislative intent, the lower courts can issue a more narrowly drawn injunction preventing enforcement of only the law's unconstitutional applications while leaving the rest of the law in force. Or, if the lower courts find that they cannot issue an injunction preventing the unconstitutional applications of the law, then they could invalidate the law in its entirety as long as the courts find that such an action was within the state legislature's intent. The crucial question for the First Circuit to answer on remand was legislative intent: whether the state legislature would have preferred a law with an exception for pregnant minors in medical emergencies, or no requirement for parental notification at all.

The Court vacated the First Circuit's decision and returned the case to determine whether a remedy exists that would correct the constitutional flaw without invalidating the entire law. Most significantly, the Court avoided addressing its controversial abortion precedents and decided *Ayotte* on the grounds of choice of remedy. Precedents include: *Stenberg*, 530 U.S. 914 (holding a Nebraska law prohibiting dilation and extraction abortions unconstitutional because it imposed an undue burden on a woman's right to choose abortion); *Planned Parenthood of Southeastern Pennsylvania*, 505 U.S. 833 (rejecting the trimester framework established in *Roe v. Wade* and establishing an undue burden test for when a state may regulate abortions while reaffirming *Roe*'s central holding that a state may not prohibit any woman from making the decision to terminate her pregnancy before viability); and *Roe*, 410 U.S. 113 (holding a Texas law prohibiting abortions except for lifesaving procedures unconstitutional and establishing a trimester framework for when a state may regulate abortions).

Rule of Law: New Hampshire's parental notification law could be applied unconstitutionally in certain situations, such as when a pregnant minor's health is at risk, and thus required revision.

References discussing this court decision: Fore, 2014; Forsythe, 2014; Gray & Holden, 2014; Jayadevan, 2015; Pruitt & Vanegas, 2015; Scaldo, 2013; Wardle, 2013; Young, 2014.

In deciding *Ayotte*, the U.S. Supreme Court reaffirmed that state legislatures may require parental involvement in abortion decisions involving minors, but that restrictions on abortions must have an emergency health exception (*See Planned Parenthood of Southeastern Pennsylvania*, 505 U.S. 833 and *Roe*, 410 U.S. 113). The decision broke little new ground on the abortion issue as the Court declined to go beyond its established abortion precedents.

The Court's limited decision merely addressed the question of what remedies a court may choose when faced with an unconstitutional application of an abortion law. Response to this ruling has been mixed. The ruling may remind state legislatures that an emergency health exception must be included in state abortion laws. The decision may also make courts less likely to invalidate entire abortion laws. Yet another consequence of the decision may be an increase in abortion litigation. What is certain is that the status quo has been preserved in the abortion controversy (Hardwick & Hodsdo, 2012).

Consent of Foster Parents for an Abortion

The volume of legislation and judicial decisions regarding women's reproductive health over the past several years demonstrates the lingering contentiousness surrounding this issue, particularly when it comes to a minor's right to obtain an abortion (Armstrong, 2015). Currently, 39 states mandate some type of parental involvement before a minor obtains an abortion; eight require written consent that is notarized (Rahders, 2015). Some states' parental consent laws provide an exception for minors who either elect not to seek or do not obtain consent from their parent or legal guardian. In this case, the difficulty in obtaining consent as a ward of the state may have imposed a substantial obstacle on the minor's right to an abortion.

COURT DECISION
Consent of Foster Parents for an Abortion

In re Petition of Anonymous 5
[Minor v. State of Nebraska]
838 N.W.2d 226 (Supreme Court of Nebraska 2013)

Facts: Anonymous was a woman 16 years of age, who was 10 weeks pregnant. Nebraska's Abortion Parental Consent Law requires a minor seeking an abortion to obtain the written consent of one of her parents or a legal guardian. While the U.S. Supreme Court has upheld the rights of states to pass **parental consent laws**, the laws must include certain exceptions. For instance, states must include a judicial bypass whereby a minor can seek judicial permission to forgo parental consent. When granting permission, a judge must consider and determine whether the minor is sufficiently mature to obtain an abortion or that an abortion would be in her best interest.

Issue: Who should be required to consent to an abortion when a minor is a ward of a state?

Holding and Decision: A minor, if she cannot be determined to be sufficiently mature, must obtain consent from her foster parents before she can choose to obtain an abortion, despite her legal status as a ward of the State of Nebraska.

Analysis: Nebraska's law satisfies the U.S. Supreme Court's constitutional standard by providing three types of judicial bypass: for a medical emergency, victim of abuse, and mature minor exceptions to the parental consent requirement. In this case, the 16-year old contended she did not need to obtain consent because she was a victim of abuse from her biological parents and that she was sufficiently mature to proceed with the abortion without parental consent. In this instance, the court found the minor did not establish she was sufficiently mature and well-informed enough to decide whether to have an abortion. The court decided she needed her foster parent's consent for an abortion.

Rule of Law: While a state may impose parental consent requirements for minors, there must be adequate judicial bypass procedures that are not a substantial obstacle to the minor's right to choose.

References discussing this court decision: Armstrong, 2015; Rahders, 2015; Shainwald, 2013.

The hardship imposed on minors who are wards of the state, including the confusion of who to turn to for consent and the legal validity of such consent if obtained from nonlegal guardians, may occur in other states with parental consent requirements. To avoid federal constitutional challenges, states should explicitly include consent requirements for minor wards of the state in their parental consent laws. By doing this, states will properly balance their interest in regulating abortions with the federal constitutional protections afforded to minors.

Judicial Bypass of Parental Consent

One aspect of the current debate on abortion centers on the issue of whether minors have the maturity to independently make decisions about abortion. Although it may be logically inconsistent to maintain minors lack the maturity to

MANAGEMENT AND LAW ISSUES

7. If a minor is not deemed sufficiently mature and well enough informed to decide whether to have an abortion without parental notice, can the minor logically be deemed sufficiently mature to raise a child?

make decisions about abortion, while considering the same minors mature enough to raise children, this part of the abortion debate may indicate some discussion is moving away from the focus on whether abortion should be legal to a more economic discussion of whether minors are prepared to accept responsibility for raising children (Cahn & Carbone, 2015).

Mandatory In-Person, Informed Consent Meetings

Although the following court decisions do not alter the abortion law battleground, they do suggest that state efforts to delay abortions by requiring informed consent meetings will be reviewed carefully if challenged.

COURT DECISION

Judicial Bypass of Parental Consent and Mandatory In-Person, Informed Consent Meetings

Cincinnati Women's Services, Inc. v. Taft
[Reproductive Clinic v. Governor]
468 F.3d 361 (U.S. Court of Appeals for the 6th Circuit 2006)

Facts: Ohio law required that minors receive informed consent of a parent or guardian before receiving an abortion. The law, however, allowed minors to petition a juvenile court for a judicial bypass of the parental consent requirement so the court could decide whether the minor was sufficiently mature and well enough informed to decide whether to have an abortion or whether notification of her parents was not in her best interest. The law did not impose any limitations on the number of times a minor could petition a court for such a bypass.

Additionally, Ohio law mandated that women seeking an abortion receive information about the procedure from a physician at least 24 hours prior to the abortion (*See* Ohio Rev. Code Ann. § 2919.12(B)(1)(a)(i)). The informed consent provision required that a physician inform the pregnant woman, verbally or by other nonwritten means of communication, about the procedure. This was interpreted to mean that videotaped or audiotaped physician statements would be an adequate means of imparting the necessary information to those seeking abortions.

The judicial bypass and informed consent provisions of Ohio's abortion regulations consist of two rules.

- In-person rule: required that the informed consent meeting take place in person (*See* Ohio Rev. Code Ann. § 2317.56(B)(1))
- Single petition rule: limited a minor to only one judicial bypass petition during the term of each pregnancy (*See* Ohio Rev. Code Ann. § 2919.121(c)(4) providing that no juvenile court shall have jurisdiction to rehear a petition concerning the same pregnancy once a juvenile court has granted or denied the petition)

The U.S. Supreme Court has ruled such bypass procedures are required if a state wishes to enact a parental informed consent requirement (*See Lambert v. Wicklund*, 520 U.S. 292 (U.S. Supreme Court 1997) and *Bellotti v. Baird*, 443 U.S. 622 (U.S. Supreme Court 1979)). Cincinnati Women's Services, a health care provider that offers family planning services, brought a pre-enforcement facial attack against the single petition and in-person rules, claiming that the rules were unconstitutionally vague and therefore invalid.

Issue: Can a state law limit minors to only one petition for judicial bypass of the parental consent requirement for an abortion and require minors to attend an in-person meeting with a physician at least 24 hours before receiving an abortion?

Holding and Decision: No, limiting minors to only one petition for judicial bypass of a parental consent requirement for an abortion was an unconstitutional undue burden, and yes, minors may be required to attend an in-person meeting with a physician at least 24 hours prior to receiving an abortion.

Analysis: The court began its analysis by determining that the proper standard to apply to facial challenges of abortion restrictions is the **large fraction test** (*See Planned Parenthood of Southeastern Pennsylvania*, 505 U.S. 833). The large fraction test requires a reviewing court to determine whether a large fraction of the women for whom the law is a restriction will be deterred from procuring an abortion as surely as if the government has outlawed abortion in all cases. The court explicitly rejected application of the more demanding 'no set of circumstances' test, noting that every federal circuit except one has opted instead to apply the large fraction test to facial challenges of abortion laws (*See U.S. v. Salerno*, 481 U.S. 739 (U.S. Supreme Court 1987) (constitutional challenges to a law must establish that no set of circumstances exists under which the law would be valid)); the court recognized that its own practice of applying the large fraction test in similar situations made it the obvious choice for analyzing the two challenged provisions.

Applying the large fraction test to the **single petition rule**, the court held that the regulation created an unconstitutional undue burden to a large fraction of women who are initially refused a judicial bypass but later experience changes entitling them to a bypass. The court reasoned that the single petition rule affected those women who were denied a bypass at first, but who would be bypass eligible if they were to reapply because of changed circumstances in their life (for instance, increased maturity or discovery of medical anomalies with the fetus). The court concluded that the single petition rule was facially unconstitutional because it would form a substantial obstacle to obtaining an abortion for most women who had experienced changes in their circumstances.

Next, the court sustained the in-person rule, holding that the number of abortion seekers likely to be frustrated by the regulation was not a large enough number of women to justify overturning the provision. In determining the number of women who would be unduly burdened by the in-person rule, the court noted that 25% of the women excused from the in-person meetings were in abusive relationships. Of this 25%, only half would be completely unable to obtain an abortion if they were forced to have a separate in-person meeting 24 hours prior to an abortion for reasons ranging from geographic and financial constraints to fear of repercussion given their abusive relationships. The court held that an undue burden on 12% was not enough to consider the law unconstitutional.

Rule of Law: In-person, informed consent meetings may be required before abortions may be performed and minors must be granted more than one opportunity to seek a judicial bypass of the parental consent requirement.

References discussing this court decision: *E.g.*, Duane, 2013; Glass, 2016; Gray & Holden, 2014; Huddleston, 2016; Toscano & Reiter, 2014.

This decision reinforces the large fraction test which has been criticized as being vague and subjective as the legislative and judicial branches struggle to identify groups for whom abortion laws are an impermissible restriction (Pruitt & Vanegas, 2015). Additionally, while the court acknowledged that the term *large fraction* is more of a concept than an algebraic application, what constitutes a large fraction remains unclear (Cohen & Bingenheimer, 2016). In refusing to clearly identify the boundaries for impermissible restrictions on abortions, the judicial branch is seeking at least the possibility of common ground with the legislative branch (Glass, 2016). The refusal by the courts to expand upon the large fraction test since it was created acknowledges recognition of the fact that the two sides of the abortion issue will most likely never agree on the underlying question of whether abortion should be legal (Huddleston, 2016).

Informed Consent for Abortions

Although informed consent information must be truthful and nonmisleading to inform women's free choice to have an abortion, states have passed numerous laws that are arguably misleading. Decisions on the constitutionality of such laws have varied in the lower courts. State laws communicating information about the development of the fetus appear to be consistent (*See Doe v. Planned Parenthood/Chicago Area*, 956 N.E.2d 564, 572 (Appellate Court of Illinois, First District, Sixth Division 2011) (holding that physicians have no duty to inform patients that abortion kills a human being), *appeal denied*, 962 N.E.2d 481 (Supreme Court of Illinois 2011)).

COURT DECISION

Informed Consent for Abortions

Acuna v. Turkish
[Pregnant Woman v. Gynecologist]
930 A.2d 416 (Supreme Court of New Jersey 2007),
cert. denied, 555 U.S. 813 (U.S. Supreme Court 2008);
followed by Doe v. Planned Parenthood/Chicago Area,
956 N.E.2d 564 (Appellate Court of Illinois, First District, Sixth Division 2011),
appeal denied, 962 N.E.2d 481 (Supreme Court of Illinois 2011)

Facts: Rosa Acuna, a married mother of two young children, consulted her gynecologist of five years, Dr. Sheldon Turkish, about abdominal pains. After Turkish informed her that she was six to eight weeks pregnant, Acuna decided to terminate the pregnancy. Turkish performed the operation, but, after complications relating to the abortion, Acuna was sent to a local hospital, where an additional procedure was performed. When she asked a nurse why the second procedure had been performed, the nurse responded that Turkish had left parts of the baby inside of her. It was only at this point Acuna claims that she started to realize there was a baby inside her and not just blood. This realization led to a decline in her mental health and a diagnosis of posttraumatic stress disorder.

The facts of the information exchange prior to the decision to terminate were disputed. Acuna maintained that Turkish told her that due to a complication with her kidneys, she would have to terminate the pregnancy or die in three months. Acuna further claimed she asked Turkish if it was the baby in there, to which Turkish replied, it is only blood. Turkish, on the other hand, asserted that Acuna suggested the option of abortion and that he had never encouraged her to terminate her pregnancy to preserve her health. Turkish could not remember the conversation but believed he would have told her that a seven-week pregnancy is not a living human being, but merely tissue at that time. Acuna filed a lawsuit alleging a lack of informed consent. She claimed that had Turkish provided her with the necessary medical and factual information surrounding the nature of abortion and the fact that her child was a complete, separate, and unique human being, she would not have had the abortion procedure.

Issue: Are physicians required to inform patients that their embryos are living human beings in order to properly obtain informed consent for abortion procedures?

Holding and Decision: No. Physicians are not required to inform patients seeking abortions that the procedure will kill an actual existing human being.

Analysis: The court dismissed Acuna's informed consent claim and ruled there was no common law duty for a physician to inform a patient seeking an abortion that the abortion would kill an actual existing human being. According to the court, the instructions sought were opinion and not medical fact; they were, therefore, a departure from the doctrine of informed consent. The court emphasized it would only compel physicians to provide medical information, not moral information. Negligence actions predicated on lack of informed consent must demonstrate that a physician withheld medical information that a reasonably prudent pregnant woman would have considered material before consenting to a termination of pregnancy. The knowledge Acuna sought cannot be compelled from a physician who may have a different scientific, moral, or philosophical viewpoint on the issue of when life begins.

Physicians might be required to convey information that reflects a consensus from the New Jersey medical community, the New Jersey legislature, or the New Jersey people. However, without such a consensus, instructions cannot be required that are not the medical norm. The court also found the instructions were at odds with current state abortion law, suggesting that both the physician and the patient would be complicit in committing the equivalent of murder. This in turn would have contradicted the New Jersey legislature's choice to exclude a fetus from within the definition of a person in the Wrongful Death Act.

Rule of Law: While potential parents should be provided sufficient medical information to make an informed decision whether or not to continue a pregnancy to term, physicians have no duty to provide moral guidance as well.

References discussing this court decision: "Physically intrusive abortion restrictions," 2015; Olson, 2013; Schlueter, 2013; Zabel, 2015.

Per Se Medical Exceptions

While Ohio became the first state to restrict an FDA-approved abortion drug for use by physicians, the courts have refused to sanction this restriction in other states.

COURT DECISION
Per Se Medical Exceptions

Planned Parenthood Cincinnati Region v. Taft
[Reproductive Clinic v. Governor]
444 F.3d 502 (U.S. Court of Appeals for the 6th Circuit 2006)

Facts: The FDA approved the use and manufacture of mifepristone (RU-486), a drug that medically induces abortion without surgical intervention. The treatment regimen that the FDA approved was to be taken within seven weeks of a pregnancy: oral administration of mifepristone followed two days later by the oral administration of misoprostol. Referred to as the medical abortion drugs, mifepristone is an abortifacient that terminates the pregnancy by detaching the gestational sac from the uterine wall; misoprostol is a prostaglandin that induces the contractions necessary to expel the fetus and other products of conception from the uterus.

Generally, once the FDA has approved a drug, physicians have the legal authority to prescribe it for **off-label use** unless state regulations require otherwise. An off-label use of RU-486 was the so-called **Schaff protocol** (named after the physician whose research primarily led to its development), which allowed for the administration of RU-486 within up to nine weeks of a pregnancy. The Schaff protocol provided for the oral administration of mifepristone followed one to three days later by misoprostol administered vaginally. Off-label use does not violate federal law because the FDA regulates the marketing and distribution of drugs in the United States, not the practice of medicine, which had always been the exclusive realm of individual states until 2007 (*contra Gonzales v. Carhart*, 550 U.S. 124 (U.S. Supreme Court 2007)).

The Ohio legislature enacted legislation that prohibited the off-label use of RU-486 in Ohio. *See* Ohio Rev. Code Ann. § 2919.123(A) (2004). Various Ohio chapters of Planned Parenthood and two physicians challenged the constitutionality of this law.

Issue: Do all state laws regulating abortions need a per se medical exception?

Holding and Decision: No. Not all state laws regulating abortions are required to contain a medical exception.

Analysis: The court first addressed and rejected the claim that all statutes regulating abortion must include an exception to preserve the life and health of the mother. The court found that medical exceptions are only required when a law regulating abortion poses a significant health risk to a woman. The court bolstered this conclusion by maintaining that a **per se requirement** of medical exceptions would preclude judicial review of whether regulations lacking such exceptions were unconstitutional. The court then undertook to summarize U.S. Supreme Court decisions to support its application of medical exception jurisprudence. *See Ayotte*, 546 U.S. 320 (state may not restrict access to abortions that are necessary for preservation of the life or health of the mother); *Stenberg*, 530 U.S. 914 (medical exceptions are required where it is necessary for the preservation of the life or health of the mother).

The court then described the standard for medical exceptions. Where substantial medical authority supports that an abortion-regulating law could endanger women's health, a medical exception is required when the procedure is necessary for the preservation of the life or health of the mother. The court emphasized that medical exemptions are required when RU-486 is safer than available alternatives (surgery), but then partially closed the door on women by restricting the use of RU-486 to situations where alternative procedures posed a significant medical risk.

To determine whether the medical exception standard had been met, the court deferred to physician experts who established that the law would pose a significant risk to women's health in narrow circumstances. Specifically, the physicians claimed the seven-week time limit on RU-486 could potentially harm certain pregnant women to whom physicians administered RU-486 in accordance with the Schaff protocol, whose time limit is nine weeks. Without the Schaff protocol as an option, physicians risk the health of the pregnant women by prescribing or administering other more dangerous treatments, including surgical abortion or methotrexate, a cancer agent.

The final issue that the court decided was the severability of the law. The court here held that when evaluating the severability of an abortion law that lacks a constitutionally necessary medical exception, the court is to defer to legislative intent. The court should ask whether the legislature would prefer what is left of its law to no law at all. If the court answers in the affirmative, then the court should prohibit enforcement of the unconstitutional provisions and leave the balance of the law intact. If, however, the court answers in the negative, then the court may invalidate the entire law. The question of severability was remanded.

Rule of Law: Only state abortion regulations that pose a significant risk to a woman's health or life are required to have medical exceptions.

References discussing this court decision: *E.g.*, Jayadevan, 2015; Kelso, 2015; Robertson, 2015; Samuels, 2014; Wardle, 2013.

State interests in the health of mothers become compelling at approximately the end of the first trimester, prior to which mortality in abortion is less than mortality in normal child birth (*Planned Parenthood of Southeastern Pennsylvania v. Casey*, 505 U.S. 833 (U.S. Supreme Court 1992)). The implications of this decision are twofold:

- Medical exceptions are not always required in abortion regulations.
- States may restrict off-label uses of abortion-inducing drugs if a medical exception is included in the restriction, given the risks of unapproved uses of such drugs for women.

This decision could inhibit physician autonomy and medical innovativeness. Following this decision, the FDA regulations on marketing and labeling may become substantive law if a state legislature acts similarly to the Ohio legislature. Thus, state law may prevent physicians from prescribing FDA-approved abortion drugs off-label (Samuels, 2014).

Freedom of Expression to Oppose Abortions

The U.S. Supreme Court places a high value on freedom of expression, especially on public sidewalks, which historically have been used for the exchange of ideas.

COURT DECISION
Buffer and Bubble Zones Around Abortion Clinics

McCullen v. Coakley
[Sidewalk Counselors v. State of Massachusetts]
134 S.Ct. 2518 (U.S. Supreme Court 2014)

Facts: This case originated when Eleanor McCullen, and other self-styled **sidewalk counselors**,[LN1] brought First Amendment challenges against the Massachusetts Reproductive Health Care Facilities Act. The sidewalk counselors wanted to engage women entering abortion clinics to offer information about alternatives to abortion; they claimed that the buffer zones significantly impaired their ability to engage women in speech about alternatives to abortion. They also objected to the practice of abortion clinics having employees escort women into the clinics, claiming that this hampered their counseling efforts. In addition, McCullen, a 76-year-old grandmother, claimed she was a sidewalk counselor and not an abortion protestor.

McCullen and other sidewalk counselors wanted to have one-on-one discussions and prayers (sidewalk counseling sessions) with women entering abortion clinics. The sidewalk counselors claimed that the law prevented them from having these personal conversations because the buffer zones forced them to remain a significant distance from the clinics. Additionally, the sidewalk counselors contended that the law was discriminatory because it allowed clinic employees to remain within the **buffer zones** around entrances and exits of abortion facilities while excluding them.

This is the third effort by Massachusetts to create an enforcement scheme that strikes the right balance between ensuring women's reproductive freedom and guaranteeing First Amendment rights. The original version of the law provided for an 18-foot buffer zone around entrances and driveways of abortion clinics and prohibited anyone from coming within 6 feet of another person in that zone without that person's consent, known as **bubble zones**. The law was enacted to address confrontations between opponents and advocates of abortion rights that occurred outside clinics. An amendment replaced bubble zones, which protected a distance around individual patients and staff entering or exiting abortion facilities, with a blanket 35-foot buffer zone that protected abortion facilities as a whole. The buffer zone applied only during business hours. Exceptions to the buffer zone include:

- Clinic employees
- Law enforcement, ambulance, firefighting, construction, utility, public works, and other municipal agents
- People entering or leaving a clinic
- People using the public sidewalk or street right-of-way adjacent to such clinic solely for the purpose of reaching a destination other than a clinic

People were prohibited from knowingly obstructing the entrance of abortion clinics. Criminal penalties were brought against anyone who interfered with the constitutionally protected rights of others.

Issue: Are the courts placing too high a value on First Amendment protections, or should buffer zones to maintain public safety and preserve access to abortion clinics be severely restricted if they impermissibly discriminate against both abortion protestors and sidewalk counselors?

Holding and Decision: Buffer and bubble zones around abortion clinics are constitutional if it can be demonstrated these zones are narrowly tailored enough so as to closely fit the circumstances, and if there are alternative means for abortion protesters and sidewalk counselors to express their opinions.

Analysis: This decision reversed, but did not explicitly overrule, an earlier decision that upheld a similar Colorado law that created 100-foot buffer zones around abortion clinics and eight-foot bubble zones around individual people within the buffer zones. That same year, Massachusetts enacted the original Reproductive Health Care Facilities Act with 18-foot buffer zones and six-foot bubble zones. The purpose of the law was:

- Patient access to health care
- Public safety
- Unobstructed use of public sidewalks and roadways

The issue addressed by this decision is whether a law creating a 35-foot buffer zone around abortion clinics is in violation of the First Amendment when the law makes it a crime to knowingly stand within the buffer zone but does not, on its face, regulate speech. The Court found that the Massachusetts law was content-neutral, noting that a neutral law does not become content-based merely because it affects some speech more than other speech. Even in a public forum, the government may impose reasonable restrictions on the time, place, or manner of protected speech, provided the restrictions meet three criteria: the restrictions are justified without reference to the content of the regulated speech; they are narrowly tailored to serve a significant governmental interest; and they leave open ample alternative channels for normal speech. Interestingly, while the Court agreed that the Massachusetts amendment was content-neutral because it prohibited everyone, not just abortion protestors and sidewalk counselors, from remaining within the buffer zone. It was exactly that breadth in content that caused the law to fail the narrow tailoring test. The Court discussed the burdens on speech imposed by the law and found that the Massachusetts law burdened substantially more speech than necessary to meet the state's interests of ensuring public safety outside abortion clinics.

Although the Court rejected the argument that, by exempting certain persons from the buffer zone restrictions, the law was content-based; the Court assumed that sidewalk counselors are different from abortion protestors. The purpose of the original Massachusetts law was maintaining public safety; the law applied equally to everyone regardless of whether they actually posed a public safety threat. Knowing that the amendment with a 35-foot buffer zone was passed in reaction to the difficulty of policing the six-foot bubble zones within the 18-foot buffer zones, the Court stressed that the First Amendment was too important to be compromised simply to make the job of law enforcement easier.

While the Court determined that the Massachusetts law had no discriminatory purpose, it nevertheless found that its burdensome effects on speakers were not justified. The Court found that the law was not narrowly tailored to meet a significant government interest. Although the Court acknowledged that the safety concerns of the government were significant, it found that the law was not narrowly tailored to meet these interests.

The Court further found that the Massachusetts legislature failed to consider a number of alternative measures that could have potentially addressed the goal of maintaining public safety without creating a heavy burden on freedom of expression by sidewalk counselors. For instance, the Court suggested that Massachusetts could have enacted a law modeled on the federal Freedom of Access to Clinic Entrances Act or New York City's antiharassment ordinance, two laws geared toward harassment outside of abortion clinics. The Court emphasized that it was not guaranteeing that such harassment laws would survive a constitutional challenge if one were to be brought in the future. Additionally, the Court pointed out that the unchallenged provisions of the Massachusetts law that prohibited obstruction of access to abortion clinics adequately addressed the state's public safety concerns. The Court also noted that the state's concerns could be addressed through existing criminal ordinances.

Rule of Law: A law creating 35-foot buffer zones around abortion clinics is in violation of the First Amendment, the principle that the government has no power to restrict speech because of its message, its ideas, its subject matter, or its content applies with full force in traditional public forums like public sidewalks.

References discussing this court decision: Barket et al., 2014; Kendrick, 2014; Miller, 2014.

Within weeks of this court decision, Massachusetts passed new legislation that seeks to protect public safety and women's access to abortions (*See* Act to Promote Public Safety and Protect Access to Reproductive Health Care Facilities of 2014, ch. 197, 2014-7 Massachusetts Advance Legislative Service 562). The new law allows law enforcement to issue written orders for the removal of anyone substantially impeding access to abortion clinics. When a removal order is issued, the removed person must remain at least 25 feet away from the abortion clinic for either eight hours or until the end of the clinic's business day.

Tension Between Religion and Science

The contraception and abortion controversies go to the very heart of debates over:

- How to define pregnancy
- What constitutes an abortion
- When life begins

This controversy highlights the tension between religion and science. On one side of the debate is religion. Advocates of religion believe life begins at conception, when a sperm unites with an egg (Smith, 2015). Fertilization, conception, and pregnancy are synonymous in this view. From this perspective, any method that prevents implantation of the fertilized egg (essentially, everything except barrier methods such as condoms) is an abortifacient (Blackman, 2016). The argument is that if implantation of a life is prevented, that is essentially an abortion (Griffin, 2015).

On the other side of the debate is science. The federal government and most of the medical community, such as the American Congress of Obstetricians and Gynecologists and the American Medical Association, disagree with the advocates of religion. In science, a pregnancy exists once a fertilized embryo has implanted in the uterus (Sawicki, 2016). Prior to implantation, there is no viable pregnancy. From this perspective, emergency contraception cannot undo implantation of a fertilized egg and is consequently not effective after implantation; therefore, it is not an abortifacient (Helfand, 2015).

The battle is the result of conception and pregnancy being defined in different ways by religion and science. Therefore, while a need exists for contraceptives, this need must be balanced with the potential burden imposed on employers who choose to operate their businesses according to their religious principles (Benedict, 2013). While a need exists for abortions, it is reasonable to place restrictions on this medical procedure (Note, 2015). In the court decisions in this chapter, the lines are not as clearly distinguishable as in the debate between religion and science.

Maternity Care Coverage

With approximately 4 million births in the United States each year, pregnancy- and childbirth-related conditions are the leading causes for hospital stays and account for almost 11% of the nation's hospitalizations (AHRQ, 2013). Yet, maternity care coverage is increasingly falling out of reach for many women. Women, including many with otherwise comprehensive health insurance, are finding themselves uncovered for one of their family's biggest health care costs: maternity care. Even women with no history of complicated births have a hard time getting **maternity coverage**. By law, employers that offer a group health insurance plan must include maternity care. But health insurers are failing to provide women reproductive services mandated by the Affordable Care Act, a problem that appears to be systemic nationwide (NWLC, 2015a).

Under the Affordable Care Act, new health insurance plans must include maternity coverage and cannot charge women higher premiums than men. However, a woman must already be enrolled in a plan that offers maternity coverage at the time she becomes pregnant; she cannot wait until she discovers she is pregnant and then enroll (Gandhi, 2016). Further, insurance plans are not required to cover:

- Labor and delivery costs
- Maternity costs for a dependent child on her parents' health care plan

(NWLC, 2015a).

This is medical coverage that many plans exclude now that they are required to cover dependents up until the age of 26 (Gandhi, 2016).

Most state insurance laws required unexpected complications during delivery (for instance an emergency cesarean) to be covered by health insurance; standard vaginal deliveries were not covered unless the woman had maternity coverage. Under the Affordable Care Act, health insurance plans must include maternity coverage for vaginal deliveries. Research supports the correlation between the nation's failure to provide basic maternity care coverage to all women and the fact that the United States has the highest rates of cesarean surgeries of any nation in the world (CIA, 2013; James & Savitz, 2011; *See* Sommers et al., 2012).

Compelled Medical Treatment During Pregnancy

The *Burton* decision is an addition to a line of cases authorizing compelled medical treatment of pregnant women for the benefit of their unborn children. Despite recurring consideration of the issues involved, there is no consensus regarding the approach to take in cases where a woman's right to refuse medical treatment comes up against the state's interest in protecting fetal health (Goodwin, 2014). This case demonstrates the difficulty of emergency decision-making when women refused medically indicated cesarean delivery and the need for considering the interests at stake (Deshpande & Oxford, 2012).

COURT DECISION
Compelled Cesarean Surgery

Burton v. Florida
[Pregnant Woman v. State]
49 So.3d 263 (Court of Appeal of Florida, 1st District 2010)

Facts: Samantha Burton, a pregnant woman with two young children, had voluntarily sought medical treatment at Tallahassee Memorial Hospital after developing complications in the 25th week of pregnancy. Her attending physician recommended a course of care to postpone delivery, including inpatient monitored bed rest, and physician supervision of physical activity, cessation of smoking, and a diet. When Burton asked instead to be discharged from the hospital, the hospital sought assistance from the state to force her to comply with the recommended course of care. The state then filed an emergency petition seeking judicial authorization to force the recommended medical treatment on Burton.

Issue: What standards should govern the compelled medical treatment of pregnant women?

Holding and Decision: The state's interest in fetal health outweighs a pregnant woman's constitutional rights based on medical evidence of what the interests of the baby require.

Analysis: The risk of severe injury or death to Burton's unborn child was found to be substantial and unacceptable unless she complied with her physician's recommended treatment. The court thus authorized Burton's health care providers to provide such medical care and treatment as in their reasonable professional judgment was necessary to preserve the life and health of her unborn child, including, but not limited to, restricting her to bed rest, administering appropriate drugs, and eventually performing a cesarean delivery. The court ordered Burton to comply with the attending physician's orders and denied her request to change hospitals as not being in her child's best interests. A few days later, the fetus was delivered stillborn following a cesarean section.

Rule of Law: Courts can override a pregnant woman's informed refusal to consent to medical treatment and order her to remain a hospital inpatient and submit to medical treatment.

References discussing this court decision: Beety, 2011; Bonner & Sheriff, 2013; Goodwin, 2016 and 2014; Gribow, 2013.

This case is one of many in which religion plays a central role in seeking judicial intervention to compel pregnant women to submit to unwanted medical interventions purported to be in the best interests of their unborn children (Gribow, 2013). As one might expect, given the important interests at stake and the general controversy over maternal-fetal conflicts, there is no consensus as to the correct approach to these cases. While there is no question that pregnant women have important constitutional liberty and privacy rights, courts diverge on whether and how those rights should be weighed against the state's interest in fetal health (Goodwin, 2016).

Some reject any balancing argument and maintain that a woman's competent choice to refuse medical treatment, as invasive as a cesarean section, must be honored even where the choice may be harmful to the fetus (Deshpande & Oxford, 2012). While this approach has been extended to blood transfusions that are refused on religious grounds, there is support for the position that pregnant women should always have the right to refuse treatment, especially cesarean sections. From this perspective, compelled cesarean surgery will always be unconstitutional when a woman gives her competent refusal (Goodwin, 2014).

Others are willing to acknowledge the possibility that judicial intervention could be appropriate, but set a high bar for intervention and counsel strongly against coercive intervention (ACOG, 2016; WHO, 2015). While not foreclosing the possibility that state interests could ever prevail over the wishes of a pregnant patient, there is doubt that there could ever be a situation extraordinary enough to justify a massive intrusion into a person's body, such as a cesarean section, against that woman's will. At the same time, the enhanced techniques for imaging, testing, and treating fetuses has led some to endorse the notion that fetuses are independent patients with treatment options and decisions separate from those of pregnant women (Minkoff & Marshall, 2016; Minkoff et al., 2014).

At the same time, some are willing to conclude that the state's interest in fetal health outweighs a pregnant woman's constitutional rights. Indeed, some favor the trend toward criminal punishment of pregnant women who harm fetal interests (Goodwin, 2016). This side tends to favor compulsory treatment over a woman's right to protect her own bodily integrity (Paltrow & Flavin, 2013). Given these three positions on compelled cesarean surgery, it is unsurprising that health care providers occasionally seek judicial authorization for compulsory medical treatment they believe is necessary to save the life of a viable unborn child (ACOG, 2014a). Petitions for compelled medical intervention during pregnancy will almost inevitably be decided in emergency hearings (HHS, 2013). Yet when pregnant women are competent adults, capable of giving informed consent, emergency hearings may not be an effective safeguard against infringements of women's constitutional rights (ACOG, 2014b, 2014c).

MANAGEMENT AND LAW ISSUES

8. What fetal protection policy addresses the concerns of the state regarding the unborn while affording pregnant women autonomous choice and the right to bodily integrity?
9. Does the criminalization of women's conduct during pregnancy (from falling down steps to refusing bed rest to smoking) support the values of society in protecting threats posed to fetuses?

Wrongful Life, Birth, and Pregnancy

Prenatal testing to avoid serious birth defects or diseases has made use of reproductive screening technologies very much a part of the culture of pregnancy (Lou, 2015). Nevertheless, health care providers still face the risk of wrongful life actions, as distinguishable from actions for wrongful birth and wrongful pregnancy, whenever a child is born with serious abnormalities. The distinctions are as follows:

- **Wrongful birth**: parent sues for failing to detect the defect that is present at birth
- **Wrongful pregnancy**: parent sues for an unplanned pregnancy, usually resulting from negligent sterilization or abortion procedures, or the negligent distribution or manufacture of contraceptives
- **Wrongful life**: child, born with natural defect, sues on their own behalf for negligence that deprived their parents of information during gestation that would have prompted them to terminate the pregnancy

(*See* Kitchen, 2015; Lou, 2015).

COURT DECISION

Wrongful Life

Willis v. Wu
[Mother on Behalf of Her Minor Disabled Son v. Physician]
607 S.E.2d 63 (Supreme Court of South Carolina 2004)

Facts: Jennie Willis, on behalf of her minor son, Thomas Willis, brought an action for wrongful life against Dr. Donald Wu. Thomas Willis was born with maximal hydrocephalus and will not develop cognitive functions beyond those of an infant. Jennie Willis claimed Dr. Wu was negligent when he failed to detect this congenital defect during a prenatal ultrasound procedure. According to Willis, had she known about the defect, she would have terminated the pregnancy.

Issue: Should South Carolina recognize a common law cause of action for wrongful life brought on behalf of children born with congenital defects?

With this decision, the Supreme Court of South Carolina joined the majority of courts that refuse to recognize an action for wrongful life. While some courts have fashioned arguments that life may not always be preferable to nonlife, they have not been able to determine damages. Thus, children seeking to bring an action for wrongful life in a jurisdiction that has yet to decide the issue must establish that the severity of their condition would make nonexistence preferable to life with their health condition. Children must then argue that the impossibility of arriving at an accurate assessment of damages should not be a fatal defect. Instead, damages can be set at the extraordinary expenses associated with treating their condition. In the end, however, children pursuing a cause of action for wrongful life face a daunting task, especially when considering the mounting precedents set by courts refusing to recognize such actions.

Holding and Decision: No. Children cannot have a cause of action for wrongful life because being born does not constitute an injury.

Analysis: Some courts reject wrongful life actions because physicians do not actually cause a congenital defect, which makes it improper under established tort principles to hold physicians liable for damages. The Supreme Court of South Carolina dispensed with this argument, however, since Willis did not claim Dr. Wu caused her son's defects. Instead, Willis claimed Dr. Wu's negligence deprived her of knowledge that would have led her to terminate the pregnancy.

In actions for wrongful life, children do not contend that they should have been born without defects, but rather that they should not have been born at all. Thus, most courts that reject actions for wrongful life hold that being born is not a legally cognizable injury. The typical rationale for these holdings is that life, whether experienced with or without a major physical handicap, is more precious than nonlife. These courts maintain that societal values serve as the foundation for this principle and that to recognize an action for wrongful life would contradict the widely held belief that all life has value.

Courts adjudicating actions for wrongful life also face the difficult task of assessing damages. Courts that refuse to recognize wrongful life actions need not reach the issue of damages, but many are willing to do so in order to expose what they believe to be a second fatal flaw in arguments for wrongful life. These courts hold that even if life may not always be preferable to nonlife, it would be impossible to determine damages based on the difference in value between life in an impaired condition and nonlife. The Supreme Court of South Carolina agreed, stating that the inability to determine a proper damage award should further preclude a cause of action for wrongful life.

The few courts that have recognized an action for wrongful life generally concede the impossibility of an accurate measure of damages. For instance, California recognizes wrongful life actions, but only allows damage awards for the extraordinary expenses associated with treating the child's condition. The few other jurisdictions that recognize actions for wrongful life also limit damage awards to such extraordinary expenses.

The South Carolina Supreme Court was unable to reconcile the inherent difficulties in recognizing an action for wrongful life. Instead, the court adopted the majority rationale that the prospect of a child arguing that they would have been better off if they had never been born at all is untenable. The court further held that the impossibility of determining damages also precludes an action for wrongful life. In addition, the court claimed that those jurisdictions recognizing an action for wrongful life fail to properly address the issue of damages.

This case would have taken on a new dimension if Dr. Wu possessed knowledge or equipment that was capable of curing or at least ameliorating Willis's condition at the time of the failed diagnosis. Under such circumstances, Willis could bring a malpractice action against Dr. Wu for damages associated with his arguably preventable condition. However, since Willis did not present such evidence, the court could not discuss the issue.

Rule of Law: Being born does not constitute an injury for children with congenital defects.

References discussing this court decision: Janssen, 2014; Lambert, 2013.

Sexually Transmitted Infections

Women are more likely than men to contract **sexually transmitted infections** and suffer serious complications, as depicted in **FEATURE BOX 34-1**, as a simple result of their biology.[LN2] Under the Affordable Care Act, the health insurance industry is now required to provide coverage for testing for high-risk strains of the **human papillomavirus** (HPV) in all women, the most common sexually transmitted viral infection, without co-payments or other cost-sharing requirements (NWLC, 2013). Sexually transmitted infections caused by bacteria or parasites can be treated with antibiotics; but there is no cure for infections caused by viruses (Richardson, 2016).[LN3]

HPV Vaccines: Gardasil and Cervarix

The contention that surrounds the HPV vaccine is the latest skirmish in the culture wars; when the FDA first approved Gardasil, it brought with it wave of controversy (Fentiman, 2014). Merck, the manufacturer of Gardasil, lobbied heavily for mandatory vaccination laws for women as the vaccine entered the market. Gardasil was promoted as a three-dose vaccine, for use in women ages 9 to 26 for the prevention of:

- Cervical precancers and cancers
- Genital warts
- Vulvar and vaginal precancers

MANAGEMENT AND LAW ISSUES

10. As comprehensive maternity care coverage with access to the newest reproductive technologies falls out of reach for more American women, how should the U.S. health care system deal with the 13% of working-age women who do not have maternity care coverage or who do not qualify for Medicaid insurance?
11. Is life with a severe disability more precious than nonlife?

FEATURE BOX 34-1

The Impact of Sexually Transmitted Infections on Women

- HPV leads to cancer for about 17,000 women every year, of which nearly 4,000 will die from the cancer.
- One in four adolescent girls between the ages of 14 and 19 has a sexually transmitted infection (such as gonorrhea, genital herpes, HIV/AIDS, HPV, or syphilis).
- Sexually transmitted infections increase the risk of acquiring HIV.
- The rate for sexually transmitted HPV infections is highest among young women ages 20 to 24.
- Untreated sexually transmitted infections cause infertility in at least 24,000 women in the United States each year.
- Untreated syphilis in women results in infant death in up to 40% of their pregnancies.
- With a prevalence rate approaching 50%, almost all sexually active people will contract at least one form of HPV during their lives.

Data from: CDC, 2016; HHS, 2015.

Shortly after Gardasil's approval, the **Advisory Committee on Immunization Practices** recommended Gardasil for routine use with middle school girls ages 11 and 12, with catch-up immunization for adolescents 13 to 26 who had not received the vaccine.[LN4] Unfortunately, this government recommendation focused attention about Gardasil disproportionately on concerns about women as opposed to public health concerns impacting both sexes (Orenstein & Yang, 2015). One side of the ensuing debate fixated on moral concern about female adolescent sexuality. The concern was that the vaccine could encourage sexual promiscuity by making sex seem safer and undermining parental authority (Fentiman, 2014). On the other side, assumptions about women's role in HPV infections formed a backdrop for efforts to promote mandatory vaccination for women (CDC, 2016). Both sides magnified conventional attitudes about women in ways that ultimately distracted from discussions on sexual health practices and the ethics of compulsory vaccination (Orenstein & Yang, 2015). One consequence of this decade-long controversy is that the rates of HPV vaccination are low and misinformation remains widespread (NWLC, 2013).

Of the 27 states that took action to require HPV vaccination for school entry, only Virginia and the District of Columbia enacted the requirement (Virginia Code § 32,1-46; District of Columbia Code § 7-1651.04(b)(1)) (Fentiman, 2014). GlaxoSmithKline subsequently obtained FDA approval for Cervarix, a competing vaccine to Merck's vaccine. Cervarix induces a higher immune response in women against HPV than Gardasil (Aizpuru, 2015). Today, the Advisory Committee on Immunization Practices recommends that all adolescents, male and female, receive the HPV vaccine between the ages of 11 and 26.

Gender-Based HPV Vaccination Mandates

The approval of a vaccine against cancer-causing HPV is a significant public health advance (Aizpuru, 2015). Yet, the attempt to mandate the HPV vaccination for only one gender presented concerns because it required only middle school-aged girls to be vaccinated (DeBois et al., 2015). While short-term clinical trials in thousands of young women did not reveal serious adverse effects, serious adverse events reported since the vaccine's approval (especially Guillain-Barré syndrome, a neurological illness resulting in muscle weakness and sometimes in paralysis) are a reminder that rare adverse events may surface as the HPV vaccine is administered to millions of women (Fentiman, 2014). The vaccine faced a risk of causing potential adverse events as well as risk that the vaccine would not be completely protective; thus, the gender-based vaccination mandate raised equal protection issues (DeBois et al., 2015).

Laws that make gender-based distinctions are reviewed with heightened scrutiny: gender-based vaccination mandates must serve an important state interest and the gender classification must substantially relate to serving that interest. While the goal of preventing cervical cancer was an important public health objective (and while cervical cancer is not a risk factor for males since they do not have cervixes, men can still contract and transmit

---

MANAGEMENT AND LAW ISSUES

12. Were women burdened with the HPV vaccination simply because of the preponderance of women affected by the virus?
13. If so, would gender-based HPV vaccination mandates have served that interest in a nondiscriminatory manner?

HPV), the justification for burdening women with the risks of HPV vaccination, and not males, was unclear (Aizpuru, 2015). Males:

- Benefited from an aggressive vaccination program of women
- Contributed to HPV transmission
- May reduce their own risk of infections and disease through HPV vaccination

(Aizpuru, 2015; Fentiman, 2014).

Admittedly, during clinical trials of the HPV vaccine, significantly more males than females reported mild fevers after the vaccination. But whether a mild fever would justify a challenge for gender-neutral mandates, as opposed to the mandate to vaccinate only females, is debatable since the vaccine industry made this medical determination, not the government units that might mandate the medical coverage (Lobo, 2016).

Medical Products Industry

While women's health is a part of all different areas of medicine, the medical products industry has concentrated on disorders that affect the female reproductive system and other disorders where there is at least a 70% preponderance of women affected by the disorders (*See* PhRMA, 2016). The harm of accessing unsafe prescription drugs must be balanced against the harm of restricting access to effective drugs when nearly two-thirds of women who gave birth take prescription drugs during pregnancy (Donley, 2015). Pregnant women are increasingly taking new drugs for cancer, depression, and other problems (Grigoriadis et al., 2013). Unfortunately, the overwhelming majority of pregnant women are using off-label prescriptions and medical devices that lack scientific support, and thus placing themselves and their fetuses at risk of harm without adequate knowledge of the therapeutic risks and benefits (Abbott & Ayres, 2014; FDA, 2014). More than 30 **drug registries** now track outcomes of pregnant women on various prescription drugs (Donley, 2015).

Restrictive Enrollment Criteria in Clinical Trials

Women consume more prescription drugs than men and disproportionately suffer a greater number of side effects from these drugs (Temming et al., 2016). On average, women are taking three prescription drugs in pregnancy with over half using four or more (Ramoz & Patel-Shori, 2014; Temming et al., 2016). Yet many drugs on the market have never been clinically tested in women, much less pregnant women; the reason for this is FDA regulatory restrictions (FDA, 2016 and 2014; Grigoriadis et al., 2013).

While federal law explicitly calls for the FDA to develop appropriate guidance on the inclusion of women in clinical trials, the FDA still places restrictive enrollment criteria on women participating in clinical trials of investigational products (Oppenheim, 2016). The influence of menstrual status (whether women are pre- or postmenopausal) and menstrual cycle on the pharmacokinetics of investigational drugs should be explored, as should the effects of

---

MANAGEMENT AND LAW ISSUES

14. Does the FDA cross the line when it requires women to undergo periodic pregnancy testing and use contraceptives as a condition of access to drugs known to cause birth defects?

concomitant supplementary estrogen treatment or systemic contraceptives (Hathaway, 2012). Finally, the influence of the investigational drug itself on the pharmacokinetics of selected oral contraceptives should be explored.

Even though the FDA is largely passive during the **clinical trial** stage of the research and development process, the FDA grants application for investigational new drugs. The pharmaceutical industry and academic institutions generally require women to agree to undergo an abortion in the event of contraceptive failure when participating in clinical trials of potential teratogens (Hathaway, 2012). Experimental protocol restrictions must be approved by local **institutional review boards** before clinical trials get under way, but few demands have been made to counter this abortion policy (Noah, 2014). However, since institutional review boards do not generally qualify as state actors, even if women objected to the restrictive enrollment criteria in privately sponsored clinical trials, they probably could not invoke constitutional protections against discrimination (Oppenheim, 2016). Moreover, there is no recognized right to participate in clinical trials (Noah, 2014).

Economic Impact of Failing to Prioritize Women's Health

As this chapter has demonstrated, it is necessary to distinguish women from men when addressing many health care issues. Failing to prioritize women's health is costly to the U.S. health care system, and the U.S. economy as a whole. For instance, women's contraception has the potential to significantly reduce public health funding; for every one dollar spent on providing family planning services, an estimated seven dollars are saved in Medicaid insurance expenditures for intended pregnancy-related and newborn care (Guttmacher, 2016c).

Access to health care on an equal basis for men and women will also help eliminate discrimination against women as far as their education and workplace opportunities. Two issues discussed in this chapter, the refusal to grant young women over-the-counter access to emergency contraception and the requirements of parental consent or notification for an abortion, are just two examples of how young women's sexual and reproductive lives are shaped and limited by laws and public policies that constrict their education opportunities and subsequent ability to compete economically in the workplace. When so many adolescent girls have unintended pregnancies by the time they reach the age of 20, the nation is unnecessarily disadvantaging a large segment of its working-age population. Americans should really ask themselves whether it is necessary to circumscribe the health care options available to young women who experience sexual desire or sexual violence in the name of protecting the young: is this really the right road to travel given the economic costs to society by this choice? Is it time to accept the right of women to have sex without accepting the possibility of pregnancy and motherhood (Smith, 2015)?

It has been almost 50 years since the U.S. Supreme Court stated women have the right to access contraception. Yet, half a century later, the broad attack on family planning, grounded in opposition to nonprocreative sex, continues. Many American women still cannot choose when to become pregnant and how many children to have because they lack access to maternal health care. Contraception and abortion are about more than fighting economic inequalities. Women's rights and freedoms are limited by strict controls on unwanted pregnancies while at the same time little is done to ensure unintended pregnancies do not occur in the first place, nor is much done to assist women with raising the child. It is necessary to begin effectively eliminating the root causes of **gender disparities** in health.

LAW FACT

In Vitro Fertilization Restrictions

Does Congress or do state legislatures have the right to decide what to do with embryos created through in vitro fertilization?

Yes. The law of reproduction is central to the future of the family in American society. Many infertility patients are grappling over the fate of their human embryos with little support for the choices they will make. Families with leftover frozen embryos generally have four choices:

- Defer the decision and leave them in storage
- Discard them

- Donate to another couple for pregnancy
- Donate to research

An estimated 500,000 embryos are in cryopreservation in the United States (Carbone & Madeira, 2016).

In the United States, the lack of publically funded research and insurance coverage for in vitro fertilization also means less oversight and few **standards of care** for what is appropriate conduct. Women like Nadya Suleman are vulnerable to less reputable practices and to lack of protection by the medical establishment.[LN5] The decades-long failure of the medical community to determine the safety or ethical permissibility of what was happening to Suleman during her five pregnancies deserves criticism; the loss of licensure to practice medicine by her fertility physician is an inadequate response to a health care system that turned a blind eye to her situation and the plight of her children. States interested in securing the safety of their citizens need to reconsider how they can help provide support for all families, not just the traditional nuclear family. This support includes providing women with the ability to be able to choose effective ways to limit the size of their families, if they so desire, prior to the establishment of a pregnancy.

— *In re Accusation against Kamrava*, No. 06-2009-197098 (Medical Board of California, Department of Consumer Affairs 2009).

See, e.g., Calandrillo & Deliganis, 2015; Carbone & Cahn, 2015; Carbone & Madeira, 2016; Mutcherson, 2015 (discussing this decision).

CHAPTER SUMMARY

- Although advancements in women's civil rights have been made since the 1960s, continued attempts are made to restrict and carve out exceptions to those rights as evidenced by the sheer amount of litigation.
- The U.S. rate of infant mortality is high compared to other industrialized nations, in large part because many babies are born prematurely and with complications without proper prenatal care.
- Reproductive health needs are not adequately met in the United States as evidenced by the high rate of unintended pregnancies, high number of abortions, lack of access to birth control, and high rate of teen pregnancy as compared to other similarly situated countries.
- Plan B, the morning-after pill, is approved by the FDA, but women often face obstacles to obtaining it, such as hospitals and pharmacists refusing to dispense it.
- Not all health insurance plans are required to provide medical coverage for prescription contraceptives but many do for the simple reason of economics: birth control costs are less than those of a pregnancy.
- Health insurance coverage for drugs related to males' reproductive systems appears to be granted more quickly and easily than it is for drugs for females' reproductive needs, particularly newer, less invasive forms of birth control and family planning.
- It is difficult for women to obtain maternity care coverage, as offerings are limited and often unaffordable or unattainable.
- Many suspect price discrimination within the health insurance industry as it seems firms attempt to steer women toward less expensive forms of birth control, and there is little or no state or federal legislation on this topic.
- Wrongful birth and wrongful pregnancy are two kinds of lawsuits that may be brought related to childbirth; wrongful life suits are much less commonly accepted by courts.
- Although the U.S. Supreme Court ruled that women have the right to an abortion in the 1973 landmark *Roe v. Wade* decision, litigation has steadfastly continued in various states in an attempt to regulate abortion to the point where it is nearly impossible for many women to obtain one, even when their health or life is at stake.
- The safety of many drugs for use by pregnant women, and even women in general, has not been thoroughly studied; it is often assumed that drugs work the same way for women as they do for men and that there are no different risks or side effects.

LAW NOTES

1. In *McCullen*, the U.S. Supreme Court misunderstood, whether deliberately or not, the purpose of sidewalk counselors, assuming they were different from abortion protestors who engage in physical violence, including murder, attempted murder, bombing, arson, assault, battery, hate mail, and bomb threats (Cherry, 2015). Yet, sidewalk counseling is a common tactic among abortion protestors; sidewalk counselors talk to and yell at women at abortion clinics in an effort to persuade them not to have an abortion. Although the Court stated that sidewalk counseling is done in a quiet and friendly manner, the purpose of such counseling is to shame women into not having abortions.

2. There are over 100 strains of HPV, with over 30 types that can cause cervical cancer and genital warts. HPV is the major cause of cervical cancer (Aizpuru, 2015). Most sexually active adults (ages 15 to 49) will acquire HPV at some time in their lives and will never even know it since it usually has no symptoms, goes away on its own, and does not generally cause disease. Some types of HPV can infect a woman's cervix and cause the cells to change; when HPV is gone, the cervical cells go back to normal. However, sometimes HPV does not go away; instead, it persists and continues to change the cells on a woman's cervix, which can lead to cancer over time if not treated (Fentiman, 2014).

3. In addition to HPV, there are more than 20 types of sexually transmitted infections, including:

   - **Gonorrhea**, a bacterial infection that is increasingly becoming drug resistant and if untreated, can lead to pelvic inflammatory disease and problems with pregnancy and infertility (*E.g.*, Hill et al., 2015)
   - **Genital herpes**, a lifetime viral infection involving periodic blister outbreaks, for which symptoms can be lessened with prescription drugs (*E.g.*, Baang, 2015)
   - **Human immunodeficiency virus** (HIV)/**acquired immunodeficiency syndrome** (AIDS), a lifetime viral infection that damages the body's immune system; HIV can be treated as a chronic disease (*E.g.*, NIH, 2015)
   - **Syphilis**, a bacterial infection treatable with antibiotics; the syphilis sores make HIV transmission easier and the bacterial infection can cause birth defects if a woman is pregnant, otherwise, today, syphilis itself rarely causes serious health problems in those who are infected (*E.g.*, Alarcón-Cabrera et al., 2016)

4. The Advisory Committee on Immunization Practices consists of 15 experts in fields associated with immunization who have been selected by the Secretary of the U.S. Department of Health and Human Services to provide advice and guidance on the most effective means to prevent vaccine-preventable diseases.

5. Dr. Michael Kamrava provided fertility treatments to Nadya Suleman beginning when she was a teenager, resulting in the birth of 14 children. Suleman was deeply depressed and suicidal, and obsessed with having babies, but Kamrava never referred her for a mental health evaluation (Daar, 2012). During that time, Suleman suffered three miscarriages and tried artificial insemination and fertility drugs but was never successful in having a child until Kamrava started performing in vitro fertilization on her (Forman, 2011). Kamrava had one of the worst live-birth rates among fertility specialists in the United States before the Medical Board of California revoked his medical license.

REFERENCES

Abbott R., & Ayres, I. (2014). Evidence and extrapolation: Mechanisms for regulating off-label uses of drugs and devices. *Duke Law Journal, 64,* 377–435.

Abrams, K. (2015). Seeking emotional ends with legal means. *California Law Review, 103,* 1657–1678.

Abrams, P. (2013). The scarlet letter: The Supreme Court and the language of abortion stigma. *Michigan Journal of Gender and Law, 19,* 293–337.

ACOG (American Congress of Obstetricians and Gynecologists). (2016). *Committee opinion: Refusal of medically recommended treatment during pregnancy.* Washington, DC: ACOG.

___. (2014a). *Professional liability and risk management: An essential guide for obstetrician–gynecologists* (3rd ed.).

___. (2014b). Health literacy: Committee Opinion No. 585. American College of Obstetricians and Gynecologists. *Obstetrics and Gynecology, 123,* 380–383.

___. (2014c). Effective patient-physician communication. Committee Opinion No. 587. *Obstetrics and Gynecology, 123,* 389–393.

AHRQ (Agency for Healthcare Research and Quality). (2013). *Most frequent conditions in U.S. hospitals.* Rockville, MD: AHRQ.

Aizpuru, K. M. (2015). Gardasil, gendered discourse, and public health. *Georgetown Journal of Gender and the Law, 16,* 347–378.

Alarcón-Cabrera, R., et al. (2016). Disseminated red violaceous papulonodular lesions. *JAMA Dermatology, 152*(1), 83–84.

Anderson, B. J. (2015). Litigating abortion access cases in the post-*Windsor* world. *Columbia Journal of Gender and Law, 29,* 143–155.

Angela, L., et al. (2014). Complications: Abortion's impact on women. *Issues in Law and Medicine, 29,* 173–175.

Armstrong, C. J. (2015). Bypassing her constitutional rights: How the Nebraska Supreme Court set a damaging precedent for pregnant minors seeking abortion care. *American University: The Modern American, 9,* 10–15.

Armstrong, W., et al. (2012, April 23). Why we have gone to court against the Obama mandate. *The Wall Street Journal*, p. A11.

Baang, J. (2015). Pericoital application of tenofovir gel reduced risk for herpes simplex virus type 2 in HIV-negative women. *Annals of Internal Medicine, 163*(12), 163–175.

Bader, V., et al. (2014). The role of previous contraception education and moral judgment in contraceptive use. *Journal of Midwifery and Women's Health, 59*(4), 447–451.

Bagley, N. (2015). Medicine as a public calling. *Michigan Law Review, 114*, 57–106.

Bakelaar, R. (2014). The North Carolina woman's right to know act: An unconstitutional infringement on a physician's First Amendment right to free speech. *Michigan Journal of Gender and Law, 20*, 187–223.

Barket, C., et al. (2014). United States Supreme Court update. *Appellate Advocate, 27*, 124–171.

Beety, V. E. (2011). Mississippi initiative 26: Personhood and the criminalization of intentional and unintentional acts by pregnant women. *Mississippi Law Journal, 81*, 55–62.

Benedict, K. S. (2013). When might does not create religious rights: For-profit corporations' employees and the contraceptive coverage mandate. *Columbia Journal of Gender and Law, 26*, 58–122.

Blackman, J. (2016). Gridlock. *Harvard Law Review, 130*, 241–304.

Bonner, M. H., & Sheriff, J. A. (2013). A child needs a champion: Guardian ad litem representation for prenatal children. *William and Mary Journal of Women and the Law, 19*, 511–584.

Brown, E. C. F. (2015). Resurrecting health care rate regulation. *Hastings Law Journal, 67*, 85–142.

Cahill, C. M. (2013). Abortion and disgust. *Harvard Civil Rights-Civil Liberties Law Review, 48*, 409–456.

Cahn, N., & Carbone, J. (2015). Growing inequality and children. *American University Journal of Gender, Social Policy and the Law, 23*, 282–317.

Calandrillo, S. P., & Deliganis, C. V. (2015). In vitro fertilization and the law: How legal and regulatory neglect compromised a medical breakthrough. *Arizona Law Review, 57*, 311–342.

Callaghan, W. M., Acting Chief, Maternal and Infant Health Branch, Centers for Disease Control and Prevention. (2010, May, 12). CDC Congressional Testimony: Prematurity and infant mortality: What happens when infants are born too early? Hearing before the Subcommittee on Health Committee on Energy and Commerce, U.S. House of Representatives, Washington, DC.

Carbone, J., & Cahn, N. (2015). Intersections in reproduction: Perspectives on abortion and assisted reproductive technologies: The triple system for regulating women's reproduction. *Journal of Law, Medicine and Ethics, 43*, 275–300.

Carbone, J., & Madeira, J. L. (2016). Buyers in the baby market: Toward a transparent consumerism. *Washington Law Review, 91*, 71–107.

Case, M. A. (2015). Why live-and-let-live is not a viable solution to the difficult problems of religious accommodation in the age of sexual civil rights. *Southern California Law Review, 88*, 463–492.

CDC (Centers for Disease Control and Prevention). (2016). *Fact sheet, Genital HPV infection.* Atlanta, GA: CDC.

____. (2015). *Abortion surveillance.*

Cherry, A. L. (2015). Shifting our focus from retribution to social justice: An alternative vision for the treatment of pregnant women who harm their fetuses. *Journal of Law and Health, 28*, 6–61.

CIA (Central Intelligence Agency). (2013). *The world factbook, rank.* Washington, DC: CIA.

Cohen, D. S., & Bingenheimer, J. B. (2016). Abortion rights and the largeness of the fraction 1/6. *University of Pennsylvania Law Review, 164*, 115–134.

Corbin, C. M. (2015). Corporate religious liberty. *Constitutional Commentary, 30*, 277–308.

Daar, J. (2012). Federalizing embryo transfers: Taming the wild west of reproductive medicine? *Columbia Journal of Gender and Law, 23*, 257–325.

Deboer, M. J. (2015). Legislating morality progressively: The contraceptive coverage mandate, religious freedom, and public health policy and ethics. *Journal of Law and Health, 28*, 62–120.

DeBois, W., et al. (2015). Anticipating HIV vaccines; Sketching an agenda for public health ethics and policy in the United States. *Saint Louis University Journal of Health Law and Policy, 8*, 225–257.

Del Negro, P. H., & Aronson, S. W. (2015). Religious accommodations for employees in the health care workplace. *Journal of Health and Life Sciences Law, 8*(3), 72–99.

Deshpande, N. A., & Oxford, C. M. (2012). Management of pregnant patients who refuse medically indicated cesarean delivery. *Reviews in Obstetrics and Gynecology, 5*(3–4), 144–150.

Donley, G. (2015). Encouraging maternal sacrifice: How regulations governing the consumption of pharmaceuticals during pregnancy prioritize fetal safety over maternal health and autonomy. *New York University Review of Law and Social Change, 39*, 45–88.

____. (2013). Does the Constitution protect abortions based on fetal anomaly? Examining the potential for disability-selective abortion bans in the age of prenatal whole genome sequencing. *Michigan Journal of Gender and Law, 20*, 291–328.

Drobac, J. A., & Wesley, J. L. (2014). Religion and employment antidiscrimination law: Past, present, and post *Hosanna-Tabor. New York University Annual Survey of American Law, 69*, 761–835.

Duane, M. (2013). The disclaimer dichotomy: A First Amendment analysis of compelled speech in disclosure ordinances governing crisis pregnancy centers and laws mandating biased physician counseling. *Cardozo Law Review, 35*, 349–389.

Duke, J. (2015). Religious freedom and the little corporation that could: *Burwell v. Hobby Lobby Stores, Inc. Mississippi College Law Review, 34*, 89–112.

Epstein, R. A. (2013). The defeat of the contraceptive mandate in *Hobby Lobby*: Right results, wrong reasons. *Cato Supreme Court Review, 14*, 34–69.

FDA (U.S. Food and Drug Administration). (2016). *The inclusion of women in clinical trials.* Bethesda, MD: FDA.

____. (2014). *Evaluation of sex-specific data in medical device clinical studies: Guidance for industry and FDA staff.*

Fentiman, L. C. (2014). Sex, science, and the age of anxiety. *Nebraska Law Review, 92*, 455–502.

Finer, L. B., & Zolna, M. R. (2016). Declines in unintended pregnancy in the United States, 2008–2011. *New England Journal of Medicine, 374*(9), 843–852.

Fischer, C., & Kasper, J. (2014). Access to contraception. *The Georgetown Journal of Gender and the Law, 15*, 37–55.

Fore, W. (2014). A joyful heart is good medicine: Sexuality conversion bans in the courts. *Michigan Journal of Gender & Law, 21*, 311–340.

Forman, D. L. (2011). When bad mothers make worse law: A critique of legislative limits on embryo transfer. *University of Pennsylvania Journal of Law and Social Change, 14,* 273–312.

Forsythe, C. (2014). The medical assumption at the foundation of *Roe v. Wade* and its implications for women's health. *Issues in Law and Medicine, 29,* 183–214.

Forte, D. F. (2013). Life, heartbeat, birth: A medical basis for reform. *Ohio State Law Journal, 74,* 121–148.

Fram, A. (2015, April 30). GOP Congress wants to let DC bosses fire women for having abortions. *Associated Press.*

Franzonello, A. (2013). Reproductive healthcare legislation: Where we've been and where we're going. *Albany Law Journal of Science and Technology, 23,* 519–529.

Friedman, A. D. (2013). Reproductive justice: Bad medicine: Abortion and the battle over who speaks for women's health. *William and Mary Journal of Women and the Law, 20,* 45–72.

Gandhi, N., Executive Vice President and Chief Population Health Officer of the Mount Sinai Health System. (2016, February 19). Remarks at the panel discussion on Payer-Provider Convergence: From Volume to Value; New Frontiers in Payer Provider Collaboration at the 2016 Wharton Health Care Business Conference on the Innovation Game; The Race Between Entrants+Incumbents, Philadelphia, PA.

Gedicks, F. M., & Van Tassel, R. G. (2014). RFRA exemptions from the contraception mandate: An unconstitutional accommodation of religion. *Harvard Civil Rights-Civil Liberties Law Review, 49,* 343–380.

Glass, D. J. (2016). Not in my hospital: The future of state statutes requiring abortion providers to maintain admitting privileges at local hospitals. *Akron Law Review, 49,* 249–284.

Goldsmith, L. M. (2014). Redefining viability: Why the state must ensure viable alternatives to pregnancy and motherhood. *Cardozo Journal of Law and Gender, 20,* 579–875.

Goodwin, M. (2016). The pregnancy penalty. *Health Matrix: Journal of Law-Medicine, 26,* 17–57.

___. (2014). Fetal protection laws: Moral panic and the new constitutional battlefront. *California Law Review, 102,* 781–839.

Gray, S., & Holden, A. (2014). Fifteenth annual gender and sexuality law: Annual review article: Abortion. *The Georgetown Journal of Gender and the Law, 15,* 3–36.

Greendorfer, M. A. (2015). Blurring lines between churches and secular corporations: The compelling case of the benefit corporation's right to the free exercise of religion (with a post-*Hobby Lobby* epilogue). *Delaware Journal of Corporate Law, 39,* 819–860.

Gregory, E. C. W., et al. (2014). *NCHS data brief: Trends in infant mortality in the United States, 2006–2012.* Hyattsville, MD: Centers for Disease Control and Prevention, National Center for Health Statistics (NCHS).

Gribow, G. (2013). Forced obstetrical intervention: The role of religion and culture, and the woman's autonomous choice. *Hastings Women's Law Journal, 24,* 177–195.

Griffin, L. C. (2015). *Hobby Lobby:* The crafty case that threatens women's rights and religious freedom. *Hastings Constitutional Law Quarterly, 42,* 641–693.

Grigoriadis, S., et al. (2013). Antidepressant exposure during pregnancy and congenital malformations: Is there an association? A systematic review and meta-analysis of the best evidence. *Journal of Clinical Psychiatry, 74*(4), 293–308.

Grindlay, K., et al. (2013). Prescription requirements and over-the-counter access to oral contraceptives: A global review. *Contraception, 88*(1), 91–96.

Guttmacher Institute. (2016a). *Refusing to provide health services.* New York, NY: Guttmacher.

___. (2016b). *Insurance coverage of contraceptives.*

___. (2016c). *Publicly funded family planning services in the United States.*

___. (2015a). *Fact sheet: Unintended pregnancies in the United States.*

___. (2015b). *State policies in brief: Insurance coverage of contraceptives.*

Hale, P. R. (2015). It is hard to make everyone happy: The rights gained and lost by companies and employees in the context of the Affordable Care Act contraception mandate. *Southern Illinois University Law Journal, 39,* 323–345.

Hansen, R., & Newman, R. (2015). Health care: Access after health care reform. *The Georgetown Journal of Gender and the Law, 16,* 191–227.

Hardwick, T., & Hodsdo, H. (2012). Abortion. *The Georgetown Journal of Gender and the Law, 13,* 109–144.

Hathaway, C. (2012). A patent extension proposal to end the underrepresentation of women in clinical trials and secure meaningful drug guidance for women. *Food and Drug Law Journal, 67,* 143–176.

Heinzerling, L. (2014). The FDA's plan B fiasco: Lessons for administrative law. *Georgetown Law Journal, 102,* 927–989.

Helfand, M. A. (2016). Identifying substantial burdens. *University of Illinois Law Review, 16,* 1771–1807.

HHS (U.S. Department of Health and Human Services. (2015). *Sexually transmitted infections.* Rockville, MD: HHS, Office on Women's Health.

___. (2013). *National standards for culturally and linguistically appropriate services in health and health care: A blueprint for advancing and sustaining CLAS (culturally and linguistically appropriate services) policy and practice.* Rockville, MD: HHS, Office of Minority Health.

Hill, B. J. (2012). What is the meaning of health? Constitutional implications of defining "medical necessity" and "essential health benefits" under the Affordable Care Act. *American Journal of Law and Medicine, 38,* 445–470.

Hill, M. G., et al. (2015). Screening for chlamydia and gonorrhea cervicitis and implications for pregnancy outcome: Are we testing and treating at the right time? *Journal of Reproductive Medicine, 60*(7–8), 301–308.

Hrobak, R. M., & Wilson, R. F. (2014). Emergency contraceptives or abortion-inducing drugs? Empowering women to make informed decisions. *Washington and Lee Law Review, 71*(2), 1386–1428.

Huberfeld, N. (2013). With liberty and access for some: The ACA's disconnect for women's health. *Fordham Urban Law Journal, 40,* 1357–1393.

Huddleston, K. (2016). Border checkpoints and substantive due process: Abortion rights in the border zone. *Yale Law Journal, 125,* 1744–1803.

James, B. C., & Savitz, L. A. (2011). How Intermountain trimmed health care costs through robust quality improvement efforts. *Health Affairs, 30*(6), 1–7.

Janssen, W. M. (2014). A duty to continue selling medicines. *American Journal of Law and Medicine, 40,* 330–392.

Jayadevan, V. R. (2015). Dying in original sin vis-à-vis living in disgrace—In defense of the right to socioeugenic abortion as personal liberty. *Hamline Law Review, 38,* 85–125.

Johnsen, D. (2015). State court protection of reproductive rights: The past, the perils, and the promise. *Columbia Journal of Gender and Law, 29,* 41–84.

Jones, R. K., & Jerman, J. (2014). Abortion incidence and service availability in the United States. *Perspectives on Sexual and Reproductive Health, 46*(1), 3–14.

Jordan, K. A. (2015). The contraceptive mandate: Compelling interest or ideology? *Journal of Legislation, 41,* 1–64.

Kaiser Family Foundation. (2014). *Emergency contraception.* Menlo Park, CA: Kaiser.

Kapp, M. B. (2011). Public health reform: Patient Protection and Affordable Care Act implications for the public's health: Conscripted physician services and the public's health. *Journal of Law, Medicine and Ethics, 39,* 414–420.

Kelso, R. R. (2015). The structure of *Planned Parenthood v. Casey* abortion rights law: Strict scrutiny for substantial obstacles on abortion choice and otherwise. *Quinnipiac Law Review, 34,* 76–139.

Kendrick, L. (2014). Nonsense on sidewalks: Content discrimination in *McCullen v Coakley. The Supreme Court Review, 2014,* 215–242.

Kitchen, R. K. (2015). Holistic pregnancy: Rejecting the theory of the adversarial mother. *Hastings Constitutional Law Quarterly, 26,* 207–269.

Koss, K. K. (2014). Constitutional law: Judge Posner got it right: Requiring abortion physicians to have hospital admitting privileges places an undue burden on a woman seeking an abortion. *The Seventh Circuit Review, 9,* 263–300.

Lambert, W. B. (2013). The price of life: A prediction of South Carolina's approach to expert testimony on hedonic damages using the willingness-to-pay method. *South Carolina Law Review, 64,* 1037–1060.

Lang, D. (2014). Truthful but misleading? The precarious balance of autonomy and state interests in *Casey* and second-generation physician-patient regulation. *University of Pennsylvania Journal of Constitutional Law, 16,* 1353–1416.

Laycock, D. (2014). Religious liberty and the culture wars. *University of Illinois Law Review, 2014,* 839–878.

Lepard, K. (2013). Standing their ground: Corporations' fight for religious rights in light of the enactment of the Patient Protection and Affordable Care Act contraceptive coverage mandate. *Texas Tech Law Review, 45,* 1041–1070.

Lobo, J. (2016). Vindicating the vaccine: Injecting strength into mandatory school vaccination requirements to safeguard the public health. *Boston College Law Review, 57,* 261–296.

Lou, H. (2015). Eugenics then and now: Constitutional limits on the use of reproductive screening technologies. *Hastings Constitutional Law Quarterly, 42,* 393–414.

Mac Dougall, S. (2015). Over-the-counter access to oral contraception: Reproductive autonomy on pharmacy shelves or a political Trojan horse? *Columbia Journal of Gender and Law, 30,* 204–253.

Madeira, J. L. (2014). Aborted emotions: Regret, relationality, and regulation. *Michigan Journal of Gender and Law, 21,* 1–66.

Mattingly, E. P. (2013). "Hobby-Lobby"-ing for religious freedom: Crafting the religious employer exemption to the PPACA. *Kentucky Law Journal, 102,* 183–209.

Melling, L. (2015). Religious refusals to public accommodations laws: Four reasons to say no. *Harvard Journal of Law and Gender, 38,* 177–192.

____. (2014). Lift the scarlet letter from abortion. *Cardozo Law Review, 35,* 1715–1727.

Melone, M. A. (2015). Corporations and religious freedom: *Hobby Lobby Stores* - A missed opportunity to reconcile a flawed law with a flawed health care system. *Indiana Law Review, 48,* 461–508.

Mendelson, N. A. (2010). Disclosing political oversight of agency decision making. *Michigan Law Review, 108*(7), 1127–1178.

Miller, J. B. (2014). The buffer zone: Where we've been and where we're going. *Boston Bar Journal, 58,* 31–34.

Minkoff, H., & Marshall, M. F. (2016). Fetal risks, relative risks, and relatives' risks. *American Journal of Bioethics, 16,* 3–11.

Minkoff, H., et al. (2014). The fetus, the potential child, and the ethical obligations of obstetricians. *Obstetrics and Gynecology, 123,* 1100–1103.

Moreno, J. A. (2015). Extralegal Supreme Court policy-making. *William and Mary Bill of Rights Journal, 24,* 451–518.

Morse, E. A. (2013). Lifting the fog: Navigating penalties in the Affordable Care Act. *Creighton Law Review, 46,* 207–256.

Mutcherson, K. M. (2015). Procreative Pluralism. *Berkeley Journal of Gender, Law and Justice, 30,* 22–75.

NCHS (National Center for Health Statistics). (2015). *National vital statistics report: Deaths: Final data for 2013.* Hyattsville, MD: Centers for Disease Control and Prevention, NCHS.

____. (2013). *Use of emergency contraception among women aged 15–44.*

New, M. J. (2015). Analyzing the impact of state level contraception mandates on public health outcomes. *Ave Maria Law Review, 13,* 345–367.

NIH (National Institute on Drug Abuse). (2015). *Drug and alcohol use: A significant risk factor for HIV.* Bethesda, MD: NIH.

Noah, B. A. (2014). The future of health law: Exemplary insight into trending topics; The inclusion of pregnant women in clinical research. *Saint Louis University Journal of Health Law and Policy, 7,* 353–388.

Norris, C., & Turk, W. (2013). Equal protection. *The Georgetown Journal of Gender and the Law, 14,* 397–448.

Note. (2015). Physically intrusive abortion restrictions as Fourth Amendment searches and seizures. *Harvard Law Review, 128,* 951–972.

NWLC (National Women's Law Center). (2016). *Fact sheet: Nondiscrimination protection in the Affordable Care Act; Section 1557.* Washington, DC: NWLC.

____. (2015a). *State of women's coverage: Health plan violations of the Affordable Care Act.*

____. (2015b). *Pharmacy refusals 101.*

____. (2015c). *State of birth control coverage: Health plan violations of the Affordable Care Act.*

____. (2013). *Women's preventive services in the Affordable Care Act.*

Oleske, J. M. (2014). The public meaning of RFRA versus legislators' understanding of RLPA: A response to Professor Laycock. *Vanderbilt Law Review En Banc, 67,* 125–134.

Olson, J. R. (2013). Defining fetal life: An establishment clause analysis of religiously motivated informed consent provisions. *Indiana Law Journal, 88,* 1113–1145.

Oman, N. B. (2015). The need for a law of church and market. *Duke Law Journal, 64,* 141–160.

Oppenheim, S. F. (2016). Jack & Jill take lots of pills, but Jill comes tumbling after: Gender inequality in privately funded early phase clinical trials. *William and Mary Journal of Women and the Law, 22,* 393–418.

Orenstein, D. G., & Yang, T. (2015). Intersection of law, policy and prevention: From beginning to end: The importance of evidence-based policymaking in vaccination mandates. *Journal of Law, Medicine and Ethics, 43,* 99–108.

Ouellette, A. (2013). Health reform and the Supreme Court: The ACA survives the battle of the broccoli and fortifies itself against future fatal attack. *Albany Law Review, 76,* 87–119.

Paltrow, L. M., & Flavin, J. (2013). Arrests of and forced interventions on pregnant women in the United States: Implications for women's legal status and public health. *Journal of Health Politics, Policy and Law, 38*, 299–343.

Pergament, D. (2013). What does choice really mean? Prenatal testing, disability, and special education without illusions. *Health Matrix: Journal of Law-Medicine, 23*, 55–117.

PhRMA (Pharmaceutical Research and Manufacturer's Association). (2016). *Industry profile.* Washington, DC: PhRMA.

Prior, K. A. (2014). The ultra sound-off: The ultrasound mandate debate and a litigator's guide to overcoming obstacles to a woman's right to abortion. *Suffolk Journal of Trial and Appellate Advocacy, 19*, 155–175.

Pruitt, L. R., & Vanegas, M. R. (2015). Urbanormativity, spatial privilege, and judicial blind spots in abortion law. *Berkeley Journal of Gender, Law and Justice, 30*, 76–153.

Quast, P. C. (2014). Respecting legislators and rejecting baselines: Rebalancing *Casey. Notre Dame Law Review, 90*, 913–939.

Rahders, S. L. (2015). Do as I say, not as I do: Sexual health education and the criminalization of teen sexuality in the United States. *Hastings Women's Law Journal, 26*, 147–182.

Ramoz, L. L., & Patel-Shori, N. M. (2014). Recent changes in pregnancy and lactation labeling: Retirement of risk categories. *Pharmacotherapy, 34*(4), 389–395.

Richardson, J. (2016). Criminal transmission of HIV laws: Are they outdated or are they still useful? *Houston Law Review, 53*, 1179–1207.

Richters, S. (2013). The moral interception of oral contraception: Potential constitutional claims against the FDA's prescription requirement for a progestin-only birth control pill. *Journal of Law and Policy, 22*, 393–432.

Robertson, J. A. (2015). *Science challenges for law and policy: Science disputes in abortion law. Texas Law Review, 93*, 1849–1883.

Rudary, D. J. (2013). Drafting a sensible conscience clause: A proposal for meaningful conscience protections for religious employers objecting to the mandated coverage of prescription contraceptives. *Health Matrix: Journal of Law-Medicine, 23*, 353–394.

Rutledge, T. E. (2014). A corporation has no soul: The business entity law response to challenges to the PPACA contraceptive mandate. *William and Mary Business Law Review, 5*, 1–53.

Samuels, L. J. (2014). Mifepristone protocol legislation: The anti-choice movement's disingenuous method of attack on the reproductive rights of women and how courts should respond. *Columbia Journal of Gender and Law, 26*, 316–342.

Sawicki, N. N. (2016). Mandating disclosure of conscience-based limitations on medical practice. *American Journal of Law and Medicine, 42*, 85–128.

Sawyer, H. (2015). The role of Congress in advancing civil rights: Lessons from two movements. *Columbia Journal of Gender and Law, 29*, 165–176.

Scaldo, S. A. (2013). Deadly dicta: *Roe*'s "unwanted motherhood", *Gonzalez*'s "women's regret" and the shifting narrative of abortion jurisprudence. *Drexel Law Review, 6*, 87–131.

Schlueter, L. L. (2013). 40th anniversary of *Roe v. Wade*: Reflections past, present and future. *Ohio Northern University Law Review, 40*, 105–249.

Sepinwall, A. (2015). Corporate piety and impropriety: *Hobby Lobby*'s extension of RFRA rights to the for-profit corporation. *Harvard Business Law Review, 5*, 173–204.

___. (2014). Conscience and complicity: Assessing pleas for religious exemptions in *Hobby Lobby*'s wake. *University of Chicago Law Review, 82*(4), 101–188.

Sepper, E. (2015). Free exercise *Lochner*ism. *Columbia Law Review, 115*, 1453–1519.

___. (2015b). Gendering corporate conscience. *Harvard Journal of Law and Gender, 38*, 193–233.

___. Associate Professor, Washington University School of Law. (2014, December 9). Remarks at the Harvard Law School Symposium on Religious Accommodation in the Age of Civil Rights: Gendering Corporate Conscience, Cambridge, MA.

Shainwald, S. (2013). Reproductive justice: Reproductive injustice in the new millennium. *William and Mary Journal of Women and the Law, 20*, 123–171.

Siegel, N. S., & Siegel, R. B. (2013). Equality arguments for abortion rights. *UCLA Law Review Discourse, 60*, 160–170.

Siegel, R. B. (2013). Equality and choice: Sex equality perspectives on reproductive rights in the work of Ruth Bader Ginsburg. *Columbia Journal of Gender and Law, 25*, 63–80.

Smith, P. J. (2015). Contraceptive comstockery: Reasoning from immorality to illness in the twenty-first century. *Connecticut Law Review, 47*, 971–1023.

Sommers, B. D., et al. (2012). Mortality and access to care among adults after state Medicaid expansions. *New England Journal of Medicine, 367*(11), 1025–1034.

Stopler, G. (2015). Biopolitics and reproductive justice: Fertility policies between women's rights and state and community interests. *University of Pennsylvania Journal of Law and Social Change, 18*, 169–207.

Strasser, M. (2014). The new frontier? IVF's challenges for state courts and legislatures. *SMU Science and Technology Law Review, 17*, 125–159.

Suter, S. M. (2013). The politics of information: Informed consent in abortion and end-of-life decision making. *American Journal of Law and Medicine, 39*, 7–61.

Taub, J. S. (2015). Is *Hobby Lobby* a tool for limiting corporate constitutional rights? *Constitutional Commentary, 30*, 403–429.

Temming, L. A., et al. (2016). Clinical management of medications in pregnancy and lactation. *American Journal of Obstetrics and Gynecology, 214*(6), 698–702.

Tenenbaum, E. M. (2013). The union of contraceptive services and the Affordable Care Act gives birth to First Amendment concerns. *Albany Law Journal of Science and Technology, 23*, 539–580.

Teufel, J., et al. (2015). Legal aid inequities predict health disparities. *Hamline Law Review, 38*, 329–360.

Toscano, V., & Reiter, E. (2014). Upholding a 40-year-old promise: Why the Texas sonogram act is unlawful according to *Planned Parenthood v. Casey. Pace Law Review, 34*, 128–184.

Trussell, J., et al. (2016). Emergency contraception: A last chance to prevent unintended pregnancy. *Contemporary Readings in Law and Social Justice, 6*(2), 1–32.

Wardle, L. D. (2013). Instilling pro-life moral principles in difficult times: The experience of one faith community. *Ave Maria Law Review, 11*, 299–363.

West, R. (2016). *Hobby Lobby*, birth control, and our ongoing cultural wars: Pleasure and desire in the crossfires. *Health Matrix: Journal of Law-Medicine, 26*, 67–107.

Wharton Business School, University of Pennsylvania. (2015). After Hobby Lobby, is there a limit to corporate religious freedom? *Knowledge@ Wharton.*

WHO (World Health Organization). (2015). *The prevention and elimination of disrespect and abuse during facility-based childbirth.* Geneva, Switzerland: WHO.

Will, J. F. (2013). Beyond abortion: Why the personhood movement implicates reproductive choice. *American Journal of Law and Medicine, 39,* 573–616.

Winters, D. R. (2015). Intractable delay and the need to amend the petition provisions of the FDCA. *Indiana Law Journal, 90,* 1047–1089.

Wisanskoonwong, P., et al. (2011). The effectiveness of medical interventions aimed at preventing preterm birth: A literature review. *Women and Birth, 24,* 141–147.

Young, L. (2014). Falling into the TRAP: The ineffectiveness of undue burden analysis in protecting women's right to choose. *Pace Law Review, 34,* 947–981.

Zabel, S. (2015). Docs v. glocks: The need for first amendment protection in preventative care. *Temple Political and Civil Rights Law Review, 24,* 483–505.

Ziegler, M. (2015). The (non)-right to sex. *University of Miami Law Review, 69,* 631–683.

CHAPTER 35

© Andy Dean Photography/ShutterStock, Inc.

Nutrition and Food Safety

"Tell me what kind of food you eat, and I will tell you what kind of person you are."

— **Jean Anthelme Brillat-Savarin** (1755–1826), French attorney and politician who studied the relationship between culture and food, from "The Physiology of Taste"

IN BRIEF

This chapter examines the debate between the food industry and public health advocates over junk food, advertising, and food safety in general. What this food fight means to already strained health care systems struggling to battle diabetes, high blood pressure, heart disease, and other weight- and diet-related illnesses is addressed. Also reviewed are federal legislation from the Personal Responsibility in Food Consumption Act that would protect the food industry from obesity-related lawsuits, similar so-called cheeseburger bills on the state level, and citizen groups like the Alliance for American Advertising that persuade legislators not to introduce bills that would restrict food advertising targeted to children.

LEARNING OBJECTIVES

Upon completion of this chapter readers should be able to:

1. Distinguish between the food and tobacco industries with regard to need for and ability to regulate each.
2. Describe the quandaries involved in defining healthy and unhealthy foods.
3. Explain the influence of advertising on demand for unhealthy foods.
4. Outline the limitations of food labeling laws.
5. Contrast obesity-related lawsuits and cheeseburger legislation with the proposed Personal Responsibility in Food Consumption Act.
6. Describe the basis for more stringent advertising regulation regarding marketing foods to children.
7. Discuss the problems of trans-fats, genetically modified foods, additives, and contaminants.
8. Present both the consumer/regulator position and the industry position on the need for government regulation as opposed to voluntary regulation of foods.

KEY TERMS

Administrative Procedure Act of 1946
Adverse health effects
Alliance for American Advertising
American Sugar Alliance
Animal fats
Animal identification system
Calorie compensation and reward
Causal link
Cheeseburger legislation

Consumer value
Dietary guidelines
Dietary supplements
Federal sugar subsidy program
First Amendment
Food advertising restrictions
Food and Drug Administration
Food safety
Food safety recalls
Free Exercise Clause

Functional foods
Generally recognized as safe
Genetic engineering
Genetically modified foods
Genetics-related litigation
Global Good Agricultural Practice
Health warnings
High-Calorie fast food
Highly processed
Hydrogenated fat

FACT OR FICTION

Food Labeling

Should the producers and sellers of milk be required to warn consumers of the risks of sickness from lactose intolerance on their packaging?

    A group of lactose-intolerant consumers purchased milk and suffered the consequences of its consumption. Before they were aware of their lactose intolerance, they suffered temporary flatulence, bloating, cramps, and diarrhea as a result of drinking milk. They filed suit claiming the producers and sellers breached their duty of reasonable care; in other words, dairy processors and grocery store retailers that sold milk knew about lactose intolerance but failed to warn consumers about those effects. The lactose-intolerant individuals sought damages and a permanent injunction requiring the milk producers and sellers to include warnings on their packaging.

— *See* Law Fact at the end of this chapter for the answer.

Principles and Applications

Faced with political leaders saying the current **food safety** system is a hazard to public health and the possibility of civil as well as regulatory actions, members of the food industry are seeking to demonstrate that they are concerned about consumer health (Weimholt, 2015). Consider just a few, some would say confusing, developments resulting from the political debate over **junk food**, advertising, and food safety:

- The Institute of Medicine points to the large-scale consumption of sugar-laden fruit juice by preschool children as the likely culprit in the recent rise in childhood **obesity**. U.S. **dietary guidelines** suggest parents give their children fresh fruit, water, or milk instead.
- When Kraft Foods was accused of misleading advertising about the fat content of its Oreo cookies from consumers who mistook them as health food, it tried to forestall a lawsuit by promoting its commitment to healthy foods and announced it was taking steps to reduce obesity by reducing the portion sizes of some products and introducing various healthier products with **reduced fat** content. Kraft then eliminated its extensive in-school marketing programs and banned its popular Weinermobiles from schoolyards. While some claim this was all designed to ward off government regulation, Kraft's moves were also made in part to reduce the risk of legal action, although thus far dismissed as frivolous. Even as fat is reduced in Dairylea and Angel Delight, Kraft fears food could be the new tobacco. Kraft knows that by producing nutritionally good foods and marketing them in a responsible way, there is no real case against the firm.
- After pressure from consumer groups, Kellogg Company decided to phase out food advertising aimed at children under 12. Not to be outdone, Kraft agreed to stop advertising Oreos, Chips Ahoy cookies, Kool-Aid, and other non-nutritional snack foods on television to children under 12.

- General Mills replaced refined grains with whole grains in many of its cereals. Then, it launched a new Berry Lucky Charms brand with brightly colored marbits, the artificially flavored marshmallows laden with sugar and corn syrup.
- Soft drink firms voluntarily pulled sugary sodas and other high-Calorie drinks out of schools when research showed that American children on average were drinking three 12-ounce cans per day. Pepsi said it would eliminate **trans-fats** from Doritos, Tostitos, and Cheetos, and promised to broaden its portfolio of reduced-fat and **low-Calorie** products.
- Ever since Nestlé was attacked for promoting powdered milk to mothers in emerging economies, it is more sensitive than ever and invests heavily to make sure that its food avoids controversy. Pick up a Nestlé Crunch or a Baby Ruth and see that Nestlé puts **health warnings** on most of its chocolate bars to remind consumers of the importance of exercise.
- Cadbury Schweppes began emphasizing its move into **natural products** after analysts at JPMorgan predicted the firm faced the highest risk of being sued because of the predominance of unhealthy products in its portfolio.
- When the *Super Size Me* documentary exposed the health risks of eating a McDonald's-only diet, the firm advised French consumers to eat in its restaurants only once per week. Meanwhile, McDonald's now buys about 54 million pounds of fresh apples per year, up from zero several years ago, making the firm the largest global wholesale purchaser of apples. Apples now show up on the McDonald's menu in salads and desserts, alongside the double quarter-pounders with cheese, chicken selects premium breast strips with sauce, deluxe McGriddles breakfasts, large french fries, and triple-thick chocolate shakes.

(AHG, 2006a and 2006b; IOM, 2010; Wharton, 2005; Zhang, 2005).

If one researches food safety, it is likely that the only common point of agreement to be found is that the problem is critical (Wharton, 2005). Consumer health is a problem that has long occupied the brightest minds in the food industry. Every firm in the food industry is looking at its complete product portfolio and looking to develop lower Calorie, lower fat, and more natural products. By using different ingredients and careful marketing, the food industry likely hopes a legal time bomb of consumer litigation can be defused. State governments have successfully sued the tobacco industry for billions in health care costs. Food firms may be next as a result of the fat, sugar, and cholesterol content in many of their products (Schwartz & Silverman, 2015). Many consumers are trying to find a scapegoat, even though the increasingly sedentary lifestyle of many Americans has contributed to the rising level of **weight-related chronic illnesses** (Wicker, 2015). If exposés of the fast food and meatpacking sectors, like turn-of-the-20th-century *Fast Food Nation* (Schlosser, 2001) and turn-of-the-19th-century *The Jungle* (Sinclair, 2006/1906), remain bestsellers, the food industry may have to become more accountable and go further than it has already gone in addressing food safety and nutrition (Linnekin & Leib, 2014).

Distinction or Similarity Between the Food and Tobacco Industries

A major difference between tobacco- and food-related litigation is in the products themselves. Cigarettes are extremely hazardous to health. The only way to completely eliminate the hazard is to eliminate the commodity. Obviously, humans cannot eliminate their consumption of food. With food, the **obesity-promoting characteristics** involve not just product content, but:

- Consumers' lifestyles
- Genetics
- Labeling
- Marketing
- Packaging

Foods are not harmful when used in moderation, whereas cigarettes are. Moreover, while it may be possible to prove that smoking caused a particular lung cancer, it may be difficult to determine how much of a role obesity played in a heart attack death, and impossible to specify the responsibility of the sources of high-fat and high-Calorie foods that might have led to the obesity. Most important, the actions of the tobacco industry have no direct counterpart within the food industry. While food advertising usually does not stress the dangers of overeating, tobacco firms went far beyond a mere failure to disclose by deliberately lying and actively concealing evidence (Browne et al., 2015).

Under the federal **Nutrition Labeling and Education Act of 1990**, some foods are exempt from **nutrition labeling**. These include:

- Food served for immediate consumption, such as that served in cafeterias and that sold by food service vendors
- Ready-to-eat food not for immediate consumption but prepared primarily on site (such as at a bakery)
- Food shipped in bulk, as long as it is not for sale in bulk form to consumers
- **Medical foods**, such as those used to address the nutritional needs of patients with certain diseases
- Plain coffee and tea and some spices
- Foods containing no significant amounts of any **nutrients** or **dietary supplements** in the product (insignificant nutrients, Calories, cholesterol, or fiber)

(*See* 21 U.S.C.A. § 343-1).

Choices: Healthy Versus Unhealthy Foods

Food safety is routinely described as a global problem affecting children and adults, not only in the United States and Western Europe, but also in emerging economies (Wiley, 2016). Public health officials warn of a coming health crisis in already struggling health care systems soon to be hit by even more patients with:

- Diabetes
- Heart disease
- High blood pressure
- Other chronic illnesses directly attributable to obesity and weight-related health conditions

(Wharton, 2005).

Statistics from the **National Health and Nutrition Examination Survey**, a nationally representative sample of the U.S. population, are disturbing:

- About one-third of American adults are considered obese, meaning they are at least 30 pounds overweight
- Almost 40% of America's preschoolers are overweight or are at risk of being overweight
- Obesity rates for elementary school students have tripled since the 1980s
- Obesity and related illnesses are now costing society $135 to $184 billion a year
- Obesity causes 300,000 premature deaths every year
- Obesity may soon be responsible for as many deaths as cigarette smoking
- **Type 2 diabetes** has become so common in children that it is no longer called adult-onset diabetes

(CDC, 2015a and 2015b; Harris, 2011; IOM, 2010; Solar & Irwin, 2010).

America's sudden explosion of chronic illnesses due to obesity and weight-related conditions cannot be attributed simply to genetics. Further, there is no evidence American consumers have suddenly become less responsible about their health over the past two decades. Rather, what has changed is that Americans are now eating one-third of their Calories outside the home; nowadays, **high-Calorie fast food** and chain restaurant meals are consumed at a higher level than ever before (FDA, 2015c). Today, only about 5% of the meals eaten inside the home consist of fresh food (USDA, 2016).

Nutritional State of Affairs

Americans are getting more than half of their daily dietary intake from **highly processed**, prepackaged, and prepared meals high in carbohydrates and sodium (Card & Abela, 2015). The U.S. Department of Agriculture finds that frozen prepared meals have been one of the fastest growing categories of food in American supermarkets every year over the past decade. The question is whether this change in consumer eating habits is contributing to weight-related chronic illnesses (Currey, 2016).

MANAGEMENT AND LAW ISSUES

1. How should the U.S. food industry that manufactures, sells, and advertises high-Calorie foods respond to food safety and nutrition concerns?
2. Should the marketing strategies for food products continue to be self-regulated?
3. Should the food industry be obligated to promote healthier products and reduce or eliminate less healthy foods and beverages, regardless of consumer demand?
4. Who is responsible for what American children and adults eat?
5. Are overweight and obesity conditions an individual and family responsibility, or do government and public health agencies have a role?

One research organization, the National Bureau of Economic Research, says 65% of America's obesity is due to fast foods and ready-prepared meals (Alkerwi et al., 2015). If this is so, who exactly is responsible for this nutritional state of affairs?

- Cereal and juice manufacturers that add sugar to their products?
- Government agencies that publish dietary guidelines but take no regulatory action to limit junk food advertising targeted at children (*See* 7 U.S.C.A. §§ 5301, *et seq.*; the *Dietary Guidelines for Americans* are a joint effort of the U.S. Department of Health and Human Services and the U.S. Department of Agriculture)?
- Overweight and obese individuals who keep spooning the food into their bodies, one bite at a time?
- Parents, who relinquish their responsibilities to provide healthy, nutritional meals and promote exercise?
- Powerful lobbies that have kept the **federal sugar subsidy program** in place since the Great Depression in the 1920s?
- Schools that fail to offer healthy eating alternatives in cafeterias and vending machines?
- The fast food sector, with its high-Calorie menus and advertising that seems to be everywhere at once?
- All the above or some combination thereof?

These are very challenging public health concerns, with weight-related illnesses very much an issue for the U.S. health care system in particular.

Subsidizing Healthy Foods and Taxing Unhealthy Foods

The **American Sugar Alliance** is a trade association that represents domestic producers, processors, and refiners of sugar. It has ensured that the sugar industry has long been one of the most protected sectors in American agriculture (USDA, 2016). Government support to some of the wealthiest Americans includes special loans to producers and a program designed to prop up prices by controlling the amount of sugar put on the market through **import limits** and **production allotments** granted to farmers with gross incomes up to $2.5 million (Giessel, 2015; *See* Hitt, 2008).

In some ways, the food industry is faced with a choice between two adverse and contrary alternatives toward nutrition. Consumers say they want healthier foods, but if consumer behavior is examined, many consumers choose unhealthy foods over healthy ones. Indeed, fast food and restaurant chains that have tried to reduce the size of their meal portions and even reduce prices have been criticized and often reinstate their original serving sizes and return to their original pricing in response to consumer demand (Wharton, 2005). When restaurant chain Ruby Tuesday tried to reduce the size of its portions, consumers soundly criticized the move and the restaurant chain quickly reinstated original serving sizes (Wong, 2014). At the same time, consumers say they want healthy options that are just as fast and cheap as the unhealthy ones. How does the food industry navigate its way through this nutritional maze? The food industry in general wants to offer healthier alternatives, in part because of all the dire warnings about the relationship between food safety and health; it simply does not have many other choices if it still wants to respond to contradictory consumer demands (Esterl, 2016).

The food industry maintains it is always looking to lower fat levels and sugar levels, but it is not always possible to get ingredients to the recommended levels. It is impossible to make chocolate without more than 30% of the Calories coming from fat, which is the recommended dietary amount (Gilhooley, 2005). It would not be chocolate anymore. It is possible that altering the composition of chocolate could lead to litigation to restore it, given its immense, unwavering popularity. In response to attacks on chocolate, and over the years, some chocolate manufacturers and sellers have responded by putting health warnings on their chocolate bars to remind consumers of the need to exercise or to include chocolate as part of a balanced diet (Wong, 2014). Nevertheless, more is required of the food industry than quick-fix changes to its packaging and labeling (Esterl, 2016).

Food Marketing and Advertising

The decision by Kraft and Kellogg to stop advertising to children has caused concern within the food industry (Wharton, 2005). When advertising to children is stopped in response to demands from public health advocates, it implies an acknowledgment that there is something wrong with that advertising (Kunkel et al., 2004). Does this suggest culpability, or did Kraft and Kellogg act responsibly? It is not easy to change food products or to predict what the effect of such changes will be. There is always the risk of altering a product and then losing customers because of the change. Coke faced this peril when it attempted to introduce a new Coca-Cola and was forced to return to the original formula in less than three months. The *New Coke* with high-fructose corn syrup was withdrawn and the sugar-sweetened *Coca Cola Classic* returned to shelves post-haste following a public outcry for the original product (*See* Dery & Evaro, 2013).

The food industry has changed the word *supersize* because the meaning has changed in popular culture from denoting something positive to denoting something negative (Wharton, 2005). When McDonald's dropped the word, it substituted the words *deluxe* and *premium* in its menu; the marketing association, however, remained the same: excessive and extremely large. One could ask whether this word choice is designed to move product or whether it has different meanings.

Beyond marketing, there is a distinction between giving consumers what they want and saying, in essence, *We know what you want, but we know it is not healthy, and we are not willing to offer it* (Making, 2005). There may be a joint responsibility between the food industry and consumers. If so, this makes it harder to determine what should be done. It is always much easier for the food industry to go through a systematic, rigorous process of segmentation, targeting, and positioning—a long-standing approach to marketing—than it is to really know what consumers want and why they want it (Wharton, 2005). If the food industry simply makes projections based on what it thinks is healthy based on its own experience and intuition, it may deliver one type of food product (Dery & Evaro, 2013). However, simply because the food industry thinks one type of food is not healthy does not mean everybody else will think it is unhealthy (Esterl, 2016). The industry's assumptions may not be true.

When healthy food becomes a tough sell, it is because consumers have obvious objections to it (Barnhill, 2015). The goal of marketing, therefore, is to frame and offer to do away with the objection. For instance, it may be as simple as consumers wanting healthy food that is as fast, cheap, and readily available as traditional fast food (Harvey, 2015). Consumers also want healthy food to be just as appetizing and delicious as less-healthy options (Barnhill, 2015). At first, that may seem impossible, but palates can be retrained over time. This is one example of where consumers could accept some responsibility for change along with the food industry.

The food industry goes after **consumer value**, which includes offering products consumers are willing to pay for. The industry is not making consumers eat unhealthy foods (Wharton, 2005). The industry argues it is just delivering foods consumers want. The counterargument to this contention is that consumers never knew they wanted Ben & Jerry's ice cream or McDonald's french fries until they existed and everyone found out about them. Consumers are always ready to indulge themselves when marketers are able to get their message through (Esterl, 2016). Food products are not about what is needed, but about wants and desires (Barnhill, 2015). In the case of McDonald's, some customers would be more satisfied with the menu offerings if they did not cause weight gain. So McDonald's keeps some fast food customers by offering healthier choices like the Fruit 'n Yogurt Parfait and salads. Still, there are other customers who do not care if they gain weight, at least some of the time, and some marketers aim to appeal to that segment (Esterl, 2016). Marketing, as the term itself implies, responds to the free market to increase responses from its intended audiences (Wharton, 2005).

MANAGEMENT AND LAW ISSUES

6. Should advice about food safety and protection from unhealthy foods by the food industry or government ever give way to individual choice and individual responsibility?

Functional Foods

The marketing spin in the food industry hides a deeper concern about increasing levels of fat and sugar. As a consequence, the food industry is remarketing its products in light of health fears (Gunter, 2014). The issue of healthy food is at the top of the food industry's agendas (PwC, 2009).

The food industry realizes it takes more than simply tinkering around with products (Barnhill, 2015). A completely new way of thinking is needed. Strategy has changed in the food industry in the past five years; by offering healthy food options, such as more fruits and salads, business is increasing and driving growth for the food industry as a whole (Buttrick & Hatch, 2016).

Functional foods, or foods that provide health benefits beyond basic nutrition, are being aggressively marketed by pharmaceutical and consumer goods firms. Although large multinational companies remain the key functional food players (Danone, Coca-Cola, General Mills, Kellogg, Kraft, Nestle, PepsiCo, and Unilever), smaller participants are also successfully occupying niches in the market (PwC, 2009). The global market for functional foods and beverages now exceeds $170 billion, accounting for 5% of the overall food market (Hoffmann & Schwartz, 2016). Grocery aisles are stacked with rows of whole-grain breakfast cereals, enhanced salad dressings, and fortified snacks and drinks (primarily enhanced water and energy drinks) that promise to fight heart disease, osteoporosis, and other ailments. In some cases, products with dietary supplements are billed as alternatives to medicine. Consumers like these healthy options (Buttrick & Hatch, 2016). Moreover, by having options, the food industry avoids dictating to consumers (Gunter, 2014).

Food Labeling Laws

Giving consumers options raises the question of whether consumers have enough information about the foods they choose to eat. While federal legislation requires easy-to-read **nutrition facts labels** on almost all packaged foods, the drug labeling rules from the **Food and Drug Administration** (FDA) focus solely on format (*See* Nutrition Labeling and Education Act of 1990, 21 U.S.C.A. § 343-1). There is an ongoing policy debate as to whether consumers have the right information to decide what to eat at fast food restaurants like McDonald's or what to drink at Starbucks or how to calculate Calories at Weight Watchers (Schwartz & Silverman, 2015).

The good news is that Dasani water is now on McDonald's menu with no Calories, and Starbucks offers skim milk in its lattes and asks whether whipped cream should be added. One fact is certain: many consumers do not know how much to eat (Barnhill, 2015). They do not eat to satisfy hunger. Most adults do not stop eating when they are no longer hungry. The same is not true for children. When children are not hungry, they will not eat. They will stop in the middle of a bite. Somehow, adults have lost or unlearned this skill (Wharton, 2005). What adults eat is largely dictated by environmental cues, not internal cues. The notion is that it is not hunger driving how much adults eat; it is perceptual cues, like portion amounts, plate size, or the sense of variety (Wong, 2014).

Adults do not always eat for fullness (Barnhill, 2015). They often unconsciously eat for these other rules. Weight Watchers has developed a business model that encourages its clients to stop eating when they are satisfied, but this alone does not help the fact that overweight and obese people often cannot detect satiety signals anyway, giving in instead to emotional triggers or social pressures to eat, or not realizing they are full until they are too full because it takes the brain 20 minutes to signal that the stomach is full (Wharton, 2005). Therefore, Weight Watchers also attempts to teach its clients to handle the psychological and environmental contributors to weight problems (Noel, 2015).

Moreover, many adults are not aware of how many Calories they consume (Wharton, 2005). Researchers note that when it comes to a plethora of food choices, the problem is not simply that consumers make bad choices. The sheer amount of available choices actually drives individuals to eat more. Other research shows that simply labeling a food as healthy makes the item unappealing (Wharton, 2005). Just the mindset that something is going to be healthy turns off some consumers. Consumers taste what they think; they believe if it is healthy, it is not going to be as good. To complicate matters even more, consumers who think they are eating healthy actually tend to reward themselves with more food (Wong, 2014). This concept is called **Calorie compensation and reward** in restaurant studies (Wansink, 2007).

As consumers become more cognizant of how much they are eating and realize they could be satisfied with less, there may again be a reduction in supersizing. The move toward downsizing or changing eating habits in the United States in general suggests Americans may be willing to assume **individual responsibility** for their actions. This is another predominant issue in the food safety debate (Wharton, 2005).

The restaurant chain T.G.I. Fridays offers a "right portion, right price" menu with smaller portions at lower prices for select dishes. This seemingly consumer-health driven effort, however, has a headline over the downsized entrees on its website that promises, "Smaller Portions Allow More Room for Dessert", and dessert is a higher profit-margin item. This may be T.G.I. Fridays's application of the Calorie compensation and reward concept (Wansink, 2007). This concept might explain why there has been a sharp rise in sales of low-fat foods as obesity levels have soared (Schwartz & Silverman, 2015).

Ideally, consumers should be responsible for making their own life decisions. What the food industry tries to do is provide choices so that consumers can make the right decisions based on their own needs, including price, portability, and convenience (Barnhill, 2015). If consumers do not buy the choices offered, then these items are pulled from the marketplace (Wharton, 2005). For instance, there are veggie burgers in some markets, but they do not sell as well as meat burger products. Almost every decision the food industry makes is based on what consumers indicate they want to eat (Hoffmann & Schwartz, 2016). McDonald's had the McLean deluxe burger, but it did not stay on the menu for long. Salads have been on McDonald's menu since 1984. McDonald's tried a salad shaker in a cup that could be eaten on the run, but the product failed. Milk was sold for years, but when low-fat milk was put in a Ronald McDonald reusable plastic container, sales increased dramatically. Wendy's offers chili, a side salad, or a Caesar side salad with its classic sandwiches, which have become popular menu options instead of french fries. Despite the consequences, research shows that when consumers go to a fast food restaurant, they want to splurge (Carpenter & Tello-Trillo, 2015).

Obesity-Related Lawsuits and Cheeseburger Legislation

Others in the food fight, however, contend that individual responsibility only goes so far. Two teenagers filed a lawsuit blaming McDonald's food and advertising for causing obesity. After being tossed out twice, the case was reinstated on a technicality. Although many consider the lawsuit frivolous, it raises the specter of additional suits against other fast food chains on similar grounds (Wharton, 2005). Public health advocates maintain most restaurant chain food is misleadingly advertised as healthy; the chains say the advocates' view is based on incomplete information and outdated material (Barnhill, 2015).

COURT DECISION
Liability for Weight-Related Illnesses

Pelman v. McDonald's Corp.
[Minor Consumers v. Fast-Food Chain]
237 F.Supp.2d 512 (U.S. District Court for the Southern District of New York 2003),
class certification denied, Pelman v. McDonald's Corp.
272 F.R.D. 82 (U.S. District Court for the Southern District of New York 2010)

Facts: Two New York City teenagers sought to hold McDonald's liable for their obesity and obesity-related illnesses. McDonald's advertises its food as nutritious and part of a healthy lifestyle, while failing to warn its consumers of the health-related risks and adverse health effects associated with consumption of foods high in cholesterol, fat, salt, sugar, and other additives. They claimed McDonald's persuaded its consumers to ingest unhealthy quantities of fattening, highly processed food substantially less healthy than represented in advertisements. In addition, McDonald's represents it provides nutritional information in all of its stores, when in fact such beneficial information is often not available.

The teenagers claimed McDonald's engaged in deceptive marketing that enticed them to eat unhealthy food with substantial frequency. Therefore, they now face a higher likelihood of developing diabetes, heart disease, and a host of obesity-related conditions as a direct result of eating at McDonald's. For instance, they pointed to advertising that sodium was reduced across the McDonald's menu, and then cited products whose sodium content had not been reduced in years.

Issue: Should McDonald's be responsible for the obesity-related illnesses of its consumers?

Holding and Decision: No, if consumers know, or should know that eating McDonald's supersized food orders is unhealthy and may result in weight gain, it is not the place of the law to protect them from their own excesses.

Analysis: The court rejected the argument that McDonald's should have warned its consumers about the **adverse health effects** associated with foods high in fat, salt, and sugar, reasoning that such information is well known to the average consumer. Nothing suggests McDonald's food is any less nutritious than the average consumer expects it to be. In addition, the court did not find any specific advertisements or public statements by McDonald's to be deceptive. The court also found that McDonald's failure to provide nutritional information could not be considered deceptive because consumers could reasonably obtain such information. Additionally, there was no causal link between McDonald's food and the obesity-related illnesses of its consumers. The court noted that heredity, sedentary lifestyles, and other health-related factors must be eliminated to show McDonald's food is a substantial factor in consumers' weight gain.

The court did not find consumers were addicted to McDonald's food, and no **causal link** was established between the consumption of McDonald's food and obesity. The court conceded a discrepancy existed between the advertising around McDonald's use of 100% vegetable oil and the fact that beef tallow was also used, but dismissed this disparity as irrelevant to the obesity-related illnesses of its consumers. The court found the plaintiffs did not allege the beef tallow contained cholesterol, and thus there was no evidence to support the claim that McDonald's acted deceptively in stating its fries were cholesterol-free.

The fact that the vegetable oil contained trans-fatty acids responsible for raising detrimental blood cholesterol levels was deemed irrelevant because the contents of food and the effects of food are different. In dismissing the case with prejudice, the court indicated the claims could not be refiled.

Rule of Law: There are substantial obstacles to liability for obesity-related illnesses allegedly brought on by consumption of fast food.

References discussing this court decision: *E.g.,* Linnekin & Leib, 2014; Schwartz & Appel, 2014; Wilking & Daynard, 2013.

In a separate lawsuit four years after the first *Pelman* decision, another court did find a discrepancy between the advertising around McDonald's use of 100% vegetable oil and the fact that beef tallow was also used. McDonald's publicly apologized and reached a $10 million settlement on behalf of vegetarians and other individuals opposed to eating beef products (Mortazavi, 2016). In an effort to ridicule the litigation against fast food firms, a restaurant in Seattle created the most fattening and delicious dessert imaginable. In order to indulge in the restaurant's delectable deep fried, ice cream anointed banana, consumers had to sign a waiver that read, in part: "I will not impose any sort of **obesity-related lawsuits** [boldface added] against the 5 Spot or consider any similar type of frivolous legislation created by a hungry trial lawyer" (Harden, 2003, p. A3). Unfortunately, some attorneys engage in a complex game of legal arbitrage in order to force the health care industry (as well as other industries) to negotiate immediate settlements with them in order to avoid the risk of litigation (Schwartz & Silverman, 2015). It is debatable whether this behavior by attorneys should be tolerated, since it hampers investment and stifles innovation (Schwartz & Appel, 2014).

Meanwhile, the food industry claims eating smaller portions and healthier foods will do more to counter the spread of weight-related illnesses than obesity-related lawsuits aimed at the fast food industry (Wilking & Daynard, 2013). Food can hold only part of the blame for the growing levels of obesity (Wicker, 2015). Food is an important factor, but not the only factor.

Still, the food industry's fear of obesity-related lawsuits is one reason why Congress is debating the **Personal Responsibility in Food Consumption Act**, federal legislation that would protect the food industry whose products are in compliance with existing laws and regulations from obesity-related lawsuits.[LN1] Similar so-called **cheeseburger legislation** (or commonsense consumption legislation) has been introduced on the state level as well. Such bills aim to remove responsibility from food manufacturers and place it back on the consumer. Passage of such legislation is a legislative priority, and industry proponents are expected to keep pushing for its passage. Others disagree and claim that eliminating the threat of litigation against the food industry also eliminates one point of pressure encouraging the industry to take responsibility for its role in combating obesity and weight-related illnesses (Buttrick & Hatch, 2016).

Food Advertising to Children

In addition to forestalling litigation, the **Alliance for American Advertising** (consisting of the American Advertising Federation, the American Association of Advertising Agencies, the Association of National Advertising, and the Grocery Manufacturers Association) was established to persuade legislators not to introduce legislation restricting food advertising targeted to children. The group maintains the issue is a **First Amendment** concern because attempts to restrict advertising violate the right to free speech. Others differ and point to current bans on cigarette and alcohol advertising (Wharton, 2005).

Critics of the food industry's push to sell unhealthy foods find as much to criticize in the advertisements as in the products themselves (Kersh & Elbel, 2015). Advertising is not only on television, but increasingly on the Internet, in video games, and on cell phones. Many nutritionists already claim there is ample evidence linking advertising to childhood obesity (IOM, 2010). One case argued that McDonald's should warn consumers that Chicken McNuggets contain more fat than burgers. Some commentators claim the food industry spends more effort warning consumers not to let their children choke on the plastic toys they give away than they do on warning of the dangers of eating too much sugar or fat (Kunkel et al., 2004).

Members of the fast food sector claim healthy options are on their menus and that they provide nutritional information about consumer items, all in order to inform consumers about what is available. They say they are not in the business of taking away individual choice and point to the fact that fat levels in food have declined since the 1970s. They argue there is increased pressure on marketers to compete on Calorie content when advertising is not restricted; **food advertising restrictions** inhibit such competition (Kersh & Elbel, 2015).

The trouble is, though, that many advertisements for food products are targeted at children (IOM, 2010). As soon as cartoon characters are used and products are tied in with children's movies and so forth, the question becomes whether consumers really make fully informed choices or whether they are flooded with marketing material that alters their behavior (Barnhill, 2015). The food industry's response to this is that children do not make the purchasing decisions; it is their parents (Kunkel et al., 2004).

Nevertheless, children can be persuasive. In fact, many of the obesity-related lawsuits against the fast food industry have been brought by parents of minors because of the health effects on their children and because children often cannot make educated food decisions. Also, there has been a big push to ensure schools contain healthy snacks in their vending machines and fewer Calorie-laden beverages (Disiena, 2015). Fast food restaurants and school systems are rethinking ways in which they can influence the debate about food (Wharton, 2005). Most schools will sell only water, certain fruit juices, and low-fat or fat-free milk in schools, with diet or low-Calorie sodas, teas, and sports drinks for sale only in high schools. Portion sizes in school cafeterias are also being tailored to each age group (Barnhill, 2015).

McDonald's promotes the idea that it is cool to be active through associations with, for instance, Olympic athletes and sports celebrities. Healthy eating versus unhealthy eating information is placed on McDonald's tray liners, on store posters, and its packaging. Kraft, for its part, advertises sugar-free Crystal Light drink mixes and whole-grain Triscuits crackers and labels foods and beverages that meet federal nutritional guidelines. There are many marketing vehicles to communicate these kinds of healthy messages beyond **paid advertising** (Wharton, 2005). The food industry should not walk away from advertising to children but should instead be a part of the solution (IOM, 2010).

Healthy Options and Nutraceutical Advertising

There is also the issue of advertising seemingly healthy options that are actually worse for consumers. Salads can be drowned in dressing with bacon bits. This contributes to consumers' confusion and lack of knowledge about what they are eating. They are choosing the healthy salad, but overlooking the unhealthy things added to make it appetizing. A lot of packaged goods seem healthier than they really are as well (Wharton, 2005). In addition, **nutraceuticals** and nutritional supplements are added to products, such as calcium to chocolate syrup and vitamin C to soda, to make foods more appealing to health-conscious consumers (*See* FDA's Food Fortification Policy, 21 C.F.R. § 104.20). Makers of children's food have rolled out yogurt and soy milk products enhanced with DHA omega-3 fatty acid, which Beech-Nut and Dannon say can aid in brain and vision development, but pediatricians question their benefit (Disiena, 2015). Coca-Cola and PepsiCo have carbonated drinks fortified with vitamins and minerals. Milk, breads, cereals, and other products have been nutrient fortified for years.

Nutritionists maintain fortified junk food is still junk food. Adding supplements does not address the larger issue of how to encourage changes in eating habits (Wharton, 2005). McDonald's response to the *Super Size Me* documentary (Rhode, 2015), which is that no one is suggesting that consumers eat at McDonald's all day, every day, ignores the fact that it advertises with an "all day, every day" theme and tries to create demand at every meal and snack time. There is clearly some inherent tension between the food industry and its critics (Barnhill, 2015). Hardee's sells its Loaded Breakfast Burrito, a menu item consisting of eggs, diced ham, bacon bits, and a sausage patty with shredded cheddar cheese and salsa. If Hardee's is responding to demand for such a product, that is one thing. However, if Hardee's is creating a demand, and if consumers would not otherwise be eating 780 calories and 51 grams of fat for breakfast, then this is a gray area and may call for changes in the way the food industry should operate (*See* Browne, 2015).

The Center for Science in the Public Interest claims the food industry tries to create demand for its products, often at the expense of healthier options. A number of firms claim marketing is intended to simply move customers from one brand to another, but this is not always the case (Wharton, 2005). For instance, "fruit" snacks are a whole new category of product not in existence years ago. Food firms compete not only with other similar products, but with real fruit (Buttrick & Hatch, 2016). So a parent may pack "fruit" gummies in a child's lunchbox instead of an apple or bag of grapes. When a child wants to go to McDonald's for dinner, that choice is competing not only with Saladworks, but with a meal cooked at home. Marketing works. That is why the food industry does it and why health advocates are concerned about it (Barnhill, 2015).

The food industry is very concerned about being blamed for the rising obesity rate, and it should be, because many of its products and practices are significant contributors (Wharton, 2005). The industry is also nervous about new regulations, legislation, and obesity-related lawsuits and is moving to head these off (Wicker, 2015). Kraft's decision to limit certain kinds of advertising is a meaningful step forward. PepsiCo is trying to add healthier versions of its products in schools, although it still markets and sells a lot of regular soda.[LN2] All the fast food restaurants have real fruit options: Wendy's has mandarin oranges, Burger King has applesauce, and McDonald's has apples in its salads and desserts (Carpenter & Tello-Trillo, 2015). However, in most cases, an overwhelming number of the entrees remain unhealthy (Barnhill, 2015). Red Lobster's Lighthouse menu advertises seafood with fewer than 500 calories, but each dish is surrounded by high-Calorie accompaniments, sides, and dipping sauces not included in the nutritional content advertisements. Indeed, hamburgers and french fries will continue to be at the core of fast food menus for the long term, although salads and deli-style sandwiches are being added (Esterl, 2016).

Voluntary Marketing Guidelines

The Center for Science in the Public Interest developed guidelines for responsible food marketing, calling on the food industry to use its power to create and market healthy foods consumers will ask for and enjoy. The industry claims it wants to respond to consumer demand, but this does not happen in a vacuum. Many interested in consumer protection believe marketers have the power to influence wants and needs as much as they respond to wants and needs (Wharton, 2005). But while consumers say they want to eat healthy, often what they really want is chips (Esterl, 2016). The assumption of consumer protection advocates is that marketers could determine that the food industry is making consumers unhealthy and that there are costs for the United States (Carpenter & Tello-Trillo, 2015). PepsiCo, however, says it wants to make more healthy snacks (like its new fiber-filled nut and fruit bar called Init), but much of its revenue growth comes from high-fat, high-salt standbys such as Doritos and Cheetos (Esterl, 2016). Thus, PepsiCo presents consumers with new products like Mac N' Cheetos, frozen cheese sticks resembling Cheetos, and Top N Go Doritos, a portable meal high in salt and fat. But why not influence consumer preferences in ways that favor healthy choices? For instance, when marketers began advertising the link between fiber in cereals and the reduced risk of cancer, there was a consumer shift to high-fiber diets. Such changes in food labeling rules could play an important role in bringing information to consumers and adding to food industry incentives to focus on the Calorie profiles of their foods (FDA, 2016a). Another such change could be decreased pre-portioned sizes of fresh ingredients of full home-cooked meals delivered to consumers at their homes on a subscription basis (like the Internet-based Blue Apron start-up). Although portion sizes today almost always greatly exceed those offered 25 to 35 years earlier (Sivin, 2015); Blue Apron offers two-person or family meal plans with fuller portions for a higher price.

Food Industry and Public Health Sector Viewpoints

There is significant controversy on whether the food industry should be expected to change their practices if is not profitable to do so. The food industry can accomplish profitability by, for instance, retraining consumers to be proactive and encouraging them to gravitate toward healthy foods. In a free market economy, the food industry maintains that healthy as well as unhealthy foods should be offered. Food retailers should offer consumers options, rather than erode or dictate choices, and give consumers more information on nutrition. As is, consumers are not fully informed or aware of the Calories and fat in food (Wharton, 2005).

The biggest challenge is developing a concerted effort across disciplines and across fields (Gunter, 2014). Natural and organic foods and beverages are growing fast—23% to $41 billion the past two years in the United States—but are still a small slice of the country's $425 billion in overall sales (Esterl, 2016). The **public health sector** is skeptical that the food industry is trying to promote healthy foods when its major concern is profits. The food industry views public health advocates as unaware of how businesses operate (Harvey, 2015); natural and organic products are often costlier to develop and harder to scale up (Esterl, 2016). To complicate the issue, the available evidence to support any proffered link between food advertising and obesity is quite limited and often contrary to the thesis. Although many European firms have limited advertising to children, evidence suggests advertising does not appear to be a significant factor in the rise of childhood obesity; this does not, however, mean that advertising, marketing, and government policies cannot be part of the solution to the problem of obesity (Wiley, 2015).

Consumer Purchasing and Parental Responsibility

Consumers are a large part of the problem as well, in terms of **purchasing patterns** and **parental responsibility**. A multi-domain effort is required across the public and private sectors (Wharton, 2005). Public health scholars and physicians in several countries have called for a broad system of taxes on unhealthy foods, possibly combined with subsidies for certain healthy foods (Taylor et al., 2014). The World Health Organization (WHO) recommends limits on sugar consumption and advertising targeted to children. WHO also encourages governments to discourage advertising that promotes the consumption of unhealthy foods by children. The European Union has threatened to restrict advertising aimed at children if the food industry fails to take action on its own (Taylor et al., 2014).

Regulation of Trans-Fats

There are two types of trans-fats (or trans-fatty acids). The food processing industry switched from **animal fats** to mixing vegetable fat with hydrogen and creating **hydrogenated fat** or partially hydrogenated oils, believing that this cheaper raw material might be healthier. However, after more than a decade of use, the FDA announced that partially hydrogenated oils from chemically altered trans-fats maybe the worst type of fat humans can consume (FDA, 2016a; *See* Federal Register, 68 FR 41433, July 11, 2003: Food labeling: *Trans fat*ty acids in nutrition labeling, nutrient content claims, and health claims).

Hydrogenated fat, used in many biscuits, chocolate, and other products, has now proven to be just as bad as animal fats for clogging arteries (Mortazavi, 2015). The most dramatic new regulatory change for the food industry

MANAGEMENT AND LAW ISSUES

9. Should the federal government mandate that the food industry change its formulation practices for unhealthy foods, even if is not profitable to do so in the short term?

10. Is government advertising about the risks of obesity more politically feasible than direct regulation of food or food consumption, given the anti-paternalistic sentiments of the American public?

occurred when the FDA issued a rule requiring food labels to list the amount of trans-fats in their products (Dhyani, 2016). Food labels and packaging must now reveal how much trans-fat they contain (*See* Nutrition Labeling of Dietary Supplements, 21 C.F.R. § 101.36(b)(2)(i)). In the realm of dietary dangers, hydrogenated trans-fats rank very high. The FDA estimates that merely revealing trans-fat content on labels could save between 2,000 and 5,600 lives a year (FDA, 2016a). Still, trans-fats are responsible for an estimated 30,000 early deaths per year in the United States (Dhyani, 2016). Worldwide, the toll of premature deaths is in the millions (Mortazavi, 2015).

Though trans-fats are found naturally in meats and some dairy products, Americans ingest far greater amounts of them through the chemical process of hydrogenation of oils found in crackers, cookies, chips, and other snack foods. **Hydrogenation** is a chemical process used to solidify oils, vegetable shortenings, and margarines, and to increase the shelf life and flavor stability of foods; it also creates hydrogenated trans-fats. Nearly all fried and baked goods have hydrogenated trans-fats, including food labeled as low fat. Nutritionists claim trans-fats are so harmful that no level is entirely safe. Not only do trans-fats raise bad cholesterol, but they also lower good cholesterol helpful in reducing the risk of clogged arteries.

The new FDA requirements force the food industry to add nutrition labels showing how many grams of trans-fats are included in each serving (FDA, 2016a). Beyond requiring that some labels list the amount of trans-fats in food, the FDA also defined the term **trans-fat free** and limited use of certain nutrient or health claims related to fat content, such as lean and low saturated fat (*See* Federal Register, 68 FR 41433, July 11, 2003: Food labeling: *Trans fatty* acids in nutrition labeling, nutrient content claims, and health claims). Together, these regulations could affect the food industry as well as consumer eating habits, just as requiring warning labels on cigarettes led some consumers to give up smoking and resulted in the tobacco industry developing lower-nicotine products. New York City became the first major American city to enact a nearly complete ban on trans-fats (Mortazavi, 2015). There are ways to reduce trans-fats while keeping the familiar taste and texture in popular food products, as shown in **FEATURE BOX 35-1**.

Genetically Modified Foods

In the United States, over 300 million consumers have spent more than a decade consuming **genetically modified foods**, without any known adverse effects (FDA, 2016b, 2015a). It is estimated that 75 to 80% of processed foods in supermarkets contain genetically modified ingredients (Wong, 2014). The first genetically modified food, a genetically engineered tomato, was sold in the U.S. market in 1995 (EPA, 2012). Since then, agricultural biotechnology has received

FEATURE BOX 35-1

Reducing Trans-Fats

- Avoid foods containing partially hydrogenated oils that sound healthy, like soybean oil.
- Select foods low in saturated fats (because trans-fats and saturated fats act similarly in the body and generally come together).
- Use olive or canola oil.
- Restrict buttery spread use to products that use only natural fats that are completely free of hydrogenated or partially hydrogenated oils, such as Smart Balance.
- Avoid all deep-fried foods, which are prime culprits in purveying trans-fats.

both unproven praise and unproven attacks. Myths on both sides of the issue of genetically modified foods need to be debunked. The U.S. policy is that genetically modified foods, derived from genetically engineered plants and animals, should be permitted to flourish in the absence of proven hazards (FDA, 2015c).

Genetically engineered plants used in industrial agriculture isolate specific genes from virtually any organism and insert them into the genetic material of crops (FDA, 2016c). On one hand, this offers tremendous benefits with increased crop yields and reduction in the use of dangerous pesticides. On the other hand, the engineering process must be monitored because it has the potential to create foods containing new toxins and previously unknown allergens. At least three human health risks associated with genetically modified foods are:

- Novel proteins
- Potential allergies
- Risk that antibiotic resistance could be spread

(Nunziato, 2014).

In addition, genetically engineered crops protected from insects and herbicides may have unforeseen adverse impacts on wildlife and plants (Wong, 2014).

The United States has not established GM-specific requirements; rather, modified foods are regulated under the existing framework of the FDA, the Environmental Protection Agency, and the U.S. Department of Agriculture. Currently, the regulatory process on what constitutes **genetic engineering** in plants is voluntary (Nunziato, 2014). The existing regulatory scheme has led to widespread consumer demand for the labeling of genetically modified foods. The issue reached the Federal Circuit in *Alliance for Bio-Integrity v. Shalala*.

COURT DECISION
Labeling of Genetically Modified Foods

Alliance for Bio-Integrity v. Shalala
[Coalition Concerned about Genetically Modified Foods v. FDA]
116 F.Supp.2d 166 (U.S. District Court for the District of Columbia 2000);
followed by Humane Society of the United States v. Johanns, 520 F.Supp.2d 8
(U.S. District Court for the District of Columbia 2007)

Facts: The FDA presumes that foods produced through **rDNA technology** are **generally recognized as safe**. Therefore, labeling of **rDNA developed foods** is not required. The Alliance for Bio-Integrity filed suit to invalidate this FDA policy based on two concerns: first, that new breeds of genetically modified foods contain unexpected allergens and toxins and second, that some religions forbid consumption of foods produced by rDNA technology.

Issue: Is labeling of genetically modified organisms in food required?

Holding and Decision: No, scientific applications of FDA policies that do not require labeling of genetically modified foods will not be second-guessed by the courts.

Analysis: The Alliance challenged the FDA policy on grounds that the:

- FDA violated the Environmental Protection Act of 1969 by not performing an environmental assessment or an environmental impact statement in conjunction with the policy (*See* 42 U.S.C.A. §§ 4321 *et seq.*)
- Policy failed to require labeling of genetically modified foods in violation of the:
  ° Food, Drug, and Cosmetic Act of 1938
  ° **Free Exercise Clause** of the U.S. Constitution
  ° Religious Freedom Restoration Act of 1993 (*See* 42 U.S.C.A. §§ 2000bb - bb-4)

- Policy was not subjected to notice-and-comment procedures as required by the **Administrative Procedure Act of 1946** (*See* 5 U.S.C.A. §§ 551-559)
- Presumption that genetically modified foods are generally accepted as safe was arbitrary and capricious

The court rejected each of the Alliance's arguments and granted summary judgment in favor of the FDA, meaning that the case did not proceed to a full trial. The FDA was not required to conduct notice-and-comment procedures because the policy merely created a presumption as opposed to a substantive rule. In addition, the FDA did not violate the Environmental Protection Act because the policy was not a major federal action and, therefore, was neither subject to an environmental assessment nor an environmental impact statement. Finally, the court determined that scientific applications of law were within the expertise of the FDA and that principles of administrative law prevented the court from overriding the FDA without just legal cause, such as if an FDA policy was indeed unconstitutional.

The court also deferred to the FDA's decision not to require the labeling of genetically modified foods. The Food, Drug, and Cosmetic Act provides that the FDA shall take action for the misbranding of food. The FDA may only consider consumer demand for labeling if genetically modified food differs materially from unmodified food. Because the FDA had concluded that genetic modification of a food was not a material change in the food, the court deferred to that conclusion.

The court concluded its analysis by further noting that the failure of the FDA to require labeling violated neither the Free Exercise Clause nor the Religious Freedom Restoration Act. In support of this conclusion, the court reasoned that the FDA policy was neutral and did not substantially burden religious practices.

Rule of Law: Genetically modified food is not materially different from unmodified food; therefore, labeling of foods as such is not required.

References discussing this court decision: *E.g.*, Miller, 2016; Tai, 2012; Walberg, 2016.

The *Alliance for Bio-Integrity* case remains one of the first reported opinions to address the safety concerns associated with genetically modified foods, mainly that biotechnology allows scientists to manipulate a variety of factors in our environment through genetic engineering. Nevertheless, the food industry expects additional **genetics-related litigation** (Dhyani, 2016). Litigation has already begun regarding genetically engineered seeds by Monsanto (*See, e.g.*, Complaint, *Grocery Manufacturer's Association. v. Sorrell*, Case No. 15-1504 (U.S. Court of Appeals 2nd Circuit, 2015).[LN3]

In addition, most of Europe refuses to import any meat from the United States containing hormones used to promote growth in cattle, creating a major dispute within the World Trade Organization. Europe takes the opposite policy position to the United States, namely that where potential health effects are serious and the relevant science is inadequate to draw a conclusion, a ban is warranted until definitive research is performed (Wiley, 2015).[LN4] Unfortunately, significant disagreement remains among scientific experts about the safety of genetically engineered foods (*See American Meat Institute v. U.S. Department of Agriculture*, 760 F.3d 18 (U.S. Court of Appeals for DC, 2014). There are numerous unanswered questions because important safety studies have not been done (Davis, 2015).

Additives and Contaminants

Over the past several decades, Congress and the FDA have increasingly turned to disclosure regulations on food safety (Noah, 2014). Beginning in the 1980s, the FDA banned sulfite preservatives from fresh fruits and vegetables and required better, more informative labeling on packaged foods. Sodium nitrites, dyes, and other chemicals are more clearly labeled or more restricted than ever (CFSAN, 2006).

Still, other harmful levels of additives remain in processed foods without monitoring for potential long-term chemical toxicity (Wiley, 2015), albeit with warnings:

- Acrylamide (probable carcinogen found in many processed foods that forms in carbohydrate-containing foods that are baked, fried, or broiled, like breads, cereals, potato chips, and coffee)
- Olestra (fat substitute that can cause diarrhea and stomach cramps)
- Quorn (fungus-based meat substitute that can cause severe vomiting and anaphylactic reactions)
- Sorbitol (sugar substitute added to diet drinks and ice cream)

(Lin, 2012; U.S. Pharmacopeia, 2016; Wiley, 2015).

Four additives recognized by the Institute of Medicine, the U.S. Pharmacopeia, the FDA, and international food regulatory authorities as being generally recognized as safe are excluded from this list, even though some public health advocates maintain they are harmful and question their long-term safety:

- Artificial sweetener acesulfame K
- Aspartame (artificial sweetener also sold under the brand names NutraSweet and Equal)

MANAGEMENT AND LAW ISSUES

11. Should genetically engineered foods be subjected to a mandatory approval process that would ensure such food is safe to eat, as opposed to assuming food is generally recognized as safe unless a hazard is proven to exist?

- Potassium bromate (used in bread)
- Saccharin (artificial sweetener used in diet drinks, fruit juices, and alcoholic beverages)

(FDA, 2016; IOM, 2006; Taylor et al., 2015; U.S. Pharmacopeia, 2016).

In several large European studies conducted at the European Mamazzini Foundation in Italy, researchers found that feeding rats aspartame, at simulated doses at or below levels considered safe for humans, increased the rats' risk of leukemia, lymphoma, and breast cancer (Soffritti et al., 2007). The U.S. Environmental Protection Agency has affirmed the European research and called for a reevaluation of its guidelines on the use of aspartame (Noah, 2014). The oldest artificial sweetener, saccharin, was almost banned in 1977 after studies in rats linked it to cancer (Hodge & Scanlon, 2014). But research in humans largely failed to turn up that risk, with the possible exception found in one study of people consuming six or more servings a day.[LN5] In 2000, the government's National Toxicology Program delisted saccharin as a possible carcinogen.

Emerging Issues

There are calls for regulatory consolidation of the government agencies that are responsible for food safety, with broader regulation of industrial livestock and poultry farming, and new restrictions on using antibiotics for growth promotion have been instituted (Halden & Schwab, 2008). A public consensus appears to be requiring much stronger protection of the U.S. meat and poultry sectors, which have had an extraordinary number of recent **food safety recalls** (Marks, 2016).

Fragmented Regulatory System

Food safety in the United States is fragmented; some health care advocates even characterize the regulatory fragmentation as broken. More than a dozen expert panels inside and outside the government have called for the consolidation of the government agencies that exercise and share food safety responsibility (Holden, 2015). Apart from the FDA and the U.S. Department of Agriculture, about 10 more federal agencies have some food safety responsibility under some 35 federal laws (Linnekin & Leib, 2014). This federal oversight is in addition to the 50 separate state agricultural agencies and 50 intersecting state environmental protection agencies, with all their overlapping state laws and related agencies (Marks, 2015). Some agencies and laws have similar regulations, others are contradictory, but all have the common mandate of food security and consumer protection (Hodge & Scanlon, 2014) (*See generally* Holden, 2015; Marks, 2016).

Voluntary Identification and Tracking Systems

The United States does not have a mandatory **animal identification system**. For instance, mad cow disease can jump to humans who eat contaminated meat and can cause rare, but always fatal brain damage. At this time, public health officials cannot trace infected cattle back to originating farms so other herd cattle can be tested; they have to rely on voluntary recalls by the industry (Halden & Schwab, 2008; Liu, 2014).

For instance, government inspections of U.S. slaughterhouses routinely find significant problems with *Escherichia coli* contamination and the treatment of cattle at the largest beef processors. Audits at Westland/Hallmark Meat Co. in California led to the largest beef recall in U.S. history in 2007 (Negowetti, 2015). About 150 million pounds of beef were recalled. If this quantity is difficult to imagine, picture it as the equivalent of about 40 continuous miles of livestock trailers filled with cattle. This would be enough beef to supply every McDonald's in the country with hamburgers for two months.

Westland, a major supplier of ground beef to the National School Lunch Program, was closed indefinitely after the National Humane Society videotaped slaughterhouse workers shoving and kicking sick, crippled cattle, and forcing them to stand using electric prods, forklifts, and water hoses. The stunning of cattle by air injection rifles as they are driven from holding pens is now prohibited. This was a common practice that was contaminating meat with potentially infective brain tissue until just recently. Until the practice was prohibited, electrical stun guns were used to pull cattle through restrainers to be shackled, hung, and bled. The issue here was the fact that downer cows that could not stand on their own presented a higher risk of bovine spongiform encephalopathy (or mad cow disease) and related phenomena before they were slaughtered and entered the nation's food supply. Both General Mills and Nestlé were forced to recall products after using Westland meat. Investigation of Westland is ongoing, while two videotaped slaughterhouse workers are facing criminal charges (*See generally, e.g.,* Negowetti, 2015; Shea, 2015).

Federal Inspections

Another concern is that the federal meat and poultry inspection agency is so understaffed that some inspectors are assigned to as many as 24 plants or facilities in a geographic region too large to traverse for the required daily inspections. A survey by the National Joint Council of Food Inspection Local Unions found that 75% of inspectors did not visit their plants daily, as required, and when they did, the processing lines often moved so quickly that contamination was difficult to detect (*E.g.,* Cooper, 2013; *Continuing Problems*, 2010). The National Joint Council of Food Inspection Local Unions claims that inspectors who blow the whistle on slaughterhouse violations often find themselves targets of retaliation within the federal Food Safety and Inspection Service. In addition, inspectors are told not to record violations, giving firms time to fix problems instead (Cooper, 2013).

Private Sector Standards

What private sector standards mean for U.S. food safety is another emerging question. Amid growing fears about food safety and impatience with lack of or slow government response times, standards set by the private sector are starting to emerge in the United States. In a key move, Wal-Mart, McDonald's, and Wegmans Food Markets are now buying produce, meat, and seafood only from suppliers accredited by private inspection offices (Marks, 2016). The largest private regulator, **Global Good Agricultural Practice**, is based in Germany. Additionally, many sellers, including grocery store chains, have established their own certification programs that go beyond the standards set by the FDA and the U.S. Department of Agriculture. The table appears set to make changes in U.S. food safety. After all, as Jean Anthelme Brillat-Savarin implied at the beginning of this chapter, we are what we eat.

LAW FACT

Food Labeling

Should the producers and sellers of milk be required to warn consumers of the risks of sickness from lactose intolerance on their packaging?

No. The law does not provide protection from obvious and widely known risks of consuming particular foods. Milk producers are not required to warn consumers of the risks of sickness from lactose intolerance on their packaging. The risk that milk may cause temporary flatulence and related stomach discomfort is well known, even if lactose intolerance as the cause may not be known to everyone who experiences a brief fit of indigestion.

— *Mills v. Giant of Maryland*, 508 F.3d 11 (U.S. Court of Appeals for the D.C. Circuit 2007).

See Makielski, 2014 (discussing this decision).

CHAPTER SUMMARY

- The recent increase in weight-related chronic illnesses in the United States coincides with the change in American eating habits, with dietary intake consisting mostly of highly processed, prepackaged, and ready-made meals high in carbohydrates and sodium content.
- Fully one-third of the daily Calories Americans eat are eaten outside the home at high-Calorie fast food and chain restaurants.
- Federal legislation requires easy-to-read nutrition facts labels on almost all packaged foods, with few exceptions.
- Proposed federal and state legislation would protect the food industry from obesity-related lawsuits when products are in compliance with existing laws and regulations.
- Marketers in the food industry have the power to influence wants and needs as much as they respond to wants and needs.
- Food labeling rules could play an important role in bringing information to consumers and adding to food industry incentives to focus on the nutritional profiles of its foods.
- The most dramatic new regulatory change for the food industry occurred when the FDA required the amount of trans-fatty acids or trans-fats to be listed on almost all food labels and packaging.
- Though trans-fats are found naturally in meats and some dairy products, far greater amounts are ingested as hydrogenated oils added to food to increase shelf life and flavor stability.
- Nutritionists claim trans-fats are so harmful in raising bad cholesterol and lowering good cholesterol, which reduces the risk of clogged arteries, that no level is entirely safe.
- Nearly all fried and baked goods have hydrogenated trans-fats, including foods labeled as low fat.
- Over 300 million U.S. consumers have spent more than a decade consuming genetically modified foods without any known adverse effects.
- Genetically modified foods, derived from genetically engineered plants and animals, are permitted in the United States in the absence of proven health hazards.
- Potentially harmful levels of additives are in many highly processed, prepackaged foods in the United States, albeit with warnings.
- The United States does not have a mandatory animal identification system to trace infected meat and poultry products, public health officials have to rely on voluntary recalls by the industry.
- The federal meat and poultry inspection agency is so understaffed, plant and facility contamination is difficult, and generally impossible, to detect.
- Amid growing fears about food safety and lack of government oversight, private sector standards are starting to emerge in the United States.

LAW NOTES

1. The National Restaurant Association reports that at least 26 states have enacted legislation that either blocks obesity-related lawsuits by mandating dismissal at the **summary judgment** stage without a full presentation of the facts to a jury or have provided immunity from obesity-related claims: Alabama, Arizona, Colorado, Florida, Georgia, Idaho, Illinois, Indiana, Kansas, Kentucky, Louisiana, Maine, Michigan, Missouri, Montana, North Dakota, Ohio, Oklahoma, Oregon, South Dakota, Tennessee, Texas, Utah, Washington, Wisconsin, and Wyoming. Similar legislation is pending in six states: Minnesota, Nebraska, New York, New Jersey, Pennsylvania, and South Carolina (*See generally* Carpenter & Tello-Trillo, 2015; Wicker, 2015; Wilking & Daynard, 2013).

2. The question always arises: which is preferable, diet or regular beverages? An eight-ounce individual serving of Coca-Cola Classic packs 97 calories, while a Pepsi has 100 calories, compared to zero calories for a Diet Coke or a Diet Pepsi. So, fewer calories, but what about the artificial sweeteners? Ever since 1982, when the government first approved aspartame for use in diet sodas, debate has raged about its possible long-term health risks. Whether aspartame, one of the most contentiously debated substances ever added to beverages, contributes to cancer is proving to be very controversial in the United States and Europe (National Cancer Institute, 2009). So the jury is out with regards to the safety of today's diet sodas.

3. Monsanto opposes current state initiatives, like the Vermont Right to Know GMOs, to mandate labeling of ingredients developed from genetically modified seeds in the absence of any demonstrated risks (Davis, 2015).

Monsanto is concerned that mandatory labeling could imply that food products containing genetically modified ingredients are somehow inferior to their conventional or organic counterparts (Ghoshray, 2015). Yet, the issue of how pervasive or how cursory genetically modified food labeling becomes, it is here to stay. Monsanto is also facing state and local legislation on its production of genetically modified seeds that require heavy application of pesticides and herbicides (Wiley, 2016). Hawaii is seeking to require farms and agricultural companies to disclose the use of Monsanto seeds and create pesticide buffer zones to prohibit the use of pesticides within specified distances from homes, roadways, and bodies of water (Wiley, 2015). Litigation by Monsanto to thwart this legislation is ongoing.

4. Before Representative Dennis Kucinich lost his seat in 2012, he spent over ten years trying to pass federal legislation concerning genetically modified food, which received varying levels of support, but ultimately never passed (Peck, 2013).

5. Although a Canadian study demonstrated saccharin caused cancer in laboratory rats, a human would have to drink 800 cans of diet soda each day to reach the level of exposure as that of the Canadian rats (Hodge & Scanlon, 2014). Regardless, diet soda manufacturers risk lawsuits complaining that sugar substitutes carry cancer risks and demanding medical monitoring to ensure early detection (Schwartz & Silverman, 2015).

REFERENCES

AHG (Alliance for a Healthier Generation). (2006a, October 6). Press release, statement from AHG & Centers for Disease Control and Prevention (CDC) concerning agreement by five U.S. food firms to meet nutritional guidelines for food sold in schools. Washington, DC: AHG.

___. (2006b, May 3). Press release, Clinton Foundation and American Heart Association and industry leaders set healthy school beverage guidelines for U.S. schools. Washington, DC: AHG.

Alkerwi, A., et al. (2015). Consumption of ready-made meals and increased risk of obesity: Findings from the Observation of Cardiovascular Risk Factors in Luxembourg (ORISCAV-LUX) study. *British Journal of Nutrition, 113*(2), 270–277.

Barnhill, A. (2015). Choice, respect and value: The ethics of healthy eating policy. *Wake Forest Journal of Law and Policy, 5*, 1–37.

Browne, M. N., et al. (2015). Protecting consumers from themselves: Consumer law and the vulnerable consumer. *Drake Law Review, 63*, 157–191.

Buttrick, H. G., & Hatch, C. D. (2016). Pomegranate juice can do that? Navigating the jurisdictional landscape of food health claim regulation in a post-Pom Wonderful world. *Indiana Law Review, 49*, 267–304.

Card, M. M., & Abela, J. F. (2015). Just a spoonful of sugar will land you six feet underground: Should the Food and Drug Administration revoke added sugar's GRAS status? *Food and Drug Law Journal, 70*, 395–408.

Carpenter, C. S., & Tello-Trillo, D. S. (2015). Do cheeseburger bills work? Effects of tort reform for fast food. *Journal of Law and Economics, 58*, 805–826.

CDC (Centers for Disease Control and Prevention. (2015a) State-specific prevalence of current cigarette smoking among adults and secondhand smoke rules and policies in homes and workplaces. *U.S. Morbidity and Mortality Weekly Report, 64*(19), 532–536.

___. (2015b). *Chronic diseases: The leading causes of death and disability in the United States.* Atlanta, GA: U.S. Department of Health and Human Services: CDC.

CFSAN (Center for Food Safety and Applied Nutrition), U.S. Food and Drug Administration. (2006). *Approaches to establish thresholds for major food allergens and gluten in food.* Silver Spring, MD: CFSAN.

Continuing Problems in USDA's Enforcement of the Humane Methods of Slaughter Act: Hearing Before the Oversight and Government Reform Committee, 111th Congress 2nd Session (2010) (statement of Stanley Painter, Chairman, National Joint Council of Food Inspection Locals).

Cooper, J. S. (2013). Slaughterhouse rules: How AG-gag laws erode the constitution. *Temple Journal of Science, Technology and Environmental Law, 32*, 233–254.

Currey, C. (2016). Despite what you've been sold; unwrapping the falsities surrounding food labels. *West Virginia Law Review, 118*, 1279–1312.

Davis, C. (2015). A right to know about GMOS: What American Meat Institute v. USDA means for vermont's food labeling law. *North Carolina Journal of Law and Technology, 16*, 32–72.

Dery, G. M., & Evaro, R. (2013). The court loses its way with the global positioning system: *United States v. Jones* retreats to the "classic trespassory search". *Michigan Journal of Race and Law, 19*, 113–150.

Dhyani, J. (2016). Science-based food labels: Improving regulations and preventing consumer deception through limited information disclosure requirements. *Albany Law Journal of Science and Technology, 26*, 1–43.

Disiena, 'L. (2015). Practice what you preach: Does the national school lunch program meet nutritional recommendations set by other USDA programs? *Journal of Law and Health, 28*, 164–199.

EPA (Environmental Protection Agency). (2012). *Major crops grown in the United States.* Washington, DC: EPA.

Esterl, M. (2016, December 11). PepsiCo wants to sell healthy food, consumers want chips. *Wall Street Journal,* B1.

FDA (U.S. Food and Drug Administration). (2016a). *Guidance for industry: Trans fatty acids in nutrition labeling, nutrient content claims, and health claims; Small entity compliance guide.* Silver Spring, MD: FDA.

___. (2016b). *News release: FDA takes several actions involving genetically engineered plants and animals for food.*

___. (2016c). *Guidance for industry: Voluntary labeling indicating whether foods have or have not been derived from genetically engineered plants.*

___. (2015a). *Labeling of foods derived from genetically engineered plants.*

___. (2015b). *Questions and answers on food from genetically engineered plants.*

___. (2015c). *Overview of FDA labeling requirements for restaurants, similar retail food establishments and vending machines.*

Ghoshray, S. (2015). Genetically modified foods at the intersection of the regulatory landscape and constitutional jurisprudence. *American Journal of Law and Medicine, 41*, 223–239.

Giessel, K. (2015). On the permanence of permanent law: An argument for the continued presence of the permanent law provisions in The Farm Bill. *Cardozo Public Law, Policy and Ethics, 13*, 765–796.

Gilhooley, M. (2005). The impact and limits of the constitutional deregulation of health claims on foods and supplements: From dementia to nuts to chocolate to saw palmetto. *Mercer Law Review, 56*, 683–714.

Gunter, T. D. (2014). Can we trust consumers with their brains? Popular cognitive neuroscience, brain images, self-help and the consumer. *Indiana Health Law Review, 11*, 483–553.

Halden, R. U., & Schwab, K. J. (2008). *Report: Environmental impact of industrial farm animal production.* Baltimore, MD: Pew Commission on Industrial Farm Animal Production at the Johns Hopkins Bloomberg School of Public Health.

Harden, B. (2003, September 20). Eatery joins battle with "the bulge"; Obesity lawsuits spur dessert protest. *Washington Post*, p. A3.

Harris, M., Chief Information Officer, Information Technology Division, Cleveland Clinic. (2011, February 25). Capstone speaker on Leadership in an Evolving Global Market at the 2011 Wharton Health Care Business Conference, Philadelphia, PA.

Harvey, H. H. (2015). Nudging the public's health: The political psychology of public health law intervention. *DePaul Law Review, 65*, 57–103.

Hitt, G. (2008, May 5). Farm bill stuck on sugar-support proposal. *Wall Street Journal*, p. A3

Hodge, J. G., & Scanlon, M. (2014). The legal anatomy of product bans to protect the public's health. *Annals of Health Law, 23*, 161–182.

Hoffmann, D., & Schwartz, J. (2016). Stopping deceptive health claims: The need for a private right of action under federal law. *American Journal of Law and Medicine, 42*, 53–103.

Holden, M. (2015). FDA-EPA public health guidance on fish consumption: A case study on informal interagency cooperation in "shared regulatory space". *Food and Drug Law Journal, 70*, 101–141.

IOM (Institute of Medicine). (2010). *Bridging the evidence gap in obesity prevention: A framework to inform decision making.* Washington, DC: National Academies Press.

___. (2006). *Food chemicals codex: First supplement* (5th ed.). Washington, DC: IOM.

Kersh, R., & Elbel, B. (2015). Public policy and obesity: Overview and update. *Wake Forest Journal of Law and Policy, 5*, 105–123.

Kunkel, D., et al. (2004). *Report of the American Psychological Association (APA) Task Force on Advertising and Children.* Washington, DC: APA.

Linnekin, B. J., & Leib, E. M. B. (2014). Food law and policy: The fertile field's origins and first decade. *Wisconsin Law Review, 2014*, 555–611.

Liu, P. (2014). WTO dispute: United States; Certain Country of Origin Labelling (COOL) requirements (complaint by Canada). *Asper Review of International Business and Trade Law, 14*, 223–249.

Makielski, K. S. (2014). May contain unvaccinated children: Imposing a duty to warn in the context of nonmedical childhood vaccine exemptions. *Case Western Reserve Law Review, 64*, 1867–1895.

Making, D. (2005). The elephant in the room: Evolution, behavioralism, and counter-advertising in the coming war against obesity. *Harvard Law Review, 116*, 1161–1184.

Marks, A. B. (2016). A new governance recipe for food safety regulation. *Loyola University Chicago Law Journal, 47*, 907–966.

Miller, C. (2016). Spiritual but not religious: Rethinking the legal definition of religion. *Virginia Law Review, 102*, 833–893.

Mortazavi, M. (2016). Tainted: Food, identity, and the search for dignitary redress. *Brooklyn Law Review, 81*, 1463–1492.

___. (2015). Tort as democracy: Lessons from the food wars. *Arizona Law Review, 57*, 929–976.

National Cancer Institute. (2009). *Artificial sweeteners and cancer.* Silver Spring, MD: National Institutes of Health, National Cancer Institute.

Negowetti, N. E. (2015). Opening the barnyard door: Transparency and the resurgence of ag-gag and veggie libel laws. *Seattle University Law Review, 38*, 1345–1398.

Noah, L. (2014). Governance by the backdoor: Administrative law(lessness?) at the FDA. *Nebraska Law Review, 93*, 89–138.

Noel, A. A. (2015). America's growing problem: How the Patient Protection and Affordable Care Act failed to go far enough in addressing the obesity epidemic. *Connecticut Insurance Law Journal, 21*, 485–519.

Nunziato, T. (2014). "You say tomato, I say solanum lycopersicum containing beta-ionone and phenylacetaldehyde": An analysis of Connecticut's GMO labeling legislation. *Food and Drug Law Journal, 69*, 471–490.

Otite, F. O., et al. (2013). Trends in trans fatty acids reformulations of U.S. supermarket and brand-name foods from 2007 through 2011. *Centers for Disease Control and Prevention: Preventing Chronic Disease, 10*, 1201–1298.

Peck, A. (2013). Does regulation chill democratic deliberation? The case of GMOS. *Creighton Law Review, 46*, 653–705.

Posner, S. F., et al. (2014). Considering trends in sodium, *trans* fat, and saturated fat as key metrics of cardiometabolic risk reduction. *Centers for Disease Control and Prevention: Preventing Chronic Disease, 11*, 1405–1461.

PwC (PricewaterhouseCoopers). (2009). *Leveraging growth in the emerging functional foods industry: Trends and market opportunities.* New York, NY: PwC.

Rhode, D. L. (2015). Obesity and public policy: A roadmap for reform. *Virginia Journal of Social Policy and the Law, 22*, 491–524.

Schlosser, E. (2001). *Fast-food nation: The dark side of the all-American meal.* New York, NY: Houghton Mifflin (compares and makes various references to Upton Sinclair's *The Jungle*).

Schwartz, V. E., & Silverman, C. (2015). Where should tort law draw the line? *Brooklyn Law Review, 80*, 599–676.

___., & Appel, C. E. (2014). Government regulation and private litigation: The law should enhance harmony, not war. *Boston University Public Interest Law Journal, 23*, 185–218.

Shea, M. (2015). Punishing animal rights activists for animal abuse: Rapid reporting and the new wave of ag-gag laws. *Columbia Journal of Law and Social Problems, 48*, 337–371.

Sinclair, U. (2006). *The jungle.* New York, NY: Penguin Classics (Original work published 1906) (classic novel on food safety that led to the passage of the Meat Inspection Act and the Pure Food and Drug Act of 1906, which established the FDA.)

Sivin, A. (2015). Striking the soda ban: The judicial paralysis on the department of health. *Journal of Law and Health, 28*, 247–263.

Soffritti, M., et al. (2007) Life-span exposure to low doses of aspartame beginning during prenatal life increases cancer effects in rats. *Environmental Health Perspective, 115*, 1293–1297.

Solar, O., & Irwin, A. (2010). *A conceptual framework for analysis and action on the social determinants of health.* Geneva, Switzerland: World Health Organization, Commission on Social Determinants of Health.

Tai, S. (2012). The rise of U.S. food sustainability litigation. *Southern California Law Review, 85*, 1069–1134.

Taylor, A. L., et al. (2015). The increasing weight of regulation: Countries combat the global obesity epidemic. *Indiana Law Journal, 90*, 257–290.

Urban, L. E., et al. (2014). Temporal trends in fast-food restaurant energy, sodium, saturated fat, and *trans* fat content, United States, 1996–2013. *Centers for Disease Control and Prevention: Preventing Chronic Disease, 11*, 140–202.

USDA. (U.S. Department of Agriculture). *USDA increases FY 2016 U.S. sugar overall allotment quantity and raw cane sugar import access*. Washington, DC: USDA.

___. (2015). *Dietary guidelines for Americans* (8th ed).

U.S. Pharmacopeia. (2016). *Food chemicals codex* (10th ed.). Rockville, MD: USP Convention.

Walberg, G. (2016). Certified organic and UNICAP compliant? The capitalization of certification costs. *Virginia Tax Review, 35*, 387–436.

Wansink, B. (2007). *Mindless eating: Why we eat more than we think*. New York, NY: Bantam.

Weimholt, J. (2015). "Bringing a butter knife to a gun fight"? Salience, disclosure, and FDA's differing approaches to the tobacco use and obesity epidemics. *Food and Drug Law Journal, 70*, 501–551.

Wharton School of the University of Pennsylvania. (2005). Food fight: Obesity raises difficult marketing questions. *Knowledge@Wharton.*

___. (2004). Biotechnology in Chile: Looking for a boost from copper and fruits.

Wicker, C. S. (2015). The not so "sweet surprise": Lawsuits blaming big sugar for obesity-related health conditions face an uphill battle. *Journal of Law and Health, 28*, 264–307.

Wiley, L. F. (2016). From patient rights to health justice: Securing the public's interest in affordable, high-quality health care. *Cardozo Law Review, 37*, 833–889.

___. (2015). Deregulation, distrust, and democracy: State and local action to ensure equitable access to healthy, sustainably produced food. *American Journal of Law and Medicine, 41*, 284–314.

Wilking, C. L., & Daynard, R. A. (2013). Beyond cheeseburgers: The impact of commonsense consumption acts on future obesity-related lawsuits. *Food and Drug Law Journal, 68*, 229–239.

Wong, T. B. (2014). Playing politics with food: Comparing labeling regulations of genetically engineered foods across the North Atlantic in the United States and European Union. *San Joaquin Agricultural Law Review, 23*, 243–283.

Violence and Gun Injury Prevention*

"A strong body makes the mind strong. As to the species of exercises, I advise the gun. While this gives moderate exercise to the body, it gives boldness, enterprise and independence to the mind. Games played with the ball, and others of that nature, are too violent for the body and stamp no character on the mind. Let your gun therefore be your constant companion of your walks."

— **Thomas Jefferson** (1743–1826), Third President of the United States, to his nephew, Peter Carr (1795)

IN BRIEF

This chapter addresses one aspect of the quandary of the modern U.S. health care system: while it is the most expensive health care system in the world, Americans are neither healthier nor do they live longer than citizens in other countries. The violence stemming from firearms assaults and suicides is highlighted based on the medical and financial impact of guns on American society. The focus of this chapter is on the data and research on decreased life expectancy as a result of gun violence and how this information might be used in Second Amendment jurisprudence. This chapter examines the social costs of gun violence and calls for stronger legislation and enforcement of laws relevant for gun injury prevention that still allow for the exercise of Second Amendment rights.

LEARNING OBJECTIVES

Upon completion of this chapter readers should be able to:

1. Discuss the extensive statistical information demonstrating the cost of gun violence in the United States.
2. Distinguish between gun rights adherents' use of "people" and gun safety adherents' use of "militia" within the Second Amendment to support their respective positions.
3. Explain the current state of U.S. Supreme Court cases on restriction of firearms.
4. List the basis for concluding that gun violence is an epidemic.
5. Describe the "substitution effect" as it relates to the level of violence in society before and after restriction of firearms.
6. Outline the insurance and health care costs associated with gun violence.

KEY TERMS

Civic violence	Defective family genes	Gun crime trace data
Common good	Executive orders	Injury Statistics Query and
De facto right	Fallacious position	Reporting System

---

*Contributor: Jim Bryce, JD, Co-Chair, Tower Memorial Committee (University of Texas at Austin); survivor of the 1966 Texas Tower mass murder, the first mass murder on a university campus in the United States.

FACT OR FICTION

Gun Violence

Can the risk of gun violence be reduced on college and university campuses?

The first mass shooting on a university campus occurred at the University of Texas in Austin more than half a century ago on August 1, 1966. University student Charles Whitman, a junior, gunned down 49 students and bystanders, killing 17 before being shot and killed by Austin police. Earlier that same morning, after killing his wife and his mother, Whitman bought over 700 rounds of ammunition, a shotgun he sawed off to an illegal length, and a 30 caliber M-1 carbine with 15- and 30-round magazines. He took firearms he already owned: a 35 Remington pump action deer rifle, a Remington 6 mm bolt action deer rifle with a four power scope, and three pistols up into the University of Texas Tower. The 6 mm bolt-action rifle was the most accurate of the three. He laid siege to the campus for over 90 minutes. None of these weapons would be characterized as an assault weapon in today's parlance. The closest was the M-1 carbine, a World War II lightweight **semiautomatic rifle** used by soldiers such as paratroopers, radiomen, and officers, as opposed to the much heavier 30-06 M-1 Garand used by infantrymen. Four months earlier, Whitman had seen a general physician at the University of Texas Student Health Center. He was referred to a psychiatrist there who saw Whitman only once. During that session the psychiatrist observed Whitman "... seemed to be oozing with hostility." It was up to Whitman to make follow-up appointments, and he never did. Assertions at the time that his actions were attributable to a small tumor in his brain have generally been discounted by more recent medical experts.

The Tower shooting in Austin was the deadliest shooting on a U.S. university campus until the mass shooting at Virginia Tech when another university student, senior Seung Hui Cho, murdered 32 and injured 25 students and faculty in two related incidents before committing suicide on April 16, 2007. Cho also used high-powered handguns with high-capacity ammunition clips for the **mass murders**, despite the fact that it was unlawful for him to have a handgun at all due to having been diagnosed as mentally unstable some four months earlier.

See Law Fact at the end of this chapter for the answer.

Principles and Applications

The emotions surrounding the gun debate are volatile. This chapter attempts to rationally depict what each side has in common by discussing credible facts one cannot reasonably disagree with.[LN1] With approximately 34,000 Americans dying each year from gun violence, the United States faces a public health crisis unrivaled in any developed country (AMA, 2016a; CDC, 2016a).

Background and Context

Despite its status as an advanced, high-income country, the United States has some remarkable characteristics. While the United States is considered among the safest countries in the world in terms of avoiding personal harm or injury, gun death rates are astoundingly high (CDF, 2015). Since the early 1960s when national data on gun violence were first collected:

- Four to five times as many people suffer from firearms injuries as are killed by firearms, both from homicides and suicides.
- Gun violence has killed nearly 177,000 children and teens under the age of 18; over 3,400 children and teens are killed by guns every year.
- Three times more children and teens have died from gun violence on American soil than U.S. soldiers were killed in the Vietnam, Persian Gulf, Afghanistan, and Iraq wars.

(CDC, 2014; CDF, 2015; WHO, 2015).

Beginning in early 2015, the nation's 50 largest cities have experienced an alarming increase in the number of homicides and shootings, mostly committed with firearms. These are disparate cities in disparate parts of the country that have little in common except for being American cities:

- Baltimore, a city of 600,000, is averaging over one homicide a day.
- In Washington, DC, there has been a 20% increase in murders.
- Milwaukee's homicide rate has nearly doubled.
- Multiple guns are being recovered in nearly all these violent incidents.

(Comey, 2015).

The debate surrounds what to do with these facts when the United States has as many guns as people.

- Civilian gun ownership is as high as 330 million—about one gun per person; in contrast, U.S. military and law enforcement personnel possess approximately 4 million guns.
- The firearms and ammunition industry manufactures enough ammunition every year to fire 31 bullets into every man, woman, and child in the United States.
- The United States has less than 5% of the global population; its citizens own 35 to 50% of all civilian-owned guns in the world.

(CDF, 2015; FBI, 2014; Karp, 2012; NRA, 2013; NSSF, 2016).

Social Costs of Firearm Assaults

The total real cost of fatal gun violence in the United States could be as high as $174 billion a year (McClurg, 2015). The annual direct cost for health care and the criminal justice system (law enforcement plus jail and prison costs) for fatal firearm assaults is in the range of $19 billion to $21 billion.

Health Care Costs

Americans pay significantly more for their health insurance as a result of gun violence. Victims of firearm assaults are more likely to need medical treatment requiring high payouts from the health insurance industry. The high payouts, in turn, raise government costs and the cost of private insurer **risk pools**,[LN2] thereby raising costs for everyone that is insured.

- About half of these health insurance costs are borne by Medicaid insurance, and therefore the American taxpayer.
- An additional $4.2 billion to $5.6 billion in health care costs is incurred by injured victims of firearm assaults each year.
- The average health care costs for each fatal firearm assault are about $42,000 a year.
- The nation's risk pools must absorb over $1.4 billion to cover the anticipated costs of treating the victims of fatal firearm assaults every year.

(CDF, 2015; Cook & Ludwick, 2002; McClurg, 2015; Miller, 2012).

MANAGEMENT AND LAW ISSUES

1. Can restriction of firearms be an effective strategy in reducing health care costs in the United States?

Other Social Costs

The annual bill for health care costs is estimated to be as low as $5.6 billion or as high as $7 billion as a result of gun violence (CDC, 2014). The following costs are in addition to the health care costs:

- The criminal justice system spends $13.6 billion addressing gun violence cases every year, including incarceration costs for the perpetrators of the violence.
- Lost lifetime earnings for fatal firearm assaults are between $16 billion and $20 billion.
- The largest social cost by far is for lost quality of life, bringing the total costs per firearm assault to $5.1 million, a figure that may be questioned but not belittled.

(McClurg, 2015; Miller, 2012; WHO, 2014).

Premium Adjustments for Health Insurance

There are opportunities in how the health insurance industry can better price, and perhaps more equitably distribute, the cost of the risks associated with gun ownership. Just owning a handgun significantly increases the chance of dying from gun violence, even when neighborhood variables are controlled for (Langley & Sugarmann, 2013). One logical thread to pursue is the risk calculations the insurance industry makes in pricing health insurance premiums. Demographics and lifestyle choices are the bread and butter of risk calculations, but gun ownership is not a factor in their risk calculations (Wharton, 2005). Yet, firearms assaults in the United States:

- Kill about 34,000 adults and children every year (93 deaths per day)
- Result in 80,000 nonfatal, often disabling, injuries each year (9-10 injuries every hour)

(AMA, 2016a; CDC, 2014; McClurg, 2015).

The increased **insurance premiums** paid by all Americans as a result of gun violence are probably of a similar order of magnitude as the increased tax dollars collected to cover the total health care costs due to gunshots or the increased costs of administering the criminal justice system due to gun crime (Lemaire, 2005; Miller, 2012). With the cost of gun violence to the criminal justice system estimated at $13.6 billion, the increased insurance premiums could be this low, or as high as $16.6 billion (McClurg, 2015).

Environmental Safety

Every gun in our society increases the odds that someone will be killed by gun violence (Wharton, 2005). New York City, decided to attack the so-called **iron pipeline** of illegal guns on the basis of environmental safety. The evidence indicates that litigation to disrupt gun trafficking originating from states with lax gun laws is having a positive effect on gun violence. New York City is one of the few American cities not experiencing an increase in the number of homicides and shootings since the start of 2015 (Comey, 2015).

A court filing in the *A-1 Jewelry III* case shows a 75% drop in illegal guns coming from a sample of the dealers sued. There has been a corresponding 16% drop in the number of guns used in crimes in New York City traced to any dealers in the states where the sued dealers were located. New York City's success may provide a model for other jurisdictions and may serve to influence Second Amendment **jurisprudence**, or philosophy of the law. The litigation settlement is functioning effectively to preserve fundamental gun rights in the context of a feasible regulatory gun safety scheme (Spitzer, 2015).

COURT DECISION
Illegal Gun Sales

City of New York v. A-1 Jewelry & Pawn (A-1 Jewelry III)
[City v. Gun Dealers]
252 F.R.D. 130 (U.S. District Court for the Eastern District of New York 2008),
case dismissed upon settlement of the parties, City of New York v. Adventure Outdoors,
2015 U.S.Dist.LEXIS 75447 (U.S. District Court for the Eastern District of New York 2015)

Facts: New York City sued 27 gun dealers in Georgia, South Carolina, Virginia, Pennsylvania, and Ohio, claiming their lax screening practices and illegal gun sales created a public nuisance in the city.

Issue: Does gun violence constitute a public nuisance? If so, does such a public nuisance exist in New York City, and should gun dealers be held responsible for this nuisance as a result of illegal gun sales?

Holding and Decision: There was enough evidence to go forward with the case.

Analysis: After 8 years of litigation, 26 dealers settled with New York City, agreeing to court appointment of a federal monitor to oversee gun sales at their stores. The federal monitoring provides for unlimited review of firearms-related records (including trace requests and multiple handgun sales reports) and unrestricted inspection of all firearm inventories, plus videotaping of their sales activities and continued undercover surveillance. The oversight will ensure that the dealers conduct legal firearm sales and identify and refuse to sell to **straw purchasers**, who purchase guns on behalf of others who, for various reasons, cannot legally purchase guns themselves. The settlement also provides for penalties for noncompliance with any laws regulating the sale and purchase of firearms, including $10,000 for a first violation, $15,000 for a second violation, and $20,000 for a third violation. The federal monitoring will expire after three consecutive years without a reported violation; the three-year clock will be reset with each violation.

The 27th dealer moved for summary judgment, essentially arguing that there was not enough evidence to proceed to a full-blown trial, but this motion was denied in part because extensive evidence obtained during discovery revealed at least 72 guns sold by this dealer were recovered in connection with criminal activity. This dealer was subsequently indicted on federal charges arising out of the conduct on which this lawsuit was based. A subsequent piece of the litigation found:

> A public nuisance exists in the City of New York, in the form of large numbers of illegally possessed firearms. Illegally possessed guns interfere with the health and safety of a large number of persons within the City.

Rather than proceed to trial, however, the last dealer opted to settle the case instead.

Rule of Law: The sales practices of firearms dealers can be considered a public nuisance, and there was enough evidence to move forward with a trial to determine whether the conduct of this particular deal contributed to that nuisance.

References discussing this court decision: Kendall, 2013; Morley, 2014.

Protection of Lawful Commerce in Arms Act

Congress passed the **Protection of Lawful Commerce in Arms Act of 2005** (*See* 15 U.S.C.A. §§ 7901-7903 and 8 U.S.C.A. Ch. 44 §§ 921, 922, 924) in response to New York City's attack on illegal guns. This legislation shields gun manufacturers, distributors, and dealers from civil liabilities arising from gun violence by protecting them being held liable when crimes have been committed with their products. *Contra A-1 Jewelry II*, 247 F.R.D. 296, 349-354 (U.S. District Court for the Eastern District of New York 2007) (denying a motion to dismiss on the grounds that this lawsuit was prohibited by the federal Protection of Lawful Commerce in Arms Act). While this law may be successful for temporarily delaying and weakening litigation on illegal gun sales, history will eventually prove Congress was misguided (Spitzer, 2015).

MANAGEMENT AND LAW ISSUES

2. Should Congress be permitted to use its appropriation strategies to restrict the collection of and access to federal databases used in injury prevention research and environmental safety litigation?

For decades, car manufacturers resisted requiring seat belts to reduce vehicular deaths and injuries; yet today, New Hampshire is the only state not to require seat belt use, and most states allow law enforcement to stop vehicles for seat belt law violations (IIHS & HLDI, 2016).

Tiahrt Amendment

In response to New York City's attack on illegal guns, Congress began attaching the **Tiahrt Amendment** to appropriations bills, blocking access to federal databases that trace guns used in crime back to particular gun dealers (Lowy & Sampson, 2016). For more than a decade, the Amendment has:

- Barred (perhaps unconstitutionally) the use of gun-tracing data in court
- Blocked funding for computerizing firearms transactions records
- Prohibited the Bureau of Alcohol, Tobacco, Firearms and Explosives from releasing gun-tracing data to the public

(McClurg, 2015).

New York City was able to file its *A-1 Jewelry* civil lawsuit using trace data collected before the Congressional ban. As time passes, that data will become less and less useful, making it harder to stop gun dealers whose conduct results in gun violence. While there is concern that the Tiahrt Amendment restricts information needed by the public to control gun violence in their communities, Congress has not repealed the legislation.

Second Amendment Jurisprudence

The flashpoint in the long running debate over restriction of firearms is the **Second Amendment** to the U.S. Constitution, which states: "A well-regulated **militia** [boldface added], being necessary to the Security of a free state, the **right of the people** [boldface added] to keep and bear arms shall not be infringed." Gun safety adherents read the Amendment as permitting restriction of firearms possession; advocates of gun rights read it as enshrining in law an individual's unfettered right to own guns (Wharton, 2005). Although the right to own guns is not absolute, there are ways to achieve common goals without sacrificing the Second Amendment. There is not an absolute trade-off between gun safety and gun rights.

Individual Right to Gun Ownership

While the concept of the **common good** is often used to justify gun safety, political trade-offs involving Second Amendment rights, indeed involving any of the people's fundamental rights, are rarely simple. Gun safety laws remain controversial. While the assertion of an absolute right to guns often creates political deadlock, this stalemate changed slightly in favor of gun rights advocates with the U.S. Supreme Court decision in *Heller*. Gun rights adherents rely on the fact that the Second Amendment mentions "people," while those espousing gun safety rely on the presence of "militia" to limit individual rights. As gun violence in America with its attendant costs of health care continues to escalate, Americans may ultimately decide their individual right to be armed should be balanced against the costs to society arising from unfettered exercise of that right.

COURT DECISION
Safety Restrictions on Firearms

District of Columbia v. Heller
[Local Government v. Citizen]
554 U.S. 570 (U.S. Supreme Court 2008), *rehearing denied*, 2016 U.S.App.LEXIS 3678
(U.S. Court of Appeals for the D.C. Circuit 2016)[LN3]

Facts: A District gun ban prohibited ownership of guns without a license and required all registered firearms to be kept in an **inoperable condition**. Dick Heller, a special police officer, was denied a license to keep a handgun at his home based on the District's gun ban. He claimed he had a Second Amendment right to possess guns for self-defense in his home.

Issue: Did the local gun ban violate the Second Amendment right of individuals who wish to keep guns for private use in their homes?

Holding and Decision: Yes. The District's gun ban violated the rights bestowed on individuals under the Second Amendment.

Analysis: Heller, who had no association with any militia, challenged the District's gun ban. He did not assert a right to carry weapons outside his home, nor did he challenge the District's authority to require the registration of firearms. As a special police officer, he was authorized to carry a handgun while on duty, but he also wanted to keep a gun in his home for self-defense purposes.

The Court extensively analyzed the precedent, text, and history of the Second Amendment and held that the Amendment granted an individual right to bear arms, subject to reasonable restrictions. The District gun ban was struck down as unconstitutional. The District ban reduced some modern-day categories of guns to the point of being useless and unconstitutionally prohibited the lawful use of guns for self-defense.

Rule of Law: General gun bans on private possession of handguns for self-defense violate the Second Amendment. However, gun safety laws may:

- Prohibit felons or the mentally disabled from possessing firearms
- Prohibit possession of firearms in sensitive areas such as schools and government buildings
- Regulate sales of firearms

References discussing this court decision: *E.g.*, Adams, 2013; Bindbeutel, 2014; Burns, 2013; Colvin, 2014; Crane, 2014; Curtis, 2015; Daniels, 2013; DeMitchell, 2014; DePalo, 2013; Dulan, 2014; Duquette, 2014; Fair, 2014; Foody, 2013; Forsey, 2013; Fox & DeLateur, 2014; Giles, 2014; Hardy, 2014; Hubbard, 2014; Lamartina, 2013; McNamara, 2014; Moeller, 2014; Moran, 2013; Pelaez, 2014; Pinals, 2014; Record & Gostin, 2014; Renneker, 2015; Rose, 2014; Ruebsamen, 2013; Salvin, 2014; Stidham, 2015; Stowell, 2014; Sturzenegger, 2013; Vasek, 2014; West, 2014; Whitney, 2014.

This ruling made clear that individuals bore arms before the Second Amendment was ever adopted (NRA, 2008). This right to be armed pre-existed like all individual rights in the Bill of Rights. The **Tenth Amendment** speaks explicitly about the allocation of governmental power. It reads as follows: "The powers not delegated to the United States by the Constitution, nor prohibited by it to the states, are reserved to the states respectively, or to the people." The ruling in *Heller* may help move the gun violence debate forward. If the nation as a whole should ultimately decide an individual right to be armed is ill advised, it can then amend the U.S. Constitution to acknowledge that Americans have the **right to be free of any harm from violence** (*E.g.*, Kopel, 2010).

Community Safety Restrictions

As gun violence and its attendant health care costs continue to escalate, one side of this debate maintains that the individual right to possess guns should be balanced against the costs to society arising from exercise of that right. The other side maintains that the common good should never influence individual rights (Blackman, 2011). The debate after *Heller* is whether states and local governments should be permitted to place reasonable restrictions on the individual right to possess guns. While gun restrictions should not depend exclusively on their effects on individuals' welfare (Zamir & Medina, 2008), the next battleground is determining how the safety of local communities can be emphasized so as to restore balance with the individual right to possess guns.

COURT DECISION
State and Local Restrictions on Guns Possession

McDonald v. City of Chicago
[Residents of Chicago v. City of Chicago]
561 U.S. 742 (U.S. Supreme Court 2010), *encompassing NRA, Inc.*, 567 F.3d 856
(U.S. Court of Appeals for the 7th Circuit 2009)[LN4]

Facts: Chicago residents would like to keep handguns in their homes for safety and **self-defense**, but they are prohibited from doing so by Chicago's firearms laws. In *Heller*, the U.S. Supreme Court held that the Second Amendment protected the right to possess guns for the purpose of self-defense and struck down a similar local law that banned the possession of handguns in the home. Chicago and the village of Oak Park, a Chicago suburb, have laws effectively banning handgun possession by almost all private citizens. Chicago and Oak Park maintained their local laws were constitutional because the Second Amendment has no application to the States. After *Heller*, this federal lawsuit was filed by Chicago residents alleging that their local handgun ban has left them vulnerable to criminals.

Holding and Decision: The Second Amendment right to own and possess handguns applies at the state and local level; state and local governments may not improperly restrict the individual rights granted by the Second Amendment.

Analysis: Local laws effectively banned ownership of handguns by law-abiding private citizens. The U.S. Supreme Court held that the Second Amendment protected the right to possess guns for self-defense and that the Second Amendment was fully applicable to the states. Self-defense is a basic right and the central component of the Second Amendment. This Second Amendment right applies to handguns, which are the preferred firearm to keep and use for protection of one's home and family.

Rule of Law: The Second Amendment gives individuals the right to possess firearms for self-defense, a right implicit in the concept of ordered **liberty** and the right to be free of any harm from violence.

References discussing this court decision: *E.g.*, Bindbeutel, 2014; Burns, 2013; Campbell, 2013; Colvin, 2014; Crane, 2014; Curtis, 2015, Daniels, 2013; DePalo, 2013; Fair, 2014; Forsey, 2013; Fox & DeLateur, 2014; Hubbard, 2014; Moeller, 2014; Moran, 2013; Pelaez, 2014; Pratt, 2014; Record & Gostin, 2014; Renneker, 2015; Ruebsamen, 2013; Stidham, 2015; Stowell, 2014; Vasek, 2014.

The gun violence issue has evolved to the issue of whether the recently confirmed right of individuals to possess guns is a limitation on states and local communities when addressing their need to ban handguns (Bindbeutel, 2014; Ruebsamen, 2013). According to the individual rights approach of this U.S. Supreme Court, the right to be free of any harm from violence does not have priority over the right of individuals who wish to keep guns in their homes for self-defense (Fair, 2014; Stowell, 2014). Gun safety adherents maintain that restrictions on guns will improve safety and reduce the incidence of gun injuries (Fox & DeLateur, 2014; Renneker, 2015). On the other hand, advocates of gun rights argue that law-abiding citizens will be made less safe by their inability to defend themselves against criminal violence (Burns, 2013; Forsey, 2013).

Both sides perceive risks associated with gun safety (Hubbard, 2014). There is either too little restriction that will inevitably lead to intentional shootings and accidents involving guns, or too much restriction that disarms responsible, law-abiding citizens and leaves them subject to violence (Colvin, 2014; Moeller, 2014). The debate now centers on the issue of whether Americans are willing to transfer some of their Second Amendment rights to the government in order to protect their right to be free of any harm from violence (Campbell, 2013).

The contour of the nation's gun debate definitively changed with the *McDonald* decision (Daniels, 2013; Moran, 2013). The freedom to think and act without being constrained by the government is a fundamental right of all U.S. citizens independent of any laws (Crane, 2014; Pelaez, 2014). At the same time, the government exists as a result of a **social contract** whereby citizens consent to transfer some of their powers and individual rights to the government (Record & Gostin, 2014; Stidham, 2015). The question facing everyone today is what will Americans consent to in order to be safe in their homes and their communities?

Restrictions on Gun Safety Research

Gun safety researchers (and cynics alike) note that federal databases suddenly became severely restricted to the public after the *Heller* decision. The U.S. Supreme Court ruling in *Heller* left the door open for accepting reasonable gun safety legislation, if supported by findings of fact regarding the epidemiology of gun violence. But almost overnight, gun safety researchers and the public alike were denied access to information from the:

- Bureau of Alcohol, Tobacco, Firearms and Explosives within the U.S. Department of Justice
- **National Electronic Injury Surveillance System** within the Centers for Disease Control and Prevention

(GAO, 2008).[LN5]

Since *Heller*, the U.S. Supreme Court has rejected more than 60 cases seeking to expand the very limited right defined in *Heller* (Law Center to Prevent Gun Violence, 2015). Rather than engaging in an expansive national debate on gun violence, gun safety viewpoints are foreclosed before a civil conversation has ever begun. The Court has consistently reconfirmed that the limitations of the Second Amendment are not an obstacle to gun safety laws supported by findings of fact. The problem is that this is a **fallacious position**; although the Court's position appears on its face to be valid, under scrutiny it is logically invalid (McClurg, 2015). The fallacy is that gun safety researchers and the public no longer have access to facts on the epidemiology of gun violence. "Mistakes" in reasoning that would be more readily understood as deliberate misunderstandings illustrate that fallacious arguments usually have the deceptive appearance of being good arguments (Damer, 2012). The result of this fallacy by the Court is that the nation is completely stuck in a rigor mortis of public debate about gun violence with arbitrary narrow bounds of the range of disagreement (McClurg, 2015). Public debates about the epidemiology of gun violence are stagnant if the country lacks facts with credible standards of accuracy upon which to base the discussion.

The Epidemiology of Gun Violence

Research studies of gun violence in the United States come at this subject from a number of health care perspectives, including the costs of health care (AMA, 2016a). Yet, other costs are more difficult to quantify, including:

- Cost of pain and fear, which must not be belittled
- Emotional costs to the forced adaptation to increased risk
- Expenditure of public resources devoted to law enforcement
- Limitations in hours of operation of retail establishments
- Limits on freedom to live or work in certain places
- Lost productivity of victims and changes in the quality of life

- Private investment by individuals in protection and avoidance
- Restrictions on residential and commercial location decisions

(Lee, 2012; Lemaire, 2005;).

The aggregate cost of gun violence (from fatal and nonfatal firearm assaults) is estimated at approximately $500 billion annually, or approximately $1,600 per capita (IOM, 2012; Lee, 2012; McClurg, 2015). This is the same aggregate cost as smoking, obesity, and other unhealthy behaviors that lead to preventable illnesses and conditions (CDC, 2015a, 2015b; HHS, 2014b). Put another way, every American spends about $3,200 each year that could be avoidable with healthier lifestyle choices.

Reduced Life Expectancy

Life expectancy is considered one of the best measures of quality of life when evaluating health care decisions. This measure summarizes in a single number all individual and external damages affecting a person. Life expectancy is influenced by numerous individual and external factors, for instance:

- Accident history
- **Civic violence**
- **Defective family genes** that, theoretically, should make future generations ill or more likely to die younger
- High-risk sexual behavior
- Limited access to high-quality health care
- Poor socioeconomic status
- Proximity to environmental degradation
- Unhealthy nutrition
- Wars

(Bezruchka, 2012; WHO, 2014).

The life expectancy measure is not affected by age distribution, so it is an appropriate epidemiological tool for comparing different populations with dissimilar age structures (WHO, 2014).

The question is how Americans compare to people in other countries in terms of life expectancy. The unfortunate answer is that Americans do not measure up very well. As illustrated in **TABLE 36-1**, the life expectancy of Americans is 79 years; 5 years less than that of the citizens in Japan and Hong Kong. From a country with one of the world's highest expenditures on health care (over $9,400 annual per capita), as shown in **TABLE 36-2**, the United States ranks 33rd in life expectancy (World Bank, 2016).

Firearms are not used uniformly in the United States. Evidence of this can be derived from the striking data on the life expectancy of Black males in the United States. Black males live 11 years less than most Americans: 67 versus 78 years (CDC, 2016b). This begs the question: what creates this difference in life expectancies? Is there the possibility that firearm assaults influence life expectancy in the United States? Several respected research studies have analyzed the impact on typical American life expectancy due to violent behavior, specifically violence from firearms.

TABLE 36-1 Global Life Expectancies

Developed Countries	Average Age of Death
Japan and Hong Kong (SAR-China)	84
Australia, Iceland, Italy, Singapore, Spain, Switzerland	83
Canada, Chile, France, Israel, Luxembourg, Norway, Sweden	82
Austria, Belgium, Finland, Germany, Greece, Ireland, Macao (SAR-China); Portugal, Virgin Islands, United Kingdom	81
Costa Rica, Cuba, Cyprus, Lebanon, Puerto Rico, St. Martin (French part)	80
Brunei Darussalam, Czech Republic, Guam, Qatar, United States	79

Data from: World Bank. (2016). *Life expectancy at birth, total (years)*. Washington, DC: World Bank.

TABLE 36-2 Global Health Expenditures Per Capita

Developed Countries	Health Expenditures Per Capita
Switzerland	$9,700
Norway	$9,500
United States	$9,400
Japan	$3,700

Note: Switzerland and Norway's national health insurance plans cover spa therapies and alternative medicine, including homoeopathy and traditional Chinese medicine like acupuncture.

Data from: World Bank. (2016). *Life expectancy at birth, total (years)*. Washington, DC: World Bank.

Availability of Firearms in Relationship to Life Expectancy

Although both life expectancies and firearm deaths are unevenly dispersed throughout the U.S. population, the disparity in firearm deaths for Black males is prominent (FBI, 2015). Combined, firearm homicides and suicides reduce overall life expectancy by an average of 96 to 104 days. Broken down by race and gender, however, there are notable gaps in how Black males fare.

- Black men face more than four times the rate of death from firearm assaults as other groups of Americans (17 deaths per 100,000 compared to four deaths per 100,000).
- Black men lose more than 10 times the days lost by White women (361 versus 3 days of life).
- Black men lose more than twice as many days of life as White men (361 versus 151 days of life).

(FBI, 2015; HHS, 2014a).

In addition, firearm homicides and suicides kill mostly young people:

- Black males are killed by guns at a younger average age than White males.
- Black males commit suicide, on average, when they are 37 years of age, as compared to 49 for White males.
- Black men on average are 31 years of age at the time of their deaths from firearm homicides.

(FBI, 2015; HHS, 2014a; VPC, 2016).

To put these statistics into context among all fatal injuries, only motor vehicle accidents have a greater effect on life expectancy than firearm deaths (CDC, 2016b).

The Substitution Effect

One objection to the idea that reducing firearm deaths would increase life expectancy and reduce health care costs is the argument that guns are simply a means to an end. In other words, people who are intent on violence, either toward themselves or others, will find a way to achieve that objective with whatever tools are available. This is called the **substitution effect** (Hardy, 2015). The question then becomes whether Americans are necessarily more violent than citizens of other nations. Certainly history shows violence is not unique to Americans.

For instance, while Japan generated more than its fair share of violence in the 20th century, today it is among the safest countries in the world and has some of the world's strictest gun safety restrictions (*E.g.*, Wolitz, 2014). With few handguns in Japan, crimes committed with firearms are low. Japan also has an extremely low rate of thefts and burglaries. This is a counterweight to the gun rights adherents' substitution effect argument that guns at home reduce property crimes. The failure of the substitution effect is apparent in Japan and might also be in the United States; at least, there is no obvious reason why it should not be.

Of course, some will argue it is the cultural differences in these two affluent democracies accounting for the difference in violence between Japan and the United States, not simply the lack of accessibility to guns in Japan. Japan is very much a paternalistic, collective society, and American society is more individualistic with a deeply ingrained sense of a right to self-defense and obligation to protect property (Wolitz, 2014). No gun safety restrictions are going to change this cultural difference. The question remains, however, what cultural factors explain the cross-country differences in violence between the United States and Japan? There is empirical support for many economic and social factors (demographics, ethnic diversity, education, income, inequality, deterrence, and the like), but it is not clear why such cultural factors would explain the large difference in violence between the United States and Japan, nor is it clear how these factors can explain the existing patterns of gun availability, gun safety, and violence (WHO, 2014; *See* Wharton, 2005).

The Substitution Effect Does Not Affect Firearm Homicides

A number of research studies show that in the area of homicides there is little or no substitution effect. There is a positive correlation between the rate of household gun ownership and the national rate of homicides as well as the proportion of homicides committed with a gun (Goode, 2016). One study by the University of Washington's Department of Surgery contrasted two cities with nearly identical climates, populations, unemployment levels, and average income: Seattle, Washington, with relaxed gun safety laws, and Vancouver, British Columbia, with strict gun safety. The comparisons show the following:

- Assault rates with a firearm: Seattle's rate is seven times higher than Vancouver's
- Burglary, robbery, homicide, and assault rates without a gun: The same between Seattle and Vancouver
- Gun ownership by residents: 12% in Vancouver compared to 41% in Seattle[LN6]
- Homicide rates with a handgun: Seattle's rate is almost five times higher

(Killias et al., 2001; *See, e.g.*, Goode, 2016).

The conclusions of this research study were threefold:

- Restrictive handgun laws reduced the homicide rate in Vancouver.
- The availability of handguns does not decrease the rate of crimes without guns.
- The increased availability of handguns in Seattle increased the assault and homicide rates with a gun.

(Killias et al., 2001; *See, e.g.*, Goode, 2016).

A Swiss study from the University of Lausanne comparing gun ownership in 21 countries, including Canada and the United States, suggests gun ownership increases the likelihood of homicides, but found little or no substitution effect in the area of homicides. The research concluded:

- There is a high correlation between gun ownership rates and homicide rates, as well as the proportions of homicides committed with handguns.
- There is little or no correlation between guns and the rates of homicide committed by other means.
- Other means were not used in homicides to compensate for the absence of guns in countries with a lower rate of gun ownership.

(Killias et al., 2001 (confirming the original research of 11 countries and comparing an additional 10 countries)).

A third comparative study by the Pacific Institute for Research and Evaluation also found the substitution effect does not affect firearm crimes. Firearms were involved in 50% of the assaults in the United States, compared to only 8% in New Zealand where there is strict restriction of guns (Spicer, 2005).

Finally, researchers at the Firearm and Injury Center at the University of Pennsylvania's Department of Surgery found gun violence generally declines after implementation of strict gun safety laws (Macinko & Marinho de Souza, 2007). When the Penn researchers looked at evidence from Brazil, a country with even greater levels of gun violence than before Brazil strictly regulated handguns, they found that:

- A significant portion of the declines in firearm-related deaths and hospitalizations in Brazil were reasonably attributed to measures reducing the availability of firearms.
- Strengthening the capacity of local law enforcement to enforce gun safety measures affected the decline in gun violence.
- These improvements were not offset by homicides committed using other weapons.

(Macinko & Marinho de Souza, 2007).

With recent gun legislation and other handgun reduction policies in Brazil reducing gun violence, Brazil may serve as an important example of how the United States might address pervasive gun violence while maintaining private ownership of firearms. The Supreme Court of Brazil looked to the plain meaning of its constitution, the original intent of their founders, and even background norms and principles on gun ownership; the Court then analyzed its gun legislation by looking at the text, the legislative history, and again at background norms and principles, this time with respect to handgun restrictions to ensure that the country's gun reduction policies comported with the basic principles of government written into their national constitution (Martin, 2014). Brazil made gun violence a federal issue; it decided to require universal federal background checks on all handgun purchasers versus the state and local law enforcement checks in the United States (Larkin, 2015). Although Brazil once had one of the highest murder rates in the world, Brazil has faced no major public backlash from its gun control laws and people are still able to obtain guns to protect themselves (*See* UNESCO, 2015).

Evidence of a Substitution Effect for Suicides

In the case of suicides, there is some evidence of a substitution effect. The reduced availability of one **method of suicide** prompts an increase in other methods. The reduced availability of handguns prompted an increase in suicides by poisoning, suffocation, cuts, crashes, and jumps (Killias, 2001). Indeed, in places like Japan and Hong Kong, suicide rates exceed the U.S. suicide rate, despite strictly limited access to firearms. Fewer than 1% of suicides in Japan and Hong Kong are committed with a firearm, whereas more than half the suicides in the United States are committed with a firearm. However, Norway, the United Kingdom, Canada, Australia, and New Zealand all experienced a decline in firearm suicides since the 1980s as the level of gun ownership continued to decline with stricter gun restrictions in place (Ajdacic-Gross et al., 2006). Universal gun background checks have expanded and owner licensing and registration of guns are the norm outside the United States; many countries require licensees to demonstrate a genuine need for a gun, while countries like Britain and Norway ban handguns altogether (Masters, 2016).

The Substitution Effect Does Not Affect Life Expectancy

Nevertheless, the substitution effect hardly changes the number of life expectancy days lost due to guns in the United States. The average American loses from 96 to 104 days of life due to guns (Lemaire, 2005). At the same time, the U.S. health care industry spends billions to extend lives, often for medical treatments that sometimes offer Americans less than 96 to 104 extra days of life (Calfo et al., 2016). Most Americans are willing to pay a lot for this extra life expectancy; many are willing to pay anything (Wharton, 2005). When debates about extending life expectancy center on the costs of gun violence, however, emotional debates about the Second Amendment keep Americans from seeking common ground on the question of how to best address this public health problem.

The evidence on life expectancies should stimulate further debate over whether restriction of firearms can be an effective strategy in reducing gun violence in the United States. With more than 310 million guns in America, it is extremely unlikely anyone will move to confiscate guns, nor should the United States necessarily ban guns (FBI, 2015). Therefore, the question for public health officials is how the United States can best reasonably and responsibly regulate and safely control the use of guns.

The Cost Controversy: Individual Rights Versus Community Safety

Firearm assaults have reached epidemic proportions with an increasing sense of public urgency to find workable solutions to reduce the culture of horrific violence and mass shootings in the United States (AMA, 2016b). Apart from the assault weapon and high-capacity magazine ban that Congress allowed to expire, the last major federal gun legislation came nearly a half century ago following the assassinations of President John F. Kennedy, Martin Luther King, and presidential candidate Robert Kennedy. The Gun Control Act of 1968:

- Expanded gun licensing requirements to include more dealers and more detailed record keeping
- Further restricted shotguns and rifles sales
- Increased restrictions on people who were banned from possessing firearms (including convicted felons, those found mentally incompetent, and drug users)

- Outlawed mail order sales of rifles and shotguns
- Restricted handgun sales over state lines

(*See* 18 U.S.C.A. §§ 921 *et seq.*).

Even after each mass murder, with a newly engaged media and public opinion aligned to take action, nothing really changes. Proposals to impose universal background checks for gun purchases and suggestions to renew the federal ban on assault weapons and high-capacity ammunition magazines meet with political deadlock. Either the nation seriously debates and agrees to balance individual rights and community safety interests with both sides compromising, or the nation's inaction confers a **de facto right** for everyone to act without reasonable care in the manufacture, distribution, and possession of firearms (McClurg, 2015). What will it take? Are Americans content with the currently reality of more terrorism, mass murders, gang violence, attacks on law enforcement, and suicides, or does the nation strive for a better way?

The Second Amendment right to bear arms comes with a high price; someone must pay the multibillion dollar cost of gun violence. The question is how to best balance this cost between gun rights adherents and gun safety adherents, and within the national debate on health care expenditures and reform. Gun violence is a public health issue that can be resolved; the question is how. This is one national debate that will ideally continue until it is satisfactorily resolved.

LAW FACT

Gun Safety

Can the risk of gun violence be reduced on college and university campuses?

No. Risk of gun violence cannot be reduced unless there is a radical change in the political climate. After each mass shooting, some believe the latest killings may lead the nation to address U.S. violence. The introduction of a gun into any act of aggression makes the resulting violence potentially lethal regardless of what gun safety laws are in place.

Government has an obligation to its citizens to enforce the gun safety laws preventing the purchase of handguns by those suffering from mental illness; yet only 30 states report mental health information to the FBI's National Instant Check System for firearms transactions (FBI, 2015). The present laws adopted in the late 1980s mandating waiting periods before purchasing any form of firearm and requiring background checks for all handgun purchasers should be more strictly enforced.

— *Adapted based upon the mass shootings at the* University of Texas at Austin, 1966 and Virginia Tech, 2007. *E.g.*, AMA, 2016a; Blocher & Miller, 2016a; Eden, 2014; Oblinger, 2013; Smith, 2013; Virginia Tech Review Panel, 2007 (discussing firearm assaults on college and university campuses and the right to carry); *See* Lavergne, 1997 (discussing the University of Texas at Austin assaults).

CHAPTER SUMMARY

- The individual practice of bearing arms existed long before the right to be armed was (arguably) made explicit in the Second Amendment of the U.S. Constitution.
- Whereas the Second Amendment right to own guns is not absolute, gun rights adherents read the Amendment as enshrining an individual's right to own guns, while gun safety adherents read it as permitting the restriction of firearms possession, and neither side of the debate identifies or acknowledges goals in common with the other side.
- The aggregate cost of gun violence (from fatal and nonfatal firearm assaults) in the United States is approximately $500 billion annually, while smoking, obesity, and other unhealthy behaviors that cause preventable health conditions cost another $500 billion annually; these are expenditures that could be avoided simply by healthier lifestyle choices.

- Life expectancy is one of the best epidemiological measures of quality of life when evaluating health care decisions; it measures all the individual and external damages affecting a person.
- Although the United States spends more on health care than any other country in the world, Americans rank 33rd in life expectancy at 79 years.
- Life expectancies and firearm deaths are unevenly distributed throughout the U.S. population; the disparity in firearm deaths for Black males is striking, with Black males living an average of 13 years less than other Americans.
- Black men are four times more likely to die from gun violence than other groups of Americans, at the rate of 17 deaths per 100,000, compared to the U.S. average of four.
- Firearm homicides and suicides reduce life expectancy in the United States by an average of 96 to 104 days.
- There are notable gaps in how various groups fare when comparing life expectancies, with firearm homicides and suicides killing mostly young people; only motor vehicle accidents have a stronger effect on life expectancy than firearm deaths.
- Americans pay more for their health benefits as a result of reduced life expectancy from gun violence; victims of gun violence are more likely to need medical treatment requiring high payouts from the health insurance industry, which in turn raises the costs for everyone.
- One objection to the suggestion that reducing gun violence would increase life expectancy and reduce the costs of health benefits, is the argument that guns are simply a means to an end; people intent on violence will achieve their objective with or without firearms, a phenomenon called the substitution effect.
- Rates of household gun ownership are proportional to the rates of both homicides and homicides committed with a gun.
- There is some evidence of a substitution effect on suicides; the reduced availability of handguns prompts an increase in suicides by other methods.
- The substitution effect hardly changes the number of life expectancy days lost due to guns in the United States.

LAW NOTES

1. Most of the data presented in this chapter are from the:

    - Federal Bureau of Investigation's Supplementary Homicide Reports and its **Uniform Crime Reporting Program** (one-year time lag on crimes data from the **National Incident-Based Reporting System** with about one-third of the states and local law enforcement agencies reporting)
    - Centers for Disease Control and Prevention's **National Vital Statistics System** at the National Bureau for Health Statistics (more than a 30-month time lag on deaths)
    - Centers for Disease Control and Prevention's **Injury Statistics Query and Reporting System** (more than a five-year time lag) that provides injury, violent death, and cost of injury data
    - Bureau of Justice Statistics **National Crime Victimization Survey** in the U.S. Department of Justice (two-year time lag)
    - The Consumer Product Safety Commission's **National Electronic Injury Surveillance System** that collects hospital emergency data on nonfatal firearm injuries, firearm assaults, and firearm suicides

2. Risk pools are special programs created by most state legislatures to provide a safety net for the medically uninsurable population (McGill & MacNaughton, 2016). Prior to the Affordable Care Act, victims of gun violence were often denied health insurance coverage because of their pre-existing gun-related injuries or could only access private health insurance coverage that was restricted or had extremely high rates (Cook, 2013). Some state-owned, not-for-profit associations assessed the health insurance industry to cover their costs; others provided an appropriation from state general tax revenue; some states shared funding of loss subsidies with the health insurance industry, using an assessment and providing them a tax credit for the assessment; while other states had a special funding source such as a tobacco tax or a hospital or health care provider surcharge (Wiley, 2016). For the 16 states without risk pools, the medically uninsured were part of the uninsured population facing financial devastation in the event of catastrophic injuries (McGill & MacNaughton, 2016). Now that the consumer protections in the Affordable Care Act have been fully implemented, risk pools are no longer necessary the way they were in the past (Wiley, 2016). People are no longer denied health insurance because of

their medical history, and people are no longer offered policies with increased premiums or exclusions based on pre-existing conditions.

3. Litigation following this U.S. Supreme Court case continued for another eight years until the U.S. Court of Appeals for the District of Columbia Circuit finally denied any more rehearings on what they characterized as difficult policy judgments. Although the Second Amendment protects an individual right to keep and bear arms, this is not a right to keep and carry any firearms whatsoever, in any manner whatsoever, and for whatever purpose. *See, e.g., Heller v. District of Columbia*, 801 F.3d 264 (U.S. Court of Appeals for the District of Columbia Circuit 2015) (holding the following):

   - Registration of long guns and the fingerprinting and photographing of everyone registering a gun were not unconstitutional
   - Requirement that firearms be made available for inspection and that gun owners reregister their firearm every three years were not upheld
   - Safety training requirements are constitutional but tests for legal knowledge are not

   See also Heller v. District of Columbia, 670 F.3d 399 (U.S. Court of Appeals for the District of Columbia Circuit 2015) (upholding the ban on assault weapons and large-capacity magazines); *See, e.g.,* Blocher & Miller, 2016b.

4. Chicago and Oak Park replaced their local gun laws with laws that do not contain a total ban on handguns. *See NRA v. Village of Oak Park*, 755 F.Supp.2d 982 (U.S. District Court for the Northern District of Illinois 2010).

5. National data is severely restricted on nonfatal injuries resulting from gun violence. Congress prohibited the Centers for Disease Control and Prevention from conducting the very research that would help explore the problems associated with gun violence and determine how to reduce the high rate of firearm-related deaths and injuries (AMA, 2016a). During the George W. Bush administration (2001-2009), the federal Consumer Product Safety Commission's National Electronic Injury Surveillance System advised hospital emergency rooms to discontinue collecting data on nonfatal firearm injuries, firearm assaults, and attempted suicides with firearms. Hospitals were advised that the Centers for Disease Control and Prevention would be collecting this information, yet the data was only collected on children under the age of 18 (Cook, 2013). Eventually, the National Electronic Injury Surveillance System returned to collecting this gun violence information, but this attempt to stop the collection of nonfatal injury data illustrates the politicized nature of gun violence research (AMA, 2016a).

   It should be noted that following failed attempts to eliminate the Centers for Disease Control and Prevention's National Center for Injury Prevention and Control, Congress effectively gagged funding for injury prevention research for years. Similar appropriation strategies also restricted access to **gun crime trace data** and data on federal firearms licenses from the Bureau of Alcohol, Tobacco, Firearms and Explosives. The Obama administration achieved a measure of progress through the issuance of 23 **executive orders** overturning Congressional restrictions to:

   - End the freeze on injury prevention research
   - Improve the national instant background check system
   - Increase tracing of illegal gun sales

   (White House, 2013).

6. In 2013, Seattle became the first city in the nation to fund research into the public health impacts of gun violence in the community, which were found to cost the city approximately $12 million in direct medical costs annually (*See* Benfer, 2015). Two years later, in 2015, Seattle passed an ordinance which created an excise tax on firearms ($25 per gun) and ammunition (five cents per round) in response to the need to cover the $181 million cost of gun violence per year (Fleischer, 2015).

REFERENCES

Adams, C.-M. (2013). Grandparents, guns, and guardianship: Incapacity and the right to bear arms. *The Florida Bar Journal, 87*, 48–51.

Ajdacic-Gross, V., et al. (2006). Changing times: A longitudinal analysis of international firearm suicide data. *American Journal of Public Health, 96*(10), 1752–1755.

AMA (American Medical Association). (2016a). *AMA calls gun violence a public health crisis; will actively lobby Congress to lift ban on Centers for Disease Control gun violence research*. Chicago, IL: AMA.

___. (2016b). *Gun violence prevention*.

Benfer, E. A. (2015). Health justice: A framework (and call to action) for the elimination of health inequity and social injustice. *American University Law Review, 65*, 275–351.

Bezruchka, S. S. (2012). The hurrider I go the behinder I get: The deteriorating international ranking of U.S. health status. *Annual Review of Public Health, 33*, 157–173.

Bindbeutel, B. (2014). Domestic tranquility: The goals of home protection. *Southern Illinois University Law Journal, 39*, 1–21.

Blackman, J. (2011). The constitutionality of social cost. *Harvard Journal of Law and Public Policy, 34*, 951–1042.

Blocher, J., & Miller, D. A.-H. (2016a). Lethality, public carry, and adequate alternatives. *Harvard Journal on Legislation, 53*, 279–301.

___. (2016b). What is gun control? Direct burdens, incidental burdens, and the boundaries of the Second Amendment. *University of Chicago Law Review, 83*, 295–354.

Burns, B. (2013). Holding fire: Why long waiting periods to buy a gun violate the Second Amendment. *Charleston Law Review, 7*, 379–410.

Calfo, S., et al. (2016). *Last year of life study.* Woodlawn, MD: Centers for Medicare and Medicaid Services, Office of the Actuary.

Campbell, K. M. (2013). Can rights be different? Justice Stevens' dissent in *McDonald v. City of Chicago. Texas Wesleyan Law Review, 19*, 733–759.

CDC (Centers for Disease Control and Prevention). (2016a). *All injuries.* Atlanta, GA: U.S. Department of Health and Human Services, CDC, National Center for Health Statistics.

___. (2016b). *Life expectancy.*

___. (2015a) State-specific prevalence of current cigarette smoking among adults and secondhand smoke rules and policies in homes and workplaces. *U.S. Morbidity and Mortality Weekly Report, 64*(19), 532–536.

___. (2015b). *Chronic diseases: The leading causes of death and disability in the United States.*

___. (2014). *Injury Statistics Query and Reporting System.*

CDF (Children's Defense Fund). (2015). *Fact sheet: Protect children, not guns.* Washington, DC: CDF.

Colvin, L. (2014). History, *Heller*, and high-capacity magazines: What is the proper standard of review for Second Amendment challenges? *Fordham Urban Law Journal, 41*, 1041–1083.

Comey, J. B., Director, Federal Bureau of Investigation. (2015, October 26). Remarks at the International Association of Chiefs of Police Conference, Chicago, IL.

Cook, P. J. (2013). The great American gun war: Notes from four decades in the trenches. *Crime and Justice, 42*, 19–66.

___. & Ludwick, J. (2002). *Gun violence: The real costs.* New York, NY: Oxford University Press.

Crane, Jr., K. T. (2014). Replacing the Second Amendment is the only way to preserve the individual right to self-defense while reducing gun violence. *New England Journal on Criminal and Civil Confinement, 40*, 427–454.

Curtis, K. (2015). A wiki weapon solution: Firearm restriction for the management of 3d printing in the American household. *Rutgers Computer and Technology Law Journal, 41*, 74–107.

Damer, T. E. (2012). *Attacking faulty reasoning* (7th ed.). Belmont, CA: Cengage Learning, Wadsworth Publishing.

Daniels, K. L. (2013). Keys, wallet, and pistol: The Seventh Circuit establishes a constitutional right to carry firearms outside of the home. *The Seventh Circuit Review, 8*, 339–373.

DeMitchell, T. A. (2014). Locked down and armed: Security responses to violence in our schools. *Connecticut Public Interest Law Journal, 13*, 275–299.

DePalo, A. C. (2013). The doctor will see you now: An argument for amending the licensing process for handguns in New York City. *Touro Law Review, 29*, 867–902.

Dulan, S. W. (2014). State of madness: Mental health and gun regulations. *Thomas M. Cooley Law Review, 31*, 1–14.

Duquette, M. (2014). The RX and the AR [Automatic/Assault Rifles]: A products liability approach to the mass shooting problem. *Nova Law Review, 38*, 359–385.

Eden, J. W. (2014). Don't take your guns to school (in Nebraska): Assessing the constitutionality of the private universities' exemption from the Concealed Handgun Permit Act. *Creighton Law Review, 48*, 113–144.

Fair, M. (2014). Dare defend: Standing for stand your ground. *Law and Psychology Review, 38*, 153–176.

FBI (Federal Bureau of Investigation). (2015). *Fact sheet: National Instant Criminal Background Check System.* Washington, DC: U.S. Department of Justice, FBI.

___. (2014). *Uniform crime reports.*

Fleischer, V. (2015). Curb your enthusiasm for pigovian taxes. *Vanderbilt Law Review, 68*, 1673–1711.

Foody, M. (2013). Docs versus glocks: NRA takes aim at Florida physicians' freedom of speech: Leaving patients' health, safety, and welfare at risk. *Cardozo Law Review de novo, 2013*, 228–257.

Forsey, L. A. (2013). State legislatures stand up for Second Amendment gun rights while the U.S. Supreme Court refuses to order a cease fire on the issue. *Seton Hall Legislative Journal, 37*, 411–436.

Fox, J. A., & DeLateur, M. J. (2014). Weapons of mass (murder) destruction. *New England Journal on Criminal & Civil Confinement, 40*, 313–343.

GAO (U.S. Government Accounting Office). (2008). *Centers for Disease Control and Prevention: Changes in obligations and activities before and after fiscal year 2005 budget reorganization.* Washington, DC: GAO.

Giles, M. G. (2014). The path to full incorporation of the Second Amendment: An individual right. *Nevada Lawyer, 22*, 18–20.

Goode, E. (2016). *Deviant behavior* (11th ed.). Abingdon, UK: Taylor and Francis, Routledge.

Hardy, D. T. (2015). Criminology, gun control and the right to arms. *Howard Law Journal, 58*, 679–713.

___. (2014). Gun owners, gun legislation, and compromise. *Thomas M. Cooley Law Review, 31*, 33–50.

HHS (U.S. Department of Health & Human Services). (2014a). *Healthy People 2020 leading health indicators: Injury and violence.* Washington, DC: HHS.

___. (2014b). *The health consequences of smoking—50 years of progress: A report of the Surgeon General.*

Hubbard, F. P. (2014). The value of life: Constitutional limits on citizens' use of deadly force. *University of California Law Review, 21*, 1–34.

IIHS (Insurance Institute for Highway Safety) & HLDI (Highway Loss Data Institute). (2016). *Safety belt laws.* Arlington, VA: IIHS & HLDI.

IOM (Institute of Medicine). (2012). *Social and economic costs of violence: Forum on global violence prevention.* Washington, DC: National Academies Press.

Jefferson, T. (1785, August 19). *Letters of Thomas Jefferson: Letter to Peter Carr from Paris*. New Haven, CN: Yale Law School Avalon Project (Documents in Law, History, and Diplomacy).

Karp, A. (2012). *Estimated civilian gun ownership: Measurement and use of statistical data to analyze small arms in the United States*. New York, NY: United Nations Office on Drugs and Crime, Center of Excellence in Statistical Information on Government, Crime, Victimization and Justice.

Kendall, G. A. (2013). Defendants' burdens under Fed. R.Civ.P. 55: Post-answer defaults and jurisdictional waivers in *City of New York v. Mickalis Pawn Shop*. *University of Cincinnati Law Review, 81*, 1079–1102.

Killias, M., et al. (2001). Guns, violent crime, and suicide in 21 countries. *Canadian Journal of Criminology, 11*, 429–448.

Kopel, D. B. (2010). The right to arms in the living constitution. *Cardozo Law Review de novo, 2010*, 99–138.

Lamartina, D. (2013). The Firearms Safety Act and the future of Second Amendment debate. *University of Baltimore Law Forum, 44*, 75–84.

Langley, M., & Sugarmann, J. (2013). *Justifiable homicides and non-fatal self-defense gun use: An analysis of Federal Bureau of Investigation and National Crime Victimization Survey Data*. Washington, DC: Violence Policy Center.

Larkin, P. J. (2015). The dynamic incorporation of foreign law and the constitutional regulation of federal lawmaking. *Harvard Journal of Law and Public Policy, 38*, 337–436.

Lavergne, G. M. (1997). *Sniper in the Tower*. Denton, Texas: University of North Texas Press.

Law Center to Prevent Gun Violence. (2015). *Protecting strong gun laws: The Supreme Court leaves lower court victories untouched*. San Francisco, CA: Law Center to Prevent Gun Violence.

Lee, J. (2012). Ringing fieldwork back in: Contemporary urban ethnographic research: Wounded: Life after the shooting. *Annals of the American Academy of Political and Social Science, 642*, 244–256.

Lemaire, J. (2005). The cost of firearm deaths in the United States: Reduced life expectancies and increased insurance costs. *Journal of Risk and Insurance, 72*(3), 359–374.

Lowy, J., & Sampson, K. (2016). The right not to be shot: Public safety, private guns, and the constellation of constitutional liberties. *Georgetown Journal of Law and Public Policy, 14*, 187–205.

Macinko, J., & Marinho de Souza, M. (2007). Reducing firearm injury: Lessons from Brazil. *Leonard Davis Institute Issue Brief, 12*(7), 1–4.

Martin, H. (2014). Legislating judicial review: An infringement on separation of powers. *New York University Journal of Legislation and Public Policy, 17*, 1097–1127.

Masters, J. (2016). *U.S. gun policy: Global comparisons*. New York, NY: Council on Foreign Relations.

McClurg, A. J. (2015). In search of the golden mean in the gun debate. *Howard Law Journal, 58*, 779–808.

McGill, M., & MacNaughton, G. (2016). The struggle to achieve the human right to health care in the United States. *Southern California Interdisciplinary Law Journal, 25*, 625–684.

McNamara, C. (2014). Finally, actually saying "no": A call for reform of gun rights legislation and policies to protect domestic violence survivors. *Seattle Journal for Social Justice, 13*, 649–689.

Miller, T. (2012). *The costs of firearm violence*. Waltham, MA: Children's Safety Network and Pacific Institute for Research and Evaluation.

Moeller, N. (2014). The Second Amendment beyond the doorstep: Concealed carry post-*Heller*. *University of Illinois Law Review, 2014*, 1401–1430.

Moran, C. L. (2013). Under the gun: Will states' one-gun-per-month laws pass constitutional muster after *Heller* and *McDonald*? *Seton Hall Legislative Journal, 38*, 163–188.

Morley, M. T. (2014). Consent of the governed or consent of the government? The problems with consent decrees in government-defendant cases. *University of Pennsylvania Journal of Constitutional Law, 16*, 637–696.

NRA (National Rifle Association. (2013). *Firearm safety in America*. Fairfax, VA: NRA.

___. (2008). *Right-to-carry-2008 fact sheet*.

NSSF (National Shooting Sports Foundation). (2016). *Firearms and ammunition industry economic impact report*. Newtown, CT: NSSF.

Oblinger, L. H. (2013). The wild, wild west of higher education: Keeping the campus carry decision in the university's holster. *Washburn Law Journal, 53*, 87–117.

Pelaez, D. D. (2014). Second Amendment right to bear arms: The cost to carry; New York State's restriction on firearm registration. *Touro Law Review, 30*, 1007–1025.

Pinals, D. A. (2014). Firearms and mental illness: Preventing fear and stigma from overtaking reason and rationality. *New England Journal on Criminal and Civil Confinement, 40*, 379–402.

Pratt, J. E. (2014). Uncommon firearms as obscenity. *Tennessee Law Review, 81*, 1–40.

Record, K. L., & Gostin, L. O. (2014). What will it take? Terrorism, mass murder, gang violence, and suicides: The American way, or do we strive for a better way? *University of Michigan Journal of Law Reform, 47*, 555–574.

Renneker, A. (2015). Chalk talks: Packing more than just a backpack. *Journal of Law and Education, 44*, 273–282.

Rose, L. A. (2014). Constitutional law: Don't take your guns to town: Maryland's good-and-substantial-reason requirement for handgun permits passes intermediate scrutiny - *Woollard v. Gallagher*, 712 F.3d 865 (4th Cir. 2013). *Suffolk Journal of Trial and Appellate Advocacy, 19*, 245–260.

Ruebsamen, M. (2013). The gun-shy commonwealth: Self-defense and concealed carry in post-*Heller* Massachusetts. *Suffolk Journal of Trial and Appellate Advocacy, 18*, 55–83.

Salvin, D. J. (2014). Landmark change in California firearms law. *Orange County Lawyer, 56*, 32–36.

Smith, M. L. (2013). Second Amendment challenges to student housing firearms bans: The strength of the home analogy. *UCLA Law Review, 60*, 1046–1080.

Spicer, R. (2005). Comparison of injury case fatality rates in the United States and New Zealand. *Injury Prevention, 11*(2), 71–76.

Spitzer, R. J. (2015). New York State and the New York Safe Act: A case study in strict gun laws. *Albany Law Review, 78*, 749–787.

Stidham, D. A. (2015). You have the right to bear arms, but not the ability? The evanescence of the Second Amendment. *New England Journal on Criminal and Civil Confinement, 41*, 137–158.

Stowell, E. T. (2014). Top gun: The Second Amendment, self-defense, and private property exclusion. *Regent University Law Review, 26*, 521–555.

Sturzenegger, T. L. B. (2013). The Second Amendment's fixed meaning and multiple purposes. *Southern Illinois University Law Journal, 37*, 337–393.

UNESCO (United National Educational, Scientific and Cultural Organization). (2015). *The map of violence*. Paris, France: UNESCO.

Vasek, B. (2014). Rethinking the Nevada Campus Protection Act: Future challenges & reaching a legislative compromise. *Nevada Law Journal, 15*, 389–430.

Virginia Tech Review Panel. (2007). *Mass shootings at Virginia Tech: Report of the review panel presented to Governor Timothy M. Kaine, Commonwealth of Virginia.* Richmond, VA.

West, R. (2014). Has the constitution fostered a pathological rights culture? The right to bear arms: A tale of two rights. *Boston University Law Review, 94,* 893–912.

Wharton School at the University of Pennsylvania. (2005). Insurance, life expectancy and the cost of firearm deaths in the United States. *Knowledge@Wharton.*

White House, The. (2013). *Now is the time: The president's plan to protect our children and our communities by reducing gun violence.* Washington, DC: The White House.

Whitney, C. R. (2014). A liberal's case for the Second Amendment. *Thomas M. Cooley Law Review, 31,* 15–31.

WHO (World Health Organization). (2015). *Global WHO mortality database.* Geneva, Switzerland, WHO.

___. (2014). *World report on violence and health.*

Wiley, L. F. (2015). From patient rights to health justice: Securing the public's interest in affordable, high-quality health care. *Cardozo Law Review, 37,* 833–897.

Wolitz, D. (2014). Second amendment realism. *Tennessee Law Review, 81,* 539–550.

World Bank. (2016). *Life expectancy at birth, total (years).* Washington, DC: World Bank.

Zamir, E., & Medina, B. (2008). Law, morality, and economics: Integrating moral constraints with economic analysis of law. *California Law Review, 96,* 323–391.

OUR FUTURE HEALTH CARE SYSTEM

Part XII, "Our Future Health Care System," briefly overviews health care management and the law within the context of health care reforms in the United States.

© Andy Dean Photography/ShutterStock, Inc.

CHAPTER 37

Future Prospects: Health Care Management and the Law

"We will restore science to its rightful place and wield technology's wonders to raise health care's quality and lower its cost. All this we can do. All this we will do."

— **Inaugural Address to the Nation by President Barack Obama**, 44th President of the United States (January 20, 2009)

IN BRIEF

This last chapter comprises two parts concerning how the U.S. health care system may be revised and refurbished, which is one of the most important issues the nation is confronting in terms of politics, economics, and the law. The first part provides an overview of the shifts required to develop policy frameworks for instituting changes in each of the major health care sectors: life sciences, health care delivery, and medical products. The second part emphasizes the principle of individual responsibility in maintaining one's health.

LEARNING OBJECTIVES

Upon completion of this chapter readers should be able to:

1. Distinguish among private health insurance plans, government health insurance plans, health insurance exchange plans, and single-payer insurance plans.
2. Discuss whether the real problem in U.S. health care might be market distortions of the equitable delivery of health care amidst competition for limited financial and human resources.
3. Present the supposition that health law and regulations are becoming so complex and nuanced that the health care industry is shifting its legal strategies away from complying with them and toward finding ways to avoid them.
4. Explain why the piecemeal method of regulations affecting the health care industry over the better part of a century has broken down.
5. Describe the primary elements of the Affordable Care Act's across-the-board reform of the entire health care system.
6. Outline the concept of a national health board based on the model of the Federal Reserve Board.
7. Explain why evidence-based medicine is so vital to the fundamental reform and overall success of the U.S. health care system.
8. List the elements of the three-tiered approach to regulatory reform.
9. Discuss the principle of individual responsibility in maintaining one's health.
10. Describe the societal impact of nicotine addiction, obesity, and individual noncompliance with treatment regimens.
11. Explain the role of individual responsibility in sexually transmitted disease, immunization coverage, and firearms ownership.

KEY TERMS

Administrative costs
Adverse selection
Affordable Care Act of 2010
Capital
Cellular therapeutics
Centers for Medicare and Medicaid
   Services
Comparative-effectiveness research
Comprehensive reform
Cost-shifting
Delivery systems
Employer-provided health insurance
Essential health care
Evidence-based medicine
Federal Open Market Committee
Fixed payments
Food and Drug Administration
Food, Drug, and Cosmetic Act of
   1938
Fragmented regulatory environment
Free market private industry
   program
Generics
Genomics
Gross domestic product
Health care delivery reform

Health care regulatory system
Health care sectors
Health insurance exchanges
Health risk
Individual responsibility
Individual responsibility paradigm
Investment returns
Liberty interests
Lifelong wellness regimens
Lifetime health insurance packages
Market distortions
Marketing operations
Medical innovation
Medical products
Medical quackery
Medical technology
Medically necessary care
Medically needed care
Medicare insurance rates
Medicare/Medicaid insurance
   plans
Mental models
Monetary policy
National health board
Overhead expenses
Oversight venue

Paradigms of preventive health
Partial capitation
Partial reform
Patient-centered model
Pharmacy benefit managers
Precision medicine
Preventive care services
Private health insurance plans
Provider network
Public health paradigm
Regenerative medicine
Regulatory infrastructure
Regulatory schemes
Risk adjustment
Secondary prevention
Single-payer system
Slippery slope argument
Social determinants of health
Stakeholders
Tax exemptions
Tertiary prevention
Three-tiered approach to regulatory
   reform
Treatment regimens
Variable payment
Vertically integrate

FACT OR FICTION

Implementation of Health Care Reforms

Can health insurance exchange plans compete with employer-provided health insurance plans?

There are various points of view about how to reform the nation's insurance system, but there are basically two views on competition in the health insurance sector. One view claims equal competition between health insurance exchange plans and **employer-provided health insurance** plans is impossible; the exchange plans will inevitably crowd out employer-provided plans, leading to a **single-payer system**. Another view claims that **health insurance exchanges** could achieve significant savings in administrative costs and prevent excessive profits by private insurers.

The health insurance industry claims that a significant proportion of its **administrative costs** are incurred for creating and maintaining **provider networks**, and for monitoring payments. There is only an incentive to spend a dollar as long as the expected savings are at least a dollar. The challenge is for the federal and state insurance exchanges to have comparable incentives. While profits are needed to earn normal returns on the **capital** the health insurance industry invests to back the sale of medical coverage, insurance profits have not been excessive compared with other industries.

Federal and state insurance exchanges, on the other hand, do not have to hold amounts of capital comparable to private plans; the exchanges are backed by the federal or state governments. Similarly, the federal and state insurance exchanges are not subject to the same taxes that the health insurance industry pays, including those on **investment returns** from holding capital. Competition on this level is only possible with legislative reforms by Congress and state legislatures because the largest share of total health care spending is the government (45%); the employer-provided share of health spending accounted for only 20% in 2015 (CMS, 2015).

Equal competition in reimbursing health care providers is another area of debate. One proposal is for the insurance exchanges to pay **Medicare rates**. But because Medicare payments involve substantial cost-shifting to **private health insurance plans**, any expansion of Medicare rates would further shift costs to private plans and accelerate their crowd-out. Whether rate markups by Medicare insurance could resolve this cost-shifting is debatable. The alternatives to having private plans reimburse health care providers at Medicare rates would require significantly higher Medicare payments. This approach would most likely produce universal price controls on health care costs and raise the obvious question: why bother with employer-provided insurance plans? Having the federal and state insurance exchanges instead pay private health insurance plan rates could challenge a major objective of health care reform: reducing health care costs. This approach would need to address complex design and administrative challenges to benchmark payment rates negotiated between thousands of health care providers and numerous employer-provided health insurance plans.

— *See* Law Fact at the end of this chapter for the answer.

Principles and Applications

The many forces that can advance the delivery of health care, such as innovative practices among providers that effectively restrain prices while improving quality of care, have been presented in this text. This chapter concludes by asking whether the real problem with U.S. health care is **market distortions** of the foundation underlying the delivery of health care amidst competition for limited financial and human resources in each of the **health care sectors** (Gavil & Koslov, 2016). The question may not be whether any intrinsic market failure could be fixed by more regulation, but whether a more just and comprehensive system of regulation is required to ensure access to medically needed care for every member of society.

Transforming U.S. Health Care

The greatest obstacle to transforming the U.S. health care system may be the nation's collective thinking. The nation's **mental models** create and limit opportunities; Americans' perception of individual and social responsibility has always been unique. Yet today, different perceptions about health care may be one of the biggest obstacles to implementing reform of the U.S. health care system. As illustrated in **FEATURE BOX 37-1**, progress regarding the role of government and how to balance individual and social responsibilities will be hindered until Americans accept responsibility for understanding and reconciling their common perceptions about health care. Comprehensive reform of the U.S. health care system may require acknowledging that everyone has different perceptions of what will benefit them and what it means to give others their just due.

Aftermath of the Affordable Care Act

The nation's health laws and regulations must be reworked in order to create an affordable high-quality system that works as intended, especially as the many health care sectors are rapidly converging and therefore defying the laws and regulations already in place (Wiley, 2016). This is true as:

- **Medically necessary care** is increasingly seen as a right for every member of society
- Health care systems and firms from different sectors merge and **vertically integrate**
- New medical products and advanced medical technologies that do not fall under any existing regulatory scheme emerge

(Christensen, 2009; Hugin, 2014; Ostroff, 2015; Wiley, 2016).

This progress is spurred by advancements in **medical technology** that are requiring the American legal system to expand the boundaries of health law to encompass the essential and best components of the U.S. health care system.

What Is the Meaning of These Data-Driven Health Care Facts?

- What is the explanation underlying the facts presented in this text, and what needs further investigation?
  - The United States spends more on health care than any other country in the world, yet ranks 33rd in life expectancy: is this because we are the only industrialized nation in the world that does not provide **medically needed care** for everyone, or could it be the immigration, economic, or gun policies of the United States?
  - Should the United States bear the highest burden in the world for research and development of **medical products** because it has one of the world's highest incomes per capita?

- Is there a single, coherent hypothesis that makes sense of all the assorted facts presented in this text?
  - If the nation's health laws and regulations are complex, exceedingly nuanced, and incomplete, does this regulatory complexity drive up health care costs and compliance overhead? If so, is this one reason why at least one-third of the U.S. health care costs are the result of management and administrative **overhead expenses**, or is this one-third ratio the norm for U.S. service industries in general?
  - Should the United States spend $770 billion every year to administer a heavily regulated, private-based health care system, where the government covers almost half the costs?

- Should the nation's leaders examine the hypotheses underlying some of these facts as they undertake implementation of reform of the U.S. health care system, or would they simply be reinventing the wheel based on prior reform efforts and the **Affordable Care Act**?
  - Should the nation grant hospitals over $51.8 billion in **tax exemptions** each year, while their executives are paid multimillion-dollar salaries and granted lavish benefits?
  - Are hospital administrators at the nation's leading tax-exempt health care systems being paid a rate comparable to executives in other sectors of the economy, and if so, is health care different?

- Is the United States being mindful of the process of transforming its health care system?
  - The United States has one of the highest infant mortality rates in the world; is this because reproductive services are not available to many women or because more babies survive high-risk pregnancies?
  - If **evidence-based medicine** is not being used by most health care providers, is this why one-third of the nation's medical spending is devoted to services that do not improve health or the quality of care, and may make things worse, or is this a faulty association?

- Should the United States rush to implement health care reforms given the rapidly escalating costs of a stressed health care system?
  - When the United States decided to provide access to affordable medical coverage to every member of society (except undocumented immigrants) with adoption of the Affordable Care Act, what happened as tens of millions of people were suddenly added to the health care system?
  - Did the Affordable Care Act greatly increase the need for primary care physicians, physician assistants, nurse practitioners, and advance practice nurses?

Data from: Gregory et al., 2014; Hugin, 2014; IMS Institute for Healthcare Informatics, 2016; IRS, 2015; NCCS, 2016; Johnson & Stukel, 2016; World Bank, 2016.

Some of this health care progress fits within established legal principles and rules of law, or the principles and rules can be adapted to include it. However, health laws and regulations are becoming so complex and nuanced that the health care industry, as well as employers and consumers, are shifting their strategies away from complying with them and toward finding ways to evade them (Flood, 2015; Pomeranz & Adler, 2015).

In the past, Americans have resisted any limits on health care. However, going forward, as health care costs continue to increase, particularly regarding life-prolonging and end-of-life care, some Americans question whether health law can be used to set limits on available care (Hugin, 2014). This is especially true as Americans continue to struggle with the question of whether everyone should be entitled to medically needed health care, and if so, how much care and how to fund it (Wiley, 2016).

Our Future: Precision Medicine

Today, with improved medical technology, it is becoming easier than ever to identify better response strategies for **precision medicine**. Health care providers and professionals are able to compare medical options quickly and cost-effectively and obtain detailed health information on experiences from elsewhere, and will soon be able to determine which personalized interventions will be most successful (Ostroff, 2015). Medical decisions can now be made using more data-driven and analytically rigorous underpinnings.

Across-the-Board Regulatory Reform

Despite the advances in medicine, calls for new regulatory scrutiny of health care remain, notwithstanding enactment of the Affordable Care Act. One might ask why there is this continuous demand for **comprehensive reform**. One reason may be that the United States spends more than any other developed nation on health care: $2.6 trillion (CMS, 2015). This disparity in expenditures between the United States and other similarly developed nations cannot, however, be solely attributed to Americans having access to the latest medical innovations with higher price tags for treatment. Although perhaps it can be partially attributed to lack of universal medical coverage, since 32 million are still uninsured (Kaiser, 2015) with another 31 million underinsured (Commonwealth Fund, 2013). Furthermore, of the Americans who are insured, many suffer from preventable health conditions that needlessly developed into chronic illnesses and diseases, costing more than $1.5 trillion annually as a result (*E.g.*, CDC, 2015a, 2015b).

After decades of cat-and-mouse games between the regulated parts of the health care industry and the regulators, a dramatic overhaul of the U.S. health care system finally occurred with the Affordable Care Act. A depression-era like reform of the complete **health care regulatory system** was needed; much like the nation experienced from the Roosevelt era's New Deal (Copeland, 2012). As opposed to the incremental reforms of the past 70 years, reform of every government agency involved in health care was reformed across the board (*See* Christensen, 2009). The reforms that are being implemented are enormously complex and require continued long and careful consideration by all **stakeholders**, including the:

- Health care providers: physicians and other licensed health care professionals
- **Delivery systems**: hospitals, home health care providers, nursing, and long-term care facilities
- Health insurers: private insurance providers, government insurance programs (Medicare/Medicaid insurance, military entitlement programs (TRICARE), the Civilian Health and Medical Program of the Department of Veteran Affairs (CHAMPVA), and other public hospital/physician coverage programs)
- Providers of medical products: pharmaceuticals, biotechnology, medical devices, and health information technology firms
- Consumers of health care: insured by private and government health insurance plans and the uninsured

Not all the reforms are working and some may have to be repealed; others will withstand the test of time.

Comprehensive Review of the Federal Food, Drug, and Cosmetic Act

For the past 80 years, Congress has sought to patch, rather than cure, a fractured regulatory system (Christensen, 2009). The **Food, Drug, and Cosmetic Act of 1938** (21 U.S.C.A. §§ 301 *et seq.*) replaced the earlier Pure Food and Drug Act of 1906 in response to a mass poisoning that resulted in more than 100 children dying from an error in formulating a medicine. The so-called Elixir Sulfanilamide disaster involved the sulfanilamide drug where diethylene glycol, a solvent related to radiator antifreeze, was used to dissolve the drug and make a liquid form (Starr, 1983). At the time, **medical quackery** was the major concern of Congress, including proprietary medicines mixed by homeopathic and allopathic physicians for individual patients.

Since 1938, Congress has amended the Food, Drug, and Cosmetic Act several hundred times, word by word, provision by provision, to the point where the complexity of the law has resulted in inconsistencies in both its terms and scope.[LN1] Despite these regulatory inconsistencies and legal contradictions affecting virtually every provider of health care, the federal agency charged with implementing the Food, Drug, and Cosmetic Act has seen the significance of its role in the U.S. economy continue to expand; today, the **Food and Drug Administration (FDA)** regulates:

- More than 25% of the total U.S. economy
- Almost $3.5 trillion in U.S. economic activities
- About 80% of the U.S. food supply

(Emmanuel, 2008).

Although the Food, Drug, and Cosmetic Act was largely successful, the U.S. pharmaceutical industry has evolved from 1938 into a $530 billion regulated industry today. The evolution of medicine over the past 80 years demands new approaches and a legal overhaul of its regulatory regime.[LN2] For instance, although the pharmaceutical industry is the most regulated industry in the United States, parts of the rapidly developing biotechnology industry remains virtually unregulated. In addition, any reform should likely include regulation of **genomics**, much of which until now have been relatively free of government oversight, as have stem cell research and **regenerative medicine**, as well as **cellular therapeutics** and precision medicine.

Balancing Transparency and Protections for Consumers of Health Care with Medical Innovations

Americans want a better health care system than currently exists. If they get it, it may not be a pure single-payer government-run system, nor is it likely to be a **free market private industry program**, but it may be a hybrid. Only time will tell what kind of hybrid it may be. One principle is, however, inviolate: any new health care regulations should balance the need to provide transparency and protections for consumers of health care while also allowing the health care industry to continue to innovate and generate the capital required for economic growth. The American public consistently ranks health care as one of the nation's top priorities (Noush, 2014).

Consolidated Health Care System

With the rate of health care costs rapidly outpacing the nation's **gross domestic product**, Americans can no longer afford to maintain the nation's fragmented delivery of care. The health care industry's current posture, however, often puts it at odds with consumers' needs. Patient care between physicians, hospitals, pharmacies, and a host of other providers and related health care services remains uncoordinated with few exceptions (Cleveland, 2015).

Technology has transformed other industries: Airbnb, Alibaba, Amazon, Apple, and Uber disrupted their markets to become billion dollar enterprises. Information is at the center of the health care industry and is ripe for similar transformations. Pharmaceutical innovation has already shifted from in-house research and development to open innovation (*See generally* Parker et al., 2016).

Perhaps the medical products industry should begin to align itself more closely with the consumers who take its drugs and use its medical device products (*See* Crossley, 2016). By looking beyond providing products and services to addressing the needs of consumers for quality outcomes, the medical products industry could connect directly with care to individual patients and focus on population-level wellness. This would be a natural sweet spot of the pharmaceutical, biotechnology, and medical devices sectors: at the center of the health care system where the industry achieves its profits. Health care may seem like a service industry, but it is powered by information. Whoever connects all the providers of health care with consumers in a hyper-efficient platform will revolutionize U.S. health care (Parker et al., 2016).

Preventive care is an emerging model that is eclipsing traditional disease-based care. The emergence of this new patient-centered model of care has the potential to impact the health care landscape. The way evidence-based medicine will apply emerging technology has yet to be determined. One goal of big data is to erase the boundaries between what occurs inside and outside of the health care system by promoting increased information flow (Hiller, 2016). For instance, with the right model, pharmaceutical firms could facilitate interactions among an enormous group of participants (from providers, hospitals, pharmacies, health insurers, to millions of consumers). Expanding this patient-centered approach would help shift the health care system from managing illnesses to preventing them. Apple is already looking at this with the Mayo Clinic and the Cleveland Clinic (Khan, 2016).

Patient-Centered Model

Encouraging wellness is one way alliances are being created in a consolidated health care system. Another possibility would be to link the medical products and health insurance industries. Medical products firms could offer **lifetime health insurance packages** to individuals who guaranteed they would follow **lifelong wellness regimens**, including drugs for chronic illnesses and diseases, abstaining from smoking, and controlling health with regular exercise and a well-balanced diet (*See* Biebl, 2013; Satz, 2015). Enrollees could be accepted into the lifelong health insurance program during their college years, at ages 19 to 24, and monitored for their lifetimes.

Skeptics state the health care industry has not moved toward this **patient-centered model** because the old one has created entrenched stakeholders. But strong and innovative leadership could take the medical products and insurance industries down a new path. The change must, however, amount to a new business model for the medical products and insurance industries, not just an offshoot of **marketing operations** (Khan, 2016).

National Health Board

Another possible model might be a consolidated system, in which health care providers, the health insurance industry, and regulators are closely aligned to recommend coverage decisions based on comparative effectiveness research (Smith & Gallena, 2014). A **national health board** could be created, similar to the Federal Reserve System and similar to the British National Institute for Health and Clinical Excellence, whose structure, functions, and enforcement capability would be largely insulated from politics. Like President Roosevelt did on **monetary policy** with the creation of the Federal Reserve System, decision-making on the immensely complex topics of health care policy and **health care delivery reform** could be delegated to a presidentially appointed panel of experts and consumers of health care (Jost, 2011).

A national health board could be structured with a central board and several regional boards. As an independent body, it could recommend medical coverage under **Medicare/Medicaid insurance plans** for only those drugs and treatment procedures backed by evidence-based medicine, not marketing. The board would determine what health conditions would be covered by Medicare/Medicaid insurance based on evidence-based practices. Exactly how the board would be organized, including how it would control costs, assure universal, equal access to health care, and guarantee quality of care is standardized, monitored, evaluated, and improved across the nation would have to be determined. The idea of creating a board to regulate health care policy would allow an impartial group of experts to improve health care at the federal policy level (*Contra* Cohen & Cannon, 2012).

The Affordable Care Act took an initial step toward a national health board when it created the Patient Centered Outcomes Research Institute to promote **comparative-effectiveness research** (Orentlicher, 2011). The Institute will compare the benefits and risks of different medical treatments so physicians will have better data on the value of treatment alternatives when making choices for their patients. While the Institute is prohibited from making medical coverage recommendations, Medicare/Medicaid insurance and the health insurance industry may take the Institute's analyses into account when making their own medical coverage decisions.

Unintended Consequences of Regulation

Often, enacted health care regulations create more problems than they solve (Pantelaki & White, 2014). The nation could easily adopt regulations that would create a more orderly health care system, but those changes could also stifle innovation. Any change should occur in a carefully considered way; reforms should be more likely to have an impact over the long term, as opposed to dousing the multiple fires that are now burning (Gavil & Koslov, 2016).

There are many examples of how the health care industry and regulators have been engaged in a dance, with the largest providers leading and regulators one step behind. Today's **fragmented regulatory environment** often allows shrewd industry players to choose an **oversight venue** where government agencies are more likely to approach their role with a narrow focus that prevents them from considering larger trends shaping the U.S. health care system (*See* Garslian, 2016).

For instance, the convergence of many health care sectors is rapidly changing the laws governing provider competition and regulation (Gavil & Koslov, 2016). Pharmaceutical firms are coupling with biotechnology firms, while emerging biopharmaceutical products that do not fit into any existing **regulatory schemes** are developing. Separate regulatory schemes made sense when drugs were pharmaceuticals and the biotechnology industry was practically nonexistent. Today, providers of health care products learn how to package a product and choose its regulators, which means that neither actually regulates or controls what is going on. Similarly, the Federal Trade Commission regulates hospital and medical products matters, while the Justice Department handles health insurance issues. Again, all sorts of improper things can take place.

Redefining the Mission of the U.S. Department of Health and Human Services

When the number one cause for bankruptcy in the United States is medical bills, this cannot be reflective of a good system of health care (*E.g.*, Zimmon, 2015). Within the U.S. Department of Health and Human Services, the missions of the two agencies with the most direct impact on the health care industry need to be redefined: the FDA and the **Centers for Medicare and Medicaid Services**.

U.S. Food and Drug Administration

The original mission of the FDA is no longer in line with the realities of the market. The FDA was created in 1938 to protect individual consumers from unsafe drugs. Now, large institutional consumers and several prominent **pharmacy benefit managers** dominate the market, but the FDA's structure remains geared toward individual consumers of health care (Carpenter, 2010). The FDA is not as effective as it could be in regulating institutional problems (Berndt et al., 2015).

Any framework for new forms of health care regulation needs to address the role of the FDA, whose primary mission has been to manage the pharmaceutical industry, and to a lesser degree, the medical devices and biotechnology industries (Christensen, 2009). However, a sole dedication to assuring the safety, efficacy, and security of medical products leaves out important considerations, leading to harsh consequences for the health care system when those issues are not comprehensively addressed, such as with drug pricing (IMS, 2016). While it would have to be determined what levers directly affect the U.S. health care system, this does not mean the FDA could not have an opinion that is not necessarily consequential. For instance, a new regulatory system could include research and discussion of conditions in the health care system as part of open committee meetings, without the FDA taking any actions in response (*See* Barkow, 2010). This could be modeled after the **Federal Open Market Committee** meetings on raising or lowering interest rates by the Federal Reserve (Carpenter, 2010).

Centers for Medicare and Medicaid Services

While the recent expansion of Medicaid insurance is applauded by some, others want the program restricted to the truly deserving. One issue that has not been addressed is that Medicaid insurance provides amongst the lowest payments for providers. Many medical treatments and procedures simply cannot be performed at the Medicaid payment level, such that major academic centers with federal support take a loss when doing business with these patients (Self, 2015). In fairness, any expansion of Medicaid insurance should increase government payment rates so that:

- Providers may recoup the actual costs of providing health care, as opposed to operating at a loss
- Private-insured consumers are not paying higher health insurance premiums to cross-subsidize Medicaid insurance

Risk-Adjusted Insurance

The concept of **risk adjustment** has merit, provided it can be used without encouraging unhealthy behavior (Sage, 2014). Under risk adjustment, and for those who joined health plans, Medicare/Medicaid insurance would pay more for predictably sicker people than for predictably healthier people. The difficulty is operational; the problem is how to define sicker individuals for medical coverage purposes. Under current law, Medicare payment adjustments are based upon certain hospitalizations in the preceding year. The concern is how individuals with health insurance coverage can be defined as sick or healthy only in terms of a previous year's hospitalization(s); this policy could encourage hospitalizations and penalize providers that attempt to reduce hospitalizations.

Partial Capitation

Partial capitation under the Medicare/Medicaid shared savings programs are another health care reform with merit. Under partial capitation, **fixed payments** for Medicare/Medicaid insured services are replaced by combining a fixed payment with a payment that reflects actual use of services (Werbelow, 2015). While the relative weights attached to the fixed payment versus the **variable payment** to health care providers are a policy judgment, the advantages of a partial capitation measure are twofold:

- Acknowledging the important ability to measure **health risk**
- Eliminating incentives to withhold treatment by paying more for people who use more services

(Jacobi, 2015; Werbelow, 2015).

Reorganizing Congressional Oversight

There should be some consolidation in oversight of the U.S. health care system, but it will take a great deal of thought on how to do this (*See* Renan, 2015). Politically, it will be very difficult to consolidate because power in congressional committees is at stake. Health care regulation remains fragmented because separate committees in Congress control different regulatory bodies, and no congressional committee is likely to give up power easily.

Three-Tiered Approach to Regulatory Reform

Congress may have to start from scratch and think about how health care should be regulated while allowing it to thrive and not taking any undue risks for which society as a whole must pay. It would be a balancing act to achieve this goal and would require everything be put on the table. One way to start might be to adopt a **three-tiered approach to regulatory reform**:

- Issues that clearly require addressing
- Issues that are a major departure from current practices, but have strong cases
- Fundamental questions

(*See* Christensen, 2009; Garslian, 2016).

Issues That Clearly Require Addressing

The first tier would aim at issues that clearly require addressing. For instance, the number of underinsured Americans who do not have access to medically necessary health care is an issue requiring immediate attention. The issue of the uninsured remains a problem despite recent reforms.

Issues That Are a Major Departure from Current Practices, but Have Strong Cases

The second tier would address issues in ways that seem like a major departure from current practices, but have strong cases nevertheless. One example is excessive executive compensation in an industry broadly subsidized by society, particularly at tax-exempt hospitals and within the health insurance industry. It is difficult to understand why presidents and chief executive officers in health care systems are allowed to earn multimillion-dollar performance bonuses when almost half of the three million aides are working for poverty wages, as are one in four of their support staff (BLS, 2016a), and meanwhile, the health care systems are not even performing particularly well.

Moreover, it is debatable whether executive compensation in the health care industry should be based on a single year's results, when it is so easy for executives to take actions that enhance their performance one year, but may harm the delivery of health care for years into the future (Wharton, 2012). Now, however, executive compensation is viewed as a corporate governance issue as opposed to a regulatory issue (Wharton, 2015). It is not clear whether executive compensation in the health care industry requires attention in a regulatory fashion at some point.

Fundamental Questions

A third tier would address the more fundamental question of balancing the benefits of medical innovation against the risk of creating new products within the federal regulatory structure. Great enthusiasm is expressed for **generics**, which in retrospect may not always be in the best interest of the consumers of health care (Kesselheim & Darrow, 2015). When $93 billion of U.S. brand sales are projected to face generic competition from 2016 to 2020 (Vernon, 2010), the balance between regulation and medical innovation obviously needs to be redefined.[LN3]

Redefining the Balance Between Regulation and Medical Innovations

If the United States wants to continue reaping the fruits of **medical innovation**, Americans must support the policies that encourage investment in the providers of medical products where it costs more than $1.2 billion to develop a pharmaceutical drug and $1.3 billion to develop a biopharmaceutical drug over 10-15 years (PhRMA, 2014; Tufts, 2014). In recent years, the balance between regulation and medical innovation has shifted toward regulation (Christensen, 2009).

The FDA must redefine how it regulates the providers of medical products that are among the nation's most important industries. For instance, with more than 1,500 public and private biopharmaceutical firms employing 854,000 highly trained people, the United States is universally considered to be the global leader in biopharmaceuticals (TEConomy, 2016). Yet:

- Only seven biopharmaceuticals were approved by the FDA and only four ever saw the market
- Just two in ten approved pharmaceuticals produce revenues that exceed average research and development costs
- The pharmaceutical industry is expending some $59 billion on research and development each year, and yet less than two dozen are being approved by the FDA each year

(PhRMA, 2016; Vernon, 2010).

The question that begs for asking is whether any of these numbers are acceptable to anyone. Alternatively, is it acceptable for regulation to replace medical innovation?

Comprehensive Regulatory Infrastructure

A careful approach must be taken to new health care regulations as the nation decides how to go about setting up a better health care system. The current **regulatory infrastructure** was created in piecemeal fashion. In the wake of the current demand to take action, perhaps there is a need to start over with a comprehensive approach to regulation (LaRocca, 2014). In the end, the most pressing thing that nearly everyone agrees on is that the time to make changes in the U.S. health care system is now (Hansen & Newman, 2015).

The Duality of American Citizenship

The nation needs to better understand and acknowledge the benefits of preventive care and the social stakes involved in providing affordable health insurance and access to medically needed care to every member of society.

Every Citizen's Individual Responsibility

Albert Einstein observed that the problems most individuals face cannot be solved with the same level of thinking as was employed when they created them (Einstein, 2015/1923). Today, a paradigm shift in U.S. health care is rapidly evolving. Everyone now has to accept responsibility for obtaining and maintaining basic health insurance coverage.

While health has always been an **individual responsibility** in the United States (compared to other advanced economies where individual health is a shared obligation), there is now a significant focus on prevention of disease as opposed to treatment of disease (Noush, 2014; Ostroff, 2015). Although individual responsibility for one's health has always been viewed as an unrestricted choice to accept or deny, the focus has shifted to emphasizing the obligation to manage one's health, while stressing personal accountability for maintaining a healthy lifestyle and avoiding preventable ill health (Emmanuel, 2008). With the newest health care reforms, the greatest power consumers of health care possess is their ability to choose healthy lifestyles (Hugin, 2014). At the same time, everyone is individually responsible for using **preventive care services** to prevent diseases from ever occurring or to delay their onset or reduce their severity.

Individual Responsibility and Self-Reliance

It is human nature to act and not be acted upon; by choosing how to respond to life, individuals can create the conditions of their lives (Covey, 2014/1990). In regard to health care, everyone has an individual and shared obligation to make healthy decisions (Jost, 2011). Everyone is responsible for their health via their lifestyle choices, and often also responsible for their illnesses, suffering, and death (*See* Starr, 1983). The vision of autonomous individuals is deeply ingrained in American culture, and consequently, health care policies are generally framed around this individualistic archetype that anyone can do whatever they want regardless of the consequences to one's health (Crossley, 2016; Tyler, 2012). This 20th century approach to health is no longer acceptable to most Americans; no one can do whatever they want regardless of the consequences to their health and then expect society to subsidize their irresponsible choices (Jacobi, 2015).

Application of Individual Responsibility in Health Care Reform

The U.S. Supreme Court recognizes the power of Congress to compel Americans to accept individual responsibility for the nation's health care resources (*See Florida, et al. v. U.S. Department of Health and Human Services*, 648 F.3d 1235 (U.S. Court of Appeals for the 11th Circuit 2011), *affirmed in part and reversed in part, National Federation of Independent Business, et al. v. Sebelius, et al.*, 132 S.Ct. 2566 (U.S. Supreme Court 2012)).[LN4] The $2.6 trillion the United States spends on health care every year are resources borne by the wider economy (CMS, 2015); the trillion dollar costs are societal resources (Moncrieff, 2013).

Individual Liberty and the Affordable Care Act

The individual responsibility debate— regarding responsible and irresponsible consumers of medical care, the insured and the uninsured—concerns the fundamental nature of **liberty interests** and the proper role of government in the United States (Hall, 2014). The legitimacy of any health care reform is based on the limitations of how Congress may set social policy and allocate the nation's resources to address age and illness. With the Affordable Care Act, Congress attempted to address a complex market failure of the U.S. health care system by addressing the sustainability problems of **cost-shifting** and **adverse selection**[LN5] in the health care and insurance industries. In its legislative findings for the Affordable Care Act, Congress acknowledged that the obligations to provide emergency care to the uninsured results in over $49 billion in uncompensated consumption of health care services annually and that this translates into an average cost-shifting of $1,000 in health insurance premiums for responsible families that are insured (Thide, 2012). In other words, the health care industry must charge more for its medical care in order to subsidize the care that is provided at or below cost; costs are shifted from the uninsured to the insured.

On one side of this debate on individual liberty, opponents of the Affordable Care Act stress the **slippery slope argument** that if Congress can require everyone to purchase and maintain health insurance during their lifetimes, then there is no limit on federal power (Blumstein, 2014). Opponents argue that if Congress can mandate that everyone purchase health insurance because their lack of insurance may, at some point in the future, impose costs on the wider economy, then on the same theory, future federal mandates can require the purchase of virtually any other product, since the failure to have any product can always be said to have some economic impact (Manheim, 2015; McCullough, 2013).

On the other side of the debate on individual liberty, proponents of the Affordable Care Act maintain that Congress recognized the existence of a fundamental economic right to **essential health care** and simply expanded federal protection of that right (Noush, 2014). The Affordable Care Act not only expanded access to basic health insurance; more importantly, it created a presumption in favor of near-universal access to affordable health insurance (Zietlow, 2011). In addressing opponents' arguments, proponents of the Affordable Care Act maintain that society can rely on individual resources, private bargains, or the government to address age and illness needs (Maher, 2011). The Affordable Care Act mandates that virtually every adult member of society make insurance bargains because decisions to not buy health insurance materially increases the costs for the insured (Auerbach, 2014).

The health care industry is unique and therefore can be regulated in ways other markets cannot (Grusin, 2015). The purpose of the Affordable Care Act is to avoid extreme cost-shifting and underwriting costs, two forces that distort the health care market and disrespect state borders (Biebl, 2013). By compelling Americans to accept individual responsibility to be insured, such wasteful forms of **competition** can be reduced and the efficiency of the health and insurance markets can be improved (Copeland, 2012).

Aligning Health Status with Health Care Costs

The U.S. health care system defines itself in terms of individual responsibility. With 55% of health status determined by lifestyle choices, it is time that health care costs be imposed proportionately, based on the health risks and day-to-day lifestyle choices of every member of society (Schoen et al., 2015). The nation will be closer to achieving economic fairness in access to health care when health status is more closely aligned with health care costs. People who:

- Are not compliant with their **treatment regimens**
- Have casual sex with multiple partners
- Smoke tobacco
- Abuse drugs and alcohol
- Refuse vaccinations
- Partake in dangerous activities such as extreme sports
- Fail to maintain healthy weights, or other measures of good health, such as low blood pressure and cholesterol numbers

Everyone must accept responsibility for the consequences of their day-to-day choices (Hall, 2014). People have an individual responsibility to remain healthy and delay the onset of preventable diseases and illness as opposed to expecting their communities or the government to subsidize their unhealthy lifestyle choices (Bryant, 2013).

Adopting Comprehensive Paradigms of Prevention

While everyone bears individual responsibility for their own health, two different, but nonexclusive, **paradigms of preventive health** prevail in the United States. The **public health paradigm** focuses on population-based primary prevention by reviewing social determinants of health (Solar & Irwin, 2010).[LN6] Such interventions seek to prevent illness or injury from ever occurring by preventing public exposure to risk factors. For instance, food security is addressed by regulating non-nutritious foods.

By contrast, the **individual responsibility paradigm** focuses on secondary and tertiary preventive health once an individual is ill (Tyler, 2012). **Secondary prevention** focuses on expanding access to health care by screening, testing, and detection of early risk factors in individuals before disease becomes symptomatic (such as hypertension), and early treatment (such as adherence to blood pressure treatment regimens). **Tertiary prevention** seeks to prevent a worsening of symptoms in individuals already suffering from a disease by encouraging healthy lifestyle choices and aggressive symptom management (Pomeranz & Adler, 2015) (*See generally* Solar & Irwin, 2010).

Choosing Healthy Lifestyles

Extra health care costs must be imposed on anyone who chooses unhealthy lifestyles that result in otherwise preventable health conditions (Synderman & Williams, 2013). Nicotine addiction, morbid obesity, and medication noncompliance are important societal issues that justify surcharges on anyone who smokes, or is exceedingly overweight, or refuses to adhere to their evidence-based treatment regimens (Wharton, 2009). The roles of individual responsibility in sexually transmitted disease, immunization coverage, and firearms ownership are also lifestyle issues. When people make unhealthy choices that expose themselves and others to significant risk and then expect everyone else to pay for their lifestyle decisions, this expectation is often met. This behavior creates incentives for others to act irresponsibly, or at least does not encourage others to act responsibly. It also violates most Americans' understanding of individual responsibility (Hall, 2014).

At the same time and while the burden of preventable disease and illness brought on by poor lifestyle choices should be borne by the individual (Tyler, 2012), no one knows with certainty how much illness is due to a breach of individual responsibility and how much is unavoidable. For instance, no one knows how much obesity is due to a breach of individual responsibility and how much is due to or the result of blameworthy food industry practices, such as overeating of non-nutritious food, or even to biological or environmental factors, as science is beginning to investigate (Wharton, 2013; WHO, 2015).

MANAGEMENT AND LAW ISSUES

1. Is it economically fair to align individual health status with the costs individuals are required to pay for their health insurance?

Ongoing Health Care Reforms

The objective of this text was to identify the perennial issues in management and the law that are confronting a health care industry in the midst of flux and change. There is a moral imperative that is intrinsic in the nation's ongoing health care reform efforts.

LAW FACT

Implementation of Health Care Reforms

Can health insurance exchange plans compete with employer-provided health insurance plans?

Yes. The Affordable Care Act has substantially changed the dimensions on which health insurance plans compete. Given the need to control the costs of health care, there are new constraints on risk pools, benefit design, marketing, and perhaps eventually, profitability of the health insurance industry itself.

— Gavil & Koslov, 2016; OMB 2016, 2015 and 2009.

CHAPTER SUMMARY

- The real problem with health care may be the conflict between theoretical ideals and market limitations, thereby requiring the development of a more equitable system with the financial resources available.
- Intrinsic in the reform of health care is the reform of the nation's health laws and regulations, which are complex, exceedingly nuanced, and incomplete.
- The future of the U.S. health care system likely involves increasingly personalized care.
- One reason comprehensive regulatory reform is clearly needed is because Americans spend more on health care than any other developed nation, yet they are neither healthier nor likely to live longer; further, the United States is the only industrialized nation that does not provide medically needed care for all of its citizens, thereby impeding its economic competitiveness.
- The current regulatory scheme encourages evasion and avoidance as opposed to compliance.
- Reform will require cooperation between health care providers and consumers of health care; it will also require more transparency and protection for consumers, while allowing for industry innovation and capital generation.
- One health care reform would reward patients who take the initiative for their own wellness, thereby decreasing their health care costs.
- Another suggested method of reform would be the creation of a national health board responsible for determining what Medicare/Medicaid insurance would cover and that would be insulated from politics.
- The mission of the U.S. Department of Health and Human Services must be redefined, including reforming the role of the FDA away from individual consumers and toward regulating institutional providers of health care, as well as the role of the Centers for Medicare and Medicaid Services in reimbursing providers.
- The United States could take a three-tiered approach to regulatory reform, addressing issues that require immediate attention, issues that depart from current practices, and fundamental questions.
- The balance between regulation and innovation must be examined so that the United States can remain competitive in the global health care arena.

LAW NOTES

1. Since 1975, no fewer than 28 amendments have been incorporated into the Federal Food, Drug, and Cosmetic Act of 1938 (21 U.S.C.A. §§ 301 *et seq.*). Many of the following acts are not independent laws; rather they amend other, already existing laws, and thus the citations provided are to the laws they amend:
Ford Administration (1974-1977)
    - Medical Device Amendments of 1975, 21 U.S.C.A. §§ 321 *et seq.*; 42 U.S.C.A. § 3512

Carter Administration (1977-1981):

- Infant Formula Act of 1980, 21 U.S.C.A. §§ 321 *et seq.*

Reagan Administration (1981-1989):

- Orphan Drug Act of 1983, 15 U.S.C.A. §§ 1274 *et seq.*; 21 U.S.C.A. §§ 360aa *et seq.*; 26 U.S.C.A. §§ 44H *et seq.*; 35 U.S.C.A. § 155; 42 U.S.C.A. §§ 209 *et seq.*
- Drug Price Competition and Patent Term Restoration Act of 1984 (Hatch-Waxman Act), 15 U.S.C.A. §§ 68b, 68c, and 70b; 21 U.S.C.A. §§ 355 and 360cc; 28 U.S.C.A. § 2201; 35 U.S.C.A. §§ 156, *et seq.*
- Prescription Drug Marketing Act of 1987, 21 U.S.C.A. §§ 331, 333, 353, and 381
- Generic Animal Drug and Patent Term Restoration Act of 1988, 21 U.S.C.A. §§ 321, 353, and 360b; 28 U.S.C.A. § 2201; 35 U.S.C.A. §§ 156 and 271

George H.W. Bush Administration (1989-1993)

- Nutrition Labeling and Education Act of 1990, 21 U.S.C.A. §§ 321 *et seq.*; 42 U.S.C.A. § 263b
- Safe Medical Devices Act of 1990, 21 U.S.C.A. §§ 321 *et seq.*; 42 U.S.C.A. §§ 263b-263n
- Prescription Drug User Fee Act of 1992, 21 U.S.C.A. §§ 321 *et seq.*
- Prescription Drug Amendments of 1992, 21 U.S.C.A. §§ 333, 353, and 381
- Medical Device Amendments of 1992, 21 U.S.C.A. §§ 321 *et seq.*; 42 U.S.C.A. § 262

Clinton Administration (1993-2001):

- Food Quality Protection Act of 1996, 21 U.S.C.A. §§ 321, 331, 333, 342, and 346a
- FDA Export Reform and Enhancement Act of 1996, 21 U.S.C.A. §§ 331, 381 and 382; 42 U.S.C.A. § 262
- Animal Drug Availability Act of 1996, 21 U.S.C.A. § 331, 353, 354, and 360b
- Food and Drug Administration Modernization Act of 1997, 21 U.S.C.A. §§ 321 *et seq.*; 26 U.S.C.A. §§ 45C; 35 U.S.C.A. § 156; 38 U.S.C.A. § 8126; 42 U.S.C.A. §§ 247b-8 *et seq.*
- Medical Device User Fee and Modernization Act of 2002, 21 U.S.C.A. §§ 321 *et seq.*; 42 U.S.C.A. § 289g-3
- Animal Drug User Fee Act of 2003, 21 U.S.C.A. §§ 379j-11 and 379j-12
- Pediatric Research Equity Act of 2003, 21 U.S.C.A. §§ 355c and 355d
- Food Allergen Labeling and Consumer Protection Act of 2004, 21 U.S.C.A. §§ 321, 343, 343-1, and 374a; 42 U.S.C.A. §§ 242r, 243, and 300d-2
- Minor Use and Minor Species Animal Health Act of 2004, 21 U.S.C.A. §§ 321, 331, 352-354, 360b, and 360ccc-ccc2.
- Dietary Supplement and Nonprescription Drug Consumer Protection Act of 2006, 21 U.S.C.A. §§ 331, 343, 352, 379aa-aa-1, and 381
- Best Pharmaceuticals for Children Act of 2007, 21 U.S.C.A. §§ 355a; 42 U.S.C.A. §§ 284m, 285g-10. 288-6, and 290b
- Food and Drug Administration Amendments Act of 2007, 21 U.S.C.A. §§ 321 *et seq.*; 42 U.S.C.A. §§ 247d-3b *et seq.*

Obama Administration (2009-2017):

- Family Smoking Prevention and Tobacco Control Act of 2009, 15 U.S.C.A. §§ 1333 and 4402; 21 U.S.C.A. §§ 321 *et seq.*
- Food Safety Modernization Act of 2011, 7 U.S.C.A. § 7625; 21 U.S.C.A. 331 *et seq.*; 42 U.S.C.A. § 241b-20
- Food and Drug Administration Safety and Innovation Act of 2012, 21 U.S.C.A. §§ 335a *et seq.*; 42 U.S.C.A. §§ 213, 262, 282, 284, and 290
- Medical Device User Fee and Modernization Act of 2012, 21 U.S.C.A. §§ 321 *et seq.*; 42 U.S.C.A. § 289g-3
- Drug Quality and Security Act of 2013, 21 U.S.C.A. §§ 331 *et seq.*

2. In addition to the Federal Food, Drug, and Cosmetic Act of 1938, a minimum of 25 additional federal laws affect the FDA:

Teddy Roosevelt Administration (1901-1909):

- Federal Meat Inspection Act of 1907, 21 U.S.C.A. §§ 601 *et seq.*

Woodrow Wilson Administration (1913-1921):

- Federal Trade Commission Act of 1914, 15 U.S.C.A. §§ 41-58

Calvin Coolidge Administration (1923-1929):

- Filled Milk Act of 1923, 21 U.S.C.A. §§ 61-64
- Import Milk Act of 1927, 21 U.S.C.A. §§ 141-149
- Public Health Service Act of 1944, 42 U.S.C.A. §§ 201 *et seq.* (2009) (containing over one thousand sections of law)

Harry Truman Administration (1945-1953):

- Trademark Act of 1946 (Lanham Act), 15 U.S.C.A. §§ 1051 *et seq.*

Dwight Eisenhower Administration (1953-1961):

- Reorganization Plan No. 1 of 1953, 5 U.S.C.A. §§ 901 *et seq.*
- Poultry Products Inspection Act of 1957, 21 U.S.C.A. §§ 451-472

Lyndon Johnson Administration (1963-1969):

- Fair Packaging and Labeling Act of 1966, 15 U.S.C.A. §§ 1451-1461

Richard Nixon Administration (1969-1974):

- National Environmental Policy Act of 1969, 42 U.S.C.A. §§ 4321 *et seq.*
- Controlled Substances Act of 1970, 21 U.S.C.A. §§ 801 *et seq.*
- Controlled Substances Import and Export Act of 1970, 21 U.S.C.A. §§ 951 *et seq.*
- Egg Products Inspection Act of 1970, 21 U.S.C.A. §§ 1031-1056
- Lead-Based Paint Poisoning Prevention Act of 1971, 42 U.S.C.A. §§ 4821 *et seq.*
- Federal Advisory Committee Act of 1972, 5 U.S.C.A. App. 2 §§ 1-15

Gerald Ford Administration (1974-1977):

- Government in the Sunshine Act of 1976, 5 U.S.C.A. § 552b

George H.W. Bush Administration (1989-1993)

- Federal Anti-Tampering Act of 1983, 18 U.S.C.A. § 1365
- Sanitary Food Transportation Act of 1990, 49 U.S.C.A. §§ 5701-5714
- Mammography Quality Standards Act of 1992, 42 U.S.C.A. § 263b

George W. Bush Administration (2001-2009):

- Agricultural Bioterrorism Protection Act of 2002, 7 U.S.C.A. § 8401
- Food Allergen Labeling and Consumer Protection Act of 2004, 21 U.S.C.A. §§ 321, 343, 343-1, 374a; 42 U.S.C.A. §§ 242r and 300d-2
- Designer Anabolic Steroid Control Act of 2004, 21 U.S.C.A. §§ 802, 811, 825, 842, and 960
- Project BioShield Act of 2004, 6 U.S.C.A. §§ 312-313 and 320; 21 U.S.C.A. § 360bbb-3; 42 U.S.C.A. §§ 247d-6, 247d-6a, 247d-6b, 247d-6c, 287a-2, and 1320b-5
- Sanitary Food Transportation Act of 2005, 21 U.S.C.A. §§ 331, 342, 373, and 350e

Barack Obama Administration (2009-2017):

- Pandemic and All-Hazards Preparedness Reauthorization Act of 2013, 21 U.S.C.A. §§ 355, 355-1, 355a, and 360bbb-3-4; 38 U.S.C.A. § 8117; 42 U.S.C.A. §§ 247d, 247d-1, 247d-3a-247d-4, 247d-6-247d-6b, 247d-6d, 247d-7b, 247d-7e, 247d-7f, 284m, 284m-1, 300hh-1, 300hh-10, 300hh-11, 300hh-15, and 300hh-16300hh-10a

In order to get the most up-to-date and complete citations of all of the sections of the U.S. Code that a particular law creates, repeals, or amends, always refer to the most recent version of the U.S. Code itself.

3. The research and development investments required to bring new drugs to patients in the future rely on revenues from existing approved innovative drugs. Continued declines in average lifetime revenues from new medicines could reduce the ability of the pharmaceutical industry to maintain their historically high levels of innovation (*See generally* Berndt et al., 2015).

4. Debate before the U.S. Supreme Court centered on the issue of whether the Affordable Care Act can require almost every member of society to have health insurance. While Congress imposed the requirement in accordance with its constitutional power to regulate interstate commerce, the mandate is not limited to those who engage in any economic activity (Faizer, 2013). Rather, the mandate applies to every U.S. resident who does not fall within one of the Affordable Care Act's limited exclusions.

Under the U.S. Constitution, only states have the authority to impose health and safety regulations on individuals; the federal government does not have general police power. Federal legislation must be grounded in one of the enumerated powers the Constitution grants to Congress, such as the power to regulate interstate commerce. Although the U.S. Supreme Court has interpreted the Commerce Clause powers broadly since the Roosevelt era's New Deal, this power is still limited (Bryant, 2013; Copeland, 2012). The U.S. Constitution limits the power of the federal government by granting Congress authority in certain defined areas, such as the regulation of commerce. Powers not expressly vested in the federal government by the Constitution are reserved to the states (Adler & Cannon, 2013). (*See generally National Federation of Independent Business v. Sebelius*, 132 S.Ct. 2566 (U.S. Supreme Court 2012); Reynolds & Denning, 2013).

5. Health insurers strive to maintain risk pools whose health, on average, is the same as the general population (Cogan, 2016). Adverse selection arises when less healthy people disproportionately enroll in a risk pool. The tendency is for sick people who are poorer risks (more likely to incur health care costs) to seek health insurance to a greater extent than do healthier people who are better risks (less likely to incur health care costs) (Hall, 2014). This situation occurs when price increases or reduced benefits make insurance no longer price-effective, taking those who make fewer and less expensive claims out of the risk pool, leaving only higher risk individuals (Turk, 2015).

6. The **social determinants of health**, or the living conditions people experience, include: access to health care, early childhood development, education, employment and working conditions, food security, housing, income and income distribution, social exclusion, social safety network, unemployment and job security, gender, race, and disability status (Solar & Irwin, 2010).

REFERENCES

Adler, J. H., & Cannon, M. F. (2013). Taxation without representation: The illegal IRS rule to expand tax credits under the PPACA. *Health Matrix: Journal of Law-Medicine, 23*, 119–195.

Auerbach, D. (2014). Assessing the true impact of the ACA: Revisiting the CBO's initial predictions. *American Journal of Law and Medicine, 40*, 231–236.

Barkow, R. E. (2010). Insulating agencies: Avoiding capture through institutional design. *Texas Law Review, 89*, 15–79.

Berndt, E. R., et al. (2015). Decline in economic returns from new drugs raises questions about sustaining innovations. *Health Affairs, 34*(2), 245–252.

Biebl, H. (2013). Re-thinking health insurance. *University of Michigan Journal of Law Reform, 2*, 62–66.

BLS (Bureau of Labor Statistics). (2016a). *Economic news release: Union members' survey*. Washington, DC: U.S. Department of Labor, BLS.

Blumstein, J. F. (2014). Understanding the faulty predictions regarding the challenges to health reform. *University of Illinois Law Review, 2014*, 1251–1263.

Bryant, A. C. (2013). Institutional newspeak: Learning to love the Affordable Care Act decision. *Journal of Legislation, 39*, 15–42.

Carpenter, D. (2010). *Reputation and Power: Organizational Image and Pharmaceutical Regulation at the FDA*. Princeton, NJ: Princeton University Press.

CDC (Centers for Disease Control and Prevention). (2015a). State-specific prevalence of current cigarette smoking among adults and secondhand smoke rules and policies in homes and workplaces. *Morbidity and Mortality Weekly Report, 64*(19), 532–536.

____. (2015b). *Chronic diseases: The leading causes of death and disability in the United States*. Atlanta, GA: U.S. Department of Health and Human Services: CDC.

Christensen, C. M. (2009). *The innovator's prescription: A disruptive solution for health care*. New York, NY: McGraw Hill.

CMS (Centers for Medicare and Medicaid Services). (2015). *National health expenditure data fact sheet*. Baltimore, MD: CMS.

Cogan, J. A. (2016). Health insurance rate review. *Temple Law Review, 88*, 411–471.

Cohen, D., & Cannon, M. F. (2012). *Policy analysis: The independent payment advisory board: PPACA's anti-constitutional and authoritarian super-legislature*. Washington, DC: Cato Institute.

Commonwealth Fund. (2013). *Health insurance survey*. New York, NY: Commonwealth Fund.

Copeland, C. C. (2012). FDR and Obama: Are there constitutional law lessons from the new deal for the Obama administration? Beyond separation in federalism enforcement: Medicaid expansion, coercion, and the norm of engagement. *University of Pennsylvania Journal of Constitutional Law, 15*, 91–182.

Covey, S. (2013). *The 7 habits of highly effective people: Powerful lessons in personal change*. New York, NY: Simon & Schuster. (Original work published 1990.)

Crossley, M. (2016). Health and taxes: Hospitals, community health and the IRS. *Yale Journal of Health Policy, Law and Ethics, 16*, 51–110.

Einstein, A. (2015). *The world as I see it*. New York, NY: Simon & Schuster. (Original work published 1923.)

Emmanuel, E. (2008). *Healthcare guaranteed: A simple, secure solution for America*. New York, NY: Perseus Books Group, Public Affairs.

Flood, A. (2015). Substance use disorder parity under the Patient Protection and Affordable Care Act: Improvements made, but further government action needed to guarantee full parity in the private insurance market. *Health and Biomedical Law Society, 10*, 363–402.

Garslian, L. (2016). Towards a universal model regulatory framework for derivatives: Post-crisis conclusions from the United States and the European Union. *University of Pennsylvania Journal of International Law, 37*, 941–1026.

Gavil, A. I., & Koslov, T. I. (2016). A flexible health care workforce requires a flexible regulatory environment: Promoting health care competition through regulatory reform. *Washington Law Review, 91*, 147–197.

Gregory, E. C. W., et al. (2014). *NCHS data brief: Trends in infant mortality in the United States, 2006–2012.* Hyattsville, MD: Centers for Disease Control and Prevention, National Center for Health Statistics (NCHS).

Hall, M. A. (2014). Evaluating the Affordable Care Act: The eye of the beholder. *Houston Law Review, 51,* 1029–2015.

Hansen, R., & Newman, R. (2015). Health care: Access after health care reform. *The Georgetown Journal of Gender and the Law, 16,* 191–227.

Hiller, J. S. (2016). Healthy predictions? Questions for data analytics in health care. *American Business Law Journal, 54,* 251–314.

Hugin, R. J., Chairman and Chief Executive Officer of Celgene Corporation. (2014, February 21). Keynote Speaker at the Wharton Health Care Business Conference: Reimagining Healthcare: Driving Change in a Patient-Centered World, Philadelphia, PA.

IMS Institute for Healthcare Informatics. (2016). *Avoidable costs in U.S. healthcare: The $200 billion opportunity from using drugs more responsibly.* Plymouth Meeting, PA: IMS Health.

IRS (Internal Revenue Service). (2015). *Report to Congress on private tax-exempt, taxable, and government-owned hospitals.* Washington, DC: U.S. Department of Treasury, IRS.

Jacobi, J. V. (2015). Multiple Medicaid missions: Targeting, universalism, or both? *Yale Journal of Health Policy, Law and Ethics, 15,* 89–109.

Johnson, A., & Stukel, T. A. (2016). *Medical practice variations.* New York, NY: Springer.

Jost, T. S. (2011). The independent Medicare Advisory Board. *Yale Journal of Health Policy, Law and Ethics, 11*(1), 21–31.

Khan, F. (2016). The "uberization" of healthcare: The forthcoming legal storm over mobile health technology's impact on the medical profession. *Health Matrix, 26,* 123–172.

Kaiser Family Foundation. (2015). *Key facts about the uninsured population.* Menlo Park, CA: Kaiser.

Kesselheim, A. S., & Darrow, J. J. (2015). Hatch-Waxman turns 30: Do we need a re-designed approach for the modern era? *Yale Journal of Health Policy, Law and Ethics, 15,* 293–345.

Maher, B. S. (2011). The benefits of opt-in federalism. *Boston College Law Review, 52,* 1733–1793.

Manheim, K. (2015). The health insurance mandate: A tax or a taking? *Hastings Constitutional Law Quarterly, 42,* 323–391.

McCullough, R. L. (2013). What is all the fuss about? The United States Congress may impose a tax (it's called the "individual mandate"). *Southern California Interdisciplinary Law Journal, 22,* 729–780.

Moncrieff, A. R. (2013). The individual mandate as healthcare regulation: What the Obama administration should have said in *NFIB v. Sebelius. American Journal of Law and Medicine, 39,* 539–572.

NCCS (National Center for Charitable Statistics). (2016). *Guidestar: NCCS national nonprofit research database.* Washington, DC: Urban Institute.

Noush, S. (2014). A storied past demands greater access to health care now and into the future. *Annals of Health Law, 24,* 53–70.

Obama, B. H. (2009, January 20). Inaugural Address to the Nation by President Barack Obama, 44th President of the United States. Washington, DC.

OMB (Office of Management and Budget). (2016). *The president's fiscal year 2017 budget proposal.* Washington, DC: Office of Management and Budget.

___. (2015). *The budget for fiscal year 2016: Investing in America's future.*

___. (2009). *The president's fiscal year 2010 budget proposal.*

Orentlicher, D. (2011). Controlling health care costs through public, transparent processes: The conflict between the morally right and the socially feasible. *The Journal of Corporation Law, 36,* 807–821.

Ostroff, S. (2015). Remarks of the FDA Commissioner: The Food and Drug Law Institute's 58th annual conference. *Food and Drug Law Journal, 70,* 237–244.

Pantelaki, M. I., & White, C. (2014). Health care: Access after health care reform. *The Georgetown Journal of Gender and the Law, 15,* 95–121.

Parker, G. G. (2016). *Platform revolution.* New York, NY: W. W. Norton and Company.

PhRMA (Pharmaceutical Research and Manufacturers of America). (2016). *PhRMA profile.* Washington, DC: PhRMA.

___. (2014). *Drug discovery and development: Understanding the R&D process.*

Pomeranz, J. L., & Adler, S. (2015). Intersection of law, policy and prevention: Defining commercial speech in the context of food marketing. *Journal of Law, Medicine and Ethics, 43,* 40–43.

Renan, D. (2015). Pooling powers. *Tulane Law Review, 115,* 211–291.

Reynolds, G. H., & Denning, B. P. (2013). *National Federation of Independent Business v. Sebelius:* Five takes. *Hastings Constitutional Law Quarterly, 40,* 807–832.

Sage, W. M. (2014). Putting insurance reform in the ACA's rear-view mirror. *Houston Law Review, 51,* 1081–1113.

Satz, A. B. (2015). Fragmentation after health care reform. *Houston Journal of Health Law and Policy, 15,* 171–228.

Schoen, C., et al. (2015). *State trends in the cost of employer health insurance coverage.* New York, NY: The Commonwealth Fund.

Self, L. (2015). Money in the bank and boots on the ground: A law-policy proposal to make the Affordable Care Act work in Louisiana. *Louisiana Law Review, 76,* 547–581.

Smith, II, G. P., & Gallena, R. P. (2014). Re-negotiating a theory of social contract for universal health care in America or, securing the regulatory state? *Catholic University Law Review, 63,* 423–463.

Solar, O., & Irwin, A. (2010). *A conceptual framework for analysis and action on the social determinants of health.* Geneva, Switzerland: World Health Organization, Commission on Social Determinants of Health.

Starr, P. (1983). *The social transformation of American medicine.* New York, NY: Basic Books.

Synderman, R., & Williams, R. S. (2013). Prospective medicine: The next health care transformation. *Academic Medicine, 78*(11), 1079–1084.

TEConomy Partners. (2016). *The economic impact of the U. S. biopharmaceutical industry.* Columbus, OH: TEConomy Partners.

Thide, F. (2012). In search of limiting principles: The Eleventh Circuit invalidates the individual mandate in *Florida v. U.S. Department of Health and Human Services. Boston College Law Review, 53,* 359–372.

Tufts Center for the Study of Drug Development. (2014). *Cost of developing a new drug.* Boston, MA: Tufts.

Turk, M. C. (2015). The convergence of insurance with banking and securities industries, and the limits of regulatory arbitrage in finance. *Columbia Business Law Review, 2015,* 967–1072.

Tyler, E. T. (2012). Aligning public health, health care, law and policy: Medical-legal partnership as a multilevel response to the social determinants of health. *Health and Biomedical Law Society, 8,* 211–247.

Vernon, J. A., et al. (2010). Drug development costs when financial risk is measured using the Fama-French three-factor model. *Health Economics, 19*(8), 1002–1005.

Werbelow, S. E. (2015). Rule of reason without a rhyme: Using big data to better analyze accountable care organizations under the Medicare shared savings program. *Tulane Law Review, 90*, 361–395.

Wharton at the University of Pennsylvania. (2015). The uncomfortable questions you should be asking about pay equity. *Knowledge@Wharton.*

___. (2013). Using the hunger games to encourage healthier choices.

___. (2012). Revisiting the American dream: Is the U.S. providing fewer opportunities to get ahead?

___. (2009). One way to lower health costs: Pay people to be healthy.

WHO (World Health Organization). (2015). *The global burden of disease.* Geneva, Switzerland: WHO.

Wiley, L. F. (2016). From patient rights to health justice: Securing the public's interest in affordable, high-quality health care. *Cardozo Law Review, 37*, 833–889.

World Bank. (2016). *Life expectancy at birth, total (years).* Washington, DC: World Bank.

Zietlow, R. E. (2011). Democratic constitutionalism and the Affordable Care Act. *Ohio State Law Journal, 72*, 1367–1405.

Zimmon, A. J. (2015). RX for costly credit: Deferred interest medical credit cards do more harm than good. *Boston College Journal of Law and Social Justice, 35*, 319–353.

List for Feature Boxes

List for Figures

List of Tables

Index